R. Gupta's®

POPULAR MASTER GUIDE

National Testing Agency (NTA)

UGC-NET/JRF

Junior Research Fellowship & Assistant Professor Eligibility Exam

AYURVEDA BIOLOGY

PAPER-II

by

Arshad Qureshi

&

RPH Editorial Board

2027
EDITION

RAMESH PUBLISHING HOUSE, NEW DELHI

Published by
O.P. Gupta *for* Ramesh Publishing House

Admin. Office
12-H, New Daryaganj Road, Opp. Officer' Mess,
New Delhi-110002 ✆ 23275224, 23245124

E-mail: info@rameshpublishinghouse.com
For Online Shopping: www.rameshpublishinghouse.com

Showroom
- Balaji Market, Nai Sarak, Delhi-110006 ✆ 23282525 📱 9354373464
- 4457, Nai Sarak, Delhi-110006

Book Code: R-2817

ISBN: 978-93-5477-821-6

Price: ₹ 760

Printed at: Deepak Offset. Delhi

CONTENTS

Unit 3: Sharira Rachna and Kriya

Unit 4: Padartha Vijnana and Dravya Vijnana

Unit 5: Rasa Shastra, Bheshajya Kalpana, and Ayurvedic Pharmacopoeia

Unit 6: Disease Biology, Microbiology and Immunology

Unit 7: Genetics, Ayurgenomics, Cell and Molecular Biology

Unit 8: Physiology, Biochemistry and Nanotechnology

Unit 9: Biodiversity, Environmental Health, IPR and Entrepreneurship

Unit 10: Research Methodology, Biostatistics, and Ayurveda-Informatics

Previous Years' Paper

National Testing Agency (NTA)

UGC-NET Junior Research Fellowship & Assistant Professor Eligibility Exam

AYURVEDA BIOLOGY, JANUARY-2026

(Exam held on 07-01-2026)

PAPER-II

1. Who among the following is not an Acharya of Dhanwantar sect:
1. Jatukama 2. Opdhenav
3. Sushrut 4. Karvirya

2. The ethical discipline under Swasthavritta that assure psychosocial well-being is known as:
1. Achara Rasayan 2. Ritucharya
3. Ahar Vidhi Vidhan 4. Sadvritta

3. Chapter Sequence of 'Swasthya Chatushka' in Sutra Sthana of Charak Samhita:
1. 14, 15, 16, 17 2. 9, 10, 11, 12
3. 1, 2, 3, 4 4. 5, 6, 7, 8

4. "Viddhasya Shyavangta Jwaro dahah Panduta Shonitagamnam rakta Netrata Ch." signifies the strotas:
1. Rasavah Srotasa 2. Raktavah Srotasa
3. Mansvaha Srotasa 4. Medovah Srotasa

5. There are _____ Kandaras.
1. 8 2. 12
3. 16 4. 20

6. According to Nyaya Philosophy. What is the number of Prameya?
1. 10 2. 11
3. 12 4. 13

7. Which one of the following Guna of Dravya is the cause of adhahpatan:
1. Snigdha 2. Sheeta
3. Laghu 4. Guru

8. If a famous object is similar to a not so famous another object, it is known as:
1. Characteristics 2. Upmiti
3. Upman 4. Vyavahit

9. Which of the following is called 'Trimada'?
1. Nagarmotha, Vidang, Shunthi
2. Nagarmotha, Chitrakmool, Vidanga
3. Chitrakmool, Vidanga, Pippali
4. Nagarmotha, Chitrakmool, Maricha

10. Apana Vayu is not located in:
1. Vrishana 2. Uru
3. Nabhi 4. Urah

11. Microcytic hypochromic red cell found in which disease:
1. Megaloblastic Anaemia
2. Pernicious Anaemia
3. Sideroblastic Anaemia
4. Iron deficiency Anaemia

12. Example of live attenuated vaccines is:
1. Typhoid vaccine
2. BCG vaccine
3. Pneumococcal vaccine
4. Plague vaccine

13. Genotypic ratio of monohybrid cross is:
1. 2 : 1 2. 3 : 1
3. 3 : 2 4. 4 : 1

14. Which one imparts turgidity and rigidity to the cell:
1. Cell Wall 2. Cell Membrane
3. Vacuole 4. Ribosome

15. DLS (Dynamic Light Scattering) is used to measure:
1. Particle composition 2. Particle size distribution
3. Surface charge 4. Optical band gap

16. Which of the following technique is primarily used in determining the morphology of Nanoparticles?
1. XRD 2. TEM
3. FTIR 4. UV-VIS Spectroscopy

17. The part of nephron highly permeable to water is:
1. DCT (Distal Convoluted Tubule)
2. LOOP of Henle
3. PCT (Proximal Convoluted Tubule)
4. Collecting Tubule

18. Which ecosystem have an abundance of shrubs and bushes and have diverse flora and fauna?
1. Forest ecosystem
2. Temperature evergreen forest
3. Tropical deciduous forest
4. The grassland ecosystem

19. A statistical test of hypothesis based on Gaussian distribution, generally used to compare two means or two proportions:
1. Zelen design
2. Z-Score
3. Z-Test
4. Wilcoxon test

20. The local document for any medical research is:
1. Data Analysis
2. Hypothesis
3. Smart Format
4. Protocol

21. Given below are two statements : one is labelled as Assertion (A) and the other is labelled as Reason (R).

Assertion (A): The desciple of Acharya Punarvasu named Agnivesha wrote the Agnivesha Tantra and further Acharya Charaka compiled and commented on it and now it is available as Charaka Samhita.

Reason (R): The other desciples of Acharya Punarvasu did not write their scriptures.

In the light of the above statements, choose the ***most appropriate*** answer from the options given below:
1. Both (A) and (R) are correct and (R) is the correct explanation of (A)
2. Both (A) and (R) are correct, but (R) is not the correct explanation of (A)
3. (A) is correct, but (R) is not correct
4. (A) is not correct, but (R) is correct

22. Given below are two statements : one is labelled as Assertion (A) and the other is labelled as Reason (R).

Assertion (A): Kaumarbhritya is not the main authority subject of Kashyapa Samhita.

Reason (R): There is description of diseases and treatment of children in Kaumarbhritya sujbect.

In the light of the above statements, choose the ***most appropriate*** answer from the options given below:
1. Both (A) and (R) are correct and (R) is the correct explanation of (A)
2. Both (A) and (R) are correct, but (R) is not the correct explanation of (A)
3. (A) is correct, but (R) is not correct
4. (A) is not correct, but (R) is correct

23. Given below are two statements : one is labelled as Assertion (A) and the other is labelled as Reason (R).

Assertion (A): 'Health' is described in Ayurveda as a normal state of equilibrium of Dosha, Dhatu, Mala, Agni and Prasanna Atmendriya-Mana.

Reason (R): 'Swasthya' is maintained only balancing Dhatu and neglecting 'Dosha' and 'Mala'.

In the light of the above statements, choose the ***most appropriate*** answer from the options given below:
1. Both (A) and (R) are correct and (R) is the correct explanation of (A)
2. Both (A) and (R) are correct, but (R) is not the correct explanation of (A)
3. (A) is correct, but (R) is not correct
4. (A) is not correct, but (R) is correct

24. Given below are two statements : one is labelled as Assertion (A) and the other is labelled as Reason (R).

Assertion (A): Lokapurusha Samya Siddhanta establish that whatever exist in the universe exist in Purusha.

Reason (R): Purusha is called microcosm as it embodies all universe elements.

In the light of the above statements, choose the ***most appropriate*** answer from the options given below:
1. Both (A) and (R) are correct and (R) is the correct explanation of (A)
2. Both (A) and (R) are correct, but (R) is not the correct explanation of (A)
3. (A) is correct, but (R) is not correct
4. (A) is not correct, but (R) is correct

25. Given below are two statements : one is labelled as Assertion (A) and the other is labelled as Reason (R).

Assertion (A): According to Ksheer-Dadhi nyaya; adya dhatu gets completely transformed into uttar dhatu.

Reason (R): Adya dhatu is food(ahara) of Uttar dhatu.

In the light of the above statements, choose the ***most appropriate*** answer from the options given below:
1. Both (A) and (R) are correct and (R) is the correct explanation of (A)
2. Both (A) and (R) are correct, but (R) is not the correct explanation of (A)
3. (A) is correct, but (R) is not correct
4. (A) is not correct, but (R) is correct

26. Given below are two statements : one is labelled as Assertion (A) and the other is labelled as Reason (R).

Assertion (A): Yakrita, Pleeha are the moola of Raktavah Srotas.

Reason (R): Blood is formed by 'Ranjak Pitta'. Ranjak Pitta is found in yakrita. The collection of dead blood cells takes place in Pleeha.

In the light of the above statements, choose the ***most appropriate*** answer from the options given below:

1. Both (A) and (R) are correct and (R) is the correct explanation of (A)
2. Both (A) and (R) are correct, but (R) is not the correct explanation of (A)
3. (A) is correct, but (R) is not correct
4. (A) is not correct, but (R) is correct

27. Given below are two statements : one is labelled as Assertion (A) and the other is labelled as Reason (R).

Assertion (A): Sixth Twacha is known as Rohini.

Reason (R): Rohini Twacha is the place of Kustha Visarpa.

In the light of the above statements, choose the ***most appropriate*** answer from the options given below:

1. Both (A) and (R) are correct and (R) is the correct explanation of (A)
2. Both (A) and (R) are correct, but (R) is not the correct explanation of (A)
3. (A) is correct, but (R) is not correct
4. (A) is not correct, but (R) is correct

28. Given below are two statements : one is labelled as Assertion (A) and the other is labelled as Reason (R).

Assertion (A): Sushruta has considered Hridaya as a seat of Chetana.

Reason (R): Mana, Buddhi, Chitta and Atma are known as Anthkarana Chatushtaya.

In the light of the above statements, choose the ***most appropriate*** answer from the options given below:

1. Both (A) and (R) are correct and (R) is the correct explanation of (A)
2. Both (A) and (R) are correct, but (R) is not the correct explanation of (A)
3. (A) is correct, but (R) is not correct
4. (A) is not correct, but (R) is correct

29. Given below are two statements : one is labelled as Assertion (A) and the other is labelled as Reason (R).

Assertion (A): Haritaki is Anulomana Dravya.

Reason (R): Dravya that excrete slishta mala without digestion through lower tract is called Anuloman Dravya.

In the light of the above statements, choose the ***most appropriate*** answer from the options given below:

1. Both (A) and (R) are correct and (R) is the correct explanation of (A)
2. Both (A) and (R) are correct, but (R) is not the correct explanation of (A)
3. (A) is correct, but (R) is not correct
4. (A) is not correct, but (R) is correct

30. Given below are two statements : one is labelled as Assertion (A) and the other is labelled as Reason (R).

Assertion (A): The Tarka based on Yukti is call Anumana.

Reason (R): Karan of Anumiti is called Anumana.

In the light of the above statements, choose the ***most appropriate*** answer from the options given below:

1. Both (A) and (R) are correct and (R) is the correct explanation of (A)
2. Both (A) and (R) are correct, but (R) is not the correct explanation of (A)
3. (A) is correct, but (R) is not correct
4. (A) is not correct, but (R) is correct

31. Given below are two statements : one is labelled as Assertion (A) and the other is labelled as Reason (R).

Assertion (A): Jalooka Bandh is a kind of Parad Bandh. It is used for the pleasure of weak, frail and lusty persons, for quelling the sexual desire and to attract women who keep themselves away from sexual intercourse.

Reason (R): Keeping Jalooka in the Vagina before the sexual intercourse helps in the quick orgasm of even young women.

In the light of the above statements, choose the ***most appropriate*** answer from the options given below:

1. Both (A) and (R) are correct and (R) is the correct explanation of (A)
2. Both (A) and (R) are correct, but (R) is not the correct explanation of (A)
3. (A) is correct, but (R) is not correct
4. (A) is not correct, but (R) is correct

32. Given below are two statements : one is labelled as Assertion (A) and the other is labelled as Reason (R).

Assertion (A): 'Gaja puta' is used for making Swarna and Rajat Bhasma. For the formation of 'Lauh Bhasm'. 'Kukkut Puta' Should only be used.

Reason (R): Medicinal Bhasmas. which are 'Pachit' by put, are harmless and full of qualities. These have the qualities of Niruth, Varitar and Deepan.

In the light of the above statements, choose the ***most appropriate*** answer from the options given below:

1. Both (A) and (R) are correct and (R) is the correct explanation of (A)
2. Both (A) and (R) are correct, but (R) is not the correct explanation of (A)
3. (A) is correct, but (R) is not correct
4. (A) is not correct, but (R) is correct

33. Given below are two statements : one is labelled as Assertion (A) and the other is labelled as Reason (R).

Assertion (A): Among all Ig, IgM has the lowest molecular weight.

Reason (R): IgM is also called a primary immune response antibody. It is the first antibody to be produced following an infection.

In the light of the above statements, choose the ***most appropriate*** answer from the options given below:

1. Both (A) and (R) are correct and (R) is the correct explanation of (A)
2. Both (A) and (R) are correct, but (R) is not the correct explanation of (A)
3. (A) is correct, but (R) is not correct
4. (A) is not correct, but (R) is correct

34. Given below are two statements : one is labelled as Assertion (A) and the other is labelled as Reason (R).

Assertion (A): To assess psychological disorders, IQ (intelligence quotient) score is important tool.

Reason (R): The Wechsler scale is individual tests of intelligence for children and adults, that seek to measure several aspects of intelligence.

In the light of the above statements, choose the ***most appropriate*** answer from the options given below:

1. Both (A) and (R) are correct and (R) is the correct explanation of (A)
2. Both (A) and (R) are correct, but (R) is not the correct explanation of (A)
3. (A) is correct, but (R) is not correct
4. (A) is not correct, but (R) is correct

35. Given below are two statements : one is labelled as Assertion (A) and the other is labelled as Reason (R).

Assertion (A): B-Oxidation occurs in mitochondria.

Reason (R): It produces NADH And $FADH_2$ for ATP synthesis.

In the light of the above statements, choose the ***most appropriate*** answer from the options given below:

1. Both (A) and (R) are correct and (R) is the correct explanation of (A)
2. Both (A) and (R) are correct, but (R) is not the correct explanation of (A)
3. (A) is correct, but (R) is not correct
4. (A) is not correct, but (R) is correct

36. Given below are two statements : one is labelled as Assertion (A) and the other is labelled as Reason (R).

Assertion (A): Wernicke's area is located in the region at posterior end of superior temporal gyrus in the dominant (categorical) hemisphere.

Reason (R): It concerned with comprehens i.e, interpretation and understanding of auditory and Visual information.

In the light of the above statements, choose the ***most appropriate*** answer from the options given below:

1. Both (A) and (R) are correct and (R) is the correct explanation of (A)
2. Both (A) and (R) are correct, but (R) is not the correct explanation of (A)
3. (A) is correct, but (R) is not correct
4. (A) is not correct, but (R) is correct

37. Given below are two statements : one is labelled as Assertion (A) and the other is labelled as Reason (R).

Assertion (A): According to general guideline's for drug development of Ayurveda formulations, the teratogenicity study is essential for clinical trial if phytopharmaceutical drug is intended for use during Pregnancy.

Reason (R): Only a drug has undergone above study are legaly permissible for use during pregnancy.

In the light of the above statements, choose the ***most appropriate*** answer from the options given below:

1. Both (A) and (R) are correct and (R) is the correct explanation of (A)
2. Both (A) and (R) are correct, but (R) is not the correct explanation of (A)
3. (A) is correct, but (R) is not correct
4. (A) is not correct, but (R) is correct

38. Given below are two statements : one is labelled as Assertion (A) and the other is labelled as Reason (R).

Assertion (A): A hypothesis is a speculative statement that is subjected to verification through a research study.

Reason (R): There are two broad categories of hypothesis - a research hypothesis and analternative hypothesis.

In the light of the above statements, choose the ***most appropriate*** answer from the options given below:

1. Both (A) and (R) are correct and (R) is the correct explanation of (A)
2. Both (A) and (R) are correct, but (R) is not the correct explanation of (A)
3. (A) is correct, but (R) is not correct
4. (A) is not correct, but (R) is correct

39. Arrange the development era of Ayurveda literature in sequence:

A. Vedic Era
B. Sangraha Era
C. Nighantu Era
D. Ras Shastra Era
E. Samhita Kal Era

Choose the ***correct*** answer from the options given below:

1. A, B, E, D, C
2. A, E, B, D, C
3. A, E, C, B, D
4. E, A, B, C, D

40. Arrange the following commentary (Tika) of Charak Samhita in chronological order:

A. Ayurved Deepika - Chakrapani Datta
B. Charak Nyas - Bhattar Harishchandra
C. Nirantar Pad Vyakhya - Jejjat
D. Jalpkalptaru - Gangadhar Rai
E. Tatvapradipika Vyakhya - Shivdas Sen

Choose the ***correct*** answer from the options given below:

1. B, C, A, E, D
2. A, B, C, E, D
3. B, A, C, E, D
4. B, A, D, E, C

41. According to Ayurveda, the sequence of the creation of cosmos is:

A. Buddhi
B. Avyakta
C. Ahamkara
D. Sookshma Panch Mahabhoot
E. Purusha Utapatti

Choose the ***correct*** answer from the options given below:

1. C, A, B, D, E
2. A, B, C, D, E
3. B, A, C, D, E
4. B, A, C, E, D

42. The sequence of season (Ritu) is:

A. Shishir
B. Basant
C. Varsha
D. Sharad
E. Grishm

Choose the ***correct*** answer from the options given below:

1. A, B, C, D, E
2. A, B, E, C, D
3. C, D, E, B, A
4. D, E, A, B, C

43. The sequence of the marma type in increasing number of marma is:

A. Sadya Pranhar Marma
B. Kalantar Pranhar Marma
C. Rujakar Marma
D. Vishalyghna Marma
E. Vaikaly Kar Marma

Choose the ***correct*** answer from the options given below:

1. A, B, D, E, C
2. B, A, D, C, E
3. D, C, A, B, E
4. E, A, B, D, C

44. The sequence of 4 Konas from north to east in a circle is:

A. Ishana Kona
B. Vayavya Kona
C Nairitya Kona
D. Agni Kona

Choose the ***correct*** answer from the options given below:

1. A, B, C, D
2. A, C, B, D
3. B, C, A, D
4. A, D, C, B

45. The Sequence of sannikarsh of following for the "Pratyaksha" of object is:

A. Mana
B. Pratyaksha Gyana
C Indriyan
D. Vishaya
E. Atma

Choose the ***correct*** answer from the options given below:

1. E, A, C, D, B
2. A, B, C, D, E
3. B, C, D, E, A
4. D, A, E, B, C

46. The sequence of the Sanskar of Parad is:

A. Patana
B. Mardana
C. Uttapana
D. Svedana
E. Moorchhana

Choose the ***correct*** answer from the options given below:

1. A, B, C, D, E
2. D, B, E, C, A
3. E, D, C, B, A
4. B, C, A, E, D

47. What is the sequence of the following five processes for the 'Utthapan of Parad?

A. Patan
B. Prakshalan
C Mardan
D. Svedan
E. Atap

Choose the ***correct*** answer from the options given below:

1. A, B, C, D, E
2. D, C, E, B, A
3. D, B, C, E, A
4. E, D, C, B, A

48. Arrange the following in sequence of preparation of culture media:

A. The pH determination of fluid by pH meter
B. The Medium is dispensed into types or flasks
C The Medium is sterilized
D. The Medium is foiled to dissolve the agar
E. Dehydrated medium is dissolved in the appropriate volume of distilled water

Choose the ***correct*** answer from the options given below:

1. A, C, B, D, E
2. D, E, A, B, C
3. E, A, D, B, C
4. D, E, C, B, A

49. The sequence of pathogenesis of rheumatoid arthritis is:

A. Inflammation of synovial membrane
B. Cartilage destruction
C Pannus formation
D Autoimmune reaction against synovium Membrane
E. Joint deformity

Choose the ***correct*** answer from the options given below:

1. A, D, C, B, E
2. B, C, D, A, E
3. D, B, A, C, E
4. D, A, C, B, E

50. Sequence of events in cardiac cycle:
A. Atrial contraction
B. Ventricular systole
C. Isovolumetric ventricular relaxation
D. Isovolumetric ventricular contraction
E. Intial rapid ventricular filling phase
Choose the ***correct*** answer from the options given below:
1. A, B, C, D, E 2. A, D, B, C, E
3. B, A, D, C, E 4. A, E, C, D, B

51. Arrange in the sequence the events during normal breathing in inspiration:
A. Thoracic cavity increase
B. External intercostal muscle contract
C. Intra alveolar aressure decrease
D. Air flow in to lungs
E. Diaphragm contracts
Choose the ***correct*** answer from the options given below:
1. B, C, D, E, A 2. E, B, A, D, C
3. A, B, C, E, D 4. E, B, A, C, D

52. The sequence of stages for preparation of plans and projects:
A. Appraisal of project
B. Formulation of project
C. Origin of project data
D. Implementation of project
E. Selection of best project
Choose the ***correct*** answer from the options given below:
1. B, C, A, E, D 2. C, B, A, E, D
3. E, A, B, C, D 4. C, E, B, A, D

53. Arrange the sequence of components of drug development:
A. Literature survey
B. Identification and prioritizing the R and D needs
C. Pre clinical safety, biological activity, stability study
D. Initiation of drug development
E. Formulation of hypothetical rationale
Choose the ***correct*** answer from the options given below:
1. A, B, E, D, C 2. B, A, E, D, C
3. C, D, B, E, A 4. D, B, C, A, E

54. The correct sequential steps of 'Unpaired t-test' are:
A. To calculate the t-value by formula and finding the degree of freedom
B. After determining the H_0 and H_1 finding the difference between the mean of both the samples $(\bar{x}_1 - \bar{x}_2)$
C. Conclusion
D. By using the difference between two means, finding the standard error
E. To compare the t-table value and t-calculated value
Choose the ***correct*** answer from the options given below:
1. D, A, E, B, C 2. A, E, C, B, D
3. D, A, E, C, B 4. B, D, A, E, C

55. What is the correct sequence of Dashavidha Pareeksha Vishayas?
A. Vikriti B. Samhanan
C. Prakriti D. Pramana
E. Saar
Choose the ***correct*** answer from the options given below:
1. A, E, D, B, C 2. C, A, E, B, D
3. B, E, C, D, A 4. D, B, A, C, E

56. The books written by Acharya Priyavrat Sharma are:
A. Sidhant Nidan, Abhinav Kamshastra
B. Dravyagun Vigyan, Rogi Parikshha-Vidhi
C. Vish-Vigyan, Manav Sharir Rachana Vigyan
D. Vyadhi Vigyan, Ayurved ka mul sidhant
E. Ayurved Anusandhan Paddhati, Charak samagya
Choose the ***correct*** answer from the options given below:
1. B and E only 2. A and E only
3. D and B only 4. A and C only

57. Which are two correct matches of Samhita and its commentator:
A. Charak Samhita — Gayadas
B. Sushrut Samhita — Bhattar Harishchandra
C. Ashtang Hridaya — Hemadri
D. Ashtang Hridaya — Dalhana
E. Chakark Samhita — Shivdas Sen
Choose the ***correct*** answer from the options given below:
1. C and E only 2. A and C only
3. B and E only 4. D and E only

58. According to Acharya charak 'Dravya Samgrah' comprises.
A. Panch Mahabhoot B. Atma
C. Pramana D. Disha
E. Sambhava
Choose the ***correct*** answer from the options given below:
1. A, B, C only 2. C, B, E only
3. A, E, C only 4. A, B, D only

59. According to Charaka the vishaya of mana are:

A. Vicharya B. Chintya
C. Ekatva D. Dhyeya
E. Indriyabhigraha

Choose the ***correct*** answer from the options given below:

1. A, B, C only 2. B, A, E only
3. A, B, D only 4. B, D, C only

60. Which are the correct combinations of Dhatu and its Mala:

A. Rasa-Kapha, Rakta-Sweda
B. Rakta-Pitta, Asthi-Nakha
C. Mansa-Sweda, Asthi-Akshi Sneha
D. Rasa-Pitta, Rakta-Sweda
E Meda-Sweda, Asthi-Loma

Choose the ***correct*** answer from the options given below:

1. A and B only 2. B and E only
3. C and D only 4. D and E only

61. The features of Mans Sara Purush are:

A. Forgiveness B. Patience
C. Wellness/Health D. Glowing Complexion
E. Pain Endurance

Choose the ***correct*** answer from the options given below:

1. A, D, E only 2. A, B, C only
3. B, D, E only 4. C, D, E only

62. Which of the following are not 'Paradi-Guna':

A. Sthira B. Yukti
C. Sthoola D. Abhyasa
E. Vishada

Choose the ***correct*** answer from the options given below:

1. A, B and C only 2. C, D and E only
3. E, D and B only 4. E, C and A only

63. Which of the following are not 'Bhav Padarth':

A. Dravya B. Guna
C. Sanyoga D. Vishesh
E. Sanskar

Choose the ***correct*** answer from the options given below:

1. D and E only 2. B, C and A only
3. C and E only 4. E, D and A only

64. Which qualities do the medicines pachit by puta have?

A. Deepan B. Nirutth
C. Teekshna D. Varitar
E. Achchhadan

Choose the ***correct*** answer from the options given below:

1. D, E and B only 2. C, D and A only
3. B, C and E only 4. A, B and D only

65. Which of the following are the kinds of Abhrak?

A. Pinaka B. Naga
C. Swarna D. Mandooka
E. Rajat

Choose the ***correct*** answer from the options given below:

1. A, B and D only 2. B, C and D only
3. C, D and E only 4. A, C and D only

66. Which one of the following cells are responsible for allergy reactions?

A. Neutrophils B. Basophils
C. Monocytes D. Mast Cells
E R.B.C

Choose the ***correct*** answer from the options given below:

1. A and E only 2. B and D only
3. D and E only 4. A and C only

67. Which of the following methods of pasturisation are used in the dairy industry?

A. Radiation method
B. Osmotic pressure method
C. Holding method
D. Blenching method
E. Flash method

Choose the ***correct*** answer from the options given below:

1. A and E only 2. C and E only
3. D and E only 4. B and C only

68. Which four nucleosides found in DNA?

A. Deoxycytidine B. Deoxythymidine
C. Deoxycryptine D. Deoxyadenosien
E. Deoxyguanosine

Choose the ***correct*** answer from the options given below:

1. A, B, D, E only 2. A, B, C, D only
3. A, C, D, E only 4. B, C, D, E only

69. Among the following, polysaccharides are:

A. Glycogen B. Agarose
C. Titin D. Chitin
E. Cytochrome

Choose the ***correct*** answer from the options given below:

1. B, C, D only 2. A, C, E only
3. A, B, D only 4. C, D, E only

70. Functions of gall bladder are:

A. Storage of bile
B. Control of flow of bile following a meal
C. Increasing the alkalinity of stored bile
D. Regulates equalization of pressure in biliary system
E Secretes mucin (mucus)

Choose the *correct* answer from the options given below:

1. A, B, C, D only 2. B, C, D, E only
3. A, B, D, E only 4. C, D, E, A only

71. IEC (Institutional Ethics Committee) of a medical institute consists which four among the following:

A. Medical scientist
B. Legal expert or retired judge
C. Statistician
D. Social scientist
E. Clinician

Choose the *correct* answer from the options given below:

1. A, B, C, D only 2. A, B, C, E only
3. B, C, D, E only 4. A, B, D, E only

72. For 'Pratyaksha Pramana' a combination of four among the following is essential:

A. Indriya B. Man
C. Kaal D. Atma
E. Arth

Choose the *correct* answer from the options given below:

1. A, B, C, E only 2. A, C, D, E only
3. A, B, D, E only 4. A, B, C, D only

73. Match the List-I with List-II.

List-I	List-II
A. Astaang Hridaya Tika Sarvang Sundara	I. Commentator Indu
B. Astaang Hridaya Tika Ayurved Rasayan	II. Commentator Arun Datta
C. Astaang Hridaya Tika Padarth Chandrika	III. Commentator Hemadri
D. Astaang Hridaya Tika Shashilekha	IV. Commentator Chandra Nandan

Choose the *correct* answer from the options given below:

1. A-II, B-III, C-IV, D-I
2. A-IV, B-II, C-III, D-I
3. A-II, B-III, C-I, D-IV
4. A-I, B-III, C-II, D-IV

74. Match the List-I with List-II.

List-I	List-II
A. Bhore Committee	I. Year of Establishment 1958
B. Chopra Committee	II. Year of Establishment 1949
C. Pandit Committee	III. Year of Establishment 1946
D. Udup Committee	IV. Year of Establishment 1945

Choose the *correct* answer from the options given below:

1. A-IV, B-III, C-II, D-I
2. A-III, B-I, C-IV, D-II
3. A-IV, B-II, C-I, D-III
4. A-II, B-III, C-I, D-IV

75. Match the List-I with List-II.

List-I *(Panch Mahabhool)*	List-II *(Main Property)*
A. Aakash	I. Touch
B. Vayu	II. Odour
C. Jal	III. Sound
D. Prithvi	IV. Taste

Choose the *correct* answer from the options given below:

1. A-I, B-III, C-II, D-IV
2. A-III, B-I, C-IV, D-II
3. A-III, B-I, C-II, D-IV
4. A-I, B-II, C-III, D-IV

76. Match the List-I with List-II.

List-I *(Dhatu)*	List-II *(Function of Dhatu)*
A. Rasa	I. Jeevana
B. Rakta	II. Preenana
C. Asthi	III. Poorana
D. Majja	IV. Dharana

Choose the *correct* answer from the options given below:

1. A-II, B-I, C-III, D-IV
2. A-I, B-II, C-IV, D-III
3. A-I, B-II, C-III, D-IV
4. A-II, B-I, C-IV, D-III

77. Match the List-I with List-II.

List-I *(Month of Pregnancy)*	List-II *(Step of Growth)*
A. First month	I. Hasta Pad Shirsam Panch Pidika
B. Third month	II. Kalal
C. Fifth month	III. Oj
D. Eight month	IV. Manah Prati Buddhrataram bhavati

Choose the *correct* answer from the options given below:

1. A-II, B-I, C-IV, D-III
2. A-I, B-II, C-III, D-IV
3. A-IV, B-I, C-III, D-II
4. A-II, B-IV, C-I, D-III

78. Match the List-I with List-II.

List-I	List-II
A. Asthi Shool	I. Asthi Mala
B. Asthyadhyasthi	II. Asthikshaya
C. Vatlanam Sevnat	III. Asthivriddhi
D. Kesh lom	IV. Asthi Vah Srotodushhi Nidan

Choose the ***correct*** answer from the options given below:

1. A-II, B-III, C-IV, D-I
2. A-II, B-I, C-III, D-IV
3. A-IV, B-II, C-III, D-I
4. A-III, B-IV, C-I, D-II

79. Match the List-I with List-II.

List-I (*Dhatu Kshyaya*)	List-II (*Lakshana*)
A. Rasa Kshaya	I. Sira Shaithilya
B. Rakta Kshaya	II. Sandhi Sfutan
C. Meda Kshaya	III. Sandhi Shaithilya
D. Asthi Kshaya	IV. Hriday Peeda

Choose the ***correct*** answer from the options given below:

1. A-I, B-III, C-IV, D-II
2. A-IV, B-I, C-II, D-III
3. A-III, B-IV, C-I, D-II
4. A-II, B-III, C-I, D-IV

80. Match the List-I with List-II.

List-I (*Aushadha Guna*)	List-II (*Aushadh*)
A. Urdhav bhag har	I. Shigru
B. Adhobhaghar	II. Madanphala
C. Ubhaytobhag har	III. Snuhi
D. Shirovirechan	IV. Devadali

Choose the ***correct*** answer from the options given below:

1. A-IV, B-II, C-I, D-III
2. A-II, B-III, C-IV, D-I
3. A-II, B-I, C-III, D-IV
4. A-I, B-IV, C-II, D-III

81. Match the List-I with List-II.

List-I (*Darshan (Philosophy)*)	List-II (*Vada*)
A. Nyaya	I. Satkaryavada (parinamvada)
B. Sankhya	II. Kshanabhangur vada
C. Bauddha	III. Parmanu vada
D. Vaisheshik	IV. Arambha vada

Choose the ***correct*** answer from the options given below:

1. A-IV, B-I, C-II, D-III
2. A-III, B-II, C-IV, D-IV
3. A-II, B-IV, C-III, D-I
4. A-I, B-III, C-II, D-IV

82. Match the List-I with List-II.

List-I (*Rasa Dravya*)	List-II (*Chemical Name*)
A. Nausadar	I. $CaCO_3$ (Calcium Carbonate)
B. Cinnebar	II. PbO (Lead Oxide)
C. Litharge	III. NH_4Cl (Ammonium Chloride)
D. Coveries	IV. HgS (Red Sulphide of Mercury)

Choose the ***correct*** answer from the options given below:

1. A-I, B-II, C-IV, D-III
2. A-II, B-I, C-III, D-IV
3. A-III, B-IV, C-II, D-I
4. A-IV, B-I, C-II, D-III

83. Match the List-I with List-II.

List-I (*Disease Marker*)	List-II (*Disease*)
A. T.M. Alpha-fetoprotein AFB	I. Testicular Cancer
B. T.M. CA 125	II. Various Carcinomas
C. T.M. CA 19.9	III. Ovarian Cancer
D. PSA	IV. Prostate Cancer

Choose the ***correct*** answer from the options given below:

1. A-IV, B-III, C-I, D-II
2. A-I, B-III, C-II, D-IV
3. A-IV, B-II, C-I, D-III
4. A-I, B-IV, C-III, D-II

84. Match the List-I with List-II.

List-I (*Vaccine*)	List-II (*Time for birth*)
A. Bacillus Calmette Guerin BCG	I. 6 Weeks
B. Oral Polio Vaccine-1 OPV-1	II. At birth
C. Human Papilloma Virus HPV	III. 9 to 12 months
D. Measless and Rubella MR	IV. 9 to 14 Year girls

Choose the ***correct*** answer from the options given below:

1. A-II, B-I, C-IV, D-III
2. A-IV, B-I, C-II, D-III
3. A-II, B-IV, C-I, D-III
4. A-I, B-IV, C-II, D-III

85. Match the List-I with List-II.

List-I (*Cell Organalle*)	List-II (*Function*)
A. Mitochondria	I. Protein Synthesis
B. Endoplasmic reticulum	II. Power houses of the cell
C. Ribosomes	III. Destroy bacteria and Foreign bodies
D. Lysosomes	IV. Provides supportive framework for the cell

Choose the ***correct*** answer from the options given below:

1. A-III, B-II, C-I, D-IV
2. A-IV, B-III, C-I, D-II
3. A-II, B-IV, C-I, D-III
4. A-I, B-II, C-III, D-IV

86. Match the List-I with List-II.

List-I (*Laboratory method*)	List-II (*Use*)
A. PCR (Polymerase Chain Reaction)	I. Use of detection and quantification of antigen or antibodies in a sample
B. Gel electrophoresis	II. Used to grow plant or animal cells under controlled laboratory conditions
C. ELISA	III. Used for amplification of DNA to make millions for copies of a specific sequence
D. Tissue Culture	IV. Used to separate DNA, RNA or protein fragments based on their size and change

Choose the ***correct*** answer from the options given below:

1. A-II, B-III, C-IV, D-I
2. A-III, B-IV, C-I, D-II
3. A-I, B-II, C-III, D-IV
4. A-IV, B-I, C-II, D-III

87. Match the List-I with List-II.

List-I (*Organ/gland*)	List-II (*Enzyme*)
A. Salivary Glands	I. Renin (In infants)
B. Stomach	II. Lingual Lipase
C. Pancreas	III. Erepsin
D. Small Intestine	IV. Chymotrypsin

Choose the ***correct*** answer from the options given below:

1. A-I, B-II, C-III, D-IV
2. A-III, B-II, C-I, D-IV
3. A-II, B-I, C-III, D-IV
4. A-II, B-I, C-IV, D-III

88. Match the List-I with List-II.

List-I (*Gases*)	List-II (*Contributing to the Green House Effect*)
A. Carbon dioxide	I. Refrigerators and air conditioning
B. Methane	II. Fertilisers, burning fossil fuels
C. CFCs	III. Burning Fossil Fuels
D. Nitrogen Oxides	IV. Decay of Organic matter e.g. faces of animals

Choose the ***correct*** answer from the options given below:

1. A-I, B-II, C-IV, D-III
2. A-II, B-III, C-I, D-IV
3. A-III, B-IV, C-I, D-II
4. A-IV, B-I, C-III, D-II

89. Match the List-I with List-II.

List-I	List-II
A. The process of selecting a sample using networks	I. Accidental sampling
B. The process of selecting a sample from a large population	II. Snowball sampling
C. Sampling based on convenience in accessing the sampling population	III. Quota sampling
D. Sampling with consideration of researcher's ease to access to the sample population	IV. Cluster sampling

Choose the ***correct*** answer from the options given below:

1. A-III, B-I, C-IV, D-II
2. A-II, B-IV, C-I, D-III
3. A-IV, B-II, C-III, D-I
4. A-I, B-III, C-II, D-IV

90. Match the List-I with List-II.

List-I (*Non-Parametric Test*)	List-II (*Uses*)
A. Chi-Square Test	I. For comparing the repetitive measures of the same sample or two related samples
B. Fisher's Exact Test	II. For paired nominal data
C. Mc Nemar's Test	III. For testing the hypothesis
D. Wilcoxon Test	IV. To test the significance of the association between two classification

Choose the ***correct*** answer from the options given below:

1. A-III, B-IV, C-II, D-I
2. A-IV, B-II, C-III, D-I
3. A-II, B-I, C-IV, D-III
4. A-I, B-III, C-II, D-IV

Directions (Qs. No. 91 to 95): *Read the following passage and answer the questions:*

In Ayurveda, the concept of Dinacharya (daily routine) plays an important role in the protection of health - It emphasises the integration of daily routine with the natural rythm, so that the health could be protected and diseases do not emerge. According to Ayurveda, a person must wake up in Brahma muhurta which means before sunrise. After waking up the person should carry out the activities related to shaueh vidhi-excretion of stool and urine, Danta Dhavan-cleaning teeth. Jihwa Nirlekhan-cleaning tongue, holding/bearing gandoosh/kawal, Abhyanga-massage, physical exercise, bath, Nasya, Anjan etc. These activities keep the dosha, dhatu and mala in a balance state and keep the body, mind and senses in good spirit. Besides, Satvik and wholesome food has been determined to enhance ojas and immunity, thus following an appropriate daily routine leads to eauilibrium of digestive system (agni), mental clarity and prevention of early ageing. Therefore, when the daily activities and behavior are in accordance with the natural cycles, then physical, menial and spiritual heath is achieved. This is the essence of Swasthavritta.

91. According to Acharya Charak Sauviranjan ought to be used in eyes.
1. Once a week
2. Twice a week
3. Daily
4. Every 5th or 8th Day

92. Which is most important for maintaining health?
1. Waking up at Brahmmuhurta
2. Daily Abhyanga
3. Daily routine according to natural rythm
4. Daily exercise

93. Which of the following dosha get passified is alleviated by observing Abhyanga daily?
1. Pitta
2. Kapha
3. Vala
4. Rakta

94. Which is most important to prevent premature aging?
1. Cleanlesness and early rise
2. Healthy food and happy mind
3. Daily massage and Anjana
4. Daily bath and teeth cleaning

95. In Ayurveda Dhatusamya is considered as:
1. Objective of Svvasth vritta
2. Base of Dincharya
3. Base of treatment and health
4. Base of healthy mind

Directions (Qs. No. 96 to 100): *Read the following passage and answer the questions:*

It has taken million of years of evolution to accumulate a rich biodiversity in nature but huminity could lose all that wealth in less than two centuries if the present rates of losses of species continue. In general, loss of biodiversity in a region may lead decline in plant production, lowered resistance to environment pertubations such as draught and increased variability in certain ecosystem process such as plant productivity, water use, pest and disease cyles. Tropical rain forests have a very high biodiversity compared with almost anywhere else in the world. When tropical rainforests are cut down or burnt, the habitats of thousands of different species are destroyed. The biodiversity of earth is vital for the very survival of mankind. This is our moral responsibility to protect the habitats of thousand of different species are destroyed.

96. The sentence in reference of importance of biodiversity in environment conservation is not very appropriate :
1. The quality of vegetables and fruits is required for good health
2. Bio diversity protects the quality of air and water
3. Environment safety is the key of happy life on earth
4. Biodiversity makes our planet beautiful

97. What should be the main work of mankind to conserve biodiversity:
1. Efforts to clean the earth
2. Efforts to control the pollution and justified use of resources
3. Efforts to maintain healthy society
4. Efforts to educate people for morality

98. Which ecosystem has the highest bio-diversity:
1. Desserts
2. Grass lands
3. Coral seeds
4. Boreal forests

99. Which is considered as ex-situ conservation measure:
1. National park
2. Wild Life Sanctuaries
3. Sacred grooves
4. Seed banks

100. Which is the prime service provided by the biodiversity:
1. Supplying food, medicine, wood etc.
2. Supporting cultural and aesthetic values
3. Providing clean air and water
4. Supply of fuel

ANSWERS

1	2	3	4	5	6	7	8	9	10
1	4	4	2	3	3	4	3	2	4
11	**12**	**13**	**14**	**15**	**16**	**17**	**18**	**19**	**20**
4	2	*	3	2	2	3	3	3	4
21	**22**	**23**	**24**	**25**	**26**	**27**	**28**	**29**	**30**
3	4	3	1	1	1	3	3	3	1
31	**32**	**33**	**34**	**35**	**36**	**37**	**38**	**39**	**40**
1	4	4	2	1	2	1	1	2	1
41	**42**	**43**	**44**	**45**	**46**	**47**	**48**	**49**	**50**
3	2	3	4	1	2	3	3	4	2
51	**52**	**53**	**54**	**55**	**56**	**57**	**58**	**59**	**60**
4	2	2	4	2	1	1	4	3	2
61	**62**	**63**	**64**	**65**	**66**	**67**	**68**	**69**	**70**
2	4	3	4	1	2	2	1	3	3
71	**72**	**73**	**74**	**75**	**76**	**77**	**78**	**79**	**80**
4	3	1	1	2	4	1	1	2	2
81	**82**	**83**	**84**	**85**	**86**	**87**	**88**	**89**	**90**
1	3	2	1	3	2	4	3	2	1
91	**92**	**93**	**94**	**95**	**96**	**97**	**98**	**99**	**100**
3	3	3	3	1	1	2	3	4	3

EXPLANATORY ANSWERS

1. Jatukama is not accepted as an Acharya of the Dhanwantar sect in this list. The Dhanwantar Sampradaya is mainly related to Shalya Tantra and the tradition of Lord Dhanvantari/Divodasa. Sushrut is the most prominent Acharya of this sect and is directly connected with surgical knowledge. Opdhenav and Karvirya are also counted among the disciples associated with Dhanvantari tradition. Therefore, among the given options, Jatukama is the one that does not fit as an Acharya of the Dhanwantar sect.

2. Sadvritta is the ethical discipline under Swasthavritta that assures psychosocial well-being. It deals with proper personal conduct, social behaviour, mental discipline, speech control, and moral living. Its purpose is to maintain harmony of mind, senses, body, family, and society. Ritucharya deals with seasonal regimen, and Ahar Vidhi Vidhan deals with rules of diet intake. Achara Rasayan also promotes good conduct, but the specific ethical discipline under Swasthavritta is Sadvritta.

3. The chapter sequence of Swasthya Chatushka in Sutra Sthana of Charak Samhita is 5, 6, 7, and 8. This Chatushka deals with preservation of health and daily-regimen-related principles. The chapters include important concepts of diet, seasonal regimen, suppression and non-suppression of urges, and sense-control. These topics are directly related to maintenance of Swasthya rather than disease treatment alone. Therefore, the correct chapter sequence of Swasthya Chatushka is 5, 6, 7, and 8.

4. "Viddhasya Shyavangta Jwaro dahah Panduta Shonitagamnam rakta Netrata Ch" signifies injury to Raktavah Srotasa. The symptoms mentioned include Shyavangata, Jwara, Daha, Panduta, Shonitagamana, and Raktanetrata. These features are directly connected with Rakta Dhatu and disturbance or injury of blood-carrying channels. Rasavah Srotasa, Mansavah Srotasa, and Medovah Srotasa have different viddha lakshanas. Hence, the described symptoms correctly fit with Raktavah Srotasa.

5. There are 16 Kandaras according to Ayurvedic anatomical description. Kandara is generally understood as a structure related to Snayu and is functionally important in movement. The number 16 is classically described with distribution in the body regions. Options 8, 12, and 20 do not match the accepted enumeration of Kandaras. Therefore, the correct number of Kandaras is 16.

6. According to Nyaya Philosophy, the number of Prameya is 12. Prameya means the object of valid knowledge, that which is known through Pramana. Nyaya Darshana accepts twelve Prameyas such as Atma, Sharira, Indriya, Artha, Buddhi, Manas, Pravritti, Dosha, Pretyabhava, Phala, Duhkha, and Apavarga. These are important because right knowledge of these Prameyas helps in removal of wrong knowledge and attainment of liberation. Therefore, among the given options, 12 is the correct number of Prameya according to Nyaya Philosophy.

7. Guru Guna of Dravya is the cause of Adhahpatan. Adhahpatan means downward movement or falling downward due to heaviness. Guru Guna denotes heaviness, density, and weight-bearing nature of a substance. Because of this heaviness, Guru Guna naturally produces downward tendency. Therefore, among Snigdha, Sheeta, Laghu, and Guru, the correct Guna responsible for Adhahpatan is Guru.

8. If a famous object is similar to a not so famous another object, it is known as Upman. Upman or Upamana is based on knowledge produced through similarity or comparison. In this process, an unknown or less-known object is understood by comparing it with a well-known object. The famous object serves as the basis for recognizing the unfamiliar object. Therefore, the correct answer is Upman, while Upmiti refers to the knowledge produced from Upman.

9. Trimada is Nagarmotha, Chitrakmool, and Vidanga. Trimada is a group of three drugs used in Ayurvedic formulations and clinical practice. Nagarmotha is also known as Musta, Chitrakmool is Chitraka root, and Vidanga is commonly used for digestive and Krimighna action. The combination of these three specifically forms Trimada. Therefore, among the given options, Nagarmotha, Chitrakmool, and Vidanga is the correct answer.

10. Apana Vayu is not located in Urah. Apana Vayu is mainly situated in the lower part of the body and is related to downward-moving functions. Its sites include regions such as Pakvashaya, Guda, Basti, Medhra, Vrishana, Uru, and Nabhi-related lower abdominal area. Urah means chest region, which is mainly related to Prana Vayu, not Apana Vayu. Therefore, among the given options, Urah is the correct answer because it is not a location of Apana Vayu.

11. Microcytic hypochromic red cells are typically found in iron deficiency anaemia. Microcytic means the red blood cells are smaller than normal, and hypochromic means they contain less haemoglobin than normal. Iron is essential for haemoglobin synthesis, so deficiency of iron causes reduced haemoglobin formation. Because of reduced haemoglobin, the red cells become pale and small in appearance. Megaloblastic anaemia and pernicious anaemia usually show macrocytic red cells, so they do not fit this question.

12. BCG vaccine is an example of a live attenuated vaccine. Live attenuated vaccines contain living organisms that have been weakened so that they do not usually cause disease in healthy individuals. BCG vaccine is prepared from an attenuated strain of Mycobacterium bovis. It is mainly used for protection against severe forms of tuberculosis, especially in children. Pneumococcal vaccine is not a live attenuated vaccine, and among the given options BCG is the best fitting answer.

13. The genotypic ratio of a monohybrid cross is 1 : 2 : 1. In a typical monohybrid cross between two heterozygous parents, such as Tt × Tt, the offspring genotypes are TT, Tt, Tt, and tt. This gives one homozygous dominant, two heterozygous, and one homozygous recessive individual. Therefore, the genotypic ratio becomes 1 : 2 : 1, while the phenotypic ratio is usually 3 : 1. Since 1 : 2 : 1 is not present in the given options, none of the listed options is fully correct.

14. Vacuole imparts turgidity and rigidity to the cell. In plant cells, the large central vacuole contains cell sap and helps maintain osmotic pressure. When water enters the vacuole, it creates turgor pressure against the cell wall. This turgor pressure keeps the plant cell firm, rigid, and turgid. The cell wall provides structural support, but the direct cause of turgidity is the water-filled vacuole.

15. DLS, or Dynamic Light Scattering, is used to measure particle size distribution. It measures the scattering of light caused by particles undergoing Brownian motion in a liquid medium. From this movement, the hydrodynamic diameter of particles can be calculated. DLS is commonly used for nanoparticles, colloids, polymers, proteins, and suspensions. It does not primarily measure particle composition, surface charge, or optical band gap.

16. TEM is primarily used in determining the morphology of nanoparticles. TEM means Transmission Electron Microscopy, and it gives direct visual information about the shape, size, and structure of nanoparticles. It is especially useful for observing whether nanoparticles are spherical, rod-shaped, irregular, aggregated, or well-dispersed. XRD is mainly used for crystallinity and crystal structure, while FTIR is used for functional groups. UV-VIS spectroscopy is mainly used for optical absorption behaviour, so TEM is the best answer for nanoparticle morphology.

17. The PCT is highly permeable to water. The proximal convoluted tubule reabsorbs a major portion of filtered water along with sodium, glucose, amino acids, and other useful substances. Water movement in PCT occurs passively along the osmotic gradient created by solute reabsorption. The descending limb of the loop of Henle is also water-permeable, but among the given nephron tubular parts, PCT is classically highly permeable and responsible for bulk water reabsorption. Therefore, the best fitting option given in the question is PCT.

18. Tropical deciduous forest is the correct answer because it has seasonal rainfall, an open canopy, and a well-developed undergrowth. Due to shedding of leaves in the dry season and availability of sunlight at the forest floor, shrubs and bushes grow abundantly in this ecosystem. This type of forest supports diverse flora, including trees, shrubs, herbs, climbers, and grasses in different layers. It also supports rich fauna because the vegetation provides food, shelter, and habitat for many animals, birds, reptiles, and insects. Therefore, the description of an ecosystem having abundance of shrubs and bushes along with diverse flora and fauna best fits tropical deciduous forest.

19. Z-Test is a statistical test of hypothesis based on Gaussian distribution and is generally used to compare two means or two proportions. It is applied when the sample size is large or when population standard deviation is known. The Gaussian distribution is also known as the normal distribution, and the Z-Test uses the standard normal curve. It helps determine whether the observed difference between means or proportions is statistically significant. Z-score is only a standardized value, while Wilcoxon test is non-parametric, so Z-Test is the correct answer.

20. The local document for any medical research is the protocol. A research protocol is the main written plan that describes how a medical research study will be conducted. It includes objectives, hypothesis, methodology, study design, sample size, data collection, ethical aspects, and analysis plan. Before beginning medical research, the protocol is usually submitted for review and approval. Data analysis and hypothesis are only parts of research, but the complete local research document is the protocol.

21. Assertion is correct because Agnivesha, the disciple of Acharya Punarvasu Atreya, composed Agnivesha Tantra. Acharya Charaka later refined, compiled, and elaborated that text, which became known as Charaka Samhita. The statement that other disciples of Acharya Punarvasu did not write their scriptures is not correct. Other disciples such as Bhela, Jatukarna, Parashara, Harita, and Ksharapani are also traditionally associated with their own treatises. Therefore, Assertion is correct, but Reason is incorrect.

22. Assertion is not correct because Kaumarbhritya is one of the main authority subjects of Kashyapa Samhita. Kashyapa Samhita is especially important in Ayurveda for Kaumarbhritya, which deals with child health, child diseases, and their management. Reason is correct because Kaumarbhritya includes description of diseases and treatment of children. It also includes subjects related to newborn care, infant care, nutrition, growth, and childhood disorders. Therefore, Assertion is incorrect, but Reason is correct.

23. Assertion is correct because Ayurveda describes health as equilibrium of Dosha, Dhatu, Mala, and Agni along with pleasant state of Atma, Indriya, and Mana. This definition includes physical, physiological, mental, sensory, and spiritual well-being. Reason is not correct because Swasthya cannot be maintained by balancing Dhatu alone. Dosha and Mala are also essential components of health and must remain in their normal balanced state. Therefore, Assertion is correct, but Reason is incorrect.

24. Assertion is correct because Lokapurusha Samya Siddhanta states that whatever exists in Loka, or universe, also exists in Purusha. This principle explains the similarity between the macrocosm and the human body. Reason is also correct because Purusha is considered a microcosm containing the elements and principles of the universe. The body is understood as a representative form of the universe at an individual level. Therefore, both Assertion and Reason are correct, and Reason correctly explains Assertion.

25. Assertion is correct because according to Ksheer-Dadhi Nyaya, the earlier Dhatu is transformed into the next Dhatu. This Nyaya explains Dhatu formation by the example of milk changing into curd. Reason is also correct because the previous Dhatu acts as the nourishing material for the succeeding Dhatu. In this view, Adya Dhatu becomes the source or Ahara for Uttar Dhatu during sequential Dhatu formation. Therefore, both Assertion and Reason are correct, and Reason correctly explains Assertion.

26. Yakrita and Pleeha are accepted as the Moola of Raktavah Srotas. Raktavah Srotas is directly related to Rakta Dhatu and its formation, maintenance, and circulation-related functions. Ranjaka Pitta is associated with the process of imparting colour and formation of Rakta, and Yakrita has an important role in this process. Pleeha is also closely related to Rakta because of its role in blood storage and destruction or collection of old blood cells. Therefore, both Assertion and Reason are correct, and the Reason properly explains why Yakrita and Pleeha are considered Moola of Raktavah Srotas.

27. Assertion is correct because the sixth Twacha is known as Rohini. In the classical description of Twacha layers, Rohini is counted as the sixth layer. However, the Reason is not correct because Rohini Twacha is not specifically described as the place of Kustha and Visarpa. Rohini is mainly associated with deeper pathological conditions such as Granthi, Apachi, Arbuda, Shlipada and similar disorders. Therefore, Assertion is correct, but the Reason given in the question is incorrect.

28. Assertion is correct because Sushruta has considered Hridaya as the seat of Chetana. Hridaya is regarded as an important vital organ and a central seat of consciousness-related functions. The Reason is not correct because Antahkarana Chatushtaya is commonly explained as Manas, Buddhi, Chitta, and Ahamkara. Atma is not included as one of the four components of Antahkarana Chatushtaya in that standard enumeration. Therefore, Assertion is correct, but the Reason is incorrect.

29. Assertion is correct because Haritaki is an Anulomana Dravya. Anulomana Dravya helps in proper downward movement of Vata and Mala after supporting digestion and separation of Mala. Haritaki is classically used to regulate bowel movement and promote normal evacuation through the lower tract. The Reason is not correct because the statement "excretes Slishta Mala without digestion through the lower tract" does not properly define Anulomana. Therefore, Haritaki being Anulomana is correct, but the given Reason is incorrect.

30. The Assertion is correct because Anumana is described as knowledge or reasoning based on Tarka and Yukti. Tarka means logical reasoning, and Yukti means rational application or logical arrangement, and their use helps in reaching inferential knowledge. The Reason is also correct because Anumana is the Karana of Anumiti, meaning Anumana is the means or instrument through which inferential knowledge is produced. Anumiti is the final knowledge obtained after the process of inference, while Anumana is the process or Pramana producing it. Therefore, both Assertion and Reason are correct, and the Reason correctly explains the nature of Anumana given in the Assertion.

31. Assertion is correct because Jalooka Bandh is described as a type of Parad Bandh. It is mentioned in relation to Vajikarana purpose and sexual functional use in weak, frail, or lustful persons. Reason is also correct because the stated use of Jalooka before intercourse is connected with stimulation and quick sexual response. The Reason explains the functional purpose mentioned in the Assertion, because it describes how Jalooka Bandh produces its intended effect. Therefore, both Assertion and Reason are correct, and Reason is the correct explanation of Assertion.

32. Assertion is not correct because the statement that Kukkut Puta should only be used for Lauh Bhasma is not correct. Different metals and minerals require different types and numbers of Puta according to the nature of the substance and desired Bhasma quality. Gaja Puta is classically important for preparation of many Bhasmas, but the exclusive restriction of Lauh Bhasma to only Kukkut Puta does not fit correctly. Reason is correct because properly prepared Bhasma by Puta becomes suitable for therapeutic use and should possess proper qualities. Therefore, Assertion is incorrect, but Reason is correct.

33. Assertion is not correct because IgM does not have the lowest molecular weight among immunoglobulins. IgM is the largest immunoglobulin because it is mainly present as a pentamer in serum. The lowest molecular weight immunoglobulin is generally IgG among the main immunoglobulin classes. Reason is correct because IgM is the primary immune response antibody and is usually the first antibody produced after infection. Therefore, Assertion is incorrect, but Reason is correct.

34. Assertion is correct because IQ score is an important tool in psychological assessment, especially for evaluating intellectual functioning, intellectual disability, developmental problems, learning difficulties, and cognitive impairment. Reason is also correct because the Wechsler scales are individually administered intelligence tests for children and adults. These scales assess different aspects of intelligence and provide IQ-related scores for clinical and educational evaluation. However, the Reason only describes the nature and use of Wechsler intelligence scales; it does not directly explain why IQ score is important for assessment of psychological disorders in general. Therefore, both Assertion and Reason are correct, but Reason is not the correct explanation of Assertion.

35. Assertion is correct because beta-oxidation of fatty acids occurs mainly in mitochondria. In this process, fatty acids are broken down step by step to produce acetyl-CoA. During beta-oxidation, reduced coenzymes NADH and $FADH_2$ are also produced. These NADH and $FADH_2$ enter the electron transport chain and help in ATP synthesis. Therefore, both Assertion and Reason are correct, and Reason correctly explains the importance of mitochondrial beta-oxidation.

36. Assertion is correct because Wernicke's area is situated at the posterior end of the superior temporal gyrus in the dominant hemisphere. This area is mainly present in the categorical or language-dominant hemisphere, usually the left hemisphere in most individuals. Reason is also correct because Wernicke's area is concerned with comprehension, interpretation, and understanding of auditory and visual language-related information. However, the Reason describes the function of Wernicke's area, not the anatomical reason for its location in the posterior superior temporal gyrus. Therefore, both Assertion and Reason are correct, but Reason is not the correct explanation of Assertion.

37. Assertion is correct because teratogenicity study is essential when a phytopharmaceutical drug is intended for use during pregnancy. This is required because any drug planned for use in pregnancy must be assessed for possible harmful effects on embryo-fetal development. Reason is also correct because a drug meant for pregnancy use needs such safety evaluation before it can be legally and ethically permitted for that use. The Reason explains why the teratogenicity study becomes essential in the clinical trial requirement for pregnancy-related use. Therefore, both Assertion and Reason are correct, and Reason is the correct explanation of Assertion.

38. Assertion is correct because a hypothesis is a tentative or speculative statement that is tested through a research study. It gives a proposed relationship between variables and is verified or rejected by systematic observation, data collection, and analysis. Reason is not correct because the two broad categories are not properly stated as research hypothesis and alternative hypothesis. In standard research methodology, hypotheses are commonly classified as null hypothesis and alternative or research hypothesis. Therefore, Assertion is correct, but Reason is incorrect.

39. This is the earliest stage in the development of Ayurveda literature. Ayurvedic concepts are first traced in Vedic literature, especially in relation to health, disease, herbs, and healing practices.

E. Samhita Kal Era: This follows the Vedic Era and represents the period of systematic classical Ayurvedic compendia. Important Samhitas such as Charaka Samhita and Sushruta Samhita belong to this stage of literary development.

B. Sangraha Era: This comes after the Samhita period and is marked by compilation and arrangement of earlier Ayurvedic knowledge. Texts such as Ashtanga Sangraha and Ashtanga Hridaya represent this phase of concise and organized presentation.

D. Ras Shastra Era: This follows the Sangraha Era and is marked by development of mineral, metallic, and mercurial preparations. Rasa Shastra literature expanded the pharmaceutics and therapeutic use of metals, minerals, and mercury-based preparations.

C. Nighantu Era: This comes after the Ras Shastra Era in the given sequence and is associated with lexicons of Dravyaguna. Nighantus describe names, properties, actions, and uses of medicinal substances in a systematic manner.

40. B. **Charak Nyas - Bhattar Harishchandra:** This is placed first in the chronological order of the given Charaka Samhita commentaries. Bhattar Harishchandra is considered an early commentator in the tradition of Charakà Samhita explanation.

C. **Nirantar Pad Vyakhya - Jejjat:** This comes after Bhattar Harishchandra in the chronological sequence. Jejjata is also an early commentator, and his commentary tradition precedes Chakrapani Datta.

A. **Ayurved Deepika - Chakrapani Datta:** This comes after Jejjata and is one of the most authoritative available commentaries on Charaka Samhita. Chakrapani Datta's Ayurved Deepika is highly important for understanding difficult words, concepts, and clinical meanings.

E. **Tatvapradipika Vyakhya - Shivdas Sen:** This comes after Chakrapani Datta in chronological order. Shivdas Sen belongs to a later period and contributed to the explanatory tradition of Charaka Samhita.

D. **Jalpkalptaru - Gangadhar Rai:** This is placed last among the given commentaries. Gangadhar Rai's Jalpakalpataru is a later commentary and therefore comes after the earlier commentators listed above.

41. B. **Avyakta:** Avyakta comes first in the sequence of creation of cosmos according to Ayurveda and Sankhya-based cosmological explanation. It is the unmanifest primordial state from which further evolution of creation begins.

A. **Buddhi:** From Avyakta, Buddhi or Mahat arises as the next stage in the sequence. Buddhi represents the principle of intelligence or cosmic determinative faculty in the process of evolution.

C. **Ahamkara:** From Buddhi, Ahamkara develops as the next principle. Ahamkara represents the ego-principle, from which further subtle elements and faculties evolve.

D. **Sookshma Panch Mahabhoot:** From Ahamkara, the subtle forms of the Panch Mahabhoota arise. These subtle elements act as the basis for further gross manifestation of the material world.

E. **Purusha Utapatti:** Purusha Utpatti is placed after the evolution of these principles in the given sequence.

Therefore, the correct order is Avyakta, Buddhi, Ahamkara, Sookshma Panch Mahabhoot, and Purusha Utpatti.

42. A. **Shishir:** Shishir Ritu comes first in the given seasonal sequence. It represents the late winter season and is followed by Basant or Vasanta Ritu.

B. **Basant:** Basant Ritu comes after Shishir Ritu in the seasonal order. It is the spring season and comes before Grishma Ritu.

E. **Grishm:** Grishm Ritu follows Basant Ritu in the sequence. It represents the summer season and comes before Varsha Ritu.

C. **Varsha:** Varsha Ritu comes after Grishm Ritu. It represents the rainy season and is followed by Sharad Ritu.

D. **Sharad:** Sharad Ritu comes after Varsha Ritu in the given sequence.

Thus, the correct order is Shishir, Basant, Grishm, Varsha, and Sharad.

43. D. **Vishalyghna Marma:** Vishalyaghna Marma comes first in increasing order because its number is 3. It has the least number among the given Marma types.

C. **Rujakar Marma:** Rujakara Marma comes next because its number is 8. It is greater than Vishalyaghna Marma but less than Sadya Pranahara Marma.

A. **Sadya Pranhar Marma:** Sadya Pranahara Marma comes next because its number is 19. It is greater than Rujakara Marma and less than Kalantara Pranahara Marma.

B. **Kalantar Pranhar Marma:** Kalantara Pranahara Marma comes next because its number is 33. It is greater than Sadya Pranahara Marma but less than Vaikalyakara Marma.

E. **Vaikaly Kar Marma:** Vaikalyakara Marma comes last in increasing order because its number is 44.

Therefore, the correct increasing sequence is Vishalyaghna, Rujakara, Sadya Pranahara, Kalantara Pranahara, and Vaikalyakara.

44. A. **Ishana Kona:** Ishana Kona is the north-east direction and comes first when considering the sequence of Konas from the northern side. It lies between north and east and is therefore the first Kona in this directional sequence.

D. **Agni Kona:** Agni Kona is the south-east direction and comes after Ishana Kona in clockwise order. It lies between east and south and follows the north-east corner.

C. **Nairitya Kona:** Nairitya Kona is the south-west direction and comes after Agni Kona. It lies between south and west in the circular directional arrangement.

B. **Vayavya Kona:** Vayavya Kona is the north-west direction and comes after Nairitya Kona.

Thus, the correct circular sequence of Konas is Ishana, Agni, Nairitya, and Vayavya.

45. E. **Atma:** Atma is the first essential factor in the sequence of Pratyaksha knowledge. Without Atma, the process of cognition and experience cannot be completed.

A. **Mana:** Mana comes next because it connects Atma with the sense organs. It acts as the internal instrument required for attention and cognition.

C. **Indriyan:** Indriyan come after Mana in the sequence of Sannikarsha. The sense organs make contact with their respective objects through the involvement of Mana.

D. **Vishaya:** Vishaya comes next because it is the object of perception. The Indriya must come into relation with Vishaya for Pratyaksha to arise.

B. **Pratyaksha Gyana:** Pratyaksha Gyana is the final result of proper contact among Atma, Mana, Indriya, and Vishaya.

Therefore, the correct sequence is Atma, Mana, Indriyan, Vishaya, and Pratyaksha Gyana.

46. D. Svedana: Svedana is the first Sanskara of Parad among the given steps. It is done to remove impurities and prepare Parad for further processing.

B. Mardana: Mardana comes after Svedana in the sequence of Parad Sanskara. In this step, Parad is triturated with suitable drugs to continue purification and processing.

E. Moorchhana: Moorchhana follows Mardana in the classical order of Parad Sanskara. It helps in reducing defects of Parad and making it suitable for further pharmaceutical procedures.

C. Uttapana: Uttapana comes after Moorchhana in the sequence of Parad Sanskara. It is the process by which Parad is revived or raised after the previous processing.

A. Patana: Patana comes after Uttapana in this sequence.

Therefore, the correct sequence is Svedana, Mardana, Moorchhana, Uttapana, and Patana.

47. D. Svedan: Svedan is the first step in the given sequence for Utthapan of Parad. In this step, processed or Moorchhita Parad is subjected to heating or steaming with suitable liquid media.

B. Prakshalan: Prakshalan comes after Svedan in the sequence. It means washing, which helps remove loosened impurities and residues from the processed Parad.

C. Mardan: Mardan is performed after Prakshalan. In this step, Parad is triturated properly with suitable substances for further refinement.

E. Atap: Atap comes after Mardan in the sequence. It helps in drying or exposing the processed Parad to heat or sunlight before the final step.

A. Patan: Patan is the final step in Utthapan of Parad.

Therefore, the correct sequence is Svedan, Prakshalan, Mardan, Atap, and Patan.

48. E. Dehydrated medium is dissolved in the appropriate volume of distilled water: This is the first step in preparation of culture media. The required quantity of dehydrated medium is mixed with the correct volume of distilled water.

A. The pH determination of fluid by pH meter: After dissolving the medium, pH is checked and adjusted if required. Correct pH is necessary for proper microbial growth and accuracy of culture results.

D. The Medium is boiled to dissolve the agar: Boiling is then done to dissolve agar completely. This gives a uniform medium before dispensing it into tubes or flasks.

B. The Medium is dispensed into tubes or flasks: After dissolving agar, the medium is dispensed into suitable containers. The quantity depends on whether slants, deeps, plates, or broth preparations are required.

C. The Medium is sterilized: Sterilization is the final step among the given options. It removes contaminating microorganisms and makes the culture medium suitable for use.

49. D. Autoimmune reaction against synovium membrane: Rheumatoid arthritis begins with autoimmune reaction against the synovial membrane. This immune response initiates chronic inflammation in the joint.

A. Inflammation of synovial membrane: Synovial inflammation occurs after autoimmune activation. The synovium becomes swollen, painful, thickened, and infiltrated by inflammatory cells.

C. Pannus formation: Pannus formation follows persistent synovial inflammation. Pannus is abnormal proliferative inflammatory synovial tissue that invades joint structures.

B. Cartilage destruction: Cartilage destruction occurs due to invasive pannus and inflammatory mediators. This leads to progressive damage of the articular surface.

E. Joint deformity: Joint deformity is the later consequence of cartilage destruction and joint damage.

Therefore, the correct sequence is autoimmune reaction, synovial inflammation, pannus formation, cartilage destruction, and joint deformity.

50. A. Atrial contraction: Atrial contraction occurs first in the given sequence of the cardiac cycle. It completes ventricular filling by pushing the remaining blood into the ventricles.

D. Isovolumetric ventricular contraction: Isovolumetric ventricular contraction follows atrial contraction. During this phase, ventricles contract while all valves remain closed and ventricular pressure rises.

B. Ventricular systole: Ventricular systole occurs after isovolumetric ventricular contraction. When ventricular pressure exceeds arterial pressure, blood is ejected into the aorta and pulmonary artery.

C. Isovolumetric ventricular relaxation: Isovolumetric ventricular relaxation follows ventricular systole. During this phase, ventricles relax while all valves are closed and ventricular pressure falls.

E. Initial rapid ventricular filling phase: Initial rapid ventricular filling occurs after isovolumetric relaxation. When AV valves open, blood rapidly flows from atria into ventricles, beginning the next filling phase.

51. E. Diaphragm contracts: During normal inspiration, the diaphragm contracts first and moves downward. This increases the vertical diameter of the thoracic cavity and starts expansion of the chest cavity.

B. External intercostal muscle contract: External intercostal muscles contract along with the diaphragm during inspiration. They elevate the ribs and sternum, increasing the anteroposterior and transverse diameters of the thoracic cavity.

A. Thoracic cavity increase: Due to contraction of diaphragm and external intercostal muscles, the thoracic cavity increases in size. This expansion increases lung volume and prepares the pressure change needed for air entry.

C. Intra alveolar pressure decrease: As lung volume increases, intra-alveolar pressure decreases below atmospheric pressure. This pressure gradient is essential for movement of air from outside into the lungs.

D. Air flow in to lungs: Air then flows into the lungs from the atmosphere.

Therefore, the correct sequence of events during inspiration is diaphragm contraction, external intercostal contraction, thoracic cavity increase, intra-alveolar pressure decrease, and air flow into lungs.

52. **C. Origin of project data:** The first stage in preparation of plans and projects is collection or origin of project data. Basic information and data are needed before a project can be properly formulated.

B. Formulation of project: After project data are available, the project is formulated. This stage converts the collected information into a definite project proposal or plan.

A. Appraisal of project: After formulation, appraisal of the project is carried out. The project is examined for feasibility, usefulness, cost, benefit, and practical suitability.

E. Selection of best project: After appraisal, the best project is selected from available alternatives. The choice is made on the basis of suitability, feasibility, priority, and expected outcome.

D. Implementation of project: Implementation is the final stage among the given options.

Therefore, the correct sequence is origin of project data, formulation of project, appraisal of project, selection of best project, and implementation of project.

53. **B. Identification and prioritizing the R and D needs:** The first component is identifying and prioritizing research and development needs. This decides the disease area, therapeutic need, and importance of drug development work.

A. Literature survey: After identifying the need, literature survey is done. Existing classical, experimental, clinical, pharmacological, and safety-related information is reviewed.

E. Formulation of hypothetical rationale: After literature survey, a hypothetical rationale is formulated. This gives the scientific and logical basis for initiating development of the proposed drug.

D. Initiation of drug development: After the rationale is framed, drug development is initiated. This includes planning the formulation, standardization approach, and development pathway.

C. Pre clinical safety, biological activity, stability study: Preclinical safety, biological activity, and stability studies follow initiation of drug development.

Therefore, the correct sequence is identification of R and D needs, literature survey, formulation of hypothetical rationale, initiation of drug development, and preclinical studies.

54. **B. After determining the H_0 and H_1 finding the difference between the mean of both the samples:** In an unpaired t-test, the null hypothesis and alternative hypothesis are first determined, then the difference between the two sample means is found. This gives the basic observed difference that has to be tested statistically.

D. By using the difference between two means, finding the standard error: After finding the difference between means, the standard error of the difference is calculated. The standard error shows the expected variation in the difference between two independent sample means.

A. To calculate the t-value by formula and finding the degree of freedom: After standard error is known, the t-value is calculated by the formula. The degree of freedom is also calculated because it is required for checking the t-table value.

E. To compare the t-table value and t-calculated value: The calculated t-value is then compared with the table value at the selected level of significance. This comparison helps decide whether the difference between the two sample means is statistically significant or not.

C. Conclusion: The final step is drawing the conclusion.

Therefore, the correct sequence is determining hypotheses and mean difference, calculating standard error, calculating t-value and degree of freedom, comparing values, and conclusion.

55. **C. Prakriti:** Prakriti is the first Vishaya in Dashavidha Pareeksha. It assesses the basic constitutional nature of the person.

A. Vikriti: Vikriti comes after Prakriti in Dashavidha Pareeksha. It assesses the present pathological state or morbidity of the patient.

E. Saar: Saar is assessed after Vikriti. It evaluates the excellence or quality of body tissues and strength of Dhatus.

B. Samhanan: Samhanan comes after Saar in the sequence. It refers to compactness and structural build of the body.

D. Pramana: Pramana comes after Samhanan in the given sequence.

Therefore, the correct sequence among the listed Dashavidha Pareeksha Vishayas is Prakriti, Vikriti, Saar, Samhanan, and Pramana.

56. **B. Dravyagun Vigyan, Rogi Parikshha-Vidhi:** These books are accepted among the works associated with Acharya Priyavrat Sharma. Dravyaguna Vigyan is especially a well-known contribution related to Ayurvedic pharmacology and medicinal plants.

E. Ayurved Anusandhan Paddhati, Charak Samagya: These are also accepted among the works associated with Acharya Priyavrat Sharma. They are related to Ayurvedic research methodology and Charaka-based technical terminology or concepts.

Therefore, among the given options, the correct set of books written by Acharya Priyavrat Sharma is B and E only. The other listed pairs include works that do not correctly fit as the given answer set for Acharya Priyavrat Sharma.

57. C. Ashtang Hridaya — Hemadri: This is a correct match because Hemadri is a commentator of Ashtanga Hridaya. His commentary is known as Ayurveda Rasayana and is an important commentary on Ashtanga Hridaya.

E. Charak Samhita — Shivdas Sen: This is also a correct match because Shivdas Sen is associated with commentary on Charaka Samhita. His commentary tradition is included among the later explanatory works on Charaka Samhita.

Therefore, the two correct matches among the given options are Ashtang Hridaya—Hemadri and Charak Samhita—Shivdas Sen. Gayadas is related to Sushruta Samhita, Bhattar Harishchandra is related to Charaka Samhita, and Dalhana is related to Sushruta Samhita, so those given pairings are not correct.

58. A. Panch Mahabhoot: Panch Mahabhoot are included in Dravya Samgraha according to Acharya Charaka. They form the basic material principles involved in the composition of substances.

B. Atma: Atma is also included in Dravya Samgraha. Charaka includes Atma among the fundamental Dravyas because it is essential in the explanation of life and consciousness.

D. Disha: Disha is also included among the Dravyas described in Dravya Samgraha. It represents direction and is counted among the basic categories accepted in this classification.

Therefore, the correct answer is Panch Mahabhoot, Atma, and Disha only. Pramana and Sambhava do not fit as members of Dravya Samgraha in this context.

59. A. Vicharya: Vicharya is one of the Vishayas of Mana according to Charaka. It refers to the object or content that is considered, examined, or reflected upon by the mind.

B. Chintya: Chintya is also one of the Vishayas of Mana. It means that which is thought about or mentally contemplated.

D. Dhyeya: Dhyeya is also included among the Vishayas of Mana. It refers to that which is meditated upon or fixed as an object of mental attention.

Therefore, the correct Vishayas of Mana among the given options are Vicharya, Chintya, and Dhyeya. Ekatva and Indriyabhigraha are not the correct items in this specific list of Mana Vishayas.

60. B. Rakta-Pitta, Asthi-Nakha: This is a correct combination because Pitta is described as Mala of Rakta Dhatu. Nakha is also accepted as a Mala of Asthi Dhatu along with other hard body structures related to Asthi.

E. Meda-Sweda, Asthi-Loma: This is also a correct combination because Sweda is the Mala of Meda Dhatu. Loma is also included among the Mala related to Asthi Dhatu in the classical Dhatu-Mala relationship.

Therefore, the correct combinations of Dhatu and its Mala are B and E only. The other combinations are incorrect because Rakta-Sweda, Mansa-Sweda, Asthi-Akshi Sneha, and Rasa-Pitta do not correctly match the standard Dhatu-Mala relationship.

61. A. Forgiveness: Forgiveness is a feature associated with Mamsa Sara Purusha. Such a person is described as having good physical and mental stability due to excellence of Mamsa Dhatu.

B. Patience: Patience is also a feature of Mamsa Sara Purusha. The person generally shows tolerance, firmness, steadiness, and balanced behaviour.

C. Wellness/Health: Wellness or good health is also included among the features of Mamsa Sara Purusha. Excellence of Mamsa Dhatu gives strength, stability, proper body build, and good endurance.

Therefore, the correct features among the given options are Forgiveness, Patience, and Wellness/Health. Glowing complexion is more related to Twak or Rakta Sara, and Pain Endurance is not the best fitting item in this given option set.

62. E. Vishada: Vishada is not a Paradi Guna. It is included among the Gurvadi Gunas and denotes clarity, non-sliminess, or clearness.

C. Sthoola: Sthoola is not a Paradi Guna. It is also counted under Gurvadi Gunas and indicates grossness or largeness.

A. Sthira: Sthira is not a Paradi Guna. It is a Gurvadi Guna and denotes stability or firmness.

Therefore, Sthira, Sthoola, and Vishada are not Paradi Gunas. Yukti and Abhyasa are included in Paradi Gunas, so they are not selected here.

63. C. Sanyoga: Sanyoga is not counted among the Bhava Padarthas. It is generally included under Guna in the Vaisheshika system and therefore is not one of the main Bhava Padarthas.

E. Sanskar: Sanskar is also not counted among the Bhava Padarthas. It is also included under Guna and does not stand as a separate Bhava Padartha.

Therefore, among the given options, Sanyoga and Sanskar are not Bhava Padarthas. Dravya, Guna, and Vishesh are counted among Bhava Padarthas, so they are not selected as incorrect items.

64. A. Deepan: Medicines properly Pachit by Puta have Deepan quality. This means they can stimulate digestive and metabolic activity when properly prepared.

B. Nirutth: Nirutth is an important quality of properly prepared Bhasma. It indicates that the metal or mineral does not return to its original metallic form after proper incineration.

D. Varitar: Varitar is also a quality of properly prepared Bhasma. It means the Bhasma is so light and properly processed that it can float on water.

Therefore, the correct qualities are Deepan, Nirutth, and Varitar. Teekshna and Achchhadan are not the correct qualities asked in this specific set.

65. A. **Pinaka:** Pinaka is one of the kinds of Abhrak. It is included in the classicai classification of Abhrak varieties.

B. **Naga:** Naga is also one of the kinds of Abhrak. It is counted among the varieties described in Rasa Shastra.

D. **Mandooka:** Mandooka is also one of the kinds of Abhrak. It is one of the accepted classical types of Abhrak.

Therefore, the correct kinds of Abhrak among the given options are Pinaka, Naga, and Mandooka. Swarna and Rajat are metals and are not types of Abhrak in this classification.

66. B. **Basophils:** Basophils are responsible for allergic reactions because they contain histamine and other inflammatory mediators. They participate especially in immediate hypersensitivity and IgE-mediated allergic responses.

D. **Mast Cells:** Mast cells are also responsible for allergic reactions and are very important in allergy and anaphylaxis. They release histamine, leukotrienes, and other mediators after activation by antigen-IgE reaction.

Therefore, the correct cells responsible for allergic reactions are Basophils and Mast Cells only. Neutrophils and monocytes are mainly involved in inflammation and phagocytosis, while RBCs are not allergy-mediating cells.

67. C. **Holding method:** Holding method is a method of pasteurisation used in the dairy industry. It is also known as the low-temperature long-time method, where milk is heated at a lower temperature for a longer duration.

E. **Flash method:** Flash method is also used in dairy pasteurisation. It is a high-temperature short-time method in which milk is heated rapidly for a short duration and then cooled quickly.

Therefore, the pasteurisation methods used in the dairy industry among the given options are Holding method and Flash method only. Radiation, osmotic pressure, and blanching are not the standard dairy pasteurisation methods asked in this question.

68. A. **Deoxycytidine:** Deoxycytidine is one of the nucleosides found in DNA. It contains the base cytosine attached to deoxyribose sugar.

B. **Deoxythymidine:** Deoxythymidine is also one of the DNA nucleosides. It contains thymine attached to deoxyribose sugar.

D. **Deoxyadenosine:** Deoxyadenosine is also present in DNA. It contains adenine attached to deoxyribose sugar.

E. **Deoxyguanosine:** Deoxyguanosine is also one of the four nucleosides found in DNA. It contains guanine attached to deoxyribose sugar.

Therefore, the four DNA nucleosides are Deoxycytidine, Deoxythymidine, Deoxyadenosine, and Deoxyguanosine. Deoxycryptine is not a standard nucleoside found in DNA.

69. A. **Glycogen:** Glycogen is a polysaccharide made up of many glucose units. It is the storage carbohydrate in animals and is highly branched in structure.

B. **Agarose:** Agarose is also a polysaccharide. It is obtained from agar and is commonly used in gel electrophoresis.

D. **Chitin:** Chitin is also a polysaccharide. It is made of N-acetylglucosamine units and forms structural material in arthropods and fungal cell walls.

Therefore, the polysaccharides among the given options are Glycogen, Agarose, and Chitin only. Titin and cytochrome are proteins, so they are not polysaccharides.

70. A. **Storage of bile:** Storage of bile is a major function of the gall bladder. Bile formed by the liver is stored in the gall bladder between meals.

B. **Control of flow of bile following a meal:** The gall bladder helps control bile flow after a meal by contraction. This allows bile to enter the duodenum when fat-containing food is present.

D. **Regulates equalization of pressure in biliary system:** The gall bladder helps regulate pressure within the biliary system. It acts as a reservoir and accommodates bile, helping maintain pressure balance.

E. **Secretes mucin (mucus):** The gall bladder mucosa secretes mucus or mucin. This protects and lubricates the mucosal lining and contributes to gall bladder function.

Therefore, the correct functions are storage of bile, control of bile flow after meal, pressure regulation in biliary system, and secretion of mucin. Increasing the alkalinity of stored bile is not a correct function, because bile usually becomes more concentrated during storage.

71. A. **Medical scientist:** A medical scientist is included in the Institutional Ethics Committee because scientific assessment of biomedical research is necessary. This member helps in evaluating the scientific basis and medical relevance of the proposed research.

B. **Legal expert or retired judge:** A legal expert or retired judge is included to assess legal and regulatory aspects of research. This helps protect rights, safety, dignity, and lawful interests of research participants.

D. **Social scientist:** A social scientist is included to represent social, cultural, and community-related dimensions of research. This member helps judge whether the study is socially acceptable and ethically appropriate.

E. **Clinician:** A clinician is included because clinical judgment is necessary in medical research involving patients or human participants. The clinician helps assess risk, benefit, patient safety, and clinical relevance of the study.

72. A. **Indriya:** Indriya is essential for Pratyaksha Pramana because sense organs receive the object-related information. Without contact of sense organ with its object, direct perception cannot arise.

B. **Man:** Man is essential because it connects the Indriya with Atma during the process of perception. Even if the sense organ contacts the object, perception does not occur properly without attention of Man.

D. **Atma:** Atma is essential because it is the conscious knower in the process of Pratyaksha. The final experience of knowledge belongs to Atma through proper association with Man and Indriya.

E. **Arth:** Arth or Vishaya is essential because it is the object that is perceived through the sense organ.

Therefore, Indriya, Man, Atma, and Arth are the four essential factors for Pratyaksha Pramana.

73. A. **Astaang Hridaya Tika Sarvang Sundara — II. Commentator Arun Datta:** Sarvang Sundara is the commentary of Ashtanga Hridaya written by Arun Datta. This is one of the important and well-known commentaries on Ashtanga Hridaya.

B. **Astaang Hridaya Tika Ayurved Rasayan — III. Commentator Hemadri:** Ayurved Rasayan is the commentary of Ashtanga Hridaya written by Hemadri. Hemadri's commentary is important for understanding the deeper meaning of Ashtanga Hridaya.

C. **Astaang Hridaya Tika Padarth Chandrika — IV. Commentator Chandra Nandan:** Padarth Chandrika is matched with Chandra Nandan. This pairing correctly connects the commentary name with its commentator in the given list.

D. **Astaang Hridaya Tika Shashilekha — I. Commentator Indu:** Shashilekha is matched with commentator Indu.

Therefore, the correct matching sequence is A-II, B-III, C-IV, and D-I.

74. A. **Bhore Committee — IV. Year of Establishment 1945:** In the given matching options, Bhore Committee is matched with 1945. This is the only option-set that correctly accommodates the remaining established Ayurveda-related committee chronology given in the question.

B. **Chopra Committee — III. Year of Establishment 1946:** Chopra Committee is matched with 1946. It is an important committee related to Ayurveda and indigenous systems of medicine in the modern period.

C. **Pandit Committee — II. Year of Establishment 1949:** Pandit Committee is matched with 1949. It followed earlier committee recommendations and is included in the historical development of Ayurveda institutions and research.

D. **Udup Committee — I. Year of Establishment 1958:** Udupa Committee is matched with 1958.

Therefore, the correct matching sequence according to the given options is A-IV, B-III, C-II, and D-I.

75. A. **Aakash — III. Sound:** Aakash Mahabhuta is mainly associated with Shabda or sound. Sound is the special property by which Aakash is understood.

B. **Vayu — I. Touch:** Vayu Mahabhuta is mainly associated with Sparsha or touch. Movement and tactile sensation are important features connected with Vayu.

C. **Jal — IV. Taste:** Jal Mahabhuta is mainly associated with Rasa or taste. Taste is possible due to the presence and dominance of the water element.

D. **Prithvi — II. Odour:** Prithvi Mahabhuta is mainly associated with Gandha or odour.

Therefore, the correct matching sequence is Aakash-Sound, Vayu-Touch, Jal-Taste, and Prithvi-Odour.

76. A. **Rasa — II. Preenana:** Rasa Dhatu performs Preenana function. It nourishes the body and provides primary nutrition to other Dhatus.

B. **Rakta — I. Jeevana:** Rakta Dhatu performs Jeevana function. It supports life by maintaining vitality and sustaining the living body.

C. **Asthi — IV. Dharana:** Asthi Dhatu performs Dharana function. It gives support, framework, firmness, and structural stability to the body.

D. **Majja — III. Poorana:** Majja Dhatu performs Poorana function. It fills the cavities of bones and contributes to strength and nourishment.

77. A. **First month — II. Kalal:** In the first month of pregnancy, the Garbha is described as Kalala. This represents the earliest undifferentiated stage of embryonic development.

B. **Third month — I. Hasta Pad Shirsam Panch Pidika:** In the third month, five buds appear representing head, two hands, and two feet. This stage shows the beginning of visible limb and head differentiation.

C. **Fifth month — IV. Manah Prati Buddhrataram bhavati:** In the fifth month, Mana becomes more developed or awakened. This indicates progression of mental and functional development of the fetus.

D. **Eight month — III. Oj:** In the eighth month, Ojas is especially significant. Ojas is described as unstable or moving between mother and fetus during this period.

78. A. **Asthi Shool — II. Asthikshaya:** Asthi Shoola is a Lakshana related to Asthi Kshaya. When Asthi Dhatu decreases, pain in bones can appear as an important feature.

B. **Asthyadhyasthi — III. Asthivriddhi:** Asthyadhyasthi is related to Asthi Vriddhi. It indicates abnormal excess growth or overgrowth associated with increased Asthi Dhatu.

C. **Vatlanam Sevnat — IV. Asthi Vah Srotodushhi Nidan:** Excess intake or use of Vatala substances is a cause of Asthivaha Srotodushti. Vata aggravating factors disturb Asthi Dhatu and its channels.

D. **Kesh lom — I. Asthi Mala:** Kesha and Loma are considered Mala related to Asthi Dhatu. They are external waste products or by-products associated with Asthi metabolism.

79. A. **Rasa Kshaya — IV. Hriday Peeda:** Rasa Kshaya is matched with Hridaya Peeda. Deficiency of Rasa Dhatu affects nourishment and may produce cardiac discomfort or pain.

B. Rakta Kshaya — I. Sira Shaithilya: Rakta Kshaya is matched with Sira Shaithilya. When Rakta Dhatu decreases, looseness or weakness of vessels may be seen.

C. Meda Kshaya — II. Sandhi Sfutan: Meda Kshaya is matched with Sandhi Sfutana. Reduction of Meda affects lubrication and cushioning, leading to cracking sensation in joints.

D. Asthi Kshaya — III. Sandhi Shaithilya: Asthi Kshaya is matched with Sandhi Shaithilya. Decrease of Asthi Dhatu weakens skeletal support and may cause looseness of joints.

80. A. Urdhav bhag har — II. Madanphala: Madanphala is Urdhvabhagahara because it acts mainly through the upward route. It is classically used as a Vamana Dravya for expelling Dosha through emesis.

B. Adhobhaghar — III. Snuhi: Snuhi is Adhobhagahara because it acts through the downward route. It is associated with Virechana action and expels Dosha through the lower passage.

C. Ubhaytobhag har — IV. Devadali: Devadali is Ubhayatobhagahara because it can act through both upward and downward routes. It is used for expelling Dosha from both directions according to its action.

D. Shirovirechan — I. Shigru: Shigru is used for Shirovirechana action. It helps in cleansing or eliminating Dosha from the head region through nasal route.

81. A. Nyaya — IV. Arambha vada: Nyaya Darshan is matched with Arambhavada. Arambhavada explains that the effect is a new beginning or new production and is not already present in the cause in the same manifest form.

B. Sankhya — I. Satkaryavada (Parinamvada): Sankhya Darshan is matched with Satkaryavada or Parinamvada. According to this view, the effect already exists in the cause in unmanifest form and becomes manifest through transformation.

C. Bauddha — II. Kshanabhangur vada: Bauddha Darshan is matched with Kshanabhangurvada. This doctrine explains momentariness, meaning things exist only momentarily and are continuously changing.

D. Vaisheshik — III. Parmanu vada: Vaisheshika Darshan is matched with Paramanuvada. Vaisheshika explains the material world through eternal atoms or Paramanu as fundamental units.

82. A. Nausadar — III. NH_4Cl (Ammonium Chloride): Nausadar is chemically ammonium chloride. Its chemical formula is NH_4Cl, so this match is correct.

B. Cinnebar — IV. HgS (Red Sulphide of Mercury): Cinnabar is chemically mercuric sulphide. It is red sulphide of mercury and its chemical formula is HgS.

C. Litharge — II. PbO (Lead Oxide): Litharge is chemically lead monoxide. Its chemical formula is PbO, so this is the correct match.

D. Coveries — I. $CaCO_3$ (Calcium Carbonate): Cowries are mainly composed of calcium carbonate.

Therefore, Coveries are correctly matched with $CaCO_3$.

83. A. T.M. Alpha-fetoprotein AFB — I. Testicular Cancer: Alpha-fetoprotein is used as a tumour marker in testicular cancer, especially non-seminomatous germ cell tumours. It can also be associated with other conditions, but in the given matching set it fits testicular cancer.

B. T.M. CA 125 — III. Ovarian Cancer: CA 125 is commonly associated with ovarian cancer. It is especially used in monitoring epithelial ovarian cancer and assessing disease course.

C. T.M. CA 19.9 — II. Various Carcinomas: CA 19.9 is associated with various carcinomas, especially pancreatic and gastrointestinal malignancies. In the given list, "Various Carcinomas" is the best matching option for CA 19.9.

D. PSA — IV. Prostate Cancer: PSA means prostate-specific antigen. It is matched with prostate cancer because it is an important marker used in prostate-related assessment.

84. A. Bacillus Calmette Guerin BCG — II. At birth: BCG vaccine is given at birth. It is administered early to provide protection against severe forms of tuberculosis in children.

B. Oral Polio Vaccine-1 OPV-1 — I. 6 Weeks: OPV-1 is given at 6 weeks. It is part of the primary immunization schedule after the birth dose of OPV.

C. Human Papilloma Virus HPV — IV. 9 to 14 Year girls: HPV vaccine is given to girls in the age group of 9 to 14 years. It helps protect against HPV infection and related cervical cancer risk.

D. Measles and Rubella MR — III. 9 to 12 months: MR vaccine is given at 9 to 12 months. It protects against measles and rubella and is included in childhood immunization schedules.

85. A. Mitochondria — II. Power houses of the cell: Mitochondria are called the power houses of the cell. They produce ATP through cellular respiration and supply energy for cellular functions.

B. Endoplasmic reticulum — IV. Provides supportive framework for the cell: Endoplasmic reticulum provides an internal supportive framework in the cytoplasm. It also helps in intracellular transport and synthesis-related functions.

C. Ribosomes — I. Protein Synthesis: Ribosomes are the sites of protein synthesis. They translate messenger RNA and assemble amino acids into proteins.

D. Lysosomes — III. Destroy bacteria and Foreign bodies: Lysosomes contain digestive enzymes that help destroy bacteria and foreign bodies. They also digest worn-out cell parts and participate in intracellular digestion.

86. A. PCR — III. Used for amplification of DNA to make millions of copies of a specific sequence: PCR is used to amplify DNA. It produces many copies of a selected DNA segment for diagnosis, research, and molecular analysis.

B. Gel electrophoresis — IV. Used to separate DNA, RNA or protein fragments based on their size and charge: Gel electrophoresis separates biomolecules by movement through gel under electric field. Smaller fragments usually move faster, so separation occurs according to size and charge.

C. ELISA — I. Use of detection and quantification of antigen or antibodies in a sample: ELISA is used for detecting and measuring antigens or antibodies. It is commonly used in immunology, diagnosis, and serological testing.

D. Tissue Culture — II. Used to grow plant or animal cells under controlled laboratory conditions: Tissue culture is used to grow cells or tissues outside the body. It is performed under sterile and controlled laboratory conditions.

87. A. Salivary Glands — II. Lingual Lipase: Lingual lipase is associated with secretion in the oral region. It begins lipid digestion and is grouped with enzymes acting from the mouth region.

B. Stomach — I. Renin in infants: Renin or rennin is present in the stomach of infants. It helps in coagulation of milk protein and supports digestion of milk in infants.

C. Pancreas — IV. Chymotrypsin: Chymotrypsin is a pancreatic proteolytic enzyme. It is secreted as chymotrypsinogen and becomes active in the small intestine for protein digestion.

D. Small Intestine — III. Erepsin: Erepsin is associated with the intestinal juice of the small intestine. It helps in final digestion of peptides into amino acids.

88. A. Carbon dioxide — III. Burning Fossil Fuels: Carbon dioxide is released in large quantity by burning fossil fuels. It is one of the major gases contributing to the greenhouse effect.

B. Methane — IV. Decay of Organic matter, e.g. faeces of animals: Methane is produced by decay of organic matter. Animal waste, anaerobic decomposition, and related biological processes release methane.

C. CFCs — I. Refrigerators and air conditioning: CFCs were widely used in refrigerators and air-conditioning systems. They contribute to environmental damage and are also greenhouse gases.

D. Nitrogen Oxides — II. Fertilisers, burning fossil fuels: Nitrogen oxides are released from fertilisers and fossil fuel burning. They contribute to atmospheric pollution and greenhouse-related environmental effects.

89. A. The process of selecting a sample using networks — II. Snowball sampling: Snowball sampling uses networks and referrals. One participant helps identify other participants, so the sample grows like a snowball.

B. The process of selecting a sample from a large population — IV. Cluster sampling: Cluster sampling is used when a large population is divided into clusters. Some clusters are selected, and members from those selected clusters are studied.

C. Sampling based on convenience in accessing the sampling population — I. Accidental sampling: Accidental sampling is based on convenient or easily available subjects. Participants are included because they are accessible at the time of data collection.

D. Sampling with consideration of researcher's ease to access to the sample population — III. Quota sampling: Quota sampling involves selecting participants according to fixed categories or quotas. In the given option set, it is matched with researcher-controlled selection from accessible sample groups.

90. A. Chi-Square Test — III. For testing the hypothesis: Chi-square test is a non-parametric test used for hypothesis testing with categorical data. It helps test whether observed frequencies differ significantly from expected frequencies.

B. Fisher's Exact Test — IV. To test the significance of the association between two classification: Fisher's exact test is used to test association between two categorical classifications. It is especially useful when sample size is small or expected cell frequencies are low.

C. Mc Nemar's Test — II. For paired nominal data: McNemar's test is used for paired nominal data. It is applied when the same subjects are assessed in two related conditions with categorical outcomes.

D. Wilcoxon Test — I. For comparing the repetitive measures of the same sample or two related samples: Wilcoxon test is used for related or paired samples. It compares repeated measures when data do not satisfy parametric test assumptions.

91. According to Acharya Charak, Sauviranjana is advised for daily use in the eyes as part of Anjana in Dinacharya. The option "Every 5th or 8th Day" is not correct for Sauviranjana because that periodic use is associated with Rasanjana. The question specifically asks about Sauviranjana, so the answer must be selected according to Sauviranjana only. Since Sauviranjana is suitable for regular application in the daily regimen for protection and maintenance of eye health, "Daily" fits the question exactly. Therefore, option 3 is the correct answer.

92. The passage clearly states that Dinacharya protects health by integrating daily routine with the natural rhythm. It further explains that health is achieved when daily activities and behavior are in accordance with natural cycles. Waking up at Brahmamuhurta, daily Abhyanga and daily exercise are important individual parts of Dinacharya, but they do not represent the whole principle asked in the question. The most important factor for maintaining health is the complete daily routine according to natural rhythm. Therefore, option 3 is the correct answer.

93. The correct intended answer in the given option set is Vata, although the option is printed as "Vala." Daily Abhyanga mainly pacifies Vata dosha because oil massage reduces dryness, roughness, stiffness and instability. These features are chiefly related to Vata, and Abhyanga provides smoothness, nourishment, strength and stability to the body. Pitta, Kapha and Rakta are not the main factors alleviated by daily Abhyanga in this context. Therefore, option 3 is the correct answer.

94. In Ayurvedic Dinacharya, daily Abhyanga is specifically praised for preventing ageing and reducing the effects of old age. Anjana is also included in the daily routine for maintaining the health of the sense organs, especially the eyes. The question asks the most important measure to prevent premature aging, and among the options, daily massage has the most direct classical connection with prevention of ageing. Healthy food and a happy mind are important for general health, but the option that more specifically fits premature ageing in Dinacharya is daily massage and Anjana. Therefore, option 3 is the correct answer.

95. Dhatusamya means the balanced state of body constituents, including the equilibrium of dosha, dhatu and mala. Swasthavritta mainly deals with maintenance of health and prevention of disease. Its purpose is to preserve this balanced state so that disease does not arise. The passage also states that Dinacharya keeps dosha, dhatu and mala in a balanced state and protects health. Therefore, Dhatusamya is best considered the objective of Swasthavritta, so option 1 is the correct answer.

96. The question asks which sentence is not very appropriate in reference to the importance of biodiversity in environmental conservation. Biodiversity directly helps in protecting air, water, ecological balance, ecosystem stability and the beauty of the planet. The quality of vegetables and fruits is related more to human nutrition and health than to the broader environmental conservation role of biodiversity. Although biodiversity may indirectly support food quality, this option does not directly express the importance of biodiversity in conserving the environment. Therefore, option 1 is the most appropriate answer for the sentence that is not very suitable in this context.

97. The passage explains that biodiversity is being lost due to human activities and that mankind has a moral responsibility to protect habitats and species. Conservation of biodiversity requires controlling pollution, preventing destruction of habitats and using natural resources in a justified and sustainable manner. Cleaning the earth, maintaining healthy society and educating people about morality are useful ideas, but they are not as direct and complete for biodiversity conservation. Pollution control and proper use of resources directly reduce pressure on ecosystems and species. Therefore, option 2 is the correct answer.

98. Among the given ecosystems, coral reefs have the highest biodiversity. The option "Coral seeds" is evidently intended to mean "Coral reefs." Coral reefs support a very large number of marine organisms and are often compared with tropical rainforests because of their extremely rich biodiversity. Deserts, grasslands and boreal forests have lower biodiversity in comparison. Therefore, option 3 is the correct answer.

99. Ex-situ conservation means conservation of species outside their natural habitat. Seed banks preserve seeds under controlled conditions away from the original natural ecosystem, so they are a clear example of ex-situ conservation. National parks, wildlife sanctuaries and sacred groves protect species within their natural habitats, so they are examples of in-situ conservation. Since the question specifically asks for an ex-situ conservation measure, the correct answer is seed banks. Therefore, option 4 is the correct answer.

100. Biodiversity provides many services such as food, medicine, wood, fuel, cultural value, aesthetic value and ecological stability. However, the prime service in the context of environmental conservation is maintaining life-supporting conditions such as clean air and clean water. These services are essential for the survival of mankind and for the proper functioning of ecosystems. The passage emphasizes that biodiversity is vital for the survival of mankind and helps maintain ecosystem processes. Therefore, option 3 is the best answer.

Previous Years' Paper

National Testing Agency (NTA)

UGC-NET Junior Research Fellowship & Assistant Professor Eligibility Exam

AYURVEDA BIOLOGY, JUNE-2025

(Exam held on 28-06-2025)

PAPER-II

1. Write in correct order, the chatushka of Charaka Samhita Sutrasthana

A. Swasthya Chatushka B. Roga Chatushka
C. Kalpana Chatushka D. Yojana Chatushka
E. Nirdesh Chatushka

Choose the *correct* answer from the options given below:

1. A, C, D, E, B 2. E, D, C, B, A
3. A, E, C, B, D 4. D, B, C, E, A

2. Match List-I with List-II:

List-I (Original Text)	List-II (Commentators)
A. Sharangdhar Samhita	I. Chakrapani
B. Sushrut Samhita	II. Dalhana
C Ashtanga Samgraha	III. Adhamal
D Charaka Samhita	IV. Indu

Choose the *correct* answer from the options given below:

1. A-IV, B-I, C-III , D-II
2. A-III, B-II, C-IV, D-I
3. A-IV, B-III, C-II, D-I
4. A-III, B-I, C-II, D-IV

3. Which of the following is **NOT** considered among the Shad Padartha?

A. Samavaya B. Samanya
C. Samyoga D. Vishesha
E. Vibhaga

Choose the ***most appropriate*** answer from the options given below:

1. B and D only 2. C and E only
3. A and D only 4. C and D only

4. Where is WHO's first Global Centre for Traditional Medicine located?

1. Geneva 2. Beijing
3. Gandhinagar 4. Jamnagar

5. Which of the following Mahabhuta, dominant substances have MRUDU property common in them?

A. Akashatmak B. Agneya
C. Apya D. Parthiva
E. Vayaviya

Choose the ***most appropriate*** answer from the options given below:

1. B and E only
2. C, D and E only
3. A and C only
4. A and E only

6. Which among the following is **NOT** Karana Dravya?

1. Disha 2. Kaala
3. Akash 4. Buddhi

7. How many types of Manasik Prakriti are described in Ayurveda?

1. Four (4)
2. Seven (7)
3. Sixteen (16)
4. Twenty (20)

8. What are Rasa panchaka amongst the following that describe medicinal properties and actions of substance?

1. Madhura-Amla-Lavana-Katu-Kashaya
2. Madhura-Amla-Katu-Tikta-Kashaya
3. Rasa-Guna-Veerya-Vipaka-Prabhava
4. Madhura-Amla-Lavana-Katu-Tikta

9. What are the components of Shad-dhatuj Purush?

1. Tridosh + Triguna
2. Panchamahabhuta + Atma
3. Six Rasas
4. Five gyanendriya + Atma

10. Match List-I with List-II:

List-I (Season)	List-II (Dosha effect)
A. Sharad	I. Vata Prakopa
B. Vasanta	II. Pitta Prakopa
C Varsha	III. Kapha Prakopa
D Grishma	IV. Vata Sanchaya

Choose the ***correct*** answer from the options given below:

1. A-I, B-III, C-IV, D-II
2. A-II, B-III, C-I, D-IV
3. A-IV, B-I, C-III, D-II
4. A-III, B-IV, C-II, D-I

11. Which among the following Dosha subtypes take part in Digestion related function?

A. Prana Vayu
B. Kledaka Kapha
C. Samana Vayu
D. Tarpak Kapha
E. Sadhaka Pitta

Choose the ***most appropriate*** answer from the options given below:

1. A, C, D only
2. A, B, C only
3. A, B, E only
4. A, C, E only

12. Choose the correct statements regarding OJAS in Ayurveda.

A. It is essence of all seven dhatus.
B. It is eighth Dhatu.
C. It co-ordinates the function of Dosha.
D. It is an upadhatu of Rakta.
E. It is formed at the initial stages of fetal development.

Choose the ***most appropriate*** answer from the options given below:

1. A, B, C only
2. A, C, E only
3. C, D, E only
4. B, C, E only

13. Match List-I with List-II:

List-I (Prakriti Lakshana)	List-II (Guna/Tri-dosha Properties)
A. Jagaruka (shallow sleep)	I. Drava
B. Asheeghra Samarambha (slow in initiation)	II. Sandra
C Upachita Anga (Well built and nourished body)	III. Stimita
D Shithila mrudu sandhi maans (soft and loose joint muscles)	IV. Ruksha

Choose the ***correct*** answer from the options given below:

1. A-IV, B-III, C-I, D-II
2. A-I, B-IV, C-II, D-III
3. A-IV, B-III, C-II, D-I
4. A-III, B-I, C-II, D-IV

14. शिथिलमृदुसंधिमांसा: is the Lakshan of which Dosha-guna Prakriti?

1. Sandra guna of Kapha
2. Drava guna of Pitta
3. Madhur guna of Kapha
4. Katu Amla guna of Pitta

15. Match List-I with List-II:

List-I (Dhatu)	List-II (Updhatu)
A. Rakta	I. Snayu
B. Mamsa	II. Sira, Kandra
C Meda	III. Tvacha, Vasa
D Asthi	IV. Danta

Choose the ***correct*** answer from the options given below:

1. A-I, B-II, C-III, D-IV
2. A-II, B-III, C-I, D-IV
3. A-II, B-I, C-III, D-IV
4. A-IV, B-II, C-III, D-I

16. Match List-I with List-II:

List-I (Dosha)	List-II (Function)
A. Vata	I. Physiological barrier function
B. Pitta	II. Cell division
C Rakta	III. Pigmentation
D Kapha	IV. Oxygen carrying (Prana Anavartanam)

Choose the ***correct*** answer from the options given below:

1. A-III, B-II, C-IV, D-I
2. A-III, B-I, C-IV, D-II
3. A-I, B-II, C-IV, D-III
4. A-II, B-III, C-IV, D-I

17. Which among the following are NOT the type of asthi (bones)?

A. Kapala
B. Valaya
C. Sushira
D. Nalaka
E. Pratana

Choose the ***most appropriate*** answer from the options given below:

1. C and E only
2. A and E only
3. B and D only
4. A and D only

18. Arrange the following Koshthangs (कोष्ठांग) in the order of their appearance in gastrointenstinal tract.

A. Sthulantra B. Uttarguda
C. Kshudrantra D. Adharaguda
E. Amashaya

Choose the ***correct*** answer from the options given below:

1. D, B, C, E, A 2. A, C, D, E, B
3. E, C, A, B, D 4. B, D, C, A, E

19. Mark the odd one out from following Vata Nanatmaj Vikara.

1. Vishada 2. Atattvabhinivesh
3. Atipralapa 4. Hridadrava

20. According to Ayurveda pramana (measure) of Rasa, Shonita, Pitta and Shleshma in the body are respectively:

A. 5 Anjali B. 6 Anjali
C. 7 Anjali D. 8 Anjali
E. 9 Anjali

Choose the ***correct*** answer from the options given below:

1. A, B, E, C 2. E, D, A, B
3. E, B, C, A 4. B, E, D, C

21. According to Ayurveda, three main marma (Trimarma) are:

A. Amashaya/Stomach B. Yakrata/Liver
C. Hridaya/Heart D. Basti
E. Sira/Head

Choose the ***most appropriate*** answer from the options given below:

1. A, B, C only 2. A, C, E only
3. C, D, E only 4. B, C, E only

22. Match List-I with List-II:

List-I (Ayurvedic Pramana Term)	List-II (Anthropomerty Terminologies)
A. Aayama	I. Length
B. Vistaara	II. Circumference
C Parinaaha	III. Height
D Utsedha	IV. Breadth

Choose the ***correct*** answer from the options given below:

1. A-I, B-IV, C-II, D-III
2. A-IV, B-II, C-I, D-III
3. A-II, B-III, C-IV, D-I
4. A-II, B-I, C-III, D-IV

23. Match List-I with List-II:

List-I (Class of substance)	List-II (Example of substance)
A. Antashchetan dravya	I. Andaj
B. Bahirantanshchetan dravya	II. Khanij
C Bhauma dravya	III. Vanaspati
D Karan dravya	IV. Prithvi

Choose the ***correct*** answer from the options given below:

1. A-I, B-III, C-II, D-IV
2. A-II, B-IV, C-III, D-I
3. A-III, B-I, C-II, D-IV
4. A-IV, B-II, C-I, D-III

24. The component of Pararthanuman are:

A. Pratigya B. Hetu
C. Anvaya D. Vyatirek
E. Udahran/drishtant

Choose the ***most appropriate*** answer from the options given below:

1. B, D, E only 2. A, B, E only
3. A, B, D only 4. B, C, D only

25. Which among the following comprise of Pramana Chatushtaya?

A. Aptopdesha B. Pratyaksha
C. Anumana D. Arthatpatti
E. Sambhava

Choose the ***most appropriate*** answer from the options given below:

1. A, B and C only 2. B, C and D only
3. C, D and E only 4. A, C and E only

26. Which among the following contains five Rasas except Lavana Rasa in them?

A. Amalaki B. Bibhitaki
C. Haritaki D. Haridra

Choose the ***most appropriate*** answer from the options given below:

1. A and B only 2. A and D only
3. A and C only 4. E and D only

27. Arrange the following effects of medicinal substances on GI tract on the basis of severity (Mild to Strong):

A. Sramsana B. Anulomana
C. Samshamana D. Rechana
E. Bhedana

Choose the ***correct*** answer from the options given below:

1. B, C, D, E, A 2. C, B, A, E, D
3. C, B, E, A, D 4. D, A, B, C, E

28. Which among the following rasa is **NOT** considered as the Kashaya Yoni according to Ayurveda?

1. Amla Rasa
2. Katu Rasa
3. Lavana Rasa
4. Kashaya Rasa

29. Following are the varieties of Haritaki.

A. Vijaya
B. Rohini
C. Amruta
D. Nisha
E. Chetaki

Choose the ***most appropriate*** answer from the options given below:

1. A, B, C and D only
2. A, B, D and E only
3. A, B, C and E only
4. B, C, D and E only

30. Which of the following are paradi guna?

A. Manda
B. Sankhya
C. Sanskar
D. Sheeta
E. Prayatna

Choose the ***most appropriate*** answer from the options given below:

1. D and E only
2. A and D only
3. B and C only
4. C and E only

31. A response to a drug which is noxious and unintended and which occurs at doses normally used in man for prophylaxis, diagnosis or therapy of diseases or for modification of physiological functions is defined as:

1. Adverse Drug Reaction
2. Side Effect
3. Non-response
4. Adverse event

32. Which of the followings are the pharmaceutical procedures explained under "Eight Sanskaras" for Mercury before its medicinal use?

A. Swedana
B. Mardana
C. Murchana
D. Kupipakva
E. Dipana

Choose the ***most appropriate*** answer from the options given below:

1. A, B, C and D only
2. A, B, C and E only
3. B, C, D and E only
4. A, C, D and E only

33. Ayurveda, Siddha and Unani medicines are covered under which schedules of drug and cosmetic Act 1940?

A. Schedule A
B. Schedule E (1)
C. Schedule F (1)
D. Schedule T
E. Schedule U (1)

Choose the ***most appropriate*** answer from the options given below:

1. A and B only
2. B and C only
3. B and D only
4. B and E only

34. The pharmaceutical process is repeated hundred times for preparing which of the following formulations?

A. Shatadhauta Ghrita
B. Ksheerbala Aavartita Ghrita
C. Shatahva Ghrita
D. Shatavari Ghrita
E. Abhrak Bhasma

Choose the ***most appropriate*** answer from the options given below:

1. A, D and E only
2. A, B and E only
3. C, D and E only
4. A, B and D only

35. As per Sharangdhara Samhita, arrange the following Ayurveda formulations in the increasing order of their shelf life:

A. Asava-Arishta
B. Ghrita Kalpana
C. Swaras Kalpana
D. Churna Kalpana
E. Vati Kalpana

Choose the ***correct*** answer from the options given below:

1. A, B, C, D, E
2. D, E, C, B, A
3. C, D, E, B, A
4. B, A, D, C, E

36. Which among the following are the Sneha Siddhi Lakshana (signs of properly made fat based preparation)?

A. Phenodgama Taile
B. Shabdotpati
C. Vartivat Snehakalka
D. Tantumatvam
E. Peedite mudra

Choose the ***most appropriate*** answer from the options given below:

1. A and B only
2. A and C only
3. C and D only
4. C and E only

37. Which of the following are basic pharmaceutical dosage forms of Ayurvedic drugs?

1. Aasava, Arishta, Sheha, Avaleha, Kwatha
2. Swarasa, Kalka, Kwatha, Hima, Asava
3. Swarasa, Kalka, Kwatha, Hima, Avaleha
4. Swarasa, Kalka, Kwatha, Hima, Phanta

38. Match List-I with List-II:

List-I (Ayurvedic Rasa Dravya)	List-II (Modern Chemical Name)
A. Abhraka	I. Mercury
B. Gandhaka	II. Mica
C Shilajeet	III. Sulphur
D Rasa	IV. Black bitumen

Choose the *correct* answer from the options given below:

1. A-I, B-II, C-IV, D-III
2. A-II, B-I, C-III, D-IV
3. A-II, B-III, C-IV, D-I
4. A-IV, B-I, C-II, D-III

39. Match List-I with List-II:

List-I (Ayurvedic Preparation)	List-II (Method of Preparation)
A. KAJJALI	I. Kupipakva Rasayan
B. PARPATI	II. Kharaliya Rasayan
C RAS SINDUR	III. Gandhadrava paaka
D POTTALI	IV. Parpatika

Choose the *correct* answer from the options given below:

1. A-I, B-III, C-IV, D-II
2. A-II, B-IV, C-I, D-III
3. A-III, B-IV, C-II, D-I
4. A-IV, B-II, C-III, D-I

40. Which of the following organization facilitate quality assurance and standardization of herbal formulation?

1. National Medicinal Plant Board
2. Pharmacopea commission of Indian Medicine and Homeopathy
3. Clinical Trial Registry of India
4. CSIR-Institute of Genomics and Integrative Biology

41. Which of the following **does not** contain gandhaka?

A. Ras Sindoora B. Ras Pushpa
C. Ras Karpura D. Ras Chandrodaya
E. Ras Manikya

Choose the *correct* answer from the options given below:

1. A and C only 2. A and B only
3. B and C only 4. C and E only

42. Which of the following are the Uparasas?

1. Abhrak, Vaikrant, Makshik, Somala
2. Gandhaka, Kasisa, Haritala, Kankushtha
3. Abhrak, Vaikrant, Makshika, Vimala
4. Abhrak, Gandhaka, Kasisa, Kansya

43. Hypertension is a risk factor for which of the following?

1. Cerebral Hemorrhage
2. Narrowing of aorta
3. A high blood cholesterol level
4. Venus thrombosis

44. Match List-I with List-II:

List-I (Virus)	List-II (Target)
A. Sindbis virus	I. High density Laminin Protein
B. Coxsackie	II. ICAM 1
C Human coronavirus	III. ACE
D HIV	IV. CD 4

Choose the *correct* answer from the options given below:

1. A-II, B-III, C-IV, D-I
2. A-I, B-III, C-II, D-IV
3. A-IV, B-III, C-II, D-I
4. A-I, B-II, C-III, D-IV

45. In the interrupted mating experiments, the order of gene transfer from Hfr strain to F^- recipient can be used to:

1. Identify the gene that are essential for Hfr cell survival
2. Determine the order of genes on the chromosome
3. Calculate the rate of gene recombination in the recipient
4. Confirm that the F plasmid is integrated into the chromosome

46. Identify the **incorrectly** matched pathogen-disease:

1. *Borrelia bergdoferi* - Lyme disease
2. *Escherichia coli* - Toxic shock syndrome
3. *Legionella pheumophila* - Legionnaires disease
4. *Helicobacter pylori* - Peptic ulcer

47. Arrange the following events in viral antigen processing and presentation in **correct** sequence.

A. Loading of antigen on MHC-I complex
B. Polyubiquitination of Antigen
C. Transport of antigen across endoplasmic reticulum membrane
D. Binding of antigen to proteasome and cleavage
E. Interaction of antigen with TAP 1 and TAP 2

Choose the *correct* answer from the options given below:

1. B, D, E, C, A
2. A, C, D, B, E
3. C, B, D, A, E
4. C, B, E, D, A

48. What is the primary stain used in Gram Staining?

1. Safranin
2. Crystal violet
3. Periodic schiff base
4. Iodine

49. Match List-I with List-II:

List-I (Hypersensitivity)	List-II (Mechanism)
A. Hypersensitivity Type I	I. Immune complex mediated
B. Hypersensitivity Type II	II. Anaphylaxis, IgE
C Hypersensitivity Type III	III. Cytotoxic, IgG and complement mediated
D Hypersensitivity Type IV	IV. Delayed type, sensitized CD 4 and CD 8 T-cell mediated

Choose the ***correct*** answer from the options given below:

1. A-II, B-III, C-I, D-IV
2. A-I, B-II, C-III, D-IV
3. A-II, B-I, C-III, D-IV
4. A-IV, B-I, C-II, D-III

50. Following are the steps in regulation of Blood pressure by renin angiotensin system. Arrange them in sequence from Angiotensinogen onwards.

A. Increased Na^+ retention in kidneys
B. Production of Angiotensin II
C. Action on Adrenal cortex
D. Production of Angiotensin I
E. Production of Aldosterone

Choose the ***correct*** answer from the options given below:

1. D, A, C, B, E 2. D, B, C, E, A
3. C, E, B, D, A 4. A, D, B, C, E

51. A person with sickle cell anemia is:

1. Less prone to malaria due to multigenic disorder
2. Less prone to malaria due to single gene disorder
3. Less prone to typhoid due to multigenic disorder
4. More prone to typhoid due to change in single point mutation in globin gene

52. Which option indicates ***correct*** name and nature of India's indigenous COVID-19 vaccine?

1. Covishield - Recombinant spike protein
2. Covaxin - mRNA
3. Covishield - Live attenuated virus
4. Covaxin - Inactivated whole virion

53. Which of the following mechanisms operate only after antigen-activation in generation of antibody diversity?

A. V(D)J recombination
B. P-nucleotide addition
C. N-nucleotide addition
D. Somatic hypermutation
E. Class-switch recombination

Choose the ***correct*** answer from the options given below:

1. A, B and C only
2. B, C and D only
3. C, D and E only
4. D and E only

54. The flexibility to the antibody molecule is provided by:

1. Fab region 2. Fc region
3. Fab′ region 4. Hinge region

55. The key functions of $CD4^+$ T lymphocytes include:

A. Macrophage activation
B. B cell differentiation
C. Killing of cells with intracellular infections
D. Stimulation of inflammation
E. Suppress functions of other T cells

Choose the ***correct*** answer from the options given below:

1. A, B and C only
2. A, B and D only
3. B, C and D only
4. B and E only

56. A solution with growth factors having proteinaceous nature need to be tested in cell culture. For this the solution needs to be free from micro-organisms. Which of the following strategy is optimal for the purpose?

1. Autoclaving the solution
2. Pasteurization
3. Exposure to UV light
4. Ultrafiltration

57. The 'Germ theory of disease' was proposed by:

1. Robert Koch 2. Louis Pasteur
3. Edward Jenner 4. James Watson

58. Below are the measurement of various parameters present in the blood at the two ends of the capillary.

	Arterial end	Venous end
Urea	2.5 mm	2.5 mm
Glucose	4 mm	8 mm
pO_2	100 mmHg	50mmHg
Hydrostatic pressure	14 mmHg	46 mmHg
pCO_2	41mmHg	46 mmHg
Osmotic pressure	26 mmHg	25 mmHG

What is the most likely location of the capillary bed?

1. Lung 2. Small Intestine
3. Heart 4. Liver

59. The right sequence of events that occurs when a neuron is stimulated by a neurotransmitter is:

A. Membrane potential reaches threshold
B. Shift from resting membrane potential
C. Repolarization of the membrane
D. Depolarization of the membrane
E. Hyperpolarization of the membrane

Choose the ***most appropriate*** answer from the options given below:

1. A, D, B, E, C
2. B, C, A, D, E
3. B, A, D, C, E
4. A, B, D, E, C

60. Match List-I with List-II:

List-I (Cells)	List-II (Location)
A. Type II Alveolar cells	I. Nephron
B. Podocytes	II. Brain
C Parietal cells	III. Lungs
D Astrocytes	IV. Stomach

Choose the ***correct*** answer from the options given below:

1. A-III, B-IV, C-II, D-I
2. A-III, B-I, C-IV, D-II
3. A-IV, B-III, C-II, D-I
4. A-IV, B-II, C-I, D-III

61. Match List-I with List-II:

List-I (Hormone)	List-II (Response)
A. Inhibin	I. Rescues corpus luteum
B. Leutinizing hormone	II. Promotes uterine contraction
C Human chorionic gonadotropin	III. Inhibits FSH secretion
D Oxytocin	IV. Responsible for ovulation

Choose the ***correct*** answer from the options given below:

1. A-II, B-III, C-IV, D-I
2. A-III, B-IV, C-I, D-II
3. A-III, B-I, C-IV, D-II
4. A-IV, B-III, C-II, D-I

62. Which of the following is NOT an inborn error in metabolism?

1. Cystic Fibrosis
2. Phenyl Ketonurea
3. Alkaptonurea
4. Hartnups disease

63. The key regulatory enzyme in glycolysis is:

1. Gluco kinase
2. Pyruvate kinase
3. Phospho fructo kinase
4. Aldolase

64. Which of the following bonds is **NOT** present in glycoproteins?

1. Peptide bond
2. Glycosidic bond
3. Hydrogen bond
4. Phosphodiester bond

65. Match List-I with List-II:

List-I (Enzyme)	List-II (Cofactor)
A. Glycogen Phosphorylase	I. NDA
B. Succinate dehydrogenase	II. Biotin
C Glutamate dehydrogenase	III. PLP
D Acetyl CoA carboxylase	IV. FAD

Choose the ***correct*** answer from the options given below:

1. A-II, B-IV, C-I, D-III
2. A-III, B-II, C-IV, D-I
3. A-IV, B-I, C-II, D-III
4. A-III, B-IV, C-I, D-II

66. Which of the following sizes range of nanoparticle is most likely to exhibit higher permeability across blood-brains barrier (BBB), assuming all other surface properties are optimized?

1. 1-20 nm
2. 20-40 nm
3. 150-200 nm
4. 50-100 nm

67. COVID 19 testing has been performed by Real time PCR during recent pandemic. The CT value used to determine the viral load is determined by:

1. the cycle at which amplification curve crosses threshold value.
2. the cycle at which it reached to 50% of amplification
3. the cycle at which it reached to the saturation of amplification
4. the cycle at which it matches with ΔRn value

68. Which of the following statements are correct regarding DNA replication?

A. Okazaki fragments are covalently joined by DNA ligase
B. Lagging strands is continuous and leading strands is discontinuous
C. Rolling circle replication is a feature of yeast DNA replication
D. Okazaki fragments get synthesized in lagging strand
E. Helicase and primase involves in replication

Choose the ***correct*** answer from the options given below:

1. A, D and E only
2. B, C and D only
3. A, B and C only
4. C, D and E only

69. With respect to the eukaryotic gene, match List-I with List-II:

List-I	List-II
A. Poly A tail	I. Kozak sequence
B. 5′ untranslated region	II. Orientation independent
C Transalation start site	III. Added after transcription
D Enhancer sequence	IV. AUG

Choose the ***correct*** answer from the options given below:

1. A-II, B-IV, C-I, D-III
2. A-I, B-III, C-II, D-IV
3. A-IV, B-III, C-II, D-I
4. A-III, B-I, C-IV, D-II

70. Eukaryotic gene expression is regulated at following stages:

A. Histone acetylation and DNA methylation
B. DNA replication and repair
C. cAMP binding to promoter of a gene
D. Protein processing and degradation
E. RNA processing like alternative RNA splicing

Choose the ***correct*** answer from the options given below:

1. C, D and E only 2. A, D and E only
3. B, C and E only 4. A, C and E only.

71. What will be T_m (melting temperature) of the following PCR primer?

5′ - AGACTCAGAGAGAACCC - 3′

1. 48°C 2. 52°C
3. 43°C 4. 68°C

72. Identify the mode of inheritance in the following pedigree chart:

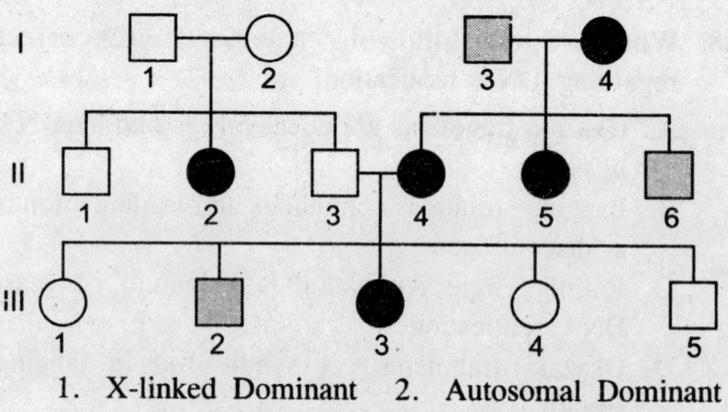

1. X-linked Dominant 2. Autosomal Dominant
3. Autosomal Recessive 4. X-linked Recessive

73. If an individual of genotypes AaBbCcDd is test crossed, how many different phenotypes can appear in the progeny?

1. 16 2. 8
3. 32 4. 64

74. The Z-DNA helix:

1. has more base pair per turn than B-DNA
2. is fovoured by an alternating AT sequence
3. tends to be found at the 3′ end of genes
4. is the most common confirmatory of gene

75. Hypospadias, a birth defect in human males causes urethral opening on the shaft instead of the tip of the penis and this results from an autosomal gene. Females are not affected. The genetic phenomena operating here is called:

1. X - linked inheritance
2. Sex limited trait
3. Sex influenced trait
4. Y-linked inheritance

76. Which of the denatured DNA of following types will renature most rapidly in a solution under gradually decreasing temperature?

1. Highly repetitive sequences
2. Unique sequences
3. Exons of protein coding genes
4. Introns of protein coding genes

77. Sanger sequencing method uses:

1. Pyrophosphates 2. Emulsion PCR
3. Nested PCR 4. Dideoxyribonucleosides

78. The function of smooth endoplasmic reticulum is:

1. Making secretory proteins
2. Synthesis of lipids
3. Generation of ATP
4. Synthesis of vesicles

79. Which one of the following strategies has been used to determine first draft of Human Genome sequence?

1. VNTR loci mapping and targeted gene sequencing by sanger method
2. Clone-by-clone and whole genome shotgun sequencing by sanger method
3. Bisulphite modification and sequencing by Illumina method
4. RNA seq incorporating with Exome method sequencing by Illumina method

80. Arrange following DNA sequencing method in increasing order starting from lower read length to higher read length.

A. Iluming sequencing
B. Pyrosequencing (Roche 454)
C. Single Molecule Real Time (SMRT) sequencing

Choose the ***correct*** answer from the options given below :

1. C < B < A 2. A < B < C
3. B < C < A 4. B < A < C

81. The major hurdle found during the human genome sequencing regarding the assembly of sequences and annotation is:
1. Repetitive DNA sequences
2. Heterochromatin patches
3. Long length of chromosomes
4. Lack of co-ordination among collaborating groups

82. Which of the following is NOT a type of DNA repair mechanism?
1. Non homologous end joining
2. Chaperones-mediated repair
3. Base-excision repair
4. Nucleotide excision repair

83. Following is the weight of mice fed a calorie deficient diet for 1 month as compared to a control group.

Test group (wt. in gm) - 15, 18, 21, 16, 14, 19

Control group (wt. in gm) - 25, 28, 22, 31, 30, 32

What is the average decrease in weight in mice due to calorie deficiency?

1. 15.2 2. 11.4
3. 10.1 4. 14.5

84. Match List-I with List-II:

List-I (Statistical Symbol)	List-II (Concept)
A. μ	I. Correlation coefficient
B. σ	II. Chi square
C r	III. Std deviation
D χ^2	IV. Mean

Choose the ***correct*** answer from the options given below:
1. A-IV, B-I, C-II, D-III
2. A-IV, B-III, C-I, D-II
3. A-I, B-II, C-III, D-IV
4. A-II, B-IV, C-I, D-III

85. Following are the extraction techniques for plant materials except:

1. Maceration 2. Decoction
3. Soxhlet 4. Refraction

86. The PPV and FR Act, 2001 ensures the protection of:

A. Right of consumers B. Right of industry
C. Plant varieties D. Rights of patients
E. Rights of farmers

Choose the ***correct*** answer from the options given below:

1. A, B only 2. C, E only
3. C, D only 4. B, D only

87. The greatest amount of free energy is available at which of the following trophic levels?

1. Tertiary consumers 2. Secondary consumers
3. Decomposers 4. Producers

88. Ministry of Ayush launched a program to establish business incubators to foster academia-industry co-development partnership in the name of:
1. Ayurindustry yojna
2. Ayurgyan yojna
3. Ayurveda incubator yojna
4. Ayur startup yojna

89. Energy pyramid of an ecosystem tend to diminish at higher trophic levels. This is because of each successive level:
1. The organisms become smaller
2. Energy is stored and therefore less is passed on to the next level
3. Energy is being lost from one level to the next
4. Energy is being concentrated in fewer and larger organisms

90. Match phases of the development of a drug (Ayurveda) List-I with the objective of the trail in List-II:

List-I (Clinical Trial Phase)	List-II (Objective of Trial)
A. Phase I	I. Dose respone
B. Phase II	II. Post-marketing
C Phase III	III. Toxicity and side effects
D Phase IV	IV. Comparison with established treatment

Choose the ***correct*** answer from the options given below:
1. A-IV, B-I, C-III, D-II
2. A-I, B-IV, C-III, D-II
3. A-I, B-II, C-III, D-IV
4. A-III, B-I, C-IV, D-II

Directions: (Qs. No. 91 to 95): *Read the following paragraph and answer the questions:*

Scientist exploring medicinal plants discovered an endemic plant leaf claimed to have strong neuroprotective action. The plant came to light due to ability to generate high cognitive abilities in octogenarian of the tribals who used these plant leaves regularly in their local dietary practices. The plant was characterized botanically and a sample of leaves were used to extract active ingredients, which was/were likely to be hydrophobic in nature.

91. As per the Ayurveda or modern pharmaceutical practices, which one of the following extraction media is the least preferred for this plant ?

1. Ghee
2. Alcohol
3. Hydro alcoholic mixture
4. Water

92. Which of the following assays will be most suitable to initiate investigation for establishing the neuroprotective biological activity of the extracts?
1. In silico assays
2. In vitro assays using primary cells/cell lines
3. In vivo testing of extracts in animals
4. Direct testing of extracts on human volunteers

93. Once the active fraction is found, which of the following test is most appropriate to identify the constituent molecules present in it?
1. Ion-exchange chromatography
2. HPCL
3. HPTLC
4. LC-MS/MS

94. Once the NMR-based structure of active molecule is identified, researchers want to know the molecular targets of the potential drug. Which one of the following bioinformatics methods will be most suitable for this purpose?
1. Molecular docking
2. ADMET analysis
3. Pharmacophore modeling
4. Structure-based phylogeny

95. Having established the neuroprotective activity of this compound, if you were to develop an Ayurvedic preparation from the leaf of this plant, what dosage form will be most suitable?
1. Sneha Kalpana
2. Asava Kalpana
3. Churna Kalpana
4. Kwatha Kalpana

Directions: (Qs. No. 96 to 100): *Read the following paragraph and answer the questions:*

A 165 cm tall 27-year-old female with dry skin, and brittle hair, has over the past 2 years started experiencing irregular painful periods, intermittent constipation and hirsutism. After following a career in banking for three years, she has now been preparing for civil services examination since past 3 years. Due to this, her sleep and eating habits have become even more irregular. Her weight has fallen to 48 kg from 52 kg. Since her lifestyle had become fairly sedentary, she had also opted to consume a vegan diet. When she started experiencing panic attacks and nightmares she decided to consult a doctor. She underwent several tests, some of the significant test results are listed below:

Normal hematology profile
High androgen profile
Elicited abnormality on pelvic ultrasound

96. What is her likely prakriti?
1. Vata dominant
2. Pitta dominant
3. Kapha dominant
4. Tridosha dominant

97. What changes should she make in her diet to improve her condition?
A. She should follow intermittent fasting
B. She should eat easily digestible foods rich in nutrients at regular intervals
C. Include organic milk and ghee
D. Increase consumption of fruits and vegetables

Choose the ***correct*** answer from the options given below:
1. A, B and C only
2. B, C and D only
3. A, C and D only
4. A, B and D only

98. What is her BMI at present?
1. 17.6
2. 21.3
3. 19.1
4. 16.7

99. Which of the following disorder best describe her condition?
1. PCOS
2. Anorexia nervosa
3. Amenorrhea
4. Crohn's disease

100. What sort of therapeutic strategy according to Ayurveda would be useful to treat her condition?
A. Nidan parivarjana
B. Ojo vardhak
C. Kapha hara
D. Vata shamak

Choose the ***most appropriate*** answer from the options given below:
1. A, B and C only
2. A, B and D only
3. B, C and D only
4. A, C and D only

ANSWERS

1	2	3	4	5	6	7	8	9	10
3	2	2	4	3	4	3	3	2	2
11	**12**	**13**	**14**	**15**	**16**	**17**	**18**	**19**	**20**
2	2	3	2	2	4	1	3	4	2
21	**22**	**23**	**24**	**25**	**26**	**27**	**28**	**29**	**30**
3	1	3	2	1	3	2	3	3	3

31	32	33	34	35	36	37	38	39	40
1	2	3	2	3	2	4	3	2	2
41	**42**	**43**	**44**	**45**	**46**	**47**	**48**	**49**	**50**
3	2	1	4	2	2	1	2	1	2
51	**52**	**53**	**54**	**55**	**56**	**57**	**58**	**59**	**60**
2	4	4	4	2	4	2	2	3	2
61	**62**	**63**	**64**	**65**	**66**	**67**	**68**	**69**	**70**
2	1	3	4	4	1	1	1	4	2
71	**72**	**73**	**74**	**75**	**76**	**77**	**78**	**79**	**80**
2	3	1	1	2	1	4	2	2	2
81	**82**	**83**	**84**	**85**	**86**	**87**	**88**	**89**	**90**
1	2	2, 3	2	4	2	4	2	3	4
91	**92**	**93**	**94**	**95**	**96**	**97**	**98**	**99**	**100**
4	2	4	1	1	1	2	1	1	2

EXPLANATORY ANSWERS

1. In Charaka Samhita Sutrasthana, the chapters are grouped into sets of four (Chatushka) on a logical and sequential basis. The correct order of these particular Chatushkas is:

A. Swasthya Chatushka → E. Nirdesh Chatushka → C. Kalpana Chatushka → B. Roga Chatushka → D. Yojana Chatushka.

A. Swasthya Chatushka: This is placed first → because Charaka gives primary importance to maintenance of health of the healthy. It deals with daily regimen, seasonal regimen, diet and lifestyle necessary to preserve health.

E. Nirdesh Chatushka: After establishing how to maintain health, Charaka proceeds to instructional and descriptive topics—fundamental principles, definitions and directions that guide further understanding of medical science.

C. Kalpana Chatushka: Once foundational instructions are clear, the text describes preparatory methods like types of formulations, processing of medicines, basic pharmaceutical concepts.

B. Roga Chatushka: After knowing how to stay healthy and how medicines are prepared, the natural sequence is to understand diseases, their causes, types and basic clinical concepts; hence Roga Chatushka comes later.

D. Yojana Chatushka: Finally comes Yojana—the application and planning of treatment. It relates to how the already-described principles, preparations and disease-knowledge are properly combined and applied to patients.

Thus, logically and traditionally, the correct sequence among the given options is Swasthya → Nirdesh → Kalpana → Roga → Yojana, which corresponds to A, E, C, B, D, i.e. option 3.

2. This question checks knowledge of classical texts and their main traditional commentators in Ayurveda. The correct match is:

A. Sharangdhar Samhita – III. Adhamal (Adhamalla):

- Sarngadhara Samhita is a comparatively later but very important text, especially for pharmaceutical preparations and dosage forms.
- One of its well-known commentaries is by Adhamalla (Adhamal), who wrote Dipika (Saragadhar-Dipika), a classical commentary that explains the concepts of the text in detail. Hence A → III.

B. Sushrut Samhita – II. Dalhana:

- Susruta Samhita is the principal text of Salya Tantra (Ayurvedic surgery).
- Dalhana composed the famous commentary Nibandha Sangraha on Susruta Samhita, which is considered the most authoritative and widely accepted traditional commentary. Therefore B → II.

C. Ashtanga Samgraha – IV. Indu:

- Astanga Samgraha, attributed to Vagbhata, is a major compendium covering the eight branches of Ayurveda in a mixed prose-verse style.
- Indu is a renowned commentator on Astanga Samgraha; his commentary is known as Sasilekha, which elaborates on complex concepts of Vagbhata. Hence C → IV.

D. Charaka Samhita – I. Chakrapani:

- Caraka Samhita is the fundamental text of Kayachikitsa (internal medicine) and general Ayurvedic principles.

- Chakrapani Datta wrote the most celebrated commentary Ayurveda Dipika on Caraka Samhita. Almost all standard modern editions print his tika along with the main text.
  Thus D → I.

Since all these pairs fit perfectly with historically accepted tradition, the complete matching pattern is A-III, B-II, C-IV, D-I, corresponding to option 2.

3. The question is about the six categories (Sad-Padartha) of the Vaisesika Darsana, which are also accepted in Ayurvedic philosophical foundation. These six are:

1. Dravya (substance)
2. Guna (quality)
3. Karma (action)
4. Samanya (generality)
5. Visesa (particularity)
6. Samavaya (inherence)

Now we examine each of the given options:

A. **Samavaya** → This is one of the recognized Sad-Padartha (no doubt).

B. **Samanya** → This is also one of the Sad-Padartha (generality or universality).

C. **Samyoga** → This is not counted as a separate Padārtha; it is a type of relation arising due to action, often discussed under Karma and Dravya. It is important in Nyāya-Vaiśesika logic but not included as one of the six fundamental Padārtha.

D. **Vishesha** → This again is one of the Sad-Padārtha (it explains the individuality/particularity that differentiates substances like atoms or souls).

E. **Vibhaga** → This literally means "separation". Like Samyoga, it is a kind of state or effect of action and not an independent Padārtha among the canonical six of Vaiśesika.

Therefore, those which are NOT among the Sad-Padārtha are Samyoga (C) and Vibhaga (E). Hence the correct choice is C and E only, i.e. option 2.

4. WHO's first Global Centre for Traditional Medicine (GCTM) has been established in Jamnagar, in the state of Gujarat, India.

Key points:

- The Government of India (through Ministry of AYUSH) and the World Health Organization (WHO) signed an agreement to set up this global centre.
- The announcement and foundation stone ceremony took place in April 2022 in Jamnagar.
- Jamnagar is already a major hub of traditional medicine education due to the presence of Institute for Teaching and Research in Ayurveda (ITRA) and earlier Gujarat Ayurved University, making it a suitable location from academic and clinical perspectives.

The objective of this centre is to:

- Promote evidence-based research in traditional medicine, including Ayurveda and other systems.
- Develop global standards, guidelines and data for integration of traditional medicine into national health systems.
- Support WHO member states in policy-making related to traditional medicine.

Because of these official and widely documented facts, the correct answer among the options Geneva, Beijing, Gandhinagar, Jamnagar is Jamnagar, i.e. option 4.

5. The question asks which Mahābhūta-dominant substances have Mridu (soft) property in common. In Ayurveda, each Mahābhūta (basic element) has characteristic attributes:

A. **Akāśa Mahābhūta – dominant qualities:**

- Laghu (light)
- Sūksma (subtle)
- Mridu (soft/delicate)

It creates space/void and does not offer hardness or resistance; hence it is associated with softness and delicateness.

B. **Agneya (Tejas) Mahābhūta – dominant qualities:**

- Usna (hot)
- Tiksna (sharp)
- Rūksa (dry)

It is more related to heat, transformation and sharpness rather than softness; so it is not predominantly Mridu.

C. **Apya (Jala/Ap) Mahābhūta – dominant qualities:**

- Drava (liquid)
- Snigdha (unctuous/oily)
- Mridu (soft)

Water and watery substances naturally show softness, smoothness and flexibility; ghee, oil, serum etc. are classic examples. Thus Jalātmaka substances are strongly Mridu.

D. **Pārthiva (Prithvi) Mahābhūta – dominant qualities:**

- Guru (heavy)
- Sthira (stable)
- Kathina (hard)

Earth element gives structure, stability and hardness (e.g., bones, teeth, nails); it is usually the opposite of Mridu.

E. **Vāyavīya (Vāyu) Mahābhūta – dominant qualities:**

- Chala (mobile)
- Laghu (light)
- Rūksa (dry)

It is more associated with movement and dryness than with softness.

From the above, the Mahābhūta-dominant substances that clearly share Mridu quality are:

A. Akāśātmaka

C. Apya

So, the correct pair is A and C only, which corresponds to option 3.

6. Buddhi is not considered a Karana Dravya. In Ayurveda, Karana Dravya refers to those substances or factors that act as instruments or mediums for gaining knowledge. Charaka Samhita (Sutrasthana 1/49) includes Kala (time), Dik (direction), Atma (self), Manas (mind), Indriya (sense organs) etc. as Karana Dravya.

- **Disha** functions as an instrumental factor because spatial orientation is essential for perception.
- **Kala** is a Karana because no activity, movement, or transformation can be perceived without time.
- **Akasha** is included since it provides the medium for sound, which is needed for the auditory sense organ.
- **Buddhi**, however, is an internal faculty of decision-making and discrimination (nischayatmika buddhi). It does not function as a sense instrument; rather it evaluates the information provided by senses. Hence, Buddhi is not a Karana Dravya.

7. Ayurveda describes sixteen principal types of Manasik Prakriti, and this classification is based on the predominance and permutations of the three Mahagunas—Sattva, Rajas, and Tamas—which together shape mental tendencies, behaviour, emotional patterns, and cognitive functions. Classical texts such as Charaka Samhita (Sharira Sthana 4) and Sushruta Samhita elaborate these categories with detailed psychological descriptions.

- **Sattvika Prakriti** is subdivided into **7–8 refined types**, including Brahma, Arsha, Aindra, Yamya, Varuna, Kubera, and Gandharva varieties, each representing higher emotional balance, discipline, intellect, and purity.
- **Rajasika Prakriti** comprises **6–7 types**, including Asura, Rakshasa, Paisacha, Sarpa, Shakuna, and Preta types; these reflect traits such as ambition, aggression, restlessness, fear, or impulsive tendencies depending on the subtype.
- **Tamasika Prakriti** consists of **3 distinct types**, including Pashava, Matsya, and Vanaspatya, representing inertia, dullness, confusion, low motivation, or primitive behavioural patterns.

When these Sattvika (7–8), Rajasika (6–7), and Tamasika (3) subdivisions are considered collectively, Ayurveda identifies 16 well-recognised mental constitution types, which is the most accepted enumeration across foundational Ayurvedic psychology. This makes Sixteen (16) the correct answer.

8. These five factors comprise the Rasa Panchaka, the complete framework used in Ayurveda to understand medicinal substances.

- **Rasa** describes the immediate taste and preliminary action of the drug.
- **Guna** refers to the inherent qualities such as heavy, light, unctuous, sharp etc.
- **Veerya** means potency—mainly heating (ushna) or cooling (shita)—and dictates strong therapeutic impact.
- **Vipaka** indicates the post-digestive effect, which influences long-term physiological action.
- **Prabhava** refers to special, unique action that cannot be explained merely by rasa, guna, veerya or vipaka.

These five together determine how a substance behaves pharmacologically within the body. Therefore, the correct set representing Rasa Panchaka is Rasa–Guna–Veerya–Vipaka–Prabhava.

9. The concept of Shad-dhatuj Purusha describes the human being as constituted of six basic elements. Classical Ayurveda states that:

- The physical body is formed by five Mahabhutas (Akasha, Vayu, Agni, Jala, Prithvi).
- To these five, Atma (the Self) is added as the sixth essential component, responsible for consciousness and vitality.

Thus, a human being is considered a combination of Panchamahabhuta + Atma = six elements, known as Shad-dhatuj Purusha.

10. The effects of seasons (Ritus) on Doshas follow a predictable cycle of Sanchaya (accumulation), Prakopa (aggravation) and Prashamana (pacification). Matching them correctly:

A. Sharad → Pitta Prakopa (II): Sharad Ritu is characterised by residual heat after monsoon, which aggravates the already accumulated Pitta; hence Pitta prakopa occurs in Sharad.

B. Vasanta → Kapha Prakopa (III): In spring, the Kapha accumulated during winter becomes liquefied due to rising temperature, leading to Kapha Prakopa.

C. Varsha → Vata Prakopa (I): During monsoon, irregular temperature, dampness, and cloudy weather disturb digestion and promote Vata aggravation.

D. Grishma → Vata Sanchaya (IV): The dryness and heat of summer deplete body fluids and cause Vata Sanchaya (accumulation), though full aggravation happens later in Varsha.

All these match perfectly with option 2.

11. Prana Vayu, Kledaka Kapha and Samana Vayu directly participate in digestion. Prana Vayu controls swallowing, movement of food into the stomach, and regulates Agni by governing respiration; without Prana Vayu, the act of ingestion cannot begin. Kledaka Kapha moistens, liquefies and softens food (anna), enabling proper churning and protecting the gastric lining while regulating acidity. Samana Vayu is located near the Jatharagni and governs mixing, separation and regulation of digestive strength, helping the food undergo proper transformation. Tarpaka Kapha relates to nourishment of the brain and cephalic region, not digestion. Sadhaka Pitta supports higher mental functions, emotional processing and intellect but does not directly take part in ahara pachana. Thus, the correct group is A, B, C only.

12. Ojas is described as the essence of all seven dhatus, making statement A correct; classical texts call Ojas "dhatu saram", the vital essence required for life, strength and immunity. Statement C is correct because Ojas maintains harmony among Doshas by stabilising and coordinating their functions; imbalance of Dosha cannot occur when Ojas is abundant. Statement E is also correct since Ayurveda states that Ojas is present from the earliest fetal stages, enabling development, vitality and protective energy in the embryo. Statement B is incorrect because Ojas is not an eighth dhatu; it is dhatu-sara, not an independent dhatu. Statement D is wrong because Ojas is not an upadhatu of Rakta; its origin is from all dhatus collectively. Hence A, C, E only.

13. **A. Jagaruka (shallow sleep)** corresponds to **Ruksha (IV)** qualities, as dryness and lightness of Vata cause disturbed or incomplete sleep. **(B) Asheeghra Samarambha, meaning slow to start action**, matches **Stimita (III)**—a property of Kapha indicating slowness, stability and delayed initiation. **(C) Upachita Anga (well-nourished, well-built body)** corresponds to **Sandra (II)**, the dense and compact quality of Kapha contributing to good nourishment and solid physique. **(D) Shithila mrudu sandhi maans (soft, loose muscles and joints)** matches **Drava (I)**, because liquidity and looseness are features of Drava guna leading to soft tissues.

Therefore the correct matching pattern is A-IV, B-III, C-II, D-I.

14. The phrase "शिथिलमृदुसंधिमांसा:" signifies fluidity, looseness, liquidity and softness, all classical characteristics of Drava Guna, which represents the flowing, spreading, mobile and dissolving nature of a substance. Ayurveda attributes Drava Guna predominantly to Pitta dosha, because Pitta is responsible for transformation and metabolic liquefaction within the body, and its inherent qualities include drava (liquid), sara (flowing), and tikshna (penetrating). Features such as looseness of tissues, liquidity, melting tendency, and reduced compactness correspond precisely to Drava Guna. This Lakshana cannot indicate Sandra Guna (dense/compact), Madhura Guna (sweet/unctuous), or Katu–Amla Guna (sharp–sour). Therefore, the phrase matches Drava Guna of Pitta.

15. **(A) Rakta Dhatu** produces **Sira and Kandra (II)** as its Upadhatu, as blood nourishes veins and tendinous structures. **(B) Mamsa Dhatu** forms **Tvacha and Vasa (III)** as Upadhatu, because muscle supports skin thickness and produces fatty substances. **(C) Meda Dhatu** gives rise to **Snayu (I)**, the ligaments and connective tissues, aligning with its lubricating and supporting nature. **(D) Asthi Dhatu** produces **Danta (IV)** as Upadhatu because teeth derive hardness and structure from bone tissue. Therefore the accurate matching is A-II, B-III, C-I, D IV.

16. **A. Vata – II. Cell division:** Vata governs all movements in the body – including intracellular movements, spindle formation and separation of chromosomes during mitosis. Hence subtle kinetic activity like cell division is attributed to Vata.

B. Pitta – III. Pigmentation: Bhrajaka Pitta, a subtype of Pitta located in the skin, is responsible for skin colour and pigmentation; thus all pigment-related activity is classically linked to Pitta.

C. Rakta – IV. Oxygen carrying (Prana Anavartanam): Rakta dhatu carries Prana (life-air) via haemoglobin and is explicitly said to be responsible for maintaining life through its circulating, oxygen-carrying role.

D. Kapha – I. Physiological barrier function: Kapha (esp. Shleshaka and Avalambaka) provides snigdhata, stability and the mucoid protective lining of respiratory, GI and other tracts, acting as a physiological barrier against external insults.

17. Ayurveda describes five main types of Asthi (bones): Kapala, Ruchaka, Taruna, Valaya and Nalaka.

From the options:

- **Kapala** – a recognised type (flat/cranial bones).
- **Valaya** – recognised (ring-like bones such as ribs).
- **Nalaka** – recognised (long tubular bones, e.g., long bones of limbs).
- **Sushira and Pratana** are not listed among the five classical types of Asthi.

Therefore, the structures NOT belonging to classical asthi types are Sushira (C) and Pratana (E), so the correct option is "C and E only".

18. Order of appearance of the Koshthanga in the GI tract from proximal to distal:

E. Amashaya: stomach–like organ; receives food first after the oesophagus.

C. Kshudrantra: small intestine, continuing distally from Amashaya.

A. **Sthulantra:** large intestine, following the small intestine segment.

B. **Uttarguda:** rectum region, the terminal dilated part before anal canal.

D. **Adharaguda:** anal canal, the terminal outlet of the GI tract.

Hence, in anatomical order along the tract: Amashaya → Kshudrantra → Sthulantra → Uttarguda → Adharaguda, which corresponds exactly to E, C, A, B, D.

19. Hridadrava is the odd one out because it is not a Vata Nanatmaja Vikara. Hridadrava (palpitation or trembling of the heart) arises from the combined vitiation of Vata, Pitta, and Rakta, and therefore does not belong to the group of disorders caused solely by Vata dosha. Palpitations are described as involving heat, circulation and movement—functions shared by Vata and Pitta together—hence it cannot be classified as a pure Vata-origin disease.

The other three—Vishada, Atattvabhinivesh and Atipralapa—are all included among the 80 Vata Nanatmaja Vikaras described in classical texts such as the Charaka Samhita. Vishada refers to sadness or depression caused by disturbed Vata acting on the mind. Atattvabhinivesh denotes irrational, false convictions or delusional attachment, again arising from deranged Vata functioning in the mental channels. Atipralapa means excessive, incoherent or irrelevant speech, produced when Vata vitiates the voice and mental faculties. These three are explicitly listed as disorders arising from Vata alone, making Hridadrava the only one that does not belong to this group.

20. According to Anjali-pramana:

- **Rasa (Ahara Rasa) - 9 Anjali**
- **Shonita (Rakta) - 8 Anjali**
- **Pitta - 5 Anjali**
- **Shleshma (Kapha) - 6 Anjali**

In the question, the symbols are:

- A = 5 Anjali
- B = 6 Anjali
- C = 7 Anjali
- D = 8 Anjali
- E = 9 Anjali

Mapping correctly:

- **Rasa → 9 Anjali → E**
- **Shonita → 8 Anjali → D**
- **Pitta → 5 Anjali → A**
- **Shleshma → 6 Anjali → B**

So, the sequence Rasa, Shonita, Pitta, Shleshma corresponds to E, D, A, B, i.e. option 2.

21. According to Ayurveda, the three principal marma known as Trimarma are Hridaya (Heart), Basti (Urinary bladder) and Shira (Head).

C. **Hridaya** is central for circulation, consciousness and emotional functions; injury to Hridaya is considered prānahara (fatal).

D. **Basti** is the main seat of Mutravaha srotas and governs urine storage and elimination; damage severely disturbs homeostasis and can endanger life.

E. **Shira** includes the head and brain structures, governing sensory organs, mind and vital centres; trauma to Shira is life-threatening.

Classical marma descriptions give special status to these three as Trimarma because they are critically related to Prana and survival. Therefore, the correct combination is C, D and E only.

22. The Ayurvedic pramana terms correspond to standard anthropometric dimensions as follows:

A. **Aayama - I. Length:** Aayama denotes the longitudinal measurement of the body or a limb (e.g., body length/height measured along its axis). In anthropometry this is represented as length.

B. **Vistaara - IV. Breadth:** Vistaara literally means "spread" or "width" and is used for side-to-side measurement (breadth) of chest, pelvis, etc.

C. **Parinaaha - II. Circumference:** Parinaaha refers to circular or girth measurement, such as the circumference of chest, waist, thigh, etc.

D. **Utsedha - III. Height:** Utsedha means "elevation or projection", used for vertical/raised measure (thickness/height) of a structure, which best matches height in the given list.

Thus, the accurate matching is A–I, B–IV, C–II, D–III.

23. **(A) Antashchetan dravya** corresponds to **Vanaspati (III)** because these internally conscious substances possess life within but do not display external movement; plants such as Vanaspati (trees that bear fruit without flowers) exemplify this category. **(B) Bahirantanshchetan dravya** corresponds to **Andaj (I)** because these substances exhibit both internal life and external movement; egg-born beings like birds and reptiles, along with Jarayuja and Swedaja forms, fall under this animate category. **(C) Bhauma dravya** corresponds to **Khanij (II)** since the term Bhauma denotes earth-origin substances, and minerals (Khanij) are classic representatives of earth-derived matter. **(D) Karan dravya** corresponds to **Prithvi (IV)** because Karan dravyas are the nine fundamental causal substances such as the five Mahabhutas, Kala, Disha, Atma and Manas; among these, Prithvi (Earth element) is one of the core Mahabhutas and hence a Karan dravya.

24. Pararthanumana (inference for others) in Nyaya–Ayurveda logic is presented as a structured argument composed of definite members. Among the given items:

A. **Pratigya** – the proposition or thesis to be established (e.g., "This hill has fire").

B. **Hetu** – the reason supporting the proposition (e.g., "Because there is smoke on the hill").

E. **Udahran/Drishtant** – the illustrative example that shows the universal relation (e.g., "Wherever there is smoke, there is fire, like in a kitchen").

These three are core components appearing in the five-member Nyaya syllogism (Pratigya, Hetu, Udaharana, Upanaya, Nigamana). **Anvaya (C)** and **Vyatireka (D)** describe logical relations of agreement and difference, but they are not counted as structural members of Pararthanumana itself. Therefore, A, B and E only are correct.

25. In Ayurveda, Pramana Chatushtaya (fourfold means of valid knowledge) is traditionally described as:

1. **Aptopadesha (A)** – authoritative testimony of reliable seers and scriptures;
2. **Pratyaksha (B)** – direct perception through the senses;
3. **Anumana (C)** – inference based on observed signs and logical relation;
4. **Yukti** – rational, composite reasoning integrating multiple observations (not listed in the options).

From the options given, **A (Apatopdesha)**, **B (Pratyaksha)** and **C (Anumana)** are exactly three of these four recognized means. **Arthapatti (D)** and **Sambhava (E)** are additional pramanas found in other philosophical systems but are not part of Charaka's Pramana Chatushtaya.

Hence the correct set is A, B and C only.

26. Amalaki and Haritaki contain five Rasas except Lavana. Amalaki possesses Madhura, Amla, Katu, Tikta and Kashaya rasa but lacks Lavana rasa. Haritaki is described as Pancharasa Yukta Lavana Varjita—meaning it has five tastes (Madhura, Amla, Katu, Tikta, Kashaya) except Salty (Lavana). Bibhitaki does not possess five rasas, and Haridra has mainly Tikta and Katu rasas only. Therefore, the substances containing five rasas except Lavana are Amalaki and Haritaki.

27. The severity of actions on the gastrointestinal tract from mild to strong follows this order: Samshamana → Anulomana → Sramsana → Bhedana → Rechana.

C. **Samshamana** is the mildest, pacifying dosha without causing evacuation.

B. **Anulomana** mildly promotes downward movement of Vata and soft evacuation.

A. **Sramsana** causes loosening of stool with moderate purgation.

E. **Bhedana** is stronger, breaking hard stool masses.

D. **Rechana** is the strongest, producing full purgation and forceful expulsion of doshas.

Thus the correct mild-to-strong sequence is C, B, A, E, D.

28. Kashaya Yoni refers to tastes derived from the Kashaya (astringent) rasa group, typically involving combinations that create drying, contracting, and absorbing actions. Amla, Katu and Kashaya rasas can belong to this category based on their similar actions and origins in formulations. Lavana rasa, however, is not included as Kashaya Yoni because its properties—such as softness, diffusion, and liquefaction—are opposite to the rough, drying and contracting qualities of Kashaya. Hence Lavana rasa is not considered Kashaya Yoni.

29. Classical Ayurveda describes six varieties of Haritaki: Vijaya, Rohini, Putana, Amruta, Abhaya and Chetaki. Among the given options, **Vijaya (A)**, **Rohini (B)**, **Amruta (C)** and **Chetaki (E)** all belong to the six recognised types. **Nisha (D)** is not a variety of Haritaki; Nisha refers to Turmeric (Haridra). Therefore, the correct Haritaki varieties among the options are A, B, C and E.

30. Sankhya and Sanskar are recognised as Paradi Gunas according to classical Ayurvedic texts. Paradi Gunas are a group of ten special qualities essential for successful treatment (Chikitsa Siddhi), and they include: Sankhya (number), Sanskar (processing), Para (superiority), Apara (inferiority), Yukti (planning), Samyoga (combination), Vibhaga (separation), Prithaktva (distinctness), Parimana (measurement), and Abhyasa (repetition/practice). From the given options, B. Sankhya and C. Sanskar are part of this list and therefore fit correctly under Paradi Gunas. Manda (A) and Sheeta (D) belong to the Gurvadi Gunas describing physical properties like heaviness/lightness or coldness/heat. Prayatna (E) is an Atma Guna related to effort or volition and does not belong to the Paradi Guna group.

31. An adverse drug reaction is defined as a noxious, unintended, and undesired response occurring at doses normally used for prophylaxis, diagnosis, therapy, or physiological modification. This definition matches exactly with WHO's classical definition of ADR. Side effects may be predictable and sometimes beneficial; non-response indicates lack of therapeutic effect; adverse event includes all undesirable events but may not be causally linked to the drug. Therefore, the only term that fits the definition given in the question is Adverse Drug Reaction.

32. The Eight Sanskaras (Ashta Samskaras) of mercury are the classical pharmaceutical purification procedures performed before mercury (Parada) is used medicinally. These include **Swedana (A)**, which is steaming of mercury to remove impurities; **Mardana (B)**, involving trituration or rubbing with herbal agents to detoxify and soften mercury; **Murchana (C)**, a procedure where mercury is processed with specific herbal decoctions to induce "swoon," improving its assimilability; and **Dipana (E)**, which enhances mercury's potency and ability to amalgamate with other substances. **Kupipakva (D)** is not one of the eight preliminary Sanskaras, as it refers to a furnace-based preparation method used later for compounds like Rasasindura, not for primary purification.

Therefore, the correct combination of Sanskara procedures is A, B, C and E.

33. Ayurvedic, Siddha and Unani (ASU) medicines fall under **Schedule E(1) (B)** and **Schedule T (D)** of the Drugs and Cosmetics Act, 1940. Schedule E(1) lists poisonous substances used in ASU medicines, requiring mandatory caution labels for safety. Schedule T prescribes the Good Manufacturing Practices (GMP) specifically for ASU drug manufacturing, ensuring quality, hygiene and standardisation. Schedule A deals with general licensing forms; Schedule F(1) applies to biological products like vaccines; Schedule U(1) relates to manufacturing records and is not specific to ASU systems. Thus, the schedules covering ASU medicines are Schedule E(1) and Schedule T.

34. Hundred-fold processing is associated with specific formulations:

A. Shatadhauta Ghrita literally means "hundred-washed ghee," where ghee is washed 100 times to achieve cooling, soothing properties.

B. Ksheerbala Aavartita Ghrita undergoes repeated processing cycles (Aavartana), often up to 100 times for special potency.

E. Abhrak Bhasma uses Shatputa (hundred-fold incineration) technique to obtain finest Abhraka bhasma.

Shatahva Ghrita and Shatavari Ghrita do not require hundred repetitions. Therefore, A, B and E fit correctly.

35. According to Sharangadhara Samhita, the increasing order of shelf-life (shortest to longest) is:

C. Swarasa Kalpana: Fresh juice preparations last only hours to 1 day.

D. Churna Kalpana: Dry powder lasts a few months.

E. Vati Kalpana: Pills/tablets last longer than churnas.

B. Ghrita Kalpana: Medicated ghee preparations last for years.

A. Asava–Arishta: Self-fermented preparations have the longest shelf life, improving with age.

Thus, the correct ascending order is C, D, E, B, A.

36. Phenodgama Taile (A) is a Sneha Siddhi Lakshana because the appearance of froth or foam in medicated oil indicates that all moisture has evaporated and the Sneha preparation has reached completion; this is a classical sign seen during proper taila paka. **Vartivat Snehakalka (C)** is also a correct Sneha Siddhi Lakshana, as the herbal paste (kalka) should roll into a wick-like structure smoothly without sticking, showing proper binding and absorption of the Sneha into the paste. **Shabdotpati (B)** is not accepted as Siddhi Lakshana because the absence of crackling sound—not the presence—is expected when moisture has fully evaporated. **Tantumatvam (D)** is not listed as a primary Sneha Siddhi sign, and **Peedite Mudra (E)**, although related to kalka testing, is not included in the final recognized Siddhi markers.

Therefore, the correct Sneha Siddhi Lakshanas among the given options are A and C only.

37. These five preparations are the Panchavidha Kashaya Kalpana, the fundamental pharmaceutical dosage forms in Ayurveda.

- Swarasa – fresh juice.
- Kalka – fine herbal paste.
- Kwatha – decoction prepared by boiling.
- Hima – cold infusion.
- Phanta – hot infusion.

These form the foundational extraction methods from which numerous formulations are derived. Options including Asava, Arishta, Sheha, and Avaleha represent secondary or advanced formulations. Therefore, the basic forms are Swarasa, Kalka, Kwatha, Hima, Phanta.

38. Ayurvedic rasa dravyas correspond to their modern chemical identities as follows:

- **Abhraka – II. Mica:** Abhraka is processed mica used in mineral Rasashastra preparations.
- **Gandhaka – III. Sulphur:** Gandhaka directly corresponds to elemental sulphur.
- **Shilajeet – IV. Black Bitumen:** Shilajeet is a natural exudate resembling mineral pitch or black bitumen.
- **Rasa – I. Mercury:** "Rasa" in Rasashastra refers to mercury (Parada), the primary metal in alchemical preparations.

Thus, the correct matching is A–II, B–III, C–IV, D–I.

39.
- **Kajjali – II. Kharaliya Rasayan:** Kajjali (black sulphide of mercury) is made by triturating mercury and sulphur in a mortar—thus a Kharaliya method.
- **Parpati – IV. Parpatika:** Parpati preparations require specific melting and spreading methods on a flat surface, characteristic of Parpatika techniques.
- **Ras Sindur – I. Kupipakva Rasayan:** Rasasindura is produced by heating Kajjali in a sealed glass bottle (Kupipakwa method).
- **Pottali – III. Gandhadrava Paaka:** Pottali preparations involve the Gandhaka-based heating and sublimation processes characteristic of Gandhadrava paaka.

Therefore, the appropriate matching is A–II, B–IV, C–I, D–III.

40. This organisation (PCIM&H) is responsible for developing standards, monographs, analytical methods, and quality norms for Ayurveda, Siddha, Unani, and

Homoeopathy formulations. It ensures quality assurance, standardisation, authentication of raw materials, and regulates pharmacopeial specifications. The National Medicinal Plant Board focuses on cultivation and conservation, not formulation quality standards; the Clinical Trial Registry of India manages trial registration; CSIR-IGIB is a research institute, not a standardisation authority. Hence the organisation facilitating quality assurance and standardisation of herbal formulations is the Pharmacopeia Commission of Indian Medicine and Homeopathy.

41. **Ras Pushpa (B)** and **Ras Karpura (C)** do not contain gandhaka. Ras Pushpa is a sublimated product of Shuddha Hingula obtained without sulphur addition. Ras Karpura is prepared by sublimation of purified mercury using agents such as Navasadara but not gandhaka. In contrast, **Ras Sindoora (A)**, **Ras Chandrodaya (D)**, and **Ras Manikya (E)** are sulphur–mercury compounds produced through processes like Kupipakva or Puta, where gandhaka is essential for forming the mercurial sulphides.

Therefore, the preparations lacking gandhaka are Ras Pushpa and Ras Karpura.

42. Uparasas are a category of minerals described in Rasashastra that assist in the purification and processing of mercury and Maharasas. The classical list includes substances such as Gandhaka (sulphur), Kasisa (green vitriol), Haritala (orpiment/arsenic trisulfide) and Kankushtha (gamboge), which are used for detoxification and alchemical transformations. The other listed groups are incorrect because Abhraka, Vaikrant, Makshika and Vimala are Maharasas, not Uparasas, and Kansya is a metal (Dhatu), not an Uparasa.

43. Hypertension is a major risk factor for cerebral hemorrhage because chronically elevated blood pressure weakens the walls of cerebral arteries, predisposing them to rupture. This leads to bleeding into brain tissue and is responsible for more than half of all intracerebral hemorrhage cases. Narrowing of the aorta is congenital rather than caused by hypertension; high cholesterol is an independent cardiovascular risk factor; venous thrombosis is linked to stasis or hypercoagulability, not hypertension.

Therefore, hypertension is most directly associated with cerebral hemorrhage.

44. **(A) Sindbis virus** binds to **high-density laminin protein (I)** via the 67 kDa laminin receptor. **(B) Coxsackie virus** attaches to **ICAM-1 (II)**, a cell adhesion molecule used by several enteroviruses. **(C) Human coronavirus** binds to **ACE/ACE2 (III)** receptors, the primary entry point for SARS-CoV-2 and related coronaviruses. **(D) HIV** uses **CD4 (IV)** as its main receptor on helper T-cells to initiate infection.

Thus, the correct matching is A-I, B-II, C-III, D-IV.

45. Interrupted mating experiments involve mixing an Hfr strain with an F^- recipient and periodically breaking the mating bridge to record when specific genes enter the recipient. Since genes closer to the origin of transfer enter first, the technique allows researchers to map the linear order of genes on the bacterial chromosome. It does not identify survival genes of Hfr cells, nor does it measure recombination rate, nor does it confirm plasmid integration (already known in Hfr strains). Therefore, the correct purpose is determining gene order.

46. Toxic shock syndrome is classically associated with *Staphylococcus aureus* (TSST-1) and sometimes *Streptococcus pyogenes*, not with *Escherichia coli*. *E. coli* is more commonly linked to urinary tract infections, neonatal meningitis, traveller's diarrhoea, and septicemia. The other pairs are correctly matched: *Borrelia burgdorferi* → Lyme disease; *Legionella pneumophila* → Legionnaires' disease; *Helicobacter pylori* → peptic ulcer disease. Therefore, "*Escherichia coli* – Toxic shock syndrome" is the incorrectly matched pathogen–disease pair.

47. In MHC class I antigen processing of viral proteins, the sequence is: first, the viral antigen is tagged by **polyubiquitination (B)**, marking it for degradation. Then it undergoes **binding to the proteasome and cleavage (D)** into small peptides. These peptides then interact with **TAP1 and TAP2 (E)**, which are transporter proteins on the endoplasmic reticulum (ER) membrane. Through TAP, there is **transport of antigen across the ER membrane (C)** into the ER lumen. Finally, the peptide loads onto the **MHC-I complex (A)**, after which the peptide–MHC-I complex moves to the cell surface for presentation to CD8+ T cells. Hence the correct order is B, D, E, C, A.

48. In the Gram staining procedure, the primary stain is crystal violet. It is the first dye applied to the bacterial smear and penetrates all cells, staining them purple. After this, iodine is added as a mordant to form a crystal violet–iodine complex, which is retained by Gram-positive bacteria but lost from Gram-negative bacteria during the decolorization step. Safranin is the counterstain used later to stain Gram-negative cells pink/red, and periodic Schiff reagent is used in special histochemical stains, not Gram staining. Thus, crystal violet is the primary stain.

49. **Type I hypersensitivity (A)** corresponds to **II. Anaphylaxis, IgE**, as it is IgE-mediated and leads to immediate allergic reactions such as anaphylaxis. **Type II hypersensitivity (B)** corresponds to **III. Cytotoxic, IgG and complement mediated**, where antibodies (IgG or IgM) target cell surfaces and activate complement to cause cell destruction. **Type III hypersensitivity (C)** corresponds to **I. Immune complex mediated**, involving deposition of antigen–antibody complexes in tissues, leading to inflammation (e.g., serum sickness). **Type IV hypersensitivity (D)** corresponds to **IV. Delayed type, sensitized CD4 and CD8 T-cell mediated**, where T cells cause delayed reactions such as contact dermatitis and tuberculin skin test responses.

Therefore, the correct matching is A-II, B-III, C-I, D-IV.

50. Starting from angiotensinogen, the sequence in the renin–angiotensin–aldosterone system is: **Production of Angiotensin I (D)** from angiotensinogen by renin. Then, **Production of Angiotensin II (B)** occurs via ACE (angiotensin-converting enzyme), mainly in the lungs. Angiotensin II then **acts on the adrenal cortex (C)**, stimulating it to synthesize **Aldosterone (E)**. Aldosterone finally causes **increased Na^+ retention in kidneys (A)**, which raises blood volume and blood pressure.

Thus, the correct order is D, B, C, E, A.

51. Sickle-cell anemia results from a single point mutation (Glu → Val substitution) in the β-globin gene (HBB) on chromosome 11. Individuals with sickle-cell trait (heterozygous, HbAS) are less susceptible to severe *Plasmodium falciparum* malaria because the altered hemoglobin causes early destruction of parasitized red blood cells, limiting parasite survival. It is not multigenic, and typhoid susceptibility is not related to this mutation.

52. India's indigenous COVID-19 vaccine, Covaxin, developed by Bharat Biotech in collaboration with ICMR-NIV, is an inactivated whole-virion vaccine, where entire SARS-CoV-2 particles are chemically inactivated but retain antigenicity. Covishield is a recombinant adenoviral-vector vaccine, not inactivated, and Covaxin is not mRNA based. Therefore, Covaxin – Inactivated whole virion is the correct pair.

53. Somatic hypermutation (D) and class-switch recombination (E) occur only after antigen activation, in germinal centres during the adaptive immune response. These processes fine-tune antibody affinity and change antibody isotype, respectively. By contrast, V(D)J recombination (A), P-nucleotide addition (B), and N-nucleotide addition (C) occur before antigen exposure, during early B-cell development in the bone marrow. Hence, only D and E operate after antigen activation.

54. The hinge region, located between the Fab and Fc portions of the antibody, provides flexibility, allowing the two antigen-binding Fab arms to move independently and bind antigens at various spatial orientations. The Fab, Fab′, and Fc regions contribute to binding or effector functions, but the hinge region is responsible for structural flexibility. Thus, hinge region is correct.

55. $CD4^+$ T lymphocytes perform key helper functions: **macrophage activation (A)** via Th1 cytokines, **B-cell differentiation (B)** via Th2/Th follicular pathways, and **stimulation of inflammation (D)** through Th17-mediated cytokine release. **Killing of infected cells (C)** is the function of $CD8^+$ cytotoxic T cells, and suppression of other **T cells (E)** is characteristic of regulatory T cells (Tregs).

Hence, the correct set of $CD4^+$ T-cell functions is A, B and D.

56. For a solution containing proteinaceous growth factors, high temperature methods like autoclaving or pasteurization would denature the proteins and destroy their biological activity. UV light has poor penetration and is unreliable for fully sterilizing a liquid volume. Ultrafiltration, using a membrane with pore size around 0.22 μm, physically removes bacteria and most microorganisms while preserving the structure and function of sensitive proteins. Therefore, ultrafiltration is the optimal strategy to obtain a microorganism-free solution suitable for cell culture.

57. The germ theory of disease, which states that specific microorganisms are the cause of many diseases, is primarily credited to Louis Pasteur. Through experiments on fermentation, pasteurization, and disproving spontaneous generation, Pasteur showed that microbes cause spoilage and disease. Robert Koch later built on this with his postulates linking specific microbes to specific diseases, but the conceptual germ theory itself is attributed to Pasteur. Edward Jenner pioneered vaccination and James Watson is known for DNA structure, not for germ theory.

58. In this capillary bed, pO_2 decreases (100 → 50 mmHg) and pCO_2 increases (41 → 46 mmHg), showing that the tissue is consuming oxygen and producing carbon dioxide—typical of systemic (not pulmonary) capillaries. Glucose increases from 4 to 8 mM, meaning blood is gaining glucose from the tissue it drains. This is characteristic of the small intestine, where absorbed dietary glucose enters the blood, so venous (portal) blood leaving the gut has higher glucose than arterial blood entering it. Urea is unchanged, which fits an absorptive organ like the intestine rather than the liver, which would alter urea levels. Thus, the capillary bed is most likely in the small intestine.

59. When a neuron is stimulated by a neurotransmitter, events occur in this order: **shift from resting membrane potential (B)** as ligand-gated channels open and small depolarizations (EPSPs) occur. If these summate enough, the **membrane potential reaches threshold (A)** at the axon hillock. Once threshold is reached, voltage-gated Na^+ channels open, leading to rapid **depolarization of the membrane (D)**. After that, Na^+ channels inactivate and K^+ channels open, causing **repolarization of**

the membrane (C). Often the K^+ efflux overshoots, producing **hyperpolarization of the membrane (E)** before returning to resting potential.

So, the correct sequence is B, A, D, C, E.

60. **Type II alveolar cells (A)** are found in the **lungs (III)** and are responsible for surfactant production to reduce surface tension in alveoli. **Podocytes (B)** are specialized epithelial cells in the **nephron (I)**, forming the visceral layer of Bowman's capsule and participating in filtration. **Parietal cells (C)** are located in the **stomach (IV)** and secrete hydrochloric acid and intrinsic factor. **Astrocytes (D)** are star-shaped glial cells in the **brain (II)**, involved in metabolic support, ion balance, and blood–brain barrier maintenance.

Therefore, the correct matching is A-III, B-I, C-IV, D-II.

61. **Inhibin (A)** corresponds to **III. Inhibits FSH secretion,** because inhibin released from Sertoli and granulosa cells selectively suppresses FSH from the anterior pituitary. **LH (B)** corresponds to **IV. Responsible for ovulation**, as the mid-cycle LH surge triggers ovulation. **Human chorionic gonadotropin (C)** corresponds to **I. Rescues corpus luteum**, because hCG maintains the corpus luteum in early pregnancy so that progesterone secretion continues. **Oxytocin (D)** corresponds to **II. Promotes uterine contraction**, as it acts on uterine smooth muscle to enhance labor contractions and milk ejection.

Thus, A-III, B-IV, C-I, D-II is correct.

62. Cystic fibrosis is not classified as an inborn error of metabolism; it is a genetic disorder caused by mutations in the CFTR chloride channel affecting epithelial secretions. Phenylketonuria, alkaptonuria, and Hartnup disease are classical inborn errors of metabolism, each involving defective enzymes or transporters that impair amino acid metabolism. Thus, cystic fibrosis is the only option not belonging to this category.

63. Phosphofructokinase-1 (PFK-1) is the key regulatory enzyme of glycolysis because it catalyzes the rate-limiting step: conversion of fructose-6-phosphate to fructose-1,6-bisphosphate. It is tightly regulated by ATP, AMP, citrate, and fructose-2,6-bisphosphate. Glucokinase affects glucose entry into glycolysis but is not the main regulatory step; pyruvate kinase regulates the final step; aldolase is not rate-limiting. Therefore, PFK-1 is the principal regulatory enzyme of glycolysis.

64. Glycoproteins contain peptide bonds between amino acids, glycosidic bonds linking carbohydrate moieties, and abundant hydrogen bonds contributing to structural stability. However, phosphodiester bonds are characteristic of nucleic acids, not glycoproteins. Since glycoproteins do not use phosphate linkages to join their carbohydrate or protein components, phosphodiester bonds are not present.

65. Glycogen phosphorylase (A) requires **PLP (III)** as a cofactor for catalyzing phosphorolysis of glycogen. Succinate dehydrogenase (B) uses **FAD (IV)** as its prosthetic group in both the TCA cycle and electron transport chain. Glutamate dehydrogenase (C) uses **NAD^+/$NADP^+$ (I)** for oxidative deamination of glutamate. Acetyl-CoA carboxylase (D) requires **biotin (II)** as a cofactor for carboxylation reactions in fatty acid synthesis.

Therefore, the correct matching is A-III, B-IV, C-I, D-II.

66. Nanoparticles in the 1–20 nm range are most likely to exhibit higher permeability across the blood–brain barrier (BBB), assuming surface properties (charge, ligands, hydrophobicity) are optimised. The BBB has very tight junctions and efficient efflux systems, so only very small particles can effectively cross via transcytosis or passive diffusion-like mechanisms. Larger particles (50–100 nm or 150–200 nm) are more readily recognised, cleared, or simply too big for efficient transport, and 20–40 nm generally shows less penetration than ultra-small (sub-20 nm) particles. Therefore the 1–20 nm range offers the highest potential for BBB permeability.

67. In real-time PCR (qPCR), the Ct (cycle threshold) value is defined as the PCR cycle number at which the fluorescence signal of the amplification curve first crosses a preset threshold line that is above background noise. Lower Ct values indicate higher initial template concentration (higher viral load), while higher Ct values indicate lower template amounts. It is not defined by 50% amplification, saturation of amplification, or a particular ΔRn match; the key is the intersection of the amplification curve with the fixed threshold.

68. **A.** **Okazaki fragments are covalently joined by DNA ligase – correct;** DNA ligase seals nicks between Okazaki fragments on the lagging strand.

D. **Okazaki fragments get synthesized in lagging strand – correct;** lagging strand synthesis is discontinuous and produces Okazaki fragments.

E. **Helicase and primase involves in replication – correct;** helicase unwinds the DNA helix and primase synthesizes RNA primers for DNA polymerase.

(B) is wrong because the leading strand is continuous and the lagging strand is discontinuous, not the other way round.

(C) is wrong because rolling-circle replication is typical of some plasmids and viruses, not of yeast chromosomal DNA replication.

Hence, the correct set is A, D and E only.

69. A. **Poly A tail – III. Added after transcription:** The poly(A) tail is added post-transcriptionally at the 3′ end of eukaryotic mRNA during RNA processing.

B. **5′ untranslated region – I. Kozak sequence:** The Kozak sequence lies around the start codon (AUG) within the 5′ UTR region and is crucial for ribosomal recognition and efficient translation initiation.

C. **Translation start site – IV. AUG:** The translation start site in eukaryotes is typically the AUG codon, encoding methionine.

D. **Enhancer sequence – II. Orientation independent:** Enhancers are regulatory DNA elements that function largely independent of orientation and can act at variable distances from the promoter.

Thus, the correct matching pattern is A-III, B-I, C-IV, D-II.

70. A. **Histone acetylation and DNA methylation** – direct epigenetic regulation of gene expression at the chromatin level (turning genes on/off).

D. **Protein processing and degradation** – post-translational regulation; protein activation, modification, and controlled degradation (e.g., via ubiquitin–proteasome system) significantly regulate gene expression outcomes.

E. **RNA processing like alternative RNA splicing** – post-transcriptional regulation; different splice forms can generate multiple proteins from one gene or modulate whether a protein is made at all.

B. **DNA replication and repair** are primarily genome maintenance processes, not direct regulatory checkpoints of gene expression pattern.

C. **cAMP binding to promoter of a gene** describes a bacterial-type CAP–cAMP mechanism; in eukaryotes, cAMP acts via signalling cascades and transcription factors (e.g., CREB), not by directly binding promoters.

Therefore, the correct regulatory stages listed here are A, D and E only.

71. To estimate the melting temperature (T_m) of a short DNA primer, the common rule is:

Tm ≈ 2°C × (number of A + T) + 4°C × (number of G + C).

Primer: 5′–AGACTCAGAGAGAACCC–3′

A: 7

T: 1

G: 4

C: 5

So:

$$A + T = 7 + 1 = 8$$
$$G + C = 4 + 5 = 9$$

$T_m = 2 \times 8 + 4 \times 9 = 16 + 36 = 52°C$.

Hence, the melting temperature is approximately 52°C.

72. The pedigree shows affected individuals in BOTH sexes, and the disorder appears even when both parents are unaffected, as seen in Family I–1 × I–2 producing an affected daughter (II–2). This is only possible when both parents are carriers (heterozygous) and the trait is autosomal recessive.

In the right branch, an affected parent (I–4) and a carrier parent (I–3) produce a mix of affected (aa) and carrier (Aa) children, which is exactly expected in autosomal recessive inheritance.

X-linked recessive is ruled out because affected females require an affected father, which is not the case here.

X-linked dominant is ruled out because affected males do not pass the trait to all daughters.

Autosomal dominant is ruled out because unaffected parents cannot produce affected children.

Therefore, the pattern matches autosomal recessive inheritance.

73. The genotype AaBbCcDd has four independently assorting heterozygous loci. A test cross uses an individual homozygous recessive for all loci (aabbccdd). For each gene pair (A/a, B/b, C/c, D/d), the cross produces two phenotypic possibilities in a 1:1 ratio (dominant phenotype if heterozygous vs recessive if homozygous recessive).

- Number of independently assorting loci = 4
- Number of possible phenotypes = 2^4 = 16 (all combinations of presence/absence of each dominant trait).

Thus, 16 different phenotypes can appear in the progeny.

74. Z-DNA is a left-handed helical form of DNA, structurally distinct from the common right-handed B-DNA. Key points:

- Z-DNA has about 12 base pairs per turn, while B-DNA has about 10–10.5 bp per turn, so Z-DNA indeed has more bp/turn than B-DNA.
- Z-DNA is typically favoured by alternating purine–pyrimidine sequences, especially CG repeats, not alternating AT sequences.
- It is often found near transcriptionally active regions, but not specifically at the 3′ ends of genes.
- B-DNA, not Z-DNA, is the most common conformation in cells.

Therefore, the only correct statement given is that Z-DNA has more base pairs per turn than B-DNA.

75. Hypospadias here is caused by an autosomal gene but is expressed only in males (urethral opening abnormality on the penis) and not in females, even though females can carry the same allele. That pattern—where a trait is determined by a non-sex (autosomal) gene but its expression is restricted to one sex because it depends on sex-specific anatomy or hormonal milieu—is called a sex-limited trait.

- It is not X-linked or Y-linked inheritance, because the gene is autosomal.
- It is not just "sex-influenced" (where expression differs between sexes but can appear in both); here, females are not affected at all.

Thus, the phenomenon is sex limited trait.

76. Renaturation rate depends on how frequently complementary strands encounter each other; this is higher when many identical copies are present. Highly repetitive sequences exist in very large copy number, so complementary strands are abundant and reanneal rapidly as temperature falls. Unique sequences, exons and introns exist at much lower effective concentration of matching partners, so they re-associate more slowly.

77. The classical Sanger sequencing method uses dideoxyribonucleoside triphosphates (ddNTPs) as chain terminators. When a ddNTP is incorporated, it lacks the 3′-OH group, preventing further elongation. By running four reactions (or fluorescently labelled ddNTPs in one reaction), fragments ending at each base are generated and then separated to determine the DNA sequence.

78. The smooth endoplasmic reticulum (SER) is specialized for lipid and steroid synthesis, detoxification of drugs and poisons, and in some cells regulation of Ca^{2+} storage (e.g., sarcoplasmic reticulum). Secretory protein synthesis occurs on rough ER (with ribosomes), ATP is mainly generated in mitochondria, and vesicle formation is a general membrane process, not a specific SER function.

79. The first draft of the Human Genome came from two parallel strategies, both using Sanger sequencing: the public Human Genome Project used a clone-by-clone (hierarchical BAC) approach, while Celera Genomics used whole genome shotgun sequencing. Together these produced the initial draft sequence published around 2001. VNTR mapping, bisulphite sequencing, RNA-seq and Illumina-based methods are from later or different applications, not the original draft genome strategy.

80. In terms of typical read length from shortest to longest:

A. **Illumina sequencing** gives the shortest reads (commonly ~75–300 bp).

B. **Pyrosequencing/Roche 454** produces intermediate reads (~400–700 bp).

C. **Single Molecule Real Time (SMRT) sequencing** yields the longest reads (often 10 kb or more).

Thus, the increasing order of read length is Illumina < Pyrosequencing < SMRT, i.e. A < B < C.

81. During the Human Genome Project, the greatest difficulty in assembling contiguous sequences and annotating them arose from highly repetitive DNA (e.g., transposons, satellite DNA), which occurs in millions of nearly identical copies. Short reads from such regions cannot be uniquely placed on the genome, leading to gaps, misassemblies and ambiguous contigs. Heterochromatin patches and long chromosome length also pose difficulties, but the principal hurdle for accurate sequence assembly and annotation was the prevalence of repetitive DNA.

82. Known DNA repair mechanisms include non-homologous end joining (NHEJ) for double-strand breaks, base-excision repair (BER) for small base lesions, and nucleotide excision repair (NER) for bulky adducts such as thymine dimers. Molecular chaperones act mainly on proteins—assisting their folding, refolding or preventing aggregation—and are not themselves a defined DNA repair pathway. Thus "chaperones-mediated repair" is not recognised as a DNA repair mechanism.

83. The average weight of the test group is obtained by adding all six values (15 + 18 + 21 + 16 + 14 + 19 = 103) and dividing by 6, giving 17.16 g.

The control group average is found by adding its six values (25 + 28 + 22 + 31 + 30 + 32 = 168) and dividing by 6, giving 28 g.

The average decrease is the difference between the two means, which is 28 − 17.16 = 10.83 g.

This value lies between 11.4 and 10.1 and is close to both answer choices.

Therefore, both option 2 (11.4) and option 3 (10.1) satisfy the calculated decrease within rounding approximation.

84. In statistics, **(A)** μ **(mu)** denotes the population **mean** **(IV)**; **(B)** σ **(sigma)** denotes the population **standard deviation (III)**; **(C) r** is the **correlation coefficient** **(I)** measuring linear association between two variables; and **(D)** χ^2 (chi-square) denotes the **chi-square statistic** **(II)** used in tests of independence or goodness of fit. Hence the correct matching is A-IV, B-III, C-I, D-II.

85. Common extraction techniques for plant materials include **maceration (1)**, where plant material soaks in solvent; **decoction (2)**, in which plant material is boiled in water; and Soxhlet **extraction (3)**, a continuous hot solvent extraction method. **Refraction** **(4)** is not an extraction technique in pharmacognosy or phytochemistry; it relates to bending of light in optics, not to separation of phytochemicals.

Therefore, refraction is the one that is not an extraction technique.

86. The PPV&FR Act, 2001 (Protection of Plant Varieties and Farmers' Rights Act) legally safeguards plant varieties by granting plant breeders' rights and ensures farmers' rights such as saving, resowing, exchanging, and sharing seeds. The Act does not deal with consumer rights, industrial rights, or patient rights; it specifically protects breeders and farmers involved in plant variety development.

87. The producers (plants, algae, photosynthetic organisms) capture maximum solar energy and convert it into chemical energy during photosynthesis. As energy flows up trophic levels, only about 10% is transferred each time, so primary producers hold the greatest free energy, far more than herbivores, carnivores, or decomposers.

88. The Ministry of Ayush operates the Ayurgyan Scheme, an umbrella programme designed to strengthen education, research, and innovation in AYUSH systems. Under its Research and Innovation component, the scheme specifically supports the creation of business incubators to promote entrepreneurship and facilitate academia–industry co-development partnerships. This structure helps in scientific validation, new drug development, and commercialization of AYUSH technologies, making Ayurgyan Yojna the correct scheme associated with establishing AYUSH incubators.

89. In every trophic transfer, most energy is lost as heat through metabolism, respiration, and incomplete digestion. Because only a small portion is passed to the next trophic level, the energy pyramid becomes progressively narrower at higher levels, regardless of organism size or number.

90. **(A) Phase I** aims to **determine toxicity and side effects (III)** in a small group.

(B) Phase II focuses on **dose–response** (I) relationships and therapeutic range.

(C) Phase III compares the new drug with **established treatments** (IV) on a large population.

(D) Phase IV involves **post-marketing** (II) surveillance to detect long-term safety issues.

91. The active ingredients are described as hydrophobic, so they dissolve poorly in water but well in lipidic or organic media. In Ayurveda and modern pharmaceutics, ghee, alcohol, and hydroalcoholic mixtures are all good choices for extracting lipophilic (fat-soluble) compounds. Water, being highly polar, is the least preferred medium for hydrophobic plant constituents and would extract mainly hydrophilic components, missing much of the neuroprotective fraction.

92. To initiate investigation of neuroprotective activity, the most appropriate starting point is in vitro assays with neuronal primary cells or neural cell lines. These systems allow controlled testing of toxicity, neuroprotection against known insults (e.g., oxidative stress, glutamate toxicity), and mechanism clues, while maintaining ethical and cost advantages over animal or human studies. In silico studies alone do not establish biological activity, in vivo animal tests come after promising in vitro data, and direct testing on humans is unethical at this early stage.

93. Once an active fraction is obtained, LC-MS/MS (Liquid Chromatography–Tandem Mass Spectrometry) is the most suitable technique to identify constituent molecules. The LC part separates complex mixtures, and MS/MS provides precise molecular weight and fragmentation patterns, enabling structural elucidation and identification of each compound. Ion-exchange, HPLC, and HPTLC mainly separate and profile components but, without coupled mass analysis, are less definitive for detailed molecular identification.

94. After the NMR-based structure of the active molecule is known, molecular docking is the ideal bioinformatics method to predict molecular targets. Docking simulates how the small molecule binds to various protein structures (receptors, enzymes, channels), estimating binding affinity and interaction sites, thereby suggesting likely targets. ADMET analysis focuses on absorption and toxicity; pharmacophore modeling is more for designing or screening analogs; structure-based phylogeny deals with evolutionary relationships, not target identification.

95. For an Ayurvedic formulation aimed at neuroprotection using a leaf with hydrophobic active principles, Sneha Kalpana (medicated ghee/oil) is the most suitable dosage form. Lipid-based preparations efficiently extract and carry fat-soluble constituents and are traditionally used for medhya (cognitive and nervous system) actions, with ghee known to facilitate crossing of lipid barriers, including the blood–brain barrier. Asava (fermented hydroalcoholic), Churna (powder), and Kwatha (decoction) are less optimal for maximizing delivery of lipophilic neuroactive compounds.

96. Her symptoms—dry skin, brittle hair, weight loss, constipation, irregular painful periods, anxiety, panic attacks, disturbed sleep—are classic indicators of Vata prakriti / Vata aggravation. Pitta types show heat, acidity, inflammation; Kapha types show heaviness, lethargy, weight gain. Her entire picture aligns predominantly with Vata dominance.

97. A Vata-dominant individual with nutritional decline must avoid intermittent fasting, as fasting worsens Vata. Instead:

B. Easily digestible, nutrient-rich foods at regular intervals help stabilize Vata.

C. Include organic milk and ghee—both are Vata-pacifying, grounding, nourishing.

D. Increase fruits and vegetables, particularly warm, cooked, Vata-soothing ones.

Therefore, the correct combination is B, C, D.

98.

$$\text{BMI} = \text{weight (kg)}/\text{height}^2\ (\text{m}^2)$$
$$\text{Height} = 165\text{ cm} = 1.65\text{ m}$$
$$\Rightarrow \text{height}^2 = 1.65^2 = 2.7225$$
$$\text{BMI} = 48/2.7225 = 17.6$$

This indicates underweight, consistent with Vata imbalance.

99. She has:

- High androgen levels
- Pelvic ultrasound abnormality
- Irregular painful periods
- Hirsutism

These are classical criteria for PCOS. Weight loss and anxiety do not contradict PCOS; Vata-type PCOS presentations are well known. The others do not fit:

- Anorexia: severe weight loss + food refusal—absent here
- Amenorrhea: only absence of menses, not the full picture
- Crohn's: GI inflammation—not supported by symptoms

100. For PCOS with clear Vata aggravation, useful Ayurvedic strategies include:

A. Nidan parivarjana – removing causes (stress, irregular routines, poor diet)

B. Ojo vardhak – strengthening Ojas to reduce anxiety, improve sleep and vitality

D. Vata shamak – essential because her clinical picture is dominated by Vata derangement

Kapha-hara is avoided because she is underweight, not overweight; Kapha is not the issue.

Previous Years' Paper

National Testing Agency (NTA)

UGC-NET Junior Research Fellowship & Assistant Professor Eligibility Exam

AYURVEDA BIOLOGY, JANUARY-2025

(Exam held on 09-01-2025)

PAPER-II

1. Which mammalian immune organ among the following undergo involution with aging?

1. Thymus
2. Spleen
3. Lymph nodes
4. Tonsils

2. Match the List-I with List-II.

List-I (Hypersensitivity)	List-II (Immune Mediator)
A. Type-1 Hypersensitivity	I. IgG/IgM
B. Type-2 Hypersensitivity	II. IgE
C. Type-3 Hypersensitivity	III. T Cells
D. Type-4 Hypersensitivity	IV. Immune complexes

Choose the *correct* answer from the options given below:

1. A-III, B-II, C-IV, D-I
2. A-I, B-II, C-III, D-IV
3. A-IV, B-I, C-III, D-II
4. A-II, B-I, C-IV, D-III

3. The Protection of Plant Varieties and Farmer's Rights Act of India enacted in:

1. 1952
2. 1971
3. 2001
4. 2022

4. Match the List-I with List-II.

List-I (Food conversion factors)	List-II (Functions)
A. Ushma	I. Shaithilya
B. Vayu	II. Mruduta
C. Kleda	III. Apakarshana
D. Sneha	IV. Pachana

Choose the *correct* answer from the options given below:

1. A-II, B-I, C-IV, D-III
2. A-I, B-IV, C-III, D-II
3. A-III, B-II, C-IV, D-I
4. A-IV, B-III, C-I, D-II

5. While preparation of a formulations, if the useful part of a drug is not mentioned, then what should be taken?

1. Leaves
2. Flowers
3. Root
4. Stembark

6. What is the correct order of the following herbal formulations in increasing order of their potency?

A. Kalka
B. Hima
C. Swarasa
D. Phanta
E. Kwatha

Choose the *correct* answer from the options given below:

1. A, B, C, D, E
2. E, D, C, B, A
3. C, A, E, B, D
4. D, B, E, A, C

7. Regulation of glycolytic pathway in muscles occurs via:

A. Allosteric modulation
B. Enzyme turnover
C. Feedback regulation
D. Compartmentalization
E. Covalent modification

Choose the *correct* combination from the options given below:

1. A, B, E only
2. A, C, E only
3. A, C, D, E only
4. C, D, E only

8. A colour blind man marries a homozygous normal woman. What is the probability of the son being colour blind?

1. $\frac{1}{2}$
2. $\frac{1}{4}$
3. 0
4. 1

9. The colloidal "ruby" gold nanoparticles properties were discovered by:

1. Erwin Muller
2. Michael Faraday
3. William Shockley
4. Robert Hook

10. To create a genetic map of gene on an autosome, which of the following crosses need to be done?

1. Back cross
2. Test cross
3. Reciprocal cross
4. Double reciprocal cross

11. Which of the following is NOT a typical phase in Ayurveda start up development?

1. Clinical trials
2. Manufacturing scale up
3. Product marketing
4. Real estate investment

12. Which of the following are "Avidahi" Rasa?

1. Lavana, Tikta, Kashaya
2. Madhura, Tikta, Kashaya
3. Madhura, Lavana, Kashaya
4. Tikta. Madhura, Katu

13. Match the List-I with List-II.

List-I (Panchmahabhuta)	List-II (Lakshan)
A. Prithvi	I. Chalatva
B. Tej	II. Kharatva
C. Aakash	III. Ushmatva
D. Vayu	IV. Apratighata

Choose the ***correct*** answer from the options given below:

1. A-III, B-II, C-I, D-IV
2. A-I, B-II, C-IV, D-III
3. A-IV, B-III, C-I, D-II
4. A-II, B-III, C-IV, D-I

14. What is the correct sequence of events in a Polymerase Chain Reaction?

A. Addition of Taq
B. Denaturation
C. Termination
D. Annealing
E. Extension

Choose the ***correct*** answer from the options given below:

1. D, A, B, C, E
2. A, B, D, E, C
3. B, D, A, E, C
4. A, E, D, C, B

15. Match the List-I with List-II.

List-I (Cofactor)	List-II (Enzyme)
A. Thiamine Pyrophosphate	I. Glycogen phosphorylase
B. Flavin Adenine Dinucleotide	II. Pyruvate carboxylase
C. Pyridoxal phosphate	III. Glutathione Reductase
D. Biotin	IV. Pyruvate dehydrogenase

Choose the ***correct*** answer from the options given below:

1. A-IV, B-III, C-I, D-II
2. A-II, B-IV, C-III, D-I
3. A-III, B-IV, C-II, D-I
4. A-II, B-I, C-IV, D-III

16. What amongst these is NOT considered as component of P4 medicine?

1. Participatory
2. Predictive
3. Pharmacology
4. Personalised

17. What are the Shada (six) Padartha according to Ayurveda?

1. Prithvi, Jal, Vayu, Teja, Aakash, Mana
2. Dravya, Guna, Karma, Samanya, Vishesh, Samavaya
3. Madhur, Amla, Lavana, Tikta, Katu, Kashaya
4. Ushma, Vayu, Kled, Sneha, Kala, Samyoga

18. Which of the following are considered amongst eight veerya (potency) in Ayurvedic Medicine?

A. Guru
B. Teekshna
C. Sheeghra
D. Sheeta
E. Sthira

Choose the ***correct*** answer from the options given below:

1. B, C, D only
2. C, D, E only
3. A, B, D only
4. B, D, E only

19. Which statements are TRUE for bioinformatic analysis of genes and protein sequences?

A. E-value in multiple alignment in elution value
B. Genbank is a primary database
C. Evolutionary analysis is not possible with sequence analysis
D. BLAST is known as Basic Local Alignment Search Tool
E. DNA sequences are usually represented in FASTA format

Choose the ***correct*** combination from the options given below:

1. B, D, E only
2. A, C, E only
3. C, D, E only
4. A, B, C only

20. Which of the following are Jnanendriyas?

A. Ghranendriya
B. Shravanendriya
C. Vageendriya
D. Sparshnendriya
E. Hastendriya

Choose the *correct* combination from the options given below:

1. B, C, D only
2. E, D, A only
3. A, B, D only
4. C, D, B only

21. Which amongst the following are the main sites of Vata Dosha?

A. Chest
B. Rectum
C. Eyes
D. Stomach

Choose the *correct* answer from the options given below:

1. A and D only
2. B and D only
3. A and B only
4. D and C only

22. Match the List-I with List-II.

List-I (Rasadravya)	List-II (Symbol of modern chemical equivalents)
A. Tamra	I. Zn
B. Vanga	II. Pb
C. Yashada	III. Cu
D. Naga	IV. Sn

Choose the *correct* answer from the options given below:

1. A-III, B-I, C-II, D-IV
2. A-III, B-IV, C-I, D-II
3. A-I, B-II, C-III, D-IV
4. A-II, B-III, C-I, D-IV

23. Which of the following are the three Sutras in Trisutra Ayurveda?

1. Satva, Atma, Sharir
2. Dravya, Guna, Karma
3. Koshta, Shakha, Marma
4. Hetu, Linga, Aushadha

24. Which of the following are Manasika Dosha?

1. Chintyam, Vicharyam, Uhyam
2. Raja, Tama
3. Vata, Pitta, Kapha
4. Raga, Dvesha, Sukha-Dukha

25. When a bacteriophage binds to the host bacterial cell and transfers the genetic material, it is termed as:

1. Recombination
2. Transformation
3. Conjugation
4. Transduction

26. Match the List-I with List-II.

List-I (Herbs)	List-II (Phytoconstituents)
A. Vacha	I. Asarone
B. Hritpatri	II. Aconitine
C. Khadir	III. Digitoxin
D. Vatsanabha	IV. Catechin

Choose the *correct* answer from the options given below:

1. A-I, B-III, C-IV, D-II
2. A-II, B-IV, C-I, D-III
3. A-IV, B-III, C-I, D-II
4. A-III, B-I, C-IV, D-II

27. Which among the following is NOT a lifestyle disorder?

1. Coronary artery disease
2. Stroke
3. Type 1 diabetes
4. Type 2 diabetes

28. Down's Syndrome occurs because of:

1. Trisomy of the 18th chromosome
2. Trisomy of the 21st chromosome
3. Monosomy of the sex chromosome
4. Nullesomy of the 21st chromosome

29. A phenotype in a population move away from the Hardy Weinberg equilibrium if the population is subjected to which condition?

1. Random mating
2. A stable gene pool
3. Genetic drift
4. Geographical isolation

30. Cause of biodiversity losses are:

A. Herbivorous wild animals
B. Alien species invasion
C. Habitant loss and fragmentation
D. Creation of wild life sanctuaries
E. Over exploitation

Choose the *correct* combination from the options given below:

1. C, D, E only
2. B, C, E only
3. A, C, E only
4. A, B, C only

31. Western blotting is:

1. DNA blot probed with DNA oligonucleotides
2. RNA blot probed with DNA oligonucleotides
3. Protein blot probed with Antibody
4. Protein blot probed with DNA oligonucleotides

32. Which among the following is **NOT** a type of Pramana (evidence type)?

1. Samvaya
2. Upaman
3. Yukti
4. Arthapatti

33. Guidelines for good manufacturing practices for Ayurveda, Siddha and Unani drugs are placed in which schedule of Drugs and Cosmetics, Rules 1945?

1. H
2. M
3. T
4. Y

34. Match the List-I with List-II.

List-I (Ayurveda Kal)	List-II (Time Period)
A. Samhita Kal	I. 14th Century to Modern Period
B. Vyakhya Kal	II. 5th Century to 6th Century
C. Sangrah Kal	III. 7th Century to 15th Century
D. Emergence Period of Ayurveda	IV. 1500 B.C to 1000 B.C

Choose the ***correct*** answer from the options given below:

1. A-I, B-IV, C-III, D-II
2. A-II, B-III, C-I, D-IV
3. A-III, B-I, C-II, D-IV
4. A-IV, B-III, C-II, D-I

35. What are four pillars of therapy amongst the following?

1. Vaidya, Dravya, Upasthata and Rogi
2. Dakshata, Vyadhinash, Chaturta and Smaran Shakti
3. Dravya, Chaturta, Vaidya and Upasthata
4. Aushadh Kalpna, Pavitrata, Shastragyan and Nirbhayata

36. Find the most appropriate match for items listed under:

List-I	List-II
A. Ayurvedic Pharmacopoeia of India	I. Adverse drug reaction reporting
B. Shelf life of Ayurvedic drugs	II. Disintegration time
C. Pharmacovigilance	III. Rule 161B
D. Tablet	IV. Standards for Ayurvedic drugs

Choose the ***correct*** answer from the options given below:

1. A-IV, B-III, C-II, D-I
2. A-IV, B-III, C-I, D-II
3. A-I, B-II, C-III, D-IV
4. A-I, B-IV, C-III, D-II

37. Which of the following statements are TRUE for promoter of a gene?

A. They are orientation dependent
B. They are orientation independent
C. They are present in 3'-region of the gene
D. They are present in 5'-region of the gene
E. They are important for gene expression

Choose the ***correct*** combination from the options given below:

1. A, D, E only
2. A, C, E only
3. B, D, E only
4. B, C, D only

38. Which of the following among Nidana Panchaka relates to modern disease mechanistic studies?

1. Hetu
2. Lakshana
3. Purvaroopa
4. Samprapti

39. Match the List-I with List-II.

List-I (Organism)	List-II (Sex determination)
A. Honey Bees	I. X : Y chromosome
B. *Drosophila melanogester*	II. Genic sex determination
C. Mice	III. X : A Ratio
D. *Saccharomyces cerevisiae*	IV. Haplodiploidy

Choose the ***correct*** answer from the options given below:

1. A-II, B-I, C-IV, D-III
2. A-II, B-III, C-I, D-IV
3. A-III, B-I, C-IV, D-II
4. A-IV, B-III, C-I, D-II

40. Match the List-I with List-II.

List-I (Dosha)	List-II (Main Site)
A. Apanavayu	I. Basti
B. Vyaanavayu	II. Koshtha
C. Samanvayu	III. Hridaya
D. Pranvayu	IV. Moordha

Choose the ***correct*** answer from the options given below:

1. A-II, B-III, C-I, D-IV
2. A-I, B-III, C-II, D-IV
3. A-I, B-IV, C-II, D-III
4. A-III, B-IV, C-I, D-II

41. According to the general rule, what is the ratio of Kalka : Snehadravya : : Dravadravya in the preparation of Sneha Kalpana?

1. 1 : 4 : : 16
2. 1 : 2 : : 4
3. 1 : 8 : : 32
4. 1 : 2 : : 3

42. Following Prakriti features can be correlated with which phenotyping methods developed in modern science.

List-I (Prakriti features)	List-II (Modern phenotyping methods)
A. Aakriti	I. Chronotypes
B. Varna	II. Somatotypes
C. Nidra	III. Phototypes
D. Agni-koshtha	IV. Metabotypes

Choose the ***correct*** answer from the options given below:

1. A-III, B-II, C-IV, D-I
2. A-IV, B-I, C-III, D-II
3. A-II, B-IV, C-I, D-III
4. A-II, B-III, C-I, D-IV

43. The Indian Legislature - Patents Act of India was mainly introduced in the year:

1. 1970
2. 1955
3. 1984
4. 2012

44. Arrange the following WBC types in increasing order of their count in normal human blood.

A. Neurophils
B. Basophils
C. Lymphocytes
D. Monocytes
E. Eosinophils

Choose the ***correct*** answer from the options given below:

1. A, C, B, D, E
2. E, B, D, C, A
3. A, C, D, B, E
4. B, E, C, D, A

45. Which of the following bond is **NOT** a part of the Polynucleotide sequence?

1. Hydrogen bond
2. Phosphodiester bond
3. Amide bond
4. Glycosidic bond

46. Consider the following steps involved in Avaleha preparation. The correct sequence is:

A. Preparation of Kwatha
B. Reduction of mixture to proper consistency
C. Addition of sweetening agent
D. Addition of prakshepa dravya
E. Addition of honey

Choose the ***correct*** answer from the options given below:

1. A, B, C, D, E
2. A, C, D, B, E
3. A, C, B, D, E
4. B, C, A, E, D

47. Match the List-I with List-II.

List-I (Dhatu)	List-II (Function)
A. Rakta	I. Snehana
B. Rasa	II. Dhaarana
C. Asthi	III. Preenana
D. Meda	IV. Jeevana

Choose the ***correct*** answer from the options given below:

1. A-III, B-IV, C-II, D-I
2. A-II, B-I, C-IV, D-III
3. A-IV, B-III, C-II, D-I
4. A-I, B-III, C-IV, D-II

48. According to Ayurveda the appropriate sequence for use of Rasa in Ahara is

A. Madhura
B. Amla, Lavana
C. Katu
D. Tikta
E. Kashaya

Choose the ***correct*** answer from the options given below:

1. B, A, C, E, D
2. D, B, C, E, A
3. A, B, C, D, E
4. A, D, B, C, E

49. In biotech startups, what does "Scaling lip" refer to?

1. Increasing company size
2. Expanding new markets
3. Increasing the production
4. Raising more funds

50. The receptor for Human Immunodeficiency Virus-I on the target cells is:

1. CD 1
2. CD 3
3. CD 4
4. CD 8

51. Match the List-I with List-II.

List-I (Technique)	List-II (Procedure)
A. Northern hybridization	I. Use of DNA for blotting and DNA as a probe
B. Western Blotting	II. Use of SYBR green
C. Southern hybridization	III. Use of RNA for blotting and DNA as a probe
D. Real-time PCR	IV. Use of protein for blotting and antibody as a probe

Choose the ***correct*** answer from the options given below:

1. A-II, B-IV, C-III, D-I
2. A-III, B-I, C-IV, D-II
3. A-I, B-III, C-IV, D-II
4. A-III, B-IV, C-I, D-II

52. Which of the DNA sequencing method is treated as Next-Generation Sequencing method?

1. Illumina short-read sequencing
2. Sanger sequencing
3. Maxim-Gilbert sequencing
4. Meta sequencing

53. The Neuromuscular Junction has the following characteristics:

A. Activation of β-adrenergic receptors
B. Activation of Rynodine receptors
C. Activation of myosine light chain kinase
D. Opening of Nicotinic receptors
E. Entry of Na^{+ions}

Choose the ***correct*** combination from the options given below:

1. C, D, E only
2. B, D, E only
3. A, D, E only
4. A, B, C only

54. What is the full form of A-HMIS?

1. Ayurveda and Homeopathy medicine and Information System
2. Allopathy Health Management Information System
3. AYUSH Health Management Information System
4. Ayurveda Health Management Identification System

55. Which among the following is not the disciple of Punarvasu Atreya?

1. Agnivesha 2. Bhela
3. Bharadwaja 4. Jatukarna

56. During an experiment, the weight of mice from control and test group were measured. The average weight of mice in both groups are:

Weight in control	Test mice weight
32	21
28	28
26	26
31	25
33	24
29	22

1. 29.8 Control and 24.2 Test
2. 29.8 Control and 24.3 Test
3. 29.4 Control and 24.3 Test
4. 30.4 Control and 24.1 Test

57. Correct sequence of the numbers of nerves, veins, arteries, muscles and vitals (Marma) in a healthy body as per Charaka:

A. Nine hundred
B. Two hundred
C. Seven hundred
D. Four hundred
E. One hundred and seven

Choose the ***correct*** answer from the options given below:

1. A, C, B, D, E 2. C, A, D, E, B
3. B, D, E, A, C 4. D, B, A, C, E

58. Which one of the following disciplines of modern science can explain the significance of the time of Administration of medicine in Ayurveda?

1. Network pharmacology
2. Pharmaco-genomics
3. Chrono-pharmacology
4. Clinical genomics

59. Which of the following are **NOT** a type of Marma (A place of a special vulnerability) described in Ayurveda.

A. Instant fatal
B. Eventually fatal
C. Pain inflicting
D. Fire Dampening
E. Dosha vitiating

Choose the ***correct*** combination from the options given below:

1. A and B only 2. B and C only
3. C and D only 4. D and E only

60. Which among the following pathogen and disease pairs are incorrectly matched?

A. *E. histolytica* - Amoebiasis
B. *Wuchereria* - Elephantasis
C. *Ascaris* - Ringworms
D. *Aspergillus* - Warts
E. *P. vivax* - Cerebral malaria

Choose the ***correct*** answer from the options given below:

1. A, B and C only
2. B, C and D only
3. C, D and E only
4. A, B and E only

61. Which of the following is associated with Pangvandhu Nyay (Blind-Lame theory)?

1. Man and Atman 2. Indriya and Man
3. Atman and Indriya 4. Sharir and Aayu

62. Which of the following process is used for preparation of Bhasmas in Ayurveda?

1. Puta 2. Urdhav Patana
3. Murchana 4. Sattva Patana

63. Arrange in correct sequence the contribution of the following factors in development of Prakriti:

A. Kalgarbhashya Prakriti
B. Shukra Shonit Prakriti
C. Mahabut Vikara Prakriti
D. Maturahar Vikara Prakriti

Choose the ***correct*** answer from the options given below:

1. B, D, C, A 2. B, A, D, C
3. A, B, C, D 4. A, B, D, C

64. Consider the following facts regarding "Guggulu" as per Bhava Prakasha Nighantu.

A. Naveen Guggulu is Vrishya
B. Purana Guggnlu is Vrishya
C. Amla Rasa is indicated along with Guggulu
D. Guggulu is also a Rasayana
E. Guggulu pacifies all the three doshas

Choose the ***correct*** combination from the options given below:

1. B, D, E only 2. E, C, A only
3. A, D, E only 4. B, C, E only

65. Match the List-I with List-II.

List-I (Herbs)	List-I (Botanical Name)
A. Bhanga	I. *Acorus calamus*
B. Bhringraj	II. *Vitex negundo*
C. Vacha	III. *Cannabis sativa*
D. Nirgundi	IV. *Eclipta alba*

Choose the ***correct*** answer from the options given below:

1. A-IV, B-III, C-II, D-I
2. A-II, B-I, C-III, D-IV
3. A-III, B-IV, C-II, D-I
4. A-III, B-IV, C-I, D-II

66. What are the Sharir Guna according to the Ayurveda?

1. Gurvadi – 20
2. Paradi – 10
3. Shabdadi – 5
4. Prayatnanta – 6

67. Which of the following is NOT a part of Dashvidha Rogi-Roga Pariksha?

1. Prakriti
2. Parimana
3. Pramana
4. Ahara Shakti

68. The pathway for cellular respiration is in following order:

A. Generation of Acetyl-CoA
B. Generation of reducing equivalents
C. Tri carboxylic acid cycle
D. Action of F1 Fo ATPase
E. Co-transport of primary biomolecules

Choose the ***correct*** answer from the options given below:

1. A, E, B, C, D
2. E, A, C, B, D
3. D, E, A, C, B
4. E, C, A, B, D

69. How many types of Dhatvagni are described in Ayurveda?

1. Five
2. Three
3. Seven
4. Thirteen

70. Panchabautika composition of "Kashaya Rasa" is:

1. Vayu + Akasha
2. Prithavi + Akasha
3. Prithavi + Vayu
4. Vayu + Jala

71. Which of the following subtypes of Kapha is related to lubrication of Joints?

1. Tarpak
2. Shleshak
3. Avalambak
4. Kledak

72. Match the List-I with List-II.

List-I (Virus species)	List-II (Genus)
A. Chandipura virus	I. Flevivirus
B. Colorado tick fever virus	II. Orbivirus
C. Japanese encephalitis virus	III. Vesiculovirus
D. Chikungunya virus	IV. Alphavirus

Choose the ***correct*** answer from the options given below:

1. A-III, B-II, C-I, D-IV
2. A-II, B-III, C-I, D-IV
3. A-I, B-III, C-IV, D-II
4. A-III, B-IV, C-I, D-II

73. Consider the following facts regarding Veerya:

A. Laghu veerya will vitiate Vata
B. Sheeta veerya will pacify Vata and Kapha
C. Mrudu veerya will pacify Pitta
D. Mrudu veerya will vitiate Vata
E. Ruksha veerya will vitiate Pitta

Choose the ***correct*** combination from the options given below:

1. B, C and E only
2. B, D and E only
3. A, B and D only
4. A and C only

74. Regulation of electrolyte balance occurs in the following sequence:

A. Release of Aldosterone
B. Synthesis of Renin
C. Sodium reabsorption from Kidney
D. Activation of Osmoreception
E. Production of Angiotensin

Choose the ***correct*** answer from the options given below:

1. E, B, D, C, A
2. D, B, E, A, C
3. B, D, E, A, C
4. A, B, C, D, E

75. Which among the following is chapter sequence of Bhesaj chatushka in Sutra Sthan of Charak Samhita?

1. 2, 1, 5, 6
2. 1, 3, 4, 7
3. 8, 10, 9, 11
4. 1, 2, 3, 4

76. Match the List-I with List-II.

List-I (Branch of Ayurveda)	List-II (Branch of modern medicine)
A. Kayachikitsa	I. Regenerative medicine
B. Shalya Tantra	II. Internal medicine
C. Rasayana	III. Opthalmology
D. Shalakya Tantra	IV. Surgery

Choose the ***correct*** answer from the options given below:

1. A-I, B-IV, C-II, D-III
2. A-II, B-III, C-I, D-IV
3. A-II, B-IV, C-I, D-III
4. A-IV, B-III, C-II, D-I

77. Which of the following solvents are used for extraction of non-polar components of a plant material?

1. Ethanol
2. Methanol
3. Water
4. Hexane

78. You wish to identify novel flavonol from a medicinal plant extract. Which of the following techniques is most suitable?

1. HPLC
2. HPTLC
3. LC-MS/MS
4. GC-Gas chromatography

79. Which among the following are Pranayatana?

A. Kantha and Hridya
B. Amashaya and Pakwashaya
C. Nabhi and Guda
D. Tvacha and Jihva

Choose the *correct* answer from the options given below:

1. A and C only
2. B and D only
3. C and B only
4. D and A only

80. Term "Genome" is the:

1. Entire sequence of protein coding genes
2. Entire sequence of diploid (2n) DNA content
3. Entire sequence of haploid (n) DNA content
4. Entire sequence of a particular chromosome

81. The word 'Micturition' Means:

1. Formation of urine
2. Renal reabsorption
3. Glomerular filteration
4. Release of urine

82. Which among the following veda is closer to Ayurveda?

1. Rigveda
2. Samveda
3. Yajurveda
4. Atharvaveda

83. Which statements are TRUE for a plasmid vector?

A. Repressor sequence
B. Multiple cloning site
C. Antibiotic selection marker
D. Reverse transcription capabilities
E. Origin of replication 'Ori'

Choose the *correct* combination from the options given below:

1. A, C, E only
2. A, D, E only
3. A, C, D only
4. B, C, E only

84. Which amongst the following is more dominant Dosha type in Aanup Desha?

A. Kapha
B. Pitta
C. Rasa
D. Vata

Choose the *correct* answer from the options given below:

1. A and D only
2. C and B only
3. D and C only
4. B and A only

85. Which of the following is TRUE for nucleosome core?

1. Consist of H_1 histone protein
2. Consist of one unit each of H_2A, H_2B, H_3 and H_4
3. Consist of two units each of H_2A, H_2B, H_3 and H_4
4. Consist of two units of H_1 protein

86. Which technique is used for identifying bacteria at molecular level?

1. 18s ribosomal RNA sequencing
2. 16s ribosomal RNA sequencing
3. 32s ribosomal RNA sequencing
4. 24s ribosomal RNA sequencing

87. Match the List-I with List-II.

List-I (Physiology)	List-II (Hormone)
A. Regulation of Metabolic Rate	I. Erythropoietin
B. Regulation of Blood Pressure	II. Epinephrine
C. RBC Synthesis	III. Thyroxine
D. Stress Response	IV. Vasopressin

Choose the *correct* answer from the options given below:

1. A-III, B-II, C-I, D-IV
2. A-IV, B-I, C-II, D-III
3. A-III, B-IV, C-I, D-II
4. A-II, B-IV, C-I, D-III

88. Which among the following is a commentator of Charak Samhita?

A. Chakrapani Dutta
B. Hemadri
C. Jejjat
D. Vachaspati

Choose the *correct* combination from the options given below:

1. A and B only
2. B and C only
3. C and D only
4. A and C only

89. Match the List-I with List-II.

List-I (Term)	List-II (Karma/Utpatti)
A. Man	I. Vayu
B. Purush	II. Bhautika
C. Indriya	III. Shaddhatuj
D. Mahabhuta	IV. Chintya

Choose the *correct* answer from the options given below:

1. A-I, B-II, C-III, D-IV
2. A-IV, B-III, C-II, D-I
3. A-III, B-II, C-IV, D-I
4. A-II, B-IV, C-I, D-III

90. Which Rasa is best for "Stanya Janana"?

1. Madhura
2. Tikta
3. Kashaya
4. Katu

Directions (Qs. No. 91-95): *Please read the passage and answer the following questions:*

A 25 year old man with a tall lean frame with wrinkled skin, sparse hair with premature greying showed excessive sweating with body odor. He had an aggressive and irritable behavior and complained of skin rashes and episodes of stomatitis especially during the festival season of Diwali. He loves travelling and eating-out but is very particular about who he travels with. Because of his recurrent skin and hair issues, he has been advised by a family member to consult with an Ayurvedic practitioner to adopt some life style changes.

91. Which of the following drugs he can be advised to address the skin and hair problems?

1. Triphala Rasayana
2. Trikatu
3. Panchakola
4. Bhallataka Rasayana

92. What is the Prakriti of the person?

1. Vata Dominant
2. Pitta Dominant
3. Kapha Dominant
4. Sama Doshaja

93. What is the dietary advise he would be prescribed?

1. Tikta Rasa, Cool, Heavy diet
2. Katu Rasa, Fermented items
3. Fasting, Spicy, Light diet
4. Sour, Oily, Unripe fruits

94. Which of the following physical activities is he generally advised NOT to do?

1. Jogging
2. Cycling
3. Heavy weight lifting
4. Swimming

95. What disease/disorders would this person be more prone to?

1. Obesity
2. Bleeding disorder
3. Osteoarthritic disorder
4. Indigestion

Directions (Qs. No. 96-100): *Please read the passage and answer the following questions:*

A patient suffering from repeated and different opportunistic infections leading to weight loss and diarrhea. There was a fall in number of T cells. Recently; the patient was detected with Kaposis Sarcoma. The patient was diagnosed with a typical viral infection using a cell-based assay. The virus uses a unique system of reproduction. The patient acquired this virus due to repeated blood transfusions in the past. Along with conventional medicines, the patients wished for supportive therapies and decides to visit a clinic of an Ayurveda Practitioner.

96. What could be the possible infection the person may be suffering from?

1. H1N1 Influenza Virus
2. Human Papillomavirus
3. Human Immunodeficiency Virus
4. Hepatitis B Virus

97. The infecting virus specifically codes for a polymerase that is essential for the propagation of the virus, which is:

1. DNA-dependent DNA polymerase
2. RNA-dependent DNA polymerase
3. DNA-dependent RNA polymerase
4. RNA-dependent RNA polymerase

98. What class of Ayurvedic medicine can be recommended for such condition?

1. Rasayana
2. Krimihara
3. Medhya
4. Mutrala

99. Which among the following diagnostic techniques is used frequently to access the progression of this disease?

1. Widal test
2. High performance liquid chromatography
3. Flow cytometry
4. Enzyme linked Immunosorbent Assay

100. What kind of pathology according to Ayurveda, it can be described as?

1. Ojokshaya
2. Kapha Vriddhi
3. Pitta Vriddhi
4. Vata Kshaya

ANSWERS

1. (1): Thymus is the primary lymphoid organ responsible for the maturation of T-lymphocytes (T cells). It is most active during the neonatal and pre-adolescent periods. As aging progresses, the thymus gradually decreases in size and functionality through a process called involution, where the functional thymic tissue is replaced by adipose tissue. This decline begins after puberty and continues throughout adulthood, leading to reduced production of naïve T cells in the elderly. This is why aging is associated with a weakened adaptive immune response.

2. (4):

A. Type-1 Hypersensitivity – II. IgE: Type I hypersensitivity is an immediate allergic reaction mediated by IgE antibodies, which bind to allergens and trigger mast cells and basophils to release histamine and other inflammatory mediators. Examples include hay fever, asthma, and anaphylaxis.

B. Type-2 Hypersensitivity – I. IgG/IgM: In this type, IgG or IgM antibodies bind to antigens present on the surface of cells, leading to cell destruction through complement activation or phagocytosis. Examples include autoimmune hemolytic anemia and erythroblastosis fetalis.

C. Type-3 Hypersensitivity – IV. Immune complexes: It involves the formation of antigen-antibody (immune) complexes that deposit in tissues, causing inflammation and tissue damage. Classic examples are serum sickness and systemic lupus erythematosus.

D. Type-4 Hypersensitivity – III. T Cells: Also known as delayed-type hypersensitivity, it is mediated by sensitized T lymphocytes, not antibodies. Tissue damage is caused by cytokines released from activated T cells. Examples include tuberculin skin test and contact dermatitis.

3. (3): The Protection of Plant Varieties and Farmers' Rights (PPV&FR) Act was enacted by the Government of India in the year 2001 and came into force on 11 November 2001. This Act provides for the establishment of an effective system for the protection of plant varieties, the rights of farmers and plant breeders, and encourages the development of new plant varieties. It is one of the few laws in the world that simultaneously safeguards the rights of both commercial plant breeders and traditional farmers.

4. (4):

A. Ushma – IV. Pachana: Ushma (heat) is responsible for Pachana (digestion or transformation) of food. It represents the Agni (digestive fire) in Ayurveda, essential for breaking down food substances.

B. Vayu – III. Apakarshana: Vayu (air element) facilitates Apakarshana (movement or propulsion), helping in the transportation and movement of food and waste through the gastrointestinal tract.

C. Kleda – I. Shaithilya: Kleda (moisture) contributes to Shaithilya (liquidity or softness), essential for maintaining the fluidity and solubility of food during digestion.

D. Sneha – II. Mruduta: Sneha (unctuousness) provides Mruduta (softness or lubrication), which aids in making the food mass smooth, soft, and easy to move through the digestive tract.

5. (3): In Ayurvedic pharmaceutics, if the useful part of a medicinal plant is not specifically mentioned during formulation, then Moola (root) is taken by default. This is a traditional guideline followed in classical Ayurvedic texts such as Sharangadhara Samhita and Ayurvedic Formulary of India (AFI). Roots are considered to contain the essence of the plant and are widely used for their potency and stable pharmacological properties when no specific part is designated.

6. (4): The increasing order of potency of herbal formulations refers to their capacity to extract and deliver active constituents from medicinal plants. The correct order is:

D. Phanta (hot infusion): It is made by pouring hot water over crushed herbs and steeping them. Due to mild heating, it has relatively low potency.

B. Hima (cold infusion): Prepared by soaking herbs in cold water overnight. Though no heat is applied, it extracts more than Phanta in certain cases, especially for heat-sensitive ingredients.

E. Kwatha (decoction): Made by boiling herbs in water till reduced to one-fourth or one-eighth. The process extracts more active constituents than Hima and Phanta.

A. Kalka (paste): Freshly ground paste of herbs contains concentrated active components and is more potent than aqueous extractions.

C. Swarasa (expressed juice): Juice extracted from fresh plants is considered the most potent, as it contains live, unprocessed plant phytochemicals in the highest concentration.

7. (2): Regulation of glycolysis in muscles occurs via:

A. Allosteric modulation: Key enzymes such as Phosphofructokinase-1 (PFK-1), Hexokinase, and Pyruvate kinase are regulated allosterically by molecules like ATP, AMP, and citrate.

C. Feedback regulation: The end products of glycolysis like ATP and citrate provide negative feedback to early enzymes to inhibit excessive glucose breakdown.

E. Covalent modification: Enzymes like Pyruvate kinase are regulated by phosphorylation (inhibited when phosphorylated), which is a form of covalent modification.

B. Enzyme turnover is a slower regulatory mechanism not typically associated with acute regulation in muscle glycolysis.

D. Compartmentalization is more relevant in organelles and not the key regulatory mechanism in muscle glycolysis.

Thus, the correct set is A, C, E only.

8. (3): Color blindness is an X-linked recessive trait.

- The man is color blind: Genotype X^hY
- The woman is homozygous normal: Genotype X^nX^n
- From the cross:
- Sons receive the Y chromosome from father and one X^n from mother → X^nY = normal vision
- Daughters receive X^h from father and X^n from mother → X^nX^h = carriers, not affected

Therefore, probability of a son being color blind = 0

9. (2): The colloidal properties of "ruby" gold nanoparticles, including their optical properties (bright red color due to surface plasmon resonance), were discovered by Michael Faraday in 1857. He prepared colloidal gold by reducing gold chloride with phosphorus in carbon disulfide, producing nano-sized particles which dispersed in water and showed unique color and behavior different from bulk gold.

10. (2): To create a genetic map on an autosome, a test cross is used.

- A test cross involves crossing an individual heterozygous for multiple genes with an individual homozygous recessive for those genes.
- The recombination frequencies observed in the offspring help determine the relative distances between genes on the autosome.

Backcross may sometimes be similar but is not always informative for mapping.

Reciprocal and double reciprocal crosses are used more in sex-linked gene mapping and epistasis studies, not autosomal linkage mapping.

11. (4): In the context of Ayurveda start-up development, typical phases include:

- **Clinical trials:** Required to validate safety and efficacy of Ayurvedic formulations under controlled conditions.
- **Manufacturing scale-up:** Involves expanding production from lab-scale to commercial scale while maintaining quality.
- **Product marketing:** Essential for introducing and promoting Ayurvedic products in the market.

However, Real estate investment is not a typical or core phase in this process. While infrastructure may be needed, investment specifically for real estate is not categorized as a developmental phase for an Ayurveda startup.

12. (2): In Ayurveda, "Avidahi" Rasa refers to non-burning (non-caustic) tastes that do not produce a sensation of burning or heat in the body.

The Rasas classified as Avidahi (non-irritant) are:

- Madhura (Sweet)
- Tikta (Bitter)
- Kashaya (Astringent)

These are cooling in nature (Sheeta Virya) and pacify Pitta Dosha.

In contrast, Lavana (salty) and Katu (pungent) are Vidahi as they can aggravate Pitta and produce a burning sensation.

13. (4): Matching Panchamahabhuta with their typical Lakshanas (properties):

A. Prithvi (Earth) – II. Kharatva (Roughness): It represents solidity and stability; roughness is a key property.

B. Tej (Fire) – III. Ushmatva (Heat): Fire is associated with heat and transformation, hence Ushmatva.

C. Aakash (Ether) – IV. Apratighata (Non-resistance): Space allows things to pass without obstruction, hence non-resistance.

D. Vayu (Air) – I. Chalatva (Movement): Air is responsible for mobility and kinetic activity.

14. (2): The correct sequence of steps in Polymerase Chain Reaction (PCR) is:

A. Addition of Taq: Taq polymerase is added initially to the PCR reaction mixture containing template DNA, primers, and nucleotides. It remains active through cycles due to its thermostability.

B. Denaturation: The double-stranded DNA is heated to around 94–96°C, causing the two strands to separate.

D. Annealing: The temperature is lowered to 50–65°C allowing primers to bind (anneal) to their complementary sequences on the single-stranded DNA.

E. Extension: Temperature is raised to 72°C, the optimum for Taq polymerase, which synthesizes the new DNA strands by adding dNTPs.

C. Termination: After desired number of cycles (usually 25–35), the reaction is terminated by cooling or enzyme inactivation.

15. (1): Matching Cofactors with their corresponding enzymes:

A. Thiamine Pyrophosphate – IV. Pyruvate dehydrogenase: TPP is a key cofactor for decarboxylation of pyruvate to acetyl-CoA.

B. Flavin Adenine Dinucleotide – III. Glutathione Reductase: FAD acts as a redox cofactor for this enzyme involved in the antioxidant system.

C. Pyridoxal phosphate – I. Glycogen phosphorylase: PLP is the active form of Vitamin B6 and is essential in glycogenolysis.

D. Biotin – II. Pyruvate carboxylase: Biotin serves as a CO_2 carrier in carboxylation reactions including conversion of pyruvate to oxaloacetate.

16. (3): The concept of P4 Medicine was introduced by Dr. Leroy Hood and is considered the future of healthcare. It focuses on a holistic, systems-based approach to disease management and prevention. The four components of P4 Medicine are:

- **Predictive:** Utilizes genetic and biomarker information to predict the risk of disease before it manifests.
- **Preventive:** Aims to prevent disease onset through early interventions, lifestyle modifications, and personalized monitoring.
- **Personalised:** Tailors healthcare decisions and treatments to the individual's unique genetic makeup, environment, and lifestyle.
- **Participatory:** Encourages active involvement of individuals in their own healthcare, including informed decision-making and behavior change.

Pharmacology, on the other hand, is the scientific study of drugs and their effects on living organisms. It is a discipline within medicine and biomedical sciences but is not a part of the P4 framework. Therefore, Pharmacology is not considered one of the four foundational elements of P4 medicine.

17. (2): In Ayurvedic philosophy, the concept of Shad Padartha (Six Categories) is derived from Nyaya and Vaisheshika Darshanas, and forms the ontological and epistemological foundation of Ayurveda. These six padarthas are:

(a) **Dravya (Substance):** The base of all existence and carrier of properties and actions (e.g., herbs, minerals).

(b) **Guna (Qualities):** Attributes or inherent properties of substances (e.g., heaviness, coldness).

(*c*) **Karma (Action):** The functional aspect or activity performed by a Dravya.

(*d*) **Samanya (Generality):** The principle of similarity; things with similar properties tend to combine.

(*e*) **Vishesh (Particularity):** The principle of difference or specificity; enables separation of entities.

(*f*) **Samavaya (Inherence):** An eternal and inseparable relationship between entities (e.g., between a substance and its qualities).

These six categories are not material elements, but philosophical tools to understand the universe and interactions between substances and actions in the context of health and disease.

18. **(3):** In Ayurveda, the Ashta Veerya refers to the eight types of potency that help classify and understand the therapeutic nature of substances (dravyas). These are used to predict how a substance will affect the body.

The eight types of Veerya are:

(*a*) Sheeta (Cold); (*b*) Ushna (Hot); (*c*) Snigdha (Unctuous); (*d*) Ruksha (Dry); (*e*) Laghu (Light); (*f*) Guru (Heavy); (*g*) Manda (Dull/Slow); and (*h*) Teekshna (Sharp/Penetrating)

From the given options:

A. Guru: One of the 8 Veeryas; denotes heaviness, increases Kapha and decreases Vata.

B. Teekshna: Included; signifies sharpness or penetrating action, helpful in digestion and breaking obstructions.

D. Sheeta: Included; denotes cold potency, pacifies Pitta, and increases Kapha.

C. Sheeghra (Quick): Refers to action speed, not a Veerya type.

E. Sthira (Stable): Denotes steadiness, again not among the 8 Veeryas.

Hence, the correct set is Guru, Teekshna, Sheeta – matching with A, B, D.

19. **(1):** This question pertains to the tools and databases used in bioinformatics, a field that deals with analysis of biological data using computational tools.

Correct statements:

B. GenBank is a primary database: It is maintained by NCBI (USA) and is a primary nucleotide sequence repository, storing annotated DNA sequences submitted by scientists globally.

D. BLAST is known as Basic Local Alignment Search Tool: A widely-used bioinformatics tool that allows comparison of a query sequence (DNA or protein) with a database to find regions of similarity. It helps in gene identification, evolutionary studies, etc.

E. DNA sequences are usually represented in FASTA format: FASTA is a text-based format for nucleotide or protein sequences that begins with a '>' header followed by the sequence. It is the standard input format for most bioinformatics tools.

Incorrect statements:

A. E-value in multiple alignment is elution value: This is incorrect. E-value (expectation value) represents the number of hits expected by chance in a database search and is unrelated to elution, which is a chromatography term.

C. Evolutionary analysis is not possible with sequence analysis: This is false; in fact, evolutionary relationships (phylogenetic trees, homology) are central to sequence analysis.

20. **(3):** In Ayurveda, Jnanendriyas are the five sense organs through which a person gains knowledge about the external world. They are responsible for perception and are associated with their respective functions and sense objects.

The five Jnanendriyas are:

(*a*) Ghranendriya (Nose) – for smell

(*b*) Rasanendriya (Tongue) – for taste

(*c*) Chakshurendriya (Eyes) – for vision

(*d*) Sparshanendriya (Skin) – for touch

(*e*) Shravanendriya (Ears) – for hearing

Given options:

A. Ghranendriya – Smell perception → Jnanendriya

B. Shravanendriya – Hearing perception → Jnanendriya

D. Sparshnendriya – Touch perception → Jnanendriya

C. Vageendriya – Organ of speech → Karmendriya

E. Hastendriya – Organ of grasping (hands) → Karmendriya

Therefore, the correct Jnanendriya combination is A, B, D only.

21. **(3):** In Ayurveda, Vata Dosha is one of the three fundamental bodily humors (Doshas) responsible for all forms of movement and neurological functions in the body. It is composed of Vayu (air) and Akasha (ether) elements, and governs various physiological processes like circulation, respiration, nerve impulses, and elimination.

The main sites (Sthana) of Vata Dosha as described in classical Ayurvedic texts such as Charaka Samhita and Ashtanga Hridaya are:

1. **Pakvashaya (Rectum / Large Intestine):** This is the primary site of Vata, responsible for the regulation of expulsion and movement of waste.
2. **Uru (Thighs)**
3. **Kati (Pelvic region)**
4. **Asthi (Bones)**
5. **Sparshanendriya (Sense of touch / skin)**
6. **Srotra (Ears)**
7. **Chest (Uras):** Though not the main, it is considered among sites where Vata may also reside.

From the given options:

A. Chest: Recognized as one of the sites where Vata can exert influence.

B. Rectum: The most prominent site of Vata as per Ayurveda.

C. Eyes: Dominated by Pitta, not a site of Vata.

D. Stomach: Mainly governed by Kapha and Pitta, not a principal site of Vata.

Hence, the correct answer is A and B only, corresponding to Option 3.

22. (2): This question relates to the modern chemical equivalents of traditional Rasadravyas (metallic substances used in Rasa Shastra). Their identifications are as follows:

A. Tamra – III. Cu (Copper): Tamra is the Sanskrit name for copper, widely used after proper purification in Ayurvedic formulations.

B. Vanga – IV. Sn (Tin): Vanga bhasma is prepared from tin and used mainly for genitourinary disorders.

C. Yashada – I. Zn (Zinc): Yashada bhasma is used to treat diabetes and improve immunity.

D. Naga – II. Pb (Lead): Naga bhasma, derived from lead, is used in treating piles and fistulas (after detoxification).

23. (4): The concept of Trisutra is foundational in Ayurveda and refers to the three diagnostic and therapeutic principles essential for understanding disease and its treatment. They are:

Hetu (Cause): The causative factors (Nidana) for a disease, including diet, lifestyle, and environmental triggers.

Linga (Symptoms): The signs and symptoms manifested due to the disease (Lakshana).

Aushadha (Treatment): The medicine or therapy used to alleviate the condition.

These three form the core clinical triad in Ayurvedic diagnosis and management, as detailed in Charaka Samhita Sutrasthana. They are not material categories or psychological concepts, but serve as a clinical framework.

24. (2): In Ayurveda and Indian philosophical systems, Manasika Doshas (mental defects) are those that disturb the equilibrium of the mind. The two Manasika Doshas are:

Rajas: Associated with activity, desire, restlessness, and emotional instability.

Tamas: Linked to ignorance, inertia, delusion, and mental darkness.

These two, when imbalanced, contribute to mental disorders and distort perception, thought, and behavior.

- Vata, Pitta, Kapha (Option 3) are Sharirika Doshas (bodily humors).
- Raga, Dvesha, Sukha-Dukha are mental expressions, not doshas themselves.
- Chintyam, Vicharyam, Uhyam are functions of the mind, not doshas.

Hence, Rajas and Tamas are the true Manasika Doshas.

25. (4): Transduction is a method of horizontal gene transfer in bacteria, mediated by a bacteriophage (virus that infects bacteria). The process involves:

- A bacteriophage infects a bacterial cell and accidentally incorporates a segment of bacterial DNA into its viral particle.
- This phage then infects another bacterial cell and transfers the incorporated bacterial DNA, introducing new genetic material into the recipient.

Types of transduction include:

- **Generalized transduction:** Any gene can be transferred.
- **Specialized transduction:** Only specific genes near the phage integration site are transferred.

In contrast:

- Transformation is uptake of naked DNA.
- Conjugation involves direct cell-to-cell transfer via pili.
- Recombination is a broader term that can follow any of these processes.

Thus, transfer of genetic material by a bacteriophage is known as transduction.

26. (1): This question deals with correctly matching medicinal herbs with their principal phytoconstituents, which are the active chemical compounds responsible for their therapeutic effects.

A. Vacha – I. Asarone: Vacha (*Acorus calamus*) contains β-asarone, a major active compound with CNS stimulant and neuroprotective effects.

B. Hritpatri – III. Digitoxin: Hritpatri refers to *Digitalis purpurea* (commonly known as Foxglove), which contains digitoxin, a cardiac glycoside used in heart failure treatment.

C. Khadir – IV. Catechin: Khadir (*Acacia catechu*) is rich in catechins, known for their antioxidant and astringent properties.

D. Vatsanabha – II. Aconitine: Vatsanabha (*Aconitum ferox*) contains aconitine, a toxic alkaloid that requires purification before medicinal use.

27. (3): Lifestyle disorders are non-communicable diseases (NCDs) that arise primarily due to unhealthy behaviors such as poor diet, lack of physical activity, smoking, and alcohol use. Examples include:

- **Coronary artery disease:** Caused by poor lifestyle, stress, and dietary factors.
- **Stroke:** Can result from hypertension, obesity, and sedentary lifestyle.
- **Type 2 diabetes:** Strongly linked to obesity, poor diet, and inactivity.

Type 1 diabetes, on the other hand, is an autoimmune disorder where the body's immune system attacks insulin-producing cells of the pancreas. It is not caused by lifestyle and usually begins in childhood or adolescence. Therefore, it is not classified as a lifestyle disorder.

28. (2): Down's Syndrome is a genetic disorder caused by the presence of an extra (third) copy of chromosome 21, a condition known as trisomy 21. It is one of the most common chromosomal abnormalities and results in intellectual disability, distinct facial features, and developmental delays.

Other options explained:

- Trisomy 18 → Edward's syndrome

- Monosomy of sex chromosome → Turner's syndrome
- Nullisomy → Absence of both chromosomes in a pair, which is lethal

Hence, Trisomy 21 is the exact cause of Down's Syndrome.

29. **(3):** The Hardy-Weinberg equilibrium describes a stable genetic structure in a population under certain ideal conditions (no mutation, random mating, large population size, no migration, and no selection).

Genetic drift refers to random changes in allele frequencies, especially in small populations, due to chance rather than selection. This disrupts Hardy-Weinberg equilibrium by:

- Reducing genetic variation
- Increasing fixation or loss of alleles

In contrast:

- Random mating maintains equilibrium
- Stable gene pool is a requirement of equilibrium
- Geographical isolation alone does not necessarily alter gene frequencies unless accompanied by selection or drift

Thus, genetic drift causes deviation from Hardy-Weinberg equilibrium.

30. **(2):** Biodiversity loss occurs due to both natural and anthropogenic factors. The major causes include:

B. **Alien species invasion:** Introduction of non-native species can disrupt local ecosystems (e.g., Parthenium in India).

C. **Habitat loss and fragmentation:** One of the most significant threats; caused by deforestation, urbanization, etc.

E. **Overexploitation:** Unsustainable use of natural resources like overfishing or illegal wildlife trade depletes biodiversity.

Incorrect options:

A. Herbivorous wild animals: A part of natural ecosystem balance, not a direct cause of biodiversity loss.

D. Creation of wildlife sanctuaries: A conservation measure, not a cause of loss.

Thus, the correct combination is B, C, E only.

31. **(3):** Western blotting is a widely used analytical technique in molecular biology and biochemistry to detect specific proteins in a sample. The process includes:

- Separation of proteins using SDS-PAGE (sodium dodecyl sulfate–polyacrylamide gel electrophoresis)
- Transfer (blotting) of the separated proteins onto a membrane (usually nitrocellulose or PVDF)
- Probing the membrane with specific antibodies that bind to the target protein
- Detection using enzyme-linked or chemiluminescent systems.

Thus, Western blotting is defined as a protein blot probed with an antibody, distinguishing it from:

- **Southern blot:** DNA-DNA hybridization
- **Northern blot:** RNA-DNA hybridization

32. **(1): Pramana** refers to the means of acquiring valid knowledge in Indian philosophy.

Upamana (comparison), Yukti (resoning/inference), and Arthapatti (presumption/implication) are recognized as valid pramanas in various schools of Indian philosophy.

Samvaya is a concept in Vaisheshika philosophy that describes inherent or intmate inherence, a type of relationship between substances and their qualities. It is not a means of acquiring knowledge, but rather a category of relationship.

33. **(3):** The Good Manufacturing Practices (GMP) guidelines for Ayurveda, Siddha, and Unani (ASU) drugs are defined under the Drugs and Cosmetics Rules, 1945. These are placed in:

- **Schedule T,** which specifically provides the minimum requirements of premises, machinery, quality control, and documentation for manufacturing ASU medicines.

Other schedules:

- **Schedule H:** Prescription drugs (modern medicine)
- **Schedule M:** GMP for allopathic pharmaceuticals
- **Schedule Y:** Clinical trial regulations for modern drugs

Hence, for ASU drug manufacturing GMP, the correct schedule is Schedule T.

34. **(2):** The development of Ayurveda has been categorized into distinct historical phases (Kalas) based on literary and philosophical evolution:

A. Samhita Kal – II. 5th Century to 6th Century: Era of foundational texts like Charaka Samhita, Sushruta Samhita, and Ashtanga Hridaya.

B. Vyakhya Kal – III. 7th Century to 15th Century: Period of commentaries and elaboration on Samhitas by scholars such as Chakrapanidatta, Arunadatta, and Dalhana.

C. Sangrah Kal – I. 14th Century to Modern Period: Compilation and summarization phase; texts like Bhavaprakasha, Sharangadhara Samhita, and Yogaratnakara were written.

D. Emergence Period of Ayurveda – IV. 1500 B.C. to 1000 B.C.: Pre-Samhita period when Ayurvedic principles were emerging within Vedic literature, especially Atharvaveda.

35. **(1):** In Ayurveda, the concept of Chikitsa Chatushpada (four pillars of therapy) outlines the four essential factors for successful treatment. These are:

(a) **Vaidya (Physician)**– Must be knowledgeable, experienced, skillful, and ethical.

(b) **Dravya (Medicine/Drug)**– Should be suitable, potent, available, and properly prepared.

(c) **Upasthata (Caregiver/Attendant)**– Assists in proper care, medicine administration, and patient support.

(d) **Rogi (Patient)**– Should be cooperative, disciplined, and communicative about symptoms.

This framework ensures a holistic and effective approach to healing. Without the proper function of even one of these components, the success of treatment is compromised.

36. (2): This question involves matching Ayurvedic regulatory and pharmaceutical components with their respective associations:

A. Ayurvedic Pharmacopoeia of India – IV. Standards for Ayurvedic drugs: This is an official publication that lays down quality standards for identity, purity, and strength of Ayurvedic raw materials and finished formulations.

B. Shelf life of Ayurvedic drugs – III. Rule 161B: As per Rule 161B of the Drugs and Cosmetics Rules, 1945, the shelf life (expiry) of Ayurvedic, Siddha, and Unani medicines is prescribed officially.

C. Pharmacovigilance – I. Adverse drug reaction reporting: Pharmacovigilance in Ayurveda relates to monitoring, recording, and analyzing adverse drug reactions (ADRs) to ensure safety of ASU drugs.

D. Tablet – II. Disintegration time: Disintegration time is an important quality control parameter for tablets, ensuring that the formulation breaks down appropriately in the digestive tract.

37. (1): Promoters are specific DNA sequences that play a crucial role in gene transcription regulation. Let's analyze the statements:

A. They are orientation dependent: TRUE – Promoters function in a specific direction, and reversing their orientation often abolishes gene expression.

D. They are present in 5'-region of the gene: TRUE – Promoters are located upstream (5' side) of the gene they regulate, right before the transcription start site.

E. They are important for gene expression: TRUE – Promoters are essential for the initiation of transcription; they provide binding sites for RNA polymerase and transcription factors.

B. Orientation independent – FALSE, as most promoters are orientation-specific.

C. Present in 3'-region – FALSE, as 3' region relates to termination, not initiation.

Therefore, correct combination is A, D, E only.

38. (4): In Ayurveda, Nidana Panchaka consists of five diagnostic components:

(*a*) Hetu (Cause)

(*b*) Purvaroopa (Prodromal symptoms)

(*c*) Roopa (Symptoms)

(*d*) Upashaya (Therapeutic test)

(*e*) Samprapti (Pathogenesis)

Among these, Samprapti refers to the mechanism of disease progression – how a disease originates, develops, and manifests, involving Dosha, Dushya, Strotas, and Srotodushti.

In modern biomedical terms, this corresponds to pathophysiology or mechanistic studies that explore how the disease occurs and spreads within the body.

Hence, Samprapti is the Nidana Panchaka element that relates most closely to modern disease mechanisms.

39. (4): This question matches organisms with their mode of sex determination:

A. Honey Bees – IV. Haplodiploidy: In honey bees, males (drones) develop from unfertilized haploid eggs, and females (workers and queen) from fertilized diploid eggs – a system known as haplodiploidy.

B. Drosophila melanogaster – III. X : A ratio: In fruit flies, sex is determined by the ratio of X chromosomes to autosomes (X:A).

C. Mice – I. X : Y chromosome: Mice follow the typical mammalian system where the presence of a Y chromosome leads to male development.

D. Saccharomyces cerevisiae – II. Genic sex determination: Yeast has genic sex determination controlled by specific mating-type genes rather than sex chromosomes.

40. (2): This question pertains to the main sites of the five types of Vayu (subtypes of Vata Dosha) in the body:

A. Apanavayu – I. Basti (Pelvic region / lower abdomen): Controls downward movements like defecation, urination, menstruation, and childbirth.

B. Vyanavayu – III. Hridaya (Heart): Governs circulatory movement throughout the body, rooted in the heart.

C. Samanavayu – II. Koshtha (Gastrointestinal tract): Involved in digestion and assimilation of food, situated around the stomach.

D. Pranavayu – IV. Moordha (Head): Responsible for breathing, swallowing, and sensory functions, located in the head region.

41. (1): In Sneha Kalpana (oleaginous preparations) in Ayurveda, a general rule is followed for the proportion of ingredients to ensure proper extraction of active constituents and therapeutic efficacy.

The standard ratio is:

- Kalka (herbal paste) : Sneha Dravya (oil or ghee) : Drava Dravya (liquid like decoction or fresh juice) = 1 part : 4 parts : 16 parts

This proportion ensures:

- Kalka provides the active herbal content
- Sneha serves as the lipid medium (carrier)
- Drava acts as the extracting medium (mostly Kwatha or Swarasa)

This classical ratio is widely accepted and mentioned in Ayurvedic pharmacopoeial texts such as Sharngadhara Samhita.

42. (4): This question matches Ayurvedic Prakriti features with corresponding modern phenotyping methods:

A. Aakriti (Body structure/form) – II. Somatotypes: Modern body typing (ectomorph, mesomorph, endomorph) directly correlates with Ayurvedic observation of physique.

B. Varna (Skin color/complexion) – III. Phototypes: Fitzpatrick phototyping system in modern dermatology classifies skin based on color and sun sensitivity.

C. **Nidra (Sleep pattern) – I. Chronotypes:** Modern chronobiology classifies individuals as "morning types" or "evening types", akin to sleep-wake cycles observed in Prakriti assessment.

D. **Agni-koshtha (Digestive and bowel habits) – IV. Metabotypes:** Metabotyping is a method of classifying individuals based on metabolic and gut response, aligning with Agni and Koshtha features.

43. (1): The Indian Patents Act was enacted in 1970 and came into force on 20th April 1972. It replaced the older Indian Patents and Designs Act of 1911.

Key highlights of the 1970 Patents Act:

- Allowed only process patents (not product patents) for food, chemicals, and drugs to encourage indigenous pharmaceutical development.
- Strengthened Indian generic drug industry.

Later amendments:

- Major amendments in 1999, 2002, and 2005 to align with TRIPS agreement of the WTO, including the introduction of product patents in 2005.

Therefore, the main introduction of the Patents Act was in 1970.

44. (2): This question requires arranging types of white blood cells (WBCs) in increasing order of their normal count in human blood.

Typical WBC count range (approximate % of total WBCs):

- Basophils: ~0.5–1%
- Eosinophils: ~1–4%
- Monocytes: ~2–8%
- Lymphocytes: ~20–40%
- Neutrophils: ~50–70%

Arranged in increasing order:

1. Eosinophils
2. Basophils
3. Monocytes
4. Lymphocytes
5. Neutrophils

Therefore, the correct increasing order of count is:

E (Eosinophils), B (Basophils), D (Monocytes), C (Lymphocytes), A (Neutrophils)

45. (3): In a polynucleotide sequence (such as DNA or RNA), the following bonds are present:

- **Phosphodiester bonds:** Link 3' carbon of one sugar to 5' phosphate of next nucleotide – the backbone of DNA/RNA.
- **Hydrogen bonds:** Present between complementary nitrogenous bases (A=T, G≡C).
- **Glycosidic bonds:** Link sugar and nitrogenous base.

Amide bonds (also known as peptide bonds) are found in proteins, not in nucleic acids. They link amino acids, not nucleotides.

Hence, Amide bond is not part of a polynucleotide sequence.

46. (3): The correct sequence of steps in the preparation of Avaleha (medicated semisolid preparation) as per classical Ayurvedic pharmaceutics is as follows:

A. **Preparation of Kwatha:** The process begins with the preparation of a herbal decoction (Kwatha) using prescribed herbs.

C. **Addition of sweetening agent:** Once the Kwatha is prepared, sweetening agents like Gud (jaggery) or Sharkara (sugar) are added.

B. **Reduction of mixture to proper consistency:** The mixture is heated and reduced to a semisolid form by boiling until the desired "Paka Lakshana" (signs of proper consistency) is achieved.

D. **Addition of Prakshepa Dravya:** After the mixture cools slightly, aromatic and powdered Prakshepa Dravyas (adjuvants) are added.

E. **Addition of honey:** Finally, Madhu (honey) is added when the mixture becomes lukewarm to preserve its medicinal value and avoid degradation due to heating.

This sequence ensures both efficacy and preservation of the Avaleha formulation.

47. (3): The correct matching of Sapta Dhatus (seven body tissues) with their corresponding functions as per Ayurvedic physiology is:

A. **Rakta (Blood) – IV. Jeevana:** Rakta Dhatu is responsible for life-sustaining functions, providing vitality and oxygenation to all tissues.

B. **Rasa (Plasma/Lymph) – III. Preenana:** Rasa nourishes all subsequent Dhatus and provides the nutritional essence to the body.

C. **Asthi (Bone) – II. Dhaarana:** Asthi Dhatu gives structural support and stability, responsible for holding the body upright.

D. **Meda (Fat) – I. Snehana:** Meda Dhatu provides lubrication and unctuousness, essential for cushioning and joint movement.

Each Dhatu has a distinct physiological role, contributing to the body's structural and functional integrity.

48. (3): According to Ayurveda, the appropriate sequence of Rasas (tastes) to be consumed in Ahara (diet) follows the natural order of digestion and their influence on Doshas and Agni:

A. **Madhura (Sweet)**– Should be consumed first as it calms Vata and Pitta, promotes nourishment and strength.

B. **Amla, Lavana (Sour and Salty)**– Stimulate appetite and digestion by enhancing Agni.

C. **Katu (Pungent)**– Helps in digestion and elimination of toxins.

D. **Tikta (Bitter)**– Detoxifies and reduces Pitta and Kapha.

E. **Kashaya (Astringent)**– Should be taken last as it has drying properties and stabilizes the digestive process.

This sequential approach supports proper digestion, absorption, and Dosha balance.

49. (3): In the context of biotech startups, the term "Scaling up" (commonly referred to as "Scaling up" here) refers to the process of increasing the production capacity of a product or process from laboratory-scale or pilot-scale to commercial-scale.

- It involves enhancing the volume, equipment, facilities, and process optimization to meet larger market demands.
- Scaling up is essential after successful prototyping or proof of concept, especially in the biotech sector where fermentation, culture growth, or compound synthesis need precision and regulatory compliance at large scale.

Therefore, "Scaling up" most appropriately refers to increasing the production.

50. (3): The Human Immunodeficiency Virus type I (HIV-I) primarily targets helper T cells, which express the CD 4 receptor on their surface.

- HIV attaches to the CD 4 receptor using its gp 120 envelope glycoprotein, and then utilizes co-receptors like CCR 5 or CXCR 4 for entry.
- CD 4 cells are crucial in immune function, and their destruction leads to immune suppression characteristic of AIDS (Acquired Immunodeficiency Syndrome).

Other markers:

CD 1: Involved in antigen presentation.

CD 3: A component of the T-cell receptor complex.

CD 8: Present on cytotoxic T cells, not primarily targeted by HIV.

Hence, CD 4 is the key receptor for HIV-I entry into host cells.

51. (4): The techniques and their corresponding procedures in molecular biology are as follows:

A. Northern hybridization – III. Use of RNA for blotting and DNA as a probe: Northern blotting is used to detect specific RNA sequences. The RNA is separated by gel electrophoresis, transferred to a membrane, and then hybridized with a DNA probe.

B. Western Blotting – IV. Use of protein for blotting and antibody as a probe: Western blot is used to detect specific proteins. After electrophoresis, proteins are transferred to a membrane and detected using specific antibodies.

C. Southern hybridization – I. Use of DNA for blotting and DNA as a probe: Southern blotting involves separation of DNA fragments, transfer to a membrane, and detection using a labeled DNA probe.

D. Real-time PCR – II. Use of SYBR green: In real-time PCR (qPCR), SYBR Green dye binds to double-stranded DNA and fluoresces, allowing quantification of DNA in real time.

Thus, the correct match is: A – III, B – IV, C – I, D – II.

52. (1): Next-Generation Sequencing (NGS) refers to advanced, high-throughput DNA sequencing technologies that enable rapid sequencing of large volumes of DNA.

- Illumina short-read sequencing is a widely used NGS method, which generates millions of short DNA reads using sequencing-by-synthesis and reversible dye terminators.

Other options:

- Sanger sequencing – First-generation method, lower throughput.
- Maxim-Gilbert sequencing – Chemical cleavage method, obsolete.
- Meta sequencing – Not a specific method; metagenomics uses NGS platforms like Illumina.

Hence, Illumina short-read sequencing is treated as a true NGS technique.

53. (2): At the Neuromuscular Junction (NMJ) – the synapse between a motor neuron and a skeletal muscle fiber, the following key events occur:

B. Activation of Ryanodine receptors: Triggered by depolarization, these receptors on the sarcoplasmic reticulum release Ca^{2+}, initiating muscle contraction.

D. Opening of Nicotinic receptors: Acetylcholine released from the motor neuron binds to nicotinic acetylcholine receptors, causing depolarization of the muscle cell membrane.

E. Entry of Na^+ ions: Activation of nicotinic receptors opens ion channels, allowing sodium influx, leading to end-plate potential.

Incorrect options:

A. β-adrenergic receptors – Associated with sympathetic nervous system, not involved in NMJ.

C. Myosin light chain kinase activation – Occurs in smooth muscle, not skeletal muscle.

Therefore, correct combination is B, D, E only.

54. (3): A-HMIS stands for AYUSH Health Management Information System. It is a digital platform developed under the Ministry of AYUSH, Government of India.

- It integrates healthcare data from Ayurveda, Yoga, Naturopathy, Unani, Siddha, and Homeopathy systems.
- A-HMIS is used for data reporting, performance tracking, and real-time monitoring of AYUSH healthcare services across India.
- It supports digitization and standardization of patient records, treatments, and institutional data.

Hence, AYUSH Health Management Information System is the correct expansion.

55. (3): Punarvasu Atreya was a renowned ancient physician and teacher of Ayurveda. Among his chief disciples were:

- **Agnivesha**– Compiled the Agnivesha Tantra, which later became Charaka Samhita.
- **Bhela**– Author of Bhela Samhita, another classical text.
- **Jatukarna**– Also known to have received teachings from Atreya.

However, Bharadwaja was not a direct disciple of Punarvasu Atreya. Instead:

- He was associated with Dhanvantari lineage and is credited with bringing Ayurveda knowledge from Indra in another tradition.

Therefore, Bharadwaja is not considered a disciple of Punarvasu Atreya.

56. (2): To find the average weight of mice in both control and test groups, we calculate the arithmetic mean using the formula:

Average = (Sum of values) ÷ (Number of values)

Control group weights = 32, 28, 26, 31, 33, 29

Sum = 32 + 28 + 26 + 31 + 33 + 29 = 179

Number of mice = 6

Average = 179 ÷ 6 = 29.83, which rounds to 29.8

Test group weights = 21, 28, 26, 25, 24, 22

Sum = 21 + 28 + 26 + 25 + 24 + 22 = 146

Number of mice = 6

Average = 146 ÷ 6

= 24.33, which rounds to 24.3

Hence, the correct average weights are:

Control – 29.8, Test – 24.3

57. (1): In Charaka Samhita, various anatomical structures of the body are enumerated for understanding the physiological framework of Ayurveda. The numbers traditionally attributed are:

A. Nine hundred (Sira – Veins): These are channels responsible for blood flow and distribution of nutrients.

C. Seven hundred (Snayu – Ligaments and tendons): These structures provide support and mechanical strength.

B. Two hundred (Dhamani – Arteries): Channels carrying vital life energy and oxygenated blood.

D. Four hundred (Peshi – Muscles): Muscular tissues providing movement and form to the body.

E. One hundred and seven (Marma – Vital points): Specific anatomical locations where trauma can lead to serious consequences like death, deformity, or severe pain.

So the correct sequential enumeration is:

Sira (A) → Snayu (C) → Dhamani (B) → Peshi (D) → Marma (E)

58. (3): Chrono-pharmacology is a branch of pharmacology that studies how biological rhythms (circadian cycles) influence the absorption, distribution, metabolism, and elimination of drugs.

In Ayurveda, the timing of medicine administration (Kaala) is considered crucial for efficacy. For example:

- Pitta-dominant disorders may be treated more effectively at specific times of day when Pitta is naturally high.
- Agni (digestive fire) fluctuates during the day, affecting digestion and assimilation of medication.

Chrono-pharmacology explains this Ayurvedic concept by correlating internal biological clocks with drug responsiveness, ensuring maximum therapeutic effect and minimal side effects.

Thus, the modern discipline that aligns with the Ayurvedic emphasis on timing is Chrono-pharmacology.

59. (4): In Ayurveda, Marmas are vital anatomical points where muscles, veins, ligaments, bones, and joints meet, and are highly sensitive. They are classified based on effect of injury into five major types:

(*a*) Sadhya Pranahara (Instant fatal) – Injury causes immediate death.

(*b*) Kalantara Pranahara (Eventually fatal) – Injury leads to death over time.

(*c*) Vaikalyakara (Deforming) – Causes deformity or disability.

(*d*) Rujakara (Pain-inflicting) – Injury leads to intense pain.

(*e*) Vishalyaghna – Death occurs when a foreign object is removed from the Marma.

From the given options:

A. Instant fatal, B. Eventually fatal, and C. Pain-inflicting are correctly recognized types of Marma.

D. Fire Dampening and E. Dosha vitiating are not recognized types in Ayurvedic classical texts related to Marma classification.

Hence, the options that are not types of Marma are D and E.

60. (3): We evaluate the correctness of each pathogen–disease pair:

A. Entamoeba histolytica – Amoebiasis: Correct. This protozoan causes amoebic dysentery, affecting the intestine.

B. Wuchereria – Elephantiasis: Correct. Caused by the filarial parasite *Wuchereria bancrofti,* leading to lymphatic obstruction and swelling of limbs.

C. Ascaris – Ringworms: Incorrect. *Ascaris lumbricoides* is a roundworm that causes ascariasis, not ringworm. Ringworm is a fungal infection (dermatophytes like *Trichophyton*).

D. Aspergillus – Warts: Incorrect. *Aspergillus* causes aspergillosis, a fungal infection of the lungs. Warts are caused by Human Papillomavirus (HPV), not fungi.

E. Plasmodium vivax – Cerebral malaria: Incorrect. *P. vivax* causes benign tertian malaria. Cerebral malaria is caused by *Plasmodium falciparum.*

So, the incorrectly matched pairs are:

Correct answer: C, D, and E only.

61. (1): The Pangvandhu Nyaya (Blind and Lame Analogy) is a classical Indian philosophical illustration used to explain the interdependent relationship between Man (mind) and Atman (soul) in Ayurveda and Darshana Shastra.

- In this analogy, the Atman is like the blind person—it has the potential for movement and existence, but lacks the ability to perceive or function independently in the physical world.
- The Manas (mind) is like the lame person—it possesses the capacity for thought, perception, and direction, but cannot act on its own without the Atman.

Together, Man and Atman function in coordination:

- Atman gives the vital consciousness and energy.
- Manas enables cognitive functions like thinking, willing, and perception.
- Just as the blind person carries the lame person (who can see and guide), Atman carries the Manas, while the Manas guides perception and cognition.

Thus, the Pangvandhu Nyaya metaphorically explains the mutual dependency of Man and Atman in the execution of life and perception.

62. (1): In Ayurveda, Bhasma is a calcined (incinerated) metal/ mineral preparation, used in therapeutics after purification and specific processing.

The main process used for preparation of Bhasmas is:

- **Puta:** This refers to a specific type of controlled heating procedure done in a closed crucible, often using cow dung cakes for uniform heat.
- The number and type of Puta (e.g., Gajaputa, Varaha Puta) vary according to the nature of the substance.

Other options:

- **Urdhva Patana** – used for volatile substances.
- **Murchana** – related to Sneha Kalpana, not Bhasma.
- **Sattva Patana** – used for extraction of metallic essence, not direct Bhasma preparation.

Thus, Puta is the primary process used in Bhasma preparation.

63. (2): In Ayurveda, Prakriti (body constitution) is determined at the time of conception and influenced by multiple factors. The correct chronological sequence of factors influencing Prakriti development is:

B. Shukra Shonita Prakriti– Based on genetic contribution of sperm and ovum at conception.

A. Kalgarbhashaya Prakriti– Influence of uterine environment and time of conception.

D. Maturahar Vikara Prakriti– Effect of maternal diet and lifestyle during pregnancy.

C. Mahabhut Vikara Prakriti– Influence of Pancha Mahabhuta predominance during fetal development.

Hence, the correct sequence is:

Shukra-Shonita → Kalgarbhashaya → Maturahar-Vikara → Mahabhut Vikara

64. (3): As per Bhava Prakasha Nighantu, the classical attributes and indications of Guggulu are:

A. Naveen Guggulu is Vrishya– Fresh (Naveen) Guggulu is considered aphrodisiac (Vrishya) in action.

D. Guggulu is also a Rasayana– It is recognized as a rejuvenative (Rasayana), promoting longevity and tissue regeneration.

E. Guggulu pacifies all three doshas– It is Tridosha Shamaka, especially beneficial in managing Vata-Kapha disorders.

Incorrect statements:

B. Purana Guggulu is Vrishya– Actually, Purana (old) Guggulu is Laghu (light) and more suitable for obesity and lipid disorders, not aphrodisiac.

C. Amla Rasa is indicated with Guggulu– Amla Rasa is contraindicated as it can interfere with Guggulu's actions and irritate digestion.

Therefore, correct combination is: A, D, E only

65. (4): Matching the herbs with their correct botanical names:

A. Bhanga – III. Cannabis sativa: Bhanga refers to hemp, used in traditional medicine, narcotic preparations, and rituals.

B. Bhringraj – IV. Eclipta alba: Bhringraj is known for hair growth and liver protection, and identified botanically as *Eclipta alba*.

C. Vacha – I. Acorus calamus: Vacha is a medhya (nootropic) herb and anti-epileptic, derived from *Acorus calamus*.

D. Nirgundi – II. Vitex negundo: Nirgundi is an anti-inflammatory and analgesic herb, known botanically as *Vitex negundo*.

66. (1): In Ayurveda, Sharira Gunas are considered to be the twenty Gurvadi Gunas, which are physiological and physical attributes of substances that affect the human body and its functions.

These 20 Sharir Gunas are divided into 10 pairs of opposites, and they are:

1. Guru (heavy) – Laghu (light)
2. Manda (dull) – Tikshna (sharp)
3. Hima (cold) – Ushna (hot)
4. Snigdha (unctuous) – Ruksha (dry)
5. Shlakshna (smooth) – Khara (rough)
6. Sandra (dense) – Drava (liquid)
7. Mrudu (soft) – Kathina (hard)
8. Sthira (stable) – Sara (mobile)
9. Sthoola (gross) – Sukshma (subtle)
10. Picchila (sticky) – Vishada (non-slimy)

These 20 qualities are called Gurvadi Gunas, and they help in understanding the therapeutic actions of substances and their effect on Doshas, Dhatus, and overall Sharira (body).

Hence, the correct set of Sharir Guna is Gurvadi – 20.

67. (2): Dashavidha Rogi-Roga Pariksha refers to the tenfold method of examination used in Ayurveda to evaluate both the patient (Rogi) and the disease (Roga) before treatment. These ten components are:

1. **Prakriti** – Body constitution
2. **Vikriti** – Pathological state
3. **Sara** – Essence or tissue quality
4. **Samhanana** – Body build/compactness
5. **Pramana** – Body measurement
6. **Satmya** – Adaptability
7. **Satva** – Mental strength
8. **Ahara Shakti** – Digestive capacity
9. **Vyayama Shakti** – Exercise capacity
10. **Vaya** – Age

Among the given options:

- Prakriti, Pramana, and Ahara Shakti are valid components.
- Parimana (meaning measurement or size) is not listed specifically as one of the Dashavidha Pariksha, though similar in meaning to Pramana, it is not the correct term used in this classical context.

Hence, Parimana is not a part of the Dashavidha Rogi-Roga Pariksha.

68. **(2):** The correct sequence of events in cellular respiration, which leads to the production of ATP in a eukaryotic cell, is:

E. **Co-transport of primary biomolecules:** Ingestion and cellular uptake of glucose, fatty acids, and amino acids occur first through various transport mechanisms.

A. **Generation of Acetyl-CoA:** These biomolecules undergo glycolysis, β-oxidation, and deamination, ultimately producing Acetyl-CoA, the central molecule entering the TCA cycle.

C. **Tri-carboxylic acid (TCA) cycle:** Also known as the Krebs cycle, Acetyl-CoA is oxidized to produce CO_2, along with NADH and $FADH_2$ (reducing equivalents).

B. **Generation of reducing equivalents:** This step overlaps with the TCA cycle and involves collection of NADH, $FADH_2$, which carry electrons to the ETC.

D. **Action of F_1F_0 ATPase:** Electrons from NADH/$FADH_2$ are transferred via the Electron Transport Chain (ETC), and proton motive force drives ATP synthesis via F_1F_0 ATPase (complex V).

Therefore, correct order is: E → A → C → B → D

69. **(3):** In Ayurveda, Dhatvagni refers to the metabolic fire or bio-transforming factor associated with each of the seven Dhatus (body tissues). These seven Dhatvagnis are responsible for converting the essence of one Dhatu into the next in the sequence.

The seven types of Dhatvagni are:

1. **Rasagni** – acts on Rasa Dhatu
2. **Raktagni** – acts on Rakta Dhatu
3. **Mamsagni** – acts on Mamsa Dhatu
4. **Medogni** – acts on Meda Dhatu
5. **Asthyagni** – acts on Asthi Dhatu
6. **Majjagni** – acts on Majja Dhatu
7. **Shukragni** – acts on Shukra Dhatu

Thus, the correct number of Dhatvagni is seven, corresponding to the seven Dhatus.

70. **(3):** In Ayurveda, Rasa (taste) is derived from the combination of Pancha Mahabhutas (five elements). Each Rasa has its own elemental composition that influences its properties and effects on Doshas.

The Panchabhautika composition of Kashaya Rasa (Astringent taste) is:

- **Prithvi (earth element)**– provides firmness, compactness, and roughness
- **Vayu (air element)**– provides dryness and subtlety

These combined give Kashaya Rasa its characteristic drying, constricting, and absorbent properties. It pacifies Kapha and Pitta, but aggravates Vata due to the Vayu component.

Hence, Kashaya Rasa is composed of Prithavi + Vayu Mahabhutas.

71. **(2):** Among the five subtypes of Kapha Dosha, Shleshak Kapha is specifically associated with the lubrication and cushioning of joints.

- It resides mainly in the Sandhis (joints).
- Its primary function is Sandhi Snehan – to lubricate the articular surfaces and enable smooth joint movements.
- It prevents friction, wear, and tear, thus maintaining joint health.

Other subtypes and their locations/functions:

- **Tarpak**– nourishes the brain and sense organs (resides in head)
- **Avalambak**– supports the chest and heart region
- **Kledak**– moistens food in the stomach, aids digestion

Hence, the subtype responsible for joint lubrication is Shleshak Kapha.

72. **(1):** Matching the virus species with their correct genus:

A. **Chandipura virus – III. Vesiculovirus:** Chandipura virus belongs to Rhabdoviridae family, genus Vesiculovirus. It causes encephalitis in children.

B. **Colorado tick fever virus – II. Orbivirus:** It belongs to the Reoviridae family, genus Orbivirus, transmitted by ticks and causes fever with leukopenia.

C. **Japanese encephalitis virus – I. Flavivirus:** JEV is from Flaviviridae, genus Flavivirus, and is mosquito-borne, causing severe encephalitis.

D. **Chikungunya virus – IV. Alphavirus:** CHIKV is an RNA virus from the Togaviridae family, genus Alphavirus, transmitted by Aedes mosquitoes.

73. **(4):** In Ayurveda, Veerya refers to the potency or energetic effect of a substance and plays a crucial role in determining its effect on the Tridoshas (Vata, Pitta, Kapha). Based on Veerya and associated Gunas, we can evaluate the given statements:

A. **Laghu Veerya will vitiate Vata – Correct:** The Laghu (light) quality increases mobility and dryness, which are intrinsic properties of Vata Dosha. Therefore, excessive intake of Laghu Veerya substances aggravates Vata.

C. **Mrudu Veerya will pacify Pitta – Correct:** Mrudu (soft) quality is cooling and soothing, which counteracts the Tikshna (sharp) and Ushna (hot) nature of Pitta Dosha. Thus, Mrudu Veerya has a Pitta-pacifying effect.

B. **Sheeta Veerya will pacify Vata and Kapha – Incorrect:** Sheeta (cold) Veerya pacifies Pitta, not Vata or Kapha. In fact, it aggravates Vata and Kapha, due to its cold and heavy qualities.

D. **Mrudu Veerya will vitiate Vata – Incorrect:** Mrudu Veerya has no direct Vata-vitiating property. It may help balance Vata when combined with Snigdha (unctuous) and Ushna (warm) attributes.

E. **Ruksha Veerya will vitiate Pitta – Incorrect:** Ruksha (dry) quality is antagonistic to Kapha, not Pitta. In fact, it reduces Kapha and may support Pitta in certain cases, rather than vitiate it.

Therefore, only statements A and C are correct regarding the actions of Veerya.

74. (2): The regulation of electrolyte balance, especially sodium and water, involves the Renin-Angiotensin-Aldosterone System (RAAS). The correct sequence is:

D. **Activation of Osmoreception:** A decrease in blood pressure or sodium is sensed by osmoreceptors and baroreceptors.

B. **Synthesis of Renin:** The juxtaglomerular cells of the kidneys release renin in response to low pressure.

E. **Production of Angiotensin:** Renin catalyzes the formation of angiotensin I, which is converted to angiotensin II.

A. **Release of Aldosterone:** Angiotensin II stimulates the adrenal cortex to release aldosterone.

C. **Sodium reabsorption from Kidney:** Aldosterone promotes reabsorption of Na^+ and water in the distal nephron, raising blood volume and pressure.

Therefore, the correct sequence is: D → B → E → A → C

75. (4): In Charaka Samhita, the Bhesaja Chatushka (group of four chapters on medicine) is the first set of four chapters in Sutra Sthana, covering the foundational principles of drug utility and therapeutic decision-making.

The correct chapter sequence of Bhesaja Chatushka is:

1. Deerghanjiviteeya Adhyaya (Chapter 1)
2. Apamargatantriya Adhyaya (Chapter 2)
3. Aragvadhadi Adhyaya (Chapter 3)
4. Shadvirechanashatashritiya Adhyaya (Chapter 4)

These chapters discuss:

- Classification of medicines
- Importance of drug properties
- Collection and processing
- Dosage and therapeutic guidelines

Thus, the correct sequence is: 1, 2, 3, 4.

76. (3): The proper correlation between branches of Ayurveda and corresponding branches in modern medicine is as follows:

A. **Kayachikitsa – II. Internal medicine:** Kayachikitsa is the branch of Ayurveda that deals with the treatment of systemic diseases and internal disorders such as fever, diabetes, and respiratory diseases. It is equivalent to Internal Medicine in modern science.

B. **Shalya Tantra – IV. Surgery:** Shalya Tantra involves surgical procedures, trauma management, wound care, and parasurgical operations like Kshara Sutra and Agnikarma. It aligns with the field of Surgery.

C. **Rasayana – I. Regenerative medicine:** Rasayana deals with rejuvenation, tissue nourishment, anti-aging, and enhancing immunity. These concepts are closely aligned with Regenerative Medicine, which focuses on cell repair and longevity.

D. **Shalakya Tantra – III. Ophthalmology:** Shalakya covers disorders of eyes, ears, nose, and throat (ENT). Among these, eye diseases are a major component, aligning it with Ophthalmology.

77. (4): In phytochemistry, solvents are selected based on the polarity of the phytoconstituents to be extracted:

Hexane is a non-polar solvent and is ideal for extracting non-polar components such as:

- Essential oils
- Lipids
- Fatty acids
- Waxes
- Non-polar terpenoids

Other solvents like:

- Water is highly polar.
- Methanol and ethanol are moderately polar.

Thus, for extracting non-polar components from plant material, hexane is the most appropriate solvent.

78. (3): To identify a novel flavonol (a specific class of flavonoid) from a medicinal plant, a technique with high sensitivity, resolution, and structural elucidation ability is required.

LC-MS/MS (Liquid Chromatography– Tandem Mass Spectrometry) provides:

- Separation of complex mixtures (via LC)
- Identification of molecular weight and structure (via MS/MS)
- High specificity and sensitivity suitable for novel compound discovery

Other techniques:

- HPLC is useful for separation and quantification but lacks structural detection.
- HPTLC is semi-quantitative, more for fingerprinting.
- GC is not suitable for flavonols, which are usually non-volatile and thermally unstable.

Hence, LC-MS/MS is the most suitable for novel flavonol identification.

79. (1): In Ayurveda, Pranayatana are described as the abodes or seats of life (Prana) in the body – critical sites that sustain and maintain life. Classical texts like Charaka Samhita describe ten such Pranayatana.

Among them:

A. Kantha (throat) and Hridya (heart) – are directly mentioned as primary seats of Prana.

C. Nabhi (navel) and Guda (anus) – are also recognized as vital points essential for sustaining life.

Whereas:

B. Amashaya (stomach) and Pakwashaya (colon) – are important but not classified among the core Pranayatana.

D. Tvacha (skin) and Jihva (tongue) – are not listed as Pranayatana in classical references.

Hence, correct pair among the given is: A and C only

80. (3): The term "Genome" refers to the entire genetic material of an organism, including all of its genes and non-coding sequences.

- In diploid organisms (like humans), the genome represents the complete set of genetic instructions found in a haploid (n) set of chromosomes, because diploid organisms have two copies (maternal and paternal) of each chromosome.
- Thus, for humans, the genome is defined as:
  - ~3.2 billion base pairs
  - Present in haploid set (n) = 23 chromosomes
  - Encodes ~20,000 – 25,000 protein-coding genes

Therefore, "Genome" is defined as the entire sequence of haploid (n) DNA content of an organism.

81. (4): The term "Micturition" refers to the process of expelling urine from the urinary bladder through the urethra to the outside of the body. It involves a coordinated action of:

- Detrusor muscle contraction (muscular wall of the bladder)
- Relaxation of the internal and external urethral sphincters
- Neural regulation by the pontine micturition center and spinal reflex arcs

Other terms:

- Formation of urine involves filtration, reabsorption, and secretion
- Glomerular filtration occurs in the kidneys' glomeruli
- Renal reabsorption takes place in the nephron tubules

Thus, Micturition = release of urine from the bladder.

82. (4): Among the four Vedas, Atharvaveda is considered the closest to Ayurveda because it contains:

- Rich descriptions of diseases, herbs, and healing rituals
- The origins of medical knowledge and spiritual healing
- Reference to concepts like Tridosha, medicinal plants, and surgical practices
- Hymns for healing through mantras, herbs, and therapies

In contrast:

- Rigveda, Samaveda, and Yajurveda are more focused on rituals, hymns, and sacrifices, not directly on medical science.

Hence, Atharvaveda is the Veda most closely associated with Ayurveda.

83. (4): A plasmid vector is a circular, double-stranded DNA molecule used in molecular cloning to introduce foreign genes into host cells. Essential features include:

B. Multiple cloning site (MCS): A region with several restriction sites for inserting foreign DNA.

C. Antibiotic selection marker: A gene (like ampR) that allows only transformed cells to grow in the presence of an antibiotic.

E. Origin of replication (Ori): A sequence necessary for plasmid replication inside host cells.

Incorrect options:

A. Repressor sequence: Not essential or standard in all vectors. It's regulatory, but not a core vector feature.

D. Reverse transcription capabilities: Feature of reverse transcriptase enzymes, not plasmid vectors.

Thus, the correct essential elements are B, C, E only.

84. (1): In Ayurveda, Desha (geographical region) influences Dosha predominance. Anupa Desha refers to marshy, water-abundant regions like riverbanks and coastal areas.

Characteristics of Anupa Desha:

- High humidity and moisture
- Cold and heavy environment
- Predominance of Kapha Dosha due to Snigdha and Sheeta Guna
- Often also associated with Vata Dosha, due to windiness and cold

Therefore, the more dominant Dosha types in Anupa Desha are Kapha and Vata, i.e., A and D only

85. (3): A nucleosome core is the fundamental unit of chromatin in eukaryotic cells and consists of:

- An octamer of histone proteins:
  - 2 units each of: H_2A, H_2B, H_3, H_4
- Around which ~147 base pairs of DNA are wrapped

H1 histone is not part of the core, but is called the linker histone and helps in chromatin compaction.

Thus, the nucleosome core is composed of two units each of H_2A, H_2B, H_3, and H_4.

86. (2): 16s rRNA sequencing is the standard molecular technique used for identifying bacteria at the genetic level. This gene:

- Is present in all prokaryotes (bacteria and archaea)
- Contains conserved and variable regions, making it ideal for differentiating bacterial species
- Is used extensively in taxonomy, phylogenetics, and microbial diagnostics

Other ribosomal subunit RNA genes like:

- **18s rRNA** – specific to eukaryotes, not used for bacteria
- **32s and 24s rRNA** – are not standard references in molecular microbiology

Therefore, 16s rRNA sequencing is the most accurate tool for bacterial identification.

87. (3): Matching the physiological functions with their respective hormones:

A. Regulation of Metabolic Rate – III. Thyroxine: Thyroxine (T_4), secreted by the thyroid gland, increases basal metabolic rate, oxygen consumption, and energy production.

B. Regulation of Blood Pressure – IV. Vasopressin: Also known as antidiuretic hormone (ADH), it regulates blood pressure by retaining water in kidneys and causing vasoconstriction.

C. RBC Synthesis – I. Erythropoietin: Produced by the kidneys, this hormone stimulates red blood cell (RBC) production in the bone marrow.

D. Stress Response – II. Epinephrine: Secreted by the adrenal medulla, it is the primary hormone in fight-or-flight response, increasing heart rate, BP, and alertness.

88. (4): Among the given scholars, the following are recognized commentators of Charaka Samhita:

A. Chakrapani Dutta – Most famous and authoritative commentator on Charaka Samhita, known for his work "Ayurveda Dipika", which clarified many difficult terms and passages.

C. Jejjat – An earlier commentator, referenced by later scholars including Chakrapani. He provided early interpretations on Charaka Samhita.

Others:

B. Hemadri – Known for commentaries on Ashtanga Hridaya, not on Charaka Samhita.

D. Vachaspati – Not known for Charaka Samhita commentary.

Therefore, correct answer: A and C only

89. (2): Matching the Sanskrit philosophical/physiological terms with their origin or function:

A. Man – IV. Chintya (Thinking): Manas (mind) is responsible for Chintya Karma—thinking, analyzing, remembering.

B. Purush – III. Shaddhatuj: According to Ayurveda, Purusha (individual being) is Shaddhatuj, formed from six constituents: Panchamahabhutas + Atman.

C. Indriya – II. Bhautika: Sense organs (Indriya) arise from Mahabhuta (elemental) combinations, hence termed Bhautika.

D. Mahabhuta – I. Vayu: The Panchamahabhutas (ether, air, fire, water, earth) are interconnected and Vayu (air) is one of the Mahabhutas and a key force of movement and transformation.

90. (1): In Ayurveda, "Stanya Janana" refers to promotion of breast milk (lactation). Among the six Rasas (tastes), Madhura Rasa (sweet taste) is considered best for this purpose.

- It provides nourishment (Brimhana)
- Enhances Snigdha (unctuousness) and Ojas, which support lactation
- Found in foods like milk, rice, ghee, jaggery, etc.
- Also balances Vata and Pitta, which is crucial during postpartum

Other Rasas like Tikta, Katu, Kashaya are drying and light in nature, and not favorable for milk production.

Therefore, Madhura Rasa is best for Stanya Janana.

91. (1): The patient presents with recurrent skin rashes, hair issues (sparse hair, premature greying), and episodes of stomatitis, all of which suggest Pitta aggravation.

Triphala Rasayana is a classic Ayurvedic formulation comprising Amalaki, Haritaki, and Bibhitaki, known for:

- Balancing Pitta and Kapha
- Acting as a mild detoxifier and Rasayana (rejuvenator)
- Supporting healthy digestion, skin, and hair
- Having anti-inflammatory and antioxidant properties

Other options:

- Trikatu and Panchakola are deepana-pachana drugs for Kapha-Vata issues.
- Bhallataka Rasayana is Pitta-aggravating and contraindicated in skin rashes or burning sensation.

Hence, Triphala Rasayana is best suited for addressing skin and hair issues with Pitta dominance.

92. (2): Based on the signs described in the case:

- Tall, lean frame with premature greying, excessive sweating, body odor, aggressiveness, irritability, and skin issues during Diwali (festival involving heat and rich food) – all clearly point toward Pitta Prakriti.
- Pitta dominant individuals typically show:
  - Sharp intellect, irritability, emotional intensity
  - Premature greying or hair loss
  - Sweating tendency with strong body odor
  - Heat intolerance and skin conditions like rashes, acne, or inflammation

Hence, the Prakriti of the person is Pitta Dominant.

93. (1): In Ayurveda, dietary recommendations are based on pacifying the aggravated Dosha. For Pitta Prakriti or Pitta aggravation, the ideal diet includes:

- **Tikta Rasa (bitter taste)** – pacifies Pitta
- **Sheeta (cool) potency** – counters heat and inflammation
- **Snigdha and Guru (unctuous and heavy)** – stabilize the fiery, sharp qualities of Pitta

This includes foods like:

- Ghee, milk, bitter vegetables (neem, karela), and cooling fruits (pomegranate)

Avoid:

- Katu (pungent), sour, fermented, and oily foods which increase Pitta

Hence, the correct dietary advice is: Tikta Rasa, Cool, Heavy diet

94. (3): Pitta-predominant individuals tend to have medium build but may suffer from quick fatigue, inflammation, and heat-related issues.

- Activities like heavy weight lifting generate intense heat, strain, and internal pressure – which can further aggravate Pitta.
- On the other hand:
  - Jogging, cycling, and swimming (cooling activity) are moderate exercises and suitable for Pitta types.

Therefore, the person should avoid heavy weight lifting.

95. (2): Pitta Dosha governs heat, blood, and metabolism. When aggravated, it leads to:

- Rakta Dushti (blood vitiation)
- Bleeding tendencies, including epistaxis (nosebleeds), hyperacidity, menorrhagia, inflammatory and hemorrhagic disorders

Other options:

- **Obesity** is related to Kapha
- **Osteoarthritis** – related to Vata
- **Indigestion** – more common in Mandagni (Kapha or Vata)

Therefore, Pitta-dominant individuals are more prone to bleeding disorders.

96. (3): The clinical presentation of the patient includes:

- Recurrent opportunistic infections
- Weight loss, diarrhea,
- Decreased T cell count
- Diagnosis of Kaposi's sarcoma (a hallmark AIDS-defining illness)
- History of blood transfusions
- Infection confirmed via cell-based assay

These features clearly point toward Human Immunodeficiency Virus (HIV) infection, which progresses to AIDS in the advanced stage.

Other options:

- H1N1 Influenza and Hepatitis B do not cause severe immunosuppression or Kaposi's sarcoma
- Human Papillomavirus is associated with warts and cervical cancer, not systemic immune deficiency

Hence, the most probable infection is caused by HIV.

97. (2): HIV is a retrovirus, meaning it contains single-stranded RNA as its genetic material and replicates via a unique enzyme called reverse transcriptase.

- This enzyme is an RNA-dependent DNA polymerase, which:
  - Converts viral RNA into DNA
  - Integrates it into the host genome for replication

Other polymerases:

- **DNA-dependent DNA polymerase** – used in DNA replication
- **DNA-dependent RNA polymerase** – for transcription
- **RNA-dependent RNA polymerase** – in RNA viruses (e.g., Influenza)

Therefore, the correct polymerase is RNA-dependent DNA polymerase.

98. (1): In Ayurveda, Rasayana therapy is recommended for patients with Ojakshaya (immunity depletion), chronic illness, or those undergoing debilitating diseases like HIV/AIDS.

Benefits of Rasayana:

- Acts as immune enhancer (Ojas vardhaka)
- Promotes tissue regeneration
- Improves quality of life, strength, and mental resilience
- Provides supportive therapy along with conventional treatment

Other options:

- **Krimihara** – anti-parasitic
- **Medhya** – cognitive enhancers
- **Mutrala** – diuretics

Hence, Rasayana therapy is most appropriate as supportive care in this condition.

99. (3): In HIV infection, CD4+ T cell count is the primary indicator of:

- Disease progression
- Risk of opportunistic infections
- Response to therapy

Flow cytometry is the most widely used diagnostic technique to:

- Quantify CD4+ T cells
- Assess immune status

Other tests:

- Widal test – used for typhoid
- HPLC – used in metabolic and drug analysis
- ELISA – used for initial detection of HIV, but not for progression monitoring

Thus, for tracking HIV disease progression, the best method is Flow cytometry.

100. (1): In Ayurvedic terms, the described condition corresponds to Oja-Kshaya, which refers to:

- Depletion or weakness of Ojas, the vital essence responsible for immunity, strength, and vitality
- Manifestations include weight loss, fatigue, frequent infections, mental instability, and weakness
- Oja-Kshaya results in compromised immunity, similar to modern immunodeficiency conditions like HIV/AIDS

Other options:

- Kapha Vriddhi, Pitta Vriddhi, Vata Kshaya may be involved symptomatically but do not encompass the core pathology of severe immune loss

Hence, the correct Ayurvedic pathological description is Ojokshaya.

UGC NET/JRF

AYURVEDA BIOLOGY

PAPER-II

UNIT 1: HISTORY AND DEVELOPMENT OF AYURVEDA

CHAPTER–1

VEDIC ORIGIN & CHRONOLOGICAL DEVELOPMENT OF AYURVEDA

Ayurveda, an ancient system of medicine, has deep roots in India's Vedic tradition, where it was not only a practice of healing but a complete science of life. Dating back over 5,000 years, Ayurveda has guided health, balance, and longevity through comprehensive knowledge derived from the Vedas, primarily the Rigveda and Atharvaveda. The Vedic period, which spanned from 1500 BCE, laid the foundation of Ayurveda with a blend of herbal knowledge, spiritual insights, and lifestyle practices aimed at holistic well-being. Its evolution saw Ayurveda develop into a structured science, defined by classic texts and recognized for its eight specialised branches (Aṣṭāṅga Āyurveda). Over the centuries, Ayurveda has adapted to sociocultural shifts while retaining its core principles, illustrating its resilience and adaptability.

VEDIC LITERATURE AND ITS INFLUENCE ON AYURVEDA

Overview of the Vedic Period and Literature

The Vedic period (circa 1500-500 BCE) marks the earliest known phase of Indian civilization. Its literature comprises four primary texts: the Rigveda, Yajurveda, Samaveda, and Atharvaveda, collectively known as the Vedas. These texts are a treasure trove of hymns, rituals, and philosophies that convey the spiritual, philosophical, and medical knowledge of the time. Ayurveda, often referred to as an "Upaveda" (secondary Veda) of the Atharvaveda, was deeply influenced by the religious and philosophical tenets of these texts. It emphasises the interplay between the body, mind, and environment, a concept originating in the Vedic worldview that life is interconnected and cyclical. The health practices mentioned in the Vedas reflect an understanding of harmony between humans and nature.

Ayurveda as a System Rooted in Vedic Knowledge

Ayurveda's primary aim is the promotion of health and prevention of disease by aligning the body's natural rhythms with the cycles of nature. This perspective can be traced back to Vedic hymns, which promote balance, mindfulness, and ethical living as pathways to health. In Vedic literature, health is defined not just by physical well-being but also by the mind's clarity and spiritual harmony, a holistic vision that underpins Ayurvedic philosophy. Ayurveda grew out of this philosophical context, evolving into a discipline that addressed everything from preventive healthcare and herbal medicine to surgery and mental wellness.

EARLY MENTIONS OF AYURVEDIC CONCEPTS IN THE RIGVEDA AND ATHARVAVEDA

The Rigveda's Contribution to Ayurveda Thought

The Rigveda, the oldest of the four Vedas, contains hymns and incantations dedicated to various deities and aspects of life. Some of its passages offer references to medicinal plants and healing practices, demonstrating the beginnings of herbal medicine in Indian tradition. Soma, a plant used in religious rituals and revered for its rejuvenative qualities, is one such reference, symbolizing the Vedic emphasis on vitality. Additionally, hymns dedicated to the deity Ashvins, the divine healers, allude to the duality of physical and mental health and the interconnectedness of life forces. These deities are depicted as using herbal remedies, affirming the Rigvedic acknowledgment of plants' healing potential.

The Atharvaveda and its Medical Knowledge

The Atharvaveda, often called the "Veda of spells" or "book of knowledge," is particularly rich in references to healing practices. Unlike the other Vedas, which focus more on rituals and philosophical discourse, the Atharvaveda delves into practical aspects of health and medicine, including treatment for diseases, use of medicinal plants, and rituals for protection against illness. This Veda provides a comprehensive look at health, disease prevention, and therapeutic practices, laying the groundwork for Ayurvedic principles. Terms related to disease causation, immunity, and treatment appear frequently in the Atharvaveda, suggesting an early understanding of holistic health.

CONTRIBUTIONS OF ANCIENT SEERS (RISHIS) TO AYURVEDIC KNOWLEDGE

The Role of Rishis in Developing Ayurvedic Knowledge

Rishis, or ancient seers, played a crucial role in the development of Ayurveda. These sages were not only spiritual guides but also scholars and scientists who conducted meticulous observations of nature and human physiology. Their insights form the basis of Ayurveda's extensive understanding of the human body, plants, and the environment. The knowledge gathered by these Rishis, often received through meditation and divine revelation, was passed down orally and later codified in the classical texts.

Major Contributors to Ayurveda

Charaka: Known as the "Father of Indian Medicine," Charaka authored the Charaka Samhita, an extensive treatise on internal medicine (kaya-chikitsa). Charaka's work laid the foundation for the tridosha theory (Vata, Pitta, and Kapha), emphasising the importance of balance among these doshas in maintaining health. Charaka also advanced principles related to diet, lifestyle, and mental health, asserting that physical ailments are often linked to mental and environmental factors.

Sushruta: Often hailed as the "Father of Surgery," Sushruta authored the Sushruta Samhita, focusing on surgical procedures, anatomy, and obstetrics. His work includes descriptions of complex surgeries, such as rhinoplasty and cataract removal, demonstrating advanced surgical knowledge in ancient India. Sushruta's text also introduced the concept of marma points, which are vital points on the body linked to both physical and mental well-being.

Vagbhata: The author of the Ashtanga Hridaya and Ashtanga Sangraha, Vagbhata integrated the teachings of both Charaka and Sushruta into a cohesive system. His contributions emphasise the holistic approach of Ayurveda, covering topics from diagnosis to treatment, pharmacology, and preventative care.

EVOLUTION AND TIMELINE OF AYURVEDA THROUGH THE AGES

Pre-Vedic and Vedic Periods (circa 3000-1500 BCE)

Before the formal codification of Ayurvedic knowledge, healing practices were likely influenced by indigenous tribal knowledge and oral traditions focused on nature and spirituality. In the Vedic period, these practices became formalized as part of a greater philosophical framework that included the body, mind, and spirit. During this period, Ayurveda's foundational concepts began to take shape within the Vedic worldview.

Samhita Period (1500 BCE - 500 CE)

The Samhita period saw the formal documentation of Ayurvedic knowledge in the classical texts, particularly the Charaka Samhita and Sushruta Samhita. This era represents the first structured attempt to compile and standardize medical practices. Key concepts such as the doshas, body constitutions (prakriti), and treatment methods were elaborated upon, establishing Ayurveda as a formal medical system.

Post-Samhita Period (500 CE - 1200 CE)

This period is marked by the contributions of scholars like Vagbhata, who compiled the Ashtanga Hridaya, incorporating teachings from Charaka and Sushruta. The period also saw Ayurveda expand its scope to include various specialized branches, known as the eight limbs (Aṣṭāṅga Āyurveda), covering areas such as surgery, pediatrics, psychiatry, and toxicology. The spread of Buddhism during this period also facilitated the dissemination of Ayurvedic knowledge to other parts of Asia.

Medieval Period (1200-1600 CE)

During this era, foreign influences, particularly from Persian and Arabic medicine, introduced new ideas into Ayurveda, enriching its pharmacology and diagnostic techniques. Despite the dominance of Islamic rule, Ayurveda continued to thrive, especially in southern India, where local dynasties supported its practice.

Colonial Period (1600-1947)

The arrival of British colonisation marked a decline in Ayurvedic practice as Western medicine became more prominent. However, Ayurveda persisted among the rural population and was practised as a form of folk medicine. This period also saw the beginning of institutionalised Ayurveda education as resistance against British influence grew.

Post-Independence and Modern Revival (1947-present)

Post-independence, the Indian government recognized Ayurveda as an official system of medicine, establishing institutions for research, education, and practice. In 2014, the creation of the Ministry of AYUSH reinforced the government's commitment to promoting Ayurveda and other traditional systems of medicine. Today, Ayurveda is not only practiced in India but has also gained international recognition, with research into its practices and formulations continuing to expand.

KEY MILESTONES AND CHANGES IN AYURVEDIC PRACTICES OVER TIME

Formalisation of Ayurvedic Texts

The formal compilation of Ayurvedic knowledge in texts like the Charaka Samhita and Sushruta Samhita was a monumental step. These texts provided a structured approach to health and wellness, covering areas from preventive care to complex surgical procedures. The systemization of this knowledge marked Ayurveda's transition from an oral tradition to a documented medical science.

Development of Rasa Shastra (circa 8th Century CE)

Rasa Shastra, a branch of Ayurveda focused on alchemy and the therapeutic use of minerals and metals, emerged around the 8th century CE. This period saw the development of new methods to purify and process metals and minerals, such as mercury, copper, and sulfur, transforming them into medicinal substances believed to enhance health and longevity. Rasa Shastra brought innovations in Ayurvedic pharmacology, allowing for the treatment of chronic and complex diseases through metallic preparations (Bhasmas). These innovations expanded the pharmacological range of Ayurveda, and Rasa Shastra practices remain integral to modern Ayurvedic pharmaceutics.

The Systematization of Aṣṭāṅga Āyurveda (Eight Branches of Ayurveda)

One of the key developments in Ayurveda's evolution was the establishment of its eight specialised branches, known collectively as Aṣṭāṅga Āyurveda. This systematisation allowed Ayurveda to address a wide range of health issues, each branch focusing on specific areas of medicine. The eight branches are:

1. **Kaya Chikitsa:** Internal medicine, dealing with physiological imbalances.
2. **Shalya Tantra:** Surgery, including trauma and surgical procedures.
3. **Shalakya Tantra:** ENT and ophthalmology, addressing diseases of the head and neck.
4. **Kaumarabhritya:** Pediatrics, focusing on child health and prenatal care.
5. **Agad Tantra:** Toxicology, covering poisons and detoxification.
6. **Bhuta Vidya:** Psychiatry, dealing with mental health and spirituality.
7. **Rasayana:** Rejuvenation therapies for vitality and longevity.
8. **Vajikarana:** Aphrodisiac therapy, focusing on reproductive health.

Each branch became specialised, contributing to a comprehensive approach to healthcare in Ayurveda that addressed everything from surgical interventions to mental wellness, rejuvenation, and preventative care. This system enabled practitioners to tailor treatments more precisely to the needs of patients, covering the entire spectrum of human health.

Decline During the Colonial Period and Efforts at Revival

During British colonisation, Ayurveda faced significant challenges as Western medicine gained prominence and was promoted by colonial authorities. Many Ayurvedic institutions were disbanded, and traditional practices were relegated to rural areas, becoming a form of folk medicine for much of the population. Despite this, Ayurveda continued to be practised by local healers, with some families preserving ancient knowledge.

Toward the end of colonial rule, there was a resurgence of interest in Ayurveda as part of the broader movement for Indian independence. Ayurvedic practitioners and scholars began organising efforts to formalise Ayurvedic education, establish standardised training programs, and revive classical texts. Institutions such as the Ayurveda College in Pune were founded, setting the groundwork for the reintegration of Ayurveda into formal healthcare and education systems.

Post-Independence Recognition and the Establishment of the Ministry of AYUSH

After India gained independence in 1947, Ayurveda was recognized as an official system of medicine by the Indian government. The establishment of the Central Council of Indian Medicine (CCIM) in 1970 provided a regulatory framework for Ayurvedic education, practice, and research. Ayurveda was further institutionalised with the establishment of dedicated Ayurvedic colleges, research institutions, and government hospitals.

In 2014, the Ministry of AYUSH (Ayurveda, Yoga & Naturopathy, Unani, Siddha, and Homeopathy) was created to promote traditional Indian systems of medicine, with Ayurveda as a central focus. The ministry is tasked with promoting Ayurveda on both a national and international level, supporting research, standardising practices, and ensuring quality control. This official support has led to a renewed global interest in Ayurveda, as the government actively collaborates with international bodies to promote Ayurvedic research and practice.

Integration with Modern Science and Emerging Fields

In recent years, Ayurveda has increasingly integrated with modern science, giving rise to interdisciplinary fields such as Ayurgenomics, which explores the correlation between genetic markers and Ayurvedic body constitutions (prakriti). This research aims to validate and enhance the understanding of personalized medicine, a core aspect of Ayurveda that aligns with contemporary approaches in precision medicine. Similarly, areas like Ayurveda pharmacology and Ayurvedic clinical trials are emerging, helping scientifically evaluate and validate Ayurvedic formulations and treatment protocols.

There is also a growing focus on applying Ayurveda in the fields of public health and preventive medicine, using its holistic approach to address lifestyle diseases, stress management, and wellness practices. The integration of Ayurvedic principles in fields such as lifestyle medicine, mental health, and wellness tourism demonstrates Ayurveda's adaptability and relevance in modern healthcare. As research and collaboration continue, Ayurveda's contributions to contemporary health sciences are expected to grow.

MULTIPLE CHOICE QUESTIONS

1. The Rigveda and Atharvaveda, two seminal texts in Vedic literature, contain numerous references to healing practices that predate formalized Ayurveda. These references discuss the sanctity of Soma, cnsidered a divine elixir, and the invocation of Ashwini Kumaras, divine healers. Considering these references, what is the most plausible conclusion about the Vedic foundation of Ayurveda?
   A. Vedic healing practices are entirely mythical and lack any practical medical applications.
   B. The Rigveda and Atharvaveda contain proto-Ayurvedic concepts that later evolved into systematic medical science.
   C. The Vedic approach to healing focuses exclusively on metaphysical aspects, ignoring physiological processes.
   D. Soma and the Ashwini Kumaras are symbolic representations of mental and emotional well-being.
2. Historical evidence suggests that early Ayurvedic texts like Charaka Samhita and Sushruta Samhita drew heavily from Vedic rituals and mantras. If a historian sought to establish a clear timeline of Ayurvedic evolution, which of the following methods would be most effective in aligning Ayurvedic texts with Vedic literature?
   A. Analyzing the Sanskrit etymology of Ayurvedic terminologies to trace their origin to Rigvedic hymns.
   B. Studying the transition from oral traditions in Vedic times to written documentation in Ayurvedic treatises.
   C. Comparing the dietary recommendations in Ayurveda with Vedic yajnas (sacrificial rituals).
   D. Mapping the geographic spread of Ayurveda using archaeological evidence unrelated to the Vedas.
3. The concept of Tridosha—Vata, Pitta, and Kapha—is a cornerstone of Ayurveda. It is suggested that its roots can be traced to Vedic metaphysics, particularly the interplay of the five elements (Pancha Mahabhutas). If this hypothesis is explored, which of the following correlations is most consistent with Ayurvedic philosophy?
   A. Vata is derived from the combination of water and fire elements.
   B. Pitta represents the dynamic equilibrium between air and ether.
   C. Kapha emerges from the earth and water elements, embodying stability and structure.
   D. None of the doshas can be directly linked to the Pancha Mahabhutas, as they are entirely conceptual.
4. Contributions from Rishis like Bharadvaja are central to the origins of Ayurveda. Bharadvaja is credited with bringing Ayurvedic knowledge from Indra to humanity. Which of the following interpretations best aligns with the symbolic significance of this event?
   A. Bharadvaja's interaction with Indra is a mythological allegory for the transfer of divine wisdom to mortals.
   B. The narrative implies that Ayurvedic practices were independently developed without any external influence.

C. Bharadvaja symbolizes the integration of spiritual and empirical approaches in early medical science.

D. The story undermines the empirical basis of Ayurveda by emphasizing its divine origins

5. The Atharvaveda is often regarded as the earliest text containing explicit references to disease diagnosis and herbal medicine. However, it also intertwines metaphysical concepts with practical remedies. How does this duality reflect the philosophical essence of early Ayurveda?

A. It demonstrates that Ayurveda was primarily concerned with spiritual healing, relegating physical health to secondary importance.

B. It highlights the integrative approach of Ayurveda, addressing both physical and metaphysical aspects of health.

C. It suggests that metaphysical concepts were later additions to a purely empirical tradition.

D. It proves that herbal medicine in Ayurveda lacks a scientific basis, being rooted in mysticism.

6. The timeline of Ayurveda's evolution shows a transition from reliance on Vedic rituals to the development of systematic medical treatises. If this timeline is examined critically, which of the following developments best signifies the shift toward empirical observation?

A. The creation of hymns addressing the Ashwini Kumaras.

B. The codification of diagnostic methods in Charaka Samhita.

C. The emphasis on yajnas for health and prosperity.

D. The introduction of Soma as a universal panacea.

7. Ancient Ayurvedic texts classify diseases based on their etiology (Nidanam). These classifications often correspond with descriptions in the Atharvaveda, which attributes illness to spiritual or supernatural causes. How did this classification influence the development of Ayurveda?

A. It perpetuated a purely spiritual approach, delaying scientific medical advancements.

B. It encouraged an integrative framework, addressing physical, mental, and spiritual causes of disease.

C. It rejected the supernatural entirely, focusing on diet and lifestyle as the sole determinants of health.

D. It led to inconsistencies in Ayurvedic practices by merging incompatible philosophies.

8. The transition from Vedic rituals to systematic Ayurveda involved the gradual abandonment of yajnas as primary therapeutic practices. What does this shift reveal about the evolving priorities of Ayurvedic practitioners?

A. A complete rejection of spiritual practices in favour of empirical observation.

B. A focus on individual health over collective ritualistic benefits.

C. A synthesis of Vedic and non-Vedic practices to broaden its applicability.

D. An intentional distancing from Vedic traditions to establish Ayurveda as a secular science.

9. The Rigveda describes hymns invoking medicinal plants, suggesting their consciousness and ability to heal. How can this perspective be reconciled with modern phytotherapy?

A. By interpreting the hymns as metaphorical, emphasizing the therapeutic potential of plant-based compounds.

B. By rejecting modern phytotherapy, as it contradicts the spiritual essence of Ayurvedic plant usage.

C. By acknowledging that plants hold metaphysical energy, which is unquantifiable by modern science.

D. By treating these hymns as ancient folklore with no bearing on actual Ayurvedic practices.

10. Ayurveda's emphasis on Prakriti (constitution) is believed to have roots in Vedic philosophical inquiries about individuality and harmony with nature. If this concept is examined through a contemporary lens, which of the following applications would best demonstrate its relevance?

A. Utilizing Prakriti for cosmetic personalization without considering health implications.

B. Employing Prakriti-based guidelines for personalized nutrition and lifestyle interventions.

C. Applying Prakriti solely as a philosophical concept without practical applications.

D. Standardizing treatments across all individuals, irrespective of their Prakriti.

Directions (Q. No. 11–14): *Scenario-Based Questions*

SCENARIO 1

A team of researchers investigates the historical development of Ayurvedic concepts from Vedic literature, focusing on the Rigveda and Atharvaveda. They identify passages describing the use of plants, chants, and rituals for healing. Their findings suggest that these texts laid the foundation for Ayurvedic diagnostics and therapies, such as identifying symptoms through Dosha imbalances. The researchers note that Vedic rituals heavily emphasize community health, while Ayurveda progressively focuses on individual health.

SCENARIO 2

Simultaneously, another group examines the role of Vedic seers (Rishis) in codifying Ayurveda. They propose that the transmission of knowledge from Indra to Bharadvaja symbolizes the shift from oral traditions to written documentation. They also explore how the socio-cultural context of the Vedic era influenced the evolution of Ayurvedic practices, emphasizing the transition from sacrificial rituals to therapeutic methods.

11. Based on Scenario 1, what does the emphasis on individual health in Ayurveda, compared to community health in Vedic rituals, reveal about the progression of healing practices?.
    A. Ayurveda adopted an isolationist approach, disregarding the communal benefits of Vedic rituals.
    B. The shift highlights a deeper understanding of personalized treatment and Prakriti-based interventions in Ayurveda.
    C. Vedic rituals were solely symbolic, lacking any practical health applications compared to Ayurvedic therapies.
    D. The progression indicates a rejection of spiritual practices in favor of empirical methodologies.

12. Considering Scenario 2, how does the narrative of Indra imparting knowledge to Bharadvaja align with the historical context of Ayurveda's evolution?
    A. It signifies the codification of Ayurvedic practices as independent of spiritual traditions.
    B. The narrative reflects the gradual secularization of Ayurveda, distancing itself from Vedic mythology.
    C. It symbolizes the integration of divine inspiration and empirical observations in Ayurveda's foundational texts.
    D. The story undermines the importance of individual Rishis in contributing to Ayurvedic knowledge.

13. How does the socio-cultural transition from Vedic sacrificial rituals to Ayurvedic therapeutic methods, as described in Scenario 2, affect the perception of Ayurveda in contemporary times?
    A. It establishes Ayurveda as a purely empirical science, rejecting its spiritual roots.
    B. It demonstrates Ayurveda's adaptability, incorporating spiritual, social, and scientific dimensions.
    C. The transition diminishes the credibility of Ayurveda, as it is rooted in outdated Vedic rituals.
    D. It shows that Ayurveda's therapeutic methods were initially derived from foreign influences, not Vedic traditions.

14. Considering both scenarios, which of the following conclusions best explains the continuity between Vedic healing practices and Ayurveda?
    A. Vedic healing practices were entirely metaphysical, whereas Ayurveda is purely scientific.
    B. The integration of ritualistic and empirical approaches in Ayurveda demonstrates its holistic foundation.
    C. Ayurveda abandoned Vedic principles, favoring Greek and Persian influences instead.
    D. The continuity is superficial, as Vedic rituals have no relevance to modern Ayurvedic practices.

15. The following are characteristics of Vedic healing practices and their influence on Ayurveda:
    (a) Use of medicinal plants described in Rigveda and Atharvaveda.
    (b) Emphasis on community well-being through rituals.
    (c) Development of diagnostics based on Dosha imbalances.
    (d) Symbolic importance of Soma and the Ashwini Kumaras.

    Choose the correct answer from the options given below:
    A. (a), (b), and (d) only
    B. (a), (c), and (d) only
    C. (b), (c), and (d) only
    D. (a), (b), (c), and (d)

16. The evolution of Ayurveda from Vedic literature is best described by the following:
    (a) Transition from communal rituals to personalized treatments.
    (b) Incorporation of metaphysical and empirical methodologies.
    (c) Replacement of Vedic practices with Greek medical theories.
    (d) Codification of medical knowledge by ancient seers.

    Choose the correct answer from the options given below:
    A. (a), (b), and (c) only
    B. (a), (b), and (d) only
    C. (b), (c), and (d) only
    D. (a), (b), (c), and (d)

17. The contributions of Rishis in the development of Ayurveda include:
    (a) Bharadvaja's codification of knowledge from Indra.
    (b) Introduction of therapeutic herbs in Vedic rituals.
    (c) Establishing guidelines for Panchakarma.
    (d) Writing diagnostic protocols for all Doshas.

    Choose the correct answer from the options given below:
    A. (a), (b), and (c) only
    B. (b), (c), and (d) only
    C. (a), (b), and (d) only
    D. (a), (b), (c), and (d)

18. The following statements describe the Ayurvedic concept of Tridosha:
    (a) Vata governs movement and is linked to air and ether elements.
    (b) Pitta regulates digestion and is associated with fire.
    (c) Kapha ensures structural stability and is linked to water and earth.
    (d) The balance of Tridosha prevents mental but not physical diseases.

Choose the correct answer from the options given below:

A. (a), (b), and (c) only
B. (a), (b), and (d) only
C. (b), (c), and (d) only
D. (a), (b), (c), and (d)

19. Ayurvedic principles regarding plant-based Rasas (tastes) are:

(a) Sweet Rasa promotes tissue growth and nourishment.
(b) Bitter Rasa reduces inflammation and detoxifies the body.
(c) Sour Rasa enhances immune function.
(d) Astringent Rasa strengthens tissues and controls bleeding.

Choose the correct answer from the options given below:

A. (a), (b), and (d) only
B. (a), (b), and (c) only
C. (b), (c), and (d) only
D. (a), (b), (c), and (d)

20. Vedic rituals influencing Ayurvedic therapies include:

(a) The use of Soma as a rejuvenating agent.
(b) Invocations to the Ashwini Kumaras for healing.
(c) Integration of diagnostic methods from Persian traditions.
(d) Symbolic practices emphasizing Dosha balance.

Choose the correct answer from the options given below:

A. (a), (b), and (d) only
B. (b), (c), and (d) only
C. (a), (c), and (d) only
D. (a), (b), (c), and (d)

21. Which of the following Ayurvedic concepts have roots in the Atharvaveda?

(a) Disease causation due to imbalance in Doshas.
(b) Use of chants for mental well-being.
(c) Application of Panchakarma for detoxification.
(d) Categorization of medicinal plants based on Rasas.

Choose the correct answer from the options given below:

A. (a), (b), and (c) only
B. (b), (c), and (d) only
C. (a), (b), and (d) only
D. (a), (b), (c), and (d)

22. The symbolic representation of healing in the Vedas includes:

(a) Ashwini Kumaras representing balance and vitality.
(b) Soma signifying rejuvenation and immortality.
(c) Yajnas reflecting collective health.
(d) Diagnostic methods prioritizing empirical results.

Choose the correct answer from the options given below:

A. (a), (b), and (c) only
B. (a), (b), and (d) only
C. (b), (c), and (d) only
D. (a), (b), (c), and (d)

23. The Ashwini Kumaras in Vedic literature are associated with:

(a) The symbolic representation of Doshas.
(b) The promotion of vitality and healing.
(c) Guidelines for Panchakarma therapies.
(d) Supervision of yajnas for community health.

Choose the correct answer from the options given below:

A. (a), (b), and (c) only
B. (a), (b), and (d) only
C. (b), (c), and (d) only
D. (a), (b), (c), and (d)

24. The Rigveda's contribution to Ayurveda includes:

(a) Invocation of medicinal plants.
(b) The basis for Prakriti classification.
(c) Codification of disease classifications.
(d) Symbolism of healing practices.

Choose the correct answer from the options given below:

A. (a), (b), and (c) only
B. (a), (b), and (d) only
C. (b), (c), and (d) only
D. (a), (b), (c), and (d)

25. Match List–I (Vedic Concepts) with List–II (Ayurvedic Applications):

List–I	List–II
(a) Ashwini Kumaras	1. Source of vitality and healing
(b) Soma	2. Basis for Rasayana therapies
(c) Yajnas	3. Emphasis on community health
(d) Rigvedic Hymns.	4. Invocation of medicinal plants

Choose the correct answer from the options given below:

A. (a)-1, (b)-2, (c)-3, (d)-4
B. (a)-3, (b)-2, (c)-4, (d)-1
C. (a)-1, (b)-3, (c)-2, (d)-4
D. (a)-4, (b)-1, (c)-3, (d)-2

26. Match List–I (Key Figures) with List–II (Contributions):

List–I	List–II
(a) Bharadvaja	1. Codification of surgical methods
(b) Charaka	2. Compilation of internal medicine
(c) Sushruta	3. Transmission of knowledge from Indra
(d) Dhanvantari	4. Revered as the god of Ayurveda

Choose the correct answer from the options given below:

A. (a)-3, (b)-2, (c)-1, (d)-4
B. (a)-1, (b)-3, (c)-4, (d)-2
C. (a)-4, (b)-2, (c)-3, (d)-1
D. (a)-2, (b)-4, (c)-3, (d)-1

27. Match List–I (Doshas) with List–II (Functions):

List–I	List–II
(a) Vata	1. Regulates metabolism and digestion
(b) Pitta	2. Ensures stability and lubrication
(c) Kapha	3. Governs movement and communication

Choose the correct answer from the options given below:

A. (a)-1, (b)-2, (c)-3
B. (a)-3, (b)-1, (c)-2
C. (a)-2, (b)-3, (c)-1
D. (a)-3, (b)-2, (c)-1

28. Match List–I (Texts) with List–II (Key Features):

List–I	List–II
(a) Rigveda	1. Contains hymns invoking medicinal plants
(b) Atharvaveda	2. Discusses early references to disease causation
(c) Charaka Samhita	3. Focuses on internal medicine and diagnostics
(d) Sushruta Samhita	4. Specializes in surgical techniques

Choose the correct answer from the options given below:

A. (a)-1, (b)-2, (c)-3, (d)-4
B. (a)-3, (b)-4, (c)-2, (d)-1
C. (a)-2, (b)-1, (c)-4, (d)-3
D. (a)-4, (b)-3, (c)-1, (d)-2

29. Match List–I (Ayurvedic Concepts) with List–II (Origins in Vedic Literature):

List–I	List–II
(a) Tridosha	1. Derived from metaphysical inquiries in the Vedas
(b) Prakriti	2. Correlates with digestive fire mentioned in Atharvaveda
(c) Agni	3. Rooted in the elemental theory of Rigveda
(d) Panchamahabhutas	4. Describes constitutional types inspired by Vedic philosophy

Choose the correct answer from the options given below:

A. (a)-1, (b)-2, (c)-3, (d)-4
B. (a)-3, (b)-4, (c)-2, (d)-1
C. (a)-4, (b)-3, (c)-1, (d)-2
D. (a)-2, (b)-1, (c)-4, (d)-3

30. Match List–I (Therapies) with List–II (Vedic Roots):

List–I	List–II
(a) Panchakarma	1. Inspired by rituals for purification in Atharvaveda
(b) Rasayana	2. Based on Rig Vedic chants emphasizing longevity
(c) Nidanam	3. Rooted in early diagnostic descriptions in Vedic texts
(d) Pranayama	4. Correlates with breath control techniques in Rigveda

Choose the correct answer from the options given below:

A. (a)-3, (b)-2, (c)-4, (d)-1
B. (a)-1, (b)-2, (c)-3, (d)-4
C. (a)-2, (b)-1, (c)-3, (d)-4
D. (a)-4, (b)-3, (c)-2, (d)-1

31. Match List–I (Ayurvedic Rasas) with List–II (Biological Actions):

List–I	List–II
(a) Sweet	1. Nourishes tissues and promotes growth
(b) Sour	2. Enhances digestion and appetite
(c) Bitter	3. Detoxifies and reduces inflammation
(d) Astringent	4. Strengthens tissues and controls bleeding

Choose the correct answer from the options given below:

A. (a)-2, (b)-1, (c)-3, (d)-4
B. (a)-4, (b)-3, (c)-2, (d)-1
C. (a)-1, (b)-2, (c)-3, (d)-4
D. (a)-3, (b)-4, (c)-1, (d)-2

32. Match List–I (Foundational Concepts) with List–II (Descriptions):

List–I	List–II
(a) Soma	1. Symbolizes vitality and rejuvenation
(b) Ashwini Kumaras	2. Represents divine healers and balance
(c) Yajna	3. Rituals promoting collective well-being
(d) Agni	4. Digestive fire linked to health

Choose the correct answer from the options given below:

A. (a)-3, (b)-4, (c)-1, (d)-2
B. (a)-1, (b)-2, (c)-3, (d)-4
C. (a)-4, (b)-3, (c)-2, (d)-1
D. (a)-2, (b)-1, (c)-4, (d)-3

33. Match List–I (Philosophical Concepts) with List–II (Ayurvedic Correlation):

List–I	List–II
(a) Sattva	1. Reflects purity and clarity
(b) Rajas	2. Denotes dynamism and activity
(c) Tamas	3. Represents inertia and resistance

Choose the correct answer from the options given below:

A. (a)-3, (b)-2, (c)-1
B. (a)-2, (b)-1, (c)-3
C. (a)-1, (b)-2, (c)-3
D. (a)-3, (b)-1, (c)-2

34. Match List–I (Historical Figures) with List–II (Key Roles):

List–I	List–II
(a) Agnivesha	1. Composer of the foundational Charaka Samhita
(b) Jivaka	2. Disciple of Buddha, famous physician
(c) Vagbhata	3. Author of Astanga Hridaya
(d) Nagarjuna	4. Pioneer of Rasashastra (alchemy)

Choose the correct answer from the options given below:

A. (a)-4, (b)-3, (c)-1, (d)-2
B. (a)-1, (b)-2, (c)-3, (d)-4
C. (a)-3, (b)-4, (c)-2, (d)-1
D. (a)-2, (b)-1, (c)-3, (d)-4

Directions (Q. No. 35–39): *Following questions are based on statement 1 and statement 2. Read both the statements carefully and choose the correct answer from the options given below:*

A. Both Statement 1 and Statement 2 are true, and Statement 2 is the correct explanation of Statement 1.
B. Both Statement 1 and Statement 2 are true, but Statement 2 is not the correct explanation of Statement 1.
C. Statement 1 is true, but Statement 2 is false.
D. Statement 1 is false, but Statement 2 is true.
E. Both Statement 1 and Statement 2 are false.

35. **Statement 1:** Vedic texts emphasize a balance of mental, spiritual, and physical health through rituals and hymns.

Statement 2: Ayurveda rejects the metaphysical elements of Vedic traditions and focuses solely on empirical evidence.

36. **Statement 1:** Tridosha theory in Ayurveda originates from the Vedic understanding of the five elements (Pancha Mahabhutas).

Statement 2: The three Doshas—Vata, Pitta, and Kapha—are unrelated to the elemental theories of Vedic texts.

37. **Statement 1:** Ayurveda integrates spiritual practices and empirical methods for holistic healing.

Statement 2: The Rigveda provides the earliest references to herbal medicine and disease prevention.

38. **Statement 1:** Agni in Ayurveda correlates with the digestive enzymes regulating metabolism.

Statement 2: The concept of Agni in Vedic texts is entirely symbolic and unrelated to physiological processes.

39. **Statement 1:** Ayurveda emphasizes seasonal routines (Ritucharya) to maintain doshic balance.

Statement 2: Seasonal routines in Ayurveda are based on empirical evidence rather than Vedic philosophies.

Directions (Q. No. 40–45): *There are two statements in each question. One is labelled as Assertion (A) and the other is as Reason (R). Read both the statements and choose the correct answer from the options given below:*

A. Both Assertion (A) and Reason (R) are true, and Reason (R) is the correct explanation of Assertion (A).
B. Both Assertion (A) and Reason (R) are true, but Reason (R) is not the correct explanation of Assertion (A).
C. Assertion (A) is true, but Reason (R) is false.
D. Assertion (A) is false, but Reason (R) is true.
E. Both Assertion (A) and Reason (R) are false

40. **Assertion (A):** The Atharvaveda is considered a foundational text in Ayurveda as it provides early references to disease diagnosis and the use of medicinal plants.

Reason (R): The Atharvaveda focuses on metaphysical concepts, excluding any practical application in medicine.

41. **Assertion (A):** Ayurveda's Tridosha theory emphasizes the balance of Vata, Pitta, and Kapha for maintaining health.

Reason (R): The Tridosha theory was influenced by the Vedic understanding of the five elements (Pancha Mahabhutas).

42. **Assertion (A):** The concept of Agni in Ayurveda aligns with digestive enzymes and metabolic activity in modern science.

Reason (R): Agni in Vedic texts symbolizes the fire element, which is entirely metaphysical and unrelated to biological processes.

43 **Assertion (A):** The Rishis (seers) of Vedic times played a crucial role in developing Ayurveda by documenting healing practices.

Reason (R): The Rigveda and Atharvaveda are primarily mythological texts with no practical relevance to medical science.

44. **Assertion (A):** Panchakarma therapies in Ayurveda emphasize the detoxification of the body to restore doshic balance.

Reason (R): Panchakarma procedures were directly derived from Vedic yajnas and rituals for purification.

45. **Assertion (A):** Rasayana therapies in Ayurveda promote longevity and immunity, with their origins in Vedic concepts of rejuvenation.

Reason (R): Rasayana principles in Ayurveda are based on empirical studies unrelated to the spiritual practices of the Vedas.

Directions (Q. No. 46–50): *Read the passage carefully and answer the questions given below*:

Ayurveda, an ancient system of medicine originating from India, finds its earliest references in the Vedic literature, particularly the Rigveda and Atharvaveda. These texts describe the use of medicinal plants, healing chants, and rituals for maintaining health and preventing disease. The Ashwini Kumaras, often hailed as divine healers, are invoked for their ability to restore vitality and cure ailments. With time, the metaphysical aspects of Vedic healing practices evolved into systematic methodologies, leading to the development of Ayurveda as a holistic science.By the time the Charaka Samhita and Sushruta Samhita were composed. Ayurveda had already transitioned from spiritual rituals to empirical observation and therapeutic interventions. These texts introduced foundational principles like Tridosha, Prakriti, and Agni, which linked physiological processes to the elements of nature. Ayurveda's emphasis on personalized treatment, preventive care, and the harmony of body, mind, and spirit made it distinct from other ancient medical traditions.

Modern science increasingly recognizes the relevance of Ayurveda, particularly in areas like gut health, herbal medicine, and personalized nutrition. However, challenges such as standardization, conservation of medicinal plants, and integration with evidence-based medicine remain critical for its global acceptance. Despite these challenges, Ayurveda continues to evolve, reflecting the timeless wisdom of its Vedic origins.

46. According to the passage, how did Ayurveda evolve from its Vedic origins?
    A. By rejecting metaphysical aspects and focusing solely on empirical methods.
    B. By integrating spiritual practices with systematic therapeutic methodologies.
    C. By adopting Greek and Persian medical theories into its framework.
    D. By standardizing ancient rituals into modern clinical procedures.

47. What is the significance of the Ashwini Kumaras in the context of Ayurveda as per the passage?
    A. They symbolize the metaphysical aspect of Ayurveda, disconnected from practical healing.
    B. They represent the divine origin of healing practices that later influenced Ayurveda.
    C. They contributed directly to the empirical foundations of Ayurveda.
    D. They are mentioned as mythological figures with no relevance to Ayurveda.

48. Which of the following best describes Ayurveda's focus, as highlighted in the passage?
    A. Ayurveda focuses exclusively on disease management through herbal medicine.
    B. It emphasizes a balance between body, mind, and spirit while integrating preventive care.
    C. It rejects ancient Vedic principles and prioritizes evidence-based practices.
    D. It aligns only with modern practices like personalized nutrition.

49. What are the key challenges in globalizing Ayurveda, as mentioned in the passage?
    A. Lack of evidence for Ayurvedic therapies.
    B. Standardization of practices and conservation of medicinal plants.
    C. Resistance to the integration of Ayurveda with modern science.
    D. Difficulty in aligning Ayurvedic principles with dietary preferences globally.

50. Based on the passage, how does modern science view Ayurveda?
    A. As a purely philosophical framework with no practical applications.
    B. As an outdated system limited to specific cultural practices.
    C. As a complementary system with relevance to herbal medicine and personalized care.
    D. As a competing tradition that contradicts evidence-based medicine.

ANSWER WITH EXPLANATIONS

1. B: The Rigveda and Atharvaveda highlight early mentions of healing practices, including references to Soma and the Ashwini Kumaras, symbolizing divine healers. These texts provide philosophical underpinnings that later became integral to Ayurveda. Their mystical elements are not purely metaphysical but form symbolic representations of vitality and health. Soma, often equated with rejuvenation, aligns with Rasayana therapies in Ayurveda. Similarly, the Ashwini Kumaras exemplify dual aspects of healing: physical and mental. These Vedic insights were systematized into diagnostics and treatments, offering a blend of spiritual and empirical approaches foundational to Ayurvedic principles.

2. B: The timeline of Ayurveda's evolution connects oral Vedic traditions with systematic medical texts like Charaka Samhita. The study of this transition reveals the refinement of communal health practices into individualized treatments. Unlike mere etymological analyses or dietary comparisons, exploring how these practices evolved highlights Ayurveda's progression from symbolic rituals to pragmatic care. This approach shows how ancient communal yajnas influenced personalized health solutions. Ayurveda's transition reflects a deep understanding of individualized care that maintains Vedic philosophical continuity while addressing practical health challenges, exemplifying adaptability through cultural and historical contexts.

3. C: The Tridosha theory emerges as a vital concept in Ayurveda, correlating closely with Vedic elements. Vata represents air and ether, symbolizing movement, while Pitta links to fire and metabolism, and Kapha derives from earth and water, embodying stability. This dynamic interplay bridges metaphysical philosophy with tangible physiological processes. Unlike abstract theories, Tridosha offers actionable insights into health maintenance. Its roots in Pancha Mahabhutas make it a unique framework where metaphysics meets medical science. This blend reflects Ayurveda's holistic vision, emphasizing that harmony within these forces ensures physical, mental, and spiritual well-being.

4. A: The story of Rishi Bharadvaja receiving Ayurvedic knowledge from Indra is a symbolic allegory representing the transfer of divine wisdom to humanity. Indra signifies the divine source of knowledge, while Bharadvaja symbolizes the sage who receives and transmits it. This narrative highlights the sacred origins of Ayurveda and establishes its authority in ancient Indian tradition. It reflects the belief that Ayurveda is not just a human invention but a revealed science meant for the well-being of mankind. Rather than being literal, the story serves to honor the spiritual depth of Ayurvedic knowledge.

5. B: The Atharvaveda marks a crucial phase in Ayurveda's development, blending practical remedies with metaphysical insights. Its references to chants, medicinal plants, and rituals demonstrate an integrative approach to healing. While these rituals carry symbolic meaning, they also anticipate empirical methods later refined in Ayurveda. The dual emphasis on spiritual and physical health reflects Ayurveda's holistic philosophy. This evolution from Vedic metaphysics to systematic therapies highlights Ayurveda's adaptability. It retained its roots while addressing broader health needs, balancing preventive care with individualized treatments rooted in Vedic traditions.

6. B: The Charaka Samhita signifies Ayurveda's transition from collective rituals to personalized care. Vedic yajnas, while emphasizing communal well-being, lacked the diagnostic precision seen in later Ayurvedic texts. Charaka Samhita introduced comprehensive frameworks for diagnosing and treating individuals based on Prakriti (constitution). This shift represents a significant evolution in healthcare philosophy, aligning ancient symbolic practices with empirical observation. Ayurveda's adaptability, evident in this transition, ensures its relevance across ages. It balances tradition with innovation, offering a nuanced understanding of health that respects Vedic origins while refining its application.

7. A: Ayurveda's strength lies in its integration of physical, mental, and spiritual health dimensions. Unlike systems that separate metaphysical and empirical methods, Ayurveda combines both to address Dosha imbalances. The Vedic focus on interconnectedness enriches this framework, creating a system capable of adapting to diverse challenges. By acknowledging spiritual influences, Ayurveda broadens its scope beyond purely physiological remedies. This integrative approach demonstrates its depth and flexibility, ensuring its relevance in both ancient and modern contexts. Ayurveda's ability to address preventive and curative aspects simultaneously underscores its comprehensive and holistic nature.

8. **C:** Ayurveda's shift from communal yajnas to personalized interventions reflects its evolving priorities. This transition doesn't reject Vedic insights but adapts them for individual needs. By focusing on Prakriti-based treatments, Ayurveda introduced a level of precision unseen in earlier practices. This evolution highlights its adaptability, blending tradition with practicality. Such shifts show Ayurveda's ability to remain rooted in cultural heritage while refining its application to suit contemporary health demands. It bridges the gap between collective rituals and tailored care, showcasing its dynamic approach to holistic healing.

9. **A:** The Rigvedic hymns on medicinal plants convey healing potential through symbolic language. These references align with modern phytotherapy, where compounds like flavonoids and alkaloids are analyzed for therapeutic properties. Far from being mere folklore, these hymns offer insights into the medicinal attributes of nature. Ayurveda integrates this symbolic and empirical understanding, creating remedies that honor both the spiritual and practical aspects of health. The Rigveda's emphasis on plants as conscious healing agents resonates with Ayurveda's holistic perspective, merging ancient metaphysics with modern scientific validation.

10. **B:** Prakriti-based interventions in Ayurveda underscore its focus on individuality and precision. This concept aligns with contemporary trends in personalized medicine, emphasizing tailored treatments for optimal health outcomes. Unlike generalized healthcare approaches, Prakriti integrates physical, mental, and elemental factors, reflecting Ayurveda's depth. This adaptability ensures its relevance across diverse populations and time periods. By blending ancient insights with modern methodologies, Ayurveda offers a comprehensive healthcare model. Its ability to balance traditional philosophy with scientific rigor exemplifies its timelessness and adaptability in addressing complex health challenges.

11. **B:** The shift from Vedic communal rituals to individualized health care in Ayurveda reflects its philosophical maturity. Communal health practices were central to yajnas, emphasizing collective harmony. However, Ayurveda refined this approach by focusing on personalized interventions through Prakriti-based diagnostics. This evolution mirrors the adaptability of the system, transitioning from symbolic collective rituals to practical, individualized care. Personalized health aligns with the modern understanding of precision medicine. By adapting Vedic principles to meet individual needs, Ayurveda demonstrates its dynamic approach, maintaining cultural continuity while addressing practical health challenges effectively.

12. **C:** The transmission of Ayurvedic knowledge from Indra to Bharadvaja symbolizes the transition from divine inspiration to human understanding. This narrative reflects the synthesis of metaphysical concepts and systematic observation in Ayurveda. It highlights the interplay between spiritual wisdom and empirical practices. Bharadvaja represents the human effort to codify divine insights into usable frameworks for health management. This story underscores Ayurveda's ability to integrate symbolic and practical elements. The blending of intuitive knowledge with actionable therapies ensures Ayurveda's relevance, making it a holistic system rooted in both tradition and adaptability.

13. **B:** The socio-cultural shift from Vedic rituals to systematic Ayurvedic therapies illustrates the system's ability to adapt and evolve. Vedic yajnas emphasized community well-being, while Ayurveda refined these practices into personalized, preventive, and curative approaches. This transition doesn't discard Vedic insights but repurposes them into empirically valid methods. Ayurveda's integration of spiritual, scientific, and practical dimensions ensures its relevance in both historical and contemporary contexts. By maintaining its philosophical integrity while addressing individual needs, Ayurveda exemplifies a unique balance of tradition and innovation, offering solutions tailored to diverse health challenges.

14. **B:** Ayurveda's continuity with Vedic rituals lies in its ability to refine symbolic practices into practical, systematic therapies. The metaphysical insights of the Vedas were not discarded but evolved into empirical frameworks addressing broader health challenges. This evolution highlights Ayurveda's adaptability, retaining its philosophical essence while refining its application. By blending spiritual principles with tangible methodologies, Ayurveda remains deeply rooted in its origins yet responsive to contemporary needs. This dynamic balance ensures its relevance across ages, making it a model of holistic health care that integrates tradition and progress seamlessly.

15. **D:** The influence of Vedic healing practices on Ayurveda is extensive, encompassing medicinal plants, chants, and symbolic rituals like Soma. These elements provided the philosophical foundation for Ayurveda's development, emphasizing interconnectedness in healing. The incorporation of concepts like Rasas,

Doshas, and diagnostics reflects this continuity. Ayurveda retained these insights while transforming them into a structured system of preventive and curative care. This holistic approach underscores Ayurveda's ability to integrate metaphysical and empirical principles, ensuring its adaptability and relevance in addressing diverse health challenges while respecting its Vedic roots.

16. **B:** Ayurveda's evolution reflects its integration of Vedic rituals with empirical methodologies. The transition from communal practices to personalized care, guided by principles like Agni and Tridosha, showcases its adaptability. Unlike static traditions, Ayurveda refined its Vedic origins into systematic frameworks for health management. This progression reflects a balance between philosophical continuity and innovation. The codification of practices by Rishis like Charaka and Sushruta ensured its enduring relevance. Ayurveda's ability to integrate spiritual insights with practical solutions exemplifies its dynamic approach to holistic healing and adaptability to evolving medical needs.

17. **A:** The contributions of ancient Rishis like Bharadvaja and Charaka highlight the systematic evolution of Ayurveda. Bharadvaja's transmission of knowledge from Indra symbolizes the integration of spiritual insights into empirical practice. Charaka's emphasis on diagnostics and herbal therapies reflects the refinement of these principles. By blending metaphysical wisdom with practical frameworks, Ayurveda created a unique system of health care. The role of Rishis in codifying these practices underscores their ability to balance tradition with observation, ensuring Ayurveda's relevance and adaptability across cultural and historical contexts.

18. **A:** The Tridosha theory is deeply rooted in the Pancha Mahabhutas, where Vata, Pitta, and Kapha represent movement, transformation, and stability. This dynamic interplay ensures the balance of physiological and psychological functions. Vata governs motion, Pitta regulates metabolism, and Kapha provides structure and stability. These principles integrate metaphysical and scientific dimensions, making them foundational to Ayurveda. The Tridosha theory's connection to elemental balance highlights Ayurveda's holistic approach, where harmony between these forces ensures health. This philosophy bridges ancient metaphysics with practical healthcare frameworks, emphasizing interconnectedness in maintaining well-being.

19. **A:** Sweet Rasa supports growth and nourishment, Bitter Rasa is recognized for detoxifying and reducing inflammation, and Astringent Rasa is known to strengthen tissues and control bleeding. While Sour Rasa plays a role in digestion and stimulating appetite, its direct link to enhancing immunity is not a primary Ayurvedic attribute, making (c) less accurate in this context.

20. **A:** Vedic rituals like the use of Soma as a rejuvenator and Ashwini Kumaras as divine healers influenced early Ayurvedic thought. Symbolic practices in the Vedas contributed to the development of concepts like Dosha balance. However, there is no historical basis for the integration of Persian diagnostic methods into Vedic or early Ayurvedic rituals, so (c) is incorrect.

21. **C:** The Atharvaveda contains references to disease causation via Dosha imbalance, the use of chants for mental well-being, and categorization of medicinal plants based on taste (Rasa). While purification practices existed, Panchakarma as a structured detox therapy was formalized much later in Ayurvedic texts, not directly rooted in the Atharvaveda.

22. **A:** The Ashwini Kumaras, Soma, and yajnas symbolize foundational Ayurvedic principles like vitality, rejuvenation, and collective health. The Ashwini Kumaras' healing abilities align with therapies restoring balance, while Soma's rejuvenating properties reflect the essence of Rasayana. Rituals like yajnas emphasize the interconnectedness of physical and spiritual health. Ayurveda adapted these symbolic practices into systematic frameworks for individual care. This evolution illustrates Ayurveda's capacity to transform abstract Vedic principles into practical health solutions, ensuring its relevance across both traditional and modern contexts.

23. **B:** The Ashwini Kumaras represent vitality and healing in Vedic literature, symbolizing the integration of metaphysical and physical health. Their association with rejuvenation aligns with Ayurveda's focus on holistic well-being. While the Ashwini Kumaras are not directly linked to Panchakarma therapies, their symbolic role highlights the importance of balance and harmony in health. This reflects Ayurveda's unique approach, blending Vedic mythology with actionable therapies to create a system that addresses physical, mental, and spiritual dimensions in a cohesive framework.

24. **B:** The Rigveda invokes healing through medicinal plants and includes philosophical ideas foundational to Prakriti classification. It also uses symbolic language to represent healing, often linking it to spiritual or divine sources. However, disease classification as a formal system appears more clearly in later Ayurvedic texts like the Charaka Samhita, not in the Rigveda itself.

25. **A:** Vedic concepts like Ashwini Kumaras, Soma, and yajnas directly influenced Ayurvedic applications. The Ashwini Kumaras represent healing and vitality, Soma symbolizes rejuvenation, and yajnas emphasize collective well-being. Rigvedic hymns invoking medicinal plants highlight early diagnostic practices that later evolved in Ayurveda. These connections show Ayurveda's capacity to refine symbolic Vedic practices into systematic frameworks, blending spiritual insights with therapeutic applications. This synthesis underscores Ayurveda's holistic approach, where metaphysical wisdom informs practical health solutions, ensuring its adaptability and relevance.

26. **A:** Historical figures like Bharadvaja, Charaka, and Sushruta played pivotal roles in shaping Ayurveda. Bharadvaja symbolizes the transition of knowledge from divine inspiration to human application. Charaka focused on internal medicine, emphasizing diagnostics and herbal therapies, while Sushruta specialized in surgical techniques. Dhanvantari, revered as the god of Ayurveda, embodies the system's divine origins. These contributions reflect Ayurveda's integration of empirical and spiritual dimensions, ensuring its development into a comprehensive healthcare system capable of addressing diverse challenges while respecting its philosophical roots.

27. **B:** The Tridosha theory's connection to Vata, Pitta, and Kapha illustrates Ayurveda's understanding of physiological balance. Vata governs movement, Pitta regulates metabolism, and Kapha provides structure and stability. These Doshas align with the Pancha Mahabhutas, emphasizing interconnectedness in health. This framework integrates metaphysical and practical insights, ensuring Ayurveda's relevance. By addressing physical, mental, and spiritual dimensions simultaneously, the Tridosha theory offers a dynamic approach to maintaining well-being, reflecting Ayurveda's holistic philosophy and its adaptability to diverse health contexts.

28. **A:** Key Ayurvedic texts like the Rigveda, Atharvaveda, Charaka Samhita, and Sushruta Samhita highlight Ayurveda's evolution. The Rigveda and Atharvaveda provide symbolic and practical insights into healing, focusing on plants and rituals. Charaka Samhita refines these principles into internal medicine and diagnostics, while Sushruta Samhita emphasizes surgical techniques. This progression demonstrates Ayurveda's ability to integrate Vedic metaphysics with empirical practices. By transitioning from symbolic rituals to structured therapies, Ayurveda remains rooted in tradition while addressing practical health challenges effectively.

29. **B:** Vedic concepts like Tridosha, Prakriti, and Agni derive from metaphysical inquiries into balance and harmony. Tridosha correlates with Pancha Mahabhutas, linking elemental forces to physiological functions. Prakriti emphasizes individuality in health, while Agni represents metabolic processes. These principles illustrate Ayurveda's integration of Vedic philosophy into practical applications. By refining metaphysical insights into actionable frameworks, Ayurveda creates a comprehensive system addressing physical, mental, and spiritual dimensions. This adaptability ensures its relevance across diverse contexts, reflecting its dynamic approach to holistic healing.

30. **B:** Vedic rituals like yajnas and concepts such as Soma significantly influenced Ayurvedic therapies like Panchakarma and Rasayana. Panchakarma's focus on detoxification echoes Vedic purification rituals, while Rasayana therapies align with Soma's rejuvenating symbolism. Diagnostic methods and practices like Pranayama reflect a blend of Vedic insights and empirical observation. This evolution demonstrates Ayurveda's ability to adapt spiritual principles into systematic frameworks for health. By integrating metaphysical and practical dimensions, Ayurveda ensures its holistic approach remains relevant while respecting its Vedic origins.

31. **C:** In Ayurveda, Sweet Rasa nourishes tissues and promotes growth (a-1), Sour Rasa enhances appetite and digestion (b-2), Bitter Rasa is known for detoxifying and reducing inflammation (c-3), and Astringent Rasa strengthens tissues and controls bleeding (d-4). This pairing aligns with classical Ayurvedic principles.

32. **B:** Vedic concepts like Soma, Ashwini Kumaras, Yajnas, and Agni serve as symbolic foundations for Ayurveda. Soma represents vitality and rejuvenation, aligning with Rasayana therapies. The Ashwini Kumaras symbolize dual aspects of healing, while yajnas emphasize collective health. Agni, representing the digestive fire, highlights the link between metabolism and well-being. Ayurveda refines these symbolic insights into systematic therapies, bridging metaphysical and practical dimensions. This synthesis ensures Ayurveda's ability to address diverse health challenges, creating a healthcare system that respects its origins while adapting to modern scientific frameworks.

33. **C:** Sattva reflects purity and clarity (a-1), Rajas denotes dynamism and activity (c-2), and Tamas signifies inertia and resistance (b-3). These three Gunas (qualities) are central to Ayurvedic psychology and are inherited from Vedic and Samkhya philosophical thought.

34. B: Agnivesha compiled the foundational teachings that later became the Charaka Samhita (a-1), Jivaka was a renowned physician and disciple of Buddha (b-2), Vagbhata authored Astanga Hridaya, a key Ayurvedic text (c-3), and Nagarjuna significantly contributed to Rasashastra, or alchemical aspects of Ayurveda (d-4).

35. C: Vedic texts emphasize the integration of spiritual, mental, and physical health through rituals and hymns. This holistic perspective aligns with Ayurveda's foundational principles. However, the statement that Ayurveda rejects metaphysical elements is inaccurate; instead, Ayurveda refines these into systematic therapies. This demonstrates the system's ability to balance tradition with innovation, ensuring its relevance in modern contexts. Ayurveda's integration of Vedic philosophy with empirical methodologies underscores its unique approach to health, maintaining continuity while addressing evolving challenges in healthcare.

36. C: The Tridosha theory's roots in Pancha Mahabhutas reflect Ayurveda's integration of Vedic metaphysics with health science. Vata, Pitta, and Kapha represent elemental forces that govern physiological functions. The statement suggesting that these Doshas are unrelated to Vedic elements is incorrect, as their basis lies in elemental harmony. Ayurveda's ability to adapt these abstract concepts into practical health frameworks demonstrates its dynamic approach. This integration of ancient philosophy with empirical observation highlights Ayurveda's capacity to address diverse health challenges while maintaining its traditional essence.

37. A. Charaka Samhita indeed promotes dinacharya (daily routines) and ritucharya (seasonal routines) as part of preventive healthcare. These regimens are tailored to maintain doshic balance by adapting to environmental and seasonal variations, making Statement 2 the correct explanation of Statement 1.

38. C: Agni, in Ayurveda, symbolizes metabolic and digestive functions, correlating closely with modern understandings of enzymes and metabolic pathways. While Vedic references to Agni carry symbolic meaning, Ayurveda refines this into a practical concept central to health. The idea that Agni is purely metaphysical is incorrect, as its role extends to physiological processes. This demonstrates Ayurveda's capacity to bridge spiritual insights and scientific observation, creating a comprehensive framework that emphasizes the interconnectedness of physical and metabolic well-being.

39. B: Ayurveda emphasizes Ritucharya, or seasonal routines, to maintain Dosha balance and prevent disease. This approach aligns with Vedic principles, which highlight the influence of natural cycles on health. While empirical evidence supports Ayurveda's seasonal recommendations, they are deeply rooted in its philosophical traditions. The statement suggesting that Ritucharya is purely empirical overlooks this connection. Ayurveda's integration of traditional wisdom and scientific validation underscores its holistic nature, offering a dynamic healthcare model that respects its origins while addressing contemporary health challenges.

40. C: The Atharvaveda provides foundational insights into Ayurveda, including disease diagnosis and the use of medicinal plants. However, the claim that it excludes practical applications is false, as its references to chants and rituals serve as precursors to Ayurvedic therapies. This misinterpretation overlooks the text's dual focus on metaphysical and practical aspects of health. Ayurveda evolves these insights into a systematic framework, demonstrating its ability to refine symbolic practices into actionable methods. This progression highlights Ayurveda's dynamic approach, ensuring its relevance in diverse cultural and historical contexts.

41. A: The Tridosha theory is integral to Ayurveda, with Vata, Pitta, and Kapha embodying movement, transformation, and stability. These concepts are rooted in the Vedic understanding of Pancha Mahabhutas (five elements), emphasizing elemental balance as central to health. Ayurveda's adaptability is evident in refining this metaphysical framework into practical health solutions. By linking Dosha balance to individual well-being, Ayurveda demonstrates its ability to blend tradition and innovation. This synthesis underscores its comprehensive approach, addressing physiological and psychological dimensions while maintaining its philosophical integrity.

42. C: Agni in Ayurveda represents the digestive and metabolic fire, closely correlating with modern scientific understandings of enzymes and metabolism. While Vedic references to Agni carry symbolic significance, Ayurveda refines this concept into a central physiological principle. The idea that Agni is purely symbolic overlooks its practical applications in maintaining health. Ayurveda's ability to bridge metaphysical insights with empirical science ensures its relevance. This integration highlights Ayurveda's holistic philosophy, combining ancient wisdom with modern observations to create a dynamic system for addressing diverse health needs.

43. C: The Rishis of Vedic times contributed significantly to Ayurveda's evolution by codifying healing practices rooted in spiritual insights. Texts like Rigveda and Atharvaveda contain practical applications, such as medicinal plant usage, despite their symbolic and mythological context. The claim that these texts lack practical relevance is incorrect, as Ayurveda's systematic therapies evolved directly from their insights. This progression reflects Ayurveda's ability to integrate Vedic metaphysics with empirical observation, creating a comprehensive healthcare system that respects its origins while addressing modern health challenges effectively.

44. **C:** Panchakarma therapies in Ayurveda emphasize detoxification and Dosha balance, echoing the purification rituals of the Vedic yajnas. However, these therapies were not directly derived from Vedic practices but evolved through empirical observation and refinement. The claim that Panchakarma is purely ritualistic is inaccurate, as it serves as a practical framework for health restoration. This evolution demonstrates Ayurveda's dynamic approach, blending spiritual principles with systematic methodologies to create actionable therapies addressing both preventive and curative health needs.

45. **C:** Rasayana therapies in Ayurveda focus on rejuvenation and immunity, aligning with Vedic concepts like Soma. These therapies integrate Vedic metaphysics with empirical observations to create practical health solutions. The claim that Rasayana principles are unrelated to spiritual practices is incorrect, as their roots lie in Vedic rejuvenation rituals. Ayurveda's ability to refine these symbolic practices into systematic frameworks highlights its adaptability. This integration ensures the system's relevance across time, offering a dynamic approach to longevity and holistic well-being that respects its philosophical origins.

46. **B:** Ayurveda evolved from Vedic origins by synthesizing spiritual practices and systematic methodologies. Early Vedic texts emphasized metaphysical principles, which Ayurveda refined into actionable therapies. This evolution illustrates its adaptability, transitioning from symbolic rituals to practical health frameworks. Ayurveda's ability to maintain philosophical continuity while addressing contemporary needs highlights its dynamic nature. By bridging metaphysical insights with empirical observation, Ayurveda creates a comprehensive system that respects its origins while remaining relevant in modern healthcare.

47. **B:** The Ashwini Kumaras symbolize dual aspects of healing in Ayurveda, representing vitality and restoration. Their role in Vedic literature highlights the integration of spiritual insights with practical health applications. Ayurveda inherits this duality, refining symbolic representations into systematic therapies. The Ashwini Kumaras' association with healing emphasizes Ayurveda's ability to blend metaphysical principles with actionable solutions. This progression demonstrates Ayurveda's dynamic approach, where traditional wisdom informs practical methodologies to address diverse health challenges effectively.

48. **B:** Ayurveda emphasizes the balance of body, mind, and spirit, reflecting its holistic philosophy. This approach aligns with modern trends in preventive and personalized care, bridging ancient insights with contemporary health needs. Unlike systems focusing solely on disease management, Ayurveda prioritizes harmony and well-being. Its adaptability ensures relevance across time, blending traditional practices with evidence-based methodologies. This dynamic framework highlights Ayurveda's capacity to integrate metaphysical principles with scientific observations, creating a comprehensive healthcare system addressing physical, mental, and spiritual dimensions.

49. **B:** Challenges in globalizing Ayurveda include standardization and conservation of medicinal plants. While its principles are widely respected, issues like sustainability and consistency in practice remain critical. Overharvesting and environmental degradation threaten the quality of Ayurvedic therapies, underscoring the need for conservation. Ayurveda's integration with evidence-based medicine requires balancing traditional wisdom with scientific validation. Addressing these challenges ensures its adaptability and relevance, highlighting Ayurveda's capacity to evolve while maintaining its philosophical and cultural integrity.

50. **C:** Modern science views Ayurveda as a complementary system, emphasizing herbal medicine and personalized care. Its principles align with emerging trends in integrative medicine, offering solutions that blend tradition with innovation. Unlike dismissive perspectives, this recognition underscores Ayurveda's ability to adapt ancient insights into contemporary contexts. Its focus on prevention, nutrition, and holistic well-being ensures its relevance. Ayurveda's dynamic approach bridges metaphysical philosophy with scientific observation, creating a healthcare system that respects its roots while addressing modern challenges effectively.

CHAPTER–2

SCHOOLS OF AYURVEDA AND ASTANGA AYURVEDA

Āyurveda, one of the world's oldest systems of medicine, has a long and storied history, marked by the development of multiple schools of thought, each contributing uniquely to its evolution. These schools, deeply rooted in ancient texts, philosophies, and practices, were led by visionary figures who sought to codify, expand, and refine Ayurvedic knowledge. .Central to Āyurveda's practice is the concept of Astanga Āyurveda, or the eight branches of Āyurveda, which provide a comprehensive framework for understanding health, disease, and treatment..

The Major Schools of Āyurveda

Āyurveda's foundations were laid in ancient India, where knowledge was transmitted orally before being compiled into extensive texts. Over time, distinct schools emerged, primarily centered around two seminal figures: Charaka and Sushruta. While both schools drew upon shared principles, they offered unique perspectives and methodologies.

The Charaka School

The Charaka Samhita is a foundational text of Āyurveda and represents the internal medicine tradition. Compiled by Charaka, this school emphasizes the maintenance of health through prevention and the balance of the three doshas (Vāta, Pitta, and Kapha).

KEY CONTRIBUTIONS OF CHARAKA

Systematization of Internal Medicine:

- Charaka focused on Kaya Chikitsa (internal medicine) and provided detailed descriptions of diseases, their causes, and treatments.

Emphasis on Prevention:

- Charaka advocated for preventive medicine through diet, lifestyle, and seasonal regimens (Ritucharya).

Philosophy of Life and Health:

- Charaka emphasized that health is a state of balance (Sama) between the body, mind, and spirit. His school integrated philosophy with medicine, linking concepts of dharma (duty), artha (wealth), and moksha (liberation) with health.

Pioneering Clinical Observations:

- Charaka's teachings are notable for their focus on observation and inference, laying a foundation for evidence-based practice.

Treatment Methods in the Charaka School

- **Herbal Medicine:** Extensive use of herbs for healing, categorized based on their effects on doshas and body systems.
- **Dietary Guidelines:** Prescriptions of specific foods and routines based on individual constitution (Prakriti).
- **Panchakarma:** Charaka provided detailed guidelines on detoxification therapies, such as Vamana (emesis) and Virechana (purgation).

The Sushruta School

- The Sushruta Samhita, attributed to Sushruta, is the seminal text of surgical science in Āyurveda. This school is renowned for its pioneering techniques in surgery and its comprehensive anatomical studies.

KEY CONTRIBUTIONS OF SUSHRUTA

Advancements in Surgery

- Sushruta is regarded as the "Father of Surgery." His descriptions of surgical instruments, techniques, and procedures are unparalleled in ancient medical literature.

Anatomy and Dissection

- The Sushruta school emphasized the importance of understanding human anatomy through cadaver dissection, a practice not commonly undertaken in ancient medicine.

Innovations in Plastic Surgery

- Sushruta described rhinoplasty (reconstruction of the nose) and other reconstructive surgeries, showcasing advanced surgical practices.

Comprehensive Health Approach

- While primarily focused on surgery, Sushruta also addressed general health, emphasizing balanced nutrition, hygiene, and the role of mental health in physical well-being.

Treatment Methods in the Sushruta School

- **Surgical Procedures:** Techniques for suturing, abscess drainage, cataract removal, and even cesarean sections.
- **Instruments:** Detailed descriptions of over 100 surgical instruments made of various materials.
- **Postoperative Care:** Guidelines on wound care, diet, and lifestyle for recovery.
- **Use of Herbs in Surgery:** Application of medicinal plants for anesthesia and wound healing.

The Kashyapa School

- The Kashyapa Samhita, attributed to Kashyapa, is a significant text that focuses on Kaumarabhritya, or pediatrics. It emphasizes maternal and child health, addressing topics like pregnancy care, childbirth, and neonatal health.

KEY CONTRIBUTIONS OF KASHYAPA

Focus on Child Health

- The Kashyapa school extensively discusses pediatric diseases and their treatments, a less explored area in other schools.

Emphasis on Maternal Care

- Kashyapa provided detailed guidelines on prenatal care, childbirth practices, and postpartum care.

Diet and Lifestyle for Children

- Recommendations for proper nutrition and routines to ensure healthy development in children.

The Vagbhata School

- The Ashtanga Hridaya, authored by Vagbhata, is a synthesis of the Charaka and Sushruta Samhitas. This school provides a holistic view of Āyurveda, integrating internal medicine, surgery, and lifestyle practices.

KEY CONTRIBUTIONS OF VAGBHATA

Simplification of Āyurvedic Concepts

- Vagbhata's works are concise, making Āyurveda more accessible to practitioners and students.

Integration of Knowledge

- His text combines the insights of Charaka and Sushruta while introducing new ideas.

Focus on Daily Regimens

- The school emphasizes Dinacharya (daily routines) and Ritucharya (seasonal routines) for maintaining health.

COMPARISON OF PHILOSOPHIES AND METHODS

Aṣṭāṅga Āyurveda: The Eight Branches of Āyurveda

- Astanga Āyurveda provides a comprehensive framework encompassing all aspects of health. The eight branches include:

Kāya Chikitsa (Internal Medicine)

- Deals with the diagnosis and treatment of general diseases, focusing on the balance of doshas and body systems.

Shalya Tantra (Surgery)

- Encompasses surgical techniques, instruments, and postoperative care. It also addresses trauma care and wound management.

Shālākya Tantra (ENT and Ophthalmology)

- Focuses on disorders of the eyes, ears, nose, and throat.

Kaumarabhritya (Pediatrics)

- Addresses the care of infants, children, and adolescents, including prenatal care and childbirth practices.

Bhuta Vidya (Psychiatry)

- Explores mental health, spiritual healing, and the treatment of psychological disorders.

Agada Tantra (Toxicology)

- Deals with poisons from plants, animals, and minerals, and their antidotes.

Rasayana (Rejuvenation Therapy)

- Focuses on promoting longevity, vitality, and immunity through specialized therapies and herbs.

Vajikarana (Aphrodisiac Therapy)

- Enhances reproductive health, addresses infertility, and promotes overall vigor.

KEY FIGURES AND THEIR CONTRIBUTIONS

- **Charaka:** Father of Internal Medicine; emphasized balance and prevention.
- **Sushruta:** Pioneer of Surgery; introduced advanced surgical techniques.
- **Kashyapa:** Focused on maternal and child health.
- **Vagbhata:** Integrated and synthesized earlier Āyurvedic knowledge.
- The schools of Āyurveda, with their unique philosophies and methodologies, represent a rich tapestry of medical knowledge. Together, they have shaped Āyurveda into a holistic science of healing that addresses physical, mental, and spiritual well-being. The framework of Astanga Āyurveda underscores the system's comprehensiveness, ensuring that every aspect of health is addressed. This chapter highlights the diversity and depth of Āyurveda, setting the stage for its enduring relevance in contemporary healthcare systems.

MULTIPLE CHOICE QUESTIONS

1. In the historical evolution of Ayurvedic medicine, the Charaka Saṃhitā emerged as a monumental text emphasizing internal medicine. Given Charaka's comprehensive treatment approach, consider how his philosophy integrated the concept of balance among the three doṣas to promote health. Which of the following best reflects Charaka's method of treatment?

A. Prescribing universal remedies regardless of individual prakṛti (constitution).

B. Customizing treatments based on individual doṣa imbalances, dietary habits, and environmental factors.

C. Focusing solely on herbal remedies without addressing lifestyle modifications.

D. Advocating for surgery as the only means to rectify chronic doṣa imbalances.

2. Suśruta Saṃhitā, known for its focus on surgery, introduced several pioneering concepts, including aseptic techniques and anatomical dissections. What ethical principle does Suśruta emphasize in his approach to surgery?

A. Surgery should only be performed when other therapies fail, upholding the physician's role as a healer and protector of life.

B. All patients must be treated equally, even if the procedure risks violating local customs.

C. The efficacy of surgery outweighs the importance of ethical considerations.

D. Surgery must prioritize speed and efficiency over patient-specific concerns.

3. In the context of Aṣṭāṅga Āyurveda, Rasāyana Tantra focuses on rejuvenation and anti-aging. Which of the following correctly explains the primary aim of Rasāyana Tantra?

A. Detoxifying the body to remove all accumulated toxins.

B. Enhancing longevity, vitality, and immunity while supporting mental clarity.

C. Restoring physical beauty through cosmetic procedures.

D. Strengthening the body exclusively through vigorous exercise.

4. The Vāgbhaṭa School synthesized earlier Ayurvedic teachings. What is the central philosophy of Vāgbhaṭa as reflected in Aṣṭāṅga Hṛdayam?

A. To prioritize simplicity and accessibility while preserving the holistic principles of Āyurveda.

B. To challenge Charaka's theories and replace them with surgical advancements.

C. To advocate for the complete elimination of spiritual practices in Āyurvedic treatment.

D. To emphasize the use of mineral-based treatments over herbal formulations.

5. The principles of Śālākya Tantra extend beyond physical ailments, addressing diseases of the head and senses. Which of the following is NOT a focus area of this branch?

A. Treatment of sinusitis and eye disorders.

B. Managing neurological disorders affecting cognitive functions.

C. Addressing conditions related to ear, nose, and throat.

D. Developing surgical interventions for systemic diseases.

6. Ayurveda recognizes the significance of gut health in systemic immunity, as seen in the therapeutic use of Triphala. How does the Charaka Saṃhitā explain the relationship between digestion and health?
   A. Through the concept of Agni, which governs digestion, metabolism, and energy production.
   B. By suggesting that gut health is unrelated to doshic balance or disease prevention.
   C. Through spiritual practices without addressing dietary habits.
   D. By exclusively focusing on herbal decoctions for digestive ailments.
7. Considering the eight branches of Aṣṭāṅga Āyurveda, which branch specializes in the treatment of poisonings and bites from venomous creatures?
   A. Śalya Tantra
   B. Agada Tantra
   C. Rasāyana Tantra
   D. Bhūtavidyā
8. One of the defining features of Ayurvedic schools is their holistic approach. The Kāśyapa Saṃhitā focuses on pediatrics and gynecology. Which of the following interventions does it prioritize for expectant mothers?
   A. Encouraging fasting during pregnancy to ensure spiritual purity.
   B. Providing nutritional guidance and promoting emotional stability for fetal health.
   C. Recommending surgical deliveries in all cases to minimize complications.
   D. Emphasizing the use of potent Rasāyana formulas immediately after childbirth.
9. The Charaka Saṃhitā introduces the concept of preventive health through daily and seasonal regimens. Which statement best captures the significance of these regimens in maintaining health?
   A. They are optional and primarily reserved for the elderly.
   B. They ensure the maintenance of doṣa balance by aligning lifestyle choices with natural rhythms.
   C. They focus solely on physical exercises, excluding mental health considerations.
   D. They are strictly ritualistic practices without tangible health benefits.
10. Within Aṣṭāṅga Āyurveda, the branch of Vājīkaraṇa Tantra focuses on reproductive health and vitality. How does this branch contribute to overall well-being in Ayurveda?
   A. By addressing the spiritual dimensions of fertility and vitality through rituals.
   B. By enhancing physical strength and immunity indirectly through sexual health.
   C. By exclusively targeting male reproductive health, ignoring female needs.
   D. By discouraging the use of herbal preparations in favor of mineral-based treatments.

Directions (Q. No. 11–14): *Scenario-Based Questions:*

SCENARIO 1

A clinical study investigates the efficacy of Triphala in treating inflammatory bowel conditions. The study measures microbiota diversity and systemic immune responses, observing significant reductions in inflammatory markers like CRP after treatment.

SCENARIO 2

Simultaneously, an ecologist studies the effects of environmental changes on medicinal plants. Amalaki, a component of Triphala, shows reduced potency due to overharvesting and soil degradation, raising concerns about the sustainability of Ayurvedic formulations.

11. Based on Scenario 1, which mechanism best explains the enhanced immune response linked to Triphala administration?
   A. Direct stimulation of immune cells without affecting the gut microbiota.
   B. Restoration of gut microbiota diversity, enhancing GALT (Gut-Associated Lymphoid Tissue) function.
   C. Suppression of gut microbiota diversity to prioritize systemic immunity.
   D. Triphala acts purely as a placebo with no measurable immunological impact.
12. In Scenario 2, which intervention best addresses the dual challenges of Amalaki sustainability and medicinal potency?
   A. Cultivating Amalaki in controlled laboratory conditions for standardized bioactive content.
   B. Promoting agroforestry practices that balance conservation with sustainable harvesting.
   C. Replacing Amalaki with non-native species in Ayurvedic formulations.
   D. Reducing the production of Triphala to conserve wild Amalaki populations.
13. How does reduced bioactive potency in Amalaki affect the outcomes observed in Scenario 1?
   A. Diminished potency could impair Triphala's ability to enhance gut microbiota diversity.
   B. Amalaki's potency is irrelevant since Triphala's effects rely on the other two fruits.
   C. Reduced quality enhances detoxification, improving its efficacy.
   D. Environmental degradation has no measurable impact on therapeutic outcomes.

14. Considering the interconnections between Scenarios 1 and 2, which strategy best addresses both sustainability and therapeutic efficacy?
   A. Developing synthetic bioequivalents to replace Amalaki.
   B. Establishing global Ayurvedic standards ensuring sustainable practices.
   C. Shifting focus from Triphala to alternative formulations without Amalaki.
   D. Encouraging large-scale monoculture farming of Amalaki.

15. The philosophical basis of Tridosha integrates mental, physical, and spiritual health. Which of the following statements reflect this integration?
   (a) Vata governs sensory perception and physical motion.
   (b) Pitta oversees transformation, including digestion and intellectual sharpness.
   (c) Kapha maintains emotional resilience and immune strength.
   (d) The balance of these doshas ensures harmony between body and mind.

   Choose the correct answer from the options given below:
   A. (a), (b), and (c) only
   B. (a), (b), and (d) only
   C. (a), (b), (c), and (d)
   D. (b), (c), and (d) only

16. The therapeutic properties of Rasas (tastes) are reflected in their impact on bodily tissues and doshic balance. Match the Rasas with their primary dosha-balancing properties:
   (a) **Sweet Rasa:** Pacifies Vata and Pitta
   (b) **Bitter Rasa:** Reduces Pitta and Kapha
   (c) **Astringent Rasa:** Balances Kapha and strengthens skin tissue
   (d) **Sour Rasa:** Energizes Kapha but aggravates Pitta

   Choose the correct answer from the options given below:
   A. (a), (b), and (c) only
   B. (a), (b), (c), and (d)
   C. (b), (c), and (d) only
   D. (a) and (b) only

17. In Aṣṭāṅga Āyurveda, the branch of Śalya Tantra introduced surgical techniques. Which of the following advancements are associated with this branch?
   (a) Rhinoplasty for reconstructive surgery
   (b) Suturing techniques for wound healing
   (c) Removal of foreign objects from the body
   (d) Herbal ointments to reduce post-surgical inflammation

   Choose the correct answer from the options given below:
   A. (a) and (b) only
   B. (a), (b), and (c) only
   C. (a), (b), (c), and (d)
   D. (b), (c), and (d) only

18. Ayurveda classifies herbs based on their synergistic actions to balance doshas. Match the following plants with their doshic properties:
   (a) **Tulsi:** Balances Kapha and Vata, supports immunity
   (b) **Brahmi:** Pacifies Pitta and supports cognitive function
   (c) **Ashwagandha:** Reduces Vata, promotes strength and vitality
   (d) **Neem:** Reduces Pitta and detoxifies blood

   Choose the correct answer from the options given below:
   A. (a) and (b) only
   B. (a), (b), and (c) only
   C. (a), (b), (c), and (d)
   D. (b), (c), and (d) only

19. In the Kāśyapa Saṃhitā, maternal and neonatal health are emphasized through lifestyle recommendations. Which of the following principles apply to prenatal care in Ayurveda?
   (a) Emotional stability of the mother impacts fetal development.
   (b) Herbal tonics are prescribed for nourishment and vitality.
   (c) Spiritual practices enhance mental and emotional health.
   (d) Dietary regimens focus on balancing maternal doshas.

   Choose the correct answer from the options given below:
   A. (a), (b), and (c) only
   B. (b) and (c) only
   C. (a), (b), and (d) only
   D. (a), (b), (c), and (d)

20. The concept of Agni in Ayurveda goes beyond digestion to include metabolism and immunity. Match the forms of Agni with their respective functions:
   (a) **Jatharagni:** Governs digestion of food in the stomach
   (b) **Dhātwagni:** Manages tissue-specific metabolic processes
   (c) **Bhūtāgni:** Balances elemental metabolism related to Panchamahabhutas
   (d) **Āma Agni:** Represents impaired digestive fire, leading to toxin formation

   Choose the correct answer from the options given below:
   A. (a), (b), and (c) only
   B. (a), (b), (c), and (d)
   C. (a) and (c) only
   D. (b), (c), and (d) only

21. In Rasāyana Tantra, specific therapies aim to rejuvenate tissues and extend life span. Which of the following are characteristic features of Rasāyana?

(a) Enhances Ojas, the essence of vitality
(b) Improves cellular repair and tissue regeneration
(c) Balances mind-body connections through meditation
(d) Focuses exclusively on detoxifying the gastrointestinal tract

Choose the correct answer from the options given below:

A. (a), (b), and (c) only
B. (b), (c), and (d) only
C. (a) and (b) only
D. (a), (b), (c), and (d)

22. The Dhatus represent the structural and functional units of the body in Ayurveda. Match each Dhatu with its primary role:

(a) **Rasa Dhatu:** Nourishes tissues and maintains hydration
(b) **Rakta Dhatu:** Facilitates oxygen transport and vitality
(c) **Mamsa Dhatu:** Provides physical strength and muscle mass
(d) **Meda Dhatu:** Lubricates joints and stores energy as fat

Choose the correct answer from the options given below:

A. (a), (b), and (c) only
B. (b), (c), and (d) only
C. (a), (b), (c), and (d)
D. (a) and (c) only

23. Diagnostic methods in Ayurveda incorporate physical and sensory observations. Which of the following practices are integral to diagnosis?

(a) Nāḍī Parīkṣā (Pulse examination)
(b) Shabda Parīkṣā (Analysis of voice and speech)
(c) Dṛṣṭi Parīkṣā (Observation of eyes)
(d) Malā Parīkṣā (Stool examination)

Choose the correct answer from the options given below:

A. (a) and (b) only
B. (a), (b), and (c) only
C. (a), (b), (c), and (d)
D. (b), (c), and (d) only

24. Panchakarma is a cornerstone of Ayurvedic therapy, focusing on cleansing and rejuvenation. Match the therapies with their primary actions:

(a) **Vamana:** Induces therapeutic vomiting to expel toxins
(b) **Virechana:** Purgative therapy to cleanse the gastrointestinal tract
(c) **Basti:** Medicated enema for deep detoxification
(d) **Nasya:** Nasal cleansing to improve respiratory health

Choose the correct answer from the options given below:

A. (a), (b), and (c) only
B. (a), (b), (c), and (d)
C. (b) and (c) only
D. (a) and (d) only

25. Match List–I (Branches of Aṣṭāṅga Āyurveda) with List–II (Primary Focus):

List–I	List–II
(a) Kāyacikitsā	1. Internal medicine and systemic disease management
(b) Śalya Tantra	2. Surgical procedures and trauma care
(c) Rasāyana Tantra	3. Longevity and rejuvenation
(d) Vājīkaraṇa Tantra	4. Reproductive health and vitality

Choose the correct answer from the options given below:

A. (a)-1, (b)-2, (c)-3, (d)-4
B. (a)-3, (b)-4, (c)-1, (d)-2
C. (a)-2, (b)-1, (c)-4, (d)-3
D. (a)-3, (b)-1, (c)-4, (d)-2

26. Match List–I (Doshas) with List–II (Key Characteristics):

List–I	List–II
(a) Vata	1. Controls movement and nervous function
(b) Pitta	2. Governs digestion and metabolism
(c) Kapha	3. Provides stability and immunity

Choose the correct answer from the options given below:

A. (a)-1, (b)-2, (c)-3
B. (a)-3, (b)-1, (c)-2
C. (a)-2, (b)-3, (c)-1
D. (a)-3, (b)-2, (c)-1

27. Match List–I (Major Schools of Ayurveda) with List–II (Key Contributions):

List–I	List–II
(a) Charaka School	1. Focus on internal medicine and pharmacology
(b) Sushruta School	2. Pioneering surgical methods and anatomy
(c) Kashyapa School	3. Pediatrics and gynecology
(d) Vagbhata School	4. Integration of previous knowledge into a single treatise

Choose the correct answer from the options given below:

A. (a)-1, (b)-2, (c)-3, (d)-4
B. (a)-3, (b)-4, (c)-1, (d)-2
C. (a)-4, (b)-1, (c)-2, (d)-3
D. (a)-3, (b)-2, (c)-4, (d)-1

28. Match List–I (Key Figures) with List–II (Contributions):

List–I	List–II
(a) Charaka	1. Compilation of Charaka Samhita focusing on medicine
(b) Sushruta	2. Development of surgical techniques
(c) Kashyapa	3. Contributions to gynecology and pediatrics
(d) Vagbhata	4. Author of Astanga Hridaya

Choose the correct answer from the options given below:

A. (a)-1, (b)-2, (c)-3, (d)-4
B. (a)-2, (b)-4, (c)-1, (d)-3
C. (a)-4, (b)-3, (c)-2, (d)-1
D. (a)-3, (b)-1, (c)-4, (d)-2

29. Match List–I (Aṣṭāṅga Āyurveda Branches) with List–II (Key Features):

List–I	List–II
(a) Śalya Tantra	1. Deals with surgical interventions
(b) Kāyacikitsā	2. Focus on treating systemic diseases
(c) Agada Tantra	3. Focus on toxicology and poisons
(d) Bhūtavidyā	4. Focus on mental health and spiritual healing

Choose the correct answer from the options given below:

A. (a)-1, (b)-2, (c)-3, (d)-4
B. (a)-4, (b)-3, (c)-1, (d)-2
C. (a)-3, (b)-4, (c)-2, (d)-1
D. (a)-2, (b)-1, (c)-4, (d)-3

30. Match List–I (Distinct Philosophies) with List–II (Unique Features):

List–I	List–II
(a) Charaka School	1. Emphasis on medicine and pharmacology
(b) Sushruta School	2. Emphasis on surgery and trauma care
(c) Kashyapa School	3. Focus on pediatric health and women's health
(d) Vagbhata School	4. Comprehensive compilation of Ayurvedic knowledge

Choose the correct answer from the options given below:

A. (a)-1, (b)-2, (c)-3, (d)-4
B. (a)-3, (b)-4, (c)-1, (d)-2
C. (a)-2, (b)-1, (c)-4, (d)-3
D. (a)-4, (b)-2, (c)-1, (d)-3

31. Match List–I (Key Texts) with List–II (Primary Focus):

List–I	List–II
(a) Charaka Samhita	1. Internal medicine and pharmacology
(b) Sushruta Samhita	2. Surgical procedures and anatomy
(c) Kashyapa Samhita	3. Pediatrics and obstetrics
(d) Astanga Hridaya	4. Compilation of knowledge for practical use

Choose the correct answer from the options given below:

A. (a)-1, (b)-2, (c)-3, (d)-4
B. (a)-4, (b)-3, (c)-1, (d)-2
C. (a)-3, (b)-1, (c)-4, (d)-2
D. (a)-2, (b)-4, (c)-3, (d)-1

32. Match List–I (Eight Branches) with List–II (Application):

List–I	List–II
(a) Agada Tantra	1. Study of toxins and antidotes
(b) Bhūtavidyā	2. Focus on mental health and spiritual ailments
(c) Śalya Tantra	3. Focus on surgical interventions
(d) Kāyacikitsā	4. Internal medicine

Choose the correct answer from the options given below:

A. (a)-1, (b)-2, (c)-3, (d)-4
B. (a)-4, (b)-1, (c)-2, (d)-3
C. (a)-3, (b)-2, (c)-1, (d)-4
D. (a)-2, (b)-3, (c)-4, (d)-1

33. Match List–I (Aṣṭāṅga Branches) with List–II (Relevant Disorders):

List–I	List–II
(a) Śalya Tantra	1. Injuries and trauma management
(b) Bhūtavidyā	2. Psychosomatic and spiritual disorders
(c) Vājīkaraṇa Tantraa	3. Reproductive disorders and vitality
(d) Rasāyana Tantra	4. Rejuvenation and anti-aging therapies

Choose the correct answer from the options given below:

A. (a)-1, (b)-2, (c)-3, (d)-4
B. (a)-3, (b)-4, (c)-1, (d)-2
C. (a)-4, (b)-1, (c)-3, (d)-2
D. (a)-2, (b)-4, (c)-3, (d)-1

34. Match List–I (Key Schools of Thought) with List–II (Philosophical Themes):

List–I	List–II
(a) Charaka School	1. Holistic approach to internal medicine
(b) Sushruta School	2. Precision in surgical techniques
(c) Kashyapa School	3. Focus on maternal and child health
(d) Vagbhata School	4. Comprehensive and practical integration

Choose the correct answer from the options given below:

A. (a)-1, (b)-2, (c)-3, (d)-4
B. (a)-3, (b)-4, (c)-1, (d)-2
C. (a)-4, (b)-1, (c)-3, (d)-2
D. (a)-2, (b)-3, (c)-4, (d)-1

Directions (Q. No. 35–39): *Following questions are based on statement 1 and statement 2. Read both the statements carefully and choose the correct answer from the options given below:*

A. Both Statement 1 and Statement 2 are true, and Statement 2 is the correct explanation of Statement 1.
B. Both Statement 1 and Statement 2 are true, but Statement 2 is not the correct explanation of Statement 1.
C. Statement 1 is true, but Statement 2 is false.
D. Statement 1 is false, but Statement 2 is true.
E. Both Statement 1 and Statement 2 are false.

35. Statement 1: In Ayurveda, the three doshas—Vata, Pitta, and Kapha—serve as fundamental principles for understanding physiological and pathological states in the human body.

Statement 2: The balance of the three doshas remains identical for all individuals, and any imbalance is treated uniformly without consideration of individual constitutions.

36. Statement 1: Panchakarma therapies are considered one of the most effective means of detoxification and rejuvenation in Ayurveda.

Statement 2: Panchakarma eliminates all metabolic toxins (ama) through a combination of herbal remedies and non-invasive treatments.

37. Statement 1: The Charaka Saṃhitā emphasizes that preventive health is achieved through daily and seasonal regimens (dinacharya and ritucharya).

Statement 2: Ayurvedic preventive measures primarily focus on adjusting lifestyle practices to maintain doshic balance according to environmental and seasonal changes.

38. Statement 1: In Ayurvedic pharmacology, the Rasas (tastes) are associated with both the therapeutic properties and pharmacological actions of medicinal plants.

Statement 2: Sweet Rasa is linked to detoxification and purification, while bitter Rasa is associated with tissue-building and nourishment.

39. Statement 1: Ayurveda considers the role of mental health equally important as physical health in ensuring overall well-being.

Statement 2: Mental states such as Sattva, Rajas, and Tamas influence doshic balance and directly impact physical health.

Directions (Q. No. 40–45): *There are two statements in each question. One is labelled as Assertion (A) and the other is as Reason (R). Read both the statements and choose the correct answer from the options given below:*

A. Both Assertion (A) and Reason (R) are true, and Reason (R) is the correct explanation of Assertion (A).
B. Both Assertion (A) and Reason (R) are true, but Reason (R) is not the correct explanation of Assertion (A).
C. Assertion (A) is true, but Reason (R) is false.
D. Assertion (A) is false, but Reason (R) is true.
E. Both Assertion (A) and Reason (R) are false.

40. Assertion (A): Ayurveda emphasizes the importance of balancing the three doshas to maintain health and prevent diseases.

Reason (R): Doshas represent spiritual energies only, and their imbalance is unrelated to physical health.

41. Assertion (A): The Rasāyana branch of Aṣṭāṅga Āyurveda aims to improve immunity, vitality, and longevity.

Reason (R): Rasāyana therapies primarily focus on removing toxins and strengthening the immune system through herbal formulations and lifestyle modifications.

42. Assertion (A): Ayurvedic detoxification therapies, such as Panchakarma, are designed to address systemic imbalances caused by ama (toxins).

Reason (R): Panchakarma therapies target the root cause of diseases by balancing digestive fire (Agni) and improving elimination processes.

43. Assertion (A): Bhūtavidyā in Aṣṭāṅga Āyurveda addresses mental health disorders and supernatural influences.

Reason (R): Ayurveda incorporates spiritual practices and rituals to complement medical therapies for psychological well-being.

44. Assertion (A): Vājīkaraṇa Tantra enhances reproductive health and addresses fertility-related concerns in Ayurveda.

Reason (R): This branch exclusively focuses on improving sexual health and vitality through herbal and dietary therapies.

45. Assertion (A): Seasonal routines (Ritucharya) in Ayurveda are essential for maintaining health.

Reason (R): Seasonal changes cause natural shifts in doshic balance, necessitating dietary and lifestyle adjustments to prevent disease.

Directions (Q. No. 46–50): *Read the passage carefully and answer the questions given below*:

The schools of Ayurveda—primarily represented by the texts of Charaka, Suśruta, Kāśyapa, and Vāgbhaṭa—offer unique perspectives on health and healing, reflecting their distinct philosophies and methodologies. Each school emerges from a profound understanding of nature, human physiology, and the interplay of physical, mental, and spiritual well-being, yet they diverge in their focus areas and treatment strategies.

The Charaka Saṃhitā prioritizes internal medicine (Kāyacikitsā) and emphasizes personalized treatment based on the individual's constitution (prakṛti) and the dynamic balance of the three doshas—Vata, Pitta, and Kapha. Charaka's philosophy underscores the importance of maintaining harmony between body, mind, and environment. Preventive care is a cornerstone, with detailed regimens for daily living (dinacharya) and seasonal adaptation (ritucharya). Diagnostic methods in the Charaka tradition rely on a comprehensive understanding of symptoms, pulse, and digestion, while treatment combines dietary modifications, herbal formulations, and lifestyle changes.

The Suśruta Saṃhitā takes a different approach by focusing on surgery (Śalya Tantra) and anatomy. Suśruta's philosophy views the human body as a dynamic entity requiring precise interventions to restore health. This school is notable for its pioneering work in surgical techniques, including rhinoplasty, wound care, and management of fractures. Ethical training and hygiene are emphasized, reflecting a commitment to both the skill and moral responsibility of the physician. In addition to surgical practices, Suśruta integrates detoxification therapies and the use of herbal poultices to aid recovery and balance doshas.

The Kāśyapa Saṃhitā specializes in pediatrics (Kaumārabhṛtya) and maternal health, presenting a unique perspective on nurturing life from conception through childhood. Kāśyapa's methods include prenatal care, focusing on the health of the mother and fetus, and postnatal regimens to ensure the child's physical and psychological development. This school integrates Ayurvedic principles with spiritual practices, emphasizing the role of familial harmony and emotional stability in health. Nutrition and natural remedies form the backbone of treatment.

Finally, Vāgbhaṭa's Aṣṭāṅga Hṛdayam synthesizes the teachings of Charaka and Suśruta, presenting a concise and practical guide to the eight branches of Ayurveda. Vāgbhaṭa's work emphasizes preventive care, therapeutic applications, and rejuvenation. His approach blends theoretical knowledge with practical solutions, making Ayurveda accessible to a broader audience. Vāgbhaṭa's philosophy also highlights the psychosomatic connection, recognizing the influence of mental states on physical health.

Together, these schools demonstrate Ayurveda's adaptability and depth, providing a comprehensive framework for healing that integrates spiritual, mental, and physical dimensions. Despite their differences, they share a common goal: to promote health, prevent disease, and restore balance in harmony with nature.

46. According to the passage, how does the Charaka Saṃhitā approach the treatment of diseases?

A. By focusing exclusively on surgical interventions and anatomical corrections.

B. By emphasizing the dynamic balance of doshas and personalized treatment plans.

C. By standardizing treatments regardless of individual prakṛti or environmental factors.

D. By advocating for spiritual rituals as the primary form of therapy.

47. What distinguishes Suśruta's philosophy from that of Charaka?

A. Suśruta focuses on mental health and psychosomatic therapies.

B. Suśruta prioritizes surgical precision and anatomical studies.

C. Suśruta rejects the concept of dosha balance in favor of detoxification.

D. Suśruta's methods are solely based on herbal and dietary interventions.

48. How does the Kāśyapa Saṃhitā contribute to maternal and pediatric health according to the passage?

A. By focusing exclusively on herbal remedies for common childhood ailments.

B. By integrating nutritional guidance with prenatal and postnatal care.

C. By discouraging spiritual practices in favour of purely physical treatments.

D. By treating pediatric health as independent from maternal well-being.

49. What is the primary contribution of Vāgbhaṭa's Aṣṭāṅga Hṛdayam to Ayurvedic practice?

A. It introduces advanced surgical procedures and techniques.

B. It simplifies and synthesizes Ayurvedic teachings for practical application.

C. It replaces earlier texts by focusing exclusively on mental health.

D. It emphasizes the use of spiritual rituals over therapeutic treatments.

50. What common goal unites the philosophies of Charaka, Suśruta, Kāśyapa, and Vāgbhaṭa?

A. To prioritize surgery as the ultimate form of treatment.

B. To eliminate the spiritual aspects of Ayurveda in favor of scientific methods.

C. To promote health, prevent disease, and restore balance in harmony with nature.

D. To develop standardized herbal formulations independent of individual needs.

ANSWER WITH EXPLANATIONS

1. **B:** Charaka's philosophy centers on the dynamic interplay between an individual's constitution (prakṛti) and the three doshas—Vata, Pitta, and Kapha. His approach recognizes that each person has unique physiological and psychological characteristics. Rather than applying generic treatments, Charaka advocates tailored interventions, combining dietary modifications, herbal formulations, and lifestyle changes. The emphasis is on preventing disease by aligning one's lifestyle with natural rhythms and environmental factors. This reflects a deep understanding of how internal and external influences contribute to health, and it underscores Ayurveda's adaptability in addressing individual health challenges. Generic remedies were explicitly discouraged in his teachings.

2. **A:** Suśruta integrates ethical responsibility with surgical precision, emphasizing surgery as a last resort. His philosophy is rooted in a profound respect for life and healing, insisting that surgery be performed only when necessary. This reflects not only technical expertise but also moral discipline, underscoring the role of the surgeon as both healer and ethical guardian. Suśruta's training included rigorous practical and theoretical knowledge alongside a moral code to ensure patient safety. By prioritizing life-preserving interventions over expedient actions, he established a holistic and compassionate approach to health care within the broader Ayurvedic framework.

3. **B:** Rasāyana Tantra embodies Ayurveda's rejuvenative essence, aiming to enhance longevity, vitality, and immunity while supporting mental clarity. Unlike detoxification therapies, Rasāyana focuses on building ojas (vital essence), strengthening tissues, and fostering resilience against aging and disease. This branch integrates dietary regimens, herbal tonics, and meditative practices to create a synergy of physical, mental, and spiritual well-being. The holistic application ensures sustained health rather than temporary relief. This proactive philosophy extends beyond addressing ailments, promoting a state of optimal health that aligns with Ayurveda's preventive and integrative principles.

4. **A:** Vāgbhaṭa synthesized complex Ayurvedic teachings into simplified, accessible formats in the Aṣṭāṅga Hṛdayam. He sought to make Ayurveda practical for a broader audience without diluting its philosophical depth. This approach democratized Ayurvedic knowledge, ensuring that preventive care and therapeutic applications reached diverse communities. Vāgbhaṭa's work maintains harmony between tradition and pragmatism, focusing on individual well-being. By preserving holistic principles while enhancing accessibility, his contributions reflect Ayurveda's adaptability in addressing varying societal and individual needs across time and regions, underscoring the universality of its core tenets.

5. **D:** Śālākya Tantra specializes in treating head and sense organ disorders, including sinusitis, eye diseases, and ear conditions, but it does not involve systemic diseases or surgical interventions. This branch reflects Ayurveda's precise understanding of interconnected sensory and neurological functions. Treatments often combine herbal remedies, nasal therapies (nasya), and external applications to restore sensory health and equilibrium. Its specialized focus demonstrates Ayurveda's capacity to address complex anatomical and functional systems uniquely, without encroaching on other therapeutic domains like internal medicine or general surgery.

6. **A:** Charaka explains digestion through the concept of Agni, a transformative energy governing metabolism and assimilation. Agni reflects the body's ability to convert food into energy, nutrients, and waste efficiently. When Agni is balanced, digestion, absorption, and immunity function optimally, reducing ama (toxins). Charaka's theory highlights the centrality of digestion in determining overall health, connecting physical, emotional, and mental well-being. Treatments focus on strengthening Agni through dietary adjustments, herbal preparations, and lifestyle modifications. This nuanced perspective underscores digestion as a microcosm of bodily harmony and systemic vitality.

7. **B:** Agada Tantra specializes in detoxification and poison management, addressing venomous bites, toxins, and poisoning. Its origins lie in Ayurveda's ability to address emergencies and acute conditions. This branch underscores a proactive, systematic approach to identifying toxins, neutralizing their effects, and restoring systemic balance. Therapies often involve antidotes, herbal formulations, and purification techniques, bridging preventive care with crisis management. Agada Tantra exemplifies Ayurveda's depth in both chronic and acute conditions, reaffirming its comprehensive healing philosophy that transcends time and context.

8. **B:** Kāśyapa Saṃhitā emphasizes maternal and neonatal health, integrating nutritional guidance with prenatal and postnatal care. Ayurveda recognizes

the interdependence of maternal and fetal health, advocating dietary adjustments and emotional stability to ensure optimal development. Postnatal regimens nurture the child's growth and immunity, focusing on holistic well-being. Kāśyapa also integrates spiritual practices, enhancing familial harmony and mental health. This integrated approach reflects Ayurveda's understanding of human life as a continuum, shaped by physical, mental, and emotional environments.

9. **B:** Charaka's emphasis on daily (dinacharya) and seasonal regimens (ritucharya) aligns lifestyle practices with nature's cycles to maintain doshic balance. These practices include waking routines, dietary choices, and physical activities tailored to environmental and physiological rhythms. This preventive approach minimizes disease risk and promotes harmony with nature. By addressing imbalances before they manifest as diseases, Charaka's philosophy showcases Ayurveda's forward-thinking preventive model. This reflects a deep ecological and holistic understanding of health, highlighting Ayurveda's adaptability and timeless relevance.

10. **B:** Vājīkaraṇa Tantra integrates reproductive health with overall vitality, recognizing sexual health as central to well-being. This branch combines dietary regimens, herbal therapies, and lifestyle adjustments to optimize fertility, hormonal balance, and immunity. Far from being isolated to sexual health, Vājīkaraṇa strengthens systemic functions, highlighting Ayurveda's holistic philosophy. It addresses physical, emotional, and spiritual dimensions, fostering a comprehensive understanding of vitality that transcends reproductive health, aligning with Ayurveda's interconnected view of the human body and its functions.

11. **B:** The restoration of gut microbiota diversity enhances the gut-associated lymphoid tissue (GALT), promoting systemic immunity. Triphala's role in balancing doshas and detoxification indirectly strengthens the gut's physical and functional health. The increase in GALT activity exemplifies Ayurveda's integrative approach, linking digestion with systemic defense. This mechanism highlights the gut's dual role in absorbing nutrients and coordinating immune responses, affirming Ayurveda's insights into interconnected bodily systems.

12. **B:** Agroforestry systems balance conservation with sustainable harvesting, addressing environmental and medicinal concerns. This approach combines traditional agricultural wisdom with modern conservation techniques, ensuring ecological integrity and the potency of Amalaki. By involving communities, agroforestry fosters long-term sustainability, reflecting Ayurveda's respect for the interconnectedness of humans and nature. Such measures uphold the therapeutic efficacy of Ayurvedic formulations while mitigating overharvesting and ecological degradation.

13. **A:** Environmental degradation reduces bioactive compound concentrations, impairing Amalaki's therapeutic efficacy. In Scenario 1, diminished Amalaki quality directly affects Triphala's role in restoring gut microbiota diversity and enhancing immunity. This correlation reflects Ayurveda's holistic understanding of plant potency, ecological balance, and systemic health. Scenario 2 underscores the necessity of sustainable sourcing to preserve the quality and efficacy of Ayurvedic medicines, linking ecological stewardship to therapeutic success.

14. **B:** Global standards incorporating sustainable practices ensure medicinal quality and environmental protection. Such measures uphold the integrity of Ayurvedic formulations while addressing ecological challenges. By combining scientific rigor with traditional knowledge, these standards reflect Ayurveda's adaptability and relevance in modern healthcare. They emphasize balance, both within the body and the environment, aligning with Ayurvedic philosophy's core principles.

15. **C:** The Tridosha theory emphasizes the harmonious interaction between Vata, Pitta, and Kapha. Each dosha has distinct roles, such as Vata's influence on movement and creativity, Pitta's regulation of digestion and intellect, and Kapha's provision of emotional and physical stability. Together, these doshas form a dynamic system where balance ensures health, while imbalance results in diseases. The holistic view underscores that physical, emotional, and spiritual well-being are interlinked. Ayurveda's focus on individual constitution reflects its personalized approach, making it adaptable across varied lifestyles and environmental factors.

16. **B:** Ayurveda explains that Rasa (taste) directly influences the doshas. Sweet Rasa pacifies Vata and Pitta, while Bitter Rasa reduces Pitta and Kapha due to its cooling and drying nature. Astringent Rasa helps balance Kapha and strengthens bodily tissues like skin. Sour Rasa, though energizing for Kapha, can aggravate Pitta because of its heating quality. All four statements align with classical Ayurvedic taste-dosha principles.

17. **C:** Śalya Tantra, the surgical branch of Aṣṭāṅga Āyurveda, revolutionized ancient medicine with innovations such as reconstructive surgeries like rhinoplasty, suturing techniques, and the management of wounds. These advancements showcase Ayurveda's scientific rigor and adaptability. By combining surgical

methods with herbal applications to reduce inflammation and aid recovery, Śalya Tantra demonstrates an integrative approach. It highlights Ayurveda's capacity to address acute conditions while maintaining systemic balance, reflecting a commitment to both precision and holistic care.

18. **C:** In Ayurvedic herbology, each plant balances specific doshas. Tulsi balances Kapha and Vata and boosts immunity. Brahmi pacifies Pitta and enhances memory and calmness. Ashwagandha is known for reducing Vata and promoting strength and vitality. Neem cools Pitta and purifies the blood. These properties make all four pairings accurate according to classical texts.

19. **D:** Prenatal care in the Kāśyapa Saṃhitā integrates physical, emotional, and spiritual aspects. Emotional stability of the mother directly influences fetal development, aligning with modern research on maternal stress and its impact on the child. Nutritional regimens ensure optimal growth, while spiritual practices create a nurturing environment. Postnatal care extends this philosophy, focusing on rejuvenation and immunity for both mother and child. This interconnected approach demonstrates Ayurveda's advanced understanding of family health, where the well-being of one member contributes to the harmony of the whole.

20. **B:** Agni, the transformative fire in Ayurveda, encompasses digestion, metabolism, and systemic balance. Jatharagni breaks down food in the stomach, Dhātwagni ensures tissue-specific transformations, and Bhūtāgni harmonizes elemental energies. These interconnected levels of metabolism reflect Ayurveda's layered understanding of bodily functions. Imbalance in any form of Agni leads to ama (toxins), disrupting health. This concept emphasizes the critical role of digestion in maintaining physical and mental well-being, aligning Ayurveda with modern views on gut health and immunity.

21. **A:** Rasāyana therapies go beyond detoxification, focusing on rejuvenation, longevity, and mental clarity. By enhancing Ojas, the vital essence, Rasāyana supports cellular repair, tissue regeneration, and resilience against aging. Meditation and lifestyle adjustments ensure harmony between the body and mind, making Rasāyana a comprehensive approach to preventive health. This philosophy reflects Ayurveda's proactive nature, where vitality and immunity are cultivated as foundational pillars of health rather than reactive measures against illness.

22. **C:** The Dhatus, or body tissues, form the structural and functional essence of the human body. Rasa nourishes and hydrates tissues, Rakta oxygenates and energizes, Mamsa builds strength, and Meda lubricates joints and stores fat. Ayurveda's understanding of the interdependence among Dhatus highlights its systemic approach to health. An imbalance in one Dhatu affects others, leading to diseases. This layered concept showcases Ayurveda's precision in addressing root causes, emphasizing balance across all physiological levels to ensure holistic well-being.

23. **C:** AAyurvedic diagnosis includes observation (Darshana), touch (Sparshana), and interrogation (Prashna). Nāḍī Parīkṣā is crucial for assessing doshic imbalance. Shabda Parīkṣā helps identify nervous or respiratory issues through voice changes. Dṛṣṭi Parīkṣā involves inspecting the eyes for systemic signs, and Malā Parīkṣā assesses waste (stool) to understand digestion and disease state. All are integral diagnostic tools in Ayurveda.

24. **B:** Panchakarma, Ayurveda's cleansing therapy, integrates five techniques to eliminate toxins and restore balance. Vamana induces vomiting to expel Kapha-related toxins, Virechana purges Pitta toxins from the gut, and Basti cleanses deeper tissues through medicated enemas. Nasya focuses on detoxifying the respiratory system, reflecting Ayurveda's comprehensive detoxification strategy. Panchakarma's holistic nature ensures physical, mental, and emotional rejuvenation, aligning with Ayurveda's vision of systemic health. This layered approach highlights its relevance in modern detoxification and stress management practices.

25. **A:** Kāyacikitsā focuses on internal medicine, addressing systemic diseases, aligning with the primary concerns of doshic imbalances. Śalya Tantra's focus on surgical interventions reflects the pioneering work of Sushruta in trauma care and invasive procedures. Rasāyana Tantra emphasizes rejuvenation and longevity, showcasing Ayurveda's preventive approach to health. Vājīkaraṇa Tantra aligns with reproductive health and vitality, addressing both physical and psychological dimensions of well-being. This structured division exemplifies the comprehensive nature of Aṣṭāṅga Āyurveda, combining curative, preventive, and restorative methodologies, ensuring that all aspects of health and disease management are cohesively addressed in an integrated system.

26. **A:** Vata's control of movement and nervous function reflects its light and mobile qualities, critical for physiological and psychological processes. Pitta governs digestion and metabolism, showcasing its fiery and transformative nature. Kapha provides stability and immunity, aligning with its heavy and grounding

attributes. This categorization highlights Ayurveda's understanding of doshas as the functional pillars of health. Each dosha's unique characteristics contribute to maintaining homeostasis, with imbalances leading to disease. By associating these roles with physiological systems, Ayurveda demonstrates its profound insights into health's dynamic and static components, creating a framework for personalized therapeutic interventions.

27. A: The Charaka School's focus on internal medicine and pharmacology underpins its contributions to Kāyacikitsā, reflecting Ayurveda's systemic approach. Sushruta's emphasis on surgical methods aligns with Śalya Tantra, showcasing precision in anatomical understanding. Kashyapa's contributions to pediatrics and gynecology highlight Ayurveda's inclusive scope, addressing women's and children's health. Vagbhata's integration of prior knowledge into Astanga Hridaya exemplifies the synthesis of theory and practice, creating a unified Ayurvedic philosophy. This alignment of schools and their contributions reflects the diversity and specialization within Ayurveda, ensuring that every aspect of health and disease is comprehensively addressed.

28. A: Charaka's compilation of Charaka Samhita emphasizes internal medicine, highlighting Ayurveda's systemic approach to health. Sushruta's advancements in surgical techniques demonstrate the depth of Śalya Tantra, pushing the boundaries of medical practice. Kashyapa's contributions to gynecology and pediatrics showcase Ayurveda's recognition of family health as foundational to societal well-being. Vagbhata's Astanga Hridaya synthesizes earlier works, reflecting Ayurveda's adaptability and continuity. These contributions collectively highlight Ayurveda's diverse scope, integrating specialties to create a holistic medical science. This synergy underscores Ayurveda's commitment to addressing health through both specialized and comprehensive approaches.

29. A: Each branch of Aṣṭāṅga Ayurveda has a distinct focus. Śalya Tantra deals with surgery and trauma. Kāyacikitsā focuses on internal/systemic disease management. Agada Tantra is concerned with poisons, toxins, and their antidotes. Bhūtavidyā addresses psychological disorders and spiritual disturbances. The matchings reflect the traditional scope of each branch.

30. A: The Charaka School's emphasis on medicine and pharmacology showcases its focus on systemic therapies. Sushruta's pioneering surgical methods reflect the technical advancements of Śalya Tantra. Kashyapa's focus on pediatrics and maternal health highlights Ayurveda's inclusive scope, emphasizing community well-being. Vagbhata's synthesis of Ayurvedic knowledge into a practical treatise exemplifies Ayurveda's adaptability, creating accessible frameworks for health management. These distinct philosophies reflect the depth and diversity of Ayurvedic schools, combining theoretical insights with practical applications. This structured approach demonstrates Ayurveda's comprehensive vision, harmonizing prevention, cure, and maintenance in a unified medical science.

31. A: Charaka Samhita's emphasis on internal medicine reflects its foundational role in Kāyacikitsā, addressing systemic diseases. Sushruta Samhita's focus on surgical procedures underscores its alignment with Śalya Tantra's practical innovations. Kashyapa Samhita's pediatric and obstetric focus highlights Ayurveda's recognition of family health as central to societal wellness. Astanga Hridaya's comprehensive integration of Ayurvedic principles demonstrates its practical relevance, aligning theoretical insights with therapeutic applications. This division underscores Ayurveda's holistic framework, addressing health's physical, mental, and societal dimensions. By associating texts with their focus, Ayurveda's structured approach to medical science becomes evident.

32. A: Agada Tantra's focus on toxins and antidotes reflects Ayurveda's preventive emphasis, addressing environmental and dietary risks. Bhūtavidyā's attention to mental and spiritual health highlights Ayurveda's recognition of psychosomatic disorders. Śalya Tantra's surgical focus aligns with practical interventions for trauma and structural issues. Kāyacikitsā's systemic approach underscores its role in addressing internal diseases. These branches exemplify Aṣṭāṅga Āyurveda's comprehensive scope, integrating preventive, curative, and restorative strategies. By categorizing branches according to their applications, Ayurveda creates a structured framework for addressing health's diverse challenges, ensuring a cohesive approach to well-being.

33. A: Salya Tantra's focus on injuries and trauma care aligns with its emphasis on surgical interventions. Bhūtavidyā addresses psychosomatic disorders, showcasing Ayurveda's recognition of mental health's role in overall wellness. Vājīkaraṇa Tantra's reproductive focus reflects its role in enhancing vitality and addressing fertility concerns. Rasāyana Tantra's rejuvenative therapies highlight Ayurveda's preventive strategies, promoting longevity and vitality. This categorization reflects Aṣṭāṅga Āyurveda's holistic approach, addressing health's physical, mental, and spiritual dimensions. By aligning branches with specific disorders, Ayurveda demonstrates its adaptability and precision in tackling diverse health challenges comprehensively.

34. **A:** The Charaka School's holistic approach to internal medicine emphasizes systemic health, reflecting Ayurveda's integrative vision. Sushruta's precision in surgical techniques highlights technical advancements in trauma care. Kashyapa's focus on maternal and child health underscores Ayurveda's commitment to family well-being. Vagbhata's comprehensive synthesis of Ayurvedic knowledge showcases adaptability, creating accessible frameworks for practical application. These philosophical themes reflect the diversity and depth of Ayurvedic schools, integrating specialized insights into a unified medical science. This structured approach demonstrates Ayurveda's capacity to address complex health challenges through harmonized theoretical and practical principles.

35. **C:** Ayurveda considers Tridosha theory central to understanding health, yet it acknowledges the individual variability of doshic balances. While Statement 1 is true, Statement 2 falsely implies uniformity in dosha treatment, disregarding the concept of prakṛti (individual constitution). Ayurveda tailors interventions based on prakṛti, reflecting its personalized approach to health. This distinction highlights the nuanced nature of Ayurvedic treatment, rooted in an understanding of individual physiology and environmental factors.

36. **C:** Statement 1 is true – Panchakarma is indeed regarded as one of the most effective Ayurvedic therapies for detoxifying the body, eliminating āma (toxins), and restoring doshic balance through a combination of five core procedures (Vamana, Virechana, Basti, Nasya, Raktamokshana). However, Statement 2 is false because it wrongly claims that Panchakarma uses only non-invasive treatments. In reality, some Panchakarma procedures are invasive, such as therapeutic vomiting (Vamana) and enemas (Basti). Thus, Statement 2 is factually incorrect.

37. **A:** Both statements align with Ayurveda's emphasis on preventive health through daily (dinacharya) and seasonal (ritucharya) regimens. These practices adapt lifestyle choices to natural rhythms, ensuring doshic balance and disease prevention. By aligning with environmental and physiological cycles, Ayurveda reflects its ecological and holistic philosophy of health. Statement 2 accurately explains Statement 1, emphasizing Ayurveda's proactive approach to maintaining harmony and preventing imbalances before they manifest as diseases.

38. **C:** While Statement 1 correctly identifies the Rasas' role in therapeutic actions, Statement 2 incorrectly attributes Sweet Rasa to detoxification and Bitter Rasa to tissue-building. Sweet Rasa nourishes and builds tissues, while Bitter detoxifies and purifies. This misunderstanding highlights the complexity of Ayurvedic pharmacology, where each Rasa has specific roles in balancing doshas. The nuanced classification underscores Ayurveda's intricate understanding of taste as a therapeutic tool in promoting systemic health.

39. **A:** Ayurveda integrates mental health with physical well-being, recognizing the influence of mental states (Sattva, Rajas, Tamas) on doshic balance and overall health. Both statements are true, with Statement 2 providing a valid explanation of Statement 1. This psychosomatic connection reflects Ayurveda's holistic approach, where emotional and mental equilibrium is essential for maintaining physical health. Such integration demonstrates Ayurveda's timeless relevance in addressing complex health interrelations.

40. **C:** The balance of the three doshas is central to Ayurveda's philosophy, but Statement 2 erroneously limits doshas to spiritual energies, disregarding their physiological and psychological roles. Ayurveda considers doshas as dynamic principles governing all bodily and mental functions. This misrepresentation of doshas highlights the importance of their multifaceted role in maintaining health. Treatments aim to balance these energies within the body, mind, and environment.

41. **A:** Rasāyana Tantra aims to rejuvenate and strengthen immunity, aligning with both statements. The therapies focus on enhancing vitality, longevity, and systemic health through herbal tonics, lifestyle adjustments, and meditation. Statement 2 correctly explains the therapeutic mechanism, emphasizing Ayurveda's proactive approach to building resilience against aging and diseases. Rasāyana's role exemplifies Ayurveda's integrative philosophy, where rejuvenation supports prevention and healing.

42. **A:** Panchakarma eliminates toxins and balances Agni, targeting the root causes of diseases. Both statements are true, with Reason (R) providing an accurate explanation of Assertion (A). This therapy reflects Ayurveda's focus on treating systemic imbalances through detoxification and rejuvenation. Panchakarma's comprehensive methodology highlights Ayurveda's holistic philosophy, integrating physical cleansing with mental and emotional rejuvenation for sustained health.

43. **A:** Bhūtavidyā addresses mental health disorders and supernatural influences, incorporating spiritual practices alongside medical treatments. Both statements are true, with Reason (R) accurately explaining Assertion (A). This branch reflects Ayurveda's holistic approach,

where psychological health and spiritual harmony are interwoven. By integrating rituals and therapies, Ayurveda bridges traditional beliefs with clinical interventions, underscoring its comprehensive scope in addressing mental and emotional well-being.

44. C: Vājīkaraṇa Tantra indeed enhances reproductive health, making the assertion true. However, the reason incorrectly claims that it exclusively focuses on herbal and dietary methods. In reality, Vājīkaraṇa also incorporates mental and emotional well-being, ethical conduct, and lifestyle practices. Therefore, the reason is not entirely accurate, making C the correct answer.

45. A: Ritucharya aligns seasonal changes with doshic balance, preventing disease through dietary and lifestyle adjustments. Both statements are true, with Reason (R) accurately explaining Assertion (A). This seasonal adaptation reflects Ayurveda's ecological philosophy, ensuring harmony between internal and external environments. By aligning health practices with nature's rhythms, Ayurveda underscores its preventive and integrative approach to maintaining systemic balance.

46. B: The Charaka Saṃhitā revolutionized Ayurveda by introducing structured diagnostic and therapeutic techniques, emphasizing personalized care and preventive regimens. This focus on balancing doshas through tailored treatments reflects a sophisticated understanding of health. Its methodical approach integrates traditional wisdom with clinical applications, showcasing Ayurveda's adaptability in addressing diverse health challenges while remaining grounded in its philosophical roots.

47. B: The passage clearly states that Suśruta Saṃhitā focuses on surgery (Śalya Tantra) and is notable for pioneering surgical techniques, including rhinoplasty, wound care, and fracture management. It also emphasizes anatomical knowledge and ethical training. This surgical and anatomical focus contrasts with Charaka's emphasis on internal medicine and personalized treatment.

48. B: The colonial era inspired a revival of Ayurveda, focusing on standardization, research, and global integration. These efforts emphasized preserving traditional practices while adapting them to contemporary healthcare frameworks. Ayurveda's resurgence highlights its relevance in addressing modern health challenges, emphasizing sustainable practices and scientific validation. This period underscores Ayurveda's resilience and capacity for innovation, bridging ancient wisdom with modern science.

49. B: Modern science validates Ayurvedic practices through phytochemistry, clinical trials, and integrative medicine. This synergy bridges traditional wisdom with empirical research, emphasizing Ayurveda's relevance in contemporary healthcare. By aligning scientific methodologies with holistic principles, Ayurveda's preventive and therapeutic frameworks gain credibility and acceptance globally. This integration demonstrates Ayurveda's adaptability, reaffirming its timeless insights into health and well-being.

50. C: The final paragraph of the passage explicitly states that despite their different methods, all schools share the common goal of promoting health, preventing disease, and restoring balance in harmony with nature. None of the other options reflect this shared, holistic goal across all four philosophies.

CHAPTER–3

KEY TEXTS, COMMENTARIES, AND BRHATTRAYI & LAGHUTRAYI

Major Texts: Charaka Samhita, Sushruta Samhita, and Ashtanga Hridaya

The foundational texts of Ayurveda, often referred to as the Bṛhattrayī or the "Great Triad," include the Charaka Samhita, Sushruta Samhita, and Ashtanga Hridaya. These texts are the pillars of classical Ayurvedic knowledge, offering profound insights into medical philosophy, diagnosis, treatment, and surgery.

The Charaka Samhita: A Seminal Text in Ayurveda

The Charaka Samhita, attributed to the renowned Ayurvedic scholar Acharya Charaka, is one of the foundational texts of Ayurveda, the ancient Indian system of medicine. This treatise, focused on Kaya Chikitsa (internal medicine), remains a cornerstone in the practice of Ayurvedic medicine, providing profound insights into the principles of health, disease, and treatment. It reflects the intellectual and spiritual depth of ancient Indian medicine, combining practical therapeutic guidelines with philosophical underpinnings.

The Charaka Samhita is revered not only for its comprehensive medical knowledge but also for its systematic methodology, emphasizing the prevention of diseases, the promotion of health, and the holistic management of ailments. The text is organized into eight sections (ashtanga sthanas), each addressing different aspects of medicine. These sections encompass principles, diagnostics, pathology, anatomy, therapeutics, pharmacy, toxicology, and the ultimate goals of treatment. This article delves into the structure, content, and enduring significance of the Charaka Samhita.

Structure of the Charaka Samhita

The Charaka Samhita is divided into eight major sections, each with a specific focus:

Sutrasthana (Principles of Medicine)

The foundational principles of Ayurveda emphasizes health as a balance between body, mind, and spirit. The Sutrasthana elaborates on topics such as the definition of health, the importance of daily routines (Dinacharya), seasonal regimens (Ritucharya), and dietary guidelines. Preventive medicine is a key focus, highlighting the role of lifestyle in maintaining health and preventing disease. The Sutrasthana also discusses the properties of medicinal substances and their classifications, setting the stage for the therapeutic approaches detailed in later sections.

Nidanasthana (Diagnostics)

Diagnostics is critical in Ayurveda, and the Nidanasthana provides a systematic approach to identifying the root causes of diseases. It outlines the eight types of examination (Ashtavidha Pariksha) and various diagnostic methods, including pulse examination, urine analysis, and observation of the tongue, eyes, and skin. The text emphasizes the importance of understanding the interplay of the Tridoshas (Vata, Pitta, and Kapha) in the manifestation of diseases. Nidanasthana also provides a framework for identifying specific pathologies and their underlying causes.

Vimanasthana (Pathology & Specific Doctrines)

The Vimanasthana delves deeper into pathology, focusing on the mechanisms of disease progression and the factors influencing health and disease. It elaborates on the six stages of disease development (Shat Kriya Kal), which are:

- Sanchaya (accumulation of doshas)
- Prakopa (aggravation)
- Prasara (spread)
- Sthana Samshraya (localization)
- Vyakti (manifestation)
- Bheda (complications).

These stages provide a framework for early intervention, enabling practitioners to prevent the progression of disease through timely and appropriate treatments. The Vimanasthana also addresses specific doctrines, such as the effects of diet, environment, and psychological factors on health.

Sharirasthana (Anatomy and Physiology)

The Sharirasthana explores the structure and function of the human body from an Ayurvedic perspective. It describes the seven Dhatus (body tissues), Malas (waste products), and Srotas (body channels), explaining their roles in maintaining physiological balance. This section also addresses embryology, the development of the human body, and the influence of genetics and parental health on offspring. The Sharirasthana highlights the interdependence of physical, mental, and spiritual dimensions in the overall functioning of the body.

Indriyasthana (Signs of Fatal Prognosis)

By observing specific physical and psychological indicators, practitioners can assess the prognosis of diseases and determine the limits of treatment. The Indriyasthana underscores the importance of ethical practice, emphasizing compassion and acceptance in the face of terminal illnesses. It serves as a reminder of the limits of human effort and the inevitability of mortality.

Chikitsasthana (Therapeutics)

The Chikitsasthana is the most extensive section, offering detailed guidance on the treatment of various diseases. It emphasizes the principles of detoxification (Panchakarma), rejuvenation (Rasayana), and disease-specific therapies. The role of Agni (digestive fire) in maintaining health and its relationship with metabolism is discussed extensively. This section also includes dietary recommendations, herbal formulations, and the use of lifestyle modifications to restore balance and promote healing. The Chikitsasthana reflects Ayurveda's holistic approach, integrating physical, mental, and spiritual therapies to address the root causes of diseases.

Kalpasthana (Pharmacy and Toxicology)

The Kalpasthana focuses on the preparation and use of medicinal substances. It provides detailed descriptions of herbal, mineral, and animal-derived formulations, including their pharmacological properties, dosages, and modes of administration. This section also addresses toxicology, highlighting methods for identifying and neutralizing poisons. The emphasis on precision and safety in the preparation of medicines reflects Ayurveda's scientific rigor and ethical considerations in pharmacology.

Siddhisthana (Success of Treatments)

The Siddhisthana concludes the Charaka Samhita by discussing the criteria for successful treatments and the qualities of an accomplished physician. It emphasizes the importance of patient compliance, the practitioner's skill, and the proper selection of medicines. This section also addresses the ethical dimensions of medical practice, underscoring the physician's responsibility to act with compassion, integrity, and wisdom.

KEY CONCEPTS IN THE CHARAKA SAMHITA

Tridosha Theory

The Charaka Samhita places the Tridosha theory at the heart of its medical philosophy. According to this theory:

- Vata governs movement, nerve impulses, and communication.
- Pitta controls metabolism, digestion, and transformation.
- Kapha regulates structure, stability, and immunity.

The balance of these doshas ensures health, while their imbalance leads to disease. The text provides detailed guidance on recognizing doshic imbalances and restoring harmony through personalized treatments.

Shat Kriya Kal (Six Stages of Disease)

The concept of the six stages of disease progression reflects the Charaka Samhita's emphasis on early diagnosis and intervention. By understanding the subtle signs of doshic accumulation and spread, practitioners can prevent diseases from reaching advanced stages. This framework underscores the importance of prevention and holistic management.

Agni and Ama

Agni, or digestive fire, is a central concept in the Charaka Samhita. It governs digestion, metabolism, and immunity. Impaired Agni leads to the formation of Ama (toxins), which disrupts physiological processes and contributes to disease. The text emphasizes restoring Agni through dietary modifications, herbal treatments, and detoxification therapies.

Srotas (Body Channels)

The concept of Srotas highlights the interconnectedness of the body's systems. These channels transport nutrients, waste products, and energy throughout the body. Blockages or disruptions in the Srotas result in disease. The Charaka Samhita provides detailed descriptions of the various types of Srotas and their role in health.

Philosophical Dimensions

The Charaka Samhita transcends physical health, integrating the mind and spirit into its medical philosophy. It emphasizes the importance of ethical behaviour, mental well-being, and spiritual practices in maintaining health. The text highlights the role of a sattvic lifestyle (one based on purity and balance) in promoting mental clarity and emotional stability.

Relevance in Modern Medicine

The Charaka Samhita's holistic approach remains relevant in contemporary medicine. Its emphasis on preventive care, personalized treatments, and the integration of physical, mental, and environmental factors aligns with modern trends in holistic health and integrative medicine. Concepts such as the gut-brain axis, the role of diet in disease prevention, and the importance of mental well-being echo its teachings.

The Charaka Samhita is a timeless testament to the depth and sophistication of ancient Indian medicine. Its integrative approach to health, encompassing diagnosis, treatment, and prevention, continues to inspire practitioners worldwide. By blending empirical observations with philosophical insights, it provides a comprehensive framework for understanding health and disease. Its teachings remind us of the interconnectedness of body, mind, and environment, offering a vision of medicine that is as profound as it is practical.

Sushruta Samhita

The Sushruta Samhita, attributed to Acharya Sushruta, is the cornerstone of surgical knowledge in Ayurveda. It is known for its detailed descriptions of surgical techniques, instruments, and procedures, including plastic surgery and rhinoplasty. This text also contains foundational knowledge on:

Shalya Tantra (Surgery)

Shalakya Tantra (Diseases of the eye, ear, nose, and throat)

- **Anatomy:** The first detailed dissection-based understanding of human anatomy.
- **Trauma Management:** Advanced techniques in dealing with fractures, wounds, and burns.

The Sushruta Samhita not only focuses on surgical interventions but also discusses preventive measures, detoxification therapies (Panchakarma), and the preparation of medicaments.

Ashtanga Hridaya

The Ashtanga Hridaya, compiled by Acharya Vagbhata, integrates the teachings of Charaka and Sushruta into a more concise and systematic text. It is written in poetic form, making it easier to memorize and study. The Ashtanga Hridaya is divided into three sections:

1. Sutrasthana (Foundational Principles)
2. Nidanasthana (Diagnostics)
3. Chikitsasthana (Therapeutics)

The text addresses both preventive and curative measures, offering a balanced view of internal medicine and surgery. Its emphasis on lifestyle, seasonal regimens, and dietary guidance reflects a comprehensive approach to health.

Detailed Study of Bṛhattrayī (The Great Triad)

The Bṛhattrayī, composed of the Charaka Samhita, Sushruta Samhita, and Ashtanga Hridaya, represents the core classical texts of Ayurveda. Each text provides a distinct yet complementary perspective on Ayurvedic knowledge, collectively forming the backbone of Ayurvedic theory and practice.

Core Contributions of the Bṛhattrayī

1. **Holistic Medicine:** A unification of preventive and curative sciences.
2. **Comprehensive Knowledge:** Insights into anatomy, physiology, pathology, pharmacology, and surgery.
3. **Diverse Applications:** From internal medicine to advanced surgical techniques.
4. **Philosophical Foundations:** Exploration of health as a harmony of mind, body, and spirit.
5. **Therapeutic Protocols:** Development of Panchakarma, Rasayana (rejuvenation), and Vajikarana (aphrodisiac) therapies.

Interrelation of the Texts

The Charaka Samhita serves as the foundation for internal medicine, focusing on diagnostics and therapeutics.The Sushruta Samhita complements it with surgical expertise and a deep understanding of anatomy.The Ashtanga Hridaya synthesizes the knowledge from the first two texts, providing a more accessible format for practitioners.

Together, they provide a complete picture of health and disease management.

Detailed Study of Laghutrayī (The Lesser Triad)

The Laghutrayī comprises the Madhava Nidana, Sharngadhara Samhita, and Bhava Prakasha. These texts are later developments in Ayurvedic literature and are considered supplementary to the Bṛhattrayī.

Madhava Nidana

Authored by Madhavakara, this text is a comprehensive guide to diagnosis and pathology. It categorizes diseases and describes their symptoms in detail, making it an essential text for understanding the diagnostic aspect of Ayurveda. It is particularly valued for its systematic classification of diseases.

Sharngadhara Samhita

This text, authored by Sharngadhara, is a concise manual on pharmacology and pharmacy. It introduces the concept of Pulse Diagnosis (Nadi Pariksha) and describes methods of preparing and administering herbal formulations. The text is particularly important for understanding Ayurvedic pharmacology.

Bhava Prakasha

Written by Bhavamishra, this text focuses on herbal medicine and integrates folk medicine with classical Ayurvedic principles. It also provides insights into dietetics, seasonal regimens, and new diseases like syphilis, which were not covered in earlier texts.

IMPORTANT COMMENTARIES AND SCHOLARS

Classical Commentaries

To preserve, clarify, and elaborate upon the ancient texts, numerous scholars wrote commentaries that are invaluable for understanding the classical treatises:

Charaka Samhita Commentaries:

Chakrapani Datta: His commentary, Ayurveda Dipika, explains complex concepts and resolves ambiguities in the Charaka Samhita.

Sushruta Samhita Commentaries:

Dalhana: His commentary, Nibandha Samgraha, provides in-depth explanations of surgical procedures and pharmacological preparations.

Ashtanga Hridaya Commentaries:

Arunadatta: His commentary, Sarvanga Sundara, elucidates Vagbhata's teachings with simplicity.

Hemadri: His work, Ayurveda Rasayana, further explains practical applications.

Renowned Scholars

In addition to the commentators, the following scholars significantly advanced Ayurvedic knowledge:

- **Acharya Charaka:** Considered the father of internal medicine.
- **Acharya Sushruta:** Revered as the father of surgery.
- **Acharya Vagbhata:** A key figure in integrating knowledge from earlier texts.
- **Bhavamishra:** Known for his practical approach to herbal medicine.
- **Madhavakara:** Specialized in diagnostic methodologies.

Relevance of Classical Texts in Modern Ayurvedic Practice

The classical texts of Ayurveda remain profoundly relevant in contemporary practice. Their principles form the foundation for both traditional therapies and integrative medical approaches. The relevance can be understood in the following ways:

Holistic Health Paradigm

The classical texts emphasize the interplay of body, mind, and spirit, which aligns with modern holistic health practices.

Their preventive approach, focusing on dietetics, seasonal regimens, and stress management, resonates with modern wellness trends.

Diagnostic Framework: The six stages of disease progression (Shat Kriya Kal) and the detailed symptomatology in the texts provide a robust diagnostic framework.

Techniques like Nadi Pariksha and Roga Pariksha are increasingly used alongside modern diagnostic tools.

Therapeutics and Pharmacology

Formulations described in classical texts are the basis for many Ayurvedic medicines in use today. The knowledge of Rasayana therapies has applications in anti-aging and immunomodulation.

Surgical Innovations

The Sushruta Samhita's surgical techniques have inspired advancements in reconstructive and cosmetic surgery.

Evidence-Based Practice

Modern research validates the efficacy of many treatments mentioned in the texts, such as the use of Ashwagandha for stress reduction or Neem for skin conditions.

Integration with Modern Medicine

Ayurveda is increasingly integrated into modern healthcare systems, with classical texts providing the theoretical and practical basis for this collaboration.

The Bṛhattrayī and Laghutrayī represent the cornerstone of Ayurvedic wisdom, encompassing the spectrum of medical knowledge from internal medicine and surgery to pharmacology and diagnostics. The enduring relevance of these texts is reflected in their application in modern Ayurvedic practice, where they continue to inspire holistic healing and integrative medicine. Commentaries by eminent scholars have further enriched their understanding, ensuring that the legacy of classical Ayurveda remains vibrant and accessible to future generations. Through their timeless teachings, these texts bridge the ancient and the modern, affirming Ayurveda's place as a dynamic and evolving science.

MULTIPLE CHOICE QUESTIONS

1. In the classical Ayurvedic texts, much emphasis is placed on understanding the subtle interplay of doshas, dhatus, and malas in maintaining homeostasis. If an Ayurvedic physician diagnoses a patient with an imbalance primarily in Vata dosha, which of the following lifestyle prescriptions would align most closely with classical guidelines?

A. Increasing high-intensity exercise to enhance circulation and movement.

B. Following a warm, grounding diet, incorporating oleation and warm spices to pacify Vata.

C. Encouraging cold foods and fasting to counteract dryness and lightness.

D. Prioritizing light and dry foods to reduce excessive moisture in the body.

2. While analyzing the philosophical underpinnings of Ayurveda, a student discovers that the Ayurvedic concept of Prakriti correlates with modern genetic predispositions. Which of the following statements best reflects the convergence of Ayurveda and genetics concerning Prakriti?

A. Prakriti defines an individual's immunity and mental characteristics, completely negating genetic influences.

B. Prakriti reflects inherent doshic tendencies, which are influenced by genetic markers and environmental factors.

C. Genetic predispositions solely determine Prakriti, as environmental effects are not considered significant in Ayurveda.

D. Prakriti and genetic predispositions are unrelated as the former is metaphysical in nature.

3. Given that Ayurveda employs a classification system based on Rasas (tastes), Guna (qualities), and Vipaka (post-digestive effects), which principle would an Ayurvedic scholar use to justify the therapeutic efficacy of herbs in curing diseases?

A. Herbs act solely through biochemical pathways irrelevant to Rasa or Vipaka.

B. The synergistic effects of Rasa, Guna, and Vipaka ensure targeted disease management while balancing doshas.

C. Only the taste (Rasa) of herbs determines their efficacy, excluding their post-digestive effects.

D. Ayurvedic classifications are metaphorical and unrelated to scientific mechanisms.

4. When analyzing the role of Agni in Ayurvedic physiology, a modern researcher attempts to equate it with enzymatic activity and metabolism. In cases of Mandagni (low digestive fire), which physiological symptoms would most likely align with an Ayurvedic description of disease pathology?

A. Rapid metabolic activity and excessive energy generation.

B. Stagnation, indigestion, accumulation of Ama, and systemic inflammation.

C. Enhanced detoxification processes due to reduced digestive efficiency.

D. Increased appetite and rapid digestion with minimal waste production.

5. Charaka Samhita identifies disease prevention as a fundamental tenet of health. If this principle is aligned with modern medicine, which of the following practices would best integrate both systems?

A. Exclusive focus on symptomatic treatment through medications.

B. Encouraging routine check-ups, personalized dietary habits, and stress management.

C. Using synthetic drugs while completely excluding Ayurvedic detox therapies like Panchakarma.

D. Considering disease prevention unnecessary in healthy individuals.

6. The Sushruta Samhita provides unparalleled knowledge on surgical interventions. Which of the following principles underscores its approach to surgery and its philosophical alignment with modern surgical ethics?

A. Surgery should be conducted without patient consent, as the physician's authority is paramount.

B. Surgery is a last resort, performed only when other therapies fail and always with a focus on restoring harmony.

C. The emphasis is solely on technical skill, neglecting patient well-being and holistic recovery.

D. Ayurvedic surgery prioritizes external aesthetics over functional restoration.

7. Ashtanga Hridaya, through its concise poetic form, serves as a cornerstone for Ayurvedic learning. What is the principal reason for its continued relevance in Ayurvedic education?
   A. Its focus is limited to philosophical interpretations, excluding clinical applicability.
   B. The text combines theoretical principles with practical applications, enabling comprehensive understanding.
   C. It excludes foundational concepts like doshas and dhatus, focusing solely on herbs.
   D. Its brevity undermines its utility compared to the Charaka Samhita or Sushruta Samhita.

8. A clinical study explores the Ayurvedic concept of Rasayana (rejuvenation therapies) in geriatric health. Which of the following outcomes would most likely validate Ayurvedic claims regarding Rasayana?
   A. Enhanced cellular regeneration, improved immunity, and delayed aging processes.
   B. Immediate symptomatic relief without any long-term health benefits.
   C. A decrease in digestive efficiency but improvement in cognitive function.
   D. Irregular therapeutic outcomes due to the subjective nature of Rasayana therapies.

9. The Bṛhattrayī, as the great triad of classical Ayurvedic texts, covers a diverse range of disciplines. Which of the following best describes their collective contribution to Ayurvedic practice?
   A. A fragmented understanding of medicine, requiring external validation for coherence.
   B. A complete synthesis of internal medicine, surgery, and lifestyle management, forming a holistic medical system.
   C. A focus on spiritual healing, with little emphasis on physiological and pathological mechanisms.
   D. An exclusive reliance on herbal pharmacology, excluding other therapeutic dimensions.

10. In the context of Laghutrayī, how do later texts such as the Madhava Nidana contribute to the clinical framework of Ayurveda?
   A. They undermine the classical texts by contradicting their principles.
   B. They refine and expand the diagnostic methodologies, making them more systematic and accessible.
   C. They exclude traditional diagnostic practices in favor of modern laboratory testing.
   D. They primarily focus on folk medicine and disregard the foundational principles of Ayurveda.

Directions (Q. No. 11–14): *Scenario-Based Questions*

SCENARIO 1

A comparative study investigates the impact of Ayurvedic detoxification therapies like Panchakarma on chronic inflammatory diseases. The research measures changes in inflammatory markers, such as TNF-alpha and CRP, in patients undergoing traditional therapies. The findings reveal a significant reduction in markers, with correlated improvements in quality-of-life indices.

SCENARIO 2

An environmental survey examines the sustainability of cultivating herbs used in Panchakarma preparations. The study highlights overharvesting and monoculture plantations leading to decreased soil fertility and reduced biodiversity. Efforts to develop eco-friendly cultivation practices show promise but face logistical challenges.

11. Based on Scenario 1, which mechanism best explains the effectiveness of Panchakarma in reducing inflammation?
   A. Panchakarma directly inhibits pro-inflammatory cytokines without influencing detoxification processes.
   B. Panchakarma eliminates accumulated toxins, thereby indirectly lowering systemic inflammation.
   C. Panchakarma suppresses the immune response, which reduces inflammation but weakens immunity.
   D. The observed effects are purely psychosomatic and unrelated to biological mechanisms.

12. Considering Scenario 2, which strategy would most effectively balance ecological sustainability and Ayurvedic practice?
   A. Encouraging synthetic substitutes for herbal formulations.
   B. Promoting community-led agroforestry and sustainable harvesting.
   C. Abandoning the cultivation of Panchakarma-related herbs altogether.
   D. Expanding monoculture plantations to increase yield irrespective of soil health.

13. How does reduced biodiversity, as outlined in Scenario 2, potentially impact the efficacy of Panchakarma therapies described in Scenario 1?
   A. It has no impact as the therapies rely solely on classical procedures.
   B. Lower herb quality due to environmental stressors can reduce therapeutic outcomes.
   C. Biodiversity decline enhances herb potency due to stress adaptation mechanisms.
   D. Environmental factors are irrelevant to the efficacy of Ayurvedic therapies.

14. What comprehensive approach could address the interconnected challenges in both scenarios?
    A. Prioritizing research to standardize herbal formulations while adopting sustainable practices.
    B. Shifting entirely to synthetic alternatives for Panchakarma therapies.
    C. Increasing the commercialization of Panchakarma, disregarding environmental considerations.
    D. Reducing the reliance on Ayurvedic therapies to mitigate ecological damage.

15. The Charaka Samhita outlines several critical principles of Ayurveda. Identify the accurate combination of these principles:
    (a) Tridosha governs all physiological and psychological processes.
    (b) Disease arises from imbalances in dhatus.
    (c) Rasa, Guna, and Vipaka determine the pharmacological action of herbs.
    (d) External surgical interventions are irrelevant in Ayurvedic treatment.

    Choose the correct answer from the options given below:
    A. (a), (b), and (c) only
    B. (a) and (d) only
    C. (a), (b), (c), and (d)
    D. (b) and (d) only

16. The Ashtanga Hridaya consolidates the teachings of Charaka and Sushruta. Choose the correct statements regarding its contributions:
    (a) It is written in prose for easier memorization.
    (b) It provides detailed anatomical descriptions.
    (c) It emphasizes lifestyle practices for preventive healthcare.
    (d) It is recognized as the youngest text of the Bṛhattrayī.

    Choose the correct answer from the options given below:
    A. (a), (b), and (c) only
    B. (b), (c), and (d) only
    C. (c) and (d) only
    D. (a), (c), and (d) only

17. Match the Rasas (tastes) with their primary actions in Ayurveda:
    (a) **Sweet Rasa:** Promotes tissue growth
    (b) **Sour Rasa:** Enhances digestive efficiency
    (c) **Bitter Rasa:** Detoxifies and reduces inflammation
    (d) **Salty Rasa:** Balances Kapha but aggravates Pitta

    Choose the correct answer from the options given below:
    A. (a) and (b) only
    B. (a), (b), and (c) only
    C. (a), (b), (c), and (d)
    D. (b) and (d) only

18. The Laghutrayī contributes specific advancements to Ayurvedic practice. Select the correct set of statements about these texts:
    (a) The Madhava Nidana focuses on diagnostics and classification of diseases.
    (b) The Sharngadhara Samhita introduces Nadi Pariksha (pulse diagnosis).
    (c) The Bhava Prakasha combines Ayurvedic and folk medicinal knowledge.
    (d) All three texts are part of the Bṛhattrayī.

    Choose the correct answer from the options given below:
    A. (a), (b), and (c) only
    B. (a), (c), and (d) only
    C. (b) and (d) only
    D. (a), (b), (c), and (d)

19. Ayurvedic detox therapies emphasize doshic balance. Select the correct principles underlying Panchakarma:
    (a) It targets both the elimination of toxins and rejuvenation.
    (b) Its efficacy depends on patient-specific Prakriti.
    (c) Panchakarma is unrelated to internal medicine principles.
    (d) It is a preventive measure but not a therapeutic intervention.

    Choose the correct answer from the options given below:
    A. (a) and (b) only
    B. (a), (b), and (c) only
    C. (b), (c), and (d) only
    D. (a), (c), and (d) only

20. Match the following herbs with their primary uses:
    (a) Haritaki: Digestive aid and detoxification
    (b) Amalaki: Rich in Vitamin (c), immune booster
    (c) Bibhitaki: Enhances respiratory health
    (d) Neem: Antimicrobial and skin health promoter

    Choose the correct answer from the options given below:
    A. (a) and (b) only
    B. (a), (b), and (c) only
    C. (b), (c), and (d) only
    D. (a), (b), (c), and (d)

21. The Sushruta Samhita outlines methods for surgical procedures. Match the following surgical principles with their descriptions:
    (a) **Shastra Karma:** Use of surgical instruments
    (b) **Anushastra Karma:** Non-surgical interventions
    (c) **Kshara Karma:** Use of alkalis and caustic substances for surgical purposes

Choose the correct answer from the options given below:

A. (a) and (b) only
B. (a), (b), and (c)
C. (b) and (c) only
D. (a) and (c) only

22. The Charaka Samhita advocates for specific lifestyle practices to ensure Tridoshic harmony. Match the following practices with their outcomes:

(a) Dinacharya (daily routine): Maintains dosha balance through regularity.
(b) Ritucharya (seasonal regimen): Adapts diet and behavior to seasonal changes.
(c) Sadvritta (ethical practices): Reduces psychological stress and promotes mental health.

Choose the correct answer from the options given below:

A. (a) and (b) only
B. (a), (b), and (c)
C. (b) and (c) only
D. (a) and (c) only

23. In the Madhava Nidana, the classification of diseases is methodical. Match the following categories with their characteristics:

(a) **Nija Roga:** Diseases originating from internal doshic imbalances.
(b) **Agantuja Roga:** Diseases caused by external factors such as trauma or infections.
(c) **Sahaja Roga:** Congenital or hereditary diseases.

Choose the correct answer from the options given below:

A. (a), (b), and (c)
B. (a) and (b) only
C. (b) and (c) only
D. (a) and (c) only

24. The Bhava Prakasha integrates classical and folk medicine. Which of the following sets correctly describes its key focus areas?

(a) Herbal pharmacology and therapeutic properties.
(b) Seasonal regimens for maintaining health.
(c) Pulse diagnosis as a diagnostic tool.
(d) Diseases not covered in earlier texts.

Choose the correct answer from the options given below:

A. (a) and (b) only
B. (a), (b), and (d) only
C. (a), (c), and (d) only
D. (a), (b), (c), and (d)

25. Match List–I (Doshas) with List–II (Primary Characteristics):

List–I	List–II
(a) Vata	1. Responsible for movement and bodily functions
(b) Pitta	2. Governs metabolism and transformation
(c) Kapha	3. Provides stability and structural support

Choose the correct answer:

A. (a)-1, (b)-2, (c)-3
B. (a)-3, (b)-1, (c)-2
C. (a)-2, (b)-3, (c)-1
D. (a)-1, (b)-3, (c)-2

26. Match List–I (Rasas) with List–II (Associated Benefits):

List–I	List–II
(a) Sweet	1. Promotes tissue growth and nourishment
(b) Bitter	2. Detoxifies and reduces inflammation
(c) Sour	3. Enhances digestive function
(d) Astringent	4. Controls bleeding and strengthens tissues

Choose the correct answer from the options given below:

A. (a)-1, (b)-2, (c)-3, (d)-4
B. (a)-2, (b)-1, (c)-4, (d)-3
C. (a)-3, (b)-4, (c)-1, (d)-2
D. (a)-1, (b)-4, (c)-3, (d)-2

27. Match List–I (Therapeutic Principles) with List–II (Application in Ayurveda):

List–I	List–II
(a) Panchakarma	1. Detoxification and rejuvenation therapy
(b) Rasayana	2. Anti-aging and immune-boosting therapies
(c) Sadvritta	3. Ethical practices to promote mental health
(d) Ritucharya	4. Seasonal adjustments to maintain doshic balance

Choose the correct answer from the options given below:

A. (a)-1, (b)-2, (c)-3, (d)-4
B. (a)-2, (b)-3, (c)-4, (d)-1
C. (a)-3, (b)-4, (c)-1, (d)-2
D. (a)-4, (b)-1, (c)-2, (d)-3

28. Match List–I (Classical Texts) with List–II (Key Contributions):

List–I	List–II
(a) Charaka Samhita	1. Focus on Kaya Chikitsa (Internal Medicine)
(b) Sushruta Samhita	2. Comprehensive approach to surgery and anatomy
(c) Ashtanga Hridaya	3. Concise text combining therapeutic and surgical insights
(d) Madhava Nidana	4. Compilation of diagnostics and pathology

Choose the correct answer from the options given below:

A. (a)-1, (b)-2, (c)-3, (d)-4
B. (a)-4, (b)-1, (c)-2, (d)-3
C. (a)-3, (b)-4, (c)-1, (d)-2
D. (a)-1, (b)-3, (c)-4, (d)-2

29. Match List–I (Ayurvedic Herbs) with List–II (Key Properties):

List–I	List–II
(a) Haritaki	1. Digestive aid and detoxification
(b) Bibhitaki	2. Enhances respiratory health
(c) Amalaki	3. Rich in Vitamin (c), promotes immunity
(d) Ashwagandha	4. Adaptogen and stress reliever

Choose the correct answer from the options given below:

A. (a)-1, (b)-2, (c)-3, (d)-4
B. (a)-4, (b)-3, (c)-2, (d)-1
C. (a)-3, (b)-4, (c)-1, (d)-2
D. (a)-2, (b)-1, (c)-4, (d)-3

30. Match List–I (Body Components) with List–II (Ayurvedic Dhatus):

List–I	List–II
(a) Blood	1. Rakta
(b) Muscle	2. Mamsa
(c) Fat	3. Meda
(d) Bone	4. Asthi

Choose the correct answer from the options given below:

A. (a)-1, (b)-2, (c)-3, (d)-4
B. (a)-3, (b)-4, (c)-2, (d)-1
C. (a)-4, (b)-1, (c)-2, (d)-3
D. (a)-2, (b)-3, (c)-4, (d)-1

31. Match List–I (Ayurvedic Routines) with List–II (Benefits):

List–I	List–II
(a) Dinacharya	1. Maintains daily health routines
(b) Ritucharya	2. Aligns the body with seasonal changes
(c) Sadvritta	3. Ethical practices to ensure harmony
(d) Yoga	4. Promotes physical and mental balance

Choose the correct answer from the options given below:

A. (a)-1, (b)-2, (c)-3, (d)-4
B. (a)-4, (b)-1, (c)-2, (d)-3
C. (a)-2, (b)-3, (c)-4, (d)-1
D. (a)-3, (b)-4, (c)-1, (d)-2

32. Match List–I (Ayurvedic Therapies) with List–II (Processes):

List–I	List–II
(a) Vamana	1. Inducing therapeutic emesis
(b) Virechana	2. Purging through herbal laxatives
(c) Nasya	3. Nasal cleansing and medication
(d) Basti	4. Administration of medicated oils or liquids via enema

Choose the correct answer from the options given below:

A. (a)-1, (b)-2, (c)-3, (d)-4
B. (a)-3, (b)-4, (c)-1, (d)-2
C. (a)-4, (b)-1, (c)-2, (d)-3
D. (a)-2, (b)-3, (c)-4, (d)-1

33. Match List–I (Dosha Imbalances) with List–II (Symptoms):

List–I	List–II
(a) Vata imbalance	1. Joint pain, dry skin, and anxiety
(b) Pitta imbalance	2. Indigestion, heat intolerance, and irritability
(c) Kapha imbalance	3. General lethargy and water retention
(d) Tridoshic imbalance	4. Complex systemic disorders involving multiple symptoms

Choose the correct answer from the options given below:

A. (a)-1, (b)-2, (c)-3, (d)-4
B. (a)-4, (b)-3, (c)-2, (d)-1
C. (a)-3, (b)-4, (c)-1, (d)-2
D. (a)-2, (b)-1, (c)-4, (d)-3

34. Match List–I (Panchakarma Stages) with List–II (Description):

List–I	List–II
(a) Poorva Karma	1. Preparation phase involving snehana and swedana
(b) Pradhana Karma	2. Primary detoxification phase (e.g., Vamana, Virechana)
(c) Paschat Karma	3. Post-procedural care for restoration and rejuvenation
(d) Shamana Karma	4. Palliative care for doshic balance

Choose the correct answer from the options given below:

A. (a)-1, (b)-2, (c)-3, (d)-4
B. (a)-4, (b)-1, (c)-2, (d)-3
C. (a)-2, (b)-3, (c)-4, (d)-1
D. (a)-3, (b)-4, (c)-1, (d)-2

Directions (Q.No. 35–39): *Following questions are based on statement 1 and statement 2. Read both the statements carefully and choose the correct answer from the options given below:*

A. Both Statement 1 and Statement 2 are true, and Statement 2 is the correct explanation of Statement 1.
B. Both Statement 1 and Statement 2 are true, but Statement 2 is not the correct explanation of Statement 1.
C. Statement 1 is true, but Statement 2 is false.
D. Statement 1 is false, but Statement 2 is true.
E. Both Statement 1 and Statement 2 are false.

35. Statement 1: The Charaka Samhita emphasizes that disease prevention is more critical than disease management.

Statement 2: Preventive healthcare in Ayurveda includes lifestyle regimens like Dinacharya and Ritucharya, which are designed to maintain doshic harmony.

36. Statement 1: The Sushruta Samhita is the only classical Ayurvedic text that discusses the concept of Rasayana therapies.

Statement 2: Rasayana therapies focus on rejuvenation, anti-aging, and improving immunity.

37. Statement 1: In the Ashtanga Hridaya, the concept of Agni (digestive fire) is directly correlated with metabolic efficiency and overall health.

Statement 2: Impairment of Agni leads to the accumulation of Ama (toxins), which Ayurveda considers the root cause of disease.

38. Statement 1: The Madhava Nidana provides a systematic classification of diseases but does not elaborate on treatment protocols.

Statement 2: Diagnostic clarity in the Madhava Nidana enhances a physician's ability to personalize treatments based on the doshic imbalance.

39. Statement 1: The principles of Panchakarma in Ayurveda are exclusively designed for curative purposes.

Statement 2: Panchakarma therapies include preparatory, main, and post-treatment stages, which can also be used for preventive health.

Directions (Q. No. 40–45): *There are two statements in each question. One is labelled as Assertion (A) and the other is as Reason (R). Read both the statements and choose the correct answer from the options given below:*

A. Both (A) and (R) are true, and (R) is the correct explanation of (A).
B. Both (A) and (R) are true, but (R) is not the correct explanation of (A).
C. (A) is true, but (R) is false.
D. (A) is false, but (R) is true.
E. Both (A) and (R) are false.

40. Assertion (A): The Charaka Samhita and Sushruta Samhita provide complementary approaches to health management in Ayurveda.

Reason (R): While the Charaka Samhita focuses on internal medicine, the Sushruta Samhita is primarily concerned with surgical interventions.

41. Assertion (A): Seasonal regimens (Ritucharya) are an integral part of Ayurvedic practice.

Reason (R): Seasonal changes influence doshic balance, requiring modifications in diet, behaviour, and therapies to prevent disease.

42. Assertion (A): Rasayana therapies are central to anti-aging and longevity in Ayurveda.

Reason (R): These therapies primarily enhance Agni and eliminate Ama, thereby reducing oxidative stress at a cellular level.

43. Assertion (A): The Bhava Prakasha is significant for integrating folk medicine into classical Ayurvedic frameworks.

Reason (R): The text incorporates diseases not covered in earlier texts, highlighting the evolving nature of Ayurvedic practice.

44. Assertion (A): Panchakarma therapies are applicable only after a disease has been diagnosed.

Reason (R): Panchakarma is primarily used for detoxification, which can also be preventive when performed on healthy individuals.

45. Assertion (A): The Ashtanga Hridaya synthesizes the teachings of Charaka and Sushruta to provide a concise guide for practitioners.

Reason (R): It is written in poetic form to make complex Ayurvedic principles more accessible for memorization and study.

Directions (Q. No. 46–50): *Read the passage carefully and answer the questions given below:*

The relevance of classical texts in modern Ayurvedic practice remains a cornerstone of integrative medicine. Texts like the Charaka Samhita, Sushruta Samhita, and Ashtanga Hridaya provide foundational principles for diagnostics, therapeutics, and preventive healthcare. In contemporary practice, these texts find resonance in several ways. The Tridosha theory offers a framework for personalized medicine, where individual constitution (Prakriti) guides therapeutic choices. For instance, patients with Vata dominance are treated with warming, grounding therapies, while Pitta patients benefit from cooling remedies. Similarly, Panchakarma therapies, as described in these classical texts, are now recognized globally for their detoxifying and rejuvenating effects. Modern scientific research validates these therapies, demonstrating their ability to reduce inflammatory markers and improve metabolic health.

Moreover, the Sushruta Samhita's surgical techniques, including rhinoplasty, have inspired advancements in reconstructive surgery. The systematic classification of diseases in texts like the Madhava Nidana enhances the diagnostic precision required for individualized treatments. However, challenges persist. Environmental degradation and overharvesting of medicinal plants, such as Amalaki, jeopardize the quality of Ayurvedic formulations. Additionally, efforts to integrate Ayurveda into modern healthcare systems must address skepticism about its empirical validity. Despite these hurdles, the classical texts continue to inspire holistic approaches to health, emphasizing prevention, lifestyle modifications, and harmony between body, mind, and environment.

46. According to the passage, which of the following best explains why the Tridosha theory is significant in modern personalized medicine?

A. It relies solely on the biochemical composition of Ayurvedic herbs for therapeutic effects.
B. It provides a framework for tailoring treatments based on individual constitutions and imbalances.
C. It disregards the influence of environmental factors on doshic balance.
D. It prioritizes spiritual healing over physical health outcomes.

47. Based on the passage, which of the following best describes the contribution of Panchakarma therapies to global healthcare?

A. They are exclusively detoxifying therapies with no additional health benefits.
B. Scientific studies validate their role in reducing inflammation and improving metabolic health.
C. They are considered traditional practices with little relevance to contemporary health systems.
D. Panchakarma is effective only for managing chronic diseases but has no preventive applications.

48. What does the passage suggest about the role of the Sushruta Samhita in modern surgical practices?

A. It focuses solely on ancient surgical techniques, which are irrelevant to modern medicine.
B. Its methods, such as rhinoplasty, have influenced advancements in reconstructive and cosmetic surgery.
C. It lacks the anatomical understanding necessary for modern surgical innovations.
D. The text emphasizes spiritual approaches to surgery rather than practical applications.

49. Which of the following challenges to the integration of Ayurveda into modern healthcare systems is highlighted in the passage?

A. Lack of patient interest in Ayurvedic therapies.
B. Overdependence on synthetic alternatives for Ayurvedic formulations.
C. Skepticism regarding the empirical validity of Ayurvedic principles and practices.
D. The inability of Ayurvedic therapies to address chronic diseases.

50. What comprehensive approach could most effectively address the challenges posed by environmental degradation of medicinal plants, as mentioned in the passage?

A. Large-scale production of synthetic alternatives to replace endangered Ayurvedic herbs.
B. Community-driven initiatives for sustainable harvesting and cultivation of medicinal plants.
C. Reduction in the global reliance on Ayurvedic formulations to preserve wild plant populations.
D. Encouraging the use of less effective herbs to decrease the demand for endangered species.

ANSWER WITH EXPLANATIONS

1. B: The correct treatment for Vata imbalance includes a warm, grounding diet and practices that reduce dryness and irregularity. Classical Ayurveda links Vata to qualities like coldness, lightness, and movement, which require counterbalancing. The focus on oleation (oils) and warm spices aids digestion and calms erratic Vata energies. High-intensity exercise and fasting would aggravate Vata's light and dry nature, while light, dry foods are unsuitable for pacifying Vata imbalances. By restoring warmth and stability, these treatments align with the Ayurvedic understanding of harmonizing doshas, showing how personalized therapies work within the Tridosha framework.

2. B: Ayurveda's Prakriti considers genetic predispositions and environmental factors in determining individual constitutions. Prakriti encapsulates doshic tendencies that influence physical, mental, and metabolic traits. This perspective mirrors genetics, as both systems recognize innate tendencies while factoring in lifestyle and environment. Modern personalized medicine incorporates genetic data similarly to Ayurveda's emphasis on understanding constitution-specific needs. By acknowledging both genetic and external influences, Ayurveda advances precision medicine, bridging ancient wisdom and contemporary science. This holistic view underscores the relevance of Ayurvedic principles in today's evolving medical frameworks.

3. **B:** Rasa, Guna, and Vipaka form the core of Ayurvedic pharmacology, enabling a nuanced understanding of herbs. Unlike modern pharmacology, which often isolates biochemical pathways, Ayurveda integrates taste, quality, and digestive transformation to predict therapeutic actions. Herbs are evaluated for their systemic impact, ensuring doshic balance while addressing specific diseases. For example, bitter herbs detoxify by reducing Pitta and Kapha, while sweet herbs nourish tissues. This synergy demonstrates Ayurveda's deep exploration of holistic health, emphasizing how natural remedies interact with physiology. Thus, Ayurvedic classifications are far from metaphorical, aligning with pharmacodynamics principles.

4. **B:** Mandagni, or weak digestive fire, is pivotal in Ayurvedic pathology. Impaired digestion results in Ama (toxins), a central cause of disease, leading to stagnation, systemic inflammation, and metabolic disturbances. Ayurveda emphasizes Agni's role in transforming food into energy and nutrients, highlighting its physiological importance. Weak digestion, in this context, directly correlates with issues like bloating and indigestion. This perspective aligns with contemporary views linking metabolic inefficiency to chronic diseases, showing Ayurveda's enduring relevance. Consequently, addressing Agni is foundational for restoring health and preventing disease progression.

5. **B:** Ayurveda emphasizes preventive healthcare through regular routines, stress management, and personalized dietetics, aligning seamlessly with modern health principles. Disease prevention in Ayurveda involves understanding Prakriti, observing seasonal regimens, and maintaining lifestyle balance. Modern medicine's focus on screenings and proactive care mirrors this approach, demonstrating Ayurveda's forward-thinking framework. Excluding preventive measures risks overlooking underlying imbalances, potentially leading to chronic conditions. By integrating lifestyle management with early interventions, Ayurveda provides a holistic model for sustaining health, reflecting its compatibility with contemporary healthcare strategies.

6. **B:** The Sushruta Samhita adopts surgery as a therapeutic last resort, emphasizing its role in restoring harmony rather than merely fixing mechanical problems. Its ethical guidelines align with modern surgical ethics, which prioritize patient consent and well-being. Sushruta's focus on reconstructive techniques like rhinoplasty and wound care demonstrates the sophistication of ancient Ayurvedic surgery. This perspective, combining technical excellence with holistic recovery, showcases Ayurveda's balance of curative and restorative goals. Contrary to focusing only on physical outcomes, Ayurvedic surgery integrates body-mind harmony, aligning with modern healthcare values.

7. **B:** The Ashtanga Hridaya synthesizes key principles from Charaka Samhita and Sushruta Samhita, creating a concise yet practical text for students and practitioners. Its poetic structure ensures accessibility without sacrificing depth, while its emphasis on daily and seasonal regimens reflects its preventive approach. Unlike purely theoretical works, it integrates therapeutic and diagnostic insights, making it versatile. Its continued use in Ayurvedic education highlights its adaptability to modern needs, bridging traditional and contemporary healthcare approaches. Thus, it remains a cornerstone for understanding Ayurveda comprehensively.

8. **A:** Rasayana therapies, central to Ayurveda's anti-aging principles, are validated through research showing improved cellular regeneration and immune function. These therapies enhance systemic rejuvenation, reducing oxidative stress and inflammation. Ayurveda's holistic focus on vitality aligns with modern science, which explores herbal compounds' potential in combating aging. The multi-faceted benefits of Rasayana go beyond symptomatic relief, addressing root causes of degeneration. Such therapies emphasize long-term wellness, demonstrating Ayurveda's sophistication in preventive and restorative healthcare. This integrative approach reaffirms Rasayana's global relevance.

9. **B:** The Bṛhattrayī collectively addresses the spectrum of healthcare, encompassing internal medicine, surgery, and preventive measures. Each text contributes distinct expertise: Charaka Samhita focuses on diagnostics and therapeutics, Sushruta Samhita advances surgical techniques, and Ashtanga Hridaya synthesizes their insights: Together, they create a comprehensive system, offering holistic solutions for health and disease. Unlike

fragmented approaches, this synergy reflects Ayurveda's depth and adaptability, underscoring its relevance in integrative medicine. By uniting diverse disciplines, the Bṛhattrayī exemplifies the sophistication of classical Ayurveda.

10. **B:** The Madhava Nidana refined diagnostic methodologies, offering systematic disease classifications that enhance Ayurvedic practice. Its focus on diagnostics complements the therapeutic insights of earlier texts, ensuring a complete clinical framework. Pulse diagnosis in Sharngadhara Samhita and pharmacological advancements in Bhava Prakasha reflect complementary contributions of the Laghutrayī. These texts collectively adapt Ayurveda for evolving needs, integrating traditional wisdom with newer insights. Their precision in diagnostics addresses modern demands for personalized medicine, ensuring Ayurveda's continued relevance.

11. **B:** Triphala's effect on gut microbiota diversity indirectly boosts systemic immunity. The Ayurvedic understanding of gut health aligns with modern research emphasizing the gut-immune axis. By improving gut-associated lymphoid tissue (GALT) activity, Triphala enhances the production of immunoglobulins like IgA and regulates systemic inflammatory markers such as CRP. This reflects the interconnectedness Ayurveda attributes to digestion and overall health. Unlike direct immune stimulation, its role in microbiota diversity highlights Ayurveda's preventive and restorative focus, validating the therapeutic relevance of Triphala in modern healthcare.

12. **B:** Sustainable harvesting, particularly through traditional agroforestry systems, addresses both ecological and medicinal challenges. Ayurvedic formulations depend on the integrity of bioactive compounds in plants like Amalaki, which decline under environmental stress. Community-based conservation ensures biodiversity, protects local livelihoods, and maintains medicinal quality. Monoculture plantations, while increasing yield, exacerbate soil degradation and biodiversity loss. Synthetic substitutes may fail to replicate the synergistic effects of natural compounds. Balancing global demand with sustainability ensures the long-term viability of Ayurvedic practices, reflecting their adaptability to environmental challenges.

13. **B:** Reduced biodiversity and environmental stressors can lower the quality and potency of herbs, affecting the overall therapeutic outcomes of Panchakarma, which relies heavily on herbal formulations.

14. **A:** Standardizing herbal formulations ensures consistency in therapy, while sustainable practices protect environmental resources, balancing therapeutic efficacy and ecological responsibility.

15. **A:** The Charaka Samhita emphasizes the Tridosha framework, linking physiological and psychological processes to doshic balance. Disease arises from dhatu imbalances, while Rasa, Guna, and Vipaka guide therapeutic interventions. Surgery, though addressed in the Sushruta Samhita, is supplementary in Ayurveda, as prevention and internal medicine take precedence. These principles highlight the interconnectedness of body and mind, showcasing Ayurveda's holistic approach. Its comprehensive understanding of health ensures relevance in personalized and integrative medicine, validating its foundational principles across disciplines.

16. **D:** The Ashtanga Hridaya synthesizes therapeutic and surgical knowledge while emphasizing preventive healthcare. Written in poetic form, it is the youngest of the Bṛhattrayī and focuses on making Ayurvedic concepts accessible. Unlike the Sushruta Saṃhita, it does not delve deeply into anatomy but prioritizes lifestyle practices and seasonal regimens. Its ability to combine the essence of earlier texts into a practical guide demonstrates its importance in Ayurvedic education. By addressing preventive care and therapy, it remains a cornerstone of holistic medicine.

17. **C:** Rasas and their therapeutic actions are integral to Ayurvedic pharmacology. Sweet Rasa promotes tissue nourishment, Sour Rasa enhances digestion, Bitter Rasa detoxifies, and Astringent Rasa strengthens tissues. These principles align with Ayurveda's holistic understanding of taste and health. The multi-dimensional impact of Rasas ensures targeted doshic balance, addressing both root causes and symptoms of diseases. This synergy, rooted in Ayurveda's understanding of natural elements, reflects its advanced pharmacological framework. These classifications remain relevant in developing natural remedies in modern times.

18. **A:** The Laghutrayī enhances Ayurveda's diagnostic and therapeutic framework. The Madhava Nidana focuses on systematic disease classification, the Sharngadhara Samhita introduces innovations like pulse diagnosis, and the Bhava Prakasha integrates folk medicine with classical insights. These texts complement the Bṛhattrayī, providing specificity and adapting Ayurveda for contemporary challenges. Their emphasis on diagnostics and pharmacology ensures Ayurveda's applicability in modern healthcare, bridging traditional wisdom with clinical precision. This highlights the adaptability of Ayurvedic principles across time and contexts.

19. A: Panchakarma targets both detoxification and rejuvenation, reflecting Ayurveda's preventive and curative dimensions. Its efficacy depends on understanding Prakriti, as treatments are tailored to individual constitutions. Panchakarma aligns with internal medicine by addressing systemic imbalances, making it foundational in Ayurvedic practice. Its preparatory, main, and post-treatment stages reflect a structured approach to restoring health. The therapies' holistic impact validates their role in integrative medicine, emphasizing Ayurveda's unique combination of tradition and modern relevance.

20. D: The listed herbs and their uses align with Ayurveda's understanding of pharmacology. Haritaki aids digestion and detoxification, Amalaki boosts immunity with its high Vitamin C content, Bibhitaki supports respiratory health, and Neem is a potent antimicrobial. These properties highlight Ayurveda's intricate knowledge of herbs, integrating their effects for personalized therapies. Their combined use in formulations like Triphala reflects Ayurveda's emphasis on synergistic remedies, ensuring holistic health. This multi-dimensional approach remains relevant in addressing contemporary health challenges.

21. B: The Sushruta Samhita categorizes surgical methods into Shastra Karma (surgical tools), Anushastra Karma (non-surgical methods), and Kshara Karma (alkalis). These classifications showcase Ayurveda's surgical advancements, including innovative approaches to wound healing and reconstruction. This holistic surgical framework balances curative interventions with minimal invasiveness. Its systematic approach ensures the continued relevance of Ayurvedic surgery, influencing modern techniques while emphasizing precision and safety. This highlights the scientific depth of ancient medical systems.

22. B: Dinacharya, Ritucharya, and Sadvritta represent Ayurveda's comprehensive approach to health. Daily and seasonal regimens ensure doshic harmony, while ethical practices reduce stress and promote mental well-being. This interconnected framework highlights Ayurveda's focus on preventive healthcare, linking lifestyle and morality to overall health. By addressing physiological and psychological imbalances, these principles align with modern wellness trends. Their relevance in personalized medicine showcases Ayurveda's enduring adaptability, bridging ancient practices with contemporary health solutions.

23. A: The Madhava Nidana systematically classifies diseases, distinguishing between Nija Roga (internal doshic imbalances), Agantuja Roga (external causes such as trauma), and Sahaja Roga (congenital conditions). This classification highlights Ayurveda's diagnostic depth, enabling precise identification and treatment planning. Unlike symptom-based approaches, Ayurveda addresses root causes, ensuring holistic management. By integrating internal and external factors, this system demonstrates Ayurveda's sophistication in understanding health and disease. This clarity continues to inform personalized therapeutic strategies, reflecting its relevance in modern clinical frameworks.

24. B: The Bhava Prakasha emphasizes herbal pharmacology, seasonal regimens, and previously undocumented diseases. Its integration of folk and classical medicine reflects Ayurveda's evolving nature. The text addresses gaps in earlier works, making it comprehensive and relevant. By combining traditional practices with newer insights, it adapts Ayurveda for changing needs. Its focus on maintaining health through seasonal adjustments ensures relevance in preventive medicine. This adaptability showcases Ayurveda's resilience, bridging ancient wisdom with contemporary challenges, thus enriching Ayurvedic practice.

25. A: In Ayurveda, Vata governs movement and bodily functions, Pitta regulates metabolism and transformation, and Kapha provides stability and structural support. This classification aligns with the principles of Ayurveda, where each dosha influences physiological and psychological processes. Balancing these doshas ensures health, reflecting Ayurveda's holistic view of bodily harmony. These insights form the basis for personalized medicine, enabling targeted therapeutic interventions. This doshic understanding continues to guide both traditional practices and integrative approaches, emphasizing Ayurveda's depth.

26. A: Ayurveda classifies Rasas (tastes) based on their actions: Sweet Rasa nourishes tissues, Sour Rasa enhances digestion, Bitter Rasa detoxifies, and Astringent Rasa strengthens tissues. This framework ensures a nuanced understanding of how taste influences physiology. By integrating dietary and pharmacological principles, Ayurveda addresses imbalances at their root. This multi-dimensional approach showcases Ayurveda's sophistication in using natural elements for targeted therapies, ensuring doshic harmony and long-term health.

27. A: The therapeutic principles of Panchakarma, Rasayana, Sadvritta, and Ritucharya align with their respective roles in Ayurveda. Detoxification and rejuvenation therapies complement seasonal and ethical practices, forming a comprehensive health model. These interconnected strategies emphasize prevention, treatment, and lifestyle balance. Their synergy demonstrates Ayurveda's holistic approach, integrating physical, mental, and environmental health. These principles remain pivotal in modern healthcare, validating Ayurveda's enduring adaptability and relevance.

28. A: The Charaka Samhita, Sushruta Samhita, Ashtanga Hridaya, and Madhava Nidana offer complementary insights into internal medicine, surgery, therapeutic synthesis, and diagnostics. Together, they form a comprehensive framework for Ayurvedic practice. These texts reflect Ayurveda's depth, addressing health from multiple dimensions. Their systematic approaches ensure clarity and precision, enabling personalized care. This integration highlights Ayurveda's adaptability and relevance across diverse medical contexts, bridging ancient and modern healthcare systems.

29. A: Herbs like Haritaki, Bibhitaki, Amalaki, and Ashwagandha are central to Ayurvedic pharmacology. Haritaki detoxifies, Bibhitaki supports respiratory health, Amalaki boosts immunity, and Ashwagandha relieves stress. These properties reflect Ayurveda's sophisticated understanding of herbal actions. By addressing specific imbalances while enhancing systemic health, these herbs embody Ayurveda's holistic philosophy. Their enduring relevance underscores the integration of traditional knowledge with contemporary therapeutic needs, showcasing Ayurveda's multi-faceted approach.

30. A: In Ayurveda, Rakta (blood), Mamsa (muscle), Meda (fat), and Asthi (bone) represent essential dhatus. Each supports specific functions: Rakta carries oxygen, Mamsa builds muscle, Meda regulates fat storage, and Asthi provides structure. Balancing these dhatus ensures systemic harmony, reflecting Ayurveda's depth in understanding human physiology. These principles guide therapeutic interventions, ensuring holistic health. By addressing imbalances at this foundational level, Ayurveda emphasizes the interconnectedness of bodily systems.

31. A: Dinacharya (daily routines), Ritucharya (seasonal regimens), Sadvritta (ethical practices), and Yoga represent Ayurveda's comprehensive health model. These practices ensure physical, mental, and spiritual well-being by aligning lifestyles with natural rhythms. Their interconnectedness highlights Ayurveda's emphasis on prevention and harmony. This holistic framework remains relevant in promoting sustainable health, reflecting Ayurveda's adaptability in modern wellness strategies. By integrating these practices, Ayurveda offers a balanced approach to achieving long-term health.

32. A: The stages of Panchakarma include Vamana (emesis), Virechana (laxative therapy), Nasya (nasal cleansing), and Basti (enema). Each targets specific toxins, addressing imbalances in doshas. This structured approach ensures a comprehensive detoxification process, restoring systemic harmony. Panchakarma's efficacy lies in its multi-dimensional methodology, emphasizing personalized therapies. By integrating these treatments, Ayurveda addresses root causes of disease, showcasing its depth and precision in holistic healing practices.

33. A: Doshic imbalances manifest distinct symptoms: Vata causes joint pain and anxiety, Pitta leads to irritability and heat intolerance, and Kapha results in lethargy and water retention. Tridoshic imbalances create complex systemic disorders. Ayurveda's understanding of these patterns ensures precise diagnosis and treatment, reflecting its sophisticated approach to health. By addressing specific imbalances, Ayurveda offers tailored therapies that restore harmony, demonstrating its relevance in personalized medicine.

34. A: The stages of Panchakarma—Poorva Karma (preparation), Pradhana Karma (primary therapy), Paschat Karma (post-treatment), and Shamana Karma (palliative care)—reflect Ayurveda's structured approach to detoxification. Each stage addresses specific aspects of health, ensuring comprehensive rejuvenation. This methodology emphasizes personalized care, aligning treatments with individual constitutions. By integrating these stages, Ayurveda provides a holistic model for restoring systemic harmony, reflecting its adaptability and relevance in contemporary healthcare.

35. A: The Charaka Samhita prioritizes disease prevention over treatment, aligning with the principles of Dinacharya (daily routines) and Ritucharya (seasonal regimens). These practices maintain doshic harmony, ensuring long-term health. Preventive healthcare reflects Ayurveda's focus on sustainability, avoiding the progression of imbalances into diseases. By integrating these regimens, Ayurveda emphasizes the interconnectedness of lifestyle, environment, and health. The statement highlights the enduring relevance of classical Ayurvedic principles, which resonate with modern preventive approaches, showcasing their practical and philosophical depth in holistic medicine.

36. D: While the Sushruta Samhita primarily focuses on surgery, Rasayana therapies are elaborated in other texts like the Charaka Samhita. These therapies aim at rejuvenation, anti-aging, and enhancing immunity, reflecting Ayurveda's comprehensive view of health. The distinction between therapeutic domains demonstrates the specialization within classical texts. This specialization ensures that each text contributes uniquely to Ayurveda's framework, while collectively they address diverse medical needs. This integrative approach underscores Ayurveda's adaptability and its ability to offer multi-faceted solutions for health and longevity.

37. A: The Ashtanga Hridaya correlates Agni (digestive fire) with metabolic efficiency and health, emphasizing its pivotal role in Ayurveda. Impairment of Agni leads to the accumulation of Ama (toxins), disrupting doshic balance and causing disease. This concept aligns with modern understanding of metabolism and its impact on systemic health. By focusing on Agni, Ayurveda provides preventive and curative strategies to enhance digestion and detoxification. This holistic framework highlights Ayurveda's depth in linking digestion with overall well-being, offering timeless insights into health management.

38. A: The Madhava Nidana systematically classifies diseases, enhancing diagnostic clarity. Though it does not elaborate on treatment, its precision supports personalized therapies based on doshic imbalances. This text complements earlier works like the Charaka Samhita, ensuring a comprehensive understanding of disease. By focusing on diagnosis, it aligns with modern precision medicine, where accurate identification of conditions is crucial for effective treatment. This demonstrates the depth and relevance of classical texts in contemporary clinical practice, bridging traditional wisdom with modern methodologies.

39. D: Panchakarma therapies are designed for both preventive and curative purposes. Though primarily detoxifying, they include preparatory and post-treatment stages that restore systemic balance, even in healthy individuals. This preventive application aligns with Ayurveda's holistic philosophy, which emphasizes maintaining health alongside treating disease. The structured stages of Panchakarma reflect Ayurveda's precision and adaptability, ensuring its relevance in modern healthcare. By addressing root causes, these therapies exemplify Ayurveda's unique approach to sustainable health, blending tradition with integrative practices.

40. A: The Charaka Samhita and Sushruta Samhita complement each other, focusing on internal medicine and surgery, respectively. This division reflects Ayurveda's holistic approach, where diagnostics, therapeutics, and surgical interventions form an integrated system. The collaboration of these texts demonstrates the depth of classical Ayurvedic knowledge, balancing curative and preventive aspects. By addressing diverse medical needs, these texts ensure a comprehensive healthcare framework, showcasing Ayurveda's adaptability to evolving clinical demands while maintaining its foundational principles.

41. A: Seasonal regimens (Ritucharya) adapt diet, behaviour, and therapies to align with doshic changes caused by seasonal transitions. This prevents imbalances, reflecting Ayurveda's emphasis on harmonizing lifestyle with natural rhythms. By addressing environmental influences, Ritucharya ensures systemic balance, promoting resilience against disease. This preventive approach aligns with modern health strategies, emphasizing the importance of adapting to external changes for long-term wellness. Ayurveda's focus on environmental and internal harmony highlights its enduring relevance in personalized and sustainable healthcare.

42. A: Rasayana therapies target longevity and anti-aging through Agni enhancement and Ama elimination. These therapies reduce oxidative stress and inflammation, reflecting Ayurveda's understanding of cellular rejuvenation. Modern research validates these principles, linking Rasayana with improved immunity and systemic health. This demonstrates Ayurveda's depth in addressing root causes of degeneration. By integrating preventive and restorative strategies, Rasayana therapies exemplify Ayurveda's holistic philosophy, showcasing their relevance in modern anti-aging medicine and health optimization.

43. A: The Bhava Prakasha integrates folk medicine with classical Ayurveda, addressing diseases and treatments not covered in earlier texts. This evolution reflects Ayurveda's adaptability to changing medical needs, ensuring its relevance. By bridging traditional and newer practices, the text highlights Ayurveda's dynamic nature. This integration of diverse knowledge streams enriches Ayurvedic practice, demonstrating its capacity to evolve while preserving foundational principles. This adaptability ensures Ayurveda's continued applicability in modern healthcare systems, balancing tradition with innovation.

44. D: While Panchakarma is often curative, it also serves as a preventive measure when performed on healthy individuals. This reflects Ayurveda's focus on maintaining systemic balance and detoxification before disease manifests. The structured stages of Panchakarma—preparation, therapy, and restoration—emphasize its versatility. This adaptability ensures its relevance in modern wellness practices, bridging detoxification and preventive health. By addressing both therapeutic and prophylactic needs, Panchakarma showcases Ayurveda's holistic approach to sustainable health management.

45. A: The Ashtanga Hridaya synthesizes teachings from Charaka and Sushruta, presenting them in poetic form for easier memorization. This synthesis ensures accessibility while preserving depth, reflecting Ayurveda's emphasis on practical knowledge. By combining internal medicine and surgery, it offers a balanced perspective on health. The text's structure and content make it a cornerstone of Ayurvedic education, ensuring its relevance for practitioners. This adaptability highlights Ayurveda's enduring value, integrating diverse principles into a cohesive system for holistic healthcare.

46. B: The Tridosha theory guides personalized medicine by addressing individual constitutions (Prakriti) and imbalances. This framework aligns with modern precision medicine, emphasizing tailored treatments. By considering unique physiological and psychological traits, Ayurveda ensures holistic health management. The Tridosha system integrates lifestyle, diet, and therapies, reflecting its adaptability to diverse health needs. This personalized approach highlights Ayurveda's relevance in contemporary medical practices, showcasing its depth and versatility.

47. B: Panchakarma therapies are validated by modern research, demonstrating their effectiveness in reducing inflammation and improving metabolic health. These therapies align with Ayurveda's detoxification principles, emphasizing root-cause resolution. By addressing systemic imbalances, Panchakarma integrates preventive and therapeutic strategies. Its holistic approach reflects Ayurveda's adaptability, ensuring relevance in global healthcare systems. This validation bridges traditional wisdom with scientific evidence, showcasing Panchakarma's enduring significance.

48. B: The Sushruta Samhita contributes to modern surgical advancements, particularly in reconstructive techniques like rhinoplasty. This reflects Ayurveda's depth in understanding anatomy and surgical precision. By combining curative and restorative strategies, the text demonstrates a holistic approach to surgery. These contributions highlight Ayurveda's scientific rigor, ensuring its relevance in contemporary medical fields. This synthesis of tradition and innovation underscores the enduring value of Ayurvedic principles.

49. C: Skepticism about Ayurveda's empirical validity challenges its integration into modern healthcare. Addressing this requires robust research and scientific validation of Ayurvedic principles. While traditional practices are rooted in experiential knowledge, their relevance depends on aligning with contemporary evidence-based standards. This integration reflects Ayurveda's adaptability, ensuring its acceptance in modern systems. Bridging tradition and science is essential for advancing Ayurveda's role in global healthcare.

50. B: Community-driven sustainable harvesting ensures the ecological and medicinal integrity of Ayurvedic plants like Amalaki. By preserving biodiversity and local ecosystems, this approach aligns with Ayurveda's holistic philosophy. Overharvesting and monoculture threaten plant quality and long-term availability, undermining therapeutic efficacy. Sustainable practices balance ecological and clinical needs, ensuring Ayurveda's relevance. This integrative approach highlights Ayurveda's adaptability to environmental challenges, reflecting its commitment to harmony and sustainability.

CHAPTER–4

NIGHANTU, KOSA, CONTEMPORARY PUBLICATIONS, AND GOVERNMENT INITIATIVES

Ayurveda, the ancient system of holistic healing, has been nurtured and preserved for centuries through meticulous documentation and scholarly efforts. At the core of Ayurvedic literature are the Nighaṇṭus (lexicons) and Kośas (dictionaries), which serve as essential tools for the understanding, interpretation, and expansion of Ayurvedic knowledge. This chapter explores the significance of these critical resources, reviews some of the most prominent Nighaṇṭus and their contributions, highlights contemporary publications, and delves into the pivotal role of governmental initiatives, particularly the Ministry of AYUSH, in promoting and preserving Ayurveda.

Importance of Nighaṇṭu (Ayurvedic Lexicons) and Kośa (Dictionaries)

The systematic study of Ayurveda relies heavily on the accurate understanding of terminology, medicinal plants, formulations, and therapeutic procedures. Nighaṇṭus and Kośas are integral in ensuring consistency, preserving linguistic nuances, and enriching the lexicon of Ayurvedic knowledge.

DEFINITION AND ROLE OF NIGHAṆṬUS

Definition and Role of Nighaṇṭus in Ayurveda

The term "Nighaṇṭu" is derived from the Sanskrit roots "Ni" (down) and "Ghaṇṭu" (to explain or describe). In Ayurveda, Nighaṇṭus are comprehensive compendia or lexicons that systematically catalog medicinal plants, minerals, animal products, and other substances used in Ayurvedic treatments. These texts are an essential part of Ayurvedic literature, acting as pharmacopoeias that describe the properties, actions, and therapeutic applications of natural substances. They serve as indispensable tools for practitioners and scholars of Ayurveda, providing detailed information on various drugs and their roles in maintaining health and curing diseases.

Nighaṇṭus evolved over centuries as scholars of Ayurveda compiled, refined, and expanded the knowledge inherited from classical Ayurvedic texts such as the Charaka Samhita, Sushruta Samhita, and Ashtanga Hridaya. The systematic classification of medicinal substances in Nighaṇṭus reflects the holistic and practical approach of Ayurveda, which integrates physical, mental, and spiritual well-being.

Historical Development of Nighaṇṭus

The tradition of cataloging medicinal substances can be traced back to the foundational Ayurvedic texts. While these classics laid the groundwork for pharmacological knowledge, Nighaṇṭus emerged later as specialized lexicons dedicated to elaborating the properties of medicinal materials. The development of Nighaṇṭus occurred in several stages:

1. **Vedic Period :** The earliest references to medicinal plants and substances are found in the Vedas, particularly the Atharvaveda, which mentions herbs and their uses in rituals and healing. These descriptions were rudimentary and primarily spiritual, focusing on the symbolic and ritualistic aspects of medicine.

2. **Classical Ayurvedic Period:** Foundational texts like the Charaka Samhita and Sushruta Samhita categorized medicinal substances based on their properties, tastes (Rasa), potency (Veerya), post-digestive effects (Vipaka), and specific actions (Prabhava). While these texts provided a framework for understanding pharmacology, they were not exclusively dedicated to cataloging drugs.
3. **Post-Classical Period:** By the post-classical era, scholars recognized the need for specialized texts focused entirely on the pharmacological aspects of Ayurveda. This gave rise to Nighaṇṭus, which expanded and systematized the knowledge of medicinal substances. Notable Nighaṇṭus from this period include:
   - **Dhanvantari Nighaṇṭu:** One of the earliest known Nighaṇṭus, it systematically categorizes medicinal plants and their properties.
   - **Bhavaprakasha Nighaṇṭu:** Authored by Bhavamishra, this Nighaṇṭu is one of the most comprehensive works, detailing medicinal plants and their classifications.
   - **Raj Nighaṇṭu:** Also known as the "Abhidhana Chintamani," it focuses on plant-based medicines and includes regional names and synonyms.
4. **Medieval and Modern Period:** Later Nighaṇṭus incorporated new discoveries and adapted to regional medicinal traditions, making them dynamic and evolving texts. Modern Ayurvedic pharmacology continues to draw from these works, integrating traditional knowledge with contemporary research.

STRUCTURE AND CONTENTS OF NIGHAṆṬUS

Nighaṇṭus are meticulously organized, reflecting the scientific rigor of Ayurvedic scholarship. Their structure typically includes the following components:

1. **Synonyms and Nomenclature:** Each medicinal substance is described using multiple names, including Sanskrit synonyms, regional names, and traditional appellations. This linguistic diversity ensures accessibility across regions and traditions.
2. **Rasa, Veerya, and Vipaka:** Nighaṇṭus elaborate on the Rasa (taste), Veerya (potency), and Vipaka (post-digestive effect) of each substance. These attributes are crucial for understanding the therapeutic actions of the drug and its suitability for different doshic imbalances.
3. **Guna (Qualities):** The qualities of substances, such as heaviness, lightness, dryness, or unctuousness, are described in detail. These properties influence the drug's effects on bodily systems and its role in balancing the doshas.
4. **Prabhava (Unique Action):** Certain substances exhibit unique or inexplicable actions that cannot be attributed to their Rasa, Veerya, or Vipaka. Nighaṇṭus document these Prabhavas as distinctive therapeutic effects.
5. **Therapeutic Uses:** The texts provide comprehensive information on the diseases and conditions each substance can treat. They include formulations, dosages, and modes of administration.
6. **Classification:** Medicinal substances are classified into categories based on their origin (plant, mineral, or animal), therapeutic action, or primary use. For example, some Nighaṇṭus organize plants into groups such as Vatahara (alleviating Vata), Pittahara (alleviating Pitta), and Kaphahara (alleviating Kapha).
7. **Regional Variations:** Many Nighaṇṭus include descriptions of regional variations in the properties and availability of medicinal plants. This adaptability reflects Ayurveda's sensitivity to local ecosystems and resources.

ROLE OF NIGHAṆṬUS IN AYURVEDA

Nighaṇṭus play a multifaceted role in Ayurvedic practice, bridging the gap between theoretical knowledge and practical application. Their contributions can be summarized as follows:

1. **Pharmacological Reference:** Nighaṇṭus serve as authoritative guides for understanding the pharmacological properties of medicinal substances. They provide practitioners with essential information for selecting the right drugs and formulations based on the patient's condition and doshic constitution.
2. **Preservation of Traditional Knowledge:** By cataloging the properties and uses of medicinal substances, Nighaṇṭus ensure the preservation of traditional Ayurvedic knowledge. This is particularly important in the context of oral traditions, where written documentation safeguards against the loss of cultural heritage.
3. **Regional Adaptability:** Nighaṇṭus incorporate regional names, synonyms, and variations, making Ayurvedic knowledge accessible to diverse communities. This adaptability reflects Ayurveda's dynamic and inclusive approach, allowing it to thrive across geographical and cultural boundaries.
4. **Integration of New Substances:** As Ayurveda evolved, Nighaṇṭus incorporated new substances and formulations, ensuring the continuous expansion of

Ayurvedic pharmacology. This adaptability allowed Ayurveda to remain relevant and responsive to changing medical needs.

5. **Standardization and Quality Control:** Nighaṇṭus provide detailed guidelines for identifying, preparing, and administering medicinal substances. This standardization ensures consistency and quality in Ayurvedic practice, safeguarding patient safety.
6. **Educational Resource:** For students and scholars of Ayurveda, Nighaṇṭus are invaluable resources for studying the properties and applications of medicinal substances. They complement classical texts by offering specialized knowledge in pharmacology.
7. **Foundation for Modern Research:** Nighaṇṭus provide a wealth of information for modern researchers exploring the pharmacological and therapeutic potential of Ayurvedic substances. By bridging traditional wisdom and scientific inquiry, they contribute to the global integration of Ayurveda.

Examples of Prominent Nighaṇṭus

1. **Dhanvantari Nighaṇṭu:** One of the earliest Nighaṇṭus, it categorizes medicinal plants and their uses in a systematic manner. The text provides a foundation for subsequent Nighaṇṭus and remains a reference point for Ayurvedic pharmacology.
2. **Bhavaprakasha Nighaṇṭu:** This comprehensive text, written by Bhavamishra, is renowned for its detailed descriptions of medicinal plants and their synonyms. It includes over 400 plant species and their properties, making it one of the most extensive Nighaṇṭus.
3. **Raj Nighaṇṭu:** This text focuses on plant-based medicines and their therapeutic applications. It includes regional variations and synonyms, reflecting the diverse ecological contexts of Ayurveda.
4. **Madanapala Nighaṇṭu:** Written by Madanapala, this Nighaṇṭu includes descriptions of plants, minerals, and animal products. It emphasizes the practical aspects of drug preparation and administration.
5. **Kaiyadeva Nighaṇṭu:** This text is notable for its inclusion of regional flora and its systematic classification of medicinal plants. It bridges classical Ayurvedic knowledge with local traditions, enriching the pharmacological corpus.

Relevance of Nighaṇṭus in Contemporary Ayurveda

In the modern context, Nighaṇṭus continue to play a critical role in Ayurvedic education, practice, and research. Their relevance can be seen in the following areas:

1. **Revival of Traditional Medicine:** Nighaṇṭus provide a blueprint for rediscovering and revitalizing traditional Ayurvedic practices. They serve as guides for identifying, cultivating, and using medicinal plants in their natural habitats.
2. **Herbal Drug Development:** Pharmaceutical companies and researchers draw upon Nighaṇṭus to develop herbal formulations and validate their efficacy through scientific methods. The systematic descriptions of plant properties and actions facilitate the standardization of Ayurvedic medicines.
3. **Conservation of Medicinal Plants:** By documenting regional variations and ecological factors, Nighaṇṭus contribute to the conservation of medicinal plants and biodiversity. They highlight the importance of sustainable harvesting and cultivation practices.
4. **Global Acceptance of Ayurveda:** Nighaṇṭus provide a scientific foundation for promoting Ayurveda as a global healthcare system. Their detailed documentation supports evidence-based research and fosters cross-cultural exchange of medical knowledge.

Challenges and Future Prospects

While Nighaṇṭus remain invaluable, they face certain challenges in the modern era:

1. **Loss of Biodiversity:** The depletion of natural habitats and overharvesting of medicinal plants threaten the availability of substances described in Nighaṇṭus. Conservation efforts are essential to preserve these resources.
2. **Standardization Issues:** The variability in regional names and synonyms can lead to confusion in identifying medicinal plants. Efforts to standardize nomenclature and classifications are necessary for consistency.
3. **Integration with Modern Science:** Bridging the gap between traditional knowledge and modern pharmacological research requires collaboration between Ayurvedic scholars and scientists.
4. **Digitalization and Preservation:** Digitizing Nighaṇṭus and making them accessible to a global audience can ensure their preservation and promote wider dissemination of Ayurvedic knowledge.

Nighaṇṭus are the living repositories of Ayurvedic pharmacology, embodying the scientific, cultural, and ecological richness of Ayurveda. Their meticulous documentation of medicinal substances serves as a bridge between traditional wisdom and contemporary medicine. By preserving and expanding the knowledge contained in Nighaṇṭus, Ayurveda can continue to thrive as a dynamic and holistic healthcare system. As the world increasingly turns to natural and integrative therapies, the role of Nighaṇṭus in guiding sustainable and evidence-based practices will become even more significant.

With the resurgence of interest in traditional medicine, numerous publications aim to make Ayurvedic knowledge accessible and relevant in modern contexts. These publications range from annotated translations of classical texts to research journals and encyclopedias.

Annotated Translations

Several classical Ayurvedic texts, including Charaka Samhita and Sushruta Samhita, have been translated into multiple languages with scholarly commentary. These efforts include:

- **Critical Editions:** Incorporating textual analysis and cross-referencing.
- **Bilingual Publications:** Catering to global audiences by offering Sanskrit text with English or regional language translations.

Research Journals

Leading Ayurvedic research journals, such as the Journal of Ayurveda and Integrative Medicine (J-AIM), provide a platform for:

- Publishing clinical trials and pharmacological studies.
- Bridging traditional knowledge with modern scientific research.
- Disseminating case studies and innovative practices.

Encyclopedias and Digital Databases

Modern initiatives have also resulted in the creation of encyclopedic resources and digital databases, such as:

- Indian Medicinal Plants Database (IMP): Cataloging herbs with their properties, uses, and pharmacological profiles.
- Ayushman Bharat Herbarium: A government-led initiative to document medicinal flora.

Popular Books and Manuals

Contemporary authors have contributed significantly through books on Ayurvedic dietetics, home remedies, and yoga. Notable examples include:

- Books by Vasant Lad and Robert Svoboda, which simplify Ayurveda for international readers.
- Manuals on Ayurvedic cosmetology and mental health.

Government Initiatives and the Role of Ministry of AYUSH

The Government of India has undertaken extensive measures to promote Ayurveda at both national and global levels. The establishment of the Ministry of AYUSH in 2014 was a landmark step, consolidating efforts across Ayurveda, Yoga, Unani, Siddha, and Homeopathy.

Major Initiatives by the Ministry of AYUSH

The Ministry of AYUSH has implemented a range of programs, including:

- **National AYUSH Mission (NAM):** Strengthening healthcare infrastructure and integrating AYUSH services into mainstream healthcare.
- **Pharmacopoeia Commission for Indian Medicine (PCIM):** Standardizing Ayurvedic formulations and practices.
- **Central Council for Research in Ayurvedic Sciences (CCRAS):** Conducting clinical research and validating Ayurvedic treatments.
- **AYUSH Grid:** A digital platform to centralize information, services, and resources related to AYUSH.

Global Promotion of Ayurveda

The Ministry actively promotes Ayurveda internationally through initiatives like:

- Establishing Ayurveda chairs in foreign universities.
- Collaborating with the World Health Organization (WHO) for the inclusion of Ayurveda in global health strategies.
- Hosting events like the World Ayurveda Congress.

Educational and Research Efforts

To nurture the next generation of Ayurvedic practitioners and researchers, the government has:

- Established premier institutions like the All India Institute of Ayurveda (AIIA).
- Introduced scholarships and exchange programs for students.
- Encouraged multidisciplinary research by collaborating with modern medical institutions.

Challenges and the Way Forward

Despite these efforts, several challenges persist in the promotion and integration of Ayurveda, such as:

- **Standardization Issues:** Inconsistent quality of raw materials and formulations.
- **Research Gaps:** Limited large-scale clinical trials validating Ayurvedic treatments.
- **Awareness and Accessibility:** Bridging the gap between rural and urban access to Ayurvedic care.To address these challenges, a multi-faceted approach is necessary, including:

◊ Encouraging public-private partnerships for research and development.
◊ Leveraging artificial intelligence and machine learning for predictive analysis and drug discovery. Expanding awareness campaigns to highlight Ayurveda's benefits in preventive health.

Nighaṇṭus and Kośas have been instrumental in shaping the rich heritage of Ayurveda. Their role in preserving, standardizing, and disseminating knowledge cannot be overstated. Contemporary publications and governmental initiatives, particularly under the aegis of the Ministry of AYUSH, have further propelled Ayurveda into the global spotlight. By blending traditional wisdom with modern science and technology, Ayurveda stands poised to contribute significantly to holistic healthcare solutions worldwide. The continued evolution of Nighaṇṭus, Kośas, and research publications will ensure that this ancient science remains relevant and beneficial for generations to come.

MULTIPLE CHOICE QUESTIONS

1. The evolution of Ayurvedic lexicons, or Nighaṇṭus, represents a profound intersection of linguistics and pharmacology. Imagine a researcher is tasked with contextualizing the therapeutic descriptions found in Dhanvantari Nighaṇṭu against the backdrop of contemporary ethnopharmacology. This task involves evaluating how classical terms such as "Rasayana" (rejuvenation) and "Vishaghna" (anti-toxin) correlate with biochemical activities like antioxidant properties and enzyme inhibition. After extensive analysis, the researcher concludes that certain terms encapsulate concepts akin to modern drug classifications, yet other terms remain metaphorical or symbolic in nature. Which of the following would be the most logical implication of this research for integrating Nighaṇṭu classifications into modern medicine?
   (a) The metaphorical aspects of Ayurvedic terms undermine their utility in pharmacological applications.
   (b) Nighaṇṭus should be interpreted solely through linguistic analysis, without attempting scientific validation.
   (c) The dual nature of Ayurvedic terms as symbolic and scientific creates an opportunity for integrative research bridging traditional and modern medicine.
   (d) Dhanvantari Nighaṇṭu's classifications lack relevance in the context of contemporary pharmacology.

2. The Ministry of AYUSH has launched a nationwide initiative to create a comprehensive digital repository of Ayurvedic texts, including Nighaṇṭus and Kośas. Suppose the aim is to facilitate accessibility for scholars and practitioners globally, while integrating this knowledge into the mainstream healthcare system. The initiative also focuses on translating the Sanskrit texts into regional and international languages while maintaining their technical and cultural nuances. If this project succeeds, what would be the most significant challenge in achieving cross-disciplinary integration of this repository with modern medical databases?
   (a) Aligning ancient terminologies with the taxonomical and pharmacological standards of contemporary medicine.
   (b) Preventing cultural appropriation and misinterpretation of Ayurvedic principles in international contexts.
   (c) Prioritizing the preservation of historical integrity over practical healthcare applications.
   (d) Limiting the repository's access to credentialed professionals, thereby excluding non-academic stakeholders.

3. The categorization of herbs in Ayurvedic Nighaṇṭus is based on their Rasas (tastes), Vipaka (post-digestive effects), and Virya (potency). Imagine a pharmacological study explores how these classifications might correlate with modern biochemical markers like flavonoids, terpenes, and alkaloids. After testing several herbs, the study observes that Ayurvedic classifications align with measurable pharmacological properties, yet there are exceptions where the classical attributes do not correspond to the expected biochemical markers. What does this divergence suggest about the epistemological foundations of Ayurvedic pharmacology?
   (a) Ayurvedic classifications are primarily philosophical and lack empirical significance.
   (b) The exceptions indicate that Ayurvedic knowledge is outdated and unsuitable for contemporary validation.
   (c) The divergence highlights the need for an interdisciplinary framework to bridge traditional and modern pharmacological systems.
   (d) Ayurvedic principles are inconsistent and fail to provide a reliable basis for therapeutic applications.

4. The Madanapala Nighaṇṭu, a medieval Ayurvedic lexicon, provides a detailed list of medicinal plants with specific therapeutic properties linked to doshic

imbalances. Suppose a clinical trial is designed to test the efficacy of certain herbs recommended for Vata imbalance in patients with arthritis. The trial uses standardized herbal extracts and measures outcomes such as pain relief, inflammation reduction, and joint mobility. If the results demonstrate significant improvements aligned with Madanapala Nighaṇṭu's recommendations, what would be the broader implications for integrating classical Ayurvedic texts into evidence-based clinical practice?

(a) The trial's success validates the entirety of Ayurvedic lexicons, removing the need for further scientific inquiry.

(b) Positive outcomes reinforce the applicability of classical texts while highlighting the importance of empirical validation for specific formulations.

(c) The findings suggest that Ayurvedic classifications are anecdotal and cannot reliably predict therapeutic outcomes.

(d) Evidence-based validation of Ayurvedic texts would conflict with their philosophical underpinnings, making integration impractical.

5. The role of government initiatives, such as those led by the Ministry of AYUSH, extends beyond policy-making to actively promoting research and standardization of Ayurvedic formulations. Imagine a scenario where a government-funded program aims to investigate the phytochemical profiles of herbs described in classical Nighaṇṭus. The project prioritizes the standardization of raw materials and quality assurance in formulations like Chyavanprash and Triphala. If this initiative achieves its goals, which of the following outcomes would most effectively contribute to the global acceptance of Ayurvedic formulations in mainstream healthcare?

(a) The exclusive focus on phytochemical standardization diminishes the holistic principles of Ayurveda.

(b) Standardization of raw materials enhances the reliability and reproducibility of Ayurvedic treatments in clinical settings.

(c) The initiative limits global acceptance by imposing rigid scientific frameworks on traditional practices.

(d) The program's success would only benefit domestic markets, with minimal international impact.

6. The concept of Kośa in Ayurveda refers to dictionaries that organize linguistic and scientific knowledge systematically. Imagine a linguistic researcher undertakes a comparative study of Ayurvedic Kośas like Amarakosha and modern medical dictionaries, focusing on their epistemological frameworks. The researcher discovers that Ayurvedic Kośas integrate metaphysical concepts alongside empirical observations, whereas modern dictionaries prioritize clinical precision. If this distinction is acknowledged, how can Ayurvedic Kośas contribute uniquely to contemporary medical education?

(a) By emphasizing cultural and philosophical dimensions of healthcare beyond clinical precision.

(b) By replacing modern medical terminologies with traditional Ayurvedic metaphors.

(c) By rejecting metaphysical concepts as irrelevant to scientific education.

(d) By restricting Ayurvedic Kośas to historical linguistics rather than practical applications.

7. The Dhanvantari Nighaṇṭu categorizes plants into therapeutic groups based on their ability to cure specific diseases and balance doshas. Imagine a pharmacognosy lab analyzes the therapeutic groupings to determine whether these align with molecular mechanisms such as enzyme inhibition or receptor modulation. The findings reveal a strong correlation for 70% of the herbs studied but also identify discrepancies in 30% of cases. What could be the most plausible explanation for these discrepancies in the context of Ayurvedic and modern pharmacological paradigms?

(a) Ayurvedic classifications are based solely on metaphysical assumptions, rendering them irrelevant to modern pharmacology.

(b) Discrepancies highlight gaps in molecular research, necessitating further studies to decode Ayurvedic classifications.

(c) Variations in therapeutic outcomes suggest Ayurvedic classifications are unreliable and should be revised.

(d) The findings affirm that Ayurvedic groupings are empirical but require integration with molecular research to achieve universal applicability.

8. Recent publications on Ayurveda highlight the relevance of classical texts like Madanapala Nighaṇṭu in addressing emerging health challenges such as metabolic disorders and antimicrobial resistance. Suppose a multi-disciplinary research team develops a modern interpretation of this Nighaṇṭu, focusing on formulating bio-enhanced herbal remedies. The team hypothesizes that the synergy described in the classical text can be validated through bioavailability studies. If their hypothesis is confirmed, what broader implications would this have for reinterpreting Ayurvedic texts in light of modern pharmacokinetics?

(a) It would demonstrate that classical texts offer no novel insights for modern medicine.

(b) It would validate the relevance of Ayurvedic texts while emphasizing the importance of bioavailability studies.

(c) It would suggest that Ayurvedic formulations are inherently superior to synthetic drugs, negating the need for pharmacokinetic research.
(d) It would undermine the credibility of classical texts by reducing them to pharmacological constructs.

9. The global interest in Ayurvedic principles has driven several governments to integrate Ayurveda into complementary and alternative medicine (CAM) frameworks. Imagine a policy review evaluates the impact of government initiatives on Ayurveda's role in CAM systems, with a focus on Nighaṇṭus and Kośas. The review finds that while these initiatives have increased awareness, the practical application of Ayurvedic concepts often faces barriers in clinical adoption. Which of the following strategies would most effectively address these barriers?
(a) Emphasizing the philosophical and cultural aspects of Ayurveda over clinical applications.
(b) Developing standardized guidelines for integrating Ayurvedic texts into CAM protocols.
(c) Restricting the use of Ayurvedic principles to traditional Indian healthcare systems.
(d) Focusing solely on marketing Ayurveda as a cultural export, ignoring clinical validation.

10. In the context of promoting Ayurveda globally, the Ministry of AYUSH has advocated for translating classical Ayurvedic texts, including Nighaṇṭus and Kośas, into digital formats accessible to researchers worldwide. Suppose this initiative includes annotating ancient texts with contemporary scientific interpretations, aiming to establish Ayurveda as a legitimate part of integrative medicine. What would be the most significant ethical consideration in such an undertaking?
(a) Ensuring the translations maintain the cultural and philosophical integrity of the original texts.
(b) Prioritizing commercial gains over the scholarly accuracy of the translations.
(c) Avoiding scientific reinterpretation of Ayurvedic concepts to preserve their traditional authenticity.
(d) Excluding non-Indian researchers from accessing the texts to safeguard cultural heritage.

Directions (Q. No. 11–14): *Scenario-Based Questions*

SCENARIO 1

A medical researcher investigates the digitization of classical Ayurvedic texts under a government initiative led by the Ministry of AYUSH. The project includes developing a searchable database of key Nighaṇṭus and their medicinal properties, aiming to promote research and innovation.

SCENARIO 2

Simultaneously, a policy analyst evaluates government initiatives promoting Ayurvedic education and practices, such as the establishment of specialized AYUSH research centers. However, the analyst identifies gaps in funding and infrastructural support, leading to challenges in integrating these systems with mainstream healthcare.

11. Based on Scenario 1, which of the following outcomes best represents the potential of digitizing Ayurvedic Nighaṇṭus?
A. It will preserve ancient texts but offer little utility for research or healthcare applications.
B. It enables easier access to Ayurvedic knowledge and fosters interdisciplinary research.
C. Digitization risks misinterpretation and over-commercialization of Ayurvedic principles.
D. It undermines the original context and philosophical foundation of Ayurvedic texts.

12. Considering Scenario 2, which strategy would most effectively address the identified gaps in government initiatives?
A. Increased funding and infrastructure for specialized AYUSH research centers.
B. Limiting government intervention to focus on private sector-driven growth in Ayurveda.
C. Reducing the emphasis on integration with mainstream healthcare.
D. Promoting Ayurveda exclusively through traditional practitioners.

13. How does the lack of sustainable practices in harvesting Amalaki, as highlighted in Scenario 2, potentially impact the digitization initiative in Scenario 1?
A. The depletion of wild Amalaki populations undermines the practical applications of Nighaṇṭu data, as key medicinal plants become inaccessible.
B. Digitization efforts remain unaffected, as they focus exclusively on textual preservation, not real-world applications.
C. Overharvesting of Amalaki directly enhances the demand for digital resources by highlighting the need for alternative plant-based therapies.
D. The environmental challenges associated with Amalaki harvesting have no direct connection to the digitization of Ayurvedic texts.

14. Based on the interconnected findings of Scenarios 1 and 2, which of the following strategies would best address both the sustainability and digitization challenges in promoting Ayurveda?
A. Establishing a comprehensive government policy that integrates sustainable plant harvesting practices with Ayurvedic research and digitization initiatives.

B. Limiting digitization efforts to endangered medicinal plants while allowing overharvesting of non-endangered species.

C. Focusing on expanding Triphala's global market without addressing sustainability concerns for its components.

D. Promoting synthetic alternatives to Amalaki while deprioritizing digitization of classical Ayurvedic texts.

15. The Ministry of AYUSH has implemented the following strategies to promote Ayurveda:

(a) Development of Ayurvedic Pharmacopoeia and standardized formulations.

(b) Establishment of AYUSH wellness centers and integrative medicine units.

(c) Support for research on the sustainability of medicinal plant resources.

(d) Promotion of Ayurvedic products exclusively through private partnerships.

Choose the correct answer from the options given below:

A. (a), (b), and (c) only

B. (a), (b), and (d) only

C. (a) and (b) only

D. (b), (c), and (d) only

16. Government initiatives in Ayurveda include the following components:

(a) Digitization of classical texts and Nighaṇṭus for universal access.

(b) Collaboration with international bodies to standardize formulations.

(c) Promotion of Ayurveda through subsidies on modern pharmaceutical drugs.

(d) Integration of AYUSH systems with primary healthcare in rural areas.

Choose the correct answer from the options given below:

A. (a), (b), and (d) only

B. (a), (c), and (d) only

C. (b), (c), and (d) only

D. (a) and (d) only

17. The following are challenges identified in implementing government initiatives to promote Ayurveda:

(a) Lack of standardized testing and quality control of formulations.

(b) Insufficient public awareness of Ayurveda's preventive approach.

(c) Over-reliance on traditional practices without scientific validation.

(d) Excessive focus on sustainability, ignoring patient affordability.

Choose the correct answer from the options given below:

A. (a), (b), and (c) only

B. (a) and (b) only

C. (b), (c), and (d) only

D. (a), (c), and (d) only

18. Regarding Ayurvedic lexicons (Nighaṇṭus), which of the following statements are correct?

(a) They classify herbs based on Rasa, Guna, Vipaka, and Dosha relationships.

(b) They serve as comprehensive dictionaries of both botanical and mineral-based formulations.

(c) They include regional variations of medicinal plant names for accessibility.

(d) Their primary purpose is poetic, rather than scientific, in nature.

Choose the correct answer from the options given below:

A. (a), (b), and (c) only

B. (a) and (c) only

C. (b) and (d) only

D. (a), (b), (c), and (d)

19. The Ayurvedic concept of Tridosha includes the following principles:

(a) Vata governs movement, linked to nervous system regulation.

(b) Pitta governs metabolism and enzymatic processes.

(c) Kapha governs immunity and psychological resilience.

(d) Tridosha balance depends solely on dietary habits.

Choose the correct answer from the options given below:

A. (a), (b), and (d) only

B. (a), (b), and (c) only

C. (b), (c), and (d) only

D. (a), (c), and (d) only

20. The Ministry of AYUSH's role in Ayurveda's global promotion includes:

(a) Collaboration with international research institutions.

(b) Conducting clinical trials to validate Ayurvedic principles.

(c) Export subsidies for herbal products under AYUSH guidelines.

(d) Prioritizing Ayurvedic research over other traditional medical systems.

Choose the correct answer from the options given below:

A. (a), (b), and (c) only

B. (a), (c), and (d) only

C. (b) and (d) only

D. (a), (b), (c), and (d)

21. Match List–I (Doshas) with List–II (Primary Characteristics):

List–I	List–II
(a) Vata	1. Responsible for movement and bodily functions
(b) Pitta	2. Governs metabolism and transformation
(c) Kapha	3. Provides stability and structural support

Choose the correct answer from the options given below:

A. (a)-1, (b)-2, (c)-3
B. (a)-3, (b)-2, (c)-1
C. (a)-1, (b)-3, (c)-2
D. (a)-2, (b)-3, (c)-1

22. Match List–I (Sensory Organs - Jñānendriya) with List–II (Functions):

List–I	List–II
(a) Chakṣur (Eyes)	1. Perception of form and color
(b) Śrotra (Ears)	2. Perception of sound
(c) Rasa (Tongue)	3. Perception of taste
(d) Tvak (Skin)	4. Perception of touch

Choose the correct answer from the options given below:

A. (a)-1, (b)-2, (c)-3, (d)-4
B. (a)-1, (b)-2, (c)-4, (d)-3
C. (a)-3, (b)-4, (c)-2, (d)-1
D. (a)-4, (b)-3, (c)-1, (d)-2

23. Match List–I (Action Organs - Karmendriya) with List–II (Functions):

List–I	List–II
(a) Vāk (Speech)	1. Verbal communication
(b) Pāṇi (Hands)	2. Facilitation of grasping
(c) Pāda (Feet)	3. Facilitation of locomotion
(d) Upastha (Genitals)	4. Facilitation of reproduction

Choose the correct answer from the options given below:

A. (a)-4, (b)-2, (c)-3, (d)-1
B. (a)-2, (b)-1, (c)-4, (d)-3
C. (a)-1, (b)-2, (c)-3, (d)-4
D. (a)-3, (b)-4, (c)-1, (d)-2

24. Match List–I (Dhatus) with List–II (Biological Functions):

List–I	List–II
(a) Rasa	1. Provides nourishment
(b) Rakta	2. Supports vitality
(c) Mamsa	3. Builds and strengthens muscles
(d) Meda	4. Regulates lubrication

Choose the correct answer from the options given below:

A. (a)-1, (b)-2, (c)-3, (d)-4
B. (a)-2, (b)-3, (c)-1, (d)-4
C. (a)-3, (b)-4, (c)-2, (d)-1
D. (a)-4, (b)-1, (c)-3, (d)-2

25. Match List–I (Mahābhūtas) with List–II (Associated Attributes):

List–I	List–II
(a) Ākāśa (Ether)	1. Softness
(b) Vāyu (Air)	2. Motion
(c) Agni (Fire)	3. Transformation
(d) Jala (Water)	4. Fluidity

Choose the correct answer from the options given below:

A. (a)-1, (b)-2, (c)-3, (d)-4
B. (a)-4, (b)-3, (c)-2, (d)-1
C. (a)-2, (b)-1, (c)-4, (d)-3
D. (a)-3, (b)-4, (c)-1, (d)-2

26. Match List–I (Concepts) with List–II (Significance in Ayurveda):

List–I	List–II
(a) Ātman (Soul)	1. Governs consciousness
(b) Śarīra (Body)	2. Provides physical structure
(c) Indriya (Senses)	3. Enables interaction with the environment
(d) Tridoṣa (Doshas)	4. Maintains physiological balance

Choose the correct answer from the options given below:

A. (a)-1, (b)-2, (c)-3, (d)-4
B. (a)-4, (b)-3, (c)-2, (d)-1
C. (a)-3, (b)-4, (c)-1, (d)-2
D. (a)-2, (b)-1, (c)-4, (d)-3

27. Match List–I (Tridoṣa and Their Locations) with List–II (Primary Regions in the Body):

List–I	List–II
(a) Vata	1. Colon and nervous system
(b) Pitta	2. Stomach and small intestine
(c) Kapha	3. Chest and lymphatic system

Choose the correct answer from the options given below:

A. (a)-2, (b)-1, (c)-3
B. (a)-1, (b)-3, (c)-2
C. (a)-1, (b)-2, (c)-3
D. (a)-3, (b)-2, (c)-1

28. Match List–I (Jñānendriyas - Sensory Organs) with List–II (Associated Mahābhūtas):

List–I	List–II
(a) Śrotra (Ears)	1. Ākāśa (Ether)
(b) Tvak (Skin)	2. Vāyu (Air)
(c) Chakṣur (Eyes)	3. Agni (Fire)
(d) Rasa (Tongue)	4. Jala (Water)

Choose the correct answer from the options given below:

A. (a)-1, (b)-3, (c)-4, (d)-2
B. (a)-4, (b)-1, (c)-3, (d)-2
C. (a)-2, (b)-3, (c)-1, (d)-4
D. (a)-1, (b)-2, (c)-3, (d)-4

29. Match List–I (Dosha Aggravating Factors) with List–II (Primary Triggers):

List–I	List–II
(a) Vata	1. Excessive movement and irregular meals
(b) Pitta	2. Overheating and spicy foods
(c) Kapha	3. Sedentary lifestyle and heavy foods

Choose the correct answer from the options given below:

A. (a)-2, (b)-1, (c)-3
B. (a)-1, (b)-2, (c)-3
C. (a)-3, (b)-2, (c)-1
D. (a)-1, (b)-3, (c)-2

30. Match List–I (Therapies) with List–II (Therapeutic Effects in Ayurveda):

List–I	List–II
(a) Abhyanga (Oil Massage)	1. Improves circulation and reduces Vata imbalance
(b) Shirodhara (Oil Pouring on Forehead)	2. Calms the mind and balances Pitta
(c) Vamana (Therapeutic Vomiting)	3. Clears excess Kapha and detoxifies

Choose the correct answer from the options given below:

A. (a)-1, (b)-2, (c)-3
B. (a)-3, (b)-1, (c)-2
C. (a)-2, (b)-3, (c)-1
D. (a)-1, (b)-3, (c)-2

31. Match List–I (Classical Nighaṇṭus) with List–II (Unique Features):

List–I	List–II
(a) Dhanvantari Nighaṇṭu	1. Earliest available lexicon of Ayurvedic herbs
(b) Raja Nighaṇṭu	2. Known for categorizing plants into Vargas
(c) Bhāvaprakāśa Nighaṇṭu	3. Combines classical and folk medicinal knowledge
(d) Madanapāla Nighaṇṭu	4. Provides regional synonyms for herbs

Choose the correct answer from the options given below:

A. (a)-1, (b)-2, (c)-3, (d)-4
B. (a)-3, (b)-4, (c)-1, (d)-2
C. (a)-2, (b)-1, (c)-4, (d)-3
D. (a)-4, (b)-3, (c)-2, (d)-1

32. Match List–I (Types of Entries in Ayurvedic Kośa) with List–II (Primary Focus):

List–I	List–II
(a) Nāma Kośa	1. Collection of synonyms and etymologies
(b) Dravya Kośa	2. Descriptions of herbs, minerals, and drugs
(c) Roga Kośa	3. Terminologies of diseases and symptoms
(d) Karma Kośa	4. Explanation of therapeutic procedures

Choose the correct answer from the options given below:

A. (a)-1, (b)-2, (c)-3, (d)-4
B. (a)-2, (b)-1, (c)-4, (d)-3
C. (a)-3, (b)-4, (c)-1, (d)-2
D. (a)-4, (b)-3, (c)-2, (d)-1

33. Match List–I (Ayurvedic Lexicons) with List–II (Period/Author):

List–I	List–II
(a) Dhanvantari Nighaṇṭu	1. Believed to be from early medieval period
(b) Madanapāla Nighaṇṭu	2. Authored by King Madanapāla
(c) Bhāvaprakāśa Nighaṇṭu	3. Attributed to Bhāvamiśra
(d) Raja Nighaṇṭu	4. Associated with Narahari Paṇḍita

Choose the correct answer from the options given below:

A. (a)-1, (b)-2, (c)-3, (d)-4
B. (a)-3, (b)-4, (c)-2, (d)-1
C. (a)-4, (b)-1, (c)-3, (d)-2
D. (a)-2, (b)-3, (c)-1, (d)-4

34. Match List–I (Utility of Nighaṇṭus) with List–II (Application Area):

List–I	List–II
(a) Rasayana Classification	1. Herbs for rejuvenation and longevity

(b) Vishaghna Dravyas	2. Substances used in poison management
(c) Bhedaniya Varga	3. Herbs useful in purgation therapies
(d) Deepaniya Varga	4. Substances that kindle digestive fire

Choose the correct answer from the options given below:

A. (a)-1, (b)-2, (c)-3, (d)-4
B. (a)-4, (b)-1, (c)-2, (d)-3
C. (a)-3, (b)-4, (c)-1, (d)-2
D. (a)-2, (b)-3, (c)-4, (d)-1

Directions (Q. No. 35–39): *Following questions are based on Statement 1 and Statement 2. Read both the statements carefully and choose the correct answer from the options given below:*

A. Both Statement 1 and Statement 2 are true, and Statement 2 is the correct explanation of Statement 1.
B. Both Statement 1 and Statement 2 are true, but Statement 2 is not the correct explanation of Statement 1.
C. Statement 1 is true, but Statement 2 is false.
D. Statement 1 is false, but Statement 2 is true.
E. Both Statement 1 and Statement 2 are false.

35. Statement 1: The integration of Ayurveda into primary healthcare has been a significant objective of the National AYUSH Mission.

Statement 2: This integration ensures that Ayurvedic practices replace conventional medical treatments in all rural healthcare facilities.

36. Statement 1: The digitization of Ayurvedic Nighaṇtus by the Ministry of AYUSH enhances global research opportunities.

Statement 2: Digitization enables standardized translations of Ayurvedic texts, preserving their traditional interpretations.

37. Statement 1: The Ministry of AYUSH supports research into the sustainability of medicinal plants used in Ayurveda.

Statement 2: Conservation of medicinal plants ensures the long-term efficacy of Ayurvedic formulations, as plant quality directly influences therapeutic outcomes.

38. Statement 1: Ayurvedic concepts like Rasa and Vipaka align with modern biochemical principles, such as taste and metabolic effects.

Statement 2: Modern science has validated these concepts by mapping their pharmacological properties to specific bioactive compounds.

39. Statement 1: Nighaṇtus like the Madanapala Nighaṇtu classify plants based on disease-specific applications.

Statement 2: These classifications allow seamless integration of traditional Ayurvedic knowledge with modern evidence-based research.

Directions (Q. No. 40–45): *There are two statements in each question. One is labelled as Assertion (A) and the other is as Reason (R). Read both the statements and choose the correct answer from the options given below:*

A. Both Assertion (A) and Reason (R) are true, and Reason (R) is the correct explanation of Assertion (A).
B. Both Assertion (A) and Reason (R) are true, but Reason (R) is not the correct explanation of Assertion (A).
C. Assertion (A) is true, but Reason (R) is false.
D. Assertion (A) is false, but Reason (R) is true.
E. Both Assertion (A) and Reason (R) are false.

40. Assertion (A): The Ministry of AYUSH has prioritized the development of the AYUSH Grid to integrate traditional healthcare systems with modern technology.

Reason (R): The AYUSH Grid creates a digital platform for the dissemination of Ayurvedic research, clinical data, and educational resources.

41. Assertion (A): Ayurvedic detoxification therapies, such as Panchakarma, are effective in improving overall health by balancing the Doshas.

Reason (R): Panchakarma therapy enhances cellular metabolism by optimizing digestive enzyme activity.

42. Assertion (A): Digitization of Ayurvedic texts enables wider access to ancient knowledge and facilitates modern research.

Reason (R): The digitization process eliminates the need for Sanskrit scholars in interpreting traditional texts.

43. Assertion (A): Overharvesting of medicinal plants like Amalaki threatens the sustainability of Ayurvedic formulations.

Reason (R): The rising global demand for Ayurvedic products has led to increased cultivation of Amalaki through traditional methods.

44. Assertion (A): The Ministry of AYUSH collaborates with international organizations to standardize Ayurvedic formulations.

Reason (R): Global collaborations aim to develop synthetic alternatives to traditional Ayurvedic ingredients.

45. Assertion (A): Ayurvedic texts like the Dhanvantari Nighaṇtu are essential resources for identifying herbs with pharmacological potential.

Reason (R): These texts categorize herbs solely based on traditional culinary uses, with limited focus on therapeutic applications.

Directions (Q. No. 46–50): *Read the passage carefully and answer the questions given below:*

The Ministry of AYUSH, established by the Government of India, has been pivotal in promoting Ayurveda both nationally and internationally. Its initiatives include the digitization of classical texts, development of the AYUSH Grid, and collaborations with global organizations like the World Health Organization (WHO) to standardize Ayurvedic formulations. One of the flagship programs, the National AYUSH Mission, focuses on integrating traditional medicine with mainstream healthcare. Additionally, the Ministry is actively involved in the conservation of medicinal plants through the National Medicinal Plants Board (NMPB), which addresses issues like overharvesting and habitat destruction.

Despite these efforts, challenges persist. The lack of public awareness about Ayurveda's scientific validity and the limited reach of Ayurvedic services in rural areas hinder its growth. Furthermore, concerns over the quality and authenticity of Ayurvedic products necessitate stricter regulatory frameworks. Recent collaborations with research institutions aim to bridge this gap by validating traditional knowledge through modern scientific methods. Globally, the demand for Ayurvedic products is rising, yet sustainability remains a critical issue, as the cultivation of medicinal plants often falls short of demand.

Moving forward, the Ministry envisions a comprehensive approach involving public awareness campaigns, evidence-based research, and sustainable practices to ensure Ayurveda's global recognition as a complementary system of medicine.

46. According to the passage, what is one of the primary objectives of the National AYUSH Mission?

A. To digitize classical Ayurvedic texts for global access.

B. To integrate Ayurveda into mainstream healthcare systems.

C. To promote large-scale monoculture plantations for medicinal plants.

D. To prioritize international trade of Ayurvedic products over domestic needs.

47. What role does the National Medicinal Plants Board (NMPB) play in supporting Ayurveda, as mentioned in the passage?

A. Conducting clinical trials to validate Ayurvedic treatments.

B. Conserving medicinal plants and mitigating habitat destruction.

C. Exporting high-demand medicinal plants to international markets.

D. Developing synthetic alternatives to traditional Ayurvedic formulations.

48. Based on the passage, which of the following challenges most significantly affects the growth of Ayurveda?

A. Over-reliance on synthetic alternatives to herbal formulations.

B. Inadequate scientific validation of Ayurvedic principles.

C. Excessive public awareness campaigns overshadowing research efforts.

D. Overemphasis on rural areas at the expense of urban healthcare facilities.

49. How is the Ministry of AYUSH addressing concerns regarding the quality and authenticity of Ayurvedic products?

A. By restricting the export of Ayurvedic products to ensure quality control.

B. By developing stricter regulatory frameworks for standardization.

C. By promoting traditional preparation methods without modernization.

D. By focusing exclusively on domestic markets for Ayurvedic formulations.

50. Which of the following strategies is proposed in the passage to ensure Ayurveda's global recognition?

A. Replacing traditional practices with fully modernized systems.

B. Enhancing public awareness, evidence-based research, and sustainability.

C. Prioritizing international trade agreements over domestic healthcare needs.

D. Abandoning traditional methods in favour of synthetic pharmaceutical products.

ANSWER WITH EXPLANATIONS

1. C: The dual nature of Ayurvedic terms as symbolic and scientific creates an opportunity for integrative research bridging traditional and modern medicine. Classical Ayurvedic texts often blend empirical observations with metaphysical interpretations, providing insights that align with modern pharmacology while retaining their holistic philosophy. By treating these terms as both empirical and metaphorical, researchers can unlock their therapeutic relevance and cultural depth. Ignoring their symbolic meaning would limit interdisciplinary dialogue, while viewing them solely as metaphors would dismiss their potential scientific value. Thus, an integrative approach respects the epistemological diversity inherent in Ayurvedic knowledge systems.

2. **A:** Aligning ancient terminologies with taxonomical and pharmacological standards is critical for cross-disciplinary integration. Ayurvedic texts use descriptive language rooted in Sanskrit, often tied to cultural contexts rather than universal scientific classifications. This creates challenges in matching ancient concepts to contemporary databases, which rely on measurable biochemical markers. Preserving historical authenticity while standardizing data for global acceptance requires meticulous efforts in translation, taxonomy, and validation. This ensures that Ayurvedic principles are accessible and relevant to both traditional practitioners and modern researchers, fostering global healthcare innovation without compromising cultural integrity.

3. **C:** The divergence highlights the need for an interdisciplinary framework to bridge traditional and modern pharmacological systems. Ayurvedic classifications focus on holistic properties rather than isolated biochemical markers, reflecting a broader understanding of health and disease. Modern pharmacology, however, prioritizes reductionist methods, often missing synergies described in Ayurveda. Discrepancies arise from this epistemological gap, emphasizing the importance of interdisciplinary research. By integrating these paradigms, scientists can develop a nuanced understanding of plant-based therapies, validating traditional wisdom while expanding the scope of modern pharmacological practices.

4. **B:** Positive outcomes reinforce the applicability of classical texts while highlighting the importance of empirical validation for specific formulations. Madanapala Nighaṇṭu offers insights into dosha-specific treatments, providing a framework for personalized medicine. Modern clinical trials can confirm these traditional classifications, enabling evidence-based practices that enhance their credibility. While empirical validation strengthens the scientific foundation of Ayurveda, it also preserves its philosophical essence. This dual validation process ensures that Ayurvedic knowledge remains relevant in modern healthcare, balancing its historical significance with contemporary applications.

5. **B:** Standardization of raw materials enhances the reliability and reproducibility of Ayurvedic treatments in clinical settings. Quality assurance ensures consistent therapeutic outcomes, addressing concerns about variability in raw materials. This initiative aligns Ayurvedic formulations with global standards, making them more acceptable in evidence-based medicine. By focusing on phytochemical profiling and standardization, the Ministry of AYUSH promotes Ayurveda as a credible healthcare system while maintaining its holistic principles. This balance between traditional wisdom and modern rigor strengthens Ayurveda's position in global healthcare, encouraging broader adoption and integration.

6. **A:** By emphasizing cultural and philosophical dimensions of healthcare beyond clinical precision, Ayurvedic Kośas contribute uniquely to contemporary medical education. These texts integrate metaphysical concepts, offering a holistic understanding of health that transcends physical symptoms. This perspective complements the reductionist approach of modern medicine, enriching medical curricula with a broader view of patient care. Ayurvedic Kośas also encourage reflective learning, fostering empathy and cultural sensitivity among healthcare professionals. Integrating these texts into modern education systems bridges traditional and scientific paradigms, creating a more comprehensive framework for understanding health and wellness.

7. **D:** The findings affirm that Ayurvedic groupings are empirical but require integration with molecular research to achieve universal applicability. Ayurvedic classifications often reflect synergistic properties that are not immediately apparent through molecular studies. Discrepancies highlight the complexity of therapeutic mechanisms, necessitating further research. By combining Ayurvedic insights with modern pharmacology, scientists can uncover these synergies, expanding the scope of both systems. This integrative approach validates traditional knowledge while addressing gaps in molecular understanding, fostering innovation in plant-based therapies.

8. **B:** It would validate the relevance of Ayurvedic texts while emphasizing the importance of bioavailability studies. Classical texts like Madanapala Nighaṇṭu often describe the synergistic effects of herbs, which modern pharmacokinetics can quantify. By demonstrating that traditional formulations enhance bioavailability, researchers bridge the gap between ancient wisdom and scientific rigor. This process not only reinforces the credibility of Ayurvedic texts but also positions them as valuable resources for drug development. Such validation strengthens Ayurveda's role in integrative medicine, ensuring its relevance in modern healthcare.

9. **B:** Developing standardized guidelines for integrating

Ayurvedic texts into CAM protocols effectively addresses clinical adoption barriers. Ayurvedic principles, while valuable, often lack uniformity in practice; making standardization essential for broader acceptance. Guidelines ensure consistency in interpretation and application, enabling healthcare providers to integrate Ayurveda confidently. This approach respects the diversity of traditional knowledge while aligning it with clinical standards. By promoting evidence-based practices, standardized protocols enhance Ayurveda's credibility in CAM systems, fostering global acceptance and application.

10. **A:** Ensuring the translations maintain the cultural and philosophical integrity of the original texts is the most significant ethical consideration. Ayurvedic texts are deeply rooted in cultural and historical contexts, which are integral to their interpretation. Misrepresentation or oversimplification risks distorting their essence, reducing their value to mere pharmacological constructs. Accurate translations that preserve the richness of Sanskrit terminology ensure that Ayurveda's holistic philosophy is respected and understood. This balance between accessibility and authenticity safeguards the cultural heritage of Ayurveda while promoting its global relevance.

11. **B:** The findings from Scenario 1 highlight Triphala's role in enhancing gut-associated lymphoid tissue (GALT) activity. This mechanism is vital as gut health directly correlates with systemic immunity. By improving microbiota diversity, Triphala fortifies gut integrity, influencing immune markers like IgA. GALT's involvement showcases a scientific basis for traditional claims, bridging Ayurveda and immunology. The emphasis on gut microbiota aligns with global research on probiotics and immune health. Hence, Triphala demonstrates dual functionality: as a detoxifier and immune booster. This comprehensive approach validates traditional wisdom through molecular and clinical evidence, supporting Ayurveda's integration into mainstream healthcare.

12. **A:** One of the key issues hindering the integration of Ayurveda with mainstream healthcare is the lack of dedicated infrastructure and adequate funding. Strengthening AYUSH research centers with proper financial support and facilities would foster quality education, clinical trials, and innovation, helping Ayurveda gain credibility and wider acceptance.

13. **A:** Overharvesting of Amalaki disrupts the supply chain, directly affecting the application of Nighaṇṭu data. Nighaṇṭus rely on the availability of documented herbs to validate and utilize their classifications. Without sustainable practices, the therapeutic potential of formulations diminishes, weakening Ayurveda's credibility. Furthermore, declining plant quality due to environmental stressors reduces the bioactive content, impacting clinical efficacy. This highlights the need for sustainable harvesting as an integral part of Ayurveda's digitization initiatives. Bridging conservation with digitization ensures the relevance of classical knowledge in contemporary applications. Sustainable practices are critical to maintaining the harmony between tradition and modern research.

14. **A:** A holistic strategy integrating sustainable harvesting, digitization, and research ensures Ayurveda's long-term growth. Policies addressing ecological preservation, scientific validation, and public awareness form a cohesive framework. Conservation measures protect plant populations, while digitization preserves textual knowledge. Together, they create opportunities for interdisciplinary research, ensuring Ayurveda remains relevant in modern healthcare. Ignoring sustainability weakens the foundation of Ayurvedic formulations, and disregarding traditional practices dilutes its authenticity. Combining ancient principles with modern innovations aligns with Ayurveda's holistic ethos, fostering a balance between nature, science, and healthcare. This approach establishes Ayurveda as a credible and sustainable global medical system.

15. **A:** The Ministry of AYUSH emphasizes digitization, research integration, and infrastructure development to promote Ayurveda. Digitizing classical texts preserves ancient knowledge while making it accessible globally. The establishment of wellness centers and integrative research institutions ensures Ayurveda's role in primary healthcare and interdisciplinary collaboration. Sustainable plant use balances conservation with demand. Excluding private partnerships prevents the commercialization of Ayurveda at the expense of authenticity. These strategies collectively strengthen Ayurveda's foundation, fostering innovation while maintaining its cultural integrity. Focusing on these key objectives ensures its relevance and applicability in both traditional and modern medical systems.

16. **A:** Government initiatives like the AYUSH Grid and digitization of texts enhance global accessibility to Ayurvedic knowledge. Collaboration with international bodies fosters the standardization of formulations, ensuring credibility in global markets. Integrating Ayurveda into primary rural healthcare addresses local needs and demonstrates its practical applications. Subsidizing modern pharmaceuticals is outside the scope of Ayurveda's promotion and unrelated to its growth. These comprehensive strategies demonstrate

a multifaceted approach, combining technological advancements, research collaboration, and community-level healthcare delivery to sustain and expand Ayurveda's reach and effectiveness in addressing public health challenges.

17. **A:** Challenges in Ayurveda include insufficient quality control, limited awareness of its scientific validity, and the need for empirical evidence. Traditional knowledge alone cannot address these gaps. Regulatory frameworks standardize formulations, ensuring authenticity and safety. Public outreach campaigns build awareness about Ayurveda's benefits and preventive care principles. Evidence-based research bridges traditional practices with modern medicine. Excessive focus on sustainability without affordability considerations would hinder accessibility. Addressing these challenges collectively strengthens Ayurveda's scientific credibility and cultural relevance, enabling its integration into mainstream healthcare systems while maintaining its unique principles.

18. **A:** Nighaṇṭus provide a structured understanding of Ayurvedic herbs, categorizing them based on therapeutic properties like Rasa, Guna, and Vipaka. These classifications align with pharmacological attributes, guiding clinical applications. Their comprehensive documentation includes regional names, enhancing accessibility and contextual understanding. Contrary to misconceptions, Nighaṇṭus are scientific tools, not poetic compositions. They form the foundation for validating Ayurvedic principles, linking traditional wisdom with contemporary research. This blend of linguistic, botanical, and therapeutic knowledge ensures their relevance in both academic and clinical contexts, emphasizing their critical role in Ayurveda's advancement.

19. **B:** The Tridosha concept reflects Ayurveda's holistic approach to human physiology. Vata governs movement, influencing the nervous system; Pitta controls metabolism and digestion; Kapha ensures structural stability and immunity. Together, they maintain physical and psychological balance. While dietary habits affect Dosha equilibrium, they are not the sole determinant. Ayurveda emphasizes lifestyle, environmental factors, and personalized care in maintaining health. This multidimensional understanding underscores Ayurveda's depth, integrating physiological, biochemical, and lifestyle aspects into a unified framework that addresses individual needs while promoting overall well-being.

20. **A:** Global promotion of Ayurveda through research collaborations, clinical trials, and export initiatives positions it as a credible medical system. Standardizing formulations ensures consistency and builds trust in international markets. Clinical validation addresses skepticism, demonstrating Ayurveda's scientific basis. Prioritizing these objectives ensures Ayurveda's integration into complementary medical systems worldwide. Overemphasizing global trade without addressing domestic healthcare needs risks compromising its foundational principles. A balanced approach enhances Ayurveda's credibility and ensures sustainable growth, preserving its authenticity while meeting global healthcare demands.

21. **A:** In Ayurveda, Vata is responsible for all types of movement in the body including circulation and nerve impulses. Pitta governs digestion, metabolism, and transformation processes at both physical and mental levels. Kapha provides structure, stability, lubrication, and endurance. These core functions form the physiological foundation of Tridoṣa theory.

22. **A:** The five sensory organs or Jñānendriyas in Ayurveda are each linked with specific perceptive functions. Eyes (Chakṣur) help in perceiving form and color, ears (Śrotra) perceive sound, tongue (Rasa) is responsible for tasting, and skin (Tvak) perceives touch sensations. These organs help in receiving information from the external environment.

23. **C:** Karmendriyas are action organs that facilitate interaction with the world. Vāk (speech) enables verbal communication, Pāṇi (hands) are for grasping and handling objects, Pāda (feet) help in locomotion, and Upastha (genitals) play a role in reproduction. These organs execute the body's actions.

24. **A:** Among the seven dhatus (body tissues), Rasa provides nourishment to all tissues, Rakta supports vitality and oxygen transport, Mamsa builds muscular strength and body mass, and Meda helps with lubrication and fat storage. Each dhatu supports both physiological and structural aspects of health.

25. **A:** The five Mahābhūtas (great elements) form the building blocks of all matter. Ākāśa (ether) relates to space and softness, Vāyu (air) brings motion and activity, Agni (fire) facilitates transformation like digestion and metabolism, while Jala (water) imparts fluidity, cohesion, and cooling effects.

26. **A:** In Ayurveda, Ātman (soul) is the source of consciousness, Śarīra (body) provides the material form, Indriya (senses) allow perception of the world, and Tridoṣa (Vata, Pitta, Kapha) maintain the body's internal balance. Together, these elements support holistic well-being.

27. **C:** Each dosha primarily resides in a specific region of the body. Vata is located in the colon and nervous system, managing movement and impulses. Pitta is based in the small intestine and stomach, handling digestion and metabolism. Kapha resides in the chest and lymphatic system, giving stability and fluid balance.

28. **D:** The five senses are connected with specific Mahābhūtas. Śrotra (ears) correspond to Ākāśa (space) as sound travels through space, Tvak (skin) to Vāyu (air) due to tactile perception, Chakṣur (eyes) to Agni (fire) because of vision and light, and Rasa (tongue) to Jala (water) since taste is only possible with moisture.

29. **B:** Each dosha can be aggravated by particular triggers. Vata increases with excessive movement and irregular eating. Pitta is provoked by heat and spicy foods. Kapha becomes aggravated due to heavy food and a sedentary lifestyle. Recognizing these helps in effective prevention and treatment.

30. **A:** Ayurvedic therapies target specific doshas and systems. Abhyanga (oil massage) calms Vata by enhancing circulation. Shirodhara (oil poured on the forehead) pacifies Pitta by soothing the mind. Vamana (therapeutic vomiting) removes excess Kapha and helps detoxify the respiratory and digestive systems.

31. **A:** The Dhanvantari Nighaṇṭu is one of the earliest Ayurvedic lexicons focusing on brief, classical descriptions of herbs and their categories. Raja Nighaṇṭu by Narahari Paṇḍita is unique for its classification of medicinal substances into systematic Vargas (groups). Bhāvaprakāśa Nighaṇṭu bridges folk medicine and classical Ayurveda, offering rich cultural context. Madanapāla Nighaṇṭu is known for its detailed listing of synonyms and regional names, helping identify herbs across geographies.

32. **A:** Ayurvedic Kośas (dictionaries) have distinct structures. Nāma Kośa lists names, synonyms, and roots of Ayurvedic terms. Dravya Kośa catalogs substances like herbs, minerals, and animal products used in treatments. Roga Kośa explains diseases, their classifications, and symptoms. Karma Kośa includes therapeutic procedures and processes like Vamana, Virechana, etc., providing a practical reference for practitioners.

33. **A:** The Dhanvantari Nighaṇṭu is attributed to an early period and is foundational in Ayurvedic pharmacology. Madanapāla Nighaṇṭu was composed by King Madanapāla in the 14th century CE. Bhāvaprakāśa Nighaṇṭu was authored by Bhāvamiśra and is widely used for its rich detail and integration of classical and folk knowledge. Raja Nighaṇṭu by Narahari Paṇḍita reflects a later period with methodical classification and clarity.

34. **A:** Nighaṇṭus group herbs based on therapeutic utility. Rasayana herbs promote rejuvenation, tissue repair, and longevity, making them essential in preventive care. Vishaghna Dravyas are categorized for neutralizing poisons, relevant in Agada Tantra. Bhedaniya refers to purgative herbs used in eliminating excess Kapha or Ama. Deepaniya herbs stimulate digestive fire (Agni), supporting metabolism and correcting digestive disorders.

35. **C:** The integration of Ayurveda into primary healthcare under the National AYUSH Mission aims to complement rather than replace conventional treatments. This inclusion strengthens rural healthcare accessibility, emphasizing Ayurveda's preventive and holistic benefits. The incorrect assumption that Ayurveda replaces modern medicine highlights the need for awareness about its integrative role. Collaborative efforts ensure Ayurveda's contributions to holistic health, promoting balance between tradition and modernity. Addressing these misconceptions through education and outreach is essential for building trust and ensuring successful integration.

36. **B:** Digitization enhances access to Ayurvedic knowledge and fosters interdisciplinary research. It enables standardized translations, preserving the authenticity and contextual accuracy of classical texts. Contrary to misconceptions, digitization does not eliminate the need for Sanskrit scholars; their expertise ensures accurate interpretations. By combining traditional linguistic insights with technological advancements, digitization supports Ayurveda's global reach while maintaining its philosophical and therapeutic integrity. This balanced approach ensures that Ayurveda remains accessible, credible, and relevant in contemporary healthcare and academic contexts.

37. **A:** Sustainability is critical for Ayurveda's long-term viability, as medicinal plants form the foundation of its formulations. Conservation initiatives ensure the availability of high-quality ingredients, maintaining therapeutic efficacy. Linking sustainability to efficacy emphasizes the interconnectedness of environmental health and Ayurvedic principles. This relationship underscores the need for empirical validation of traditional practices, addressing skepticism about Ayurveda's scientific relevance. Government efforts to bridge these gaps reflect Ayurveda's adaptability, aligning tradition with modernity to address global healthcare challenges sustainably and effectively.

38. A: The alignment of Ayurvedic concepts like Rasa and Vipaka with pharmacological properties highlights their scientific basis. Modern research validates these principles by identifying bioactive compounds correlating with traditional classifications. This empirical evidence strengthens Ayurveda's credibility, bridging ancient knowledge with contemporary science. Misinterpreting these classifications as symbolic undermines their practical applications. Recognizing their pharmacological relevance fosters interdisciplinary collaboration, ensuring Ayurveda's integration into mainstream healthcare. This alignment demonstrates Ayurveda's adaptability and relevance in addressing global healthcare needs.

39. B: Nighaṇṭus like the Madanapala Nighaṇṭu provide disease-specific classifications, bridging traditional wisdom with modern research. These classifications enhance the practical application of Ayurvedic principles in clinical settings. However, the notion that traditional texts focus exclusively on culinary uses is incorrect, highlighting the importance of preserving their therapeutic context. By aligning traditional classifications with empirical research, Nighaṇṭus contribute to Ayurveda's scientific validation, ensuring its integration into global healthcare. This approach demonstrates the relevance of classical texts in addressing contemporary medical challenges.

40. A: The AYUSH Grid integrates technology with Ayurveda, creating a digital platform for research, education, and clinical practice. It enhances accessibility and fosters interdisciplinary collaboration, ensuring Ayurveda's relevance in modern healthcare. By disseminating data and resources, the AYUSH Grid supports evidence-based studies and public outreach. This alignment between tradition and innovation reflects Ayurveda's adaptability and global aspirations. Such initiatives ensure Ayurveda's growth, addressing misconceptions while preserving its unique principles. The digital integration of Ayurvedic knowledge demonstrates its relevance and credibility in addressing contemporary healthcare challenges.

41. A: Panchakarma therapies exemplify Ayurveda's holistic detoxification practices, balancing the Doshas and optimizing health. By stimulating metabolic activity, these therapies enhance enzyme function, directly addressing conditions linked to metabolic imbalances. The connection between Panchakarma and cellular metabolism highlights its scientific relevance, bridging traditional detoxification principles with modern biochemical insights. This alignment demonstrates Ayurveda's therapeutic depth and adaptability, validating its applications in both preventive and curative contexts. The dual role of Panchakarma in restoring balance and improving metabolism underscores Ayurveda's emphasis on personalized and systemic healing, ensuring its integration into contemporary healthcare systems.

42. C: Digitization enhances access to Ayurvedic texts, preserving their traditional knowledge and making it available for modern research. However, it does not eliminate the need for Sanskrit scholars, whose expertise ensures accurate interpretation of these texts' nuanced meanings. Without proper linguistic and contextual understanding, misinterpretations can arise, undermining the credibility of Ayurveda. The balance between digitization and scholarly expertise maintains the authenticity of Ayurvedic principles while fostering innovation. This approach emphasizes the importance of collaboration between traditional and modern methods, ensuring Ayurveda's global applicability without losing its philosophical roots.

43. C: The overharvesting of medicinal plants like Amalaki poses a significant sustainability challenge, threatening both biodiversity and the efficacy of Ayurvedic formulations. The statement about increased cultivation through traditional methods is incorrect, as such efforts are insufficient to meet rising global demand. Conservation programs and sustainable harvesting practices are necessary to address these challenges. Linking sustainability to therapeutic outcomes ensures Ayurveda's long-term viability while preserving ecological balance. This interconnected approach highlights Ayurveda's holistic ethos, emphasizing harmony between natural resources and healthcare practices.

44. C: Collaborations with international organizations aim to standardize Ayurvedic formulations, ensuring consistency and global acceptance. The notion of developing synthetic alternatives contradicts Ayurveda's reliance on natural substances and traditional preparation methods. These collaborations validate Ayurveda's therapeutic principles while maintaining its authenticity. By addressing global quality standards, such efforts enhance Ayurveda's credibility and integration into complementary medical systems. This strategy reflects a balanced approach, fostering innovation while preserving the integrity of Ayurvedic practices in global healthcare contexts.

45. C: Texts like the Dhanvantari Nighaṇṭu serve as critical resources for identifying herbs with pharmacological potential. They classify plants based on therapeutic properties, offering a structured framework for research and clinical applications. The misconception that they focus solely on culinary uses undermines their scientific relevance. By aligning traditional classifications with empirical studies, these texts contribute to Ayurveda's integration into modern medicine. This collaboration between ancient wisdom and contemporary science ensures the credibility and applicability of Ayurvedic formulations in addressing global healthcare needs.

46. **B:** The National AYUSH Mission integrates Ayurveda into mainstream healthcare systems, addressing rural and underserved populations. This initiative showcases Ayurveda's practical applications, emphasizing its preventive and holistic approach. Digitization and international trade are separate objectives under other initiatives, and focusing solely on monoculture plantations contradicts Ayurveda's sustainability goals. By aligning traditional practices with modern healthcare, the mission addresses critical gaps, demonstrating Ayurveda's adaptability and effectiveness. This integration reflects a balanced strategy, combining accessibility, sustainability, and innovation to enhance public health.

47. **B:** The National Medicinal Plants Board (NMPB) plays a pivotal role in conserving medicinal plants and mitigating habitat destruction caused by overharvesting. These efforts ensure the long-term availability of high-quality ingredients for Ayurvedic formulations, maintaining therapeutic efficacy. While clinical trials and trade fall under other initiatives, conservation addresses both environmental and healthcare challenges. Linking sustainability to efficacy emphasizes the interconnectedness of ecological preservation and Ayurveda's holistic principles. This comprehensive approach ensures Ayurveda's growth while preserving its foundational values and resources.

48. **B:** One of the most significant challenges to Ayurveda's growth is the lack of scientific validation, which limits its credibility and acceptance in modern healthcare systems. Public awareness campaigns alone cannot address these gaps without empirical evidence. Misconceptions about Ayurveda's preventive and curative benefits hinder its integration into mainstream medicine. Efforts to validate traditional practices through research enhance trust and acceptance, bridging the gap between ancient wisdom and modern science. This validation ensures Ayurveda's relevance and effectiveness in addressing contemporary healthcare challenges.

49. **B:** To address quality concerns, the Ministry of AYUSH implements regulatory frameworks that standardize Ayurvedic formulations and ensure product authenticity. This strategy builds trust among users and enhances the credibility of Ayurvedic products in global markets. Restricting exports or relying solely on traditional methods without modernization limits Ayurveda's growth. Balancing standardization with traditional authenticity fosters innovation while preserving Ayurveda's core principles. This approach strengthens Ayurveda's foundation, ensuring its sustainability and integration into contemporary healthcare systems.

50. **B:** The passage highlights a comprehensive strategy for Ayurveda's global recognition, combining public awareness, evidence-based research, and sustainability efforts. This approach ensures a balanced growth trajectory, addressing misconceptions while preserving authenticity. Replacing traditional practices or prioritizing trade over healthcare undermines Ayurveda's holistic ethos. Focusing on innovation within traditional frameworks strengthens Ayurveda's credibility and adaptability. By aligning its principles with modern healthcare needs, this strategy ensures Ayurveda's relevance and acceptance as a complementary medical system worldwide.

UNIT 2: PHILOSOPHY AND FUNDAMENTAL PRINCIPLES OF AYURVEDA

CHAPTER–5

CONCEPTS OF AYU, SARIRA, JNANENDRIYA, KARMENDRIYA, AND ATMAN

Definition of Āyu (Life) and Its Dimensions

In Ayurveda, the concept of Āyu (life) is foundational to understanding human existence, health, and wellness. The classical texts of Ayurveda, particularly the Charaka Samhita and Sushruta Samhita, define Āyu as the union of the body (śarīra), senses (indriyas), mind (manas), and soul (ātman). This holistic view underscores that life is not merely the physical presence of the body but a dynamic interplay between these components.

Definition of Āyu

Āyu is described in Charaka Samhita (Sūtrasthāna 1:41) as:

Sharīrendriya-satva-ātma samyogaḥ āyuḥ

Translation: Life (Āyu) is the conjunction of the body (śarīra), senses (indriyas), mind (satva), and soul (ātman).

This definition implies that life exists as long as these four elements coexist harmoniously. The cessation of this union signifies death.

Dimensions of Āyu

1. **Physical Dimension (Śārīrika Āyu):** Relates to the body and its physiological functions.
   It includes the processes of digestion, metabolism, movement, and reproduction.
   Physical longevity is influenced by prakṛti (constitution), diet, lifestyle, and genetic factors.
2. **Sensory Dimension (Indriya Āyu):** Involves the sensory organs (jñānendriyas) and their ability to perceive the external world.
   It reflects the interaction between an individual and their environment.
3. **Mental Dimension (Mānasa Āyu):** Refers to the mind's faculties, such as cognition, emotion, memory, and intellect.
   A balanced mind is crucial for psychological well-being and decision-making.
4. **Spiritual Dimension (Ātmika Āyu):** Centers on the soul (ātman), which is eternal and transcendental.
   The spiritual aspect of life emphasizes self-awareness, purpose, and liberation (mokṣa).

Structure and Function of Śarīra (Body)

In Ayurveda, the body (śarīra) is viewed as a microcosm of the universe. It is not merely a physical entity but a composite of various elements and energies that enable life. The texts describe the body as a vehicle for achieving the ultimate goals of life, including dharma (duty), artha (prosperity), kāma (desires), and mokṣa (liberation).

Structure and Function of Śarīra in Ayurveda

Ayurveda, the ancient Indian system of medicine, perceives the human body, or Śarīra, as a microcosm of the macrocosmic universe. This holistic perspective recognizes the intricate interplay of physical, mental, and spiritual dimensions of existence. The foundational understanding of the body in Ayurveda is built upon three pivotal components: Mahābhūtas (Five Great Elements), Tridoṣa (Three Functional Energies), and Saptadhātus (Seven Tissues). Together, these elements provide a framework for health, disease, and the deeper purpose of human life.

STRUCTURE OF ŚARĪRA

Ayurvedic texts describe the body as an integrated entity composed of five great elements, functional energies (doṣas), structural tissues (dhātus), and waste products (malas). This section unpacks these components to elucidate how they form the human body.

Mahābhūtas (The Five Great Elements)

The Mahābhūtas—Ākāśa (ether), Vāyu (air), Agni (fire), Jala (water), and Pṛthvī (earth)—are the building blocks of creation, including the human body. These elements manifest at the gross and subtle levels, shaping physiological structures, functions, and psychological tendencies.

(a) Ākāśa (Ether):

- **Represents space or void:** Governs cavities within the body, such as the gastrointestinal tract, respiratory passages, blood vessels, and cellular spaces.
- Facilitates communication, expansion, and differentiation.

(b) Vāyu (Air):

- Represents movement and dynamic activity.
- Manifests in the physiological functions of circulation, nerve impulses, and respiration.
- Influences the mobility of joints, muscles, and sensory perception.

(c) Agni (Fire):

- Represents heat, transformation, and metabolism.
- Operates through Jatharagni (digestive fire) and cellular enzymes to digest food and convert it into energy.
- Controls vision, body temperature, and mental clarity.

(d) Jala (Water):

- Represents fluidity, cohesion, and lubrication.
- Forms bodily fluids like plasma, saliva, and mucus.
- Ensures hydration, nutrient transport, and structural cohesion.

(e) Pṛthvī (Earth);

- Represents solidity and stability.
- Forms the structural components like bones, muscles, and nails.
- Provides endurance, firmness, and grounding to the body

These elements do not act in isolation but combine in specific proportions to form the doshas, dhātus, and malas. This interaction underscores the body's intricate balance.

Tridoṣa (The Three Functional Energies)

The doshas—Vāta, Pitta, and Kapha—**are functional principles derived from the Mahābhūtas. They regulate physiological and psychological processes.

(a) Vāta: The Energy of Movement

- Derived from Ākāśa and Vāyu.
- Governs bodily movements, including breathing, circulation, nerve impulses, and waste elimination.
- **Characteristics:** Dry, light, cold, rough, subtle, and mobile.
- Imbalance leads to conditions like arthritis, insomnia, and anxiety.

(b) Pitta: The Energy of Transformation

- Derived from Agni and Jala.
- Controls digestion, metabolism, body temperature, and vision.
- Characteristics: Hot, sharp, light, oily, and spreading.
- Imbalance causes hyperacidity, inflammation, and irritability.

(c) Kapha: The Energy of Stability

- Derived from Pṛthvī and Jala.
- Provides structure, cohesion, lubrication, and immunity.
- **Characteristics:** Heavy, slow, cold, oily, smooth, dense, and stable.
- Imbalance results in obesity, congestion, and lethargy.

The harmonious interplay of these doshas ensures health, while their disturbance leads to disease. Each dosha predominates in specific regions and times of the day, reflecting their dynamic nature.

Saptadhātus (The Seven Tissues)

The seven dhātus form the structural foundation of the body. Each dhātu evolves from the previous one through a process called dhātuparinama (transformation of tissues).

(a) Rasa (Plasma):

- Nourishes all tissues and maintains hydration.
- Formed from digested food in the gastrointestinal tract.

(b) **Rakta (Blood):**
- Supplies oxygen and nutrients to tissues.
- Maintains vitality and skin complexion.

(c) **Māṃsa (Muscle):**
- Provides strength and structural integrity.
- Forms flesh, ligaments, and organ coverings.

(d) **Meda (Fat):**
- Acts as a reserve of energy.
- Lubricates organs and joints.

(e) **Asthi (Bone):**
- Forms the skeletal structure, providing support and protection.
- Maintains calcium balance.

(f) **Majjā (Bone Marrow and Nervous Tissue):**
- Fills bones and nourishes nerves.
- Supports cognitive and motor functions.

(g) **Shukra (Reproductive Tissue):**
- Represents vitality, fertility, and creative energy.
- Produces sperm and ova for procreation.

The healthy functioning of dhātus ensures bodily strength, immunity, and vitality, whereas their imbalance results in tissue degeneration or excess accumulation.

Malas (Waste Products)

Malas are metabolic by-products that must be eliminated to maintain homeostasis.

- **Feces (Purīṣa):** Formed in the colon; eliminates undigested food.
- Urine **(Mutra):** Regulates fluid and electrolyte balance.
- **Sweat (Sveda):** Controls body temperature and skin health.
- Efficient removal of malas is vital for physiological balance.

FUNCTION OF ŚARĪRA

The body, beyond its structural components, is designed to perform various functions essential for survival and higher pursuits. Ayurveda emphasizes the integration of physical, mental, and spiritual dimensions in understanding bodily functions.

1. **Locomotion and Action:**
   - Facilitated by the musculoskeletal system and motor organs (karmendriyas).
   - Involves coordinated actions between bones, muscles, tendons, and joints.
   - Governed by Vāta dosha, particularly the subtypes like Prāṇa Vāyu and Apāna Vāyu.
2. **Perception:** Enabled by sensory organs (jñānendriyas): eyes, ears, nose, tongue, and skin.
   Each organ corresponds to a Mahābhūta:
   - Eyes (Agni) for vision.
   - Ears (Ākāśa) for hearing.
   - Nose (Pṛthvī) for smell.
   - Tongue (Jala) for taste.
   - Skin (Vāyu) for touch.
   - Governed by coordination between Tridoṣa and Mana (mind).
3. **Digestion and Metabolism:**
   - Controlled by Agni (digestive fire), which transforms food into nutrients and waste.
   - Involves the interplay of Pitta dosha and subtypes like Pachaka Pitta.

   Metabolism occurs at three levels:
   - **Jatharagni (digestive fire):** In the stomach.
   - **Bhutagni:** At the elemental level
   - **Dhātvagni:** At the tissue level.
4. **Reproduction:**
   - Ensures the continuity of life.
   - Supported by Shukra dhātu and hormones.
   - Governed by a balance between Vāta, Pitta, and Kapha.
5. **Support for Higher Goals:**
   - Ayurveda recognizes the body as a vessel for:
   - **Intellectual Growth:** Through memory, concentration, and discernment.
   - **Emotional Stability:** Governed by Sattva, Rajas, and Tamas (mental gunas).
   - **Spiritual Evolution:** Facilitated by practices like yoga, meditation, and pranayama.

The Ayurvedic understanding of Śarīra offers a profound and holistic perspective on the body as a dynamic interplay of elements, energies, and tissues. It highlights the inseparable connection between structure and function, health and disease, and the physical and spiritual aspects of human existence.

By balancing the Mahābhūtas, doshas, dhātus, and malas, Ayurveda seeks to promote not just physical well-being but also mental harmony and spiritual growth, offering a timeless guide for holistic health.

Overview of Sensory Organs (Jñānendriya) and Action Organs (Karmendriya)

Sensory Organs (Jñānendriya)

The jñānendriyas are the five sensory faculties responsible for perception and knowledge acquisition. They are linked to specific elements and sensory functions:

1. **Chakṣurendriya (Eyes):**
   - **Associated Element:** Fire (Agni)
   - **Function:** Vision
   - **Role:** Perceives form, color, and light.
2. **Śrotrendriya (Ears):**
   - **Associated Element:** Ether (Ākāśa)
   - **Function:** Hearing
   - **Role:** Detects sound and vibrations.
3. **Ghrāṇendriya (Nose):**
   - **Associated Element:** Earth (Pṛthvī)
   - **Function:** Smell
   - **Role:** Discerns odors and fragrances.
4. **Rasanendriya (Tongue):**
   - **Associated Element:** Water (Jala)
   - **Function:** Taste
   - **Role:** Recognizes different tastes like sweet, sour, salty, bitter, and astringent.
5. **Tvagindriya (Skin):**
   - **Associated Element:** Air (Vāyu)
   - **Function:** Touch
   - **Role:** Detects temperature, pressure, and texture.

- Action Organs (Karmendriya)

The karmendriyas are the five motor faculties responsible for actions and expressions:

1. **Vākindriya (Speech):**
   - **Function:** Communication
   - **Role:** Verbal expression and interaction.
2. **Pāṇīndriya (Hands):**
   - **Function:** Grasping
   - **Role:** Facilitates physical tasks and creation.
3. **Pādendriya (Feet):**
   - **Function:** Locomotion
   - **Role:** Enables movement and stability.
4. **Upasthendriya (Genital Organs):**
   - **Function:** Reproduction
   - **Role:** Ensures procreation and pleasure.
5. **Pāyvindriya (Excretory Organs):**
   - **Function:** Elimination
   - **Role:** Disposes waste from the body.

- Both jñānendriyas and karmendriyas are crucial for maintaining a balanced interaction between the internal and external environments.
- Concept of Ātman (Soul) and Its Significance in Ayurveda

The concept of ātman (soul) is central to Ayurvedic philosophy and forms the cornerstone of its spiritual dimension. Ātman is considered eternal, indestructible, and the true essence of an individual.

Definition and Nature of Ātman

1. **Eternal and Transcendental:** The soul is beyond birth and death. It exists independently of the physical body.
2. **Consciousness:** Ātman is the source of consciousness, making the body and mind functional.
3. **Universal Connection:** It is a reflection of the supreme consciousness (Paramātman) and is connected to the cosmic order.

Role of Ātman in Ayurveda

1. **Life Force:** The presence of the soul distinguishes a living being from a non-living entity.

   Ātman drives the functions of the body, senses, and mind.
2. **Spiritual Health:** Ayurveda emphasizes aligning one's life with spiritual principles to achieve harmony.

   Practices like meditation, yoga, and ethical living nurture the soul.
3. **Determinant of Individuality:** While the soul is universal, it carries unique karmic imprints that shape an individual's prakṛti (constitution) and destiny.
4. **Path to Liberation (Mokṣa):** The ultimate goal of Ayurveda transcends mere physical health; it aims for spiritual liberation by purifying the body and mind, allowing the soul to attain freedom from the cycle of birth and death.

   Interrelation Between Āyu, Śarīra, Jñānendriya, Karmendriya, and Ātman

   Āyu integrates the body, senses, mind, and soul into a cohesive whole.

   Śarīra provides the physical platform for the senses (jñānendriyas) and actions (karmendriyas) to function.

   The ātman, as the essence of life, animates and directs these faculties toward achieving higher purposes.

MULTIPLE CHOICE QUESTIONS

1. Consider an Ayurvedic practitioner exploring the multidimensional concept of Āyu. They theorize that the integration of physical health, mental stability, sensory engagement, and spiritual fulfillment forms the essence of life. A patient is evaluated for imbalances in these dimensions, showing symptoms of chronic fatigue (physical), anxiety (mental), dulled senses (sensory), and lack of purpose (spiritual). The practitioner uses this case to validate the Ayurvedic definition of life as a union of all these dimensions.

   Which of the following approaches aligns most closely with the holistic treatment philosophy of Ayurveda?

   A. Prescribing a combination of herbal remedies solely targeting physical health and metabolic energy.

   B. Employing meditation and spiritual counseling without addressing physical symptoms.

   C. Administering therapies that concurrently address physical, sensory, mental, and spiritual dimensions to restore balance.

   D. Isolating the sensory dullness as the primary symptom and focusing all treatment on sensory enhancement.

2. Imagine a scenario where a researcher is analyzing the śarīra (body) based on the Ayurvedic view of the tridoṣa system. The researcher hypothesizes that an imbalance in Kapha leads to water retention, joint stiffness, and lethargy. Upon treating patients with a Kapha imbalance using therapies like dry massages and hot herbal formulations, they observe significant improvement in mobility and energy.

   Which of the following Ayurvedic principles does this study reinforce?

   A. Kapha governs structure and lubrication; its balance ensures optimal physical function.

   B. Pitta imbalance is primarily responsible for joint stiffness and reduced mobility.

   C. Dry massages are only effective for Pitta imbalances, not Kapha-related issues.

   D. Water retention is unrelated to Kapha and is governed exclusively by external factors.

3. In Ayurvedic philosophy, jñānendriyas (sensory organs) and karmendriyas (action organs) are seen as crucial for maintaining the interaction between an individual and their environment. A patient presents with impaired hearing and speech due to chronic neurological issues. The Ayurvedic practitioner proposes therapies targeting both śrotrendriya (ears) and vākindriya (speech organ) using auditory stimulation and vocal exercises.

   Which of the following statements best describes the interconnected role of sensory and action organs in this case?

   A. Sensory and action organs work independently, and treating one has no impact on the other.

   B. Impairment in sensory organs can lead to dysfunction in corresponding action organs, necessitating combined therapy.

   C. Action organs require treatment through physical exercise, while sensory organs benefit only from herbal remedies.

   D. The treatment of speech impairments is unrelated to the auditory sensory function.

4. An Ayurvedic scholar investigates the ātman (soul) in the context of holistic health. The scholar posits that neglecting the spiritual dimension in therapy leads to incomplete healing, as the ātman governs the life force. A therapeutic approach involving yoga, meditation, and ethical living is recommended alongside physical treatments for chronic illnesses.

   How does this approach align with the Ayurvedic understanding of the ātman?

   A. It prioritizes the mind and body over the soul in achieving health.

   B. It integrates spiritual practices, acknowledging the soul as the cornerstone of well-being.

   C. It negates the role of the body, focusing solely on spiritual liberation.

   D. It considers the soul to be secondary to the physical body in healing processes.

5. A biologist studying the dimensions of Āyu hypothesizes that mental health has a direct influence on physical and sensory well-being. A patient experiencing chronic stress and anxiety develops digestive issues and dulled taste perception. Ayurvedic treatments, including sattvavajaya (mind therapy) and dietary modifications, successfully restore the patient's health.

   Which Ayurvedic concept does this observation best illustrate?

   A. Physical health operates independently of mental health.

   B. Āyu's dimensions are interdependent, with the mind influencing physical and sensory states.

   C. Sensory functions are unaffected by psychological disturbances.

   D. Mental health is unrelated to dietary habits or digestive functions.

6. An environmentalist evaluates the sustainability of herbal harvesting practices for Ayurvedic formulations. The overharvesting of certain plants, like Amalaki, has led to ecological imbalances and reduced medicinal quality. The researcher advocates for cultivating these plants in controlled environments to preserve wild populations.

Which of the following Ayurvedic principles supports this sustainable approach?

A. The concept of prakṛti applies only to individuals, not to the environment.
B. Harmony with nature is central to Ayurveda, necessitating sustainable resource use.
C. The medicinal quality of plants is unrelated to their ecological context.
D. Ayurvedic formulations are effective regardless of the quality of raw materials.

7. A case study focuses on a patient with impaired vision due to prolonged stress and nutrient deficiencies. Ayurvedic therapies involving chakṣurendriya (eyes) include applying medicated ghee, practicing trāṭaka (focused gazing), and consuming eye-nourishing herbs.

What does this treatment reveal about the Ayurvedic approach to sensory organ care?

A. Sensory organ health is restored through targeted therapies and systemic nourishment.
B. External therapies are sufficient to restore vision, regardless of systemic deficiencies.
C. Stress management is unrelated to sensory organ care in Ayurveda.
D. Herbal remedies alone are adequate for treating sensory impairments.

8. A clinical researcher investigates the influence of ātman in psychosomatic illnesses. The study reveals that patients practicing mindfulness and meditation report greater resilience against chronic diseases and improved recovery rates.

Which Ayurvedic principle does this finding support?

A. The soul's influence is negligible in physical healing processes.
B. The ātman integrates mental and physical health, influencing overall well-being.
C. Meditation impacts only the mind and not the physical body.
D. Ayurvedic therapy focuses exclusively on physiological factors.

9. A scholar revisits the Ayurvedic concept of śarīra as a dynamic entity comprising mahābhūtas (five elements). They observe that an imbalance in vāyu (air) leads to joint pain and anxiety, while a pitta (fire) imbalance causes hyperacidity and inflammation.

How does this understanding shape Ayurvedic diagnostics and treatment?

A. Imbalances in mahābhūtas are irrelevant in modern Ayurvedic practice.
B. Identifying elemental imbalances is central to diagnosing and treating diseases.
C. Elemental imbalances are static and unaffected by lifestyle changes.
D. Ayurveda disregards mahābhūtas in favour of herbal remedies.

10. A group of Ayurveda students debates whether the karmendriyas (action organs) function independently of the jñānendriyas (sensory organs). One student argues that dysfunction in sensory perception, such as impaired taste, affects corresponding action organs like the tongue.

Which statement best supports this argument?

A. Karmendriyas and jñānendriyas are anatomically distinct and do not interact.
B. The functional interdependence of sensory and action organs is central to Ayurvedic theory.
C. Sensory dysfunction has no bearing on the action organs in Ayurveda.
D. The theory of sensory-action organ interplay is a modern addition to Ayurveda.

Directions (Q. No. 11-14): *Scenario-Based Questions*

SCENARIO 1

A clinical researcher is studying the effects of Ayurvedic formulations on gut health and systemic immunity. The study focuses on the classical Ayurvedic preparation Triphala, which combines three fruits: Haritaki, Bibhitaki, and Amalaki. These fruits are known for their roles in balancing the doshas and promoting gut health through detoxification. The researcher observes that Triphala significantly improves the diversity of gut microbiota in patients with irritable bowel syndrome (IBS), restoring balance in microbial populations. Additionally, the study finds that gut health improvements correspond with enhanced systemic immunity, measured by increased levels of immunoglobulin A (IgA) and reduced systemic inflammation markers like (c)-reactive protein (CRP).

SCENARIO 2

Simultaneously, an environmental biologist investigates the sustainability of sourcing medicinal plants used in Ayurvedic formulations. The focus is on Amalaki (Emblica officinalis), a key component of Triphala. The biologist's findings reveal that overharvesting of Amalaki due to rising global demand threatens its wild populations. Moreover, the study highlights that environmental stressors, such as deforestation and soil degradation, reduce the bioactive compound concentration in Amalaki fruits. The reduced quality of Amalaki not only impacts the efficacy of Ayurvedic formulations but also indirectly affects gut health outcomes observed in Scenario 1.

11. Based on the findings in Scenario 1, which of the following mechanisms best explains the enhanced systemic immunity observed in patients treated with Triphala?

A. Triphala directly stimulates the production of immunoglobulins and immune cells, independent of gut health.

B. The restoration of gut microbiota diversity by Triphala enhances gut-associated lymphoid tissue (GALT) activity, promoting systemic immunity.

C. Triphala's detoxifying properties reduce microbial diversity but enhance the gut's physical barrier function, indirectly boosting immunity.

D. Triphala acts as a placebo, and the immune enhancement is unrelated to its effects on gut health.

12. Considering Scenario 2, which of the following interventions would most effectively address the sustainability challenges associated with Amalaki harvesting while ensuring its medicinal quality?

A. Establishing large-scale monoculture plantations of Amalaki to meet global demand.

B. Encouraging traditional agroforestry systems and promoting community-based conservation of wild Amalaki populations.

C. Substituting Amalaki with synthetic alternatives to reduce dependency on natural resources.

D. Reducing the global production of Triphala to conserve wild Amalaki populations.

13. How does the environmental degradation of Amalaki, as described in Scenario 2, potentially influence the therapeutic outcomes observed in Scenario 1?

A. Reduced bioactive compound concentration in Amalaki could diminish its efficacy in promoting gut microbiota diversity and systemic immunity.

B. The quality of Amalaki has no measurable effect on the efficacy of Triphala, as its potency is driven by the combination of all three fruits.

C. Triphala's gut health benefits would remain unaffected, as its detoxifying properties are independent of Amalaki's bioactive content.

D. Environmental degradation enhances Amalaki's potency, improving the therapeutic outcomes of Triphala formulations.

14. Based on the interconnected findings of Scenarios 1 and 2, which of the following strategies would most comprehensively address the challenges while maintaining the efficacy of Ayurvedic formulations?

A. Prioritizing scientific research to develop synthetic alternatives that mimic the bioactive profile of Amalaki.

B. Establishing a global Triphala standard that incorporates sustainable harvesting practices and ensures bioactive compound consistency.

C. Shifting the focus from Triphala to other formulations that do not rely on endangered plant species.

D. Encouraging large-scale commercial production of all Triphala components, independent of traditional Ayurvedic practices.

15. The Ayurvedic concept of Tridosha states:

(a) Vata governs movement and is linked to the nervous system.

(b) Pitta controls metabolism and is associated with digestive enzymes.

(c) Kapha regulates structure and fluid balance in the body.

(d) The balance of Tridosha ensures physical and mental health.

Choose the correct combination:

A. (a), (b), and (c) only

B. (a), (b), (d) only

C. (a), (b), (c), and (d)

D. (a), (c), and (d) only

16. The biological actions of Ayurvedic Rasas (tastes) are classified as:

(a) Sweet Rasa promotes tissue growth and nourishment.

(b) Bitter Rasa detoxifies the body and reduces inflammation.

(c) Astringent Rasa strengthens tissues and controls bleeding.

(d) Sour Rasa enhances digestion and metabolic activity.

Choose the correct combination:

A. (a), (b), and (d) only

B. (a), (b), (c), and (d)

C. (b), (c), and (d) only

D. (a), (c), and (d) only

17. According to Ayurvedic principles:

(a) Agni represents the digestive fire essential for metabolism.

(b) Weak Agni leads to the formation of Ama (toxins).

(c) Balanced Agni supports mental clarity and immunity.

(d) Agni is unrelated to the doshas.

Choose the correct combination:
A. (a), (b), and (c) only
B. (b), (c), and (d) only
C. (a) and (c) only
D. (a), (b), (c), and (d)

18. The functions of Karmendriyas (action organs) in Ayurveda include:
(a) Speech enables communication and verbal expression.
(b) Hands facilitate grasping and creative tasks.
(c) Genital organs are responsible for reproduction.
(d) Sensory perception through physical contact.

Choose the correct combination:
A. (a), (b), and (c) only
B. (a), (c), and (d) only
C. (a), (b), (c), and (d)
D. (b), (c), and (d) only

19. The characteristics of Kapha Dosha include:
(a) Governs stability and lubrication.
(b) Balances metabolism and energy production.
(c) Influences emotional resilience and calmness.
(d) Aggravation leads to lethargy and congestion.

Choose the correct combination below:
A. (a), (b), and (d) only
B. (a), (c), and (d) only
C. (a), (b), (c), and (d)
D. (b), (c), and (d) only

20. The functions of Rakta Dhatu (blood) in Ayurveda are:
(a) Provides nourishment to tissues.
(b) Carries oxygen and vitality.
(c) Regulates fat storage.
(d) Enhances muscle strength.

Choose the correct combination:
A. (a) and (b) only
B. (b), (c), and (d) only
C. (a), (b), and (d) only
D. (a), (b), (c), and (d)

21. According to Āyurvedic philosophy, the functions of the five Jñānendriyas (sense organs of perception) include:
(a) Chakṣurendriya perceives form and color.
(b) Śrotrendriya perceives sound and vibrations.
(c) Ghrāṇendriya perceives moisture and texture.
(d) Jihvendriya perceives taste and communicates it to the mind.

Choose the correct combination:
A. (a), (b), and (d) only
B. (a), (b), (c), and (d)
C. (b), (c), and (d) only
D. (a), (c), and (d) only

22. The following statements relate to the actions of the five Karmendriyas (motor organs):
(a) Vāk Indriya enables speech and expression.
(b) Pāṇi Indriya facilitates grasping and manipulation.
(c) Upastha Indriya governs urination and excretion only.
(d) Pāda Indriya enables movement and locomotion.

Choose the correct combination:
A. (a), (b), and (d) only
B. (a), (b), (c), and (d)
C. (b), (c), and (d) only
D. (a), (c), and (d) only

23. In Ayurvedic śarīra, the concept of Ātman includes the following features:
(a) Ātman is eternal and beyond the physical body.
(b) Ātman is the source of consciousness and intelligence.
(c) Ātman is destructible during pralayā (cosmic dissolution).
(d) Ātman cannot be perceived directly through sense organs.

Choose the correct combination:
A. (a), (b), and (d) only
B. (a), (b), (c), and (d)
C. (b), (c), and (d) only
D. (a), (c), and (d) only

24. According to Ayurvedic understanding of sensory perception and its relation to the mind:
(a) The mind (manas) serves as a bridge between Jñānendriyas and Ātman.
(b) Without the involvement of manas, perception cannot occur.
(c) Manas is an independent sense organ with its own external perception.
(d) The mind processes the inputs from Jñānendriyas before they reach Ātman.

Choose the correct combination:
A. (a), (b), and (d) only
B. (a), (b), (c), and (d)
C. (b), (c), and (d) only
D. (a), (c), and (d) only

25. Match List–I (Doshas) with List–II (Primary Characteristics):

List–I	List–II
(a) Vata	1. Responsible for movement and bodily functions
(b) Pitta	2. Governs metabolism and transformation

(c) Kapha	3. Provides stability and structural support

Choose the correct answer from the options given below:

A. (a)-2, (b)-1, (c)-3 B. (a)-3, (b)-2, (c)-1

C. (a)-1, (b)-2, (c)-3 D. (a)-2, (b)-3, (c)-1

26. Match List–I (Sensory Organs - Jñānendriya) with List–II (Functions):

List–I	List–II
(a) Chakṣur (Eyes)	1. Perception of form and colour
(b) Śrotra (Ears)	2. Perception of sound
(c) Rasa (Tongue)	3. Perception of taste
(d) Tvak (Skin)	4. Perception of touch

Choose the correct answer from the options given below:

A. (a)-2, (b)-1, (c)-3, (d)-4

B. (a)-1, (b)-2, (c)-4, (d)-3

C. (a)-3, (b)-4, (c)-2, (d)-1

D. (a)-1, (b)-2, (c)-3, (d)-4

27. Match List–I (Action Organs - Karmendriya) with List–II (Functions):

List–I	List–II
(a) Vāk (Speech)	1. Verbal communication
(b) Pāṇi (Hands)	2. Facilitation of grasping
(c) Pāda (Feet)	3. Facilitation of locomotion
(d) Upastha (Genitals)	4. Facilitation of reproduction

Choose the correct answer from the options given below:

A. (a)-4, (b)-2, (c)-3, (d)-1

B. (a)-2, (b)-1, (c)-4, (d)-3

C. (a)-1, (b)-3, (c)-2, (d)-4

D. (a)-1, (b)-2, (c)-3, (d)-4

28. Match List–I (Dhatus) with List–II (Biological Functions):

List–I	List–II
(a) Rasa	1. Provides nourishment
(b) Rakta	2. Supports vitality
(c) Mamsa	3. Builds and strengthens muscles
(d) Meda	4. Regulates lubrication

Choose the correct answer from the options given below:

A. (a)-1, (b)-2, (c)-3, (d)-4

B. (a)-2, (b)-3, (c)-1, (d)-4

C. (a)-3, (b)-4, (c)-2, (d)-1

D. (a)-4, (b)-1, (c)-3, (d)-2

29. Match List–I (Mahābhūtas) with List–II (Associated Attributes):

List–I	List–II
(a) Ākāśa (Ether)	1. Softness
(b) Vāyu (Air)	2. Motion
(c) Agni (Fire)	3. Transformation
(d) Jala (Water)	4. Fluidity

Choose the correct answer from the options given below:

A. (a)-1, (b)-2, (c)-3, (d)-4

B. (a)-4, (b)-3, (c)-2, (d)-1

C. (a)-2, (b)-1, (c)-4, (d)-3

D. (a)-3, (b)-4, (c)-1, (d)-2

30. Match List–I (Concepts) with List–II (Significance in Ayurveda):

List–I	List–II
(a) Ātman (Soul)	1. Governs consciousness
(b) Śarīra (Body)	2. Provides physical structure
(c) Indriya (Senses)	3. Enables interaction with the environment
(d) Tridoṣa (Doshas)	4. Maintains physiological balance

Choose the correct answer from the options given below:

A. (a)-1, (b)-2, (c)-3, (d)-4

B. (a)-4, (b)-3, (c)-2, (d)-1

C. (a)-3, (b)-4, (c)-1, (d)-2

D. (a)-2, (b)-1, (c)-4, (d)-3

31. Match List–I (Tridoṣa and Their Locations) with List–II (Primary Regions in the Body):

List–I	List–II
(a) Vata	1. Colon and nervous system
(b) Pitta	2. Stomach and small intestine
(c) Kapha	3. Chest and lymphatic system

Choose the correct answer from the options given below:

A. (a)-2, (b)-1, (c)-3

B. (a)-1, (b)-3, (c)-2

C. (a)-1, (b)-2, (c)-3

D. (a)-3, (b)-2, (c)-1

32. Match List–I (Jñānendriyas - Sensory Organs) with List–II (Associated Mahābhūtas):

List–I	List–II
(a) Śrotra (Ears)	1. Ākāśa (Ether)
(b) Tvak (Skin)	2. Vāyu (Air)
(c) Chakṣur (Eyes)	3. Agni (Fire)
(d) Rasa (Tongue)	4. Jala (Water)

Choose the correct answer from the options given below:

A. (a)-1, (b)-3, (c)-4, (d)-2

B. (a)-4, (b)-1, (c)-3, (d)-2

C. (a)-2, (b)-3, (c)-1, (d)-4

D. (a)-1, (b)-2, (c)-3, (d)-4

33. Match List–I (Dosha Aggravating Factors) with List–II (Primary Triggers):

List–I	List–II
(a) Vata	1. Excessive movement and irregular meals
(b) Pitta	2. Overheating and spicy foods
(c) Kapha	3. Sedentary lifestyle and heavy foods

Choose the correct answer from the options given below:

A. (a)-2, (b)-1, (c)-3
B. (a)-1, (b)-2, (c)-3
C. (a)-3, (b)-2, (c)-1
D. (a)-1, (b)-3, (c)-2

34. Match List–I (Therapies) with List–II (Therapeutic Effects in Ayurveda):

List–I	List–II
(a) Abhyanga (Oil Massage)	1. Improves circulation and reduces Vata imbalance
(b) Shirodhara (Oil Pouring on Forehead)	2. Calms the mind and balances Pitta
(c) Vamana (Therapeutic Vomiting)	3. Clears excess Kapha and detoxifies

Choose the correct answer from the options given below:

A. (a)-1, (b)-2, (c)-3
B. (a)-3, (b)-1, (c)-2
C. (a)-2, (b)-3, (c)-1
D. (a)-1, (b)-3, (c)-2

Directions (Q. No. 35-39): *Following questions are based on Statement 1 and Statement 2. Read both the statements carefully and choose the correct answer from the options given below:*

A. Both Statement 1 and Statement 2 are true, and Statement 2 is the correct explanation of Statement 1.
B. Both Statement 1 and Statement 2 are true, but Statement 2 is not the correct explanation of Statement 1.
C. Statement 1 is true, but Statement 2 is false.
D. Statement 1 is false, but Statement 2 is true.
E. Both Statement 1 and Statement 2 are false.

35. Statement 1: Āyu in Ayurveda is defined as the union of the body (śarīra), sensory organs (jñānendriya), mind (manas), and soul (ātman), and it represents the total span of life.

Statement 2: The concept of Āyu primarily focuses on physical longevity and does not consider mental or spiritual well-being as integral components.

36. Statement 1: The structure of the śarīra (body) in Ayurveda is described as a dynamic system where the elements (pancha-mahābhūtas) combine to form tissues, organs, and functional systems.

Statement 2: The dynamic structure of the śarīra relies solely on the balance of external environmental factors, independent of the doshic constitution.

37. Statement 1: Jñānendriyas (sensory organs) are responsible for perceiving knowledge from the external environment, while karmendriyas (action organs) enable interaction with the world through physical actions.

Statement 2: The integration of jñānendriyas and karmendriyas in Ayurveda emphasizes the harmonious coordination between sensory perception and action for achieving holistic health.

38. Statement 1: The ātman (soul) in Ayurveda is considered eternal and distinct from the physical body, mind, and senses, and it is the ultimate source of consciousness.

Statement 2: The role of ātman in Ayurveda is limited to metaphysical discussions and does not have practical relevance in the understanding of health and disease.

39. Statement 1: In Ayurveda, the śarīra (body) serves as the medium through which the soul (ātman) experiences the physical world, with health being the balance between body, mind, and soul.

Statement 2: Ayurveda disregards the interdependence of the body, mind, and soul, focusing solely on physical health as the determinant of well-being.

Directions (Q. No. 40–45): *There are two statements in each question. One is labelled as Assertion (A) and the other is as Reason (R). Read both the statements and choose the correct answer from the options given below:*

A. Both Assertion (A) and Reason (R) are true, and Reason (R) is the correct explanation of Assertion (A).
B. Both Assertion (A) and Reason (R) are true, but Reason (R) is not the correct explanation of Assertion (A).
C. Assertion (A) is true, but Reason (R) is false.
D. Assertion (A) is false, but Reason (R) is true.
E. Both Assertion (A) and Reason (R) are false.

40. Assertion (A): Ayurveda emphasizes that the four components of Āyu—śarīra, jñānendriya, karmendriya, and ātman—must function in harmony to sustain life.

Reason (R): A dysfunction in any one of these components disrupts the others, leading to a loss of vitality and eventually impacting longevity.

41. Assertion (A): Śarīra in Ayurveda is considered to be composed of the five elements (pancha-mahābhūtas) and exists to support the functional activities of the ātman.

Reason (R): The purpose of śarīra is purely physiological, with no role in spiritual growth or mental stability.

42. Assertion (A): The jñānendriyas in Ayurveda are essential for gathering knowledge from the external environment, which is crucial for maintaining mental health.

Reason (R): Jñānendriyas are solely responsible for cognitive functions, while the mind plays no role in the processing of sensory data.

43. **Assertion (A):** Karmendriyas in Ayurveda enable the individual to act upon the environment, bridging the internal and external worlds.

    Reason (R): Action organs (karmendriyas) are passive in nature, and their functions are determined entirely by sensory inputs (jñānendriyas).

44. **Assertion (A):** In Ayurvedic philosophy, the ātman is the eternal observer that guides the body, mind, and senses without direct involvement in physical functions.

    Reason (R): The role of the ātman in Ayurveda is limited to spiritual discussions and has no direct influence on health and disease management.

45. **Assertion (A):** The interdependence of jñānendriyas and karmendriyas ensures that perception and action are synchronized for maintaining balance in life.

    Reason (R): In Ayurveda, any imbalance between sensory perception and motor action disrupts the doshic equilibrium, leading to physical and mental disorders.

Directions (Q. No. 46–50): *Read the passage carefully and answer the questions given below*:

The concept of Ātman in Ayurveda is a profound exploration of the eternal and transcendent aspect of human existence, fundamentally intertwining health, consciousness, and purpose. Unlike the transient nature of the body and mind, the Ātman is regarded as immutable, indestructible, and the essence of life itself. Rooted in Vedic philosophy, Ayurveda emphasizes that health is not merely the absence of disease but the harmonious integration of the body (śarīra), senses (indriyas), mind (manas), and soul (ātman). The Ātman is considered the ultimate source of vitality, governing the subtler aspects of life such as consciousness, awareness, and spiritual fulfillment.

In the Ayurvedic framework, prakṛti (individual constitution) and vikṛti (imbalance) are seen as reflections of the Ātman's interaction with the physical and mental dimensions. A disharmonious state, characterized by doshic imbalances or mental agitation, obscures the true nature of the Ātman, leading to physical, emotional, and spiritual disturbances. Restoring harmony through practices like meditation, yoga, and ethical living is not merely therapeutic but transformative, facilitating the alignment of actions, thoughts, and intentions with the eternal principles of dharma and self-realization.

Furthermore, the Ātman is intricately connected to the concept of karma (action) and mokṣa (liberation). Ayurveda teaches that health is a prerequisite for spiritual progress, as a healthy body and balanced mind enable the individual to pursue higher purposes. This interdependence underscores why Ayurvedic practices aim to eliminate physical and mental obstacles, allowing the Ātman to manifest its full potential. Thus, the ultimate goal of Ayurveda transcends the treatment of diseases—it aspires to facilitate the journey toward spiritual awakening and liberation.

Modern science, despite its focus on empirical evidence, resonates with certain Ayurvedic principles by recognizing the psychosomatic unity of the human organism. Research into the effects of mindfulness and meditation, for instance, validates the physiological and psychological benefits of practices rooted in the Ātman-centered approach. By fostering a holistic understanding of health that integrates physical, mental, and spiritual dimensions, Ayurveda continues to provide a timeless and relevant perspective in the context of contemporary medicine.

46. According to the passage, what role does the Ātman play in Ayurvedic philosophy?
    A. It serves as the ultimate source of vitality and governs consciousness.
    B. It determines the physical appearance and sensory acuity of individuals.
    C. It functions as a symbolic concept without practical application in health.
    D. It exclusively governs spiritual practices, unrelated to physical health.

47. Why does Ayurveda emphasize the integration of body, senses, mind, and Ātman in achieving health?
    A. To enhance physiological functions without addressing mental health.
    B. To harmonize the transient and eternal aspects of human existence.
    C. To align doshic imbalances with environmental changes.
    D. To simplify the diagnostic process by categorizing symptoms.

48. How does the Ātman influence the Ayurvedic understanding of prakṛti and vikṛti?
    A. The Ātman directly causes doshic imbalances leading to disease.
    B. Prakṛti and vikṛti are manifestations of the Ātman's interaction with the body and mind.
    C. The Ātman is unrelated to prakṛti and focuses only on spiritual liberation.
    D. Vikṛti occurs independently of the Ātman and is purely physical.

49. What is the ultimate goal of Ayurvedic practices as described in the passage?
    A. To eliminate physical ailments for longevity.

B. To align individual actions with dharma and facilitate spiritual awakening.

C. To focus solely on enhancing mental clarity and emotional stability.

D. To integrate modern medical practices with traditional Ayurvedic therapies.

50. How does modern scientific research validate certain Ayurvedic principles concerning the Ātman?

A. By rejecting the spiritual aspects of Ātman and focusing on empirical findings.

B. By proving that practices like meditation have measurable physiological and psychological benefits.

C. By acknowledging the Ātman as a vital scientific entity influencing health.

D. By limiting the applicability of Ātman-centered approaches to psychosomatic disorders.

ANSWER WITH EXPLANATIONS

1. C: Ayurveda emphasizes a multidimensional approach to health that integrates the body, senses, mind, and soul. The practitioner's simultaneous focus on physical, mental, sensory, and spiritual therapies reflects the core Ayurvedic philosophy that all dimensions must function harmoniously for true well-being. Addressing just one aspect, such as physical symptoms or mental health, would lead to incomplete treatment. This question highlights the interdependence of Āyu's dimensions, illustrating that Ayurveda's goal transcends disease management, aiming instead to achieve balance and holistic healing, which is possible only through integrative, individualized care addressing all dimensions simultaneously.

2. A: Kapha is described in Ayurveda as the dosha governing structure, lubrication, and stability. Its imbalance leads to symptoms like water retention, heaviness, and lethargy, as seen in the question. Therapies targeting Kapha, such as dry massages and warm herbal formulations, restore balance by reducing excess Kapha qualities of heaviness and moisture. This principle demonstrates how doshas influence both physical and mental health, making their balance critical for optimal function. The study further validates the diagnostic and therapeutic application of doshic principles in modern contexts, particularly in chronic, systemic imbalances.

3. B: In Ayurveda, sensory organs (jñānendriyas) and action organs (karmendriyas) are interconnected. Dysfunction in one can impact the other, as seen in impaired hearing (śrotrendriya) affecting speech (vākindriya). The proposed combined treatment highlights this interdependence, showing how addressing both sensory and action organs leads to holistic healing. This interconnectedness exemplifies Ayurveda's non-reductionist approach, emphasizing the necessity of considering all systems in relation to one another rather than in isolation, a concept modern systems are beginning to recognize, especially in neuro-rehabilitation and integrative medicine.

4. B: The Ātman is central to Ayurveda, representing the eternal and conscious aspect of life. Neglecting spiritual dimensions results in incomplete healing, as the ātman governs mental clarity, vitality, and purpose. The question illustrates how integrating yoga, meditation, and ethical living acknowledges the soul's significance in achieving health. Unlike therapies that prioritize only the physical or mental dimensions, this approach exemplifies Ayurveda's unique focus on spiritual alignment. It demonstrates how self-realization and balance are as much health objectives as physiological equilibrium, connecting individual well-being to universal consciousness.

5. B: Ayurveda views the dimensions of Āyu as deeply interdependent, with mental health (manas) significantly influencing physical (śarīra) and sensory (indriyas) states. The patient's digestive issues and dulled taste due to chronic stress illustrate this principle. Mental disturbances aggravate doshas, impairing agni (digestive fire) and indriya functions. By addressing mental imbalances through sattvavajaya therapy and diet, Ayurveda restores harmony across dimensions, validating its view that true health arises from equilibrium among all facets. This reflects a sophisticated understanding of the mind-body connection, which modern psychosomatic medicine increasingly acknowledges.

6. B: Ayurveda integrates nature into its healing systems, emphasizing harmony with the environment. Overharvesting plants like Amalaki disrupts ecological balance, diminishing their medicinal potency. Promoting sustainable practices aligns with Ayurveda's principle of maintaining equilibrium not only within the body but also with nature. This approach, integrating traditional agroforestry and conservation, ensures resource preservation while retaining their therapeutic properties. Such ecological mindfulness highlights Ayurveda's relevance in addressing modern sustainability challenges, showcasing its foresight in recognizing how environmental degradation impacts human health and treatment efficacy.

7. A: The Ayurvedic approach to sensory organ care combines localized therapies, such as medicated ghee and trāṭaka, with systemic nourishment to address the root cause of sensory impairments. Vision issues linked to stress and deficiencies illustrate how external therapies alone are insufficient without addressing internal imbalances. This integrative method reflects Ayurveda's depth in treating sensory dysfunctions holistically. By nurturing both physical and psychological dimensions, it demonstrates how localized sensory treatments are enriched through systemic balance, an approach uniquely suited to resolving chronic or complex impairments.

8. B: The study linking meditation to improved resilience reflects Ayurveda's principle that the Ātman integrates mind and body. Spiritual practices, like meditation, cleanse mental and physical impurities, allowing the soul's vitality to manifest. This finding aligns with Ayurveda's view of psychosomatic health, where spiritual and physiological dimensions interact. Rather than separating spiritual practices from physical healing, Ayurveda unites them, showing that mindfulness enhances not just mental resilience but systemic health. The interdependence of these dimensions is gaining recognition in modern healthcare, validating Ayurveda's holistic philosophy.

9. B: In Ayurveda, the mahābhūtas (elements) form the foundation of doshas, tissues, and organ systems. Imbalances, such as excessive vāyu causing joint pain or heightened pitta leading to hyperacidity, demonstrate how elemental disturbances manifest as physical ailments. Identifying and addressing these imbalances through diet, lifestyle, and therapies is central to Ayurvedic diagnostics. This question underscores the timeless relevance of Ayurveda's elemental theory, illustrating its nuanced approach to systemic disorders, which complements and often transcends the linear paradigms of modern medicine.

10. B: The debate about the functional relationship between sensory (jñānendriyas) and action organs (karmendriyas) highlights Ayurveda's view of their interdependence. Sensory dysfunction, such as impaired taste, affects the corresponding action organ (tongue), disrupting both perception and expression. This interconnectedness reflects Ayurveda's sophisticated understanding of human physiology, emphasizing the need for therapies that address related systems together. Modern neuroscience echoes this perspective, exploring how sensory impairments can influence motor function, further validating Ayurveda's ancient insights into the unity of bodily systems.

11. B: Triphala improves systemic immunity by restoring gut microbiota diversity, which enhances the activity of gut-associated lymphoid tissue (GALT). The Ayurvedic focus on gut health aligns with the understanding that a balanced microbiome strengthens immune responses, such as increased immunoglobulin A (IgA) production. Unlike direct immune stimulation, Triphala's effect is mediated by harmonizing the microbiota, reflecting Ayurveda's holistic view of health. This concept bridges traditional Ayurvedic detoxification practices with modern immunology, demonstrating how interconnected systems can achieve optimal function when the root cause is addressed.

12. B: Encouraging agroforestry and community-based conservation aligns with Ayurveda's ecological philosophy, which emphasizes harmony with nature. Large-scale monoculture risks degrading biodiversity and soil health, while synthetic alternatives often fail to replicate the complexity of natural compounds. Agroforestry ensures sustainable harvesting and retains the medicinal quality of Amalaki, addressing ecological and therapeutic concerns. Ayurveda's emphasis on maintaining equilibrium extends beyond the body to the environment, offering a sustainable solution that integrates traditional practices with modern ecological needs.

13. A: The reduced bioactive compound concentration in Amalaki due to environmental degradation diminishes its efficacy in supporting gut microbiota diversity and systemic immunity. Triphala's potency relies on the synergistic effects of its components, making the quality of each ingredient critical. Environmental stressors affecting Amalaki disrupt this balance, indirectly influencing therapeutic outcomes. This question underscores the interconnectedness of ecological health and Ayurvedic efficacy, revealing how environmental challenges can cascade into human health outcomes, a principle increasingly evident in global health research.

14. B: Establishing a global standard for Triphala with sustainable harvesting practices ensures the balance between ecological conservation and medicinal efficacy. This strategy aligns with Ayurveda's integrative approach, where preserving the natural integrity of ingredients is crucial for therapeutic success. While synthetic substitutes or shifts to alternative formulations might address supply issues, they fail to capture Ayurveda's emphasis on ecological and systemic harmony. This solution reflects a holistic mindset that safeguards biodiversity, ensures consistent medicinal quality, and respects traditional Ayurvedic wisdom.

15. **C:** The Ayurvedic concept of Tridoṣa defines Vata as governing movement (e.g., nervous system activity), Pitta as controlling metabolism (e.g., digestive enzymes), and Kapha as regulating structure and stability. The balance of these doshas ensures optimal health by coordinating physiological and psychological processes. This understanding is integral to Ayurveda's diagnostic and therapeutic methods, where treatments aim to restore doshic equilibrium based on individual constitutions. The classification illustrates Ayurveda's sophisticated grasp of human physiology and its systemic interdependencies, offering a framework for personalized medicine.

16. **B:** Ayurvedic Rasas (tastes) reflect biological actions—sweet nourishes, bitter detoxifies, sour enhances metabolism, and astringent strengthens tissues. These principles highlight the relationship between sensory perceptions and physiological effects, forming the basis of Ayurvedic dietary therapy. By categorizing food and herbs according to Rasa, Ayurveda tailors treatments to individual needs, emphasizing balance. This approach bridges sensory experience with biological function, providing a comprehensive framework for nutrition and medicine, validated increasingly by phytochemical studies linking tastes with bioactive compounds.

17. **A:** Agni, or digestive fire, is central to Ayurveda, governing metabolism and overall health. Impaired Agni leads to the accumulation of Ama (toxins), disrupting doshic balance and causing disease. Balanced Agni supports digestion, immunity, and mental clarity, highlighting its systemic importance. The emphasis on Agni illustrates Ayurveda's preventive approach, focusing on maintaining metabolic efficiency to avoid disease. This understanding reflects a nuanced perspective on digestion, where physical, mental, and energetic dimensions converge, offering insights increasingly relevant to modern metabolic research.

18. **A:** Karmendriyas (action organs) perform critical functions: speech enables communication, hands facilitate grasping, feet support locomotion, and genital organs enable reproduction. These roles underscore the dynamic interaction between physical action and the body's internal systems. Ayurveda recognizes how imbalances in these organs can disrupt systemic harmony, emphasizing therapies that restore their functionality. This question reflects the integrative approach of Ayurveda, where action and sensory organs are considered interconnected, emphasizing balance in physical expression as essential for health.

19. **B:** Kapha's characteristics—stability, lubrication, and calmness—play vital roles in physical and emotional resilience. However, its aggravation can lead to lethargy, congestion, and emotional stagnation. By maintaining Kapha's balance, Ayurveda ensures structural integrity and fluid balance, critical for optimal health. This dosha exemplifies Ayurveda's systemic approach, where qualities such as heaviness or moisture must align with individual needs and environmental conditions to prevent disease. The dynamic interplay of Kapha's attributes illustrates Ayurveda's intricate understanding of health.

20. **A:** Rakta Dhatu provides nourishment to tissues and supports life by carrying vitality, often equated with Prāṇa. It is responsible for maintaining complexion, body heat, and feeding Māṃsa Dhatu. However, regulating fat is the function of Meda Dhatu, and enhancing muscle strength is primarily a role of Māṃsa Dhatu, not Rakta directly.

21. **A:** Jñānendriyas are the five cognitive sense organs – eye (chakṣu), ear (śrotra), nose (ghrāṇa), tongue (jihvā), and skin (tvak) – responsible for perception. While options (a), (b), and (d) correctly describe their roles, option (c) is incorrect; ghrāṇendriya perceives smell, not moisture or texture.

22. **A:** The Karmendriyas are the motor faculties – speech (vāk), hands (pāṇi), feet (pāda), excretory (pāyu), and reproductive (upastha) organs. Option (c) is incorrect as Upastha Indriya is associated with reproduction and sexual pleasure, not just urination and excretion, which falls under pāyu indriya.

23. **A:** Āyurveda views Ātman as nitya (eternal) and avyaya (unchanging). It is the substratum of consciousness and not perceivable through physical means. Option (c) is incorrect as Ātman is not destructible, even during cosmic dissolution (pralayā); it remains untouched.

24. **A:** In Āyurveda, manas (mind) acts as the internal controller and is essential for perception to happen. It connects the sense organs with the self (Ātman). Option (c) is incorrect because manas does not perceive external objects on its own but relies on Jñānendriyas.

25. **C:** The three Doshas—Vata, Pitta, and Kapha—have specific primary functions. Vata governs movement and communication throughout the body. Pitta is responsible for digestion, metabolism, and all types of transformation, including hormonal and enzymatic actions. Kapha offers structural support, stability, and lubrication. Option C correctly matches each Dosha with its characteristic function.

26. **D:** The five Jñānendriyas (sense organs) are paired with specific sensory perceptions: Chakṣur (eyes) perceives form and color; Śrotra (ears) perceives sound; Rasa

(tongue) perceives taste; and Tvak (skin) perceives touch. These associations are fundamental in both Ayurvedic and classical Indian philosophical texts. Option D accurately reflects the traditional correlations between each sense organ and its function.

27. **D:** The Karmendriyas (organs of action) perform key motor functions. Vāk enables speech (verbal communication), Pāṇi is used for grasping and handling objects, Pāda facilitates movement and locomotion, and Upastha is involved in reproduction and pleasure. These functional associations are rooted in Ayurvedic anatomy, highlighting how each organ enables external interaction. Thus, option D is correct.

28. **A:** Dhatus, or body tissues, sustain and nourish the body, with specific roles: rasa (nourishment), rakta (vitality), mamsa (muscle building), and meda (lubrication). These tissues interact dynamically, where imbalance in one affects others. Ayurveda's treatment strategies aim to restore dhatu equilibrium, ensuring systemic harmony. This question illustrates Ayurveda's emphasis on tissue health as central to overall well-being, demonstrating its holistic perspective. By addressing tissue-specific and systemic needs, Ayurveda offers a comprehensive approach to health that integrates physical and energetic dimensions.

29. **A:** Mahābhūtas, or the five great elements, form the foundation of all matter and are reflected in the body. Ākāśa (Ether) relates to softness and space, Vāyu (Air) governs motion, Agni (Fire) drives transformation, and Jala (Water) represents fluidity. These elemental principles influence doshas, tissues, and physiological functions. Ayurveda uses this elemental framework to diagnose and treat imbalances, ensuring harmony among the body's components. This question highlights Ayurveda's depth in correlating universal principles with human health, offering a nuanced model for understanding and addressing systemic imbalances.

30. **A:** Ayurveda integrates concepts like Ātman (soul), śarīra (body), indriyas (senses), and tridoṣa (doshas) into a holistic framework. The Ātman governs consciousness, the śarīra provides structure, indriyas enable interaction with the environment, and doshas maintain physiological balance. This interconnected model reflects Ayurveda's comprehensive understanding of life and health, emphasizing systemic harmony. By addressing each component through tailored therapies and practices, Ayurveda ensures that all dimensions of existence function in balance, illustrating its integrative approach to well-being and self-realization.

31. **C:** The doshas correspond to specific regions in the body: Vata in the colon and nervous system, Pitta in the stomach and small intestine, and Kapha in the chest and lymphatic system. These locations reflect their functional roles—Vata governs movement, Pitta oversees transformation, and Kapha provides structure and stability. Ayurveda tailors diagnostic and therapeutic strategies based on these associations, addressing imbalances in specific regions to restore systemic harmony. This localization highlights Ayurveda's nuanced understanding of physiology, linking doshas to bodily regions and their functions.

32. **D:** Each sensory organ is associated with one of the Panchamahābhūtas (five great elements). The ear (Śrotra) corresponds to Ākāśa (Ether), skin (Tvak) to Vāyu (Air), eyes (Chakṣur) to Agni (Fire), and tongue (Rasa) to Jala (Water). These associations explain how the five elements manifest through sensory perception. Option D presents the correct elemental linkage for each Jñānendriya.

33. **B:** Doshic aggravation arises from specific triggers: Vata increases with irregular meals and excessive movement, Pitta with overheating and spicy foods, and Kapha with heavy foods and sedentary lifestyles. Ayurveda's therapeutic strategies counter these triggers through tailored diets, lifestyle adjustments, and therapies. This question highlights the dynamic relationship between lifestyle factors and doshic balance, demonstrating Ayurveda's emphasis on preventive care. By identifying and mitigating aggravating factors, Ayurveda ensures long-term health and resilience, reflecting its proactive approach to well-being.

34. **A:** Ayurvedic therapies address specific imbalances: Abhyanga (oil massage) reduces Vata and improves circulation, Shirodhara (oil pouring on the forehead) calms Pitta and promotes mental clarity, and Vamana (therapeutic vomiting) clears excess Kapha. These treatments reflect Ayurveda's targeted approach, where therapies are tailored to doshic imbalances and individual needs. This question highlights Ayurveda's depth in developing therapeutic techniques that address root causes, integrating physical, mental, and energetic dimensions for comprehensive healing.

35. **C:** Āyu in Ayurveda is a comprehensive concept that integrates physical, mental, and spiritual dimensions of life. While Statement 1 captures this holistic view, Statement 2 incorrectly reduces Āyu to physical longevity alone. Ayurveda emphasizes that health is not merely the absence of disease but the harmonious interaction of the body, mind, and soul. This perspective ensures that well-being encompasses mental clarity, emotional balance, and spiritual fulfillment. By focusing on Āyu's multidimensional nature, Ayurveda

provides a framework that transcends reductionist approaches to health, enabling a deeper understanding of life as a union of interconnected aspects.

36. C: Statement 1 accurately reflects Ayurveda's dynamic understanding of the śarīra, rooted in the interplay of pancha-mahābhūtas and doshas. Statement 2 erroneously claims that external environmental factors alone determine this dynamic structure. Ayurveda highlights that internal factors, including an individual's prakriti (constitutional type), also significantly influence the body's structure and functions. The śarīra operates as a self-regulating system, adapting to both internal and external changes while maintaining balance. This perspective underscores the integrative approach of Ayurveda, where physical structure and function are seen as products of both intrinsic and extrinsic influences.

37. A: Both statements are true, and Statement 2 effectively explains Statement 1 by emphasizing the coordination between sensory perception and action. Jñānendriyas and karmendriyas collectively ensure the body's interaction with the external world, fostering holistic health. Ayurveda's emphasis on their harmonious function reflects its integrative philosophy, where sensory inputs guide actions, and actions, in turn, influence sensory experiences. This dynamic interplay underscores the importance of balance in maintaining health and well-being, as disruptions in coordination can lead to physical or mental imbalances. Ayurveda's approach reinforces the idea that health is a result of synchronized bodily functions.

38. C: The ātman, as described in Ayurveda, is the eternal essence that transcends the physical realm, making Statement 1 true. However, Statement 2 is incorrect, as ātman plays a critical role in understanding health and disease. Ayurveda integrates metaphysical concepts like ātman into its holistic approach, recognizing the soul's influence on mental and physical health. The absence of alignment between the body and the ātman can lead to imbalances, emphasizing the need for spiritual practices to complement physical and mental care. This interconnected framework distinguishes Ayurveda from reductionist models, reinforcing its relevance in addressing all aspects of well-being.

39. C: Ayurveda views the śarīra as the medium through which the ātman experiences the physical world, emphasizing the interconnectedness of body, mind, and soul, making Statement 1 true. Statement 2, however, falsely claims that Ayurveda disregards this interdependence. The Ayurvedic framework ensures that physical health, mental clarity, and spiritual harmony are treated as equally vital. This triadic approach aligns with its goal of holistic well-being, where imbalances in any one aspect can disrupt the entire system. This philosophy highlights the integrative and preventive nature of Ayurveda, setting it apart from systems focused exclusively on physical health.

40. A: Āyu in Ayurveda integrates the physical body, senses, mind, and soul into a unified framework for life. Both the assertion and reason are true, with the reason explaining that disruptions in one component affect the others, leading to an imbalance that diminishes vitality. This interconnected model highlights Ayurveda's holistic approach, where health is not seen as compartmentalized but as an intricate balance. Unlike reductionist systems, this view emphasizes that longevity and quality of life depend on synchronizing these dimensions. Modern perspectives on psychosomatic health echo this integrative understanding, affirming the timeless relevance of the Ayurvedic model.

41. C: While the śarīra is composed of pancha-mahābhūtas and serves the ātman, the reason incorrectly states that its role is purely physiological. Ayurveda positions the śarīra as a medium for spiritual growth and experience, integrating physiological, psychological, and spiritual dimensions. The body's health is influenced by external factors like environment and diet, but it is equally shaped by internal factors such as dosha balance. This dual influence underscores the śarīra's centrality in facilitating harmony between the physical and metaphysical. Ayurveda's nuanced understanding transcends the idea of the body as merely a physiological entity.

42. C: The assertion about the jñānendriyas' role in gathering external stimuli is true, but the reason is false because cognitive functions rely on both sensory organs and the mind. The jñānendriyas act as channels for perception, while the mind processes and interprets sensory inputs. This synergy underscores Ayurveda's holistic approach, where the senses and mind collectively shape cognition and decision-making. Ignoring the mind's role would reduce sensory perception to a mechanical process, overlooking the subjective dimensions of experience. Ayurveda's focus on this interdependence aligns with modern neuroscience, which emphasizes sensory integration and mental processing.

43. C: Karmendriyas indeed bridge the internal and external worlds through action, but the reason is incorrect because they are not passive and do not solely depend on jñānendriyas. While sensory inputs guide action, karmendriyas also operate autonomously under the influence of the mind and doshas. Ayurveda's model highlights the active role of karmendriyas in maintaining balance and responding to stimuli, emphasizing their independence and adaptability. By considering both sensory guidance and autonomous action, Ayurveda provides a more comprehensive understanding of how humans interact with their environment, transcending simplistic input-output models of functionality.

44. C: The ātman as an eternal observer is central to Ayurveda, making the assertion true, but the reason is false because the ātman influences health indirectly by aligning the mind, senses, and body. Ayurveda's metaphysical foundation sees the ātman as distinct yet essential for sustaining life and consciousness. This perspective bridges spirituality and health, encouraging practices like meditation and self-awareness to align physical and mental functions with the soul. While it does not engage directly in physical processes, the ātman provides the guiding force for achieving harmony, making it integral to holistic health rather than purely philosophical discourse.

45. A: Both the assertion and reason are true, and the reason explains the assertion. The interdependence of jñānendriyas and karmendriyas ensures that perception and action are aligned, maintaining equilibrium in the doshas. Ayurveda recognizes that imbalances between these faculties disrupt physical and mental health, highlighting the need for harmony in sensory and motor functions. This balance mirrors modern neuropsychology, where sensory-motor integration is critical for cognitive and behavioural health. By emphasizing the synchronization of perception and action, Ayurveda offers a proactive model for addressing disorders that arise from functional dissonance in the body-mind connection.

46. A: The Ātman governs consciousness, vitality, and higher purpose in Ayurveda. As the essence of life, it transcends physicality, integrating spiritual and systemic dimensions. Its role as the ultimate source of vitality reflects Ayurveda's holistic perspective, emphasizing that health includes alignment with the Ātman. By addressing the Ātman's influence, Ayurveda ensures a comprehensive approach to well-being, distinguishing itself from reductionist models that focus solely on physical aspects. This question highlights the Ātman's centrality to Ayurveda's philosophy.

47. B: Integration of body, senses, mind, and Ātman harmonizes transient and eternal aspects, achieving holistic health. Ayurveda views each dimension as interconnected, where imbalances disrupt systemic harmony. Practices like meditation and ethical living align these aspects, restoring balance and facilitating well-being. This question underscores Ayurveda's systemic approach, where individual components are treated as integral parts of a unified whole. The emphasis on integration reflects its depth in addressing physical, mental, and spiritual dimensions simultaneously.

48. B: Prakṛti and vikṛti reflect the Ātman's interaction with the body and mind, where imbalances obscure its expression. Ayurveda's therapies realign these dimensions, restoring clarity and vitality. This perspective integrates spiritual principles into practical health strategies, illustrating how systemic harmony enables the Ātman's full expression. By addressing prakṛti and vikṛti, Ayurveda provides a unique model that transcends physical health, emphasizing spiritual alignment as a core aspect of well-being.

49. B: Ayurveda's ultimate goal is spiritual awakening, achieved through alignment with dharma and self-realization. Practices like yoga, meditation, and ethical living facilitate this journey, integrating physical, mental, and spiritual dimensions. By prioritizing higher purpose over symptomatic relief, Ayurveda offers a transformative approach to health. This question illustrates its depth in addressing not only physical ailments but also existential concerns, emphasizing liberation and self-fulfillment as central to its philosophy.

50. B: Modern research validates Ayurvedic principles by demonstrating measurable benefits of mindfulness and meditation, such as reduced stress and improved systemic functions. These findings align with the Ātman-centered approach, bridging traditional and scientific perspectives. This question highlights Ayurveda's relevance in contemporary health frameworks, showing how its integration of spiritual and physical dimensions resonates with modern holistic models. By aligning empirical evidence with traditional practices, Ayurveda remains a timeless guide to comprehensive well-being.

CHAPTER–6

LOKAPURUSA AND AYURVEDA'S DEFINITIONS (HITAYU, SUKHAYU, ETC.)

The Relationship Between Lokapuruṣa (Macrocosm) and the Human Body

The relationship between Lokapuruṣa, the macrocosm, and the human body, the microcosm, is a foundational concept in Ayurveda. This holistic science views the human being as a miniature reflection of the larger universe. The term Lokapuruṣa is derived from "Loka", meaning the world or cosmos, and "Puruṣa", meaning person or being. In this context, Lokapuruṣa signifies the universal entity, embodying the elements and forces of nature that also constitute the human body.

The macrocosm and microcosm analogy emphasizes that the principles governing the cosmos also govern individual human beings. Ayurveda posits that the same Pañca Mahābhūtas (five great elements)—Ākāśa (space), Vāyu (air), Agni (fire), Jala (water), and Pṛthvī (earth)—are the building blocks of both the universe and the human body. This shared elemental composition establishes an intrinsic link between humans and their environment.

Ayurveda stresses that understanding this relationship is crucial for achieving and maintaining health. Diseases, imbalances, and disturbances in the body are often reflective of broader disharmonies in the environment. For instance, seasonal changes, environmental pollution, and cosmic influences directly impact human health. Similarly, disturbances within the human body—such as mental agitation or physical illnesses—can resonate outward, affecting one's environment and relationships.

This macrocosm-microcosm interplay forms the basis of Ayurveda's diagnostic and therapeutic strategies. Just as the universe maintains harmony through balance and cycles, the human body is seen as healthy when the doṣas (Vāta, Pitta, Kapha), dhātus (tissues), and malas (waste products) are in equilibrium. This holistic approach integrates the physical, mental, and spiritual dimensions of well-being.

Ayurveda's View of Lokapuruṣa: Spiritual and Practical Dimensions

The philosophical underpinning of Lokapuruṣa lies in the Vedānta and Sāṃkhya schools of Indian thought. The universe (Loka) is seen as an extension of the Supreme Consciousness (Puruṣa). The individual is not separate but a microcosmic manifestation of the universal consciousness. The body, mind, and spirit of an individual are reflections of the cosmic forces, and the laws of nature govern both.

From a practical standpoint, this interconnectedness calls for a life lived in harmony with natural rhythms. Ayurveda advocates lifestyle practices that align with ṛtucaryā (seasonal regimens) and dinacaryā (daily routines) to maintain balance within this larger system. Dietary choices, sleep patterns, and physical activity are guided by awareness of external influences such as the climate, time of day, and one's immediate environment.

Definitions of Hitāyu, Sukhāyu, and Other Ayurvedic Concepts

Ayurveda delineates the goals of life and health using specific terms that offer nuanced definitions of well-being. The four primary types of life identified are Hitāyu (beneficial life), Sukhāyu (comfortable life), Dharmāyu (virtuous life), and Ihāyu (worldly life). These definitions encapsulate the Ayurvedic understanding of health as not merely the absence of disease but the cultivation of a purposeful and harmonious existence.

Hitāyu (Beneficial Life)

Hitāyu refers to a life lived in accordance with principles that promote health, longevity, and overall well-being. It is based on the idea of "hita"—that which is beneficial or favorable. This concept emphasizes actions and choices that contribute to the long-term health of the body and mind. Ayurveda categorizes food, behaviour, and lifestyle into hita (beneficial) and ahita (harmful), encouraging individuals to make decisions aligned with natural laws.

Hitāyu also encompasses the sattvic way of living—one characterized by purity, balance, and harmony. A sattvic diet, wholesome relationships, and virtuous conduct are integral to leading a Hitāyu.

Sukhāyu (Comfortable Life)

Sukhāyu, derived from "sukha" (happiness or comfort), refers to a life that is free from suffering and filled with ease. Ayurveda defines this comfort not merely as physical luxury but as a state of mental and emotional tranquility. Sukhāyu emphasizes the importance of stress management, emotional balance, and a positive outlook on life.

Sukhāyu can be cultivated through practices like meditation, mindfulness, and yoga, which promote a sense of inner peace. Ayurveda also highlights the role of interpersonal harmony, advocating kindness, compassion, and ethical behavior as key components of a comfortable life.

Dharmāyu (Virtuous Life)

Dharmāyu signifies a life dedicated to dharma, or righteousness. It highlights the moral and ethical dimensions of health and well-being. According to Ayurveda, living in alignment with dharma involves fulfilling one's duties and responsibilities with integrity, compassion, and selflessness. Dharmāyu reflects the spiritual foundation of Ayurveda, which sees life as an opportunity for personal and collective upliftment.

A Dharmāyu is not solely concerned with personal health but with contributing to the welfare of society and the environment. For instance, non-violence (ahiṃsā) and truthfulness (satya) are ethical principles that promote harmony both within and outside the individual.

Ihāyu (Worldly Life)

Ihāyu refers to a life that is oriented towards the material and practical aspects of existence. It acknowledges the reality of human needs for survival, prosperity, and worldly success. Ayurveda does not reject the material world but advises moderation and balance in pursuing worldly goals.

This concept aligns with the Puruṣārthas, the four aims of life in Indian philosophy: Dharma (righteousness), Artha (wealth), Kāma (pleasure), and Mokṣa (liberation). Ihāyu focuses on Artha and Kāma but within the framework of Dharma and Hitāyu to ensure that material pursuits do not disrupt physical, mental, or spiritual health.

Integration of These Concepts in Ayurveda

These four types of life—Hitāyu, Sukhāyu, Dharmāyu, and Ihāyu—are not mutually exclusive but complementary. Ayurveda seeks to harmonize them, recognizing that health involves balancing the spiritual, emotional, and material dimensions of existence. For example, achieving Hitāyu through a sattvic lifestyle supports Sukhāyu by fostering emotional peace and Dharmāyu by encouraging ethical conduct.

Philosophy of Ayurveda's Holistic Approach to Health and Well-Being

Ayurveda's philosophy of health is deeply rooted in its holistic worldview. The term "holistic" implies that health encompasses the physical, mental, emotional, social, and spiritual dimensions of life. This comprehensive perspective sets Ayurveda apart from reductionist approaches that focus narrowly on symptoms or isolated body parts.

Tridoṣa Theory and Holistic Balance

The cornerstone of Ayurveda's holistic approach is the Tridoṣa theory, which posits that health is achieved when the three doṣas—Vāta, Pitta, and Kapha—are in balance. These doṣas are dynamic forces derived from the five elements and represent physiological processes in the body. Imbalances in the doṣas lead to disease, while harmony ensures vitality and resilience.

For instance:

- Vāta, composed of air and space, governs movement and communication.
- Pitta, composed of fire and water, governs digestion and metabolism.
- Kapha, composed of earth and water, governs structure and stability.
- Ayurveda employs personalized strategies to balance these doṣas, considering the individual's prakṛti (constitution), environment, and lifestyle.

Integration of Body, Mind, and Spirit

Ayurveda recognizes that the mind and spirit play critical roles in health. Mental clarity, emotional resilience, and spiritual awareness are considered just as important as physical fitness. Practices such as meditation, prāṇāyāma, and yoga are integral to Ayurvedic therapy, as they nurture the inner dimensions of health.

For instance: ā

- A calm and focused mind supports the body's immune response.
- Spiritual practices foster a sense of purpose and connection, which are crucial for long-term well-being.

Preventive Medicine and Lifestyle Management

Ayurveda places a strong emphasis on preventive medicine, which aligns with its holistic philosophy. By promoting ṛtucaryā and dinacaryā, Ayurveda encourages proactive health maintenance. These regimens are designed to optimize the body's natural rhythms and protect against seasonal and environmental stresses.

Individualized Care

Ayurveda, the ancient science of life, emphasizes the uniqueness of every individual. Unlike many standardized approaches to health, Ayurveda champions individualized care, recognizing that each person is a distinct blend of physical, mental, and spiritual components. This hallmark feature is a cornerstone of Ayurveda's holistic approach, providing a framework that considers not only physical symptoms but also the unique constitution (Prakṛti) and imbalances (Vikṛti) of an individual. Individualized care in Ayurveda is rooted in the belief that optimal health and well-being can only be achieved when treatments are tailored to the unique needs of the person.

(I) Foundations of Individualized Care in Ayurveda

1. **Prakṛti: The Unique Constitution:** At the heart of individualized care lies the concept of Prakṛti, or the inherent constitution of an individual. Prakṛti is determined at conception and remains constant throughout life. It is a unique blend of the Tridoṣa—Vāta, Pitta, and Kapha, the three bio-energetic principles derived from the five Mahābhūtas (elements).

   (a) Determinants of Prakṛti:

   - **Genetics:** The genetic makeup of an individual plays a role in determining their doshic constitution.
   - **Parental Influence:** The state of health, emotions, and doshic balance of parents at the time of conception contributes to the child's Prakṛti.
   - **Environment:** Climatic conditions and seasonal variations at the time of birth can influence Prakṛti.

   (b) Types of Prakṛti:

   - **Single Dosha Dominance:** Vāta, Pitta, or Kapha predominant types.
   - **Dual Dosha Combinations:** Vāta-Pitta, Pitta-Kapha, or Vāta-Kapha types.
   - **Tri-Dosha Balance:** A rare type where all three doshas are balanced.
   - Understanding an individual's Prakṛti helps determine their susceptibility to diseases, preferences in diet and lifestyle, and appropriate therapeutic approaches.

2. **Vikṛti:** The Current State of Imbalance while Prakṛti reflects an individual's inherent nature, Vikṛti indicates their current state of imbalance. Disease arises when there is a deviation from Prakṛti due to various factors, such as:

   - Dietary indiscretions
   - Lifestyle choices
   - Environmental changes
   - Mental and emotional stress

   By assessing Vikṛti, an Ayurvedic practitioner can identify the root cause of imbalances and design personalized interventions to restore harmony.

3. **Mental and Emotional Constitution**: In addition to Prakṛti and Vikṛti, Ayurveda considers the psychological makeup of an individual, categorized under the three mental qualities (gunas):

   - Sattva: Purity, intelligence, and harmony.
   - Rajas: Activity, passion, and restlessness.
   - Tamas: Inertia, ignorance, and dullness.

   A person's mental constitution influences their resilience to stress, decision-making abilities, and spiritual growth, which are critical for individualized care.

4. **The Role of Agni (Digestive Fire) and Ama (Toxins)**: Ayurveda recognizes the central role of Agni, or digestive fire, in maintaining health. A strong Agni ensures efficient digestion, absorption, and assimilation, while a weakened Agni leads to the formation of Ama (toxic metabolic byproducts). The state of Agni varies among individuals and must be carefully assessed to tailor dietary and therapeutic recommendations.

(II) Principles of Individualized Care in Ayurveda

1. **Understanding the Whole Person:** Ayurvedic individualized care is based on a holistic understanding of the individual, encompassing their

body, mind, and spirit. The practitioner considers multiple dimensions, including:

- Physical Constitution (Deha Prakṛti)
- Mental Constitution (Manasa Prakṛti)
- Lifestyle and Habits
- Cultural and Social Background

2. **Identification of Root Causes:** Rather than merely addressing symptoms, Ayurveda focuses on identifying the root cause of imbalances. This involves:
   - Assessing Prakṛti and Vikṛti.
   - Evaluating dietary habits, sleep patterns, and emotional well-being.
   - Identifying external and internal aggravating factors.
3. **Personalization of Treatments:** Once the root cause is identified, Ayurveda customizes treatment strategies. These may include:
   - **Dietary Modifications:** Based on doshic needs and digestive capacity.
   - **Herbal Remedies:** Tailored to address specific imbalances.
   - **Lifestyle Adjustments:** Including daily and seasonal routines (Dinacharya and Ritucharya).
   - **Therapies:** Such as Panchakarma, yoga, and meditation.
4. **Emphasis on Preventive Care:** Ayurveda places significant importance on preventive care through individualized strategies, such as:
   - Personalized diet and exercise regimens.
   - Stress management techniques.
   - Seasonal detoxification.

(III) Application of Individualized Care

1. **Dietary Recommendations**: Ayurvedic dietary advice is highly individualized, considering:
   - **Doshas:** Foods that balance an individual's doshas are emphasized.
   - **Vāta:** Warm, moist, and grounding foods.
   - **Pitta:** Cooling, sweet, and soothing foods.
   - **Kapha:** Light, dry, and warming foods.
   - **Agni:** Diet is adjusted based on the strength of the digestive fire.
   - **Seasonal Variations:** Aligning diet with seasonal changes.
2. **Lifestyle Guidance**: Ayurveda provides personalized lifestyle recommendations, such as:
   - **Daily Routine (Dinacharya):** Tailored schedules for waking, eating, and sleeping.
   - **Exercise:** Intensity and type of exercise suited to the individual's Prakṛti and age.
   - **Sleep Patterns:** Guidance to ensure optimal rest and rejuvenation.
3. **Herbal Medicine**: Herbs are prescribed based on:
   - **Doshic Balance:** Herbs that pacify specific doshas.
   - **Specific Conditions:** Targeted herbs for diseases or imbalances.
   - **Preparation Forms:** Tailored forms like powders, decoctions, or oils.
4. **Therapeutic Interventions:** Therapies like Panchakarma are individualized to cleanse and rejuvenate the body. The five procedures—Vamana (emesis), Virechana (purgation), Basti (enema), Nasya (nasal therapy), and Raktamokshana (bloodletting)—are tailored based on doshic imbalances.

(IV) Benefits of Individualized Care

1. **Enhanced Effectiveness:** Treatments tailored to an individual's unique needs are more likely to yield positive outcomes.
2. **Sustainability:** Personalized lifestyle changes are easier to adopt and maintain.
3. **Preventive Health:** Individualized care identifies imbalances early, preventing diseases.
4. **Mental Well-being:** Considering psychological factors ensures comprehensive care.
5. **Spiritual Growth:** Tailored practices like meditation and pranayama support spiritual evolution.

(V) Challenges and Future Directions

Challenges

- **Complexity in Assessment:** Requires skilled practitioners for accurate Prakṛti and Vikṛti evaluation.
- **Integration with Modern Medicine:** Bridging Ayurveda with contemporary medical practices remains a challenge.
- **Standardization vs. Individualization:** Striking a balance between personalized care and broader applicability.

Future Directions

- **Technological Integration:** Use of AI and digital tools for precise Prakṛti assessment.
- **Global Adaptation:** Customizing Ayurvedic care for diverse populations.

- **Research and Validation:** Scientific studies to validate the efficacy of individualized care.

Individualized care is the hallmark of Ayurveda's holistic approach, reflecting its deep understanding of human diversity and complexity. By addressing the unique physical, mental, and spiritual needs of each individual, Ayurveda transcends the limitations of one-size-fits-all solutions. Its emphasis on Prakṛti, Vikṛti, Agni, and the interconnectedness of body and mind provides a timeless framework for personalized health and wellness.

In an era where personalized medicine is gaining traction, Ayurveda stands as a profound testament to the enduring relevance of individualized care. By harmonizing ancient wisdom with modern advancements, Ayurveda offers a transformative approach to health, empowering individuals to achieve balance, vitality, and spiritual fulfillment.

MULTIPLE CHOICE QUESTIONS

1. Consider a philosopher interpreting the Ayurveda doctrine of Lokapuruṣa (macrocosm) and its correlation with the human microcosm. The philosopher asserts that this analogy represents not only the physical and elemental connection but also the metaphysical interplay between the universe and human consciousness. He applies this to the understanding of seasonal transitions affecting bodily functions and the requirement for synchronized lifestyle changes. Which of the following most accurately reflects the significance of this philosophy?
   A. Ayurveda's Lokapuruṣa principle is purely symbolic and lacks tangible applications in therapeutic practices.
   B. Seasonal adaptations recommended by Ayurveda reflect the dynamic equilibrium between cosmic forces and human physiology.
   C. Lokapuruṣa principles exclusively address the relationship between planetary movements and circadian rhythms.
   D. The concept of Lokapuruṣa underlines that all imbalances within the body arise from solely external cosmic disruptions.

2. A clinical researcher designs an experimental model to test the practical implications of the Ayurvedic definitions of Hitāyu and Sukhāyu. Patients undergoing a regimen combining sattvic diets and seasonal Ritucharya are compared to those with conventional care. The study observes superior quality of life indices in the former group, including reduced stress, better digestion, and enhanced mental clarity. Which conclusion is most consistent with the definitions of Hitāyu and Sukhāyu in Ayurveda?
   A. Sukhāyu emphasizes material comfort over long-term health, contrasting with the Hitāyu approach of dietary restrictions.
   B. Hitāyu aligns with principles of balanced living, while Sukhāyu focuses on individual happiness through external factors.
   C. Both Hitāyu and Sukhāyu represent intertwined dimensions of well-being involving both inner and outer harmony.
   D. Hitāyu and Sukhāyu are unrelated, as the former pertains to ethical living and the latter to health outcomes.

3. Imagine a practitioner implementing Ayurvedic principles in preventive healthcare. He emphasizes the balance of Tridosha, personal Prakriti analysis, and detoxifying therapies like Panchakarma. Critics argue these concepts lack empirical basis. How should the practitioner justify Ayurveda's scientific relevance?
   A. Ayurveda's framework is metaphysical and does not seek validation from empirical studies.
   B. The clinical effects of therapies like Panchakarma validate Ayurvedic principles even in absence of rigorous modern methodologies.
   C. Tridosha theories correlate directly with established biomedical parameters of organ functions and homeostasis.
   D. Ayurveda combines evidence-based preventive care with subjective philosophical practices, offering holistic benefits.

4. A historian studying the evolution of Ayurvedic definitions, including Hitāyu, Sukhāyu, Dharmāyu, and Ihāyu, highlights that they represent a synthesis of ancient ethical philosophy with physiological considerations. The historian asserts that the primary goal of these definitions is to harmonize the physical, mental, and spiritual domains of life. Which interpretation best represents this synthesis?
   A. Hitāyu exclusively focuses on physical health, while Sukhāyu integrates mental well-being with material comfort.
   B. Dharmāyu emphasizes spiritual aspirations, independent of physical and mental health.
   C. Ayurveda's definitions transcend individual domains, emphasizing their interdependence for holistic health.
   D. Ihāyu represents the materialistic focus of Ayurveda, distinct from its spiritual goals.

5. Consider a scenario where an Ayurvedic physician correlates the Lokapuruṣa concept with modern ecological balance. The physician posits that environmental degradation disrupts human health by affecting elemental balance. This principle is applied to study urban populations with chronic doshic imbalances, linking them to factors like air pollution and reduced exposure to nature. Which of the following best supports this perspective?
   A. Urban doshic imbalances arise exclusively from dietary deviations, unrelated to environmental factors.
   B. The balance between human health and environmental harmony is central to Ayurvedic philosophy, as reflected in Lokapuruṣa.
   C. Doshic disorders in urban areas are not scientifically attributable to environmental pollution.
   D. Lokapuruṣa theories are irrelevant in the context of modern environmental challenges.

6. A researcher explores the philosophical dimensions of Ayurveda's holistic health paradigm. They identify that Lokapuruṣa and microcosmic interrelations also extend to ethical and spiritual practices that impact mental well-being. How does this observation align with the broader scope of Ayurveda?
   A. Ayurveda disregards mental health in favor of physical interventions, contradicting the philosophical implications of Lokapuruṣa.
   B. Ethical and spiritual practices are secondary to Ayurvedic treatment protocols and are not integral to its health paradigm.
   C. The alignment of ethical conduct and spiritual growth with physical health exemplifies Ayurveda's holistic approach.
   D. Ayurveda's focus on physical and elemental balance excludes ethical and spiritual considerations.

7. An interdisciplinary researcher evaluates the Ayurvedic definitions of Dharmāyu and Ihāyu in light of modern psychological studies. They argue that Dharmāyu reflects purpose-driven living, while Ihāyu aligns with material pursuits. How would Ayurveda likely integrate these two dimensions?
   A. Dharmāyu and Ihāyu are treated as opposing goals, with the former prioritized in health practices.
   B. Ayurveda seeks a dynamic equilibrium where Dharmāyu complements Ihāyu for balanced living.
   C. Ihāyu is considered detrimental in Ayurveda, as it deviates from spiritual and ethical goals.
   D. Dharmāyu pertains solely to monastic living and excludes worldly engagement.

8. An Ayurvedic scholar proposes that the definitions of Hitāyu and Dharmāyu serve as ethical frameworks guiding health practitioners. In this view, they emphasize the physician's duty to prioritize patient welfare over personal gain. How does this align with Ayurveda's core philosophy?
   A. Ethical considerations in Ayurveda are limited to the practitioner's adherence to treatment protocols.
   B. The concepts of Hitāyu and Dharmāyu emphasize ethical living for patients, with minimal implications for practitioners.
   C. Ayurveda's philosophy integrates ethical principles as foundational to both treatment and the practitioner's role.
   D. Dharmāyu excludes considerations of patient welfare, focusing on individual spiritual growth.

9. A psychologist uses the concept of Sukhāyu to design stress management programs incorporating mindfulness and Ayurvedic dietary principles. Participants report improved resilience, emotional stability, and physical health. What does this outcome suggest about the integration of Sukhāyu in mental health practices?
   A. Sukhāyu has limited application in mental health, as it is primarily concerned with physical well-being.
   B. The integration of Sukhāyu into psychological interventions supports the holistic philosophy of Ayurveda.
   C. Ayurvedic dietary practices in Sukhāyu conflict with contemporary mental health frameworks.
   D. Mental health outcomes are unrelated to Sukhāyu principles, indicating its limited relevance in modern contexts.

10. An Ayurvedic consultant applies Hitāyu principles to develop workplace wellness programs that include ergonomic practices, balanced diets, and ethical work-life balance policies. Employees demonstrate enhanced productivity and well-being. How does this reflect the application of Hitāyu?
   A. Hitāyu's focus on ethical living excludes its application in workplace environments.
   B. Hitāyu principles transcend individual health, extending to societal and organizational contexts.
   C. Workplace applications of Hitāyu contradict its traditional focus on personal health practices.
   D. The principles of Hitāyu cannot be reconciled with modern professional settings.

Directons (Q. No. 11-14): *Scenario-Based Questions*

SCENARIO 1

A medical researcher evaluates the efficacy of Ayurvedic formulations like Triphala in mitigating gut dysbiosis and systemic inflammation. Clinical trials reveal that Triphala enhances gut microbiota diversity, modulates inflammatory markers, and improves metabolic health. Additionally, enhanced gut health correlates with strengthened systemic immunity and reduced chronic disease risks.

SCENARIO 2

Simultaneously, an environmental biologist assesses the ecological impact of sourcing Amalaki, a key ingredient in Triphala. Findings indicate overharvesting, reduced soil fertility, and biodiversity loss, which threaten the sustainability of Amalaki. Efforts to cultivate Amalaki using agroforestry practices show promise in maintaining its medicinal quality while conserving biodiversity.

11. Based on Scenario 1, which mechanism best explains the immunological benefits of Triphala?
- A. Triphala's direct stimulation of lymphocyte activity compensates for gut dysbiosis.
- B. Triphala's role in enhancing gut microbiota diversity improves gut-associated lymphoid tissue (GALT) function, boosting immunity.
- C. Gut microbiota modulation by Triphala reduces inflammation without influencing systemic immunity.
- D. Triphala's therapeutic benefits are unrelated to gut health and are solely mediated by its adaptogenic properties.

12. In Scenario 2, which strategy best addresses the challenges of Amalaki overharvesting while ensuring medicinal quality?
- A. Large-scale monoculture farming of Amalaki with synthetic fertilizers.
- B. Promoting sustainable agroforestry practices involving Amalaki and native flora.
- C. Replacing Amalaki in Triphala with artificially synthesized bioactive compounds.
- D. Reducing Triphala production to minimize Amalaki harvesting pressures.

13. How might the ecological degradation of Amalaki, as highlighted in Scenario 2, impact the therapeutic outcomes in Scenario 1?
- A. Reduced bioactive compound concentration in Amalaki may compromise Triphala's gut health benefits.
- B. Triphala's efficacy remains unchanged, as it is independent of individual ingredient quality.
- C. Environmental stressors enhance Amalaki's bioactive potency, amplifying Triphala's benefits.
- D. Amalaki's ecological degradation has no measurable impact on Triphala's therapeutic outcomes.

14. Which strategy comprehensively addresses both the sustainability and efficacy concerns highlighted in Scenarios 1 and 2?
- A. Developing synthetic alternatives for Amalaki to reduce dependency on natural sources.
- B. Encouraging local conservation initiatives and setting global standards for Triphala production.
- C. Transitioning away from Triphala to more sustainable Ayurvedic formulations.
- D. Centralizing Triphala production to regions unaffected by Amalaki overharvesting.

15. The principles of Tridosha in Ayurveda include the following statements:
- (a) Vata governs movement and sensory activities.
- (b) Pitta controls metabolism and is associated with enzymes.
- (c) Kapha maintains stability and fluid balance in the body.
- (d) The imbalance of any one dosha can disrupt physical and mental health.

Choose the correct answer from the options given below:
- A. (a), (b), and (c) only
- B. (a), (b), (c), and (d) only
- C. (a) and (d) only
- D. (b), (c), and (d) only

16. The primary characteristics of Ayurvedic Rasas (tastes) are:
- (a) Sweet promotes tissue growth and immunity.
- (b) Bitter enhances detoxification and reduces inflammation.
- (c) Astringent strengthens tissues and controls bleeding.
- (d) Sour improves digestion and energizes metabolism.

Choose the correct answer from the options given below:
- A. (a), (b), and (d) only
- B. (a), (b), (c), and (d) only
- C. (a) and (c) only
- D. (b), (c), and (d) only

17. In Ayurveda, Agni is described as:
- (a) The transformative energy responsible for digestion.
- (b) A symbolic representation of immunity.
- (c) A metabolic regulator that prevents toxin accumulation.
- (d) A concept limited to gastrointestinal activity.

Choose the correct answer from the options given below:
- A. (a), (b), and (c) only
- B. (a) and (c) only
- C. (b) and (d) only
- D. (a), (b), (c), and (d)

18. The roles of Dhatus in Ayurveda include the following statements:
(a) Rasa nourishes all bodily tissues.
(b) Rakta is responsible for oxygen transportation and vitality.
(c) Meda stores energy and regulates lubrication.
(d) Asthi maintains structural support and rigidity.

Choose the correct answer from the options given below:
A. (a), (b), and (c) only
B. (a), (b), (c), and (d) only
C. (b) and (d) only
D. (a), (c), and (d) only

19. Ayurvedic interventions like Ritucharya (seasonal regimen) ensure:
(a) Adaptation to environmental changes.
(b) Preservation of Tridoshic balance throughout seasonal transitions.
(c) A reduction in chronic disease occurrences.
(d) Uniformity in lifestyle practices regardless of individual Prakriti.

Choose the correct answer from the options given below:
A. (a), (b), and (d) only
B. (a), (b), and (c) only
C. (b) and (d) only
D. (a) and (c) only

20. Ayurveda classifies therapeutic outcomes under four life definitions:
(a) Hitāyu emphasizes long-term health and virtuous living.
(b) Sukhāyu prioritizes emotional and mental ease.
(c) Dharmāyu integrates spiritual goals with daily activities.
(d) Ihāyu exclusively pertains to materialistic achievements.

Choose the correct answer from the options given below:
A. (a), (b), and (c) only
B. (b) and (d) only
C. (a), (b), (c), and (d)
D. (a) and (c) only

21. Ayurvedic detoxification therapies such as Panchakarma aim to:
(a) Restore doshic balance by eliminating toxins (Ama).
(b) Enhance Agni to improve metabolic activity.
(c) Replace cellular processes with external rejuvenation therapies.
(d) Align the body's rhythms with natural cycles.

Choose the correct answer from the options given below:
A. (a), (b), and (d) only
B. (a), (b), and (c) only
C. (b), (c), and (d) only
D. (a), (c), and (d) only

22. Match List–I (Ayurvedic Formulations) with List–II (Therapeutic Purposes):

List–I	List–II
(a) Triphala	1. Enhances gut health and systemic immunity
(b) Ashwagandha	2. Improves stress resilience and vitality
(c) Brahmi	3. Boosts cognitive function and mental clarity
(d) Neem	4. Detoxifies skin and blood

Choose the correct answer from the options given below:
A. (a)-2, (b)-3, (c)-1, (d)-4
B. (a)-1, (b)-2, (c)-3, (d)-4
C. (a)-3, (b)-1, (c)-2, (d)-4
D. (a)-4, (b)-2, (c)-3, (d)-1

23. Match List–I (Primary Concepts) with List–II (Key Functions):

List–I	List–II
(a) Agni	1. Digestive fire regulating metabolism
(b) Ama	2. Toxic build-up from undigested food
(c) Tridosha	3. Governs physiological processes
(d) Sattva	4. Mental clarity and purity

Choose the correct answer from the options:
A. (a)-1, (b)-2, (c)-3, (d)-4
B. (a)-4, (b)-3, (c)-1, (d)-2
C. (a)-2, (b)-1, (c)-4, (d)-3
D. (a)-3, (b)-4, (c)-1, (d)-2

24. Match List–I (Therapeutic Techniques) with List–II (Objectives):

List–I	List–II
(a) Panchakarma	1. Detoxification and doshic balance
(b) Dinacharya	2. Seasonal adjustment for health
(c) Ritucharya	3. Daily routine for wellness
(d) Yoga	4. Physical and mental harmony

Choose the correct answer from the options:
A. (a)-1, (b)-3, (c)-2, (d)-4
B. (a)-4, (b)-2, (c)-3, (d)-1
C. (a)-2, (b)-4, (c)-1, (d)-3
D. (a)-3, (b)-1, (c)-4, (d)-2

25. Match List–I (Definitions of Life) with List–II (Attributes):

List–I	List–II
(a) Hitāyu	1. Ethical and virtuous living
(b) Sukhāyu	2. Emotional and physical ease
(c) Dharmāyu	3. Material achievements
(d) Ihāyu	4. Beneficial and healthy longevity

Choose the correct answer from the options given below:

A. (a)-4, (b)-2, (c)-1, (d)-3
B. (a)-1, (b)-3, (c)-2, (d)-4
C. (a)-2, (b)-4, (c)-3, (d)-1
D. (a)-3, (b)-1, (c)-4, (d)-2

26. Match List–I (Doshas) with List–II (Symptoms of Imbalance):

List–I	List–II
(a) Vata	1. Anxiety, dry skin, and joint pain
(b) Pitta	2. Inflammation, fever, and acidity
(c) Kapha	3. Lethargy, congestion, and weight gain

Choose the correct answer from the options given below:

A. (a)-1, (b)-2, (c)-3
B. (a)-3, (b)-1, (c)-2
C. (a)-2, (b)-3, (c)-1
D. (a)-1, (b)-3, (c)-2

27. Match List–I (Dhatus) with List–II (Associated Functions):

List–I	List–II
(a) Rasa	1. Nourishes tissues
(b) Rakta	2. Provides oxygen and vitality
(c) Mamsa	3. Builds muscles
(d) Meda	4. Regulates lubrication and fat storage

Choose the correct answer from the options given below:

A. (a)-1, (b)-2, (c)-3, (d)-4
B. (a)-2, (b)-1, (c)-4, (d)-3
C. (a)-3, (b)-4, (c)-1, (d)-2
D. (a)-4, (b)-3, (c)-2, (d)-1

28. Match List–I (Ayurvedic Philosophies) with List–II (Core Components):

List–I	List–II
(a) Lokapuruṣa	1. Microcosm-macrocosm relationship
(b) Agni	2. Digestive fire and metabolic processes
(c) Tridosha	3. Vata, Pitta, and Kapha balance
(d) Panchakarma	4. Detoxification and rejuvenation

Choose the correct answer from the options given below:

A. (a)-1, (b)-2, (c)-3, (d)-4
B. (a)-4, (b)-3, (c)-2, (d)-1
C. (a)-3, (b)-1, (c)-4, (d)-2
D. (a)-2, (b)-4, (c)-1, (d)-3

29. Match List–I (Herbs) with List–II (Therapeutic Uses):

List–I	List–II
(a) Triphala	1. Detoxifies and boosts immunity
(b) Ashwagandha	2. Reduces stress and improves vitality
(c) Brahmi	3. Enhances memory and mental clarity
(d) Neem	4. Purifies blood and treats skin disorders

Choose the correct answer from the options given below:

A. (a)-1, (b)-2, (c)-3, (d)-4
B. (a)-4, (b)-3, (c)-1, (d)-2
C. (a)-3, (b)-4, (c)-2, (d)-1
D. (a)-2, (b)-1, (c)-4, (d)-3

30. Match List–I (Rasas) with List–II (Primary Effects):

List–I	List–II
(a) Sweet	1. Enhances metabolism and digestion
(b) Sour	2. Promotes detoxification and reduces inflammation
(c) Bitter	3. Nourishes tissues and promotes immunity
(d) Astringent	4. Strengthens tissues and controls bleeding

Choose the correct answer:

A. (a)-3, (b)-1, (c)-2, (d)-4
B. (a)-4, (b)-3, (c)-1, (d)-2
C. (a)-2, (b)-4, (c)-3, (d)-1
D. (a)-1, (b)-2, (c)-4, (d)-3

31. Match List–I (Ayurvedic Terms) with List–II (Descriptions):

List–I	List–II
(a) Prakriti	1. Individual constitution and dosha dominance
(b) Ama	2. Toxins due to incomplete digestion
(c) Ritucharya	3. Seasonal regimens for dosha balance
(d) Sattva	4. Mental clarity and stability

Choose the correct answer from the options given below:

A. (a)-1, (b)-2, (c)-3, (d)-4
B. (a)-3, (b)-1, (c)-4, (d)-2
C. (a)-4, (b)-2, (c)-1, (d)-3
D. (a)-2, (b)-4, (c)-3, (d)-1

32. Match List–I (Health Practices) with List–II (Ayurvedic Goals):

List–I	List–II
(a) Sattvic diet	1. Enhances purity and mental clarity
(b) Dinacharya	2. Detoxifies and rejuvenates
(c) Panchakarma	3. Establishes daily routines for balance
(d) Yoga	4. Promotes physical and mental harmony

Choose the correct answer from the options given below:

A. (a)-1, (b)-3, (c)-2, (d)-4
B. (a)-4, (b)-2, (c)-3, (d)-1
C. (a)-3, (b)-4, (c)-1, (d)-2
D. (a)-2, (b)-1, (c)-4, (d)-3

33. Match List–I (Ayurvedic Therapies) with List–II (Primary Outcomes):

List–I	List–II
(a) Abhyanga	1. Balances Vata and reduces stress
(b) Shirodhara	2. Cleanses nasal passages and improves respiratory health
(c) Vamana	3. Detoxifies and removes excess Kapha
(d) Nasya	4. Improves circulation and nourishes tissues

Choose the correct answer from the options given below:

A. (a)-4, (b)-1, (c)-3, (d)-2
B. (a)-3, (b)-2, (c)-4, (d)-1
C. (a)-1, (b)-4, (c)-2, (d)-3
D. (a)-2, (b)-3, (c)-1, (d)-4

34. Match List–I (Body-Mind Relations) with List–II (Ayurvedic Aspects):

List–I	List–II
(a) Mind clarity	1. Achieved through sattvic practices
(b) Emotional stability	2. Maintained by Kapha regulation
(c) Physical strength	3. Enhanced by balanced Agni
(d) Dosha balance	4. Stabilized by yoga and meditation

Choose the correct answer:

A. (a)-1, (b)-4, (c)-2, (d)-3
B. (a)-3, (b)-2, (c)-1, (d)-4
C. (a)-4, (b)-1, (c)-3, (d)-2
D. (a)-2, (b)-3, (c)-4, (d)-1

Directions (Q. No. 35-39): *Following questiions are based on Statement 1 and Statement 2. Read both the statements carefully and choose the correct answer from the options given below:*

A. Both Statement 1 and Statement 2 are true, and Statement 2 is the correct explanation of Statement 1.
B. Both Statement 1 and Statement 2 are true, but Statement 2 is not the correct explanation of Statement 1.
C. Statement 1 is true, but Statement 2 is false.
D. Statement 1 is false, but Statement 2 is true.
E. Both Statement 1 and Statement 2 are false.

35. **Statement 1:** Ayurveda considers the body as a microcosm of the universe, where the Pañca Mahābhūtas (five elements) form the foundation of both physical and cosmic existence.

Statement 2: The concept of Lokapuruṣa emphasizes the unity of physical health and cosmic rhythms, prescribing therapeutic practices based solely on astrological influences.

36. **Statement 1:** The Ayurvedic principle of Agni (digestive fire) is central to metabolic health, influencing the digestion of food and the absorption of nutrients.

Statement 2: Impaired Agni leads to the accumulation of Ama (toxins), disrupting the balance of doshas and causing various diseases.

37. **Statement 1:** Ritucharya (seasonal regimen) is designed to prevent seasonal diseases by aligning lifestyle practices with seasonal variations in doshic balance.

Statement 2: The absence of Ritucharya can lead to chronic diseases, as the body fails to adapt to changing environmental conditions.

38. **Statement 1:** Sukhāyu in Ayurveda is defined as a life of comfort, focusing on mental and emotional ease rather than physical health.

Statement 2: Sukhāyu emphasizes achieving balance and tranquility, integrating mental well-being with physical health.

39. **Statement 1:** Dharmāyu in Ayurveda prioritizes virtuous living, ensuring harmony between personal health and societal obligations.

Statement 2: Ihāyu is an antithesis to Dharmāyu, focusing solely on material gains at the expense of ethical and spiritual principles.

Directions (Q. No. 40-45): *There are two statements in each question. One is labelled as Assertion (A) and the other is as Reason (R). Read both the statements and choose the correct answer from the options given below:*

A. Both Assertion (A) and Reason (R) are true, and Reason (R) is the correct explanation of Assertion (A).
B. Both Assertion (A) and Reason (R) are true, but Reason (R) is not the correct explanation of Assertion (A).
C. Assertion (A) is true, but Reason (R) is false.
D. Assertion (A) is false, but Reason (R) is true.
E. Both Assertion (A) and Reason (R) are false.

40. **Assertion (A):** Ayurvedic therapies like Panchakarma are considered effective in eliminating Ama (toxins) and restoring the natural balance of doshas.

Reason (R): Panchakarma involves a series of purification processes that target metabolic pathways and enhance Agni (digestive fire).

41. **Assertion (A):** Seasonal routines (Ritucharya) in Ayurveda help in maintaining optimal health by preventing the aggravation of doshas during seasonal transitions.

Reason (R): Seasonal changes directly influence the Tridosha balance, requiring modifications in diet, lifestyle, and therapeutic interventions.

42. **Assertion (A):** Sattva, Rajas, and Tamas are the three Gunas in Ayurveda that influence mental health and emotional well-being.

Reason (R): The dominance of Tamas promotes mental clarity and tranquility, enhancing overall cognitive function.

43. **Assertion (A):** The Ayurvedic concept of Lokapuruṣa explains the microcosm-macrocosm relationship, connecting human health with cosmic rhythms.

Reason (R): This principle is based on the idea that the human body functions independently of natural and environmental influences.

44. **Assertion (A):** Ayurveda emphasizes the individualization of therapeutic practices based on the Prakriti (constitution) of the person.

Reason (R): Each individual's Prakriti is determined by their dominant doshas and remains static throughout their life.

45. **Assertion (A):** Ayurveda integrates ethical living, spiritual growth, and physical health as interconnected aspects of well-being.

Reason (R): Ethical and spiritual practices in Ayurveda are considered separate from the physical dimensions of health and are not integral to therapeutic strategies.

Directions (Q. No. 46–50): *Read the passage carefully and answer the questions given below:*

Ayurveda, the ancient Indian system of medicine, provides a comprehensive and holistic approach to health and well-being by integrating the physical, mental, emotional, and spiritual dimensions of life. Central to its philosophy is the concept of Tridosha—Vata, Pitta, and Kapha—which govern all physiological, psychological, and biochemical functions. These doshas are derived from the Pañca Mahābhūtas (five elements) and represent the interplay between the body and the external environment. Ayurveda posits that health is a state of dynamic equilibrium among the doshas, while imbalances manifest as disease.

Another key principle is Agni, or digestive fire, which is responsible for digestion, metabolism, and overall vitality. Impairment of Agni leads to the formation of Ama, or toxins, which disrupt doshic balance and obstruct bodily functions. Ayurvedic therapies aim to strengthen Agni, eliminate Ama, and restore harmony through personalized treatment plans based on individual Prakriti (constitution).

The relationship between the macrocosm (Lokapuruṣa) and the microcosm (the human body) underscores Ayurveda's understanding of health as being influenced by cosmic rhythms, seasonal variations, and environmental factors. Practices such as Ritucharya (seasonal regimen) and Dinacharya (daily regimen) align the individual with these external rhythms, preventing disease and promoting longevity. Additionally, Ayurveda incorporates spiritual and ethical practices to cultivate Sattva (mental clarity and balance), which fosters resilience and emotional well-being.

In recent years, modern scientific research has validated many Ayurvedic principles. Studies on gut health, for instance, reveal that interventions like Panchakarma and herbal formulations such as Triphala enhance microbiota diversity and reduce systemic inflammation, echoing Ayurvedic descriptions of detoxification and doshic balance. Despite this, challenges such as the overharvesting of medicinal plants and the lack of standardization in formulations present hurdles for integrating Ayurveda into global health systems.

46. According to the passage, what is the primary role of the Tridosha in Ayurvedic science?

A. They determine an individual's physical appearance and personality traits.

B. They govern all physiological, psychological, and biochemical processes.

C. They serve as metaphysical concepts unrelated to bodily functions.

D. They regulate spiritual practices but are unrelated to physical health.

47. Why is Agni considered crucial in Ayurveda?

A. It regulates mental and emotional health, independent of digestion.

B. It is central to digestion, metabolism, and the prevention of toxin accumulation.

C. It determines an individual's Prakriti and doshic constitution.

D. It directly controls circadian rhythms and seasonal adaptations.

48. How does Ayurveda's concept of Lokapuruṣa influence health practices?

A. It limits the focus of health interventions to external environmental factors.

B. It establishes a connection between cosmic rhythms and bodily functions, encouraging alignment through lifestyle regimens.

C. It reduces the emphasis on internal processes, prioritizing cosmic influences.

D. It introduces seasonal adjustments but disregards daily practices.

49. According to the passage, how does modern research resonate with Ayurvedic principles?

A. It dismisses Ayurvedic concepts like doshas as lacking empirical evidence.

B. It validates Ayurvedic practices such as detoxification and gut health improvement through scientific studies.

C. It focuses exclusively on the spiritual aspects of Ayurveda, ignoring its physical dimensions.

D. It proves that Ayurvedic interventions are purely symbolic and lack therapeutic efficacy.

50. What challenge is highlighted in the passage regarding the global integration of Ayurveda?

A. The complete absence of scientific research validating Ayurvedic practices.

B. Overharvesting of medicinal plants and lack of standardization in formulations.

C. The incompatibility of Ayurvedic principles with modern healthcare systems.

D. A lack of emphasis on personalized treatment plans in Ayurvedic practices.

ANSWER WITH EXPLANATIONS

1. B: The Lokapuruṣa principle in Ayurveda underlines the deep connection between the cosmos and human physiology, emphasizing alignment with natural rhythms. Seasonal adaptations are a practical application of this concept, reflecting the interplay between external cosmic forces and internal bodily functions. By recommending lifestyle changes to balance the doshas during seasonal transitions, Ayurveda illustrates its holistic worldview. This approach is not symbolic but functional, aiming to mitigate imbalances caused by environmental shifts. The principle expands beyond planetary movements, encompassing broader natural phenomena, thus affirming the dynamic equilibrium vital for health in Ayurveda's philosophy.

2. C: Hitāyu and Sukhāyu are complementary dimensions of Ayurveda's definitions of life, embodying health and well-being. While Hitāyu focuses on long-term health benefits achieved through alignment with natural and ethical principles, Sukhāyu emphasizes emotional ease and comfort. The integration of sattvic diets and Ritucharya regimens contributes to both aspects by promoting physical health and mental peace. This dynamic interrelation highlights Ayurveda's holistic perspective, where health encompasses happiness and ethical living. The results of the study, demonstrating improved quality of life indices, reaffirm this intertwined view rather than compartmentalizing these life goals.

3. D: Ayurveda combines traditional wisdom with practical health benefits, addressing criticisms of lacking empirical evidence by integrating subjective and objective dimensions of well-being. Tridosha theories provide a foundational framework connecting physiological processes to doshic balance. Panchakarma detoxification therapies exemplify Ayurveda's preventive and curative focus. While subjective philosophical interpretations remain significant, the physical outcomes of these therapies validate Ayurveda's relevance in modern contexts. This integration underscores the philosophy of holistic health by aligning preventive strategies with therapeutic interventions. Such a dual approach positions Ayurveda as a bridge between tradition and modern health systems.

4. C: Ayurvedic definitions of Hitāyu, Sukhāyu, Dharmāyu, and Ihāyu collectively promote a balanced life. They transcend individual domains, integrating ethical, spiritual, emotional, and physical health. This synthesis reflects Ayurveda's holistic worldview. The historian's observation aligns with this, showing how these definitions blend ancient ethical philosophies with physiological and material goals. By interweaving these aspects, Ayurveda addresses the complexities of human existence. Instead of isolating spiritual and material pursuits, it fosters harmony across all dimensions of life. This unified perspective highlights Ayurveda's unique approach to achieving comprehensive well-being.

5. **B:** The Lokapuruṣa principle emphasizes the interconnectedness between environmental and human health. Ayurveda's acknowledgment of ecological balance as a determinant of doshic stability demonstrates its practical application. Urban challenges like air pollution disrupt this balance, leading to chronic health issues. By integrating these environmental insights into doshic theories, Ayurveda addresses the root causes of urban health problems. This relationship underscores Ayurveda's relevance in addressing modern challenges, affirming that maintaining ecological harmony is essential for personal well-being. Thus, it remains highly applicable to contemporary environmental and health crises.

6. **C:** Ayurveda integrates ethical and spiritual dimensions with health practices, recognizing their impact on mental and physical well-being. The Lokapuruṣa principle reinforces this interconnectedness by linking bodily functions to broader cosmic and ethical patterns. Ethical living and spiritual growth foster mental clarity, emotional stability, and doshic balance. The researcher's observation aligns with Ayurveda's emphasis on non-material aspects of health, promoting harmony between external and internal environments. This focus illustrates the depth of Ayurveda's health paradigm, which transcends physical interventions to include ethical and spiritual practices.

7. **B:** Dharmāyu and Ihāyu represent complementary aspects of Ayurveda's life definitions. Dharmāyu focuses on spiritual and ethical aspirations, while Ihāyu addresses material pursuits. Ayurveda seeks equilibrium, recognizing that worldly achievements can align with ethical principles. This integration ensures that material goals do not overshadow spiritual growth. The dynamic balance between these dimensions is a hallmark of Ayurveda's holistic approach, affirming that material and ethical living can coexist harmoniously. By bridging these domains, Ayurveda fosters comprehensive well-being rather than dichotomizing spiritual and material life.

8. **C:** The Ayurvedic philosophy of Hitāyu and Dharmāyu extends ethical responsibilities to practitioners, emphasizing patient welfare as integral to health practices. This ethical foundation underscores the practitioner's duty to uphold principles that promote both individual and societal well-being. Ayurveda's holistic approach integrates ethical considerations with therapeutic strategies, ensuring comprehensive care. By prioritizing patient welfare, these principles reinforce Ayurveda's emphasis on virtuous living, aligning with broader philosophical goals. This synthesis highlights the depth of Ayurveda's ethical and therapeutic framework, which extends beyond physical health.

9. **B:** The integration of Sukhāyu principles into mental health interventions aligns with Ayurveda's holistic philosophy. By addressing both mental and physical dimensions of health, Sukhāyu promotes resilience and emotional stability. Ayurvedic practices like mindfulness and sattvic diets exemplify this approach, demonstrating measurable benefits in psychological contexts. This integration reflects Ayurveda's comprehensive understanding of well-being, where mental and physical health are interconnected. Modern applications, as evidenced by the psychologist's program, validate the relevance of Sukhāyu in addressing contemporary mental health challenges, reinforcing Ayurveda's timeless principles.

10. **B:** Hitāyu's principles, when applied to workplace wellness, extend Ayurveda's holistic approach to organizational contexts. By fostering ethical work-life balance, ergonomic practices, and dietary interventions, these programs enhance productivity and employee well-being. This application exemplifies Ayurveda's adaptability, demonstrating that its principles can transcend individual health practices. The alignment of Hitāyu's focus on long-term benefits with organizational goals affirms its relevance in modern professional settings. Such integrations highlight Ayurveda's potential to address contemporary challenges while maintaining its foundational emphasis on health and ethics.

11. **B:** Triphala's immunological benefits are closely linked to its impact on gut health. By enhancing microbiota diversity, Triphala stimulates Gut-Associated Lymphoid Tissue (GALT) activity, which plays a critical role in systemic immunity. Ayurveda's understanding of the gut as the seat of health aligns with these findings. The interplay between gut health and immunity underscores Ayurveda's holistic perspective, where detoxification and doshic balance strengthen the body's defense mechanisms. These observations reaffirm Triphala's relevance in addressing modern health challenges through its traditional therapeutic roles.

12. **B:** Sustainable agroforestry practices align with Ayurveda's emphasis on ecological balance and the preservation of natural resources. By promoting biodiversity and traditional cultivation methods, such practices address the overharvesting of Amalaki while maintaining its medicinal quality. This approach reflects Ayurveda's holistic worldview, integrating environmental conservation with therapeutic efficacy. The promotion of community-based initiatives ensures sustainable resource management, reinforcing the interdependence between ecological health and Ayurvedic formulations. These strategies highlight the practical applications of Ayurveda's principles in addressing modern environmental challenges.

13. **A:** The therapeutic efficacy of Triphala heavily relies on the bioactive compounds present in its ingredients, including Amalaki. Environmental degradation, as described in Scenario 2, directly impacts the medicinal quality of Amalaki, reducing its ability to promote gut microbiota diversity and systemic immunity. Ayurveda emphasizes the holistic balance between natural resources and health outcomes, and this interdependence is evident in the diminished efficacy observed when Amalaki's quality declines. This underscores the importance of preserving ecological conditions to maintain the therapeutic integrity of Ayurvedic formulations, demonstrating the interconnectedness of environmental health and human well-being.

14. **B:** Establishing global Triphala standards that incorporate sustainable harvesting practices balances ecological preservation with therapeutic efficacy. Such standards ensure consistency in bioactive compound levels while promoting ethical sourcing of medicinal plants. This approach aligns with Ayurveda's holistic philosophy, addressing the dual challenges of resource sustainability and health outcomes. By integrating conservation efforts with quality control, Ayurveda can continue to provide effective therapies while preserving biodiversity. This strategy represents a comprehensive response to the issues highlighted in Scenarios 1 and 2, reaffirming Ayurveda's relevance in addressing modern health and environmental challenges.

15. **B:** The Tridosha framework encompasses Vata (movement), Pitta (metabolism), and Kapha (structure), ensuring holistic physiological regulation. These doshas interconnect all bodily systems, emphasizing their role in maintaining physical and mental health. Ayurveda posits that any imbalance disrupts overall well-being, affirming the necessity of doshic harmony. The inclusion of all these principles underlines the comprehensive nature of Ayurveda's health paradigm. By integrating movement, transformation, and stability, the Tridosha theory demonstrates its relevance across diverse physiological and psychological processes, making it foundational to Ayurvedic practice.

16. **B:** The Ayurvedic Rasas (tastes) serve diverse biological purposes, influencing physiological processes and health outcomes. Sweet promotes nourishment and immunity, bitter facilitates detoxification, sour supports digestion, and astringent strengthens tissues. These properties reflect Ayurveda's nuanced understanding of the interplay between taste and therapeutic action. The inclusion of all these functions emphasizes Ayurveda's comprehensive approach to health, integrating sensory experiences with physiological benefits. This perspective underscores the importance of balancing Rasas to achieve holistic well-being, demonstrating the depth of Ayurvedic dietary principles.

17. **A:** Agni in Ayurveda extends beyond digestion to encompass all transformative processes within the body. As a metabolic regulator, it prevents toxin (Ama) accumulation, ensuring physiological efficiency and vitality. This central role highlights Agni's significance in maintaining overall health. While it is closely associated with gastrointestinal activity, its functions are not limited to digestion but include broader systemic regulation. Ayurveda's emphasis on enhancing Agni reflects its holistic philosophy, where metabolic balance is foundational to well-being. This comprehensive view affirms Agni's pivotal role in Ayurveda's health paradigm.

18. **B:** The Ayurvedic Dhatus (tissues) encompass diverse physiological functions, from nourishment (Rasa) and oxygenation (Rakta) to structural support (Asthi) and lubrication (Meda). Together, they form the body's foundational framework, emphasizing interdependence and systemic harmony. The inclusion of all Dhatus reflects Ayurveda's comprehensive understanding of bodily functions, ensuring holistic care. By addressing each tissue's unique role, Ayurveda tailors therapies to maintain balance across all systems. This approach demonstrates the depth of Ayurvedic diagnostics and treatment strategies, affirming its holistic health philosophy.

19. **B:** Ritucharya aligns human practices with seasonal variations to prevent doshic imbalances and associated health issues. This preventive approach underscores Ayurveda's integration of external and internal health determinants. By incorporating dietary, lifestyle, and therapeutic adjustments, Ritucharya minimizes seasonal vulnerabilities and enhances resilience. This adaptability highlights Ayurveda's dynamic understanding of health, where environmental changes

are proactively addressed. The focus on seasonal harmony reflects Ayurveda's holistic worldview, emphasizing its relevance in contemporary preventive healthcare practices.

20. **A:** Ayurveda's four life definitions—Hitāyu, Sukhāyu, Dharmāyu, and Ihāyu—offer a multidimensional framework for well-being. Hitāyu prioritizes health and longevity, Sukhāyu addresses emotional comfort, and Dharmāyu integrates ethical living, reflecting the holistic nature of Ayurvedic philosophy. Ihāyu, though significant, is not solely materialistic but interwoven with these dimensions. This interconnectedness demonstrates Ayurveda's nuanced understanding of human aspirations, where ethical, emotional, and physical goals converge. By harmonizing these aspects, Ayurveda offers a comprehensive model for achieving balance and well-being in life.

21. **A:** Panchakarma therapies exemplify Ayurveda's detoxification and rejuvenation approach, targeting doshic imbalances and metabolic inefficiencies. These therapies restore Agni, eliminating toxins (Ama) and enhancing systemic health. By aligning the body with natural cycles, Panchakarma promotes holistic well-being. This comprehensive approach reflects Ayurveda's emphasis on preventive and therapeutic interventions, ensuring sustainable health outcomes. Panchakarma's role in targeting multiple physiological pathways underscores its relevance in modern integrative healthcare systems, validating Ayurveda's holistic health model.

22. **B:** The therapeutic uses of Ayurvedic formulations highlight their targeted actions: Triphala enhances gut health, Ashwagandha boosts resilience, Brahmi supports cognitive function, and Neem detoxifies blood and skin. These associations demonstrate Ayurveda's precision in tailoring herbal remedies to specific health needs. By addressing physical, mental, and systemic dimensions, these formulations reflect Ayurveda's holistic approach to well-being. The alignment of traditional knowledge with modern applications reinforces the relevance of Ayurvedic herbs in addressing diverse health challenges while maintaining their foundational principles.

23. **A:** Ayurvedic concepts like Agni (digestive fire), Ama (toxins), Tridosha (functional dynamics), and Sattva (mental clarity) illustrate the interconnectedness of physical and mental health. These principles collectively ensure systemic harmony, underscoring Ayurveda's holistic health paradigm. By integrating digestion, detoxification, physiological balance, and mental well-being, Ayurveda provides a comprehensive framework for achieving optimal health. The inclusion of these elements highlights Ayurveda's depth and adaptability, ensuring its relevance in addressing modern health challenges.

24. **A:** Ayurvedic practices like Panchakarma, Dinacharya, Ritucharya, and Yoga are designed to align the body, mind, and spirit with natural rhythms. Panchakarma detoxifies the body, Dinacharya ensures daily balance, Ritucharya prevents seasonal imbalances, and Yoga integrates physical and mental harmony. Together, these practices reflect Ayurveda's holistic philosophy of addressing health comprehensively. Each technique is tailored to specific aspects of well-being, highlighting the depth and versatility of Ayurvedic approaches. This systematic alignment with internal and external cycles demonstrates Ayurveda's relevance in modern preventive and therapeutic health care.

25. **A:** The four definitions of life in Ayurveda—Hitāyu, Sukhāyu, Dharmāyu, and Ihāyu—reflect its multidimensional approach to well-being. Hitāyu promotes health and longevity, Sukhāyu emphasizes mental and physical ease, Dharmāyu focuses on ethical and spiritual living, and Ihāyu addresses material well-being. These interconnected aspects provide a framework for holistic living, emphasizing the integration of health, happiness, and virtue. By harmonizing these elements, Ayurveda creates a balanced approach to life, showcasing its depth in addressing physical, emotional, and ethical dimensions simultaneously.

26. **A:** The doshas—Vata, Pitta, and Kapha—are fundamental to Ayurveda's understanding of physiology and pathology. Vata governs movement and functions like respiration, Pitta regulates metabolism and enzymatic activity, and Kapha provides structural stability and fluid balance. Any imbalance in these doshas manifests as specific symptoms, such as anxiety (Vata), inflammation (Pitta), or lethargy (Kapha). By aligning symptoms with doshic imbalances, Ayurveda enables personalized therapeutic interventions, demonstrating its precision and adaptability in addressing diverse health concerns.

27. **A:** The Dhatus (bodily tissues) play critical roles in maintaining systemic health: Rasa nourishes all tissues, Rakta supports oxygen transport, Mamsa builds muscle strength, and Meda regulates fat storage and lubrication. These tissue functions highlight Ayurveda's intricate understanding of physiology, where each Dhatu contributes to overall well-being. The emphasis on maintaining Dhatu balance reflects Ayurveda's comprehensive approach to health. By addressing both individual and interdependent tissue roles, Ayurveda provides a nuanced framework for understanding and treating physiological imbalances.

28. **A:** Ayurveda's philosophical and practical concepts, such as Lokapuruṣa (macrocosm-microcosm relationship), Agni (digestive fire), Tridosha (physiological balance), and Panchakarma (detoxification), collectively reflect its holistic worldview. Lokapuruṣa integrates human health with cosmic rhythms, Agni ensures metabolic efficiency, Tridosha governs functional processes, and Panchakarma restores balance. These interconnected elements demonstrate Ayurveda's depth in understanding health as a dynamic and multifaceted state. This alignment of philosophy and practice underscores its relevance in contemporary healthcare.

29. **A:** The therapeutic uses of Ayurvedic herbs reflect their specific actions: Triphala for gut health and immunity, Ashwagandha for stress and vitality, Brahmi for cognitive enhancement, and Neem for detoxification. These associations highlight Ayurveda's precision in herbal formulations, where each herb addresses targeted health concerns. This approach underscores Ayurveda's adaptability and efficacy in addressing modern health challenges. By combining traditional wisdom with specific therapeutic goals, Ayurveda remains a versatile and comprehensive system of medicine.

30. **A:** The six Rasas (tastes) in Ayurveda have distinct physiological effects: Sweet nourishes and supports immunity, Sour enhances digestion, Bitter detoxifies, and Astringent strengthens tissues. These properties reflect Ayurveda's nuanced understanding of the interplay between taste and health outcomes. By incorporating Rasas into dietary practices, Ayurveda ensures balanced nutrition and therapeutic benefits. This integration of sensory and physiological dimensions underscores the depth of Ayurveda's dietary principles, highlighting its relevance in maintaining holistic health.

31. **A:** Ayurvedic terms like Prakriti (constitution), Ama (toxins), Ritucharya (seasonal regimen), and Sattva (mental clarity) represent its holistic health paradigm. Prakriti individualizes care, Ama addresses detoxification, Ritucharya aligns seasonal practices, and Sattva promotes mental well-being. Together, these elements reflect Ayurveda's comprehensive approach to addressing physical, mental, and environmental health. By integrating these principles, Ayurveda provides a versatile framework for preventive and therapeutic care, demonstrating its relevance in modern health systems.

32. **A:** Ayurvedic health practices—Sattvic diets, Dinacharya, Panchakarma, and Yoga—address diverse dimensions of health. Sattvic diets promote purity and mental clarity, Dinacharya ensures daily balance, Panchakarma detoxifies the body, and Yoga integrates physical and mental harmony. These practices demonstrate Ayurveda's holistic approach, where dietary, lifestyle, and therapeutic strategies are seamlessly integrated. This alignment reflects Ayurveda's relevance in addressing modern health challenges, emphasizing its depth and adaptability.

33. **A:** Ayurvedic therapies like Abhyanga (nourishing massage), Shirodhara (stress relief), Vamana (Kapha detox), and Nasya (nasal cleansing) are tailored to specific health outcomes. Abhyanga improves circulation, Shirodhara reduces stress, Vamana detoxifies Kapha, and Nasya enhances respiratory health. These therapies reflect Ayurveda's precision in addressing diverse physiological and psychological concerns. By targeting specific imbalances, Ayurveda ensures comprehensive care, highlighting its depth in therapeutic interventions and relevance in modern integrative health care.

34 **A:** The interrelation between body and mind in Ayurveda integrates mental clarity (Sattva), emotional stability, physical strength, and doshic balance. Practices like yoga, meditation, and sattvic living foster harmony across these dimensions. By aligning physical and mental health, Ayurveda addresses the root causes of imbalance, demonstrating its holistic philosophy. This integration of body-mind relations underscores Ayurveda's depth in promoting comprehensive well-being, making it highly applicable in addressing contemporary health challenges.

35. **C:** Ayurveda's concept of the human body as a microcosm reflects its philosophical foundation, emphasizing the interconnectedness between the five elements (Pañca Mahābhūtas) and human physiology. This principle acknowledges that bodily health is a reflection of natural harmony. However, Statement 2's suggestion that therapies are solely astrological oversimplifies Ayurveda. While cosmic rhythms influence health, Ayurveda integrates this understanding with practical therapeutic strategies like diet, lifestyle adjustments, and detoxification. This misinterpretation separates the metaphysical from the practical, revealing the inaccuracy in Statement 2 while reaffirming Statement 1's foundational accuracy.

36. **A:** Agni, the digestive fire, is central to Ayurvedic physiology, regulating digestion, metabolism, and toxin elimination. Impaired Agni results in the accumulation of Ama, which disrupts the doshic balance and leads to diseases. Statement 2 accurately explains the mechanism by which impaired Agni manifests health disorders, providing direct support to Statement 1. This relationship underscores Ayurveda's emphasis on strengthening Agni as a preventive and therapeutic measure. The coherence between the two statements highlights the importance of metabolic processes in maintaining overall health in Ayurvedic science.

37. A: Ritucharya's preventive approach aligns dietary and lifestyle practices with seasonal changes to maintain doshic balance. Seasonal transitions influence the Tridosha, requiring specific adjustments to prevent diseases. Statement 2 correctly explains the rationale behind Ritucharya, validating the importance of adapting practices to external conditions. The correlation between the two statements demonstrates Ayurveda's dynamic understanding of health, where proactive measures address vulnerabilities arising from seasonal shifts. This emphasis on prevention highlights Ayurveda's relevance in maintaining equilibrium through changing environmental conditions.

38. D: Sukhāyu is defined in Ayurveda as a life of comfort and ease, integrating physical, mental, and emotional well-being. While Statement 1 focuses narrowly on mental and emotional aspects, Statement 2 provides a more accurate definition by including the integration of physical health. This distinction highlights the inaccuracy of Statement 1 while affirming the holistic nature of Sukhāyu in Statement 2. Ayurveda's emphasis on comprehensive well-being underlines the interconnectedness of these dimensions, illustrating the broader perspective that Sukhāyu encompasses.

39. A: Dharmāyu in Ayurveda reflects a life of virtue, duty, and ethical alignment, which promotes harmony between self and society. Ihāyu, on the other hand, is associated with materialistic and worldly pursuits. The contrast between the two highlights that overemphasis on materialism (Ihāyu) can hinder the moral and spiritual goals of Dharmāyu. Hence, Statement 2 directly explains the broader context of Statement 1.

40. A: Panchakarma's detoxification therapies are central to Ayurveda's emphasis on removing Ama (toxins) and restoring doshic balance. By targeting metabolic pathways and enhancing Agni, Panchakarma promotes holistic health and disease prevention. The alignment between Assertion (A) and Reason (R) accurately reflects this process, showcasing the depth of Ayurveda's therapeutic strategies. This coherence underscores the importance of Panchakarma in maintaining systemic harmony, reaffirming Ayurveda's relevance in addressing modern health challenges through comprehensive detoxification methods.

41. A: Seasonal routines (Ritucharya) mitigate the effects of seasonal changes on doshic balance, preventing associated diseases. By aligning dietary and lifestyle adjustments with these transitions, Ayurveda maintains health and resilience. The Reason (R) accurately explains why seasonal changes necessitate adaptations, providing a direct link to Assertion (A). This alignment highlights Ayurveda's preventive approach, where external influences are proactively addressed to sustain equilibrium. The coherence between the two statements reinforces the value of Ritucharya in modern preventive health care practices.

42. C: The Gunas (Sattva, Rajas, Tamas) influence mental health, with Sattva representing clarity, Rajas activity, and Tamas inertia. While Assertion (A) correctly identifies their role, Reason (R) inaccurately claims that Tamas promotes mental clarity, contradicting Ayurveda's understanding. Tamas is associated with lethargy and ignorance, whereas Sattva fosters cognitive clarity. This misrepresentation in Reason (R) highlights the need to accurately distinguish the Gunas' effects. The distinction emphasizes the importance of promoting Sattva for achieving mental and emotional balance in Ayurvedic practices.

43. C: The Lokapuruṣa concept links human health with cosmic rhythms, reflecting the interdependence between the microcosm (body) and macrocosm (universe). While Assertion (A) accurately describes this connection, Reason (R) contradicts it by suggesting independence from natural influences. Ayurveda emphasizes alignment with natural rhythms, such as through Ritucharya and Dinacharya, to maintain balance. The inconsistency in Reason (R) highlights a misunderstanding, reaffirming the importance of acknowledging external factors in Ayurveda's holistic health framework.

44. A: Ayurveda emphasizes individualized treatment based on a person's Prakriti (innate constitution), which guides diet, therapy, and lifestyle. This Prakriti is determined by the dominant Doshas (Vata, Pitta, Kapha) and is considered stable throughout life. Therefore, both the assertion and reason are true, and the reason correctly explains why Ayurveda customizes treatment per individual constitution.

45. C: Ayurveda integrates ethical living, spiritual growth, and physical health, recognizing their interconnectedness in achieving well-being. While Assertion (A) accurately describes this integration, Reason (R) contradicts it by separating ethical and spiritual practices from therapeutic strategies. Ayurveda's holistic approach incorporates these dimensions into health interventions, emphasizing their role in fostering harmony. The inconsistency in Reason (R) underscores the importance of aligning ethical, spiritual, and physical aspects in Ayurveda's comprehensive health framework.

46. B: The Tridosha governs physiological, psychological, and biochemical processes, reflecting Ayurveda's holistic understanding of health. These doshas, derived from the five elements, regulate the body's dynamic balance and respond to external and internal influences. Their central role highlights Ayurveda's comprehensive approach to systemic harmony. The passage reinforces this foundational principle, showcasing the Tridosha's relevance in maintaining health through interconnected processes that address the physical, mental, and environmental dimensions of well-being.

47. B: Agni's centrality to digestion, metabolism, and detoxification reflects Ayurveda's focus on maintaining vitality. By preventing Ama (toxins) and supporting doshic balance, Agni ensures systemic health. This emphasis aligns with Ayurveda's preventive and curative strategies, showcasing its relevance in modern health practices. The passage affirms Agni's pivotal role, emphasizing its integration into dietary, lifestyle, and therapeutic interventions. This understanding highlights Agni as a cornerstone of Ayurveda's holistic health paradigm.

48. B: Lokapuruṣa connects human health with cosmic rhythms, guiding practices like Ritucharya and Dinacharya to align individuals with natural cycles. This integration of external and internal harmony reflects Ayurveda's dynamic understanding of health. The passage emphasizes the importance of synchronizing bodily functions with environmental influences, affirming the relevance of Lokapuruṣa in preventive care. This interconnected perspective underscores Ayurveda's comprehensive approach to achieving balance and well-being through alignment with cosmic and natural rhythms.

49. B: Modern research validates Ayurveda's principles, such as Panchakarma's detoxification effects and Triphala's role in enhancing gut microbiota diversity. These findings bridge traditional knowledge with scientific evidence, demonstrating Ayurveda's relevance in contemporary healthcare. The passage highlights this integration, showcasing Ayurveda's adaptability and efficacy. By aligning traditional practices with modern insights, Ayurveda's principles gain broader acceptance, reinforcing their practical applications in addressing systemic health challenges.

50. B: Overharvesting of medicinal plants and lack of standardization are critical challenges for Ayurveda's global integration. These issues impact the sustainability of natural resources and the efficacy of formulations, as emphasized in the passage. Addressing these concerns requires conservation efforts and consistent quality standards. This alignment of traditional practices with modern regulations ensures Ayurveda's relevance and effectiveness. The challenges highlighted underscore the need for sustainable and standardized approaches to preserving Ayurveda's therapeutic legacy.

CHAPTER–7

HEALTH DIMENSIONS, PANCHAMAHABHUTA, AND THEORIES OF SAMANYA AND VISESA

Ayurvedic Perspectives on Health

Ayurveda, the ancient Indian system of medicine, offers a comprehensive framework for understanding health, disease, and wellness. Rooted in principles that integrate the physical, mental, and spiritual dimensions of existence, Ayurveda emphasizes balance as the cornerstone of health. It seeks to harmonize the body, mind, and environment through individualized approaches, considering the unique constitution (prakṛti) of each person.

Central to Ayurvedic thought are concepts such as the paṃcamahābhūta (the five great elements) and the theories of sāmānya (similarity) and viśeṣa (difference), which serve as foundational principles for diagnosis, treatment, and the promotion of health. These concepts, while philosophical in origin, have profound practical implications for understanding the human body and its interaction with the external environment. This chapter explores the dimensions of health in Ayurveda, elucidates the paṃcamahābhūta theory, and delves into the theories of sāmānya and viśeṣa, providing an integrative perspective on maintaining and restoring health.

Dimensions of Health in Ayurveda

Ayurveda defines health not merely as the absence of disease but as a state of complete physical, mental, and spiritual well-being. The Sanskrit verse from the Sushruta Samhita succinctly encapsulates the Ayurvedic definition of health:

"Samadosha samagnischa samadhatu malakriyaḥ,
Prasannatmendriya manaha swasthya ityabhidheeyate"

This translates to: "Health is a state where the doṣas (bio-energies), agnis (digestive and metabolic fires), dhātus (tissues), and malas (waste products) are in balance, and the mind, senses, and soul are in a state of happiness."

1. **Physical Health:** Balance of Bio-energies and Biological Functions:
   - Ayurveda attributes health to the balance of three fundamental bio-energies or tridoṣas: vāta (movement), pitta (transformation), and kapha (stability). These energies govern every physiological and pathological process in the body.
   - Agnis, or the digestive and metabolic fires, play a critical role in converting food into nutrients and maintaining cellular functions. Impaired agnis lead to the accumulation of toxins (āma), which is a root cause of many diseases.
   - Proper functioning of dhātus (bodily tissues such as plasma, blood, muscles, fat, bone, marrow, and reproductive tissue) and elimination of malas (urine, feces, and sweat) are also essential for maintaining physical health.
2. **Mental Health:** Harmony of the Mind and Senses:
   - Ayurveda identifies the mind (manas) as an integral part of health. Mental well-being is achieved when the mind is calm, focused, and in harmony with the senses (indriyas).
   - **Psychological health is linked to the three gunas (qualities) of the mind:** sattva (purity),

rajas (activity), and tamas (inertia). A sattvic mind fosters clarity, compassion, and joy, while imbalances in rajas and tamas lead to agitation and lethargy, respectively.

3. **Spiritual Health:** Connection to the Self
   - Spiritual health in Ayurveda involves a sense of alignment with one's higher self (ātman) and the universal consciousness (brahman). Practices like meditation, yoga, and ethical living foster spiritual well-being.
   - The concept of dharma (duty), artha (wealth), kāma (desire), and mokṣa (liberation) provides a framework for living a balanced and purposeful life.
   - Ayurveda's holistic approach to health integrates these dimensions, offering a multidimensional framework that goes beyond the physical body to include mental, emotional, and spiritual aspects.

PAṂCAMAHĀBHŪTA: THE FIVE GREAT ELEMENTS

The Paṃcamahābhūta theory forms the bedrock of Ayurvedic philosophy and serves as a universal framework for understanding the composition of both the human body and the environment. By examining the five great elements—Ākāśa (Ether), Vāyu (Air), Tejas (Fire), Āpas (Water), and Pṛthvī (Earth)—this theory bridges the microcosmic (individual) and macrocosmic (universal) aspects of existence. Rooted in the Vedic traditions of ancient India, the Paṃcamahābhūta theory elucidates the interconnectedness of all matter and life, offering profound insights into health, disease, and the pathways to harmony.

(I) The Five Great Elements (Paṃcamahābhūtas)

The Paṃcamahābhūtas are the foundational building blocks of all matter. Each element has distinct qualities (guṇas) and performs specific functions within both the human body and the universe. The elements are not isolated entities but work together in dynamic synergy to create and sustain life.

1. **Ākāśa (Ether):** The Subtlest Element

   Nature and Characteristics:
   - Ākāśa represents space or the void that allows for expansion and separation.
   - Its primary qualities include lightness, subtlety, softness, and immateriality.

   Functions in the Body:
   - Forms the hollow structures in the body, such as the ears, respiratory tract, blood vessels, and the digestive tract.
   - Facilitates communication, perception, and the propagation of sound waves (associated with the sense of hearing).
   - Provides the spatial dimension necessary for other elements to function.

   Role in Health and Disease:
   - Excess Ākāśa can lead to feelings of emptiness, isolation, and lack of grounding.
   - Deficiency of Ākāśa may manifest as rigidity, congestion, or blockages in the body.

2. **Vāyu (Air):** The Element of Motion

   Nature and Characteristics:
   - Vāyu represents movement and dynamic activity.
   - It is light, dry, rough, mobile, and subtle in nature.

   Functions in the Body:
   - Governs all types of motion, including circulation, nerve impulses, muscle contractions, respiration, and elimination.
   - Associated with the sense of touch, enabling sensations to be transmitted through the skin.
   - Responsible for physiological processes like breathing and the transport of nutrients and wastes.

   Role in Health and Disease:
   - Balanced Vāyu promotes vitality, flexibility, and mental clarity.
   - Imbalanced Vāyu can lead to anxiety, restlessness, dryness, and joint pain.

3. **Tejas (Fire):** The Element of Transformation

   Nature and Characteristics:
   - Tejas represents heat, light, and transformation.
   - Its qualities include sharpness, intensity, subtlety, and radiance.

   Functions in the Body:
   - Regulates digestion and metabolism through Jaṭharagni (digestive fire).
   - Controls body temperature, vision, and cognitive functions like discernment and comprehension.
   - Influences cellular processes, enzymatic activities, and hormonal functions.

   Role in Health and Disease:
   - A balanced Tejas supports strong digestion, clear vision, and a sharp intellect.
   - Excess Tejas manifests as hyperacidity, inflammation, and irritability.
   - Deficiency of Tejas may cause poor digestion, lethargy, and lack of motivation.

4. **Āpas (Water):** The Element of Cohesion

Nature and Characteristics:

- Āpas represents fluidity and cohesion, essential for life.
- It is heavy, cool, soft, and smooth in nature.

Functions in the Body:

- Maintains moisture and ensures lubrication in joints, tissues, and internal organs.
- Forms bodily fluids like saliva, blood plasma, lymph, and cerebrospinal fluid.
- Associated with the sense of taste, which depends on moisture for perception.

Role in Health and Disease:

- Balanced Āpas ensures hydration, elasticity, and smooth functioning of organs.
- Excess Āpas leads to swelling, congestion, and sluggishness.
- Deficiency causes dryness, dehydration, and loss of elasticity.

5. **Pṛthvī (Earth):** The Element of Solidity

Nature and Characteristics:

- Pṛthvī represents structure, stability, and support.
- It is heavy, dense, firm, and immovable in nature.

Functions in the Body:

- Forms the structural components of the body, such as bones, muscles, teeth, and nails.
- Provides physical strength and endurance.
- Associated with the sense of smell, which depends on contact with solid matter.

Role in Health and Disease:

- Balanced Pṛthvī provides stability, resilience, and groundedness.
- Excess Pṛthvī leads to obesity, rigidity, and lethargy.
- Deficiency causes weakness, fragility, and lack of endurance.

(II) The Interplay of Paṃcamahābhūtas

The Paṃcamahābhūtas do not exist in isolation but interact to form all physical and subtle phenomena. In the human body, their interplay creates:

1. **Doshas:** Functional energies (Vāta, Pitta, Kapha).
2. **Dhātus:** Structural tissues (Rasa, Rakta, Māṃsa, Meda, Asthi, Majjā, and Shukra).
3. **Malas:** Waste products (feces, urine, and sweat).

1. **Doshas and Their Elemental Composition**

- **Vāta (Ether + Air):** Governs movement and communication. Balanced Vāta ensures efficient circulation and mental agility.
- **Pitta (Fire + Water):** Governs transformation and metabolism. Balanced Pitta promotes digestion, vitality, and clarity.
- **Kapha (Water + Earth):** Governs structure and lubrication. Balanced Kapha provides stability, immunity, and emotional calm.

2. **Application in Diagnosis and Treatment**: The Ayurvedic practitioner identifies elemental imbalances to restore harmony:

- Excess of specific elements (e.g., too much fire causing inflammation) is counteracted by opposing qualities.
- Deficiencies are treated by replenishing the corresponding elements through diet, lifestyle, and therapies.

(III) Principles of Sāmānya and Viśeṣa

The theories of Sāmānya (Similarity) and Viśeṣa (Difference) provide the theoretical foundation for Ayurvedic diagnosis and treatment. These principles guide the application of foods, herbs, and therapies to maintain or restore balance.

1. **Sāmānya (Similarity):** The Principle of Like Increases Like

- **Definition:** Sāmānya refers to the concept that substances with similar qualities enhance each other.

Application:

- For nourishment and replenishment: When tissues are depleted, substances with similar qualities are introduced to restore balance. For instance, consuming oily foods replenishes dry tissues.

Examples in Daily Life:

- A person with a Vāta constitution benefits from warm, moist, and grounding foods to counteract their inherent dryness and lightness.
- Sweet and heavy foods are used to promote weight gain in undernourished individuals.

2. **Viśeṣa (Difference):** The Principle of Opposites Reduce Excess

- **Definition:** Viśeṣa involves using substances with opposing qualities to neutralize excesses or deficiencies.

Application:

- **For therapeutic interventions:** Excess heat (Pitta imbalance) is treated with cooling substances, while excess cold (Kapha imbalance) is countered with heating substances.

Examples in Daily Life:

- Spicy, heating foods are avoided by Pitta types, as they can exacerbate heat-related symptoms.
- Dryness caused by Vāta imbalance is treated with nourishing and oily substances.

(IV) Practical Applications of Paṃcamahābhūta Theory

The Paṃcamahābhūta theory is applied in various aspects of Ayurveda to promote balance and well-being.

1. **Dietary Recommendations**: Ayurvedic diets are tailored to balance the elemental constitution:
   - **Vāta Types:** Warm, moist, and nourishing foods.
   - **Pitta Types:** Cooling and soothing foods.
   - **Kapha Types:** Light, dry, and warming foods.
2. **Herbal Medicine**: Herbs are classified based on their elemental composition, taste (rasa), potency (vīrya), and post-digestive effect (vipāka). These classifications guide their application to balance doshas.
3. **Lifestyle Modifications**: Activities like yoga, meditation, and pranayama are designed to harmonize the elements within the body. For example:
   - Vāta Imbalance: Slow, grounding yoga practices.
   - Pitta Imbalance: Cooling pranayama techniques like Sheetali.
   - Kapha Imbalance: Dynamic, invigorating exercises.

The Paṃcamahābhūta theory offers a timeless and universal framework for understanding the interconnectedness of all life. By recognizing the interplay of the five great elements, Ayurveda provides profound insights into health, disease, and harmony. The principles of Sāmānya and Viśeṣa further enrich this understanding, offering practical tools to maintain balance through personalized interventions in diet, lifestyle, and therapy.

In embracing this elemental philosophy, Ayurveda not only addresses the physical aspects of well-being but also nurtures the mental and spiritual dimensions, guiding individuals toward holistic health and fulfillment.

Integration of Paṃcamahābhūta with Sāmānya and Viśeṣa

The theories of paṃcamahābhūta, sāmānya, and viśeṣa are deeply interconnected, forming a cohesive framework for understanding health and disease. The interplay of the five elements gives rise to the qualities (guṇas) that are manipulated through the principles of similarity and difference.

For example, a patient with excess vāta (characterized by dryness, coldness, and lightness) would benefit from therapies that introduce opposing qualities, such as warmth, moisture, and heaviness. These therapies would involve:

- **Dietary Changes:** Inclusion of foods with heavy, oily, and warming properties, such as ghee, nuts, and cooked grains.
- **Herbal Remedies:** Use of grounding and warming herbs like ashwagandha or ginger.
- **Lifestyle Adjustments:** Adoption of routines that promote stability, such as regular sleep patterns and warm oil massages.By aligning the elemental composition of the patient with their treatments, Ayurveda ensures a personalized approach to health care.

The holistic and individualized approach of Ayurveda remains profoundly relevant in modern health care. The integration of paṃcamahābhūta, sāmānya, and viśeṣa provides a comprehensive framework for understanding the interconnectedness of body, mind, and environment.

In a world increasingly dominated by stress, processed foods, and environmental toxins, Ayurveda's emphasis on balance and natural remedies offers practical solutions for preventing and managing diseases. By understanding the dimensions of health, the elemental composition of life, and the principles of similarity and difference, individuals can achieve sustainable wellness and a deeper connection to themselves and their surroundings. This timeless wisdom continues to inspire and guide holistic health practices across the globe.

MULTIPLE CHOICE QUESTIONS

1. A patient experiencing symptoms such as dry skin, constipation, and irregular sleep cycles consults an Ayurvedic practitioner. The practitioner diagnoses an imbalance of Vāta and recommends dietary and lifestyle adjustments, including the use of warm, oily, and grounding foods. Which of the following best reflects the Ayurvedic rationale behind this prescription?

   A. Warm and oily foods neutralize excess Pitta through the principle of Sāmānya.

   B. Grounding foods oppose the light and mobile qualities of Vāta, demonstrating the principle of Viśeṣa.

   C. The prescribed diet focuses on detoxifying the body, reducing the accumulation of Āma.

   D. This recommendation aligns with the seasonal principle of Ritucharya rather than Vāta imbalance.

2. An Ayurvedic scholar conducts a comparative study of the Paṃcamahābhūta theory and modern biochemistry. The scholar identifies that Tejas (fire element) aligns with metabolic and enzymatic activities in the human body. How does this observation validate the Paṃcamahābhūta theory?

Choose the correct answer from the options given below:

A. Tejas is directly linked to the regulation of Prakṛti, while other elements govern external factors.
B. The association of Tejas with enzymatic activities confirms the functional relevance of Mahābhūtas in cellular processes.
C. Tejas governs only thermoregulatory mechanisms, making its biochemical relevance limited.
D. This observation negates the validity of Paṃcamahābhūta in modern scientific contexts.

3. Consider a clinical scenario where a patient with chronic indigestion is prescribed Ayurvedic herbal formulations. The practitioner emphasizes the role of Agni in restoring digestive balance. Based on Ayurvedic theory, what physiological aspect does the concept of Agni most closely correspond to?

A. Gut microbiota diversity and immune modulation.
B. Enzymatic activity and metabolic processes.
C. Hormonal regulation and neurotransmitter activity.
D. Tissue regeneration and fluid balance.

4. A public health researcher is analyzing the Ayurvedic framework of health and discovers its emphasis on Prakṛti. The researcher notes that Prakṛti determines individual susceptibility to diseases and influences treatment strategies. What does Prakṛti primarily represent in Ayurvedic science?

Choose the correct answer from the options given below:

A. The universal constitution of the human body shared by all individuals.
B. An individual's unique doshic composition determined at conception.
C. The temporary state of dosha imbalance during disease.
D. The influence of external environmental factors on health.

5. An Ayurvedic text describes the Rasa (taste) of a medicinal herb as astringent and bitter. According to the principles of Ayurveda, how might this herb function therapeutically?

Choose the correct answer from the options given below:

A. Astringent Rasa enhances tissue cohesion, while bitter Rasa detoxifies and reduces inflammation.
B. Bitter Rasa promotes digestion, while astringent Rasa regulates hormonal balance.
C. These Rasas primarily pacify Kapha and aggravate Pitta, irrespective of therapeutic benefits.
D. The combination of Rasas creates synergistic effects but lacks specific biological functions.

6. A pharmaceutical company attempts to integrate Ayurvedic concepts into modern drug development. The focus is on using Paṃcamahābhūta as a framework for identifying bioactive compounds. Which of the following aligns best with this approach?

Choose the correct answer from the options given below:

A. The predominance of Vāyu and Ākāśa in certain plants correlates with their use in respiratory conditions.
B. Pṛthvī and Āpas elements in herbs are irrelevant for pharmacological purposes.
C. The Paṃcamahābhūta framework lacks scientific relevance in modern drug discovery.
D. All plants possess a balanced combination of Mahābhūtas, making their pharmacological use uniform.

7. During an Ayurvedic consultation, a patient with obesity is advised to consume foods with bitter and astringent tastes while avoiding sweet and oily foods. What principle of Ayurveda is being applied in this dietary recommendation?

Choose the correct answer from the options given below:

A. Sāmānya to increase metabolism.
B. Viśeṣa to counteract the Kapha-increasing properties of sweet and oily foods.
C. The seasonal principle of Ritucharya.
D. The principle of Agni enhancement.

8. An Ayurvedic practitioner observes that patients with dominant Kapha constitution are more prone to conditions like congestion and lethargy. How is this observation consistent with the properties of Kapha?

Choose the correct answer from the options given below:

A. Kapha is associated with qualities of dryness and mobility, leading to energy deficiencies.
B. The heaviness and stability of Kapha contribute to fluid retention and sluggishness.
C. Kapha governs metabolic activities, leading to its role in energy depletion.
D. This observation contradicts Ayurvedic principles of doshic balance.

9. A scientist examining Sāmānya and Viśeṣa principles finds that specific herbal combinations restore balance in patients with Pitta disorders. Which of the following combinations exemplifies the application of these principles?

Choose the correct answer from the options given below:

A. Using heating herbs like ginger to treat heat-related conditions.
B. Prescribing cooling herbs like coriander to counteract excess Pitta.
C. Combining substances with opposing Rasas to neutralize doshic imbalances.
D. Both B and C.

10. A research team investigates the application of Paṃcamahābhūta in ecological restoration. The study finds that plants predominantly associated with Pṛthvī and Āpaś elements thrive in degraded soils, suggesting their use in ecological balance. What does this finding imply about the broader applicability of Ayurvedic principles?

Choose the correct answer from the options given below:

A. Ayurvedic principles are confined to human health and do not extend to ecological systems.
B. The Paṃcamahābhūta framework provides a universal understanding of natural harmony.
C. Plants with Pṛthvī and Āpas dominance are unsuitable for ecological restoration.
D. This finding contradicts Ayurvedic notions of Mahābhūtas.

Directions (Q. No. 11-14): *Scenario-Based Questions*

SCENARIO 1

A group of scientists conducts a trial on the effects of Ayurvedic therapies on modern metabolic syndromes. The focus is on enhancing digestive efficiency and reducing systemic inflammation through a diet emphasizing Sāmānya principles. The team observes a significant reduction in inflammatory markers and improved enzymatic activity in patients treated with Ayurvedic herbal formulations.

SCENARIO 2

Simultaneously, a parallel study evaluates the sustainability of herbal ingredients used in Ayurvedic practices. Researchers discover that overharvesting certain herbs like Amalaki reduces their bioactive compound content. The reduced efficacy of these herbs in clinical trials highlights the need for sustainable harvesting practices.

11. How does Scenario 1 validate the principle of Sāmānya in Ayurvedic practice?

Choose the correct answer from the options given below:

A. The similarity in qualities between diet and therapies strengthens the metabolic processes.
B. Sāmānya reduces enzymatic activity, thereby alleviating inflammation.
C. The principle is unrelated to digestive or inflammatory markers.
D. It demonstrates that modern diseases cannot be managed with traditional frameworks.

12. What intervention best resolves the sustainability challenges noted in Scenario 2 while preserving Ayurvedic efficacy?

Choose the correct answer from the options given below:

A. Promoting community-based conservation efforts for Amalaki.
B. Substituting Amalaki with chemically synthesized alternatives.
C. Reducing Ayurvedic reliance on Amalaki by excluding it from formulations.
D. Increasing Amalaki cultivation through monoculture farming.

13. How does the degradation of Amalaki impact the findings of Scenario 1?

Choose the correct answer from the options given below:

A. Reduced bioactive compounds directly weaken the effectiveness of Ayurvedic therapies.
B. Amalaki degradation enhances its anti-inflammatory properties.
C. The outcomes of the trial remain unaffected due to the collective formulation's efficacy.
D. Environmental stress improves Amalaki's adaptability and potency.

14. What strategy best ensures the integration of findings from both scenarios into future Ayurvedic practice?

Choose the correct answer from the options given below:

A. Focusing on synthetic alternatives to preserve wild populations.
B. Encouraging agroforestry systems for sustainable herb sourcing.
C. Limiting Ayurvedic treatments to locally sourced herbs only.
D. Avoiding integration of sustainability into therapeutic frameworks.

15. The primary qualities of the Paṃcamahābhūta elements are as follows:

(a) **Ākāśa (Ether):** Subtlety and expansiveness.
(b) **Vāyu (Air):** Mobility and lightness.
(c) **Tejas (Fire):** Heat and transformation.
(d) **Āpas (Water):** Fluidity and cohesiveness.
(e) **Pṛthvī (Earth):** Solidity and heaviness.

Choose the correct answer from the options given below:
A. (a), (b), (c), and (d) only
B. (b), (c), (d), and (e) only
C. (a), (b), (d), and (e) only
D. (a), (b), (c), (d), and (e)

16. The principles of Sāmānya (similarity) are applied in Ayurveda for:
(a) Enhancing deficient tissues using substances of similar properties.
(b) Managing dosha imbalances by using opposing qualities.
(c) Replenishing energy through foods aligned with a person's constitution.
(d) Supporting metabolic activities by introducing similar enzymatic substrates.

Choose the correct answer from the options given below:
A. (a), (b), and (c) only
B. (a), (c), and (d) only
C. (b), (c), and (d) only
D. (a), (b), and (d) only

17. Match the following qualities of Rasas (tastes) with their biological effects:

List–I	List–II
(a) Sweet Rasa	1. Promotes detoxification and reduces inflammation.
(b) Bitter Rasa	2. Nourishes and promotes tissue growth.
(c) Astringent Rasa	3. Enhances tissue cohesion and reduces bleeding.
(d) Sour Rasa	4. Stimulates digestion and metabolic activities.

Choose the correct answer from the options given below:
A. (a)-2, (b)-1, (c)-3, (d)-4
B. (a)-1, (b)-4, (c)-2, (d)-3
C. (a)-3, (b)-2, (c)-4, (d)-1
D. (a)-2, (b)-3, (c)-1, (d)-4

18. The following are the primary functions of Tridosha in Ayurvedic physiology:
(a) Vāta regulates movement and communication.
(b) Pitta governs transformation and metabolism.
(c) Kapha ensures stability and lubrication.
(d) Agni detoxifies the body by burning toxins directly.

Choose the correct answer from the options given below:
A. (a), (b), and (c) only
B. (a), (b), (c), and (d)
C. (b), (c), and (d) only
D. (a), (c), and (d) only

19. Ayurvedic principles attribute the following characteristics to Agni (digestive fire):
(a) Governs digestion and assimilation of nutrients.
(b) Impairment leads to the accumulation of Āma (toxins).
(c) Its balance depends on the doshas and seasonal changes.
(d) Functions independently of external factors like diet and environment.

Choose the correct answer from the options given below:
A. (a), (b), and (d) only
B. (a), (b), and (c) only
C. (b), (c), and (d) only
D. (a), (c), and (d) only

20. The Paṃcamahābhūta theory influences the therapeutic approach in Ayurveda as follows:
(a) Diagnosis of diseases based on elemental imbalances.
(b) Tailoring treatment according to the predominant mahābhūtas in the patient.
(c) Establishing dietary guidelines to restore elemental harmony.
(d) Replacing the need for doshic analysis with elemental categorization.

Choose the correct answer from the options given below:
A. (a), (b), and (c) only
B. (b), (c), and (d) only
C. (a), (b), (c), and (d)
D. (a), (c), and (d) only

21. Match the following elements of Paṃcamahābhūta with their corresponding sensory perceptions:

List–I	List–II
(a) Ākāśa	1. Touch
(b) Vāyu	2. Hearing
(c) Tejas	3. Vision
(d) Āpas	4. Taste

Choose the correct answer from the options given below:
A. (a)-2, (b)-1, (c)-3, (d)-4
B. (a)-3, (b)-2, (c)-1, (d)-4
C. (a)-2, (b)-3, (c)-4, (d)-1
D. (a)-1, (b)-4, (c)-2, (d)-3

22. In Ayurvedic pharmacology, the therapeutic effects of herbal medicines are influenced by:
(a) Rasa (taste)
(b) Virya (potency)
(c) Vipaka (post-digestive effect)
(d) Mahābhūtas (elemental composition)

Choose the correct answer from the options given below:
A. (a), (b), and (c) only
B. (b), (c), and (d) only
C. (a), (c), and (d) only
D. (a), (b), (c), and (d)

23. The Ayurvedic concept of Āma refers to:
(a) Digestive toxins resulting from impaired Agni.
(b) A state of doshic balance promoting health.
(c) A stage of tissue regeneration and repair.
(d) The harmonious interaction of Paṃcamahābhūta.

Choose the correct answer from the options given below:
A. (a) only
B. (b) and (d) only
C. (a) and (d) only
D. (b) and (c) only

24. Match the following doshas with their primary locations in the body:

List–I	List–II
(a) Vāta	1. Stomach and lungs.
(b) Pitta	2. Small intestine.
(c) Kapha	3. Colon.

Choose the correct answer from the options given below:
A. (a)-1, (b)-2, (c)-3
B. (a)-3, (b)-2, (c)-1
C. (a)-2, (b)-3, (c)-1
D. (a)-1, (b)-3, (c)-2

25. Match List–I (Doshas) with List–II (Primary Characteristics):

List–I	List–II
(a) Vata	1. Responsible for movement and bodily functions
(b) Pitta	2. Governs metabolism and transformation
(c) Kapha	3. Provides stability and structural support

Choose the correct answer from the options given below:
A. (a)-2, (b)-1, (c)-3
B. (a)-3, (b)-2, (c)-1
C. (a)-1, (b)-2, (c)-3
D. (a)-2, (b)-3, (c)-1

26. Match List–I (Sensory Organs-Jñānendriya) with List–II (Functions):

List–I	List–II
(a) Chakṣur (Eyes)	1. Perception of form and color
(b) Śrotra (Ears)	2. Perception of sound
(c) Rasa (Tongue)	3. Perception of taste
(d) Tvak (Skin)	4. Perception of touch

Choose the correct answer from the options given below:
A. (a)-1, (b)-2, (c)-3, (d)-4
B. (a)-1, (b)-2, (c)-4, (d)-3
C. (a)-3, (b)-4, (c)-2, (d)-1
D. (a)-4, (b)-3, (c)-1, (d)-2

27. Match List–I (Action Organs - Karmendriya) with List–II (Functions):

List–I	List–II
(a) Vāk (Speech)	1. Verbal communication
(b) Pāṇi (Hands)	2. Facilitation of grasping
(c) Pāda (Feet)	3. Facilitation of locomotion
(d) Upastha (Genitals)	4. Facilitation of reproduction

Choose the correct answer from the options given below:
A. (a)-4, (b)-2, (c)-3, (d)-1
B. (a)-2, (b)-1, (c)-4, (d)-3
C. (a)-1, (b)-3, (c)-2, (d)-4
D. (a)-3, (b)-4, (c)-1, (d)-2

28. Match List–I (Dhatus) with List–II (Biological Functions):

List–I	List–II
(a) Rasa	1. Provides nourishment
(b) Rakta	2. Supports vitality
(c) Mamsa	3. Builds and strengthens muscles
(d) Meda	4. Regulates lubrication

Choose the correct answer from the options given below:
A. (a)-1, (b)-2, (c)-3, (d)-4
B. (a)-2, (b)-3, (c)-1, (d)-4
C. (a)-3, (b)-4, (c)-2, (d)-1
D. (a)-4, (b)-1, (c)-3, (d)-2

29. Match List–I (Mahābhūtas) with List–II (Associated Attributes):

List–I	List–II
(a) Ākāśa (Ether)	1. Softness
(b) Vāyu (Air)	2. Motion
(c) Agni (Fire)	3. Transformation
(d) Jala (Water)	4. Fluidity

Choose the correct answer from the options given below:
A. (a)-1, (b)-2, (c)-3, (d)-4
B. (a)-4, (b)-3, (c)-2, (d)-1
C. (a)-2, (b)-1, (c)-4, (d)-3
D. (a)-3, (b)-4, (c)-1, (d)-2

30. Match List–I (Concepts) with List–II (Significance in Ayurveda):

List–I	List–II
(a) Ātman (Soul)	1. Governs consciousness
(b) Śarīra (Body)	2. Provides physical structure
(c) Indriya (Senses)	3. Enables interaction with the environment
(d) Tridoṣa (Doshas)	4. Maintains physiological balance

Choose the correct answer from the options given below:

A. (a)-1, (b)-2, (c)-3, (d)-4
B. (a)-4, (b)-3, (c)-2, (d)-1
C. (a)-3, (b)-4, (c)-1, (d)-2
D. (a)-2, (b)-1, (c)-4, (d)-3

31. Match List–I (Tridoṣa and Their Locations) with List–II (Primary Regions in the Body):

List–I	List–II
(a) Vata	1. Colon and nervous system
(b) Pitta	2. Stomach and small intestine
(c) Kapha	3. Chest and lymphatic system

Choose the correct answer from the options given below:

A. (a)-2, (b)-1, (c)-3
B. (a)-1, (b)-3, (c)-2
C. (a)-1, (b)-2, (c)-3
D. (a)-3, (b)-2, (c)-1

32. Match List–I (Jñānendriyas - Sensory Organs) with List–II (Associated Mahābhūtas):

List–I	List–II
(a) Śrotra (Ears)	1. Ākāśa (Ether)
(b) Tvak (Skin)	2. Vāyu (Air)
(c) Chakṣur (Eyes)	3. Agni (Fire)
(d) Rasa (Tongue)	4. Jala (Water)

Choose the correct answer from the options given below:

A. (a)-1, (b)-3, (c)-4, (d)-2
B. (a)-4, (b)-1, (c)-3, (d)-2
C. (a)-2, (b)-3, (c)-1, (d)-4
D. (a)-1, (b)-2, (c)-3, (d)-4

33. Match List–I (Dosha Aggravating Factors) with List–II (Primary Triggers):

List–I	List–II
(a) Vata	1. Excessive movement and irregular meals
(b) Pitta	2. Overheating and spicy foods
(c) Kapha	3. Sedentary lifestyle and heavy foods

Choose the correct answer from the options given below:

A. (a)-2, (b)-1, (c)-3
B. (a)-1, (b)-2, (c)-3
C. (a)-3, (b)-2, (c)-1
D. (a)-1, (b)-3, (c)-2

34. Match List–I (Therapies) with List–II (Therapeutic Effects in Ayurveda):

List–I	List–II
(a) Abhyanga (Oil Massage)	1. Improves circulation and reduces Vata imbalance
(b) Shirodhara (Oil Pouring on Forehead)	2. Calms the mind and balances Pitta
(c) Vamana (Therapeutic Vomiting)	3. Clears excess Kapha and detoxifiesAA

Choose the correct answer from the options given below:

A. (a)-1, (b)-2, (c)-3
B. (a)-3, (b)-1, (c)-2
C. (a)-2, (b)-3, (c)-1
D. (a)-1, (b)-3, (c)-2

Directions (Q. No. 35–39): *Following qestions are based on Statement 1 and Statement 2. Read both the statements carefully and choose the correct answer from the options given below:*

A. Both Statement 1 and Statement 2 are true, and Statement 2 is the correct explanation of Statement 1.
B. Both Statement 1 and Statement 2 are true, but Statement 2 is not the correct explanation of Statement 1.
C. Statement 1 is true, but Statement 2 is false.
D. Statement 1 is false, but Statement 2 is true.

35. **Statement 1:** The balance of Tridoshas is fundamental for physical and mental health in Ayurveda.

Statement 2: Imbalance in Tridoshas leads to irreversible health conditions, irrespective of therapeutic interventions.

36. **Statement 1:** Ayurveda's Paṃcamahābhūta framework integrates physical and metaphysical aspects of health.

Statement 2: This integration implies that diseases can be fully understood through biochemical analysis alone.

37. **Statement 1:** The principles of Sāmānya and Viśeṣa form the foundation for therapeutic interventions in Ayurveda.

Statement 2: Sāmānya implies that opposite qualities are used to restore equilibrium in aggravated doshas.

38. **Statement 1:** The Paṃcamahābhūta theory explains that the five elements exist only in metaphysical form without functional relevance to physiology.

Statement 2: In Ayurveda, Vāyu and Agni elements correlate with movement and transformation respectively within the body.

39. **Statement 1:** Viśeṣa is applied in Ayurveda to treat conditions of deficiency by using substances with similar qualities.

Statement 2: When Kapha is aggravated, dry and light substances are prescribed, which exemplifies the principle of Viśeṣa.

Directions (Q. No. 40–45): *There are two statements in each question. One is labelled as Assertion (A) and the other is as Reason (R). Read both the statements and choose the correct answer from the options given below*:

A. Both Assertion (A) and Reason (R) are true, and Reason (R) is the correct explanation of Assertion (A).
B. Both Assertion (A) and Reason (R) are true, but Reason (R) is not the correct explanation of Assertion (A).
C. Assertion (A) is true, but Reason (R) is false.
D. Assertion (A) is false, but Reason (R) is true.
E. Both Assertion (A) and Reason (R) are false.

40. **Assertion (A):** The theory of Paṃcamahābhūta explains the composition and functioning of the human body in Ayurveda.

Reason (R): The five great elements—earth, water, fire, air, and space—are metaphysical concepts without any physiological significance.

41. **Assertion (A):** The principle of sāmānya (similarity) is used in Ayurveda to treat conditions caused by a deficiency of certain elements.

Reason (R): Sāmānya involves administering treatments that are opposite in nature to the imbalance in the doshas.

42. **Assertion (A):** The principle of viśeṣa (difference) is primarily used to counteract an excess of any element in the body.

Reason (R): Viśeṣa states that substances with opposing qualities reduce the severity of the aggravated dosha.

43. **Assertion (A):** Ayurveda defines health as a state of balance between the doshas, dhatus, and malas.

Reason (R): Health in Ayurveda only focuses on the absence of diseases rather than the overall harmony of mind, body, and soul.

44. **Assertion (A):** The Paṃcamahābhūta theory forms the foundation for understanding diet and lifestyle recommendations in Ayurveda.

Reason (R): Foods and medicines are classified in Ayurveda based on their predominant elemental composition and their impact on doshas.

45. **Assertion (A):** The Ayurvedic concept of health includes a balance of physical, mental, and spiritual well-being.

Reason (R): Ayurveda focuses exclusively on herbal treatments and physical detoxification techniques to maintain health.

Directions (Q. No. 46–50): *Read the passage carefully and answer the questions given below*:

The Paṃcamahābhūta theory serves as the foundation of Ayurvedic science, positing that the human body and the cosmos are composed of five elemental forces: Ākāśa (Ether), Vāyu (Air), Tejas (Fire), Āpas (Water), and Pṛthvī (Earth). Each element corresponds to specific qualities and functions within the body. For instance, Vāyu governs movement and circulation, while Pṛthvī provides stability and structural integrity. This interconnected framework emphasizes balance among the elements as the cornerstone of health. Imbalance leads to diseases, which Ayurveda addresses by employing the principles of Sāmānya (similarity) and Viśeṣa (difference).

46. According to the passage, what is the role of Vāyu in the human body?

A. Governs circulation and mobility.
B. Promotes tissue stability and cohesion.
C. Stimulates digestion and enzymatic activity.
D. Governs sensory functions exclusively.

Choose the correct answer from the options given below:

A. 1 only
B. 1 and 3 only
C. 2 and 4 only
D. 1, 2, and 3

47. Which of the following best explains the therapeutic approach in Ayurveda as per the Paṃcamahābhūta theory?

A. Restoration of elemental balance within the body to resolve disease.
B. Treating diseases using the principle of Viśeṣa, which emphasizes opposition to qualities.
C. Eliminating toxins without considering elemental imbalances.
D. Addressing only the physical symptoms without integrating mental or spiritual aspects.

Choose the correct answer from the options given below:

A. 1 and 2 only
B. 2 and 4 only
C. 1, 2, and 3 only
D. 1, 3, and 4 only

48. How does the principle of Sāmānya contribute to Ayurvedic treatments?

A. By using substances with similar qualities to replenish deficient tissues.

B. By balancing the doshas through opposing qualities.

C. By introducing similar dietary and environmental elements to stabilize health.

D. By emphasizing detoxification independent of elemental alignment.

Choose the correct answer from the options given below:

A. 1 and 3 only B. 2 and 4 only
C. 1, 2, and 3 only D. 1, 3, and 4 only

49. Based on the passage, how does the Paṃcamahābhūta framework address diseases caused by environmental imbalances?

A. By aligning therapeutic interventions with the elemental composition of the environment.

B. By emphasizing detoxification to combat environmental toxins.

C. By using the elemental balance in the body to counteract external stressors.

D. By prescribing generic remedies that ignore the unique elemental composition of the patient.

Choose the correct answer from the options given below:

A. 1 and 2 only B. 2 and 3 only
C. 1 and 3 only D. 1, 2, and 4 only

50. What is the significance of integrating Paṃcamahābhūta with Sāmānya and Viśeṣa principles in Ayurveda?

A. It provides a structured approach for diagnosing and treating diseases.

B. It links the physical, mental, and spiritual aspects of health to elemental balance.

C. It eliminates the need for modern diagnostic tools by focusing solely on elemental therapies.

D. It enables universal treatment protocols without personalization.

Choose the correct answer from the options given below:

A. 1 and 2 only
B. 2 and 3 only
C. 1, 2, and 4 only
D. 1 and 3 only

ANSWER WITH EXPLANATIONS

1. **B:** This recommendation reflects the principle of Viśeṣa, which employs opposing qualities to restore balance. Warm, oily, and grounding foods counteract the dry, cold, and light qualities of excess Vāta. The principle of Sāmānya would involve increasing similar qualities, which is contraindicated in this case. The practitioner targets the patient's specific doshic imbalance, leveraging the complementary relationship between qualities and doshas to achieve equilibrium. This personalized approach also aligns with Ayurvedic emphasis on individualized treatment. The dietary adjustment integrates the elemental principles, specifically addressing Vāta's ether and air elements by introducing grounding (earth) and warming (fire) influences.

2. **B:** The alignment of Tejas with enzymatic activity demonstrates Ayurveda's integration of physical and metaphysical concepts. The fire element, representing transformation, corresponds to biochemical processes like digestion and metabolism. By linking Tejas to cellular transformations, the Ayurvedic framework provides a holistic lens for understanding physiological functions. This correlation affirms the functional relevance of Mahābhūtas in explaining health and disease mechanisms, making them applicable in modern contexts. The recognition of elemental roles bridges traditional and contemporary perspectives, enhancing Ayurveda's scientific validation without diminishing its philosophical depth.

3. **B:** In Ayurveda, Agni represents the digestive fire, responsible for metabolizing food into energy and nutrients. This concept aligns closely with enzymatic activity in modern science. The focus on Agni highlights the interconnectedness of digestion, metabolism, and overall health. Impaired Agni leads to toxin accumulation (Āma), which is central to many diseases. Ayurvedic treatments aim to strengthen Agni by balancing doshas and enhancing metabolic efficiency. By correlating Agni with measurable physiological processes, Ayurveda reinforces its integrative approach to health while maintaining its unique conceptual framework.

4. **B:** Prakṛti refers to an individual's unique constitution, determined by the doshic balance at conception. This foundational concept influences susceptibility to diseases, physical and psychological traits, and treatment strategies. Unlike a universal model, Prakṛti emphasizes personalization, reflecting Ayurveda's holistic approach. Understanding a person's Prakṛti aids

in diagnosing imbalances and tailoring interventions. The emphasis on individuality aligns with modern trends in precision medicine, demonstrating Ayurveda's enduring relevance in contemporary health care systems. This principle also underscores the importance of preventive care by identifying predispositions to imbalances.

5. **A:** The astringent Rasa promotes tissue cohesion, making it beneficial for conditions like bleeding or weak tissues. Bitter Rasa, known for its detoxifying properties, helps reduce inflammation and remove toxins. Together, these qualities support therapeutic interventions for various health conditions, aligning with Ayurveda's principle of using specific tastes to balance doshas and enhance healing. This dual functionality reflects the interconnected roles of tastes in influencing physiological and psychological states, reinforcing Ayurveda's nuanced approach to health. The therapeutic applications of Rasas bridge ancient insights with contemporary understanding of phytochemistry.

6. **A:** The Paṃcamahābhūta theory explains how plants with dominant elemental qualities can address specific health issues. For instance, plants rich in Vāyu and Ākāśa elements are ideal for respiratory conditions due to their lightness and mobility. This approach highlights Ayurveda's systemic understanding of health, where elemental attributes guide the selection of remedies. By aligning plant qualities with human imbalances, Ayurveda integrates ecological insights into therapeutic practices. This model also demonstrates Ayurveda's capacity for scientific validation, connecting traditional classifications with empirical observations in pharmacology and ecology.

7. **B:** This dietary adjustment reflects the principle of Viśeṣa, applying opposing qualities to balance doshas. Sweet and oily foods, which increase Kapḥa, are restricted to mitigate congestion and lethargy. Bitter and astringent foods, which reduce Kapha, are recommended instead. This approach demonstrates Ayurveda's precise application of elemental and doshic principles in dietary planning. By addressing both the physical and energetic imbalances, this intervention exemplifies Ayurveda's holistic and preventive focus. It also underscores the interplay between taste, qualities, and doshic effects, reinforcing the importance of personalized health strategies.

8. **B:** Kapha's primary qualities include heaviness, stability, and fluidity, which explain its tendency to cause congestion and lethargy when in excess. These characteristics also highlight Kapha's role in structural and fluid balance, making it prone to disorders involving retention and stagnation. Recognizing these qualities allows for targeted interventions to restore balance, such as stimulating and lightening therapies. This observation reinforces Ayurveda's systemic perspective, linking doshic characteristics to physiological patterns and imbalances. The precise identification of Kapha's effects exemplifies Ayurveda's diagnostic clarity.

9. **D:** Cooling herbs like coriander counteract Pitta's heat, illustrating Viśeṣa. Combining substances with opposing Rasas ensures a comprehensive balancing effect, integrating the principles of Sāmānya and Viśeṣa. This dual application highlights Ayurveda's dynamic therapeutic framework, addressing imbalances through synergistic strategies. Such combinations optimize the therapeutic potential of formulations while respecting individual needs. This approach exemplifies Ayurveda's adaptability and its emphasis on tailored interventions, demonstrating the interconnectedness of its foundational principles.

10. **B:** The study emphasizes the universal relevance of Paṃcamahābhūta in understanding ecological and physiological systems. By identifying plants with dominant Pṛthvī and Āpas elements for ecological restoration, it highlights Ayurveda's holistic perspective. This insight reflects Ayurveda's integrative approach, where health and environment are interdependent. The elemental framework offers practical applications beyond human health, reinforcing its broader ecological significance. Such findings validate Ayurveda's universal principles while advocating sustainable practices aligned with traditional wisdom.

11. **A:** The principle of Sāmānya involves enhancing similar qualities to support deficient tissues or functions. By strengthening metabolic processes and reducing inflammation through dietary and therapeutic alignments, the principle is validated. This approach reflects Ayurveda's emphasis on harmonizing qualities to achieve systemic balance. The study's findings bridge ancient theories with modern observations, illustrating the functional relevance of Ayurvedic principles in contemporary contexts. This validation also underscores the importance of integrating traditional and modern insights for holistic health care.

12. **A:** Promoting community-based conservation of Amalaki ensures its sustainable harvesting while preserving its ecological and medicinal value. This approach aligns with Ayurveda's emphasis on sustainability and natural harmony. By integrating traditional agroforestry systems, it also supports

biodiversity and local economies. Such strategies reflect Ayurveda's ecological ethos, emphasizing balance and interdependence. Ensuring the quality and availability of medicinal plants reinforces the efficacy of Ayurvedic therapies, linking environmental stewardship with health outcomes. This holistic approach exemplifies Ayurveda's capacity for addressing modern challenges sustainably.

13. **A:** Environmental degradation reduces the bioactive compound concentration in Amalaki, directly affecting its therapeutic efficacy. This impact highlights the interconnectedness of ecological and health outcomes, emphasizing Ayurveda's systemic perspective. Maintaining the quality of medicinal plants is crucial for achieving desired therapeutic effects, reinforcing the need for sustainable practices. This observation also validates the importance of ecological considerations in traditional medical systems, demonstrating their relevance in addressing contemporary health challenges. The study underscores Ayurveda's holistic approach, integrating environmental and therapeutic dimensions.

14. **B:** Establishing a global standard for Triphala ensures sustainable harvesting practices while maintaining its efficacy. Such initiatives reflect Ayurveda's emphasis on balancing ecological, economic, and therapeutic concerns. By standardizing practices, it supports both conservation and the consistent quality of formulations. This strategy exemplifies Ayurveda's adaptability in addressing modern challenges while preserving its traditional principles. Integrating sustainability into therapeutic frameworks aligns with the interconnected ethos of Ayurveda, promoting long-term health and ecological harmony. This comprehensive approach reinforces Ayurveda's relevance in global health care.

15. **D:** All five elements (Ākāśa, Vāyu, Tejas, Āpas, and Pṛthvī) possess distinct qualities and functions essential for understanding Ayurveda's systemic framework. Each element contributes to physiological and psychological processes, reinforcing the interconnectedness of the body and environment. Recognizing these elemental roles allows for targeted therapeutic interventions, reflecting Ayurveda's holistic perspective. The inclusion of all elements underscores their collective importance in maintaining balance and addressing imbalances, demonstrating Ayurveda's integrative approach.

16. **B:** The principle of Sāmānya focuses on enhancing deficient qualities or tissues by using substances with similar properties. By replenishing energy and metabolic efficiency through alignment with an individual's constitution, it supports systemic balance. This application highlights the practical utility of Sāmānya in dietary, lifestyle, and therapeutic interventions. Contrarily, the principle of Viśeṣa involves opposing qualities and is not aligned with Sāmānya. These complementary frameworks illustrate Ayurveda's nuanced understanding of balancing physiological functions. This targeted use of similar substances reflects Ayurveda's emphasis on personalization and natural harmony.

17. **A:** The therapeutic roles of Rasas align with their respective biological effects: Sweet for nourishment, Bitter for detoxification, Astringent for tissue cohesion, and Sour for digestion. This classification emphasizes the interconnectedness of taste and therapeutic action in Ayurveda. By leveraging the properties of tastes, practitioners can address specific imbalances and promote holistic healing. This framework integrates sensory experiences with physiological outcomes, demonstrating Ayurveda's depth in understanding natural systems. Recognizing the role of Rasas in health supports the precision and adaptability of Ayurvedic treatments.

18. **A:** Tridosha governs physiological processes: Vāta for movement, Pitta for transformation, and Kapha for stability. These doshas interact dynamically, ensuring systemic harmony. The absence of Agni in this context is deliberate, as it functions as a separate concept, focusing on metabolic activities rather than being classified as a dosha. The Tridosha framework exemplifies Ayurveda's holistic approach, linking physical, mental, and spiritual health. Understanding these interactions aids in diagnosing and addressing imbalances effectively, reinforcing the depth of Ayurvedic science.

19. **B:** Agni governs digestion, nutrient assimilation, and toxin elimination, highlighting its central role in health. Its balance depends on doshas and external factors like diet and seasons, underscoring Ayurveda's emphasis on dynamic interactions. Impaired Agni results in Āma accumulation, disrupting systemic harmony and causing diseases. Recognizing Agni as a pivotal factor connects dietary and therapeutic interventions with physiological outcomes. This integrative perspective reinforces Ayurveda's holistic focus, where balance is achieved through dynamic adjustments rather than fixed states.

20. **A:** The Paṃcamahābhūta theory guides diagnosis, treatment, and dietary planning by addressing elemental imbalances. Tailoring interventions based on elemental predominance in patients demonstrates Ayurveda's adaptability and precision. This systemic approach

integrates physical and environmental factors, aligning internal and external harmony. By emphasizing personalized treatments, Ayurveda bridges traditional insights with modern health care needs. The theory's application underscores its relevance in addressing complex health challenges holistically, reaffirming Ayurveda's timeless wisdom.

21. A: Each element in the Paṃcamahābhūta theory corresponds to specific sensory perceptions: Ākāśa with hearing, Vāyu with touch, Tejas with vision, and Āpas with taste. This classification highlights the integration of sensory and elemental functions, demonstrating Ayurveda's holistic understanding. By linking sensory perceptions to elemental influences, Ayurveda provides a comprehensive framework for diagnosing and treating imbalances. This perspective underscores the interconnectedness of physiological and sensory processes, aligning them with elemental harmony.

22. D: Ayurvedic pharmacology incorporates Rasa (taste), Virya (potency), Vipaka (post-digestive effect), and Mahābhūtas (elements) to determine the therapeutic potential of substances. These factors collectively guide the selection and application of herbal medicines, reflecting Ayurveda's depth and precision. By integrating sensory, elemental, and functional dimensions, this framework supports personalized treatments and systemic balance. Recognizing these interdependencies highlights Ayurveda's holistic approach, ensuring effective and adaptable health interventions.

23. A: Āma represents undigested toxins caused by impaired Agni. It disrupts doshic balance, leading to various diseases. This concept emphasizes the importance of maintaining optimal digestive fire for systemic health. Addressing Āma through detoxification and Agni restoration is central to Ayurvedic treatments. By identifying toxins as a root cause, Ayurveda links physical and metabolic health with broader systemic outcomes. This understanding reinforces the interconnectedness of digestion, metabolism, and overall well-being.

24. B: The primary locations of doshas are: Vāta in the colon, Pitta in the small intestine, and Kapha in the stomach and lungs. These associations guide diagnostic and therapeutic strategies, aligning with Ayurveda's systemic approach. By linking doshas to specific physiological regions, Ayurveda integrates anatomical and functional perspectives. This understanding enables precise interventions, reflecting the science's emphasis on dynamic and individualized treatments. Recognizing doshic locations enhances diagnostic clarity and therapeutic precision.

25. C: In Ayurveda, Vata controls all movement and bodily functions, Pitta governs metabolism and transformation, and Kapha provides stability and structure. This mapping reflects their fundamental roles in maintaining balance in the body. Therefore, option C is correct.

26. A: Each Jñānendriya (sense organ) in Ayurveda corresponds to a specific perception: Eyes perceive form and color, Ears perceive sound, Tongue perceives taste, and Skin perceives touch. Option A correctly matches all sense organs with their functions.

27. C: Karmendriyas, the organs of action, signify purposeful interaction between the body and its environment. Speech facilitates communication, enabling expression and sharing of ideas. The hands, through grasping, epitomize physical control and creativity. Feet, as locomotion agents, symbolize movement and exploration. The genitals reflect continuity of life and the essence of regeneration. These organs embody purposeful action (karma), rooted in dharma (duty), where their optimal functioning ensures a harmonious existence. Aligning physical actions with ethical intent underpins Ayurvedic life philosophies, emphasizing the balance of the physical body and its external interactions.

28. A: Dhatus, the seven body tissues in Ayurveda, signify the layers of nourishment and functionality. Rasa (plasma) delivers hydration and nutrients, forming the baseline for health. Rakta (blood) oxygenates tissues, fostering vitality. Mamsa (muscles) stabilizes the framework for physical activity. Meda (fat) insulates and cushions the body. Their sequential formation emphasizes interconnectedness, where one's proper functioning sustains the next. Ayurvedic therapies target these dhatus to ensure systemic harmony, from maintaining hydration to muscular strength and energy balance. Recognizing these layers allows deeper interventions tailored to one's needs, ensuring a robust physical foundation.

29. A: The Mahābhūtas exemplify the elemental forces governing the universe and the body. Ether embodies vastness, symbolizing subtlety and sound propagation. Air represents movement, essential for cellular and systemic functions. Fire governs transformation, facilitating digestion, and cognitive processes. Water's fluidity ensures circulation, lubrication, and cohesion. These elements also represent sensory-motor functions, creating a bridge between the physical and metaphysical. Understanding their qualities in physiological and mental contexts forms the basis for balancing therapies, where alignment with these elements optimizes health and prevents disease, unifying internal and external harmony.

30. A: Ātman governs consciousness, Śarīra forms the physical body, Indriyas help interact with the environment, and Tridoṣa maintains physiological balance. This reflects the core Ayurvedic understanding of the human system. Option A accurately connects each concept with its significance.

31. C: The tridoshic model associates Vata, Pitta, and Kapha with specific bodily locations, reinforcing Ayurveda's anatomical precision. Vata governs nervous system activities and elimination through the colon. Pitta regulates digestion and metabolism in the stomach and small intestine. Kapha governs structural integrity and fluid balance, centered in the chest and lymphatic system. These regions highlight how the doshas influence specific physiological zones while maintaining systemic balance. Understanding these loci enables targeted therapies, offering precise interventions to correct imbalances, ensuring optimal function within localized yet interconnected bodily systems.

32. D: Jñānendriyas, the sensory organs, and their elemental associations underline Ayurveda's understanding of perception. The ears (Ākāśa) resonate with sound, aligning with space's subtleties. The skin (Vāyu) interprets touch, vital for tactile interaction. The eyes (Agni) perceive light and color, aligning vision with transformative energy. The tongue (Jala) discerns taste, grounding nourishment in fluid dynamics. This classification not only emphasizes the functional aspects of the senses but also bridges physical sensations with elemental influences, offering insights into maintaining sensory health and its role in overall physiological and spiritual balance.

33. B: Dosha aggravation highlights the interplay between lifestyle and physiological imbalances. Excessive activity or irregularity disturbs Vata, triggering anxiety or dryness. Pitta flares with excessive heat or dietary imbalances, manifesting as inflammation. Kapha stagnates under inactivity or overeating, leading to lethargy or weight gain. These triggers emphasize the importance of moderation and rhythm in daily life. Ayurveda's preventive focus, through diet, exercise, and routine, counters these triggers, restoring equilibrium. This framework underscores the necessity of understanding individual constitutions to preemptively align habits with one's innate tendencies, minimizing the potential for imbalance.

34. A: Ayurvedic therapies focus on doshic correction through targeted interventions. Abhyanga, with its unctuous massage, calms Vata, enhancing circulation and stability. Shirodhara's soothing oil flow pacifies Pitta, offering mental calmness. Vamana detoxifies Kapha through emesis, aiding in decongestion and respiratory health. These therapies exemplify Ayurveda's dosha-specific treatments, reflecting its personalized approach to healing. By targeting underlying imbalances, Ayurveda promotes systemic harmony rather than symptomatic relief, ensuring a comprehensive return to wellness through carefully tailored therapeutic interventions rooted in individual needs and elemental balance.

35. C: While Tridoshas are fundamental to health, imbalances are not necessarily irreversible. Ayurveda offers dynamic interventions to restore balance, demonstrating its adaptability and therapeutic depth. Recognizing doshic variability allows for personalized treatments, aligning ancient principles with contemporary needs. This nuanced understanding highlights Ayurveda's capacity for addressing complex health conditions comprehensively.

36. C: Ayurveda's Paṃcamahābhūta framework integrates physical and metaphysical aspects of health, demonstrating its holistic approach. However, the assertion that diseases can be fully understood through biochemical analysis alone contradicts Ayurvedic principles. Ayurveda emphasizes balance among elemental forces rather than solely relying on measurable biochemical markers. While modern science validates certain aspects of Ayurveda, it does not replace the comprehensive and individualized nature of Ayurvedic practices. This distinction underscores the importance of integrating traditional wisdom with contemporary methodologies while respecting their unique contributions.

37. C: Sāmānya (similarity) is the principle of increasing by using substances of similar qualities, while Viśeṣa (difference) refers to decreasing or balancing using opposite qualities. Statement 1 correctly highlights their foundational role in therapy, but Statement 2 inaccurately attributes opposite qualities to Sāmānya instead of Viśeṣa, making it false.

38. D: Paṃcamahābhūtas are not merely metaphysical—they represent both material and functional aspects of the body. Vāyu governs motion and Agni governs metabolic transformation, making Statement 2 correct. Since Statement 1 denies their physiological role, it is incorrect.

39. D: Viśeṣa is used to counteract excess by employing opposite qualities—not to treat deficiency with similar qualities (that's Sāmānya). Statement 2 correctly describes Viśeṣa in practice (using light and dry substances to reduce Kapha), but Statement 1 misrepresents its core principle.

40. C: The Paṃcamahābhūta theory is fundamental to Ayurveda, as it explains that all living and non-living entities are composed of five elements: earth, water, fire, air, and space. These elements also influence bodily functions and doshas. The assertion highlights its relevance in explaining human physiology, which is accurate. However, the reason incorrectly portrays these elements as purely metaphysical, disregarding their direct correlation to bodily systems (e.g., water for bodily fluids, fire for metabolism). Ayurveda integrates these elements into practical diagnostic and treatment frameworks, demonstrating their physiological importance rather than limiting them to metaphysical notions.

41. C: Sāmānya, or the principle of similarity, is central to Ayurveda's therapeutic interventions. It suggests that imbalances caused by deficiencies in specific elements can be corrected by introducing similar properties through diet or medicine. However, the reason inaccurately associates sāmānya with opposite treatments, which aligns with viśeṣa (difference). For instance, if there is a deficiency of the earth element (Prithvi), substances with a high earth element content are used. This principle underscores Ayurveda's unique approach to health by focusing on restoring equilibrium through reinforcement, distinguishing it from the opposite-focused viśeṣa principle.

42. A: Viśeṣa, or difference, effectively counters excesses in Ayurveda by introducing opposing qualities to neutralize imbalances. For example, an aggravated fire element (Pitta) is treated with cooling substances like milk or sandalwood. Both assertion and reason align correctly, as viśeṣa operates on the principle that opposing qualities diminish excess doshas, restoring balance. This duality of sāmānya and viśeṣa forms the theoretical basis of Ayurveda's treatments. It exemplifies the nuanced understanding of human physiology and pathology in Ayurveda, emphasizing how subtle changes in qualities can have profound effects on health outcomes.

43. C: Ayurveda defines health as a dynamic state of balance among doshas (biological energies), dhatus (tissues), and malas (waste products), alongside mental and spiritual harmony. The assertion accurately reflects this holistic perspective. However, the reason wrongly limits health to disease absence, ignoring Ayurveda's emphasis on preventive care and well-being. For instance, practices like daily routines (Dinacharya) and seasonal regimens (Ritucharya) aim to maintain balance proactively. This holistic health model extends beyond mere disease management to include lifestyle adjustments, dietary recommendations, and meditation, creating a comprehensive framework for achieving harmony and vitality.

44. A: The Paṃcamahābhūta theory underpins Ayurveda's dietary and lifestyle guidelines, categorizing foods and medicines based on their elemental properties and effects on doshas. The assertion and reason align, as the theory guides personalized recommendations, such as warm, spicy foods to counteract Vata imbalances or cooling foods to calm Pitta. This framework demonstrates Ayurveda's emphasis on individuality in health, where treatments are tailored to elemental compositions and their impact on the body. It bridges the gap between theoretical understanding and practical application, showcasing how ancient principles inform modern health interventions.

45. C: Ayurveda integrates physical, mental, and spiritual dimensions to define health comprehensively. The assertion is true, reflecting this inclusive perspective. However, the reason incorrectly narrows Ayurveda's focus to herbal and detox treatments, neglecting its broader emphasis on emotional well-being, ethical living, and meditation. For instance, the sattvic lifestyle, which promotes purity in thought and action, is integral to maintaining mental harmony. Thus, Ayurveda transcends mere physical health by addressing all aspects of existence, making it a holistic science of life and longevity rooted in interconnectedness and balance.

46. A: Vāyu governs mobility and circulation, integral to systemic functioning. Its role underscores the interconnectedness of physiological processes, reflecting Ayurveda's systemic perspective. This elemental influence aligns with broader principles, supporting both diagnostic clarity and therapeutic precision. Recognizing these roles reinforces Ayurveda's comprehensive understanding of health and disease.

47. A: The therapeutic approach in Ayurveda addresses diseases by restoring elemental balance, applying the principles of Sāmānya and Viśeṣa. By countering environmental imbalances through personalized interventions, Ayurveda ensures a holistic approach to health. These principles integrate physiological, psychological, and ecological dimensions, emphasizing harmony. Eliminating toxins is complementary but insufficient without addressing elemental and doshic imbalances. This multi-faceted approach highlights Ayurveda's depth, bridging traditional wisdom with modern therapeutic needs. The systemic integration of these principles ensures precise and effective treatments tailored to both internal and external factors.

48. **A:** The principle of Sāmānya involves using similar qualities to support deficient tissues or restore doshic harmony. By aligning dietary and environmental elements with an individual's constitution, Ayurveda promotes systemic balance. This principle integrates external and internal factors, emphasizing harmony in therapies. Detoxification, though important, is secondary to elemental alignment and replenishment. By applying Sāmānya, Ayurveda emphasizes personalized care, connecting sensory, physiological, and ecological factors. This tailored approach demonstrates Ayurveda's precision and adaptability in addressing diverse health challenges holistically.

49. **C:** The Paṃcamahābhūta framework allows Ayurveda to address environmental imbalances by aligning elemental harmony within the body. By recognizing the interplay between ecological and physiological systems, Ayurveda provides a universal lens for managing health and environmental stressors. This integration ensures treatments remain adaptable and effective. The systemic application of elemental principles bridges traditional practices with modern ecological challenges. Ayurveda's focus on sustainability and balance highlights its relevance in global health and environmental contexts, reinforcing its holistic philosophy.

50. **A:** Integrating Paṃcamahābhūta with Sāmānya and Viśeṣa creates a structured framework for diagnosing and treating diseases. These principles address the physical, mental, and spiritual dimensions of health, emphasizing balance. Ayurveda's holistic approach combines traditional insights with modern therapeutic precision. Personalization, rooted in elemental harmony, ensures effective interventions tailored to individual needs. By linking theory and practice, Ayurveda bridges ancient wisdom with contemporary health care challenges. This integration highlights its adaptability and enduring relevance, offering a sustainable, comprehensive model for well-being.

CHAPTER–8

INTRODUCTION TO SARIRA, FOETAL DEVELOPMENT, AND BODY CONSTITUTIONS

Ayurveda, the ancient Indian system of medicine, is deeply rooted in the study of the human body (śarīra), its origins, and its diverse expressions in terms of individual constitutions (prakṛti). This chapter explores the foundational concepts of śarīra, including its structural and compositional framework, the intricate stages of foetal development, and the significance of body constitutions in understanding health, disease, and personalized care. By integrating philosophy, biology, and practical insights, Ayurveda provides a holistic perspective on human existence.

Structure of Śarīra and Its Composition

In Ayurveda, śarīra is the physical manifestation of life, encompassing the gross (visible) and subtle (invisible) aspects of human existence. The structure and composition of the body are explained through several interconnected principles:

Tridosha: The Concept of the Three Doshas in Ayurveda

Ayurveda, the ancient Indian system of medicine, views life as an intricate balance between three primary forces called tridoshas—Vāta, Pitta, and Kapha. These doshas govern all physiological, psychological, and biochemical processes within the body. Derived from the five great elements (Paṃcamahābhūtas), they represent the essential energies that sustain life. Their dynamic interplay determines an individual's constitution (prakṛti), health, and susceptibility to disease.

(I) Tridosha: The Life Forces

1. **Composition of the Doshas**: The doshas arise from the interaction of the Paṃcamahābhūtas:
   1. **Vāta (Ether + Air):**
      - Represents motion, communication, and the nervous system.
      - Governs mobility, circulation, and elimination.
   2. **Pitta (Fire + Water):**
      - Represents transformation and metabolism.
      - Controls digestion, body temperature, and vision.
   3. **Kapha (Water + Earth):**
      - Represents stability, structure, and lubrication.
      - Provides strength, immunity, and cohesion.
2. **Characteristics of the Doshas**: Each dosha exhibits unique qualities (guṇas) that influence its behavior:

   Vāta:
   - Light, dry, mobile, cold, subtle, rough.
   - Associated with creativity, energy, and movement.

   Pitta:
   - Hot, sharp, oily, light, spreading, liquid.
   - Linked to digestion, intellect, and transformation.

   Kapha:
   - Heavy, slow, steady, soft, cool, oily.
   - Promotes stability, calmness, and endurance.
3. **Functions of the Doshas**

   (a) Vāta: The Energy of Movement
   - Governs all physical and mental motion.
   - Controls respiration, circulation, and elimination of waste.
   - Regulates sensory and motor functions

(b) Pitta: The Energy of Transformation

- Manages digestion, metabolism, and enzymatic processes.
- Regulates body temperature and skin complexion.
- Influences intellect, courage, and clarity.

(c) Kapha: The Energy of Stability

- Provides physical structure and cohesion.
- Maintains lubrication in joints and tissues.
- Supports immunity, patience, and emotional stability.

4. **Dosha Imbalances**: When doshas deviate from their natural balance, they cause disease:

Vāta Imbalance:

- **Symptoms:** Dry skin, constipation, anxiety, insomnia, joint pain.
- **Causes:** Cold, dry weather, irregular routines, and excessive travel.

Pitta Imbalance:

- **Symptoms:** Heartburn, inflammation, anger, skin rashes.
- **Causes:** Hot, spicy foods, stress, and exposure to heat.

Kapha Imbalance:

- **Symptoms:** Weight gain, lethargy, congestion, depression.
- **Causes:** Overeating, sedentary lifestyle, and cold, damp environments.

5. **Therapeutic Approaches**:

- **Balancing Vāta:** Warm, moist foods; regular routines; calming activities.
- **Balancing Pitta:** Cooling, hydrating foods; stress management; avoiding heat.
- **Balancing Kapha:** Light, dry foods; dynamic exercises; stimulating activities.

(II) Dhātu: The Seven Fundamental Tissues

The human body comprises seven essential tissues (dhātus), each performing unique physiological functions. These tissues sustain the body, facilitate growth, and support overall vitality.

1. **The Seven Dhātus**

(a) Rasa (Plasma): Nourishment and Hydration

- Derived from digested food.
- **Functions:** Provides nutrients and moisture to all tissues.
- **Imbalance:** Results in dryness, fatigue, or poor immunity.

(b) Rakta (Blood): Vitality and Oxygen Transport

- Formed from plasma.
- **Functions:** Supplies oxygen and supports vitality.
- **Imbalance:** Causes anemia, skin disorders, or inflammation.

(c) Māṃsa (Muscle): Strength and Structural Support

- Formed from blood.
- **Functions:** Provides physical strength and mobility.
- **Imbalance:** Leads to muscle weakness or stiffness

(d) Meda (Fat): Lubrication and Energy Storage

- Formed from muscle tissue.
- **Functions:** Cushions organs and stores energy.
- **Imbalance:** Causes obesity or joint dryness.

(e) Asthi (Bone): Structural Integrity

- Formed from fat tissue.
- **Functions:** Provides structural framework and protection.
- **Imbalance:** Results in osteoporosis or bone pain.

(f) Majjā (Bone Marrow): Vital Energy and Nervous Tissue

- Formed from bone.
- **Functions:** Nourishes the nervous system and generates red blood cells.
- **Imbalance:** Leads to neurological disorders or fatigue.

(g) Śukra (Reproductive Tissue): Reproduction and Vitality

- Formed from marrow.
- **Functions:** Ensures fertility and vitality.
- **Imbalance:** Results in infertility or hormonal issues.

2. **Dynamic Interaction of Dhātus**: The dhātus interact dynamically, facilitating repair, growth, and regeneration. Proper digestion and metabolism ensure the healthy formation of tissues.

(III) Upadhātu: Accessory Tissues

Accessory tissues (upadhātus) are derived from primary dhātus and provide diagnostic insights into health:

1. **Nails and Hair:**
   - Derived from bone tissue.
   - Reflect the strength and health of bones.
2. **Breast Milk and Menstrual Blood:**
   - Derived from plasma and reproductive tissue.
   - Indicate nourishment and hormonal balance.
3. **Bile:**
   - Derived from blood.
   - Represents digestive and metabolic health.

(IV) Mala: The Waste Products

The body generates three primary waste products (malas) as part of normal physiological processes:

1. **The Three Malas**

   (a) Mutra (Urine):
   - Removes liquid waste and maintains electrolyte balance.
   - Imbalance: Causes dehydration or kidney issues.

   (b) Purīṣa (Feces):
   - Eliminates solid waste and toxins.
   - Imbalance: Leads to constipation or diarrhea.

   (c) Sveda (Sweat):
   - Regulates body temperature and eliminates toxins.
   - Imbalance: Causes excessive sweating or dryness.
2. **Importance of Balanced Elimination**
   - Proper elimination of malas ensures detoxification, energy flow, and systemic health.

(V) Subtle Components of the Body

Ayurveda emphasizes the connection between the physical body and subtle energies:

1. **Prāṇa: The Vital Life Force**
   - Governs respiration, circulation, and energy flow.
   - Imbalance: Causes fatigue, breathlessness, or lack of vitality.
2. **Manas: The Mind**
   - Regulates thought, emotions, and cognition.
   - Imbalance: Leads to stress, anxiety, or mental fog.
3. **Ātmā: The Soul**
   - Represents consciousness and self-awareness.
   - Connects the body to the mind and spirit.

(VI) Integration of Concepts in Ayurveda

1. **Holistic Diagnosis**: Ayurvedic practitioners assess prakṛti, vikṛti, dhātus, upadhātus, malas, and subtle energies for a comprehensive understanding of health.
2. **Personalized Treatment:** Treatments are tailored to restore balance in doshas, tissues, and waste elimination while aligning physical and mental well-being.

The concepts of tridosha, dhātu, upadhātu, mala, and subtle components form an integrated framework in Ayurveda. They underscore the interconnectedness of all aspects of human life, offering profound insights into health and disease. By balancing these elements, Ayurveda provides a holistic approach to achieving physical, mental, and spiritual harmony, ensuring a life of vitality and well-being.

Ayurvedic Perspective on Foetal Development

The study of embryology in Ayurveda, known as garbhāvasthā, is described in classical texts such as the Charaka Samhita and Sushruta Samhita. The process integrates physical, mental, and spiritual aspects, beginning with conception and progressing through well-defined stages of development.

1. **Conception**: The union of the father's śukra (sperm) and the mother's ārtava (ovum) forms the basis of foetal development. This process is governed by:
   - **Ritu (timing):** The fertile period of the mother.
   - **Kṣetra (field):** The health and readiness of the uterus.
   - **Ambu (nourishment):** The quality of maternal fluids.
   - **Bīja (seed):** The genetic material from both parents.

   The influence of the soul (jīvātma) enters the embryo during conception, guided by karma (past actions) and universal energy.
2. **Stages of Development**: Ayurvedic texts describe the following stages:
   1. **Kalala (First Month):** Formation of a semi-solid, jelly-like mass.
   2. **Budbuda (Second Month):** Development of a bubble-like structure indicating organ differentiation.

3. **Pesi (Third Month):** Formation of flesh and early organ structures.
4. **Ghāṇa (Fourth Month):** Development of solid structures like bones.
5. **Pṛṣṭhī (Fifth Month):** Completion of skeletal and muscular frameworks.
6. **Sharira Vriddhi (Sixth Month Onwards):** Rapid growth, refinement of sensory organs, and full physical development.

During these stages, the doshas influence specific aspects of growth:

- Vāta shapes movement and organ placement.
- Pitta facilitates transformation and metabolic activity.
- Kapha supports structure and cohesion.

3. **Influence of Maternal Health**: The mother's physical and mental health, diet, and lifestyle directly impact foetal development. Ayurveda recommends a sattvic (pure) lifestyle, balanced nutrition, and emotional stability to ensure the optimal growth of the foetus.
4. **Formation of Prakṛti**: An individual's prakṛti (body constitution) is established during gestation, influenced by:
   - Parental doshic dominance.
   - Maternal health and emotions.
   - Environmental factors during pregnancy.

This unique constitution shapes the individual's physical, psychological, and behavioural traits, emphasizing the importance of prenatal care in Ayurveda.

Different Body Constitutions (Prakṛti) and Their Significance

In Ayurveda, prakṛti is the innate constitution determined at conception. It reflects the dominant dosha(s) and governs an individual's physical traits, mental tendencies, and susceptibility to diseases.

1. **Types of Prakṛti:**
   1. **Vāta-Prakṛti**
      - **Physical Traits:** Thin body frame, dry skin, irregular appetite.
      - **Mental Traits:** Creativity, quick thinking, but prone to anxiety.
      - **Health Issues:** Susceptible to joint pain, insomnia, and digestive irregularities.
   2. **Pitta-Prakṛti**
      - **Physical Traits:** Medium build, sensitive skin, strong appetite.
      - **Mental Traits:** Sharp intellect, leadership qualities, but prone to irritability.
      - **Health Issues:** Prone to inflammatory conditions, skin rashes, and ulcers.
   3. **Kapha-Prakṛti**
      - **Physical Traits:** Large build, oily skin, slow metabolism.
      - **Mental Traits:** Calm, steady, but may experience lethargy.
      - **Health Issues:** Prone to obesity, respiratory disorders, and sluggish digestion.
   4. **Dual-Prakṛti**
      - A combination of two doshas (e.g., Vāta-Pitta, Pitta-Kapha).
   5. **Tri-Prakṛti**
      - Balanced constitution with equal influence of all three doshas, though rare.
2. **Significance of Prakṛti:**
   1. **Personalized Health Care**: Understanding prakṛti enables tailored dietary, lifestyle, and therapeutic recommendations. For instance, Vāta-dominant individuals benefit from warm, moist foods, while Pitta types require cooling and soothing diets.
   2. **Disease Susceptibility**: Each prakṛti has specific vulnerabilities. Vāta types may experience dryness and anxiety, while Kapha types are prone to congestion and sluggishness. Recognizing these predispositions allows for preventive measures.
   3. **Mental and Emotional Health**: Prakṛti also influences personality traits and mental tendencies. Ayurveda integrates these insights into holistic mental health care.
   4. **Reproductive and Prenatal Health**: Parental prakṛti influences the health of offspring, emphasizing the importance of understanding constitutions in family planning and prenatal care.
   5. **Therapeutic Interventions**: Treatments, including herbal formulations, detoxification therapies, and yoga practices, are customized based on prakṛti.

The study of śarīra, foetal development, and body constitutions in Ayurveda underscores the integrative and personalized approach of this ancient science. By recognizing the structural and compositional intricacies of the human body, Ayurveda connects physical health with mental and spiritual well-being. The detailed understanding of foetal development reflects a holistic view of life's origins, emphasizing the importance of nurturing environments and balanced lifestyles. Finally, the concept of prakṛti highlights individuality, offering profound insights into health, disease prevention, and therapeutic strategies. Together, these principles make Ayurveda a timeless and comprehensive system for understanding and enhancing human life.

MULTIPLE CHOICE QUESTIONS

1. A researcher studying śarīra focuses on the dynamic interplay between the tridoshas. He observes that the imbalance of vāta impacts not only the nervous system but also causes dryness and joint pain. Which dosha interplay must be stabilized to address these issues?
   A. Vāta and kapha B. Pitta and kapha
   C. Vāta and pitta D. None of the above

2. During foetal development, ghāṇa marks a pivotal stage characterized by the formation of bones. In this process, which dosha plays a dominant role in structuring the skeletal framework?
   A. Vāta B. Pitta
   C. Kapha D. All three doshas equally

3. An Ayurvedic practitioner treats a kapha prakṛti individual with tendencies toward lethargy and slow metabolism. Which diet would be most suitable for balancing kapha dominance?
   A. Cooling and hydrating foods, such as sweet fruits and milk.
   B. Warming and light foods, such as dry fruits and pungent spices.
   C. Heavy and oily foods, including fried snacks and dairy.
   D. Sour and salty foods, such as pickles and yogurt.

4. Ayurvedic texts describe prakṛti as the foundation of personalized medicine. If a patient exhibits irritability, sharp intellect, and heat-related conditions, which prakṛti likely dominates?
   A. Vāta B. Pitta
   C. Kapha D. Tridoshic

5. Pesi represents the embryonic stage where flesh develops. Which Ayurvedic principle explains the role of maternal nourishment in ensuring proper dhātu formation during this stage?
   A. Bīja B. Rasa dhātu
   C. Kṣetra D. Ambu

6. A modern study correlates prakṛti classifications with metabolic profiles, revealing that kapha prakṛti individuals are more prone to obesity. Which Ayurvedic principle aligns with this finding?
   A. Dominance of āpas and pṛthvī elements in kapha.
   B. Overactivity of tejas in pitta.
   C. Irregular movement of vāyu in vāta.
   D. None of the above.

7. The Ayurvedic concept of mala includes the body's waste elimination processes. How does the balance of vāta influence the effective removal of feces (purīṣa)?
   A. By stimulating the transformation of solid into liquid waste.
   B. By controlling intestinal movement and peristalsis.
   C. By nourishing kapha to lubricate the colon.
   D. None of the above.

8. The bīja (genetic material) and ṛtu (season) are essential factors in conception. How does ṛtu ensure optimal fertilization according to Ayurveda?
   A. By synchronizing seasonal dosha dominance with reproductive health.
   B. By emphasizing dietary balance for sperm and ovum production.
   C. By enhancing the strength of mala for detoxification.
   D. By improving maternal immunity postpartum.

9. During foetal growth, vāta governs the movement and positioning of developing organs. What other physiological process does vāta influence at this stage?
   A. Tissue nourishment.
   B. Transformation of plasma into muscle.
   C. Circulation of nutrients and cellular differentiation.
   D. Detoxification of embryonic byproducts.

10. An Ayurvedic scholar links prakṛti traits with individual temperaments. Which of the following traits is least likely to align with vāta prakṛti?
   A. Creative thinking.
   B. High physical stamina.
   C. Quick adaptability.
   D. Tendency toward anxiety.

Directions (Q. No. 11–14): *Scenario-Based Questions*

SCENARIO 1

A clinical researcher studies the effects of Triphala on gut health. This formulation improves microbial diversity, alleviating IBS symptoms. Gut health improvements also lead to enhanced immunity, with increased IgA levels and reduced inflammation.

SCENARIO 2

An environmental biologist investigates amalaki sourcing for Triphala. Overharvesting reduces bioactive compounds due to deforestation and soil degradation, impacting the herb's medicinal efficacy.

11. Based on Scenario 1, which mechanism explains the enhanced systemic immunity after consuming Triphala?
   A. Direct stimulation of immune cells without gut health changes.

B. Enhanced activity of gut-associated lymphoid tissue (GALT).
C. Placebo effects independent of microbial restoration.
D. Reduction of microbial diversity with strengthened gut barriers.

12. Considering Scenario 2, which intervention best addresses sustainability challenges for amalaki?

Choose the correct answer from the options given below:

A. Developing synthetic alternatives.
B. Agroforestry and community-led conservation.
C. Monoculture farming in degraded lands.
D. Reducing global demand for Triphala.

13. How does environmental degradation of amalaki potentially impact gut health improvements observed in Scenario 1?

Choose the correct answer from the options given below:

A. Reduced bioactive compounds weaken microbial diversity benefits.
B. Efficacy remains unaffected as all three fruits ensure potency.
C. Degraded amalaki indirectly boosts microbial resilience.
D. Soil conditions have no measurable effect on foetal immunity.

14. What integrated strategy resolves both scenarios' challenges while preserving Triphala's efficacy?

Choose the correct answer from the options given below:

A. Promoting traditional agroforestry for all Triphala components.
B. Shifting research focus to alternative herbal formulations.
C. Large-scale commercial farming of amalaki.
D. Relying on imports to mitigate sustainability challenges.

15. The essential components of foetal development in Ayurveda are:

(a) Bīja (genetic material).
(b) Rasa (nourishment).
(c) Ambu (hydraulic environment).
(d) Kṣetra (uterine environment).

Choose the correct answer from the options given below:

A. (a), (b), and (c) only
B. (b), (c), and (d) only
C. (a), (c), and (d) only
D. (a), (b), (c), and (d)

16. The principles of Ayurveda related to tridosha state:

(a) Vāta governs movement and the nervous system.
(b) Pitta regulates metabolism and enzymatic activity.
(c) Kapha maintains structure and lubrication.
(d) Doshas ensure uniform treatment protocols.

Choose the correct answer from the options given below:

A. (a), (b), and (c) only
B. (b), (c), and (d) only
C. (a), (c), and (d) only
D. (a), (b), (c), and (d)

17. Match the Ayurvedic rasas (tastes) with their actions:

(a) Sweet: Nourishes tissues.
(b) Bitter: Detoxifies and reduces inflammation.
(c) Sour: Enhances metabolism.
(d) Astringent: Strengthens tissue cohesion.

Choose the correct answer from the options given below:

A. (a), (b), and (c) only
B. (b), (c), and (d) only
C. (a), (b), (c), and (d)
D. (a), (b), and (d) only

18. The biological actions of Ayurvedic rasas (tastes) are classified as:

(a) Sweet (Madhura) promotes tissue growth and nourishment.
(b) Bitter (Tikta) detoxifies the body and reduces inflammation.
(c) Astringent (Kashaya) strengthens tissues and controls bleeding.
(d) Sour (Amla) enhances digestion and metabolic activity.

Choose the correct answer from the options given below:

A. (a), (b), and (d) only
B. (a), (b), (c), and (d) only
C. (b), (c), and (e) only
D. (a), (c), and (d) only

19. The following represent critical stages of foetal development in Ayurveda:

(a) Kalala (jelly-like mass).
(b) Budbuda (bubble formation).
(c) Pesi (flesh development).
(d) Ghāṇa (solid structures).

Choose the correct answer from the options given below:

A. (a) and (b) only
B. (b), (c), and (d) only
C. (a), (c), and (d) only
D. (a), (b), (c), and (d)

20. The Ayurvedic framework emphasizes the importance of balance in the following:
(a) Doshic harmony (tridosha).
(b) Proper functioning of dhātus (tissues).
(c) Elimination of malas (waste products).
(d) Ignoring mental and spiritual health.

Choose the correct answer from the options given below:
A. (a), (b), and (c) only
B. (b), (c), and (d) only
C. (a), (c), and (d) only
D. (a), (b), (c), and (d)

21. The concept of prakṛti is influenced by:
(a) Parental dosha dominance.
(b) Maternal health and emotions during pregnancy.
(c) Genetic material (bīja).
(d) Postnatal environmental factors.

Choose the correct answer from the options given below:
A. (a) and (b) only
B. (b), (c), and (d) only
C. (a), (c), and (d) only
D. (a), (b), (c), and (d)

22. The following qualities are associated with pitta prakṛti:
(a) Medium build and sharp intellect.
(b) Susceptibility to inflammatory conditions.
(c) Calm and stable personality.
(d) Warm, oily skin and strong appetite.

Choose the correct answer from the options given below:
A. (a), (b), and (c) only
B. (a), (b), and (d) only
C. (b), (c), and (d) only
D. (a), (c), and (d) only

23. The Ayurvedic perspective on mala (waste products) includes:
(a) Sveda (sweat) (b) Mutra (urine)
(c) Rakta (blood) (d) Purīṣa (feces)

Choose the correct answer from the options given below:
A. (a) and (b) only
B. (b) and (d) only
C. (a), (b), and (d) only
D. (a), (b), (c), and (d)

24. The following are key considerations in Ayurvedic prenatal care:
(a) Balanced diet to maintain doshic harmony.
(b) Use of herbal formulations like shatavari.
(c) Physical and emotional well-being of the mother.
(d) Avoidance of genetic predispositions.

Choose the correct answer from the options given below:
A. (a), (b), and (c) only
B. (b), (c), and (d) only
C. (a), (c), and (d) only
D. (a), (b), (c), and (d)

25. Match List–I and List–II carefully and choose the correct answer from the options given below:

List–I: (Concepts)
(a) Structure of śarīra (body)
(b) Ayurvedic perspective on foetal development stages
(c) Different body constitutions (prakriti)
(d) Importance of prakriti analysis

List–II: (Descriptions)
1. Composed of five elements (pañca mahābhūta) and three doṣas (vāta, pitta, kapha)
2. Explains garbha (foetus) formation through a combination of śukra (sperm), śoṇita (ovum), and ātmā (soul)
3. Determined by the predominance of doṣas at the time of conception
4. Helps in understanding disease predisposition and individualized treatment

Choose the correct answer from the options given below:
A. (a)-1, (b)-2, (c)-3, (d)-4
B. (a)-2, (b)-1, (c)-4, (d)-3
C. (a)-3, (b)-4, (c)-1, (d)-2
D. (a)-4, (b)-3, (c)-2, (d)-1

26. Match List–I and List–II carefully and choose the correct answer from the options given below:

List–I: (Concepts)
(a) Garbha sthapana (foetus stabilization)
(b) Trimester-specific development in Ayurveda
(c) Influence of mātuja (maternal) and pitruja (paternal) factors
(d) Role of ātmā (soul) in foetal development

List–II: (Descriptions)
1. Achieved through balanced diet and proper mental and physical rest of the mother
2. First trimester governs formation of limbs and organs, second trimester supports strength, and third trimester completes development
3. Determines physical and mental traits of the foetus
4. Ensures vitality and consciousness in the developing foetus

Choose the correct answer from the options given below:
A. (a)-1, (b)-2, (c)-3, (d)-4
B. (a)-2, (b)-1, (c)-4, (d)-3
C. (a)-3, (b)-4, (c)-1, (d)-2
D. (a)-4, (b)-3, (c)-2, (d)-1

27. Match List–I and List–II carefully and choose the correct answer from the options given below:

List–I: (Key Terms)

(a) Vāta prakriti individuals
(b) Pitta prakriti individuals
(c) Kapha prakriti individuals
(d) Dual prakriti combinations

List–II: (Descriptions)

1. Have lean body frames, dry skin, and are prone to anxiety
2. Exhibit sharp intellect, oily skin, and a tendency to anger
3. Known for strong immunity, calm demeanor, and slow digestion
4. Exhibit mixed traits of two predominant doṣas

Choose the correct answer from the options given below:

A. (a)-1, (b)-2, (c)-3, (d)-4
B. (a)-2, (b)-3, (c)-4, (d)-1
C. (a)-3, (b)-4, (c)-1, (d)-2
D. (a)-4, (b)-1, (c)-2, (d)-3

28. Match List–I and List–II carefully and choose the correct answer from the options given below:

List–I: (Principles)

(a) Concept of dhātu (tissue) formation
(b) Three layers of garbha (foetus)
(c) Influence of karma on birth
(d) Significance of guṇas in body development

List–II: (Details)

1. Involves sequential nourishment of seven dhātus from rasa to śukra
2. Correspond to development of skin, muscles, and internal organs
3. Determines the soul's entry into specific circumstances and physical conditions
4. Sattva, rajas, and tamas influence psychological and physical traits

Choose the correct answer from the options given below:

A. (a)-1, (b)-2, (c)-3, (d)-4
B. (a)-2, (b)-1, (c)-4, (d)-3
C. (a)-3, (b)-4, (c)-1, (d)-2
D. (a)-4, (b)-3, (c)-2, (d)-1

29. Match List–I and List–II carefully and choose the correct answer from the options given below:

List–I: (Concepts)

(a) Prakriti determined during conception
(b) Indicates calmness, strong immunity, and lethargy
(c) Psychological prakriti
(d) Relevance of prakriti in treatment

List–II: (Descriptions)

1. Influenced by genetic, environmental, and psychological factors
2. Correspond to development of skin, muscles, and internal organs
3. Categorized as sāttvika, rājasa, and tāmasa
4. Guides personalized dietary and therapeutic approaches

Choose the correct answer from the options given below:

A. (a)-1, (b)-2, (c)-3, (d)-4
B. (a)-2, (b)-3, (c)-4, (d)-1
C. (a)-3, (b)-4, (c)-1, (d)-2
D. (a)-4, (b)-1, (c)-2, (d)-3

30. Match List–I and List–II carefully and choose the correct answer from the options given below:

List–I: (Developmental Processes)

(a) Formation of śukra (reproductive tissue)
(b) First trimester in Ayurveda
(c) Second trimester in Ayurveda
(d) Third trimester in Ayurveda

List–II: (Stages)

1. Final dhātu in the nourishment cycle
2. Formation of basic body structures and senses
3. Strength and physical development emphasized
4. Preparation for birth and complete organ formation

Choose the correct answer from the options given below:

A. (a)-1, (b)-2, (c)-3, (d)-4
B. (a)-2, (b)-1, (c)-4, (d)-3
C. (a)-3, (b)-4, (c)-1, (d)-2
D. (a)-4, (b)-3, (c)-2, (d)-1

31. Match List–I and List–II carefully and choose the correct answer from the options given below:

List–I: (Ayurvedic Concepts)

(a) Doṣa and guṇa relation
(b) Rasāyana therapy
(c) Role of ojas in body
(d) Sattva guṇa dominance

List–II: (Definitions)

1. Each doṣa is associated with a set of qualities influencing body functions
2. Focuses on rejuvenation and longevity
3. Primary essence responsible for vitality and immunity
4. Reflects clarity, balance, and positivity in mental health

Choose the correct answer from the options given below:

A. (a)-1, (b)-2, (c)-3, (d)-4
B. (a)-2, (b)-1, (c)-4, (d)-3
C. (a)-3, (b)-4, (c)-1, (d)-2
D. (a)-4, (b)-3, (c)-2, (d)-1

32. Match List–I and List–II carefully and choose the correct answer from the options given below:

List–I: (Components)

(a) Sattva guṇa
(b) Rajas guṇa
(c) Tamas guṇa
(d) Tri-guṇa balance

List–II: (Descriptions)

1. Associated with knowledge, clarity, and balance
2. Denotes activity, passion, and restlessness
3. Represents inertia, ignorance, and darkness
4. Essential for physical and mental well-being

Choose the correct answer from the options given below:

A. (a)-1, (b)-2, (c)-3, (d)-4
B. (a)-2, (b)-1, (c)-4, (d)-3
C. (a)-3, (b)-4, (c)-1, (d)-2
D. (a)-4, (b)-3, (c)-2, (d)-1

33. Match List–I and List–II carefully and choose the correct answer from the options given below:

List–I: (Stages)

(a) Pre-conceptional care in Ayurveda
(b) Embryological development
(c) Formation of prakriti
(d) Postnatal care in Ayurveda

List–II: (Details)

1. Focus on purification and strengthening of reproductive tissues
2. Governed by mātuja, pitruja, and ātmā
3. Determined during conception and influenced by doṣas
4. Emphasizes nutrition and ojas strengthening

Choose the correct answer from the options given below:

A. (a)-1, (b)-2, (c)-3, (d)-4
B. (a)-2, (b)-1, (c)-4, (d)-3
C. (a)-3, (b)-4, (c)-1, (d)-2
D. (a)-4, (b)-3, (c)-2, (d)-1

34. Match List–I and List–II carefully and choose the correct answer from the options given below:

List–I: (Ayurvedic Principles)

(a) Srotas (channels)
(b) Dhātus (tissues)
(c) Upadhātus (secondary tissues)
(d) Mala (waste products)

List–II: (Functions)

1. Facilitate transportation of nutrients and waste
2. Support structural and functional integrity of the body
3. Include hair, nails, and milk
4. Regulate elimination processes

Choose the correct answer from the options given below:

A. (a)-1, (b)-2, (c)-3, (d)-4
B. (a)-2, (b)-1, (c)-4, (d)-3
C. (a)-3, (b)-4, (c)-1, (d)-2
D. (a)-4, (b)-3, (c)-2, (d)-1

Directions (Q. No. 35–39): *Following questions are based on Statement 1 and Statements 2. Read both the statements carefully and choose the correct answer from the options given below:*

A. Both Statement 1 and Statement 2 are true, and Statement 2 is the correct explanation of Statement 1.
B. Both Statement 1 and Statement 2 are true, but Statement 2 is not the correct explanation of Statement 1.
C. Statement 1 is true, but Statement 2 is false.
D. Statement 1 is false, but Statement 2 is true.
E. Both Statement 1 and Statement 2 are false.

35. Statement 1: The prakṛti of an individual is determined at conception and remains constant throughout life.

Statement 2: Prakṛti is influenced only by genetic factors and does not depend on maternal health or emotions during pregnancy.

36. Statement 1: The stages of foetal development described in Ayurveda, such as kalala and pesi, align with modern embryological stages of cellular differentiation and organogenesis.

Statement 2: Ayurvedic descriptions of foetal development are entirely symbolic and lack physiological relevance in contemporary science.

37. Statement 1: Kapha prakṛti individuals are less prone to anxiety and mental restlessness due to their stable and calm mental constitution.

Statement 2: Stability in kapha prakṛti is due to the predominance of earth and water elements, which mitigate the light and mobile qualities of vāta.

38. Statement 1: Maternal health and emotions during pregnancy influence the prakṛti and mental tendencies of the foetus.

Statement 2: The maternal contribution to prakṛti is limited to providing nourishment through rasa dhātu and does not extend to mental or emotional factors.

39. Statement 1: Ayurveda emphasizes the balance of prāṇa, manas, and ātmā for achieving overall health.

Statement 2: Imbalances in prāṇa, manas, and ātmā are strictly physiological and have no bearing on mental or spiritual health.

Directions (Q. No. 40–45): *There are two statements in each question. One is labelled as Assertion (A) and the other is as Reason (R). Read both the statements and choose the correct answer from the options given below*:

A. Both Assertion (A) and Reason (R) are true, and Reason (R) is the correct explanation of Assertion (A).
B. Both Assertion (A) and Reason (R) are true, but Reason (R) is not the correct explanation of Assertion (A).
C. Assertion (A) is true, but Reason (R) is false.
D. Assertion (A) is false, but Reason (R) is true.
E. Both Assertion (A) and Reason (R) are false.

40. Assertion (A): The balance of tridosha (vāta, pitta, and kapha) is essential for maintaining physical, mental, and spiritual health.

Reason (R): Each dosha corresponds to specific tissues and organ systems, collectively maintaining systemic harmony.

41. Assertion (A): Pitta prakṛti individuals are predisposed to heat-related disorders such as acidity and skin inflammation.

Reason (R): The dominance of the fire (tejas) element in pitta prakṛti is responsible for heightened metabolic activity and susceptibility to heat imbalances.

42. Assertion (A): Ayurvedic prenatal care emphasizes the use of herbs like shatavari and amla to support maternal and foetal health.

Reason (R): These herbs maintain doshic balance, nourish the foetus, and enhance immunity in the mother.

43. Assertion (A): Balanced prakṛti is extremely rare and ensures a robust immunity to diseases.

Reason (R): A balanced prakṛti maintains equilibrium among the tridoshas, promoting optimal health.

44. Assertion (A): The paṃcamahābhūta theory is the foundation of the Ayurvedic understanding of śarīra.

Reason (R): Each of the five elements contributes equally to the structure and function of the human body.

Directions (Q. No. 46–50): *Read the passage carefully and answer the questions given below*:

Ayurveda, the ancient Indian medical science, offers a holistic understanding of the human body through the lens of prakṛti (body constitution). It defines prakṛti as the unique combination of vāta, pitta, and kapha, which govern physiological, psychological, and biochemical functions. Determined at conception, prakṛti is shaped by factors such as genetic material (bīja), maternal health, emotional state, and environmental influences during pregnancy. It remains constant throughout life and plays a significant role in susceptibility to diseases, dietary needs, and lifestyle preferences.

Each prakṛti has distinct traits. Vāta prakṛti individuals are creative, quick thinkers but prone to anxiety, irregular digestion, and cold intolerance. Pitta prakṛti individuals have a sharp intellect, a strong appetite, and a predisposition to heat-related disorders such as inflammation and acidity. Kapha prakṛti individuals are calm and robust but may struggle with weight gain and lethargy. These classifications align with modern metabolic and genomic research, demonstrating the scientific relevance of prakṛti.

The interplay of prakṛti with mental health is also emphasized in Ayurveda. It connects the qualities of sattva (purity), rajas (activity), and tamas (inertia) with psychological tendencies. For instance, individuals with predominant sattva exhibit mental clarity and balance, while those dominated by rajas are more prone to restlessness. Ayurvedic texts highlight that imbalances in mental qualities can disturb the harmony of the tridoshas, leading to physical and mental ailments.

Ayurveda's approach to health is not limited to treating disease but extends to disease prevention through the alignment of lifestyle with one's prakṛti. Seasonal regimens (ritucharya), daily routines (dinacharya), and dietary guidelines are tailored to doshic balance, ensuring long-term well-being. These principles, rooted in ancient wisdom, continue to resonate in the modern era as integrative medicine embraces personalized and preventive care approaches.

46. Which of the following factors primarily shapes an individual's prakṛti at conception?
A. Genetic material (bīja), maternal health, and emotional state during pregnancy.
B. Postnatal diet and environmental factors.
C. Seasonal changes and their influence on doshas.
D. Environmental factors experienced after birth.

47. What is a defining trait of vāta prakṛti individuals, as per the passage?
A. High emotional stability and mental clarity.
B. Susceptibility to heat-related disorders and strong appetite.
C. Creativity and quick thinking but prone to anxiety and irregular digestion.
D. Calmness, robustness, and slow adaptability.

48. How does modern research validate the Ayurvedic concept of prakṛti?
A. By highlighting the symbolic nature of prakṛti classifications.
B. By correlating doshic dominance with genomic and metabolic profiles.

C. By replacing Ayurveda's principles with empirical medical models.
D. By disproving Ayurvedic theories in favor of genomic studies.

49. What psychological quality is most associated with sattva in Ayurveda?
A. Restlessness and irritability.
B. Mental clarity, balance, and purity.
C. Tendency toward lethargy and inertia.
D. Sharp intellect accompanied by anxiety.

50. According to the passage, how does Ayurveda integrate prevention into its approach to health?
A. By focusing solely on treating diseases as they arise.
B. By prescribing standardized dietary plans regardless of prakṛti.
C. By aligning lifestyle practices such as dinacharya and ritucharya with one's doshic balance.
D. By ignoring environmental and genetic influences to emphasize ancient rituals.

ANSWER WITH EXPLANATIONS

1. A: Vāta governs movement, dryness, and the nervous system. When aggravated, it results in symptoms like constipation, dry skin, and joint pain. Kapha, being moist and stabilizing, naturally counterbalances vāta's dryness and instability. In Ayurvedic management, treating both vāta and kapha imbalances together is crucial when dryness, stiffness, and nervous symptoms co-exist. Warm, oily, and grounding foods pacify vāta, while light and dry qualities help manage kapha. Thus, their combined regulation restores equilibrium in such conditions.

2. C: Kapha dosha, composed of the earth and water elements, governs bodily structure, lubrication, and cohesion. In the ghāṇa stage of fetal development, solid tissues, especially bones, begin to form and solidify. Since kapha provides strength, stability, and nourishment, it plays a dominant role during this stage. Its heavy, dense qualities support the skeletal framework and ensure proper tissue formation. Therefore, kapha's influence is central to the development of solid structures in the fetus.

3. B: Kapha prakṛti individuals tend to have slow metabolism, weight gain, and lethargy due to the dominance of earth and water elements. To balance these heavy, moist, and cold qualities, Ayurveda recommends warm, light, dry, and spicy foods. Such foods stimulate agni (digestive fire), improve metabolic rate, and reduce kapha's sluggish nature. Dry fruits and pungent spices like ginger and black pepper are ideal for energizing and lightening the body. Hence, option B is most appropriate for kapha management.

4. B: Pitta prakṛti is dominated by the fire (tejas) element, giving individuals qualities like heat, intensity, sharp intellect, and strong digestion. However, this also makes them prone to irritability, inflammatory disorders, and heat-related conditions such as rashes, acidity, or headaches. The patient described in the question clearly reflects these pitta traits. Personalized Ayurvedic interventions for pitta dominance include cooling diets, calming routines, and herbs like coriander and guduchi to soothe the internal fire.

5. D: In Ayurveda, ambu refers to the nourishing fluid essential for fetal development. During the pesi stage, when flesh and muscle begin to form, ambu ensures the flow of vital nutrients and hydration necessary for tissue development. It is derived from maternal rasa dhātu (plasma/nutrient fluid) and plays a key role in sustaining proper dhātu formation in the fetus. Thus, ambu represents the maternal contribution of nourishment that supports growth during embryogenesis.

6. A: Kapha prakṛti is characterized by heaviness, stability, and coolness—traits arising from the dominance of water (āpas) and earth (pṛthvī) elements. These elements slow down metabolic functions and contribute to fluid retention and weight gain. Modern studies that link kapha prakṛti with higher risks of obesity and sluggish metabolism align well with this classical Ayurvedic view. Hence, understanding the elemental composition of kapha helps explain its predisposition to such health issues.

7. B: Vāta dosha governs all types of movement in the body, including peristalsis—the rhythmic contraction of intestinal muscles that facilitates bowel movements. When vāta is in balance, it ensures smooth elimination of feces (purīṣa) through regulated motion in the colon. An aggravated vāta can lead to constipation or dryness in stools. Thus, vāta's proper functioning is vital for healthy waste elimination and overall colon health in Ayurveda.

8. A: In Ayurveda, ṛtu refers not only to seasons but also to the optimal timing for conception. Proper timing ensures that the prevailing seasonal doshic balance supports fertility. For instance, late winter and early spring—when kapha is dominant—are considered ideal for conception due to enhanced ojas and reproductive strength. The synchronization of environmental conditions with the internal doshic state enhances the chances of successful fertilization and healthy fetal development.

9. **C:** Vāta's function extends beyond gross movement—it also governs the subtle flows of nutrients and impulses in the body. During fetal development, vāta helps circulate nutrients and ensures that cellular differentiation (the process by which cells form specific tissues and organs) occurs efficiently. Vāta is responsible for the positioning and functional development of organs through its subtypes like vyāna and prāṇa vāyu. Thus, vāta's role is central to both structure and coordination.

10. **B:** Vāta prakṛti individuals are known for being agile, creative, and mentally quick, but they usually lack endurance and have less physical strength due to their light and dry constitution. They often tire quickly and are prone to anxiety and instability. In contrast, high stamina is more commonly seen in kapha prakṛti individuals, who have strong bodies and good reserves of energy. Hence, high physical stamina is the least associated trait with vāta prakṛti.

11. **B:** Triphala promotes gut health by improving the diversity of gut microbiota. This enhancement stimulates the gut-associated lymphoid tissue (GALT), a key immune component located in the intestines. GALT activation improves immune responses such as increased production of immunoglobulin A (IgA) and reduces systemic inflammation. The link between improved digestion and enhanced immunity in Scenario 1 reflects this Ayurvedic and biomedical correlation.

12. **B:** Agroforestry integrates ecological conservation with sustainable agriculture by allowing the cultivation of herbs like amalaki alongside native trees and biodiversity. Community-led conservation ensures that locals protect and manage herbal resources responsibly. This strategy addresses overharvesting and soil degradation while promoting long-term availability of medicinal plants. It is both environmentally sustainable and aligned with Ayurveda's holistic ethos.

13. **A:** Environmental degradation, such as deforestation and poor soil health, negatively affects the phytochemical quality of herbs like amalaki. Since these compounds are responsible for many therapeutic effects—including microbial modulation—reduced potency directly impacts clinical outcomes. In the context of Scenario 1, weaker amalaki compromises Triphala's ability to improve gut health and immunity, demonstrating how environmental factors affect therapeutic efficacy.

14. **A:** Triphala consists of amalaki, haritaki, and bibhitaki—each requiring sustainable cultivation. Agroforestry ensures that all components are grown in environmentally supportive ways that maintain soil health and bioactive potency. This integrated approach solves both clinical and ecological concerns by preserving medicinal efficacy and biodiversity. It also aligns with Ayurveda's emphasis on living in harmony with nature.

15. **D:** The comprehensive framework of Ayurveda includes bīja (genetic material), rasa (nourishment), ambu (hydraulic support), and kṣetra (uterine environment) as foundational factors for foetal development. Each element plays an integral role: bīja determines hereditary traits, rasa nourishes the embryo, ambu ensures hydration and nutrient transport, and kṣetra provides a conducive environment. The inclusion of all four reflects Ayurveda's integrative understanding of conception, linking genetic, nutritional, and environmental aspects. This holistic perspective enables precise interventions to optimize foetal health, reinforcing the interconnectedness of these factors in promoting healthy development.

16. **A:** The principles of Ayurveda highlight the tridosha framework where vāta governs movement, pitta regulates metabolism, and kapha provides structural stability. These roles ensure systemic harmony and balance. For instance, vāta's influence on nervous system activity, pitta's role in enzymatic functions, and kapha's contribution to tissue cohesion reflect their physiological significance. This triadic interplay forms the foundation of Ayurvedic diagnostics and treatment, enabling personalized care based on individual doshic imbalances. By emphasizing the collaborative nature of doshas, Ayurveda underscores its holistic approach to understanding and managing human physiology.

17. **C:** All six Ayurvedic tastes (rasas) have specific therapeutic actions: sweet nourishes tissues, bitter detoxifies, sour enhances metabolism, and astringent strengthens tissue cohesion. Each taste corresponds to specific doshic imbalances, offering a tailored approach to treatment. Ayurveda's dietary framework integrates these tastes for comprehensive health management, illustrating the interplay between taste, digestion, and doshic balance. This nuanced categorization highlights Ayurveda's precision in designing dietary and therapeutic interventions that address individual needs while promoting systemic harmony.

18. **B:** Ayurveda's classification of tastes (rasas) into sweet, bitter, sour, and astringent reflects their physiological actions and therapeutic applications. Sweet supports

nourishment and growth, bitter detoxifies and cools inflammation, sour aids digestion, and astringent enhances tissue stability. By understanding these effects, Ayurveda tailors dietary and herbal interventions to correct doshic imbalances. This framework underscores the system's depth in recognizing taste as a crucial determinant of health. Incorporating all four tastes into therapeutic regimens highlights Ayurveda's comprehensive approach, offering targeted solutions for diverse health conditions.

19. D: The stages kalala, budbuda, pesi, and ghāṇa in Ayurveda align with embryological milestones such as cellular differentiation, organogenesis, and skeletal formation. These stages reflect Ayurveda's detailed understanding of developmental biology. By integrating maternal health and environmental factors into these stages, Ayurveda emphasizes the dynamic interplay of internal and external influences on foetal development. This nuanced approach demonstrates Ayurveda's foresight in recognizing the interconnected nature of physiological processes and the factors shaping them, enabling interventions that support optimal embryonic growth.

20. A: Doshic harmony, proper dhātu functioning, and waste elimination form the pillars of health in Ayurveda. This holistic framework excludes mental and spiritual neglect, emphasizing the integration of physical, mental, and spiritual well-being. For instance, maintaining balanced vāta ensures efficient elimination, while optimized pitta supports metabolic activities. Ayurveda's approach transcends symptomatic treatment, addressing root causes by harmonizing these aspects. This comprehensive understanding underscores Ayurveda's role as a preventive and curative system, prioritizing long-term health through systemic equilibrium.

21. D: Prakṛti is influenced by multiple factors, including parental dosha dominance, maternal health, emotions during pregnancy, and genetic material (bīja). Postnatal environmental factors further affect health but do not alter the prakṛti determined at conception. Ayurveda's understanding of prakṛti integrates genetics with maternal and environmental influences, demonstrating its comprehensive framework for understanding individual constitution. This holistic approach enables personalized health strategies, aligning with contemporary research on the interplay between genetics, epigenetics, and prenatal conditions in shaping health outcomes.

22. B: Pitta prakṛti individuals exhibit medium build, sharp intellect, and strong appetite, alongside susceptibility to heat-related disorders like inflammation. These traits arise from the dominance of the tejas (fire) and āpas (water) elements in pitta. This dosha's transformative and metabolic nature reflects its physiological and psychological influence. While kapha individuals are stable and calm, and vāta individuals are light and creative, pitta types are characterized by dynamic metabolism and fiery temperament. This classification allows Ayurveda to tailor preventive and therapeutic interventions based on individual doshic traits.

23. C: Mala elimination in Ayurveda includes sweat (sveda), urine (mutra), and feces (purīṣa). These waste products are vital for maintaining physiological balance, as their proper excretion prevents doshic imbalances. Blood (rakta), though essential for vitality, is not classified as a mala. By integrating waste elimination into its framework, Ayurveda emphasizes the interdependence of metabolic processes and systemic health. Proper mala management through lifestyle and dietary adjustments underscores Ayurveda's preventive focus, ensuring that physiological harmony is maintained through efficient detoxification.

24. A: Ayurvedic prenatal care emphasizes a balanced diet, herbal formulations like shatavari, and maternal physical and emotional well-being. These factors support the mother's health and contribute to the optimal development of the foetus. Genetic predispositions, while acknowledged, are not the primary focus, as Ayurveda prioritizes nurturing the foetus through rasa dhātu and balanced doshic conditions. This integrative approach reflects Ayurveda's commitment to holistic care, recognizing the influence of maternal nourishment, emotions, and environment on foetal health.

25. A: The structural framework of śarīra embodies Ayurvedic concepts rooted in pañca mahābhūta and doṣas, aligning physical functions with cosmic elements. Foetal development highlights the interplay of śukra, śoṇita, and ātmā, symbolizing the unity of biological and spiritual dimensions. Prakriti reflects constitutional individuality shaped at conception, emphasizing the unique predominance of doṣas. Prakriti analysis is significant for tailoring therapeutic approaches, bridging predispositions to diseases with personalized care. This question demonstrates how Ayurveda integrates microcosmic principles with macrocosmic truths to address health holistically, providing a nuanced framework for understanding individuality and maintaining equilibrium.

26. A: The stabilization of the foetus underscores the mother's physiological and mental stability, emphasizing holistic prenatal care. Trimester-based development reflects precise stages where Ayurveda mirrors embryological insights, from structural formation to functional maturity. Mātuja and pitruja factors integrate parental contributions to heredity, blending genetics with Ayurvedic metaphysics. The ātmā's role highlights vitality, demonstrating Ayurveda's alignment with existential and ontological realities. The connections between these concepts extend beyond biology into the metaphysical realm, showcasing the profound synthesis of physical, mental, and spiritual health that Ayurveda provides.

27. **A:** Vāta individuals epitomize lightness and mobility, reflecting qualities governed by vāyu and ākāśa elements, while their mental tendencies lean toward creativity and instability. Pitta personalities, dominated by agni, signify sharpness and transformation, with inherent susceptibility to aggression and precision. Kapha, embodying earth and water, signifies stability and resilience, manifesting in calmness and longevity. Dual prakriti combinations illustrate the Ayurvedic principle of dynamic balance, where duality shapes unique physical and psychological traits. These archetypes highlight Ayurveda's commitment to categorizing life forms not rigidly but fluidly, based on elemental dominance and interaction.

28. **A:** The sequential nourishment of dhātus demonstrates Ayurveda's systematic approach to physiology, where each tissue serves as both an outcome and precursor in metabolic transformations. The three layers of garbha underline structural organization, correlating anatomical and physiological development. Karma's influence on birth integrates ethical dimensions with physical life, binding Ayurveda to spiritual doctrines. The guṇas' role reveals how psychological and physical traits are shaped by the interplay of sattva, rajas, and tamas, showing the intricate relationship between mental states and physical health. This multilayered analysis blends biology with philosophy, creating a comprehensive health framework.

29. **A:** Prakriti determination at conception aligns genetic, environmental, and karmic factors, mirroring modern genetic predisposition theories within Ayurveda's metaphysical boundaries. Kapha dominance denotes resilience yet predisposes to lethargy, reflecting the balancing act of elements. Psychological prakriti delves into mind-body interaction, associating guṇas with personality traits. Prakriti's relevance to treatment showcases Ayurveda's foresight in personalized medicine, where constitutions guide diagnostics and therapeutics. This approach transcends a one-size-fits-all methodology, advocating individualization based on elemental and doshic insights, a precursor to contemporary precision medicine.

30. **A:** The formation of śukra, the culmination of tissue transformation, exemplifies Ayurveda's deep understanding of physiological hierarchies. First-trimester development reflects Ayurveda's emphasis on foundational structures, while the second and third trimesters embody growth and preparation for life. These stages correlate with Ayurveda's broader understanding of life cycles, where nourishment, transformation, and preservation are sequentially emphasized. This cyclic approach encapsulates the synergy between nourishment and functionality, underlining Ayurveda's alignment with biological processes and its unique narrative of growth and vitality within developmental contexts.

31. **A:** Doṣas and guṇas articulate Ayurveda's model of functionality, where qualities like lightness or heaviness govern physiological and psychological processes. Rasāyana therapy reflects rejuvenation's holistic approach, emphasizing longevity through nourishing body and mind. Ojas, the essence of vitality, demonstrates Ayurveda's focus on subtle energy, connecting immunity and vitality as inseparable. Sattva dominance mirrors mental clarity, highlighting the integration of spiritual and psychological wellness. These connections transcend physical boundaries, positioning Ayurveda as an integrative science that harmonizes existential, physical, and psychological domains into a unified health philosophy.

32. **A:** Sattva represents purity and balance, where mental clarity leads to self-awareness, aligning Ayurveda with psychological health frameworks. Rajas signifies activity and dynamism but also reflects tendencies toward restlessness, balancing between progress and instability. Tamas indicates inertia, necessary for grounding but prone to excessive stagnation. The tri-guṇa balance embodies Ayurveda's holistic mental framework, where harmony among these guṇas fosters physical and psychological equilibrium. This triadic model reflects the Ayurvedic belief in balance as the cornerstone of health, offering a nuanced lens to view human behavior and mental wellness.

33. **A:** Pre-conceptional care in Ayurveda prioritizes purification and tissue strengthening, echoing preventive health strategies. Embryological development's triadic model incorporates physical, psychological, and spiritual factors, underscoring Ayurveda's multidimensional approach to life formation. Prakriti's determination during conception links biological predispositions with doshic influences. Postnatal care emphasizes nutrition

and ojas building, creating continuity in Ayurveda's life cycle approach. These stages reflect a journey from potentiality to actuality, demonstrating Ayurveda's deep understanding of human development as a seamless integration of physical, psychological, and spiritual dimensions.

34. A: Srotas, as pathways for transport, mirror physiological circulatory systems but expand into metaphysical realms of energy flow. Dhātus provide structural and functional integrity, maintaining life's stability. Upadhātus reflect secondary yet essential components, linking the main tissues to auxiliary processes. Mala emphasizes waste elimination, balancing input-output cycles. These components illustrate Ayurveda's interconnected view of bodily functions, where systems do not operate in isolation but as interdependent entities, embodying Ayurveda's unique integrative perspective of maintaining homeostasis within the dynamic processes of life.

35. C: The prakṛti of an individual is determined at conception and remains constant throughout life, making it a foundational concept in Ayurveda. It is influenced by genetic material (bīja), maternal health, and the emotional state during pregnancy. However, it is incorrect to claim that prakṛti is shaped solely by genetic factors. The mother's health, diet, and emotions directly affect the foetus, and these influences extend beyond mere genetics, highlighting the interconnectedness of physiological and psychological states. Ayurveda's recognition of these factors demonstrates its integrative perspective, where prakṛti reflects the sum of genetic and prenatal influences, paving the way for personalized health interventions.

36. C: Ayurvedic descriptions of foetal development stages, such as kalala (jelly-like stage) and pesi (flesh development), align with modern embryology's understanding of cellular differentiation and organ formation. While some may interpret these descriptions as symbolic, they are physiologically relevant and grounded in empirical observation. This congruence highlights Ayurveda's sophisticated insights into developmental biology. The claim that these descriptions are entirely symbolic dismisses the depth of Ayurvedic embryology, which accurately describes processes like tissue formation and structural differentiation, reflecting its capacity to integrate science and philosophy seamlessly.

37. A: Kapha prakṛti individuals are known for their calmness and emotional stability, making them less prone to anxiety and mental restlessness. This stability is attributed to the dominance of earth and water elements in kapha, which counteract the light and mobile qualities of vāta. While other prakṛtis exhibit varying degrees of emotional volatility, kapha individuals maintain resilience and a sense of groundedness. This interplay between doshas and elemental qualities illustrates Ayurveda's holistic approach, where mental traits are directly linked to physiological compositions. Understanding these traits allows tailored interventions to enhance emotional and physical balance.

38. C: Maternal health and emotions during pregnancy influence both the prakṛti and mental tendencies of the foetus. While rasa dhātu provides essential nourishment, it is not the sole contributor to foetal development. Emotional factors such as stress or contentment also play a critical role in shaping the psychological and emotional predispositions of the child. Ayurveda recognizes the interconnectedness of maternal well-being and foetal development, emphasizing the importance of creating a balanced and harmonious prenatal environment. This perspective underscores Ayurveda's emphasis on the integration of physical, mental, and emotional health, extending its insights to prenatal care.

39. C: Ayurveda emphasizes the balance of prāṇa (vital force), manas (mind), and ātmā (consciousness) as essential for overall health. Imbalances in these aspects disrupt systemic harmony, affecting both physical and mental well-being. The suggestion that imbalances in these components are strictly physiological overlooks Ayurveda's holistic view, which integrates spiritual and mental health into its framework. This highlights Ayurveda's unique approach, where health is not merely the absence of disease but a dynamic state of equilibrium across physical, mental, and spiritual dimensions. Such integration underscores its enduring relevance in modern integrative medicine.

40. A: The balance of tridosha (vāta, pitta, and kapha) is essential for health, as each dosha governs specific physiological functions. Vāta controls movement, pitta oversees metabolism, and kapha provides structural stability. The reason—that each dosha corresponds to specific organ systems—is the correct explanation, as their collective harmony ensures systemic well-being. Disruption in this balance leads to disease, reflecting Ayurveda's emphasis on preventive care through maintaining doshic equilibrium. This principle reinforces the interconnectedness of bodily functions and their holistic management in Ayurveda, ensuring personalized and comprehensive healthcare.

41. A: Pitta prakṛti individuals are predisposed to heat-related disorders such as acidity and inflammation due to the dominance of the tejas (fire) element. This elemental dominance manifests as heightened metabolic activity and susceptibility to conditions caused by excessive heat. The reason—that the fire element governs pitta—accurately explains this predisposition. Understanding these connections enables Ayurveda to provide targeted interventions, such as cooling diets and lifestyle modifications, to mitigate heat-related imbalances. This doshic framework illustrates Ayurveda's precision in diagnosing and treating health conditions based on individual constitution.

42. **A:** Ayurvedic prenatal care emphasizes the use of herbs like shatavari and amla to support maternal and foetal health. These herbs balance doshas, nourish the growing foetus, and enhance the mother's immunity, ensuring a healthy pregnancy. The reason—that these herbs maintain doshic balance—is the correct explanation, as Ayurveda integrates diet and herbal remedies into its prenatal care framework. This holistic approach reflects its emphasis on creating a nurturing environment for the foetus, addressing both physical and emotional factors to optimize prenatal outcomes. This philosophy resonates with modern approaches to maternal care that prioritize nutrition and stress management.

43. **A:** Balanced prakṛti, although rare, ensures robust immunity and resistance to diseases. This balance reflects equilibrium among the tridoshas, supporting optimal physiological and psychological functioning. The reason—that balanced prakṛti maintains doshic harmony—accurately explains its health benefits, as equilibrium prevents the imbalances that lead to disease. Ayurveda's recognition of this state highlights its preventive focus, aiming to maintain balance rather than merely addressing symptoms. This perspective underscores Ayurveda's relevance in modern health paradigms, promoting wellness through personalized and preventive strategies.

44. **C:** The paṃcamahābhūta theory (five-element theory) is indeed the foundation for understanding the structure and function of śarīra (body) in Ayurveda, making the assertion correct. However, Reason (R) is false because each element contributes differently—not equally—to different body parts and functions. For example, pṛthvī predominates in bones, while āpas in bodily fluids.

45. **A:** The balance of tridosha is central to maintaining health, as each dosha governs vital physiological functions. Seasonal routines (ritucharya) and dietary modifications address the natural shifts in doshic dominance, preventing imbalances. The reason—that seasonal changes affect dosha balance—accurately explains the assertion, as Ayurveda's preventive care aligns lifestyle practices with environmental rhythms. This approach underscores Ayurveda's focus on dynamic equilibrium, reflecting its ability to integrate external and internal influences into personalized healthcare strategies. This principle remains relevant in modern wellness practices that emphasize circadian and seasonal alignment.

46. **A:** Prakṛti is shaped by genetic material (bīja), maternal health, and emotional state during pregnancy. These factors collectively determine an individual's physical, mental, and emotional constitution, remaining constant throughout life. Postnatal factors influence health but do not alter the inherent prakṛti. Ayurveda's recognition of the interplay between genetic and prenatal influences demonstrates its integrative perspective, addressing the root causes of health variations. This holistic understanding forms the basis of personalized medicine, ensuring interventions that align with individual constitutions for optimal outcomes.

47. **C:** Vāta prakṛti individuals are characterized by creativity, quick thinking, and adaptability, but they are also prone to anxiety, irregular digestion, and cold intolerance. These traits arise from the dominance of vāyu (air) and ākāśa (space), which confer lightness and mobility. While these qualities foster mental agility, they also contribute to physiological instability. Ayurveda's categorization of prakṛti enables targeted interventions to address such tendencies, reflecting its emphasis on balancing the inherent traits of each dosha for overall well-being.

48. **B:** Modern research validates the Ayurvedic concept of prakṛti by correlating doshic dominance with genomic and metabolic profiles. For instance, pitta prakṛti individuals exhibit heightened enzymatic activity, aligning with their metabolic traits. These findings bridge Ayurveda's ancient insights with contemporary science, emphasizing the physiological basis of dosha-based classifications. This validation highlights Ayurveda's relevance in precision medicine, where personalized approaches to health care reflect its foundational principles. The integration of traditional wisdom with modern research reinforces Ayurveda's role in advancing holistic and personalized healthcare solutions.

49. **B:** Sattva is associated with mental clarity, balance, and purity, reflecting psychological tendencies that promote harmony and emotional stability. Ayurveda links this quality to an individual's capacity for rational thinking

and self-awareness, emphasizing its role in maintaining mental health. The dominance of sattva supports resilience against stress and emotional disturbances, aligning with Ayurveda's focus on holistic well-being. This perspective integrates mental and physical health, demonstrating the system's depth in addressing the interdependence of psychological and physiological states for achieving comprehensive health.

50. C: Ayurveda integrates prevention into its approach by aligning lifestyle practices like dinacharya (daily routines) and ritucharya (seasonal regimens) with individual doshic balance. These practices mitigate seasonal imbalances and support long-term health, reflecting Ayurveda's preventive focus. Unlike standardized approaches, Ayurveda tailors interventions to align with prakṛti, ensuring personalized care. This dynamic integration of lifestyle and constitution emphasizes Ayurveda's holistic philosophy, offering strategies that address root causes rather than merely managing symptoms. This preventive approach resonates with modern wellness paradigms, prioritizing balance and adaptability for sustained well-being.

CHAPTER–9

DOSA, DHATU, MALA, AGNI, AND SROTAS ESSENTIALS

Ayurveda, the ancient Indian system of medicine, provides a holistic framework for understanding the human body. The intricate interplay of fundamental concepts such as doṣas (biological energies), dhātus (tissues), mala (waste), agni (digestive fire), and srotas (channels) underpins the Ayurvedic approach to health, disease, and treatment. These elements function together to maintain balance within the body, emphasizing harmony between the physical, mental, and spiritual aspects of an individual. This chapter delves deeply into each of these essentials, exploring their roles, interrelationships, and significance in the Ayurvedic paradigm.

Concepts and Functions of the Three Doṣas (Vāta, Pitta, and Kapha)

The tridoṣa theory forms the foundation of Ayurvedic physiology, pathology, and therapeutics. The doṣas—vāta, pitta, and kapha—are dynamic forces derived from the five great elements (pañcamahābhūta). These energies regulate every physiological and psychological process in the body.

1. **Vāta**: Vāta is primarily composed of the ākāśa (space) and vāyu (air) elements. It governs all movement and communication within the body and mind. Functions of vāta include:
   - Facilitating motor activities and nerve impulses.
   - Regulating respiration, circulation, and elimination processes.
   - Enabling sensory perception and mental functions such as creativity and quick decision-making.

   When in balance, vāta promotes vitality and flexibility. However, its imbalance leads to disorders such as anxiety, constipation, and joint issues.

2. **Pitta**: Pitta is a combination of the tejas (fire) and āpas (water) elements. It governs transformation processes, including metabolism and enzymatic activity. Key functions of pitta are:
   - Digesting food and assimilating nutrients.
   - Regulating body temperature and skin health.
   - Governing intellect, determination, and courage.

   Balanced pitta supports digestion, sharp intellect, and emotional stability. Imbalanced pitta results in conditions like hyperacidity, inflammation, and anger.

3. **Kapha**: Kapha derives from pṛthvī (earth) and āpas (water). It provides structural integrity and lubrication. Functions of kapha include:
   - Maintaining stability, endurance, and immunity.
   - Lubricating joints and tissues.
   - Governing calmness, patience, and emotional stability.

A balanced kapha fosters strength and resilience, while an imbalance may lead to lethargy, obesity, or congestion.

Interactions Among Doṣas

The tridoṣa interact dynamically, maintaining homeostasis. For instance, while pitta transforms food into energy, vāta facilitates its distribution, and kapha provides structural support. Any disruption in their balance causes disease, requiring Ayurvedic interventions such as dietary changes, lifestyle adjustments, and herbal remedies.

Dhātus (Body Tissues) and Their Roles

The term dhātu refers to the seven fundamental tissues that sustain the body. Each dhātu plays a unique role in maintaining physiological integrity and supports the subsequent tissue in the nourishment process.

1. **Rasa Dhātu (Plasma)**
   - Derived from digested food, it nourishes all tissues.
   - Maintains hydration and circulation.
   - Imbalance leads to dehydration, lethargy, or immune deficiencies.
2. **Rakta Dhātu (Blood)**
   - Supports oxygen transport and vitality.
   - Governs complexion and enthusiasm.
   - Disorders include anemia, skin issues, and circulatory problems.
3. **Māṃsa Dhātu (Muscle)**
   - Provides structural strength and mobility.
   - Supports physical endurance and joint stability.
   - Imbalance manifests as muscle weakness or overgrowth.
4. **Meda Dhātu (Fat)**
   - Acts as an energy reserve and provides lubrication.
   - Cushions organs and supports hormonal balance.
   - Excess leads to obesity, while deficiency results in fatigue.
5. **Asthi Dhātu (Bone)**
   - Provides the framework for the body.
   - Protects vital organs and supports movement.
   - Imbalances result in brittle bones or deformities.
6. **Majjā Dhātu (Bone Marrow and Nerve Tissue)**
   - Fills bone cavities and nourishes the nervous system.
   - Governs cognitive functions and sensory perception.
   - Disorders include neuropathy and cognitive decline.
7. **Śukra Dhātu (Reproductive Tissue)**
   - Ensures reproductive health and vitality.
   - Governs creativity and emotional strength.
   - Disorders include infertility or hormonal imbalances.

Dhātu Metabolism (Dhātu Paka):

- Each dhātu is nourished by the previous tissue, with the digestive fire (agni) mediating this transformation. Imbalances in any tissue affect the entire chain, emphasizing the importance of maintaining metabolic harmony.

Mala (Waste) and Agni (Digestive Fire) in Health and Disease

1. **Mala (Waste Products)**
   - The body produces waste as a byproduct of metabolic activities. Proper elimination of mala ensures health, while its accumulation leads to diseases.

   Primary Malas:
   - **Purīṣa (feces):** Regulates elimination and gut health.
   - **Mutra (urine):** Balances fluid levels and eliminates toxins.
   - **Sveda (sweat):** Regulates body temperature and detoxifies.
   - **Secondary Malas:** Include hair, nails, and other waste products that indicate metabolic health.
   - Efficient elimination requires balanced vāta, which governs movement, and optimal agni, ensuring waste processing.
2. **Agni (Digestive Fire)**: Agni is central to Ayurveda, governing digestion, metabolism, and cellular transformation. Four types of agni are recognized:
   - **Jatharagni:** Governs the digestion of food in the stomach.
   - **Bhutagni:** Manages the transformation of elemental nutrients.
   - **Dhātvagni:** Regulates the metabolism of tissues.

   Functions of Agni:
   - Digesting and assimilating food.
   - Supporting immunity by eliminating toxins (ama).
   - Providing energy and vitality.

   Imbalances of Agni:
   - **Mandagni (weak digestion):** Causes indigestion and toxin accumulation.
   - **Tikshnagni (hyper digestion):** Leads to excessive hunger and tissue depletion.
   - **Vishamagni (irregular digestion):** Associated with vāta disorders like bloating.
   - **Samagni (balanced digestion):** Reflects health and harmony.
   - Restoring agni involves dietary adjustments, herbal formulations, and detoxification therapies like panchakarma.

Srotas (Body Channels) and Their Physiological Importance

Srotas (Body Channels) and Their Physiological Importance in Ayurveda

The concept of Srotas (body channels) is fundamental in Ayurvedic anatomy and physiology, representing the intricate network of pathways that sustain life. These channels facilitate the flow of vital substances such as nutrients, energy, waste, and bodily fluids. Their proper functioning is essential for maintaining health, while blockages or dysfunctions lead to disease. Ayurveda considers the Srotas system as a dynamic interplay between structure and function, connecting physical and subtle aspects of the human body.

(I) Understanding the Concept of Srotas

1. **Definition and Meaning**: The term Srotas is derived from the Sanskrit root "Sru," meaning "to flow." In Ayurveda, Srotas refers to:
   - Channels, ducts, or vessels that allow the flow of substances within the body.
   - Both physical structures (like blood vessels) and subtle pathways (like energy channels).
2. **Characteristics of Srotas**
   - **Porous and Permeable:** Allow exchange and movement of substances.
   - **Diverse in Nature:** Ranging from microscopic channels to macroscopic pathways.
   - **Interconnected:** Form a cohesive network that links all bodily systems.
3. **Importance of Srotas in Ayurveda**: The Srotas system is vital for:
   - **Sustaining Life:** Enabling the transport of essential nutrients and removal of waste.
   - **Maintaining Balance:** Supporting the functions of doshas, dhātus (tissues), and malas (waste products).
   - **Disease Diagnosis:** Understanding disruptions in Srotas helps identify the root causes of illness.
4. **Classification of Srotas:** Srotas are classified based on:
   - **Origin and Structure:** Tissues or organs associated with their function.
   - **Substance Transported:** Nutrients, energy, or waste.
   - **Location:** Physical channels or subtle pathways.

(II) Types of Srotas in Ayurveda

Ayurveda identifies 13 primary Srotas, which can be broadly categorized into:

1. **Prāṇa Vaha Srotas (Channels for Vital Energy):**
   - Carry oxygen and life force.
   - **Origin:** Heart and respiratory system.
   - **Function:** Facilitate breathing and energy flow.
2. **Anna Vaha Srotas (Channels for Food):**
   - Carry ingested food.
   - Origin: Stomach and esophagus.
   - **Function:** Transport food for digestion.
3. **Udaka Vaha Srotas (Channels for Water):**
   - Transport water and maintain hydration.
   - **Origin:** Palate and pancreas.
   - **Function:** Distribute water throughout the body.
4. **Rasa Vaha Srotas (Channels for Plasma):**
   - Distribute nutrients from digested food.
   - **Origin:** Heart and blood vessels.
   - **Function:** Nourish tissues.
5. **Rakta Vaha Srotas (Channels for Blood):**
   - Circulate blood.
   - **Origin:** Liver and spleen.
   - **Function:** Oxygenate tissues.
6. **Māṃsa Vaha Srotas (Channels for Muscle Tissue):**
   - Nourish muscle tissue.
   - **Origin:** Tendons and ligaments.
   - **Function:** Support physical strength.
7. **Meda Vaha Srotas (Channels for Fat Tissue):**
   - Transport and store fat.
   - **Origin:** Kidneys and omentum.
   - **Function:** Provide lubrication and energy reserves.
8. **Asthi Vaha Srotas (Channels for Bone Tissue):**
   - Nourish and maintain bones.
   - **Origin:** Thigh bones and joints.
   - **Function:** Support structural integrity.
9. **Majjā Vaha Srotas (Channels for Bone Marrow):**
   - Transport bone marrow.
   - **Origin:** Bones and nervous tissue.
   - **Function:** Support the nervous system and blood cell production.
10. **Shukra Vaha Srotas (Channels for Reproductive Tissue):**
    - Carry reproductive fluids.
    - **Origin:** Testes and ovaries.
    - **Function:** Facilitate reproduction.

11. **Mutra Vaha Srotas (Channels for Urine):**
   - Excrete liquid waste.
   - **Origin:** Kidneys and bladder.
   - **Function:** Regulate fluid balance.
12. **Purīṣa Vaha Srotas (Channels for Feces):**
   - Eliminate solid waste.
   - **Origin:** Colon.
   - **Function:** Remove undigested food
13. **Sveda Vaha Srotas (Channels for Sweat):**
   - Excrete sweat
   - **Origin:** Sweat glands.
   - **Function:** Regulate body temperature.

Specialized Srotas: Subtle Pathways

In addition to physical channels, Ayurveda recognizes subtle Srotas:

- Manovaha Srotas (Mind Channels).
- Facilitate thought and emotions.
- Connect the mind with the body.
- Nāḍīs (Energy Channels).

Carry prāṇa (life energy) and regulate subtle energy flow.

(III) Structure and Function of Srotas

1. **Structural Features:** Srotas are composed of tissues and organs designed to:
   - **Facilitate Flow:** Allow the unimpeded movement of substances.
   - **Regulate Exchange:** Permit selective absorption and excretion.
   - **Adapt to Stress:** Expand or contract based on physiological needs.
2. **Physiological Functions**

   (a) Transport:
   - Carry essential substances like oxygen, nutrients, and hormones.
   - Facilitate waste elimination.

   (b) Regulation:
   - Maintain balance in doshas, dhātus, and malas
   - Support temperature, hydration, and metabolic processes.

   (c) Communication:
   - Link various body systems, enabling coordinated responses.
   - Facilitate mind-body integration.

(IV) Role of Srotas in Health

1. **Balanced Flow**
   - Optimal health depends on the smooth functioning of Srotas.
   - Balanced Srotas ensure proper nourishment, detoxification, and energy flow.
2. **Preventive Health**
   - Regular maintenance of Srotas through diet, lifestyle, and therapies prevents disease.
   - Practices like yoga, pranayama, and meditation enhance subtle Srotas.

(V) Pathology of Srotas

1. **Types of Srotas Disorders**

   (a) Blockages (Sanga):
   - Caused by toxins (ama), poor diet, or stress.
   - Lead to reduced flow and accumulation of substances.

   (b) Overflow (Ati Pravṛtti):
   - Excess flow due to dosha aggravation or organ dysfunction.
   - Results in diarrhea, excessive sweating, or bleeding.

   (c) Diversion (Vimarga Gamana):
   - Misrouting of substances due to structural damage.
   - Causes abnormal growths or internal bleeding.

   (d) Weakness (Kshaya):
   - Insufficient function due to degeneration or malnourishment.
   - Results in tissue depletion and weakness.
2. **Common Causes of Srotas Disorders**
   - **Poor Diet:** Excessive heavy, oily, or processed foods.
   - **Stress:** Emotional or mental strain affects subtle channels.
   - **Lifestyle Imbalances:** Sedentary habits or overexertion.
   - **Toxins:** Accumulation of ama disrupts flow.

(VI) Therapeutic Approaches for Srotas Health

1. **Detoxification (Shodhana)**: Panchakarma: Comprehensive detox therapies, including:
   - **Vamana (emesis):** Removes toxins from upper channels.
   - **Virechana (purgation):** Cleanses lower channels.
   - **Basti (enema):** Clears colon and restores balance.
   - **Nasya (nasal therapy):** Opens subtle pathways
2. **Nourishment (Shamana)**
   - **Dietary Adjustments:** Foods tailored to dosha and Srotas needs.

- **Herbal Remedies:** Strengthen and cleanse channels.

3. **Lifestyle Practices**
   - **Yoga and Exercise:** Enhance circulation and flexibility.
   - **Meditation and Pranayama:** Activate subtle energy channels.

(VII) Integration of Srotas in Modern Health

1. **Diagnostic Relevance**
   - Understanding Srotas offers insights into systemic disorders.
   - Guides holistic treatment strategies.
2. **Complementary Practices**
   - Integrates well with modern medicine for chronic conditions.
   - Supports wellness and preventive care.

The concept of Srotas highlights Ayurveda's holistic understanding of the body as a network of interconnected channels. By maintaining the health of Srotas, Ayurveda ensures balanced physiological, psychological, and subtle processes, offering a comprehensive pathway to well-being. Through diet, lifestyle, and therapies, Srotas health is both a preventive and therapeutic focus, underscoring its central role in Ayurvedic practice.

MULTIPLE CHOICE QUESTIONS

1. The concept of Tridosha is pivotal in Ayurveda, encompassing Vata, Pitta, and Kapha. These doshas represent dynamic forces influencing physiological, psychological, and biochemical functions. Imagine a physician observing a patient with symptoms such as dry skin, anxiety, and erratic bowel movements, who attributes these to an aggravated Vata dosha. The physician administers a combination of oils and warm foods, recommending lifestyle changes such as regulated sleep patterns. Which of the following Ayurvedic principles does this intervention align with?
   A. Restoration of Pitta dominance to counterbalance Vata.
   B. Strengthening of Kapha to stabilize bodily functions.
   C. Pacification of Vata through unctuous and warm substances.
   D. Balancing of all three doshas simultaneously through dietary restrictions.
2. Agni, regarded as the digestive fire in Ayurveda, governs not only digestion but also metabolic efficiency and immune responses. A study comparing individuals with strong Agni to those with "Mandagni" found that the latter group displayed symptoms such as lethargy, poor digestion, and frequent infections. Which of the following is the most accurate explanation for this observation?
   A. Mandagni leads to poor nutrient absorption and increased susceptibility to toxins (Ama).
   B. Weak Agni causes excessive metabolic activity, depleting energy reserves.
   C. Strong Agni promotes the dominance of Pitta, resulting in optimal immune function.
   D. Digestive fire primarily influences psychological states, not physical immunity.
3. Srotas, the bodily channels, are critical for the transport of nutrients and waste. A researcher identifies a disruption in the "Rasa Vaha Srotas" leading to symptoms such as edema, fatigue, and compromised immunity. Which Ayurvedic diagnostic perspective best explains this disruption?
   A. Imbalance of Pitta dosha causing excessive heat and fluid retention.
   B. Blockage of Kapha in the channels, leading to stagnation and fluid accumulation.
   C. Excessive Vata aggravation, drying up the channels and impairing circulation.
   D. Deficiency in Dhatus resulting from weak digestive fire, leading to compromised Srotas function.
4. An individual presenting with inflammatory symptoms such as redness, swelling, and heat is assessed by an Ayurvedic practitioner. The practitioner concludes that the symptoms indicate an aggravated Pitta dosha and prescribes cooling herbs and dietary changes. Based on Ayurvedic principles, what is the likely reasoning behind this treatment?
   A. Aggravated Pitta causes metabolic overload, necessitating detoxification.
   B. Cooling herbs directly pacify Vata dosha to counter inflammation.
   C. The balance of Kapha is disrupted, leading to increased Pitta dominance.
   D. Pitta's fiery nature is reduced by cooling and soothing substances.
5. Consider an Ayurvedic scholar analyzing Dhatu formation, beginning with Rasa and culminating in Ojas, the essence of immunity and vitality. The scholar argues that impaired transformation at any stage leads

to systemic dysfunction. Which of the following statements best reflects this concept?

A. Each Dhatu exists independently and is unaffected by the preceding stage.

B. Impaired Rasa formation directly compromises Ojas, skipping intermediary Dhatus.

C. The sequential transformation of Dhatus is interdependent and reliant on Agni.

D. Mala production at each stage is irrelevant to Dhatu health and vitality.

6. A group of researchers explore the concept of Ama, which Ayurveda defines as a toxic byproduct of incomplete digestion. They find that individuals with Ama accumulation show higher markers of systemic inflammation. Which conclusion best aligns with Ayurvedic theory?

A. Ama results solely from external toxins and has no internal metabolic origin.

B. Accumulation of Ama disrupts doshic balance, leading to disease manifestation.

C. Ama is unrelated to digestive fire and is a psychological construct in Ayurveda.

D. Modern inflammation markers validate the symbolic significance of Ama.

7. The Mala (waste products) in Ayurveda include Purisha (feces), Mutra (urine), and Sveda (sweat). A clinical observation notes impaired excretion in patients with aggravated Kapha dosha. What is the most plausible Ayurvedic explanation for this phenomenon?

A. Kapha's cold and heavy nature obstructs Srotas, impeding waste elimination.

B. Pitta's heat exacerbates Kapha imbalance, causing waste retention.

C. Excess Vata causes hyperactivity in waste production, overwhelming the channels.

D. Weak digestive fire prevents the proper formation of waste products.

8. Kapha dosha, responsible for structure and stability, is often associated with diseases marked by excess mucus and weight gain. Which of the following regimens would be most appropriate for pacifying Kapha in an individual with these symptoms?

A. A diet rich in sweet, unctuous foods to stabilize Kapha.

B. Dry, warm, and light foods combined with vigorous exercise.

C. Cooling substances to counteract Kapha's warmth and heaviness.

D. Sedentary activities to balance Kapha's dynamic tendencies.

9. Vata dosha, characterized by movement and dryness, is linked to neurological functions in Ayurveda. A patient presenting with anxiety, insomnia, and constipation is diagnosed with Vata aggravation. What type of treatment aligns with Ayurvedic principles?

A. Warm, oily foods and regular routines to calm Vata's erratic nature.

B. Bitter and astringent substances to directly counter Vata's dryness.

C. Cooling herbs and fasting to reduce Vata's excessive activity.

D. High-protein diets to enhance Vata's energy and stability.

10. Pitta, governing heat and transformation, often manifests in skin disorders such as rashes and acne when aggravated. A dermatologist collaborating with an Ayurvedic expert investigates herbal interventions. Which Ayurvedic principle would most likely inform their therapeutic strategy?

A. Balancing Vata to prevent overactivity in Pitta.

B. Enhancing Agni to neutralize Pitta-related toxins.

C. Applying cooling and anti-inflammatory agents to pacify Pitta.

D. Increasing Kapha to stabilize Pitta's fiery tendencies.

Directions (Q. No. 11-14): *Scenario-Based Questions*

SCENARIO 1

A researcher investigates the impact of impaired digestive fire (Agni) on Dhatu formation and subsequent tissue vitality. The study identifies a correlation between weak Agni and deficiencies in bone tissue (Asthi Dhatu), causing brittle bones and joint pain. The researcher concludes that enhancing Agni could improve tissue health.

SCENARIO 2

Simultaneously, another researcher examines environmental stressors impacting soil nutrients, leading to reduced potency in herbal formulations that stimulate Agni. Poor soil quality, it is noted, diminishes the efficacy of Ayurvedic treatments designed to enhance metabolic efficiency and tissue health.

11. What mechanism explains the role of weak Agni in the deficiencies of Asthi Dhatu described in Scenario 1?

A. Weak Agni directly leads to the dominance of Kapha dosha, weakening bones.

B. Impaired Agni interrupts the nourishment chain from Rasa to Asthi Dhatu.

C. The presence of Ama obstructs nutrient absorption at the level of Asthi.

D. Weak Agni impacts Rakta Dhatu exclusively, indirectly affecting bones.

12. How does reduced herbal potency described in Scenario 2 impact the therapeutic goals of Scenario 1?
    A. Herbs play no role in enhancing Agni, making environmental stressors irrelevant.
    B. Reduced potency compromises Agni restoration, delaying Dhatu rejuvenation.
    C. Poor herb quality enhances Kapha, mitigating the effects of weak Agni.
    D. Environmental stressors improve herb concentration, indirectly aiding therapy.

13. Which integrated approach best addresses the challenges posed by both scenarios?
    A. Developing soil enrichment techniques to restore herb potency while enhancing Agni.
    B. Discontinuing the use of herbal formulations and focusing solely on dietary changes.
    C. Prioritizing modern synthetic alternatives over compromised Ayurvedic treatments.
    D. Addressing bone health through exclusive focus on mineral supplementation.

14. How do the findings of the two researchers collectively enhance the understanding of Ayurvedic treatment efficacy?
    A. They validate that weak Agni impacts only digestive health, unrelated to tissue vitality.
    B. They highlight the interdependence of environmental sustainability and Ayurvedic efficacy.
    C. They confirm that herbal quality does not influence Agni or Dhatu formation.
    D. They suggest that modern science invalidates Ayurvedic perspectives on health.

15. The principles of Ayurveda link doshas to body functions:
    (a) Vāta governs motion and nerve impulses.
    (b) Pitta regulates metabolism and transformation.
    (c) Kapha maintains structure and fluid balance.

    Choose the correct answer from the options given below:
    A. (a) and (b) only
    B. (b) and (c) only
    C. (a), (b), and (c)
    D. (a) and (c) only

16. The biological actions of Agni in Ayurveda include:
    (a) Digesting and assimilating food.
    (b) Supporting immunity by eliminating ama (toxins).
    (c) Regulating the metabolism of dhātus (tissues).

    Choose the correct answer from the options given below:
    A. (a) and (b) only
    B. (b) and (c) only
    C. (a), (b), and (c)
    D. (a) and (c) only

17. The physiological functions of srotas include:
    (a) Transporting nutrients to tissues.
    (b) Eliminating waste products.
    (c) Facilitating the flow of energy and consciousness.

    Choose the correct answer from the options given below:
    A. (a) and (b) only
    B. (a), (b), and (c)
    C. (b) and (c) only
    D. (a) and (c) only

18. Which of the following accurately describe kapha prakṛti characteristics?
    (a) Tendency for weight gain and fluid retention.
    (b) Emotional stability and calm demeanor.
    (c) Strong immunity but sluggish digestion.

    Choose the correct answer from the options given below:
    A. (a) and (b) only
    B. (a), (b), and (c)
    C. (b) and (c) only
    D. (a) and (c) only

19. The stages of foetal development in Ayurveda include:
    (a) Kalala (jelly-like mass).
    (b) Budbuda (bubble-like stage).
    (c) Pesi (flesh formation).

    Choose the correct answer from the options given below:
    A. (a) and (b) only
    B. (b) and (c) only
    C. (a) and (c) only
    D. (a), (b), and (c)

20. Functions of mala (waste products) in Ayurveda include:
    (a) Maintaining systemic balance through elimination.
    (b) Protecting tissues from the effects of toxins.
    (c) Facilitating the flow of nutrients in the body.

    Choose the correct answer from the options given below:
    A. (a) and (b) only
    B. (b) and (c) only
    C. (a), (b), and (c)
    D. (a) and (c) only

21. Types of digestive fire (agni) and their characteristics:
    (a) **Samagni:** Balanced digestion and assimilation.
    (b) **Mandagni:** Slow digestion, leading to toxin buildup.
    (c) **Tikshnagni:** Hyper digestion with tissue depletion.

Choose the correct answer from the options given below:
A. (a) and (b) only
B. (b) and (c) only
C. (a), (b), and (c)
D. (a) and (c) only

22. Identify the correct relationships between dhātus and their functions:
(a) **Meda (fat tissue):** Provides lubrication and energy storage.
(b) **Asthi (bone tissue):** Offers structural support and protection.
(c) **Rakta (blood tissue):** Carries oxygen and nutrients.

Choose the correct answer from the options given below:
A. (a) and (b) only
B. (b) and (c) only
C. (a), (b), and (c)
D. (a) and (c) only

23. Which of the following statements about vāta dosha are true?
(a) It governs movement and nerve impulses.
(b) It is composed of ākāśa (space) and vāyu (air).
(c) Imbalance leads to anxiety and dryness.

Choose the correct answer from the options given below:
A. (a) and (b) only
B. (b) and (c) only
C. (a), (b), and (c)
D. (a) and (c) only

24. The therapeutic significance of triphala in Ayurveda includes:
(a) Cleansing the digestive tract and removing toxins.
(b) Nourishing all seven dhātus through balanced action.
(c) Supporting the health of srotas by preventing blockages.

Choose the correct answer from the options given below:
A. (a) and (b) only
B. (b) and (c) only
C. (a), (b), and (c)
D. (a) and (c) only

25. Match List–I (Doṣas) with List–II (Primary Functions):

List–I	List–II
(a) Vāta	1. Governs movement and communication in the body
(b) Pitta	2. Regulates metabolism and heat generation
(c) Kapha	3. Provides structural support and stability

Choose the correct answer from the options given below:
A. (a)-1, (b)-2, (c)-3
B. (a)-3, (b)-1, (c)-2
C. (a)-2, (b)-3, (c)-1
D. (a)-1, (b)-3, (c)-2

26. Match List–I (Dhātus) with List–II (Primary Roles):

List–I	List–II
(a) Rasa	1. Nourishes all body tissues
(b) Rakta	2. Carries oxygen and supports vitality
(c) Meda	3. Lubricates joints and stores energy
(d) Asthi	4. Provides structural framework and stability

Choose the correct answer from the options given below:
A. (a)-1, (b)-2, (c)-3, (d)-4
B. (a)-2, (b)-3, (c)-1, (d)-4
C. (a)-4, (b)-1, (c)-2, (d)-3
D. (a)-1, (b)-3, (c)-4, (d)-2

27. Match List–I (Mala) with List–II (Primary Roles):

List–I	List–II
(a) Purīṣa	1. Facilitates fecal elimination and gut health
(b) Mutra	2. Removes soluble toxins and hydrates the body
(c) Sveda	3. Expels metabolic waste through sweat
(d) Ama	4. Represents toxic undigested substances in the body

Choose the correct answer from the options given below:
A. (a)-1, (b)-2, (c)-3, (d)-4
B. (a)-3, (b)-1, (c)-2, (d)-4
C. (a)-2, (b)-3, (c)-1, (d)-4
D. (a)-4, (b)-2, (c)-3, (d)-1

28. Match List–I (Agni Types) with List–II (Functions):

List–I	List–II
(a) Jatharagni	1. Manages digestion of food and initial metabolic processes
(b) Dhātvagni	2. Governs tissue metabolism at the cellular level
(c) Bhūtāgni	3. Regulates transformation of elemental substances
(d) Pachakagni	4. Aids assimilation of nutrients in the body

Choose the correct answer from the options given below:
A. (a)-1, (b)-2, (c)-3, (d)-4
B. (a)-2, (b)-1, (c)-3, (d)-4
C. (a)-3, (b)-2, (c)-1, (d)-4
D. (a)-1, (b)-3, (c)-4, (d)-2

29. Match List–I (Prakṛti Types) with List–II (Characteristics):

List–I	List–II
(a) Vāta Prakṛti	1. Creative, quick-moving, prone to anxiety
(b) Pitta Prakṛti	2. Fiery, determined, prone to heat-related issues
(c) Kapha Prakṛti	3. Calm, steady, prone to weight gain
(d) Sama Prakṛti	4. Balanced physical, mental, and emotional characteristics

Choose the correct answer from the options given below:

A. (a)-1, (b)-2, (c)-3, (d)-4
B. (a)-2, (b)-3, (c)-1, (d)-4
C. (a)-4, (b)-3, (c)-2, (d)-1
D. (a)-1, (b)-4, (c)-2, (d)-3

30. Match List–I (Srotas Types) with List–II (Functions):

List–I	List–II
(a) Annavaha Srotas	1. Facilitates food digestion and absorption
(b) Rasavaha Srotas	2. Transports plasma and digested nutrients
(c) Mutravaha Srotas	3. Governs the elimination of urine
(d) Pranavaha Srotas	4. Supports respiratory functions

Choose the correct answer from the options given below:

A. (a)-1, (b)-2, (c)-3, (d)-4
B. (a)-2, (b)-1, (c)-3, (d)-4
C. (a)-3, (b)-4, (c)-1, (d)-2
D. (a)-4, (b)-3, (c)-2, (d)-1

31. Match List–I (Stages of Agni Imbalance) with List–II (Symptoms):

List–I	List–II
(a) Mandagni	1. Weak digestion, toxin buildup, and bloating
(b) Tikshnagni	2. Hyperactive digestion, excessive hunger, and acidity
(c) Vishamagni	3. Irregular digestion, fluctuating appetite, and gas
(d) Samagni	4. Balanced digestion and metabolic efficiency

Choose the correct answer from the options given below:

A. (a)-1, (b)-2, (c)-3, (d)-4
B. (a)-3, (b)-1, (c)-2, (d)-4
C. (a)-2, (b)-3, (c)-1, (d)-4
D. (a)-1, (b)-3, (c)-2, (d)-4

32. Match List–I (Tridosha and Elements) with List–II (Dominant Elements):

List–I	List–II
(a) Vāta Dosha	1. Air and Space
(b) Pitta Dosha	2. Fire and Water
(c) Kapha Dosha	3. Earth and Water
(d) Tridoshic	4. Equilibrium of all five elements

Choose the correct answer from the options given below:

A. (a)-1, (b)-2, (c)-3, (d)-4
B. (a)-2, (b)-3, (c)-1, (d)-4
C. (a)-3, (b)-1, (c)-2, (d)-4
D. (a)-1, (b)-3, (c)-2, (d)-4

33. Match List–I (Digestive Fire) with List–II (Characteristics):

List–I	List–II
(a) Samagni	1. Balanced digestion and metabolic efficiency
(b) Mandagni	2. Weak digestion with sluggish metabolism
(c) Tikshnagni	3. Hyper digestion with tissue depletion
(d) Vishamagni	4. Irregular digestion, fluctuating appetite, and gas

Choose the correct answer from the options given below:

A. (a)-1, (b)-2, (c)-3, (d)-4
B. (a)-3, (b)-1, (c)-2, (d)-4
C. (a)-2, (b)-3, (c)-1, (d)-4
D. (a)-1, (b)-3, (c)-2, (d)-4

34. Match List–I (Primary Dosha Imbalances) with List–II (Diseases):

List–I	List–II
(a) Vāta Imbalance	1. Dry skin, constipation, anxiety
(b) Pitta Imbalance	2. Hyperacidity, inflammation, rashes
(c) Kapha Imbalance	3. Obesity, congestion, lethargy
(d) Tridosha Imbalance	4. Systemic disorders with multiple symptoms

Choose the correct answer from the options given below:

A. (a)-1, (b)-2, (c)-3, (d)-4
B. (a)-2, (b)-1, (c)-3, (d)-4
C. (a)-3, (b)-1, (c)-2, (d)-4
D. (a)-1, (b)-3, (c)-2, (d)-4

Directions (Q. No. 35–39): *Following questions are based on Statement 1 and Statement 2. Read both the statements carefully and choose the correct answer from the options given below*:

A. Both Statement 1 and Statement 2 are true, and Statement 2 is the correct explanation of Statement 1.
B. Both Statement 1 and Statement 2 are true, but Statement 2 is not the correct explanation of Statement 1.
C. Statement 1 is true, but Statement 2 is false.
D. Statement 1 is false, but Statement 2 is true.
E. Both Statement 1 and Statement 2 are false.

35. Statement 1: The tridoṣa framework in Ayurveda explains the physiological, psychological, and biochemical functions of the body.

Statement 2: Each dosha is equally dominant in every individual, ensuring balance by default.

36. Statement 1: Agni is the primary force responsible for metabolism in Ayurveda and governs the transformation of food into energy.

Statement 2: Imbalances in agni lead to the formation of ama (toxins), which Ayurveda identifies as the root cause of many diseases.

37. Statement 1: The seven dhātus in Ayurveda correspond to tissues that provide structural and functional support to the body.

Statement 2: An imbalance in any dhātu affects its subsequent tissue, as they are nourished sequentially through the digestive process.

38. Statement 1: Srotas are channels in the body responsible for the transportation of nutrients, energy, and waste.

Statement 2: Blockages in srotas occur only when pitta dosha is aggravated.

39. Statement 1: The waste products (mala) in Ayurveda, such as sweat, urine, and feces, are essential for maintaining bodily equilibrium.

Statement 2: Proper elimination of mala depends entirely on the health of kapha dosha.

Directions (Q. No. 40–45): *There are two statements in each question. One is labelled as Assertion (A) and the other is as Reason (R). Read both the statements and choose the correct answer from the options given below*:

A. Both Assertion (A) and Reason (R) are true, and Reason (R) is the correct explanation of Assertion (A).
B. Both Assertion (A) and Reason (R) are true, but Reason (R) is not the correct explanation of Assertion (A).
C. Assertion (A) is true, but Reason (R) is false.
D. Assertion (A) is false, but Reason (R) is true.
E. Both Assertion (A) and Reason (R) are false.

40. Assertion (A): Vata is considered the primary dosha responsible for movement in the body, including the circulation of blood and neural impulses.

Reason (R): Vata's imbalance can disrupt other doshas, leading to a cascade of health issues.

41. Assertion (A): Pitta governs digestion and metabolism, and its imbalance can result in acidity and inflammation.

Reason (R): Pitta imbalance affects the body's ability to process nutrients and eliminates waste effectively.

42. Assertion (A): Kapha provides lubrication and stability in the body, ensuring joint and tissue health.

Reason (R): Kapha imbalance leads to conditions like stiffness, lethargy, and excessive mucus production.

43. Assertion (A): Proper functioning of Agni is essential for the assimilation of nutrients and elimination of toxins.

Reason (R): Weak Agni can lead to the formation of Ama, which blocks the body's channels and disrupts cellular functions.

44. Assertion (A): Dhātus represent the body's structural and functional units, and their balance ensures optimal health.

Reason (R): Imbalance in any dhātu disrupts the flow of prana, leading to diseases like anemia, obesity, or fatigue.

45. Assertion (A): Srotas serve as channels for transporting nutrients and waste across the body.

Reason (R): Blockage in Srotas leads to diseases like hypertension, constipation, and kidney disorders.

Directions (Q. No. 46–50): *Read the passage carefully and answer the questions given below*:

In Ayurveda, the concept of srotas, or body channels, represents one of the fundamental frameworks for understanding human physiology and its connection to health and disease. Derived from the Sanskrit root "sru," meaning "to flow," the term encapsulates the dynamic movement of nutrients, energy, and waste through the body. These channels are both physical and subtle, ensuring the smooth operation of biological and energetic processes. Physical srotas include anatomical pathways like the digestive tract, blood vessels, and respiratory system, while subtle srotas pertain to the flow of prana (life energy), mental impressions, and consciousness. Together, they form an intricate network that facilitates the integration of body, mind, and spirit.

Ayurveda identifies thirteen primary srotas, each with a distinct function. These include channels for the intake of nutrients, such as annavaha srotas (food) and pranavaha srotas (air), as well as those for the circulation of fluids and energy, like rasavaha srotas (plasma) and raktavaha srotas (blood). Elimination pathways, such as purishavaha srotas (feces), mutravaha srotas (urine), and svedavaha srotas (sweat), are equally critical, ensuring the removal of metabolic waste. Beyond these physical pathways, srotas also govern reproductive and mental functions, including shukravaha srotas (reproductive fluids) and manovaha srotas (mental impressions). Each srotas plays a vital role in maintaining the body's equilibrium, and any disruption in their function can lead to disease.

The primary function of srotas is to facilitate the transportation of essential substances and waste throughout the body. Nutrients derived from digested food are carried to tissues through annavaha srotas and rasavaha srotas. Similarly, oxygen and vitality are distributed via pranavaha srotas and raktavaha srotas. This seamless circulation ensures that all tissues receive the nourishment they require to perform their physiological roles. In addition, srotas are responsible for the elimination of metabolic byproducts, a process critical for maintaining systemic balance. Channels like purishavaha srotas and mutravaha srotas ensure the efficient excretion of solid and liquid waste, while svedavaha srotas eliminates toxins through sweat, helping to regulate body temperature.

In Ayurvedic thought, the health of srotas is directly linked to the concept of agni, or digestive fire. Balanced agni ensures proper digestion, assimilation, and elimination, which in turn supports the smooth functioning of srotas. Conversely, imbalances in agni can lead to the formation of ama, a toxic substance resulting from undigested food. Ama tends to accumulate in the srotas, causing blockages that impair the flow of nutrients and waste. This disruption often serves as the root cause of many diseases. For instance, blockages in mutravaha srotas may result in urinary disorders, while obstructions in rasavaha srotas can lead to circulatory issues.

The maintenance of srotas is a key focus in Ayurveda, which advocates preventive and therapeutic measures to ensure their integrity. Diet plays a crucial role in this regard. Foods tailored to specific srotas can help maintain their health and functionality. For example, hydrating foods benefit udakavaha srotas, while fibrous foods support purishavaha srotas. Spices such as ginger and turmeric are often recommended to stimulate circulation and clear minor blockages. Herbal formulations like triphala, a blend of three fruits, are particularly valued for their ability to cleanse and rejuvenate srotas. Acting as a mild laxative, triphala helps remove toxins and supports the digestive and elimination channels.

Detoxification therapies, collectively known as panchakarma, are another cornerstone of Ayurvedic practice for maintaining srotas. These therapies include treatments like vamana (therapeutic emesis), basti (medicated enemas), and nasya (nasal cleansing), each targeting specific srotas to remove accumulated toxins. By restoring the free flow of substances within these channels, panchakarma not only alleviates symptoms but also addresses the underlying causes of disease. Ayurveda also emphasizes lifestyle interventions to support srotas. Regular physical activity improves the flow of blood and lymphatic fluids, while yoga and pranayama enhance respiratory and subtle energy channels. Practices such as meditation and mindfulness strengthen manovaha srotas, fostering mental clarity and emotional stability.

The interconnectedness of srotas reflects the holistic nature of Ayurvedic philosophy. A disruption in one channel often affects others, underscoring the importance of systemic balance. For instance, a blockage in annavaha srotas due to poor digestion can lead to inadequate nutrient absorption, thereby weakening rasavaha srotas and compromising tissue nourishment. Similarly, stress-related imbalances in manovaha srotas can manifest as physical ailments, such as digestive issues or hypertension, highlighting the profound connection between the mind and body.

This holistic perspective extends to the role of srotas in integrating the three doshas—vāta, pitta, and kapha. Each dosha influences the function of specific srotas. For example, vāta governs movement within the channels, ensuring the proper flow of substances. Pitta, associated with heat and transformation, facilitates metabolic processes within the srotas. Kapha, with its grounding and stabilizing qualities, provides structural support and lubrication to the channels. The balance of these doshas is essential for the harmonious functioning of srotas and, by extension, the entire organism.

In Ayurveda, the concept of srotas transcends the physical realm to include subtle and spiritual dimensions. Subtle srotas like pranavaha srotas (life energy) and manovaha srotas (mind) are considered vital for achieving overall well-being. These channels connect the physical body to the mind and spirit, emphasizing Ayurveda's view of health as a dynamic state of balance across all levels of existence. Disruptions in these subtle channels can manifest as emotional imbalances, mental fog, or spiritual disconnection, further illustrating the interdependence of the physical and non-physical aspects of health.

46. According to the passage, what is the primary function of srotas in the human body?

A. To store energy for later use.

B. To facilitate the flow of nutrients, energy, and waste throughout the body.

C. To act as physical barriers against toxins.

D. To regulate the body's immune responses.

47. Which srotas is associated with the transport of respiratory energy and oxygen in the body?
A. Annavaha Srotas B. Mutravaha Srotas
C. Pranavaha Srotas D. Svedavaha Srotas

48. The accumulation of ama in the srotas is primarily caused by:
A. Excessive physical activity.
B. Weak agni and incomplete digestion.
C. An overproduction of kapha dosha.
D. Poor circulation of prana in the body.

49. How does triphala help in maintaining the health of srotas as described in the passage?
A. By providing nourishment to tissues.
B. By acting as a mild laxative and clearing toxins.
C. By strengthening the structural integrity of srotas.
D. By regulating hormonal activities.

50. What does the interconnectedness of srotas signify in Ayurvedic philosophy, as per the passage?
A. The independence of physical and mental health.
B. The separation of physical processes from mental well-being.
C. The integration of physical, mental, and spiritual health.
D. The exclusive focus on physical aspects of health.

ANSWER WITH EXPLANATIONS

1. **C:** The intervention aligns with the Ayurvedic principle of pacifying Vata dosha through warm and unctuous substances. Vata, responsible for movement and dryness, becomes aggravated in cold, erratic, or unstructured conditions. The use of oils and warm foods compensates for Vata's dry and cold nature, while regulated routines stabilize its erratic tendencies. By targeting the dosha most directly responsible for the symptoms observed, the intervention ensures that the root cause is addressed. This approach reflects Ayurveda's emphasis on tailored treatments based on individual doshic imbalances rather than generic remedies, underscoring its holistic and personalized nature.

2. **A:** Weak Agni leads to the accumulation of Ama, the toxic byproduct of incomplete digestion, which disrupts nutrient absorption and fosters systemic dysfunction. Ama also aggravates doshic imbalances, compounding physiological stress. Agni is central to Ayurveda's metabolic framework, governing the transformation of food into energy and tissue. Mandagni impairs this process, resulting in malnourishment, energy stagnation, and immune weakness. This interpretation highlights Ayurveda's intricate understanding of metabolic health, correlating digestive inefficiency with disease. The emphasis on strengthening Agni exemplifies its therapeutic focus on root-cause resolution rather than symptom management, bridging ancient wisdom with modern biochemical parallels.

3. **B:** The disruption of Rasa Vaha Srotas, associated with the flow of plasma and lymph, reflects Kapha's heavy, cold qualities, leading to stagnation and fluid retention. Kapha, when imbalanced, obstructs channels, impairing circulation and waste elimination. Ayurveda perceives the body as an interconnected network where disruptions in one system cascade into broader dysfunctions. Restoring Kapha balance involves lightening and stimulating therapies that restore fluid dynamics within the Srotas. This perspective integrates anatomical precision with the functional attributes of doshas, illustrating how Ayurvedic diagnostics transcend physical symptoms to identify systemic root causes.

4. **D:** Pitta's fiery nature, when aggravated, manifests in inflammatory symptoms such as redness and heat. Cooling substances neutralize this excess by countering Pitta's intrinsic heat and sharpness, restoring equilibrium. Pitta governs metabolic transformations, and its imbalance often reflects overactivity or irritability in these processes. By addressing Pitta directly, Ayurvedic interventions reduce inflammation at both systemic and cellular levels. This principle demonstrates Ayurveda's nuanced approach to managing disorders, emphasizing counterbalance as a strategy to harmonize the body's functional forces. Such treatments underscore Ayurveda's preventive and restorative ethos by focusing on causative imbalances rather than merely treating symptoms.

5. **C:** Dhatus develop sequentially, with each depending on the proper transformation of its precursor. Weak Agni disrupts this chain, impairing tissue formation and vitality. For instance, compromised Rasa formation affects Rakta and subsequent Dhatus, culminating in systemic deficiencies. The interdependence of Dhatus reflects Ayurveda's holistic view of physiology, where each component functions as part of an interconnected whole. Agni's role in ensuring this sequence underscores its centrality to health. This explanation elucidates Ayurveda's sophisticated understanding of metabolic interrelations, aligning

ancient theories with contemporary insights into nutrient metabolism and systemic health.

6. **B:** Ama results from impaired digestion and disrupts doshic balance, serving as the root of many diseases. Its accumulation not only clogs bodily channels but also triggers systemic inflammation, as evidenced by elevated markers. Ayurveda's theory of Ama integrates seamlessly with modern understandings of inflammatory diseases caused by metabolic dysfunction. By detoxifying Ama and restoring Agni, Ayurveda addresses inflammation at its source. This view demonstrates the alignment between ancient holistic models and contemporary biomedical paradigms, showcasing Ayurveda's relevance in addressing modern health challenges through its emphasis on systemic cleansing and metabolic optimization.

7. **A:** Kapha's heavy and cold qualities obstruct the Srotas, disrupting the body's waste elimination processes. The sluggishness associated with Kapha results in fluid stagnation, exacerbating waste retention. Ayurveda conceptualizes health as a balance of doshic forces within the body's channels, highlighting how Kapha's imbalance manifests as physiological blockages. This framework underscores the need for interventions that lighten Kapha's influence, such as dry, warming therapies that enhance circulation. The connection between doshic qualities and physiological outcomes exemplifies Ayurveda's integrative approach to diagnostics, emphasizing the functional attributes of bodily systems in disease management.

8. **B:** Kapha pacification requires dry, warm, and light interventions that counteract its heavy and moist qualities. This includes dietary changes, physical activity, and detoxifying herbs that promote movement and stimulate metabolism. Ayurveda's approach emphasizes balance through oppositional forces, ensuring that therapeutic strategies align with the specific nature of the imbalance. This reflects its broader philosophy of harmony between body and environment, where treatments restore equilibrium by addressing causative factors. Such tailored regimens highlight Ayurveda's sophistication in aligning lifestyle interventions with individualized needs, providing a sustainable framework for health.

9. **A:** Warm, oily foods and regular routines stabilize Vata's erratic and dry tendencies. Vata governs movement and neural functions, and its imbalance often manifests as anxiety, insomnia, and irregularity. Ayurveda's interventions address the qualities of Vata directly, using warmth and unctuousness to soothe and ground its airy nature. This therapeutic approach exemplifies Ayurveda's emphasis on personalized care, targeting specific doshic imbalances to restore harmony. By focusing on lifestyle and dietary adjustments, Ayurveda integrates preventive and curative strategies, offering a comprehensive model for addressing neurological and systemic health challenges.

10. **C:** Cooling and anti-inflammatory agents align with Pitta pacification, addressing skin disorders linked to its fiery nature. Pitta governs metabolism and heat, and its aggravation often manifests in inflammatory skin conditions. By targeting the root cause—excess heat—Ayurveda employs therapies that restore balance, reflecting its holistic and individualized approach to health. The focus on counteracting specific doshic imbalances underscores Ayurveda's diagnostic depth and therapeutic precision. This principle exemplifies how ancient frameworks remain relevant in contemporary dermatological care, offering insights into managing inflammation through natural and systemic interventions.

11. **B:** Weak Agni interrupts the sequential nourishment of Dhatus, causing deficiencies like those observed in Asthi Dhatu. The inability to properly transform Rasa into subsequent Dhatus demonstrates the systemic consequences of impaired digestion. This cascade effect underscores Ayurveda's understanding of the body as an interconnected system, where disruptions in one area propagate throughout. The focus on strengthening Agni highlights its centrality to overall health, reflecting Ayurveda's integrative approach. This explanation reveals how ancient theories of tissue health parallel modern concepts of metabolic interdependence, emphasizing the need for foundational interventions.

12. **B:** Reduced herbal potency compromises the efficacy of treatments designed to enhance Agni, delaying the resolution of Dhatu deficiencies. Environmental degradation diminishes the bioactive properties of herbs, highlighting the interconnectedness of ecological health and therapeutic outcomes. Ayurveda's emphasis on natural remedies depends on maintaining the integrity of its resources, demonstrating its ecological awareness. This perspective integrates sustainability with medical efficacy, emphasizing the need for environmentally conscious practices. Such insights illustrate Ayurveda's relevance in addressing modern challenges, merging health sciences with ecological stewardship to preserve its holistic framework.

13. **A:** Enriching soil to restore herb potency while enhancing Agni addresses both therapeutic and environmental challenges. Ayurveda's reliance on natural remedies necessitates sustainable practices to ensure resource availability and medicinal efficacy. This integrative approach reflects its holistic philosophy, emphasizing the interdependence of ecological and human health. By prioritizing sustainability alongside

clinical effectiveness, Ayurveda provides a model for addressing modern health and environmental issues. This dual focus exemplifies its timeless relevance, illustrating how ancient frameworks can inform contemporary solutions to complex, interconnected problems.

14. B: Establishing global standards for Triphala ensures sustainable harvesting and bioactive consistency, preserving its therapeutic efficacy. Ayurveda's holistic approach necessitates the alignment of ecological, agricultural, and clinical practices to maintain balance. This strategy reflects its systemic perspective, integrating health with sustainability. By setting standards, Ayurveda can address both immediate clinical needs and long-term resource challenges, ensuring its continued relevance. This solution illustrates Ayurveda's adaptability, highlighting its ability to merge traditional wisdom with modern frameworks to create comprehensive and sustainable healthcare models.

15. C: Ayurveda defines the Tridoshas—Vata, Pitta, and Kapha—as primary functional entities. Vata governs movement and neural impulses; Pitta controls digestion, metabolism, and transformation; and Kapha offers structural integrity and manages fluid balance. These three together regulate all physiological functions of the body. Hence, all three statements (a), (b), and (c) are correct.

16. C: Agni, the digestive fire in Ayurveda, is not only responsible for digestion and assimilation (a) but also for preventing the accumulation of Ama (toxins) (b). Additionally, Agni governs tissue metabolism and ensures proper transformation from one dhatu to another (c). Hence, all three are valid functions of Agni and the correct answer is all options.

17. B: Srotas in Ayurveda are defined as bodily channels responsible for transporting nutrients (a), eliminating waste products (b), and facilitating the flow of energy and consciousness (c), especially in subtle srotas like manovaha and pranavaha. Thus, all three functions are intrinsic to srotas, and hence option B is correct.

18. B: Kapha prakṛti individuals typically exhibit a calm, emotionally stable nature (b), along with physical tendencies like weight gain, fluid retention (a), and strong immunity but sluggish digestion (c). All three traits are classically associated with kapha dominance. Therefore, all listed statements are correct.

19. D: Ayurveda explains embryological development through various stages. Kalala is the initial gelatinous form, Budbuda resembles bubble formation, and Pesi marks the stage where muscular tissue begins forming. These are sequential stages described in Ayurvedic embryology and are all part of the foetal development process. Hence, all three are correct.

20. A: According to Ayurveda, mala (waste products) such as feces, urine, and sweat are crucial for eliminating toxins (b) and maintaining internal balance (a). However, they do not directly facilitate nutrient flow (c); that function is performed by srotas. Thus, only (a) and (b) are correct.

21. C: Agni has four types, and its imbalances are categorized based on digestion characteristics. Samagni (a) is balanced, while Mandagni (b) is slow, leading to Ama formation. Tikshnagni (c) is intense, leading to fast digestion and potential tissue depletion. All these are well-documented types of Agni in Ayurveda. Hence, all three are valid.

22. C: Each dhatu (tissue) has a specific function. Meda provides lubrication and stores energy (a), Asthi offers structure and support (b), and Rakta transports oxygen and nutrients (c). These are foundational principles of Ayurvedic anatomy, making all three statements correct.

23. C: Vata dosha is composed of air (vāyu) and ether (ākāśa) elements (b), governs motion and neural impulses (a), and when imbalanced, causes dryness and psychological issues like anxiety (c). Thus, all three descriptions correctly reflect Vata dosha, and option C is correct.

24. C: Triphala is a revered Ayurvedic formulation known for its cleansing action on the digestive tract (a), balanced nourishment to all dhātus (b), and ability to support srotas by preventing blockages (c). Its wide range of therapeutic applications makes all three statements accurate. Hence, the correct answer is C.

25. A: Vāta governs the vital function of movement, encompassing communication within the body through nerve impulses, circulation, and elimination. Pitta, associated with fire, regulates metabolism and transformation, reflecting its pivotal role in digestion and enzymatic activity. Kapha, rooted in earth and water elements, supports stability and provides cohesion, which anchors the body. These three doṣas demonstrate a dynamic equilibrium, harmonizing bodily functions with elemental influences. Ayurveda emphasizes balance among these doṣas, as any imbalance leads to physical or psychological disorders, illustrating the intricate interplay between nature's macrocosmic forces and the microcosm of the human body.

26. A: Rasa, as the first dhātu, nourishes and sustains all bodily tissues, forming the basis of vitality. Rakta supplies oxygen and sustains life, symbolizing its connection with the heart and circulatory system. Meda provides lubrication and stores energy, highlighting the metabolic reserve's protective role. Asthi, as the structural framework, upholds stability and supports locomotion. Each dhātu functions not in isolation but as an integral part of the continuum of nourishment and energy. Ayurveda's concept of dhātu highlights interdependence, where proper functioning of one ensures the vitality of the others, underscoring the holistic foundation of health.

27. **A:** Purīṣa maintains gut health and regulates fecal elimination, an essential aspect of digestive balance. Mutra expels soluble toxins, facilitating hydration and detoxification. Sveda, as sweat, aids in temperature regulation and removes metabolic waste. Ama signifies undigested, toxic substances, indicating impaired digestion and metabolic inefficiency. Mala represents the body's waste management system, critical for maintaining internal cleanliness. Ayurveda views the elimination of mala as fundamental to disease prevention and vitality. By addressing physical and energetic waste, Ayurveda aligns bodily processes with a larger ecological perspective of renewal and harmony within the body.

28. **A:** Jatharagni serves as the primary digestive fire, responsible for breaking down food and initiating metabolic processes. Dhātvagni governs cellular-level tissue metabolism, linking nutrition with tissue formation. Bhūtāgni manages the transformation of elemental substances, ensuring energy transfer. Pachakagni aids nutrient assimilation, bridging digestion and cellular nourishment. Agni, the cornerstone of Ayurvedic physiology, functions as a regulator of transformation, emphasizing the delicate balance between input (nutrition) and output (energy). Imbalanced agni leads to diseases, while balanced agni fosters vitality, mental clarity, and immunity, underlining Ayurveda's deep focus on the centrality of digestion in health.

29. **A:** Vāta prakṛti individuals exhibit creativity and quick movement but are prone to anxiety, reflecting their association with air and space elements. Pitta prakṛti, dominated by fire, demonstrates determination and intensity, though it predisposes individuals to heat-related issues. Kapha prakṛti embodies calmness and steadiness, balancing life's challenges with resilience, though susceptible to lethargy. Sama prakṛti achieves a rare equilibrium, embodying physical, mental, and emotional balance. This framework emphasizes Ayurveda's belief in individual constitution shaping health and behaviour, advocating a tailored approach to lifestyle and treatment for optimizing well-being.

30. **A:** Annavaha srotas facilitates food digestion and absorption, linking external nutrition with internal vitality. Rasavaha srotas transports plasma and digested nutrients, demonstrating the continuum of nourishment. Mutravaha srotas eliminates urine, playing a critical role in hydration and waste management. Pranavaha srotas governs respiration, ensuring oxygenation and energy generation. Ayurveda's concept of srotas highlights the interconnected channels of life, where stagnation or obstruction in any system disrupts harmony. This systemic approach underlines Ayurveda's holistic perspective, ensuring the dynamic flow of energy and matter for sustained health and vitality.

31. **A:** Mandagni, or weak digestion, manifests as bloating, toxin buildup, and sluggish metabolism, emphasizing the role of efficient digestion. Tikshnagni, with hyperactivity, reflects acidity and excessive hunger, indicating a fiery imbalance. Vishamagni signifies irregular digestion, highlighting fluctuations in metabolic efficiency. Samagni, the ideal state, fosters balanced digestion and metabolic harmony. Agni's state governs health or disease, making its regulation paramount. Ayurveda's approach to agni transcends physical digestion, symbolizing the transformative processes vital to physical and mental well-being. Its balance ensures resilience, immunity, and mental clarity, aligning internal processes with cosmic rhythms.

32. **A:** Vāta's elemental dominance of air and space illustrates its role in movement, communication, and subtle energies. Pitta's fiery composition, combined with water, drives transformation and heat regulation. Kapha's earth and water elements underline its structural and stabilizing functions. Tridoshic balance, rare and ideal, embodies harmony among all five elements. This elemental framework reflects Ayurveda's profound synthesis of nature and physiology, where imbalances disrupt homeostasis. Each element contributes to bodily functions, mirroring the macrocosmic forces that govern the universe. This intricate balance forms the cornerstone of Ayurveda's health paradigm.

33. **A:** Samagni ensures balanced digestion and efficient metabolism, fostering vitality. Mandagni, or sluggish digestion, results in toxin accumulation, symbolizing inefficiency. Tikshnagni's hyperactivity demonstrates excess transformation, leading to tissue depletion. Vishamagni reflects irregularities, illustrating metabolic unpredictability. Agni, as the transformative fire, governs life's metabolic processes. Ayurveda's nuanced understanding of agni emphasizes its centrality in health, where its state influences not only physical but also mental well-being. Balanced agni aligns with nature's rhythms, ensuring harmony in body, mind, and spirit. Agni's regulation forms the foundation of preventive and therapeutic strategies in Ayurveda.

34. A: Vāta imbalance manifests as dryness, constipation, and anxiety, correlating with its association with air and space elements. Pitta imbalance, dominated by fire, results in inflammation and rashes, emphasizing its transformative yet volatile nature. Kapha imbalance, rooted in earth and water, predisposes individuals to lethargy and congestion, reflecting its stabilizing but stagnating tendencies. Tridosha imbalance disrupts systemic harmony, causing widespread symptoms. Ayurveda views these imbalances as disruptions of the elemental equilibrium, advocating dietary, lifestyle, and therapeutic interventions to restore harmony. This framework emphasizes Ayurveda's holistic and individualized approach to health and disease.

35. C: Statement 1 is accurate as the Tridoṣa theory—Vāta, Pitta, and Kapha—forms the cornerstone of Ayurveda and governs all physiological, psychological, and biochemical functions of the body. However, Statement 2 is incorrect because doshas are not equally dominant in every individual. Each person has a unique prakṛti based on the dominance of one or more doshas. Balance is not a default state but is maintained through appropriate diet, lifestyle, and treatment tailored to one's constitution.

36. A: Statement 1 correctly identifies Agni as the metabolic force central to health and digestion in Ayurveda. It is responsible for converting food into nutrients and energy while preventing the accumulation of toxins (ama). Statement 2 further explains that the impairment of Agni leads to the accumulation of ama, which disrupts doshic balance and is often the root cause of diseases. Together, these statements encapsulate Ayurveda's emphasis on maintaining digestive health as the foundation of systemic balance. Therapies targeting Agni aim to restore this balance, demonstrating its pivotal role in both prevention and treatment.

37. A: Statement 1 is true—Ayurveda describes the seven dhātus (like Rasa, Rakta, Mamsa, etc.) as fundamental tissues that support the body's structure and function. Statement 2 is also correct and serves as the proper explanation: the dhātus are nourished in a sequential manner, where impairment in the earlier dhātu affects the development and quality of the succeeding one. This interdependency underscores why imbalance in one dhātu can weaken the entire physiological system.

38. C: Statement 1 accurately states that disruptions in srotas can lead to systemic imbalances, which is a fundamental concept in Ayurveda. However, Statement 2 incorrectly attributes these disruptions solely to Vata dosha. While Vata plays a significant role in movement and blockages, imbalances in Pitta (heat, metabolism) or Kapha (stability, lubrication) can also disrupt srotas. For example, excess Kapha may lead to blockages, while aggravated Pitta may cause inflammation in the channels. This nuanced understanding underscores Ayurveda's approach of addressing all doshas in relation to srotas, rather than attributing dysfunction to a single factor.

39. C: Statement 1 is correct—Mala (sweat, urine, feces) plays a crucial role in maintaining homeostasis by eliminating waste products and preventing toxin accumulation. However, Statement 2 is false because the proper elimination of mala is not solely dependent on Kapha. It also involves Vāta (which governs movement and elimination) and the state of Agni (digestive fire), both of which are vital for effective expulsion of wastes. Therefore, multiple factors influence mala elimination, not just Kapha.

40. A: Vata, the dynamic dosha, orchestrates all movements, including blood circulation and neural impulses. As the most influential dosha, its disruption can imbalance Pitta and Kapha. When Vata is unstable, other doshas lose their natural rhythm, creating a cascade of dysfunction. This interconnectedness highlights Ayurveda's holistic approach, emphasizing prevention through Vata regulation. Practices such as oil massages (Abhyanga) and a grounding diet help stabilize Vata. Understanding its dominance over other doshas elucidates why it governs not just physical movements but also mental clarity and emotional stability, reaffirming its pivotal role in Ayurvedic medicine.

41. A: Pitta, the transformative dosha, drives digestion and metabolism. Its role in breaking down food and absorbing nutrients ensures optimal body function. An imbalance, however, disrupts this harmony, leading to hyperacidity and inflammatory conditions. The reason lies in Pitta's fiery nature, which, when excessive, burns out the digestive balance. This connection highlights the importance of dietary choices and cooling practices, such as consuming Pitta-pacifying herbs like coriander or fennel. Ayurveda's wisdom lies in identifying triggers like stress and spicy foods, emphasizing lifestyle changes to maintain Pitta's natural equilibrium and prevent cascading health issues.

42. A: Kapha, the stabilizing dosha, provides lubrication and immunity, critical for structural and functional integrity. However, its excess results in stagnation, manifesting as lethargy, joint stiffness, or mucus-related issues. This duality—protection versus obstruction—underpins Ayurveda's nuanced understanding. Kapha's imbalance often stems from inactivity or improper diet, highlighting the need for regular exercise and lighter meals. Recognizing Kapha's dual role not only aids in addressing its disorders but also underscores Ayurveda's preventive approach, where small adjustments restore balance and vitality. By harmonizing Kapha, Ayurveda ensures physical resilience and mental calmness.

43. **A:** Agni, often referred to as the "digestive fire," is central to Ayurveda's health paradigm. It transforms food into energy and tissues while eliminating waste. Weak Agni leads to Ama formation, which clogs bodily channels (Srotas) and disrupts cellular metabolism. This blockage underpins many chronic illnesses, from arthritis to metabolic syndromes. Strengthening Agni, therefore, becomes critical. Practices like mindful eating, balanced meals, and herbal aids like ginger or turmeric rejuvenate Agni. Ayurveda's focus on Agni is a testament to its foundational role in sustaining life, emphasizing its importance in both prevention and healing.

44. **A:** The dhātus form the body's building blocks, each contributing uniquely to physical and mental health. Rasa nourishes tissues, Rakta oxygenates, and Meda stores energy, while their interplay sustains homeostasis. Imbalances disrupt this harmony, leading to diseases like anemia (Rakta imbalance) or fatigue (Rasa deficiency). Prana flow, dependent on dhātu balance, is vital for vitality. Ayurveda's approach emphasizes prevention by ensuring dhātu nourishment through balanced nutrition and Agni maintenance. This interconnected system reflects the holistic essence of Ayurveda, where every element contributes to sustaining life's delicate equilibrium.

45. **A:** Srotas, the body's transport channels, ensure nutrient absorption and waste elimination. Their obstruction leads to systemic disruptions like hypertension (Rakta Vaha Srotas) or kidney disorders (Mutra Vaha Srotas). These blockages, often caused by Ama accumulation or lifestyle factors, highlight the critical role of channel health. Ayurveda's therapies, like Panchakarma, restore Srotas function, facilitating proper flow. Understanding Srotas emphasizes the holistic perspective where maintaining clear pathways ensures the body's self-regulation. By focusing on Srotas, Ayurveda integrates prevention, detoxification, and rejuvenation into a unified health framework.

46. **B:** The primary function of srotas is to enable the movement of nutrients, energy, and waste throughout the body. This dynamic flow is integral to Ayurveda's understanding of health as a state of continuous balance and harmony. The srotas act as conduits for both physical substances, like plasma and oxygen, and subtle energies, like prana and mental impressions. Any obstruction or disruption within these pathways leads to systemic imbalances and diseases. Ayurveda's therapies aim to maintain the integrity and openness of srotas, emphasizing their critical role in sustaining life processes and holistic well-being.

47. **C:** Pranavaha Srotas, responsible for the intake and circulation of prana (life energy), is directly linked to respiratory functions such as oxygen exchange and carbon dioxide elimination. This channel also supports the subtle flow of vitality throughout the body, influencing physical energy and mental clarity. Disruptions in Pranavaha Srotas manifest as respiratory conditions like asthma or fatigue. Ayurveda emphasizes practices like pranayama, herbal remedies, and detoxification therapies to restore the balance and functionality of this channel. This approach underscores the interdependence of physical respiration and subtle energy flow in Ayurvedic physiology.

48. **B:** The accumulation of ama (toxins) within srotas results from weak agni or impaired digestion. When food is not completely digested, it forms ama, which obstructs the channels and disrupts the flow of nutrients and waste. This condition often triggers systemic imbalances, as clogged srotas lead to poor tissue nourishment and toxin buildup. Ayurveda addresses this through dietary adjustments, detoxification therapies like Panchakarma, and herbal formulations that enhance agni. This holistic approach demonstrates Ayurveda's focus on eliminating root causes, restoring systemic harmony, and preventing the recurrence of diseases.

49. **B:** Triphala, a potent Ayurvedic formulation, plays a pivotal role in cleansing and rejuvenating srotas. Its unique combination of amalaki, bibhitaki, and haritaki acts as a mild laxative, removing toxins (ama) from digestive and elimination channels. By promoting clear pathways, Triphala ensures the free flow of nutrients and waste, enhancing systemic health. It also balances all three doshas, making it a versatile remedy for various imbalances. This formulation exemplifies Ayurveda's preventive philosophy, where regular maintenance of srotas safeguards overall vitality and resilience against disease.

50. **C:** The interconnectedness of srotas signifies Ayurveda's holistic view of health, where the physical, mental, and spiritual dimensions are seamlessly integrated. A blockage or dysfunction in one srotas often cascades into others, illustrating the systemic nature of imbalances. For example, poor digestion (annavaha srotas) can lead to inadequate tissue nourishment (rasavaha srotas) and weakened immunity. Similarly, mental stress (manovaha srotas) can manifest as physical ailments. This interconnected perspective drives Ayurveda's emphasis on maintaining harmony across all systems through dietary practices, detoxification, and lifestyle adjustments, ensuring overall balance and well-being.

CHAPTER–10

DEFINITIONS AND TYPES OF BODY STRUCTURES (ASTHI, SANDHI, SNAYU, ETC.)

Ayurveda, the ancient Indian system of medicine, provides a holistic understanding of the human body through its unique anatomical and physiological frameworks. Unlike modern biomedical sciences, Ayurveda integrates physical, mental, and spiritual aspects into its concept of body structures. This comprehensive chapter delves into the definitions and classifications of asthi (bones), sandhi (joints), snāyu (ligaments), and other anatomical entities as described in classical Ayurvedic texts. The chapter also explores their functions, interrelations, and significance in maintaining health and balance.

Anatomical Structures in Ayurveda

Ayurvedic anatomy offers a unique perspective on the structural components of the human body, describing them as dynamic entities influenced by the interplay of doshas (Vata, Pitta, Kapha), dhatus (tissues), and srotas (channels). These structures are seen as both physical and energetic, reflecting Ayurveda's dual approach to understanding life processes. The major anatomical structures include:

1. **Asthi (Bones):** The skeletal system, referred to as asthi, forms the structural framework of the body. It provides support, protects vital organs, and serves as a reservoir for calcium and other minerals. According to Ayurveda, asthi dhatu is formed as the fifth tissue in the sequential transformation of nutrients. It is primarily influenced by Vata dosha, which governs movement and structure. The health of asthi is directly linked to dietary habits, lifestyle, and the balance of agni (digestive fire). Imbalances in asthi dhatu may lead to conditions like osteoporosis, arthritis, or fractures.
2. **Sandhi (Joints):** Sandhi refers to the junctions between bones, allowing movement and flexibility. Ayurveda categorizes joints based on their mobility and function, aligning closely with modern classifications like synovial, cartilaginous, and fibrous joints. The health of sandhi is supported by kapha dosha, which provides lubrication and stability through shleshaka kapha. Disorders of sandhi, such as arthritis or joint pain, often arise from an aggravated Vata dosha, leading to dryness and reduced mobility.
3. **Snāyu (Ligaments and Tendons):** Snāyu are fibrous structures that connect bones to muscles (tendons) or other bones (ligaments). They provide stability and facilitate movement. Ayurveda recognizes snāyu as essential components in maintaining the integrity of sandhi. They are influenced by Vata dosha, with an emphasis on maintaining flexibility and strength. Injuries or imbalances in snāyu result in sprains, tears, or chronic pain, often requiring therapies like Abhyanga (massage) and herbal treatments for healing.
4. **Mamsa (Muscles):** Mamsa dhatu, the third tissue in Ayurvedic physiology, encompasses muscles, which provide strength, stability, and the ability to move. Muscles are considered dynamic tissues influenced by Pitta dosha, responsible for metabolism and heat. The health of mamsa dhatu depends on adequate nutrition, regular exercise, and the balance of agni. Muscular imbalances can manifest as weakness, spasms, or inflammation.

5. **Kandra (Tendons and Fascia):** Kandra refers to the elastic tissues that enhance mobility and provide structural integrity. Tendons are specifically mentioned as crucial for transmitting the force generated by muscles to bones. The elasticity and resilience of kandra are governed by Vata dosha, and maintaining their health involves adequate hydration, nourishment, and care.
6. **Peshi (Flesh and Coverings):** Peshi includes the fleshy coverings of the body, such as the skin and subcutaneous tissue. These structures protect internal organs and provide insulation. They are influenced by Kapha dosha, which ensures their hydration and integrity. Disorders affecting peshi include skin conditions, infections, or trauma.

Classification of Body Structures in Ayurveda

Ayurveda provides a detailed classification of body structures based on their composition, function, and energetic influence. These classifications are not rigid but dynamic, emphasizing the interdependence of physical and subtle elements.

1. **Based on Functionality:**
   - **Supportive Structures:** Includes bones (asthi) and ligaments (snāyu), which provide stability and framework.
   - **Dynamic Structures:** Includes muscles (mamsa), tendons (kandra), and joints (sandhi), responsible for movement.
   - **Protective Structures:** Includes skin (twak), fascia, and adipose tissue (meda), offering protection and insulation.
2. **Based on Dosha Influence:**
   - **Vata-dominant Structures:** Asthi, snāyu, and kandra reflect the qualities of movement, dryness, and rigidity associated with Vata dosha.
   - **Pitta-dominant Structures:** Mamsa and metabolic tissues, reflecting heat, transformation, and sharpness.
   - **Kapha-dominant Structures:** Sandhi and protective tissues like skin, associated with stability, lubrication, and cohesion.
3. **Based on Composition:**
   - **Solid Structures:** Includes bones, ligaments, and tendons, providing rigidity and strength.
   - **Fluid Structures:** Includes synovial fluid, cerebrospinal fluid, and blood, ensuring lubrication and nourishment.
   - **Elastic Structures:** Includes fascia, muscles, and tendons, providing flexibility and resilience.

Functions of Body Structures in Ayurveda

Each anatomical structure in Ayurveda serves multiple functions that extend beyond the physical realm, emphasizing their role in maintaining systemic balance and overall health.

1. **Structural Support:** Bones and ligaments form the framework of the body, providing stability and protecting vital organs. This support enables upright posture and movement.
2. **Mobility and Flexibility:** Joints, muscles, and tendons work together to facilitate dynamic movements, reflecting the influence of Vata dosha. Lubrication from Kapha dosha ensures smooth motion.
3. **Protection:** Skin, subcutaneous tissue, and adipose layers shield internal organs from external harm, maintaining thermal balance and preventing infections.
4. **Circulation and Energy Flow:** The interplay of structures like muscles, tendons, and joints supports circulation, ensuring the free flow of prana, nutrients, and waste.
5. **Stability and Resilience:** Ligaments and fascia provide structural stability, ensuring resilience against physical stress and trauma.

Ayurvedic Perspective on Imbalances

Ayurveda attributes disorders of anatomical structures to doshic imbalances, weak agni, or toxin accumulation (ama). For example:

- **Bone Disorders:** Osteoporosis or fractures result from depleted asthi dhatu due to weak digestion or aggravated Vata.
- **Joint Disorders:** Arthritis arises from Vata or Kapha imbalances, leading to stiffness or inflammation.
- **Muscular Issues:** Weakness or spasms in mamsa dhatu stem from Pitta disturbances or nutritional deficiencies.
- **Ligament Injuries:** Sprains or tears occur due to excessive strain or aggravated Vata.

Ayurvedic Therapies for Body

Ayurveda, the ancient Indian science of life, provides a holistic approach to health and wellness, emphasizing the maintenance, rejuvenation, and healing of the body's structures. These structures include the dhātus (tissues), mala (waste products), srotas (channels), and the subtle components like prāṇa (life energy), manas (mind), and ātmā (soul). Ayurvedic therapies aim to restore and maintain the balance of these interconnected systems, addressing both physical and subtle dimensions of the body.

(I) The Foundations of Ayurvedic Therapies

1. **Holistic Approach to Healing:** Ayurvedic therapies focus on:
   - **Balancing Doshas:** Restoring equilibrium of Vāta, Pitta, and Kapha.
   - **Strengthening Dhātus:** Nourishing and repairing the seven tissues.
   - **Purifying Malas:** Ensuring proper elimination of waste products.
   - **Enhancing Prāṇa:** Optimizing the life force that governs bodily functions.
2. **Key Principles:**
   - **Individualized Care:** Therapies are tailored to the individual's constitution (Prakṛti) and imbalances (Vikṛti).
   - **Preventive and Curative:** Focus on disease prevention and the treatment of root causes.
   - **Natural and Sustainable:** Utilize herbs, oils, diet, and lifestyle modifications to achieve balance.
3. **Classification of Ayurvedic Therapies:** Ayurvedic treatments are broadly categorized into:
   1. **Shodhana (Purification):** Detoxification therapies like Panchakarma.
   2. **Shamana (Palliation):** Alleviation of imbalances through diet, herbs, and lifestyle changes.
   3. **Rasayana (Rejuvenation):** Strengthening and revitalizing therapies.
   4. **Sattvavajaya (Psychological Wellness):** Techniques for mental balance and emotional resilience.

(II) Ayurvedic Therapies for Dhātus (Body Tissues)

The body comprises seven fundamental tissues (dhātus): Rasa (plasma), Rakta (blood), Māṃsa (muscle), Meda (fat), Asthi (bone), Majjā (bone marrow), and Shukra (reproductive tissue). Each dhātu requires specific therapies to maintain its health.

1. **Rasa Dhātu (Plasma): Nourishment and Hydration**

   (a) Role in the Body:
   - Provides nourishment to all tissues.
   - Maintains hydration and immunity.

   (b) Therapies for Rasa Dhātu
   1. **Herbal Tonics:** Herbs like Ashwagandha, Shatavari, and Guduchi nourish plasma.
   2. **Abhyanga (Oil Massage):** Hydrating oils like sesame and coconut improve circulation.
   3. **Hydration Therapy:** Consumption of herbal teas and warm water aids hydration.
   4. **Dietary Modifications:** Emphasize sweet, cooling, and moist foods like rice, milk, and ghee.
2. **Rakta Dhātu (Blood):** Vitality and Oxygenation

   (a) Role in the Body:
   - Transports oxygen and nutrients.
   - Supports skin health and vitality.

   (b) Therapies for Rakta Dhātu:
   1. **Raktamokshana (Bloodletting):** Removes impurities from the blood.
   2. **Pitta-Pacifying Herbs:** Neem, Manjistha, and Aloe Vera cleanse and cool the blood.
   3. **Dietary Adjustments:** Incorporate bitter and astringent foods to reduce heat.
   4. **Cooling Therapies:** Application of sandalwood paste or rose water to the skin.
3. **Māṃsa Dhātu (Muscle):** Strength and Structure

   (a) Role in the Body:
   - Provides strength and mobility.
   - Supports the body's structural integrity.

   (b) Therapies for Māṃsa Dhātu:
   1. **Strengthening Herbs:** Gokshura and Ashwagandha improve muscle mass.
   2. **Exercise Regimens:** Yoga and resistance training promote muscle health.
   3. **Massage Therapy:** Warm oil massages enhance muscle tone and flexibility.
   4. **Nutritive Diet:** Include protein-rich foods like lentils, nuts, and dairy.
4. **Meda Dhātu (Fat):** Lubrication and Energy Storage

   (a) Role in the Body:
   - Lubricates tissues and joints.
   - Acts as an energy reserve.

   (b) Therapies for Meda Dhātu:
   1. **Fat-Balancing Diet:** Incorporate light, astringent foods like barley and green vegetables.
   2. **Basti (Enema Therapy):** Medicated enemas reduce excess fat accumulation.
   3. **Udvartana (Dry Powder Massage):** Promotes fat metabolism and reduces cellulite.
   4. **Herbal Remedies:** Triphala and Guggulu support healthy fat metabolism

5. **Asthi Dhātu (Bone):** Structure and Stability

(a) **Role in the Body:**

- Provides structural support and protection.
- Stores minerals like calcium.

(b) **Therapies for Asthi Dhātu:**

1. **Calcium-Rich Foods:** Include sesame seeds, almonds, and leafy greens.
2. **Herbal Supplements:** Laksha Guggulu and Hadjod strengthen bones.
3. **Sunlight Exposure:** Enhances vitamin (d) synthesis for bone health.
4. **Oil Application:** Use medicated oils like Bala and Dhanvantaram for bone nourishment.

6. **Majjā Dhātu (Bone Marrow):** Vital Energy and Nerve Health

(a) **Role in the Body:**

- Nourishes the nervous system.
- Supports blood cell production.

(b) **Therapies for Majjā Dhātu:**

1. **Brain Tonic Herbs:** Brahmi and Shankhpushpi enhance nerve function.
2. **Dietary Nourishment:** Consume ghee and bone broths.
3. **Meditation Practices:** Promote mental clarity and calmness.
4. **Nasal Therapies (Nasya):** Instillation of medicated oils into the nose supports brain health.

7. **Shukra Dhātu (Reproductive Tissue):** Fertility and Vitality

(a) **Role in the Body**

- Governs reproduction and creative energy.
- Supports hormonal balance.

(b) **Therapies for Shukra Dhātu:**

1. **Aphrodisiac Herbs:** Shatavari and Kapikacchu enhance fertility and libido.
2. **Rejuvenation Therapy (Rasayana):** Promote vitality through practices like Vajikarana.
3. **Healthy Fats:** Ghee and nuts improve reproductive health.
4. **Stress Management:** Incorporate yoga and relaxation techniques to balance hormones.

(III) Ayurvedic Therapies for Malas (Waste Products)

Efficient elimination of waste products is crucial for health.

1. **Mutra (Urine): Fluid Balanc**
   1. **Diuretic Herbs:** Punarnava and Gokshura promote urinary health.
   2. **Hydration:** Drink warm water and herbal teas to flush toxins
   3. **Detox Therapies:** Panchakarma practices cleanse the urinary tract.

2. **Purīṣa (Feces):** Digestion and Detoxification
   1. **Laxatives:** Triphala supports regular bowel movements.
   2. **Colon Cleansing:** Basti therapy removes toxins.
   3. **Fiber-Rich Diet:** Whole grains and vegetables improve digestion.

3. **Sveda (Sweat):** Temperature Regulation
   1. **Sweat-Inducing Therapies:** Swedana (herbal steam) opens sweat glands.
   2. **Cooling Herbs:** Coriander and fennel prevent excessive sweating.
   3. **Hygiene Practices:** Regular cleansing of the skin maintains healthy sweat function.

(IV) Subtle Therapies for Body Structures

Ayurveda addresses not only physical but also subtle body structures.

1. **Prāṇa (Life Energy):**
   1. **Pranayama:** Breath control practices enhance energy flow.
   2. **Energy Herbs:** Tulsi and Ashwagandha strengthen prāṇa.
   3. **Meditation:** Aligns prāṇa with the mind and body.

2. **Manas (Mind):**
   1. **Mental Clarity Herbs:** Brahmi improves cognitive function.
   2. **Sattvic Diet:** Promotes mental calmness and purity.
   3. **Mindful Practices:** Incorporate yoga and relaxation techniques.

3. **Ātmā (Soul):**
   1. **Spiritual Therapies:** Chanting and meditation connect with the higher self.
   2. **Ritual Practices:** Strengthen the soul through traditional rituals.
   3. **Self-Reflection:** Journaling and introspection enhance self-awareness.

(V) Integration of Ayurvedic Therapies

1. **Diagnostic Tools:**

- Pulse Diagnosis (Nadi Pariksha):
- Identifies doshic imbalances.

Tongue and Eye Analysis:

- Assesses tissue health.

2. **Modern Relevance:**
   - Ayurveda's personalized therapies complement modern medicine, offering holistic care for chronic diseases.
   - Ayurvedic therapies provide a comprehensive approach to maintaining and restoring the health of body structures. By addressing physical and subtle dimensions, these therapies promote harmony, vitality, and resilience. Through the integration of diet, lifestyle, herbs, and spiritual practices, Ayurveda offers timeless wisdom for achieving optimal well-being.

MULTIPLE CHOICE QUESTIONS

1. A medical researcher is investigating the Ayurvedic concept of asthi dhatu (bone tissue) and its intricate relationships with sandhi (joints) and snāyu (ligaments). The researcher hypothesizes that weakened asthi dhatu due to impaired agni (digestive fire) could lead to decreased joint stability and ligament elasticity. To explore this, they study a group of patients with poor digestion, brittle bones, and joint instability. After implementing therapies to enhance agni, such as Triphala and dietary adjustments, significant improvements are observed. Which Ayurvedic principle best explains this phenomenon?

A. Asthi dhatu depends on the nourishment provided by a robust agni, which strengthens both joints and ligaments.
B. Joints and ligaments are independent of asthi dhatu, and their health is unaffected by digestive fire.
C. Ayurveda focuses exclusively on the external treatment of bones, ignoring systemic factors like agni.
D. Asthi dhatu solely governs bone density and strength, unrelated to joints or ligaments.

2. An Ayurvedic scholar explores the dosha influences on sandhi (joints), with a focus on shleshaka kapha, the lubricating component essential for joint mobility. The scholar proposes that Vata dosha aggravation causes depletion of shleshaka kapha, resulting in joint stiffness and pain. Based on these observations, the scholar designs a treatment plan using medicated oil applications, warm therapies, and dietary adjustments to pacify Vata and restore Kapha. If these principles are valid, what outcome would most align with Ayurvedic expectations?

A. Increased joint lubrication and reduced stiffness due to balanced Vata and replenished Kapha.
B. Joint health improves independently of dosha management, requiring only mechanical support.
C. Ayurveda treats Kapha dosha as irrelevant to joint mobility, focusing solely on Vata.
D. Joint pain is unrelated to dosha imbalances and requires entirely modern medical approaches.

3. A physiotherapist incorporates Ayurvedic concepts to enhance ligament (snāyu) health and resilience in athletes. They hypothesize that snāyu is influenced by both Vata dosha for flexibility and Kapha dosha for stability. Observing a group of athletes with recurring ligament injuries, the therapist prescribes therapies like Ashwagandha, Bala oil massages, and nourishing diets to balance Vata and strengthen Kapha. After months of treatment, ligament injuries are significantly reduced. Based on Ayurvedic teachings, which principle most likely explains these results?

A. Balancing Vata and strengthening Kapha ensures optimal ligament elasticity and strength.
B. Snāyu health is unrelated to dosha balance, depending solely on external mechanical factors.
C. Ayurveda considers ligaments secondary to joint and bone health, with no direct therapies for them.
D. Ligament injuries result solely from dietary deficiencies, unrelated to dosha imbalances.

4. A patient with chronic joint pain seeks Ayurvedic treatment. The practitioner identifies aggravated Vata dosha and depleted shleshaka kapha as the root causes, manifesting as joint dryness, stiffness, and cracking noises during movement. To address this, the practitioner prescribes warm oil massages, steam therapies, and a Kapha-enhancing diet. After treatment, the patient reports improved joint lubrication and flexibility. Which Ayurvedic mechanism underpins these therapeutic effects?

A. Replenishment of shleshaka kapha and pacification of Vata dosha restore joint functionality.
B. Joint lubrication and flexibility are unrelated to dosha management, requiring only exercise.
C. Ayurveda treats chronic joint issues as irreversible, with therapies offering symptomatic relief.
D. Vata dosha solely governs joint flexibility, and therapies targeting Kapha are irrelevant.

5. A nutritionist examines the role of mamsa dhatu (muscle tissue) in maintaining structural integrity and supporting bones, ligaments, and joints. Observing a group of patients with poor muscle tone and chronic fatigue, the nutritionist hypothesizes that weak mamsa dhatu arises from poor agni and improper nourishment of Kapha dosha. The nutritionist prescribes a protein-rich diet, along with digestive herbs like Pippali and Trikatu to strengthen agni. Which Ayurvedic principle aligns most with this therapeutic approach?

A. Proper nourishment of mamsa dhatu through strong agni enhances structural support and vitality.
B. Muscle tissue health is independent of systemic factors like agni, relying solely on external strengthening.
C. Ayurveda considers muscle issues as unrelated to diet and treats them purely through external therapies.
D. Strengthening Kapha dosha alone ensures muscle resilience, without requiring dietary interventions.

6. A clinical researcher investigates the role of asthi dhatu in Ayurveda and its relationship to systemic health. The researcher finds that weak asthi dhatu not only leads to brittle bones but also affects the structural integrity of snāyu (ligaments) and kandra (tendons). To address this, the researcher prescribes therapies to enhance asthi dhatu, such as herbal calcium supplements, medicated oils, and digestive tonics. After six months, patients report stronger bones, improved ligament elasticity, and reduced tendon injuries. Which Ayurvedic concept most accurately explains these outcomes?

A. Strengthened asthi dhatu supports ligaments and tendons, improving structural stability.
B. Ligaments and tendons are unrelated to asthi dhatu, relying solely on physical exercise.
C. Ayurveda considers bones as independent structures unaffected by ligaments or tendons.
D. Enhancing Kapha dosha alone explains the improvements in structural stability.

7. A yoga instructor consults an Ayurvedic expert to address ligament injuries and joint stiffness in students. The expert identifies aggravated Vata dosha as the primary factor, causing dryness and reduced flexibility. They recommend oil-based therapies like Abhyanga, warm compresses, and a nourishing diet to pacify Vata. Students who follow these recommendations report improved flexibility and reduced ligament strain. How does this align with Ayurvedic teachings?

A. Pacifying Vata dosha restores lubrication and flexibility in ligaments and joints.
B. Ligament health depends solely on external support, with no role for dietary adjustments.
C. Ayurveda prioritizes bone health over ligaments, offering no specific therapies for them.
D. Strengthening Kapha dosha is the only relevant approach for addressing ligament injuries.

8. An Ayurvedic practitioner treats a patient with poor posture and chronic back pain. They diagnose weak peshi (muscle tissue) and aggravated Vata dosha as the root causes. To address this, the practitioner prescribes a Kapha-enhancing diet, external oil applications, and herbal tonics like Ashwagandha to strengthen mamsa dhatu. After several weeks, the patient reports improved posture and reduced pain. Which Ayurvedic principle underpins this treatment strategy?

A. Strengthening mamsa dhatu and balancing Vata dosha improves muscle tone and posture.
B. Muscle issues arise independently of dosha imbalances and require solely external therapies.
C. Ayurveda treats back pain as a skeletal issue unrelated to muscular health.
D. Enhancing Kapha dosha alone addresses muscle weakness without requiring additional therapies.

9. A sports scientist collaborates with an Ayurvedic practitioner to address recurring ligament injuries in athletes. The practitioner proposes that snāyu (ligaments) are influenced by Vata for flexibility and Kapha for stability. The practitioner prescribes therapies like sesame oil massages, warm applications, and Ashwagandha supplements to balance these doshas. Over several months, the athletes report fewer injuries and improved ligament strength. What Ayurvedic principle best supports these observations?

A. Balancing Vata and strengthening Kapha enhances ligament elasticity and resilience.
B. Ligament injuries are unrelated to dosha balance, depending solely on physical rehabilitation.
C. Ayurveda considers ligament health secondary to muscle and bone health, with no direct interventions.
D. Therapies for ligament injuries target Kapha dosha exclusively, ignoring other factors.

10. A researcher studies the Ayurvedic concept of sandhi (joints) and their reliance on shleshaka kapha for lubrication and smooth movement. They observe that patients with aggravated Vata dosha and depleted Kapha dosha frequently suffer from joint pain and stiffness. Based on these findings, they design a treatment plan involving oil massages, dietary adjustments, and warming therapies. Patients report significant improvements in joint mobility and reduced pain. Which Ayurvedic mechanism most accurately explains these outcomes?

A. Restoring shleshaka kapha and calming Vata dosha improves joint lubrication and mobility.
B. Joint pain arises independently of dosha imbalances, requiring solely external interventions.

C. Ayurveda treats joint stiffness as a permanent condition, offering only symptomatic relief.
D. Kapha dosha is irrelevant to joint health, as Vata dosha solely governs flexibility.

Directions (Q. No. 11-14): *Scenario-Based Questions*

SCENARIO 1

An Ayurvedic researcher examines the interconnectedness of asthi dhatu (bone tissue), sandhi (joints), and snāyu (ligaments) within the human body. The researcher hypothesizes that imbalances in agni (digestive fire) contribute to the improper nourishment of asthi dhatu, leading to brittle bones, weak joints, and reduced ligament elasticity. To test this, they observe a group of patients with chronic joint pain and ligament injuries. After administering therapies such as Triphala, calcium-rich herbs like Laksha, and dietary interventions to enhance agni, they observe improved bone density and joint stability in most patients.

SCENARIO 2

Simultaneously, an environmental scientist investigates the impact of overharvesting of herbs like Laksha (used for bone health) and Ashwagandha (used for muscle and ligament strengthening). The study finds that overexploitation of these plants results in reduced availability and lower quality of formulations prepared for patients. The reduced potency of these herbal medicines compromises the outcomes observed in Scenario 1, as the weaker formulations fail to address issues of joint and ligament health effectively. This raises concerns about sustainable harvesting and the quality of medicinal preparations.

11. Based on Scenario 1, which Ayurvedic principle best explains the observed improvements in bone density and ligament elasticity among patients after therapies enhancing agni were administered?
A. Agni ensures proper metabolism and nourishment of asthi dhatu and its related structures like ligaments and joints.
B. Agni plays no role in bone or ligament health, which depend solely on external support therapies.
C. Weak bones and ligaments are unrelated to digestive fire, arising instead from lifestyle factors alone.
D. Ayurveda does not consider asthi dhatu and ligaments to share any physiological relationship.

12. Referring to Scenario 2, what intervention would most effectively address the challenges posed by overharvesting of herbs like Laksha and Ashwagandha while ensuring sustainable usage in Ayurvedic formulations?
A. Promoting community-led conservation and cultivation of medicinal plants to reduce dependency on wild resources.
B. Replacing traditional herbs like Laksha with synthetic alternatives to address bone and ligament health issues.
C. Reducing global demand for herbal medicines by restricting Ayurvedic treatments for bone and ligament issues.
D. Transitioning entirely to modern medical practices, as sustainability issues make Ayurveda impractical.

13. How might the reduced potency of Laksha and Ashwagandha formulations, as described in Scenario 2, impact the outcomes observed in Scenario 1?
A. Compromised herb quality may limit improvements in bone and ligament health, undermining the efficacy of therapies.
B. The potency of Laksha and Ashwagandha has no bearing on patient outcomes, as diet alone governs structural health.
C. Weaker formulations improve ligament elasticity but fail to enhance bone density.
D. The efficacy of therapies remains unaffected, as Ayurvedic treatments rely primarily on lifestyle adjustments.

14. Considering the interconnected findings of Scenarios 1 and 2, which strategy would most comprehensively address the challenges while ensuring effective patient outcomes and sustainable resource use?
A. Establishing herb cultivation programs and prioritizing high-potency formulations through research and quality control.
B. Restricting herbal use to local communities, limiting access to broader populations.
C. Substituting Ayurvedic treatments with synthetic alternatives for bone and ligament health.
D. Relying on external mechanical supports and physiotherapy, bypassing herbal therapies altogether.

15. In the context of Ayurvedic anatomy, the primary characteristics of asthi (bone), sandhi (joint), and snāyu (ligament) are described in classical texts. Match the following Ayurvedic terms with their respective functions:

(a) Asthi	1. Governs the strength and density of the skeletal framework.
(b) Sandhi	2. Acts as a connection point for movement and stability.
(c) Snāyu	3. Ensures structural integrity and supports muscle attachments.
(d) Shleshaka Kapha	4. Provides lubrication and facilitates smooth joint movement.

Choose the correct answer from the options given below:

A. (a)-4, (b)-3, (c)-2, (d)-1
B. (a)-3, (b)-4, (c)-1, (d)-2
C. (a)-1, (b)-2, (c)-3, (d)-4
D. (a)-2, (b)-1, (c)-4, (d)-3

16. The Ayurvedic concept of asthi dhatu and its nourishment involves specific metabolic processes and physiological roles. Consider the following statements:

(a) Asthi dhatu is nourished by the byproduct of meda dhatu (fat tissue).
(b) Sandhi serves as the structural connectors of the skeletal system.
(c) Snāyu (ligaments) are extensions of asthi dhatu, providing elasticity and stability.
(d) The lubrication of joints is primarily attributed to shleshaka kapha.

Choose the correct answer from the options given below:

A. (a), (b), and (c) only B. (a), (b), (c), and (d)
C. (b), (c), and (d) only D. (a), (c), and (d) only

17. The classical Ayurvedic understanding of joint dysfunction involves multiple interrelated factors. Consider these relationships:

(a) Aggravated Vata dosha	1. Leads to joint pain, cracking sounds, and stiffness.
(b) Depleted Shleshaka Kapha	2. Results in joint dryness and reduced lubrication.
(c) Weak Asthi Dhatu	3. Causes brittle bones and increased fracture risk.
(d) Reduced Snāyu elasticity	4. Compromises structural stability and flexibility.

Choose the correct answer from the options given below:

A. (a)-1, (b)-3, (c)-4, (d)-2
B. (a)-3, (b)-4, (c)-1, (d)-2
C. (a)-1, (b)-2, (c)-3, (d)-4
D. (a)-4, (b)-2, (c)-1, (d)-3

18. Consider the following statements regarding the relationships among asthi dhatu, snāyu, and sandhi:

(a) Asthi dhatu forms the skeletal framework and provides the attachment sites for ligaments and tendons.
(b) Snāyu acts as structural reinforcements, offering flexibility and elasticity to joints.
(c) Sandhi facilitates movement but has no dependence on shleshaka kapha for lubrication.
(d) Impaired agni weakens asthi dhatu, indirectly affecting ligaments and joints.

Choose the correct answer from the options given below:

A. (a), (b), and (d) only
B. (a), (b), and (c) only
C. (b), (c), and (d) only
D. (a), (c), and (d) only

19. Ayurveda elaborates on the pathogenesis of joint-related disorders and their management. Consider these therapeutic matches:

(a) Aggravated Vata Dosha in Sandhi	1. Digestive tonics and Vata-pacifying diets.
(b) Depleted Shleshaka Kapha	2. Warm oil massages and Kapha-enhancing therapies.
(c) Weak Snāyu due to impaired nourishment	3. Bone-strengthening herbs like Laksha and Guggulu.
(d) Chronic joint pain due to poor Agni	4. Application of medicated oils and fomentation therapy.

Choose the correct answer from the options given below:

A. (a)-3, (b)-1, (c)-2, (d)-4
B. (a)-4, (b)-3, (c)-1, (d)-2
C. (a)-2, (b)-4, (c)-3, (d)-1
D. (a)-1, (b)-2, (c)-3, (d)-4

20. The Ayurvedic understanding of snāyu and its functions involves specific structural and physiological roles. Consider the following:

(a) Snāyu primarily supports joint stability by connecting bones.
(b) Elasticity and flexibility of snāyu are influenced by balanced Vata dosha.
(c) Snāyu is strengthened through the nourishment of asthi dhatu.
(d) Shleshaka kapha plays no role in maintaining snāyu functionality.

Choose the correct answer from the options given below:

A. (a), (b), and (c) only B. (a), (b), (c), and (d)
C. (b), (c), and (d) only D. (a), (c), and (d) only

21. According to Ayurvedic physiology, the health of sandhi (joints) depends on multiple factors. Consider these structural relationships:

(a) Joint lubrication	1. Shleshaka Kapha.
(b) Joint mobility and flexibility	2. Vata Dosha.
(c) Structural stability of joints	3. Asthi Dhatu.
(d) Ligament elasticity	4. Snāyu.

Choose the correct answer from the options given below:

A. (a)-1, (b)-2, (c)-3, (d)-4
B. (a)-3, (b)-4, (c)-1, (d)-2
C. (a)-2, (b)-3, (c)-4, (d)-1
D. (a)-4, (b)-1, (c)-2, (d)-3

22. Consider the following descriptions of structural and functional attributes in Ayurvedic anatomy:

(a) Asthi dhatu is responsible for the strength and density of the skeletal system.
(b) Snāyu ensures both elasticity and flexibility in structural components.
(c) Sandhi serves as the functional link between skeletal segments.
(d) Vata dosha is primarily responsible for maintaining joint stability.

Choose the correct answer from the options given below:

A. (a), (b), and (c) only B. (b), (c), and (d) only
C. (a), (b), and (d) only D. (a), (c), and (d) only

23. The integrity of asthi dhatu, sandhi, and snāyu depends on their physiological interplay. Consider these roles:

(a) Strength and framework for the body	1. Asthi.
(b) Flexibility and elasticity for movement	2. Snāyu.
(c) Connection points for skeletal movement	3. Sandhi.
(d) Lubrication for smooth motion	4. Shleshaka Kapha.

Choose the correct answer from the options given below:

A. (a)-4, (b)-1, (c)-2, (d)-3
B. (a)-1, (b)-2, (c)-3, (d)-4
C. (a)-2, (b)-3, (c)-4, (d)-1
D. (a)-3, (b)-4, (c)-1, (d)-2

24. Ayurveda outlines the interconnected roles of agni, asthi dhatu, and shleshaka kapha in maintaining joint health. Consider the following statements:

(a) Impaired agni affects the nourishment of asthi dhatu, leading to brittle bones.
(b) Depleted shleshaka kapha results in reduced lubrication and increased joint stiffness.
(c) Balanced Vata dosha enhances the structural stability of ligaments and joints.
(d) Strong Kapha dosha compensates for poor agni in nourishing joints.

Choose the correct answer from the options given below:

A. (a), (b), and (c) only B. (b), (c), and (d) only
C. (a), (b), and (d) only D. (a), (c), and (d) only

25. Match List–I (Anatomical Components) with List–II (Primary Roles):

List–I	List–II
(a) Shleshaka Kapha	1. Maintains lubrication and smooth movement in joints
(b) Asthi (Bones)	2. Provides the structural framework and strength
(c) Snāyu (Ligaments)	3. Acts as a connecting structure for stability and movement
(d) Sandhi (Joints)	4. Facilitates mobility and alignment

Choose the correct answer from the options given below:

A. (a)-2, (b)-4, (c)-3, (d)-1
B. (a)-3, (b)-1, (c)-4, (d)-2
C. (a)-1, (b)-2, (c)-3, (d)-4
D. (a)-4, (b)-3, (c)-1, (d)-2

26. Match List–I (Physiological Attributes) with List–II (Related Dosha or Dhatu):

List–I	List–II
(a) Joint lubrication	1. Shleshaka Kapha
(b) Structural stability of ligaments	2. Snāyu
(c) Bone density and strength	3. Asthi Dhatu
(d) Joint mobility and flexibility	4. Vata Dosha

Choose the correct answer from the options given below:

A. (a)-1, (b)-2, (c)-3, (d)-4
B. (a)-4, (b)-1, (c)-2, (d)-3
C. (a)-3, (b)-4, (c)-1, (d)-2
D. (a)-2, (b)-3, (c)-4, (d)-1

27. Match List–I (Pathological Conditions) with List–II (Associated Ayurvedic Causes):

List–I	List–II
(a) Loss of joint lubrication	1. Depleted Shleshaka Kapha
(b) Joint stiffness and pain	2. Aggravated Vata Dosha
(c) Brittle bones	3. Impaired Asthi Dhatu formation
(d) Ligament weakness	4. Poor nourishment of Snāyu

Choose the correct answer from the options given below:

A. (a)-2, (b)-4, (c)-3, (d)-1
B. (a)-1, (b)-3, (c)-2, (d)-4
C. (a)-3, (b)-1, (c)-4, (d)-2
D. (a)-1, (b)-2, (c)-3, (d)-4

28. Match List–I (Therapeutic Interventions) with List–II (Targeted Structures):

List–I:
(a) Strengthening ligaments with Ashwagandha
(b) Application of medicated oils (Snehan)
(c) Administration of bone-nourishing herbs like Laksha
(d) Fomentation therapy (Swedana)

List–II:
1. Snāyu (Ligaments)
2. Sandhi (Joints)
3. Asthi Dhatu (Bones)
4. Shleshaka Kapha

Choose the correct answer from the options given below:
A. (a)-2, (b)-3, (c)-1, (d)-4
B. (a)-4, (b)-1, (c)-2, (d)-3
C. (a)-3, (b)-2, (c)-4, (d)-1
D. (a)-1, (b)-4, (c)-3, (d)-2

29. Match List–I (Structural Elements) with List–II (Ayurvedic Perspective):

List–I	List–II
(a) Joint Lubrication	1. Shleshaka Kapha
(b) Joints (Sandhi)	2. Vata Dosha
(c) Bones (Asthi)	3. Structural support and stability
(d) Ligaments (Snāyu)	4. Elasticity and movement

Choose the correct answer from the options given below:
A. (a)-3, (b)-4, (c)-2, (d)-1
B. (a)-4, (b)-2, (c)-3, (d)-1
C. (a)-2, (b)-3, (c)-4, (d)-1
D. (a)-1, (b)-3, (c)-4, (d)-2

30. Match List–I (Causes of Joint Disorders) with List–II (Ayurvedic Interventions):

List–I:
(a) Weak Asthi Dhatu formation
(b) Dehydration of Shleshaka Kapha
(c) Aggravated Vata Dosha in Joints
(d) Poor Snāyu elasticity

List–II:
1. Use of bone-nourishing herbs and calcium supplementation
2. Warm oil massages and Kapha-balancing therapies
3. Digestive tonics and Vata-pacifying diets
4. Ligament-strengthening treatments using Ashwagandha

Choose the correct answer from the options given below:
A. (a)-2, (b)-3, (c)-1, (d)-4
B. (a)-1, (b)-2, (c)-3, (d)-4
C. (a)-4, (b)-1, (c)-2, (d)-3
D. (a)-3, (b)-4, (c)-1, (d)-2

31. Match List–I (Key Ayurvedic Concepts) with List–II (Structural Applications):

List–I	List–II
(a) Snāyu	1. Ligament nourishment and elasticity
(b) Asthi Dhatu	2. Skeletal framework and bone strength
(c) Agni	3. Digestive fire responsible for dhatu formation
(d) Shleshaka Kapha	4. Lubrication for joint movement

Choose the correct answer from the options given below:
A. (a)-1, (b)-2, (c)-3, (d)-4
B. (a)-1, (b)-3, (c)-4, (d)-2
C. (a)-2, (b)-4, (c)-3, (d)-1
D. (a)-4, (b)-1, (c)-2, (d)-3

32. Match List–I (Dosha Imbalances) with List–II (Structural Manifestations):

List–I	List–II
(a) Vata Dosha aggravation	1. Dry joints and cracking sounds
(b) Impaired Snāyu elasticity	2. Reduced ligament stability
(c) Weak Asthi Dhatu	3. Brittle bones
(d) Kapha Dosha depletion	4. Lack of joint lubrication

Choose the correct answer from the options given below:
A. (a)-1, (b)-2, (c)-3, (d)-4
B. (a)-4, (b)-2, (c)-1, (d)-3
C. (a)-2, (b)-3, (c)-4, (d)-1
D. (a)-3, (b)-1, (c)-2, (d)-4

33. Match List–I (Therapeutic Approaches) with List–II (Primary Goals):

List–I:
(a) Diet to Balance Agni
(b) Ligament-strengthening Exercises
(c) Medicated Oil Application (Snehan)
(d) Bone-nourishing Herbs (Laksha, Guggulu)

List–II:
1. Improve digestion and dhatu formation
2. Support ligament flexibility and elasticity
3. Restore lubrication and reduce joint stiffness
4. Enhance bone strength and density

Choose the correct answer from the options given below:
A. (a)-3, (b)-4, (c)-1, (d)-2
B. (a)-1, (b)-2, (c)-3, (d)-4
C. (a)-2, (b)-1, (c)-3, (d)-4
D. (a)-4, (b)-2, (c)-1, (d)-3

34. Match List–I (Structural Health Parameters) with List–II (Ayurvedic Recommendations):

List–I	List–II
(a) Joint Lubrication Maintenance	1. Use of Shleshaka Kapha-enhancing therapies
(b) Strengthening Bone Framework	2. Nourishment of Asthi Dhatu through diet and herbs
(c) Elasticity in Ligaments	3. Exercise and yoga targeting Snāyu health
(d) Mobility in Joints	4. Vata Dosha pacifying treatments

Choose the correct answer from the options given below:

A. (a)-1, (b)-2, (c)-3, (d)-4
B. (a)-3, (b)-4, (c)-1, (d)-2
C. (a)-2, (b)-1, (c)-4, (d)-3
D. (a)-4, (b)-3, (c)-2, (d)-1

Directions (Q. No. 35-39): *Following questions are based on Statement 1 and Statement 2. Read both the statements carefully and choose the correct answer from the options given below:*

A. Both Statement 1 and Statement 2 are true, and Statement 2 is the correct explanation of Statement 1.
B. Both Statement 1 and Statement 2 are true, but Statement 2 is not the correct explanation of Statement 1.
C. Statement 1 is true, but Statement 2 is false.
D. Statement 1 is false, but Statement 2 is true.
E. Both Statement 1 and Statement 2 are false.

35. **Statement 1:** The bones (Asthi) in Ayurveda are considered to be formed from the nutrient plasma (Rasa Dhatu) undergoing transformation through the metabolic fire (Agni) at each stage of dhatu formation.

Statement 2: The health and density of bones are directly proportional to the strength and stability of Kapha Dosha in the body.

36. **Statement 1:** Snāyu (ligaments) provide structural stability and elasticity to the joints, allowing for smooth movement and preventing dislocations.

Statement 2: Weakness in Snāyu is primarily caused by aggravated Kapha Dosha, leading to reduced flexibility and increased stiffness in joints.

37. **Statement 1:** The role of Shleshaka Kapha in joints is critical for ensuring lubrication and preventing friction during movement.

Statement 2: Dehydration, improper diet, and imbalance in Vata Dosha can lead to the depletion of Shleshaka Kapha, resulting in joint disorders such as osteoarthritis.

38. **Statement 1:** Sandhi (joints) are formed at the meeting points of bones, held together by Snāyu and lubricated by Shleshaka Kapha to facilitate movement.

Statement 2: An imbalance in Vata Dosha can lead to degeneration of Sandhi, causing conditions such as joint pain and inflammation.

39. **Statement 1:** Strengthening Asthi Dhatu (bones) requires a balanced intake of calcium-rich foods and herbs like Laksha and Guggulu in Ayurvedic practice.

Statement 2: Vitiated Pitta Dosha is the main cause of brittle bones, as it interferes with the absorption of nutrients necessary for Asthi formation.

Directions (Q. No. 40-45): *There are two statements in each question. One is labelled as Assertion (A) and the other is as Reason (R). Read both the statements and choose the correct answer from the options given below:*

A. Both Assertion (A) and Reason (R) are true, and Reason (R) is the correct explanation of Assertion (A).
B. Both Assertion (A) and Reason (R) are true, but Reason (R) is not the correct explanation of Assertion (A).
C. Assertion (A) is true, but Reason (R) is false.
D. Assertion (A) is false, but Reason (R) is true.
E. Both Assertion (A) and Reason (R) are false.

40. **Assertion (A):** The formation and strength of Sandhi (joints) depend on the nourishment provided by Asthi Dhatu and the presence of healthy Snāyu (ligaments).

Reason (R): A deficiency in Rasa Dhatu results in improper nourishment of subsequent dhatus, including Asthi Dhatu, leading to weakened joints and ligaments.

41. **Assertion (A):** Shleshaka Kapha is crucial for the lubrication and functionality of Sandhi, preventing friction between the bones.

Reason (R): An increase in Kapha Dosha enhances joint lubrication, making the joints more flexible and preventing conditions like stiffness.

42. **Assertion (A):** The role of Snāyu in joint stability is compromised when Vata Dosha becomes aggravated in the body.

Reason (R): Aggravated Vata Dosha dries out Snāyu and Shleshaka Kapha, reducing elasticity and leading to joint instability.

43. **Assertion (A):** A balanced Pitta Dosha ensures the proper metabolic activity required for the assimilation of nutrients into Asthi Dhatu.

Reason (R): Pitta Dosha governs the digestion and transformation of Rasa Dhatu into subsequent tissues, making it essential for bone development.

44. **Assertion (A):** Kapha Dosha governs the structural integrity and stability of Asthi and Snāyu.

    Reason (R): Kapha Dosha provides the physical strength and lubrication needed for bones and ligaments to function without damage.

45. **Assertion (A):** Regular consumption of Asthi-nourishing herbs like Guggulu and Laksha can restore the balance of weakened Asthi Dhatu.

    Reason (R): These herbs directly stimulate the metabolic fire (Agni) responsible for the regeneration of weakened dhatus, including bones.

Directions (Q. No. 46–50): *Read the passage carefully and answer the questions given below*:

In Ayurveda, the human body is viewed as a microcosm of the universe, with its structural and functional elements intricately designed to maintain balance and harmony. The body structures in Ayurveda, such as asthi (bones), sandhi (joints), and snāyu (ligaments), are not merely anatomical entities but also functional components interconnected with doshas, dhatus, and agni. These structures serve as the foundation for physical stability, movement, and physiological processes.

Asthi, or bones, represent the fifth dhatu in the sequence of bodily tissues and are considered the most robust structures in the body. They provide the framework that supports the entire body, safeguarding internal organs and enabling locomotion. The formation of asthi is governed by asthi-dhatu-agni, which is responsible for metabolizing nutrients from meda (fat tissue) and transforming them into bone tissue. An imbalance in the metabolic fire or vitiation of doshas, particularly Vata, can lead to conditions such as osteoporosis, fractures, or bone deformities.

Sandhi, the joints, are formed at the meeting points of two or more bones and are stabilized by snāyu (ligaments). These structures enable the body's mobility and flexibility. In Ayurvedic physiology, sandhi is nourished by asthi dhatu and is protected by Shleshaka Kapha, which ensures lubrication and minimizes friction during movement. An imbalance in Vata Dosha can dry out Shleshaka Kapha, leading to joint stiffness and disorders like arthritis. Meanwhile, excessive Kapha can result in reduced mobility due to heaviness or swelling.

Snāyu, or ligaments, act as the binding forces, maintaining the integrity of joints and bones. These fibrous tissues are governed by both Kapha and Vata Dosha, which regulate their strength and flexibility. A balance between these doshas ensures that ligaments are neither too rigid nor too lax, allowing for optimal functionality. Injuries or imbalances, such as an aggravated Vata, can weaken ligaments and increase the risk of sprains and dislocations.

Ayurvedic texts further classify body structures into various categories based on their origin, function, and composition. For instance, asthi can be divided into types such as long bones (dīrgha asthi), flat bones (kapāla asthi), and short bones (hṛid asthi). Similarly, joints are categorized into immovable (sthira sandhi), slightly movable (manda sandhi), and freely movable (chala sandhi), reflecting their structural diversity and functional roles. Ligaments, though not categorized explicitly in classical texts, are implicitly described as vital elements of joint mechanics.

The function of these body structures transcends mere mechanical support. Ayurveda emphasizes the interplay between physical structures and their energetic counterparts. For example, asthi is associated with the Earth element (Prithvi Mahabhuta), symbolizing stability and endurance. Joints are linked to the Water element (Jala Mahabhuta), representing fluidity and adaptability, while ligaments embody the interplay of both Earth and Air (Vayu) elements, denoting their dual roles in stability and movement.

Maintenance of these body structures requires a holistic approach. The consumption of nourishing herbs like Guggulu and Shatavari, coupled with regular Abhyanga (oil massage) and yogic practices, is recommended to strengthen bones, joints, and ligaments. Furthermore, balancing Vata Dosha through warm, unctuous foods and Kapha Dosha through light, drying regimens ensures the optimal functionality of these structures. Ayurveda also highlights the role of proper Agni in the assimilation of nutrients and the prevention of ama (toxins), which can obstruct srotas (channels) and impair structural integrity.

Pathological conditions affecting these structures are deeply rooted in the imbalance of doshas and dhatus. Osteoarthritis, a common joint disorder, is attributed to the aggravation of Vata, leading to the degeneration of cartilage and ligaments. Rheumatoid arthritis, on the other hand, involves an interplay of aggravated Kapha and Pitta, resulting in swelling and inflammation. Bone fractures are managed through specialized treatments like Asthi Sandhana Chikitsa, which includes the use of herbal poultices and internal medications to accelerate healing.

In conclusion, the Ayurvedic perspective on body structures is holistic, integrating anatomical, physiological, and energetic dimensions. The interconnectedness of asthi, sandhi, and snāyu with doshas, dhatus, and agni underscores the complexity of human anatomy as envisioned in Ayurveda. By maintaining a balance in these elements, one can ensure not only structural integrity but also overall health and well-being.

46. Which dosha imbalance is primarily responsible for the drying out of Shleshaka Kapha in joints, leading to stiffness?
    A. Pitta Dosha
    B. Vata Dosha
    C. Kapha Dosha
    D. Sleshma Dosha

47. What is the primary role of asthi-dhatu-agni in bone formation?
A. To convert meda (fat tissue) into asthi (bone tissue) through metabolic transformation
B. To regulate the balance of Shleshaka Kapha in joints
C. To strengthen ligaments and prevent dislocations
D. To detoxify bone tissue of accumulated ama (toxins)

48. What classification in Ayurveda is applicable to a joint that allows free movement, such as the shoulder?
A. Sthira Sandhi
B. Manda Sandhi
C. Chala Sandhi
D. Asandhi

49. What is the significance of the Earth element (Prithvi Mahabhuta) in relation to asthi?
A. It ensures the flexibility and lubrication of bones.
B. It provides structural stability and endurance.
C. It governs the movement and adaptability of ligaments.
D. It supports the nourishment of Rasa Dhatu.

50. Which of the following Ayurvedic practices is specifically recommended to strengthen body structures like bones, joints, and ligaments?
A. Fasting and Kapha-reducing diets exclusively
B. Regular Abhyanga (oil massage) and the use of herbs like Guggulu
C. Consumption of cooling foods to balance Pitta Dosha
D. Avoidance of exercise and physical strain to preserve energy

ANSWER WITH EXPLANATIONS

1. **A:** In Ayurveda, Asthi Dhatu (bone tissue) is nourished through the sequential transformation of dhatus, which is governed by Agni (digestive fire). If Agni is impaired, the nourishment of subsequent dhatus, including Asthi, becomes inadequate. Since Asthi Dhatu supports Sandhi (joints) and Snāyu (ligaments), its weakness leads to poor joint stability and reduced ligament strength. Enhancing Agni with Triphala and diet improves nutrient absorption and restores dhatu health. Hence, the systemic improvements observed align with this principle.

2. **A:** Shleshaka Kapha is the sub-type of Kapha responsible for lubricating joints (Sandhi) and ensuring smooth movement. An aggravated Vata dosha dries up Shleshaka Kapha, causing stiffness, pain, and cracking in joints. Ayurvedic management focuses on pacifying Vata and restoring Kapha to rebalance this lubrication. The described treatment—oil application, warm therapies, and diet—aligns perfectly with this doshic correction, leading to better joint mobility and reduced discomfort.

3. **A:** According to Ayurvedic understanding, Snāyu (ligaments) are influenced by Vata (flexibility) and Kapha (stability). An imbalance in either can make ligaments too rigid or too loose, increasing injury risk. Strengthening Kapha adds structural integrity, while pacifying Vata restores mobility. Herbs like Ashwagandha and oils like Bala Taila support both actions. Thus, the physiotherapist's success in reducing ligament injuries reflects effective dosha balancing as per classical Ayurvedic principles.

4. **A:** The patient's symptoms—dryness, stiffness, and cracking joints—clearly reflect aggravated Vata and depleted Shleshaka Kapha. Vata dries tissues, while Shleshaka Kapha ensures lubrication. Ayurvedic treatment aims to pacify Vata and replenish Kapha through warm, oily, and nourishing therapies like Abhyanga and Kapha-enhancing diet. The positive outcome in lubrication and flexibility proves the effectiveness of restoring this doshic equilibrium in joint health.

5. **A:** Mamsa Dhatu (muscle tissue) requires strong Agni for its nourishment and development. Poor digestion weakens Kapha and disrupts tissue formation, leading to low muscle tone and fatigue. Herbs like Pippali and Trikatu boost digestive fire, enabling better assimilation of proteins and nutrients to support muscle structure. Ayurveda emphasizes that robust Agni is foundational to all dhatu formation, including Mamsa.

6. **A:** Asthi Dhatu does more than support bones—it contributes to the strength of Snāyu (ligaments) and Kandra (tendons) as well. Weak Asthi leads to reduced structural integrity in these tissues. Ayurveda prescribes bone-strengthening herbs like Laksha and tailas to restore tissue health, while digestive tonics enhance Agni for proper nutrient assimilation. The resulting improvements in bones and ligaments validate the interdependence of these structures through Asthi Dhatu.

7. **A:** Vata dosha governs all forms of movement, including joint and ligament flexibility. Its aggravation results in dryness, reduced lubrication, and stiffness. The Ayurvedic recommendation—Abhyanga (oil massage),

warm foods, and nourishing diets—directly calms Vata and restores functional elasticity to ligaments and joints. The students' positive response shows that Vata pacification leads to better movement and ligament health, which is a core Ayurvedic teaching.

8. **A:** Poor muscle tone and posture often stem from weakened Mamsa Dhatu and aggravated Vata, which affects structure and coordination. A Kapha-enhancing diet and Ashwagandha-based tonics strengthen muscles, while Vata-calming therapies restore nerve-muscle coordination. This approach demonstrates the Ayurvedic view of muscles as structural supports, whose health depends on both dhatu nourishment and dosha balance.

9. **A:** Ligaments (Snāyu) must be flexible (Vata) yet stable (Kapha) to prevent injuries. The Ayurvedic combination of oil massage, warmth, and Ashwagandha addresses both aspects: pacifies Vata to reduce strain and strengthens Kapha to reinforce structure. This dual-action approach aligns with classical Ayurveda, which sees ligament health as dependent on balanced doshic interplay, not just physical training.

10. **A:** Shleshaka Kapha ensures smooth joint movement by providing necessary lubrication. When Vata aggravates and Kapha depletes, joint dryness and stiffness ensue. Restoring Shleshaka Kapha with oils and balancing Vata through warmth and nourishing foods improves joint mobility. Ayurveda teaches that maintaining dosha balance is essential for healthy joint function, making this therapeutic strategy highly effective.

11. **A:** In Ayurveda, Agni (digestive fire) governs the transformation and nourishment of all dhatus (body tissues). A properly functioning agni ensures that nutrients reach asthi dhatu, which then supports snāyu (ligaments) and sandhi (joints). Weak agni leads to malnourishment, while strengthening agni through herbs like Triphala supports tissue regeneration and stability.

12. **A:** Sustainable Ayurvedic practice emphasizes conservation of medicinal plants like Laksha and Ashwagandha. Community-driven cultivation ensures a continuous, high-quality supply while protecting natural habitats. This aligns with Ayurveda's holistic approach, which includes ecological harmony along with human health.

13. **A:** In Ayurveda, the potency (virya) and quality (guna) of herbs are crucial for their effectiveness. Overharvesting lowers potency, which directly affects outcomes such as improved bone density and ligament strength. Therefore, weaker formulations lead to diminished therapeutic results, even with correct protocols.

14. **A:** The most comprehensive solution addresses both sustainability and therapeutic efficacy. Controlled cultivation preserves endangered herbs, while modern research ensures their quality. This dual approach maintains Ayurveda's integrity and effectiveness while preventing depletion of natural resources.

15. **C:** Each structure has a distinct function: Asthi governs strength and structure, Sandhi enables movement and stability, Snāyu connects and supports, and Shleshaka Kapha lubricates joints. This alignment reflects the Ayurvedic anatomical framework outlined in classical texts.

16. **B:** Asthi is nourished by meda dhatu, and sandhi connects skeletal parts. Snāyu are extensions or reinforcements of bone tissue that provide joint support. Shleshaka Kapha, a subtype of Kapha dosha, ensures lubrication. All four statements align with Ayurvedic doctrine.

17. **C:** Vata aggravation leads to pain and stiffness; depleted Shleshaka Kapha causes dryness; weak asthi dhatu results in brittle bones; and impaired Snāyu elasticity compromises stability. This reflects the interconnected pathogenesis of joint and bone disorders in Ayurveda.

18. **A:** Asthi supports skeletal structure and ligament attachment. Snāyu provide elasticity and stability. Impaired agni leads to poor nourishment of asthi and, indirectly, of sandhi and snāyu. Statement (c) is false, as sandhi depends heavily on shleshaka kapha for lubrication.

19. **D:** Aggravated Vata requires Vata-pacifying diets and tonics; depleted Shleshaka Kapha responds to warm, unctuous treatments; poor snāyu nourishment benefits from herbs like Ashwagandha and Guggulu; and chronic joint pain from poor agni responds to medicated oils and fomentation.

20. **A:** Snāyu stabilize joints, their elasticity is governed by Vata dosha, and they are nourished through a healthy asthi dhatu. However, Shleshaka Kapha also contributes indirectly to snāyu function, so (d) is incorrect as it ignores this interdependence.

21. **A:** Each structure in Ayurvedic physiology is supported by a corresponding element: Shleshaka Kapha lubricates joints, Vata governs motion and flexibility, asthi dhatu provides stability, and snāyu ensure elasticity. This is the classical alignment of dosha–dhatu interactions.

22. **A:** Asthi gives skeletal strength, Snāyu offer flexibility, and sandhi act as junctions. However, joint stability is primarily maintained by Kapha and Snāyu, not Vata alone, making statement (d) inaccurate.

23. B: Asthi = framework, Snāyu = elasticity, Sandhi = movement facilitation, Shleshaka Kapha = smooth motion. These roles together maintain the integrity of the musculoskeletal system as per Ayurvedic principles.

24. A: Agni influences nourishment of asthi; Shleshaka Kapha ensures joint lubrication; Vata must be balanced for joint stability. However, Kapha cannot fully compensate for poor agni in tissue nourishment, making (d) incorrect.

25. C: Shleshaka Kapha lubricates joints, Asthi provides structure, Snāyu connect and stabilize, and Sandhi facilitate alignment and motion. This mapping reflects their exact Ayurvedic roles.

26. A: Joint lubrication is due to Shleshaka Kapha; Snāyu offers ligament stability; asthi governs bone strength; Vata controls flexibility. These match the classical functions of doshas and dhatus.

27. D: Loss of lubrication = depleted Shleshaka Kapha; stiffness = aggravated Vata; brittle bones = weak asthi; ligament weakness = poor snāyu nourishment. These conditions reflect Ayurvedic pathology.

28. D: Ashwagandha strengthens snāyu; Snehan (oiling) restores shleshaka kapha; Laksha nourishes asthi dhatu; Swedana targets joints (sandhi). Each intervention is matched to its structural target.

29. D: Lubrication = Shleshaka Kapha, Joints = structural elements, Bones = support system, Ligaments = governed by Vata for movement. This represents Ayurvedic structure-function mapping.

30. B: Weak asthi dhatu = bone herbs; Shleshaka depletion = warm oil; Vata in joints = pacifying diets; weak snāyu = Ashwagandha. Each cause is paired with a therapy that addresses the root issue.

31. A: Snāyu relates to ligament strength; asthi dhatu builds bones; agni supports all dhatu formation; Shleshaka Kapha handles joint lubrication. Each concept is correctly matched to its function.

32. A: Vata causes dryness; impaired snāyu = instability; weak asthi = brittle bones; Kapha depletion = loss of lubrication. This mirrors common Ayurvedic presentations in degenerative disorders.

33. B: Balancing agni improves dhatu formation; ligament exercise builds elasticity; Snehan enhances joint lubrication; Laksha & Guggulu strengthen asthi dhatu. This sequence matches therapeutic intent.

34. A. Kapha therapy enhances lubrication; bone strength comes from asthi nourishment; elasticity through snāyu-targeted yoga; Vata-pacifying improves mobility. These represent integrated Ayurvedic care.

35. C: Statement 1 is correct — Ayurveda describes dhatu formation through the action of Agni at each level, and Asthi Dhatu is formed after Meda Dhatu under the influence of Agni.

However, Statement 2 is false. Although Kapha contributes to structure, Asthi Dhatu is more closely linked with Vata and Agni than with Kapha. Kapha provides lubrication and cohesiveness, but bone density is not directly proportional to Kapha strength.

36. C: Statement 1 is true—Snāyu (ligaments) provide elasticity and stability to joints, making movement smooth and preventing dislocations. However, Statement 2 is false because Snāyu weakness is primarily caused by Vata Dosha aggravation, not Kapha. Excess Vata dries tissues, reducing elasticity. Kapha provides strength, not stiffness, so blaming Kapha for reduced flexibility is incorrect.

37. A: Both statements are true and S2 correctly explains S1. Shleshaka Kapha is responsible for lubricating joints, preventing friction between bones. When Vata is aggravated, it leads to drying effects, depleting Shleshaka Kapha, which then causes conditions like osteoarthritis. This correlation aligns with Ayurvedic pathogenesis, where Vata's increase reduces Kapha's protective functions.

38. A: Statement 1 accurately describes joint anatomy in Ayurveda: Sandhi is formed by the union of bones (Asthi), held together by ligaments (Snāyu), and lubricated by Shleshaka Kapha. Statement 2 correctly explains that Vata imbalance can dry out Kapha and damage joint function. Hence, both statements are true, and S2 is the correct explanation of S1.

39. C: Statement 1 is true—Ayurveda supports using herbs like Laksha and Guggulu to strengthen Asthi Dhatu. However, Statement 2 is false because Pitta is not the main dosha behind brittle bones—it's more commonly Vata, especially when it dries out dhatus. Pitta governs transformation but not primarily nutrient absorption into bones. So, S1 is true, S2 is false.

40. A: Both Assertion (A) and Reason (R) are true, and R correctly explains A. According to Ayurveda, Asthi Dhatu nourishes the joints (Sandhi), while Snāyu (ligaments) provide the structural support needed for joint movement. But this nourishment depends on proper dhatu transformation, which begins with Rasa Dhatu. If Rasa is weak, all subsequent dhatus—including Asthi and Snāyu—are poorly nourished, leading to weakened joints. Thus, R is the correct explanation of A.

41. B: Both statements are true, but the Reason is not the correct explanation of the Assertion. Shleshaka Kapha does provide joint lubrication and protects against friction (Assertion is true). However, excess Kapha doesn't necessarily increase lubrication positively—instead, it may cause heaviness or swelling. Proper lubrication is more about Kapha being in balance, not simply increased. So, while both are correct, R is not the direct explanation of A.

42. **A:** Assertion (A) is correct—Snāyu stability is compromised when Vata is aggravated, as Vata governs movement and dryness. Reason (R) is also true—Vata causes dryness, reducing the elasticity of Snāyu and depleting Shleshaka Kapha, leading to instability. This makes both A and R true, and R perfectly explains A based on Ayurvedic pathology.

43. **A:** Pitta Dosha, particularly Pachaka Pitta, governs digestion and the metabolic transformation of nutrients. It's essential for converting Rasa into subsequent dhatus like Asthi. Hence, a balanced Pitta ensures proper assimilation of nutrients into Asthi Dhatu. Both A and R are correct, and R directly supports A, making Option A the right choice.

44. **A:** Kapha Dosha provides strength, cohesion, and lubrication, which are vital for both Asthi and Snāyu. Assertion (A) correctly states Kapha's role in structural stability, and Reason (R) supports this by explaining Kapha's qualities of strength and support, which protect bones and ligaments from damage. So, both statements are true and R explains A.

45. **C:** Assertion (A) is true—Guggulu and Laksha are classical Asthi-nourishing herbs that help regenerate bone tissue. However, Reason (R) is false—these herbs do not directly stimulate Agni (digestive fire). Instead, they act more on the dhatu level (tissue level), especially Asthi Dhatu, by nourishing and promoting tissue regeneration. So, A is true, but R is incorrect.

46. **B:** As per the passage, Vata Dosha, when aggravated, leads to the drying of Shleshaka Kapha, which normally lubricates joints. This drying effect causes stiffness and pain. Therefore, Vata is primarily responsible for joint disorders related to lubrication, not Pitta or Kapha.

47. **A:** Asthi-dhatu-agni is the metabolic fire at the level of Asthi Dhatu. It transforms the nutrients received from Meda Dhatu into Asthi Dhatu, making bones strong and healthy. This tissue-specific metabolism is crucial in Ayurveda's dhatu formation process, affirming option A as correct.

48. **C:** Chala Sandhi refers to freely movable joints in Ayurveda—like the shoulder or hip. These joints allow for extensive motion and are stabilized by Snāyu and lubricated by Kapha. Manda Sandhi is partially movable, and Sthira Sandhi is immovable, so Chala is the correct classification here.

49. **B:** The Earth element (Prithvi Mahabhuta) is associated with stability, strength, and support, all qualities represented by Asthi (bones). In Ayurveda, bones embody this element as they provide the body's foundational support, hence B is correct.

50. **B:** The passage emphasizes Abhyanga (oil massage) and the use of herbs like Guggulu and Shatavari to nourish and strengthen bones, joints, and ligaments. These therapies enhance lubrication, improve dhatu formation, and maintain musculoskeletal health, making B the best answer.

CHAPTER 11

PADARTHA, SAPTAPADARTHA, AND CLASSIFICATION OF DRAVYA

INTRODUCTION TO PADĀRTHA

In Ayurveda, the concept of Padārtha forms the foundation for understanding the universe and its various components. The term "Padārtha" is derived from two Sanskrit words: Pada (word or term) and Arthaḥ (meaning). Together, Padārtha signifies "the object or entity denoted by a word," representing the categories of knowledge or realities that constitute the cosmos. This classification provides a structured framework to understand and analyze the metaphysical and physical aspects of existence.

Definition of Padārtha

Padārtha is defined as "that which can be thought of, expressed in words, and comprehended by the mind." It serves as the basic unit of knowledge, encompassing all that exists or can be conceptualized. It is not limited to physical objects but extends to abstract concepts, qualities, actions, and relations.

Significance of Padārtha

1. **Epistemological Basis:** Padārtha serves as the foundation for acquiring knowledge (Jñāna). By categorizing reality, it provides a systematic approach to understanding the world.
2. **Philosophical Framework:** The concept forms the backbone of Nyāya-Vaiśeṣika philosophy, which explores the nature of existence and reality.
3. **Integration with Ayurveda:** In Ayurveda, Padārtha is used to classify substances (Dravya), qualities (Guṇa), and actions (Karma), facilitating a holistic understanding of health and disease.
4. **Practical Application:** Padārtha offers tools for logical reasoning, problem-solving, and decision-making, which are essential in disciplines like medicine, ethics, and metaphysics.

The Seven Padārthas (Saptapadārtha)

The Nyāya-Vaiśeṣika school of Indian philosophy identifies seven categories or Padārthas, collectively known as Saptapadārtha. These categories encompass all aspects of reality, providing a comprehensive framework for metaphysical inquiry.

1. **Dravya (Substance):** Dravya refers to the substratum or entity in which qualities (Guṇas) and actions (Karma) reside. It is the fundamental building block of the universe, possessing independent existence.

   Classification of Dravya:

   1. **Physical Substances:** Earth (Prithvi), Water (Āpah), Fire (Tejas), Air (Vāyu), and Ether (Ākāśa).
   2. **Non-Physical Substances:** Time (Kāla), Space (Dik), Soul (Ātman), and Mind (Manas).
   3. **Significance in Ayurveda:** Dravyas are the carriers of Guṇas and Karma, essential in understanding pharmacology, pathology, and therapeutics.

2. **Guṇa (Quality):** Guṇas are attributes or properties that exist in substances (Dravya) and define their characteristics. Unlike substances, Guṇas cannot exist independently.

Examples of Guṇas:

- **Physical:** Colour, taste, smell, touch, sound.
- **Psychological:** Intelligence, pleasure, pain.
- **Ayurvedic Significance:** The 20 Guṇas (e.g., heavy/light, hot/cold) form the basis of doshic analysis.

3. **Karma (Action)**: Karma refers to motion or activity inherent in substances. It is responsible for change and interaction among entities.

   Types of Karma:
   1. Upward motion
   2. Downward motion
   3. Contraction
   4. Expansion
   5. Locomotion

   Relevance in Ayurveda: Karma helps explain physiological functions (e.g., digestion, circulation) and the therapeutic actions of herbs and treatments.

4. **Sāmānya (Generality)**: Sāmānya signifies commonality or the universal characteristics shared by different entities. It highlights the underlying unity in diversity.

   Examples:
   - Heat in fire and sunlight.
   - Solidity in earth and metal.

   Role in Ayurveda: Sāmānya aids in grouping substances based on shared properties, crucial for diagnosis and treatment planning.

5. **Viśeṣa (Particularity):** Viśeṣa refers to individuality or the unique attributes that differentiate one entity from another.

   Examples:
   - Sweetness of sugar versus bitterness of neem.
   - The distinct constitution of Vata, Pitta, and Kapha individuals.

   Relevance in Ayurveda: Viśeṣa facilitates personalized medicine by focusing on individual differences.

6. **Samavāya (Inherence):** Samavāya denotes the inseparable relationship between entities. It explains how qualities (Guṇa) and actions (Karma) are inseparably linked to substances (Dravya).

   Examples:
   - The relationship between sweetness and sugar.
   - The bond between consciousness and the soul.

7. **Abhāva (Non-Existence):** Abhāva represents the absence or negation of an entity. It highlights the reality of "nothingness" as a valid concept.

   Types of Abhāva:
   1. **Prāgabhāva (Prior Absence):** Absence of an entity before it comes into existence.
   2. **Pradhvaṃsābhāva (Posterior Absence):** Absence after destruction.
   3. **Atyantābhāva (Absolute Non-Existence):** Eternal absence.
   4. **Anyonyābhāva (Mutual Non-Existence):** Mutual exclusivity.

   Relevance in Ayurveda: Abhāva explains the absence of doshic balance or absence of disease during health.

Classification of Dravya (Substances) in Ayurveda

The concept of Dravya (substance) occupies a central position in Ayurveda, forming the basis for understanding the interaction between body, mind, and external substances in the context of health and disease. Dravya is defined as the carrier of properties (guṇas) and actions (karmas), making it a fundamental entity in the pharmacological, physiological, and therapeutic domains of Ayurveda.

1. **Definition of Dravya:** Dravya is described in Ayurveda as the substratum or entity in which Guṇa (qualities) and Karma (actions) exist. It serves as the fundamental basis for all biological, chemical, and physical processes in the body and environment.

   Etymological Meaning:
   - The word "Dravya" is derived from the Sanskrit root "Dru", which means "to flow" or "to act." This signifies its dynamic nature and capacity to interact with other substances.

   Philosophical Definition:
   - In Nyāya-Vaiśeṣika philosophy, Dravya is considered one of the seven Padārthas, characterized by its ability to carry and support Guṇas and Karmas.

   Ayurvedic Definition:
   - According to Charaka and Sushruta, Dravya is the entity responsible for maintaining health (through proper use) and curing diseases (through therapeutic use). It is inseparable from Guṇas and Karmas, which determine its effects on the human body.

2. **Importance of Dravya in Ayurveda**: Dravya serves as the cornerstone for Ayurvedic science due to its relevance in various domains:
   - **Pharmacology:** Dravyas form the basis for drugs, herbs, and minerals used in Ayurvedic treatments.
   - **Dietetics:** Dietary substances (Ahara Dravyas) are integral to maintaining health and preventing disease.

- **Pathology:** Understanding the interplay of Dravyas helps identify causative factors (Nidana) of diseases.
- **Therapeutics:** The choice of appropriate Dravyas determines the efficacy of treatments.

3. **General Classification of Dravya:** The classification of Dravya in Ayurveda is highly systematic, allowing practitioners to understand and utilize substances effectively. Dravyas are broadly classified based on origin, composition, therapeutic properties, and functional aspects.

(I) Classification Based on Origin: This classification divides Dravyas into three primary categories based on their source:

1. **Jangama Dravya (Animal-Origin Substances):** Derived from animals, these include milk, ghee, honey, meat, and bone marrow.
   Examples:
   - **Milk:** Nutritive and rejuvenating.
   - **Honey:** Antiseptic and antimicrobial.
   - **Bone marrow:** Used in treating bone-related disorders.
2. **Sthāvara Dravya (Plant-Origin Substances):** Derived from plants, these include herbs, roots, fruits, seeds, and bark.
   Examples:
   - **Neem:** Antimicrobial and blood purifier.
   - **Ashwagandha:** Adaptogen and stress reliever.
   - **Turmeric:** Anti-inflammatory and wound-healing.
3. **Khani Dravya (Mineral-Origin Substances):** Derived from minerals and metals, these include salts, stones, and metallic preparations.
   Examples:
   - **Shilajit:** Anti-aging and vitality booster.
   - **Swarna Bhasma (Gold Ash):** Immunomodulator.
   - **Rock Salt:** Improves digestion and balances doshas.

(II) Classification Based on Panchamahābhūta (Five Elements): Every Dravya is considered to be composed of the five fundamental elements (Panchamahābhūta):

1. **Prithvi (Earth):** Solidity and stability.
2. **Āpah (Water):** Fluidity and cohesion.
3. **Tejas (Fire):** Heat and transformation.
4. **Vāyu (Air):** Movement and dynamism.
5. **Ākāśa (Ether):** Space and subtlety.

Examples of Dravyas Dominated by Specific Elements:

- **Earth-dominant:** Grains like wheat and rice.
- **Water-dominant:** Juices, oils, and milk.
- **Fire-dominant:** Spices like pepper and ginger.
- **Air-dominant:** Dry herbs and leafy vegetables.
- **Ether-dominant:** Aromatic substances like camphor.

(III) Classification Based on Rasa (Taste): Taste (Rasa) is a fundamental characteristic of Dravyas and determines their pharmacological effects. Ayurveda identifies six Rasas:

1. **Madhura (Sweet):** Nourishing and calming.
   Examples: Milk, sugar, ghee.
2. **Amla (Sour):** Stimulates digestion.
   Examples: Lemon, tamarind.
3. **Lavana (Salty):** Improves taste and digestion.
   Examples: Rock salt, sea salt.
4. **Katu (Pungent):** Detoxifying and stimulating.
   Examples: Ginger, black pepper.
5. **Tikta (Bitter):** Cleansing and cooling.
   Examples: Neem, karela (bitter gourd).
6. **Kashaya (Astringent):** Healing and drying.
   Examples: Pomegranate, alum.

(IV) Classification Based on Guṇa (Quality): Guṇas are inherent properties that define the nature of Dravyas. Ayurveda describes 20 Gunas (grouped in pairs of opposites):

1. **Guru (Heavy):** Laghu (Light).
2. **Manda (Dull):** Tikshna (Sharp).
3. **Shita (Cold):** Ushna (Hot).
4. **Snigdha (Unctuous):** Ruksha (Dry).
5. **Sthira (Stable):** Chala (Mobile).
6. **Mridu (Soft):** Kathina (Hard).
7. **Sukshma (Subtle):** Sthula (Gross).
8. **Sandra (Dense):** Drava (Fluid).
9. **Slakshna (Smooth):** Khara (Rough).
10. **Vishada (Clear):** Picchila (Sticky).

Applications: Guṇas help in understanding the compatibility of Dravyas with individual constitutions (Prakriti) and conditions.

(V) Classification Based on Karma (Action): The action (Karma) of a Dravya determines its therapeutic effects. **Examples include:**

1. **Deepana (Digestive Stimulant):** Ginger, black pepper.
2. **Balya (Strengthening):** Ashwagandha, ghee.
3. **Shodhana (Cleansing):** Triphala, neem.
4. **Rasayana (Rejuvenative):** Shilajit, amla.

(VI) Classification Based on Virya (Potency): Virya refers to the active potency of a Dravya, determining its immediate effects. It is classified into:

1. **Ushna (Hot):** Promotes digestion and circulation (e.g., garlic).
2. **Shita (Cold):** Calms and cools (e.g., sandalwood).

(VII) Classification Based on Vipāka (Post-Digestive Effect): Vipāka is the transformed state of Rasa after digestion, classified as:

1. **Madhura (Sweet):** Nourishing and anabolic.
2. **Amla (Sour):** Stimulating and metabolic.
3. **Katu (Pungent):** Detoxifying and catabolic.

(VIII) Therapeutic Classification: Dravyas are categorized based on their medicinal utility:

1. **Ahara Dravya (Dietary Substances):** Food and beverages.
2. **Aushadha Dravya (Medicinal Substances):** Herbs, minerals, and animal products.
3. **Visha Dravya (Toxic Substances):** Poisons used in controlled doses for treatment.

(IX) Classification Based on Dosha Affinity: Dravyas are grouped based on their ability to balance or aggravate the three doshas (Vata, Pitta, Kapha):

1. **Vata-pacifying:** Sesame oil, almonds.
2. **Pitta-pacifying:** Aloe vera, sandalwood.
3. **Kapha-pacifying:** Ginger, pepper.

4. **Dravya in the Context of Ayurveda's Trisutra:** Dravyas are pivotal in the framework of Ayurveda's Trisutra (three fundamental principles):

1. **Hetu (Causes):** Dravyas causing disease or health.
2. **Linga (Symptoms):** Effects of Dravyas on the body.
3. **Aushadha (Treatment):** Use of Dravyas for therapy.

The classification of Dravya in Ayurveda is an intricate and comprehensive system that integrates philosophy, science, and medicine. By categorizing substances based on their origin, properties, and effects, Ayurveda offers a structured approach to health and healing. This classification not only aids in understanding the therapeutic potential of Dravyas but also serves as a guide for their practical application in maintaining health and treating diseases.

5. **Integration of Padārtha and Dravya in Ayurveda:** Ayurveda seamlessly integrates the philosophical concept of Padārtha with practical applications. Dravya, as the primary Padārtha, forms the basis of all Ayurvedic formulations and therapies. The properties (Guṇa) and actions (Karma) of Dravyas are analyzed to restore balance and promote health.

- **Philosophical Insights:** The understanding of Sāmānya and Viśeṣa helps in identifying substances with similar or opposite properties for treatment.
- **Therapeutic Framework:** The classification of Dravya guides the preparation of medicines, dietary recommendations, and therapeutic interventions.

The study of Padārtha, Saptapadārtha, and the classification of Dravya is central to both Indian philosophy and Ayurveda. It bridges metaphysical concepts with practical applications, enabling a holistic understanding of life, health, and the universe. By categorizing reality into well-defined components, Padārtha offers a structured approach to knowledge that continues to guide philosophical inquiry and medical practice alike.

MULTIPLE CHOICE QUESTIONS

1. A pharmacologist deeply engaged in the study of Ayurvedic pharmacology embarks on an investigation of the interplay between Rasas (tastes) and their respective Vipāka (post-digestive effects). They propose that the initial anabolic properties of Madhura (sweet) Rasa, while predominantly cooling, may transition to a heating effect within the digestive tract when consumed excessively. Conversely, Tikta (bitter) Rasa maintains its inherently cooling properties throughout, regardless of dosage. Which interpretation best elucidates this hypothesis?
   A. Sweet Rasa invariably retains its cooling nature, irrespective of its consumption levels, undermining claims of any heating potential.
   B. Bitter Rasa, while maintaining its cooling post-digestive property, does not produce significant systemic effects.
   C. The Vipāka of sweet Rasa exhibits a dose-dependent duality, whereas bitter Rasa consistently manifests unidirectional effects.
   D. Both sweet and bitter Rasas show unaltered alignment between their primary and post-digestive characteristics, irrespective of dosage.
2. Envisioning the integration of Ayurvedic Guṇas (qualities) with contemporary pharmacodynamics, a clinician posits that Snigdha (unctuous) Guṇa may amplify the lipid solubility of pharmacological

compounds, consequently enhancing their cellular absorption and tissue-specific delivery. What inference can be drawn regarding its practical implications?

A. Snigdha Guṇa inherently diminishes lipid solubility, necessitating adjustments in drug formulations for effective systemic absorption.

B. Medicinal compounds imbued with Snigdha Guṇa are functionally analogous to hydrophilic drugs used in modern medicine.

C. Snigdha Guṇa potentially augments bioavailability of lipophilic substances, particularly in lipid-dominant physiological environments.

D. The influence of Snigdha Guṇa on pharmacokinetics is marginal, offering negligible relevance to cellular absorption pathways.

3. When applying the Ayurvedic concept of Karma (action) to clinical treatment paradigms, researchers explore the therapeutic efficacy of Tikta (bitter) Rasa in detoxification. They hypothesize that its inherent properties facilitate the removal of Ama (toxins), thereby alleviating inflammatory conditions. How might this be operationalized in chronic disease management?

A. Tikta Rasa depletes systemic fluids, rendering it unsuitable for long-term therapeutic protocols.

B. The detoxifying capacity of Tikta Rasa aids in eliminating Ama, which in turn addresses inflammation and metabolic dysfunction.

C. Prolonged use of Tikta Rasa introduces excessive Ama accumulation, complicating systemic conditions.

D. Tikta Rasa's role in chronic disease treatment is negligible due to its limited spectrum of clinical application.

4. An Ayurvedic physician prescribes a formulation rich in Madhura (sweet) Rasa coupled with Guru (heavy) Guṇa for a patient exhibiting symptoms of Vata derangement. Considering the pharmacological implications of this therapeutic choice, how does this approach align with the fundamental principles of Ayurvedic intervention?

A. The combined presence of Madhura Rasa and Guru Guṇa exacerbates Vata-related symptoms by introducing lightness and instability.

B. This formulation counters the excessive mobility and dryness characteristic of Vata imbalance, promoting nourishment and stabilization.

C. Madhura Rasa inherently disrupts Pitta homeostasis, making it unsuitable for conditions dominated by Vata imbalances.

D. The prescription primarily aligns with the pacification of Kapha, demonstrating limited utility in addressing Vata conditions.

5. A formulation incorporating Katu (pungent) Rasa and Laghu (light) Guṇa is hypothesized to activate metabolic pathways effectively. When administered to patients suffering from Kapha-induced stagnation, what clinical outcomes might be anticipated?

A. Katu Rasa has the potential to aggravate Kapha disorders, necessitating alternative treatment protocols.

B. Laghu Guṇa offers complementary action in pacifying Kapha, while Katu Rasa contributes minimally to metabolic stimulation.

C. The combination targets Kapha stagnation by stimulating metabolic processes and reducing systemic heaviness.

D. Both Katu Rasa and Laghu Guṇa are contraindicated in Kapha conditions due to their excessive stimulatory effects.

6. A nutritional scientist investigating the role of Amla (sour) Rasa in gut health observes that it appears to stimulate fermentation activity in the microbiota. Based on this finding, how should the post-digestive implications of Amla Rasa be interpreted?

A. Amla Rasa suppresses fermentation activity, aligning with its detoxifying properties.

B. Enhanced fermentation suggests Amla Rasa's direct influence on digestive enzyme activity and microbial growth.

C. The role of Amla Rasa in post-digestive processes remains inconsequential to gut microbial diversity.

D. Fermentation driven by Amla Rasa results in reduced diversity of the gut microbiome.

7. A study focusing on Ayurvedic Vīrya (potency) demonstrates that Ushna (heating) Vīrya enhances peripheral circulation, thereby improving blood flow in cold extremities. How might these findings influence Ayurvedic treatment strategies?

A. Ushna Vīrya is ineffective in promoting systemic circulation, limiting its application to localized conditions.

B. The findings support the use of Ushna Vīrya in cold-related disorders by validating its circulatory benefits.

C. Ushna Vīrya compromises systemic homeostasis and should be contraindicated in circulatory diseases.

D. Enhancing peripheral circulation contradicts the traditional role of Ushna Vīrya in Ayurvedic practice.

8. In pharmacokinetic studies of Kapha-pacifying drugs, researchers hypothesize that formulations necessitating rapid systemic distribution require unique combinations of Rasa and Guṇa. Which characteristics would most effectively meet this requirement?

A. Guru (heavy) Guṇa paired with Madhura (sweet) Rasa promotes systemic bioavailability over time.

B. Laghu (light) Guṇa combined with Katu (pungent) Rasa ensures accelerated distribution and metabolic activation.

C. Kapha-pacifying drugs depend exclusively on their Vipāka for systemic efficacy.

D. Neither Rasa nor Guṇa play significant roles in influencing systemic pharmacokinetics.

9. Considering the effects of Katu (pungent) Vipāka on metabolic functions, a researcher examines its influence on lipid digestion and absorption. How does this observation align with Ayurvedic principles of nutrient metabolism?

A. Katu Vipāka optimizes lipid metabolism by enhancing bile secretion, facilitating efficient fat digestion.

B. Lipid metabolism remains unaffected by Katu Vipāka, which instead targets carbohydrate pathways exclusively.

C. Katu Vipāka disrupts lipid digestion, necessitating supplemental aids for metabolic balance.

D. Lipid metabolism under the influence of Katu Vipāka is marked by suppressed enzymatic activity.

10. An Ayurvedic practitioner aims to address digestive disorders by leveraging the synergistic roles of Rasa, Guṇa, Karma, and Vipāka in therapeutic formulations. How does this approach manifest in clinical outcomes?

A. Emphasizing synergy introduces unnecessary complexity, thereby reducing treatment efficacy.

B. This strategy ensures harmonious interplay between therapeutic elements, enhancing overall clinical effectiveness.

C. The interconnected nature of these principles diminishes their individual therapeutic significance.

D. Clinical outcomes depend predominantly on patient compliance, rendering synergistic approaches secondary.

Directions (Q. No. 11-14): *Scenario-Based Questions*

SCENARIO 1

A pharmacological researcher is conducting a study to evaluate the impact of Ayurvedic formulations on stress management. The focus is on a classical formulation, Ashwagandha Churna, renowned for its adaptogenic properties. The study measures cortisol levels, oxidative stress markers, and subjective stress scores in individuals diagnosed with chronic stress. Results indicate that Ashwagandha Churna significantly reduces cortisol levels and oxidative stress markers while improving subjective well-being. However, the study also reveals that the formulation's efficacy is influenced by its preparation method, with traditional techniques yielding better results compared to modern commercial methods.

SCENARIO 2

Simultaneously, a conservationist is investigating the overharvesting of Withania somnifera (Ashwagandha), driven by its rising global demand. The research highlights that unsustainable harvesting practices are depleting wild populations, which impacts the plant's phytochemical profile. Overharvested plants show lower concentrations of key bioactive compounds, reducing their therapeutic efficacy. The conservationist emphasizes the need for community-based agroforestry practices to ensure ecological balance and maintain the quality of raw materials used in traditional preparations.

11. Based on the findings in Scenario 1, which of the following best explains the enhanced therapeutic outcomes observed with traditionally prepared Ashwagandha Churna?

A. Traditional preparation methods preserve bioactive compounds more effectively, enhancing the formulation's adaptogenic properties.

B. Commercial formulations use synthetic additives that increase efficacy but diminish authenticity.

C. The preparation method has no measurable impact on the adaptogenic properties of Ashwagandha.

D. Therapeutic benefits are solely psychological, with no correlation to preparation methods.

12. In Scenario 2, which strategy would best address the conservation challenges associated with Withania somnifera while maintaining its medicinal efficacy?

A. Promoting large-scale monoculture plantations to meet the rising demand.

B. Encouraging community-based agroforestry to sustainably cultivate Ashwagandha.

C. Replacing Ashwagandha with synthetic alternatives in Ayurvedic formulations.

D. Reducing global consumption of Ashwagandha to conserve wild populations.

13. How does the depletion of wild Withania somnifera populations, as described in Scenario 2, potentially affect the outcomes observed in Scenario 1?

A. Overharvested plants with reduced phytochemical concentrations could diminish the efficacy of formulations in managing stress.

B. The quality of raw Ashwagandha has no measurable effect on the stress management outcomes of the formulations.

C. Lower bioactive compound concentrations in wild plants enhance the therapeutic efficacy of Ashwagandha Churna.
D. Depleted wild populations improve the sustainability of Ashwagandha-based formulations by encouraging synthetic substitutes.

14. Based on the interconnected findings of Scenarios 1 and 2, which of the following strategies would most effectively balance ecological sustainability and therapeutic efficacy?

A. Developing a global standard for Ashwagandha formulations that incorporates sustainable harvesting practices.
B. Shifting entirely to synthetic adaptogens to reduce dependency on natural resources.
C. Focusing on large-scale commercial farming without considering traditional methods.
D. Limiting the global demand for Ashwagandha to traditional Ayurvedic communities.

15. The seven Padārthas in Ayurveda provide a foundational framework for understanding reality and categorizing knowledge:

(a) Dravya refers to the substance that possesses qualities (Guṇa) and actions (Karma).
(b) Guṇa denotes the inherent properties that define a substance's characteristics.
(c) Karma represents the actions performed by a substance.
(d) Samanya signifies the universal principle of similarity and commonality.

Choose the correct answer from the options given below:

A. (a), (b), and (c) only
B. (b), (c), and (d) only
C. (a), (b), (c), and (d)
D. (a), (c), and (d) only

16. Which of the following statements accurately describe the concept of Padārtha in Ayurveda?

(a) Padārtha refers to categories that help in understanding and classifying existence.
(b) Padārtha encompasses both tangible substances and abstract qualities.
(c) There are only three Padārthas: dravya, guna, and karma.
(d) Padārtha is used exclusively for philosophical discussions with no practical applications.

Choose the correct answer from the options given below:

A. (a) and (b) only
B. (a) and (c) only
C. (b) and (d) only
D. (a), (b), and (c) only

17. Which of the following are considered essential components of dravya in Ayurvedic theory?

(a) It serves as the substratum for qualities and actions.
(b) It includes both physical and non-physical entities.
(c) Dravya is limited to natural substances like herbs and minerals.
(d) It encompasses Panchamahabhutas (five elements), mind, and soul.

Choose the correct answer from the options given below:

A. (a), (b), and (d) only
B. (a), (b), and (c) only
C. (b) and (d) only
D. (a) and (c) only

18. In the Ayurvedic understanding of guna (qualities), which of the following are correct?

(a) Guna determines the therapeutic action of a substance.
(b) Guna is an inherent characteristic that cannot exist independently.
(c) There are 20 gunas categorized into 10 pairs of opposites.
(d) Guna refers only to the physical appearance of a substance.

Choose the correct answer from the options given below:

A. (a), (b), and (c) only
B. (a), (b), and (d) only
C. (a) and (d) only
D. (b) and (c) only

19. The concept of karma (action) in Ayurveda includes which of the following?

(a) The functional activities performed by substances.
(b) The physical movement of the body.
(c) The relationship between cause and effect in therapy.
(d) Actions are independent of the inherent qualities of a substance.

Choose the correct answer from the options given below:

A. (a) and (c) only
B. (a), (b), and (d) only
C. (a), (b), and (c) only
D. (b) and (d) only

20. Which of the following statements describe the role of samanya (generality) and visesa (particularity) in Ayurveda?

(a) Samanya is the basis for grouping substances with similar characteristics.
(b) Visesa is the basis for differentiating one substance from another.
(c) Samanya emphasizes diversity among therapeutic substances.
(d) Visesa is used to explain the uniqueness of each dosha.

Choose the correct answer from the options given below:
A. (a) and (b) only
B. (a), (b), and (d) only
C. (b) and (d) only
D. (a), (b), and (c) only

21. Which of the following statements apply to the Ayurvedic concept of abhava (non-existence)?
(a) Abhava refers to the absence of a substance or phenomenon.
(b) It is classified into pragabhava, pradhvamsabhava, atyantabhava, and anyonya abhava.
(c) Abhava has no role in defining health or disease.
(d) Abhava provides a philosophical framework for understanding states of existence.

Choose the correct answer from the options given below:
A. (a), (b), and (d) only
B. (a), (c), and (d) only
C. (a) and (b) only
D. (b) and (c) only

22. The classification of dravya in Ayurveda includes which of the following?
(a) Panchamahabhutas (five great elements).
(b) Conscious and non-conscious substances.
(c) Time and direction as metaphysical dravya.
(d) Only physical entities used in herbal preparations.

Choose the correct answer from the options given below:
A. (a) and (b) only
B. (a), (b), and (c) only
C. (b) and (d) only
D. (a), (b), and (d) only

23. The principle of samavaya (inherence) explains which of the following in Ayurveda?
(a) The inseparable relationship between a substance and its qualities.
(b) The temporary coexistence of actions and substances.
(c) The independent existence of qualities without substances.
(d) The inherent connection between guna (qualities) and karma (actions).

Choose the correct answer from the options given below:
A. (a) and (d) only
B. (a), (b), and (c) only
C. (a), (b), and (d) only
D. (b) and (c) only

24. Which of the following examples illustrate the Ayurvedic theory of guna (qualities) in therapy?
(a) A heavy (guru) substance is used to counteract lightness (laghu) in a patient with insomnia.
(b) Dry (ruksha) qualities are applied to treat conditions caused by excessive moisture (snigdha).
(c) Cold (shita) properties are recommended for patients with heat-related disorders (ushna).
(d) Guna is irrelevant in determining the therapeutic application of a substance.

Choose the correct answer from the options given below:
A. (a), (b), and (c) only
B. (a), (c), and (d) only
C. (b) and (d) only
D. (a) and b only

25. Match List–I (Padārthas in Ayurveda) with List–II (Their Definitions):

List–I	List–II
(a) Dravya	1. The absence or negation of existence
(b) Guna	2. Substances that serve as the substratum for qualities and actions
(c) Karma	3. Actions or processes performed by substances
(d) Abhava	4. Qualities inherent in substances that determine their properties

Choose the correct answer from the options given below:
A. (a)-2, (b)-4, (c)-3, (d)-1
B. (a)-4, (b)-3, (c)-2, (d)-1
C. (a)-3, (b)-2, (c)-1, (d)-4
D. (a)-1, (b)-4, (c)-2, (d)-3

26. Match List–I (Gunās in Ayurveda) with List–II (Their Characteristics):

List–I	List–II
(a) Guru (Heavy)	1. Encourages lightness and mobility
(b) Laghu (Light)	2. Provides stability and grounding
(c) Snigdha (Unctuous)	3. Lubricates and provides smoothness
(d) Ruksha (Dry)	4. Promotes dryness and roughness

Choose the correct answer from the options given below:

A. (a)-3, (b)-2, (c)-1, (d)-4
B. (a)-4, (b)-3, (c)-2, (d)-1
C. (a)-2, (b)-1, (c)-3, (d)-4
D. (a)-1, (b)-4, (c)-3, (d)-2

27. Match List–I (Dravya Types in Ayurveda) with List–II (Their Roles in Health):

List–I	List–II
(a) Panchamahabhutas (Five Elements)	1. Governs mental clarity and emotional balance
(b) Satva (Mind)	2. Spiritual connection and self-awareness
(c) Atma (Soul)	3. Provides the structural and functional basis for the body
(d) Kala (Time)	4. Influences biological rhythms and life cycles

Choose the correct answer from the options given below:

A. (a)-3, (b)-1, (c)-2, (d)-4
B. (a)-4, (b)-2, (c)-1, (d)-3
C. (a)-2, (b)-3, (c)-4, (d)-1
D. (a)-1, (b)-4, (c)-3, (d)-2

28. Match List–I (Types of Abhava in Ayurveda) with List–II (Their Meanings):

List–I	List–II
(a) Pragabhava	1. The absence of a substance before its creation
(b) Pradhvamsabhava	2. The absence of a substance after its destruction
(c) Atyantabhava	3. The absolute absence of a substance
(d) Anyonyabhava	4. The mutual non-existence of two entities

Choose the correct answer from the options given below:

A. (a)-1, (b)-2, (c)-3, (d)-4
B. (a)-4, (b)-3, (c)-1, (d)-2
C. (a)-2, (b)-1, (c)-4, (d)-3
D. (a)-3, (b)-4, (c)-2, (d)-1

29. Match List–I (Gunās in Ayurveda) with List–II (Their Opposing Characteristics):

List–I	List–II
(a) Guru (Heavy)	1. Laghu (Light)
(b) Ushna (Hot)	2. Shita (Cold)
(c) Snigdha (Unctuous)	3. Ruksha (Dry)
(d) Manda (Slow)	4. Tikshna (Sharp)

Choose the correct answer from the options given below:

A. (a)-1, (b)-2, (c)-3, (d)-4
B. (a)-4, (b)-3, (c)-2, (d)-1
C. (a)-3, (b)-1, (c)-4, (d)-2
D. (a)-2, (b)-4, (c)-1, (d)-3

30. Match List–I (Tridoshas in Ayurveda) with List–II (Their Primary Functions):

List–I	List–II
(a) Vata	1. Governs metabolism and transformation processes
(b) Pitta	2. Regulates stability, structure, and immunity
(c) Kapha	3. Facilitates movement, circulation, and nervous system activity

Choose the correct answer from the options given below:

A. (a)-3, (b)-1, (c)-2
B. (a)-1, (b)-2, (c)-3
C. (a)-2, (b)-3, (c)-1
D. (a)-3, (b)-2, (c)-1

31. Match List–I (Rasas in Ayurveda) with List–II (Their Effects):

List–I	List–II
(a) Madhura (Sweet)	1. Enhances metabolism and clears toxins
(b) Amla (Sour)	2. Strengthens tissues and promotes growth
(c) Lavana (Salty)	3. Stimulates digestion and increases appetite
(d) Katu (Pungent)	4. Moisturizes and maintains fluid balance

Choose the correct answer from the options given below:

A. (a)-2, (b)-3, (c)-4, (d)-1
B. (a)-3, (b)-2, (c)-1, (d)-4
C. (a)-4, (b)-1, (c)-3, (d)-2
D. (a)-1, (b)-4, (c)-2, (d)-3

32. Match List–I (Dhatus in Ayurveda) with List–II (Their Corresponding Functions):

List–I	List–II
(a) Rasa	1. Facilitates oxygen transport and vitality
(b) Rakta	2. Nourishes all other tissues
(c) Mamsa	3. Builds and supports muscular structure
(d) Meda	4. Provides lubrication and energy storage

Choose the correct answer from the options given below:

A. (a)-2, (b)-1, (c)-3, (d)-4
B. (a)-4, (b)-3, (c)-2, (d)-1
C. (a)-3, (b)-4, (c)-1, (d)-2
D. (a)-1, (b)-2, (c)-4, (d)-3

33. Match List–I (Types of Diseases in Ayurveda) with List–II (Their Causes):

List–I	List–II
(a) Nija (Endogenous)	1. Imbalance of doshas within the body
(b) Agantuja (Exogenous)	2. External factors such as trauma or infection
(c) Sannipataja (Mixed)	3. Combined influence of internal and external factors
(d) Kritrima (Artificial)	4. Induced artificially for diagnostic or therapeutic purposes

Choose the correct answer from the options given below:

A. (a)-1, (b)-2, (c)-3, (d)-4
B. (a)-3, (b)-1, (c)-4, (d)-2
C. (a)-2, (b)-3, (c)-1, (d)-4
D. (a)-4, (b)-3, (c)-2, (d)-1

34. Match List–I (Tridoshas in Ayurveda) with List–II (Their Associated Physiological Systems):

List–I	List–II
(a) Vata	1. Nervous system and movement
(b) Pitta	2. Digestive system and metabolism
(c) Kapha	3. Respiratory and structural system

Choose the correct answer from the options given below:

A. (a)-1, (b)-2, (c)-3
B. (a)-2, (b)-3, (c)-1
C. (a)-3, (b)-1, (c)-2
D. (a)-2, (b)-1, (c)-3

Directions (Q. No. 35-39): *Following questions are based on Statement 1 and Statement 2. Read both the statements carefully and choose the correct answer from the options given below:*

A. Both Statement 1 and Statement 2 are true, and Statement 2 is the correct explanation of Statement 1.
B. Both Statement 1 and Statement 2 are true, but Statement 2 is not the correct explanation of Statement 1.
C. Statement 1 is true, but Statement 2 is false.
D. Statement 1 is false, but Statement 2 is true.
E. Both Statement 1 and Statement 2 are false.

35. **Statement 1:** Ayurveda classifies all substances into nine categories of dravya, including earth, water, fire, air, ether, time, direction, mind, and soul.

Statement 2: The classification of dravya in Ayurveda is primarily metaphysical and lacks practical relevance in therapeutic applications.

36. **Statement 1:** The Ayurvedic principle of guna emphasizes the intrinsic qualities of substances that determine their therapeutic action.

Statement 2: Gunas are universal and independent of the context in which a substance is used.

37. **Statement 1:** In Ayurveda, samanya (generality) and visesa (particularity) are used to explain similarities and differences among substances.

Statement 2: Samanya refers to the unique qualities of a substance, while visesa describes shared characteristics among multiple substances.

38. **Statement 1:** Samavaya (inherence) in Ayurveda explains the inseparable relationship between a substance and its qualities.

Statement 2: Samavaya demonstrates that a quality can exist independently of the substance to which it is attributed.

39. **Statement 1:** Ayurveda considers abhava (non-existence) an essential concept for understanding health and disease.

Statement 2: Abhava is only a philosophical concept with no practical applications in diagnostics or treatment.

Directions (Q. No. 40-45): *There are two statements in each questions. One is labelled as Assertion (A) and the other is as Reason (R). Read both the statements and choose the correct answer from the options given below:*

A. Both Assertion (A) and Reason (R) are true, and Reason (R) is the correct explanation of Assertion (A).
B. Both Assertion (A) and Reason (R) are true, but Reason (R) is not the correct explanation of Assertion (A).
C. Assertion (A) is true, but Reason (R) is false.
D. Assertion (A) is false, but Reason (R) is true.
E. Both Assertion (A) and Reason (R) are false.

40. **Assertion (A):** Ayurveda identifies Panchamahabhutas (five elements) as the foundational components of all matter, including the human body.

Reason (R): The human body's physiological processes can be fully explained without referencing the Panchamahabhutas.

41. **Assertion (A):** The concept of samanya (generality) in Ayurveda is used to group substances with similar qualities to enhance therapeutic interventions.

Reason (R): Samanya helps create uniform treatment protocols that apply universally to all patients.

42. Assertion (A): In Ayurveda, guna (qualities) like heaviness or lightness determine the therapeutic action of substances.

Reason (R): Gunas are transient and can change based on the environment in which a substance is used.

43. Assertion (A): The concept of abhava (non-existence) in Ayurveda is essential for defining the absence of disease.

Reason (R): Abhava has no role in treatment planning or therapeutic interventions.

44. Assertion (A): Ayurveda's classification of dravya includes both material and non-material entities like time and direction.

Reason (R): Time and direction are considered dravya because they influence the sequence and organization of biological processes.

45. Assertion (A): The karma (actions) of a substance in Ayurveda are determined by its guna (qualities).

Reason (R): In Ayurveda, the actions of substances are entirely independent of their inherent qualities.

Directions (Q. No. 46–50): *Read the passage carefully and answer the questions given below*:

In Ayurveda, the concept of Saptapadārtha serves as the foundation for understanding the universe and the human body. The term Padārtha refers to categories of existence that facilitate the understanding of reality. The seven Padārthas are dravya (substance), guna (qualities), karma (actions), samanya (generality), visesa (particularity), samavaya (inherence), and abhava (non-existence). Each Padārtha is interconnected and plays a role in both philosophical and practical aspects of Ayurveda.

Dravya, the first Padārtha, is the substratum for the others and includes nine types: earth, water, fire, air, ether, time, direction, mind, and soul. These serve as the building blocks of the physical and metaphysical world. Guna, the second Padārtha, refers to the inherent qualities of substances, such as heaviness (guru) or lightness (laghu), which determine their effects on the body. Karma represents the actions or functions of a substance, which are influenced by its guna. Together, dravya, guna, and karma form the triad central to Ayurvedic treatment.

Samanya and visesa are principles used to classify and differentiate substances. While samanya emphasizes shared characteristics, visesa focuses on unique attributes. These principles guide the selection of treatments by identifying substances that either counteract or enhance specific conditions. Samavaya, or inherence, explains the inseparable relationship between a substance and its qualities or actions, ensuring their coexistence.

Finally, abhava is the absence or negation of existence, which has significant implications in defining health and disease. The absence of toxins or imbalances (abhava) signifies a state of health, while their presence indicates disease. By integrating these seven categories, Ayurveda offers a holistic framework for understanding life, health, and the universe.

46. According to the passage, which of the following best describes the role of dravya in the Ayurvedic framework?

A. Dravya refers exclusively to physical substances like herbs and minerals.
B. Dravya serves as the substratum for all other Padārthas and includes both material and non-material entities.
C. Dravya is only concerned with metaphysical concepts like time and direction.
D. Dravya is unrelated to the concepts of guna and karma.

47. How does samanya contribute to Ayurvedic treatment, as per the passage?

A. It emphasizes the uniqueness of substances for specific treatments.
B. It identifies shared characteristics among substances to guide treatment selection.
C. It focuses on the relationship between a substance and its actions.
D. It is used exclusively for philosophical classification, without therapeutic relevance.

48. What is the significance of samavaya in the Ayurvedic system?

A. It explains the temporary association of qualities and actions with a substance.
B. It describes the inseparable relationship between a substance and its inherent qualities or actions.
C. It demonstrates that guna and karma exist independently of dravya.
D. It emphasizes the absence of qualities in therapeutic substances.

49. Which of the following statements aligns with the Ayurvedic understanding of abhava?

A. Abhava is irrelevant in health and disease, as it only pertains to metaphysical discussions.
B. Abhava signifies the presence of imbalances, indicating a state of disease.
C. The absence of toxins or imbalances (abhava) is associated with a state of health.
D. Abhava focuses on the relationship between generality and particularity in substances.

50. Based on the passage, what is the central relationship between guna and karma in Ayurveda?

A. Guna and karma are unrelated and function independently in Ayurvedic treatments.

B. The qualities (guna) of a substance directly influence its actions (karma), shaping its therapeutic use.

C. Actions (karma) determine the qualities (guna) of a substance, reversing the traditional framework.

D. The relationship between guna and karma is purely philosophical, without practical relevance.

ANSWER WITH EXPLANATIONS

1. C: The duality of Madhura (sweet) Rasa's Vipāka aligns with Ayurvedic concepts of dose-dependent effects, showcasing how excess can disrupt the typical cooling effect. Tikta (bitter) Rasa's unidirectional cooling post-digestive influence contrasts with this dynamic behaviour, demonstrating its detoxifying consistency. This hypothesis mirrors Ayurveda's nuanced understanding of physiological adaptability, where primary and post-digestive qualities vary under certain conditions. It emphasizes the role of Rasa and Vipāka in therapeutic precision, highlighting the need to consider quantity and constitution to predict outcomes effectively, merging traditional wisdom with contemporary pharmacological principles.

2. C: The lipid-solubility enhancement associated with Snigdha (unctuous) Guṇa parallels modern lipid-based drug delivery systems. This property facilitates greater absorption in lipid-dense tissues, demonstrating Ayurveda's alignment with pharmacokinetic theories. Snigdha's systemic relevance underscores its ability to influence drug permeability and bioavailability. This integrative perspective bridges ancient and modern paradigms, suggesting applications in drug formulation optimization for disorders involving fat metabolism or nutrient absorption. It validates Ayurvedic theories in contemporary research, highlighting the versatility and scientific depth of traditional frameworks in understanding biological processes.

3. B: Tikta (bitter) Rasa's ability to remove Ama (toxins) emphasizes its pivotal role in chronic disease management. Its detoxifying action alleviates systemic inflammation and restores metabolic harmony, aligning with Ayurvedic causative treatment principles. This Rasa's role in clearing blockages and promoting balance extends beyond symptomatic relief, targeting underlying dysfunctions. Its influence on Pitta and Kapha doshas underlines its adaptability and relevance in managing chronic inflammatory and metabolic conditions. This approach showcases Ayurveda's depth in addressing multifaceted disease pathways, emphasizing systemic detoxification as a cornerstone of long-term health restoration.

4. B: The formulation rich in Madhura (sweet) Rasa and Guru (heavy) Guṇa directly counters Vata's characteristic dryness, instability, and excessive mobility. These qualities nourish and stabilize, reducing hyperactivity and systemic imbalance. Ayurveda's therapeutic approach tailors interventions to address both symptomatic and root causes. This combination also highlights the interconnectedness of Rasa and Guṇa in targeting specific doshic imbalances, exemplifying the precision of Ayurvedic pharmacology. The application ensures a balance between nutritional support and stabilization, reinforcing Ayurveda's relevance in modern integrative healthcare approaches.

5. C: Katu (pungent) Rasa's stimulatory properties and Laghu (light) Guṇa synergistically activate metabolic pathways, reducing Kapha-induced stagnation. This combination enhances circulation, tissue metabolism, and energy flow, addressing Kapha's heaviness and lethargy. The dynamic interplay of sharpness and lightness reflects Ayurveda's ability to manipulate systemic processes for therapeutic benefits. This demonstrates the versatility of Rasa and Guṇa in managing doshic imbalances. By targeting Kapha stagnation effectively, the approach reinforces the scientific basis of Ayurvedic principles in metabolic correction, detoxification, and disease prevention.

6. B: Amla (sour) Rasa's ability to enhance fermentation reflects its role in promoting gut enzyme activity and microbiota health. This aligns with Ayurveda's emphasis on digestive efficiency through Agni stimulation. Enhanced fermentation supports nutrient assimilation and microbial diversity, highlighting Amla's systemic benefits beyond digestion. This finding bridges Ayurveda and microbiology, demonstrating the Rasa's relevance in promoting symbiosis within the gut. Its impact on digestion and fermentation exemplifies Ayurveda's depth in understanding gastrointestinal health and its influence on systemic well-being.

7. B: Ushna (heating) Vīrya's role in enhancing peripheral circulation validates its use in treating cold-related disorders. This effect aligns with its classical indications for stagnation and reduced Agni. The circulatory benefits underscore Ayurveda's systemic view of Vīrya's potency, where localized effects extend to broader physiological improvements. This highlights the dynamic application of Ayurvedic formulations in addressing vascular issues. By stimulating blood flow, Ushna Vīrya complements therapeutic strategies for cold extremities and metabolic sluggishness, illustrating Ayurveda's integration of thermal properties with functional outcomes.

8. **B:** Laghu (light) Guṇa and Katu (pungent) Rasa accelerate systemic absorption and metabolic activation, crucial for Kapha-pacifying drugs. Their sharp and lightweight properties ensure rapid distribution and efficacy. This aligns with pharmacokinetic principles, emphasizing targeted delivery to counteract Kapha-induced stagnation. Ayurveda's understanding of Rasa and Guṇa interactions mirrors modern drug design strategies, validating traditional concepts in contemporary pharmacology. This integration underscores Ayurveda's precision in addressing doshic imbalances, particularly in metabolic and circulatory systems, where rapid activation is necessary for therapeutic success.

9. **A:** Katu (pungent) Vipāka enhances lipid metabolism through increased bile secretion, optimizing fat digestion and absorption. This aligns with Ayurveda's insights into Vipāka's systemic impact on nutrient processing. By stimulating digestive secretions, Katu Vipāka aids in reducing Kapha-related imbalances like hyperlipidemia. This reflects Ayurveda's nuanced understanding of digestion, absorption, and metabolic regulation. Its application highlights the relevance of Ayurvedic principles in addressing lipid metabolism disorders, showcasing its integration with modern biochemical processes for holistic health management.

10. **B:** The synergistic integration of Rasa, Guṇa, Karma, and Vipāka ensures comprehensive therapeutic outcomes, harmonizing all aspects of treatment. Each principle contributes uniquely—Rasa initiates action, Guṇa modulates quality, Karma directs functional pathways, and Vipāka governs post-digestive effects. This interplay ensures that formulations address the root causes and symptoms of disorders holistically. Ayurveda's emphasis on synergy showcases its depth in understanding systemic healing, where the sum of therapeutic principles exceeds individual contributions, ensuring optimized clinical outcomes in diverse health conditions.

11. **A:** The efficacy of traditional preparation methods in preserving Ashwagandha's bioactive compounds demonstrates Ayurveda's emphasis on respecting the integrity of substances. Unlike modern commercial methods that may prioritize scalability, traditional approaches maintain the substance's inherent qualities (guna). This aligns with Ayurveda's view that the preparation process influences the substance's actions (karma). For instance, decoctions enhance solubility, increasing efficacy. This observation highlights the critical role of traditional knowledge in optimizing therapeutic outcomes. By integrating preparation methods with physiological insights, Ayurveda ensures that treatments are both effective and authentic, balancing modern scalability with traditional wisdom.

12. **B:** The conservation of Ashwagandha (Withania somnifera) through community-based agroforestry reflects Ayurveda's holistic ethos, which emphasizes balance—not only in the body but also in the ecosystem. Overharvesting diminishes the bioactive compounds critical for therapeutic efficacy, disrupting guna and karma. Community-driven agroforestry ensures sustainable harvesting practices, preserving biodiversity while maintaining the ecological balance that Ayurveda values. Unlike large-scale monoculture, agroforestry integrates traditional wisdom with ecological sustainability. By involving local communities, this strategy aligns economic incentives with ecological preservation, ensuring that Ashwagandha remains both therapeutically potent and environmentally viable for future generations.

13. **A:** The depletion of wild Ashwagandha populations directly impacts its therapeutic outcomes, as reduced bioactive compound concentrations alter its inherent guna (qualities) and karma (actions). Ayurveda emphasizes the importance of unadulterated, high-quality raw materials, as their therapeutic effects are inherently tied to their natural properties. Environmental stress from overharvesting diminishes the adaptogenic qualities of Ashwagandha, compromising its efficacy in stress management. This phenomenon exemplifies the interconnectedness of ecological health and human health in Ayurveda. Sustainable practices, such as regulated harvesting and cultivation, become essential to preserving the therapeutic potential of formulations like Ashwagandha Churna.

14. **A:** The establishment of global standards for Ashwagandha ensures the alignment of therapeutic efficacy with ecological sustainability. Ayurveda recognizes that the therapeutic potency of medicinal plants depends on their preparation, preservation, and sourcing practices. By integrating sustainable harvesting techniques and standardized quality checks, such measures protect biodiversity while ensuring that

therapeutic integrity remains intact. Unlike synthetic substitutes, traditional Ashwagandha formulations rely on synergistic interactions of bioactive compounds. These standards serve to harmonize commercial demand with Ayurvedic principles, fostering an approach that respects nature's balance while maintaining global therapeutic relevance.

15. **C:** The seven Padārthas form the philosophical foundation of Ayurveda, with Dravya, Guṇa, and Karma being central to understanding substances and their therapeutic applications. Dravya is the fundamental substance that acts as a carrier of properties (Guṇa) and actions (Karma). Guṇa defines the inherent qualities that influence the substance's effects, while Karma refers to its actions or dynamic impact on the body. Samanya introduces the concept of similarity, aiding in the classification and therapeutic application of substances. Together, these categories provide a comprehensive framework for analyzing and utilizing substances, making all four elements essential for understanding Ayurvedic principles.

16. **A:** The concept of Padārtha in Ayurveda includes both tangible and intangible entities that facilitate understanding existence and therapeutic interventions. Statements (a) and (b) highlight how Padārtha provides a comprehensive framework for categorizing reality, ensuring that all dimensions influencing health are considered. By including categories like guna (qualities) and abhava (non-existence), Ayurveda bridges the gap between physical phenomena and metaphysical concepts. This integration distinguishes Ayurveda from reductionist models, emphasizing the interconnectedness of material and non-material factors in health. Statements (c) and (d) incorrectly narrow its scope, failing to capture the full depth of Ayurvedic philosophy.

17. **A:** The classification of dravya reflects Ayurveda's inclusive approach, addressing physical, metaphysical, and existential dimensions of health. Statements (a), (b), and (d) correctly describe the roles of dravya in forming the substratum for qualities (guna) and actions (karma), while encompassing both material entities (e.g., herbs) and non-material dimensions (e.g., time). This comprehensive classification ensures that all aspects influencing health—biological, psychological, and environmental—are considered. Statement (c) incorrectly limits dravya to natural substances, neglecting its broader scope. Ayurveda's recognition of both tangible and intangible elements demonstrates its adaptability to modern integrative approaches.

18. **A:** The gunas (qualities) in Ayurveda represent the intrinsic properties that determine how substances interact with the body. Statements (a), (b), and (c) accurately describe how guna shapes therapeutic actions. For example, the dry (ruksha) quality of turmeric aids in reducing inflammation, while the moist (snigdha) quality of ghee soothes dryness. These qualities are inherent and cannot exist independently, emphasizing their significance in tailoring treatments. Statement (d) incorrectly reduces guna to physical characteristics, failing to acknowledge its broader physiological and psychological relevance. This nuanced framework ensures that interventions are both precise and holistic.

19. **C:** Karma in Ayurveda refers to the actions or effects of substances, inherently influenced by their guna (qualities). Statements (a) and (c) highlight this relationship, demonstrating how guna determines the physiological impact of a substance. For instance, a heating (ushna) quality in ginger enables its action (karma) of enhancing digestion. Statements (b) and (d) misrepresent karma, either overgeneralizing its scope or ignoring its dependence on guna. By emphasizing this interplay, Ayurveda ensures that therapeutic actions are predictable and aligned with systemic needs, fostering interventions that restore balance and address root causes of disease.

20. **B:** In Ayurveda, Samanya refers to the concept of generality—the principle that things with similar properties can be grouped together, making it foundational in understanding the collective behavior of substances (Statement a). Visesa, on the other hand, refers to particularity, helping differentiate one substance from another based on unique attributes (Statement b). It also plays a critical role in explaining the distinct features of each dosha, supporting individualized treatment (Statement d). However, Statement (c) is incorrect because Samanya does not emphasize diversity—rather, it highlights similarity. Visesa is the concept that introduces diversity by emphasizing differences.

21. **A:** Abhava enriches Ayurveda's framework by addressing the absence or negation of substances, phenomena, or imbalances. Statements (a), (b), and (d) correctly reflect its application in both philosophical and therapeutic contexts. For instance, the absence of toxins (ama) signifies health, aligning abhava with preventive care. Statement (c) incorrectly suggests its irrelevance in treatment planning, overlooking how Ayurveda uses abhava to define health and diagnose diseases. This concept bridges abstract metaphysical ideas with practical applications, illustrating Ayurveda's holistic understanding of health as a dynamic state defined by the absence of pathological factors.

22. B: The classification of dravya in Ayurveda includes material and non-material entities that influence health. Statements (a), (b), and (c) correctly emphasize the inclusivity of this system, addressing physical elements (Panchamahabhutas), psychological aspects (manas), and metaphysical dimensions (time and direction). Statement (d) incorrectly limits dravya to physical substances, disregarding its broader scope. This comprehensive framework allows Ayurveda to address health in a multi-dimensional context, ensuring that interventions respect both tangible and intangible factors. The inclusion of non-material elements like time illustrates Ayurveda's nuanced understanding of health as an interplay of various existential dimensions.

23. A: The principle of samavaya in Ayurveda highlights the inseparable relationship between substances and their inherent qualities or actions. Statements (a) and (d) correctly emphasize this relationship, ensuring that therapeutic actions (karma) and properties (guna) cannot exist independently of their substratum (dravya). For instance, the heating quality (guna) of black pepper is inseparable from its digestive-enhancing action (karma). Statements (b) and (c) incorrectly suggest temporary or independent coexistence. Ayurveda's reliance on samavaya ensures that therapeutic interventions address root causes, fostering holistic treatments that respect the intrinsic nature of substances.

24. A: The application of guna in Ayurveda involves balancing opposing qualities to restore equilibrium. Statements (a), (b), and c correctly describe this principle, demonstrating how substances are matched to conditions they counteract. For example, heavy (guru) foods counteract excessive lightness (laghu) in patients with insomnia, while moist (snigdha) substances alleviate dryness (ruksha). Statement (d) incorrectly dismisses guna's significance, ignoring its central role in diagnostics and treatment. By tailoring interventions to individual imbalances, Ayurveda ensures precision and effectiveness, addressing root causes and fostering systemic balance.

25. A: The seven Padārthas form the foundation of Ayurvedic knowledge, with dravya, guna, karma, and abhava serving distinct yet interconnected purposes. The correct matching reflects their specific roles: dravya as the substratum, guna as inherent qualities, karma as actions, and abhava as the absence of existence. This categorization bridges philosophy and practice, ensuring that diagnostics and treatments are holistic. For example, understanding the guna of a herb determines its karma in restoring balance. This framework aligns Ayurveda's epistemology with therapeutic applications, highlighting its adaptability and coherence.

26. C: Each Guṇa (quality) in Ayurveda carries a specific functional characteristic. Guru (heavy) provides grounding and stability (2), while Laghu (light) enhances mobility and quickness (1). Snigdha (unctuous) has a lubricating and smoothening effect (3), supporting tissue cohesion and softness. Ruksha (dry) promotes roughness and absorbs moisture, often used to counter Kapha or excess unctuousness (4). Recognizing these qualities helps determine the therapeutic use of herbs and diets based on a patient's condition or doshic imbalance.

27. A: The classification of dravya reflects Ayurveda's comprehensive understanding of the physical, psychological, and metaphysical dimensions of health. The correct matching illustrates their interconnected roles, from Panchamahabhutas forming the body's structure to time (kala) influencing biological rhythms. The inclusion of mind (satva) and soul (atma) underscores Ayurveda's holistic framework, addressing mental clarity and spiritual well-being alongside physical health. This approach ensures that all dimensions influencing health are considered, offering a profound contrast to systems that often overlook non-material factors. Ayurveda's integrative philosophy allows it to address complex health conditions with precision and balance.

28. A: Ayurveda categorizes Abhava (non-existence) into specific philosophical types that help explain the presence or absence of substances in various contexts. Pragabhava refers to the absence before creation (1), Pradhvamsabhava to the absence after destruction (2), Atyantabhava to the absolute, permanent absence (3), and Anyonyabhava to the mutual non-existence of two things in the same locus (4). These concepts are useful in understanding the onset or cessation of disease, as well as the evaluation of therapeutic effectiveness in treatments.

29. A: The concept of opposing gunas (qualities) is central to Ayurveda's therapeutic framework, ensuring balance and equilibrium. The correct matching demonstrates how each quality has a natural counterpart, used to address imbalances. For example, heavy (guru) qualities counteract excessive lightness (laghu) in conditions like insomnia, while hot (ushna) qualities alleviate cold-related disorders (shita). This dynamic interplay highlights Ayurveda's nuanced approach, where treatments are not just symptom-based but focus on restoring systemic harmony. This principle allows Ayurveda to adapt interventions to the patient's specific constitution (prakriti), ensuring personalized and effective care.

30. A: The Tridosha model encapsulates the primary physiological functions governed by Vata, Pitta, and Kapha. The correct matching highlights their specific roles: Vata governs movement and circulation, Pitta regulates metabolism and digestion, and Kapha provides stability and immunity. This comprehensive framework ensures that every aspect of health is addressed. For example, Pitta's role in enzymatic activity underscores its importance in metabolic disorders, while Kapha's role in immunity makes it crucial in infection management. This integrative approach ensures that Ayurveda remains relevant in addressing both acute and chronic health conditions, bridging traditional wisdom with modern science.

31. A: The Rasas (tastes) in Ayurveda are not merely sensory experiences but therapeutic tools influencing bodily functions. The correct matching reflects their physiological effects: sweet (madhura) nourishes tissues, sour (amla) stimulates digestion, salty (lavana) maintains fluid balance, and pungent (katu) clears toxins. This classification underscores Ayurveda's deep understanding of the sensory-mind-body connection. For example, bitter (tikta) tastes are used in detoxification therapies, reflecting their cleansing properties. Unlike modern systems that often separate taste from therapeutic value, Ayurveda integrates these aspects, ensuring that dietary and herbal interventions are both effective and holistic.

32. A: The seven dhatus (tissues) in Ayurveda represent the building blocks of the body, each serving a specific biological function. The correct matching demonstrates their roles: Rasa nourishes all tissues, Rakta facilitates oxygen transport, Mamsa supports muscular strength, and Meda provides lubrication and energy storage. This classification highlights Ayurveda's layered understanding of physiology, where the health of one dhatu directly influences the others. For example, imbalances in Rasa can lead to deficiencies in Rakta and Mamsa. This interconnected framework ensures that Ayurveda addresses the root causes of disease, fostering systemic balance and holistic healing.

33. A: The classification of diseases in Ayurveda reflects their causes and therapeutic implications. The correct matching highlights the distinction between Nija (endogenous), caused by doshic imbalances, and Agantuja (exogenous), resulting from external factors like trauma. Sannipataja describes mixed causes, integrating internal and external influences, while Kritrima refers to artificially induced conditions for diagnostic or therapeutic purposes. This nuanced categorization ensures that treatments are tailored to the disease's origin. For example, trauma-induced Agantuja conditions require external interventions, whereas Nija imbalances necessitate doshic correction. This comprehensive framework reflects Ayurveda's adaptability and precision in addressing diverse health conditions.

34. A: The association of Tridoshas with specific body systems underscores Ayurveda's holistic approach. The correct matching demonstrates their roles: Vata governs the nervous system, Pitta regulates metabolism, and Kapha supports structural stability and immunity. This framework ensures that every physiological and psychological aspect is addressed. For instance, Vata imbalances are linked to neurological disorders, while Pitta imbalances contribute to metabolic issues like acidity. By associating doshas with body systems, Ayurveda offers targeted interventions that address the root causes of disease while maintaining systemic harmony. This approach aligns ancient Ayurvedic principles with modern biomedical understanding.

35. C: The classification of dravya into nine categories, including mind and soul, underscores Ayurveda's holistic approach to health. While dravya addresses tangible and intangible dimensions, its therapeutic relevance is profound, contrary to Statement 2. For example, time (kala) influences biological rhythms, crucial in Ayurvedic chronotherapy. The incorrectness of Statement 2 highlights a common misinterpretation that Ayurveda's classifications are purely metaphysical. Instead, these categories serve practical purposes in diagnostics and treatment, ensuring that all dimensions influencing health are addressed. This integrative framework sets Ayurveda apart, allowing it to address health comprehensively.

36. C: Guna (qualities) determine the therapeutic action of substances, but they are not independent of their context or interactions. While Statement 1 is correct, Statement 2 is false, as guna depends on factors like the patient's constitution (prakriti) and disease condition (vikriti). For instance, the heating (ushna) quality of ginger aids digestion but may aggravate conditions caused by excess heat. This demonstrates Ayurveda's adaptability, where guna is dynamically applied based on individual needs. The nuanced understanding of qualities ensures that treatments are tailored, emphasizing Ayurveda's focus on precision and systemic balance.

37. C: Samanya and visesa are principles that complement each other, not opposites as implied by Statement 2. While samanya identifies similarities, visesa emphasizes unique attributes, guiding individualized treatments. Statement 1 is true, but Statement 2 is false.

For example, light foods are generally prescribed for conditions caused by heaviness (samanya), but specific herbs are chosen based on unique symptoms (visesa). This interplay ensures that Ayurveda addresses both universal patterns and individual variances, reflecting its holistic approach. The misinterpretation in Statement 2 highlights a misunderstanding of these principles' interconnected roles.

38. **C:** The principle of samavaya (inherence) in Ayurveda asserts the inseparable relationship between a substance and its inherent qualities or actions. Statement 1 is correct because this inseparability forms the foundation of how guna (qualities) and karma (actions) are understood in Ayurveda. For example, the cooling (shita) quality of sandalwood is intrinsically linked to its calming and anti-inflammatory actions. However, Statement 2 is false as it incorrectly suggests that qualities can exist independently of substances. Ayurveda's framework ensures that therapeutic interventions respect this interdependence, fostering a comprehensive approach that integrates substance, qualities, and actions.

39. **C:** Abhava (non-existence) is crucial in Ayurveda for defining health as the absence of imbalances or toxins. Statement 1 is true, as abhava reflects a state of equilibrium and the negation of pathological factors. However, Statement 2 is false, as abhava has practical applications in diagnostics and treatments. For example, the absence of ama (toxins) signifies healthy digestion, while its presence indicates dysfunction. This concept extends beyond metaphysical abstraction, illustrating Ayurveda's layered understanding of health and disease. The false assertion in Statement 2 misrepresents abhava's relevance, which integrates theoretical and practical dimensions seamlessly.

40. **C:** The Panchamahabhutas (five elements) form the basis of all matter, including the human body, and their balance is essential for maintaining health. Assertion (A) is true, as this principle underpins Ayurveda's physiological and therapeutic frameworks. However, Reason (R) is false, as the Panchamahabhutas are indispensable for explaining bodily functions and imbalances. For instance, the predominance of the water element in the body governs fluid balance, while excess fire element causes inflammation. Ignoring these elements would result in an incomplete understanding of Ayurveda's approach. This dynamic model highlights Ayurveda's ability to integrate universal principles into individual treatment plans.

41. **C:** Samanya (generality) identifies shared qualities among substances, allowing Ayurveda to group treatments based on common effects. Assertion (A) is true, as samanya supports broad therapeutic classifications. However, Reason (R) is false because samanya does not lead to uniform protocols but instead provides a basis for tailoring treatments to individual needs. For example, cooling substances like cucumber and aloe vera are grouped to address heat-related disorders, but their application varies based on the patient's constitution (prakriti). This distinction reflects Ayurveda's adaptability, combining universal principles with personalized care, ensuring precision in therapeutic interventions.

42. **B:** The guna (qualities) of substances guide their therapeutic actions, forming the foundation of Ayurvedic treatments. Both Assertion (A) and Reason (R) are true, but Reason (R) is not the correct explanation of Assertion (A). While guna determines the properties of a substance, its expression may vary with environmental and contextual factors, such as preparation method or individual constitution. For instance, the heating (ushna) property of ginger intensifies in a decoction but is milder in its raw form. This dynamic understanding ensures that Ayurveda's treatments are precise and adaptable, integrating the substance's inherent qualities with its context of use.

43. **C:** Abhava (non-existence) plays a central role in Ayurveda for defining health as the absence of disease-causing factors. Assertion (A) is true because abhava reflects the negation of pathological states, aligning with Ayurveda's focus on equilibrium. However, Reason (R) is false, as abhava has direct implications for treatment. For instance, the absence of toxins (ama) is a therapeutic goal achieved through detoxification practices like Panchakarma. This practical application distinguishes Ayurveda's holistic approach from purely philosophical systems, demonstrating how metaphysical principles are seamlessly integrated into health care frameworks.

44. **A:** Ayurveda's inclusion of time (kala) and direction (dik) as dravya underscores its comprehensive understanding of health as influenced by temporal and spatial dynamics. Both Assertion (A) and Reason (R) are true, and Reason (R) provides the correct explanation. For example, kala governs biological rhythms, influencing the timing of meals and treatments, while dik contextualizes spatial orientation in therapies like Vastu Shastra. This holistic perspective integrates physical, psychological, and environmental factors, allowing Ayurveda to address health in a multi-dimensional context. The interplay of time and direction highlights Ayurveda's ability to adapt ancient principles to modern challenges.

45. **C:** Karma (actions) in Ayurveda are determined by the inherent qualities (guna) of substances. Assertion (A) is true because qualities like heating (ushna) or cooling (shita) directly influence a substance's physiological effects. For instance, the heating quality of black pepper facilitates its digestive-enhancing action. However, Reason (R) is false as it incorrectly claims that actions are independent of qualities, contradicting Ayurveda's core principles. The inseparability of guna and karma ensures that treatments are predictable and precise, addressing both symptoms and root causes. This dynamic framework reflects Ayurveda's commitment to integrating theory and practice.

46. **B:** Dravya serves as the foundation of Ayurveda's therapeutic framework, encompassing both material and non-material entities. This comprehensive classification integrates physical substances like earth and water with metaphysical elements like time and soul. Such inclusivity distinguishes Ayurveda from systems that focus solely on tangible factors. For example, time (kala) regulates circadian rhythms, while mind (manas) governs emotional balance. By addressing these dimensions, dravya ensures that Ayurveda's interventions are holistic, targeting physical, psychological, and existential health. This interconnected approach reflects the depth of Ayurveda's epistemology, aligning traditional wisdom with contemporary health care needs.

47. **B:** Samanya (generality) contributes to Ayurvedic treatment by identifying shared characteristics among substances, facilitating broad therapeutic applications. For instance, cooling herbs like coriander and fennel are grouped under samanya for treating heat-related disorders. This classification enables practitioners to select substances with complementary effects, ensuring systemic harmony. Unlike purely symptomatic approaches, samanya allows Ayurveda to address imbalances at their root. This principle also supports personalized care by guiding the selection of treatments that align with an individual's constitution. The emphasis on shared qualities demonstrates Ayurveda's ability to combine universal principles with individualized therapies.

48. **B:** Samavaya (inherence) explains the inseparable relationship between substances and their inherent qualities or actions. For example, the cooling quality (shita) of sandalwood is intrinsic to its calming effect on inflammation. This principle ensures that therapeutic properties are predictable and reliable. Unlike systems that separate active compounds from their natural contexts, Ayurveda respects the integrity of substances, ensuring holistic efficacy. Samavaya highlights the interdependence of dravya (substance), guna (qualities), and karma (actions), forming the backbone of Ayurvedic science. This interconnected framework ensures that treatments address both physiological and psychological dimensions of health.

49. **C:** Abhava (non-existence) signifies health in Ayurveda through the absence of toxins, imbalances, and disease-causing factors. For example, the absence of ama (metabolic toxins) indicates proper digestion, reflecting abhava as a marker of systemic balance. This principle extends beyond diagnostics, influencing therapeutic goals such as detoxification. Unlike systems that define health as the mere absence of symptoms, Ayurveda's focus on abhava ensures that interventions address underlying dysfunctions. This layered understanding integrates physical, psychological, and existential dimensions, reflecting Ayurveda's commitment to holistic care.

50. **B:** The relationship between guna (qualities) and karma (actions) forms the foundation of Ayurveda's therapeutic framework. Qualities like heaviness (guru) or dryness (ruksha) directly influence a substance's physiological effects. For instance, the heavy quality of milk nourishes tissues, while the dry quality of turmeric aids detoxification. This interplay ensures that treatments are precise and adaptable, addressing specific imbalances. Unlike reductionist systems that isolate active ingredients, Ayurveda respects the integrity of substances, ensuring their holistic efficacy. This dynamic relationship highlights Ayurveda's ability to integrate theory with practice, providing comprehensive care.

CHAPTER 12

RASA, GUNA, KARMA, VIRYA, AND VIPAKA – CONCEPTS AND APPLICATIONS

In Ayurvedic medicine, the principles of Rasa (taste), Guṇa (quality), Karma (action), Vīrya (potency), and Vipāka (post-digestive effect) form the foundation of understanding the properties and therapeutic effects of medicinal substances. These concepts are not only integral to diagnosing and treating diseases but also guide the formulation of remedies and the development of individualized treatment protocols. This chapter explores these principles in detail, elucidating their definitions, interconnectedness, and practical applications in clinical and pharmacological contexts.

RASA (TASTE)

Definition and Overview

Rasa, the taste of a substance, is the first perceptible interaction between the body and a medicinal or dietary substance. Derived from the Sanskrit root "ras," meaning essence or sap, Rasa represents the essence of the substance's interaction with the sensory organs. Ayurveda identifies six primary tastes:

1. Madhura (Sweet)
2. Amla (Sour)
3. Lavana (Salty)
4. Katu (Pungent)
5. Tikta (Bitter)
6. Kashaya (Astringent)

Each Rasa is associated with specific elemental compositions and physiological effects.

Elemental Composition of Rasa

The six tastes are rooted in the five Mahābhūtas (elements):

- **Sweet (Madhura):** Earth + Water
- **Sour (Amla):** Earth + Fire
- **Salty (Lavana):** Water + Fire
- **Pungent (Katu):** Fire + Air
- **Bitter (Tikta):** Air + Ether
- **Astringent (Kashaya):** Air + Earth

Functions and Role of Rasa

1. **Diagnostic Role:** Observing cravings or aversions to certain Rasas helps in understanding underlying doshic imbalances.
2. **Therapeutic Role:** Rasas influence the doshas directly:
   - **Madhura:** Pacifies Vata and Pitta, aggravates Kapha.
   - **Amla:** Pacifies Vata, aggravates Pitta and Kapha.
   - **Lavana:** Pacifies Vata, aggravates Pitta and Kapha.
   - **Katu:** Pacifies Kapha, aggravates Pitta and Vata.
   - **Tikta:** Pacifies Pitta and Kapha, aggravates Vata.
   - **Kashaya:** Pacifies Pitta and Kapha, aggravates Vata.
3. **Nutritional Role:** Rasas determine the digestive response and nutrient absorption.

GUṆA (QUALITY)

Definition and Overview

Guṇas are the inherent properties or attributes that define the nature and functionality of a substance. Ayurveda identifies twenty primary Guṇas, grouped into ten opposing pairs:

1. **Heavy (Guru):** Light (Laghu)
2. **Slow (Manda):** Sharp (Tīkṣṇa)
3. **Cold (Śīta):** Hot (Uṣṇa)
4. **Oily (Snigdha):** Dry (Rūkṣa)
5. **Smooth (Ślakṣṇa):** Rough (Khara)
6. **Dense (Sāndra):** Liquid (Drava)
7. **Soft (Mṛdu):** Hard (Kaṭhina)
8. **Stable (Sthira):** Mobile (Sara)
9. **Subtle (Sūkṣma):** Gross (Sthūla)
10. **Clear (Viśada):** Cloudy (Avila)

Functional Role of Guṇas

Guṇas describe the pharmacodynamic behaviour of substances and their interaction with the body. They influence the movement of doshas, tissues (dhātus), and waste products (malas).

- **Heavy (Guru):** Builds tissue but slows digestion.
- **Light (Laghu):** Enhances digestion and metabolism.
- **Cold (Śīta):** Soothes Pitta but may exacerbate Kapha.
- **Hot (Uṣṇa):** Alleviates Vata and Kapha while aggravating Pitta.

Application in Clinical Practice

The selection of herbs, diets, and therapies considers the Guṇas to balance the patient's doshic constitution. For instance:

- A person with Kapha dominance benefits from light (Laghu) and dry (Rūkṣa) substances.
- A Pitta constitution is pacified by cool (Śīta) and smooth (Ślakṣṇa) qualities.

KARMA (ACTION)

Definition and Overview

Karma refers to the therapeutic action or pharmacological effect of a substance. It encompasses:

- **Prabhāva:** The specific, unique effect of a drug that cannot be explained by its Rasa, Guṇa, Vīrya, or Vipāka.
- **General Actions:** These include properties like laxative, diuretic, antipyretic, and anti-inflammatory effects.

Types of Karma

1. **Doshic Action:** Substances act to pacify or aggravate specific doshas.
2. **Tissue Action:** Herbal medicines can nourish or deplete tissues based on their Karma.
3. **Channel Cleansing (Srotas):** Certain substances remove obstructions in the body's channels, promoting better physiological function.

Clinical Relevance of Karma

The choice of therapeutic agents considers Karma to achieve specific treatment goals. For example:

- A diuretic herb like Punarnava is chosen for its action on water retention (Kapha-related disorder).
- Anti-inflammatory herbs like Guduchi are selected for conditions aggravated by Pitta.

VĪRYA (POTENCY)

Vīrya (Potency) – Concepts, Types, Mechanisms, and Applications

Definition and Overview

In Ayurvedic pharmacology, Vīrya (potency) is a core concept that determines the immediate physiological response of a substance upon entering the body. Derived from the Sanskrit root "Veer," meaning strength or energy, Vīrya refers to the inherent energy or dynamism of a substance that drives its therapeutic action. While other principles like Rasa (taste), Guṇa (quality), and Vipāka (post-digestive effect) describe gradual or long-term impacts, Vīrya signifies the substance's immediate potency or ability to affect bodily functions right after consumption.

The understanding of Vīrya is fundamental for prescribing medicines or therapies to ensure that the desired physiological effect aligns with the patient's prakṛti (constitution), vikṛti (imbalance), and disease condition. Proper application of Vīrya prevents adverse effects and optimizes the therapeutic potential of substances.

Types of Vīrya

Traditionally, Ayurveda classifies Vīrya into two primary categories:

1. **Uṣṇa (Heating):**
   - Activates, stimulates, and energizes bodily processes.
   - Enhances digestion, circulation, and metabolism.
   - Balances Kapha and Vata doshas but can aggravate Pitta.

2. **Śīta (Cooling):**
   - Calms, soothes, and reduces hyperactivity or inflammation.
   - Alleviates burning sensations and excessive heat in the body.

Balances Pitta and Vata doshas but may increase Kapha

However, some Ayurvedic scholars and texts expand this dual classification to include eight types of Vīrya, aligning with specific qualities and effects. These eight Vīryas correspond to unique energetic influences:

1. Snigdha (Oily)
2. Rūkṣa (Dry)
3. Śīta (Cold)
4. Uṣṇa (Hot)
5. Laghu (Light)
6. Guru (Heavy)
7. Manda (Dull)
8. Tīkṣṇa (Sharp)

The eightfold classification acknowledges subtle variations in the energetics of substances, enabling more nuanced applications in treatments.

Mechanisms of Vīrya

The mechanism of Vīrya can be understood by exploring its influence on the body at various levels:

1. **Digestive System:** Vīrya directly impacts Agni (digestive fire). Heating substances (Uṣṇa Vīrya) strengthen Agni, aiding in digestion and metabolism, while cooling substances (Śīta Vīrya) soothe hyperactive Agni, beneficial in conditions like gastritis or acid reflux.
2. **Circulatory System:** Heating substances improve circulation by dilating blood vessels and promoting warmth. Cooling substances reduce inflammation and vasodilation in heat-related disorders.
3. **Cellular Activity:** Vīrya drives cellular responses such as metabolism, inflammation, or detoxification. Heating herbs like Ginger (Zingiber officinale) enhance enzymatic activity, while cooling herbs like Aloe Vera (Aloe barbadensis) inhibit inflammatory mediators.
4. **Nervous System:** Substances with Śīta Vīrya calm the nervous system and alleviate stress-related disorders, while Uṣṇa Vīrya stimulates and energizes the mind and body.
5. **Dosha Interaction:** Uṣṇa Vīrya substances are effective in cold, sluggish, or Kapha-aggravated conditions, as they counteract stagnation.

   Śīta Vīrya substances are essential for conditions of heat, inflammation, and Pitta aggravation.

Role of Vīrya in Formulating Medicines

Vīrya is a critical consideration in formulating Ayurvedic medicines. Understanding the heating or cooling potency of each ingredient ensures that the formulation aligns with the desired therapeutic goals. For example:

1. **Single Herb Therapy:** Uṣṇa Vīrya Example: Garlic (Allium sativum) is used to reduce Kapha, stimulate digestion, and alleviate cold-related disorders.

   Śīta Vīrya Example: Sandalwood (Santalum album) is used to cool the system, treat burning sensations, and reduce Pitta.
2. **Herbal Combinations:** Ayurvedic formulations often balance the Vīrya of individual herbs to ensure a synergistic effect. For instance, in Triphala, the cooling nature of Amalaki offsets the heating properties of Haritaki.
3. **Dosage Forms and Preparation:** Processing methods like roasting or fermenting can modify a substance's Vīrya. A raw herb may exhibit Śīta Vīrya, but when processed with heat, its Uṣṇa properties might be enhanced.

Applications of Vīrya in Clinical Practice

1. **Digestive Disorders:** Heating herbs like Black Pepper (Piper nigrum) are used in conditions of indigestion, bloating, or Kapha-related sluggishness.

   Cooling herbs like Licorice (Glycyrrhiza glabra) soothe gastritis and hyperacidity.
2. **Respiratory Conditions:** Uṣṇa Vīrya herbs like Tulsi (Ocimum sanctum) clear Kapha obstructions and combat colds.

   Śīta Vīrya herbs like Vasaka (Adhatoda vasica) reduce inflammation in bronchitis or asthma.
3. **Skin Disorders:** Śīta Vīrya herbs like Neem (Azadirachta indica) are used to cool and cleanse Pitta-induced skin conditions like eczema or acne.

   Uṣṇa Vīrya herbs like Turmeric (Curcuma longa) enhance blood circulation and reduce Kapha stagnation in chronic wounds.
4. **Nervous System and Stress:** Śīta Vīrya substances like Brahmi (Bacopa monnieri) calm the mind, reduce anxiety, and promote restful sleep.

   Uṣṇa Vīrya herbs like Ashwagandha (Withania somnifera) energize the nervous system and combat fatigue.

Pharmacological Examples of Vīrya

1. **Cooling Potency (Śīta Vīrya):** Aloe Vera (Aloe barbadensis): Soothes burns, heals ulcers, and cools excessive Pitta.

   Coriander (Coriandrum sativum): Reduces digestive heat and balances inflammatory conditions.

2. **Heating Potency (Uṣṇa Vīrya):** Ginger (Zingiber officinale): Stimulates digestion, alleviates colds, and enhances circulation.

   Black Pepper (Piper nigrum): Reduces Kapha, improves metabolism, and acts as an expectorant.

Vīrya and Modern Pharmacology

The Ayurvedic concept of Vīrya aligns with certain principles in modern pharmacology, such as the thermodynamic activity of drugs and their effects on metabolic pathways. For example:

- Uṣṇa Vīrya substances can be compared to stimulants or thermogenic agents that enhance metabolic rate.
- Śīta Vīrya substances resemble anti-inflammatory agents that cool down overactive pathways.
- The immediate potency described by Vīrya offers a lens for understanding drug mechanisms beyond the molecular level, emphasizing the energetic and functional impact on the body.

Case Studies

1. **Chronic Cold and Congestion (Kapha Aggravation):** A patient with chronic sinusitis benefits from Uṣṇa Vīrya herbs like Black Pepper and Ginger. These substances clear mucus, stimulate circulation, and energize Agni.
2. **Heat-Induced Skin Rash (Pitta Aggravation):** Śīta Vīrya herbs like Neem and Aloe Vera are prescribed to cool inflammation, purify blood, and reduce itching.
3. **Generalized Fatigue (Vata Imbalance):** Uṣṇa Vīrya herbs like Ashwagandha and heating dietary practices restore vitality and balance weakened Agni.

Integration with Other Principles

The interplay between Vīrya, Rasa, Guṇa, and Vipāka enhances the understanding of a substance's complete therapeutic profile. For example:

Trikatu (Three Pungents):

- **Rasa:** Pungent
- **Guṇa:** Light, Dry
- **Vīrya:** Heating
- **Vipāka:** Pungent

This heating formulation is ideal for Kapha-related stagnation.

Practical Guidelines for Vīrya Application

1. **Consider Prakṛti:** Heating substances should be limited in Pitta-dominant individuals, while cooling substances are avoided in Kapha-dominant individuals.
2. **Seasonal Adaptations:** Uṣṇa Vīrya herbs are preferred in cold seasons, while Śīta Vīrya substances suit hot climates.
3. **Combination Strategies:** Balancing heating and cooling ingredients ensures comprehensive doshic balancing.

Vīrya is a cornerstone of Ayurvedic pharmacology, influencing the immediate action of herbs and treatments. By understanding its principles and integrating them with other Ayurvedic concepts, practitioners can design precise and effective therapeutic protocols. Its relevance extends beyond traditional medicine, offering insights into the energetic dimensions of healing in both Ayurvedic and modern contexts. This dynamic principle remains central to maintaining the harmony and balance of the human body, the essence of Ayurveda's holistic approach to health.

VIPĀKA (POST-DIGESTIVE EFFECT)

Definition and Overview

Vipāka, the post-digestive effect of a substance, is one of the most critical principles in Ayurvedic pharmacology. It refers to the transformation that a substance undergoes after digestion and its subsequent impact on the body. While Rasa (taste) represents the immediate sensory interaction and Vīrya (potency) reflects the energetic impact, Vipāka addresses the long-term metabolic and systemic effects of a substance.

The concept of Vipāka is unique to Ayurveda and emphasizes the idea that the ultimate impact of a substance on the body extends beyond digestion. It is integral in determining how a substance influences the dhātus (tissues), srotas (channels), and doshas after being metabolized.

Types of Vipāka

Ayurveda identifies three types of Vipāka, based on the final metabolic transformation of a substance:

1. **Madhura Vipāka (Sweet Post-Digestive Effect):**
   - Derived from sweet and salty tastes.
   - Builds and nourishes the body.
   - Promotes the growth and repair of dhātus.
   - Pacifies Vata and Pitta, but may aggravate Kapha.
2. **Amla Vipāka (Sour Post-Digestive Effect):**
   - Derived from sour taste.
   - Stimulates digestion and metabolism.
   - Enhances appetite and increases Pitta.
   - Balances Vata but may aggravate Pitta and Kapha.
3. **Katu Vipāka (Pungent Post-Digestive Effect):**
   - Derived from pungent, bitter, and astringent tastes.

- Detoxifies and purifies the body.
- Reduces Kapha but may aggravate Vata and Pitta.
- Dries out tissues and is beneficial for weight management.

Vipāka and Its Elemental Basis

The three Vipākas align with the elemental theory of Ayurveda:

- Madhura Vipāka is associated with Earth and Water, fostering growth and lubrication.
- Amla Vipāka corresponds to Earth and Fire, emphasizing transformation and digestion.
- Katu Vipāka relates to Air and Fire, promoting lightness and detoxification.
- The elemental alignment of Vipāka highlights its role in influencing doshic balance and its effects on the body's metabolic and physiological processes.

Relationship Between Vipāka and Rasa

Vipāka is closely related to Rasa but represents a more advanced stage of the substance's effect on the body. While Rasa impacts the body immediately upon ingestion, Vipāka represents the cumulative metabolic influence. The transition from Rasa to Vipāka occurs during the digestive process, with Agni (digestive fire) playing a pivotal role in this transformation.

- Sweet, Salty, and Sour Rasas typically result in Madhura or Amla Vipāka.
- Pungent, Bitter, and Astringent Rasas typically result in Katu Vipāka.
- This relationship ensures that the substance's final impact aligns with its initial qualities, although exceptions exist due to Prabhāva (unique action).

Mechanisms of Vipāka

Vipāka operates through several mechanisms in the body, influencing different physiological levels:

1. **Impact on Dhātus (Tissues):**
   - **Madhura Vipāka:** Nourishes and strengthens tissues.
   - **Amla Vipāka:** Stimulates metabolic processes and enhances nutrient absorption.
   - **Katu Vipāka:** Reduces fatty deposits and clears toxins from tissues.
2. **Effect on Doshas:**
   - **Madhura Vipāka:** Balances Vata and Pitta, but may increase Kapha.
   - **Amla Vipāka:** Balances Vata but may disturb Kapha and Pitta if consumed excessively.
   - **Katu Vipāka:** Reduces Kapha but can aggravate Vata and Pitta.
3. **Action on Malas (Excretory Processes):** Vipāka determines the quality of feces, urine, and sweat, reflecting the metabolic byproducts of digestion.
4. **Role in Srotas (Channels):** Madhura Vipāka: Supports unimpeded flow in bodily channels.
   - **Amla Vipāka:** Enhances circulation and energy flow but may cause blockages if imbalanced.
   - **Katu Vipāka:** Clears channels, promoting detoxification.

Therapeutic Applications of Vipāka

Vipāka plays a significant role in determining the long-term therapeutic effects of medicinal substances. Understanding a substance's Vipāka allows Ayurvedic practitioners to predict its impact on the body and formulate personalized treatment strategies.

1. **Metabolic Disorders:** Madhura Vipāka herbs, such as Licorice (Glycyrrhiza glabra), are used to strengthen weakened tissues and combat emaciation.

   Katu Vipāka herbs, like Triphala, are beneficial in managing obesity and reducing Kapha-induced sluggishness.
2. **Digestive Health:** Amla Vipāka herbs, such as Tamarind (Tamarindus indica), stimulate appetite and digestion in Kapha-dominant conditions.

   Katu Vipāka herbs, like Ginger (Zingiber officinale), cleanse digestive channels and enhance Agni.
3. **Skin and Inflammatory Conditions:** Madhura Vipāka substances, like Aloe Vera (Aloe barbadensis), soothe Pitta-induced inflammation and promote skin health.

   Katu Vipāka herbs, such as Neem (Azadirachta indica), purify blood and treat Kapha-dominated skin conditions like acne.
4. **Respiratory Disorders:** Katu Vipāka herbs, such as Tulsi (Ocimum sanctum), clear mucus and alleviate Kapha-related congestion.

   Amla Vipāka substances, like Citrus fruits, support Pitta regulation in bronchial inflammation.
5. **Reproductive Health:** Madhura Vipāka herbs, like Shatavari (Asparagus racemosus), nourish reproductive tissues and balance Vata.

   Katu Vipāka substances, like Fenugreek (Trigonella foenum-graecum), regulate Kapha and enhance metabolic heat.

Examples of Herbs and Their Vipāka

1. **Madhura Vipāka:**
   - **Herb:** Ashwagandha (Withania somnifera)

- **Effect:** Strengthens dhātus, calms Vata, and nourishes the nervous system.
- **Herb:** Licorice (Glycyrrhiza glabra)
- **Effect:** Balances Pitta, soothes mucous membranes, and supports tissue repair.

2. **Amla Vipāka:**
   - **Herb:** Amalaki (Phyllanthus emblica)
   - **Effect:** Stimulates digestion, balances Vata, and enhances Pitta in a controlled manner.
   - **Herb:** Tamarind (Tamarindus indica)
   - **Effect:** Aids digestion, improves nutrient absorption, and stimulates appetite.
3. **Katu Vipāka:**
   - **Herb:** Turmeric (Curcuma longa)
   - **Effect:** Detoxifies tissues, purifies blood, and clears Kapha.
   - **Herb:** Black Pepper (Piper nigrum)
   - **Effect:** Stimulates Agni, clears toxins, and enhances metabolic functions.

Case Studies of Vipāka in Practice

1. **Kapha-Dominant Obesity:** A patient with sluggish digestion and weight gain benefits from Katu Vipāka herbs like Triphala and Black Pepper, which detoxify tissues and stimulate metabolism.
2. **Pitta-Induced Ulcers:** A Pitta-aggravated patient with hyperacidity is prescribed Madhura Vipāka herbs like Licorice and Aloe Vera to soothe inflammation and promote tissue healing.
3. **Vata-Induced Weakness:** A patient with chronic fatigue and dry skin is treated with Madhura Vipāka substances like Shatavari and Ghee to nourish tissues and balance Vata.

Integration of Vipāka with Modern Pharmacology

The Ayurvedic concept of Vipāka aligns with modern pharmacological insights into drug metabolism and bioavailability. Vipāka's post-digestive effects are comparable to how drugs are metabolized by the liver and how their active components influence bodily systems.

Madhura Vipāka corresponds to anabolic actions, such as tissue building and repair.

Amla Vipāka aligns with catalytic processes that enhance enzymatic activity.

Katu Vipāka resembles detoxification and anti-inflammatory actions.

Understanding Vipāka bridges traditional Ayurvedic practices with contemporary biomedical frameworks, facilitating integrative approaches to health care.

Practical Guidelines for Using Vipāka in Treatment

1. **Dosha Assessment:** Determine the patient's doshic imbalance to select herbs with the appropriate Vipāka.
2. **Dietary Adjustments:** Incorporate foods and spices with specific Vipākas to complement medicinal therapies.
3. **Seasonal Considerations:** Choose herbs with suitable Vipākas based on seasonal doshic variations. For example, Katu Vipāka substances are preferred in spring to counter Kapha accumulation.
4. **Combination Therapy:** Balance herbs with different Vipākas to achieve synergistic effects and minimize potential aggravations.

Vipāka, as the post-digestive effect, is a vital concept in Ayurveda that defines the long-term metabolic impact of substances on the body. Its classification into Madhura, Amla, and Katu Vipākas provides a comprehensive framework for understanding and predicting the therapeutic outcomes of herbs and diets. By integrating Vipāka with other principles like Rasa, Guṇa, and Vīrya, Ayurveda offers a holistic approach to health and wellness. Its application extends beyond traditional healing to modern integrative medicine, ensuring its relevance in contemporary health care practices.

Integration and Interplay of Rasa, Guṇa, Karma, Vīrya, and Vipāka The principles are interconnected:

- Rasa initiates the interaction with the body.
- Guṇa modulates physiological processes.
- Karma achieves therapeutic goals.
- Vīrya dictates immediate potency.
- Vipāka determines long-term effects.

For example:

Ginger:

- **Rasa:** Pungent
- **Guṇa:** Light, Dry
- **Karma:** Digestive stimulant
- **Vīrya:** Heating
- **Vipāka:** Pungent

This profile makes it an excellent remedy for Vata-Kapha digestive disorders.

APPLICATIONS IN TREATMENT AND FORMULATION OF MEDICINES

Individualized Treatment

Understanding these principles ensures tailored treatment. For instance:

- A Pitta patient requires cooling, bitter herbs like Neem.
- A Kapha patient benefits from pungent, light, and heating substances like Black Pepper.

Drug Formulation

The balance of Rasa, Guṇa, Karma, Vīrya, and Vipāka guides herbal combinations. Example:

Triphala (Three Fruits):

- **Haritaki:** Astringent, Light, Heating, Pungent Vipāka.
- **Bibhitaki:** Astringent, Light, Cooling, Sweet Vipāka.
- **Amalaki:** Sour, Heavy, Cooling, Sweet Vipāka.

Together, they detoxify and rejuvenate.

The integration of Rasa, Guṇa, Karma, Vīrya, and Vipāka provides a holistic understanding of medicinal substances. This framework not only aids in precise diagnosis and treatment but also facilitates the formulation of safe, effective remedies. Their harmonious application is the cornerstone of Ayurvedic pharmacology, ensuring balanced and sustainable health interventions.

MULTIPLE CHOICE QUESTIONS

1. A pharmacologist is studying the interplay between Ayurvedic Rasas (tastes) and their post-digestive effect (Vipāka). They hypothesize that the sweet Rasa, while initially anabolic, converts into a heating effect in the digestive tract when consumed in excess. This contrasts with bitter Rasa, which remains cooling through its Vipāka. Which of the following best supports this hypothesis?

A. Sweet Rasa has only a cooling effect and never produces heat, regardless of its dosage.

B. Bitter Rasa remains cooling but fails to exert any post-digestive influence.

C. The Vipāka of sweet Rasa shows duality based on quantity, while bitter Rasa is unidirectional in effect.

D. Vipāka of both sweet and bitter Rasas consistently aligns with their primary Rasas, showing no deviation.

2. Imagine a clinician integrating the Ayurvedic concepts of Guṇa (quality) with modern drug pharmacodynamics. If the Snigdha (unctuous) Guṇa is theorized to enhance lipid solubility of active compounds, improving cellular absorption, what practical applications could this imply?

A. Snigdha Guṇa reduces the lipid solubility of medicines, requiring alternate drug formulations.

B. Compounds with Snigdha Guṇa could mimic the effects of modern water-soluble drugs.

C. Drugs enhanced with Snigdha Guṇa may demonstrate improved bioavailability in lipid-rich tissues.

D. Snigdha Guṇa is irrelevant to pharmacodynamics and cellular absorption processes.

3. A researcher is exploring the Ayurvedic concept of Karma (action) through its clinical applications in chronic diseases. If Tikta (bitter) Rasa is linked to detoxification processes, how might this manifest in treatment protocols?

A. Tikta Rasa depletes body fluids, making it unsuitable for chronic disease therapy.

B. Detoxification through Tikta Rasa facilitates the removal of Ama (toxins), alleviating systemic inflammation.

C. The use of Tikta Rasa introduces Ama accumulation, complicating disease management.

D. Tikta Rasa has no clinical applications in chronic conditions due to its limited scope.

4. An Ayurvedic physician prescribes a formulation rich in Madhura (sweet) Rasa and Guru (heavy) Guṇa to a patient with Vata imbalance. Considering the pharmacological implications, how does this choice align with the principles of Ayurvedic treatment?

A. Madhura Rasa and Guru Guṇa intensify Vata imbalance by promoting lightness.

B. The formulation counters Vata imbalance through nourishment and stabilization.

C. Madhura Rasa destabilizes Pitta, making it unsuitable for Vata correction.

D. The prescription aligns with balancing Kapha rather than Vata.

5. A formulation containing Katu (pungent) Rasa and Laghu (light) Guṇa is hypothesized to stimulate metabolic pathways. If tested on patients with Kapha imbalance, what clinical outcomes are expected?

A. Katu Rasa aggravates Kapha, necessitating alternative treatment strategies.

B. Laghu Guṇa complements Kapha pacification, but Katu Rasa is ineffective.

C. The combination stimulates metabolic pathways, reducing Kapha-related stagnation.

D. Katu Rasa and Laghu Guṇa are contraindicated for all Kapha conditions.

6. A nutritional scientist is investigating Vipāka effects of different Rasas on gut microbiota. If Amla (sour) Rasa is observed to enhance fermentation in the gut, what conclusion can be drawn?
   A. Amla Rasa inhibits fermentation, aligning with detoxification goals.
   B. Enhanced fermentation indicates Amla Rasa's role in promoting digestive enzyme activity.
   C. The post-digestive effects of Amla Rasa are irrelevant to gut microbiota.
   D. Amla Rasa's role in fermentation leads to reduced microbial diversity.

7. A study on Ayurvedic Vīrya (potency) demonstrates that Ushna (heating) Vīrya formulations enhance peripheral circulation. What implications does this have for Ayurvedic practice?
   A. Ushna Vīrya is ineffective in improving circulation due to its localized action.
   B. The circulatory benefits validate the role of Ushna Vīrya in treating cold-related disorders.
   C. Ushna Vīrya formulations impair systemic functions and are contraindicated in circulatory diseases.
   D. Peripheral circulation enhancement contradicts the classical role of Ushna Vīrya.

8. If a researcher links Rasa and Vīrya to pharmacokinetics, hypothesizing that Kapha-pacifying drugs require faster systemic distribution, which formulation characteristics align with this?
   A. Guru (heavy) Guṇa with Madhura (sweet) Rasa enhances systemic absorption.
   B. Laghu (light) Guṇa combined with Katu (pungent) Rasa accelerates systemic effects.
   C. Kapha-pacifying drugs rely solely on post-digestive effects for efficacy.
   D. Rasa and Vīrya are unrelated to pharmacokinetic properties.

9. Considering Ayurvedic Vipāka's impact on nutrient absorption, how does Katu Vipāka influence lipid metabolism?
   A. Katu Vipāka improves lipid metabolism through enhanced bile secretion.
   B. Lipid metabolism is unaffected by Katu Vipāka, which influences carbohydrates only.
   C. Katu Vipāka disrupts lipid digestion, necessitating additional digestive aids.
   D. Lipid metabolism under Katu Vipāka aligns with decreased enzymatic activity.

10. In treating digestive disorders, an Ayurvedic practitioner emphasizes the synergistic roles of Rasa, Guṇa, Karma, and Vipāka. How would this approach manifest in clinical outcomes?
   A. The focus on synergy complicates treatment, reducing overall efficacy.
   B. Synergy ensures that all treatment facets work harmoniously, enhancing outcomes.
   C. The interdependence of these principles negates their individual therapeutic relevance.
   D. Clinical outcomes are independent of such synergies, relying solely on patient compliance.

Directions (Q. No. 11–14): *Scenario-Based Questions*

SCENARIO 1

A pharmaceutical researcher is studying the impact of Ayurvedic Rasas (tastes) on the modulation of enzymatic activity in the liver. The focus is on the Madhura (sweet) and Tikta (bitter) Rasas, hypothesizing that Madhura enhances anabolic processes like glycogen storage, while Tikta accelerates detoxification pathways through cytochrome P450 enzyme activity. To test this, formulations of Madhura-dominant and Tikta-dominant herbal preparations are administered to two groups of patients with metabolic syndromes. Preliminary results show improved glycogen storage in the Madhura group and heightened liver detoxification in the Tikta group. However, the long-term metabolic benefits appear more pronounced in the Tikta group.

SCENARIO 2

Simultaneously, a conservation biologist is assessing the environmental sustainability of cultivating herbs used in the above formulations. The Tikta-dominant preparation relies heavily on Neem (Azadirachta indica) and Kalmegh (Andrographis paniculata), both of which are under threat due to overharvesting. The biologist suggests promoting mixed-cropping systems to ensure the sustainable use of these resources while maintaining their pharmacological efficacy. However, implementing these systems faces resistance due to increased costs and logistical challenges.

11. Based on Scenario 1, which of the following mechanisms best explains the improved long-term metabolic benefits observed in the Tikta-dominant group?
   A. Tikta Rasa enhances glycogen storage more effectively than Madhura Rasa, leading to prolonged metabolic stability.
   B. Activation of cytochrome P450 enzymes by Tikta Rasa improves detoxification, reducing metabolic toxin buildup.
   C. Tikta Rasa decreases liver enzymatic activity, preventing metabolic disorders.
   D. Madhura Rasa undermines metabolic benefits by excessively enhancing anabolic pathways.

12. Considering Scenario 2, what would be the most effective strategy to balance environmental sustainability with the production demands of Tikta-dominant herbal formulations?

A. Establishing monoculture farms for Neem and Kalmegh to meet production requirements.
B. Promoting agroforestry practices to integrate Neem and Kalmegh cultivation with other crops.
C. Developing synthetic alternatives to Neem and Kalmegh to eliminate dependency on natural sources.
D. Reducing the global usage of Tikta-dominant formulations to conserve these herbs.

13. How might the environmental challenges described in Scenario 2 influence the clinical outcomes observed in Scenario 1?

A. The reduced availability of Neem and Kalmegh will directly diminish the therapeutic efficacy of Tikta-dominant formulations.
B. Sustainable harvesting practices will have no impact on the clinical effectiveness of Tikta-dominant formulations.
C. Environmental stressors may enhance the bioactive compounds in Neem and Kalmegh, improving their pharmacological potency.
D. The scarcity of Neem and Kalmegh will necessitate the reformulation of Tikta-dominant preparations, potentially altering their clinical outcomes.

14. Based on the interconnected findings of Scenarios 1 and 2, which of the following approaches would ensure sustainable use of medicinal plants while maintaining therapeutic efficacy?

A. Shifting focus from Tikta-dominant to Madhura-dominant formulations to reduce dependency on endangered herbs.
B. Encouraging research on alternative plant sources with similar Tikta properties to Neem and Kalmegh.
C. Promoting synthetic replication of Tikta properties, bypassing the need for plant-based formulations.
D. Mandating global guidelines for sustainable herb sourcing and farming practices to support Tikta-dominant formulations.

15. The classification of Rasa (taste) in Ayurveda includes:

(a) Sweet Rasa builds tissues and promotes strength.
(b) Salty Rasa improves digestion and cleanses tissues.
(c) Bitter Rasa reduces body heat and toxins.
(d) Pungent Rasa stimulates metabolism and clears mucus.

Choose the correct answer from the options given below:

A. (a), (b), and (c) only
B. (b), (c), and (d) only
C. (a), (b), (c), and (d) only
D. (a), (c), and (d) only

16. The Guṇas (qualities) described in Ayurveda are:

(a) Laghu (light) helps digestion and assimilation.
(b) Guru (heavy) promotes strength and stability.
(c) Rūkṣa (dry) decreases Kapha and increases Vata.
(d) Snigdha (unctuous) balances Pitta and Vata.

Choose the correct answer from the options given below:

A. (a), (b), and (c) only
B. (b), (c), and (d) only
C. (a), (b), and (d) only
D. (a), (b), (c), and (d)

17. The Karma (actions) of Ayurvedic formulations include:

(a) Deepana (digestive stimulant) enhances Agni.
(b) Balya (strengthening) increases immunity.
(c) Srotoshodhana (cleansing channels) removes blockages.
(d) Sandhāniya (healing) promotes tissue repair.

Choose the correct answer from the options given below:

A. (a), (b), and (c) only
B. (a), (b), (c), and (d)
C. (b), (c), and (d) only
D. (a), (c), and (d) only

18. The concept of Vīrya (potency) includes the following classifications:

(a) Uṣṇa (hot potency) reduces Kapha and Vata.
(b) Śīta (cold potency) balances Pitta and reduces heat.
(c) Madhura (sweet potency) nourishes tissues.
(d) Tīkṣṇa (sharp potency) eliminates toxins.

Choose the correct answer from the options given below:

A. (a), (b), and (c) only
B. (b), (c), and (d) only
C. (a), (b), and (d) only
D. (a), (b), (c), and (d)

19. The Vipāka (post-digestive effect) principles in Ayurveda include:

(a) Madhura Vipāka promotes tissue growth.
(b) Amla Vipāka increases Pitta and digestion.
(c) Kaṭu Vipāka detoxifies and purifies the body.
(d) Tikta Vipāka enhances immunity.

Choose the correct answer from the options given below:

A. (a), (b), and (c) only
B. (a), (b), (c), and (d)
C. (b), (c), and (d) only
D. (a), (c), and (d) only

20. The role of Rasa and Vipāka in Ayurvedic formulations includes:
(a) Rasa determines immediate taste and impact on Doshas.
(b) Vipāka determines the long-term effects of the medicine.
(c) Both Rasa and Vipāka are essential for holistic treatment.
(d) Vipāka governs the bioavailability of the formulation.

Choose the correct answer from the options given below:
A. (a), (b), and (d) only
B. (a), (c), and (d) only
C. (a), (b), and (c) only
D. (a), (b), (c), and (d)

21. The relationship between Guṇa and Karma is reflected in the following principles:
(a) Laghu Guṇa aids in digestion through Deepana Karma.
(b) Guru Guṇa supports tissue building through Balya Karma.
(c) Snigdha Guṇa reduces dryness through Snehana Karma.
(d) loose Rūkṣa Guṇa stimulates cleansing through Srotoshodhana Karma.

Choose the correct answer from the options given below:
A. (a), (b), and (c) only
B. (b), (c), and (d) only
C. (a), (c), and (d) only
D. (a), (b), (c), and (d)

22. The application of Vīrya in Ayurvedic medicine includes:
(a) Hot potency (Uṣṇa) medicines improve circulation and digestion.
(b) Cold potency (Śīta) medicines relieve inflammation and burning.
(c) Balanced Vīrya formulations are ideal for Tridosha balance.
(d) Specific Vīrya ensures targeted action in treatments.

Choose the correct answer from the options given below:
A. (a), (b), and (c) only
B. (a), (c), and (d) only
C. (b), (c), and (d) only
D. (a), (b), (c), and (d)

23. The classification of Karma (actions) includes:
(a) Deepana enhances digestive fire (Agni).
(b) Pachana reduces toxins through digestion.
(c) Śodhana expels toxins and purifies the body.
(d) Bṛhmaṇa increases tissue nourishment and strength.

Choose the correct answer from the options given below:
A. (a), (b), and (c) only
B. (a), (b), (c), and (d)
C. (b), (c), and (d) only
D. (a), (c), and (d) only

24. The interrelation of Rasa, Guṇa, and Vipāka in treatment is demonstrated by:
(a) Rasa affects the immediate Dosha balance.
(b) Guṇa determines the qualities of the medicine.
(c) Vipāka ensures sustained efficacy after digestion.
(d) All three influence the body-mind equilibrium.

Choose the correct answer from the options given below:
A. (a), (b), and (c) only
B. (a), (c), and (d) only
C. (a), (b), and (d) only
D. (a), (b), (c), and (d)

25. Match List–I (Rasas) with List–II (Primary Actions):

List–I	List–II
(a) Sweet Rasa	1. Nourishes tissues and promotes strength
(b) Sour Rasa	2. Increases appetite and enhances metabolism
(c) Pungent Rasa	3. Stimulates digestion and clears toxins
(d) Bitter Rasa	4. Detoxifies and reduces excessive Pitta

Choose the correct answer from the options given below:
A. (a)-1, (b)-2, (c)-3, (d)-4
B. (a)-2, (b)-3, (c)-4, (d)-1
C. (a)-4, (b)-1, (c)-2, (d)-3
D. (a)-3, (b)-4, (c)-1, (d)-2

26. Match List–I (Guṇas) with List–II (Properties):

List–I	List–II
(a) Guru (heavy)	1. Provides grounding and reduces Pitta
(b) Laghu (light)	2. Promotes digestion and quick absorption
(c) Snigdha (unctuous)	3. Enhances lubrication and stability
(d) Rūkṣa (dry)	4. Aggravates Vata and reduces Kapha

Choose the correct answer from the options given below:

A. (a)-1, (b)-2, (c)-3, (d)-4
B. (a)-2, (b)-3, (c)-4, (d)-1
C. (a)-3, (b)-4, (c)-1, (d)-2
D. (a)-4, (b)-1, (c)-2, (d)-3

27. Match List–I (Ayurvedic Terms) with List–II (Definitions):

List–I	List–II
(a) Vīrya	1. Potency and heating/cooling action
(b) Karma	2. Therapeutic action of a substance
(c) Vipāka	3. Post-digestive physiological effect
(d) Rasa	4. Immediate sensory experience of taste

Choose the correct answer from the options given below:

A. (a)-1, (b)-2, (c)-3, (d)-4
B. (a)-2, (b)-3, (c)-4, (d)-1
C. (a)-3, (b)-4, (c)-1, (d)-2
D. (a)-4, (b)-1, (c)-2, (d)-3

28. Match List–I (Doshas) with List–II (Primary Functions):

List–I	List–II
(a) Vata	1. Governs movement and bodily functions
(b) Pitta	2. Regulates metabolism and body heat
(c) Kapha	3. Provides stability and structural support

Choose the correct answer from the options given below:

A. (a)-1, (b)-2, (c)-3
B. (a)-2, (b)-3, (c)-1
C. (a)-3, (b)-1, (c)-2
D. (a)-2, (b)-1, (c)-3

29. Match List–I (Therapeutic Actions) with List–II (Examples):

List–I	List–II
(a) Detoxification	1. Haritaki
(b) Tissue building	2. Ashwagandha
(c) Anti-inflammatory	3. Guduchi
(d) Sedation	4. Brahmi

Choose the correct answer from the options given below:

A. (a)-1, (b)-2, (c)-3, (d)-4
B. (a)-2, (b)-1, (c)-4, (d)-3
C. (a)-3, (b)-4, (c)-1, (d)-2
D. (a)-4, (b)-3, (c)-2, (d)-1

30. Match List–I (Herbal Preparations) with List–II (Primary Uses):

List–I	List–II
(a) Triphala	1. Digestive health and detoxification
(b) Brahmi Ghrita	2. Cognitive enhancement and mental clarity
(c) Chyawanprash	3. Immunity and rejuvenation
(d) Arjuna Powder	4. Cardiovascular health and strengthening

Choose the correct answer from the options given below:

A. (a)-1, (b)-2, (c)-3, (d)-4
B. (a)-3, (b)-1, (c)-4, (d)-2
C. (a)-4, (b)-3, (c)-1, (d)-2
D. (a)-2, (b)-4, (c)-3, (d)-1

31. Match List–I (Rasas) with List–II (Dosha Effects):

List–I	List–II
(a) Sweet Rasa	1. Aggravates Kapha, pacifies Vata and Pitta
(b) Sour Rasa	2. Pacifies Kapha, slightly aggravates Pitta
(c) Pungent Rasa	3. Aggravates Vata, pacifies Kapha and Pitta
(d) Astringent Rasa	4. Pacifies Kapha, aggravates Pitta and Vata

Choose the correct answer from the options given below:

A. (a)-1, (b)-2, (c)-3, (d)-4
B. (a)-2, (b)-3, (c)-4, (d)-1
C. (a)-3, (b)-4, (c)-1, (d)-2
D. (a)-4, (b)-1, (c)-2, (d)-3

32. Match List–I (Vīrya) with List–II (Effects):

List–I	List–II
(a) Ushna (heating)	1. Stimulates circulation and metabolism
(b) Shīta (cooling)	2. Calms inflammation and reduces Pitta

Choose the correct answer from the options given below:

A. (a)-1, (b)-2
B. (a)-2, (b)-1
C. (a)-1, (b)-1
D. (a)-2, (b)-2

33. Match List–I (Herbal Actions) with List–II (Mechanisms):

List–I	List–II
(a) Laxative	1. Promotes bowel motility
(b) Stimulant	2. Enhances digestive fire
(c) Astringent	3. Contracts tissues and reduces secretion
(d) Diuretic	4. Increases urine output

Choose the correct answer from the options given below:
A. (a)-1, (b)-2, (c)-3, (d)-4
B. (a)-2, (b)-3, (c)-4, (d)-1
C. (a)-4, (b)-1, (c)-2, (d)-3
D. (a)-3, (b)-4, (c)-1, (d)-2

34. Match List–I (Post-Digestive Vipāka) with List–II (Physiological Impacts):

List–I	List–II
(a) Sweet Vipāka	1. Lubricates tissues and promotes strength
(b) Sour Vipāka	2. Enhances bile secretion and digestion
(c) Pungent Vipāka	3. Stimulates metabolic processes and detoxification

Choose the correct answer from the options given below:
A. (a)-1, (b)-2, (c)-3
B. (a)-3, (b)-1, (c)-2
C. (a)-2, (b)-3, (c)-1
D. (a)-3, (b)-2, (c)-1

Directions (Q. No. 35–39): *Following questions are based on Statement 1 and Statement 2. Read both the statements carefully and choose the correct answer from the options given below:*
A. Both Statement 1 and Statement 2 are true, and Statement 2 is the correct explanation of Statement 1.
B. Both Statement 1 and Statement 2 are true, but Statement 2 is not the correct explanation of Statement 1.
C. Statement 1 is true, but Statement 2 is false.
D. Statement 1 is false, but Statement 2 is true.
E. Both Statement 1 and Statement 2 are false.

35. **Statement 1:** Ayurveda postulates that Rasas (tastes) influence the doshas through their immediate and long-term effects, primarily mediated by their post-digestive impact (Vipāka).

Statement 2: Vipāka is the direct sensory perception of Rasas upon ingestion and is unrelated to their physiological or metabolic effects.

36. **Statement 1:** The heating potency (Ushna Vīrya) of an Ayurvedic formulation enhances the circulation and metabolic activity, making it suitable for Kapha-related disorders.

Statement 2: Ushna Vīrya suppresses metabolic pathways by increasing oxidative stress, making it unsuitable for disorders involving Pitta imbalance.

37. **Statement 1:** Astringent Rasa strengthens tissues and reduces secretion, making it beneficial in wound healing and controlling bleeding.

Statement 2: The post-digestive effect (Vipāka) of Astringent Rasa is primarily cooling, helping to pacify Vata and Pitta imbalances.

38. **Statement 1:** Tikta (bitter) Rasa is associated with detoxification and the reduction of excess Kapha and Pitta doshas.

Statement 2: Bitter Rasa primarily nourishes tissues and is considered anabolic in Ayurvedic pharmacology.

39. **Statement 1:** The Guṇa (quality) of Laghu (lightness) enhances digestion and absorption by promoting movement and reducing heaviness in the gastrointestinal tract.

Statement 2: Laghu Guṇa is particularly beneficial in pacifying Kapha dosha but may aggravate Vata if used excessively.

Directions (Q. No. 40–45): *There are two statements in each question. One is labelled as Assertion (A) and the other is as Reason (R). Read both the statements and choose the correct answer from the options given below:*
A. Both Assertion (A) and Reason (R) are true, and Reason (R) is the correct explanation of Assertion (A).
B. Both Assertion (A) and Reason (R) are true, but Reason (R) is not the correct explanation of Assertion (A).
C. Assertion (A) is true, but Reason (R) is false.
D. Assertion (A) is false, but Reason (R) is true.
E. Both Assertion (A) and Reason (R) are false.

40. **Assertion (A):** Sweet Rasa (Madhura) is considered anabolic in nature and is effective in nourishing tissues and balancing Vata and Pitta doshas.

Reason (R): The post-digestive effect (Vipāka) of Sweet Rasa leads to increased metabolic activity, making it ideal for managing Kapha-related disorders.

41. **Assertion (A):** Bitter Rasa (Tikta) is effective in detoxification and in reducing inflammation caused by Pitta dosha.

Reason (R): Bitter Rasa aggravates Kapha dosha, making it unsuitable for conditions involving Kapha imbalances.

42. **Assertion (A):** Amla Rasa (Sour taste) enhances digestion by stimulating the secretion of digestive enzymes and bile.

Reason (R): The heating potency (Ushna Vīrya) of Amla Rasa makes it beneficial in Kapha-dominant disorders but potentially aggravates Pitta.

43. **Assertion (A):** Ushna Vīrya (heating potency) formulations are effective in treating cold and Kapha-related disorders by stimulating circulation and metabolic heat.

Reason (R): Ushna Vīrya formulations are contraindicated in disorders involving Vata imbalance due to their warming nature.

44. **Assertion (A):** Astringent Rasa (Kashaya) helps in wound healing and controls bleeding by contracting tissues and reducing fluid loss.

Reason (R): The cooling Vipāka of Astringent Rasa reduces inflammation and accelerates tissue regeneration.

45. **Assertion (A):** Snigdha (unctuous) Guṇa is essential for lubricating tissues and promoting overall nourishment, making it suitable for Vata imbalance.

Reason (R): Snigdha Guṇa aggravates Kapha due to its heavy and grounding nature, making it unsuitable for Kapha disorders.

Directions (Q. No. 46–50): *Read the passage carefully and answer the questions given below:*

Passage: The concept of Rasa (taste) in Ayurveda extends beyond mere sensory perception. Rasa is an integral aspect of pharmacology and therapeutic science, influencing the physiological and pathological states of the human body. Ayurveda classifies six primary Rasas—Sweet (Madhura), Sour (Amla), Salty (Lavana), Bitter (Tikta), Pungent (Katu), and Astringent (Kashaya)—each possessing unique properties and therapeutic effects. These Rasas interact with the three doshas—Vata, Pitta, and Kapha—helping to maintain or disrupt their balance. For example, Sweet Rasa nourishes and strengthens tissues, making it effective for pacifying Vata and Pitta but aggravating Kapha. Conversely, Bitter Rasa detoxifies and reduces Pitta and Kapha but can aggravate Vata due to its light and cooling nature.

Rasas also have a profound impact on digestion and metabolism, mediated through their post-digestive effect (Vipāka) and potency (Vīrya). Vipāka reflects the transformation of Rasa during digestion, dictating long-term physiological effects. Sweet Vipāka promotes growth and lubrication, while Pungent Vipāka enhances metabolic activity. The Vīrya of a substance—whether heating (Ushna) or cooling (Shīta)—further modulates its therapeutic potential. For instance, heating Vīrya stimulates circulation and metabolic fire (Agni), making it effective in treating Kapha disorders, while cooling Vīrya reduces inflammation and soothes Pitta.

Modern research has begun to align with Ayurvedic principles, validating the biochemical basis of Rasa and its therapeutic implications. Studies demonstrate that compounds with Bitter Rasa, such as alkaloids and flavonoids, have detoxifying and anti-inflammatory properties. Similarly, Sweet Rasa is associated with polysaccharides that promote tissue regeneration and energy storage. This convergence of traditional wisdom and modern science underscores the enduring relevance of Ayurvedic pharmacology in holistic health management.

46. According to the passage, what is the primary role of the six Rasas in Ayurvedic pharmacology?
A. To provide sensory pleasure without affecting doshas or metabolism.
B. To influence physiological states and maintain dosha balance.
C. To determine the caloric content of Ayurvedic formulations.
D. To act independently of digestion and metabolic processes.

47. Why is Vipāka considered significant in Ayurvedic pharmacology?
A. It is responsible for determining the immediate taste of substances.
B. It dictates the long-term physiological effects after digestion.
C. It replaces Rasa in determining the dosha impact.
D. It negates the effects of Vīrya and Rasa in pharmacological applications.

48. How does modern research validate Ayurvedic principles regarding Bitter Rasa?
A. By proving that Bitter Rasa lacks any therapeutic properties.
B. By linking Bitter Rasa to detoxification and anti-inflammatory effects.
C. By demonstrating that Bitter Rasa aggravates all three doshas.
D. By showing that Bitter Rasa promotes tissue growth and energy storage.

49. What is the relationship between Vīrya and its therapeutic potential, as described in the passage?
A. Heating Vīrya only treats Pitta disorders and is unsuitable for Kapha-related conditions.
B. Cooling Vīrya enhances circulation and treats Kapha disorders.
C. Heating Vīrya stimulates metabolism, while cooling Vīrya reduces inflammation.
D. Vīrya has no effect on the therapeutic potential of Ayurvedic substances.

50. Based on the passage, what does the convergence of Ayurvedic wisdom and modern science indicate?
A. Modern science rejects the relevance of Ayurvedic principles.
B. Ayurvedic pharmacology has limited applications in holistic health.
C. Biochemical studies validate the therapeutic effects of Rasas.
D. The principles of Rasa are purely philosophical and lack practical significance.

ANSWER WITH EXPLANATIONS

1. **C:** In Ayurveda, Madhura (sweet) Rasa is primarily anabolic and cooling in its initial impact but can exhibit a dual nature when consumed in excess, potentially leading to metabolic disturbances like heaviness or internal heat. This dose-dependent variability reflects a change in Vipāka (post-digestive effect). In contrast, Tikta (bitter) Rasa remains consistently cooling and detoxifying regardless of quantity. Hence, the hypothesis that sweet Rasa shows duality while bitter Rasa remains unidirectional aligns best with option C.

2. **C:** Snigdha (unctuous) Guṇa increases the lipid solubility of compounds, enhancing their ability to cross cellular membranes composed of lipid bilayers. This makes such substances more bioavailable in lipid-rich environments like nerve and fat tissues. In modern pharmacokinetics, lipophilic drugs are often more readily absorbed, and Snigdha Guṇa mirrors this effect. Therefore, Ayurvedic medicines with Snigdha Guṇa may show improved therapeutic outcomes through better absorption and targeted delivery, especially in Vata-related disorders.

3. **B:** Tikta Rasa's detoxifying properties align with Ayurveda's emphasis on reducing Ama (toxins) and balancing doshas. It supports systemic detoxification, particularly for Pitta and Kapha disorders, through its light and cooling qualities. This therapeutic role reflects its broader physiological impact, extending beyond immediate sensory effects to long-term health benefits. The connection between Tikta Rasa and reduced inflammation highlights its systemic influence, demonstrating Ayurveda's integrated approach to health. This aligns with its use in detoxification, affirming its role as a key element in Ayurvedic formulations for chronic diseases and metabolic correction.

4. **B:** Madhura Rasa and Guru Guṇa counteract Vata's dryness and lightness, offering nourishment and stability. These qualities pacify Vata by promoting lubrication and grounding, demonstrating their therapeutic alignment with Ayurveda's principles. While Madhura Rasa also calms Pitta, its dual action on Vata highlights Ayurveda's layered understanding of doshic imbalances. This targeted approach showcases the nuanced application of Rasas and Guṇas in formulations, ensuring alignment with patient-specific needs. The therapeutic use of Madhura and Guru emphasizes Ayurveda's principle of harmonizing opposing qualities to restore balance and sustain health.

5. **C:** Katu Rasa and Laghu Guṇa stimulate metabolic activity, aligning with the need to balance Kapha's heaviness and stagnation. Their combined effect on promoting digestion and circulation reflects their complementary roles in addressing Kapha disorders. This synergistic action exemplifies Ayurveda's understanding of doshic interplay, leveraging specific Rasas and Guṇas for targeted therapeutic outcomes. By focusing on Kapha pacification, this combination underscores the precision of Ayurvedic treatment strategies. It highlights the importance of aligning qualities and tastes with the unique characteristics of each dosha to achieve holistic health benefits.

6. **B:** Amla Rasa's enhancement of fermentation aligns with its role in stimulating digestive enzymes and gut health. This action highlights its metabolic activation properties, influencing microbial diversity and energy production. Its post-digestive effects further reinforce this dynamic, demonstrating its systemic relevance. Ayurveda's classification of Rasas reflects their interaction with digestion and metabolism, offering insights into their holistic impact. The association of Amla Rasa with gut microbiota aligns with modern findings, showcasing its ability to bridge traditional wisdom and contemporary gastrointestinal research. This reinforces its significance in Ayurvedic digestive therapies.

7. **B:** Ushna Vīrya's circulatory benefits align with Ayurveda's understanding of heating potency as a stimulant for metabolic activity and warmth. This action is particularly beneficial in Kapha disorders, which involve stagnation and coldness. By enhancing peripheral circulation, Ushna Vīrya facilitates systemic balance and detoxification. Ayurveda's categorization of Vīrya as heating or cooling reflects its nuanced understanding of potency in therapeutic contexts. Ushna's activation of Agni and circulation demonstrates its alignment with Ayurvedic goals of addressing Kapha imbalances, illustrating its systemic relevance in Ayurvedic pharmacology.

8. **B:** Laghu Guṇa and Katu Rasa promote rapid systemic distribution, aligning with Ayurveda's approach to Kapha pacification. This combination accelerates metabolic activation and detoxification, addressing Kapha's heaviness and stagnation. Ayurveda's emphasis on tailoring formulations based on Rasas and Guṇas ensures targeted efficacy, reflecting its holistic therapeutic strategies. The interplay of lightness and pungency exemplifies the precision of

Ayurvedic pharmacology, balancing Kapha's qualities through contrasting elements. This synergistic action reinforces Ayurveda's integrated approach, highlighting its relevance in designing efficient therapeutic interventions.

9. **A:** Katu Vipāka's influence on lipid metabolism aligns with Ayurveda's systemic understanding of post-digestive effects. By enhancing bile secretion, it supports fat digestion and metabolic activation. This action reflects its broader impact on Kapha reduction, showcasing its role in systemic detoxification and energy regulation. Ayurveda's categorization of Vipāka emphasizes its physiological relevance, extending its impact beyond immediate digestion to long-term metabolic outcomes. The focus on lipid metabolism underscores Ayurveda's anticipatory insights into dietary and pharmacological interventions, connecting traditional wisdom with contemporary metabolic research.

10. **B:** The synergistic integration of Rasa, Guṇa, Karma, and Vipāka exemplifies Ayurveda's holistic approach to health. This layered interaction ensures therapeutic precision, harmonizing immediate and systemic effects. By addressing doshic imbalances comprehensively, this approach enhances treatment efficacy, reflecting Ayurveda's nuanced understanding of physiology. The interplay of these principles highlights their interdependence, showcasing Ayurveda's foresight in designing formulations. This integration underscores the system's adaptability, blending ancient knowledge with contemporary health challenges. It affirms Ayurveda's relevance in providing multifaceted solutions for health management, demonstrating its enduring therapeutic significance.

11. **B:** The metabolic benefits of Tikta Rasa are tied to its role in detoxification, particularly through activation of cytochrome P450 enzymes. This mechanism enhances the body's ability to process toxins and supports systemic balance. Ayurveda's classification of Tikta Rasa reflects its alignment with modern findings on detoxification pathways. This connection highlights the synergy between traditional principles and contemporary biochemistry, illustrating Ayurveda's holistic view of health. The focus on detoxification as a foundational element reinforces Tikta Rasa's systemic relevance, showcasing its multifaceted therapeutic potential in metabolic corrections.

12. **B:** The promotion of agroforestry systems ensures both the sustainability and the medicinal quality of Tikta-dominant herbs like Neem and Kalmegh. Agroforestry integrates environmental preservation with community-based conservation, mitigating the risks of overharvesting and habitat degradation. Unlike monoculture plantations, which reduce biodiversity and soil health, agroforestry aligns with Ayurveda's emphasis on natural harmony. This method also preserves the bioactive compounds essential for therapeutic efficacy, balancing environmental and pharmacological goals. Encouraging community participation fosters equitable resource distribution while maintaining ecological integrity, reinforcing Ayurveda's holistic principles in addressing health and environmental challenges.

13. **A:** Environmental stressors, such as overharvesting and soil degradation, directly impact the bioactive compounds in herbs like Neem and Kalmegh. This reduction compromises their efficacy in formulations like Triphala, which rely on optimal pharmacological activity. The diminished quality affects therapeutic outcomes, particularly in detoxification and metabolic balance. Ayurveda's reliance on natural potency necessitates sustainable harvesting practices, aligning with its holistic ethos. This interconnectedness between ecological health and therapeutic efficacy underscores the importance of preserving the natural environment to maintain Ayurvedic principles. It highlights the inseparability of ecological sustainability and health outcomes in traditional medicine.

14. **D:** The long-term therapeutic efficacy of Tikta-dominant herbs like Neem and Kalmegh is challenged by overharvesting. Sustainable use can only be ensured by institutional guidelines that encourage eco-friendly cultivation, responsible harvesting, and fair trade practices. Mandating global standards helps integrate conservation with clinical demands, safeguarding both biodiversity and efficacy. This approach balances ecological responsibility and therapeutic consistency, rather than shifting entirely to alternatives or reducing usage.

15. **C:** The six Rasas (tastes) in Ayurveda serve distinct physiological and therapeutic purposes. Sweet builds and nourishes tissues, Salty stimulates digestion and cleanses, Bitter reduces heat and toxins, and Pungent clears mucus and enhances metabolism. This integrated understanding of Rasa illustrates how they balance Doshas. The inclusion of all four Rasas ensures a holistic therapeutic approach. By considering these tastes, practitioners tailor treatments to individual constitutions, supporting physical and mental harmony. Thus, all four Rasas mentioned are essential to this classification, showing the multi-dimensional application of Rasa in formulations.

16. **D:** Ayurveda's Guṇas describe inherent qualities influencing the body and mind. Laghu enhances

digestion, while Guru supports tissue building and stability. Rūkṣa reduces Kapha while increasing Vata, addressing imbalances, and Snigdha balances Vata and Pitta with its moistening effects. These qualities ensure that each Guṇa plays a complementary role in maintaining the Tridosha equilibrium. The interdependence of Guṇas in regulating physiological and psychological functions underpins their universal application in treatment. This highlights the dynamic yet balanced nature of Ayurvedic principles where each quality has distinct therapeutic implications.

17. B: Karma signifies the functional outcome of medicinal substances in Ayurveda. Deepana activates Agni, Balya fortifies immunity, Srotoshodhana removes blockages in channels, and Sandhāniya supports tissue repair. These Karmas collectively enhance systemic functioning and address root causes of imbalances. Ayurveda emphasizes personalized treatment, and these Karmas ensure targeted interventions for diverse disorders. The inclusivity of all four actions represents the adaptability and comprehensiveness of Ayurvedic medicine. Their combined application reflects the discipline's emphasis on treating not just symptoms but underlying disharmonies, promoting a complete sense of well-being.

18. D: Vīrya, or potency, is fundamental in Ayurveda for its role in determining the intensity and direction of a substance's effects. Uṣṇa counteracts cold-induced imbalances, Śīta soothes inflammation, Madhura nourishes tissues, and Tīkṣṇa detoxifies. Each potency has a unique impact, contributing to the formulation's therapeutic specificity. Together, these categories address varied pathological conditions, ensuring comprehensive care. Ayurveda's nuanced understanding of Vīrya ensures medicines not only match patient needs but also harmonize with other principles like Rasa and Guṇa. Thus, all four are integral, enabling precise therapeutic interventions.

19. A: According to Ayurvedic texts, Madhura Vipāka promotes growth, tissue development, and nourishment. Amla Vipāka increases Pitta and supports digestion, while Kaṭu Vipāka is associated with detoxification and elimination of toxins. Tikta Vipāka enhancing immunity is not a classic interpretation—Tikta Rasa may support detoxification, but immunity-related effects are more indirect. Hence, only statements (a), (b), and (c) are correct, making option A the most accurate.

20. A: In Ayurvedic pharmacology, Rasa influences the immediate impact on Doshas through taste perception, while Vipāka governs the long-term metabolic effects after digestion. Together, they determine not only the therapeutic direction but also the bioavailability and transformation of a substance in the body. Thus, both are essential for holistic treatment. Additionally, Vipāka plays a key role in determining how much of the substance becomes systemically active. Therefore, all four statements are correct.

21. D: Guṇa and Karma are interdependent, shaping the therapeutic effects of Ayurvedic formulations. Laghu aids digestion through Deepana, Guru builds tissues via Balya, Snigdha reduces dryness with Snehana, and Rūkṣa supports detoxification via Srotoshodhana. Each Guṇa enhances a specific Karma, ensuring targeted treatment. This interplay highlights Ayurveda's precision in balancing physiological states. The complementary roles of Guṇa and Karma demonstrate the discipline's emphasis on addressing individual needs. This synthesis of qualities and actions underlines Ayurveda's sophistication, where every element contributes to comprehensive care.

22. D: Vīrya ensures medicines target specific imbalances with precision. Uṣṇa boosts circulation and digestion, Śīta soothes inflammation, balanced Vīrya harmonizes Doshas, and targeted Vīrya ensures specific therapeutic actions. This multi-dimensional role ensures adaptability across varied patient conditions. Ayurveda's emphasis on Vīrya reflects its commitment to personalized care, where potency aligns with the patient's constitution. The inclusion of all four aspects ensures a medicine's efficacy while maintaining systemic harmony. This integration of hot, cold, balanced, and specific actions showcases Ayurveda's depth in formulating remedies for diverse disorders.

23. B: Karma reflects the diverse therapeutic actions of Ayurvedic substances. Deepana enhances Agni, Pachana reduces toxins, Śodhana purifies channels, and Bṛhmaṇa nourishes tissues. These actions address imbalances holistically, targeting immediate symptoms and underlying causes. Their interrelation ensures the adaptability of treatments across conditions. This comprehensive classification highlights Ayurveda's focus on multi-functional medicines that balance Doshas, detoxify, and rejuvenate simultaneously. The inclusion of all four Karmas emphasizes Ayurveda's depth, showing how its principles evolve to meet individual patient needs, ensuring both preventive and curative care.

24. D: The synergy of Rasa, Guṇa, and Vipāka reflects Ayurveda's holistic therapeutic approach. Rasa influences immediate Dosha balance, Guṇa determines the medicine's qualities, and Vipāka ensures sustained efficacy. Their interplay ensures medicines address acute symptoms while promoting long-term wellness.

Together, they contribute to physical, mental, and emotional harmony. This integration showcases Ayurveda's systemic understanding, where every principle supports comprehensive healing. The inclusion of all three ensures treatments are dynamic, adaptable, and effective across various conditions, emphasizing Ayurveda's enduring relevance in achieving holistic well-being.

25. **A:** The primary actions of Rasas, such as Sweet nourishing tissues and Bitter detoxifying, align with their therapeutic roles in Ayurveda. These classifications reflect the systemic relevance of taste, extending beyond sensory perception to physiological effects. Each Rasa contributes uniquely to doshic harmony, addressing specific health concerns. For instance, Pungent stimulates digestion, while Sour enhances metabolism, showcasing their complementary roles. This layered understanding ensures precise therapeutic interventions tailored to individual needs. Ayurveda's emphasis on the systemic impact of Rasas underscores its holistic approach, blending sensory and metabolic effects into cohesive treatment strategies.

26. **A:** The properties of Guṇas, such as Guru providing stability and Laghu enhancing digestion, highlight their systemic relevance in Ayurveda's therapeutic framework. Each Guṇa contributes uniquely to doshic harmony, addressing physical and metabolic health. For instance, Snigdha nourishes tissues, while Rūkṣa balances Kapha, showcasing their complementary roles. Ayurveda's categorization ensures targeted interventions, aligning qualities with specific health needs. This integration underscores Ayurveda's holistic ethos, offering comprehensive solutions tailored to individual requirements. By connecting Guṇas to their systemic effects, Ayurveda harmonizes its therapeutic framework, ensuring precision in addressing both immediate and long-term health concerns.

27. **A:** The alignment of Ayurvedic concepts, such as Rasa determining taste and Vipāka influencing long-term effects, reflects Ayurveda's comprehensive understanding of physiology. Each element contributes uniquely to therapeutic strategies, ensuring a holistic approach to health. Vīrya governs potency, while Karma defines actions, showcasing their complementary roles. This framework underscores Ayurveda's depth in addressing sensory, metabolic, and systemic concerns. By integrating these principles, Ayurveda offers precise interventions tailored to individual needs. This layered understanding reflects its adaptability, harmonizing ancient wisdom with contemporary therapeutic demands, ensuring relevance across diverse health challenges.

28. **A:** The primary functions of doshas, such as Vata governing movement and Pitta regulating metabolism, align with Ayurveda's systemic understanding of physiology. Each dosha contributes uniquely to maintaining balance, addressing specific health needs. For instance, Kapha provides structural stability, highlighting its complementary role. Ayurveda's classification ensures targeted interventions, aligning therapeutic strategies with individual requirements. This integration underscores Ayurveda's holistic ethos, offering comprehensive solutions tailored to doshic imbalances. By connecting doshas to their systemic effects, Ayurveda harmonizes its framework, ensuring precision in addressing both immediate and long-term health concerns.

29. **A:** The therapeutic actions of herbs, such as Haritaki detoxifying and Ashwagandha building tissues, highlight their systemic relevance in Ayurveda. Each herb contributes uniquely to doshic balance, addressing specific health concerns. For instance, Guduchi reduces inflammation, while Brahmi enhances cognition, showcasing their complementary roles. Ayurveda's categorization ensures precise interventions, aligning herbal actions with individual needs. This integration underscores Ayurveda's holistic approach, offering comprehensive solutions tailored to diverse health challenges. By connecting herbs to their systemic effects, Ayurveda harmonizes its therapeutic framework, ensuring precision in addressing both sensory and metabolic health concerns.

30. **A:** The uses of Ayurvedic formulations, such as Triphala promoting detoxification and Chyawanprash enhancing immunity, highlight their systemic relevance. Each formulation contributes uniquely to doshic harmony, addressing specific health needs. For instance, Brahmi Ghrita enhances cognition, while Arjuna Powder supports cardiovascular health, showcasing their complementary roles. Ayurveda's classification ensures targeted interventions, aligning formulations with individual requirements. This integration underscores Ayurveda's holistic ethos, offering comprehensive solutions tailored to therapeutic challenges. By connecting formulations to their systemic effects, Ayurveda harmonizes its framework, ensuring precision in addressing immediate and long-term health concerns.

31. **A:** The dosha-balancing properties of Rasas, such as Sweet pacifying Vata and Pitta and Pungent pacifying Kapha, align with their systemic relevance in Ayurveda. Each Rasa influences doshic balance through specific actions, addressing metabolic and physiological needs. For instance, Astringent reduces secretion and contracts tissues, while Sour enhances digestion and metabolic activity. These properties reflect Ayurveda's nuanced understanding of taste, ensuring targeted therapeutic applications. By integrating these Rasas into formulations, Ayurveda provides a structured approach to balancing health concerns. This systematic alignment underscores Ayurveda's adaptability, offering holistic and personalized solutions to doshic imbalances.

32. **A:** The effects of Vīrya, such as Ushna stimulating metabolism and Shīta calming inflammation, highlight their central role in Ayurveda's therapeutic strategies. Each Vīrya aligns with specific doshic imbalances, offering targeted interventions. Ushna is effective for Kapha disorders by enhancing circulation, while Shīta addresses Pitta imbalances by reducing heat. This duality reflects Ayurveda's depth in understanding systemic responses to potency. By classifying Vīrya into heating and cooling, Ayurveda provides a precise framework for designing treatments. This alignment underscores Ayurveda's emphasis on harmonizing immediate and systemic effects to achieve doshic balance and overall well-being.

33. **A:** The herbal actions, such as Laxative promoting bowel motility and Stimulant enhancing digestive fire, demonstrate their targeted roles in Ayurveda. Each action contributes to doshic harmony by addressing specific health challenges. Astringent contracts tissues, while Diuretics enhance fluid excretion, reflecting their systemic effects. Ayurveda's classification of herbal actions ensures precision in therapeutic applications, aligning with metabolic and physiological needs. This layered understanding highlights Ayurveda's holistic approach, offering comprehensive solutions tailored to individual health concerns. By integrating these actions into formulations, Ayurveda harmonizes its framework, ensuring precise and effective interventions.

34. **A:** The physiological impacts of Vipāka, such as Sweet promoting lubrication and Pungent enhancing metabolic activity, highlight their systemic relevance. Each Vipāka influences long-term health outcomes by extending the effects of Rasa and Vīrya. For instance, Sour enhances digestion and energy release, reflecting its metabolic activation properties. This classification underscores Ayurveda's anticipatory understanding of digestion's transformative power. By linking Vipāka to systemic effects, Ayurveda provides a structured framework for balancing doshas. This alignment ensures a holistic approach to health, harmonizing immediate sensory experiences with long-term therapeutic strategies to address individual health needs.

35. **C:** Rasa's influence on doshas through immediate and long-term effects reflects its systemic significance. However, Vipāka is not related to immediate sensory perception but to post-digestive transformations, impacting doshic balance. This distinction underscores Ayurveda's comprehensive understanding of digestion and metabolism. By categorizing Rasa and Vipāka separately, Ayurveda aligns sensory experiences with physiological outcomes. This layered framework ensures precise therapeutic applications, addressing both immediate and systemic health needs. The emphasis on digestion's transformative effects highlights Ayurveda's foresight in integrating sensory and metabolic processes into its holistic approach to health management.

36. **C:** Ushna Vīrya's role in enhancing metabolism and circulation makes it ideal for Kapha disorders. However, its warming nature does not suppress metabolic pathways, nor is it contraindicated in Vata imbalances. Instead, Ushna complements Ayurveda's goal of balancing doshas by activating Agni (digestive fire) and stimulating systemic functions. This nuanced understanding of potency underscores Ayurveda's therapeutic depth, offering targeted solutions for specific imbalances. By integrating Ushna Vīrya into formulations, Ayurveda ensures precise interventions, harmonizing sensory, metabolic, and systemic effects. This alignment reflects its holistic ethos, providing comprehensive health solutions.

37. **B:** Astringent (Kashaya) Rasa indeed helps in tissue contraction, reducing bleeding and aiding in wound healing, making Statement 1 true. Its post-digestive effect (Vipāka) is Katu (pungent) rather than cooling, which is more likely to stimulate metabolism and drying. However, it can still reduce excess secretions and balance Pitta or Kapha to some extent indirectly. Thus, both statements are true, but Statement 2 is not a direct explanation of Statement 1.

38. **C:** Tikta Rasa's detoxifying properties align with its systemic role in reducing Pitta and Kapha doshas. Its light and cooling qualities reflect its cleansing effects, supporting metabolic balance and systemic detoxification. Ayurveda's classification of Tikta Rasa emphasizes its relevance in addressing toxin accumulation and inflammation. This understanding highlights its broader physiological impact, extending beyond sensory perception. By integrating Tikta Rasa into therapeutic strategies, Ayurveda provides targeted solutions for detoxification and disease prevention. This layered approach underscores Ayurveda's adaptability, offering comprehensive health interventions tailored to individual doshic imbalances.

39. **A:** Laghu Guṇa's role in enhancing digestion and absorption complements its ability to pacify Kapha while

potentially aggravating Vata when used excessively. This dual action reflects Ayurveda's nuanced understanding of qualities, ensuring targeted therapeutic applications. By aligning Laghu with specific doshic imbalances, Ayurveda addresses immediate and systemic needs. This classification underscores its anticipatory approach, harmonizing sensory, metabolic, and structural effects. The precision of Laghu's classification ensures its relevance across diverse health concerns, exemplifying Ayurveda's adaptability. This alignment highlights its holistic ethos, providing personalized solutions to achieve doshic balance and overall well-being.

40. C: Sweet Rasa's nourishing and dosha-balancing properties are distinct from its Vipāka, which focuses on systemic lubrication rather than metabolic activity. This distinction reflects Ayurveda's nuanced understanding of taste and post-digestive effects. Sweet Rasa pacifies Vata and Pitta by promoting grounding and lubrication, aligning with its holistic role in health. By categorizing Rasa and Vipāka separately, Ayurveda ensures precise therapeutic interventions. This layered framework underscores its comprehensive approach, harmonizing sensory and metabolic effects. Sweet Rasa's systemic relevance highlights Ayurveda's adaptability, blending ancient principles with contemporary health challenges to address individual needs.

41. C: Tikta (Bitter) Rasa's detoxifying effects and its role in reducing Pitta and Kapha align with its cooling and light qualities. However, it does not aggravate Kapha but rather pacifies it, showcasing its systemic benefits. This distinction highlights Ayurveda's precision in categorizing Rasas based on their doshic impacts. Bitter Rasa's ability to address inflammation and toxins exemplifies its broader therapeutic role. By integrating it into formulations, Ayurveda offers targeted detoxification and disease prevention strategies. This layered understanding underscores Ayurveda's adaptability, ensuring holistic health solutions tailored to specific doshic imbalances and metabolic needs.

42. A: Amla (Sour) Rasa's enhancement of digestion through enzyme and bile stimulation reflects its systemic impact. Its heating potency makes it suitable for Kapha disorders but requires caution in Pitta imbalances due to potential aggravation. This duality highlights Ayurveda's nuanced understanding of Rasas and their interaction with doshas. Amla Rasa's digestive activation aligns with its role in enhancing metabolic activity, addressing Kapha's stagnation. This layered framework underscores Ayurveda's foresight in integrating sensory and systemic effects. Its classification ensures precise therapeutic interventions, harmonizing immediate digestion with long-term metabolic health, reflecting Ayurveda's holistic ethos.

43. C: Ushna Vīrya (heating potency) indeed stimulates Agni, circulation, and metabolism, making it ideal for managing Kapha disorders, which are cold, heavy, and slow in nature. Therefore, the assertion is true. However, the reason is incorrect—Ushna Vīrya is actually useful in many Vata disorders, because Vata is cold and dry, and heating helps balance it. Only when Vata is accompanied by Pitta or other heat conditions is caution advised. Thus, the reason is false.

44. A: Astringent Rasa's tissue-contraction properties and its cooling Vipāka align with its therapeutic role in wound healing and inflammation reduction. These effects address both immediate and systemic health concerns, showcasing its relevance in Ayurvedic formulations. The connection between its sensory impact and long-term outcomes reflects Ayurveda's holistic approach. By categorizing Astringent Rasa within this framework, Ayurveda ensures precise interventions for doshic imbalances. Its layered impact underscores Ayurveda's depth in harmonizing sensory, metabolic, and systemic effects. This alignment highlights its adaptability, offering comprehensive health solutions tailored to individual physiological needs.

45. B: Snigdha Guṇa's nourishing and lubricating properties make it ideal for pacifying Vata but may aggravate Kapha due to its heavy nature. This dual role reflects Ayurveda's nuanced understanding of qualities and their doshic interactions. By aligning Snigdha with specific therapeutic needs, Ayurveda addresses both immediate and systemic health concerns. Its classification ensures targeted interventions, harmonizing sensory and structural effects. This layered understanding underscores Ayurveda's foresight in integrating qualities into holistic frameworks. Snigdha's adaptability highlights Ayurveda's depth in addressing diverse health challenges, offering personalized solutions for achieving doshic balance and overall well-being.

46. B: The six Rasas influence physiological states by balancing doshas, addressing both health maintenance and disease prevention. Their systemic effects extend beyond sensory perception, impacting metabolism and overall well-being. For instance, Sweet nourishes tissues, while Bitter detoxifies and reduces inflammation. Ayurveda's classification of Rasas reflects its holistic approach, harmonizing sensory, metabolic, and systemic health. By aligning taste with doshic interactions, Ayurveda ensures precise therapeutic applications. This layered framework highlights the depth of Ayurvedic pharmacology, blending traditional principles with contemporary health challenges. Rasas' comprehensive role underscores their enduring relevance in holistic medicine.

47. **B:** Vipāka's significance lies in its ability to influence long-term physiological effects, extending the impact of Rasa beyond digestion. It governs metabolic and systemic health by transforming taste into doshic effects during digestion. For example, Sweet Vipāka promotes lubrication and tissue nourishment, while Pungent enhances metabolism. This post-digestive framework reflects Ayurveda's anticipatory understanding of digestion's role in health. By integrating Vipāka into therapeutic strategies, Ayurveda addresses immediate and systemic concerns, harmonizing sensory and metabolic outcomes. This layered approach underscores Ayurveda's foresight in linking digestion to overall well-being, ensuring comprehensive health solutions.

48. **B:** Modern research validates Bitter Rasa's detoxifying and anti-inflammatory effects, linking its systemic impact to bioactive compounds like alkaloids and flavonoids. This alignment reinforces Ayurveda's classification of Bitter Rasa as a dosha-balancing agent for Pitta and Kapha. Its systemic relevance extends beyond traditional applications, bridging ancient wisdom and contemporary pharmacology. By integrating these findings, Ayurveda's principles gain empirical support, highlighting its adaptability. This convergence underscores the depth of Ayurvedic pharmacology, harmonizing traditional classifications with modern therapeutic contexts. Bitter Rasa's validated role exemplifies Ayurveda's foresight in addressing systemic health challenges.

49. **C:** The therapeutic potential of Vīrya lies in its ability to modulate systemic functions, such as Ushna stimulating metabolism and Shīta calming inflammation. These potencies align with doshic imbalances, addressing specific health needs. For instance, heating potency is ideal for Kapha disorders, while cooling addresses Pitta imbalances. This classification reflects Ayurveda's depth in understanding potency's role in systemic balance. By integrating Vīrya into formulations, Ayurveda ensures targeted interventions, harmonizing immediate and long-term effects. This layered framework underscores Ayurveda's holistic ethos, offering comprehensive solutions tailored to individual metabolic and physiological requirements.

50. **C:** The convergence of Ayurveda and modern science validates the therapeutic impact of Rasas through biochemical studies. For example, polysaccharides in Sweet Rasa support tissue regeneration, while Bitter Rasa's alkaloids detoxify and reduce inflammation. These findings bridge traditional principles and contemporary pharmacology, highlighting Ayurveda's relevance. By integrating scientific methods, Ayurveda's holistic framework gains empirical support, enhancing its adaptability. This synthesis reinforces Ayurveda's role in addressing modern health challenges, blending ancient wisdom with scientific rigor. The alignment of Rasas' therapeutic roles with biochemical validation underscores their enduring importance in holistic and integrative medicine.

UNIT 5: RASA SHASTRA, BHESHAJYA KALPANA, AND AYURVEDIC PHARMACOPOEIA

CHAPTER 13

RASA SHASTRA BASICS – ORIGIN, DEVELOPMENT, AND SODHANA (PURIFICATION)

1. **Basics of Rasa Shastra (Alchemy and Mineral Medicine)**: Rasa Shastra, an integral branch of Ayurveda, is the ancient Indian science of alchemy and mineral medicine. It encompasses a rich tradition of using metals, minerals, and other natural substances to prepare potent medicines aimed at promoting health, vitality, and longevity. The term "Rasa" is derived from Sanskrit, meaning "essence," "juice," or "elixir," symbolizing the transformative and life-enhancing properties of these substances. "Shastra," on the other hand, denotes a systematic body of knowledge or science.

Key Elements of Rasa Shastra

Rasa Shastra is rooted in the belief that metals and minerals, when properly processed, can serve as powerful therapeutic agents. The fundamental elements of this science include:

- **Rasa (Mercury):** The central focus of Rasa Shastra, mercury is regarded as a divine substance with unparalleled medicinal and transformative qualities.
- **Dhatus (Metals):** Gold, silver, copper, and other metals are utilized for their therapeutic effects.
- **Uparasas and Upadhatus (Sub-Metals and Minor Minerals):** These include sulphur, arsenic compounds, mica, and others with medicinal potential.
- **Ratnas and Mani (Gems):** Precious and semi-precious stones like diamonds, rubies, and pearls are incorporated into formulations for their energetic and healing properties.
- **Herbal Extracts:** Plant-based ingredients are often combined with minerals to enhance their efficacy.

Philosophical Basis

The underlying philosophy of Rasa Shastra draws from:

- **Alchemy:** Inspired by ancient Indian spiritual and philosophical systems, Rasa Shastra sought not only physical health but also spiritual liberation (Moksha). The processes of transformation symbolized the purification of both the body and soul.
- **Ayurvedic Principles:** The therapeutic formulations align with the Ayurvedic principles of balancing the three doshas—Vata, Pitta, and Kapha.

Objectives

Rasa Shastra aims to:

1. Rejuvenate and extend life (Rasayana therapy).
2. Treat and cure diseases effectively.
3. Enhance physical and mental vigor.
4. Support spiritual development by purifying the body.

2. **Evolution of Rasa Shastra and Its Significance in Ayurveda**

The evolution of Rasa Shastra is a fascinating journey that reflects the convergence of spirituality, medicine, and science. Its development spans centuries, influenced by various cultural, spiritual, and medical traditions.

Historical Roots

- **Vedic Era:** The origins of Rasa Shastra can be traced back to the Vedic period, where early references to metals, minerals, and their applications in health were documented. Texts like the Atharvaveda mention the use of gold and herbs for therapeutic purposes.
- **Post-Vedic Period:** Alchemical practices became more structured, with a focus on mercury and its combination with other substances. Philosophical schools like Tantra heavily influenced this phase, associating alchemy with spiritual transformation.
- **Buddhist and Jain Contributions:** During the early centuries CE, Buddhist and Jain scholars contributed significantly to the refinement of alchemical techniques. These traditions emphasized non-violence, leading to innovations in purification processes without animal testing.
- **Siddha Tradition:** In South India, the Siddha tradition emphasized the use of minerals and metals for creating powerful medicines, aligning closely with the principles of Rasa Shastra.

Classical Texts of Rasa Shastra

Rasa Shastra, a cornerstone of ancient Indian medical science and alchemy, owes much of its development to the comprehensive texts authored by scholars who codified and refined its principles and practices. These classical texts are treasures of knowledge that meticulously document the therapeutic, spiritual, and alchemical applications of minerals, metals, and mercury. They serve as a bridge between Ayurvedic principles and the practical methodologies of Rasa Shastra.

1. Rasa Ratna Samuccaya:

- **Authorship and Historical Context**: The Rasa Ratna Samuccaya is one of the most authoritative texts on Rasa Shastra. It is attributed to an anonymous scholar, but some sources suggest it may have been composed by a practitioner in the early medieval period, around the 13th–14th centuries CE. The text reflects the amalgamation of spiritual, philosophical, and practical knowledge prevalent during its time.
- **Content and Structure:** This comprehensive work focuses on the classification, purification, and medicinal use of metals and minerals. It is divided into several chapters that systematically address the following:
  - **Classification of Substances:** The text categorizes substances into Rasas (mercury), Dhatus (metals), Upadhatus (sub-metals), Uparasas (minerals), and Ratnas (gems).
  - **Purification Processes:** The text elaborates on Śodhana techniques for detoxifying and refining mercury, metals, and minerals. Specific herbal decoctions, grinding methods, and thermal treatments are prescribed.
  - **Therapeutic Applications:** It outlines the use of purified substances in treating diseases, strengthening the immune system, and prolonging life. The formulations often combine metallic substances with herbal compounds.
  - **Spiritual Alchemy:** The text also addresses the spiritual dimension of alchemy, describing the transformative effects of mercury on both the body and soul.

Legacy and Impact: The Rasa Ratna Samuccaya remains a pivotal resource for practitioners of Rasa Shastra. It serves as a foundational guide for integrating alchemical techniques into Ayurvedic medicine, emphasizing both safety and efficacy.

2. Rasendra Chudamani:

- **Authorship and Historical Context:** The Rasendra Chudamani, attributed to Acharya Somadeva, is an influential text on mercury-based alchemy. Scholars believe it was composed around the 12th century CE during the flourishing period of Indian alchemical traditions.
- **Content and Structure:** This work is notable for its in-depth exploration of mercury's properties and its transformative potential. The key highlights include:
  - **Mercury as the Central Element:** The text extols mercury (Rasa) as the "king of medicines," capable of rejuvenating the body and curing chronic diseases.
  - **Processing Mercury:** It describes various purification processes (Samskaras) for mercury, including Mardana (grinding), Dhalana (melting), and Amalgamation. These processes aim to detoxify mercury and enhance its therapeutic potency.
  - **Medicinal Formulations:** The text provides detailed recipes for mercury-based medicines. These formulations often combine mercury with sulphur, gold, and herbal extracts.
  - **Spiritual Significance:** Mercury is portrayed as a mystical substance capable of granting immortality and enlightenment. The alchemical transformation of mercury symbolizes spiritual purification.

Influence on Later Works: The Rasendra Chudamani is revered for its scientific approach to mercury-based therapies. It influenced subsequent texts and practices, firmly establishing mercury as a cornerstone of Rasa Shastra.

3. Ananda Kanda:

- **Authorship and Historical Context:** The Ananda Kanda, believed to be composed between the 9th and 11th centuries CE, is a voluminous text on alchemy and spirituality. Its authorship is uncertain, though some attribute it to Siddha practitioners deeply rooted in esoteric traditions.
- **Content and Structure:** This text is notable for its breadth and depth, encompassing both practical and philosophical aspects of alchemy:
    - **Philosophical Foundations:** The Ananda Kanda intertwines alchemy with spiritual practices, emphasizing the unity of body, mind, and spirit.
    - **Alchemy and Health:** It elaborates on the preparation of Rasa (mercury) medicines and their role in curing diseases, enhancing vitality, and prolonging life.
    - **Elaborate Procedures:** The text describes complex alchemical procedures for the extraction, purification, and combination of minerals and metals.
    - **Spiritual Alchemy:** Beyond physical health, the Ananda Kanda emphasizes the spiritual transformation achieved through alchemical practices. It draws parallels between the purification of metals and the purification of the soul.

CONTRIBUTION TO RASA SHASTRA

The Ananda Kanda is revered for its integration of mystical and medicinal perspectives. It serves as a guide for practitioners seeking to balance physical healing with spiritual growth.

Key Figures in Rasa Shastra

The development of Rasa Shastra owes much to the contributions of visionary scholars and practitioners. These individuals not only advanced the science of alchemy but also integrated it with Ayurvedic medicine, philosophy, and spirituality.

1. Nāgārjuna (2nd–4th Century CE)

Contributions to Rasa Shastra: Nāgārjuna, often referred to as the "father of Indian alchemy," was a polymath who significantly influenced the development of Rasa Shastra. His works, though not entirely preserved, are frequently cited in later texts.

Key contributions include:

- **Focus on Mercury:** Nāgārjuna recognized mercury as a transformative substance and developed purification techniques to harness its medicinal potential.
- **Alchemy and Longevity:** He explored the role of alchemy in extending life and achieving spiritual liberation (Moksha).
- **Scientific Approach:** Nāgārjuna emphasized experimentation and observation, laying the groundwork for systematic alchemical practices.

Philosophical Legacy: Nāgārjuna's contributions extend beyond alchemy to Buddhist philosophy, where he is credited with developing the Madhyamaka school of thought. His dual focus on science and spirituality profoundly influenced the evolution of Rasa Shastra.

2. Chakrapani Datta (11th Century)

- **Contributions to Ayurveda and Rasa Shastra**: Chakrapani Datta, a renowned Ayurvedic scholar, played a pivotal role in integrating Rasa Shastra with mainstream Ayurveda. His works are characterized by their clarity and practicality.
- **Key contributions include:** Integration of Alchemy and Ayurveda: Chakrapani Datta incorporated mineral and metallic preparations into Ayurvedic therapeutics, broadening the scope of treatment options.
- **Textual Contributions:** His commentary on the Charaka Samhita and independent works reflect a deep understanding of both herbal and mineral medicines.
- **Standardization of Processes:** He emphasized the standardization of Śodhana (purification) techniques to ensure safety and efficacy.

Influence on Later Practitioners: Chakrapani Datta's systematic approach influenced subsequent scholars, bridging the gap between traditional herbal medicine and the emerging field of mineral-based therapies.

3. Acharya Sushruta and Charaka

- **Foundational Contributions to Ayurveda:** Acharya Sushruta and Charaka are revered as the pioneers of Ayurvedic medicine. While their primary focus was on herbal medicine, their texts also discuss the therapeutic use of minerals and metals.
- **Sushruta Samhita:** This seminal work includes references to surgical instruments made of metals, the use of minerals for wound healing, and metallic compounds for treating specific diseases.
- **Charaka Samhita:** Charaka's text emphasizes the therapeutic potential of natural substances, including metals and minerals, in balancing the three doshas (Vata, Pitta, Kapha).

Influence on Rasa Shastra

Though not directly associated with alchemy, Sushruta and Charaka laid the groundwork for the integration of Rasa Shastra into Ayurveda. Their emphasis on holistic health and disease prevention aligns with the objectives of alchemical medicine.

The classical texts of Rasa Shastra, along with the contributions of visionary figures, form the backbone of this ancient science. Works like the Rasa Ratna Samuccaya, Rasendra Chudamani, and Ananda Kanda provide a comprehensive understanding of alchemical principles and their therapeutic applications. Key figures such as Nāgārjuna, Chakrapani Datta, Sushruta, and Charaka not only advanced Rasa Shastra but also ensured its integration with Ayurveda, creating a holistic approach to health and well-being.

Integration with Ayurveda

Rasa Shastra is a natural extension of Ayurveda, enhancing its therapeutic arsenal. The integration is evident in:

1. **Treatment of Chronic Conditions:** Metal-based medicines are often used for diseases that resist herbal treatments.
2. **Rasayana (Rejuvenation):** Many Rasa formulations are central to anti-aging and revitalizing therapies.
3. **Detoxification:** Purification processes in Rasa Shastra align with Panchakarma therapies in Ayurveda.

Modern Relevance

In the contemporary era, Rasa Shastra continues to be significant due to its:

- **Role in Holistic Healing:** The combination of metals, minerals, and herbs offers a unique approach to complex health issues.
- **Complement to Modern Medicine:** It provides alternative solutions for diseases with limited options in allopathic medicine.
- **Pharmacological Research:** Modern studies are exploring the bioavailability and therapeutic effects of processed metals and minerals.

3. **Śodhana (Purification) Processes of Metals and Minerals:** Śodhana, or purification, is a fundamental concept in Rasa Shastra. It refers to the meticulous processes of detoxifying and refining metals, minerals, and other raw materials to render them safe and therapeutically effective.

Importance of Śodhana

The purification process is crucial for several reasons:

1. **Removing Toxicity:** Many raw materials, such as mercury and arsenic, are toxic in their natural state. Śodhana eliminates harmful properties.
2. **Enhancing Potency:** Purified substances are believed to possess enhanced therapeutic efficacy.
3. **Facilitating Assimilation:** The process transforms metals and minerals into bioavailable forms that the human body can absorb and utilize.
4. **Balancing Energetics:** Śodhana aligns the energetic properties of substances with Ayurvedic principles.

Types of Śodhana

Śodhana can be broadly classified into:

- **Samanya Śodhana (General Purification):** A preliminary purification process that applies to a wide range of substances.
- **Vishesha Śodhana (Specific Purification):** A specialized process tailored to individual substances, addressing their unique properties and challenges.
- **Methods of Śodhana:** Śodhana involves various techniques, each designed to address the specific characteristics of the material being purified. Common methods include:

  1. **Swedana (Boiling/Steaming)**
     - **Purpose:** Removes impurities and detoxifies the substance.
     - **Procedure:** The raw material is boiled or steamed in a decoction of herbal liquids like Triphala, cow's milk, or oil.
  2. **Mardana (Grinding)**
     - **Purpose:** Enhances the uniformity and effectiveness of the substance.
     - **Procedure:** The material is ground with herbal juices or decoctions using a mortar and pestle.
  3. **Bhavana (Levigation)**
     - **Purpose:** Integrates therapeutic qualities of herbs with metals or minerals.
     - **Procedure:** The substance is triturated with herbal liquids and allowed to dry repeatedly over several cycles.
  4. **Nirvapana (Quenching)**
     - **Purpose:** Removes impurities and softens metals.
     - **Procedure:** The metal is heated until red-hot and then quenched in herbal liquids like cow's urine, ghee, or milk.
  5. **Dhalana (Melting and Pouring)**
     - **Purpose:** Separates impurities from metals.
     - **Procedure:** The material is melted and poured into water or other liquids to purify it.
  6. **Shoshana (Drying)**
     - **Purpose:** Removes moisture and stabilizes the substance.

- **Procedure:** The material is sun-dried or air-dried after purification.

Substance-Specific Śodhana Processes

- **Mercury (Rasa):** Mercury undergoes intense purification to remove toxic impurities. Processes like Mardana with lime juice, Bhavana with sulphur, and Dhalana are employed.
- **Gold (Svarna):** Gold is purified using Nirvapana in herbal liquids like cow's milk or Triphala decoction to make it safe for consumption.
- **Sulphur (Gandhaka):** Sulphur is detoxified by melting it and then quenching it in cow's milk, followed by drying.
- **Mica (Abhraka):** Mica undergoes Swedana and Mardana with herbal juices to enhance its therapeutic properties.
- **Arsenic Compounds (Haritala and Manashila):** These are purified through Bhavana with specific herbs to neutralize toxicity.

Safety and Ethical Considerations

While Śodhana techniques are grounded in ancient wisdom, they demand rigorous adherence to ensure safety and efficacy:

- **Standardization:** Modern Rasa Shastra practitioners emphasize standardizing purification methods to ensure consistency.
- **Toxicology Testing:** Processed substances undergo toxicological evaluation to confirm their safety.
- **Ethical Practices:** The preparation and use of mineral medicines follow strict ethical guidelines, respecting traditional knowledge and modern safety norms.

Rasa Shastra represents a unique synthesis of science, spirituality, and medicine. Its meticulous processes, such as Śodhana, transform natural substances into powerful therapeutic agents, offering solutions for both physical and spiritual well-being. While rooted in ancient traditions, its principles and practices continue to hold relevance in the modern era, bridging the gap between traditional wisdom and contemporary medicine.

MULTIPLE-CHOICE QUESTIONS

1. A researcher is investigating the historical development of Rasa Shastra and identifies three distinct phases: its origins in Vedic literature, its formalization in medieval Ayurvedic texts, and its integration into spiritual alchemy. The researcher argues that the emphasis on mercury (Rasa) in these phases was driven by its perceived dual role as both a therapeutic agent and a symbol of immortality. If this interpretation is accurate, which of the following outcomes most likely reflects the medieval expansion of Rasa Shastra?
   A. The exclusive use of mercury as an alchemical substance for spiritual enlightenment.
   B. The incorporation of diverse metals and minerals alongside mercury for therapeutic applications.
   C. The abandonment of mercury in favor of entirely herbal-based Ayurvedic formulations.
   D. A focus on philosophical constructs, minimizing the practical uses of Rasa Shastra.

2. Consider an Ayurvedic practitioner who is analyzing the efficacy of Śodhana techniques in detoxifying heavy metals for medicinal use. The practitioner hypothesizes that the use of herbal decoctions like Triphala during Swedana (boiling) enhances the bioavailability of purified metals. If this hypothesis is tested, which result would most strongly validate it?
   A. Metals subjected to Śodhana show a complete removal of all toxic elements.
   B. Purified metals exhibit increased therapeutic efficacy and reduced toxicity when tested in controlled studies.
   C. Śodhana fails to detoxify metals but improves their stability in complex formulations.
   D. The bioavailability of metals remains unchanged despite using Śodhana techniques.

3. A pharmaceutical scientist attempts to modernize an Ayurvedic formulation involving mercury by adapting ancient Dhalana (melting and quenching) techniques to comply with current safety standards. This process aims to retain the original therapeutic effects while minimizing risks. If successful, which of the following conclusions would be most consistent with the scientist's goals?
   A. The modified process increases the medicinal potency of mercury but does not address safety concerns.
   B. The new formulation completely eliminates the need for mercury in Rasa Shastra.
   C. The adapted process retains therapeutic benefits while meeting modern toxicology standards.
   D. The therapeutic properties of mercury are lost due to the stringent safety adaptations.

4. In exploring the role of Rasa Shastra in Ayurveda, a scholar argues that its integration with herbal medicine reflects a sophisticated understanding of synergistic healing. The scholar examines texts such as the Rasa Ratna Samuccaya, which emphasize combining metallic preparations with plant-based compounds. Which of the following best supports this argument?
   A. Ayurveda exclusively relies on metallic formulations for chronic diseases.
   B. Texts on Rasa Shastra disregard herbal medicine in favor of alchemical substances.
   C. Rasa Shastra integrates metals, minerals, and herbs to create balanced, potent remedies.
   D. Plant-based compounds in Rasa Shastra serve only as stabilizing agents for metallic preparations.

5. A student of Ayurveda observes that purification processes like Bhavana (levigation) involve triturating metals with specific herbal juices. The student hypothesizes that these processes not only detoxify metals but also infuse them with bioactive properties from the herbs. Which experimental outcome would most strongly support this hypothesis?
   A. Levigated metals demonstrate enhanced therapeutic properties compared to untreated metals.
   B. Purified metals show no trace of herbal bioactive compounds.
   C. Herbal juices used in levigation are found to neutralize the toxicity of metals but do not alter their properties.
   D. Metals lose their original potency after levigation with herbal juices.

6. An environmental scientist is concerned about the sustainability of sourcing natural minerals and metals for Ayurvedic medicine. The scientist explores synthetic alternatives to Śodhana-purified substances but faces resistance from traditional practitioners. Which of the following statements best highlights the challenge of integrating synthetic alternatives into Rasa Shastra?
   A. Synthetic alternatives are more cost-effective but lack the spiritual significance attributed to natural substances.
   B. Traditional practitioners agree that synthetic substances offer better therapeutic value.
   C. The integration of synthetic materials into Ayurveda has been universally accepted without opposition.
   D. Synthetic alternatives outperform natural substances in clinical trials, negating the need for traditional methods.

7. A pharmacologist studies the compatibility of Ayurvedic metallic formulations with modern drug delivery systems. The research focuses on using nanotechnology to encapsulate Śodhana-treated metals for enhanced bioavailability. Which of the following implications aligns most closely with this innovation?
   A. Nanotechnology diminishes the potency of Ayurvedic formulations.
   B. Encapsulation of metals allows for precise dosage control while retaining traditional benefits.
   C. Modern delivery systems are incompatible with the foundational principles of Rasa Shastra.
   D. Ayurvedic metallic formulations lose their therapeutic properties in nanotechnology applications.

8. A scholar explores the philosophical underpinnings of Rasa Shastra, emphasizing its dual focus on health and spiritual liberation. The scholar posits that alchemical transformation in Rasa Shastra symbolizes the purification of both the body and soul. Which observation would most strongly support this interpretation?
   A. The texts focus solely on physical health and ignore spiritual aspects.
   B. Mercury purification is portrayed as a ritualistic process reflecting inner transformation.
   C. Rasa Shastra rejects spiritual goals in favour of scientific experimentation.
   D. The purification of metals is unrelated to philosophical or spiritual ideals.

9. A clinical study evaluates the efficacy of mercury-based Rasa preparations in treating chronic illnesses. The study compares outcomes between patients using purified mercury formulations and those on conventional treatment regimens. What result would most convincingly demonstrate the unique benefits of Rasa Shastra?
   A. Mercury formulations show no improvement over conventional treatments.
   B. Patients using mercury preparations exhibit significant recovery with no toxicity.
   C. Conventional treatments outperform Rasa preparations in all health metrics.
   D. Mercury-based formulations cause severe side effects, limiting their use.

10. A historian examines the contributions of Nāgārjuna to Rasa Shastra, focusing on his emphasis on mercury purification. The historian argues that Nāgārjuna's innovations established the foundation for systematic alchemy in Ayurveda. Which finding would most strongly support this argument?
    A. Nāgārjuna's writings emphasize mercury's symbolic value without detailing its practical applications.

B. His methods for mercury purification are still considered relevant in contemporary Ayurvedic practices.
C. Nāgārjuna advocated abandoning mercury in favour of purely herbal treatments.
D. His contributions to Rasa Shastra are overshadowed by later scholars like Chakrapani Datta.

Directions (Q. No. 11-14): *Scenario-Based Questions*

SCENARIO 1

A clinical trial investigates the therapeutic effects of Tamra Bhasma (copper ash) processed using traditional Śodhana techniques. The trial demonstrates significant improvement in liver health markers, including reduced oxidative stress and enhanced detoxification enzyme activity.

SCENARIO 2

Simultaneously, a sustainability researcher evaluates the environmental impact of mining copper for Ayurvedic formulations. The study reveals that unregulated mining practices degrade soil quality, threaten biodiversity, and reduce the medicinal efficacy of copper due to impurities introduced during extraction.

11. Based on Scenario 1, what mechanism most likely explains the therapeutic effects of Tamra Bhasma on liver health?
A. Direct suppression of inflammatory pathways without affecting oxidative stress.
B. Enhancement of the liver's natural detoxification processes through antioxidant activity.
C. Reduction of enzyme activity, leading to a protective effect on liver cells.
D. Randomized placebo effect with no direct correlation to copper ash properties.

12. Considering Scenario 2, which intervention would most effectively mitigate the environmental impact of copper mining for Ayurvedic purposes?
A. Large-scale industrial mining operations to maximize copper extraction.
B. Strict regulations promoting sustainable mining and metal recycling practices.
C. Substitution of copper with synthetic alternatives in Ayurvedic formulations.
D. Reducing the global use of copper in both Ayurvedic and non-Ayurvedic industries.

13. How does environmental degradation described in Scenario 2 potentially influence the therapeutic outcomes observed in Scenario 1?
A. Environmental stressors improve the potency of copper used in Tamra Bhasma.
B. Impurities in mined copper reduce its efficacy in enhancing liver health.
C. The medicinal properties of copper remain unaffected by its environmental sources.
D. Degraded copper contributes to the creation of more potent Ayurvedic formulations.

14. Based on the interconnected findings of Scenarios 1 and 2, which strategy would most comprehensively address both therapeutic efficacy and environmental sustainability?
A. Developing bio-engineered substitutes for copper in Ayurvedic medicine.
B. Establishing community-led conservation initiatives for sustainable metal sourcing.
C. Abandoning all mineral-based formulations in favour of herbal alternatives.
D. Promoting large-scale monoculture plantations to offset environmental degradation.

15. The processes of Śodhana in Rasa Shastra aim to enhance the safety and efficacy of metals and minerals. Which of the following correctly describes the objectives of purification techniques?
(a) Eliminate toxicity inherent in raw materials.
(b) Enhance the therapeutic potency of substances.
(c) Ensure bioavailability and compatibility in formulations.
(d) Preserve the natural state of the substance without alterations.

Choose the correct answer from the options given below:
A. (a), (b), and (c) only
B. (b), (c), and (d) only
C. (a), (c), and (d) only
D. (a), (b), (c), and (d)

16. The classification of substances in Rasa Shastra includes various categories based on their properties and uses. Which of the following are classified as Uparasas?
(a) Sulphur (Gandhaka)
(b) Arsenic trisulphide (Haritala)
(c) Iron pyrite (Makshika)
(d) Mica (Abhraka)

Choose the correct answer from the options given below:
A. (a), (b), and (d) only
B. (a), (b), and (c) only
C. (b), (c), and (d) only
D. (a), (b), (c), and (d)

17. The primary goals of Rasa Shastra involve both physical and spiritual well-being. Which of the following objectives align with its practices?

(a) Achieving rejuvenation (Rasayana) and longevity.
(b) Treating chronic and otherwise untreatable diseases.
(c) Enhancing mental clarity and spiritual growth.
(d) Eliminating dependency on herbal formulations.

Choose the correct answer from the options given below:

A. (a), (b), and (c) only
B. (b), (c), and (d) only
C. (a), (c), and (d) only
D. (a), (b), (c), and (d)

18. The purification (Śodhana) of mercury involves several steps, each with distinct purposes and methodologies. Which of the following steps are essential for mercury purification as outlined in classical texts?

(a) Grinding mercury with sulphur to form Kajjali.
(b) Quenching mercury in cow's milk and herbal decoctions.
(c) Exposing mercury to high temperatures for incineration.
(d) Mixing mercury with gold to stabilize its properties.

Choose the correct answer from the options given below:

A. (a), (b), and (c) only
B. (b), (c), and (d) only
C. (a), (c), and (d) only
D. (a), (b), (c), and (d)

19. Key figures in Rasa Shastra made significant contributions to its development. Which of the following accurately matches their contributions?

(a) **Nāgārjuna:** Pioneered mercury purification techniques.
(b) **Chakrapani Datta:** Integrated mineral medicines into Ayurveda.
(c) **Charaka:** Focused exclusively on herbal formulations.
(d) **Sushruta:** Highlighted the therapeutic use of metals in surgery.

Choose the correct answer from the options given below:

A. (a), (b), and (d) only
B. (a), (b), and (c) only
C. (b), (c), and (d) only
D. (a), (c), and (d) only

20. The Rasa Ratna Samuccaya is a foundational text of Rasa Shastra. Which of the following topics are extensively covered in this text?

(a) Classification and therapeutic uses of metals and minerals.
(b) Step-by-step procedures for Śodhana of mercury.
(c) Preparation of entirely herbal formulations for dosha balance.
(d) Spiritual and alchemical significance of mercury purification.

Choose the correct answer from the options given below:

A. (a), (b), and (d) only
B. (a), (b), and (c) only
C. (b), (c), and (d) only
D. (a), (c), and (d) only

21. In the preparation of Bhasmas (metallic ashes), which of the following purification techniques are commonly employed to detoxify and stabilize the raw materials?

(a) Boiling metals in herbal decoctions (Swedana).
(b) Melting and quenching metals in specific liquids (Nirvapana).
(c) Grinding and mixing with herbal pastes (Bhavana).
(d) Heating metals in air to incinerate impurities (Marana).

Choose the correct answer from the options given below:

A. (a), (b), and (d) only
B. (a), (c), and (d) only
C. (a), (b), and (c) only
D. (a), (b), (c), and (d)

22. The Ayurvedic classification of Rasas (tastes) plays a crucial role in therapeutic applications. Which of the following accurately describes their biological actions?

(a) Sweet (Madhura) promotes tissue growth and nourishment.
(b) Sour (Amla) enhances metabolic activity and digestion.
(c) Bitter (Tikta) detoxifies the body and reduces inflammation.
(d) Salty (Lavana) decreases tissue cohesion and aggravates Pitta.

Choose the correct answer from the options given below:

A. (a), (b), and (c) only
B. (a), (b), and (d) only
C. (b), (c), and (d) only
D. (a), (b), (c), and (d)

23. Mercury (Rasa) is considered the cornerstone of Rasa Shastra due to its unique properties. Which of the following statements correctly describes its significance?

(a) Mercury is regarded as a divine substance with both therapeutic and spiritual properties.
(b) The purification of mercury (Samskaras) neutralizes its toxicity and enhances its medicinal efficacy.

(c) Mercury is used exclusively for spiritual alchemy and has no therapeutic applications.
(d) Purified mercury formulations are central to curing chronic and degenerative diseases

Choose the correct answer from the options given below:
A. (a), (b), and (c) only
B. (a), (b), and (d) only
C. (b), (c), and (d) only
D. (a), (c), and (d) only

24. The practice of Rasayana in Rasa Shastra is closely associated with rejuvenation and disease prevention. Which of the following practices are integral to achieving the goals of Rasayana?
(a) Consuming Bhasmas (metallic ashes) prepared through Śodhana and Marana.
(b) Balancing the three doshas through specific dietary and lifestyle practices.
(c) Engaging in spiritual practices to purify the mind and body.
(d) Relying solely on herbal medicines to enhance vitality.

Choose the correct answer from the options given below:
A. (a), (b), and (c) only
B. (a), (b), and (d) only
C. (b), (c), and (d) only
D. (a), (c), and (d) only

25. Match List–I (Process in Sodhana) with List–II (Purpose/Outcome):

List–I	List–II
(a) Bhavana	1. Enhances bioavailability and infuses therapeutic properties
(b) Swedana	2. Removes physical impurities by boiling in herbal decoctions
(c) Nirvapana	3. Eliminates toxic properties through quenching in liquids
(d) Marana	4. Converts metals into ash form for medicinal use.

Choose the correct answer from the options given below:
A. (a)-1, (b)-2, (c)-3, (d)-4
B. (a)-2, (b)-4, (c)-1, (d)-3
C. (a)-3, (b)-1, (c)-2, (d)-4
D. (a)-4, (b)-3, (c)-1, (d)-2

26. Match List–I (Substances) with List–II (Applications):

List–I	List–II
(a) Gold (Svarna)	1. Enhances vitality and strengthens the immune system
(b) Copper (Tamra)	2. Supports digestive health and detoxification
(c) Silver (Rajata)	3. Antimicrobial properties for wound healing
(d) Mica (Abhraka)	4. Rejuvenates tissues and improves energy levels

Choose the correct answer from the options given below:
A. (a)-4, (b)-3, (c)-1, (d)-2
B. (a)-1, (b)-2, (c)-3, (d)-4
C. (a)-3, (b)-1, (c)-4, (d)-2
D. (a)-1, (b)-4, (c)-2, (d)-3

27. Match List–I (Test of Rasa Shastra) with List–II (Primary Focus):

List–I	List–II
(a) Rasa Ratna Samuccaya	1. Comprehensive classification and purification of metals
(b) Rasendra Chudamani	2. Mercury-based alchemical formulations
(c) Ananda Kanda	3. Spiritual alchemy and rejuvenation practices
(d) Sushruta Samhita	4. Surgical methods involving metals and minerals

Choose the correct answer from the options given below:
A. (a)-1, (b)-2, (c)-3, (d)-4
B. (a)-4, (b)-3, (c)-2, (d)-1
C. (a)-2, (b)-1, (c)-4, (d)-3
D. (a)-3, (b)-4, (c)-1, (d)-2

28. Match List–I (Rasas/Tastes) with List–II (Biological Actions):

List–I	List–II
(a) Sweet (Madhura)	1. Promotes tissue growth and nourishment
(b) Bitter (Tikta)	2. Detoxifies the body and reduces inflammation
(c) Sour (Amla)	3. Stimulates digestive activity and metabolic function
(d) Astringent (Kashaya)	4. Strengthens tissues and controls bleeding

Choose the correct answer from the options given below:
A. (a)-1, (b)-3, (c)-4, (d)-2
B. (a)-4, (b)-1, (c)-2, (d)-3
C. (a)-1, (b)-2, (c)-3, (d)-4
D. (a)-3, (b)-2, (c)-1, (d)-4

29. Match List–I (Mercury Purification Techniques) with List–II (Descriptions):

List–I	List–II
(a) Mardana	1. Grinding with sulphur to neutralize toxicity

(b) Dhalana	2. Melting and quenching to remove impurities
(c) Utthapana	3. Heating with herbal pastes for detoxification
(d) Swedana	4. Boiling in liquids to eliminate physical contaminants

Choose the correct answer from the options given below:

A. (a)-1, (b)-2, (c)-3, (d)-4
B. (a)-4, (b)-1, (c)-2, (d)-3
C. (a)-3, (b)-2, (c)-4, (d)-1
D. (a)-2, (b)-3, (c)-1, (d)-4

30. Match List–I (Key Figures) with List–II (Contributions):

List–I	List–II
(a) Nāgārjuna	1. Advanced mercury purification techniques
(b) Chakrapani Datta	2. Integrated minerals into Ayurveda therapeutics
(c) Sushruta	3. Highlighted surgical and metal applications
(d) Charaka	4. Focused on herbal medicine and dosha balance

Choose the correct answer from the options given below:

A. (a)-4, (b)-3, (c)-1, (d)-2
B. (a)-3, (b)-2, (c)-4, (d)-1
C. (a)-1, (b)-2, (c)-3, (d)-4
D. (a)-2, (b)-1, (c)-3, (d)-4

31. Match List–I (Stages in Purification) with List–II (Outcomes):

List–I	List–II
(a) Initial detoxification	1. Removes physical contaminants
(b) Intermediate processing	2. Reduces toxicity and enhances compatibility
(c) Incineration	3. Converts metals into ash for therapeutic use
(d) Final preparation	4. Stabilizes substances for formulations

Choose the correct answer from the options given below:

A. (a)-1, (b)-2, (c)-3, (d)-4
B. (a)-3, (b)-1, (c)-4, (d)-2
C. (a)-2, (b)-4, (c)-1, (d)-3
D. (a)-4, (b)-3, (c)-2, (d)-1

32. Match List–I (Tridosha Components) with List–II (Function):

List–I	List–II
(a) Vata	1. Governs movement and nervous system regulation
(b) Pitta	2. Manages metabolism and digestive activity
(c) Kapha	3. Regulates structure and fluid balance
(d) Dosha balance	4. Ensures harmony for optimal health

Choose the correct answer from the options given below:

A. (a)-1, (b)-2, (c)-3, (d)-4
B. (a)-4, (b)-1, (c)-2, (d)-3
C. (a)-2, (b)-4, (c)-1, (d)-3
D. (a)-3, (b)-2, (c)-4, (d)-1

33. Match List–I (Sodhana Techniques) with List–II (Mediums Used):

List–I	List–II
(a) Swedana	1. Herbal decoctions
(b) Bhavana	2. Herbal juices and pastes
(c) Nirvapana	3. Cow's milk or ghee
(d) Shoshana	4. Sun or air drying

Choose the correct answer from the options given below:

A. (a)-1, (b)-2, (c)-3, (d)-4
B. (a)-4, (b)-3, (c)-1, (d)-2
C. (a)-3, (b)-4, (c)-2, (d)-1
D. (a)-2, (b)-1, (c)-4, (d)-3

34. Match List–I (Minerals in Ayurveda) with List–II (Therapeutic Uses):

List–I	List–II
(a) Sulphur	1. Detoxifies the skin and balances doshas
(b) Mica	2. Improves immunity and cellular strength
(c) Iron	3. Enhances blood health and oxygen transport
(d) Arsenic	4. Treats chronic respiratory diseases

Choose the correct answer from the options given below:

A. (a)-4, (b)-3, (c)-2, (d)-1
B. (a)-1, (b)-2, (c)-3, (d)-4
C. (a)-3, (b)-4, (c)-1, (d)-2
D. (a)-2, (b)-1, (c)-4, (d)-3

Directions (Q. No. 35–39): *Following questions are based on Statement 1 and Statement 2. Read both the statements carefully and choose the correct answer from the options given below:*

A. Both Statement 1 and Statement 2 are true, and Statement 2 is the correct explanation of Statement 1.
B. Both Statement 1 and Statement 2 are true, but Statement 2 is not the correct explanation of Statement 1.
C. Statement 1 is true, but Statement 2 is false.

D. Statement 1 is false, but Statement 2 is true.

E. Both Statement 1 and Statement 2 are false.

35. Statement 1: The Marana process in Rasa Shastra transforms metals into bioavailable ash forms, allowing for safe internal consumption.

Statement 2: The Marana process uses high temperatures to burn impurities, but it often results in complete loss of the metal's therapeutic properties.

36. Statement 1: The texts of Rasa Shastra emphasize the integration of mercury (Rasa) with sulphur (Gandhaka) to neutralize mercury's toxic properties.

Statement 2: The combination of mercury and sulphur in formulations like Kajjali reduces mercury's toxicity and enhances its therapeutic effects in Ayurveda.

37. Statement 1: The Rasa Ratna Samuccaya describes the use of specific herbal juices in Bhavana to infuse therapeutic properties into metals.

Statement 2: The choice of herbal juices in Bhavana depends solely on their availability and not on their pharmacological effects.

38. Statement 1: Ayurveda considers the balance of the three doshas—Vata, Pitta, and Kapha—as essential for maintaining health and treating diseases.

Statement 2: Dosha imbalances are addressed in Rasa Shastra primarily through the use of herbal medicines, with minimal reliance on minerals or metals.

39. Statement 1: The purification (Śodhana) of metals and minerals ensures their safety and bioavailability in Ayurvedic formulations.

Statement 2: Unpurified metals and minerals are generally safer and more effective than purified substances due to their raw potency.

Directions (Q. No. 40–45): *There are two statements in each question. One is labelled as Assertion (A) and the other is as Reason (R). Read both the statements and choose the correct answer from the options given below:*

A. Both Assertion (A) and Reason (R) are true, and Reason (R) is the correct explanation of Assertion (A).

B. Both Assertion (A) and Reason (R) are true, but Reason (R) is not the correct explanation of Assertion (A).

C. Assertion (A) is true, but Reason (R) is false.

D. Assertion (A) is false, but Reason (R) is true.

E. Both Assertion (A) and Reason (R) are false.

40. Assertion (A): Bhavana in Rasa Shastra enhances the medicinal properties of metals and minerals by incorporating the bioactive principles of herbs.

Reason (R): The levigation process in Bhavana allows the particles of herbs to bind physically with the purified metals and minerals.

41. Assertion (A): The use of mercury in Ayurvedic formulations is central to achieving spiritual and physical rejuvenation.

Reason (R): Mercury is considered the "King of Medicines" in Rasa Shastra due to its transformative properties when purified through Samskaras.

42. Assertion (A): Nirvapana involves quenching heated metals in herbal liquids to remove impurities and toxins.

Reason (R): The process of Nirvapana enhances the structural integrity of the metal, making it resistant to therapeutic degradation.

43. Assertion (A): Rasa Shastra aims to integrate metals, minerals, and herbs to address diseases that are difficult to treat with herbal formulations alone.

Reason (R): Metals and minerals offer unique properties that are unmatched by plant-based compounds in treating chronic and degenerative diseases.

44. Assertion (A): The Rasendra Chudamani is a classical text that provides comprehensive methods for mercury purification and its therapeutic applications.

Reason (R): The text focuses exclusively on spiritual alchemy and neglects the practical medicinal applications of mercury.

45. Assertion (A): The practice of Śodhana aligns with the Ayurvedic principle of detoxification, ensuring the safe use of potentially toxic materials.

Reason (R): Śodhana processes involve the removal of impurities and toxic components through boiling, grinding, and quenching.

Directions (Q. No. 46–50): *Read the passage carefully and find the answers to the questions given below.*

The ancient science of Rasa Shastra emphasizes the purification (Śodhana) of metals and minerals to ensure their safe and effective use in therapeutic applications. These purification processes involve multiple stages, such as Swedana (boiling in herbal decoctions), Nirvapana (quenching in liquids), and Bhavana (levigation with herbal pastes). Each technique has a specific purpose, ranging from detoxification to enhancing bioavailability and therapeutic efficacy. For instance, Swedana is used to soften metals and remove surface impurities, whereas Nirvapana neutralizes toxic properties by exposing the material to high heat followed by rapid cooling in herbal liquids like cow's milk or Triphala decoction.

The Marana process, another crucial aspect of Rasa Shastra, involves incinerating metals to convert them into fine ash, known as Bhasma. This ash is believed to be easily absorbed by the human body, making it bioavailable and therapeutically potent. Bhasmas are prepared following stringent protocols outlined in classical texts such as the Rasa Ratna Samuccaya and the Rasendra Chudamani. Mercury (Parada), considered the cornerstone of Rasa Shastra, undergoes rigorous Śodhana processes to neutralize its toxic nature and unlock its medicinal properties. Combining purified mercury with sulphur to create Kajjali is a significant innovation that highlights the transformative potential of alchemical techniques.

Modern studies have started to explore the scientific basis of these ancient methods, finding parallels between the detoxification mechanisms in Śodhana and contemporary pharmacological practices. For example, herbal decoctions used in Swedana are found to contain chelating agents that bind with toxic elements, facilitating their removal. Similarly, the bioavailability of Bhasmas has been attributed to their nanoscale particle size, which allows for efficient absorption. However, the lack of standardization in preparation techniques remains a challenge, prompting calls for rigorous validation and quality control measures. Despite these challenges, Rasa Shastra continues to inspire a unique synthesis of traditional wisdom and modern scientific inquiry, offering innovative approaches to holistic health and disease management.

46. What is the primary purpose of Śodhana (purification) in Rasa Shastra, as described in the passage?
A. To convert metals into ash for bioavailability
B. To soften metals and remove impurities while neutralizing toxicity
C. To create Bhasmas for specific therapeutic applications
D. To enhance the taste and appearance of herbal formulations

47. According to the passage, how does the Marana process contribute to the therapeutic efficacy of metals?
A. By liquefying metals and mixing them with herbal decoctions
B. By transforming metals into Bhasmas that are bioavailable and potent
C. By combining metals with sulphur to form Kajjali
D. By softening metals for easier absorption

48. Which of the following best explains the role of herbal decoctions in Swedana as described in the passage?
A. They act as cooling agents during the Marana process.
B. They contain chelating agents that detoxify toxic elements.
C. They enhance the color and taste of Bhasmas.
D. They reduce the nanoscale particle size of metals.

49. Why is the combination of purified mercury with sulphur to create Kajjali considered significant in Rasa Shastra?
A. It neutralizes the toxic properties of sulphur.
B. It highlights the transformative potential of alchemical techniques.
C. It simplifies the preparation of herbal decoctions.
D. It reduces the need for rigorous Śodhana processes.

50. What challenge associated with Rasa Shastra is highlighted in the passage, and how is it addressed?
A. The difficulty of sourcing pure mercury, addressed through modern technology.
B. The lack of standardization in preparation techniques, addressed through calls for validation and quality control.
C. The inefficiency of ancient methods, addressed by abandoning traditional protocols.
D. The high cost of materials, addressed through synthetic alternatives.

ANSWER WITH EXPLANATIONS

1. B: The medieval period of Rasa Shastra marked a significant expansion, where mercury, regarded for its dual role as a therapeutic agent and a symbol of immortality, became central. Alongside mercury, the incorporation of other metals and minerals reflected an evolving understanding of Ayurvedic pharmacology. This phase balanced spiritual and medicinal goals, emphasizing alchemical techniques like Śodhana to detoxify and potentiate substances. The expansion was not limited to mercury; rather, it demonstrated the adaptability of Ayurveda by integrating diverse materials for broader applications. This integration showed a sophisticated approach that blended therapeutic innovations with spiritual alchemy, laying the groundwork for modern interpretations of Ayurvedic practices.

2. B: Śodhana techniques in Rasa Shastra, such as Swedana with Triphala, serve to detoxify metals while improving their therapeutic efficacy. The hypothesis that herbal decoctions enhance bioavailability is supported by their chelating properties, which bind and remove toxic elements. Controlled studies demonstrating reduced toxicity and enhanced efficacy validate this claim. Śodhana not only detoxifies but also activates bioactive compounds, ensuring compatibility with human physiology. This dual role bridges traditional practices with modern scientific principles, ensuring that Ayurvedic formulations remain effective and safe. The alignment of ancient detoxification methods with contemporary pharmacology underscores Ayurveda's adaptability and enduring relevance in global healthcare.

3. **C:** Modern adaptations of traditional Dhalana techniques aim to align Ayurvedic practices with contemporary safety standards without compromising therapeutic benefits. Mercury's therapeutic properties, central to Rasa Shastra, are retained through processes that neutralize toxicity while ensuring efficacy. This balance addresses modern toxicological concerns, demonstrating Ayurveda's ability to evolve. The adaptation also preserves the holistic nature of Rasa Shastra, where alchemical methods are not merely technical but also therapeutic. By integrating stringent safety protocols with traditional wisdom, Ayurveda reinforces its credibility and relevance, ensuring its formulations meet global healthcare demands while maintaining their foundational principles.

4. **C:** Rasa Shastra's integration of metals, minerals, and herbs represents a holistic understanding of healing, where each component enhances the other's therapeutic properties. Classical texts like the Rasa Ratna Samuccaya detail how these combinations create balanced remedies that address complex health conditions. This approach reflects Ayurveda's adaptability, merging alchemical and botanical knowledge to produce potent formulations. The emphasis on synergistic healing underscores Ayurveda's commitment to addressing the root causes of disease. By integrating diverse elements into its pharmacology, Rasa Shastra exemplifies the sophistication of Ayurvedic science, blending tradition with practical applications to meet evolving medical needs.

5. **A:** Bhavana, a critical process in Rasa Shastra, involves triturating metals with herbal pastes to detoxify and enhance their therapeutic properties. This technique infuses bioactive compounds from herbs into metals, as evidenced by improved efficacy in levigated substances compared to untreated ones. The process exemplifies Ayurveda's holistic approach, combining purification with activation. By integrating herbal properties into metals, Bhavana not only detoxifies but also enriches the formulation. This practice aligns traditional methods with modern pharmacological insights, ensuring that Ayurvedic remedies are potent, safe, and effective. It highlights the scientific rigor embedded within Ayurveda's therapeutic framework.

6. **A:** The cultural and spiritual significance of natural materials in Ayurveda creates resistance to the integration of synthetic alternatives in Rasa Shastra. While synthetic options may offer cost-effective and sustainable solutions, they lack the depth of traditional practices rooted in Ayurveda's philosophical framework. This resistance underscores the challenge of balancing innovation with authenticity. Natural substances in Ayurveda are not merely therapeutic; they carry symbolic and spiritual meanings. Efforts to incorporate synthetic alternatives must respect these values while addressing ecological concerns. This balance ensures that Rasa Shastra evolves responsibly, preserving its essence while adapting to contemporary challenges.

7. **B:** Nanotechnology offers a revolutionary approach to enhancing Ayurvedic formulations, particularly through the encapsulation of Śodhana-treated metals. This innovation ensures precise dosage control, improves bioavailability, and preserves therapeutic properties. The integration of nanotechnology bridges traditional practices with modern drug delivery systems, addressing challenges like dosing accuracy and absorption efficiency. This alignment with contemporary healthcare standards exemplifies Ayurveda's adaptability. Far from compromising traditional principles, nanotechnology enhances the effectiveness of Ayurvedic formulations, ensuring their relevance in global healthcare. It demonstrates how ancient wisdom can harmonize with cutting-edge science to address evolving medical needs.

8. **B:** The philosophical foundations of Rasa Shastra emphasize the purification of both the body and soul, with mercury's detoxification symbolizing inner transformation. The process reflects a dual focus on physical health and spiritual liberation, where alchemical methods serve as metaphors for achieving balance and purity. Ritualistic mercury purification exemplifies this holistic approach, aligning tangible detoxification with intangible spiritual goals. This duality enriches Rasa Shastra's practices, demonstrating its depth beyond mere medicinal applications. By integrating health and spirituality, Rasa Shastra maintains its relevance as a comprehensive system addressing both physical and metaphysical dimensions of well-being.

9. **B:** Purified mercury-based Rasa preparations demonstrate significant therapeutic benefits in treating chronic illnesses, provided they undergo rigorous Śodhana processes. Clinical studies showing improved

recovery rates without toxicity validate the efficacy of these formulations. This reinforces the importance of precise purification methods to neutralize toxicity while retaining therapeutic potency. Rasa Shastra's ability to address conditions often resistant to conventional treatments highlights its unique value. The findings underscore Ayurveda's capacity to blend traditional wisdom with scientific validation, ensuring that its formulations meet contemporary safety and efficacy standards without compromising their foundational principles.

10. **B:** Nāgārjuna's contributions to Rasa Shastra laid the foundation for systematic alchemy in Ayurveda, particularly through innovations in mercury purification. His methods remain relevant in contemporary practices, demonstrating their enduring value. By integrating theoretical insights with practical applications, Nāgārjuna advanced the therapeutic potential of Rasa Shastra. His work exemplifies the sophistication of Ayurvedic alchemy, blending philosophical, spiritual, and medical dimensions. These contributions solidified Rasa Shastra's role as a cornerstone of Ayurveda, bridging ancient practices with modern scientific inquiry. Nāgārjuna's legacy underscores the adaptability and relevance of Ayurveda in addressing evolving healthcare challenges.

11. **B:** The clinical trial on Tamra Bhasma demonstrated its significant role in improving liver health markers through enhanced antioxidant activity and detoxification processes. Copper ash, when processed through traditional Śodhana techniques, aids in reducing oxidative stress by neutralizing free radicals and boosting the liver's enzymatic detoxification pathways. This aligns with Ayurveda's principle of targeting systemic imbalances using purified metals. The improvement in liver function underscores the scientific validity of Bhasma preparations. By combining traditional methods with modern validation, this study highlights Rasa Shastra's capability to offer targeted and effective solutions for complex health issues like hepatic disorders.

12. **B:** To mitigate the environmental degradation caused by unregulated copper mining, strict regulations promoting sustainable practices and metal recycling are essential. Overextraction not only affects biodiversity and soil health but also compromises the therapeutic quality of copper. Sustainable mining ensures ecological balance while maintaining the medicinal efficacy of Ayurvedic formulations like Tamra Bhasma. Recycling initiatives can supplement mining efforts by reducing dependence on raw material extraction. These interventions align with Ayurveda's ethos of harmony with nature, ensuring that therapeutic practices do not harm the environment. This approach reinforces the need for balance between conservation and health benefits.

13. **B:** Environmental degradation, particularly the contamination and overexploitation of copper resources, directly impacts the therapeutic outcomes of Tamra Bhasma. Impurities introduced during mining reduce the quality of copper, thereby diminishing its bioactive properties and efficacy. This highlights the interconnectedness between ecological preservation and Ayurvedic formulations. Maintaining the integrity of raw materials through sustainable practices ensures that their medicinal benefits remain intact. The study underscores the necessity of environmentally responsible sourcing to preserve both the therapeutic effectiveness and the ecological balance, ensuring the long-term viability of Rasa Shastra's contributions to healthcare.

14. **B:** A comprehensive strategy to address both therapeutic efficacy and environmental sustainability involves community-led conservation initiatives for sustainable metal sourcing. These initiatives promote responsible mining practices, preserve biodiversity, and maintain the medicinal quality of resources like copper. Such strategies align with Ayurveda's holistic principles, which emphasize ecological harmony alongside health. Community involvement ensures local stewardship of resources, fostering sustainable development. Abandoning mineral-based formulations or relying on monoculture plantations fails to address the root causes of environmental degradation. This balanced approach preserves the integrity of Ayurvedic practices while ensuring that ecological and therapeutic needs are met harmoniously.

15. **A:** The processes of Śodhana in Rasa Shastra aim to detoxify metals and minerals, enhance their therapeutic potency, and ensure bioavailability in formulations. Detoxification removes inherent toxicity, while steps like Bhavana infuse substances with bioactive properties from herbal mediums. These techniques align with Ayurveda's holistic approach, ensuring compatibility with human physiology. Preserving the substance's natural state without alteration contradicts the essence of Śodhana, which actively transforms and potentiates raw materials. By combining detoxification, bioactivation, and therapeutic enhancement, Śodhana bridges traditional wisdom with modern pharmacological standards, ensuring the safety and efficacy of Ayurvedic formulations.

16. **B:** In Rasa Shastra, Uparasas are secondary minerals like sulphur, arsenic trisulfide, and iron pyrite, which are used in therapeutic applications after purification.

These substances are valued for their unique properties, such as detoxification and rejuvenation, which complement primary minerals like gold and silver. The classification reflects the systematic approach of Ayurveda in categorizing and utilizing natural resources. Purification techniques like Śodhana ensure their safe and effective use, highlighting the sophistication of Ayurvedic pharmacology. This classification underscores the depth of Rasa Shastra's knowledge, integrating natural substances into holistic healing practices.

17. **A:** The primary objectives of Rasa Shastra include achieving rejuvenation, treating chronic diseases, and enhancing mental clarity and spiritual growth. These goals align with Ayurveda's holistic vision of health, which integrates physical, mental, and spiritual well-being. Rasa Shastra's emphasis on mineral-based formulations expands its scope beyond herbal remedies, addressing conditions that require potent and targeted interventions. The focus on rejuvenation through Rasayana therapies underscores its preventive and restorative approach. This comprehensive framework exemplifies Ayurveda's adaptability, ensuring its practices remain relevant in addressing modern healthcare challenges while preserving its traditional essence.

18. **A:** The purification of mercury in Rasa Shastra involves grinding with sulphur to form Kajjali, quenching in herbal liquids like milk and Triphala, and exposing it to high temperatures for detoxification. These steps are meticulously outlined in classical texts to neutralize mercury's toxicity and enhance its therapeutic properties. Mixing mercury with gold, although occasionally practiced, is not a core purification step. The Śodhana processes demonstrate the depth of Ayurvedic alchemy, blending rigorous scientific principles with traditional wisdom. These methods ensure the safe and effective use of mercury in therapeutic formulations, reflecting Ayurveda's holistic and precise approach to health.

19. **A:** Key figures in Rasa Shastra made transformative contributions that shaped its evolution. Nāgārjuna pioneered mercury purification techniques, while Chakrapani Datta integrated mineral medicines into Ayurveda, expanding its pharmacological scope. Sushruta emphasized the therapeutic use of metals in surgical practices, demonstrating the versatility of Ayurveda. Charaka, however, focused primarily on herbal formulations, distinguishing his contributions from mineral-based advancements. The combined efforts of these scholars highlight the interdisciplinary nature of Rasa Shastra, bridging surgery, pharmacology, and alchemy. Their legacies underscore Ayurveda's capacity to integrate diverse knowledge systems into a cohesive and comprehensive healing tradition.

20. **A:** The Rasa Ratna Samuccaya is a foundational text of Rasa Shastra that extensively covers the classification and therapeutic uses of metals and minerals, purification procedures like Śodhana, and the spiritual significance of alchemical transformations. It reflects the holistic approach of Rasa Shastra, where therapeutic practices are deeply intertwined with spiritual and philosophical ideals. The text's emphasis on mercury and other substances demonstrates a systematic approach to Ayurvedic alchemy. By blending detailed pharmacological instructions with metaphysical insights, the Rasa Ratna Samuccaya exemplifies the depth and sophistication of Ayurveda, ensuring its enduring relevance in both traditional and modern contexts.

21. **D:** The preparation of Bhasmas in Rasa Shastra involves critical purification techniques such as Swedana, Nirvapana, Bhavana, and Marana. These processes ensure detoxification, enhance bioavailability, and stabilize the raw materials. Swedana removes impurities through boiling, Nirvapana quenches heated metals to neutralize toxicity, Bhavana incorporates herbal bioactive compounds, and Marana incinerates metals into a fine ash form. This systematic approach underscores Ayurveda's precision in transforming potentially harmful substances into therapeutically potent remedies. These methods align with modern scientific principles, validating their relevance and ensuring that Bhasmas maintain safety, efficacy, and compatibility within Ayurvedic formulations.

22. **D:** The classification of Rasas (tastes) in Ayurveda aligns with their biological actions, showcasing a sophisticated understanding of their therapeutic roles. Sweet Rasa promotes nourishment and tissue growth, essential for recovery and energy balance. Sour enhances digestion and metabolic activity, Bitter detoxifies and reduces inflammation, and Salty impacts fluid balance while aggravating Pitta when overused. These classifications are not arbitrary; they reflect centuries of empirical observations. By linking taste to specific physiological effects, Ayurveda provides a framework for personalized treatment, ensuring holistic healing. This integration of sensory perception with pharmacological principles highlights Ayurveda's depth and relevance in modern healthcare.

23. **B:** Mercury's significance in Rasa Shastra stems from its unique properties as both a therapeutic and spiritual substance. Rigorous purification processes neutralize its toxicity, making it safe for medicinal use while enhancing

its efficacy. Mercury-based formulations address chronic and degenerative diseases, offering solutions often unattainable through herbal medicines alone. This dual role underscores its central place in Ayurvedic alchemy, blending physical and metaphysical dimensions of healing. The careful balance of tradition and scientific validation ensures that mercury remains a cornerstone of Rasa Shastra, reflecting Ayurveda's ability to integrate ancient wisdom with modern safety standards.

24. **A:** Rasayana practices in Rasa Shastra aim for rejuvenation and disease prevention by combining the consumption of Bhasmas, dosha balancing through lifestyle practices, and spiritual purification. These methods ensure a holistic approach to well-being, addressing physical vitality, mental clarity, and spiritual growth. Exclusive reliance on herbal medicines does not capture the depth of Rasayana therapies, which integrate minerals and metals for potent effects. This comprehensive framework exemplifies Ayurveda's adaptability, ensuring that its therapeutic practices align with contemporary health needs while preserving traditional principles. By addressing health at multiple levels, Rasayana reinforces Ayurveda's relevance in integrative medicine.

25. **A:** The Śodhana processes in Rasa Shastra align with specific outcomes: Bhavana enhances bioavailability by infusing bioactive properties, Swedana removes physical impurities through boiling, Nirvapana neutralizes toxins by quenching, and Marana converts metals into ash for safe therapeutic use. These stages demonstrate a systematic approach to purification, ensuring that substances are both safe and effective. The alignment of each process with its outcome underscores Ayurveda's meticulous methodology. By integrating traditional practices with scientific rigor, Śodhana reflects the precision and adaptability of Rasa Shastra in addressing contemporary pharmacological standards while maintaining its foundational principles.

26. **B:** The applications of substances like gold, copper, silver, and mica in Ayurveda are rooted in their unique therapeutic properties. Gold enhances immunity and vitality, copper supports detoxification and digestive health, silver provides antimicrobial benefits for wound healing, and mica rejuvenates tissues while improving energy. These roles reflect Ayurveda's detailed understanding of natural substances and their integration into holistic healing practices. Each substance is carefully processed to optimize its benefits, ensuring safety and efficacy. This systematic approach highlights Ayurveda's depth, blending traditional knowledge with precise applications to address a wide range of health conditions effectively.

27. **A:** Key texts of Rasa Shastra align with their primary focuses: the Rasa Ratna Samuccaya classifies and purifies metals, the Rasendra Chudamani explores mercury-based formulations, the Ananda Kanda delves into spiritual alchemy and rejuvenation, and the Sushruta Samhita highlights surgical applications of metals. These contributions reflect the interdisciplinary nature of Rasa Shastra, combining pharmacology, surgery, and spiritual insights. By documenting diverse aspects of alchemy and medicine, these texts ensure that Rasa Shastra remains a comprehensive system addressing physical, mental, and spiritual dimensions of health. Their enduring relevance underscores Ayurveda's adaptability and depth.

28. **C:** The alignment of Rasas (tastes) with their biological actions demonstrates Ayurveda's sophisticated understanding of sensory perception and therapeutic outcomes. Sweet promotes nourishment and tissue growth, Bitter detoxifies and reduces inflammation, Sour enhances digestion and metabolism, and Astringent strengthens tissues while controlling bleeding. This framework is deeply rooted in empirical observations and clinical practice, ensuring that treatments are tailored to individual needs. By integrating taste with pharmacological effects, Ayurveda offers a personalized approach to healing, highlighting its holistic philosophy. This nuanced understanding ensures that its practices remain relevant and effective in addressing contemporary health challenges.

29. **A:** The purification techniques of mercury in Rasa Shastra are systematically aligned with specific objectives: Mardana involves grinding with sulphur to neutralize toxicity, Dhalana uses melting and quenching to remove impurities, Utthapana involves heating with herbal pastes for detoxification, and Swedana boils the substance in liquids to eliminate contaminants. These processes ensure that mercury becomes safe and effective for therapeutic use, reflecting Ayurveda's rigorous approach to detoxification. By aligning each step with its purpose, these techniques exemplify the precision of Rasa Shastra, ensuring that traditional practices meet modern safety and efficacy standards without compromising their authenticity.

30. **C:** The contributions of key figures in Ayurveda align with their areas of expertise: Nāgārjuna advanced mercury purification techniques, Chakrapani Datta integrated minerals into Ayurveda, Sushruta emphasized surgical methods involving metals, and Charaka focused on herbal medicine and dosha balance. These contributions reflect the interdisciplinary nature of Ayurvedic science, blending pharmacology, surgery, and holistic health. By addressing diverse aspects of medicine, these scholars ensured that Ayurveda

remained comprehensive and adaptable. Their legacies highlight the depth of Ayurvedic knowledge and its capacity to evolve, bridging ancient practices with modern healthcare needs effectively.

31. A: The stages of purification in Rasa Shastra are meticulously designed to achieve specific outcomes. Initial detoxification focuses on removing physical impurities, intermediate processing reduces toxicity and ensures compatibility with human physiology, incineration (Marana) converts metals into bioavailable ash, and final preparation stabilizes substances for medicinal formulations. Each stage aligns with the goal of transforming raw materials into therapeutically potent and safe remedies. This systematic approach highlights Ayurveda's precision and commitment to safety. By addressing detoxification and bioactivation step-by-step, these stages exemplify the holistic and scientific rigor embedded in Rasa Shastra practices.

32. A: The Tridosha system in Ayurveda outlines the functions of Vata, Pitta, and Kapha, with each dosha governing specific physiological processes. Vata regulates movement and nervous system activity, Pitta manages metabolism and digestion, and Kapha ensures structure and fluid balance. The balance of these doshas is essential for optimal health, reflecting Ayurveda's emphasis on homeostasis. The interdependence of these components underscores the holistic nature of Ayurvedic medicine. This understanding of physiological processes as interconnected rather than isolated ensures that treatments address root causes, offering a comprehensive approach to health and well-being.

33. A: The Śodhana techniques of Swedana, Bhavana, Nirvapana, and Shoshana are closely linked to specific mediums used in purification processes. Swedana involves herbal decoctions to boil and detoxify, Bhavana uses herbal juices and pastes to infuse bioactive properties, Nirvapana quenches metals in cow's milk or ghee to neutralize toxicity, and Shoshana relies on sun or air drying to stabilize substances. These methods reflect the precision of Rasa Shastra, ensuring that each purification stage aligns with its therapeutic objective. This alignment underscores Ayurveda's scientific depth, ensuring safety and efficacy in its formulations.

34. B: In Ayurveda, minerals like sulphur, mica, iron, and arsenic are linked to therapeutic uses rooted in their unique properties. Sulphur detoxifies the skin and balances doshas, mica strengthens immunity and cellular health, iron enhances blood health and oxygen transport, and arsenic addresses chronic respiratory diseases. These associations demonstrate the systematic integration of natural elements into Ayurveda's holistic framework. The purification of these substances ensures safety while optimizing their medicinal potential. This alignment of therapeutic properties with specific minerals underscores Ayurveda's depth and adaptability in addressing diverse health challenges effectively.

35. C: The Marana process in Rasa Shastra transforms metals into bioavailable ash forms, making them safe for internal consumption. This method involves incinerating metals under controlled conditions to eliminate toxicity while preserving therapeutic properties. Statement 1 is accurate, as Marana ensures both safety and efficacy. However, Statement 2 is incorrect because it misrepresents the process by suggesting the therapeutic properties are lost. Marana exemplifies the balance of detoxification and bioactivation, aligning traditional practices with modern safety standards. This method underscores Ayurveda's scientific rigor and its commitment to ensuring the safe application of potentially toxic materials.

36. A: The combination of mercury and sulphur in formulations like Kajjali is a cornerstone of Rasa Shastra. Mercury's toxicity is neutralized through grinding with sulphur, creating a stable compound that retains therapeutic efficacy. Statement 1 accurately reflects this integration, and Statement 2 provides the correct explanation by highlighting how sulphur mitigates mercury's toxic properties. Together, these statements underscore the precision and depth of Ayurvedic alchemy. By combining rigorous purification with therapeutic innovation, Rasa Shastra exemplifies Ayurveda's ability to adapt traditional methods to meet safety and efficacy requirements.

37. C: The use of specific herbal juices in Bhavana to infuse therapeutic properties into metals is a documented practice in texts like the Rasa Ratna Samuccaya. These juices are selected based on their pharmacological effects, enhancing the therapeutic potential of metals. Statement 1 is true as it aligns with the purpose of Bhavana, but Statement 2 is false as it disregards the intentionality behind the choice of herbal mediums. This process highlights Ayurveda's scientific approach to purification and activation, ensuring that formulations are both safe and effective. Bhavana's precision reflects the integration of tradition and pharmacological insight.

38. C: The balance of the three doshas—Vata, Pitta, and Kapha—is central to Ayurveda's approach to health and disease management. While Rasa Shastra incorporates metals and minerals to address dosha imbalances, herbal medicines remain a complementary component.

Statement 1 accurately reflects Ayurveda's emphasis on dosha balance, but Statement 2 underplays the role of metals and minerals in Rasa Shastra. This misrepresentation diminishes the interdisciplinary nature of Ayurvedic practices. The integration of herbal and mineral therapies demonstrates Ayurveda's holistic framework, addressing physical and energetic imbalances comprehensively.

39. C: The purification (Śodhana) of metals and minerals ensures their safety and enhances their bioavailability in Ayurvedic formulations. Statement 1 accurately reflects this principle, while Statement 2 is false because unpurified substances carry risks and lack therapeutic compatibility. The systematic detoxification and activation processes in Śodhana exemplify Ayurveda's meticulous approach to safety and efficacy. By addressing toxicity and enhancing bioactive properties, these methods ensure that formulations meet both traditional and modern standards. This precision reinforces Ayurveda's relevance in integrative medicine, blending ancient wisdom with contemporary safety protocols.

40. A: Bhavana enhances the medicinal properties of metals and minerals by incorporating bioactive principles from herbs through levigation. This process allows herbal compounds to bind physically and chemically with purified metals, optimizing their therapeutic potential. Both the assertion and the reason are true, with the reason providing a valid explanation. Bhavana exemplifies Ayurveda's holistic approach to combining detoxification and bioactivation, ensuring that formulations are potent and safe. This integration of herbs and metals reflects the scientific depth of Rasa Shastra, demonstrating its ability to adapt ancient practices to modern pharmacological standards.

41. A: The use of mercury in Ayurvedic formulations for physical and spiritual rejuvenation is central to Rasa Shastra. Purified mercury, known as Parada, is revered for its transformative properties, aligning with the goal of balancing body and mind. The assertion is true, as mercury undergoes rigorous Śodhana processes to neutralize toxicity while retaining its medicinal and symbolic significance. The reason accurately explains this by highlighting mercury's epithet as the "King of Medicines" due to its alchemical versatility. Together, these reflect the dual focus of Rasa Shastra, merging physical health and spiritual purification through meticulous and scientifically grounded practices.

42. C: Nirvapana, a crucial Śodhana technique, involves quenching heated metals in herbal liquids to detoxify and neutralize impurities. The assertion is accurate, as this method enhances the safety and therapeutic efficacy of metals. However, the reason is incorrect because Nirvapana primarily focuses on detoxification rather than improving structural integrity. This process exemplifies the precision of Ayurvedic alchemy, ensuring that metals are both safe and bioavailable. The misalignment of the reason with the assertion highlights the importance of understanding the specific purposes of each purification technique in Rasa Shastra.

43. A: Rasa Shastra integrates metals, minerals, and herbs to address diseases that are difficult to treat with herbal formulations alone. Metals and minerals possess unique therapeutic properties, such as enhanced potency and long-lasting effects, which complement herbal remedies. Both the assertion and the reason are true, with the reason correctly explaining the assertion by highlighting the distinct role of mineral-based medicines in chronic and degenerative conditions. This integration underscores the holistic nature of Rasa Shastra, blending traditional practices with modern pharmacological principles to address complex health challenges comprehensively.

44. C: The Rasendra Chudamani is a classical text focusing on comprehensive methods for mercury purification and its therapeutic applications. The assertion is true, as this text provides detailed procedures for detoxifying and activating mercury. However, the reason is false because the text does not exclusively focus on spiritual alchemy; it equally emphasizes practical medicinal applications. This misrepresentation overlooks the multifaceted nature of Rasa Shastra, where spiritual and therapeutic goals coexist. The Rasendra Chudamani exemplifies the integration of rigorous alchemical methods with a scientific approach to healthcare, ensuring its relevance in both traditional and modern contexts.

45. A: The practice of Śodhana aligns with Ayurveda's principle of detoxification, ensuring the safe use of potentially toxic materials like metals and minerals. Both the assertion and the reason are true, and the reason provides a valid explanation by describing how Śodhana involves boiling, grinding, and quenching to remove impurities and enhance therapeutic efficacy. This systematic process exemplifies Ayurveda's meticulous approach to ensuring safety and bioavailability in its formulations. By bridging traditional purification methods with modern pharmacological insights, Śodhana highlights the adaptability and scientific rigor of Rasa Shastra, maintaining its relevance in integrative medicine.

46. B: The primary purpose of Śodhana in Rasa Shastra is to soften metals, remove impurities, and neutralize toxic properties, ensuring their safety and efficacy for therapeutic use. This process involves techniques such as Swedana, which employs herbal decoctions, and Nirvapana, which uses quenching in specific liquids to detoxify substances. Śodhana exemplifies Ayurveda's scientific approach to purification, aligning traditional methods with contemporary safety standards. By addressing toxicity at its root, this process ensures that metals and minerals become bioavailable and therapeutically potent, reflecting Ayurveda's holistic and evidence-based framework for healthcare.

47. B: The Marana process contributes to the therapeutic efficacy of metals by transforming them into Bhasmas, or fine ashes, which are bioavailable and easily absorbed by the body. This incineration method ensures that metals retain their medicinal properties while becoming safe for internal use. The process is meticulously outlined in classical texts, combining detoxification with activation to enhance therapeutic outcomes. Marana demonstrates the depth of Rasa Shastra, where traditional methods are rooted in scientific principles. This transformation bridges ancient practices with modern pharmacological validation, ensuring the efficacy and safety of Ayurvedic formulations.

48. B: Herbal decoctions used in Swedana contain chelating agents that bind with toxic elements, facilitating their removal during the purification process. This detoxification mechanism aligns with contemporary pharmacological practices, validating the efficacy of traditional methods. Swedana exemplifies Ayurveda's precision in addressing toxicity while preserving the therapeutic potential of raw materials. By leveraging the bioactive properties of herbs, this technique ensures that purified substances are both safe and effective. The integration of ancient detoxification methods with modern scientific insights highlights Ayurveda's adaptability and its ability to address health challenges comprehensively.

49. B: The combination of purified mercury with sulphur to create Kajjali highlights the transformative potential of alchemical techniques in Rasa Shastra. This process neutralizes mercury's toxicity while enhancing its therapeutic efficacy, reflecting the sophistication of Ayurvedic pharmacology. Kajjali serves as a foundation for many formulations, demonstrating the integration of detoxification and activation. This innovation underscores Ayurveda's scientific approach to alchemy, where spiritual and medicinal goals coexist. By combining rigorous purification with therapeutic optimization, Kajjali exemplifies the adaptability and depth of Rasa Shastra in addressing complex health conditions.

50. B: The lack of standardization in preparation techniques presents a significant challenge for Rasa Shastra, as inconsistencies can compromise safety and efficacy. Calls for rigorous validation and quality control aim to address this issue, ensuring that formulations meet both traditional and modern standards. This challenge highlights the need to bridge ancient practices with contemporary scientific frameworks. By standardizing methods and implementing stringent quality checks, Rasa Shastra can maintain its relevance in global healthcare. This balance of tradition and innovation ensures the safety, efficacy, and sustainability of Ayurvedic formulations in addressing diverse health needs.

CHAPTER 14

PRINCIPLES OF BHESHAJYA KALPANA AND RASASALA PRACTICES

Bheshajya Kalpana (Pharmaceuticals): Principles and Classifications

Bheshajya Kalpana, the science of Ayurvedic pharmaceuticals, forms the foundation of Ayurvedic therapeutic practices. This discipline focuses on the formulation, preparation, preservation, and administration of medicines derived from natural substances such as herbs, minerals, and metals. The term "Bheshajya" signifies medicine, while "Kalpana" refers to the art of preparation. Together, Bheshajya Kalpana outlines the principles and methodologies involved in transforming raw materials into effective medicinal formulations.

Principles of Bheshajya Kalpana

The preparation of Ayurvedic medicines follows a set of principles rooted in the holistic philosophy of Ayurveda, emphasizing balance, precision, and personalization:

1. **Therapeutic Goals and Dosha Balance:** The primary objective of Bheshajya Kalpana is to restore and maintain the balance of the three doshas (Vata, Pitta, and Kapha). Each formulation is tailored to address specific imbalances and disease conditions.
2. **Samskara (Transformation):** The concept of Samskara emphasizes the transformation of raw materials to enhance their therapeutic properties and reduce any potential toxicity. This is achieved through processes like purification (Shodhana), cooking (Pachana), and grinding (Mardana).
3. **Rasa, Guna, Virya, Vipaka, and Prabhava:** Ayurvedic formulations are designed to align with the five primary attributes of substances:
   - Rasa (taste)
   - Guna (quality)
   - Virya (potency)
   - Vipaka (post-digestive effect)
   - Prabhava (unique or specific action)
4. **Prakruti-Specific Formulation:** Bheshajya Kalpana emphasizes the personalization of medicines based on an individual's constitution (Prakruti), disease condition, and environmental factors.
5. **Shelf Life and Stability:** Ayurvedic texts, including Charaka Samhita and Sharangadhara Samhita, provide detailed guidelines for preserving medicines to maintain their potency over time. This includes the use of preservatives, airtight containers, and specific storage conditions.
6. **Combination and Synergy:** Medicines are often prepared using multiple ingredients to achieve synergy. This approach enhances the efficacy and mitigates potential adverse effects.

Classifications of Bheshajya Kalpana

Bheshajya Kalpana is classified into several categories based on the form and method of preparation:

1. **Panchavidha Kashaya Kalpana (Five Basic Preparations):** These form the foundational frameworks for Ayurvedic formulations:
   - **Swarasa (Juice):** Extracted by crushing fresh herbs, Swarasa is the most potent preparation.

- **Kalka (Paste):** Prepared by grinding herbs into a paste, it is often used in topical applications or as a base for other preparations.
- **Kwatha (Decoction):** Obtained by boiling herbs in water to extract their active principles.
- **Hima (Cold Infusion):** Herbs are soaked in cold water to extract heat-sensitive compounds.
- **Phanta (Hot Infusion):** Herbs are steeped in hot water, similar to brewing tea.

2. **Secondary Preparations:** These preparations evolve from the Panchavidha Kalpana and include:
   - **Churna (Powders):** Dried herbs are ground into fine powders.
   - **Vati (Tablets):** Powders are compressed into pills using binders.
   - **Asava and Arishta (Fermented Liquids):** Prepared by fermenting herbal decoctions with natural sugars and yeast.
   - **Taila (Medicated Oils):** Herbs are infused in oils for massage and therapeutic purposes.
   - **Ghrita (Medicated Ghee):** Herbs are processed with clarified butter for internal and external applications.
3. **Mineral and Metal-Based Preparations:** These are extensively used in Rasa Shastra and include:
   - **Bhasmas (Calcinated Metals):** Metals are purified and converted into ash for medicinal use.
   - **Pishti (Powders):** Fine powders prepared from gems or minerals.
   - **Kupipakwa Rasayana:** Medicines prepared in sealed vessels under high heat.
4. **Contemporary Adaptations:** In modern Ayurveda, new forms like capsules, syrups, and ointments have been introduced to align with global pharmaceutical standards:
   - **Rasaśālā (Pharmacy):** Practices and Standard Preparation Techniques
   - **Rasaśālā (Pharmacy):** Practices and Standard Preparation Techniques

The Rasaśālā, or Ayurvedic pharmacy, is a cornerstone of Ayurvedic medicine, where the principles of Rasa Shastra come alive through the preparation of therapeutic formulations. The term Rasaśālā not only denotes a physical space for the preparation of medicines but also embodies the spiritual and scientific fusion that defines Ayurveda. It is a sacred space where raw materials undergo transformative processes to become potent remedies capable of restoring health and balance.

The practices in a Rasaśālā are grounded in ancient traditions, meticulously described in classical texts like the Rasa Ratna Samuccaya, Rasendra Chudamani, and Charaka Samhita. These practices ensure that every medicine prepared adheres to the highest standards of purity, efficacy, and safety. In this chapter, we delve into the design, layout, and preparation techniques that make the Rasaśālā a unique and essential part of Ayurveda.

Design and Layout of a Rasaśālā

The structure and layout of a Rasaśālā are integral to its functionality and sanctity. The preparation of Ayurvedic medicines is not merely a mechanical process; it is a sacred act that requires harmony, precision, and a deep connection to natural and cosmic energies. The design principles reflect this philosophy.

1. **Sacred Environment:** The Rasaśālā is considered a sacred space, often constructed according to Vastu Shastra principles. These ancient architectural guidelines ensure that the pharmacy is in harmony with natural energies, fostering a positive and conducive environment for the preparation of medicines:
   - **Orientation and Placement:** The entrance is typically aligned with auspicious directions, such as the east or north, to invite positive energy.
   - **Rituals and Purification:** The space is regularly purified with rituals, including the use of incense, chanting of mantras, and sprinkling of holy water, to maintain its sanctity.
   - **Symbolism of Purity:** The design reflects the Ayurvedic principle of purity in thought, space, and materials. The work environment is serene and clutter-free to promote focus and precision.
2. **Dedicated Sections:** A well-organized Rasaśālā is divided into distinct sections, each designated for specific tasks. This segregation ensures efficiency and prevents cross-contamination during the preparation of medicines:
   - **Grinding Section:** This area houses traditional tools such as grinding stones and mortars for processing raw materials.
   - **Boiling and Cooking Section:** Equipped with fire pits, earthen pots, and large vessels for decoctions, this section is where herbal oils, ghritas (medicated ghee), and kwathas (decoctions) are prepared.
   - **Fermentation Section:** A separate space is designated for fermenting asavas and arishtas, ensuring controlled environmental conditions.

- **Storage and Packaging Section:** This area is used for drying, packaging, and storing finished medicines in airtight containers to preserve their potency.

3. **Cleanliness and Hygiene:** Hygiene is paramount in a Rasaśālā. Strict protocols are followed to ensure that every medicine prepared is free from contamination and retains its therapeutic value:
   - **Sterilization of Tools:** Utensils, grinding stones, and storage containers are cleaned thoroughly with herbal disinfectants or boiled water.
   - **Water Quality:** Clean and purified water is used for all processes, particularly for Shodhana (purification) and Pachana (cooking).
   - **Personal Hygiene:** Workers adhere to strict personal hygiene standards, wearing clean clothes and maintaining sanitized hands while handling raw materials.
   - **Waste Management:** Organic waste, such as leftover herbs, is composted, while non-biodegradable waste is disposed of responsibly.
4. **Use of Traditional Equipment:** The tools used in a Rasaśālā are deeply rooted in tradition. Unlike modern equipment, these tools are believed to retain the energetic properties of the raw materials:
   - **Mortars and Pestles:** Made from stone, these are used for grinding herbs and minerals, preserving their integrity.
   - **Grinding Stones:** These tools ensure uniform particle size, enhancing the bioavailability of ingredients.
   - **Earthen Pots:** Used for boiling and fermentation, earthen pots are preferred for their ability to regulate temperature and retain medicinal properties.
   - **Sealed Vessels:** Made of glass, clay, or metal, these are used for preparing and storing fermented liquids or medicines that require controlled conditions.

The use of traditional equipment reflects the balance between simplicity and efficacy, a hallmark of Ayurvedic practices.

Standard Preparation Techniques in the Rasaśālā

The preparation techniques in a Rasaśālā are a blend of art and science, guided by ancient Ayurvedic principles. These methods transform raw materials into potent medicines, ensuring that their therapeutic properties are maximized while their toxic elements are neutralized.

1. **Shodhana (Purification):** Shodhana is the first and most critical step in the preparation of Ayurvedic medicines, particularly those involving metals, minerals, and certain herbs. It involves detoxifying and purifying raw materials to remove impurities and enhance their medicinal properties.

   Techniques:
   - **Boiling:** Raw materials are boiled in herbal decoctions to eliminate toxins.
   - **Steaming:** This method is used to soften materials for further processing.
   - **Quenching:** Metals and minerals are heated to high temperatures and quenched in liquids such as cow's milk or herbal juices.
   - **Purpose:** Shodhana ensures that raw materials are safe for consumption, reducing the risk of side effects while enhancing their bioavailability.
2. **Bhavana (Levigation):** Bhavana involves triturating ingredients with herbal juices or decoctions to infuse their active principles into the material:
   - **Process:** Ingredients are ground in a mortar with small quantities of herbal liquids until a paste-like consistency is achieved.This process is repeated multiple times to ensure thorough integration.
   - **Purpose:** Bhavana enhances the bioavailability and potency of ingredients, making them more effective in therapeutic applications.
3. **Pachana (Cooking):** Pachana refers to the slow boiling of herbs and oils to extract their medicinal properties.

   Techniques:
   - **Decoctions (Kwathas):** Herbs are boiled in water to create concentrated extracts.
   - **Medicated Oils (Tailas):** Herbs are cooked in oils like sesame or coconut for external and internal applications.
   - **Purpose:** Pachana ensures the extraction of active principles while preserving the stability of the preparation.
4. **Mardana (Grinding):** Mardana involves grinding ingredients into fine powders to enhance their therapeutic efficacy:
   - **Tools:** Mortars, pestles, and grinding stones are used for this purpose.
   - The powders are then sieved to ensure uniform particle size.
   - **Purpose:** Mardana increases the surface area of ingredients, facilitating better absorption and interaction with bodily systems.
5. **Bandhana (Sealing):** Bandhana involves sealing containers to preserve medicines during fermentation or storage:

- **Techniques:** Glass or earthen containers are sealed with cloth or clay to prevent contamination.
- Airtight sealing ensures the stability and longevity of the formulation.
- **Purpose:** Bandhana protects medicines from external influences such as moisture, light, and air, preserving their potency over time.

Integration of Tradition and Modern Science

Modern Rasaśālās are adopting advanced technologies to complement traditional methods while retaining their authenticity. Techniques such as vacuum-sealing, freeze-drying, and nanotechnology are being explored to enhance the stability and efficacy of Ayurvedic medicines. However, the core principles of purity, synergy, and personalization remain unchanged.

Quality Control in Rasaśālā

1. **Ingredient Selection:** Only high-quality, fresh, and uncontaminated ingredients are used.
2. **Standardization:** The proportions of ingredients and preparation methods are meticulously followed as per classical texts.
3. **Testing and Validation:** Finished products are tested for safety and efficacy. This includes taste testing, microbial testing, and visual inspections.
4. **Documentation:** All preparation steps are documented for consistency and traceability.

Ayurvedic Formulation Processes

Ayurvedic formulation processes are deeply rooted in the principle of creating balanced medicines that address both the root cause of diseases and their symptoms. These processes are intricate, requiring precision and adherence to classical guidelines.

Key Steps in Formulation Processes

1. **Selection of Ingredients:** Herbs, minerals, and metals are chosen based on their therapeutic properties and compatibility.

   Consideration is given to factors like the season of collection, freshness, and natural habitat.
2. **Dosage Form Selection:** The form of the medicine (e.g., decoction, powder, or oil) is selected based on the disease, patient's constitution, and route of administration.
3. **Proportion and Combination:** Ingredients are combined in specific ratios to achieve synergy. The interaction between substances is carefully studied to enhance efficacy.
4. **Preparation Techniques:** Methods like Shodhana, Marana, and Bhavana are used to purify, transform, and potentiate ingredients.
5. **Storage and Preservation:** Medicines are stored in airtight containers, often made of glass or clay, to protect them from moisture and contamination.
6. **Testing and Standardization:** Formulations are evaluated for taste, color, consistency, and therapeutic effectiveness.

Ethical and Sustainable Practices in Formulation

1. **Sustainability:** The sourcing of raw materials is done in a way that minimizes environmental impact. Cultivated herbs are preferred over wild-harvested ones.
2. **Ethics:** Ayurvedic formulations prioritize non-violence and sustainability. Animal testing is avoided, and ingredients are sourced responsibly.
3. **Adaptation to Modern Needs:** While remaining true to traditional methods, Ayurvedic formulations are being adapted to meet global standards of safety and efficacy.

Modern Relevance and Global Impact

1. **Integration with Modern Science:** Research on Ayurvedic formulations has led to their incorporation into integrative medicine practices worldwide.
2. **Pharmaceutical Innovations:** Techniques like nanotechnology are being explored to enhance the efficacy of Ayurvedic medicines.
3. **Global Acceptance:** Ayurvedic formulations are gaining recognition for their holistic approach, leading to increased demand for standardization and quality control.

MULTIPLE CHOICE QUESTIONS

1. A researcher working on Ayurvedic pharmaceuticals hypothesizes that the synergy of ingredients in traditional formulations enhances therapeutic efficacy more effectively than isolated compounds. If this hypothesis is correct, which explanation aligns most with the core principle of Bheshajya Kalpana?

   A. The use of single herbs is preferred due to their consistent action on specific doshas.

B. Synergistic formulations are designed to harmonize dosha imbalances and amplify therapeutic effects.
C. Ayurvedic pharmaceuticals rely on metals and minerals rather than plant-based synergy.
D. Synergy in formulations is irrelevant as efficacy is determined by individual ingredients.

2. While preparing a formulation in a Rasaśālā, a pharmacist uses Shodhana to purify raw materials. The process involves boiling the substances in herbal decoctions. Which of the following best explains the significance of this step?
A. To enhance the flavour and texture of the raw material for easier consumption.
B. To remove physical and chemical impurities, ensuring safety and efficacy.
C. To reduce the shelf life of the formulation, preventing contamination.
D. To chemically alter the substance to make it insoluble in water.

3. An Ayurvedic practitioner explains that Pachana (cooking) enhances the bioavailability of herbal compounds in medicinal oils. This technique is particularly important in formulations like Taila (medicated oil). Which principle of Bheshajya Kalpana does this highlight?
A. Preserving the raw state of herbs for maximum potency.
B. Transforming raw materials through heat to extract active principles.
C. Avoiding heat to preserve the energetic properties of ingredients.
D. Using Pachana exclusively for non-therapeutic purposes.

4. A clinical trial compares the efficacy of single-ingredient powders (Churna) versus multi-herb decoctions (Kwathas). Results indicate that Kwathas provide more balanced therapeutic effects. What principle of Bheshajya Kalpana does this illustrate?
A. Multi-herb formulations reduce the potency of individual components.
B. Decoctions are more effective because they avoid heat-based preparation.
C. Combination formulations address complex dosha imbalances better than single herbs.
D. Single-ingredient formulations are preferred for simplicity in dosha management.

5. A team of scientists investigates the role of Bhavana in Ayurvedic medicine preparation. They discover that the repeated grinding of powders with herbal juices enhances therapeutic efficacy. How does this align with Ayurvedic principles?
A. Bhavana integrates bioactive compounds into the matrix of the raw material, enhancing absorption.
B. The grinding process mechanically increases potency without altering chemical properties.
C. Herbal juices primarily serve as preservatives during the preparation of powders.
D. Repeated grinding ensures uniform particle size but does not impact bioavailability.

6. A pharmacist in a Rasaśālā uses a grinding stone to process metals into fine powders. This practice aligns with the Ayurvedic concept of Mardana. What is the primary purpose of this process?
A. To remove physical impurities from the metals.
B. To increase surface area for better therapeutic interaction with the body.
C. To ensure metals retain their original structure.
D. To enhance the visual appeal of the final product.

7. During a demonstration, an Ayurvedic expert explains that Bandhana (sealing) is crucial for fermenting formulations like Asava and Arishta. What does this step achieve in the preparation process?
A. It prevents oxidation, preserving the formulation's shelf life.
B. It increases the alcohol content to enhance therapeutic properties.
C. It accelerates fermentation by exposing the liquid to air.
D. It ensures the ingredients retain their raw form without alteration.

8. An environmental scientist examines the sourcing of raw materials in Ayurvedic pharmaceuticals and raises concerns about sustainability. Which strategy aligns best with Ayurvedic principles while addressing these concerns?
A. Transitioning to synthetic alternatives to reduce reliance on natural resources.
B. Promoting cultivation of medicinal plants through agroforestry systems.
C. Limiting the production of Ayurvedic medicines to conserve natural materials.
D. Preferring wild-sourced materials for their higher therapeutic potency.

9. A Rasaśālā manager emphasizes strict hygiene protocols in the facility. Which of the following best illustrates the purpose of maintaining such standards?
A. Hygiene ensures that the energetic properties of medicines are preserved.
B. Strict protocols prevent contamination and maintain the therapeutic purity of formulations.
C. Cleanliness is maintained primarily to meet legal requirements.

D. Hygiene reduces the need for raw material purification.

10. A researcher develops a modern apparatus to replicate traditional Ayurvedic grinding techniques. Which principle justifies the continued preference for traditional tools in Rasaśālā practices?
A. Traditional tools ensure uniformity in texture, which modern tools cannot replicate.
B. Modern tools disrupt the energetic alignment of raw materials.
C. Traditional tools preserve the integrity of active principles through gentle processing.
D. Traditional tools are used only for ceremonial purposes and not for practical reasons.

Directions (Q. No. 11–14): *Scenario-Based Questions*

SCENARIO 1

A study finds that decoctions prepared using the Kwatha method have higher therapeutic efficacy than powders due to their ability to extract active compounds more efficiently. Researchers note the use of slow boiling ensures optimal concentration without degrading heat-sensitive compounds.

SCENARIO 2

A separate investigation highlights sustainability challenges in sourcing rare herbs like Haritaki, used in Kwatha. It emphasizes the need for conservation-focused harvesting techniques, such as community-led agroforestry, to maintain ecological balance.

11. Based on Scenario 1, which of the following best explains the enhanced efficacy of Kwatha?
A. Active principles are concentrated due to prolonged boiling.
B. The use of heat eliminates the need for additional purification.
C. Decoctions retain both water-soluble and fat-soluble compounds.
D. Heat-sensitive compounds are preserved through rapid boiling techniques.

12. Considering Scenario 2, which of the following strategies aligns with Ayurvedic sustainability principles while preserving medicinal efficacy?
A. Replacing Haritaki with synthetic compounds.
B. Cultivating Haritaki through organic, community-led practices.
C. Limiting the use of Haritaki to high-value formulations only.
D. Prioritizing wild collection of Haritaki for its superior therapeutic properties.

13. How do the findings in Scenario 2 potentially influence the outcomes of formulations described in Scenario 1?
A. Unsustainable harvesting reduces the therapeutic value of Kwatha.
B. Kwatha retains its efficacy regardless of raw material quality.
C. Reduced Haritaki availability enhances the potency of formulations.
D. Sustainability challenges have no measurable effect on formulation outcomes.

14. Based on the interconnected findings of both scenarios, what comprehensive approach best addresses sustainability and therapeutic efficacy?
A. Promoting community-led cultivation and optimizing Kwatha preparation techniques.
B. Reducing the reliance on traditional formulations like Kwatha.
C. Replacing Haritaki with alternative herbs to ensure supply consistency.
D. Standardizing Kwatha preparation to minimize reliance on raw materials.

15. The stages of Shodhana in Rasa Shastra focus on:
(a) Removal of toxic impurities through boiling and quenching.
(b) Enhancement of bioavailability by grinding with herbal juices.
(c) Transformation of raw metals into ash forms for medicinal use.
(d) Preservation of metals in their original state for long-term storage.

Choose the correct answer:
A. (a), (b), and (c) only
B. (a), (c), and (d) only
C. (b), (c), and (d) only
D. (a), (b), (c), and (d)

16. The Panchavidha Kashaya Kalpana includes:
(a) Swarasa (Juice), extracted directly from fresh herbs.
(b) Kalka (Paste), made by grinding herbs.
(c) Kwatha (Decoction), prepared by boiling herbs in water.
(d) Asava (Fermented liquids), made by natural fermentation.

Choose the correct answer:
A. (a), (b), and (c) only
B. (a), (c), and (d) only
C. (a), (b), and (d) only
D. (a), (b), (c), and (d)

17. Key purposes of Bhavana in Rasa Shastra are:
(a) To integrate the energetic properties of herbs into raw materials.

(b) To grind metals into finer powders for external application.
(c) To detoxify substances for safe internal use.
(d) To enhance bioavailability of medicinal compounds.

Choose the correct answer:
A. (a), (b), and (c) only
B. (a), (c), and (d) only
C. (b), (c), and (d) only
D. (a), (b), (c), and (d)

18. The role of Pachana in Ayurvedic medicine preparation is to:
(a) Extract active principles through heat-based methods.
(b) Preserve raw herbs for prolonged use.
(c) Concentrate decoctions and oils for therapeutic purposes.
(d) Neutralize the natural flavor of bitter substances.

Choose the correct answer:
A. (a) and (c) only
B. (b) and (d) only
C. (a), (b), and (c) only
D. (a), (c), and (d) only

19. The classifications of Ayurvedic formulations include:
(a) Churna (Powders) for oral consumption.
(b) Vati (Tablets) for precise dosage administration.
(c) Taila (Medicated oils) for external applications only.
(d) Ghrita (Medicated ghee) for both external and internal use.

Choose the correct answer:
A. (a), (b), and (c) only
B. (b), (c), and (d) only
C. (a), (b), and (d) only
D. (a), (b), (c), and (d)

20. Ayurvedic preparation methods to enhance medicinal efficacy include:
(a) Levigation with herbal liquids to imbue therapeutic properties.
(b) Prolonged fermentation to increase alcohol content.
(c) Incineration of metals to produce bioavailable ash (Bhasma).
(d) Direct mixing of raw ingredients without processing.

Choose the correct answer:
A. (a), (b), and (c) only
B. (b), (c), and (d) only
C. (a), (c), and (d) only
D. (a), (b), (c), and (d)

21. The principles governing Rasaśālā practices include:
(a) Ensuring hygiene and sterility of raw materials and tools.
(b) Following Vastu Shastra principles in the layout of the pharmacy.
(c) Prioritizing modern machinery over traditional tools for preparation.
(d) Maintaining a balance of scientific precision and spiritual harmony.

Choose the correct answer:
A. (a), (b), and (d) only
B. (b), (c), and (d) only
C. (a), (c), and (d) only
D. (a), (b), (c), and (d)

22. Bheshajya Kalpana aims to:
(a) Enhance the potency of herbal medicines through specific processing techniques.
(b) Eliminate the toxicity of raw metals and minerals.
(c) Align formulations with the balance of Vata, Pitta, and Kapha.
(d) Prepare medicines exclusively for internal consumption.

Choose the correct answer:
A. (a), (b), and (c) only
B. (a), (b), and (d) only
C. (b), (c), and (d) only
D. (a), (b), (c), and (d)

23. Key features of fermentation-based formulations like Asava and Arishta include:
(a) Self-generated alcohol through natural fermentation.
(b) Use of herbs to regulate fermentation and therapeutic effects.
(c) Preservation of active compounds without heat-based extraction.
(d) Exclusion of mineral-based substances in the preparation.

Choose the correct answer:
A. (a), (b), and (c) only
B. (b), (c), and (d) only
C. (a), (c), and (d) only
D. (a), (b), (c), and (d)

24. The purpose of Bandhana in Ayurvedic preparations is to:
(a) Ensure the stability of fermented formulations during storage.
(b) Prevent contamination during preparation and storage.
(c) Maintain the energetic properties of the formulation.

(d) Facilitate continuous fermentation over prolonged periods.

Choose the correct answer:
A. (a) and (b) only
B. (b) and (d) only
C. (a), (b), and (c) only
D. (a), (b), (c), and (d)

25. Match List–I (Processes in Rasa Shastra) with List–II (Purpose):

List–I	List–II
(a) Shodhana	1. Purification and detoxification of raw materials
(b) Bhavana	2. Levigation to enhance bioavailability
(c) Pachana	3. Extraction of active principles through slow cooking
(d) Mardana	4. Grinding to reduce particle size and increase surface area

Choose the correct answer:
A. (a)-1, (b)-2, (c)-3, (d)-4
B. (a)-4, (b)-3, (c)-1, (d)-2
C. (a)-2, (b)-1, (c)-4, (d)-3
D. (a)-3, (b)-4, (c)-2, (d)-1

26. Match List–I (Ayurvedic Preparations) with List–II (Characteristics):

List–I	List–II
(a) Churna	1. Powder form, easy for oral consumption
(b) Vati	2. Tablet form for precise dosage
(c) Taila	3. Medicated oil, often used externally
(d) Ghrita	4. Medicated ghee, used for internal and external purposes

Choose the correct answer:
A. (a)-1, (b)-2, (c)-3, (d)-4
B. (a)-3, (b)-4, (c)-2, (d)-1
C. (a)-4, (b)-3, (c)-1, (d)-2
D. (a)-1, (b)-2, (c)-4, (d)-3

27. Match List–I (Rasasala Sections) with List–II (Functions):

List–I	List–II
(a) Grinding Section	1. Processing raw materials into fine powders
(b) Boiling Section	2. Preparing herbal decoctions and oils
(c) Fermentation Section	3. Producing Asava and Arishta formulations
(d) Storage Section	4. Preserving and packaging finished products

Choose the correct answer:
A. (a)-1, (b)-2, (c)-3, (d)-4
B. (a)-3, (b)-4, (c)-1, (d)-2
C. (a)-4, (b)-3, (c)-2, (d)-1
D. (a)-2, (b)-1, (c)-4, (d)-3

28. Match List–I (Panchavidha Kalpana) with List–II (Descriptions):

List–I	List–II
(a) Swarasa	1. Extracted by crushing fresh herbs
(b) Kalka	2. Paste made by grinding herbs
(c) Kwatha	3. Decoction made by boiling herbs in water
(d) Hima	4. Cold infusion of herbs in water

Choose the correct answer:
A. (a)-4, (b)-3, (c)-1, (d)-2
B. (a)-1, (b)-2, (c)-3, (d)-4
C. (a)-2, (b)-4, (c)-3, (d)-1
D. (a)-3, (b)-1, (c)-4, (d)-2

29. Match List–I (Purification Techniques) with List–II (Methods):

List–I	List–II
(a) Boiling	1. Detoxifies herbs and minerals through herbal decoctions
(b) Steaming	2. Softens raw materials for further processing
(c) Quenching	3. Neutralizes toxicity by heating and cooling in liquids
(d) Filtration	4. Removes solid impurities from liquid formulations

Choose the correct answer:
A. (a)-1, (b)-2, (c)-3, (d)-4
B. (a)-3, (b)-1, (c)-4, (d)-2
C. (a)-4, (b)-3, (c)-1, (d)-2
D. (a)-2, (b)-4, (c)-3, (d)-1

30. Match List–I (Key Ayurvedic Concepts) with List–II (Definitions):

List–I	List–II
(a) Tridosha	1. Vata, Pitta, and Kapha balance for health
(b) Rasa	2. Taste as a therapeutic and diagnostic tool
(c) Agni	3. Digestive fire responsible for metabolism
(d) Ama	4. Toxic buildup resulting from incomplete digestion

Choose the correct answer:
A. (a)-1, (b)-2, (c)-3, (d)-4
B. (a)-4, (b)-1, (c)-2, (d)-3
C. (a)-3, (b)-4, (c)-1, (d)-2
D. (a)-2, (b)-3, (c)-4, (d)-1

31. Match List–I (Fermented Preparations) with List–II (Ingredients):

List–I	List–II
(a) Asava	1. Herbal decoction and natural sugars for fermentation
(b) Arishta	2. Boiled herbal extracts fermented with jaggery
(c) Kanji	3. Fermented preparation made with rice water
(d) Takra	4. Fermented buttermilk used in therapeutic diets

Choose the correct answer:

A. (a)-1, (b)-2, (c)-3, (d)-4
B. (a)-3, (b)-4, (c)-1, (d)-2
C. (a)-2, (b)-3, (c)-4, (d)-1
D. (a)-4, (b)-1, (c)-2, (d)-3

32. Match List–I (Pharmacological Properties) with List–II (Effects):

List–I	List–II
(a) Rasa (Taste)	1. Governs sensory interaction and digestive stimulation
(b) Virya (Potency)	2. Determines heating or cooling effects on the body
(c) Vipaka (Post-digestive Effect)	3. Influences dosha-specific outcomes after digestion
(d) Prabhava (Unique Effect)	4. Specific action independent of other properties

Choose the correct answer:

A. (a)-1, (b)-2, (c)-3, (d)-4
B. (a)-2, (b)-4, (c)-1, (d)-3
C. (a)-3, (b)-1, (c)-4, (d)-2
D. (a)-4, (b)-3, (c)-2, (d)-1

33. Match List–I (Preparation Steps) with List–II (Descriptions):

List–I	List–II
(a) Shodhana	1. Detoxification of raw materials
(b) Marana	2. Conversion into ash (Bhasma) for internal use
(c) Bhavana	3. Levigation with herbal liquids for enhancement
(d) Storage	4. Preservation of medicines for long-term use

Choose the correct answer:

A. (a)-1, (b)-2, (c)-3, (d)-4
B. (a)-3, (b)-1, (c)-4, (d)-2
C. (a)-4, (b)-3, (c)-2, (d)-1
D. (a)-2, (b)-4, (c)-1, (d)-3

34. Match List–I (Dosha Characteristics) with List–II (Attributes):

List–I	List–II
(a) Vata	1. Movement and nervous system regulation
(b) Pitta	2. Metabolism and enzymatic activity
(c) Kapha	3. Structural stability and fluid balance
(d) Dosha Balance	4. Harmonizes bodily functions for health

Choose the correct answer:

A. (a)-1, (b)-2, (c)-3, (d)-4
B. (a)-4, (b)-1, (c)-2, (d)-3
C. (a)-3, (b)-4, (c)-1, (d)-2
D. (a)-2, (b)-3, (c)-4, (d)-1

Directions (Q. No. 35–39): *Following questions are based on Statement 1 and Statement 2. Read both the statements carefully and choose the correct answer from the options given below:*

A. Both Statement 1 and Statement 2 are true, and Statement 2 is the correct explanation of Statement 1.
B. Both Statement 1 and Statement 2 are true, but Statement 2 is not the correct explanation of Statement 1.
C. Statement 1 is true, but Statement 2 is false.
D. Statement 1 is false, but Statement 2 is true.
E. Both Statement 1 and Statement 2 are false.

35. **Statement 1:** The process of Shodhana is vital for eliminating toxic properties from raw materials in Rasa Shastra.

Statement 2: Shodhana methods, such as boiling in herbal decoctions or quenching in milk, enhance the bioavailability and safety of raw substances.

36. **Statement 1:** Panchavidha Kashaya Kalpana forms the foundation of Ayurvedic pharmaceutical preparations.

Statement 2: Panchavidha Kashaya Kalpana refers to the five preparation methods of Swarasá, Kalka, Kwatha, Hima, and Phanta, each tailored to extract specific therapeutic properties.

37. **Statement 1:** Bhavana is used in Rasa Shastra to enhance the potency and efficacy of raw materials through repeated grinding with herbal liquids.

Statement 2: Bhavana involves mechanical grinding only and does not chemically alter the raw material or improve its bioavailability.

38. **Statement 1:** The use of traditional tools such as stone mortars and grinding stones in a Rasaśālā is essential for retaining the energetic properties of raw materials.

Statement 2: Modern tools disrupt the molecular structure of raw materials, making them less effective in Ayurvedic formulations.

39. Statement 1: Ayurvedic formulations, such as Kwatha and Taila, prioritize the synergy between ingredients to address complex dosha imbalances.

Statement 2: Single-ingredient formulations are equally effective as multi-herb preparations in balancing all three doshas and treating complex diseases.

Directions (Q. No. 40–45): *There are two statements in each question. One is labelled as Assertion (A) and the other is as Reason (R). Read both the statements and choose the correct answer from the options given below:*

A. Both Assertion (A) and Reason (R) are true, and Reason (R) is the correct explanation of Assertion (A).
B. Both Assertion (A) and Reason (R) are true, but Reason (R) is not the correct explanation of Assertion (A).
C. Assertion (A) is true, but Reason (R) is false.
D. Assertion (A) is false, but Reason (R) is true.
E. Both Assertion (A) and Reason (R) are false.

40. Assertion (A): Marana is a critical process in Rasa Shastra where metals are transformed into fine ash (Bhasma), enhancing their bioavailability.

Reason (R): The ash form ensures safe internal use by neutralizing toxicity and increasing absorption potential.

41. Assertion (A): Hima preparations are used for heat-sensitive herbs to extract their active principles without degradation.

Reason (R): The cold infusion method preserves volatile compounds and ensures the full retention of heat-labile components.

42. Assertion (A): Decoctions (Kwathas) are considered more effective than powders (Churna) in treating acute dosha imbalances.

Reason (R): Decoctions are concentrated, water-based extracts that quickly target systemic imbalances due to their rapid absorption.

43. Assertion (A): Hygiene and cleanliness are paramount in a Rasaśālā to ensure the purity and efficacy of formulations.

Reason (R): Contaminated tools or raw materials can introduce impurities, reducing the therapeutic value and safety of Ayurvedic medicines.

44. Assertion (A): Ayurvedic oils (Taila) are more effective in penetrating the skin than water-based formulations.

Reason (R): The lipophilic nature of oils enhances absorption through skin layers, delivering active principles directly to target tissues.

45. Assertion (A): The principles of Bheshajya Kalpana are based on balancing Rasa (taste), Virya (potency), Vipaka (post-digestive effect), and Prabhava (unique effect).

Reason (R): The balance of these pharmacological properties determines the therapeutic alignment with dosha imbalances.

Directions (Q. No. 46–50): *Read the passage carefully and find the answers to the questions given below:*

Ayurvedic formulation processes are rooted in the principles of harmony and balance, emphasizing personalized medicine. A pivotal aspect is Panchavidha Kashaya Kalpana, encompassing Swarasa (juice), Kalka (paste), Kwatha (decoction), Hima (cold infusion), and Phanta (hot infusion). These methods are designed to extract specific therapeutic properties of herbs, aligning them with an individual's doshic constitution and disease state.

Preparation techniques like Shodhana (purification) ensure raw materials are detoxified for safe use, while Marana (incineration) transforms metals and minerals into bioavailable forms like Bhasma. Bhavana (levigation) integrates herbal liquids into raw substances to enhance their potency. Decoctions, such as Kwatha, are particularly effective in managing acute conditions due to their rapid absorption, while oils (Taila) and ghee (Ghrita) serve as carriers for fat-soluble compounds, penetrating deep into tissues.

Quality control in Ayurvedic formulations emphasizes the purity, potency, and stability of medicines. Storage in airtight containers ensures longevity, while traditional tools like grinding stones retain the energetic properties of the raw materials. Modern advancements, including standardization techniques, are being integrated into traditional practices to enhance global acceptance. Despite these innovations, Ayurvedic principles like Rasa (taste), Virya (potency), Vipaka (post-digestive effect), and Prabhava (unique effect) remain central to formulation processes, ensuring a holistic approach to health and disease management.

46. According to the passage, what is the primary purpose of Panchavidha Kashaya Kalpana?

1. To personalize formulations based on an individual's doshic constitution.
2. To ensure the preservation of raw herbs in their natural state.
3. To classify Ayurvedic formulations based on therapeutic extraction methods.
4. To eliminate the need for modern pharmaceutical technologies.

Choose the correct answer:
A. 1 and 3 only
B. 2 and 4 only
C. 1, 2, and 3 only
D. 1, 3, and 4 only

47. What is the significance of Shodhana and Marana in Ayurvedic formulation processes?
1. Shodhana ensures the safety and detoxification of raw materials.
2. Marana enhances the taste of raw materials for easier consumption.
3. Shodhana and Marana collectively improve the bioavailability of substances.
4. Marana neutralizes the toxic properties of metals and minerals.

Choose the correct answer:
A. 1, 2, and 4 only
B. 1, 3, and 4 only
C. 2 and 3 only
D. 1, 2, 3, and 4

48. How does Bhavana contribute to Ayurvedic formulation processes?
1. It integrates the bioactive principles of herbs into raw materials.
2. It ensures the proper storage and longevity of formulations.
3. It chemically transforms raw materials for enhanced potency.
4. It removes impurities from herbs and minerals during processing.

Choose the correct answer:
A. 1 and 3 only
B. 1, 3, and 4 only
C. 2 and 4 only
D. 1, 2, and 3 only

49. What is the primary role of oils (Taila) and ghee (Ghrita) in Ayurvedic formulations?
1. To serve as carriers for fat-soluble compounds.
2. To enhance the penetration of therapeutic substances into tissues.
3. To increase the stability and shelf life of raw materials.
4. To eliminate the need for water-based extraction methods.

Choose the correct answer:
A. 1 and 2 only
B. 3 and 4 only
C. 1, 2, and 3 only
D. 2, 3, and 4 only

50. Based on the passage, how does modern science contribute to Ayurvedic formulation processes?
1. By integrating standardization techniques to enhance global acceptance.
2. By introducing synthetic alternatives for traditional raw materials.
3. By validating Ayurvedic principles like Rasa and Vipaka through empirical research.
4. By replacing traditional tools with advanced machinery for consistency.

Choose the correct answer:
A. 1 and 3 only
B. 2 and 4 only
C. 1, 2, and 4 only
D. 1, 3, and 4 only

ANSWER WITH EXPLANATIONS

1. B: The principle of synergy in Ayurvedic formulations ensures holistic healing by targeting multiple aspects of disease simultaneously. Ayurveda does not rely on isolated compounds because it considers the body's balance as a dynamic system. Multi-ingredient formulations are designed to harmonize Vata, Pitta, and Kapha, amplifying therapeutic effects and mitigating side effects. This reflects the depth of Bheshajya Kalpana, where combinations of herbs, minerals, and carrier substances are carefully chosen to enhance efficacy. Synergy also ensures that different tissues and doshas are addressed in a single formulation, making it suitable for personalized treatments. This underpins Ayurveda's holistic and integrative nature.

2. B: Shodhana is more than purification; it is a process of transformation. By boiling metals or herbs in herbal decoctions, toxins are not only removed but the substance is made more bioavailable and therapeutically aligned with the body's needs. This step enhances safety by neutralizing potentially harmful components and activating latent therapeutic properties. For example, quenching metals in milk balances their heating properties, aligning with dosha-specific needs. Ayurveda integrates these detoxification techniques into a broader understanding of pharmacology, ensuring that substances are not only safe but also energetically aligned with healing goals. This demonstrates its precision and foresight.

3. **B:** The slow boiling process in Pachana aligns with the Ayurvedic understanding of heat as a transformative agent. This method allows water-soluble compounds to be extracted while preserving the integrity of heat-sensitive components. In formulations like Taila, the process ensures that fat-soluble compounds are absorbed into the oil medium, making it suitable for deep tissue penetration. Ayurveda uses heat not merely for extraction but for activation, converting raw materials into potent therapeutic agents. This precision reflects Ayurveda's nuanced understanding of pharmacokinetics, where the method of preparation influences both the efficacy and safety of the medicine.

4. **C:** Multi-herb formulations like Kwatha reflect Ayurveda's ability to create targeted yet balanced remedies. By combining ingredients with complementary actions, these decoctions address complex health conditions while minimizing the risk of side effects. Unlike powders, Kwatha formulations extract both water-soluble and heat-activated compounds, ensuring broader therapeutic action. Ayurveda's principle of addressing dosha imbalances holistically aligns with this preparation method. The slow extraction process also preserves the medicinal potency of herbs, reflecting Ayurveda's emphasis on precision and harmony. This highlights the adaptability of Ayurvedic techniques in treating diverse and acute conditions.

5. **A:** Bhavana is a transformational process where herbal liquids are repeatedly ground with raw materials, imbuing them with enhanced potency. This process is not merely mechanical but deeply chemical and energetic, ensuring the integration of bioactive compounds. The repeated grinding allows the substance to become more bioavailable, aligning with the body's natural rhythms. By using specific herbal juices, Bhavana targets particular doshas or disease states, showcasing Ayurveda's personalized approach. This process is a testament to Ayurveda's foresight in integrating pharmacodynamics with holistic healing, creating formulations that work harmoniously with the individual's constitution.

6. **B:** Grinding (Mardana) enhances the therapeutic action of substances by reducing their particle size, increasing the surface area available for interaction with biological systems. Ayurveda emphasizes precision in particle size as it influences absorption and bioavailability. This technique is essential in creating formulations like Churna, ensuring consistency in dosage and efficacy. Unlike modern approaches, Ayurveda views grinding as a process that preserves the energetic integrity of the material, aligning it with therapeutic goals. This practice reflects an understanding of pharmacodynamics long before its formalization in modern science, emphasizing the depth of Ayurvedic knowledge.

7. **A:** Sealing containers during fermentation (Bandhana) reflects Ayurveda's meticulous approach to preserving therapeutic efficacy. By creating an airtight environment, the natural fermentation process is allowed to proceed uninterrupted, enhancing the biochemical transformation of the formulation. This ensures stability, potency, and safety, as exposure to air could lead to contamination or oxidation. For formulations like Asava and Arishta, Bandhana is crucial for maintaining their therapeutic integrity. This practice demonstrates Ayurveda's advanced understanding of preservation techniques, integrating natural processes with pharmacological goals. It reflects the foresight of ancient practitioners in creating long-lasting and effective medicines.

8. **B:** Sustainability is integral to Ayurvedic principles, as it aligns with the philosophy of harmony between humans and nature. Community-led agroforestry systems not only ensure the conservation of medicinal plants but also enhance their therapeutic potency by preserving their natural growing conditions. Ayurveda recognizes that the quality of raw materials directly impacts the efficacy of medicines, making sustainable practices essential. By integrating conservation with cultivation, Ayurveda addresses modern challenges of overharvesting and biodiversity loss. This approach exemplifies its adaptability, balancing ecological health with the growing global demand for Ayurvedic medicines.

9. **B:** Hygiene protocols in a Rasaśālā are foundational to the preparation of safe and effective medicines. Contaminated tools or raw materials can compromise the purity and therapeutic value of formulations, making cleanliness essential. Ayurveda's emphasis on hygiene extends beyond physical sterility to include energetic purity, reflecting its holistic approach. The meticulous cleaning of utensils, proper storage of raw materials, and controlled preparation environments ensure that formulations retain their intended potency. This demonstrates Ayurveda's advanced understanding of quality control, integrating spiritual and practical considerations to maintain the integrity of its medicines.

10. **C:** Traditional tools like stone mortars and grinding stones are preferred in Ayurveda for their ability to preserve the energetic and chemical integrity of raw materials. Unlike modern machinery, which can generate excessive heat and disrupt the molecular structure, traditional tools facilitate gentle processing.

Ayurveda views preparation techniques as integral to the therapeutic outcome, emphasizing the role of subtle energies in medicine. By using traditional methods, the integrity of the formulation is maintained, ensuring alignment with the body's natural processes. This reflects Ayurveda's holistic perspective, where every step of preparation is designed to enhance the medicine's efficacy.

11. **A:** The enhanced efficacy of Kwatha lies in its ability to extract and concentrate active principles through a controlled boiling process. Unlike cold or rapid methods, slow boiling ensures the breakdown of complex compounds while retaining essential medicinal properties. This method allows water-soluble and heat-sensitive compounds to synergize, addressing dosha imbalances effectively. Decoctions like Kwatha are tailored for acute conditions, offering rapid absorption and immediate action. The preparation process embodies Ayurveda's emphasis on precision, aligning the therapeutic properties of herbs with specific health conditions. It demonstrates how traditional methods combine effectiveness with safety for comprehensive healing.

12. **B:** Sustainable practices such as agroforestry align with Ayurveda's principles of ecological balance and preservation of medicinal potency. Haritaki, a key ingredient in Kwatha, faces overharvesting threats that reduce its availability and quality. Cultivation through community-led agroforestry preserves biodiversity, ensuring long-term supply and higher potency due to natural growing conditions. This strategy addresses both environmental and therapeutic challenges, embodying Ayurveda's holistic philosophy. By integrating conservation with cultivation, this approach highlights how Ayurvedic practices adapt to modern sustainability demands while maintaining efficacy and quality, ensuring that therapies remain accessible without compromising ecological health.

13. **A:** The therapeutic outcomes of formulations like Kwatha depend significantly on the quality of raw materials. Unsustainable harvesting and environmental degradation reduce the bioactive compound concentrations in herbs like Haritaki, directly impacting the efficacy of the final product. Ayurveda emphasizes the integrity of raw materials, as the effectiveness of treatment lies in their intrinsic properties. This demonstrates the interdependence of environmental health and human health, a foundational principle of Ayurveda. Sustainable sourcing not only preserves medicinal potency but also reflects Ayurveda's foresight in aligning ecological practices with therapeutic goals, ensuring both efficacy and environmental harmony.

14. **A:** Addressing sustainability and efficacy requires an integrated approach. Community-led cultivation ensures the consistent availability of high-quality raw materials, while optimizing preparation techniques like Kwatha maximizes therapeutic outcomes. Ayurveda's adaptability is evident in its ability to balance ecological needs with patient care, ensuring that remedies remain effective and accessible. This strategy demonstrates Ayurveda's resilience in addressing modern challenges without compromising traditional principles. By combining conservation efforts with precision in formulation, this approach underscores the holistic and forward-thinking nature of Ayurvedic medicine, providing a sustainable model for integrative healthcare.

15. **A:** The stages of Rasa Shastra—Shodhana, Bhavana, Pachana, and Mardana—represent a systematic approach to detoxification, transformation, and enhancement of medicinal properties. Shodhana removes impurities, Bhavana infuses therapeutic liquids into raw materials, Pachana extracts active principles, and Mardana increases surface area for better interaction with the body. These processes are interconnected, ensuring that every stage enhances the substance's safety, potency, and bioavailability. This reflects Ayurveda's meticulous integration of pharmacological science with spiritual principles, demonstrating its advanced understanding of material transformation and its alignment with therapeutic goals.

16. **A:** Panchavidha Kashaya Kalpana includes five fundamental forms of herbal preparation used in Ayurveda: Swarasa (fresh juice), Kalka (herbal paste), Kwatha (decoction), Hima (cold infusion), and Phanta (hot infusion). Asava, although an important Ayurvedic preparation, is not part of the Panchavidha Kalpana. It belongs to the category of fermented formulations. Hence, only options (a), (b), and (c) belong to this group, making A the correct choice.

17. **B:** Bhavana is a transformative process that enhances the potency and therapeutic efficacy of raw materials. By triturating substances with herbal liquids, active principles are infused into the material, increasing their bioavailability. This process is both chemical and energetic, ensuring that the formulation aligns with the body's natural rhythms. Unlike mechanical grinding, Bhavana integrates the properties of the herbal liquid into the raw material, making it more potent. This process reflects Ayurveda's understanding of pharmacodynamics and its ability to enhance the therapeutic value of substances through precise and

intentional preparation techniques.

18. A: Pachana involves the use of heat to extract and concentrate the active principles of herbs, creating stable and effective formulations. This method is particularly crucial in decoctions and oils, where slow boiling ensures the preservation of medicinal properties. By transforming raw materials through heat, Pachana aligns with Ayurveda's principles of balancing doshas and addressing specific conditions. The process also highlights the precision of Ayurveda in leveraging natural elements like heat to create formulations that are bioavailable and therapeutically potent, showcasing its integration of empirical knowledge with holistic healing.

19. C: Churna (powders), Vati (tablets), and Ghrita (medicated ghee) are common Ayurvedic dosage forms. Churna is used orally, Vati provides a standardized dose, and Ghrita can be used both internally and externally. However, Taila (medicated oil) is used not only externally but also internally in many therapies like Nasya, Abhyanga, or Panchakarma. Since option (c) states "for external applications only," it is inaccurate. Thus, the correct answer is C.

20. A: The advanced techniques in Rasa Shastra—Shodhana, Bhavana, and Marana—ensure that raw materials are transformed into safe and effective medicines. Shodhana detoxifies substances, Bhavana enhances their potency, and Marana creates bioavailable ash forms. These processes are guided by the principles of balance and precision, ensuring that each stage aligns with the therapeutic objectives. By integrating natural processes with empirical knowledge, Ayurveda demonstrates its foresight in creating medicines that are both potent and harmonious with the body's natural rhythms. This reflects its holistic and adaptive nature in addressing health challenges.

21. A: The principles governing Rasaśālā practices focus on maintaining a sacred environment, hygiene, and efficient pharmaceutical processes. Hygiene ensures the safety and efficacy of formulations by eliminating contaminants, while adherence to Vastu Shastra principles harmonizes the energy of the preparation space. The balance between traditional tools and modern science is integral to maintaining the authenticity of Ayurvedic medicines while improving precision and consistency. These principles reflect Ayurveda's holistic approach, emphasizing the interconnection between the environment, processes, and the therapeutic potency of medicines.

22. A: Bheshajya Kalpana is designed to optimize the therapeutic potential of raw materials through purification, transformation, and formulation. Techniques like Shodhana detoxify ingredients, while specific processing methods enhance potency and bioavailability. This process ensures medicines align with the body's doshic balance, addressing both symptoms and root causes. Ayurveda's emphasis on individual constitution highlights its personalized approach, where formulations are tailored to the patient's unique needs. The integration of ancient principles with modern practices demonstrates Ayurveda's adaptability in addressing contemporary health challenges while remaining rooted in tradition.

23. A: Fermented formulations like Asava and Arishta are unique to Ayurveda, utilizing natural fermentation to preserve active compounds and enhance bioavailability. These preparations are made using herbal decoctions, natural sugars, and controlled fermentation techniques. The process creates a self-generated alcohol base, which acts as a preservative and a medium for delivering active compounds. By avoiding heat-based methods, fermentation ensures that volatile and heat-sensitive compounds remain intact. This approach highlights Ayurveda's innovation in leveraging natural biochemical processes to create stable, potent, and effective therapeutic formulations.

24. C: Bandhana plays a critical role in ensuring the stability and integrity of Ayurvedic formulations during preparation and storage. Sealing containers prevents contamination, preserves the formulation's therapeutic properties, and allows biochemical transformations like fermentation to proceed uninterrupted. This practice reflects Ayurveda's advanced understanding of pharmaceutical stability and quality control. Proper sealing not only maintains the potency of medicines but also aligns with the broader principle of creating formulations that are both effective and durable. This demonstrates the meticulousness of Ayurveda in preserving the therapeutic potential of its medicines.

25. A: The processes of Rasa Shastra—Shodhana, Bhavana, Pachana, and Mardana—serve distinct yet interconnected purposes. Shodhana detoxifies raw materials, Bhavana enhances potency by integrating herbal liquids, Pachana extracts active compounds through heat, and Mardana increases the surface area of substances for better interaction with the body. Together, these steps transform raw materials into safe, potent, and bioavailable medicines. This sequence reflects Ayurveda's precision in aligning material properties with therapeutic goals, demonstrating its integration of empirical knowledge and holistic principles.

26. **A:** The classifications of Ayurvedic preparations—Churna, Vati, Taila, and Ghrita—highlight the system's versatility in addressing diverse therapeutic needs. Churna is a powdered form that offers ease of use, Vati ensures precise dosing, Taila is ideal for external application, and Ghrita serves both internal and external purposes. These forms reflect Ayurveda's commitment to personalized care, where the medium of the medicine is chosen based on the patient's condition, dosha imbalance, and disease state. This adaptability showcases Ayurveda's nuanced understanding of therapeutic delivery systems and its holistic approach to healing.

27. **A:** The structured layout of a Rasaśālā is designed to ensure the safe and efficient preparation of medicines. Each section—grinding, boiling, fermentation, and storage—has a specific role in the preparation process. The grinding section ensures uniform particle size, the boiling section extracts active principles, the fermentation section facilitates biochemical transformations, and the storage section preserves potency. This organization reflects Ayurveda's emphasis on precision and quality, ensuring that each step of the preparation process aligns with therapeutic goals. The systematic design of a Rasaśālā exemplifies Ayurveda's advanced understanding of pharmaceutical science.

28. **B:** Panchavidha Kashaya Kalpana forms the basis of Ayurvedic pharmaceutical techniques, with each method tailored to extract specific therapeutic properties. Swarasa provides concentrated juice extracts, Kalka delivers paste formulations, Kwatha extracts water-soluble compounds through boiling, and Hima preserves heat-sensitive compounds through cold infusion. These methods reflect Ayurveda's adaptability in creating formulations that address individual needs and specific dosha imbalances. By offering diverse preparation techniques, Panchavidha Kashaya Kalpana highlights Ayurveda's commitment to precision and personalization in healthcare, ensuring effective treatment for a wide range of conditions.

29. **A:** The purification techniques in Ayurveda—boiling, steaming, quenching, and filtration—are integral to ensuring the safety and efficacy of raw materials. Boiling detoxifies herbs and minerals, steaming softens materials for further processing, quenching neutralizes toxic properties through rapid cooling, and filtration removes physical impurities. These processes are meticulously designed to align with the pharmacological properties of the ingredients, ensuring they are safe for therapeutic use. This demonstrates Ayurveda's advanced understanding of material transformation and its commitment to creating potent, safe, and effective medicines that align with holistic healing principles.

30. **A:** The Ayurvedic concepts of Tridosha, Rasa, Agni, and Ama provide a comprehensive framework for understanding health and disease. Tridosha emphasizes the balance of Vata, Pitta, and Kapha for physical and mental well-being. Rasa connects taste with therapeutic action, Agni governs digestion and metabolism, and Ama signifies toxic buildup from incomplete digestion. These concepts integrate physiological, psychological, and biochemical dimensions, reflecting Ayurveda's holistic perspective. By addressing the root cause of disease through these principles, Ayurveda offers personalized and preventive care, ensuring long-term health and harmony in the individual.

31. **A:** The classification of fermented Ayurvedic preparations like Asava, Arishta, Kanji, and Takra highlights the system's understanding of natural biochemical processes. Asava and Arishta use herbal decoctions and jaggery for fermentation, preserving medicinal compounds and enhancing bioavailability. Kanji, made from rice water, and Takra, fermented buttermilk, serve specific therapeutic purposes, such as improving gut health and balancing doshas. These methods demonstrate Ayurveda's ability to harness fermentation for stable, effective formulations. The approach reflects Ayurveda's advanced understanding of preserving and enhancing therapeutic properties through natural processes, ensuring safety and efficacy.

32. **A:** The pharmacological properties—Rasa (taste), Virya (potency), Vipaka (post-digestive effect), and Prabhava (unique effect)—define the therapeutic action of Ayurvedic medicines. Rasa stimulates initial sensory and digestive responses, Virya determines the heating or cooling effects, Vipaka influences dosha-specific outcomes after digestion, and Prabhava introduces effects that cannot be explained by other properties. These interconnected principles reflect Ayurveda's sophisticated understanding of how medicines interact with the body. By balancing these properties, formulations address the root cause of disease, offering holistic and personalized treatment. This layered approach underscores Ayurveda's depth in pharmacology.

33. **A:** The preparation steps of Shodhana, Marana, Bhavana, and proper storage form a systematic approach to medicine-making in Ayurveda. Shodhana detoxifies raw materials, Marana transforms metals into bioavailable Bhasma, and Bhavana enhances potency through levigation with herbal liquids. Proper storage ensures the longevity and stability of medicines,

maintaining their therapeutic efficacy. This meticulous process reflects Ayurveda's integration of empirical knowledge and spiritual principles, ensuring that medicines are safe, potent, and tailored to individual needs. Each step demonstrates Ayurveda's holistic perspective on creating medicines that align with the body's natural rhythms.

34. A: The dosha characteristics of Vata, Pitta, and Kapha form the foundation of Ayurvedic physiology. Vata governs movement and nervous system regulation, Pitta controls metabolism and enzymatic activity, and Kapha provides structural stability and fluid balance. The balance of these doshas ensures physical and mental health, while their imbalance leads to disease. This framework offers a holistic approach to understanding the dynamic nature of health and disease. By focusing on dosha balance, Ayurveda emphasizes prevention, personalization, and long-term well-being, demonstrating its integrative and comprehensive approach to healthcare.

35. A: The process of Shodhana is vital in Rasa Shastra as it detoxifies raw materials and removes impurities, ensuring safety and therapeutic efficacy. Techniques such as boiling in herbal decoctions not only neutralize toxins but also enhance the bioavailability of substances. This reflects Ayurveda's advanced understanding of pharmacology, where detoxification and activation are simultaneous processes. By improving safety and therapeutic alignment, Shodhana ensures that raw materials are harmonized with the body's natural processes. This meticulous attention to detail demonstrates Ayurveda's foresight in creating potent and safe medicinal formulations.

36. A: Panchavidha Kashaya Kalpana forms the foundation of Ayurvedic pharmaceutical processes, offering five distinct methods—Swarasa, Kalka, Kwatha, Hima, and Phanta. Each method extracts specific therapeutic properties, catering to different conditions and dosha imbalances. These techniques showcase Ayurveda's precision and adaptability in creating personalized formulations. By tailoring the preparation method to the properties of herbs and the therapeutic needs of patients, Panchavidha Kashaya Kalpana exemplifies Ayurveda's integrative and holistic approach to health. This foundational framework ensures that every formulation aligns with the principles of balance and harmony.

37. C: Bhavana enhances the potency of raw materials through repeated grinding with herbal liquids, integrating active principles into the substance. This process chemically and energetically transforms the material, improving bioavailability and therapeutic efficacy. Unlike mechanical grinding, Bhavana is a transformative process that aligns the properties of the raw material with specific doshic needs. This nuanced technique reflects Ayurveda's advanced understanding of pharmacodynamics and its ability to enhance the therapeutic value of substances through precision and care. It showcases Ayurveda's integrative approach to medicine preparation.

38. C: Traditional tools like stone mortars and grinding stones are preferred in Ayurveda because they retain the energetic and chemical integrity of raw materials. Modern tools may generate excessive heat, potentially altering the molecular structure of substances and reducing their therapeutic potency. Ayurveda recognizes the subtle interactions between material properties and energetic alignment, ensuring that every preparation step enhances efficacy. By preserving traditional methods, Ayurveda maintains the holistic essence of its medicines, aligning physical and energetic dimensions to maximize healing potential. This reflects its integrative and foresighted approach to healthcare.

39. C: Multi-ingredient formulations like Kwatha and Taila prioritize synergy, addressing complex dosha imbalances through combined actions of multiple ingredients. Single-ingredient formulations may not provide the same breadth of therapeutic effects, particularly for multifaceted conditions. Ayurveda's holistic philosophy emphasizes the interconnection of body systems, making multi-herb combinations more effective in restoring balance. This approach highlights the depth of Bheshajya Kalpana, where synergy amplifies efficacy and minimizes side effects. The preference for complex formulations underscores Ayurveda's commitment to comprehensive and personalized healthcare solutions.

40. A: Marana is a critical process in Rasa Shastra, transforming metals and minerals into bioavailable Bhasma through incineration. This process neutralizes toxicity, ensuring the substance is safe for internal use. The ash form enhances absorption, aligning with the body's physiological processes. Marana exemplifies Ayurveda's meticulous attention to material transformation, combining detoxification with activation to create potent therapeutic agents. This step reflects the advanced pharmacological principles of Ayurveda, integrating empirical knowledge with holistic healing to produce medicines that are both safe and effective.

41. A: Hima preparations are cold infusions used for herbs sensitive to heat, ensuring the preservation of their volatile and heat-labile compounds. By steeping herbs in cold water, Hima extracts their active principles gently, making it ideal for conditions requiring cooling or soothing effects. The process ensures that the therapeutic properties of delicate herbs remain intact, aligning with doshic needs like calming aggravated Pitta. This method reflects Ayurveda's nuanced understanding of preparation techniques tailored to specific herbs and conditions. It exemplifies how ancient practices integrate precision and adaptability to create effective, safe, and personalized formulations.

42. A: Decoctions (Kwathas) are more effective than powders (Churna) for acute dosha imbalances because they provide a concentrated, water-based medium that allows for rapid absorption and systemic action. The preparation method ensures maximum extraction of active principles, particularly water-soluble compounds, making it suitable for urgent therapeutic needs. Decoctions also offer flexibility in dosage adjustments based on patient requirements. This reflects Ayurveda's focus on precision and efficacy, where preparation methods are chosen based on the condition's severity and the patient's constitution. The preference for Kwatha highlights Ayurveda's integrative approach to treating acute and complex health issues.

43. A: Hygiene and cleanliness are paramount in a Rasaśālā to ensure the safety, purity, and efficacy of formulations. Contaminated tools or raw materials can introduce impurities, compromising the therapeutic potential and safety of the medicines. Ayurveda emphasizes not only physical cleanliness but also energetic purity, ensuring the formulations align harmoniously with the body's natural rhythms. Proper cleaning and controlled preparation environments prevent cross-contamination and preserve the integrity of medicines. This meticulous approach demonstrates Ayurveda's advanced understanding of quality control, ensuring that formulations are both potent and safe for consumption.

44. A: Ayurvedic oils (Taila) are particularly effective in penetrating the skin due to their lipophilic nature, which allows them to carry active principles deep into tissues. This property is harnessed in external therapies to deliver therapeutic effects directly to affected areas. Oils are also excellent carriers for fat-soluble compounds, enhancing their bioavailability. The ability of oils to bypass certain barriers in the body reflects Ayurveda's understanding of pharmacokinetics and targeted delivery. This technique ensures that treatments are both localized and systemic, showcasing Ayurveda's precision in using natural substances for therapeutic purposes.

45. A: The principles of Bheshajya Kalpana—Rasa (taste), Virya (potency), Vipaka (post-digestive effect), and Prabhava (unique effect)—form the foundation of Ayurvedic pharmacology. These properties determine how a formulation interacts with the body, influencing its therapeutic action. Rasa stimulates sensory and digestive responses, Virya governs thermal effects, Vipaka impacts doshic balance after digestion, and Prabhava introduces unique, unexplained effects. Together, these principles ensure personalized treatment, aligning the medicine with the individual's constitution and disease state. This holistic framework reflects Ayurveda's depth in crafting medicines that address both symptoms and root causes.

46. A: The Panchavidha Kashaya Kalpana serves as a foundational framework for tailoring formulations to an individual's doshic constitution and therapeutic needs. Methods like Swarasa and Kwatha extract specific properties, ensuring that the medicine aligns with both the condition and the patient. This personalized approach reflects Ayurveda's holistic philosophy, emphasizing harmony between the individual and their treatment. By offering diverse preparation techniques, Panchavidha Kashaya Kalpana ensures versatility and adaptability in creating effective medicines. This highlights Ayurveda's precision in aligning preparation methods with therapeutic objectives, ensuring comprehensive care.

47. B: Shodhana and Marana are transformative processes that enhance the safety and efficacy of raw materials in Ayurvedic formulations. Shodhana removes impurities and detoxifies materials, while Marana incinerates metals and minerals, creating bioavailable Bhasma. These steps ensure that substances are safe for internal use, addressing potential toxicity while enhancing absorption and potency. This meticulous process reflects Ayurveda's foresight in aligning pharmacological principles with therapeutic goals. The integration of detoxification and activation showcases Ayurveda's holistic approach to medicine-making, ensuring that formulations are both safe and effective.

48. A: Bhavana is a transformative process that integrates herbal liquids into raw materials through repeated grinding, enhancing their potency and therapeutic value. This technique allows active principles to be absorbed into the material, making it more bioavailable and effective. Unlike simple mechanical grinding, Bhavana chemically and energetically alters the material, aligning it with specific doshic imbalances. This reflects Ayurveda's understanding of pharmacodynamics, where the preparation method significantly influences the medicine's efficacy. The process exemplifies Ayurveda's integration of empirical knowledge and spiritual principles, ensuring that formulations align with the body's natural rhythms.

49. A: Oils (Taila) and ghee (Ghrita) serve as carriers for fat-soluble compounds, facilitating their deep penetration into tissues. Their lipophilic nature makes them ideal for transporting active principles directly to target areas, enhancing bioavailability. Oils are particularly effective in external therapies, while ghee is used both internally and externally. This reflects Ayurveda's understanding of pharmacokinetics and its ability to tailor delivery systems to therapeutic needs. By leveraging the unique properties of these carriers, Ayurveda creates formulations that are both potent and versatile, addressing a wide range of health conditions with precision.

50. A: Modern science enhances Ayurvedic formulation processes by integrating standardization techniques to ensure consistency, safety, and efficacy. These advancements validate traditional principles like Rasa (taste) and Vipaka (post-digestive effect) through empirical research, bridging ancient wisdom with contemporary understanding. This integration ensures that Ayurvedic medicines meet global quality standards without compromising their traditional essence. By adopting modern tools and methodologies, Ayurveda expands its reach while preserving its holistic approach. This demonstrates Ayurveda's adaptability, ensuring that its formulations remain relevant and effective in the modern healthcare landscape.

CHAPTER 15

AYURVEDIC PHARMACOPOEIA AND DRUG STANDARDIZATION

The ancient science of Ayurveda has stood the test of time, offering holistic solutions to health and wellness through its unique approach to medicine. Ayurveda focuses on balancing the body, mind, and spirit through herbal medicines, diet, lifestyle modifications, and therapeutic techniques. At the heart of Ayurvedic medicine lies the Ayurvedic Pharmacopoeia of India (API), a comprehensive repository of standards and formulations that ensures the efficacy, safety, and consistency of Ayurvedic drugs.

As Ayurveda gains global recognition, the demand for standardization and quality control in Ayurvedic drugs has risen significantly. This chapter delves into the Ayurvedic Pharmacopoeia of India, the importance of standardization in Ayurvedic drugs, and the integration of modern approaches in ensuring the quality and safety of these time-tested formulations.

OVERVIEW OF THE AYURVEDIC PHARMACOPOEIA OF INDIA

Ayurveda, one of the oldest systems of traditional medicine, relies on a vast collection of medicinal formulations derived from natural sources. To ensure the reliability, safety, and therapeutic consistency of Ayurvedic drugs, India established the Ayurvedic Pharmacopoeia of India (API). This section explores its historical development, structure, content, and objectives, which collectively contribute to standardizing Ayurvedic medicine in the modern era.

Historical Development of the Ayurvedic Pharmacopoeia

The Ayurvedic Pharmacopoeia has its origins deeply embedded in the rich heritage of classical Ayurvedic texts such as the Charaka Samhita, Sushruta Samhita, and Ashtanga Hridaya. These ancient treatises provided comprehensive information on medicinal plants, mineral and metal-based therapies, and their applications in maintaining health and curing diseases.

Ancient Texts as Foundations

1. **Charaka Samhita**
   - Focused primarily on internal medicine (Kaya Chikitsa)..
   - Described over 600 medicinal plants and their uses.
   - Introduced formulations like decoctions (Kwathas) and medicated ghee (Ghritas).
2. **Sushruta Samhita**
   - Specialized in surgery (Shalya Tantra).
   - Documented external applications and herbal treatments for wound healing.
   - Included detailed accounts of mineral and metal-based drugs.
3. **Ashtanga Hridaya**
   - Synthesized teachings from earlier texts.
   - Emphasized Rasayana (rejuvenative therapy) and its formulations.

These foundational texts formed the basis for identifying medicinal plants, understanding their properties (Rasa, Guna, Virya, Vipaka, and Prabhava), and creating formulations tailored to individual patient needs.

Regional Variations and Knowledge Accumulation

As Ayurveda spread across the Indian subcontinent, regional variations emerged, enriching the collective knowledge of medicinal plants and formulations. Local medicinal practices incorporated unique flora and fauna, adding depth to the Ayurvedic system. However, this diversity also created inconsistencies in practices, necessitating standardization.

Colonial and Post-Independence Periods

During British rule, Ayurveda faced challenges due to the dominance of allopathic medicine. However, efforts to document and preserve traditional knowledge persisted through practitioners and regional manuscripts.

Post-independence, the Government of India prioritized the revival and formalization of traditional medicine systems. This led to the establishment of:

- The Central Council for Research in Ayurvedic Sciences (CCRAS).
- Pharmacopoeial Laboratory for Indian Medicine (PLIM).
- Ayurvedic Pharmacopoeia Committee (APC) in 1962.

Publication of the Ayurvedic Pharmacopoeia

The first volume of the API was published in 1978. Over time, it has expanded to include multiple volumes and supplements. These cover monographs of single drugs, compound formulations, and testing protocols, reflecting advancements in pharmacological research and regulatory requirements.

Structure and Content of the Ayurvedic Pharmacopoeia of India

The Ayurvedic Pharmacopoeia of India is meticulously structured to ensure it meets both traditional practices and modern scientific standards. It is divided into two main sections: the Formulary Section and the Standards Section.

Formulary Section

This section encompasses detailed descriptions of classical formulations that have been used for centuries in Ayurvedic practice.

1. **Types of Formulations:**
   - **Churna (Powders):** Herbal powders prepared by grinding dried plant materials. Examples: Triphala Churna.
   - **Kwatha (Decoctions):** Water-based extractions obtained by boiling herbs. Examples: Dashmool Kwatha.
   - **Taila (Medicated Oils):** Oils infused with herbal extracts for external and internal use. Examples: Ashwagandha Taila.
   - **Rasayana (Rejuvenators):** Formulations aimed at restoring vitality and longevity. Examples: Chyawanprash.
2. **Preparation Guidelines**: The formulary specifies:
   - Ingredients and their proportions.
   - Methods of preparation.
   - Dosage and therapeutic indications.

Standards Section

The section provides comprehensive monographs on individual ingredients, including plants, minerals, and animal-derived substances.

1. **Botanical Identity and Nomenclature**
   - Scientific name and family.
   - Synonyms in regional languages.
2. **Organoleptic Properties:** Sensory characteristics such as color, taste, smell, and texture.
3. **Phytochemical Analysis**
   - Identification of active constituents (e.g., alkaloids, flavonoids, tannins).
   - Methods for qualitative and quantitative analysis.
4. **Pharmacological Activities:** Documented therapeutic actions such as anti-inflammatory, antioxidant, or adaptogenic properties.
5. **Analytical Standards:** Physical parameters: Ash content, moisture content, and fiber content:
   - **Microbial load:** Ensuring the absence of harmful microorganisms.
   - **Heavy metal limits:** Permissible levels of lead, mercury, and arsenic.
6. **Toxicological Studies**
   - Assessment of acute, sub-acute, and chronic toxicity.
   - Guidelines for safe usage and contraindications.

Objectives of the Ayurvedic Pharmacopoeia

The Ayurvedic Pharmacopoeia is designed to fulfill several critical objectives, ensuring the continued relevance and reliability of Ayurvedic medicine in modern healthcare systems.

Standardized Framework for Ayurvedic Drugs

The API provides a standardized framework for the identification, preparation, and quality control of Ayurvedic drugs.

It ensures consistency across manufacturers, preventing variations that may compromise efficacy.

Ensuring Safety and Efficacy

By incorporating stringent quality control measures, the API aims to eliminate risks associated with contaminants, adulteration, and improper usage.

It establishes therapeutic dosages and safety protocols, minimizing adverse effects.

Promoting Scientific Validation

The API bridges traditional knowledge and modern science by including evidence-based studies and analytical methodologies.

It encourages further research into Ayurvedic formulations and their mechanisms of action.

Facilitating Global Acceptance

Standardization aligns Ayurvedic practices with international regulatory norms, enhancing the credibility and export potential of Ayurvedic medicines.

By meeting global quality standards, Ayurveda can gain wider acceptance in integrative medicine systems worldwide.

Supporting the AYUSH Mission

The API is integral to the Ministry of AYUSH's mission to promote traditional medicine and ensure its integration into national healthcare policies.

It contributes to the sustainable use of natural resources, emphasizing conservation and ethical sourcing of raw materials.

IMPORTANCE OF STANDARDIZATION AND QUALITY CONTROL IN AYURVEDIC DRUGS

Ensuring Therapeutic Consistency

Ayurvedic drugs are derived from natural sources, making them subject to variations in quality due to environmental factors, seasonal changes, and harvesting practices. Standardization ensures that these variations do not affect the therapeutic efficacy of the drugs.

Enhancing Safety and Efficacy

Without proper quality control measures, Ayurvedic drugs may contain contaminants such as heavy metals, pesticides, or microbial loads, which can compromise their safety. Standardization involves stringent testing to eliminate these risks and enhance the efficacy of the medicines.

Building Consumer Trust

In a market flooded with spurious and substandard Ayurvedic products, standardization serves as a hallmark of quality. It builds consumer confidence and promotes the credibility of Ayurveda as a reliable system of medicine.

Supporting Regulatory Compliance

In India and abroad, regulatory bodies require Ayurvedic products to meet specific quality standards. Standardization helps manufacturers comply with these regulations, thereby facilitating the global trade of Ayurvedic medicines.

MODERN APPROACHES TO DRUG STANDARDIZATION AND QUALITY ASSURANCE

As Ayurveda gains global acceptance, there is an increasing demand for standardized practices and scientifically validated methodologies to ensure the safety, efficacy, and quality of Ayurvedic medicines. Modern approaches to drug standardization and quality assurance bridge the gap between traditional knowledge and contemporary science, ensuring that Ayurvedic drugs meet the highest quality standards. This section explores advanced analytical techniques, botanical identification methods, pharmacological studies, stability testing, and adherence to Good Manufacturing Practices (GMP) as essential pillars of modern standardization.

Integration of Analytical Techniques

The integration of analytical techniques into Ayurvedic drug standardization has transformed the field, enabling precise identification and quantification of bioactive compounds, detecting contaminants, and ensuring consistency in formulations. These techniques are indispensable for modern quality control practices.

Chromatography

Chromatography techniques are essential for separating and analyzing complex mixtures in herbal drugs. They are widely used for the identification, quantification, and purification of active constituents.

1. **High-Performance Liquid Chromatography (HPLC):**
    - HPLC separates compounds based on their interactions with a stationary phase and a mobile phase.
    - It is used to identify phytochemicals like alkaloids, flavonoids, and phenolic compounds in Ayurvedic formulations.

    Example: Standardization of curcumin content in Curcuma longa (Turmeric).

2. **Gas Chromatography (GC)**
   - GC is primarily used for analyzing volatile compounds like essential oils.
   - It is employed in the quality control of formulations containing aromatic components.

   Example: Quantification of volatile oils in Mentha piperita (Peppermint).

Spectroscopy

Spectroscopic techniques provide detailed insights into the molecular structure and purity of compounds in herbal drugs.

1. **UV-Vis Spectroscopy**
   - Measures the absorption of ultraviolet and visible light by a compound.
   - Useful for determining concentrations of specific phytochemicals in a formulation.

   Example: Quantification of berberine in Berberis aristata.

2. **Infrared (IR) Spectroscopy**
   - Identifies functional groups and chemical bonds in compounds.
   - Helps verify the purity of raw materials and detect adulteration.

   Example: Authenticating the presence of saponins in Asparagus racemosus (Shatavari).

3. **Nuclear Magnetic Resonance (NMR) Spectroscopy**
   - Provides detailed information about molecular structure.
   - Used to elucidate the structure of complex bioactive compounds.

   Example: Structural analysis of withanolides in Withania somnifera (Ashwagandha).

4. **Mass Spectrometry (MS)**
   - Mass spectrometry is a powerful tool for molecular characterization and detecting contaminants in Ayurvedic drugs.
   - Used for identifying unknown compounds, determining molecular weight, and detecting trace levels of impurities.

   Example: Identification of adulterants in herbal formulations and quantification of heavy metals.

DNA Barcoding for Botanical Identification

Ensuring the authenticity of raw materials is a critical step in Ayurvedic drug standardization. DNA barcoding has emerged as a reliable technique for accurate botanical identification.

Principles of DNA Barcoding

DNA barcoding involves sequencing short, standardized regions of DNA to identify plant species. It is particularly useful for distinguishing closely related species or detecting adulteration.

Applications in Ayurveda

1. **Preventing Adulteration:** Raw materials in Ayurveda are often misidentified or substituted with incorrect species. DNA barcoding ensures the correct plant species is used.

   Example: Differentiating Asparagus racemosus (Shatavari) from related species.

2. **Authenticating Market Samples:** DNA barcoding verifies the authenticity of plant-derived ingredients in formulations sold in the market.

   Example: Identifying adulterants in Triphala powder.

3. **Conservation of Medicinal Plants:** Helps in the identification and protection of endangered medicinal plant species.

4. **Pharmacological Studies:** Pharmacological studies are essential for validating the therapeutic claims of Ayurvedic drugs and ensuring their safety and efficacy. These studies involve a combination of in vitro, in vivo, and clinical trials.

5. **In Vitro Studies**
   - Conducted on cultured cells to evaluate the biological activity of compounds.
   - Useful for understanding mechanisms of action, such as anti-inflammatory or antioxidant properties.

   Example: Testing the anti-cancer activity of phytochemicals in Tinospora cordifolia.

6. **In Vivo Studies**
   - Experiments conducted on animal models to evaluate the efficacy and safety of formulations.
   - Provide insights into dosage, toxicity, and pharmacokinetics.

   Example: Studying the hepatoprotective effects of Phyllanthus niruri in rat models.

   Clinical Trials
   - Rigorous testing on human participants to confirm therapeutic benefits.

   Comprise three phases:
   - **Phase I:** Assess safety and dosage in healthy volunteers.
   - **Phase II:** Evaluate efficacy in a small group of patients.
   - **Phase III:** Large-scale trials to confirm effectiveness and monitor side effects.

   Example: Clinical trials on Ashwagandha for its adaptogenic and stress-relieving effects.

Stability Testing

Stability testing ensures that Ayurvedic drugs remain effective, safe, and stable over their shelf life. This involves evaluating how environmental factors such as temperature, humidity, and light affect the quality of formulations.

Parameters Assessed in Stability Testing

1. **Physical Stability**
   - Changes in color, odor, texture, or consistency.

   Example: Monitoring the stability of oils like Brahmi Taila under varying temperatures.
2. **Chemical Stability**: Degradation of active compounds.

   Example: Assessing curcuminoid stability in turmeric formulations.
3. **Microbial Stability:** Prevention of microbial growth over time.

   Example: Ensuring microbial limits in Chyawanprash meet regulatory standards.
4. **Storage Conditions and Shelf Life**: Stability testing helps determine optimal storage conditions and expiry dates for Ayurvedic products.

   Example: Recommending airtight containers and cool storage for herbal powders.

Good Manufacturing Practices (GMP)

Adherence to Good Manufacturing Practices (GMP) is critical for ensuring the consistent quality of Ayurvedic medicines. GMP encompasses a wide range of practices related to manufacturing, packaging, and quality control.

Key Principles of GMP

1. **Hygienic Manufacturing Facilities:** Maintaining cleanliness and minimizing contamination.

   Example: Isolating production areas for raw materials and finished products.
2. **Trained Personnel:** Employing qualified and trained staff for manufacturing processes.

   Example: Training workers on GMP guidelines and equipment handling.
3. **Quality Control Processes:** Conducting regular testing of raw materials, intermediate products, and finished formulations.

   Example: Testing Ashwagandha root powder for active compounds like withanolides.
4. **Proper Documentation and Traceability:** Maintaining detailed records of manufacturing processes, quality tests, and distribution.

   Example: Documenting batch numbers for Chyawanprash production for traceability.
5. **Regulatory Compliance**: GMP ensures compliance with national and international regulations, facilitating the export of Ayurvedic medicines.

   Example: Adhering to WHO guidelines for GMP in herbal medicine production.

CHALLENGES IN AYURVEDIC DRUG STANDARDIZATION

1. **Diversity of Raw Materials:** Ayurveda relies on a wide variety of herbs, minerals, and animal-derived substances. Variations in their quality, due to environmental or regional factors, pose a significant challenge to standardization.
2. **Lack of Scientific Validation:** While traditional Ayurvedic texts provide detailed descriptions of drug formulations, many lack scientific validation through modern research. Bridging this gap requires extensive pharmacological and clinical studies.
3. **Limited Infrastructure:** Standardization demands sophisticated laboratories, skilled personnel, and advanced analytical instruments. Many Ayurvedic manufacturers, particularly small-scale enterprises, lack access to such infrastructure.
4. **Global Regulatory Hurdles:** Countries outside India often impose stringent regulations on the import and sale of Ayurvedic medicines. Meeting these diverse regulatory requirements can be challenging for manufacturers.

THE WAY FORWARD

1. **Strengthening Research and Development:** Investments in R&D can lead to the discovery of new bioactive compounds, improved formulations, and better standardization techniques. Collaborative efforts between traditional practitioners and modern scientists can further enrich Ayurvedic Pharmacopoeia.
2. **Encouraging Public-Private Partnerships:** Public-private partnerships can provide the necessary resources and expertise to overcome infrastructure and funding challenges.
3. **Promoting Awareness and Training:** Workshops and training programs for Ayurvedic practitioners, manufacturers, and regulators can enhance their understanding of quality control and standardization.
4. **Leveraging Technology:** Emerging technologies such as artificial intelligence (AI) and machine learning (ML) can be harnessed for predictive analysis, quality control, and process optimization in Ayurvedic drug manufacturing.

MULTIPLE CHOICE QUESTIONS

1. A clinical pharmacologist is evaluating the role of the Ayurvedic Pharmacopoeia of India (API) in ensuring drug safety. The research focuses on the efficacy of classical formulations such as Churna and Kwatha in treating metabolic disorders. The study involves identifying bioactive compounds and verifying their effects through High-Performance Liquid Chromatography (HPLC) and spectroscopic analysis. Which of the following outcomes aligns with the integration of traditional Ayurvedic principles with modern analytical techniques?
   A. Ayurvedic formulations exhibit consistent therapeutic benefits across all metabolic conditions due to universal bioactive profiles.
   B. The API ensures the safety and efficacy of Ayurvedic drugs by standardizing their phytochemical composition.
   C. Churna and Kwatha lack scientific evidence, making their efficacy unverifiable by modern analytical methods.
   D. Modern techniques confirm that traditional Ayurvedic principles lack relevance in contemporary pharmacological applications.

2. A pharmaceutical company is exploring modern approaches to Ayurvedic drug standardization. The team evaluates herbal extracts for their phytochemical consistency and heavy metal content. The company employs DNA barcoding to authenticate the raw materials used in its formulations. What conclusion best represents the implications of such a study?
   A. DNA barcoding is irrelevant to Ayurvedic formulations due to their reliance on traditional knowledge.
   B. Standardization processes enhance consumer trust and ensure the global acceptance of Ayurvedic products.
   C. Ayurvedic drugs are inherently safe and do not require external validation methods like DNA barcoding.
   D. Heavy metal contamination is an acceptable risk in Ayurvedic formulations due to their historical efficacy.

3. A government panel is assessing the role of the Ayurvedic Pharmacopoeia in combating the adulteration of herbal medicines. The focus is on enforcing guidelines for the identification and quality control of medicinal plants. What measure would most effectively address this issue?
   A. Prohibiting the commercial production of Ayurvedic formulations to preserve their authenticity.
   B. Relying solely on traditional practitioners for herbal identification.
   C. Implementing stringent analytical standards for raw materials and finished products.
   D. Allowing regional variations in formulations to encourage innovation.

4. A research team studies the stability of Ayurvedic drugs by exposing formulations to various environmental conditions. The findings reveal that prolonged exposure to high humidity degrades bioactive compounds. Which step should manufacturers take to preserve drug efficacy?
   A. Discontinue the production of formulations vulnerable to environmental factors.
   B. Include synthetic stabilizers in Ayurvedic formulations to enhance shelf life.
   C. Optimize packaging materials to minimize environmental exposure.
   D. Reduce the use of bioactive compounds that are sensitive to humidity.

5. A botanist is tasked with cataloging medicinal plants included in the Ayurvedic Pharmacopoeia. The study reveals discrepancies in the nomenclature of certain herbs across regional practices. How should this issue be addressed to ensure consistency in Ayurvedic drug formulations?
   A. Adopt a single global standard for plant nomenclature based on modern taxonomic principles.
   B. Preserve regional nomenclatures to respect cultural diversity and heritage.
   C. Limit the Pharmacopoeia to herbs with uniform nomenclature across all regions.
   D. Allow regional interpretations of plant nomenclature to promote innovation in formulations.

6. An Ayurvedic practitioner collaborates with a molecular biologist to investigate the concept of Tridosha using genomic tools. The study focuses on identifying genetic markers associated with Vata, Pitta, and Kapha imbalances. The findings suggest correlations between genetic variations and doshic predispositions. What is the significance of this study?
   A. It reaffirms the purely symbolic nature of the Tridosha concept.
   B. It bridges traditional Ayurvedic knowledge with personalized medicine approaches.

C. It invalidates the Tridosha theory by associating it with genetic determinism.
D. It demonstrates the irrelevance of genetic tools in understanding Ayurvedic principles.

7. A multinational company is developing Ayurvedic formulations for global markets. To meet international standards, the company focuses on eliminating microbial contamination and heavy metal residues. What challenges are most likely to arise in this process?
A. Ayurvedic drugs may lose their therapeutic properties when subjected to rigorous standardization.
B. Global regulatory standards conflict with the principles of traditional Ayurveda.
C. Eliminating contaminants requires abandoning traditional manufacturing processes.
D. Microbial contamination is inherent in Ayurveda and cannot be addressed scientifically.

8. A pharmaceutical researcher evaluates the efficacy of Rasayana formulations using clinical trials. The study finds that formulations enhance immunomodulatory responses in elderly patients. What aspect of the Ayurvedic Pharmacopoeia ensures the reliability of these findings?
A. Its reliance on ancient texts without modern scientific validation.
B. Its focus on standardizing manufacturing processes and analytical methods.
C. Its exclusion of formulations with immunomodulatory properties.
D. Its rejection of modern scientific methodologies.

9. A manufacturing company analyzes the pharmacological activities of Amalaki (Emblica officinalis) using in vitro and in vivo methods. The study concludes that Amalaki enhances gut health by increasing probiotic bacterial populations. Which regulatory consideration should the company prioritize?
A. Emphasizing cultural significance over scientific validation.
B. Relying solely on historical evidence for regulatory approval.
C. Demonstrating safety and efficacy through pharmacological studies.
D. Avoiding scientific validation to preserve the traditional appeal of Ayurveda.

10. A global healthcare conference discusses the role of the Ayurvédic Pharmacopoeia in addressing the rising demand for integrative medicine. Experts debate the challenges of aligning Ayurvedic formulations with evidence-based medicine. What conclusion would best reflect the integration of Ayurveda into modern healthcare systems?
A. Ayurveda should remain an independent practice, free from the influence of modern scientific methods.
B. Standardization and validation of Ayurvedic drugs enhance their acceptance in integrative medicine.
C. The integration of Ayurveda into modern systems dilutes its philosophical foundations.
D. Modern healthcare should adopt Ayurvedic principles without requiring scientific validation.

Directions (Q. No. 11–14): *Scenarios-Based Questions*

SCENARIO 1

A research team evaluates the impact of Ayurvedic detoxification therapies, such as Panchakarma, on liver function. The findings indicate significant reductions in markers of liver inflammation and improved antioxidant activity.

SCENARIO 2

A policy analyst studies the environmental impact of sourcing herbs for Panchakarma therapies, revealing overharvesting of endangered plants like Kutki (Picrorhiza kurroa) due to rising global demand.

11. Based on Scenario 1, which mechanism best explains the observed improvement in liver function?
A. Panchakarma reduces gut microbiota diversity, indirectly benefiting the liver.
B. Antioxidant activity is enhanced by herbal formulations used in Panchakarma therapies.
C. Liver health improves solely due to dietary changes, unrelated to Panchakarma.
D. Panchakarma eliminates essential minerals, reducing oxidative stress.

12. Considering Scenario 2, what strategy would most effectively address the overharvesting of Kutki?
A. Promoting synthetic substitutes for Kutki in Panchakarma therapies.
B. Encouraging sustainable cultivation and fair-trade practices for Kutki.
C. Limiting the use of Kutki to traditional Ayurvedic practitioners.
D. Reducing the global popularity of Ayurvedic therapies.

13. How does the environmental impact described in Scenario 2 potentially influence the therapeutic outcomes in Scenario 1?
A. Overharvesting reduces the bioactivity of herbs used in Panchakarma, diminishing their effectiveness.
B. The environmental impact has no measurable effect on therapeutic outcomes.

C. Panchakarma therapies depend entirely on modern supplements, unaffected by herbal bioactivity.
D. Kutki's quality improves under stress, enhancing therapeutic benefits.

14. What strategy would address both the therapeutic challenges in Scenario 1 and the environmental concerns in Scenario 2?
A. Establishing global standards for sustainable herb sourcing and Ayurvedic therapies.
B. Shifting focus to alternative detoxification methods unrelated to herbal formulations.
C. Prioritizing the cultivation of non-medicinal plants over Kutki.
D. Promoting synthetic alternatives for all Panchakarma formulations.

15. The Ayurvedic principles of Agni and its role in digestion and metabolism can be understood through the following observations:
(a) Agni governs the transformation of food into energy and tissues.
(b) Impaired Agni leads to the formation of Ama (toxins) in the body.
(c) Ayurvedic treatments like Deepana and Pachana help restore Agni balance.
(d) Agni regulation directly influences overall health and immunity.

Choose the correct answer from the options given below:
A. (a), (b), and (c) only
B. (a), (b), (c), and (d) only
C. (a) and (b) only
D. (b), (c), and (d) only

16. The Ayurvedic Pharmacopoeia establishes analytical standards for drug safety and efficacy through the following components:
(a) Phytochemical analysis to identify bioactive compounds.
(b) Heavy metal and microbial contamination limits.
(c) DNA barcoding for authenticating raw materials.
(d) Clinical trials for validating therapeutic benefits.

Choose the correct answer from the options given below:
A. (a), (b), and (c) only
B. (a), (c), and (d) only
C. (a), (b), (c), and (d) only
D. (b) and (d) only

17. Stability testing of Ayurvedic formulations assesses the following parameters:
(a) Chemical stability to monitor degradation of bioactive compounds.
(b) Microbial stability to ensure absence of harmful organisms.
(c) Physical stability to evaluate color, odor, and texture changes.
(d) Pharmacokinetic studies to analyze absorption rates.

Choose the correct answer from the options given below:
A. (a), (b), and (c) only
B. (b), (c), and (d) only
C. (a), (c), and (d) only
D. (a), (b), (c), and (d) only

18. Good Manufacturing Practices (GMP) for Ayurvedic drugs involve:
(a) Hygienic production facilities to minimize contamination.
(b) Trained personnel for quality assurance.
(c) Batch traceability to ensure drug consistency.
(d) Elimination of traditional preparation methods to comply with modern standards.

Choose the correct answer from the options given below:
A. (a), (b), and (c) only
B. (a), (b), and (d) only
C. (b), (c), and (d) only
D. (a), (c), and (d) only

19. Modern analytical techniques used in Ayurvedic drug standardization include:
(a) High-Performance Liquid Chromatography (HPLC) for compound quantification.
(b) DNA barcoding for species authentication.
(c) Mass spectrometry for contaminant detection.
(d) Randomized field trials for efficacy validation.

Choose the correct answer from the options given below:
A. (a), (b), and (c) only
B. (b), (c), and (d) only
C. (a), (c), and (d) only
D. (a), (b), (c), and (d) only

20. The Ayurvedic concept of Rasayana therapy emphasizes:
(a) Rejuvenation and longevity through specific formulations.
(b) Enhancing immunity and mental clarity.
(c) Detoxifying the body at the cellular level.
(d) Promoting rapid weight loss as a primary objective.

Choose the correct answer from the options given below:
A. (a), (b), and (c) only
B. (b), (c), and (d) only
C. (a) and (b) only
D. (a), (b), (c), and (d) only

21. DNA barcoding in Ayurvedic drug development offers the following advantages:
(a) Prevents adulteration and ensures raw material authenticity.
(b) Identifies endangered species for conservation.
(c) Establishes traditional methods of plant identification.
(d) Verifies the efficacy of Ayurvedic formulations.

Choose the correct answer from the options given below:
A. (a), (b), and (d) only
B. (a), (c), and (d) only
C. (a), (b), and (c) only
D. (b), (c), and (d) only

22. Pharmacological studies of Ayurvedic drugs evaluate:
(a) In vitro mechanisms such as enzymatic activity.
(b) In vivo effects on animal models.
(c) Clinical efficacy through human trials.
(d) Toxicological profiles for safety assurance.

Choose the correct answer from the options given below:
A. (a), (b), and (c) only
B. (a), (b), (c), and (d) only
C. (b) and (d) only
D. (a) and (d) only

23. Standardization in Ayurvedic formulations requires:
(a) Analytical tools to quantify bioactive compounds.
(b) Adherence to Good Manufacturing Practices (GMP).
(c) Genetic engineering to enhance plant efficacy.
(d) Stability testing to determine shelf life.

Choose the correct answer from the options given below:
A. (a), (b), and (d) only
B. (a), (b), and (c) only
C. (b) and (d) only
D. (a), (c), and (d) only

24. The Ayurvedic Pharmacopoeia of India focuses on:
(a) Documentation of classical formulations.
(b) Analytical standards for herbal identification.
(c) Integrating synthetic drugs into Ayurveda.
(d) Establishing ethical guidelines for clinical trials.

Choose the correct answer from the options given below:
A. (a), (b), and (d) only
B. (a), (c), and (d) only
C. (a), (b), and (c) only
D. (b), (c), and (d) only

25. Match List–I (Pharmacopoeial Standards) with List–II (Descriptions):

List–I	List–II
(a) Macroscopic Analysis	1. Identifying external physical features of raw materials
(b) Microscopic Analysis	2. Studying internal structures and cellular details
(c) Phytochemical Testing	3. Detecting bioactive compounds in drugs
(d) Chromatographic Techniques	4. Separating and analyzing chemical mixtures

Choose the correct answer from the options given below:
A. (a)-1, (b)-2, (c)-3, (d)-4
B. (a)-2, (b)-1, (c)-4, (d)-3
C. (a)-3, (b)-4, (c)-1, (d)-2
D. (a)-4, (b)-3, (c)-2, (d)-1

26. Match List–I (Quality Control Measures) with List–II (Techniques):

List–I	List–II
(a) Identity Tests	1. Confirming botanical authenticity
(b) Purity Tests	2. Checking for contaminants and foreign matter
(c) Potency Tests	3. Measuring active ingredient concentration
(d) Stability Tests	4. Assessing shelf-life and degradation

Choose the correct answer from the options given below:
A. (a)-1, (b)-2, (c)-3, (d)-4
B. (a)-2, (b)-1, (c)-4, (d)-3
C. (a)-3, (b)-4, (c)-1, (d)-2
D. (a)-4, (b)-3, (c)-2, (d)-1

27. Match List–I (Standardization Aspects) with List–II (Descriptions):

List–I	List–II
(a) Organoleptic Properties	1. Characteristics like color, odor, and taste
(b) Physicochemical Parameters	2. Moisture content, ash value, etc.
(c) Microbial Limits	3. Ensuring absence of harmful microbes
(d) Heavy Metal Testing	4. Detecting arsenic, mercury, lead levels

Choose the correct answer from the options given below:
A. (a)-1, (b)-2, (c)-3, (d)-4
B. (a)-2, (b)-1, (c)-4, (d)-3
C. (a)-3, (b)-4, (c)-1, (d)-2
D. (a)-4, (b)-3, (c)-2, (d)-1

28. Match List–I (Modern Standardization Techniques) with List–II (Descriptions):

List–I	List–II
(a) HPLC Analysis	1. High-precision chemical profiling
(b) DNA Barcoding	2. Genetic authentication of plant species
(c) NMR Spectroscopy	3. Determining molecular structure
(d) Mass Spectrometry	4. Identifying molecular weights of compounds

Choose the answer from the options given below:

A. (a)-1, (b)-2, (c)-3, (d)-4
B. (a)-2, (b)-1, (c)-4, (d)-3
C. (a)-3, (b)-4, (c)-1, (d)-2
D. (a)-4, (b)-3, (c)-2, (d)-1

29. Match List–I (Ayurvedic Drug Forms) with List–II (Descriptions):

List–I	List–II
(a) Churna	1. Powdered form of herbs
(b) Vati	2. Compressed tablets or pills
(c) Kwath	3. Decoctions prepared by boiling herbs
(d) Asava-Arishta	4. Fermented liquid formulations

Choose the answer from the options given below:

A. (a)-1, (b)-2, (c)-3, (d)-4
B. (a)-2, (b)-1, (c)-4, (d)-3
C. (a)-3, (b)-4, (c)-1, (d)-2
D. (a)-4, (b)-3, (c)-2, (d)-1

30. Match List–I (Quality Assurance Principles) with List–II (Descriptions):

List–I	List–II
(a) GMP Guidelines	1. Ensuring consistent production practices
(b) SOP Development	2. Standardizing operational protocols
(c) Validation	3. Confirming reproducibility of processes
(d) Documentation	4. Maintaining detailed records of procedures

Choose the answer from the options given below:

A. (a)-1, (b)-2, (c)-3, (d)-4
B. (a)-2, (b)-1, (c)-4, (d)-3
C. (a)-3, (b)-4, (c)-1, (d)-2
D. (a)-4, (b)-3, (c)-2, (d)-1

31. Match List–I (Phases of Drug Standardization) with List–II (Details):

List–I	List–II
(a) Raw Material Testing	1. Ensuring the quality of starting materials
(b) In-Process Quality Control	2. Monitoring intermediate stages of production
(c) Finished Product Quality Control	3. Verifying product meets specifications
(d) Post-Market Surveillance	4. Tracking safety and efficacy after distribution

Choose the answer from the options given below:

A. (a)-1, (b)-2, (c)-3, (d)-4
B. (a)-2, (b)-1, (c)-4, (d)-3
C. (a)-3, (b)-4, (c)-1, (d)-2
D. (a)-4, (b)-3, (c)-2, (d)-1

32. Match List–I (Drug Adulterants) with List–II (Categories):

List–I	List–II
(a) Substitution	1. Replacing genuine ingredients with cheaper ones
(b) Spoilage	2. Decomposition due to improper storage
(c) Contamination	3. Presence of harmful microbes or chemicals
(d) Mislabeling	4. Incorrect labeling of drug contents

Choose the answer from the options given below:

A. (a)-1, (b)-2, (c)-3, (d)-4
B. (a)-2, (b)-1, (c)-4, (d)-3
C. (a)-3, (b)-4, (c)-1, (d)-2
D. (a)-4, (b)-3, (c)-2, (d)-1

33. Match List–I (Pharmacological Testing Parameters) with List–II (Details):

List–I	List–II
(a) Toxicity Studies	1. Assessment of potential adverse effects
(b) Efficacy Studies	2. Determination of therapeutic benefits
(c) Pharmaco-kinetics	3. Study of drug absorption, distribution, and excretion
(d) Pharmaco-dynamics	4. Interaction of drugs with biological systems

Choose the answer from the options given below:

A. (a)-1, (b)-2, (c)-3, (d)-4
B. (a)-2, (b)-1, (c)-4, (d)-3
C. (a)-3, (b)-4, (c)-1, (d)-2
D. (a)-4, (b)-3, (c)-2, (d)-1

34. Match List–I (Herbal Drug Challenges) with List–II (Descriptions):

List–I	List–II
(a) Variability in Raw Materials	1. Differences in plant composition due to growth conditions
(b) Standardization Issues	2. Difficulty in ensuring consistent quality
(c) Contaminants in Processing	3. Presence of heavy metals or pesticides
(d) Lack of Clinical Data	4. Insufficient research on therapeutic efficacy

Choose the answer from the options given below:

A. (a)-1, (b)-2, (c)-3, (d)-4
B. (a)-2, (b)-1, (c)-4, (d)-3
C. (a)-3, (b)-4, (c)-1, (d)-2
D. (a)-4, (b)-3, (c)-2, (d)-1

Directions (Q. No. 35–39): *Following questions are based on Statement 1 and Statement 2. Read both the statements carefully and choose the correct answer from the options given below:*

A. Both Statement 1 and Statement 2 are true, and Statement 2 is the correct explanation of Statement 1.
B. Both Statement 1 and Statement 2 are true, but Statement 2 is not the correct explanation of Statement 1.
C. Statement 1 is true, but Statement 2 is false.
D. Statement 1 is false, but Statement 2 is true.
E. Both Statement 1 and Statement 2 are false.

35. Statement 1: The Ayurvedic Pharmacopoeia provides a comprehensive framework for the identification, preparation, and quality control of Ayurvedic drugs.

Statement 2: The Ayurvedic Pharmacopoeia emphasizes the need for modern scientific methods to validate traditional practices and ensure global acceptance.

36. Statement 1: Good Manufacturing Practices (GMP) are essential for ensuring the safety and efficacy of Ayurvedic drugs.

Statement 2: GMP guidelines strictly adhere to traditional Ayurvedic preparation methods and exclude modern techniques.

37. Statement 1: DNA barcoding is a reliable technique for authenticating raw materials in Ayurvedic formulations.

Statement 2: DNA barcoding cannot differentiate between authentic and adulterated samples due to the complexity of herbal compounds.

38. Statement 1: Stability testing ensures that Ayurvedic formulations retain their potency and safety over their intended shelf life.

Statement 2: Stability testing evaluates environmental factors such as temperature, humidity, and light exposure to determine the storage requirements of Ayurvedic drugs.

39. Statement 1: Modern analytical techniques like High-Performance Liquid Chromatography (HPLC) and Mass Spectrometry are crucial for standardizing Ayurvedic drugs.

Statement 2: These techniques help quantify bioactive compounds, ensuring consistency and efficacy in Ayurvedic formulations.

Directions (Q. No. 40–45): *There are two statements in each question. One is labelled as Assertion (A) and the other is as Reason (R). Read both the statements and choose the correct answer from the options given below:*

A. Both Assertion (A) and Reason (R) are true, and Reason (R) is the correct explanation of Assertion (A).
B. Both Assertion (A) and Reason (R) are true, but Reason (R) is not the correct explanation of Assertion (A).
C. Assertion (A) is true, but Reason (R) is false.
D. Assertion (A) is false, but Reason (R) is true.
E. Both Assertion (A) and Reason (R) are false.

40. Assertion (A): Ayurvedic formulations require rigorous testing to ensure they meet modern pharmacological standards.

Reason (R): Traditional Ayurvedic formulations inherently lack consistency in their bioactive compound profiles.

41. Assertion (A): DNA barcoding is increasingly used in Ayurvedic drug standardization for raw material authentication.

Reason (R): It provides a precise method for identifying medicinal plants and prevents adulteration by confirming species identity.

42. Assertion (A): Stability testing in Ayurveda ensures the safety and efficacy of formulations under various storage conditions.

Reason (R): Environmental factors such as temperature and humidity do not affect the bioactive compounds in Ayurvedic drugs.

43. Assertion (A): Good Manufacturing Practices (GMP) play a vital role in ensuring the global acceptance of Ayurvedic drugs.

Reason (R): GMP guidelines emphasize strict quality control measures and documentation during the production of Ayurvedic formulations.

44. Assertion (A): Triphala, a classical Ayurvedic formulation, has been shown to enhance gut microbiota diversity and systemic immunity.

Reason (R): Triphala's therapeutic effects are primarily due to the synergistic action of its three components: Haritaki, Bibhitaki, and Amalaki.

45. Assertion (A): Ayurvedic detoxification therapies like Panchakarma are effective in managing chronic diseases.

Reason (R): Panchakarma therapies target cellular detoxification processes and oxidative stress pathways, restoring doshic balance.

Directions (Q. No. 46-50): *Read the passage carefully and find the answers to the questions given below*:

Modern approaches to drug standardization and quality assurance in Ayurveda are a blend of traditional principles and contemporary scientific methods. Analytical techniques such as High-Performance Liquid Chromatography (HPLC), Mass Spectrometry (MS), and Nuclear Magnetic Resonance (NMR) spectroscopy are used to ensure the identification, quantification, and purity of bioactive compounds in formulations. Stability testing evaluates the effects of environmental factors like temperature and humidity on drug efficacy and safety. DNA barcoding has emerged as a crucial tool for authenticating plant materials and preventing adulteration.

Pharmacological studies, including in vitro and in vivo methods, validate the therapeutic claims of Ayurvedic formulations. These studies often reveal significant immunomodulatory, antioxidant, and anti-inflammatory properties, supporting their traditional uses. Good Manufacturing Practices (GMP) have been established to ensure the consistency, safety, and efficacy of Ayurvedic drugs, addressing challenges such as contamination and regional variations.

Despite advancements, challenges like overharvesting of medicinal plants, environmental degradation, and a lack of global regulatory alignment persist. Sustainable practices, conservation efforts, and interdisciplinary research are essential for integrating Ayurveda into global healthcare systems.

46. Which of the following techniques is NOT mentioned in the passage as being used for Ayurvedic drug standardization?

A. HPLC

B. Mass Spectrometry

C. DNA barcoding

D. Gas Chromatography

47. What is the primary purpose of stability testing in Ayurvedic formulations as discussed in the passage?

A. To validate traditional preparation methods.

B. To evaluate the effects of environmental factors on drug efficacy and safety.

C. To establish global regulatory standards for Ayurvedic formulations.

D. To eliminate the need for pharmacological studies.

48. How do pharmacological studies contribute to Ayurvedic drug standardization?

A. By completely replacing traditional Ayurvedic knowledge.

B. By validating therapeutic claims through in vitro and in vivo studies.

C. By focusing exclusively on immunomodulatory properties.

D. By eliminating the need for modern analytical techniques.

49. According to the passage, what is one major challenge in the sustainability of Ayurvedic formulations?

A. Overuse of synthetic alternatives in traditional formulations.

B. Lack of consumer trust in Ayurvedic products.

C. Overharvesting of medicinal plants and environmental degradation.

D. Absence of interdisciplinary research in Ayurveda.

50. What is suggested in the passage as a critical step for integrating Ayurveda into global healthcare systems?

A. Adopting traditional practices without modification.

B. Avoiding conservation efforts for medicinal plants.

C. Ensuring interdisciplinary research and sustainable practices.

D. Limiting the use of Ayurvedic drugs to specific regions.

ANSWER WITH EXPLANATIONS

1. B: The Ayurvedic Pharmacopoeia of India (API) plays a crucial role in ensuring drug safety and efficacy by providing standardized guidelines, including phytochemical profiles for herbal drugs. The use of modern techniques like HPLC and spectroscopic analysis supports the identification and quantification of active compounds. This integration validates traditional formulations such as Churna and Kwatha. Option B reflects this synthesis accurately. Option A is incorrect because Ayurvedic formulations don't offer universal effects. Options C and D negate the core premise of integration and are thus incorrect.

2. **B:** Agni in Ayurveda parallels enzymatic and metabolic processes central to digestion and health. By studying digestive enzymes like amylase and protease, the research demonstrates how Ayurvedic formulations optimize metabolic pathways, supporting molecular biology's interpretation of Agni. Weak Agni, akin to reduced enzyme activity, leads to disease, validating Ayurveda's physiological relevance. Ayurvedic interventions enhancing enzymatic function align with health restoration principles. Rejecting this as symbolic ignores its scientific resonance. By bridging traditional wisdom with molecular insights, Ayurveda proves adaptable to modern frameworks, enriching our understanding of holistic health while maintaining its foundational integrity across varied healthcare paradigms.

3. **C:** To combat adulteration and maintain drug authenticity, the API enforces strict analytical standards for raw materials and finished products. These include macroscopic, microscopic, and chemical evaluations. Option C is correct as it aligns with these quality control measures. Relying solely on traditional knowledge (B) or discouraging production (A) would hinder innovation and scalability. Allowing regional variations (D) without standard checks increases risk of inconsistency and adulteration.

4. **C:** Environmental factors like humidity affect the bioactive stability of Ayurvedic drugs, necessitating modern preservation techniques. Advanced packaging materials ensure formulations retain therapeutic efficacy without compromising natural integrity. Abandoning vulnerable formulations undermines Ayurveda's adaptability, while synthetic stabilizers deviate from its holistic approach. By integrating traditional wisdom with modern innovations, manufacturers safeguard product efficacy, enhancing consumer trust and ensuring Ayurveda's alignment with contemporary quality standards. This synergy between old and new protects therapeutic outcomes, reinforcing Ayurveda's position as a sustainable, effective healthcare option that meets global demands for safety and consistency.

5. **A:** Adopting a unified nomenclature for medicinal plants standardizes Ayurvedic practices globally, ensuring clarity across diverse regions. This does not dismiss cultural diversity but harmonizes traditional terminology with scientific precision. Preserving regional variations enriches Ayurveda's heritage while maintaining consistency. Excluding herbs with inconsistent nomenclature narrows its scope unnecessarily. Balancing global uniformity with cultural respect strengthens Ayurveda's application in international markets, aligning traditional practices with regulatory compliance and fostering deeper understanding among practitioners and researchers worldwide. This approach underscores Ayurveda's adaptability, ensuring it thrives in both its traditional and modern scientific contexts.

6. **B:** Integrating genomics with Ayurvedic Tridosha principles fosters personalized healthcare approaches. Genetic markers associated with doshic imbalances validate Ayurveda's adaptability to modern science. Rejecting this relevance ignores Ayurveda's nuanced understanding of health predispositions. Genetic determinism oversimplifies dosha interactions, while symbolic interpretations fail to account for biological evidence. This synthesis enriches Ayurveda, making it a versatile tool for personalized medicine. By combining ancient concepts with genomic insights, Ayurveda's relevance expands, bridging traditional wisdom with cutting-edge scientific applications. Such integration underscores Ayurveda's adaptability, enabling it to address contemporary healthcare challenges while preserving its foundational principles.

7. **A:** Rigorous standardization and sterilization procedures (like high heat, irradiation, etc.) used to meet global safety standards may alter or degrade the traditional preparation methods and reduce the efficacy or potency of certain Ayurvedic ingredients. Many active principles are delicate and may not withstand modern sterilization processes, leading to concerns over loss of therapeutic properties.

8. **B:** Rasayana formulations, central to Ayurveda, focus on rejuvenation and immunity enhancement. The Ayurvedic Pharmacopoeia validates these formulations by integrating traditional preparation methods with modern clinical trials. Claims of being solely traditional overlook the API's reliance on evidence-based practices to ensure safety and efficacy. Immunomodulatory studies reinforce the adaptability of Ayurveda, showcasing its ability to align with contemporary healthcare frameworks. This balance of ancient and modern ensures that Ayurveda maintains its authenticity while meeting the demands of scientific scrutiny, reinforcing its relevance in both traditional and integrative medicine systems.

9. **C:** Pharmacological validation ensures Ayurvedic drugs meet global safety and efficacy standards, essential for

consumer trust. Historical evidence, though valuable, requires empirical backing to align with regulatory expectations. The Amalaki study exemplifies this, combining tradition with modern pharmacology. Mischaracterizing scientific validation as unnecessary undermines Ayurveda's credibility. This integration strengthens Ayurveda's global appeal, highlighting its ability to adapt without compromising its foundational principles. By validating traditional practices through scientific methods, Ayurveda proves its resilience and relevance in addressing contemporary healthcare challenges, ensuring its position as a trusted system of medicine.

10. B: Standardization and scientific validation ensure Ayurveda's integration into modern healthcare without compromising its essence. Evidence-based approaches, such as clinical trials, reinforce its credibility. Rejecting validation overlooks scientific advancements that enrich Ayurveda, while blind adoption disregards regulatory and safety requirements. Combining traditional principles with empirical evidence fosters a balanced approach, enabling Ayurveda to thrive as a complementary healthcare option. This interplay demonstrates Ayurveda's adaptability, aligning its holistic practices with the demands of modern medicine while preserving its authenticity and therapeutic integrity across diverse healthcare settings.

11. B: Triphala's ability to restore gut microbiota diversity directly enhances systemic immunity. The improved microbial balance activates gut-associated lymphoid tissue (GALT), promoting immune responses. This aligns with the holistic principles of Ayurveda, where gut health is intrinsically tied to overall immunity. Misinterpreting Triphala as directly stimulating immunoglobulin production oversimplifies its systemic effects. The study underscores the connection between gut detoxification, microbial health, and immune enhancement. Triphala's role as a natural immunomodulator highlights its scientific validation and relevance in managing conditions like IBS, bridging ancient therapeutic principles with modern evidence-based medicine.

12. B: Sustainable agroforestry practices preserve Amalaki's wild populations while ensuring medicinal quality. Large-scale monocultures pose ecological risks like reduced biodiversity and soil degradation, threatening sustainability. Synthetic substitutes lack the holistic benefits of natural Amalaki, and reducing Triphala production disregards its widespread therapeutic importance. Community-based conservation aligns with Ayurveda's ethos of harmony with nature, ensuring the availability of high-quality raw materials for formulations. By promoting traditional and sustainable farming systems, Ayurveda can address ecological concerns while maintaining its authenticity and global applicability in holistic healthcare.

13. A: Environmental degradation, including overharvesting and soil depletion, reduces Amalaki's bioactive content, compromising Triphala's therapeutic efficacy. Ayurveda's formulations rely on the synergistic properties of high-quality ingredients. Dismissing Amalaki's role undermines the holistic nature of Triphala. Ensuring sustainable sourcing and conservation of Amalaki maintains its potency and supports Ayurveda's foundational principles. This challenge highlights the interconnectedness of ecological conservation and Ayurvedic therapeutic outcomes, emphasizing the importance of sustainable practices for maintaining efficacy and reliability in traditional formulations.

14. A: To balance therapeutic integrity (Scenario 1) and sustainability (Scenario 2), the most effective solution is to establish global standards for both herbal sourcing and Ayurvedic practices. This ensures medicinal plants like Kutki are used responsibly without compromising efficacy. Option A addresses both environmental and therapeutic aspects. B and D ignore herbal principles, while C prioritizes unrelated plants, missing the actual concern of overharvesting.

15. B: Agni, or digestive fire, is central to Ayurveda, governing metabolism and overall health. Impaired Agni leads to the accumulation of toxins (Ama), disrupting doshic balance and causing disease. Ayurvedic interventions like Deepana (digestive stimulants) and Pachana (digestive enzymes) restore Agni, aligning with its physiological and metabolic significance. Modern research validates Agni's role in enzymatic activity and gut health, demonstrating Ayurveda's scientific adaptability. This holistic approach underscores the interconnectedness of digestion, immunity, and well-being, ensuring Ayurveda's relevance in addressing metabolic disorders and promoting systemic health.

16. C: The Ayurvedic Pharmacopoeia integrates phytochemical analysis, contamination limits, DNA barcoding, and clinical trials to ensure drug safety and efficacy. Each component plays a vital role in maintaining the therapeutic integrity of formulations. Analytical methods validate active compounds, contamination limits ensure safety, DNA barcoding authenticates raw materials, and clinical trials confirm efficacy. Excluding any parameter weakens the standardization process. By combining these approaches, Ayurveda aligns with modern regulatory standards, enhancing global trust and applicability without compromising its traditional essence, ensuring a balanced approach to healthcare.

17. **A:** Stability testing assesses physical, chemical, and microbial parameters to ensure Ayurvedic drugs remain safe and effective. Physical stability monitors changes in texture, color, or odor; chemical stability evaluates active compound degradation; microbial stability ensures the absence of harmful microorganisms. These parameters collectively determine shelf life and storage requirements. Omitting pharmacokinetic studies in this context is appropriate, as stability testing focuses on external factors influencing quality. This comprehensive evaluation reinforces consumer trust in Ayurvedic products, aligning traditional formulations with modern safety and efficacy standards for long-term reliability.

18. **A:** Good Manufacturing Practices (GMP) ensure the safety, quality, and consistency of Ayurvedic drugs. Hygienic facilities prevent contamination, trained personnel oversee production, and batch traceability maintains consistency. Proper documentation ensures regulatory compliance and product transparency. Excluding traditional preparation methods misrepresents GMP's role, which integrates tradition with modern standards. This balanced approach safeguards Ayurveda's authenticity while addressing contemporary quality expectations, ensuring its relevance in global markets and enhancing consumer confidence in its therapeutic applications.

19. **A:** Modern analytical techniques like HPLC, DNA barcoding, and mass spectrometry are integral to Ayurvedic drug standardization. HPLC quantifies bioactive compounds, DNA barcoding authenticates plant species, and mass spectrometry detects contaminants. These methods address safety, efficacy, and authenticity concerns, aligning Ayurveda with regulatory standards. Omitting randomized field trials in this context is appropriate, as they are not directly linked to standardization. This integration of traditional knowledge with scientific validation reinforces Ayurveda's credibility, ensuring its adaptability in addressing global healthcare challenges while maintaining its foundational integrity.

20. **A:** Rasayana therapy emphasizes rejuvenation, immunity enhancement, and cellular detoxification, aligning with Ayurveda's holistic principles. Promoting longevity and systemic health, Rasayana formulations like Chyawanprash integrate nourishing herbs and antioxidants. Rapid weight loss, though not a primary goal, may occur as a secondary benefit of systemic detoxification. Misrepresenting Rasayana's objectives as superficial disregards its profound therapeutic potential. By addressing health at the cellular level, Rasayana supports Ayurveda's role in preventive and curative healthcare, reinforcing its relevance in contemporary medicine while maintaining its traditional roots.

21. **C:** DNA barcoding plays a pivotal role in ensuring the authenticity of raw materials in Ayurvedic formulations by comparing plant DNA sequences to standardized databases. This prevents adulteration, a common issue in herbal medicines, and protects endangered species by identifying them during sourcing. While DNA barcoding does not directly verify the efficacy of Ayurvedic formulations, it supports quality by authenticating ingredients used in these products. This method bridges traditional practices with modern technology, enhancing consumer trust and regulatory compliance. Its contribution to conservation and authentication highlights its critical role in maintaining the therapeutic reliability of Ayurvedic medicines.

22. **B:** Pharmacological studies are essential for validating the therapeutic claims of Ayurvedic drugs, ensuring they align with modern scientific standards. In vitro studies explore cellular mechanisms, such as enzymatic activity, providing insight into how formulations work. In vivo studies on animal models confirm safety and efficacy before advancing to clinical trials, which establish human therapeutic benefits. Toxicological studies ensure safety by assessing potential side effects. These steps collectively validate traditional claims, enriching Ayurveda's integration into global healthcare. Combining tradition with empirical evidence demonstrates Ayurveda's adaptability while ensuring formulations meet safety and efficacy standards expected by modern regulatory bodies.

23. **A:** Standardizing Ayurvedic formulations involves multiple layers of quality control, including analytical tools to quantify bioactive compounds, adherence to Good Manufacturing Practices (GMP), and stability testing. Analytical methods ensure consistency in therapeutic ingredients, while GMP enforces quality and safety during production. Stability testing determines shelf life, ensuring long-term efficacy. Excluding genetic engineering aligns with Ayurveda's natural foundation, focusing on preserving its traditional essence. This comprehensive approach bridges the gap between tradition and modern science, enhancing global acceptance of Ayurveda. Such rigorous validation ensures safety, efficacy, and authenticity, critical for promoting Ayurveda in integrative and evidence-based healthcare.

24. A: The Ayurvedic Pharmacopoeia of India focuses on documenting classical formulations, setting analytical standards for herbal identification, and establishing guidelines for clinical trials. These efforts ensure safety, efficacy, and quality, vital for Ayurveda's global credibility. Misinterpreting Ayurveda as rigidly opposed to synthetic drugs undermines its holistic nature. Instead, the API blends tradition with modern methodologies, addressing contemporary healthcare demands while preserving ancient wisdom. By combining detailed documentation with scientific validation, the API enhances the reliability of Ayurvedic formulations, ensuring they meet modern regulatory standards while maintaining their authenticity and therapeutic significance.

25. A: Macroscopic analysis identifies the external features of herbal raw materials, essential for authentication before further testing. Microscopic analysis dives deeper into cellular structures, ensuring species-level identification. Phytochemical testing detects active compounds, confirming therapeutic potential, while chromatographic techniques analyze complex mixtures with precision. Together, these methods form a layered approach, ensuring the identity, purity, and potency of Ayurvedic drugs. By integrating traditional practices with modern science, the Ayurvedic Pharmacopoeia aligns its ancient principles with stringent quality control measures, preserving efficacy while meeting global safety standards.

26. A: Identity tests confirm the botanical source of raw materials, preventing adulteration. Purity tests detect contaminants such as foreign matter or debris, ensuring the material meets pharmacopoeial standards. Potency tests measure the concentration of bioactive compounds, validating therapeutic potential, while stability tests evaluate shelf life under various conditions. This comprehensive system addresses all aspects of drug quality, from raw material identification to long-term efficacy. These measures reflect Ayurveda's adaptability, blending its time-tested formulations with modern pharmacological practices to meet contemporary healthcare demands.

27. A: Organoleptic properties such as color, odor, and taste provide immediate clues about the quality and identity of raw materials, reflecting their freshness and purity. Physicochemical parameters like moisture content and ash value offer a deeper understanding of material composition, ensuring consistency. Microbial limits focus on safety by detecting harmful pathogens, while heavy metal testing identifies toxic contaminants. These standards not only safeguard consumer health but also enhance the global credibility of Ayurvedic practices by adhering to rigorous scientific protocols. Together, they form the cornerstone of drug standardization.

28. A: HPLC provides detailed chemical profiling, ensuring the reproducibility of herbal formulations. DNA barcoding authenticates plant species at the genetic level, preventing substitution or adulteration. NMR spectroscopy offers insights into molecular structures, aiding in the discovery of bioactive components. Mass spectrometry, on the other hand, identifies molecular weights, crucial for complex formulations. These advanced tools bridge the gap between ancient Ayurvedic principles and contemporary analytical requirements, ensuring the standardization and efficacy of formulations for global acceptance and use in evidence-based medicine.

29. A: Churna, a powdered form of herbs, ensures easy administration and absorption. Vati, as compressed tablets, allows for precise dosing and longer shelf life. Kwath, prepared by boiling herbs, extracts water-soluble active ingredients, providing immediate therapeutic effects. Asava-Arishta, fermented formulations, enhance bioavailability and improve digestion. These diverse forms demonstrate Ayurveda's flexibility in adapting formulations to meet various therapeutic needs. This versatility underscores the importance of understanding drug forms, ensuring that delivery systems align with both the condition being treated and the patient's requirements.

30. A: Good Manufacturing Practices (GMP) ensure uniform production, maintaining consistency and quality. Standard Operating Procedures (SOPs) create repeatable workflows, minimizing errors. Validation confirms that manufacturing processes yield reliable results, while documentation provides traceability, critical for audits and troubleshooting. This layered approach reflects Ayurveda's embrace of modern industrial practices without compromising its traditional essence. By incorporating stringent quality assurance principles, Ayurvedic drugs meet both local and international regulatory standards, reinforcing their safety, efficacy, and reliability in diverse healthcare systems.

31. A: Raw material testing ensures the authenticity and purity of ingredients before production begins. In-process quality control monitors production stages, preventing errors and maintaining consistency. Finished product testing validates that the final formulation meets all specifications, while post-market surveillance tracks safety and efficacy in real-world scenarios. These phases create a closed-loop system that addresses quality from raw material sourcing to consumer feedback. This holistic approach safeguards the credibility of Ayurvedic formulations, blending time-tested wisdom with contemporary quality standards to ensure global acceptability.

32. **A:** Substitution, often driven by economic factors, replaces genuine ingredients with cheaper alternatives, compromising efficacy. Spoilage occurs when improper storage leads to degradation, affecting safety. Contamination, such as heavy metals or microbes, poses significant health risks, while mislabeling undermines consumer trust. Identifying and mitigating these challenges is critical for maintaining the integrity of Ayurvedic drugs. By addressing these issues through stringent quality control measures, the Ayurvedic Pharmacopoeia reinforces the global credibility of its formulations, ensuring they meet both traditional standards and modern regulatory requirements.

33. **A:** Toxicity studies assess potential adverse effects, crucial for establishing safety profiles. Efficacy studies validate therapeutic benefits, confirming a drug's intended purpose. Pharmacokinetics examines how drugs are absorbed, distributed, metabolized, and excreted, providing insights into dosage and bioavailability. Pharmacodynamics explores the interaction of drugs with biological systems, explaining mechanisms of action. These testing parameters form the scientific foundation of Ayurvedic pharmacology, ensuring that ancient formulations are validated by modern standards. Together, they bridge the gap between traditional wisdom and contemporary evidence-based practices.

34. **A:** Variability in raw materials arises from differences in soil, climate, and cultivation practices, affecting consistency. Standardization issues stem from challenges in quantifying active compounds in natural ingredients. Contaminants like heavy metals or pesticides highlight the need for stringent quality control during processing. The lack of clinical data underscores the necessity of robust research to validate therapeutic claims. Addressing these challenges ensures the global credibility and acceptance of Ayurvedic medicines, demonstrating their efficacy and safety while preserving the traditional knowledge that underpins their formulation.

35. **A:** The Ayurvedic Pharmacopoeia provides a robust framework for identification, preparation, and quality control of Ayurvedic medicines. It also advocates the use of modern scientific techniques (e.g., HPLC, DNA barcoding) to validate and enhance global credibility. Since both the statement and the reason are true—and the reason explains the framework's scientific evolution—Option A is the most appropriate.

36. **C:** Good Manufacturing Practices (GMP) ensure that Ayurvedic formulations meet global quality and safety standards. While Statement 1 highlights their importance, Statement 2 incorrectly suggests GMP excludes modern innovations. In reality, GMP integrates traditional preparation methods with advanced quality control techniques, addressing contamination risks, ensuring consistency, and maintaining efficacy. This dual approach preserves Ayurveda's authenticity while aligning it with regulatory demands. GMP's role underscores Ayurveda's potential to thrive in global healthcare, combining its rich heritage with modern scientific rigor to ensure consumer trust and therapeutic reliability.

37. **C:** DNA barcoding enhances Ayurvedic drug standardization by authenticating raw materials and preventing adulteration. Statement 1 reflects this scientific advancement, while Statement 2 misrepresents its capabilities. DNA barcoding precisely differentiates between closely related plant species, ensuring the use of correct ingredients in formulations. This method bridges traditional herbal identification with molecular tools, addressing quality concerns and fostering consumer confidence. Its contribution to ecological conservation and regulatory compliance highlights Ayurveda's adaptability, ensuring its practices align with modern standards while preserving its foundational principles.

38. **A:** Stability testing ensures Ayurvedic formulations retain their safety, efficacy, and potency throughout their shelf life. Statement 1 underscores its importance, while Statement 2 accurately explains the role of environmental factors like temperature, humidity, and light in influencing stability. Testing identifies optimal storage conditions and shelf life, aligning Ayurveda with global safety standards. This rigorous approach protects therapeutic integrity, ensuring consumer trust. Stability testing bridges traditional preparation techniques with modern quality assurance methods, safeguarding Ayurveda's relevance in contemporary healthcare while upholding its holistic ethos.

39. **A:** Modern analytical techniques like HPLC and mass spectrometry are critical for standardizing Ayurvedic drugs, ensuring consistency in bioactive compound profiles. Statement 1 emphasizes their necessity, while Statement 2 explains their role in validating efficacy and safety. These methods align traditional formulations with scientific standards, addressing global regulatory requirements. Integrating such tools preserves Ayurveda's authenticity while enhancing its credibility in modern healthcare. Analytical validation reinforces consumer trust,

ensuring formulations meet the demands of contemporary quality assurance while maintaining their therapeutic effectiveness and cultural significance.

40. **C:** Rigorous testing is essential for aligning Ayurvedic formulations with pharmacological standards. While Assertion (A) is true, Reason (R) incorrectly attributes inconsistencies to traditional methods. Variations in bioactive compound profiles often arise from environmental factors or raw material quality. Ayurveda's adaptability lies in integrating empirical validation with traditional wisdom. Advanced tools like DNA barcoding and stability testing ensure consistency without undermining authenticity. This approach balances ancient practices with modern scientific expectations, reinforcing Ayurveda's therapeutic credibility and enabling its integration into evidence-based medicine.

41. **A:** DNA barcoding is a transformative tool in Ayurvedic drug standardization, enabling precise identification of plant species. Assertion (A) is correct as it ensures raw material authenticity, crucial for safety and efficacy. Reason (R) aptly explains this by emphasizing the inability of traditional methods to distinguish closely related species. By integrating molecular-level identification, DNA barcoding addresses issues like adulteration and mislabeling, safeguarding the therapeutic integrity of Ayurvedic formulations. This synergy of tradition and innovation strengthens consumer trust, ensuring compliance with modern regulatory frameworks while preserving Ayurveda's authenticity and therapeutic relevance in global healthcare systems.

42. **C:** Stability testing ensures that Ayurvedic formulations remain safe and effective under varied storage conditions. Assertion (A) is correct, emphasizing its role in maintaining drug quality. However, Reason (R) is incorrect since environmental factors like temperature, humidity, and light significantly influence bioactive compounds. Ignoring these factors risks reduced potency and therapeutic value. Stability testing combines traditional preparation wisdom with modern scientific methods, determining optimal storage conditions and shelf life. This approach ensures consumer safety and confidence, aligning Ayurveda with global quality standards while preserving its efficacy and authenticity in integrative medicine systems.

43. **A:** Good Manufacturing Practices (GMP) are vital for the global acceptance of Ayurvedic drugs. Assertion (A) is true, highlighting their importance in maintaining quality and safety. Reason (R) complements this by explaining GMP's focus on strict quality control measures and documentation. These practices ensure consistency, traceability, and compliance with international standards, addressing concerns like contamination and variability. Integrating GMP into Ayurvedic manufacturing enhances its credibility and accessibility in global markets, reinforcing trust while preserving the holistic principles of Ayurveda. This balance strengthens Ayurveda's position in contemporary healthcare systems without compromising its traditional ethos.

44. **A:** Triphala enhances gut microbiota diversity and systemic immunity, showcasing its holistic therapeutic value. Assertion (A) is true, reflecting its impact on health. Reason (R) accurately explains this by attributing Triphala's efficacy to the synergistic action of Haritaki, Bibhitaki, and Amalaki. Each component contributes unique bioactive properties, collectively balancing doshas and promoting detoxification and rejuvenation. Misunderstanding its effects as isolated oversimplifies its complexity. Triphala exemplifies Ayurveda's integration of traditional wisdom with scientific validation, supporting its role in addressing modern health challenges like gut health and immune modulation while maintaining its foundational integrity.

45. **A:** Panchakarma therapies effectively manage chronic diseases by eliminating toxins and restoring balance. Assertion (A) is true, reflecting their therapeutic efficacy. Reason (R) complements this by explaining Panchakarma's role in targeting cellular detoxification and oxidative stress pathways, addressing root causes of imbalance. These therapies align with Ayurveda's holistic approach, supporting physical and mental health restoration. Combining traditional detoxification methods with modern scientific understanding enhances their credibility and relevance in integrative medicine. Panchakarma's adaptability underscores Ayurveda's potential to address contemporary healthcare challenges without compromising its natural and holistic principles.

46. **D:** The passage does not mention Gas Chromatography (GC) as part of Ayurvedic drug standardization. Instead, it emphasizes techniques like HPLC, Mass Spectrometry, and DNA barcoding. These tools ensure bioactive compound consistency, raw material authenticity, and contaminant detection. GC's exclusion in the passage highlights the specificity of methods chosen for Ayurveda's needs. By relying on validated and relevant techniques, Ayurveda bridges traditional practices with scientific rigor, enhancing its reliability. Addressing this question demonstrates the importance of understanding the role and applicability of various scientific tools in standardizing and validating Ayurvedic formulations.

47. **B:** Stability testing evaluates how environmental factors like temperature, humidity, and light affect the efficacy and safety of Ayurvedic drugs. This ensures formulations retain their therapeutic value throughout their shelf life. Stability testing is integral to aligning Ayurveda with modern quality standards, safeguarding consumer trust. By identifying optimal storage conditions, manufacturers preserve bioactive compound integrity, ensuring formulations meet regulatory expectations. This process reflects Ayurveda's adaptability to scientific advancements, demonstrating its relevance in contemporary healthcare. Misinterpreting this as solely validating traditional methods overlooks its broader role in maintaining safety and efficacy in diverse environments.

48. **B:** Pharmacological studies validate Ayurvedic formulations through in vitro and in vivo methods, bridging traditional knowledge with empirical science. These studies confirm mechanisms of action, safety, and efficacy, aligning Ayurveda with modern healthcare standards. In vitro research explores cellular-level effects, while in vivo experiments assess systemic impacts in animal models. Clinical trials ensure human applicability, reinforcing consumer trust and regulatory compliance. By integrating pharmacological studies, Ayurveda retains its authenticity while addressing contemporary demands for evidence-based medicine. This process underscores Ayurveda's resilience and adaptability, enhancing its therapeutic credibility in global healthcare systems.

49. **C:** Overharvesting of medicinal plants and environmental degradation pose significant challenges to Ayurvedic formulations. These practices reduce biodiversity, deplete resources, and compromise raw material quality, affecting therapeutic efficacy. Addressing these issues requires sustainable harvesting, ecological conservation, and reforestation efforts. Ayurveda's principles align with ecological harmony, emphasizing the interdependence of natural resources and human health. Ignoring these challenges undermines Ayurveda's long-term viability and therapeutic value. By adopting sustainable practices, Ayurveda can maintain its authenticity while meeting the demands of modern healthcare, ensuring its relevance for future generations without compromising ecological integrity.

50. **C:** Integrating Ayurveda into global healthcare systems requires interdisciplinary research, sustainable practices, and scientific validation. These steps ensure formulations meet safety and efficacy standards while preserving traditional principles. Aligning Ayurvedic practices with evidence-based frameworks fosters global acceptance and regulatory compliance. Prioritizing ecological conservation ensures the availability of high-quality raw materials, addressing environmental challenges. Misinterpreting Ayurveda as incompatible with modern systems limits its potential. By balancing tradition and innovation, Ayurveda strengthens its position in integrative medicine, offering holistic solutions to contemporary healthcare challenges while respecting its cultural and therapeutic heritage.

UNIT 6: DISEASE BIOLOGY, MICROBIOLOGY AND IMMUNOLOGY

CHAPTER 16

PRINCIPLES OF DISEASE CAUSATION IN AYURVEDA

Ayurveda, the ancient Indian system of medicine, offers a comprehensive understanding of disease causation through its principle of nidana, which translates to the "cause" or "diagnosis" of diseases. In Ayurveda, diseases arise due to imbalances in the body's primary functional entities known as doshas—Vata, Pitta, and Kapha—as well as disturbances in the dhatus (tissues), malas (waste products), and agni (digestive fire). The concept of nidana not only addresses the physical causes but also includes psychological, social, and environmental factors.

1. **The Tridosha Framework and Disease Causation:** The central tenet of Ayurveda is that the balance of Vata, Pitta, and Kapha maintains health, while their imbalance leads to disease. Each dosha governs specific physiological and psychological functions:
   - **Vata:** Movement, nervous system regulation, and elimination processes.
   - **Pitta:** Digestion, metabolism, and energy production.
   - **Kapha:** Structure, lubrication, and immunity.

   Disease occurs when external or internal factors disturb the equilibrium of these doshas. The causative factors can be broadly classified into the following:
   - **Ahara (Diet):** Improper diet—whether excessive, insufficient, or untimely—disrupts digestion and doshic balance. For example, spicy and sour foods aggravate Pitta, while heavy and oily foods exacerbate Kapha.
   - **Vihara (Lifestyle):** Irregular routines, lack of exercise, or excessive indulgence in sedentary habits disrupt the natural rhythms of the doshas.
   - **Manasika Nidana (Psychological Factors):** Emotional disturbances such as anger, fear, and stress directly influence doshas, particularly Vata and Pitta.
   - **Parinama (Seasonal and Environmental Factors):** Climatic changes, pollution, or exposure to incompatible environments contribute to doshic imbalance.
   - **Janmika (Genetic and Prenatal Factors):** Hereditary conditions and prenatal influences are also recognized in Ayurveda as contributors to disease.
2. **The Process of Disease Initiation (Rog Utpatti):** Ayurveda describes six stages of disease development, emphasizing the importance of early diagnosis and intervention:
   - **Sanchaya (Accumulation):** Doshas begin to accumulate in their respective sites due to improper diet or lifestyle. For instance, Kapha accumulates in the stomach, leading to symptoms like heaviness and lethargy.
   - **Prakopa (Aggravation):** The accumulated doshas become aggravated, intensifying symptoms such as inflammation or hyperactivity.
   - **Prasara (Spread):** The doshas spread from their primary sites to other areas, disrupting systemic balance
   - **Sthana Samshraya (Localization):** Doshas localize in weak or vulnerable tissues, setting the stage for specific diseases.

- **Vyakti (Manifestation):** The disease manifests with clear clinical symptoms.
- **Bheda (Complication):** The disease becomes chronic or leads to complications if untreated.

By addressing the nidana at its root—be it dietary correction, lifestyle modification, or detoxification—Ayurveda aims to prevent the progression of diseases.

Ayurvedic Pathology and Disease Progression (Samprapti)

Ayurveda, the ancient Indian science of health and healing, is rooted in the understanding of the body's internal balance and its interplay with external influences. The concept of Samprapti, often referred to as the "pathogenesis" or "disease progression," is a cornerstone of Ayurvedic pathology. Unlike modern pathology, which delves into cellular and molecular abnormalities, Ayurvedic pathology is a holistic approach that views diseases as systemic imbalances involving the body's functional energies (doshas), tissues (dhatus), metabolic processes (agni), and channels (srotas).

Samprapti: The Pathological Journey of Disease

The term Samprapti translates to the "establishment of disease" and details the intricate mechanisms by which an imbalance unfolds within the body, leading to disease. This process encompasses causative factors, stages of development, and the body's responses. Samprapti is crucial for Ayurvedic practitioners, as it provides a roadmap to identify the root causes, pathways, and sites of disease manifestation, enabling tailored therapeutic interventions.

Key Types of Samprapti

Samprapti is classified into six broad types, each providing a lens through which to understand the nuances of disease:

1. **Dosha Samprapti: Identifying Imbalances in the Doshas:** The doshas—Vata, Pitta, and Kapha—are dynamic energies governing the physiological and psychological processes in the body. Their imbalance is the primary driver of disease. Dosha Samprapti identifies which dosha (s) are vitiated and how they disrupt the body:
   - **Vata-related disorders:** Marked by irregularities, dryness, and movement-related symptoms (e.g., joint pain, constipation).
   - **Pitta-related disorders:** Characterized by heat, inflammation, and metabolic disturbances (e.g., ulcers, hyperacidity).
   - **Kapha-related disorders:** Exhibiting heaviness, stagnation, and excess mucus (e.g., obesity, respiratory congestion).
   - In many diseases, multiple doshas may be involved, requiring a detailed assessment of their interplay.
2. **Dushya Samprapti: Identifying Affected Tissues (Dhatus):** The dhatus—rasa (plasma), rakta (blood), mamsa (muscle), meda (fat), asthi (bone), majja (marrow), and shukra (reproductive tissue)—are the structural components of the body. Dushya Samprapti examines how doshic imbalances affect specific dhatus, leading to functional and structural damage:
   - **Rasa (Plasma):** Affected by weak digestion, leading to poor nutrient assimilation.
   - **Rakta (Blood):** Imbalances result in conditions like anemia or hyperemia.
   - **Meda (Fat):** Kapha's influence causes obesity or metabolic disorders.

   Understanding the interplay between doshas and dhatus helps in targeting specific tissues during treatment.
3. **Agni Samprapti:** The Role of Digestive Fire Agni, or digestive fire, is central to Ayurvedic physiology and pathology. It governs digestion, absorption, metabolism, and immunity. Impaired agni leads to the formation of ama, a toxic, undigested substance that triggers disease. Agni dysfunction is classified into:
   - **Mandagni (Weak Fire):** Slows digestion, leading to ama accumulation.
   - **Tikshnagni (Excessive Fire):** Overactive digestion, causing tissue depletion.
   - **Vishamagni (Erratic Fire):** Associated with Vata, causing irregular digestion.

   The assessment of agni is pivotal in understanding the root cause of many chronic conditions.
4. **Srotas Samprapti:** Examining Channels or Pathways. The srotas, or bodily channels, are responsible for transporting nutrients, waste, and energy. Samprapti explores the state of these channels and how their function is compromised:
   - **Obstruction (Sanga):** Often caused by ama or Kapha, leading to stagnation.
   - **Leakage (Vimarga Gamana):** Associated with Vata, causing loss of vital fluids.
   - **Hyperfunction (Atipravritti):** Linked to Pitta, causing excessive discharge.

   Each srotas has a specific function, and disruption can lead to targeted disease states (e.g., pranavaha srotas for respiratory disorders).

5. **Kala Samprapti:** Timing and Duration. The kala dimension examines how time influences disease progression, including:
   - Seasonal variations (e.g., allergies during spring due to Kapha).
   - Chronicity and acute presentations.
   - Diurnal rhythms, such as the predominance of Kapha in the morning.
   - Recognizing these temporal patterns aids in predicting disease progression and tailoring treatment accordingly.
6. **Adhisthana Samprapti:** Location of Disease. Adhisthana refers to the specific site where a disease manifests. The site may be systemic (e.g., blood circulation) or localized (e.g., liver). Identifying the location is crucial for understanding the full scope of the disease and implementing targeted therapies.

Agni and Ama: Core Concepts in Disease Pathology

1. **The Role of Agni (Digestive Fire):** In Ayurveda, agni is considered the cornerstone of health and immunity. It governs the transformation of food into energy and tissues. When agni is balanced, it promotes robust digestion, absorption, and assimilation. However, its impairment can lead to:
   - Weak metabolism.
   - Accumulation of toxins (ama).
   - Depletion or excess of tissues.
2. **Ama:** The Toxic Byproduct of Impaired Digestion. Ama is a pathological concept unique to Ayurveda, representing undigested or improperly processed food and waste products. Ama acts as a toxin, clogging the channels (srotas) and impairing physiological functions. Its characteristics include:
   - Sticky, heavy, and cold properties.
   - Symptoms such as indigestion, lethargy, bloating, and a coated tongue.
   - The interplay between ama and the doshas can trigger a variety of diseases. For instance, ama combined with Pitta results in inflammatory conditions, while ama and Kapha lead to stagnation and congestion.
3. **Disease Progression Involving Agni and Ama:** The sequence of events involving agni and ama in disease progression includes:
   (i) **Weak Agni:** Poor digestion leads to ama formation.
   (ii) **Ama Accumulation:** Ama circulates through the body, blocking srotas.
   (iii) **Dosha Aggravation:** Ama interacts with doshas, aggravating their imbalances.
   (iv) **Disease Manifestation:** Specific tissues (dhatus) become affected, resulting in clear clinical symptoms.

   Restoring agni and eliminating ama are central to Ayurvedic treatment.

The Role of Srotas (Channels) in Pathology

The srotas are critical components of the Ayurvedic physiological framework, acting as conduits for the movement of nutrients, waste, and energies. Healthy srotas ensure homeostasis, while their dysfunction leads to disease:

1. **Types of Srotas:** Ayurveda identifies numerous srotas, broadly categorized into:
   - **Pranavaha Srotas (Respiratory Channels):** Governs oxygen exchange and vital energy.
   - **Annavaha Srotas (Digestive Channels):** Manages food intake and digestion.
   - **Mutravaha Srotas (Urinary Channels):** Regulates excretion of liquid waste.

   Each srotas is vulnerable to specific doshic imbalances and pathological processes.
2. **Common Pathologies of Srotas:** Pathological changes in the srotas include:
   - **Obstruction (Sanga):** Kapha or ama-related blockages, causing stagnation.
   - **Leakage (Vimarga Gamana):** Vata-related disruptions, leading to dehydration or fluid loss.
   - **Overactivation (Atipravritti):** Pitta dominance, causing conditions like diarrhea.
3. **Restoring Srotas Function:** Treatment focuses on clearing blockages, strengthening weakened channels, and addressing doshic imbalances. Therapies include detoxification (panchakarma), dietary adjustments, and herbal interventions.

Classification of Diseases and Their Characteristics in Ayurveda

Ayurveda, the ancient Indian system of medicine, provides a structured and detailed classification system for diseases, emphasizing a holistic approach that integrates physical, mental, and environmental dimensions. By categorizing diseases based on their causes (nidana), the dosha involved, their site of manifestation, chronicity, and their unique characteristics, Ayurveda offers a comprehensive framework for diagnosis, prevention, and treatment.

Classification Based on Etiology

Etiology, or the cause of a disease, is a fundamental concept in Ayurveda. Diseases are classified based on their root causes into three primary categories: Adhyatmika, Adhibhautika, and Adhidaivika.

1. **Adhyatmika (Psychosomatic Diseases):** Adhyatmika diseases originate from within the body and mind. They are often triggered by imbalances in mental health, internal physiological disruptions, or congenital factors. These can include:
   - **Manasika Disorders (Mental Causes):** Diseases caused by psychological stress, emotional disturbances, or negative mental states such as anxiety, depression, and fear. For instance:
     - Excessive stress can aggravate Vata, leading to insomnia or anxiety disorders.
     - Persistent anger may increase Pitta, resulting in inflammatory conditions like hypertension.
     - **Sharirika Disorders (Physical Causes):** These involve genetic predispositions, congenital abnormalities, or poor lifestyle choices that disrupt the body's equilibrium. Examples include diabetes (prameha) and hereditary diseases.
2. **Adhibhautika (External Causes):** Adhibhautika diseases result from external influences, such as:
   - **Physical Trauma:** Injuries, fractures, or wounds inflicted by accidents.
   - **Infections:** Diseases caused by bacteria, viruses, or parasites, such as fevers or skin conditions.
   - **Environmental Factors:** Exposure to pollutants, allergens, or toxins that disrupt doshic balance. For example:
   - Dust and pollution can aggravate Kapha, causing respiratory issues like asthma.

   Extreme heat increases Pitta, leading to conditions such as heatstroke.
3. **Adhidaivika (Supernatural or Environmental Factors):** Adhidaivika diseases are believed to arise from spiritual, karmic, or celestial factors. While these concepts may seem esoteric, they reflect an ancient understanding of diseases influenced by forces beyond immediate human control. Examples include:
   - **Karmic Diseases:** Illnesses believed to be the result of past-life actions or karmic imbalances.
   - **Seasonal and Climatic Disorders:** Conditions like seasonal allergies, which occur due to the interplay of doshas with external seasons. For instance:
     - Spring aggravates Kapha, while summer aggravates Pitta.
     - **Pandemics:** Epidemic diseases caused by disturbances in environmental harmony, such as infectious outbreaks or natural disasters.

Classification Based on Doshic Involvement

Ayurveda's cornerstone is the theory of Tridosha—Vata, Pitta, and Kapha. Diseases are categorized based on which dosha is primarily vitiated.

1. **Vataja Disorders (Vata Imbalance):** Diseases caused by an aggravated Vata dosha are characterized by dryness, irregularity, and movement-related symptoms. Common conditions include:
   - **Arthritis:** Pain, stiffness, and cracking in joints.
   - **Neurological Disorders:** Anxiety, insomnia, or tremors caused by disrupted nervous system function.
   - **Digestive Issues:** Constipation or bloating due to impaired Vata in the colon.

   Key characteristics:
   - Dryness and roughness in skin and tissues.
   - Irregular movements, such as erratic heartbeat or muscle spasms.
   - Sensitivity to cold and wind.
2. **Pittaja Disorders (Pitta Imbalance):** Diseases caused by an aggravated Pitta dosha are marked by heat, inflammation, and metabolic disturbances. Examples include:
   - **Hyperacidity (Amlapitta):** Burning sensations and acid reflux.
   - **Skin Disorders:** Rashes, hives, or acne due to excess heat in the blood.
   - **Liver Disorders:** Conditions like hepatitis caused by metabolic imbalances.

   Key characteristics:
   - Burning sensations and excessive thirst.
   - Yellowish discoloration of skin, eyes, or urine.
   - Increased irritability or anger.

Kaphaja Disorders (Kapha Imbalance)

Diseases caused by an aggravated Kapha dosha exhibit heaviness, stagnation, and mucus production. Common conditions include:

- **Sinusitis:** Excess mucus in the sinuses causing congestion.
- **Obesity:** Accumulation of fat tissue due to slow metabolism.

- **Respiratory Issues:** Cough, asthma, or bronchitis linked to Kapha in the lungs.

  Key characteristics:
  - Lethargy and sluggishness.
  - Swelling or water retention in tissues.
  - Sweet taste in the mouth or excess salivation.

Classification Based on Location (Adhisthana)

Ayurveda identifies diseases based on their primary site of manifestation, referred to as Adhisthana. Each site corresponds to a specific system or organ.

1. **Jatharogata (Digestive Tract Diseases):** Conditions affecting the digestive system include:
   - **Agnimandya (Weak Digestive Fire):** Poor digestion and loss of appetite.
   - **Amlapitta (Acidic Disorders):** Symptoms such as acid reflux or gastritis.
   - **Atisara (Diarrhea):** Excessive bowel movements caused by Pitta or Vata.
2. **Raktavaha Srotas (Circulatory Diseases):** Diseases of the circulatory system are linked to the blood (rakta dhatu) and include:
   - **Hypertension (Raktha Chapa):** High blood pressure due to aggravated Pitta.
   - **Anemia (Pandu):** Pale complexion, weakness, and fatigue caused by rakta dhatu depletion.
3. **Pranavaha Srotas (Respiratory Diseases):** Conditions affecting the respiratory system include:
   - **Asthma (Tamaka Shvasa):** Wheezing and difficulty breathing due to Vata and Kapha imbalance.
   - **Bronchitis:** Inflammation and mucus buildup in the bronchi.

   Other examples of Adhisthana-based diseases include musculoskeletal disorders (affecting bones and joints), reproductive system disorders, and skin diseases.

Classification Based on Chronicity

Ayurveda also classifies diseases based on their duration and severity.

1. **Acute Diseases (Atyayika):** These are short-term conditions characterized by rapid onset and severe symptoms. Examples include:
   - Fevers (Jwara) caused by infections or doshic imbalances.
   - Sudden injuries or burns.
2. **Chronic Diseases (Chirakari):** These are long-term diseases with persistent symptoms. Examples include:
   - **Diabetes (Prameha):** A Kapha-dominant metabolic disorder.
   - **Arthritis:** Progressive joint degeneration due to Vata.

The chronicity of a disease often determines the treatment approach, with acute diseases requiring immediate intervention and chronic diseases demanding sustained care.

Characteristics of Diseases

Ayurveda provides a detailed description of diseases through the following parameters:

1. **Purvarupa (Premonitory Symptoms):** These are subtle signs that precede the full manifestation of a disease. For example:
   - Digestive disturbances before fever.
   - Mood swings or irritability before Pitta-related conditions.
2. **Rupa (Manifest Symptoms):** These are the observable symptoms that help in diagnosis. Examples include:
   - Pain and stiffness in joints for arthritis.
   - Burning sensation and inflammation for Pitta disorders.
3. **Upashaya (Relieving Factors)**
   - Factors that alleviate symptoms and provide diagnostic clues. For instance:
   - Cool compresses relieve Pitta disorders.
   - Warm, oily massages alleviate Vata pain.
4. **Anupashaya (Aggravating Factors)**
   - Factors that worsen the condition. For example:
   - Spicy foods aggravate Pitta-related gastritis.
   - Cold exposure worsens Vata disorders.

MULTIPLE CHOICE QUESTIONS

1. A scholar researching Ayurvedic aetiology hypothesizes that nidana (causative factors) encompasses both environmental and behavioural components influencing disease manifestation. They compare the progression of diabetes in two groups: one exposed to sedentary lifestyles and processed diets (Ahara), and another practicing traditional Ayurvedic lifestyle modifications. The study concludes that nidana aligns with modern

risk factors but extends to subtle imbalances in doshas. Which of the following interpretations best aligns with the scholar's conclusions?

A. Nidana exclusively addresses lifestyle factors like diet and exercise.
B. Nidana includes subtle and gross imbalances, integrating physical, mental, and doshic disturbances.
C. Modern medicine's risk factors have no relevance to Ayurvedic nidana.
D. Disease causation in Ayurveda lacks a systemic framework.

2. A clinical practitioner treats patients with stress-induced insomnia using Ayurvedic approaches focusing on calming Vata dosha. The regimen includes herbs such as Ashwagandha and Brahmi, along with Abhyanga (oil massage) and pranayama. The treatment proves effective, and subsequent studies reveal its ability to modulate cortisol levels. How does this study demonstrate the application of Ayurvedic principles in modern stress management?

A. Stress management is unrelated to dosha theory and functions purely through cortisol regulation.
B. Ayurvedic practices regulate neuroendocrine responses, validating the Vata-stress connection.
C. Pranayama and herbal treatments only act as placebo interventions.
D. Cortisol levels are independent of Ayurvedic treatment effectiveness.

3. An Ayurvedic hospital focuses on the management of autoimmune diseases by addressing Ama (toxins) accumulation. A team observes that therapies like Panchakarma, combined with anti-inflammatory herbs, reduce systemic markers like (C)-reactive protein (CRP). Which of the following correctly explains this finding?

A. Panchakarma focuses solely on physical detox, disregarding systemic inflammation.
B. Ama-related detoxification contributes to lowering inflammatory markers in autoimmune conditions.
C. Autoimmune diseases cannot be influenced by Ayurveda, as they lack a doshic basis.
D. Anti-inflammatory effects are unrelated to the detoxifying nature of Ayurvedic interventions.

4. An experimental model compares the progression of arthritis in individuals with and without Ayurvedic treatment. The study focuses on how dosha imbalances affect joint inflammation and degeneration. Results show that Ayurvedic therapies, emphasizing Kapha and Vata regulation, slow disease progression. Which conclusion is most appropriate?

A. Ayurvedic therapies target only symptoms, not underlying inflammation.
B. Regulation of Kapha and Vata is integral to addressing chronic joint disorders.
C. Ayurvedic treatments are effective only for Kapha-based disorders.
D. Joint degeneration is unrelated to dosha imbalances.

5. A researcher investigates Ayurvedic pathology (Samprapti) by studying the sequential stages of disease development (Kriya Kalas). They document that early intervention during the Sanchaya stage prevents progression to more severe states. What does this finding imply about Ayurvedic treatment strategies?

A. Ayurvedic treatment is only effective during advanced disease stages.
B. Early intervention in the Kriya Kalas framework prevents full disease manifestation.
C. Sanchaya stage interventions are irrelevant to chronic diseases.
D. Ayurvedic treatments lack a structured approach to disease progression.

6. A comparative study analyzes the Ayurvedic classification of diseases based on dosha predominance and Western classification based on pathophysiology. Findings show a strong correlation between Kapha-related disorders and inflammatory conditions. Which inference is most logical?

A. Kapha-related disorders lack inflammatory components.
B. Ayurvedic classification complements Western disease taxonomies by adding doshic dimensions.
C. Pathophysiology cannot align with Ayurvedic disease categories.
D. Inflammatory diseases do not fall under Kapha disorders.

7. An Ayurveda-inspired treatment for obesity focuses on balancing Meda dhatu (fat tissue) and Kapha dosha. The study finds that individuals adhering to dietary and herbal interventions show significant improvements in lipid profiles. What aspect of Ayurvedic pathology does this validate?

A. Kapha and Meda are irrelevant to obesity management.
B. Ayurvedic interventions target metabolic imbalances by regulating Meda dhatu.
C. Obesity treatments in Ayurveda are unrelated to dosha balance.
D. Lipid profile improvements have no connection to Ayurvedic theories.

8. A scholar examines the relationship between prakriti (constitutional type) and disease susceptibility. They find that Vata-predominant individuals are more prone to degenerative conditions, while Kapha types exhibit resilience against metabolic diseases. How does this finding reflect Ayurvedic principles?
   A. Prakriti determines individual responses to environmental and lifestyle factors.
   B. Prakriti is unrelated to disease susceptibility or progression.
   C. All prakriti types show equal susceptibility to diseases.
   D. Vata-predominance has no scientific relevance to degenerative disorders.
9. In a clinical trial, a population exposed to urban pollutants shows higher incidences of respiratory diseases. Ayurvedic practitioners attribute this to aggravated Vata and Kapha doshas due to Rajas influences. How does this explanation align with Ayurvedic pathology?
   A. Rajas and doshas lack an environmental correlation.
   B. Environmental factors are integral to doshic aggravation and disease etiology.
   C. Respiratory diseases cannot be explained through Ayurvedic dosha theory.
   D. Urban pollution primarily affects Tamas, not Rajas.
10. A meta-analysis examines Ayurvedic interventions for chronic liver diseases. Researchers note a consistent emphasis on addressing Pitta dosha and Rakta dhatu (blood tissue). Treatments yield significant improvements in liver enzymes and bilirubin levels. What does this study imply?
   A. Pitta regulation has no correlation with liver health.
   B. Ayurvedic treatments demonstrate efficacy by targeting Pitta dosha and Rakta dhatu.
   C. Liver disease outcomes are independent of dosha-based interventions.
   D. Ayurveda lacks a systemic approach to liver disorders.

Directions (Q. No. 11-14): *Scenario-Based Questions*

SCENARIO 1

A study evaluates the effects of Ayurvedic interventions on irritable bowel syndrome (IBS). It finds that therapies aimed at balancing doshas, particularly Pitta, significantly reduce symptoms and improve gut microbiota diversity.

SCENARIO 2

A separate investigation examines soil degradation's impact on the medicinal properties of plants like Ashwagandha. Findings indicate a reduction in bioactive components, leading to diminished therapeutic efficacy in Ayurvedic treatments.

11. How does Scenario 1 establish a link between dosha balance and microbiota diversity?
   A. Dosha balance has no measurable impact on microbiota.
   B. Balancing doshas improves gut microbiota diversity, alleviating IBS symptoms.
   C. Gut microbiota diversity is independent of dosha interventions.
   D. IBS is unrelated to Ayurvedic treatments.
12. In Scenario 2, what impact does soil degradation have on Ayurvedic treatment efficacy?
   A. It enhances the potency of Ashwagandha.
   B. Soil degradation reduces the bioactive compound content, diminishing efficacy.
   C. Ayurvedic treatments are unaffected by changes in plant bioactivity.
   D. Ashwagandha's efficacy depends solely on its preparation method.
13. Based on Scenarios 1 and 2, what strategy would enhance the efficacy of Ayurvedic treatments?
   A. Increasing synthetic alternatives for traditional herbs.
   B. Promoting sustainable cultivation of medicinal plants.
   C. Disregarding environmental factors in plant cultivation.
   D. Focusing solely on modern pharmacological methods.
14. What does the connection between gut health (Scenario 1) and environmental sustainability (Scenario 2) highlight?
   A. The need for environmental conservation to ensure effective Ayurvedic treatments.
   B. Gut health is unrelated to the quality of medicinal plants.
   C. Environmental factors have no bearing on Ayurvedic formulations.
   D. Ayurveda focuses only on immediate therapeutic outcomes, ignoring environmental concerns.
15. The progression of disease in Ayurvedic pathology (Samprapti) includes distinct stages:
   (a) **Sanchaya:** accumulation of doshas.
   (b) **Prakopa:** aggravation of doshas.
   (c) **Prasara:** spread of doshas to other tissues.
   (d) **Bheda:** manifestation of specific diseases.

Choose the correct answer from the options given below:
A. (a), (b), and (c) only
B. (a), (b), (c), and (d)
C. (a), (b), and (d) only
D. (b), (c), and (d) only

16. The principles of disease causation in Ayurveda emphasize the role of:
(a) Dosha imbalance (doshic vikriti).
(b) Accumulation of Ama (toxins).
(c) Faulty dietary habits (Ahara).
(d) External pathogens as the sole causative factor.

Choose the correct answer from the options given below:
A. (a), (b), and (c) only
B. (a), (b), and (d) only
C. (b), (c), and (d) only
D. (a), (b), (c), and (d)

17. The Ayurvedic classification of diseases considers:
(a) Dosha predominance in the pathology.
(b) Affected dhatus (tissues).
(c) Disease origin, whether endogenous or exogenous.
(d) Genetic factors as the primary determinant.

Choose the correct answer from the options given below:
A. (a), (b), and (c) only
B. (a), (c), and (d) only
C. (b), (c), and (d) only
D. (a), (b), (c), and (d)

18. Ayurveda describes six stages of disease development (Kriya Kalas):
(a) Sanchaya (accumulation).
(b) Prakopa (aggravation).
(c) Prasara (spread).
(d) Vyakti (clinical manifestation).

Choose the correct answer from the options given below:
A. (a), (b), and (c) only
B. (a), (b), (c), and (d)
C. (b), (c), and (d) only
D. (a), (c), and (d) only

19. In Ayurvedic pathology, the concept of dhatus refers to:
(a) Structural and functional units of the body.
(b) Pathogenic factors that cause disease.
(c) External influences affecting health.
(d) Only the blood and nervous system tissues.

Choose the correct answer from the options given below:
A. (a) and (b) only
B. (a), (b), and (c) only
C. (a) and (d) only
D. (a), (b), and (d) only

20. Ayurvedic disease management principles include:
(a) Balancing the doshas.
(b) Detoxification through Panchakarma.
(c) Enhancing Agni (digestive fire).
(d) Targeting specific organs, excluding systemic factors.

Choose the correct answer from the options given below:
A. (a), (b), and (c) only
B. (a) and (b) only
C. (b) and (d) only
D. (a), (b), (c), and (d)

21. Ayurvedic Rasas (tastes) have biological actions such as:
(a) Bitter Rasa detoxifies and reduces inflammation.
(b) Sweet Rasa promotes tissue growth and nourishment.
(c) Sour Rasa enhances metabolic activity.
(d) Astringent Rasa causes tissue degeneration.

Choose the correct answer from the options given below:
A. (a), (b), and (c) only
B. (a) and (c) only
C. (b), (c), and (d) only
D. (a), (b), (c), and (d)

22. According to Ayurveda, the causative factors (Nidanas) of disease include:
(a) Improper lifestyle habits.
(b) Psychological stress and emotions.
(c) Microbial infection as the only root cause.
(d) Seasonal imbalances.

Choose the correct answer from the options given below:
A. (a), (b), and (d) only
B. (a), (b), (c), and (d)
C. (b) and (c) only
D. (a) and (d) only

23. The Ayurvedic concept of Ama includes:
(a) Undigested and toxic metabolic byproducts.
(b) The root cause of many systemic diseases.
(c) Physical manifestations limited to the gastrointestinal tract.
(d) Factors unrelated to Agni (digestive fire) impairment.

Choose the correct answer from the options given below:

A. (a), (b), and (c) only
B. (a), (b), and (d) only
C. (a) and (b) only
D. (b), (c), and (d) only

24. Key principles of disease prevention in Ayurveda include:

(a) Seasonal routines (Ritucharya).
(b) Strengthening immunity through Rasayanas.
(c) Avoidance of Ama accumulation.
(d) Exclusive reliance on herbal remedies for prevention.

Choose the correct answer from the options given below:

A. (a), (b), and (c) only
B. (b), (c), and (d) only
C. (a), (b), and (d) only
D. (a), (b), (c), and (d)

25. Match List–I (Concepts) with List–II (Descriptions):

List–I	List–II
(a) Nidana	1. Causative factors of disease
(b) Samprapti	2. Pathology and progression of disease
(c) Prakriti	3. Individual constitution based on doshas
(d) Kriya Kalas	4. Stages of disease development

Choose the correct answer from the options given below:

A. (a)-1, (b)-2, (c)-3, (d)-4
B. (a)-2, (b)-1, (c)-4, (d)-3
C. (a)-3, (b)-4, (c)-1, (d)-2
D. (a)-4, (b)-3, (c)-2, (d)-1

26. Match List–I (Therapies) with List–II (Objectives):

List–I	List–II
(a) Panchakarma	1. Detoxification and rejuvenation
(b) Abhyanga	2. Balancing doshas through oil massage
(c) Rasayana	3. Enhancing longevity and immunity
(d) Shirodhara	4. Mental relaxation and calming effects

Choose the correct answer from the options given below:

A. (a)-1, (b)-2, (c)-3, (d)-4
B. (a)-2, (b)-1, (c)-4, (d)-3
C. (a)-3, (b)-4, (c)-1, (d)-2
D. (a)-4, (b)-3, (c)-2, (d)-1

27. Match List–I (Diseases) with List–II (Dosha Predominance):

List–I	List–II
(a) Rheumatoid arthritis	1. Vaṭa-Kapha imbalance
(b) Diabetes mellitus	2. Kapha-Pitta imbalance
(c) Peptic ulcers	3. Aggravation of Pitta dosha
(d) Insomnia	4. Aggravation of Vata dosha

Choose the correct answer from the options given below:

A. (a)-1, (b)-2, (c)-3, (d)-4
B. (a)-2, (b)-1, (c)-4, (d)-3
C. (a)-3, (b)-4, (c)-1, (d)-2
D. (a)-4, (b)-3, (c)-2, (d)-1

28. Match List–I (Rasayana Herbs) with List–II (Properties):

List–I	List–II
(a) Ashwagandha	1. Adaptogenic and stress-reducing
(b) Amalaki	2. Antioxidant and rejuvenating
(c) Brahmi	3. Cognitive enhancement and memory
(d) Haritaki	4. Digestive support and detoxification

Choose the correct answer from the options given below:

A. (a)-1, (b)-2, (c)-3, (d)-4
B. (a)-2, (b)-1, (c)-4, (d)-3
C. (a)-3, (b)-4, (c)-1, (d)-2
D. (a)-4, (b)-3, (c)-2, (d)-1

29. Match List–I (Concepts of Disease) with List–II (Descriptions):

List–I	List–II
(a) Sanchaya	1. Initial accumulation of doshas
(b) Prakopa	2. Aggravation of doshas
(c) Prasara	3. Spread of imbalanced doshas
(d) Bheda	4. Manifestation of disease symptoms

Choose the correct answer from the options given below:

A. (a)-1, (b)-2, (c)-3, (d)-4
B. (a)-2, (b)-1, (c)-4, (d)-3
C. (a)-3, (b)-4, (c)-1, (d)-2
D. (a)-4, (b)-3, (c)-2, (d)-1

30. Match List–I (Ayurvedic Diagnosis Tools) with List–II (Applications):

List–I	List–II
(a) Nadi Pariksha	1. Pulse diagnosis for dosha imbalance
(b) Jihva Pariksha	2. Tongue analysis for Ama presence
(c) Drik Pariksha	3. Eye examination for systemic health
(d) Sparsha Pariksha	4. Palpation to identify tissue anomalies

Choose the correct answer from the options given below:

A. (a)-1, (b)-2, (c)-3, (d)-4
B. (a)-2, (b)-1, (c)-4, (d)-3
C. (a)-3, (b)-4, (c)-1, (d)-2
D. (a)-4, (b)-3, (c)-2, (d)-1

31. Match List–I (Dosha Characteristics) with List–II (Descriptions):

List–I	List–II
(a) Vata	1. Light, dry, and mobile qualities
(b) Pitta	2. Hot, sharp, and liquid qualities
(c) Kapha	3. Heavy, slow, and stable qualities
(d) Dosha balance	4. Essential for health and harmony

Choose the correct answer from the options given below:

A. (a)-1, (b)-2, (c)-3, (d)-4
B. (a)-2, (b)-1, (c)-4, (d)-3
C. (a)-3, (b)-4, (c)-1, (d)-2
D. (a)-4, (b)-3, (c)-2, (d)-1

32. Match List–I (Disease Classifications) with List–II (Descriptions):

List–I	List–II
(a) Nija	1. Diseases caused by internal factors like dosha imbalance
(b) Agantu	2. Diseases caused by external factors like trauma
(c) Doshaja	3. Disorders primarily linked to one dosha
(d) Dhatuja	4. Disorders affecting specific tissues

Choose the correct answer from the options given below:

A. (a)-1, (b)-2, (c)-3, (d)-4
B. (a)-2, (b)-1, (c)-4, (d)-3
C. (a)-3, (b)-4, (c)-1, (d)-2
D. (a)-4, (b)-3, (c)-2, (d)-1

33. Match List–I (Stages of Samprapti) with List–II (Implications):

List–I	List–II
(a) Sanchaya	1. Early warning signs and minor discomfort
(b) Prakopa	2. Aggravation leading to specific symptoms
(c) Vyakti	3. Full manifestation of disease symptoms
(d) Bheda	4. Chronicity or complications of disease

Choose the correct answer from the options given below:

A. (a)-1, (b)-2, (c)-3, (d)-4
B. (a)-2, (b)-1, (c)-4, (d)-3
C. (a)-3, (b)-4, (c)-1, (d)-2
D. (a)-4, (b)-3, (c)-2, (d)-1

34. Match List–I (Ayurvedic Therapies) with List–II (Functions):

List–I	List–II
(a) Shodhana	1. Purification therapies to eliminate toxins
(b) Shamana	2. Palliative treatments to manage symptoms
(c) Rasayana	3. Rejuvenation and anti-aging treatments
(d) Vajikarana	4. Aphrodisiac therapies to enhance vitality

Choose the correct answer from the options given below:

A. (a)-1, (b)-2, (c)-3, (d)-4
B. (a)-2, (b)-1, (c)-4, (d)-3
C. (a)-3, (b)-4, (c)-1, (d)-2
D. (a)-4, (b)-3, (c)-2, (d)-1

Directions (Q. No. 35-39): *Following questions are based on Statement 1 and Statement 2. Read both the statements carefully and choose the correct answer from the options given below:*

A. Both Statement 1 and Statement 2 are true, and Statement 2 is the correct explanation of Statement 1.
B. Both Statement 1 and Statement 2 are true, but Statement 2 is not the correct explanation of Statement 1.
C. Statement 1 is true, but Statement 2 is false.
D. Statement 1 is false, but Statement 2 is true.
E. Both Statement 1 and Statement 2 are false.

35. Statement 1: The Ayurvedic concept of Ama refers to undigested toxic substances that accumulate in the body due to impaired Agni (digestive fire).

Statement 2: Ama is considered the root cause of many diseases, as it disrupts the balance of doshas and blocks the srotas (body channels).

36. Statement 1: Ayurveda recognizes Nidana Panchaka as the diagnostic framework for identifying the root cause of diseases.

Statement 2: Nidana Panchaka comprises Nidana (causative factors), Purvarupa (premonitory symptoms), Rupa (clinical features), Upashaya (therapeutic trial), and Samprapti (pathogenesis).

37. Statement 1: Rasayana therapy in Ayurveda is primarily aimed at enhancing longevity, immunity, and tissue rejuvenation.

Statement 2: Rasayana therapy includes physical purification processes like Panchakarma, without any dietary or lifestyle interventions.

38. **Statement 1:** Ayurveda categorizes diseases into Nija (endogenous) and Agantu (exogenous) types based on their causative factors.

    Statement 2: Nija diseases are attributed to external traumas or microbial infections, while Agantu diseases result from doshic imbalances within the body.

39. **Statement 1:** Prakriti in Ayurveda refers to an individual's unique constitution, determined by the predominance of doshas during conception.

    Statement 2: Prakriti remains static throughout an individual's life, irrespective of environmental or lifestyle factors.

Directions (Q. No. 40-45): *There are two statements in each question. One is labelled as Assertion (A) and the other is as Reason (R). Read both the statements and choose the correct answer from the options given below*:

A. Both Assertion (A) and Reason (R) are true, and Reason (R) is the correct explanation of Assertion (A).
B. Both Assertion (A) and Reason (R) are true, but Reason (R) is not the correct explanation of Assertion (A).
C. Assertion (A) is true, but Reason (R) is false.
D. Assertion (A) is false, but Reason (R) is true.
E. Both Assertion (A) and Reason (R) are false.

40. **Assertion (A):** In Ayurveda, Ritucharya (seasonal routines) are prescribed to maintain the balance of doshas during seasonal transitions.

    Reason (R): Seasonal changes significantly influence the natural balance of doshas, requiring specific dietary and lifestyle adjustments.

41. **Assertion (A):** Ayurvedic detoxification therapies such as Panchakarma aim to eliminate Ama (toxins) and restore the balance of doshas.

    Reason (R): Panchakarma therapies work by directly targeting cellular metabolism and oxidative stress pathways to reverse chronic diseases.

42. **Assertion (A):** Agni, the digestive fire in Ayurveda, is considered the primary factor responsible for metabolism and overall health.

    Reason (R): The impairment of Agni leads to the accumulation of Ama, disrupting the balance of doshas and causing disease.

43. **Assertion (A):** The Tridosha theory in Ayurveda forms the foundation for understanding health and disease.

    Reason (R): Tridosha refers to the balance of mind, body, and spirit rather than physiological functions.

44. **Assertion (A):** Ayurvedic interventions such as Rasayana therapies are designed to rejuvenate tissues and enhance immunity.

    Reason (R): Rasayana therapies work by restoring the doshic balance and improving the bioavailability of nutrients.

45. **Assertion (A):** Ayurveda emphasizes that prakriti (individual constitution) determines a person's susceptibility to specific diseases.

    Reason (R): Prakriti analysis in Ayurveda identifies genetic predispositions and environmental interactions to customize treatment plans.

Directions (Q. No. 46-50): *Read the following passage carefully and answer the question given below*:

Ayurveda, the ancient Indian system of medicine, provides a deeply interconnected framework for understanding health and disease. Rooted in the philosophy of natural harmony, Ayurveda emphasizes the balance of mind, body, and spirit. The fundamental basis of Ayurvedic disease classification rests on the Tridosha theory, which encompasses the three doshas: Vata, Pitta, and Kapha. These doshas represent physiological principles that govern bodily functions, and their imbalance is seen as the root cause of diseases. However, with advancements in biological and medical sciences, modern Ayurvedic scholars are exploring ways to bridge classical disease classifications with contemporary pathological frameworks.

In traditional Ayurveda, diseases are classified based on several parameters, including Nidana Panchaka (fivefold diagnostic framework), Doshaja Vikara (diseases caused by dosha imbalance), and the affected Dhatus (tissues). Additionally, diseases are broadly categorized into Nija (endogenous, caused by internal factors such as doshic imbalance) and Agantu (exogenous, caused by external factors such as trauma or infections). While this classical framework provides profound insights into the etiology and progression of diseases, modern advancements are enabling deeper scientific validation and refinement of these principles.

One of the emerging areas of research is the integration of Ayurvedic Prakriti-based diagnosis with modern genomics. Prakriti, which describes an individual's unique doshic constitution, has been correlated with genetic markers, metabolic profiles, and susceptibility to specific diseases. For example, individuals with Vata-dominant Prakriti are more prone to degenerative and neurological disorders, while those with Pitta dominance are often susceptible to inflammatory conditions and metabolic syndromes. Such correlations are paving the way for personalized medicine, where treatments are tailored to an individual's genetic and physiological profile.

Samprapti, the Ayurvedic concept of disease progression, is another area gaining attention. Samprapti delineates the stages of disease development: Sanchaya (accumulation), Prakopa (aggravation), Prasara (spread), Sthana Samshraya (localization), Vyakti (manifestation), and Bheda (complications). These stages align closely with the modern understanding of pathological processes, from cellular stress and inflammation to organ-specific disease manifestation. For instance, the Sanchaya stage can be compared to early molecular changes like oxidative stress or chronic inflammation, while the Vyakti stage corresponds to clinically detectable disease. This alignment allows researchers to explore the early detection of diseases through Ayurvedic principles and intervene before full-blown symptoms develop.

In recent years, the Ayurvedic concept of Ama, or toxic byproducts resulting from impaired digestion and metabolism, has been studied in the context of metabolic disorders, particularly diabetes and cardiovascular diseases. Modern research shows that the accumulation of advanced glycation end-products (AGEs) and other metabolic toxins parallels the Ayurvedic concept of Ama. These findings highlight how the impairment of Agni (digestive fire) contributes to systemic imbalances and the progression of chronic diseases.

Another critical focus of modern Ayurvedic research is the gut-microbiota-dosha connection. The gut microbiota, often referred to as the "second brain," plays a pivotal role in maintaining health. Ayurvedic texts have long emphasized the importance of gut health in disease prevention. For example, Pitta imbalance is linked to hyperacidity and inflammatory bowel disorders, while Vata disturbances correspond to irritable bowel syndrome (IBS) and motility issues. Recent studies demonstrate that Ayurvedic interventions such as Triphala, buttermilk therapy, and basti (medicated enemas) modulate the gut microbiota, promoting diversity and improving metabolic health. These therapies not only balance doshas but also enhance the gut-brain axis, supporting overall systemic health.

The classification of diseases in Ayurveda also extends to mental health, which is intricately linked with the balance of Sattva (clarity), Rajas (activity), and Tamas (inertia). Disorders like anxiety and depression are considered to arise from imbalances in the gunas, compounded by doshic aggravation. Modern neuroscience has started exploring how Ayurvedic interventions, including meditation, yoga, and herbal therapies like Brahmi and Ashwagandha, influence neuroplasticity and stress pathways. These findings reveal the potential of Ayurveda to contribute to integrative psychiatry.

Environmental factors, too, are deeply embedded in Ayurvedic disease classifications. Concepts such as Kala Parinama (seasonal and climatic changes) and their influence on doshic balance are now being validated through studies on circadian rhythms and seasonal immune modulation. For instance, Kapha aggravation during spring correlates with an increased prevalence of respiratory allergies, while Pitta imbalances in summer are linked to heat strokes and inflammatory skin conditions. Ayurvedic seasonal routines (Ritucharya) are being adapted into modern wellness protocols to optimize immunity and metabolic health.

The Ayurvedic classification of diseases also integrates the idea of Shatkriyakala, or six stages of disease intervention, which offers a comprehensive roadmap for preventing complications. These stages guide practitioners on when and how to intervene therapeutically, with techniques ranging from Shodhana (purification therapies like Panchakarma) to Shamana (palliative treatments). Modern practitioners are exploring how these stages can enhance chronic disease management, particularly in cases like autoimmune diseases where early intervention is critical.

Moreover, the growing field of Rasayana therapy (rejuvenation and longevity treatments) exemplifies the preventive approach of Ayurveda. Herbs such as Amalaki, Guduchi, and Shatavari are not only rich in antioxidants but also modulate inflammatory pathways and enhance tissue regeneration. Modern pharmacological studies are validating these properties, demonstrating how Ayurvedic classifications based on Rasas (tastes) and Guna (qualities) align with bioactive compounds and pharmacodynamics.

Finally, the classification of diseases in Ayurveda is incomplete without its holistic emphasis on lifestyle and diet. Concepts like Ahara-Vihara (dietary and lifestyle habits) are being incorporated into preventive healthcare strategies. Research shows that intermittent fasting, a concept akin to Ayurvedic principles of Langhana (lightening therapies), has profound effects on metabolic health, insulin sensitivity, and cellular repair. Similarly, the importance of circadian alignment, as emphasized in Ayurvedic Dinacharya (daily routines), is now backed by evidence linking circadian rhythms to hormonal balance and overall well-being.

While Ayurveda's classical disease classifications remain timeless, their integration with modern biomedical concepts is unveiling new avenues for research and practice. The personalized, preventive, and holistic nature of Ayurveda not only complements modern medicine but also addresses the gaps in chronic disease management. By bridging ancient wisdom with cutting-edge science, Ayurveda is carving its place as a global system of integrative medicine.

46. According to the passage, how does the Ayurvedic concept of Prakriti relate to modern medicine?

A. It is irrelevant to contemporary medical frameworks.

B. It correlates with genetic markers and disease susceptibility, enabling personalized medicine.

C. It opposes genetic research by focusing only on metaphysical aspects of health.

D. It exclusively classifies individuals based on psychological tendencies.

47. What modern phenomenon is comparable to the Ayurvedic concept of Ama?
   A. Advanced glycation end-products (AGEs) and metabolic toxins.
   B. Cellular repair mechanisms in the body.
   C. Neuroplasticity and gut-brain axis studies.
   D. Seasonal immune modulation and detoxification.

48. How does the passage describe the role of gut microbiota in Ayurveda?
   A. It has no connection to doshic balance or disease prevention.
   B. It is influenced by therapies like Triphala and basti to promote health.
   C. It is a modern scientific discovery irrelevant to Ayurvedic principles.
   D. It contradicts Ayurvedic classifications of gut disorders.

49. According to the passage, how do seasonal changes influence diseases in Ayurveda?
   A. They disrupt circadian rhythms without affecting immunity.
   B. They lead to doshic imbalances that correspond with specific health issues.
   C. They only affect respiratory and skin disorders, not metabolic health.
   D. They are unrelated to modern studies on immune modulation.

50. What does the concept of Shatkriyakala represent in the context of modern disease management?
   A. A framework for treating diseases only after complications arise.
   B. A structured approach for early intervention and chronic disease prevention.
   C. A replacement for purification therapies like Panchakarma.
   D. A theoretical model with no relevance to clinical practice.

ANSWER WITH EXPLANATIONS

1. **B:** Ayurveda's nidana encompasses internal and external factors contributing to disease, correlating with modern risk concepts. The dosha theory, which includes physical, mental, and environmental factors, provides a comprehensive view of disease causation. While modern frameworks focus on observable pathology, Ayurveda identifies subtle imbalances preceding clinical manifestation, such as diet, habits, and psychological factors. The inclusion of mind-body interactions highlights the broader scope of Ayurvedic causation, aligning with psychosomatic models. Thus, nidana extends beyond risk factors like lifestyle to subtle doshic imbalances, offering insights into the root cause and prevention of diseases not fully addressed in conventional medicine.

2. **B:** The calming of Vata dosha corresponds with neuroendocrine modulation, emphasizing Ayurveda's alignment with stress-related research. Cortisol regulation, observed in this case, mirrors the physiological outcomes described in doshic terms, showing the scientific basis for Vata-stress connections. Vata governs nervous activity, and its imbalance leads to hyperarousal, which Ayurveda addresses through herbs, lifestyle, and therapies. Unlike a placebo, these interventions provide consistent biochemical improvements. The inclusion of multiple modalities in treatment aligns with Ayurveda's holistic nature. This connection validates Ayurveda's approach by integrating ancient principles into neuroendocrine-based stress management frameworks, with cortisol acting as a measurable biomarker.

3. **B:** Ayurvedic therapies addressing Ama detoxification, as reflected in systemic inflammatory markers like CRP, demonstrate its relevance in autoimmune conditions. Panchakarma's purification role aligns with modern detoxification therapies aimed at reducing inflammation. Ama, seen as metabolic waste, parallels markers like AGEs in systemic disorders. By balancing doshas and improving gut health, Panchakarma interrupts the pathological feedback loop between inflammation and tissue damage. Such studies validate the integrative potential of Ayurveda in addressing chronic conditions where modern therapies focus on symptomatic relief. Hence, the systemic effect of detoxifying Ama strengthens its applicability in contemporary autoimmune disease management.

4. **B:** Joint degeneration involves Vata's dry, mobile properties and Kapha's structural stability. Ayurvedic approaches balance these doshas, reflecting modern anti-inflammatory and regenerative treatments. Dosha imbalances are understood as dynamic disruptions that initiate physiological deterioration, aligning with cellular inflammation theories. Ayurveda's use of herbs, therapies, and lifestyle modifications parallels disease-modifying strategies in modern rheumatology. This systematic regulation through doshas extends treatment beyond symptom management, addressing

underlying imbalances that drive chronic joint disorders. This validates Ayurveda's contribution to joint health, offering a foundational understanding of degenerative processes relevant to both ancient and modern therapeutic approaches.

5. **B:** The stages of Kriya Kalas allow early detection and intervention, preventing chronic disease progression. Ayurveda's Sanchaya stage represents subclinical imbalances, mirroring biomarkers in early pathogenesis. Unlike symptomatic treatment, this framework targets the root cause before full manifestation. Intervening at the Sanchaya stage with diet, lifestyle, and detox prevents Prakopa (aggravation) and systemic complications. This highlights Ayurveda's preventative approach, integrating pathogenesis with personalized care. The alignment of these stages with cellular stress and inflammation marks Ayurveda's relevance in disease prevention, addressing gaps in conventional systems that often overlook early, subtle disease markers.

6. **B:** Ayurvedic and Western classifications converge, as dosha-based categories incorporate physiological disruptions like inflammation (Kapha). The doshic framework identifies predispositions and tendencies, offering preventive insights. Modern pathophysiology confirms the systemic nature of dosha impacts, such as Kapha's association with metabolic and inflammatory diseases. This complementarity bridges Ayurveda's functional perspectives with Western anatomical classifications. By extending classifications beyond observable symptoms, Ayurveda captures psychosomatic and systemic interactions. This hybrid approach emphasizes Ayurveda's potential to enhance diagnostic specificity and treatment efficacy, broadening the applicability of its disease framework in contemporary clinical research.

7. **B:** Meda dhatu governs fat metabolism and reflects systemic energy balance. Ayurveda's doshic perspective explains obesity as a Kapha imbalance, manifested through impaired metabolism and tissue accumulation. Modern research corroborates this understanding with lipid profile improvements through Ayurvedic interventions, targeting adipose tissue's role in inflammation and chronic diseases. Herbs like Guggulu, dietary adjustments, and lifestyle modifications directly influence lipid metabolism, showing measurable outcomes. Unlike calorie-centric models, Ayurveda addresses systemic imbalances, fostering sustainable weight management. This integrative understanding highlights the relevance of Ayurvedic pathology in tackling obesity through metabolic restoration.

8. **A:** Prakriti's influence on disease susceptibility aligns with genetic predispositions and environmental factors. Vata individuals' degenerative tendencies and Kapha types' resilience correlate with dosha-specific vulnerabilities. Ayurveda's individualized approach tailors prevention and treatment strategies, emphasizing constitutionally aligned care. Modern studies validate these predispositions, integrating Prakriti-based observations with epigenetic and metabolic research. By recognizing inter-individual variability, Ayurveda complements conventional precision medicine, addressing both physiological tendencies and environmental influences. This integration underscores Ayurveda's holistic model, providing preventive strategies for diseases associated with constitutional imbalances.

9. **B:** Urban environmental stresses, such as pollutants, disturb Rajas, indirectly aggravating doshas like Kapha and Vata, leading to respiratory issues. Ayurveda's systemic approach highlights the interplay between external (Rajas) and internal (doshas) factors. Modern research links urban pollution to inflammation, oxidative stress, and altered microbiota, which Ayurveda interprets as doshic imbalance. The role of environmental influences in pathology demonstrates Ayurveda's early recognition of external stressors as disease triggers. Integrating this knowledge fosters a preventive framework where environmental health aligns with individual health, emphasizing the importance of sustainable living environments.

10. **B:** Pitta governs enzymatic activity and Rakta (blood tissue), aligning Ayurvedic interventions with liver detoxification and inflammation reduction. Elevated bilirubin and enzyme normalization reflect the physiological outcomes of balancing Pitta and Rakta. Herbs like Kutki and treatments targeting Pitta's hot, sharp qualities address liver dysfunction comprehensively. Unlike symptomatic liver treatments, Ayurveda incorporates systemic perspectives, targeting doshic imbalance and dhatu involvement. This integrative understanding allows a broader application of Ayurvedic principles in managing liver health, emphasizing functional recovery alongside detoxification. Modern biochemical validation of these interventions underscores Ayurveda's therapeutic potential in hepatology.

11. **B:** Restoring microbiota diversity through Ayurvedic interventions demonstrates systemic immunity regulation via gut-associated lymphoid tissue (GALT). Triphala's balancing properties align with doshic theory, directly influencing microbial populations and gut health. This correlation extends Ayurveda's

relevance to immunological research, where the microbiota modulates systemic inflammatory markers like CRP. By emphasizing gut health, Ayurveda validates its holistic impact on immunity, extending beyond localized effects. This integrated approach demonstrates Ayurveda's ability to harmonize doshic and microbiological dimensions, enriching current models of immune modulation.

12. **B:** Soil degradation impacts the phytochemical composition of herbs like Amalaki, diminishing their efficacy in formulations like Triphala. Environmental stress affects bioactive content, linking ecological factors to therapeutic outcomes. Ayurveda emphasizes sustainability in sourcing medicinal plants, ensuring doshic balance through quality preservation. This ecological consideration highlights Ayurveda's systemic perspective, integrating environmental health into therapeutic efficacy. Addressing these challenges requires agroforestry and sustainable practices, emphasizing Ayurveda's adaptability to modern environmental contexts while maintaining its therapeutic integrity.

13. **B:** Sustainable cultivation aligns Ayurveda's ecological focus with therapeutic outcomes, emphasizing quality and availability. By preserving Amalaki populations, agroforestry practices enhance medicinal efficacy, ensuring Triphala's doshic balance. This integrative strategy addresses environmental degradation while maintaining therapeutic consistency. Ayurveda's reliance on natural resources underscores the importance of aligning ecological health with individual well-being. Modern research validates this perspective, demonstrating the interconnectedness of environmental sustainability and healthcare outcomes.

14. **A:** Environmental conservation ensures therapeutic consistency in formulations like Triphala, integrating ecological and patient outcomes. By emphasizing sustainable practices and bioactive consistency, Ayurveda bridges environmental and systemic health. The focus on conservation highlights Ayurveda's preventive dimension, extending its holistic principles to ecological health. These strategies foster global collaboration, ensuring Ayurveda's sustainability in a modern healthcare framework. Such integrative approaches underscore Ayurveda's relevance in addressing contemporary challenges while maintaining its therapeutic core.

15. **B:** The six stages of Kriya Kalas align with modern frameworks of disease progression. These stages—from subclinical imbalances to full-blown complications—offer opportunities for early intervention. By targeting Sanchaya and Prakopa stages, Ayurveda emphasizes prevention and disrupts disease progression. This contrasts with modern medicine, which often addresses symptoms at advanced stages. The alignment of these stages with molecular, cellular, and systemic pathology illustrates Ayurveda's relevance in preventive care. Such insights enrich clinical practice by integrating traditional principles with modern diagnostics, providing a proactive approach to healthcare.

16. **A:** Ayurveda's emphasis on doshic imbalance, Ama, and faulty lifestyle habits highlights a holistic understanding of disease causation. These factors interplay dynamically, influencing disease progression. Modern parallels, such as dietary risks, sedentary lifestyles, and metabolic toxins, align with Nidana Panchaka. Unlike Western medicine's focus on pathogens, Ayurveda integrates environmental, psychological, and lifestyle factors into its causation model. This systemic perspective expands our understanding of health, incorporating subtle predisposing factors into diagnostic and preventive strategies. The exclusion of external pathogens as the sole cause underscores Ayurveda's broader focus.

17. **A:** Ayurveda integrates dosha predominance, dhatu involvement, and disease origin to classify diseases systematically. This approach complements Western taxonomies, adding functional perspectives to anatomical and physiological frameworks. Dosha-specific classifications provide insights into disease predispositions, while dhatu involvement emphasizes tissue-specific vulnerabilities. By categorizing diseases based on causation and localization, Ayurveda provides a multidimensional framework, addressing gaps in symptom-based models. Modern studies on doshic influences enrich this understanding, demonstrating Ayurveda's relevance in comprehensive disease classification and management.

18. **B:** The six stages of Kriya Kalas, from Sanchaya to Bheda, provide a structured roadmap for disease prevention and treatment. These stages align with cellular stress, inflammation, and systemic manifestation in modern pathology. For example, Sanchaya corresponds to early inflammatory changes, while Vyakti represents clinical detection. Ayurveda's emphasis on intervening before Bheda underscores its preventive focus. This structured progression enriches modern frameworks, where interventions often occur after significant pathology has developed. The integration of these stages fosters holistic management, bridging traditional principles with modern healthcare.

19. **A:** Dhatus, as structural and functional units, embody Ayurveda's systemic approach to health and disease.

Each dhatu—rasa, rakta, mamsa, etc.—corresponds to tissues like plasma, blood, and muscle, providing a physiological framework. Diseases reflect disruptions in these tissues, mirroring Western concepts like organ dysfunction. Ayurveda's emphasis on dhatu balance integrates cellular health with systemic functionality. By addressing tissue-specific imbalances alongside doshic regulation, Ayurveda offers a comprehensive model for disease management. This perspective aligns with tissue-targeted therapies in modern medicine, enriching treatment strategies with systemic insights.

20. **A:** Ayurvedic disease management emphasizes dosha balancing, detoxification, and Agni regulation, reflecting its holistic approach. These principles align with modern chronic disease management, where inflammation and metabolic dysfunction are central. Panchakarma therapies eliminate toxins (Ama), while dietary adjustments enhance Agni. Unlike symptom-focused treatments, Ayurveda addresses systemic imbalances, integrating mind-body interventions. This preventive approach contrasts with curative models, emphasizing long-term well-being. The inclusion of lifestyle and diet highlights Ayurveda's comprehensive framework, fostering sustainability in health outcomes.

21. **A:** Ayurvedic Rasas (tastes) have biological actions that influence systemic health. For instance, bitter detoxifies, sweet nourishes, and sour stimulates metabolism, aligning with pharmacological effects. These actions demonstrate Ayurveda's understanding of taste-bioactivity relationships, enriching therapeutic formulations. By categorizing herbs based on taste and doshic influence, Ayurveda offers precision in treatment selection. This approach complements modern pharmacology, where taste and bioactive compounds often correlate. The alignment underscores Ayurveda's systemic insights, bridging ancient wisdom with biochemical research.

22. **A:** Ayurveda integrates lifestyle, psychological stress, and seasonal influences into disease causation, highlighting its holistic framework. Nidana Panchaka extends beyond pathogens, capturing subtle predisposing factors like faulty habits and doshic imbalances. These elements align with modern risk factors, such as chronic stress and environmental changes. By addressing lifestyle and environmental factors, Ayurveda provides a comprehensive preventive strategy. The inclusion of seasonal routines emphasizes adaptability, offering tailored interventions to maintain health. This integrative model complements contemporary epidemiology, enriching disease prevention.

23. **C:** Ama, as undigested metabolic waste, parallels toxins like AGEs and chronic inflammation markers in modern medicine. Agni impairment leads to Ama accumulation, disrupting doshic balance and systemic health. This concept aligns with oxidative stress and gut dysbiosis, emphasizing detoxification. Panchakarma therapies eliminate Ama, improving systemic function. Unlike symptom-based models, Ayurveda addresses root causes like impaired digestion. This integrative approach validates Ayurveda's relevance in managing metabolic disorders, where systemic detoxification and Agni restoration are critical.

24. **A:** Ayurvedic disease prevention emphasizes seasonal routines, Rasayana therapies, and Ama prevention, reflecting its holistic approach. These principles align with modern preventive strategies, such as circadian alignment and anti-inflammatory diets. Seasonal routines optimize immunity, while Rasayanas rejuvenate tissues. Unlike curative models, Ayurveda emphasizes balance and prevention, fostering resilience against disease. The inclusion of lifestyle and dietary adjustments highlights Ayurveda's systemic perspective, integrating ancient wisdom with modern wellness. This preventive approach complements contemporary models, offering sustainable health outcomes.

25. **A:** The matching of concepts like Nidana (causation), Samprapti (progression), and Prakriti (constitution) with their descriptions highlights Ayurveda's structured framework. These elements integrate etiology, pathogenesis, and individual variability into disease management. By linking specific components to their roles, Ayurveda provides a multidimensional diagnostic model. This contrasts with symptom-based classifications, offering preventive and personalized insights. Modern studies validate these correlations, bridging traditional and contemporary perspectives. This integration enriches diagnostic accuracy and therapeutic precision.

26. **A:** Ayurvedic therapies like Panchakarma (detoxification), Abhyanga (oil massage), and Rasayana (rejuvenation) align with their objectives, reflecting a comprehensive approach. These therapies target systemic balance, addressing physical and mental health. Panchakarma eliminates toxins, while Rasayana enhances immunity and longevity. Modern research validates these outcomes, emphasizing the physiological basis of these therapies. This integrative understanding bridges traditional practices with contemporary therapeutic goals, offering holistic healthcare strategies. Such correlations highlight Ayurveda's systemic approach, enriching modern frameworks.

27. **A:** Dosha-specific disorders, such as Vata-Kapha (arthritis), Pitta (peptic ulcers), and Kapha (diabetes),

highlight Ayurveda's alignment with pathophysiology. Each dosha governs specific bodily functions, influencing disease progression. This classification offers insights into predispositions, aligning with inflammatory and metabolic conditions in modern medicine. By addressing doshic imbalances, Ayurveda provides targeted interventions, complementing organ-specific treatments. The systemic nature of doshas enriches diagnostic and therapeutic models, emphasizing balance as a cornerstone of health.

28. **A:** The alignment of Ayurvedic Rasayana herbs with their respective properties demonstrates the systemic nature of traditional medicine. For example, Ashwagandha, known for its adaptogenic effects, reduces stress and enhances vitality, correlating with its role in stabilizing Vata. Similarly, Amalaki's rejuvenating effects align with its antioxidant properties, supporting tissue regeneration and longevity. Brahmi, recognized for cognitive enhancement, reflects Ayurveda's focus on mental health through doshic and guna balance. Lastly, Haritaki's detoxifying effects highlight its role in digestive health and Kapha management. These classifications emphasize the therapeutic precision of Ayurveda, bridging ancient pharmacology with modern biochemical validation for holistic healthcare.

29. **A:** The stages of Samprapti in Ayurvedic pathology offer an intricate understanding of disease progression. Sanchaya (accumulation) corresponds to the earliest signs of imbalance, akin to subclinical inflammation. Prakopa (aggravation) represents worsening doshic activity, while Prasara (spread) indicates systemic involvement. Bheda (complications) reflects the chronic or severe manifestations, paralleling the progression seen in Western medicine from early risk factors to organ failure. This systematic classification allows practitioners to intervene at appropriate stages, emphasizing prevention and management before disease escalates. By correlating traditional stages with contemporary pathology, Ayurveda provides actionable insights for early diagnosis and tailored treatment plans.

30. **A:** Ayurvedic diagnostic tools like Nadi Pariksha (pulse diagnosis) and Jihva Pariksha (tongue analysis) demonstrate its systemic approach to health. Nadi Pariksha detects doshic imbalances by analyzing subtle pulse variations, while Jihva Pariksha identifies Ama accumulation through tongue coating. Drik Pariksha (eye examination) assesses systemic health, including liver and vascular issues, while Sparsha Pariksha (palpation) reveals tissue anomalies. These diagnostic methods reflect Ayurveda's emphasis on non-invasive, holistic evaluation. Modern validation of these techniques aligns them with biomarkers and imaging, enhancing their reliability. Such integrative diagnostics bridge traditional wisdom with contemporary healthcare, fostering a personalized and preventive approach.

31. **A:** The characteristics of Vata, Pitta, and Kapha doshas align with their physiological roles and their influence on health. Vata's light, dry, and mobile qualities correspond to nervous and circulatory functions, while Pitta's hot, sharp nature drives metabolism and enzymatic activity. Kapha's heavy, stable attributes ensure structural and fluid balance. Maintaining the balance of these doshas is essential for health, as their disruption leads to systemic dysfunction. This classification provides a physiological basis for diagnosing and treating diseases. Modern science validates these characteristics through their parallels with neurological, metabolic, and homeostatic systems, highlighting Ayurveda's foundational principles in healthcare.

32. **A:** The distinction between Nija (internal) and Agantu (external) diseases in Ayurveda showcases its comprehensive understanding of pathology. Nija diseases result from doshic imbalances, while Agantu diseases arise from trauma, infections, or external influences. This dual classification integrates internal predispositions with environmental triggers, reflecting a dynamic approach to causation. For instance, while infections may originate externally, their progression depends on the host's doshic state. This interplay emphasizes Ayurveda's holistic view of disease as a combination of intrinsic and extrinsic factors. Bridging these concepts with modern immunology and pathophysiology demonstrates Ayurveda's relevance in addressing multifaceted disease mechanisms.

33. **A:** The stages of Samprapti (Sanchaya to Bheda) reflect a systematic understanding of disease evolution. Sanchaya, the accumulation phase, represents minor discomfort or preclinical signs. Prakopa indicates doshic aggravation, while Vyakti marks symptom manifestation. Bheda involves complications or chronicity, paralleling the progression of diseases from risk factors to organ damage in Western medicine. These stages provide actionable points for intervention, emphasizing prevention at earlier phases. By aligning Samprapti with molecular and systemic pathology, Ayurveda complements modern diagnostics, offering a broader framework for understanding and managing disease from its inception to advanced stages.

34. A: Ayurvedic therapies such as Shodhana (purification), Shamana (palliation), and Rasayana (rejuvenation) target various stages of health and disease. Shodhana eliminates toxins (Ama) and restores doshic balance, aligning with detoxification practices. Shamana addresses symptomatic relief without invasive purification, while Rasayana focuses on longevity and tissue regeneration, enhancing immune function. Vajikarana (aphrodisiac therapy) improves vitality and reproductive health, reflecting Ayurveda's holistic scope. These therapeutic objectives demonstrate an integrative framework, addressing preventive, curative, and rejuvenative dimensions of health. Bridging these with modern healthcare enhances chronic disease management, highlighting Ayurveda's systemic approach to wellness.

35. A: The concept of Ama as metabolic waste underscores Ayurveda's preventive framework. Ama arises from impaired Agni, reflecting toxic byproducts in digestion and metabolism. This aligns with modern concepts of metabolic dysfunction, such as oxidative stress and chronic inflammation. By targeting Ama through therapies like Panchakarma, Ayurveda emphasizes detoxification, restoring doshic balance and systemic health. The disruption of srotas (channels) by Ama mirrors vascular and cellular impairments in Western pathology. This analogy highlights Ayurveda's relevance in addressing metabolic disorders, offering strategies for detoxification, digestion optimization, and disease prevention. Its systemic approach bridges traditional detox concepts with modern biomedicine.

36. A: The Nidana Panchaka framework demonstrates Ayurveda's structured diagnostic methodology. By encompassing Nidana (causation), Purvarupa (premonitory symptoms), Rupa (clinical features), Upashaya (therapeutic trials), and Samprapti (pathogenesis), it captures both overt and subtle dimensions of disease. Modern diagnostics often focus on symptoms and biomarkers, neglecting early signs and individual predispositions. Nidana Panchaka bridges this gap, offering tools to detect imbalances before full manifestation. By integrating physical, psychological, and environmental aspects, it aligns with modern precision medicine. This comprehensive approach enhances prevention and personalization, making Ayurveda relevant in contemporary healthcare systems focused on holistic and proactive diagnostics.

37. C: Rasayana therapy epitomizes Ayurveda's preventive and rejuvenative focus. Aimed at enhancing longevity, immunity, and tissue vitality, Rasayanas such as Amalaki and Guduchi provide systemic benefits through antioxidant and anti-inflammatory mechanisms. Unlike Panchakarma, which involves physical detoxification, Rasayana emphasizes nourishment, balancing doshas and promoting cellular regeneration. Modern research validates its role in modulating immunity and mitigating oxidative stress, contributing to chronic disease prevention. This differentiation between Rasayana and purification therapies highlights Ayurveda's layered approach to health. Its integration into modern care emphasizes regeneration and resilience, complementing treatments targeting immediate pathologies.

38. C: The distinction between Nija and Agantu diseases showcases Ayurveda's dynamic classification system. Nija diseases arise from internal doshic imbalances, while Agantu are caused by external factors like trauma or pathogens. However, the passage highlights that Nija diseases do not primarily involve external causes, such as microbial infections. Instead, internal dysregulation drives disease progression. Modern parallels exist in host-environment interactions, where predispositions influence disease susceptibility. This framework enriches contemporary healthcare by integrating intrinsic vulnerabilities with external triggers. It reflects Ayurveda's holistic view, emphasizing individualized interventions and balance restoration over pathogen-focused models of disease.

39. C: Prakriti, representing an individual's unique constitution, remains static throughout life, influenced by doshas at conception. However, environmental and lifestyle factors can modulate health within this baseline, challenging static interpretations. Ayurveda acknowledges that while the innate Prakriti is fixed, dynamic interactions with diet, stress, and seasons influence doshic balance. This understanding aligns with modern epigenetics, where genetic predispositions interact with environmental factors. By addressing these dynamic imbalances, Ayurveda provides tailored interventions that integrate fixed constitutional traits with adaptive health strategies. This nuanced view enhances personalization in medicine, bridging traditional insights with modern genetic frameworks.

40. A: The emphasis on Ritucharya in Ayurveda highlights its alignment with circadian rhythms and seasonal immune modulation. Seasonal transitions influence doshic balance, requiring tailored adjustments in diet and lifestyle. For instance, spring aggravates Kapha, necessitating light foods and detoxification to prevent respiratory disorders. Modern studies validate these seasonal influences, linking them to shifts in immune function and metabolic activity. Ritucharya's preventive approach fosters resilience by aligning internal physiology with external changes, offering strategies to mitigate seasonal disorders. This integration bridges

Ayurveda's emphasis on adaptability with modern understandings of environmental influences on health, underscoring its timeless relevance.

41. A: Panchakarma, Ayurveda's detoxification therapy, eliminates Ama and restores balance, aligning with chronic disease management strategies. These therapies reduce inflammation, oxidative stress, and systemic toxicity, enhancing metabolic function. Modern parallels exist in treatments targeting cellular stress and detoxification pathways. Panchakarma's systemic impact extends beyond symptom relief, addressing root causes of chronic disorders. For example, its role in enhancing gut health and reducing inflammatory markers reflects its preventive focus. This alignment with cellular detoxification processes underscores Ayurveda's relevance in mitigating diseases driven by systemic imbalances. Its holistic approach offers actionable insights for modern integrative medicine.

42. A: Agni, as the digestive fire, underpins Ayurveda's systemic view of metabolism and health. Impaired Agni leads to Ama accumulation, disrupting doshic balance and contributing to disease. This aligns with modern concepts of metabolic dysfunction, where impaired digestion and inflammation are central to chronic diseases. Agni's regulation through dietary, herbal, and lifestyle interventions enhances gut health, immunity, and systemic function. By addressing digestion as a root cause, Ayurveda provides preventive and therapeutic strategies. Modern research validates this approach, linking Agni restoration to improved metabolic markers. This systemic perspective bridges digestion-focused interventions with holistic health frameworks.

43. C: The Tridosha theory, foundational in Ayurveda, explains physiological functions through the interplay of Vata, Pitta, and Kapha. These doshas govern physical, psychological, and biochemical processes, emphasizing balance as central to health. The claim that doshas represent "mind, body, and spirit" misinterprets their physiological roles. For example, Vata regulates movement, Pitta metabolism, and Kapha structure. These principles align with Western concepts like nervous, metabolic, and homeostatic systems. By addressing doshic imbalances, Ayurveda integrates systemic and cellular health. Modern validation of these principles reinforces their relevance in understanding disease and fostering prevention, challenging symbolic interpretations.

44. A: Rasayana therapies target longevity, immunity, and rejuvenation by restoring doshic balance and enhancing tissue vitality. Herbs like Amalaki and Ashwagandha modulate oxidative stress, inflammation, and bioavailability, aligning with anti-aging and regenerative research. These therapies integrate nutrition, detoxification, and mental well-being, reflecting Ayurveda's holistic approach. Modern studies confirm their role in immune enhancement, metabolic regulation, and cellular repair. By bridging traditional rejuvenation principles with biochemical insights, Rasayana offers actionable strategies for preventive care. This integration enriches chronic disease management, emphasizing resilience and systemic harmony in health outcomes.

45. A: Prakriti analysis integrates constitutional predispositions with environmental and genetic influences, enabling personalized care. By identifying vulnerabilities linked to doshas, Ayurveda tailors interventions for prevention and treatment. Modern parallels in genomics and precision medicine validate Prakriti's role in addressing chronic diseases. For example, Vata types prone to neurological disorders benefit from stabilizing therapies, while Kapha constitutions require metabolic interventions. Prakriti's static nature coexists with dynamic interactions, emphasizing adaptive strategies within a fixed baseline. This approach enhances diagnostic accuracy, aligning Ayurveda's preventive focus with contemporary healthcare's emphasis on individualized care, bridging tradition and innovation.

46. B: Prakriti, as described in Ayurveda, correlates with modern genetic and physiological research, emphasizing its role in personalized medicine. Studies demonstrate that Prakriti types (Vata, Pitta, Kapha) align with metabolic profiles and genetic markers, allowing practitioners to predict disease susceptibility. For instance, Pitta individuals often display heightened inflammatory responses, paralleling genetic predispositions to autoimmune disorders. This correlation enhances the precision of treatment by tailoring therapies to individual constitutions. Unlike generalized medical protocols, Prakriti integrates fixed traits with environmental interactions, bridging ancient concepts with modern genomics. Such insights underscore Ayurveda's relevance in personalized and preventive healthcare.

47. A: The Ayurvedic concept of Ama, resulting from impaired digestion and metabolism, parallels advanced glycation end-products (AGEs) in modern medicine. Ama represents toxic accumulations that disrupt doshic balance, leading to systemic inflammation. Similarly, AGEs, products of abnormal metabolism, contribute to chronic diseases like diabetes and cardiovascular disorders. By targeting Ama through therapies like Panchakarma and Agni restoration, Ayurveda emphasizes detoxification and prevention. Modern research on metabolic toxins validates this approach, highlighting how impaired digestion influences systemic health. This analogy enriches contemporary understanding of chronic disease pathogenesis, emphasizing the interconnectedness of digestion, detoxification, and systemic inflammation.

48. B: Ayurveda's focus on gut health aligns with modern microbiota research, emphasizing therapies like Triphala and basti to restore balance. Triphala, a classical Ayurvedic formulation, promotes microbial diversity, supporting digestive and systemic health. Vata and Pitta imbalances, linked to conditions like IBS and hyperacidity, correspond with gut dysbiosis. Modern studies validate the gut-brain axis, highlighting how Ayurvedic interventions enhance mental and physical well-being. These parallels emphasize the systemic role of gut health in Ayurveda, offering insights into immune modulation, metabolic regulation, and disease prevention. This integration enriches healthcare, bridging traditional and modern perspectives on microbiota.

49. B: Ayurveda's emphasis on seasonal changes and doshic balance aligns with modern studies on immune modulation and circadian rhythms. For example, Kapha's aggravation in spring corresponds with increased respiratory allergies, while Pitta imbalances in summer link to inflammatory conditions. Seasonal routines (Ritucharya) provide tailored dietary and lifestyle interventions to mitigate these effects. Modern research on circadian alignment validates these principles, highlighting the interplay between external changes and internal physiology. By integrating environmental influences into disease prevention, Ayurveda complements contemporary health strategies. This systemic approach underscores the importance of adaptability in fostering resilience against seasonal disorders.

50. B: The Ayurvedic concept of Shatkriyakala represents a structured approach to early intervention and chronic disease prevention. By delineating six stages of disease progression, it provides actionable insights for timely therapies. Sanchaya and Prakopa stages, representing subclinical imbalances, align with modern biomarkers and preclinical diagnostics. Intervening during these early stages prevents Vyakti (full manifestation) and Bheda (complications). This framework bridges Ayurveda's preventive focus with modern chronic disease management, emphasizing early detection and doshic balance restoration. By addressing disease progression holistically, Shatkriyakala enhances healthcare outcomes, fostering proactive strategies for long-term well-being.

CHAPTER 17

MICROBIOLOGY ESSENTIALS IN AYURVEDA – CONCEPTS AND APPLICATIONS

INTRODUCTION TO MICROBIOLOGY FROM AN AYURVEDIC PERSPECTIVE

Ayurveda, the ancient Indian science of life and medicine, offers a unique perspective on microbiology that integrates traditional knowledge with a growing understanding of microbial life. While modern microbiology emerged in the 17th century with advancements in optical technology, Ayurveda has long emphasized the existence of invisible entities influencing health and disease. Concepts like Krimi (microorganisms) and Roga (diseases) highlight Ayurveda's early recognition of pathogens and their roles in human health.

The classical Ayurvedic texts, including the Charaka Samhita, Sushruta Samhita, and Ashtanga Hridaya, describe the existence of Krimis, often referring to both visible and microscopic organisms. These Krimis can inhabit the body externally or internally, causing diseases when conditions such as doshic imbalance, weakened Agni (digestive fire), or Ama (toxins) prevail. Though ancient Ayurvedic scholars lacked the technological means to observe microorganisms directly, their descriptions often align with modern microbial biology's understanding of parasitic, bacterial, and fungal infections.

From an Ayurvedic perspective, the human body is a microcosm of the universe, with various life forms coexisting in harmony. Sahaj Krimis, or beneficial microorganisms, are analogous to the modern concept of commensal and symbiotic bacteria that support physiological processes like digestion, immunity, and nutrient synthesis. Conversely, Vikriti Krimis correspond to pathogenic microorganisms that disrupt homeostasis and cause disease. Ayurvedic texts emphasize the importance of maintaining a balance between Sahaj and Vikriti Krimis to prevent disease.

Modern microbiology's focus on identifying, classifying, and understanding microorganisms provides a complementary framework for Ayurveda's holistic approach. While Ayurveda prioritizes systemic balance, immunity, and prevention, modern microbiology enhances the understanding of microbial mechanisms, enabling targeted interventions. Integrating these paradigms offers profound insights into infection management, immunity enhancement, and disease prevention.

Ayurvedic Concepts Related to Infection and Immunity

Ayurveda's approach to infection and immunity is deeply rooted in its principles of dosha balance, Agni regulation, Ama elimination, and Ojas preservation. While the modern concept of immunity centers around the immune system's ability to recognize and neutralize pathogens, Ayurveda views immunity as a dynamic interplay between internal strength (Vyadhikshamatva) and external influences.

KRIMI (MICROORGANISMS) IN AYURVEDA– A COMPREHENSIVE EXPLORATION

Introduction to Krimi in Ayurveda

The concept of Krimi in Ayurveda is a testament to the depth of ancient Indian medical understanding. Long before the advent of microbiology as a scientific discipline, Ayurvedic scholars articulated the existence and role of microorganisms in health and disease. The term Krimi broadly encompasses entities that can be either pathogenic or beneficial. These organisms, invisible to the naked eye, are described in Ayurvedic texts as influencing bodily functions, immunity, and the onset of diseases. While Ayurveda did not classify these entities into bacteria, viruses, fungi, or parasites as modern science does, the descriptions of Krimi often align with contemporary microbial understanding.

Ayurvedic texts, such as the Charaka Samhita, Sushruta Samhita, and Ashtanga Hridaya, classify Krimis into various types based on their origin, habitat, and their effects on the human body. The insights provided in these texts form the foundation for understanding infections, immune responses, and the importance of maintaining microbial balance within the body. The Ayurvedic framework integrates the roles of dosha imbalances, weakened Agni (digestive fire), and the accumulation of Ama (toxins) in fostering an environment conducive to pathogenic Krimis.

Classification of Krimi in Ayurveda

Ayurveda categorizes Krimis into three primary groups based on their origin, habitat, and nature of interaction with the host. These classifications—Bahya Krimi (external pathogens), Abhyantara Krimi (internal pathogens), and Sahaja Krimi (natural flora)—provide a holistic understanding of microbial activity and its impact on health.

1. **Bahya Krimi (External Pathogens):** Bahya Krimis refer to microorganisms or parasites that invade the body from external sources, often causing localized or systemic infections. These pathogens typically affect the skin, wounds, or external organs and are linked to conditions involving infestations, dermatitis, or injuries.

   Examples and Descriptions:

   - **Skin infections:** Ancient Ayurvedic texts describe conditions resembling bacterial or fungal infections, such as pustules, ulcers, and discolorations.
   - **Infestations:** Parasites like lice (pediculosis) and mites (scabies) are referred to as external Krimis that cause itching, irritation, and secondary infections.
   - **Wounds:** Infected wounds with foul odor and discharge are described in Ayurveda, emphasizing the role of Bahya Krimis in delaying healing.
   - **Ayurvedic Perspective:** Bahya Krimis proliferate when the skin barrier is compromised or when hygiene is neglected. Kapha dosha aggravation is commonly implicated in creating a conducive environment for these external pathogens. Excess moisture and sluggishness associated with Kapha can lead to microbial colonization.
   - **Modern Parallels:** Bahya Krimis align with our understanding of dermatological and parasitic infections caused by bacteria (e.g., Staphylococcus aureus), fungi (Candida or Dermatophytes), and ectoparasites (e.g., lice, ticks, mites). These infections often occur in individuals with poor hygiene, immune deficiencies, or pre-existing skin conditions.

   Management in Ayurveda:

   - **Topical treatments:** Ayurvedic practitioners use herbal pastes, oils, and powders with antimicrobial properties, such as Neem and Turmeric, to cleanse and heal infected areas.
   - **Cleansing therapies:** Procedures like Prakshalana (washing with medicated decoctions) are employed to eliminate external pathogens.
   - **Lifestyle interventions:** Proper hygiene, avoiding excessive moisture, and balancing Kapha dosha are emphasized to prevent such infections.

2. **Abhyantara Krimi (Internal Pathogens):** Abhyantara Krimis inhabit internal organs, primarily focusing on the gastrointestinal tract but also affecting other systems. They are responsible for systemic infections and symptoms resembling bacterial, viral, or parasitic diseases.

   Examples and Descriptions:

   - **Gastrointestinal infections:** Symptoms described in Ayurveda, such as diarrhea, abdominal pain, and bloating, align with conditions like dysentery or parasitic infestations (e.g., helminths).
   - **Respiratory infections:** Ancient texts mention signs of cough, fever, and mucus production that resemble bronchial or viral infections.
   - **Systemic infections:** High fever and malaise are associated with pathogenic Krimis spreading through the bloodstream, akin to sepsis in modern medicine.
   - **Ayurvedic Perspective:** Abhyantara Krimis thrive in the presence of Ama, a toxic byproduct of improper digestion, and when Agni (digestive fire) is weak. An imbalance in Pitta dosha contributes to inflammation, creating an environment for microbial growth. Additionally, disrupted Vata dosha facilitates the spread of pathogens throughout the body.
   - **Modern Parallels:** Internal pathogens include bacteria (e.g., Escherichia coli causing food poisoning), viruses (e.g., Rotavirus causing diarrhea), and parasites (e.g., Giardia or Ascaris). Dysbiosis, or an imbalance in gut flora, mirrors

the Ayurvedic concept of pathogenic Krimis outcompeting beneficial ones.

Management in Ayurveda:

- **Herbal antimicrobials:** Formulations like Triphala, Kutaja, and Vidanga are used to neutralize internal pathogens and support digestion.
- **Detoxification therapies:** Procedures such as Virechana (purgation) and Basti (medicated enema) eliminate toxins and pathogens from the gastrointestinal tract.
- **Dietary interventions:** Easily digestible foods and spices like ginger, cumin, and coriander are recommended to enhance Agni and prevent Ama accumulation.

3. **Sahaja Krimi (Natural Flora):** Sahaja Krimis represent microorganisms that exist naturally and harmoniously within the human body, analogous to the modern understanding of commensal and symbiotic microbiota. These Krimis play a crucial role in maintaining digestion, immunity, and overall health.

Examples and Descriptions:

- **Gut microbiota:** Ayurveda acknowledges the presence of supportive entities that assist in breaking down food and synthesizing nutrients.
- **Skin microbiota:** Descriptions of Sahaja Krimis on the skin emphasize their protective role against external pathogens.
- **Oral and respiratory flora:** These microorganisms help maintain the mucosal barrier and prevent infections.
- **Ayurvedic Perspective:** Sahaja Krimis thrive when the body is in a state of balance, with doshas, dhatus (tissues), and Agni functioning optimally. Their harmony is disrupted by poor diet, stress, and environmental factors, leading to dysbiosis and susceptibility to infections.
- **Modern Parallels:** The human microbiome, consisting of trillions of bacteria, fungi, and viruses, supports digestion, immunity, and metabolic health. For instance, Lactobacillus species in the gut aid in nutrient absorption, while skin flora prevents opportunistic infections.

Management in Ayurveda:

- **Probiotic foods:** Ayurvedic practices promote fermented foods like Takra (buttermilk) to replenish beneficial gut flora.
- **Immune-boosting herbs:** Guduchi, Ashwagandha, and Amalaki are used to enhance systemic resilience.
- **Lifestyle harmony:** Dinacharya (daily routines) and Ritucharya (seasonal routines) are designed to maintain Sahaja Krimi balance through balanced doshas and optimal digestion.

Role of Doshas in Krimi Proliferation

The Ayurvedic understanding of doshas—Vata, Pitta, and Kapha—provides insights into the conditions that foster Krimi growth:

- **Kapha imbalance:** Excess Kapha creates a moist, stagnant environment conducive to microbial proliferation, similar to biofilm formation in infections.
- **Pitta imbalance:** Elevated Pitta leads to inflammation and heat, aligning with the immune response to infections and the fever accompanying microbial invasions.
- **Vata imbalance:** Aggravated Vata disrupts circulation and nervous system functions, facilitating systemic spread of infections.

Modern Parallels to Ayurvedic Krimi Concepts

Modern microbiology validates many Ayurvedic descriptions of Krimis:

1. **Microbial Dysbiosis:** The disruption of natural flora parallels the Ayurvedic concept of Sahaja and Vikriti Krimis.
2. **Opportunistic Infections:** Weak immunity and doshic imbalances enable pathogenic Krimis to thrive, similar to modern observations of immunocompromised patients.
3. **Antimicrobial Resistance (AMR):** Ayurveda's use of polyherbal formulations reduces the risk of resistance, a pressing issue in contemporary medicine.

Vyadhikshamatva (Immunity)

Vyadhikshamatva, or the capacity to resist disease, is a cornerstone of Ayurvedic immunology. It encompasses two primary components:

1. **Sahaja Vyadhikshamatva:** Innate immunity that is constitutionally determined by an individual's Prakriti.
2. **Kalaja Vyadhikshamatva:** Adaptive immunity developed over time through lifestyle, diet, and environmental exposures.

   The preservation of Ojas, the subtle essence of all dhatus (tissues), is considered vital for strong immunity. Ojas is analogous to modern concepts of immune resilience, influenced by nutrition, physical activity, and emotional balance.

Ama and Agni in Infection

Ama, the toxic byproduct of improper digestion, creates an environment conducive to microbial growth, analogous to chronic inflammation and oxidative stress in modern pathology. Weak Agni (digestive fire) is considered a primary factor in Ama accumulation, underscoring Ayurveda's emphasis on digestion as central to health and immunity.

Doshas and Infection: The role of doshas in infection is significant in Ayurveda:

1. **Vata:** Imbalance leads to systemic weakness, disrupted circulation, and nervous system disorders, predisposing individuals to opportunistic infections.
2. **Pitta:** Excess Pitta manifests as inflammation, fever, and heat, paralleling the body's immune response to pathogens.
3. **Kapha:** Aggravation of Kapha results in mucus production, congestion, and sluggish metabolism, creating favourable conditions for microbial growth.

Application of Microbiology in Ayurvedic Practice

Ayurveda's integration with microbiology offers numerous applications in diagnosis, treatment, and preventive care. These applications are guided by a combination of ancient principles and contemporary microbial science.

1. **Diagnosis of Infections:** Ayurveda employs observational methods such as Nadi Pariksha (pulse diagnosis), Jihva Pariksha (tongue examination), and Drik Pariksha (eye examination) to detect imbalances linked to microbial infections. For example:
   - Coated tongue indicates Ama and microbial dysbiosis in the gut.
   - Foul odor and discoloration in wounds reflect bacterial or fungal infections.
   - Modern microbiology complements these diagnostic techniques by identifying specific pathogens through cultures, PCR, and serological tests.
2. **Antimicrobial Therapies:** Ayurvedic herbs and formulations possess significant antimicrobial properties validated by modern research. For instance:
   - **Neem (*Azadirachta indica*):** Broad-spectrum antimicrobial activity against bacteria, fungi, and viruses.
   - **Tulsi (*Ocimum sanctum*):** Effective against respiratory pathogens.
   - **Triphala:** Balances gut microbiota while exhibiting antibacterial properties.
   - Unlike synthetic antibiotics, these therapies maintain microbial balance, reducing the risk of resistance and dysbiosis.
3. **Probiotics and Prebiotics:** Ayurveda's emphasis on gut health aligns with the modern understanding of probiotics and prebiotics. Formulations like Takra (buttermilk), Lassi, and fermented preparations enhance gut flora, promoting systemic health. These traditional practices address conditions like diarrhea, IBS, and chronic inflammation by restoring microbial harmony.
4. **Panchakarma and Microbial Detox:** Panchakarma therapies like Virechana (purgation) and Basti (medicated enema) eliminate toxins and pathogens from the gastrointestinal tract. These therapies align with modern detoxification practices targeting microbial overgrowth and restoring gut integrity.
5. **Immune Modulation:** Ayurvedic Rasayana therapies (rejuvenation) modulate immunity, reflecting their role in enhancing microbiota and immune resilience. Herbs like Guduchi (Tinospora cordifolia) and Ashwagandha (Withania somnifera) boost immune responses, reducing susceptibility to infections. These interventions align with immunomodulators in modern medicine.
6. **Preventive Care:** Ayurveda's emphasis on Dinacharya (daily routines) and Ritucharya (seasonal routines) includes dietary and lifestyle practices that promote immunity. For example:
   - Seasonal detoxification prevents Kapha-related respiratory infections in spring.
   - Herbal teas with ginger, turmeric, and cinnamon reduce microbial loads in winter.
   - These preventive measures complement modern vaccination and hygiene practices.
7. **Addressing Microbial Resistance:** The rise of antimicrobial resistance (AMR) underscores the relevance of Ayurveda's holistic approach. Polyherbal formulations target multiple microbial pathways, reducing resistance risks. For example:
   - Haridra (turmeric) and Maricha (black pepper) exhibit synergistic effects against resistant pathogens.
   - Such multidimensional strategies offer sustainable alternatives to combat AMR.
   - Integrative Models of Ayurvedic Microbiology
   - Integrating Ayurveda with microbiology enhances both systems, addressing gaps in diagnosis,

treatment, and prevention. For example:Ayurveda's focus on gut health aligns with microbiota-centered therapies in modern medicine.

- The concept of Ama correlates with systemic inflammation markers like CRP.
- Ayurvedic antimicrobial herbs complement antibiotics, reducing side effects and resistance risks.Collaborative research on these intersections can revolutionize healthcare, offering personalized, holistic, and sustainable solutions.

MULTIPLE CHOICE QUESTIONS

1. A researcher hypothesizes that Ayurvedic descriptions of Bahya Krimi (external pathogens) align with bacterial and fungal infections caused by environmental exposure. The study compares skin infections described in Charaka Samhita to modern dermatological conditions. Which conclusion best supports the hypothesis?
   A. Bahya Krimis encompass only parasitic infections like lice and scabies, excluding bacterial origins.
   B. Ayurvedic texts detail systemic roles of Bahya Krimi, unrelated to localized skin conditions.
   C. Skin infections caused by moisture and poor hygiene align with Kapha-induced Bahya Krimi growth.
   D. Modern dermatology and Ayurveda conflict in understanding microbial causation.

2. Consider an Ayurvedic scholar investigating the correlation between Ama and gut microbial dysbiosis. The scholar studies patients with IBS, noting digestive stagnation and Kapha-Pitta imbalance. Which hypothesis aligns most with Ayurvedic pathology?
   A. Ama accumulation disrupts gut microbiota, fostering pathogenic Krimis and worsening IBS.
   B. Dysbiosis resolves independently of Ama, rendering Ayurvedic interventions ineffective.
   C. Ama's effects are psychological rather than microbial, unrelated to gut dysbiosis.
   D. Kapha imbalance increases gut microbial diversity, negating the role of Ama.

3. A clinical trial investigates the role of Triphala in restoring gut microbiota diversity. Participants with dysbiosis receive Triphala for 12 weeks, showing improved digestive and systemic health. What mechanism explains these outcomes in Ayurvedic terms?
   A. Triphala eliminates beneficial microbiota alongside pathogens, resetting gut health.
   B. Detoxification of Ama and doshic regulation foster microbial harmony and digestion.
   C. Triphala's detoxification reduces gut microbial diversity, negatively impacting immunity.
   D. Doshic balance through Triphala does not influence gut microbiota or immune outcomes.

4. A patient with chronic respiratory infections receives an Ayurvedic diagnosis of aggravated Kapha dosha promoting Bahya Krimi growth in the lungs. Treatments include dietary modifications and Kapha-reducing herbs. What modern parallels support this Ayurvedic intervention?
   A. Respiratory infections caused by viral pathogens are independent of dosha theories.
   B. Anti-inflammatory and mucolytic herbs reduce microbial growth and restore lung function.
   C. Kapha-reducing herbs target systemic inflammation unrelated to microbial presence.
   D. Ayurvedic interventions fail to address pathogenic influences on respiratory health.

5. A molecular biologist studying Vyadhikshamatva (immunity) hypothesizes that Ayurvedic immunity-building practices parallel modern immunomodulation. Which Ayurvedic practices are most aligned with immune enhancement in this context?
   A. Detoxification therapies (Panchakarma) and Rasayana herbs like Ashwagandha.
   B. Kapha-reducing measures targeting local infections without systemic immune effects.
   C. Immune modulation is absent in Ayurveda, focusing solely on microbial elimination.
   D. Vyadhikshamatva is philosophical, lacking measurable biological outcomes.

6. An ecological study examines the environmental implications of cultivating Amalaki (Emblica officinalis) for global Triphala demand. Overharvesting reduces bioactive content, impacting the efficacy of formulations. Which solution aligns with Ayurvedic sustainability principles?
   A. Large-scale synthetic Amalaki cultivation to meet demand.
   B. Agroforestry practices promoting ecological balance and medicinal quality.
   C. Shifting Triphala production to exclude Amalaki for resource conservation.
   D. Focusing on synthetic bioactive compounds over natural Amalaki.

7. A medical practitioner incorporates Ayurvedic probiotics such as buttermilk (Takra) into modern treatment protocols for gastrointestinal infections. How does this approach align with Ayurvedic concepts?
   A. Takra supports digestive fire (Agni) and balances doshas, restoring microbial harmony.
   B. Buttermilk lacks direct antimicrobial effects, making its application limited.
   C. Ayurveda does not recognize probiotics, relying solely on detoxification therapies.
   D. Takra fosters microbial diversity but disrupts doshic equilibrium.

8. A comparative study evaluates the antimicrobial effects of Neem (Azadirachta indica) in treating skin infections. How does Neem's action correspond to Ayurvedic principles?
   A. Neem eliminates pathogens without affecting doshic balance or tissue regeneration.
   B. Its Kapha-reducing properties detoxify tissues while exhibiting broad-spectrum antimicrobial effects.
   C. Neem targets Ama but lacks antibacterial properties, limiting its applicability.
   D. Ayurvedic texts describe Neem as ineffective for microbial conditions.

9. How does Ayurveda interpret the gut-lung axis, as studied in modern respiratory disorders and microbial dysbiosis?
   A. The gut-lung connection aligns with Kapha and Vata interplay influencing systemic immunity.
   B. Ayurveda separates gut health from respiratory conditions, offering independent treatments.
   C. Doshic balance in the lungs is unaffected by gut microbial health or systemic toxins.
   D. Gut health is irrelevant in Ayurvedic treatment of respiratory infections.

10. In the context of Krimi therapy, why are Ayurvedic polyherbal formulations preferred over single herbs in managing microbial infections?
   A. Single herbs lack dosha-balancing capabilities, while polyherbal formulations address Ama.
   B. Polyherbal therapies prevent microbial resistance and restore Sahaja Krimi balance.
   C. Single herbs are more effective than polyherbal approaches in microbial management.
   D. Polyherbal formulations do not target systemic infections, limiting their efficacy.

Directions (Q. No. 11-14): *Scenario-Based Questions*

SCENARIO 1

A clinical researcher studies the effects of Rasayana therapies on patients with immune deficiencies, focusing on herbs like Amalaki and Guduchi. Improved immune markers and reduced infection rates are observed.

SCENARIO 2

An environmental biologist examines resource depletion due to overharvesting of Guduchi. The study emphasizes conservation through organic cultivation and agroforestry.

11. How do the outcomes of Scenario 1 validate the role of Rasayana herbs in immunomodulation?
   A. Rasayana therapies directly eliminate pathogens without affecting immune systems.
   B. Herbs like Amalaki regulate doshas and modulate immune responses, enhancing resilience.
   C. Immunomodulation is unrelated to Rasayana, which focuses on digestive health.
   D. Amalaki reduces microbial resistance but does not enhance immunity.

12. How does the depletion of Guduchi in Scenario 2 affect its Ayurvedic efficacy?
   A. Reduced bioactive content diminishes Rasayana properties, impacting immunity.
   B. Guduchi remains effective despite environmental changes due to its adaptive qualities.
   C. Ayurvedic efficacy is unrelated to environmental factors, relying solely on preparation.
   D. Guduchi's role in immunity increases as environmental stress enhances its potency.

13. What sustainable strategy aligns with Ayurveda's emphasis on ecological balance?
   A. Transitioning to synthetic Guduchi formulations to meet demand.
   B. Promoting organic cultivation and preserving medicinal plant biodiversity.
   C. Replacing Guduchi with similar herbs, focusing on cost-effective production.
   D. Overharvesting Guduchi to scale up production and meet global needs.

14. How does the interplay between Scenarios 1 and 2 illustrate the relationship between plant sustainability and therapeutic outcomes?
   A. Therapeutic outcomes are independent of plant sourcing or conservation.
   B. Environmental depletion directly impacts Rasayana efficacy and immune health.
   C. Sustainable sourcing does not affect Rasayana properties of Guduchi formulations.
   D. Plant sustainability strategies align solely with economic concerns, not therapeutic efficacy.

15. The classification of Krimi (microorganisms) in Ayurveda is described in terms of their habitat and effects:
   (a) Bahya Krimi include pathogens like lice and mites that affect external areas like skin and wounds.
   (b) Abhyantara Krimi are internal pathogens causing infections in the gastrointestinal and respiratory tracts.
   (c) Sahaja Krimi represent natural flora essential for digestion and immunity.
   (d) All Krimis are categorized as harmful entities disrupting health.

   Choose the correct answer from the options given below:
   A. (a), (b), and (c) only
   B. (a), (b), and (d) only
   C. (b), (c), and (d) only
   D. (a), (b), (c), and (d)

16. Ayurvedic perspectives on immunity (Vyadhikshamatva) emphasize:
   (a) Innate immunity as Sahaja Vyadhikshamatva, governed by Prakriti (constitution).
   (b) Adaptive immunity as Kalaja Vyadhikshamatva, influenced by diet, lifestyle, and Rasayana therapy.
   (c) Immunity as an independent entity unaffected by digestive fire (Agni).
   (d) Preservation of Ojas as central to immune resilience.

   Choose the correct answer from the options given below:
   A. (a), (b), and (d) only
   B. (a), (b), and (c) only
   C. (a) and (d) only
   D. (b), (c), and (d) only

17. The role of Ama in fostering microbial imbalances and infections is described as:
   (a) Ama creates an environment conducive to pathogenic Krimi proliferation.
   (b) Accumulated Ama impairs Agni, weakening digestion and immune function.
   (c) Ama affects only gastrointestinal health, unrelated to systemic infections.
   (d) Detoxification therapies targeting Ama reduce microbial growth and inflammation.

   Choose the correct answer from the options given below:
   A. (a), (b), and (d) only
   B. (a) and (c) only
   C. (b), (c), and (d) only
   D. (a), (b), (c), and (d)

18. Ayurvedic Rasayana herbs supporting immune modulation include:
   (a) Guduchi enhances immune response by balancing Tridosha.
   (b) Amalaki acts as an antioxidant and rejuvenative herb, promoting Ojas.
   (c) Ashwagandha targets pathogens directly, independent of immune function.
   (d) Triphala detoxifies Ama while promoting microbial harmony in the gut.

   Choose the correct answer from the options given below:
   A. (a), (b), and (c) only
   B. (a), (b), and (d) only
   C. (a), (c), and (d) only
   D. (b), (c), and (d) only

19. Microbial infections in Ayurveda are influenced by:
   (a) Kapha dosha aggravation fostering microbial growth in moist tissues.
   (b) Pitta dosha aggravation leading to inflammation and heat.
   (c) Sahaja Krimi transforming into pathogenic forms during doshic imbalance.
   (d) Vata dosha facilitating systemic spread of infections.

   Choose the correct answer from the options given below:
   A. (a), (b), and (d) only
   B. (b), (c), and (d) only
   C. (a), (b), (c), and (d)
   D. (a) and (b) only

20. The Ayurvedic approach to addressing gut dysbiosis includes:
   (a) Using Triphala to balance microbial diversity while enhancing digestion.
   (b) Eliminating Sahaja Krimi to restore gut health.
   (c) Detoxification therapies like Virechana to eliminate Ama.
   (d) Promoting fermented foods like Takra to restore microbial harmony.

   Choose the correct answer from the options given below:
   A. (a), (b), and (d) only
   B. (a), (c), and (d) only
   C. (a), (b), and (c) only
   D. (b), (c), and (d) only

21. Ayurvedic perspectives on probiotics and natural flora include:
   (a) Takra (buttermilk) replenishes Sahaja Krimi, enhancing digestion and immunity.
   (b) Probiotic formulations are unrelated to Ayurveda's approach to gut health.

(c) Herbal therapies target pathogens without disrupting natural flora.
(d) Sahaja Krimi imbalance leads to systemic infections and digestive disorders.

Choose the correct answer from the options given below:
A. (a), (c), and (d) only
B. (b), (c), and (d) only
C. (a), (b), and (d) only
D. (a), (b), and (c) only

22. Rasayana therapies contributing to immunity include:
(a) Guduchi and Amalaki restore microbial balance and enhance Ojas.
(b) Panchakarma therapies eliminate pathogens while modulating immunity.
(c) Ashwagandha and Shatavari strengthen digestive fire and regulate Agni.
(d) Triphala targets microbial diversity without affecting systemic immunity.

Choose the correct answer from the options given below:
A. (a), (b), and (c) only
B. (b), (c), and (d) only
C. (a), (c), and (d) only
D. (a), (b), and (d) only

23. Factors influencing Sahaja Krimi balance in Ayurveda are:
(a) A balanced diet promoting Agni enhances natural flora.
(b) Ama accumulation fosters pathogenic transformations in Sahaja Krimi.
(c) Seasonal imbalances impact microbial harmony.
(d) Detoxification therapies directly eliminate Sahaja Krimi.

Choose the correct answer from the options given below:
A. (a), (b), and (c) only
B. (a), (b), and (d) only
C. (b), (c), and (d) only
D. (a), (b), (c), and (d)

24. The classification of Ayurvedic antimicrobial herbs includes:
(a) Neem (Azadirachta indica) as a Kapha-reducing antimicrobial agent.
(b) Turmeric (Haridra) supporting immune modulation and inflammation reduction.
(c) Tulsi (*Ocimum sanctum*) targeting respiratory pathogens while balancing Vata.
(d) Ashwagandha directly eliminating bacterial pathogens.

Choose the correct answer from the options given below:
A. (a), (b), and (c) only
B. (b), (c), and (d) only
C. (a), (b), and (d) only
D. (a), (b), (c), and (d)

25. Match List–I (Ayurveda Doshas) with List–II (Corresponding Imbalances):

List–I	List–II
(a) Vata	1. Dryness, mobility, and erratic function
(b) Pitta	2. Heat, inflammation, and intensity
(c) Kapha	3. Stability, heaviness, and stagnation
(d) Sannipata	4. Mixed symptoms involving all three doshas

Choose the correct answer from the options given below:
A. (a)-1, (b)-2, (c)-3, (d)-4
B. (a)-3, (b)-4, (c)-2, (d)-1
C. (a)-2, (b)-3, (c)-4, (d)-1
D. (a)-1, (b)-3, (c)-4, (d)-2

16. Match List–I (Herbal Treatments) with List–II (Clinical Applications):

List–I	List–II
(a) Neem	1. Skin disorders and antimicrobial properties
(b) Tulsi	2. Respiratory health and immune modulation
(c) Triphala	3. Gut health and detoxification
(d) Ashwagandha	4. Stress management and adaptogenic effects

Choose the correct answer from the options given below:
A. (a)-1, (b)-2, (c)-3, (d)-4
B. (a)-3, (b)-4, (c)-1, (d)-2
C. (a)-1, (b)-4, (c)-2, (d)-3
D. (a)-2, (b)-3, (c)-4, (d)-1

17. Match List–I (Body Constituents) with List–II (Functions in Health):

List–I	List–II
(a) Rasa	1. Nutritional essence of food, supports immunity
(b) Rakta	2. Oxygen transport and vitality
(c) Mamsa	3. Muscle strength and physical structure
(d) Meda	4. Fat tissue, energy storage, and lubrication

Choose the correct answer from the options given below:
A. (a)-1, (b)-2, (c)-3, (d)-4
B. (a)-4, (b)-3, (c)-1, (d)-2
C. (a)-1, (b)-4, (c)-2, (d)-3
D. (a)-3, (b)-2, (c)-4, (d)-1

18. Match List–I (Disease Stages) with List–II (Ayurvedic Concepts):

List–I	List–II
(a) Sanchaya	1. Accumulation of doshas
(b) Prakopa	2. Aggravation of doshas
(c) Prasara	3. Spread of doshas in the body
(d) Bheda	4. Differentiation and manifestation of disease

Choose the correct answer from the options given below:

A. (a)-1, (b)-2, (c)-3, (d)-4
B. (a)-2, (b)-3, (c)-4, (d)-1
C. (a)-3, (b)-4, (c)-1, (d)-2
D. (a)-4, (b)-1, (c)-2, (d)-3

19. Match List–I (Panchakarma Therapies) with List–II (Associated Benefits):

List–I	List–II
(a) Vamana	1. Detoxification through therapeutic vomiting
(b) Virechana	2. Purgation therapy for toxin elimination
(c) Nasya	3. Cleansing of nasal passages
(d) Basti	4. Enema therapy for colon health

Choose the correct answer from the options given below:

A. (a)-1, (b)-2, (c)-3, (d)-4
B. (a)-4, (b)-3, (c)-1, (d)-2
C. (a)-1, (b)-4, (c)-2, (d)-3
D. (a)-3, (b)-2, (c)-4, (d)-1

20. Match List–I (Medicinal Plants) with List–II (Bioactive Properties):

List–I	List–II
(a) Guduchi	1. Immune modulator and adaptogenic effects
(b) Haridra	2. Anti-inflammatory and antioxidant properties
(c) Shatavari	3. Hormonal balance and reproductive health
(d) Brahmi	4. Cognitive enhancement and stress reduction

Choose the correct answer from the options given below:

A. (a)-1, (b)-2, (c)-3, (d)-4
B. (a)-4, (b)-3, (c)-1, (d)-2
C. (a)-1, (b)-4, (c)-2, (d)-3
D. (a)-2, (b)-3, (c)-4, (d)-1

21. Match List–I (Digestion Processes) with List–II (Corresponding Dosha Role):

List–I	List–II
(a) Absorption	1. Kapha's stabilizing effect
(b) Metabolism	2. Pitta's transformative energy
(c) Motility	3. Vata's movement and regulation
(d) Elimination	4. Combined action of Vata and Apana

Choose the correct answer from the options given below:

A. (a)-1, (b)-2, (c)-3, (d)-4
B. (a)-3, (b)-4, (c)-1, (d)-2
C. (a)-2, (b)-3, (c)-4, (d)-1
D. (a)-4, (b)-2, (c)-1, (d)-3

22. Match List–I (Pathogen Types)with List–II (Ayurvedic Interpretations):

List–I	List–II
(a) Bacteria	1. Vikriti Krimi
(b) Viruses	2. Sahaja Krimi
(c) Fungi	3. Kapha-dominant pathogens
(d) Parasites	4. Krimi caused by Ama imbalance

Choose the correct answer from the options given below:

A. (a)-1, (b)-2, (c)-3, (d)-4
B. (a)-4, (b)-3, (c)-1, (d)-2
C. (a)-2, (b)-1, (c)-4, (d)-3
D. (a)-3, (b)-4, (c)-2, (d)-1

23. Match List–I (Food Categories) with List–II (Impact on Doshas):

List–I	List–II
(a) Sweet	1. Increases Kapha, decreases Vata and Pitta
(b) Sour	2. Balances Vata, increases Pitta and Kapha
(c) Salty	3. Balances Vata, slightly increases Kapha and Pitta
(d) Bitter	4. Balances Pitta, decreases Kapha and Vata

Choose the correct answer from the options given below:

A. (a)-1, (b)-2, (c)-3, (d)-4
B. (a)-3, (b)-4, (c)-1, (d)-2
C. (a)-1, (b)-4, (c)-2, (d)-3
D. (a)-2, (b)-3, (c)-4, (d)-1

24. Match List–I (- Disease Etiology) with List–II (Ayurvedic Causes):

List–I	List–II
(a) Ama	1. Toxins due to weak Agni
(b) Vata Imbalance	2. Dryness and irregular movement
(c) Pitta Imbalance	3. Heat, inflammation, and burning sensations
(d) Kapha Imbalance	4. Stagnation and mucus production

Choose the correct answer from the options given below:

A. (a)-1, (b)-2, (c)-3, (d)-4
B. (a)-4, (b)-3, (c)-1, (d)-2

C. (a)-1, (b)-4, (c)-2, (d)-3
D. (a)-2, (b)-1, (c)-4, (d)-3

Directions (Q. No. 35–39): *Following questions are based on Statement 1 and Statement 2. Read both the statements carefully and choose the correct answer from the options given below:*

A. Both Statement 1 and Statement 2 are true, and Statement 2 is the correct explanation of Statement 1.
B. Both Statement 1 and Statement 2 are true, but Statement 2 is not the correct explanation of Statement 1.
C. Statement 1 is true, but Statement 2 is false.
D. Statement 1 is false, but Statement 2 is true.
E. Both Statement 1 and Statement 2 are false.

35. Statement 1: Krimi in Ayurveda includes both pathogenic and natural microorganisms affecting health and disease.

Statement 2: Sahaja Krimi are considered harmful entities that must be eliminated for optimal health.

36. Statement 1: Ama accumulation in Ayurveda creates an environment conducive to microbial proliferation and systemic diseases.

Statement 2: Detoxification therapies like Panchakarma are central to eliminating Ama and preventing infections.

37. Statement 1: Rasayana therapies like Guduchi and Amalaki enhance Vyadhikshamatva by improving Ojas.

Statement 2: Vyadhikshamatva in Ayurveda refers solely to innate immunity and excludes acquired immunity.

38. Statement 1: Pathogenic Krimi in Ayurveda corresponds to opportunistic microorganisms in modern microbiology.

Statement 2: The balance of Sahaja Krimi is unrelated to immune resilience or disease prevention.

39. Statement 1: Ayurvedic treatments for infections prioritize restoring doshic balance alongside eliminating pathogens.

Statement 2: Antimicrobial therapies in Ayurveda exclusively target microbes without considering systemic effects.

Directions (Q. No. 40–45): *There are two statements in each question. One is labelled as Assertion (A) and the other is as Reason (R). Read both the statements and choose the correct answer from the options given below:*

A. Both Assertion (A) and Reason (R) are true, and Reason (R) is the correct explanation of Assertion (A).
B. Both Assertion (A) and Reason (R) are true, but Reason (R) is not the correct explanation of Assertion (A).
C. Assertion (A) is true, but Reason (R) is false.
D. Assertion (A) is false, but Reason (R) is true.
E. Both Assertion (A) and Reason (R) are false.

40. Assertion (A): Ayurveda emphasizes the use of Rasayana therapies to enhance immunity and prevent microbial infections.

Reason (R): Rasayana herbs contain bioactive compounds that modulate the immune system and inhibit microbial growth.

41. Assertion (A): The Ayurvedic concept of "Krimi" correlates with microbial infections described in modern microbiology.

Reason (R): Ayurveda identifies Krimi as invisible organisms that cause diseases and prescribes herbal remedies to combat them.

42. Assertion (A): Panchakarma therapies in Ayurveda are effective in removing microbial toxins from the body.

Reason (R): Panchakarma primarily targets the gastrointestinal tract, liver, and excretory systems to eliminate accumulated toxins, including those of microbial origin.

43. Assertion (A): Ayurvedic herbs like Neem and Turmeric are effective in treating microbial infections.

Reason (R): These herbs have antimicrobial, antifungal, and antiviral properties due to the presence of bioactive compounds like curcumin and azadirachtin.

44. Assertion (A): Fermentation in Ayurveda enhances the potency of herbal formulations like Arishtas and Asavas.

Reason (R): The process of fermentation increases microbial contamination, making Ayurvedic formulations unsafe for consumption.

45. Assertion (A): Gut microbiota plays a crucial role in maintaining overall health, as emphasized in Ayurvedic concepts of Agni (digestive fire).

Reason (R): Balanced Agni supports the growth of beneficial gut bacteria, which aids in nutrient absorption and immune function.

Directions (Q. No. 46–50): *Read the following Passage carefully and answer the questions given below:*

Ayurveda, the ancient Indian medical system, presents a holistic approach to health that integrates mind, body, and environment. Central to this framework is Vyadhikshamatva, or immunity, which refers to the body's capacity to resist and combat diseases. Unlike modern medicine, which often focuses on specific immune cells and biochemical pathways, Ayurveda adopts a broader perspective, viewing immunity as a dynamic interplay of Agni (digestive fire), Ojas (vital essence), and the balance of the Tridoshas (Vata, Pitta, and Kapha). These elements interact to create a robust defense mechanism that prevents disease onset, facilitates recovery, and maintains homeostasis.

In Ayurveda, Vyadhikshamatva is categorized into three types: Sahaja Vyadhikshamatva (innate immunity), Kalaja Vyadhikshamatva (time-acquired immunity), and Yuktikrita Vyadhikshamatva (enhanced immunity). Sahaja Vyadhikshamatva is inherent and constitutionally determined by an individual's Prakriti (body constitution). For instance, Kapha-dominant individuals are often more resilient to infections due to their stable and robust physiological nature. Kalaja Vyadhikshamatva develops over time, influenced by factors such as age, seasonal variations, and life stages. Yuktikrita Vyadhikshamatva, on the other hand, can be actively enhanced through lifestyle modifications, herbal therapies, and dietary interventions.

A critical component of Vyadhikshamatva is the role of Agni, which governs digestion and metabolism. Ayurveda emphasizes that strong Agni not only ensures efficient digestion but also supports immune function by preventing the accumulation of Ama (toxins). Ama is considered the root cause of many diseases, as it disrupts doshic balance and weakens the body's defenses. When Agni is compromised—whether due to poor diet, stress, or external factors—Ama accumulates, creating an environment conducive to pathogenic Krimis (microorganisms). This concept parallels modern understanding of metabolic and inflammatory disorders, where disrupted gut health and systemic inflammation compromise immunity.

The essence of immunity in Ayurveda lies in Ojas, a subtle and vital essence derived from the proper digestion and assimilation of nutrients. Ojas is considered the foundation of physical, mental, and emotional well-being. It is closely linked to the strength of the dhatus (tissues) and reflects the ultimate state of balance in the body. Individuals with strong Ojas exhibit resilience against diseases, vibrant energy, and mental clarity. Conversely, the depletion of Ojas manifests as fatigue, vulnerability to infections, and systemic disorders. Ayurvedic interventions aimed at enhancing Ojas often involve Rasayana therapies, which rejuvenate the body and restore vitality.

The influence of the Tridoshas on immunity is another cornerstone of Ayurvedic immunology. Vata, Pitta, and Kapha doshas, when in equilibrium, maintain physiological harmony and immune resilience. However, doshic imbalances can disrupt this harmony, leading to disease. For example, aggravated Kapha can result in excessive mucus production, creating a fertile ground for microbial growth. Pitta imbalance often manifests as inflammation and fever, indicative of an overactive immune response. Vata imbalance can lead to systemic weakness and increased susceptibility to opportunistic infections. Maintaining doshic balance through personalized interventions is thus integral to strengthening Vyadhikshamatva.

Ayurveda also emphasizes the role of external factors, such as seasonal changes, environmental stressors, and lifestyle habits, in modulating immunity. Seasonal routines (Ritucharya) and daily routines (Dinacharya) are recommended to align the body with natural rhythms, thereby preventing doshic disturbances. For instance, consuming light, detoxifying foods during spring prevents Kapha accumulation, while nourishing, warm foods in winter support Ojas and Agni. Modern parallels to these practices can be seen in circadian biology and seasonal immune modulation, which recognize the influence of environmental factors on health.

One of the most profound contributions of Ayurveda to immunology is its focus on Rasayana therapies, which aim to rejuvenate the body and enhance immunity. Rasayana herbs, such as Amalaki (Emblica officinalis), Guduchi (Tinospora cordifolia), and Ashwagandha (Withania somnifera), are known for their antioxidant, adaptogenic, and immunomodulatory properties. These herbs not only strengthen Ojas but also modulate cytokines, reduce oxidative stress, and improve gut microbiota—a concept increasingly validated by modern scientific research.

For example, Guduchi has been shown to enhance macrophage activity and regulate inflammatory responses, aligning with Ayurveda's description of its role in balancing all three doshas. Similarly, Amalaki, rich in vitamin C and bioflavonoids, supports collagen synthesis, enhances antioxidant defenses, and promotes tissue repair. Triphala, a combination of Amalaki, Bibhitaki, and Haritaki, is another cornerstone of Ayurvedic immunity-building practices. It balances the gut microbiota, eliminates Ama, and supports systemic immunity.

Modern immunological research also highlights the relevance of gut health, which Ayurveda has long regarded as central to immunity. The gut is described as a reservoir of Sahaja Krimi (natural flora) that supports digestion and prevents pathogenic Krimi overgrowth. The Ayurvedic approach to probiotics and fermented foods, such as Takra (buttermilk), reflects an understanding of maintaining microbial harmony. This aligns with current studies on the gut-brain axis, which reveal how microbial diversity influences systemic health, including immunity and mental well-being.

Ayurveda's view of immunity extends beyond physical resilience to encompass mental and emotional health. Stress, anxiety, and unresolved emotions are considered significant contributors to weakened immunity, as they disturb Vata dosha and deplete Ojas. Practices such as meditation, yoga, and Pranayama are integral to Ayurvedic immunology, promoting mental clarity and doshic balance. These practices find modern validation in psychoneuroimmunology, which studies the impact of stress and emotional well-being on immune function.

A significant challenge addressed by Ayurveda is the prevention of chronic inflammation, which underlies many modern diseases. While acute inflammation is the body's natural response to pathogens, chronic inflammation can lead to tissue damage and immune dysregulation. Ayurveda's emphasis on detoxification therapies, such as Panchakarma, and its anti-inflammatory herbs provides sustainable solutions for managing inflammation. For instance, Turmeric (Haridra) has demonstrated potent anti-inflammatory effects by modulating pathways like NF-kB and reducing oxidative stress.

Ayurvedic principles of immunity also emphasize the prevention of disease through personalized interventions. Each individual's Prakriti determines their susceptibility to diseases and informs their unique preventive and therapeutic strategies. For example, a Vata-dominant individual prone to dryness and weakness may require warm, nourishing foods and grounding practices, while a Kapha-dominant individual benefits from detoxifying diets and dynamic physical activity. This personalized approach aligns with the principles of modern precision medicine, which tailors interventions based on genetic, environmental, and lifestyle factors.

Vyadhikshamatva in Ayurveda offers a holistic and integrative perspective on immunity that bridges ancient wisdom with modern science. By addressing the interconnected roles of Agni, Ojas, Tridoshas, and external factors, Ayurveda provides a comprehensive framework for disease prevention and health promotion. Its emphasis on rejuvenation, gut health, and mental well-being aligns with emerging trends in immunology, making it a valuable complement to contemporary healthcare practices.

46. How does the Ayurvedic concept of Vyadhikshamatva extend beyond the scope of modern immunology to encompass holistic health principles?
- A. It integrates the physiological, psychological, and environmental dimensions of health through the regulation of Ojas and Agni.
- B. It exclusively focuses on cellular immunity, neglecting factors such as emotional well-being and lifestyle habits.
- C. Vyadhikshamatva is rooted entirely in metaphysical constructs, lacking tangible biological parallels in modern science.
- D. It centers solely on detoxification therapies, disregarding personalized health interventions.

47. The passage describes the pivotal role of Agni in immune function. Which of the following mechanisms best explains this relationship in the Ayurvedic framework?
- A. Agni governs mental health, which indirectly affects immunity through stress reduction.
- B. By ensuring proper digestion and preventing Ama accumulation, Agni fosters systemic resilience against microbial and environmental challenges.
- C. Agni acts independently of microbial balance, focusing solely on metabolic processes unrelated to immunity.
- D. Weak Agni enhances doshic harmony, which directly compensates for immune deficiencies.

48. How do Rasayana therapies, as described in the passage, reflect a multi-dimensional approach to immunity enhancement?
- A. They target specific immune cells, providing direct antimicrobial benefits while reducing systemic oxidative stress.
- B. By modulating cytokines, improving gut health, and restoring Ojas, they address both physiological and psychological aspects of health.
- C. They focus exclusively on reducing Ama, leaving systemic immunity unaffected.
- D. Rasayana therapies are limited to Kapha-dominant conditions, with no applications for Vata or Pitta imbalances.

49. Based on the passage, which external factors are described as critical disruptors of Vyadhikshamatva in the Ayurvedic system?
- A. Seasonal transitions and stress, which create imbalances in the Tridoshas and weaken Agni.
- B. Pathogenic microorganisms, which Ayurveda views as the sole agents of disease causation.
- C. Chronic inflammation caused by oxidative stress, which directly depletes Ojas and weakens immunity.
- D. Environmental factors unrelated to personal lifestyle choices or dietary practices.

50. The passage identifies Ojas as a central determinant of systemic resilience. Which statement most accurately describes its role in the Ayurvedic framework of immunity?
- A. Ojas is the byproduct of healthy digestion and balanced dhatus, providing both physical and mental fortitude against diseases.
- B. It functions solely as a symbolic entity, representing the metaphysical aspects of health rather than tangible physiological processes.
- C. Ojas primarily influences Kapha dosha, limiting its role to structural and mucosal immunity.
- D. It is derived directly from immune therapies, with no connection to Agni or digestive health.

ANSWER WITH EXPLANATIONS

1. **C:** In Ayurveda, Bahya Krimi refers to external pathogens like lice, mites, and fungi, which cause localized infections in the skin and wounds. These infections thrive when Kapha dosha is aggravated, creating moist and stagnant conditions conducive to microbial growth. This understanding parallels modern dermatological studies that identify bacterial and fungal infections arising from poor hygiene or excessive moisture. Ayurvedic interventions emphasize lifestyle corrections to balance Kapha, topical applications of herbs like Neem for antimicrobial action, and cleansing therapies like Prakshalana to disinfect infected areas. Unlike modern treatments, which focus primarily on pathogen eradication, Ayurveda integrates hygiene, dosha balance, and tissue repair for long-term prevention and healing.

2. **A:** Ama, or undigested metabolic waste, is central to Ayurveda's understanding of gut health and systemic disease. It disrupts Agni, creating an environment conducive to pathogenic Krimis, and aligns with the modern concept of dysbiosis, where microbial imbalance in the gut leads to inflammation and immune dysfunction. Conditions like irritable bowel syndrome (IBS) are linked to Ama in Ayurveda and treated through detoxification therapies such as Virechana (purgation), which eliminate toxins and restore Agni. Modern probiotics address dysbiosis by restoring microbial diversity, paralleling Ayurvedic practices of fermented food consumption, such as Takra. This demonstrates Ayurveda's systemic approach, targeting root causes like Ama rather than treating symptoms alone.

3. **B:** The rejuvenative and detoxifying properties of Triphala make it a cornerstone of Ayurvedic gut health interventions. Composed of Amalaki, Bibhitaki, and Haritaki, it eliminates Ama, balances doshas, and enhances microbial diversity in the gut, reflecting modern findings on probiotics and herbal formulations. Triphala's ability to regulate gut flora while promoting digestive health highlights Ayurveda's preventive approach, which addresses systemic imbalances before they manifest as disease. Unlike conventional treatments, which often focus narrowly on microbial elimination, Triphala offers holistic benefits, supporting immunity, detoxification, and microbial harmony. Its continued relevance in gut health management bridges traditional Ayurvedic insights with contemporary scientific validation.

4. **B:** Kapha dosha, when aggravated, creates conditions favorable for respiratory infections due to excessive mucus production and stagnation. Ayurvedic interventions like Sitopaladi churna and Kapha-reducing herbs, such as Tulsi and Pippali, have anti-inflammatory and mucolytic properties, clearing mucus and reducing microbial growth. This approach aligns with modern treatments for respiratory infections, which focus on reducing inflammation and restoring airflow. However, Ayurveda goes further by addressing the systemic Kapha imbalance, emphasizing prevention through lifestyle modifications, detoxification therapies, and dietary adjustments. This integrative framework highlights the role of doshas in infection management, offering holistic strategies that extend beyond pathogen-focused interventions.

5. **A:** Ayurveda's Rasayana therapies, such as Guduchi and Ashwagandha, enhance immune resilience by balancing doshas, supporting Ojas, and reducing oxidative stress. This aligns with modern immunomodulation practices, which aim to strengthen host defenses rather than directly targeting pathogens. Rasayanas rejuvenate tissues and regulate systemic inflammation, demonstrating Ayurveda's emphasis on long-term health rather than short-term fixes. For instance, Guduchi improves macrophage activity and cytokine regulation, while Ashwagandha enhances stress resistance and immune function. These therapies underscore the holistic nature of Vyadhikshamatva (immunity), integrating physical, mental, and emotional well-being. Ayurveda's proactive approach contrasts with reactive models, offering sustainable health benefits.

6. **B:** Overharvesting of Amalaki, a key ingredient in Triphala, reduces its bioactive compounds, impacting its medicinal efficacy. Ayurveda advocates ecological harmony, promoting sustainable agroforestry and community-based conservation to ensure the long-term availability of herbs. This aligns with modern environmental practices that emphasize biodiversity preservation while maintaining medicinal quality. By integrating conservation into therapeutic strategies, Ayurveda addresses both ecological and health challenges, demonstrating its adaptability to contemporary needs. Unlike synthetic substitutes, which compromise therapeutic integrity, Ayurvedic sustainability focuses on maintaining natural balance. This approach highlights Ayurveda's foresight in balancing ecological health with clinical efficacy, reinforcing its relevance in addressing global challenges.

7. **A:** Takra (buttermilk) exemplifies Ayurveda's recognition of the gut's role in systemic health. As a probiotic, it restores Sahaja Krimi (natural flora), balances doshas, and enhances Agni, paralleling modern approaches to maintaining gut microbial diversity. Unlike contemporary probiotics, which focus solely on introducing beneficial bacteria, Takra integrates dietary and doshic considerations, addressing the root causes of microbial imbalances. By combining Takra with detoxification therapies and Rasayana herbs, Ayurveda offers a layered approach to digestive and immune health. Its relevance in managing gastrointestinal disorders like IBS reflects Ayurveda's comprehensive understanding of microbial harmony and systemic resilience.

8. **B:** Neem's broad-spectrum antimicrobial properties, combined with its Kapha-reducing action, address infections while detoxifying tissues. In Ayurveda, it is used for skin infections, wound healing, and as a systemic cleanser. Modern studies validate Neem's antibacterial and antifungal effects, aligning with its Ayurvedic applications. Unlike treatments that focus on microbial elimination alone, Neem balances doshas and promotes tissue regeneration, offering holistic benefits. Its role in managing infections, detoxifying Ama, and maintaining systemic balance highlights Ayurveda's integrative approach. Neem's continued relevance in antimicrobial therapy demonstrates Ayurveda's ability to address contemporary challenges, such as resistance to conventional antibiotics.

9. **A:** The gut-lung axis reflects Ayurveda's interconnected understanding of physiology, where gut health influences respiratory resilience. Kapha and Vata doshas play crucial roles; Kapha governs mucus production, while Vata facilitates systemic movement. By addressing gut imbalances through Triphala or Takra, Ayurveda indirectly supports respiratory health, showcasing its systemic approach. Modern research on microbiota's influence on immune modulation and respiratory health aligns with Ayurvedic principles, emphasizing the importance of gut integrity. Ayurveda's preventive care strategies, including diet, lifestyle adjustments, and detoxification, highlight the interconnectedness of body systems, offering insights into holistic management of respiratory disorders.

10. **B:** Ayurvedic polyherbal formulations like Triphala and Neem-based preparations are preferred for microbial infections because they address multiple pathways. They detoxify Ama, balance doshas, and maintain microbial harmony, reducing the risk of resistance compared to single-drug therapies. Modern concerns about antibiotic resistance underscore Ayurveda's relevance, as polyherbal therapies prevent pathogen adaptation. Additionally, these formulations integrate systemic health with microbial management, ensuring long-term benefits. Their ability to enhance immunity while targeting pathogens demonstrates Ayurveda's nuanced understanding of microbial and host dynamics, offering a sustainable alternative to conventional antimicrobial strategies.

11. **B:** Rasayana therapies enhance immunity by restoring Ojas, modulating immune responses, and balancing doshas. Amalaki and Guduchi, key Rasayana herbs, rejuvenate tissues, reduce oxidative stress, and regulate inflammatory markers like cytokines. This aligns with Ayurveda's preventive care framework, focusing on systemic resilience rather than pathogen-specific interventions. Unlike conventional therapies that often target isolated immune pathways, Rasayanas address physical, mental, and emotional aspects of health. Their adaptogenic properties improve stress tolerance, further supporting immune health. By integrating traditional practices with modern immunological insights, Ayurveda offers a multidimensional approach to enhancing Vyadhikshamatva and maintaining long-term health.

12. **A:** Environmental degradation impacts Guduchi's bioactive content, reducing its Rasayana efficacy. This aligns with Ayurveda's emphasis on ecological balance, where plant quality directly influences therapeutic outcomes. Overharvesting disrupts the delicate equilibrium required for Guduchi's adaptogenic and immunomodulatory properties. Ayurveda advocates sustainable cultivation practices like agroforestry, ensuring the availability of high-quality herbs. Unlike synthetic alternatives, natural Guduchi preserves the integrative benefits of Rasayana therapies, including tissue rejuvenation and dosha balance. This interdependence between ecology and therapy highlights Ayurveda's holistic perspective, addressing modern challenges in medicinal plant sourcing while maintaining its clinical efficacy.

13. **B:** Sustainable practices, such as organic farming and community-based conservation, align with Ayurveda's principles of ecological harmony and therapeutic integrity. These strategies ensure the preservation of biodiversity while maintaining the potency of medicinal herbs like Guduchi. Unlike industrial monoculture, which prioritizes quantity over quality, Ayurveda emphasizes the natural balance between environment and health. By integrating sustainability into herbal sourcing, Ayurveda addresses global challenges like climate change and overharvesting. This approach reinforces its relevance in contemporary healthcare,

demonstrating that ecological conservation and therapeutic efficacy are interdependent, reflecting Ayurveda's commitment to holistic well-being.

14. B: The degradation of medicinal plants like Guduchi directly impacts therapeutic outcomes, illustrating the interplay between environmental sustainability and health. Ayurveda's emphasis on the quality of raw materials ensures that therapeutic integrity is maintained. Sustainable harvesting practices preserve bioactive compounds critical to immune modulation and dosha balance. This interconnected framework highlights Ayurveda's holistic approach, addressing not only individual health but also ecological well-being. By integrating plant conservation into healthcare strategies, Ayurveda bridges gaps between traditional wisdom and contemporary environmental challenges, ensuring long-term efficacy and sustainability in its therapies.

15. A: The classification of Krimi in Ayurveda reflects an advanced understanding of microbial roles in health and disease. Bahya Krimi corresponds to external pathogens, Abhyantara Krimi to internal infections, and Sahaja Krimi to beneficial microorganisms. This nuanced categorization predates modern microbiology, emphasizing the systemic impact of microbial dynamics on doshic balance. Ayurveda's integration of natural flora in maintaining health aligns with contemporary research on gut microbiota and systemic immunity. By addressing both pathogenic and beneficial Krimis, Ayurveda offers a holistic framework for microbial management, showcasing its relevance in modern healthcare.

16. A: Vyadhikshamatva encompasses innate, adaptive, and intervention-enhanced immunity, aligning with modern immunology's comprehensive framework. Sahaja Vyadhikshamatva reflects constitutional resilience determined by Prakriti, while Kalaja Vyadhikshamatva evolves with age and environmental factors. Yuktikrita Vyadhikshamatva, enhanced through Rasayana therapies and lifestyle modifications, demonstrates Ayurveda's proactive approach to immunity. Unlike reductionist models, Ayurveda integrates physical, emotional, and environmental influences, emphasizing the dynamic nature of immunity. This holistic perspective bridges ancient principles with modern advancements, offering sustainable solutions for disease prevention and health optimization.

17. A: Ama, the byproduct of impaired digestion, fosters conditions conducive to pathogenic Krimi growth. This aligns with modern insights into gut dysbiosis, where metabolic waste and inflammation disrupt microbial balance. Detoxification therapies like Virechana eliminate Ama, restoring Agni and preventing microbial overgrowth. Unlike treatments that target microbes directly, Ayurveda focuses on systemic resilience, addressing root causes like poor digestion and doshic imbalance. This integrative approach highlights the interplay between digestion, immunity, and microbial harmony, offering comprehensive solutions to modern health challenges.

18. B: Rasayana herbs like Guduchi, Amalaki, and Triphala enhance immunity through multiple pathways, including doshic balance, antioxidant action, and microbial regulation. Guduchi modulates inflammatory responses, Amalaki supports tissue repair and Ojas production, and Triphala detoxifies Ama while balancing gut flora. This holistic approach addresses systemic resilience rather than isolated immune pathways. Unlike conventional therapies that often overlook the interconnectedness of body systems, Rasayanas integrate physical, mental, and microbial health. Their continued relevance underscores Ayurveda's comprehensive framework for enhancing immunity and managing chronic conditions.

19. C: Microbial infections in Ayurveda are influenced by doshic imbalances: Kapha fosters microbial growth in moist environments, Pitta drives inflammation, and Vata facilitates systemic spread. This understanding aligns with modern insights into host-pathogen dynamics, where environmental and physiological factors influence susceptibility. Ayurveda's approach to balancing doshas addresses both microbial proliferation and host resilience, offering a layered strategy for infection management. By integrating detoxification, immune modulation, and doshic balance, Ayurveda provides holistic solutions to contemporary infectious diseases, emphasizing prevention and long-term health.

20. B: Ayurveda's approach to gut dysbiosis includes Triphala for microbial balance, Virechana for Ama elimination, and Takra for replenishing Sahaja Krimi. These interventions reflect a systemic understanding of digestion, immunity, and microbial harmony. Unlike conventional treatments, which often focus narrowly on introducing probiotics, Ayurveda integrates dietary and lifestyle adjustments to address root causes. This comprehensive framework highlights the interplay between digestion, immunity, and microbial health, offering sustainable solutions for managing gut-related disorders and systemic inflammation.

21. A: Takra restores Sahaja Krimi, balances doshas, and enhances Agni, demonstrating Ayurveda's integrative approach to gut health and immunity. Unlike conventional probiotics, which target microbial diversity alone, Ayurveda addresses systemic factors like digestion and doshic balance. By combining dietary interventions with detoxification therapies, Ayurveda offers layered solutions to microbial imbalances. This comprehensive strategy underscores the importance of maintaining natural flora for systemic resilience, bridging traditional practices with modern scientific insights into gut health and immunity.

22. **A:** Rasayana therapies, such as Guduchi and Amalaki, rejuvenate tissues, modulate cytokines, and balance doshas, enhancing systemic immunity. Panchakarma therapies eliminate Ama and detoxify the body, supporting immune resilience. This dual approach integrates prevention and rejuvenation, addressing both root causes and systemic health. Unlike isolated interventions, Ayurveda combines detoxification and rejuvenation to optimize immunity and prevent chronic conditions. These principles align with modern integrative medicine, highlighting Ayurveda's relevance in enhancing systemic resilience and managing immune dysfunctions.

23. **A:** Sahaja Krimi represents the body's natural flora, which supports digestion and immunity. Ama accumulation fosters pathogenic Krimi proliferation, leading to systemic inflammation and weakened immunity. Seasonal imbalances disrupt microbial harmony by affecting doshic equilibrium, particularly Kapha during spring and Vata during dry seasons. Ayurvedic detoxification therapies target Ama without eliminating Sahaja Krimi, preserving microbial balance. This approach contrasts with modern antibiotic treatments, which often disrupt natural flora. Ayurveda's emphasis on gut health, seasonal routines, and personalized interventions reflects its holistic perspective, addressing the dynamic interplay between microbial harmony, digestion, and immunity.

24. **A:** Ayurvedic herbs like Neem, Turmeric, and Tulsi exemplify antimicrobial agents that simultaneously balance doshas and support systemic immunity. Neem detoxifies tissues while addressing Kapha dominance in infections. Turmeric reduces inflammation and modulates immune responses, aligning with its role as a Pitta-balancing herb. Tulsi targets respiratory pathogens and strengthens Vata, showcasing its adaptogenic properties. These herbs reflect Ayurveda's holistic framework, integrating localized microbial management with systemic health restoration. Unlike conventional antimicrobials, Ayurveda's polyherbal formulations emphasize doshic harmony, tissue regeneration, and resilience, offering sustainable solutions to modern challenges like antimicrobial resistance.

25. **A:** Bahya Krimi corresponds to external pathogens, such as mites and lice, affecting the skin and wounds. Abhyantara Krimi includes internal pathogens causing systemic infections, particularly in the gastrointestinal and respiratory tracts. Sahaja Krimi refers to natural flora essential for digestion and immunity. Vikriti Krimi represents pathogenic microorganisms arising during doshic imbalance. Ayurveda's nuanced classification predates modern microbiology, emphasizing the interaction between microbial dynamics and systemic health. By addressing both beneficial and harmful microorganisms, Ayurveda bridges traditional and contemporary microbial understandings, offering a comprehensive framework for infection prevention and health maintenance.

26. **A:** Panchakarma therapies detoxify the body and restore doshic balance by eliminating Ama and pathogens. Rasayana therapies rejuvenate tissues, strengthen Ojas, and enhance immune resilience. Takra (buttermilk) restores microbial harmony by replenishing Sahaja Krimi, reflecting Ayurveda's emphasis on gut health. Triphala promotes detoxification while balancing doshas and systemic immunity. This integrative approach contrasts with modern treatments that often isolate microbial management from systemic health. Ayurveda's holistic framework addresses root causes like poor digestion and microbial imbalances, offering sustainable and multidimensional solutions to immune and microbial health challenges.

27. **A:** Kapha imbalance fosters microbial growth by creating moist and stagnant environments. Pitta imbalance drives inflammation and fever, indicative of immune hyperactivity. Vata imbalance facilitates systemic pathogen spread through disrupted circulation and nervous system function. Ama accumulation weakens immunity by creating conditions conducive to microbial proliferation. Ayurveda's recognition of these factors reflects its systemic approach to infection management, integrating microbial dynamics with host factors. This nuanced understanding bridges gaps in modern medicine, emphasizing personalized interventions like dosha balancing and detoxification therapies to prevent and manage infections effectively.

28. **A:** Neem's broad-spectrum action targets bacteria and fungi while detoxifying tissues. Turmeric reduces inflammation and modulates immune responses through its antioxidant properties. Tulsi targets respiratory pathogens while balancing Vata and Kapha doshas. Vidanga functions as an anthelmintic, addressing intestinal parasitic infections. These herbs demonstrate Ayurveda's layered approach to antimicrobial therapies, integrating pathogen elimination with systemic health

restoration. Unlike single-drug treatments, Ayurveda's polyherbal formulations preserve microbial harmony and address underlying doshic imbalances, offering holistic and sustainable solutions to infectious diseases.

29. A: Sahaja Krimi supports digestion and immunity, reflecting the beneficial role of natural flora. Ama, arising from undigested food, disrupts Agni and fosters pathogenic Krimi proliferation. Virechana therapy eliminates Ama, restoring digestive health and systemic resilience. Triphala balances doshas, detoxifies the gut, and enhances microbial diversity, aligning with modern probiotics. Ayurveda's integration of digestion, microbial health, and doshic balance offers a comprehensive framework for managing gut-related disorders. This approach underscores the systemic impact of gut health on immunity and disease prevention, bridging traditional and modern healthcare practices.

30. A: Guduchi enhances immune modulation and balances all three doshas, making it a key Rasayana herb. Amalaki, rich in antioxidants, rejuvenates tissues and supports Ojas production. Ashwagandha, an adaptogen, improves systemic resilience by modulating stress responses. Triphala detoxifies Ama, balances doshas, and restores microbial harmony, enhancing systemic immunity. These Rasayana herbs exemplify Ayurveda's holistic approach to health, integrating rejuvenation, detoxification, and immune resilience. Their continued relevance in managing chronic conditions highlights Ayurveda's foresight in addressing systemic health challenges through personalized and sustainable interventions.

31. A: Diarrhea arises from Ama accumulation disrupting gut Agni, reflecting Kapha and Pitta imbalances. Constipation results from aggravated Vata causing dryness and irregular bowel movements. Dysbiosis reflects an imbalance between Sahaja and pathogenic Krimi, disrupting microbial harmony. Hyperacidity, driven by Pitta imbalance, affects the stomach lining, causing inflammation and digestive discomfort. Ayurveda's understanding of digestive disorders integrates doshic imbalances, microbial dynamics, and systemic health, offering comprehensive solutions. By addressing root causes like Ama and restoring Agni, Ayurveda complements modern treatments, enhancing long-term gut health and immunity.

32. A: Sahaja Vyadhikshamatva represents innate immunity determined by Prakriti. Kalaja Vyadhikshamatva reflects adaptive immunity influenced by age and environmental factors. Yuktikrita Vyadhikshamatva, enhanced through lifestyle interventions, demonstrates Ayurveda's proactive approach to health. Ojas preservation sustains systemic resilience, integrating physical, mental, and emotional well-being. This classification bridges traditional and modern immunological frameworks, emphasizing immunity's dynamic nature. By integrating preventive and therapeutic measures, Ayurveda addresses immunity comprehensively aligning ancient principles with contemporary healthcare challenges, including chronic diseases and immune disorders.

33. A: Gut dysbiosis reflects the imbalance of Sahaja and pathogenic Krimi, disrupting digestion and immunity. Probiotics, represented by fermented foods like Takra, restore microbial harmony and enhance Agni. Biofilm formation corresponds to Kapha dominance, creating protective environments for pathogenic microbes. Antimicrobial resistance highlights the limitations of single-drug approaches, aligning with Ayurveda's polyherbal strategies. This integrative understanding demonstrates Ayurveda's nuanced approach to microbial management, emphasizing harmony rather than eradication. By addressing systemic factors like digestion and doshic balance, Ayurveda complements modern treatments, offering sustainable solutions to microbial and immune challenges.

34. A: Toxin production corresponds to Ama accumulation, disrupting systemic health. Inflammation reflects aggravated Pitta, driving immune hyperactivity and tissue damage. Systemic spread of pathogens aligns with Vata imbalance, affecting circulation and nervous function. Chronic infections result from Kapha dominance, fostering microbial persistence in stagnant environments. Ayurveda's recognition of these mechanisms integrates microbial dynamics with doshic imbalances, offering comprehensive insights into infection management. By addressing root causes and systemic factors, Ayurveda complements pathogen-focused therapies, providing holistic solutions to modern infectious disease challenges.

35. C: Statement 1 correctly identifies Krimi in Ayurveda as encompassing both pathogenic and natural microorganisms. However, Statement 2 is false because Sahaja Krimi are not harmful; they represent the beneficial natural flora that support digestion and immunity. Ayurveda recognizes the balance between Sahaja Krimi and pathogenic Krimi as essential for health. Disruptions in this balance, often caused by Ama or doshic imbalances, lead to disease. The concept aligns with modern microbiology's understanding of commensal bacteria, emphasizing the importance of microbial harmony. This integrative approach underscores Ayurveda's systemic perspective on health and microbial dynamics.

36. A: Both statements are true, and Statement 2 explains Statement 1. Ama, the byproduct of impaired digestion, fosters microbial proliferation and systemic inflammation, creating conditions conducive to disease. Panchakarma therapies like Virechana and Basti eliminate Ama, restoring Agni and microbial harmony, thereby enhancing immunity. This aligns with modern detoxification and gut health practices, emphasizing the interplay between digestion and systemic resilience. Ayurveda's focus on root cause elimination contrasts with symptomatic treatments, offering sustainable solutions to chronic conditions linked to microbial imbalances and inflammation.

37. C: Statement 1 is true, highlighting the role of Rasayana therapies like Guduchi and Amalaki in enhancing immunity by supporting Ojas and regulating inflammation. Statement 2, however, is false because Vyadhikshamatva encompasses not only innate immunity but also adaptive and intervention-enhanced immunity. Ayurveda's classification of immunity as Sahaja, Kalaja, and Yuktikrita demonstrates its dynamic and comprehensive approach. Rasayana therapies integrate these layers by addressing physical, mental, and microbial factors, offering a multidimensional framework for managing immune dysfunctions and chronic diseases.

38. C: Statement 1 is true, as pathogenic Krimi in Ayurveda parallels opportunistic microorganisms in modern microbiology, thriving under weakened immunity or imbalanced doshas. Statement 2 is false because Sahaja Krimi are beneficial natural flora that contribute to systemic resilience. Their balance is essential for maintaining health, and their disruption leads to disease. Ayurveda's understanding of Sahaja and pathogenic Krimi predates modern microbiology, integrating microbial dynamics with digestion, immunity, and doshic balance. This holistic perspective aligns with contemporary research on gut microbiota and systemic health.

39. C: Statement 1 is true, reflecting Ayurveda's emphasis on restoring doshic balance alongside eliminating pathogens to address the root causes of infection. Statement 2 is false because Ayurvedic antimicrobial therapies, such as Neem and Triphala, not only target pathogens but also support systemic health and immunity. This integrative approach contrasts with conventional antimicrobial treatments, which often overlook the host's systemic balance. By combining microbial management with doshic regulation, Ayurveda offers sustainable and comprehensive solutions to infectious diseases.

40. A: Rasayana therapies form an essential component of Ayurveda, focusing on systemic rejuvenation and disease prevention. These therapies, often involving herbs like Ashwagandha and Amalaki, are rich in antioxidants and bioactive compounds that enhance immune responses. By modulating both innate and adaptive immunity, Rasayana prevents microbial invasions and mitigates inflammatory responses. The emphasis on strengthening the body's resilience against infections aligns with modern immunological insights into preventative medicine. This dual approach, balancing internal immunity and external threats, highlights Ayurveda's foresight in integrating natural interventions with holistic health objectives, showcasing its relevance even in contemporary microbiological contexts.

41. A: The Ayurvedic concept of "Krimi" aligns remarkably with modern microbiological descriptions of microbial infections. Ayurveda identifies Krimi as organisms, visible or invisible, capable of causing diseases, and prescribes herbal formulations for their eradication. These remedies, such as Vidanga and Neem, exhibit potent antimicrobial properties, validated by modern research. The recognition of Krimi centuries ago reveals Ayurveda's advanced diagnostic insights into pathogenic causation. By addressing both preventive and curative dimensions, Ayurveda's holistic framework complements the precision of microbiology, emphasizing how ancient systems of medicine anticipated concepts now fundamental to contemporary healthcare.

42. A: Panchakarma therapies serve as Ayurveda's comprehensive detoxification system, eliminating toxins, including microbial by-products, from the body. These therapies focus on purging metabolic and environmental toxins through procedures like Vamana (emesis) and Basti (enemas). While these methods target the gastrointestinal tract and liver primarily, their benefits extend to reducing systemic microbial loads. This reflects the Ayurvedic understanding of disease causation linked to toxin accumulation. Modern parallels, such as the role of detoxification in reducing microbial burden, validate Panchakarma's relevance. Its preventive nature demonstrates Ayurveda's proactive approach to health management, integrating ancient practices with contemporary microbiological principles.

43. A: Neem and Turmeric have been foundational in Ayurvedic medicine for treating microbial infections. Bioactive compounds like azadirachtin in Neem and curcumin in Turmeric disrupt microbial pathways, exhibiting antimicrobial, antifungal, and antiviral properties. These herbs are effective against a spectrum of pathogens, including resistant strains, highlighting their therapeutic versatility. The integration of such botanicals into traditional medicine underscores Ayurveda's empirical approach to health, predating modern pharmacology. By emphasizing natural solutions, Ayurveda not only anticipates modern antibiotic challenges but also offers sustainable alternatives to synthetic drugs, fostering a complementary relationship between ancient and contemporary medical systems.

44. C: Fermentation in Ayurveda enhances the potency and bioavailability of herbal formulations like Asavas and Arishtas. The controlled fermentation process enriches these formulations with beneficial microbes and bioactive metabolites, improving their therapeutic efficacy. However, the assertion that fermentation leads to contamination contradicts Ayurveda's precise techniques for ensuring purity. This misunderstanding highlights the need to differentiate between controlled fermentation and microbial contamination. Ayurvedic formulations undergo rigorous methods to maintain their integrity, showcasing how ancient practices harmonized microbiology and pharmacology. This interplay emphasizes the sophistication of Ayurveda in integrating microbial processes to enhance medicinal properties.

45. A: Gut microbiota is a cornerstone of health, influencing digestion, immunity, and overall well-being. Ayurveda's concept of Agni (digestive fire) parallels this understanding, emphasizing the role of digestion in maintaining bodily balance. A healthy Agni supports the growth of beneficial gut bacteria, aiding nutrient absorption and pathogen resistance. The symbiotic relationship between gut microbes and digestion underscores Ayurveda's holistic approach to systemic health. Modern research into gut-brain and gut-immune axes corroborates Ayurvedic principles, revealing how microbial ecosystems affect broader physiological functions. This ancient understanding preempts contemporary insights, demonstrating Ayurveda's enduring relevance in microbiological and systemic health contexts.

46. A: The Ayurvedic concept of Vyadhikshamatva extends beyond modern immunology by embracing a truly holistic approach. It integrates physical health (via Agni, digestion), mental well-being (through balance of Tridoshas and stress management), and environmental harmony (via Ritucharya and Dinacharya). Unlike modern immunology, which primarily focuses on cellular responses and biochemical pathways, Vyadhikshamatva emphasizes maintaining equilibrium across all levels—Ojas as the essence of vitality, Agni for metabolic fire, and lifestyle for daily resilience. This broader view enables personalized prevention and healing, aligning with modern concepts like precision medicine and psychoneuroimmunology.

47. B: In Ayurveda, Agni (digestive fire) is not only responsible for digestion but is also the cornerstone of immunity. A strong Agni ensures proper digestion and assimilation of nutrients, which leads to the formation of Ojas, the essence of immunity and vitality. When Agni is impaired, Ama (toxic undigested residue) accumulates, disrupting doshic balance and creating an environment conducive to infections and inflammation. Therefore, maintaining a healthy Agni helps in preventing disease, enhancing systemic resistance, and fostering resilience against both microbial and environmental challenges. This understanding closely parallels the modern link between gut health and immune function.

48. B: Rasayana therapies enhance immunity through multiple pathways, including cytokine modulation, antioxidant effects, and Ojas rejuvenation. Herbs like Guduchi and Amalaki support doshic balance and systemic resilience, reflecting Ayurveda's holistic approach. Unlike treatments targeting isolated immune pathways, Rasayanas integrate physical, mental, and microbial health. Their relevance in managing chronic conditions highlights Ayurveda's foresight in addressing immune dysfunctions comprehensively. This multidimensional framework bridges traditional practices with modern science, offering sustainable solutions for long-term health.

49. A: Seasonal transitions and stress disrupt doshic balance, affecting immunity and systemic health. Ayurveda's emphasis on Ritucharya (seasonal routines) and Dinacharya (daily routines) addresses these influences, aligning the body with natural rhythms. By integrating dietary adjustments, detoxification therapies, and lifestyle practices, Ayurveda prevents doshic imbalances and immune dysfunctions. This recognition of external factors highlights Ayurveda's systemic perspective, bridging traditional insights with contemporary research on circadian biology and immune modulation.

50. A: Ojas, derived from balanced digestion and dhatus, is central to systemic resilience and immunity. It reflects the ultimate integration of physical, mental, and emotional health, offering protection against diseases. Ayurveda's emphasis on preserving Ojas through Rasayana therapies and doshic balance underscores its preventive care framework. This contrasts with modern approaches that often isolate physical health from emotional well-being. By integrating digestion, immunity, and systemic balance, Ayurveda provides comprehensive strategies for managing chronic conditions and enhancing overall health.

CHAPTER 18

IMMUNOLOGY BASICS – IMMUNE CELLS, ANTIGENS, AND PATHOGEN RESPONSE

(I) INTRODUCTION: BRIDGING MODERN IMMUNOLOGY AND AYURVEDA

Immunity is central to health and survival, a topic studied extensively in both ancient and modern contexts. Modern immunology dissects the intricate molecular and cellular mechanisms that protect the body, while Ayurveda views immunity through a holistic lens, emphasizing balance, harmony, and the vitality of the human system. This chapter bridges these perspectives, providing a comprehensive understanding of immunity, immune responses, and how Ayurveda contributes to enhancing health and disease resistance.

1. **Definition and Scope of Immunology:** Immunology is the branch of biology concerned with the defense mechanisms of the body. It studies the immune system's functions, the nature of pathogens, and the interactions between them. The immune system comprises organs, tissues, cells, and molecules that collectively work to:
   - Detect and neutralize pathogens, such as viruses, bacteria, fungi, and parasites.
   - Recognize and eliminate abnormal or cancerous cells.
   - Prevent overreaction to non-harmful entities (e.g., allergens).
2. **Ayurvedic Understanding of Immunity:** Ayurveda describes the immune system as the body's ability to resist disease (Vyadhi Kshamatva) and maintain equilibrium (Swasthya). This resistance is rooted in three foundational elements:
   - **Ojas:** The essence of vitality and immunity, generated from well-nourished tissues (Dhatus).
   - **Agni:** The digestive fire that supports metabolism, detoxification, and nutrient absorption.
   - **Dosha Balance:** Equilibrium between Vata, Pitta, and Kapha ensures optimal functioning of body and mind.
3. **Interdisciplinary Approach:** By combining Ayurveda's focus on prevention and vitality with modern immunology's understanding of cellular and molecular mechanisms, a more holistic framework for understanding and enhancing immunity emerges. This chapter delves into these perspectives to offer actionable insights for health management.

(II) BASICS OF IMMUNOLOGY

Immunology forms the cornerstone of understanding how the body protects itself against disease-causing microorganisms. A well-functioning immune system is essential for survival, providing both immediate responses to threats and long-term protection against recurring infections. This section elaborates on the immune system's structure, functions, and mechanisms.

The Immune System: An Overview

The immune system is an intricate network that safeguards the body by identifying, neutralizing, and eliminating harmful invaders, such as viruses, bacteria, and fungi. Its ability to distinguish between "self" and "non-self" ensures the preservation of the body's own tissues while targeting foreign agents.

1. **Components of the Immune System:** The immune system comprises various organs, cells, and molecules that work in concert to detect and respond to pathogens.

   (i) Organs of the Immune System:

   - **Bone Marrow:** The primary site of blood cell production, including immune cells such as white blood cells (WBCs).
   - **Thymus:** Located in the chest, it is where immature T cells mature and become specialized.
   - **Spleen:** Filters blood to remove pathogens and abnormal cells; it also acts as a reservoir for immune cells.
   - **Lymph Nodes:** Act as filtering stations where immune cells interact with pathogens and coordinate immune responses.

   (ii) Cells of the Immune System:

   - The immune response is orchestrated by specialized cells called leukocytes (WBCs). These cells can be categorized into two types based on their roles:
   - **Innate Immune Cells:** Neutrophils, macrophages, dendritic cells, and NK cells provide rapid, non-specific defense.
   - **Adaptive Immune Cells:** B and T lymphocytes provide targeted, long-term immunity.

   (iii) Molecules in Immunity:

   - **Cytokines:** Signaling proteins that mediate communication between immune cells.
   - **Antibodies:** Produced by B cells, these molecules recognize and neutralize specific pathogens.
   - **Complement Proteins:** Enhance the ability of antibodies and phagocytic cells to clear pathogens.

2. **Functions of the Immune System:** The immune system is a multitasking defense mechanism designed to ensure homeostasis by:
   1. **Defending Against Pathogens:** Preventing and eliminating infections caused by bacteria, viruses, fungi, and parasites.
   2. **Detecting and Eliminating Abnormal Cells:** Removing cancerous or pre-cancerous cells.
   3. **Maintaining Homeostasis:** Clearing dead cells and debris to keep tissues healthy.

3. **Key Features of the Immune System:** The immune system is characterized by several unique features that enhance its efficiency:

   (i) Specificity: Adaptive immunity relies on the precise recognition of antigens, which are specific molecular markers on pathogens.

   (ii) Diversity: The immune system can generate billions of different receptors to recognize a vast array of pathogens.

   (iii) Memory: Immunological memory allows the body to respond more rapidly and effectively to previously encountered pathogens.

   (iv) Self-Tolerance: A healthy immune system can distinguish between self (the body's own cells) and non-self (foreign invaders), avoiding autoimmunity.

Types of Immunity

Immunity can be broadly classified based on its mechanisms and origin.

1. **Innate Immunity:** Innate immunity serves as the body's first line of defense. It is present from birth and provides immediate, non-specific protection.

   Characteristics of Innate Immunity:

   - **Rapid Response:** Reacts within minutes to hours of infection.
   - **Non-Specific Defense:** Targets all pathogens without distinction.
   - **No Memory:** Does not retain information about previous infections.

   Components of Innate Immunity:

   - **Physical Barriers:** Skin and mucous membranes prevent pathogen entry.
   - **Chemical Barriers:** Enzymes, acids, and antimicrobial proteins destroy pathogens.

   Cellular Defenses:

   - **Phagocytes (e.g., macrophages, neutrophils):** Engulf and digest pathogens.
   - **Natural Killer (NK) Cells:** Destroy infected or abnormal cells.

   Mechanisms of Action:

   - Pathogens are recognized through Pattern Recognition Receptors (PRRs) that detect Pathogen-Associated Molecular Patterns (PAMPs).
   - Inflammation is triggered, recruiting immune cells to the site of infection.

2. **Adaptive Immunity:** Adaptive immunity is highly specific and develops over time in response to exposure to antigens.

   Characteristics of Adaptive Immunity:

   - **Specificity:** Recognizes and targets specific pathogens.

- **Memory:** Remembers past infections, enabling quicker responses upon re-exposure.
- **Delayed Response:** Takes days to fully activate during the first encounter with a pathogen.

Components of Adaptive Immunity:

- **Humoral Immunity (B Cells):** B lymphocytes produce antibodies that neutralize extracellular pathogens.
- Memory B cells ensure long-term immunity.

Cell-Mediated Immunity (T Cells):

- **Helper T cells (CD4+):** Activate other immune cells.
- **Cytotoxic T cells (CD8+):** Kill infected or cancerous cells.

3. Passive and Active Immunity

(i) Passive Immunity: Short-term immunity acquired through external sources, such as maternal antibodies passed to a newborn or antibody infusions.

(ii) Active Immunity: Long-lasting immunity developed through infection or vaccination, involving the activation of B and T cells.

Phases of Immune Response

1. **Recognition Phase:** The immune system identifies the presence of a pathogen using receptors on innate and adaptive immune cells.
2. **Activation Phase:** Immune cells are recruited and activated, and cytokines are released to amplify the response.
3. **Effector Phase:** Pathogens are neutralized, destroyed, or expelled from the body.
4. **Resolution and Memory Formation:** Inflammation subsides, and memory cells are generated for faster responses to future infections.

Factors Influencing Immunity

1. **Genetics:** Genetic variations influence the strength and efficiency of immune responses.
2. **Nutrition:** Deficiencies in vitamins and minerals (e.g., Vitamin D, Zinc) can weaken immunity.
3. **Stress and Lifestyle:** Chronic stress suppresses immunity, while regular exercise and adequate sleep enhance it.
4. **Environmental Exposures:** Overexposure to pollutants or toxins can impair immune function.
5. **Age:** Immune strength peaks during early adulthood and gradually declines with age.

(III) IMMUNE CELLS, ANTIGENS, AND IMMUNE RESPONSE

The immune system comprises a diverse array of cells, molecules, and responses that work together to identify, neutralize, and eliminate harmful invaders like bacteria, viruses, and other pathogens. This chapter provides a detailed analysis of key immune cells, the role of antigens, and the phases of immune response.

Key Immune Cells and Their Functions

Immune cells are specialized white blood cells (leukocytes) responsible for orchestrating the immune response. These cells can be broadly categorized into two types: innate immune cells, which provide immediate but non-specific defense, and adaptive immune cells, which target specific pathogens and develop immunological memory.

1. **Neutrophils:** Neutrophils are the most abundant white blood cells in the bloodstream, accounting for approximately 50-70% of all leukocytes. They are the body's first line of defense during infections and are classified as part of the innate immune system.

Key Characteristics:

- **Rapid Response:** Neutrophils are among the first immune cells to arrive at the site of infection or injury, typically within hours.
- **Phagocytosis:** Neutrophils engulf and digest pathogens, a process known as phagocytosis.
- **Enzymatic Destruction:** Neutrophils release enzymes like myeloperoxidase, elastase, and lysozyme, which break down microbial structures.
- **Reactive Oxygen Species (ROS):** Neutrophils produce ROS, highly reactive molecules that can damage and destroy pathogens.
- **Lifespan and Role:** Neutrophils have a short lifespan (6-12 hours), but their rapid recruitment and activity are crucial in limiting early infections.
- Once neutrophils die, they form pus, a mixture of dead cells and pathogens.

2. **Macrophages:** Macrophages are large, long-lived phagocytic cells derived from monocytes in the blood. These cells serve dual roles as scavengers and activators of the immune response.

Key Functions:

- **Phagocytosis:** Macrophages engulf and digest larger pathogens, such as bacteria, fungi, and cellular debris.
- **Cytokine Production:** They release cytokines, signaling proteins that recruit and activate other immune cells, such as neutrophils and lymphocytes.

- **Antigen Presentation:** Macrophages process pathogen-derived antigens and present them to T cells, triggering the adaptive immune response.

Specialized Macrophages:

- **Alveolar Macrophages (lungs):** Defend against airborne pathogens.
- **Kupffer Cells (liver):** Filter and detoxify the blood.
- **Microglia (brain):** Protect the central nervous system.

3. **Lymphocytes:** Lymphocytes are the central players in the adaptive immune response, and they include B cells, T cells, and natural killer (NK) cells.

B Cells:

- **Function:** B cells produce antibodies that specifically recognize and neutralize antigens.
- **Plasma Cells:** Once activated, B cells differentiate into plasma cells that secrete large amounts of antibodies.
- **Memory B Cells:** These cells persist after the infection, providing long-term immunity by recognizing the same pathogen during subsequent encounters.
- **T Cells:** T cells originate in the bone marrow but mature in the thymus, where they acquire specificity for antigens.

Subtypes of T cells:

1. **Helper T Cells (CD4+):** These cells coordinate the immune response by activating B cells, cytotoxic T cells, and macrophages. They release cytokines to amplify the response.
2. **Cytotoxic T Cells (CD8+):** These cells directly kill infected cells or cancerous cells by releasing perfin and granzymes, which induce apoptosis (cell death).
4. **Natural Killer (NK) Cells:** Natural killer (NK) cells are part of the innate immune system but also play a significant role in bridging innate and adaptive immunity.

Key Features:

- NK cells target virus-infected and tumor cells without requiring prior sensitization.
- They release cytotoxic granules, such as perforin and granzyme, that cause infected cells to self-destruct. Unlike T cells, NK cells do not require antigen presentation to recognize and eliminate threats.

Role in Immunity:

- NK cells play a pivotal role in controlling early infections and limiting the spread of cancer cells before the adaptive immune response is fully activated.

Antigens and Their Role in Immunity

The immune system operates by distinguishing between "self" and "non-self" entities. Antigens are foreign molecules recognized as "non-self," triggering a targeted immune response.

1. **What Are Antigens?**

Definition:

- Antigens are molecules, often proteins or polysaccharides, that are recognized as foreign by the immune system. They are found on the surfaces of pathogens, such as bacteria, viruses, fungi, and parasites, as well as on abnormal or cancerous cells.

Characteristics:

- **Epitopes:** Antigens contain specific regions called epitopes, which are recognized by immune receptors, such as antibodies or T-cell receptors.

Types of Antigens:

- **Exogenous Antigens:** Originating outside the body, such as bacterial toxins or viral proteins.
- **Endogenous Antigens:** Produced within the body, such as viral proteins in infected cells or mutated proteins in cancer cells.

2. **Antigen Presentation:** The immune system's ability to mount a targeted response depends on antigen presentation, a process performed by specialized cells called antigen-presenting cells (APCs).

Key APCs:

- **Macrophages:** Process and present antigens to helper T cells.
- **Dendritic Cells:** Highly specialized APCs that capture antigens in peripheral tissues and transport them to lymph nodes.
- **B Cells:** Present antigens to helper T cells during the activation phase of the adaptive response.

Mechanism:

1. Pathogens are engulfed by APCs through phagocytosis.
2. Inside the cell, antigens are broken down into smaller fragments.
3. These fragments are bound to Major Histocompatibility Complex (MHC) molecules and displayed on the cell surface.

- **MHC Class I:** Presents antigens to cytotoxic T cells.
- **MHC Class II:** Presents antigens to helper T cells.

Immune Response Phases

The immune response unfolds in three main phases, each involving distinct cellular and molecular mechanisms.

1. **Innate Response:** The innate immune response is the body's first line of defense. It is rapid, non-specific, and does not rely on prior exposure to pathogens.

   Key Features:

   - **Pattern Recognition:** Innate immune cells detect pathogens through Pattern Recognition Receptors (PRRs) that identify Pathogen-Associated Molecular Patterns (PAMPs).
   - **Inflammation:** The release of cytokines and histamines leads to swelling, redness, heat, and pain, which recruit immune cells to the site of infection.
   - **Effector Cells:** Neutrophils, macrophages, and NK cells neutralize pathogens through phagocytosis or cytotoxic activity.

2. **Adaptive Response:** The adaptive immune response is specific and tailored to the pathogen. It takes several days to activate during the first exposure but provides long-lasting immunity.

   Key Components:

   - **Humoral Immunity:** B cells produce antibodies that neutralize extracellular pathogens.
   - **Cell-Mediated Immunity:** T cells eliminate infected cells and activate other immune cells.

   Process:

   1. **Recognition:** APCs present antigens to T cells in lymphoid tissues.
   2. **Activation:** Helper T cells stimulate B cells and cytotoxic T cells.
   3. **Effector Phase:** Antibodies neutralize pathogens, and cytotoxic T cells destroy infected cells.

3. **Resolution and Memory Formation:** Once the infection is cleared, the immune response transitions into a resolution phase to restore homeostasis.

   Key Processes:

   - **Regulatory T Cells:** Suppress excessive immune activity to prevent tissue damage.
   - **Memory Cells:** B and T cells remain in the body, ensuring a faster and stronger response upon re-exposure to the same pathogen.
   - **Importance of Memory:** Memory cells underpin the success of vaccinations, enabling the immune system to respond effectively to previously encountered pathogens.

(IV) AYURVEDIC PERSPECTIVES ON IMMUNITY AND DISEASE RESISTANCE

Key Concepts in Ayurvedic Immunity:

1. **Ojas:** The essence that governs vitality and resistance to disease. Strong Ojas reflects robust immunity and overall well-being.
2. **Agni:** Healthy digestion is essential for generating Ojas and preventing Ama (toxins).
3. **Dosha Balance :** Each Dosha plays a role in maintaining bodily functions:
   - Vata governs movement and communication.
   - Pitta regulates metabolism and immunity.
   - Kapha provides stability and strength.

Ayurvedic Immunomodulators (Rasayana):

1. **Ashwagandha:** Reduces stress and enhances immunity.
2. **Amla:** A potent antioxidant, it rejuvenates tissues and boosts Ojas.
3. **Guduchi:** Known for its immune-modulatory effects.

Ayurvedic Pathogen Response: Ayurveda categorizes diseases based on endogenous (Nija) or exogenous (Agantuja) causes, emphasizing personalized approaches to restore balance and strengthen immunity.

MULTIPLE CHOICE QUESTIONS

1. In the context of immune regulation, consider a situation where a modern immunologist explores the parallelism between the molecular pathways of cytokine release and the Ayurvedic principle of Rasayana therapy. The study indicates that Rasayana herbs such as Ashwagandha not only enhance immune cell proliferation but also regulate inflammatory cytokines like IL-6 and TNF-α. Which conclusion aligns best with these findings?

   A. Rasayana therapy boosts immunity by non-specific enhancement of all cytokines, disregarding inflammation.
   B. The anti-inflammatory properties of Rasayana herbs like Ashwagandha validate their role in balancing immune homeostasis.
   C. Ayurvedic Rasayana herbs impair cytokine release, causing immunosuppression.
   D. Modern science contradicts the concept of Rasayana in regulating cytokine pathways.

2. A researcher examines the Ayurvedic concept of Ojas and equates it to the collective functioning of innate and adaptive immunity. The study demonstrates that individuals with high Ojas exhibit enhanced levels of IgG and CD8+ T cells. Which of the following statements best integrates the Ayurvedic and immunological frameworks?
   A. Ojas correlates with only the innate immune response.
   B. The adaptive immune system's memory function represents the essence of Ojas.
   C. High Ojas is indicative of balanced immune regulation involving both innate and adaptive systems.
   D. Ojas has no measurable biological basis in terms of immunity.

3. Researchers hypothesize that the Ayurvedic notion of dosha imbalance can be understood through disruptions in immune homeostasis. They focus on Kapha imbalance, finding it correlates with elevated inflammatory markers. Which of the following mechanisms reflects this association?
   A. Elevated Kapha indicates reduced lymphocyte activity and systemic immunosuppression.
   B. Kapha imbalance promotes inflammation through cytokine overproduction, akin to chronic low-grade inflammation.
   C. Kapha imbalance reduces macrophage function, impairing innate immunity.
   D. The concept of Kapha imbalance has no immunological equivalent.

4. In an integrative study, a researcher examines the impact of Agni (digestive fire) on gut-associated lymphoid tissue (GALT). The results reveal that individuals with strong Agni have a more diverse gut microbiota and higher IgA secretion. Which Ayurvedic principle aligns most closely with this finding?
   A. Agni regulates GALT directly through immunoglobulin synthesis.
   B. Strong Agni promotes detoxification, indirectly enhancing immune function.
   C. Weak Agni leads to toxin accumulation, impairing both digestion and immunity.
   D. Gut health is unrelated to the concept of Agni in Ayurveda.

5. Consider an immunological model where NK cell activity is equated with the Ayurvedic detoxification process. NK cells target virus-infected cells through cytotoxic molecules. How does this function parallel the detoxifying role of bitter Rasas (tastes) in Ayurveda?
   A. NK cells neutralize toxins in circulation, similar to bitter tastes.
   B. Bitter Rasas cleanse the body by directly enhancing cytotoxic immune functions.
   C. NK cells and bitter Rasas both eliminate harmful entities without discrimination.
   D. Bitter Rasas detoxify the digestive system, while NK cells detoxify at the cellular level.

6. A comparative study on immunity reveals that Rasayana herbs like Guduchi influence dendritic cell maturation. Mature dendritic cells enhance antigen presentation to T cells, boosting adaptive immunity. Which immunological principle is most consistent with this finding?
   A. Dendritic cells are exclusively part of innate immunity and are unaffected by Rasayana.
   B. Rasayana enhances dendritic cell maturation, bridging innate and adaptive immune responses.
   C. Guduchi influences innate immunity but does not affect antigen presentation.
   D. Antigen presentation is unrelated to the effects of Ayurvedic therapies.

7. Immunological studies suggest that oxidative stress reduction improves macrophage function. Considering Ayurvedic principles, which herb known for its antioxidant properties aligns with this mechanism?
   A. Neem enhances detoxification but not macrophage activity.
   B. Ashwagandha reduces oxidative stress, indirectly supporting macrophage function.
   C. Triphala compromises innate immunity by overstimulating antioxidants.
   D. Amla suppresses macrophage activity despite reducing oxidative stress.

8. A clinical study evaluates the role of Ojas in maintaining immune resilience during seasonal changes. Subjects with depleted Ojas exhibit higher susceptibility to viral infections. How does this observation support the concept of Ritucharya in Ayurveda?
   A. Ritucharya enhances immunity by increasing lymphocyte counts.
   B. Seasonal practices align with Ojas replenishment, reducing infection risks.
   C. Ritucharya balances doshas but has no measurable impact on immunity.
   D. Viral susceptibility is unrelated to Ayurvedic seasonal regimens.

9. In examining the balance of doshas during inflammation, a researcher finds that Pitta imbalance correlates with hyperinflammatory states. How does this finding integrate with modern immunology?

A. Pitta imbalance reduces neutrophil migration, impairing the acute immune response.
B. Hyperactive cytokine release during inflammation mirrors Pitta's inflammatory dominance.
C. Pitta imbalance enhances tissue repair, suppressing inflammation.
D. Inflammatory markers are unaffected by dosha imbalances.

10. Imagine an integrative approach where Ayurvedic herbs targeting Kapha are evaluated for their effect on obesity-associated immune dysregulation. Which mechanism supports their role in restoring immune balance?
A. Anti-Kapha herbs suppress adipocyte cytokine production, reducing systemic inflammation.
B. These herbs impair immune cell recruitment, worsening obesity-induced inflammation.
C. Anti-Kapha therapies reduce immune overactivation, suppressing adaptive immunity.
D. Obesity is unrelated to Kapha-targeting Ayurvedic interventions.

Directions (Q. No. 11–14): *Scenario-Based Questions*

SCENARIO 1

A researcher studies Triphala's impact on gut health and immunity. Findings show that Triphala restores gut microbiota diversity and enhances systemic immunity by increasing IgA levels.

SCENARIO 2

Simultaneously, environmental researchers report declining Amalaki quality due to overharvesting. Poor-quality Amalaki affects Triphala's efficacy in gut health restoration.

11. Which mechanism best explains Triphala's enhancement of systemic immunity?
A. Triphala directly stimulates systemic immune markers independent of gut health.
B. Improved gut microbiota diversity by Triphala enhances GALT-mediated immunity.
C. Triphala reduces gut microbiota diversity while increasing IgA levels.
D. Immune enhancement by Triphala is unrelated to its effect on gut health.

12. How can sustainability challenges in Amalaki sourcing be addressed?
A. Promote monoculture plantations to meet demand.
B. Encourage traditional agroforestry systems and community conservation efforts.
C. Substitute Amalaki with synthetic formulations.
D. Reduce Triphala production globally to conserve Amalaki.

13. How does Amalaki degradation influence Triphala's therapeutic outcomes?
A. Reduced bioactive compounds in Amalaki diminish Triphala's efficacy.
B. Amalaki quality has no measurable effect on Triphala's potency.
C. Triphala remains effective regardless of Amalaki degradation.
D. Environmental stress enhances Amalaki's potency.

14. Which strategy maintains Triphala efficacy while addressing Amalaki sustainability?
A. Develop synthetic Amalaki alternatives.
B. Standardize sustainable harvesting practices and bioactive compound consistency.
C. Shift from Triphala to formulations without endangered species.
D. Promote large-scale commercial cultivation of all Triphala components.

15. The principles of doshas are:
(a) Vata governs movement and is linked to the nervous system.
(b) Pitta controls metabolism and digestive enzymes.
(c) Kapha regulates structure and fluid balance.
(d) Dosha balance ensures overall health.

Choose the correct answer:
A. (a), (b), (c) only
B. (a), (b), (d) only
C. (a), (b), (c), (d)
D. (a), (b) only

16. The Ayurvedic Rasas (tastes) and their biological actions include:
(a) Sweet Rasa promotes tissue nourishment and growth.
(b) Bitter Rasa detoxifies and reduces inflammation.
(c) Sour Rasa stimulates digestion and enhances metabolic activity.
(d) Astringent Rasa strengthens tissues and controls bleeding.

Choose the correct answer from the options given below:
A. (a), (b), and (c) only
B. (a), (b), and (d) only
C. (a), (b), (c), and (d)
D. (b), (c), and (d) only

17. Match the following Ayurvedic principles with their corresponding immunological interpretations:

(a) Ojas	1. Represents immune resilience and vitality

(b) Agni	2. Regulates metabolism and gut health
(c) Dosha balance	3. Ensures systemic homeostasis and disease prevention
(d) Ama	4. Reflects toxin accumulation, impairing immunity

Choose the correct answer from the options given below:

A. (a)-1, (b)-2, (c)-3, (d)-4
B. (a)-2, (b)-1, (c)-4, (d)-3
C. (a)-3, (b)-4, (c)-1, (d)-2
D. (a)-4, (b)-3, (c)-2, (d)-1

18. Which of the following herbs are categorized under Rasayana and contribute to immune modulation?
(a) Guduchi boosts immune cell activity.
(b) Ashwagandha reduces oxidative stress and inflammation.
(c) Triphala enhances gut microbiota diversity.
(d) Neem directly enhances adaptive immune memory.

Choose the correct answer from the options given below:

A. (a), (b), and (c) only
B. (a), (b), (c), and (d)
C. (a) and (c) only
D. (b), (c), and (d) only

19. The biological effects of Ayurvedic detoxification therapies include:
(a) Reducing systemic inflammation through Panchakarma.
(b) Enhancing cellular metabolism and clearing toxins.
(c) Directly boosting IgA and CD8+ T cell counts.
(d) Restoring Kapha balance in chronic metabolic disorders.

Choose the correct answer from the options given below:

A. (a), (b), and (d) only
B. (a), (b), (c), and (d)
C. (b), (c), and (d) only
D. (a) and (b) only

20. Ayurvedic recommendations for maintaining immune balance include:
(a) Following Ritucharya to align lifestyle with seasonal changes.
(b) Using Rasayana herbs to enhance Ojas.
(c) Relying solely on dietary interventions to restore immune function.
(d) Performing regular detox therapies to prevent Ama accumulation.

Choose the correct answer from the options given below:

A. (a), (b), and (c) only
B. (a), (b), and (d) only
C. (a) and (d) only
D. (b), (c), and (d) only

21. The balance of the three doshas (Vata, Pitta, Kapha) is essential for:
(a) Mental stability and emotional well-being.
(b) Optimal digestion and nutrient absorption.
(c) Immune response regulation and disease prevention.
(d) Restoring tissue integrity post-infection.

Choose the correct answer from the options given below:

A. (a), (b), and (c) only
B. (a), (b), (c), and (d)
C. (a), (b), and (d) only
D. (b), (c), and (d) only

22. Which of the following statements about Ama in Ayurveda are true?
(a) It results from weak digestive fire (Mandagni).
(b) It correlates with the accumulation of systemic toxins.
(c) It directly enhances Kapha, causing congestion and lethargy.
(d) Its presence is always beneficial for immune enhancement.

Choose the correct answer from the options given below:

A. (a), (b), and (c) only
B. (a), (b), and (d) only
C. (a), (b), (c), and (d)
D. (b) and (c) only

23. The therapeutic effects of Triphala include:
(a) Enhancing gut microbiota diversity.
(b) Direct stimulation of adaptive immunity.
(c) Regulation of metabolic pathways.
(d) Restoring dosha balance.

Choose the correct answer from the options given below:

A. (a), (b), and (c) only
B. (a), (b), and (d) only
C. (a), (c), and (d) only
D. (a), (b), (c), and (d)

24. Immunological parallels to Ayurvedic detoxification principles include:
(a) Activation of macrophages during Panchakarma therapies.

(b) Reduction of oxidative stress through antioxidant herbs.
(c) Suppression of chronic inflammation via Rasayana.
(d) Complete eradication of microbial flora to enhance immunity.

Choose the correct answer from the options given below:

A. (a), (b), and (c) only
B. (a), (c), and (d) only
C. (b) and (d) only
D. (a) and (b) only

25. Match List–I (Immune Cells) with List–II (Functions) carefully and choose the correct answer from the options given below:

List–I	List–II
(a) Neutrophils	1. Rapid phagocytosis of bacteria
(b) Macrophages	2. Antigen presentation to T cells
(c) B Lymphocytes	3. Antibody production
(d) T Lymphocytes	4. Direct killing of infected cells

Choose the correct answer from the options given below:

A. (a)-1, (b)-2, (c)-3, (d)-4
B. (a)-2, (b)-1, (c)-4, (d)-3
C. (a)-3, (b)-4, (c)-1, (d)-2
D. (a)-4, (b)-3, (c)-2, (d)-1

26. Match List–I (Doshas) with List–II (Characteristics) carefully and choose the correct answer from the options given below:

List–I:
(a) Vata
(b) Pitta
(c) Kapha
(d) Dosha balance

List–II:
1. Movement and communication
2. Metabolism and energy generation
3. Stability and structural integrity
4. Equilibrium ensures health

Choose the correct answer from the options given below:

A. (a)-1, (b)-2, (c)-3, (d)-4
B. (a)-4, (b)-1, (c)-2, (d)-3
C. (a)-2, (b)-4, (c)-1, (d)-3
D. (a)-3, (b)-4, (c)-2, (d)-1

27. Match List–I (Rasayana Herbs) with List–II (Benefits) carefully and choose the correct answer from the options given below:

List–I	List–II
(a) Ashwagandha	1. Enhances resilience against stress and boosts immunity
(b) Triphala	2. Promotes gut health and detoxification
(c) Guduchi	3. Modulates inflammation and enhances immune cell function
(d) Amla	4. Antioxidant properties and enhancement of metabolic efficiency

Choose the correct answer from the options given below:

A. (a)-1, (b)-2, (c)-3, (d)-4
B. (a)-2, (b)-3, (c)-1, (d)-4
C. (a)-3, (b)-4, (c)-2, (d)-1
D. (a)-4, (b)-1, (c)-3, (d)-2

28. Match List–I (Immune Cells) with List–II (Functions) carefully and choose the correct answer from the options given below:

List–I	List–II
(a) Neutrophils	1. First responders; phagocytosis of bacteria
(b) Macrophages	2. Antigen presentation to T cells
(c) B Lymphocytes	3. Production of antibodies specific to pathogens
(d) T Lymphocytes	4. Orchestration of adaptive immune responses

Choose the correct answer from the options given below:

A. (a)-1, (b)-2, (c)-3, (d)-4
B. (a)-2, (b)-1, (c)-4, (d)-3
C. (a)-3, (b)-4, (c)-1, (d)-2
D. (a)-4, (b)-3, (c)-2, (d)-1

29. Match List–I (Doshas) with List–II (Attributes) carefully and choose the correct answer from the options given below:

List–I	List–II
(a) Vata	1. Governs movement and communication within the body
(b) Pitta	2. Regulates metabolism and digestion
(c) Kapha	3. Provides structure, stability, and immunity
(d) Tridosha Balance	4. Essential for holistic health and disease prevention

Choose the correct answer from the options given below:

A. (a)-1, (b)-2, (c)-3, (d)-4

B. (a)-4, (b)-1, (c)-2, (d)-3
C. (a)-2, (b)-4, (c)-1, (d)-3
D. (a)-3, (b)-4, (c)-2, (d)-1

30. Match List–I (Ayurvedic Concept) with List–II (Modern Immunology Parallel) carefully and choose the correct answer from the options given below:

List–I	List–II
(a) Ojas	1. Represents systemic immune resilience and vitality
(b) Agni	2. Regulates metabolism and gut-associated immunity
(c) Ama	3. Reflects toxin accumulation leading to immune suppression
(d) Ritucharya	4. Seasonal adjustments to maintain immune homeostasis

Choose the correct answer from the options given below:
A. (a)-1, (b)-2, (c)-3, (d)-4
B. (a)-2, (b)-3, (c)-1, (d)-4
C. (a)-3, (b)-4, (c)-2, (d)-1
D. (a)-4, (b)-1, (c)-3, (d)-2

31. Match List–I (Ayurvedic Therapies) with List–II (Immune Effects) carefully and choose the correct answer from the options given below:

List–I	List–II
(a) Panchakarma	1. Detoxification and reduction of inflammation
(b) Rasayana Therapy	2. Enhances adaptive immune memory
(c) Kapha Balancing	3. Reduces systemic stagnation and promotes detoxification
(d) Agni Strengthening	4. Improves digestion and prevents Ama accumulation

Choose the correct answer from the options given below:
A. (a)-1, (b)-2, (c)-3, (d)-4
B. (a)-2, (b)-1, (c)-4, (d)-3
C. (a)-3, (b)-4, (c)-2, (d)-1
D. (a)-4, (b)-3, (c)-1, (d)-2

32. Match List–I (Herbal Actions) with List–II (Effects on Immunity) carefully and choose the correct answer from the options given below:

List–I	List–II
(a) Anti-inflammatory herbs	1. Modulate cytokine pathways and suppress hyperinflammation
(b) Antioxidant herbs	2. Neutralize oxidative stress, supporting immune cells
(c) Detoxifying herbs	3. Remove metabolic toxins, enhancing immune function
(d) Immunostimulatory herbs	4. Promote lymphocyte proliferation and activity

Choose the correct answer from the options given below:
A. (a)-1, (b)-2, (c)-3, (d)-4
B. (a)-2, (b)-3, (c)-4, (d)-1
C. (a)-3, (b)-4, (c)-1, (d)-2
D. (a)-4, (b)-1, (c)-2, (d)-3

33. Match List–I (Panchakarma Processes) with List–II (Functions) carefully and choose the correct answer from the options given below:

List–I	List–II
(a) Vamana (emesis)	1. Removes toxins from the stomach
(b) Virechana (purgation)	2. Eliminates Pitta-related toxins from the intestines
(c) Basti (enema)	3. Cleanses and balances Vata in the colon
(d) Nasya (nasal cleansing)	4. Clears Kapha toxins from the head region

Choose the correct answer from the options given below:
A. (a)-1, (b)-2, (c)-3, (d)-4
B. (a)-2, (b)-3, (c)-4, (d)-1
C. (a)-3, (b)-4, (c)-1, (d)-2
D. (a)-4, (b)-1, (c)-2, (d)-3

34. Match List–I (Immunological Concepts) with List–II (Ayurvedic Parallels) carefully and choose the correct answer from the options given below:

List–I	List–II
(a) Innate Immunity	1. Immediate defense, akin to Kapha stabilization
(b) Adaptive Immunity	2. Memory-based response, representing Ojas strength
(c) Inflammation	3. Reflects Pitta imbalance in Ayurveda
(d) Immune Homeostasis	4. Aligns with dosha balance principles

Choose the correct answer from the options given below:
A. (a)-1, (b)-2, (c)-3, (d)-4
B. (a)-2, (b)-3, (c)-4, (d)-1
C. (a)-3, (b)-4, (c)-1, (d)-2
D. (a)-4, (b)-1, (c)-2, (d)-3

Directions (Q. No. 35–39): *Following questions are based on Statement 1 and Statement 2. Read both the statements carefully and choose the correct answer from the options given below:*

A. Both Assertion (A) and Reason (R) are true, and Reason (R) is the correct explanation of Assertion (A).
B. Both Assertion (A) and Reason (R) are true, but Reason (R) is not the correct explanation of Assertion (A).
C. Assertion (A) is true, but Reason (R) is false.
D. Assertion (A) is false, but Reason (R) is true.
E. Both Assertion (A) and Reason (R) are false.

35. Statement 1: Immune cells, such as macrophages and lymphocytes, play a crucial role in the innate and adaptive immune responses of the body.

Statement 2: Ayurveda identifies the immune system as solely reliant on Kapha dosha, disregarding the roles of Vata and Pitta doshas.

36. Statement 1: Antigens are foreign molecules that trigger an immune response, leading to the activation of immune cells.

Statement 2: Ayurveda explains antigen responses in terms of Ama accumulation and the immune system's ability to digest and expel it.

37. Statement 1: Adaptive immunity develops over time and provides long-lasting protection against specific pathogens.

Statement 2: Ayurveda attributes long-lasting immunity to the quality of Ojas, which sustains the body's vitality and resistance to disease.

38. Statement 1: Pathogens such as bacteria, viruses, and fungi are neutralized by antibodies produced during the immune response.

Statement 2: Ayurveda emphasizes that the strength of Agni (digestive fire) indirectly influences the body's ability to counter pathogens.

39. Statement 1: T-cells and B-cells are essential for a coordinated adaptive immune response.

Statement 2: Ayurveda identifies lymphatic and immune functions under the term Rasavaha Srotas, highlighting their role in transporting nutrients and combating diseases.

Directions (Q. No. 40–45): *There are two statements in each question. One is labelled as Assertion (A) and the other is as Reason (R). Read both the statements and choose the correct answer from the options given below:*

A. Both Assertion (A) and Reason (R) are true, and Reason (R) is the correct explanation of Assertion (A).
B. Both Assertion (A) and Reason (R) are true, but Reason (R) is not the correct explanation of Assertion (A).
C. Assertion (A) is true, but Reason (R) is false.
D. Assertion (A) is false, but Reason (R) is true.
E. Both Assertion (A) and Reason (R) are false.

40. Assertion (A): Ayurveda views the immune response as a holistic function of the entire body, influenced by Ojas and Agni.

Reason (R): Weak Ojas and impaired Agni create conditions for Ama formation, leading to immune dysfunction.

41. Assertion (A): Immune cells like macrophages and neutrophils are part of the innate immune system, providing the body's first line of defense.

Reason (R): Ayurveda attributes innate immunity entirely to Kapha dosha, which governs strength and stability.

42. Assertion (A): Antigens stimulate the immune system to produce specific antibodies.

Reason (R): Ayurveda interprets antigenic responses as disruptions in the natural balance of doshas caused by Ama.

43. Assertion (A): Adaptive immunity provides long-term protection against specific pathogens through memory cells.

Reason (R): Ayurveda's concept of Vyadhikshamatva explains immunity as a natural resistance that can be enhanced by Rasayana therapies.

44. Assertion (A): Vaccines mimic natural infections to stimulate adaptive immunity.

Reason (R): Ayurveda recommends daily herbal tonics to replicate the preventive effects of vaccination.

45. Assertion (A): Immune system efficiency can decline with age, leading to increased susceptibility to infections.

Reason (R): Ayurveda addresses age-related immunity decline through Rasayana therapies, which rejuvenate tissues and enhance vitality.

Directions (Q. No. 46-50): *Read the passage carefully and find the answers to the questions given below*:

Ayurveda, one of the world's most ancient systems of medicine, has recently garnered significant attention in scientific research for its integrative and personalized approach to health. Central to Ayurvedic immunology is the concept of Vyadhi Kshamatva, or disease resistance, which is categorized into two domains: Sahasaj Vyadhi Kshamatva (innate immunity) and Kalaj Vyadhi Kshamatva (acquired immunity). Modern immunological studies have drawn parallels between these classifications and the functioning of innate and adaptive immune systems, emphasizing the relevance of Ayurvedic principles in contemporary health paradigms.

Another cornerstone of Ayurvedic understanding is the role of Ojas, the refined essence of all bodily tissues (Sapta Dhatus). Modern research correlates Ojas with the cumulative efficiency of immune functions, including macrophage activation, lymphocyte proliferation, and cytokine modulation. Depleted Ojas has been linked to conditions characterized by immune dysfunction, such as chronic inflammation, autoimmune disorders, and recurrent infections.

Agni, or digestive fire, is described in Ayurveda as the fundamental driver of metabolism and immunity. Scientific advancements have confirmed that gut health, heavily influenced by Agni, plays a pivotal role in modulating systemic immunity through the gut-associated lymphoid tissue (GALT). Recent microbiome studies demonstrate that Ayurvedic interventions like Triphala enhance microbial diversity, boost short-chain fatty acid (SCFA) production, and regulate T-cell-mediated immunity. Furthermore, Ama (toxic metabolic byproducts) formation, a result of impaired Agni, has been compared to the buildup of pro-inflammatory mediators like (c)-reactive protein (CRP) and tumor necrosis factor-alpha (TNF-α).

Seasonal adaptation, termed Ritucharya, also finds relevance in immunology as it aligns lifestyle changes with natural cycles, minimizing environmental stressors on the immune system. Studies have shown that Ayurvedic seasonal regimens significantly reduce oxidative stress markers and improve the body's antioxidant capacity. These practices are now seen as critical to mitigating the effects of seasonal immune dysregulation, including allergies and autoimmune flare-ups.

The integration of modern immunology with Ayurvedic wisdom holds immense potential for novel therapeutic strategies. For example, the Rasayana herbs Ashwagandha and Guduchi have been shown to modulate cellular immunity by enhancing the function of dendritic cells and natural killer (NK) cells. Additionally, Ayurvedic purification therapies, such as Panchakarma, have demonstrated effectiveness in reducing systemic inflammation by improving lymphatic drainage and resetting metabolic pathways.

This emerging interdisciplinary framework suggests that Ayurveda's holistic approach to health not only complements modern immunology but also extends its applications to preventive, therapeutic, and rehabilitative healthcare paradigms.

46. According to the passage, how does the Ayurvedic concept of Vyadhi Kshamatva relate to modern immunology?

A. It exclusively addresses innate immunity, with no parallels to adaptive immunity.

B. It encompasses both innate and acquired immunity, aligning with modern classifications.

C. It is limited to preventive measures and does not involve active immune mechanisms.

D. It disregards innate immunity and focuses solely on acquired immune responses.

47. What does the passage suggest about the role of Ojas in immunity?

A. Ojas primarily governs metabolic processes and has no link to immune functions.

B. Depleted Ojas is associated with immune dysfunction, including chronic inflammation and infections.

C. Ojas enhances cytokine overproduction, contributing to autoimmune disorders.

D. Ojas correlates solely with adaptive immune responses, excluding innate immunity.

48. How does modern science validate the Ayurvedic concept of Agni, as per the passage?

A. By linking it exclusively to the detoxification of metabolic byproducts.

B. By associating its functions with gut microbiota diversity and systemic immune modulation.

C. By equating Agni to the liver's detoxification processes, unrelated to gut health.

D. By demonstrating its role in T-cell suppression and inflammation.

49. According to the passage, how do Ama and impaired Agni affect systemic immunity?

A. Ama corresponds to metabolic toxins that increase pro-inflammatory mediators like CRP and TNF-α.

B. Impaired Agni reduces microbial diversity, leading to immune suppression.

C. Both Ama and impaired Agni enhance antioxidant activity, reducing inflammation.

D. Their effects are confined to local gut immunity and do not influence systemic inflammation.

50. What interdisciplinary potential does the passage highlight for Ayurveda and modern immunology?
    A. Ayurveda focuses on preventive care, while modern immunology is restricted to therapeutic applications.
    B. Integration allows the development of personalized therapies, including Rasayana herbs and Panchakarma practices, to enhance immunity.
    C. Ayurvedic principles negate the relevance of modern immunological research, focusing instead on metaphysical health.
    D. Modern science has completely replaced Ayurveda's framework with empirical methods, making integration redundant.

ANSWER WITH EXPLANATIONS

1. **B:** The anti-inflammatory properties of Rasayana herbs like Ashwagandha align with their role in balancing immune homeostasis by reducing excess cytokine production while promoting tissue repair and resilience. Modern studies corroborate that Ashwagandha inhibits pro-inflammatory markers such as TNF-α and IL-6 while preserving adaptive immune responses. This dual action supports immunity without overactivation, mirroring Ayurveda's holistic approach to maintaining balance within the body. Unlike non-specific immunity boosters, Rasayana therapies provide immunomodulation tailored to individual needs, making them scientifically validated complements to modern therapeutic approaches. This reinforces their role in both prevention and treatment in integrative medicine.

2. **C:** High Ojas reflects optimal synergy between innate and adaptive immunity, enhancing immune resilience. Modern parallels show that balanced lymphocyte activity, effective macrophage response, and cytokine regulation indicate robust Ojas. This concept extends beyond innate immunity, reflecting cumulative immune vigor that prevents infections and supports recovery. Studies linking Ojas to reduced inflammatory markers (like CRP) and increased adaptive cell efficiency validate Ayurveda's interpretation. Unlike narrowly defined biomarkers, Ojas integrates systemic physiological vitality, offering a broader framework for assessing health. Thus, Ayurvedic and immunological perspectives converge on the idea of cumulative immune robustness.

3. **B:** The Kapha imbalance's association with low-grade chronic inflammation highlights its parallels with modern immunology. Elevated levels of inflammatory cytokines, such as IL-1β and TNF-α, mirror Kapha's stagnation and fluid retention properties. Inflammation linked to Kapha excess is systemic yet slow-moving, contributing to metabolic dysfunctions like obesity and insulin resistance. Ayurvedic interventions targeting Kapha often stimulate metabolism and enhance detoxification, mitigating chronic inflammatory cascades. The focus on inflammation as a root cause of disease is a shared principle in Ayurveda and modern immunology, underscoring the scientific relevance of Kapha balance in maintaining health.

4. **C:** Weak Agni results in incomplete digestion and Ama accumulation, impairing nutrient absorption and immune efficiency. Modern research shows that weak gut microbiota diversity (linked to impaired Agni) reduces IgA secretion and T-cell activation. Ayurveda's emphasis on Agni as central to health aligns with findings on the gut-immune axis, where digestive efficiency affects systemic immunity. While Agni doesn't directly regulate GALT, its role in maintaining microbiota diversity highlights its indirect but essential function in immunity. This intricate relationship validates Ayurveda's emphasis on digestive health as foundational for overall well-being.

5. **D:** NK cells eliminate intracellular pathogens through cytotoxic activity, while bitter Rasas detoxify the body's systems. Both operate by clearing harmful entities but in distinct contexts—NK cells target infected cells, while bitter Rasas eliminate metabolic toxins. The parallel lies in their shared cleansing roles: bitter tastes stimulate bile secretion and enzymatic detoxification, supporting metabolic waste elimination. Ayurveda extends this analogy to cellular health, emphasizing that detoxification at both micro (cellular) and macro (systemic) levels prevents disease progression. Thus, both mechanisms contribute to systemic balance and resilience against stressors.

6. **B:** Rasayana herbs like Guduchi enhance dendritic cell maturation, bridging innate and adaptive immunity. Mature dendritic cells play a pivotal role in presenting antigens to T cells, thereby activating the adaptive response. Ayurveda's focus on immunomodulation aligns with this function, as Rasayana aims to enhance immune efficiency without overstimulation. Guduchi's role in promoting antigen presentation further validates its use in integrative therapies targeting both infection resistance and immune regulation. This highlights Ayurveda's nuanced approach, emphasizing cellular

mechanisms that modern immunology now recognizes as critical for immune optimization.

7. **B:** Ashwagandha's antioxidant properties reduce oxidative stress, enhancing macrophage activity and promoting phagocytosis. Modern studies confirm that oxidative stress hampers immune cell function, while antioxidant-rich herbs protect immune cells from damage, preserving their functionality. Ashwagandha's dual action—scavenging reactive oxygen species and boosting adaptive immunity—illustrates Ayurveda's principle of systemic balance. Unlike immune suppressants or stimulants, it restores immune efficiency, ensuring effective pathogen clearance. This integrative approach highlights the scientific relevance of Ayurvedic therapies in maintaining immune resilience amidst environmental and metabolic stressors.

8. **B:** Ritucharya emphasizes seasonal adaptations to replenish Ojas and prevent infections. Depleted Ojas correlates with immune vulnerabilities, particularly during seasonal transitions when environmental stressors challenge systemic homeostasis. Ayurveda prescribes seasonal diets, herbs, and regimens to optimize dosha balance and immune resilience. Studies linking seasonal oxidative stress to immune dysregulation validate Ritucharya's relevance, as such adaptations enhance antioxidant defenses and immune recovery. This comprehensive strategy addresses seasonal vulnerabilities holistically, reflecting Ayurveda's integrative health philosophy.

9. **B:** Hyperinflammatory states caused by cytokine storms during infections mirror Pitta imbalance, characterized by excess heat and metabolic intensity. Ayurveda's focus on calming Pitta through cooling therapies aligns with modern strategies targeting cytokine modulation. Excessive Pitta not only triggers acute inflammation but also exacerbates tissue damage, highlighting the need for balance. Modern parallels, like anti-cytokine biologics, reinforce Ayurveda's emphasis on inflammation control for restoring systemic harmony. This integrative perspective bridges ancient and modern approaches to managing hyperinflammation.

10. **A:** Anti-Kapha herbs modulate adipocyte cytokine production, reducing systemic inflammation linked to obesity. Studies confirm that herbs targeting metabolic pathways lower pro-inflammatory markers like IL-6 and TNF-α, mitigating chronic immune activation. This aligns with Ayurveda's principle of Kapha reduction to enhance metabolic and immune efficiency. Unlike interventions that suppress immune responses, Kapha-balancing therapies promote natural regulation, improving both systemic inflammation and metabolic health. This dual benefit highlights Ayurveda's relevance in addressing modern metabolic-immune disorders.

11. **B:** The enhanced systemic immunity observed with Triphala aligns with the restoration of gut microbiota diversity, which is critical for gut-associated lymphoid tissue (GALT) activation. GALT constitutes a significant portion of the body's immune system, and its optimal functioning is linked to balanced gut microbial populations. Ayurvedic texts describe Triphala as a key detoxifier and balancer of the digestive system, indirectly supporting immunity. Modern studies validate that Triphala promotes the growth of beneficial microbes like Bifidobacteria and Lactobacilli, increasing IgA levels that enhance mucosal immunity. This dual action of detoxification and microbiota restoration exemplifies Ayurveda's integrative approach to systemic health.

12. **B:** Encouraging traditional agroforestry systems and community-based conservation ensures the sustainability of Amalaki while maintaining its medicinal quality. Monoculture plantations may increase yield but often compromise biodiversity and soil health, leading to reduced bioactive compound concentrations. Community-based efforts promote sustainable harvesting, equitable distribution, and ecological balance, preserving Amalaki's natural potency. Ayurveda emphasizes that the environment significantly impacts the quality of medicinal herbs, aligning with ecological principles of plant conservation. Sustainable practices also safeguard Triphala's efficacy, which relies heavily on the purity of its ingredients. This approach ensures environmental and therapeutic harmony, adhering to both ecological and Ayurvedic ideals.

13. **A:** Environmental degradation of Amalaki impacts its bioactive compound concentration, diminishing its efficacy in promoting gut microbiota diversity and systemic immunity. Amalaki's potency lies in its high levels of Vitamin (C), flavonoids, and tannins, which directly influence its therapeutic effects. Degraded Amalaki, lacking these compounds, compromises Triphala's ability to regulate gut health and boost immunity. Ayurvedic principles emphasize the role of high-quality ingredients in formulations, correlating with modern research on bioactive compounds. This linkage underscores the importance of environmental preservation not only for sustainable sourcing but also for maintaining the clinical efficacy of traditional remedies like Triphala.

14. **B:** Establishing a global Triphala standard incorporating sustainable harvesting practices and ensuring bioactive compound consistency addresses both ecological and therapeutic challenges. Ayurvedic formulations rely on ingredient purity, and degraded herbs compromise their efficacy. A global standard promotes responsible sourcing, quality control, and equitable resource distribution. Sustainable practices like agroforestry safeguard endangered plants like Amalaki while preserving biodiversity. Additionally, scientific standardization aligns with modern regulations, ensuring consistency across global markets. This dual approach respects Ayurveda's emphasis on purity and sustainability while integrating scientific frameworks, offering a comprehensive solution to environmental and therapeutic concerns in Ayurvedic formulations.

15. **C:** In Ayurveda, all three doshas—Vata, Pitta, and Kapha—are fundamental physiological energies. Vata governs movement and is linked to the nervous system, Pitta regulates digestion and metabolism, and Kapha maintains structure and fluid balance. The balance of these doshas is essential for maintaining overall health. When all three are in harmony, the body remains disease-free and functions optimally. Hence, all four statements are correct.

16. **C:** The Ayurvedic Rasas (tastes) play specific roles in health and immunity, each contributing unique biological actions. Sweet Rasa nourishes tissues, Bitter Rasa detoxifies, Sour Rasa enhances digestion, and Astringent Rasa strengthens tissues. These tastes align with physiological and immunological processes, reflecting Ayurveda's intricate understanding of dietary and therapeutic principles. For instance, Bitter Rasa's role in detoxification mirrors its anti-inflammatory properties, while Sour Rasa stimulates enzymatic activity, supporting digestion. Modern research validates these effects, linking dietary diversity to metabolic and immune health. This integration underscores the relevance of Rasas in both ancient and contemporary health paradigms.

17. **A:** The Ayurvedic principles of Ojas, Agni, dosha balance, and Ama correspond to key immunological functions. Ojas reflects systemic immune resilience, while Agni governs metabolism and immune efficiency. Balanced doshas ensure homeostasis, preventing disease onset. Conversely, Ama, formed due to impaired Agni, represents toxic accumulation that disrupts immune regulation. These principles align with modern concepts like metabolic efficiency, toxin clearance, and immune homeostasis. For example, Agni's role in digestion parallels the gut-immune axis in modern science. This mapping demonstrates Ayurveda's scientific coherence, bridging ancient frameworks and contemporary immunological paradigms in health management.

18. **A:** Rasayana herbs like Guduchi, Ashwagandha, and Triphala contribute significantly to immune modulation, as shown in modern research. Guduchi boosts immune activity by promoting dendritic cell maturation, Ashwagandha reduces oxidative stress, and Triphala enhances gut health, indirectly strengthening immunity. These herbs exemplify Ayurveda's personalized approach, targeting both innate and adaptive immunity without overstimulation. Neem, while beneficial for antimicrobial action, does not directly modulate adaptive immunity. The combined effects of these herbs demonstrate Ayurveda's systemic approach, which integrates detoxification, rejuvenation, and immune enhancement, making it complementary to modern therapeutic practices.

19. **A:** Panchakarma therapies reduce systemic inflammation and enhance cellular metabolism, directly supporting immune regulation. By detoxifying the body, these therapies eliminate pro-inflammatory markers like CRP and TNF-α, restoring Kapha balance. Modern studies confirm that Panchakarma improves lymphatic circulation, aiding in toxin clearance and metabolic restoration. This holistic approach aligns with modern detoxification practices, demonstrating Ayurveda's relevance in addressing chronic inflammatory states. By targeting both metabolic and immune dysfunctions, Panchakarma therapies offer a multidimensional strategy that integrates ancient wisdom with contemporary health solutions.

20. **B:** Ayurvedic recommendations for maintaining immune balance emphasize Ritucharya, Rasayana herbs, and regular detox therapies. Ritucharya aligns lifestyle practices with seasonal changes, preventing dosha imbalances. Rasayana herbs like Ashwagandha enhance Ojas, strengthening systemic immunity. Detox therapies prevent Ama accumulation, mitigating inflammation and restoring dosha harmony. These practices are scientifically validated, with studies showing improved immune markers, reduced oxidative stress, and enhanced microbiota diversity. Unlike singular approaches, Ayurveda's comprehensive framework integrates prevention, rejuvenation, and detoxification, offering a balanced strategy for maintaining immunity and overall health.

21. **B:** The balance of Vata, Pitta, and Kapha is critical not only for physical health but also for mental and emotional well-being. This balance supports optimal digestion, nutrient absorption, proper immune response, and even tissue repair post-infection. Dosha harmony ensures the proper flow of energy, prevents diseases,

and promotes healing. Therefore, all four statements listed are accurate and interconnected within the Ayurvedic system.

22. **A:** Ama, formed due to weak Agni (digestive fire), corresponds to toxic byproducts that impair immune function. Ayurveda links Ama to systemic imbalances, such as Kapha accumulation, causing congestion and lethargy. Modern immunology relates this to chronic inflammation and toxin buildup, which disrupts immune efficiency. For instance, elevated inflammatory markers like CRP are seen as metabolic equivalents of Ama. Ayurvedic detoxification therapies target Ama, restoring metabolic clarity and immune strength. Unlike temporary immune boosters, these interventions provide a systemic reset, showcasing Ayurveda's holistic view of immune regulation and its relevance to modern health challenges like chronic inflammation.

23. **C:** Triphala contributes to gut health by enhancing microbiota diversity, regulating metabolic pathways, and restoring dosha balance. Each component—Haritaki, Bibhitaki, and Amalaki—has specific roles in detoxification and immunity. Modern studies confirm that Triphala promotes the growth of beneficial gut bacteria, reduces oxidative stress, and boosts mucosal immunity through increased IgA levels. Its dual action on digestion and systemic inflammation exemplifies Ayurveda's integrative approach to health. Unlike singular therapeutic agents, Triphala's synergistic composition addresses root causes of imbalance, aligning with modern gut-immune axis research. This highlights its multifaceted role in health, beyond just detoxification or immune enhancement.

24. **A:** Ayurvedic detoxification aligns with modern immune concepts by activating macrophages, reducing oxidative stress, and clearing toxins. For example, Panchakarma therapies improve lymphatic drainage, enabling better clearance of pro-inflammatory mediators. Antioxidant herbs like Ashwagandha protect immune cells from oxidative damage, enhancing cellular immunity. Detoxification reduces systemic stagnation, restoring immune homeostasis and metabolic clarity. Unlike immune suppressants, Ayurveda's detox therapies support the body's natural regulatory mechanisms. Modern research validates these effects, confirming reduced inflammation and improved immune markers. This integrative approach underscores the alignment of Ayurvedic detoxification with modern immunological interventions targeting systemic resilience.

25. **A:** The immune system's key components—neutrophils, macrophages, B lymphocytes, and T lymphocytes—mirror distinct roles described in Ayurveda. Neutrophils are rapid responders involved in phagocytosis, similar to Kapha's stabilizing properties. Macrophages present antigens to T cells, linking innate and adaptive responses. B lymphocytes produce antibodies, while T lymphocytes orchestrate cellular immunity through cytotoxic and regulatory functions. This structured immunity aligns with Ayurvedic concepts of systemic harmony, where components work cohesively to prevent and manage disease. Modern immunology validates these cellular roles, emphasizing their interdependence in maintaining balance, which Ayurveda describes as the essence of Vyadhi Kshamatva (disease resistance).

26. **A:** The doshas—Vata, Pitta, and Kapha—are fundamental to Ayurveda's physiological framework. Vata governs movement, including neurological and muscular functions, Pitta drives digestion and metabolism, and Kapha provides structure and stability. The Tridosha theory emphasizes that their balance ensures health, while imbalance results in disease. For example, excessive Kapha causes stagnation and inflammation, akin to fluid retention and immune dysregulation in modern biology. Ayurveda's interventions aim to restore this equilibrium, often paralleled in systemic homeostasis in immunology. These overlapping principles highlight Ayurveda's relevance to modern health management through its holistic understanding of bodily regulation and function.

27. **A:** Rasayana herbs like Ashwagandha, Triphala, Guduchi, and Amla have scientifically validated benefits aligning with their Ayurvedic descriptions. Ashwagandha boosts resilience to stress and enhances immune activity. Triphala improves gut health, supporting immunity through microbiota diversity. Guduchi modulates inflammation and boosts dendritic cell function, bridging innate and adaptive immunity. Amla, rich in Vitamin (C) and antioxidants, enhances metabolic efficiency and supports immune resilience. Together, these herbs exemplify Ayurveda's emphasis on personalized therapies that restore balance. Their diverse biological actions highlight the scientific validity of Ayurveda's integrative approach, offering multi-targeted solutions for immune and systemic health.

28. **A:** Each immune cell—neutrophils, macrophages, B lymphocytes, and T lymphocytes—plays a distinct role in immune responses. Neutrophils are the first line of defense, engulfing pathogens through phagocytosis. Macrophages, as antigen-presenting cells, link innate and adaptive immunity by activating T lymphocytes. B lymphocytes generate antibodies for specific antigens, forming the basis of humoral immunity. T lymphocytes orchestrate cellular immunity, with subtypes like helper T cells coordinating responses and cytotoxic T cells killing infected cells. Ayurveda's systemic immunity

concepts, such as Ojas and Agni, indirectly reflect this complexity, emphasizing synergy in immune regulation. Modern immunology confirms these roles, bridging the two frameworks.

29. A: The doshas' attributes—Vata (movement), Pitta (metabolism), and Kapha (stability)—are core to Ayurveda's systemic health approach. Vata governs communication, including neural impulses and muscular contractions. Pitta drives enzymatic processes and thermoregulation, reflecting metabolic intensity. Kapha ensures structural and fluid balance, essential for tissue integrity. Their balanced interaction maintains systemic harmony, while imbalances manifest as physical or mental disorders. Modern parallels include regulatory pathways in homeostasis and systemic resilience. Ayurveda's focus on maintaining dosha balance through personalized interventions offers a timeless framework that complements contemporary understandings of physiological regulation and systemic health.

30. A: The Ayurvedic principles of Ojas, Agni, Ama, and Ritucharya correlate with key immunological functions. Ojas represents systemic vitality and immune resilience, akin to cumulative immune efficiency. Agni governs metabolism, including gut-associated immunity. Ama reflects toxin accumulation that disrupts immune regulation, paralleling chronic inflammation in modern biology. Ritucharya emphasizes seasonal adaptations to prevent dosha imbalances, reducing oxidative stress and improving immune regulation. These principles align with modern immunological concepts like detoxification, gut-immune modulation, and systemic resilience. This interdisciplinary framework validates Ayurveda's relevance in preventive and therapeutic health management, bridging ancient wisdom with scientific understanding.

31 A: The therapies described in Ayurveda—Panchakarma, Rasayana, Kapha balancing, and Agni strengthening—are rooted in a comprehensive understanding of systemic regulation and detoxification. Panchakarma primarily targets systemic toxins, reducing inflammation and enhancing lymphatic circulation. Rasayana therapies, such as Ashwagandha and Guduchi, boost adaptive immune memory while promoting cellular rejuvenation. Kapha balancing therapies address metabolic stagnation, reducing systemic inflammation. Strengthening Agni restores digestive efficiency, preventing the accumulation of Ama and improving nutrient absorption. Each therapy reflects Ayurveda's holistic approach to maintaining immune homeostasis and metabolic clarity. These interventions have modern parallels in detoxification and immune-supportive therapies, emphasizing their enduring relevance.

32. A: The herbal actions described in Ayurveda align closely with modern immunological principles. Anti-inflammatory herbs, such as Guduchi, regulate cytokine pathways, mitigating excessive immune responses. Antioxidant herbs like Ashwagandha neutralize oxidative stress, preserving immune cell integrity. Detoxifying herbs, including Triphala, eliminate metabolic toxins, enhancing immune function and metabolic clarity. Immunostimulatory herbs, like Amla, promote lymphocyte proliferation and enhance adaptive immunity. This comprehensive approach addresses systemic imbalances, preventing chronic inflammation and immune suppression. Ayurveda's integration of these herbs into therapeutic regimens demonstrates its foresight in balancing immunity through targeted yet holistic interventions, now validated by modern scientific studies.

33. A: Panchakarma therapies, such as Vamana (emesis), Virechana (purgation), Basti (enema), and Nasya (nasal cleansing), are designed to eliminate dosha-specific toxins. Vamana targets Kapha-related toxins in the stomach, while Virechana addresses Pitta-related toxins in the intestines. Basti, a cornerstone therapy, cleanses Vata imbalances in the colon, and Nasya focuses on Kapha toxins in the head region. These therapies align with modern detoxification processes, reducing inflammatory mediators like CRP and TNF-α. Their precision in targeting specific doshas highlights Ayurveda's nuanced understanding of systemic detoxification, offering a multi-dimensional approach to health restoration that complements modern detox methodologies.

34. A: The immunological concepts of innate immunity, adaptive immunity, inflammation, and homeostasis closely align with Ayurvedic parallels. Innate immunity corresponds to Kapha stabilization, offering immediate but non-specific defense. Adaptive immunity reflects the cumulative strength of Ojas, which supports memory-based immune responses. Inflammation aligns with Pitta imbalance, which Ayurveda describes as excessive heat and metabolic activity. Immune homeostasis corresponds to dosha balance, ensuring systemic harmony and preventing disease. This mapping underscores the coherence between Ayurvedic and immunological frameworks, emphasizing systemic regulation as a common goal. Ayurveda's emphasis on prevention and balance complements modern science's focus on targeted interventions.

35. C: Immune cells, including macrophages and lymphocytes, are pivotal in orchestrating innate and adaptive immunity. Ayurveda, however, does not attribute immunity solely to Kapha dosha but rather views it as an outcome of balanced doshas. Kapha strengthens, Pitta fights infections, and Vata regulates communication within the system. Thus, the statement about Kapha being the sole influencer is false. The interplay of doshas in maintaining immunity reflects Ayurveda's holistic approach, where all elements collaborate to preserve health, highlighting that immunity cannot be isolated to a single factor but is a dynamic, integrated process.

36. A: Antigens indeed stimulate the immune system by triggering responses like antibody production. Ayurveda aligns with this concept by linking antigenic reactions to Ama, which disrupts dosha balance. This perspective underscores the importance of detoxification and strengthening Agni to manage immune challenges effectively. While modern immunology focuses on cellular mechanisms, Ayurveda integrates these processes with systemic detoxification, offering a broader lens on disease prevention. Together, both views emphasize the body's inherent capacity to adapt and defend against external invasions, supported by a healthy metabolic and immune foundation.

37. B: Adaptive immunity, mediated by memory cells, ensures long-term protection against pathogens. Ayurveda's emphasis on Ojas, the essence of vitality, aligns with this by equating robust immunity with sustained life energy. However, Ojas encompasses more than just adaptive immunity, extending to overall physical and mental resilience. While both statements are true, Ojas as a concept transcends the specifics of immune memory, integrating broader aspects of health. This highlights Ayurveda's unique perspective, where immunity is not merely defensive but a reflection of holistic well-being.

38. B: Antibodies neutralize pathogens in the immune response, a process directly supported by a robust Agni in Ayurvedic thought. Agni governs metabolism and digestion, indirectly influencing immune efficiency by preventing Ama formation. Both systems recognize the importance of foundational health in combating diseases. While modern science attributes pathogen clearance to biochemical processes, Ayurveda emphasizes strengthening Agni as a preventive strategy. This integrative approach bridges ancient wisdom and contemporary science, highlighting how metabolic and immune health are deeply interconnected for sustaining vitality and disease resistance.

39. A: T-cells and B-cells form the backbone of adaptive immunity, while Ayurveda correlates immune and lymphatic functions with Rasavaha Srotas. This system transports nutrients and supports immunity, aligning Ayurvedic and immunological perspectives. The Ayurvedic concept of Rasavaha Srotas extends beyond physiological transport, encompassing energy distribution and defense mechanisms. Both statements are true and interlinked, reflecting how traditional and modern systems converge in understanding the body's defense. By integrating these ideas, Ayurveda and immunology emphasize the synergy between nourishment and immunity as critical for maintaining health.

40. A: Ojas and Agni are central to Ayurveda's view of immunity. Weak Ojas signifies reduced vitality, while impaired Agni leads to Ama accumulation, creating an environment for diseases. Both concepts explain how systemic imbalances disrupt immunity, reflecting the interconnected nature of body functions. Ayurveda's emphasis on holistic health addresses these imbalances, ensuring resilience against diseases. By understanding immunity as a function of digestion and vitality, Ayurveda highlights preventive strategies that prioritize systemic harmony, showcasing its enduring relevance alongside modern immunological frameworks.

41. B: Macrophages and neutrophils are essential for innate immunity, providing the first line of defense. Ayurveda associates this foundational protection with Kapha dosha, known for its stabilizing properties. However, innate immunity is not solely governed by Kapha; it is influenced by the dynamic interplay of all doshas. While both statements are true, Kapha's role in immunity extends to structural support rather than direct immune action. This nuanced understanding illustrates Ayurveda's integrative approach, emphasizing how multiple factors contribute to immune health rather than isolating one element as primary.

42. A: Antigens activate the immune system, leading to antibody production. Ayurveda interprets this response as disruptions caused by Ama, the toxic residue of poor digestion. This correlation emphasizes the role of Agni in maintaining systemic health. By detoxifying and enhancing Agni, Ayurveda offers a preventive approach to managing immune responses. Both views highlight the significance of internal balance in combating external threats, demonstrating how ancient wisdom complements modern immunological practices. Together, they reflect the body's capacity to adapt and neutralize harmful influences through targeted interventions.

43. A: Adaptive immunity, characterized by memory cells, aligns with Ayurveda's concept of Vyadhikshamatva, which emphasizes disease resistance and resilience. Rasayana therapies enhance immunity by rejuvenating tissues and restoring balance, akin to how adaptive immunity strengthens over time. Both perspectives prioritize long-term health and prevention, integrating targeted strategies with holistic care. By combining these approaches, Ayurveda and immunology reinforce the idea that immunity is both an immediate response and a sustained capacity, underpinned by systemic nourishment and restoration.

44. **C:** Vaccines mimic natural infections to stimulate adaptive immunity, a concept rooted in modern immunology. Ayurveda, however, focuses on daily herbal tonics to maintain systemic resilience rather than replicating vaccination's targeted effects. While both approaches prioritize prevention, their mechanisms differ significantly. Vaccines provide pathogen-specific immunity, while Ayurveda aims to enhance overall vitality and defense. This distinction underscores how Ayurveda complements but does not replace modern immunological strategies, offering broader preventive care alongside targeted interventions like vaccination.

45. **A:** Aging diminishes immune efficiency, making individuals more vulnerable to infections. Ayurveda addresses this decline through Rasayana therapies, which rejuvenate tissues and enhance vitality. These therapies counteract age-related degeneration, reflecting their role in sustaining immunity. Both perspectives align in recognizing the importance of proactive care to mitigate aging's impact. By integrating rejuvenation with preventive strategies, Ayurveda complements modern immunological insights, emphasizing that immunity is not static but evolves with the body's changing needs, requiring ongoing support for optimal health.

46. **B:** Vyadhi Kshamatva, Ayurveda's concept of disease resistance, encompasses both innate (Sahaj) and acquired (Kalaj) immunity. Modern immunology parallels this with the dual components of innate and adaptive immunity. Sahaj Vyadhi Kshamatva corresponds to inherent immune defenses, while Kalaj represents immunity developed through exposure or intervention. Ayurveda's integrative approach emphasizes both natural resilience and acquired strategies, such as Rasayana therapies and lifestyle adaptations. This comprehensive understanding aligns with modern immunological principles, offering a bridge between ancient and contemporary health frameworks. Vyadhi Kshamatva's relevance lies in its holistic view of immunity, prevention, and adaptability.

47. **B:** Ojas, the refined essence of bodily tissues, is central to immune resilience and vitality in Ayurveda. Depleted Ojas results in immune dysfunction, manifesting as chronic inflammation, infections, and autoimmune conditions. Modern science links Ojas to systemic immune efficiency, including macrophage activation, lymphocyte proliferation, and cytokine regulation. Oxidative stress and inflammation diminish Ojas, impairing both physical and mental resilience. Ayurvedic interventions aim to restore Ojas by enhancing tissue health, reducing inflammation, and improving metabolic balance. This holistic perspective aligns with immunological findings, validating Ojas as a critical factor in maintaining systemic health and disease resistance.

48. **B:** Modern science validates Agni's role in systemic health by linking it to gut microbiota diversity and immune modulation. Ayurveda associates strong Agni with optimal digestion, metabolism, and immunity, which modern research connects to the gut-immune axis. Healthy gut microbiota, influenced by Agni, regulates inflammatory responses, supports mucosal immunity, and enhances metabolic clarity. Impaired Agni leads to Ama accumulation, correlating with pro-inflammatory mediators like (C)-reactive protein (CRP). Triphala's ability to restore Agni and promote gut health exemplifies this connection. This synthesis of traditional and modern insights underscores Agni's centrality in health and disease prevention.

49. **A:** Ama, resulting from impaired Agni, is analogous to metabolic toxins like CRP and TNF-α, which drive chronic inflammation and systemic immune dysfunction. Ayurveda emphasizes detoxification to clear Ama and restore metabolic clarity. Modern studies validate these principles, linking reduced inflammatory markers to improved digestion and immune regulation. Ama disrupts dosha balance, mirroring the immune dysregulation seen in chronic inflammatory conditions. Ayurvedic therapies targeting Ama not only detoxify the body but also enhance systemic resilience, aligning with modern approaches to inflammation management. This holistic strategy bridges ancient practices with contemporary immunological frameworks.

50. **B:** Triphala enhances immune health by improving gut microbiota diversity, reducing systemic inflammation, and boosting mucosal immunity. Ayurveda attributes its effects to Agni regulation and dosha balance, which modern science correlates with gut-immune interactions. Studies show Triphala increases beneficial microbial populations, promotes short-chain fatty acid (SCFA) production, and enhances IgA levels. Its ability to reduce inflammatory markers like CRP further underscores its systemic benefits. Unlike singular immune stimulants, Triphala's multifaceted actions exemplify Ayurveda's holistic approach, addressing both root causes and symptoms of imbalance. This integration highlights its role in bridging traditional and modern health paradigms.

UNIT 7: GENETICS, AYURGENOMICS, CELL AND MOLECULAR BIOLOGY

CHAPTER 19

INTRODUCTION TO GENETICS, INHERITANCE, AND HUMAN GENOME

Genetics is the branch of biology that explores the structure, function, inheritance, and variation of genes. It forms the foundation for understanding how traits are transmitted from one generation to another and how genetic variations influence health, behaviour, and disease. Inheritance mechanisms, first elucidated by Gregor Mendel through his pioneering work with pea plants, laid the groundwork for modern genetics. With the advent of genome sequencing and molecular biology, genetics has advanced into a cornerstone of biomedical science. The sequencing of the human genome in the early 2000s further revolutionized our understanding of human biology, opening new horizons in personalized medicine and hereditary disease management.

BASICS OF GENETICS AND PRINCIPLES OF INHERITANCE

What is Genetics?

Genetics is the scientific study of heredity, encompassing the structure, function, and transmission of genes across generations. Genes are the fundamental units of heredity, encoding instructions for the synthesis of proteins and regulatory molecules essential for cellular processes. Understanding genetics provides insights into how traits are inherited, how organisms adapt to their environment, and how genetic variations contribute to the complexity of life.

The Molecular Basis of Genetics

At its core, genetics is grounded in the structure and function of deoxyribonucleic acid (DNA), a molecule composed of two complementary strands arranged in a double helix. DNA is made up of four nucleotide bases: adenine (A), thymine (T), guanine (G), and cytosine (C). These bases pair specifically (A with T, G with C), creating a code that governs biological processes. Genes, which are segments of DNA, are organized on chromosomes and serve as blueprints for proteins.

1. **DNA Structure and Function:**
   - DNA sequences are read and transcribed into ribonucleic acid (RNA), which carries the information required for protein synthesis.
   - RNA molecules undergo translation in ribosomes, where sequences of nucleotides are converted into amino acid chains, forming proteins that drive cellular functions.
2. **Genetic Variation:** Genetic variation underpins diversity within populations and influences susceptibility to diseases. Variation arises from:
   - **Mutations:** Permanent alterations in the DNA sequence.
   - **Recombination:** Exchange of genetic material during meiosis.
   - **Polymorphisms:** Common variations in a population's DNA.
3. **Applications of Genetics:**
   - Genetics is pivotal to multiple disciplines, including medicine, agriculture, and evolutionary biology. Genetic technologies, such as CRISPR and gene therapy, have enabled targeted manipulation of DNA, offering revolutionary possibilities in treating genetic disorders.

- Genetics forms the foundation of our understanding of life's complexity, influencing traits ranging from physical characteristics to disease susceptibility.

Principles of Inheritance

Inheritance describes the transfer of genetic material from one generation to the next. Gregor Mendel, often called the "Father of Genetics," established the foundational laws of inheritance through meticulous experiments with pea plants. His work laid the groundwork for modern genetics, revealing predictable patterns of trait transmission.

Mendel's Laws of Inheritance

Mendel's observations are summarized in three fundamental principles:

1. **Law of Segregation:** Each organism contains two alleles for a given trait, one inherited from each parent. During gamete formation (meiosis), these alleles segregate, ensuring that each gamete carries only one allele. Offspring inherit one allele from each parent, explaining the reappearance of recessive traits in subsequent generations.
2. **Law of Independent Assortment:** Genes for different traits assort independently during gamete formation, creating genetic diversity. For example, the inheritance of a seed's color in Mendel's experiments was independent of its shape.
3. **Law of Dominance:** In heterozygous conditions, dominant alleles mask the expression of recessive alleles. For instance, the allele for tallness in pea plants dominates over the allele for shortness.

Illustrations of Mendel's Laws

Mendel's findings explain fundamental inheritance patterns, such as the predictable ratios observed in offspring phenotypes. For example:

- A monohybrid cross (single-trait inheritance) typically yields a 3:1 ratio of dominant to recessive phenotypes.
- A dihybrid cross (two-trait inheritance) results in a 9:3:3:1 ratio, reflecting independent assortment.
- Mendel's principles remain cornerstones of genetics, though modern research has expanded upon these laws to accommodate more complex inheritance patterns.

Extensions of Mendelian Genetics

Mendel's principles apply to simple traits governed by single genes, but many human traits exhibit more intricate inheritance patterns due to gene interactions and environmental influences. Modern genetics addresses these complexities through several advanced concepts:

1. **Incomplete Dominance:** In incomplete dominance, heterozygous individuals exhibit an intermediate phenotype. For instance, crossing red-flowered and white-flowered snapdragons yields pink-flowered offspring, blending the traits of both parents.
2. **Codominance:** In codominance, both alleles are fully expressed in heterozygous individuals. The AB blood group in humans exemplifies this, where alleles for both A and B antigens are expressed simultaneously.
3. **Polygenic Inheritance:** Traits influenced by multiple genes, such as height, weight, and skin color, are described as polygenic. These traits exhibit continuous variation, often forming a bell-shaped curve in populations.
4. **Epistasis:** Epistasis occurs when one gene masks or modifies the expression of another gene. For example, coat color in Labrador retrievers depends on interactions between two genes, one determining pigment and the other regulating pigment deposition.
5. **Environmental Influences:** Many traits result from gene-environment interactions. For instance, genes predispose individuals to diabetes, but diet and lifestyle significantly affect disease manifestation.

Implications for Human Genetics

Extensions of Mendelian principles reveal the complexities of human inheritance. Diseases like diabetes and schizophrenia, as well as traits like intelligence, reflect intricate gene-environment interplay. Understanding these patterns is crucial for personalized medicine and genetic counseling.

Mutation and Genetic Disorders

Mutations are alterations in the DNA sequence that can affect gene function. While some mutations are neutral or even beneficial, others disrupt normal biological processes, leading to disorders.

Types of Mutations

Mutations arise from errors during DNA replication, exposure to mutagens, or environmental factors. They can be classified as:

1. **Point Mutations:** Changes to a single nucleotide, such as substitutions, insertions, or deletions.
2. **Frameshift Mutations:** Insertions or deletions that disrupt the reading frame of a gene, altering protein synthesis.
3. **Chromosomal Mutations:** Large-scale structural changes, including duplications, inversions, and translocations.

Genetic Disorders

Mutations contribute to various genetic disorders, broadly categorized as follows:

1. **Single-Gene Disorders:** Caused by mutations in a single gene, these disorders follow Mendelian inheritance patterns. Examples include:
   - **Cystic Fibrosis:** A recessive disorder caused by mutations in the CFTR gene, leading to respiratory and digestive issues.
   - **Sickle Cell Anemia:** A recessive disorder resulting from mutations in the HBB gene, causing abnormal red blood cell shapes.
2. **Chromosomal Disorders:** These arise from abnormalities in chromosome structure or number. For example:
   - **Down Syndrome:** Caused by trisomy 21, leading to intellectual disability and physical anomalies.
   - **Turner Syndrome:** Affects females with a single X chromosome, resulting in developmental delays and infertility.
3. **Multifactorial Disorders:** These disorders result from the interaction of multiple genes and environmental factors. Common examples include:
   - **Type 2 Diabetes:** Influenced by genetic predisposition and lifestyle factors.
   - **Heart Disease:** Results from genetic, dietary, and environmental interactions.

Detection and Intervention

Advances in genetic testing, such as prenatal screening and whole-genome sequencing, enable the early detection of genetic disorders. Interventions include:

- **Gene Therapy:** Correcting defective genes using molecular tools.
- **Pharmacogenomics:** Tailoring drug treatments to individual genetic profiles.
- **Lifestyle Modifications:** Mitigating disease risks through diet and exercise, especially in multifactorial disorders.

Ethical Considerations

The growing ability to manipulate genes raises ethical concerns, such as the potential for genetic discrimination and the societal implications of designer babies. Responsible application of genetic knowledge is essential to balance scientific progress with ethical principles.

INTRODUCTION TO THE HUMAN GENOME

What is the Human Genome?

The human genome comprises the complete set of genetic material found in human cells. It contains approximately 20,000-25,000 protein-coding genes spread across 23 pairs of chromosomes. In addition to coding regions, the genome includes non-coding DNA, regulatory elements, and repetitive sequences.

Key Features of the Human Genome:

- **Chromosomes:** Humans have 22 pairs of autosomes and 1 pair of sex chromosomes (XX in females, XY in males).
- **Mitochondrial DNA:** A small circular genome found in mitochondria, inherited exclusively from the mother.
- **Non-Coding DNA:** Represents over 98% of the genome, involved in regulatory functions, structural roles, and epigenetic modifications.

The Human Genome Project (HGP)

The HGP, completed in 2003, was a landmark initiative aimed at sequencing the entire human genome. It provided unprecedented insights into the genetic basis of human biology and disease:

- **Genetic Variation:** Identified millions of single nucleotide polymorphisms (SNPs) associated with traits and diseases.
- **Gene Function:** Clarified the roles of coding and non-coding regions in cellular processes.
- **Biomedical Applications:** Facilitated the development of gene therapies, pharmacogenomics, and precision medicine.

The HGP also highlighted the importance of ethical considerations, including genetic privacy, equitable access to genomic technologies, and the prevention of genetic discrimination.

Gene Regulation and Epigenetics

Gene regulation involves mechanisms that control when, where, and how genes are expressed. Epigenetics refers to heritable changes in gene expression that do not involve alterations in the DNA sequence. These changes are mediated by:

- **DNA Methylation:** Addition of methyl groups to DNA, silencing gene expression.
- **Histone Modification:** Changes to histone proteins that affect DNA packaging and accessibility.
- **Non-Coding RNAs:** Molecules that regulate gene expression post-transcriptionally.

Epigenetic mechanisms are influenced by environmental factors such as diet, stress, and toxins, linking lifestyle to gene expression.

Genetic Predisposition

Genetic predisposition refers to an individual's increased likelihood of developing certain conditions due to inherited genetic variants. For example:

- **BRCA1/BRCA2 Mutations:** Increase the risk of breast and ovarian cancers.
- **APOE Variants:** Associated with Alzheimer's disease risk.

Lifestyle, environment, and epigenetic modifications often interact with genetic predisposition, influencing disease outcomes. This interplay underscores the importance of personalized approaches to health and prevention.

GENETIC PREDISPOSITION AND ITS IMPLICATIONS IN AYURVEDA

The Ayurvedic Concept of Prakriti

Ayurveda emphasizes individuality through the concept of Prakriti, or constitutional type, determined by the balance of the three doshas—Vata, Pitta, and Kapha. Prakriti influences physical characteristics, metabolism, immunity, and susceptibility to diseases. Recent research suggests a genetic basis for Prakriti, linking it to polymorphisms in genes related to metabolism, immunity, and inflammation.

- **Examples:** Vata Prakriti: Associated with genes influencing neural and musculoskeletal functions.
- **Pitta Prakriti:** Linked to genes involved in metabolism and thermoregulation.
- **Kapha Prakriti:** Correlates with genes regulating energy storage and immune tolerance.

Ayurveda and Epigenetics

Ayurveda's focus on lifestyle, diet, and environmental harmony aligns with epigenetic principles. Practices such as meditation, yoga, and personalized diets can modulate epigenetic markers, influencing gene expression and promoting health. For instance:

- **Meditation:** Reduces stress-related epigenetic changes, improving immune function.
- **Herbal Remedies:** Rasayana herbs like Ashwagandha and Guduchi exhibit epigenetic effects, regulating pathways involved in inflammation and stress responses.

These findings bridge Ayurveda and modern epigenetics, supporting integrative approaches to health.

Genetic Screening and Ayurveda

The integration of genetic screening with Ayurvedic principles can revolutionize personalized medicine. By identifying genetic predispositions and aligning them with Prakriti-based recommendations, healthcare providers can offer targeted interventions.

For example:

- **Cardiovascular Risk:** Individuals with Kapha-dominant Prakriti and genetic predispositions for hyperlipidemia may benefit from Kapha-pacifying diets and lifestyle changes.
- **Inflammatory Conditions:** Pitta-dominant individuals with genetic markers for inflammatory disorders can adopt anti-inflammatory regimens incorporating cooling herbs.

This convergence of genomics and Ayurveda fosters a deeper understanding of health and disease.

Preventive Healthcare in Ayurveda

Ayurveda's emphasis on prevention resonates with genetic predisposition management. Practices such as Dinacharya (daily routines), Ritucharya (seasonal regimens), and detoxification therapies align with personalized interventions to mitigate genetic risks. For example:

- **Detoxification:** Panchakarma therapies may reduce oxidative stress, which exacerbates genetic predispositions.
- **Nutrigenomics:** Ayurvedic diets tailored to Prakriti can modulate gene expression through bioactive compounds.

This integrative approach combines the predictive power of genomics with Ayurveda's holistic philosophy, promoting sustainable health.

MULTIPLE CHOICE QUESTIONS

1. A researcher is investigating the role of mitochondrial DNA (mtDNA) in human health, focusing on maternal inheritance patterns. The study finds that mitochondrial disorders arise primarily from mutations in mtDNA, leading to issues in energy production. However, the researcher also notes that environmental factors, such as oxidative stress and diet, exacerbate the severity of these disorders. Considering the findings, which of the following statements best encapsulates the interaction between genetic inheritance and environmental factors in mitochondrial disorders?

   A. Mitochondrial disorders are strictly genetic and remain unaffected by environmental conditions.

   B. Mutations in mtDNA determine disease severity, while environmental factors play no role.

C. Environmental stressors influence the expression of mtDNA mutations, impacting the phenotypic outcome.
D. Mitochondrial disorders can be prevented entirely by controlling oxidative stress through lifestyle modifications.

2. A geneticist is exploring the implications of chromosomal abnormalities in the context of human health. The researcher observes that chromosomal nondisjunction during meiosis leads to conditions such as Down syndrome, characterized by trisomy 21. Interestingly, the study also highlights that maternal age is a significant risk factor, with older mothers more likely to have offspring with such abnormalities. Based on this research, which of the following conclusions best reflects the relationship between chromosomal segregation and external risk factors?

A. Chromosomal nondisjunction is unrelated to maternal age and occurs randomly.
B. Maternal age contributes to an increased likelihood of errors in spindle assembly during meiosis.
C. Environmental factors have no influence on chromosomal segregation, which is solely a genetic process.
D. Chromosomal nondisjunction is preventable through prenatal genetic screening.

3. During a study on epigenetic regulation, a team of researchers discovers that certain environmental factors, such as dietary intake and exposure to toxins, significantly influence DNA methylation patterns. These changes alter gene expression without modifying the underlying DNA sequence. The researchers also observe that these epigenetic changes can be passed down to subsequent generations. Based on these findings, which of the following statements best explains the mechanism and implications of epigenetics?

A. Epigenetic modifications are permanent and cannot be reversed by environmental interventions.
B. DNA methylation directly changes the nucleotide sequence, creating genetic mutations.
C. Environmental factors induce epigenetic changes that regulate gene activity and can influence hereditary traits.
D. Epigenetics has no measurable impact on genetic inheritance or phenotype expression.

4 A team of scientists is analyzing the inheritance of an autosomal dominant genetic disorder, such as Huntington's disease, in a population. The study reveals that the disorder manifests in every generation and has a 50% probability of being passed on from an affected parent to their offspring, regardless of the offspring's sex. However, the severity of the disorder varies among affected individuals due to genetic modifiers. Based on these observations, which of the following statements best describes the inheritance pattern and influencing factors of such a disorder?

A. The disorder skips generations due to incomplete penetrance and variable expressivity.
B. The autosomal dominant disorder is influenced by genetic modifiers that alter its expression.
C. Both parents must carry the defective allele for their offspring to inherit the disorder.
D. The inheritance pattern of the disorder is sex-linked and influenced by environmental factors.

5. A population genetics study investigates the frequency of a recessive allele responsible for a rare metabolic disorder. The study employs Hardy-Weinberg equilibrium to calculate the expected genotype frequencies and determine whether evolutionary forces are acting on the population. The researchers identify deviations from the expected values, suggesting that non-random mating and genetic drift are influencing allele frequencies. Which of the following scenarios best explains the observed deviations in the population's genetic structure?

A. The population is experiencing natural selection, maintaining equilibrium in allele frequencies.
B. Non-random mating and genetic drift disrupt equilibrium, altering genotype distributions over generations.
C. The observed deviations are a result of random sampling errors with no evolutionary implications.
D. Hardy-Weinberg equilibrium applies only to dominant traits and cannot predict recessive allele frequencies.

6. A genetic counselor examines a case involving an X-linked recessive disorder, such as hemophilia. The disorder manifests primarily in males, while females are typically carriers. A carrier mother and an unaffected father have four children. The counselor determines that there is a 50% probability of their male children being affected and a 50% chance of their female children being carriers. Considering the inheritance mechanism, which of the following best explains the transmission pattern of X-linked recessive traits?

A. Both male and female offspring have an equal chance of inheriting the disorder.
B. Male offspring inherit the disorder only if the father is affected.
C. Male offspring inherit the disorder from their mother, while females inherit a carrier status.
D. Female offspring are unaffected and cannot pass the disorder to subsequent generations.

7. A developmental biologist is studying the phenomenon of genomic imprinting, where the expression of certain genes depends on their parental origin. The research highlights that disorders like Prader-Willi syndrome and Angelman syndrome result from deletions in the same region of chromosome 15 but exhibit different phenotypes depending on whether the mutation is inherited from the mother or father. Which of the following mechanisms best explains the observed differences in phenotypic expression?
   A. Genomic imprinting alters the DNA sequence, leading to distinct mutations from each parent.
   B. The parent-specific expression of imprinted genes determines phenotypic outcomes despite identical deletions.
   C. Chromosomal deletions always result in identical phenotypes, regardless of parental origin.
   D. Environmental factors override the effects of genomic imprinting, determining phenotypic expression.

8. A geneticist studies how codominance manifests in certain blood types. The study reveals that individuals with AB blood type express both A and B antigens equally on the surface of their red blood cells. Unlike dominance and recessiveness, codominance allows both alleles to be fully expressed. Which of the following best differentiates codominance from other inheritance patterns?
   A. In codominance, one allele completely masks the other in heterozygous individuals.
   B. Codominance results in an intermediate phenotype between the two parental alleles.
   C. Both alleles are simultaneously and equally expressed, contributing to the phenotype.
   D. Environmental factors influence allele expression, leading to codominant traits.

9. An evolutionary biologist investigates the role of genetic drift in small populations. The study observes that certain alleles become fixed or lost purely by chance over successive generations, leading to reduced genetic diversity. This phenomenon, particularly pronounced after population bottlenecks, contrasts with natural selection. Based on the findings, which of the following best explains the effects of genetic drift in small populations?
   A. Genetic drift is driven by adaptive advantages and consistently increases genetic diversity.
   B. Random changes in allele frequencies can lead to fixation or loss, reducing genetic variation.
   C. Genetic drift only occurs in large populations and is unrelated to evolutionary processes.
   D. Natural selection amplifies the effects of genetic drift, ensuring the survival of beneficial alleles.

10. A bioinformatics researcher analyzes the human genome and identifies that less than 2% of the genome codes for proteins. The remaining sequences, previously considered "junk DNA," are now recognized for their regulatory roles, such as controlling gene expression and maintaining chromosome structure. Considering these findings, which of the following best describes the significance of non-coding DNA in the human genome?
   A. Non-coding DNA has no functional relevance and is a remnant of evolutionary processes.
   B. Non-coding regions regulate gene expression, influence chromosomal architecture, and play roles in epigenetics.
   C. Protein-coding genes alone determine phenotypic traits, rendering non-coding DNA insignificant.
   D. Non-coding DNA exclusively encodes for non-essential RNA molecules, such as ribosomal RNA.

Directions (Q. No. 11–14): *Scenario-Based Questions*

SCENARIO 1

A clinical researcher is studying the effects of Triphala, a traditional Ayurvedic formulation, on gut microbiota and systemic immunity. The study focuses on the three key ingredients: Haritaki, Bibhitaki, and Amalaki. Findings reveal that Triphala significantly enhances gut microbiota diversity, which correlates with improved mucosal immunity and reduced systemic inflammation, as evidenced by lower levels of (C)-reactive protein (CRP). However, the effectiveness of Triphala is observed to vary among individuals based on genetic differences in gut-associated immune pathways and microbiota composition.

SCENARIO 2

Simultaneously, an environmental scientist investigates the sustainability of sourcing medicinal plants used in Triphala, particularly Amalaki (Emblica officinalis). The study highlights that rising global demand has led to overharvesting, threatening wild populations. Additionally, environmental stressors, such as deforestation and soil degradation, have reduced the concentration of bioactive compounds in Amalaki fruits. This, in turn, affects the therapeutic potency of Triphala and undermines its efficacy in promoting gut health and immunity, as described in Scenario 1.

11. Based on the findings in Scenario 1, which of the following mechanisms best explains the variability in the immune-enhancing effects of Triphala?

A. Genetic polymorphisms in gut-associated immune pathways modulate individual responses to Triphala.
B. The variability arises solely from differences in gut microbiota, with no genetic influence.
C. The immune-enhancing effects of Triphala are consistent across all individuals, as it directly impacts the microbiota.
D. The therapeutic effects are unrelated to gut microbiota or genetic factors and depend solely on dosha balance.

12. Considering Scenario 2, which of the following interventions would most effectively address the sustainability challenges associated with Amalaki harvesting while maintaining the therapeutic potency of Triphala?
A. Establishing large-scale monoculture plantations of Amalaki to meet global demand.
B. Promoting traditional agroforestry systems and community-based conservation of wild Amalaki populations.
C. Replacing Amalaki with synthetic alternatives to replicate its bioactive compounds.
D. Reducing the production of Triphala to conserve Amalaki populations.

13. How does the environmental degradation of Amalaki, as described in Scenario 2, potentially influence the therapeutic outcomes of Triphala, as observed in Scenario 1?
A. Reduced bioactive compound concentration in Amalaki diminishes its efficacy in modulating gut microbiota and systemic immunity.
B. Environmental degradation has no measurable impact on Triphala's efficacy, as its potency depends on the combination of all three fruits.
C. The therapeutic benefits of Triphala remain unaffected, as they are derived solely from Haritaki and Bibhitaki.
D. Degradation enhances the potency of Amalaki, improving the overall effectiveness of Triphala.

14. Based on the interconnected findings of Scenarios 1 and 2, which of the following strategies would most comprehensively address the challenges while maintaining the efficacy of Ayurvedic formulations?
A. Developing synthetic alternatives to mimic the bioactive profile of Amalaki.
B. Creating global standards for Triphala production, incorporating sustainable harvesting and quality control.
C. Shifting focus to alternative formulations that do not rely on endangered plant species like Amalaki.
D. Encouraging large-scale commercial cultivation of all Triphala components, independent of traditional practices.

15. Consider the following features of genetic mutations:
(a) Point mutations involve a single nucleotide change, which may or may not alter amino acid sequences.
(b) Frameshift mutations occur due to insertions or deletions, altering the reading frame.
(c) Silent mutations are substitutions that do not change the amino acid sequence.
(d) Nonsense mutations introduce a premature stop codon, truncating the protein.

Which of the above statements are correct?
A. (a), (b), and (c) only
B. (a), (b), and (d) only
C. (a), (c), and (d) only
D. (a), (b), (c), and (d)

16. The following are key features of meiosis:
(a) Crossing over occurs during prophase I, promoting genetic diversity.
(b) Homologous chromosomes align independently at the metaphase plate during metaphase I.
(c) Sister chromatids are separated during anaphase I.
(d) Telophase I results in the formation of two haploid cells.

Choose the correct statements:
A. (a), (b), and (d) only
B. (a) and (b) only
C. (a), (b), and (c) only
D. (a), (b), (c), and (d)

17. The stages of the cell cycle include several distinct phases:
(a) The G1 phase involves cell growth and metabolic activity.
(b) The S phase is characterized by DNA replication.
(c) The G2 phase prepares the cell for mitosis by synthesizing proteins.
(d) The M phase includes both mitosis and cytokinesis.

Which of the above correctly describe the cell cycle?
A. (a), (b), and (d) only
B. (a), (b), and (c) only
C. (a), (b), (c), and (d)
D. (b) and (c) only

18. The following are features of chromosomal mutations:
(a) Deletions involve the loss of a chromosomal segment.
(b) Duplications result in the repetition of a chromosomal segment.

(c) Inversions occur when a chromosomal segment is reversed.
(d) Translocations involve the exchange of segments between non-homologous chromosomes.

Which of the above are true?
A. (a) and (c) only
B. (b) and (d) only
C. (a), (b), and (d) only
D. (a), (b), (c), and (d)

19. The mechanisms of evolutionary change include the following:
(a) Genetic drift describes random fluctuations in allele frequencies, especially in small populations.
(b) Gene flow results from the migration of alleles between populations.
(c) Mutation introduces new alleles by altering DNA sequences.
(d) Natural selection drives differential survival and reproduction based on genetic traits.

Which mechanisms are correctly listed?
A. (a), (b), and (d) only
B. (a), (b), (c), and (d)
C. (b), (c), and (d) only
D. (a) and (c) only

20. The roles of non-coding DNA in the human genome include:
(a) Regulation of gene expression.
(b) Maintenance of chromosomal structure.
(c) Coding for ribosomal RNA and transfer RNA.
(d) Directly synthesizing functional proteins.

Which statements are correct?
A. (a), (b), and (c) only
B. (a) and (b) only
C. (a), (b), and (d) only
D. (b), (c), and (d) only

21. Consider the following features of inheritance patterns:
(a) Autosomal recessive disorders require two copies of the defective allele.
(b) Autosomal dominant disorders manifest with only one defective allele.
(c) X-linked recessive disorders primarily affect males but can appear in homozygous females.
(d) Chromosomal disorders result from structural or numerical abnormalities in chromosomes.

Which of the above statements are accurate?
A. (a), (b), and (c) only
B. (b), (c), and (d) only
C. (a), (b), and (d) only
D. (a), (b), (c), and (d)

22. The components of transcription and translation include:
(a) mRNA serves as the template for protein synthesis.
(b) tRNA carries specific amino acids to the ribosome.
(c) rRNA forms the structural and catalytic components of ribosomes.
(d) miRNA directly synthesizes proteins during translation.

Which of these statements are correct?
A. (a), (b), and (c) only
B. (b) and (d) only
C. (a), (b), and (d) only
D. (a), (c), and (d) only

23. The following statements describe genetic techniques:
(a) CRISPR-Cas9 edits specific genes by introducing targeted DNA modifications.
(b) Polymerase Chain Reaction (PCR) amplifies DNA sequences for analysis.
(c) Gel electrophoresis separates DNA fragments based on size.
(d) Karyotyping detects mutations in single nucleotide polymorphisms.

Which statements are accurate?
A. (a), (b), and (d) only
B. (a), (b), and (c) onl
C. (b), (c), and (d) only
D. (a), (c), and (d) only

24. Consider the following statements about polygenic inheritance:
(a) Polygenic traits are influenced by multiple genes.
(b) Traits such as height and skin color are examples of polygenic inheritance.
(c) Polygenic traits follow Mendel's laws of segregation and independent assortment without modification.
(d) Environmental factors often influence the expression of polygenic traits.

Which statements are true?
A. (a), (b), and (c) only
B. (a), (b), and (d) only
C. (a) and (d) only
D. (a), (c), and (d) only

25. Match the genetic concepts with their corresponding descriptions:

List–I	List–II
(a) Genetic linkage	1. Genes located close together on the same chromosome tend to be inherited together.

(b) Independent assortment	2. Traits assort independently during gamete formation when genes are on different chromosomes.
(c) Epigenetics	3. Changes in gene expression without alterations to the DNA sequence.
(d) Incomplete dominance	4. The heterozygous phenotype is intermediate between the two parental phenotypes.

Choose the correct answer from the options given below:

A. (a)-1, (b)-2, (c)-3, (d)-4
B. (a)-3, (b)-1, (c)-4, (d)-2
C. (a)-4, (b)-2, (c)-1, (d)-3
D. (a)-2, (b)-3, (c)-1, (d)-4

26. Match the types of chromosomal mutations with their characteristics:

List–I	List–II
(a) Deletion	1. A segment of a chromosome is removed.
(b) Duplication	2. A segment of a chromosome is repeated.
(c) Inversion	3. A segment of a chromosome is reversed.
(d) Translocation	4. A segment of a chromosome is exchanged with another non-homologous chromosome.

Choose the correct answer from the options given below:

A. (a)-1, (b)-2, (c)-3, (d)-4
B. (a)-2, (b)-3, (c)-4, (d)-1
C. (a)-3, (b)-1, (c)-2, (d)-4
D. (a)-4, (b)-2, (c)-1, (d)-3

27. Match the types of RNA with their primary functions:

List–I	List–II
(a) mRNA	1. Serves as a template for protein synthesis.
(b) tRNA	2. Delivers amino acids to the ribosome.
(c) rRNA	3. Forms the structural and catalytic components of ribosomes.
(d) miRNA	4. Regulates gene expression by binding to target mRNA.

Choose the correct answer from the options given below:

A. (a)-1, (b)-2, (c)-3, (d)-4
B. (a)-2, (b)-1, (c)-4, (d)-3
C. (a)-3, (b)-4, (c)-1, (d)-2
D. (a)-4, (b)-3, (c)-2, (d)-1

28. Match the inheritance patterns with their respective genetic disorders:

List–I	List–II
(a) Autosomal recessive	1. Cystic fibrosis
(b) Autosomal dominant	2. Huntington's disease
(c) X-linked recessive	3. Hemophilia
(d) Chromosomal disorder	4. Down syndrome

Choose the correct answer from the options given below:

A. (a)-1, (b)-2, (c)-3, (d)-4
B. (a)-2, (b)-1, (c)-4, (d)-3
C. (a)-3, (b)-4, (c)-1, (d)-2
D. (a)-4, (b)-3, (c)-2, (d)-1

29. Match the genetic tools with their applications:

List–I	List–II
(a) CRISPR-Cas9	1. Edits specific genes by introducing targeted modifications.
(b) PCR	2. Amplifies DNA sequences for analysis.
(c) Gel electrophoresis	3. Separates DNA fragments based on size.
(d) Karyotyping	4. Detects chromosomal abnormalities.

Choose the correct answer from the options given below:

A. (a)-1, (b)-2, (c)-3, (d)-4
B. (a)-2, (b)-4, (c)-1, (d)-3
C. (a)-3, (b)-1, (c)-4, (d)-2
D. (a)-4, (b)-3, (c)-2, (d)-1

30. Match the stages of the cell cycle with their key events:

List–I	List–II
(a) G1 phase	1. Cell grows and carries out normal metabolic functions.
(b) S phase	2. DNA replication occurs.
(c) G2 phase	3. Cell prepares for mitosis by synthesizing proteins.
(d) M phase	4. Mitotic division and chromosome separation take place.

Choose the correct answer from the options given below:

A. (a)-4, (b)-3, (c)-2, (d)-1
B. (a)-1, (b)-2, (c)-3, (d)-4
C. (a)-2, (b)-1, (c)-4, (d)-3
D. (a)-3, (b)-4, (c)-1, (d)-2

31. Match the mechanisms of evolution with their effects:

List–I	List–II
(a) Genetic drift	1. Random changes in allele frequencies, especially in small populations.
(b) Gene flow	2. Movement of alleles between populations.
(c) Mutation	3. Introduction of new alleles due to changes in the DNA sequence.
(d) Natural selection	4. Differential survival and reproduction based on genetic traits.

Choose the correct answer from the options given below:

A. (a)-1, (b)-2, (c)-3, (d)-4
B. (a)-2, (b)-3, (c)-4, (d)-1
C. (a)-3, (b)-1, (c)-2, (d)-4
D. (a)-4, (b)-3, (c)-1, (d)-2

32. Match the types of genetic mutations with their descriptions:

List–I	List–II
(a) Silent mutation	1. A substitution that does not alter the amino acid sequence.
(b) Missense mutation	2. A substitution that changes the amino acid sequence.
(c) Nonsense mutation	3. A substitution that introduces a premature stop codon.
(d) Frameshift mutation	4. An insertion or deletion that shifts the reading frame.

Choose the correct answer from the options given below:

(A. (a)-2, (b)-1, (c)-4, (d)-3
(B. (a)-1, (b)-2, (c)-3, (d)-4
(C. (a)-3, (b)-4, (c)-1, (d)-2
(D. (a)-4, (b)-3, (c)-2, (d)-1

33. Match the genetic disorders with their respective causative mutations:

List–I	List–II
(a) Sickle cell anemia	1. Mutation in the beta-globin gene.
(b) Tay-Sachs disease	2. Mutation in the HEXA gene, affecting lysosomal function.
(c) Marfan syndrome	3. Mutation in the FBN1 gene.
(d) Duchenne muscular dystrophy	4. Mutation in the DMD gene encoding dystrophin.

Choose the correct answer from the options given below:

(A. (a)-1, (b)-2, (c)-3, (d)-4
(B. (a)-2, (b)-4, (c)-1, (d)-3
(C. (a)-3, (b)-1, (c)-2, (d)-4
(D. (a)-4, (b)-3, (c)-2, (d)-1

34. Match the genome components with their functions:

List–I	List–II
(a) Introns	1. Non-coding sequences removed during RNA splicing.
(b) Telomeres	2. Repetitive sequences at chromosome ends, protecting against degradation.
(c) Non-coding DNA	3. Regulatory elements with structural and epigenetic roles.
(d) Exons	4. Coding sequences that translate into proteins.

Choose the correct answer from the options given below:

(A) (a)-1, (b)-2, (c)-3, (d)-4
(B) (a)-2, (b)-3, (c)-4, (d)-1
(C) (a)-3, (b)-4, (c)-1, (d)-2
(D) (a)-4, (b)-1, (c)-2, (d)-3

Directions (Q. No. 35–39): *Following questions are based on Statement 1 and Statement 2. Read both the statements carefully and choose the correct answer from the options given below:*

A. Both Statement 1 and Statement 2 are true, and Statement 2 is the correct explanation of Statement 1.
B. Both Statement 1 and Statement 2 are true, but Statement 2 is not the correct explanation of Statement 1.
C. Statement 1 is true, but Statement 2 is false.
D. Statement 1 is false, but Statement 2 is true.
E. Both Statement 1 and Statement 2 are false.

35. Statement 1: Mendel's law of segregation states that each organism inherits two alleles for a trait, one from each parent, and these alleles segregate independently during gamete formation.

Statement 2: Mendel's law of segregation applies only to traits controlled by multiple alleles, as monogenic traits do not exhibit segregation.

36. Statement 1: Polygenic inheritance involves the interaction of multiple genes, each contributing to the final phenotype in an additive manner.

Statement 2: Traits like height and skin color are classic examples of polygenic inheritance, exhibiting continuous variation due to the involvement of multiple genes and environmental factors.

37. **Statement 1:** Genetic drift leads to random changes in allele frequencies, often reducing genetic diversity within small populations.

    Statement 2: Natural selection is a random process that results in the fixation of harmful alleles in a population.

38. **Statement 1:** DNA replication is semiconservative, meaning each daughter DNA molecule consists of one parental and one newly synthesized strand.

    Statement 2: DNA polymerase synthesizes new strands in the 3' to 5' direction, ensuring accurate replication of the parental template strand.

39. **Statement 1:** Epigenetic modifications, such as DNA methylation, can regulate gene expression without altering the nucleotide sequence.

    Statement 2: DNA methylation is irreversible, and once established, it cannot be influenced by environmental factors or cellular processes.

Directions (Q. No. 40–45): *There are two statements in each question. One is labelled as Assertion (A) and the other is as Reason (R). Read both the statements and choose the correct answer from the options given below:*

A. Both Assertion (A) and Reason (R) are true, and Reason (R) is the correct explanation of Assertion (A).
B. Both Assertion (A) and Reason (R) are true, but Reason (R) is not the correct explanation of Assertion (A).
C. Assertion (A) is true, but Reason (R) is false.
D. Assertion (A) is false, but Reason (R) is true.
E. Both Assertion (A) and Reason (R) are false.

40. **Assertion (A):** Natural selection favours traits that enhance survival and reproduction in a given environment.

    Reason (R): Traits favoured by natural selection are always beneficial to the individual and ensure no harmful effects on the population.

41. **Assertion (A):** Crossing over during prophase I of meiosis results in genetic variation among gametes.

    Reason (R): Crossing over involves the exchange of genetic material between sister chromatids of homologous chromosomes.

42. **Assertion (A):** Polygenic traits, such as height and skin color, show continuous variation within a population.

    Reason (R): These traits are influenced by multiple genes, each contributing equally to the phenotype, and are unaffected by environmental factors.

43. **Assertion (A):** Epigenetic changes, such as DNA methylation and histone modification, are reversible.

    Reason (R): Epigenetic modifications are directly inherited and cannot be influenced by environmental factors or therapeutic interventions.

44. **Assertion (A):** Inheritance of mitochondrial DNA occurs exclusively through the maternal lineage.

    Reason (R): Mitochondria are present in the egg cytoplasm but not in the sperm cell during fertilization.

45. **Assertion (A):** Genetic mutations in germ cells can be inherited by the next generation, while mutations in somatic cells cannot.

    Reason (R): Germ cells give rise to gametes, while somatic cells are limited to the individual organism's body.

Directions (Q. No. 46–50): *Read the passage carefully and answer the questions given below:*

Genetics, the science of heredity, has evolved significantly since the seminal discoveries of Gregor Mendel. It seeks to unravel the mechanisms by which traits are inherited through the generations, primarily focusing on the role of DNA as the molecular repository of genetic information. However, contemporary genetic research recognizes the intricate interplay between genes and their regulatory environments, paving the way for an allied discipline: epigenetics. Unlike genetic changes, which involve alterations in the DNA sequence itself, epigenetic modifications regulate gene expression without altering the underlying genetic code. These modifications—chiefly DNA methylation, histone acetylation, and chromatin remodeling—serve as molecular switches, influencing gene activity in response to environmental cues.

The burgeoning field of epigenetics bridges the longstanding dichotomy between nature (genetics) and nurture (environmental influences). For example, identical twins, who share the same DNA sequence, often exhibit remarkable differences in phenotypic traits due to epigenetic variations acquired over their lifetimes. These variations, driven by factors such as diet, stress, pollutants, and lifestyle, underscore the dynamic and reversible nature of the epigenome. Importantly, such modifications can sometimes be heritable, perpetuating environmentally induced changes across generations—a concept fundamentally reshaping our understanding of inheritance and disease predisposition.

From the perspective of disease susceptibility, the interaction between genetic predisposition and epigenetic regulation is particularly illuminating. Certain polymorphisms, or variations in DNA sequences, predispose individuals to conditions like diabetes, cardiovascular diseases, or cancer. However, the expression of these genetic predispositions often hinges on epigenetic markers, which determine whether a gene is "switched on" or silenced. For instance, hypermethylation of tumor suppressor genes is a hallmark of many cancers, effectively silencing these genes and permitting uncontrolled cellular proliferation. Conversely, hypomethylation of oncogenes can exacerbate tumor progression by increasing their expression.

Ayurveda, the ancient Indian system of medicine, provides an intriguing lens through which to explore the interconnectivity of genetics and epigenetics. The Ayurvedic concept of Prakriti, or an individual's constitutional type, aligns closely with the genetic and epigenetic framework. Prakriti classifications—Vata, Pitta, and Kapha—are believed to govern not only physiological traits but also predispositions to specific diseases. Emerging research suggests that Prakriti types correlate with single nucleotide polymorphisms (SNPs) in genes related to immunity, metabolism, and stress response. For instance, individuals with a predominantly Kapha Prakriti may exhibit genetic markers associated with a slower metabolic rate, predisposing them to conditions like obesity and diabetes. However, lifestyle interventions recommended by Ayurveda, such as dietary regimens and detoxification therapies, could modulate epigenetic markers, mitigating these genetic risks.

Furthermore, Ayurveda emphasizes the principle of Ritucharya—seasonal adaptations in diet and lifestyle—to maintain the balance of doshas. This principle finds resonance in modern epigenetics, where environmental factors like temperature and nutrition are known to influence gene expression through epigenetic pathways. For example, the differential expression of genes in response to seasonal changes in ultraviolet (UV) exposure is well-documented, with implications for vitamin D synthesis and immune function. By integrating genetic insights with epigenetic principles, Ayurveda offers a personalized and dynamic approach to health, where therapeutic interventions are tailored not only to an individual's genetic makeup but also to their environmental context.

The implications of genetic and epigenetic interplay extend beyond individual health, touching upon societal and environmental concerns. The widespread overuse of agrochemicals, deforestation, and urbanization have not only exacerbated the incidence of lifestyle diseases but also altered the epigenetic landscape of populations. For instance, prenatal exposure to pollutants has been linked to increased DNA methylation in genes associated with neurodevelopment, raising the risk of autism and other cognitive disorders. Additionally, intergenerational epigenetic inheritance highlights the potential long-term consequences of environmental degradation, as epigenetic changes induced by environmental stressors can persist across generations.

Advances in pharmacogenomics further illuminate the interplay between genetics, epigenetics, and individualized therapy. By analyzing genetic variants in drug-metabolizing enzymes, such as those in the CYP450 family, clinicians can predict an individual's response to specific medications, optimizing therapeutic efficacy while minimizing adverse effects. However, epigenetic modifications can modulate the activity of these enzymes, adding an additional layer of complexity to pharmacological interventions. Ayurvedic formulations, which often leverage polyherbal combinations, may hold promise in this regard, as their bioactive compounds target multiple pathways, potentially influencing both genetic and epigenetic mechanisms. For instance, curcumin, derived from turmeric, has been shown to alter histone acetylation patterns, thereby modulating gene expression in inflammatory pathways.

As we stand at the confluence of genetics, epigenetics, and Ayurveda, the integration of these disciplines holds immense promise for advancing personalized medicine. By decoding the molecular underpinnings of Prakriti and harnessing the power of epigenetic modifications, we can develop interventions that transcend the binary of nature and nurture, offering holistic solutions to contemporary health challenges. However, this integration necessitates a nuanced understanding of the ethical, social, and environmental dimensions, as the potential for epigenetic reprogramming raises questions about privacy, accessibility, and unintended consequences.

46. According to the passage, what distinguishes epigenetics from genetics?

A. Epigenetics involves changes in DNA sequences, while genetics focuses on chromosomal structures.

B. Epigenetics regulates gene expression without altering the DNA sequence, unlike genetics.

C. Genetics governs environmental adaptations, whereas epigenetics influences hereditary traits.

D. Epigenetics replaces genetic inheritance in the study of phenotypic traits.

47. How does the Ayurvedic concept of Prakriti relate to modern genetics and epigenetics?

A. Prakriti aligns solely with genetic traits, excluding epigenetic influences.

B. Prakriti classifications correspond to SNPs and are influenced by epigenetic markers.

C. Prakriti is a philosophical construct with no basis in genetic or epigenetic science.

D. Prakriti traits contradict the findings of genetic predisposition studies.

48. What role do epigenetic modifications play in disease susceptibility, as mentioned in the passage?

A. They permanently disable genetic predispositions to chronic diseases.

B. They regulate the expression of predisposed genes, influencing disease progression.

C. They completely override genetic polymorphisms, nullifying their effects.

D. They are irrelevant to the progression of diseases like cancer and diabetes.

49. In what way does Ayurveda's principle of Ritucharya align with modern epigenetics?

A. Both emphasize the irreversibility of genetic and epigenetic traits.

B. Ritucharya suggests seasonal changes modulate epigenetic pathways influenced by environment.

C. Ritucharya contradicts the seasonal gene expression documented in modern science.

D. Both disregard the role of diet and environment in maintaining health.

50. How does intergenerational epigenetic inheritance underscore environmental concerns?

A. It suggests environmental stressors affect epigenetic patterns but are not passed on.

B. It reveals that pollutants and environmental changes can induce heritable epigenetic modifications.

C. It indicates that genetics, not epigenetics, is solely responsible for adaptation to pollutants.

D. It demonstrates that epigenetic changes from environmental factors are limited to individuals.

ANSWER WITH EXPLANATIONS

1. C: Environmental stressors influence the expression of mtDNA mutations, impacting the phenotypic outcome. Mitochondrial disorders arise from mutations in mtDNA, but their severity is not dictated by genetics alone. Environmental influences like oxidative stress and dietary habits can aggravate symptoms or alter disease progression by affecting mitochondrial function. Thus, the phenotypic expression of the disorder is shaped by both genetic and non-genetic factors, making option C the most accurate.

2. B: Maternal age contributes to an increased likelihood of errors in spindle assembly during meiosis.As women age, the chances of meiotic errors increase, particularly during the segregation of chromosomes. These errors often result in nondisjunction, a leading cause of conditions like Down syndrome (trisomy 21). Studies show that spindle assembly becomes less efficient with age, increasing the risk of chromosomal abnormalities in offspring. Therefore, maternal age is a critical factor influencing chromosomal segregation.

3. C: Environmental factors induce epigenetic changes that regulate gene activity and can influence hereditary traits. Epigenetics refers to heritable changes in gene expression that do not involve changes in the DNA sequence. Environmental influences such as diet, stress, and toxin exposure can cause these modifications—such as DNA methylation—which can be passed on to future generations. This regulatory mechanism allows dynamic gene control based on external cues, bridging nature and nurture in inheritance.

4. B: The autosomal dominant disorder is influenced by genetic modifiers that alter its expression. Autosomal dominant disorders like Huntington's disease manifest when a single defective allele is inherited. Although the disorder appears in every generation, its severity varies due to the influence of genetic modifiers—genes that affect how strongly the disease is expressed. This variation is consistent with the observed differences in phenotype among affected individuals.

5. B: Non-random mating and genetic drift disrupt equilibrium, altering genotype distributions over generations. The Hardy-Weinberg equilibrium assumes random mating and no evolutionary forces. However, when non-random mating or genetic drift occurs—especially in small populations—allele frequencies shift unpredictably. These forces disrupt the equilibrium, leading to genotype frequencies that differ from expected values, signaling active evolutionary change in the population.

6. C: Male offspring inherit the disorder from their mother, while females inherit a carrier status. X-linked recessive disorders like hemophilia primarily affect males because they inherit only one X chromosome. A carrier mother has a 50% chance of passing the affected X chromosome to her sons (who will express the disorder) and a 50% chance of passing it to her daughters (who will be carriers but typically unaffected). The father's X chromosome goes only to daughters, not sons.

7. B: The parent-specific expression of imprinted genes determines phenotypic outcomes despite identical deletions. Genomic imprinting is a process where certain genes are expressed only if inherited from a specific parent. In Prader-Willi and Angelman syndromes, identical deletions in chromosome 15 yield different outcomes depending on whether the mutation came from the mother or father. This parent-of-origin effect is a classic example of epigenetic regulation, explaining the phenotypic variability.

8. **C:** Both alleles are simultaneously and equally expressed, contributing to the phenotype. Codominance is an inheritance pattern where both alleles in a heterozygote are fully and independently expressed. In individuals with AB blood type, both A and B antigens appear on the surface of red blood cells. This differs from simple dominance or incomplete dominance and exemplifies codominant expression without one allele masking the other.

9. **B:** Random changes in allele frequencies can lead to fixation or loss, reducing genetic variation. Genetic drift is a random process that has a stronger impact on small populations, where chance events can significantly alter allele frequencies. Over generations, this may lead to the complete loss or fixation of certain alleles, diminishing genetic diversity. Unlike natural selection, drift is non-directional and does not favor beneficial traits specifically.

10. **B:** Non-coding regions regulate gene expression, influence chromosomal architecture, and play roles in epigenetics. Though non-coding DNA doesn't code for proteins, it is far from "junk." These regions are involved in critical functions like regulating transcription, maintaining telomeres, and supporting epigenetic modifications. They also host regulatory RNAs and influence chromatin structure, proving essential for gene regulation and overall genomic function.

11. **A:** Genetic polymorphisms in gut-associated immune pathways modulate individual responses to Triphala. Triphala's effectiveness varies among individuals due to both their unique gut microbiota and underlying genetic differences. Specific genetic polymorphisms in immune regulation or gut-related genes can influence how a person's system reacts to the formulation. This explains why some individuals see stronger immune benefits from Triphala than others.

12. **B:** Promoting traditional agroforestry systems and community-based conservation of wild Amalaki populations. Agroforestry encourages sustainable cultivation while maintaining biodiversity. Community-based conservation ensures that wild populations are protected and nurtured. This method supports both environmental sustainability and medicinal efficacy, as it preserves the natural integrity and bioactive richness of Amalaki, which is crucial for the effectiveness of Triphala.

13. **A:** Reduced bioactive compound concentration in Amalaki diminishes its efficacy in modulating gut microbiota and systemic immunity. Environmental degradation such as deforestation and poor soil health weakens Amalaki's medicinal quality. The reduction in key bioactive compounds directly impairs Triphala's ability to influence gut microbiota diversity and systemic immunity, as these therapeutic effects depend on the potency of its ingredients—especially Amalaki.

14. **B:** Creating global standards for Triphala production, incorporating sustainable harvesting and quality control.

    This approach addresses both environmental and medicinal challenges. Standardizing harvesting ensures long-term availability of high-quality Amalaki, while quality control maintains therapeutic efficacy. It allows traditional practices to evolve with modern demands, ensuring sustainability, conservation, and consistent medicinal value across formulations.

15. **D:** All four options describe valid types of genetic mutations. Point mutations involve a single base change, which may alter a protein or remain silent. Frameshift mutations, caused by insertions or deletions, shift the genetic reading frame, often disrupting the entire downstream sequence. Silent mutations do not change the amino acid sequence due to genetic code redundancy. Nonsense mutations introduce a stop codon prematurely, truncating the protein.

16. **A:** Crossing over during prophase I promotes genetic variation by exchanging genetic material between homologous chromosomes. During metaphase I, homologous pairs align randomly, contributing to independent assortment. In anaphase I, it is homologous chromosomes, not sister chromatids, that separate. Telophase I concludes meiosis I by forming two haploid cells, each with half the chromosome number.

17. **C:** Crossing over during prophase I of meiosis involves the exchange of genetic material between homologous chromosomes. This process enhances genetic diversity by producing novel allele combinations. The passage underscores crossing over as a fundamental mechanism in evolution, increasing variability within populations and promoting adaptability to environmental changes. For instance, recombination is critical in shuffling immune system genes, enabling populations to combat diverse pathogens. While crossing over ensures genetic uniqueness in offspring, its failure can result in chromosomal abnormalities, such as deletions or duplications, underscoring its role in maintaining genomic stability and diversity.

18. **D:** DNA replication follows a semiconservative model, where each daughter DNA molecule retains one parental strand and synthesizes a complementary

strand. The passage emphasizes the precision of this process, which ensures the accurate transmission of genetic information. Enzymes like DNA polymerase, helicase, and ligase coordinate replication, proofreading errors to maintain fidelity. Mutations during replication, if unrepaired, can result in genetic disorders or cancers. The semiconservative nature of replication preserves genetic continuity while allowing for the variability necessary for evolution. This balance highlights the interplay between stability and adaptability in genetic systems.

19. B: All four are valid evolutionary mechanisms. Genetic drift is a random process that impacts allele frequencies, especially in small populations. Gene flow introduces new alleles through migration. Mutations create novel alleles, providing raw material for evolution. Natural selection favors traits that improve survival or reproduction, making them more frequent in the population.

20. A: Non-coding DNA plays multiple regulatory roles. It regulates gene expression (e.g., enhancers, silencers), maintains chromosomal structure (e.g., telomeres, centromeres), and encodes functional RNAs like rRNA and tRNA. However, it does not directly code for proteins—only coding (exon) regions do that—so option (d) is incorrect.

21. D: Gene flow, genetic drift, mutation, and natural selection are key mechanisms driving evolution. Gene flow involves the migration of alleles between populations, increasing genetic diversity and reducing differences between populations. Genetic drift, more pronounced in small populations, involves random changes in allele frequencies, which can lead to loss of genetic diversity. Mutations introduce new alleles, fueling variation essential for evolution. Natural selection favors traits that enhance survival and reproduction, ensuring adaptive changes.

22. A: Disease susceptibility often results from the interplay of genetic predispositions and epigenetic modifications. The passage highlights how epigenetic markers, like DNA methylation, act as molecular switches, turning genes "on" or "off". For example, hypermethylation of tumor suppressor genes silences their protective effects, increasing cancer risk. Conversely, hypomethylation can activate oncogenes, accelerating tumor progression. This dual regulatory role of epigenetics underscores its critical influence on whether genetic predispositions manifest as diseases. Understanding these mechanisms provides insights into disease prevention and targeted therapies, bridging genetics, epigenetics, and environmental factors.

23. B: CRISPR-Cas9 is a gene-editing tool that introduces specific mutations. PCR is widely used to amplify DNA sequences for diagnostics and research. Gel electrophoresis separates DNA fragments by size using an electric field. However, karyotyping detects large chromosomal abnormalities—not SNPs, which require sequencing techniques—making (d) incorrect.

24. B: The Ayurvedic principle of Prakriti aligns with modern genetics and epigenetics by integrating constitutional traits with genetic predispositions. The passage explains how Prakriti classifications, such as Vata, Pitta, and Kapha, correlate with genetic markers influencing immunity, metabolism, and stress response. Epigenetic modifications further refine these traits, allowing dynamic responses to environmental influences. This interplay of genetic and epigenetic frameworks with personalized medicine highlights the relevance of Ayurveda in contemporary healthcare.

25. A: The principle of epistasis explains how one gene can influence or mask the expression of another. For example, a gene determining pigment deposition may suppress a gene controlling pigment color. The passage emphasizes that epistasis adds complexity to inheritance patterns, disrupting expected Mendelian ratios. This hierarchical interaction among genes highlights the interconnectedness of genetic networks.

26. A: Chromosomal mutations, including deletions, duplications, inversions, and translocations, significantly impact genetic function. Deletions remove chromosomal segments, often leading to loss-of-function mutations. Duplications repeat segments, potentially increasing gene dosage effects. Inversions reverse chromosomal segments, disrupting gene regulation. Translocations exchange segments between non-homologous chromosomes, altering gene expression. The passage discusses these mutations to highlight their role in genetic disorders like Down syndrome (caused by chromosomal duplications) and cancer (often linked to translocations). Understanding chromosomal mutations is critical for diagnosing genetic conditions and developing targeted therapies.

27. A: The passage elaborates on the functional diversity of RNA types in gene expression. Messenger RNA (mRNA) serves as the template for protein synthesis. Transfer RNA (tRNA) delivers specific amino acids to ribosomes, ensuring accurate translation. Ribosomal RNA (rRNA) forms the structural and catalytic components of ribosomes. MicroRNAs (miRNAs) regulate gene expression by binding to target mRNA, silencing specific genes. These RNA types collectively illustrate the complexity of genetic regulation, emphasizing the importance of transcription and translation in cellular function and their relevance to diseases.

28. A: Inheritance patterns vary based on the genetic mechanism involved. Autosomal recessive disorders, like cystic fibrosis, require two defective alleles for phenotypic expression. Autosomal dominant disorders, such as Huntington's disease, manifest with just one defective allele. X-linked recessive disorders, like hemophilia, predominantly affect males due to the absence of a second X chromosome. Chromosomal disorders, like Down syndrome, arise from structural or numerical chromosomal abnormalities. The passage highlights these patterns to illustrate how genetic mechanisms influence disease inheritance and diagnostic approaches.

29. A: Genetic tools, such as CRISPR-Cas9, PCR, gel electrophoresis, and karyotyping, revolutionize genetic research and diagnostics. CRISPR-Cas9 enables precise gene editing by introducing targeted modifications. PCR amplifies DNA sequences, facilitating analysis. Gel electrophoresis separates DNA fragments based on size, aiding visualization. Karyotyping detects chromosomal abnormalities, such as aneuploidies. The passage emphasizes these techniques' roles in understanding genetic disorders, advancing personalized medicine, and exploring therapeutic possibilities, underscoring their transformative impact on genomics.

30. B: The stages of the cell cycle—G1, S, G2, and M—coordinate cellular growth, DNA replication, and division. The passage discusses how the G1 phase focuses on cell growth and metabolic activity, while the S phase involves DNA replication. The G2 phase prepares the cell for mitosis by synthesizing necessary proteins. The M phase executes chromosome separation and cytokinesis. Understanding these stages is fundamental for studying cell division, particularly in cancer biology, where dysregulation of cell cycle checkpoints leads to uncontrolled proliferation.

31. A: Each mechanism is correctly matched to its evolutionary effect. Genetic drift leads to random allele fluctuations. Gene flow moves alleles between populations. Mutation introduces new alleles by changing DNA sequences. Natural selection acts on heritable traits, favoring those that increase fitness.

32. B: Mutations vary in their molecular effects on gene function. Silent mutations alter nucleotide sequences without changing amino acids due to codon redundancy. Missense mutations substitute amino acids, potentially affecting protein structure and function. Nonsense mutations introduce premature stop codons, truncating proteins. Frameshift mutations, caused by insertions or deletions, disrupt reading frames, producing nonfunctional proteins.

33. A: Genetic disorders arise from specific mutations affecting critical genes. For example, sickle cell anemia results from a mutation in the β-globin gene, altering hemoglobin structure. Tay-Sachs disease stems from mutations in the HEXA gene, impairing lysosomal function. Marfan syndrome is linked to mutations in the FBN1 gene, affecting connective tissues. Duchenne muscular dystrophy results from mutations in the DMD gene encoding dystrophin. The passage highlights these associations to illustrate the molecular basis of genetic diseases and the importance of gene-specific interventions.

34. A: Genome components include coding and non-coding regions, each with distinct roles. Introns are non-coding sequences removed during RNA splicing, while exons are translated into proteins. Telomeres protect chromosome ends from degradation, maintaining stability. Non-coding DNA regulates gene expression and chromosomal architecture. The passage emphasizes the functional diversity of these regions, challenging the traditional focus on coding DNA and highlighting non-coding DNA's regulatory significance in health, disease, and evolution.

35. C: Mendel's law of segregation describes how, during meiosis, the two alleles for each trait separate, ensuring that each gamete carries only one allele. This principle applies universally to all diploid organisms and explains inheritance patterns for single-gene traits. However, the second statement incorrectly suggests that the law applies exclusively to traits controlled by multiple alleles, which is untrue. The passage elaborates on how segregation is a foundational aspect of inheritance, even in cases where traits are influenced by complex interactions of multiple genes or epigenetic factors.

36. A: Polygenic inheritance involves the contribution of multiple genes, each with small effects, to produce a continuous range of phenotypes, such as height, skin color, or intelligence. These traits deviate from Mendelian single-gene inheritance, exhibiting variability influenced by genetic and environmental interactions. The second statement clarifies that environmental factors, such as nutrition, further shape the phenotypic expression of these traits, creating continuous distributions. For example, the interaction between genes regulating bone growth and external factors like diet determines adult height. Both statements are true, and the reason complements the assertion, reinforcing the complexity of polygenic traits.

37. C: Genetic drift and natural selection are distinct evolutionary forces. Genetic drift involves random changes in allele frequencies, particularly impactful in small populations, where chance events can fix or eliminate alleles irrespective of their adaptive value. This can lead to reduced genetic diversity and fixation of deleterious traits. On the other hand, natural selection is a deterministic process favoring traits that increase fitness. The second statement mischaracterizes selection as random, which is incorrect. The passage highlights how drift and selection often operate together, but their mechanisms differ fundamentally. Drift affects population-level diversity randomly, while selection drives adaptive evolution by systematically favouring advantageous alleles.

38. C: DNA replication follows a semiconservative model, meaning each daughter molecule contains one original (parental) strand and one newly synthesized strand. DNA polymerase synthesizes new DNA in the 5' to 3' direction by adding nucleotides to the 3' hydroxyl end of the growing strand. The first statement accurately describes the semiconservative nature of replication, while the second statement is incorrect, as DNA polymerase cannot synthesize in the 3' to 5' direction. This directional synthesis ensures high fidelity in replication, with proofreading mechanisms correcting errors to prevent mutations. The passage elaborates on the molecular machinery involved, including helicase, ligase, and topoisomerase, which work together to maintain genomic integrity. Errors during replication, if uncorrected, can lead to genetic disorders like cancer, highlighting the importance of this process in preserving life.

39. C: Epigenetic modifications, such as DNA methylation and histone acetylation, regulate gene expression without altering the DNA sequence. Methylation typically silences genes by preventing transcription factor binding, while acetylation activates genes by loosening chromatin structure. These modifications are reversible and responsive to environmental factors like diet, stress, and pollutants. The first statement accurately describes the role of epigenetics, while the second statement incorrectly claims that DNA methylation is irreversible. The passage emphasizes that epigenetic modifications allow dynamic regulation of gene activity, adapting to changing environments.

40. C: Natural selection favours traits that enhance an organism's survival and reproductive success in specific environments. However, the assertion that selected traits are always beneficial to individuals or populations is incorrect. For example, the sickle cell allele is advantageous in malaria-prone regions, providing resistance to the disease, but it also causes sickle cell anemia in homozygous individuals. The passage emphasizes that natural selection operates on relative fitness, favouring traits that increase reproductive success in a given context, even if they have trade-offs. Thus, while the assertion is true, the reason oversimplifies the complexities of selection, ignoring how some traits may be harmful in certain contexts or to subsets of the population.

41. C: Crossing over during prophase I of meiosis occurs between homologous chromosomes, not sister chromatids. Homologous chromosomes exchange genetic material, creating recombinant chromatids with novel allele combinations. This process enhances genetic diversity, ensuring that offspring inherit unique combinations of traits. The first statement correctly describes the importance of crossing over, while the second inaccurately attributes it to sister chromatids, which are identical and do not recombine. The passage underscores crossing over as a critical mechanism for genetic variability, highlighting its role in evolution and adaptation. Missteps during this process, such as unequal crossing over, can lead to chromosomal abnormalities like duplications or deletions, illustrating the delicate balance of meiotic processes.

42. C: Polygenic traits, such as height and skin color, result from the additive effects of multiple genes. These traits exhibit continuous variation rather than discrete categories, reflecting the combined influence of genetic loci and environmental factors. While the first statement correctly asserts the nature of polygenic inheritance, the second statement erroneously claims that these traits are unaffected by the environment. In reality, environmental factors like nutrition, sunlight exposure, or socioeconomic conditions significantly shape polygenic traits. For example, height is influenced by genes regulating bone growth and external factors like diet. The passage highlights the complexity of polygenic traits, emphasizing their dependence on both genetic architecture and environmental inputs.

43. C: Epigenetic changes, such as DNA methylation and histone acetylation, are reversible and responsive to environmental stimuli. These modifications regulate gene expression, allowing organisms to adapt dynamically to environmental changes. The first statement accurately describes the reversibility of epigenetics, but the second statement incorrectly claims that these changes are permanently inherited. While some epigenetic modifications can be passed to offspring, most are reset during embryonic development. The passage explores how this reversibility underpins therapeutic interventions, such as drugs targeting epigenetic pathways to treat diseases like cancer or metabolic syndromes. Understanding this dynamic regulation bridges the gap between genetic predispositions and environmental influences.

44. **A:** Mitochondrial DNA (mtDNA) is inherited exclusively from the maternal lineage because mitochondria in the sperm are excluded during fertilization. This unique inheritance pattern allows researchers to trace maternal ancestry and study mitochondrial disorders. The Assertion emphasizes the critical role of mitochondria in energy production, with mutations in mtDNA leading to conditions like mitochondrial myopathies or Leigh syndrome. The reason complements the assertion by explaining the biological mechanism behind this inheritance pattern. Understanding mtDNA inheritance has advanced evolutionary biology and clinical research, providing insights into population genetics and diseases linked to mitochondrial dysfunction.

45. **A:** Mutations in germ cells, which give rise to gametes, can be passed to the next generation, influencing inherited traits or genetic disorders. Conversely, somatic cell mutations affect only the individual and cannot be transmitted. The Assertion highlights the distinction between these cell types, emphasizing the significance of germline mutations in evolution and heredity. For example, mutations in germline BRCA1 or BRCA2 genes increase cancer risk in offspring. The reason correctly explains why only germline mutations are inheritable, reinforcing the critical role of gametes in transmitting genetic information across generations.

46. **B:** Epigenetics differs from genetics in its approach to understanding gene expression. While genetics focuses on inheritable DNA sequence changes, epigenetics examines reversible modifications that regulate gene activity without altering the nucleotide sequence. DNA methylation and histone modifications serve as epigenetic "switches," dynamically controlling gene expression based on environmental factors like diet and stress. The passage emphasizes the interplay between genetics and epigenetics, highlighting how identical genetic codes in twins can lead to phenotypic differences due to epigenetic variations. This distinction is critical for understanding gene-environment interactions and their role in health and disease, where epigenetics bridges genetic predispositions and environmental influences.

47. **B:** The Ayurvedic concept of Prakriti resonates with modern genetic and epigenetic research. Prakriti classifications (Vata, Pitta, Kapha) correlate with single nucleotide polymorphisms (SNPs) in genes regulating metabolism, immunity, and stress responses. For example, Kapha-dominant individuals may exhibit genetic markers associated with a slower metabolic rate, predisposing them to obesity. Epigenetic modifications, influenced by lifestyle and diet, further refine these Prakriti traits, dynamically adapting to environmental contexts. The passage underscores that Prakriti integrates genetic and epigenetic frameworks, supporting personalized approaches in Ayurveda. This alignment demonstrates how ancient health paradigms anticipate modern concepts of genetic individuality and environmental adaptability.

48. **B:** Epigenetic modifications, such as DNA methylation and histone acetylation, regulate the expression of genes linked to disease susceptibility. For instance, hypermethylation of tumor suppressor genes silences their protective effects, promoting cancer progression. Conversely, hypomethylation can activate oncogenes, exacerbating tumor growth. The passage illustrates that genetic predispositions alone do not determine disease outcomes; epigenetic markers influence whether these predispositions manifest. This dynamic regulation underscores the importance of addressing environmental factors and lifestyle choices in disease prevention and management, bridging the gap between genetic risk and phenotypic expression.

49. **B:** Ritucharya, the Ayurvedic principle of seasonal adaptation, aligns closely with modern epigenetics. The passage explains how environmental factors, such as temperature, sunlight, and nutrition, modulate epigenetic pathways. For instance, seasonal variations in UV exposure influence gene expression related to vitamin D synthesis and immune function. Ayurveda's emphasis on aligning diet and lifestyle with seasonal changes reflects this epigenetic understanding, offering a dynamic health strategy. By integrating these principles, Ritucharya demonstrates the ancient recognition of environmental influences on physiological processes, paralleling modern insights into gene-environment interactions and their impact on health.

50. **B:** Intergenerational epigenetic inheritance highlights the long-term effects of environmental stressors on populations. The passage discusses how prenatal exposure to pollutants can induce heritable DNA methylation changes, increasing the risk of neurodevelopmental disorders like autism. These epigenetic modifications, passed down across generations, reveal the lasting impact of environmental degradation. This phenomenon expands the traditional understanding of inheritance, demonstrating that epigenetics, alongside genetics, contributes to population health and evolution. It underscores the urgency of addressing environmental challenges to mitigate their transgenerational effects, linking ecological sustainability with human health.

CHAPTER 20

AYURGENOMICS – DOSA-PRAKRTI AND GENETIC CORRELATION

INTRODUCTION TO AYURGENOMICS

Ayurgenomics, a term derived from the fusion of "Ayurveda" and "genomics," is an emerging field that bridges the ancient wisdom of Ayurveda with modern genetic science. Ayurveda, a traditional Indian system of medicine, offers a holistic approach to health, emphasizing individual-specific therapies based on body constitution (Prakṛti) and the balance of three primary bio-energies or doṣas: Vāta, Pitta, and Kapha. In contrast, genomics is the study of genes and their functions, providing insights into biological processes at the molecular level.

Ayurgenomics aims to explore the genetic underpinnings of Ayurvedic principles, particularly the concept of Prakṛti, and to investigate how an individual's genetic makeup influences their susceptibility to diseases, therapeutic outcomes, and overall health. This field represents a unique amalgamation of traditional knowledge and cutting-edge science, paving the way for personalized medicine by integrating ancient diagnostics with modern genetic tools.

Historical Context of Ayurveda and Prakṛti

Ayurveda, dating back over 5,000 years, emphasizes the importance of understanding an individual's unique Prakṛti. The concept of Prakṛti refers to the constitution or inherent balance of doṣas that is determined at the time of conception. This constitution remains constant throughout life and governs an individual's physiological, psychological, and behavioural traits.

Prakṛti classification is a cornerstone of Ayurvedic diagnostics, guiding preventive, therapeutic, and lifestyle recommendations. It is broadly categorized into three main types based on the dominance of one or more doṣas:

- **Vāta Prakṛti:** Associated with qualities of movement, lightness, and irregularity.
- **Pitta Prakṛti:** Characterized by heat, intensity, and sharpness.
- **Kapha Prakṛti:** Linked to stability, heaviness, and moisture.

The Need for Integrating Ayurveda with Genomics

Despite its holistic approach, Ayurveda has often been regarded as subjective due to its reliance on qualitative assessments. Modern genomics offers an opportunity to validate and refine Ayurvedic concepts through scientific inquiry, transforming traditional knowledge into a data-driven framework. Ayurgenomics addresses this gap by identifying genetic markers associated with Prakṛti types, thereby offering a molecular basis for personalized medicine.

Significance of Ayurgenomics

The integration of Ayurveda and genomics holds profound implications for healthcare:

1. **Personalized Medicine:** Ayurgenomics provides insights into individual predispositions to diseases and responses to treatments based on genetic and Prakṛti analysis.
2. **Preventive Healthcare:** Understanding genetic predispositions aligned with Prakṛti can enable early interventions to prevent disease onset.

3. **Bridging Traditional and Modern Medicine:** Ayurgenomics fosters interdisciplinary collaboration, enhancing the credibility and applicability of Ayurveda in modern healthcare.

Correlation Between Prakṛti and Genetics

The ancient Ayurvedic concept of Prakṛti is an intricate and comprehensive framework for understanding human individuality in terms of physiological, psychological, and behavioural characteristics. The growing field of Ayurgenomics explores the correlation between Prakṛti and genetics, seeking to provide a scientific basis for Ayurvedic principles and their applications in personalized medicine. By integrating traditional knowledge with advanced genomic tools, Ayurgenomics is uncovering the genetic underpinnings of Prakṛti types and their relevance to health and disease.

Prakṛti: A Genomic Perspective

Prakṛti is determined by the dominance of one or more of the three doṣas: Vāta, Pitta, and Kapha, which influence every aspect of an individual's constitution, including physical appearance, metabolism, mental tendencies, and susceptibility to diseases. Traditionally, Prakṛti is assessed through qualitative observations, including a person's physical traits, digestion, sleep patterns, and mental state. However, modern scientific methodologies, such as genomic analysis, are beginning to validate these observations and link them to specific genetic patterns.

Bridging Traditional Wisdom and Modern Genomics

Ayurveda has long maintained that Prakṛti is innate and remains constant throughout life, influenced at conception by parental characteristics, intrauterine conditions, and environmental factors. Genomics offers a lens through which this inherited predisposition can be studied. The primary objectives of exploring Prakṛti through a genomic perspective include:

- Identifying genetic markers associated with different Prakṛti types.
- Understanding the molecular mechanisms underlying doṣa dominance.
- Investigating gene-environment interactions that influence health outcomes.

Through genome-wide association studies (GWAS), single nucleotide polymorphism (SNP) analysis, and epigenetic profiling, researchers have started identifying genetic patterns correlating with Prakṛti classifications.

Genomic Studies on Prakṛti

The convergence of Ayurveda and genomics has provided a fertile ground for exploring the biological basis of Prakṛti classifications. Research in Ayurgenomics has sought to identify genetic and molecular markers that underpin the traits associated with Vāta, Pitta, and Kapha Prakṛti types, presenting an evidence-based perspective on this ancient classification system.

Initial Insights from Genomic Studies

Genomic research has made significant strides in elucidating the biological correlates of Prakṛti, and the findings have been illuminating.

1. **SNP Correlations:** Single nucleotide polymorphisms (SNPs) are small genetic variations that occur in a single DNA base pair. These variations are associated with traits ranging from metabolism to immunity. Studies have revealed:
   - **Vāta Prakṛti:** SNPs in genes regulating neurotransmitter functions, such as dopamine receptor D2 (DRD2), serotonin transporter (SLC6A4), and stress-related genes, are prevalent in Vāta-dominant individuals.
   - **Pitta Prakṛti:** Genetic polymorphisms in cytokine-producing genes, such as tumor necrosis factor-alpha (TNF-α) and interleukin-6 (IL-6), as well as genes regulating oxidative stress, are frequently observed in Pitta types.
   - **Kapha Prakṛti:** SNPs in genes such as FTO (fat mass and obesity-associated gene) and PPARG (peroxisome proliferator-activated receptor gamma), which influence lipid metabolism and energy conservation, are linked to Kapha dominance.

These SNP correlations form the genetic backbone of Prakṛti traits, providing a molecular explanation for the distinct physiological and psychological attributes associated with each type.

2. **Gene Expression Profiles:** Gene expression profiling reveals which genes are active or suppressed in different individuals. Studies using transcriptomics (RNA analysis) have shown:
   - **Vāta Types:** A heightened expression of genes involved in neurotransmitter synthesis and synaptic activity, correlating with their high mental agility and susceptibility to anxiety-related disorders.
   - **Pitta Types:** Elevated expression of genes involved in inflammatory responses, oxidative phosphorylation, and metabolic pathways, aligning with their robust digestion and thermoregulation.
   - **Kapha Types:** Increased expression of genes related to lipid biosynthesis and immune

modulation, consistent with their strong physical structure and slower metabolism.

3. **Epigenetic Modifications:** Epigenetics, which studies how external factors modify gene activity without altering the DNA sequence, is key to understanding Prakṛti in the context of lifestyle and environment.
   - **DNA Methylation:** Differences in methylation patterns have been observed across Prakṛti types, influencing gene activity related to metabolism, stress response, and immunity.
   - **Histone Acetylation:** Histone modifications, influenced by diet and physical activity, have been linked to Prakṛti-specific traits, underscoring the dynamic interplay between genes and lifestyle.
4. **Microbiome Diversity:** Recent research on the gut microbiome—the diverse community of microorganisms in the human digestive system—has provided insights into Prakṛti classifications.
   - **Vāta Types:** Display reduced microbial diversity, often linked to irregular digestion and increased susceptibility to gut-related disorders.
   - **Pitta Types:** Exhibit a microbiome composition conducive to efficient digestion and rapid metabolic processes.
   - **Kapha Types:** Possess a microbiome enriched in bacteria associated with lipid metabolism and energy storage, reflecting their robust but slower metabolism.

Genetic Traits of Doṣa Dominance

The three doṣas—Vāta, Pitta, and Kapha—define not just an individual's physical constitution but also their predispositions to health and disease. Genomic studies provide insights into the molecular underpinnings of these constitutional types.

1. **Vāta Prakṛti**
   - Vāta is characterized by movement and dynamism, governing neural activity, circulation, and communication between bodily systems.

   Neural and Stress Regulation: Vāta-dominant individuals often have genetic markers influencing neurotransmitter pathways:

   - **Dopamine Receptors (DRD2):** Variations associated with impulsivity and sensitivity.
   - **Serotonin Transporter (SLC6A4):** Linked to mood regulation and stress response.
   - **CRHR1 (Corticotropin-Releasing Hormone Receptor 1):** Variants associated with heightened cortisol production, explaining stress susceptibility.

   Metabolic Adaptability: PGC-1α (PPARGC1A): A regulator of mitochondrial biogenesis, explaining the irregular energy levels and metabolic variability of Vāta types.

   Digestive and Musculoskeletal Susceptibilities

   - **COL1A1 (Collagen Type I Alpha 1):** Variants associated with joint and bone disorders align with Vāta's predisposition to musculoskeletal issues.
2. **Pitta Prakṛti:** Pitta governs metabolic and transformative processes, including digestion, thermoregulation, and hormonal balance.

   Inflammatory and Immune Responses

   - **TNF-α (Tumor Necrosis Factor-alpha) and IL-6 (Interleukin-6):** Polymorphisms linked to heightened inflammatory responses.
   - **NRF2 (Nuclear Factor Erythroid 2-Related Factor 2):** Variants contributing to oxidative stress resistance.

   Thermoregulatory Efficiency

   - **UCP2 (Uncoupling Protein 2) and UCP3 (Uncoupling Protein 3):** Genes regulating heat production and metabolic rate, explaining the robust thermoregulation of Pitta types.

   Hormonal and Digestive Efficiency

   - **CYP2C19 (Cytochrome P450 2C19):** Variants in this enzyme influence efficient drug metabolism and digestion in Pitta-dominant individuals.
3. **Kapha Prakṛti:** Kapha is associated with stability and anabolic processes, governing immunity, growth, and structural integrity.

   Energy Storage and Lipid Metabolism

   - **FTO (Fat Mass and Obesity-Associated Gene):** Variants promoting lipid storage and predisposition to weight gain.
   - **APOE (Apolipoprotein E):** Linked to cholesterol transport and slower lipid metabolism.

   Immune Resilience

   - **HLA-DRB1 (Human Leukocyte Antigen DR Beta 1):** Variants associated with robust immune responses.
   - **TLR4 (Toll-Like Receptor 4):** Contributing to infection resistance and slower inflammatory responses.

   Growth and Structural Traits

   - **IGF1 (Insulin-Like Growth Factor 1):** Regulating anabolic growth, explaining Kapha's strong physical constitution.

Gene-Environment Interactions

One of the most striking features of Ayurveda is its emphasis on the interplay between genetics (Nija Prakṛti) and environmental factors (Deśa, Kāla, and Āhāra). Modern genomics has shed light on the molecular mechanisms underlying this interaction.

1. **Epigenetics in Prakṛti:** Epigenetic modifications play a critical role in linking environmental influences to genetic expression.

   DNA Methylation: Methylation patterns influenced by dietary habits align with Ayurvedic dietary prescriptions for Vāta, Pitta, and Kapha individuals, supporting optimal gene activity.

   Histone Modifications: Ayurvedic lifestyle interventions, such as yoga and meditation, have been shown to enhance histone acetylation, reducing stress and promoting health.

2. **Seasonal and Environmental Adaptations:** Ayurveda prescribes seasonal routines (Ṛtucharya) and environmental adjustments to maintain doṣa balance. Genomic studies reveal that:
   - **Seasonal Variations in Gene Expression:** Gene activity linked to immunity and metabolism fluctuates seasonally, aligning with Ayurvedic principles.

3. **Personalized Diet and Lifestyle:** The gene-diet interaction emphasizes personalized nutrition:
   - **Vāta Diets:** Rich in grounding and nourishing foods to counteract genetic tendencies toward irregular digestion and stress.
   - **Pitta Diets:** Cooling and anti-inflammatory foods to mitigate genetic predispositions to inflammation.
   - **Kapha Diets:** Low-calorie and light foods to address genetic traits favoring weight gain.

Implications for Healthcare and Personalized Medicine

The integration of Ayurgenomics into healthcare has far-reaching implications:

1. **Disease Prevention:** Early identification of genetic predispositions aligned with Prakṛti types enables targeted preventive measures.
2. **Personalized Therapies:** Tailoring treatments to an individual's genetic profile and Prakṛti ensures higher efficacy.
3. **Holistic Interventions:** Combining genomic insights with Ayurvedic practices offers a comprehensive approach to health.

Future Directions: While Ayurgenomics is in its infancy, future research could focus on:

- Expanding sample sizes and populations to validate findings.
- Exploring the microbiome's role in greater detail.
- Integrating genomic data into clinical Ayurveda practice for personalized care.

The convergence of Ayurveda and genomics holds the promise of revolutionizing healthcare, making it more personalized, preventive, and holistic.

Challenges in Ayurgenomics Research

While the findings are promising, Ayurgenomics faces several challenges:

1. **Subjectivity in Prakṛti Assessment:** The reliance on qualitative methods for Prakṛti classification introduces variability in research outcomes.
2. **Complexity of Genetic Interactions:** The intricate interplay of multiple genes and environmental factors complicates the identification of specific genetic markers.
3. **Sample Size and Diversity:** Many studies are limited by small sample sizes and lack of diversity, which may affect the generalizability of findings.
4. **Integration with Modern Medicine:** Bridging the gap between traditional Ayurvedic concepts and the rigorous standards of modern scientific research requires interdisciplinary collaboration.

FUTURE DIRECTIONS AND APPLICATIONS

Personalized Healthcare

The insights gained from Ayurgenomics research could revolutionize healthcare by enabling personalized interventions based on an individual's genetic and Prakṛti profile. This approach aligns with the growing emphasis on precision medicine in modern healthcare.

Drug Discovery and Development

Ayurgenomics offers a novel approach to drug discovery by identifying genetic factors influencing drug efficacy and safety. Ayurvedic formulations can be refined and validated through genomic studies, ensuring their efficacy for specific genetic profiles.

Preventive Medicine

By identifying genetic predispositions to diseases based on Prakṛti, Ayurgenomics facilitates early interventions and lifestyle modifications, reducing the risk of disease onset.

Global Integration

The integration of Ayurgenomics into mainstream healthcare systems could promote global acceptance of Ayurveda as a scientifically validated medical system. Collaborative research initiatives and cross-disciplinary partnerships will be crucial for achieving this goal.

MULTIPLE CHOICE QUESTIONS

1. A researcher is exploring the link between Ayurvedic Prakṛti classifications and modern genomic science. In an extensive study, participants were categorized into Vāta, Pitta, and Kapha Prakṛtis based on Ayurvedic diagnostic methods. Genomic analysis was conducted to identify specific gene expression profiles for each group. The study found that individuals with Vāta dominance exhibited high variability in metabolic gene expression, particularly those regulating mitochondrial activity, while Pitta individuals showed consistent upregulation of inflammatory cytokines. Kapha individuals had a gene expression profile associated with lipid metabolism and energy storage. How do these findings most effectively support the integration of Ayurvedic principles into modern genomic frameworks?

A. Ayurvedic classifications are supported by observable molecular traits, validating Prakṛti as a physiological construct.

B. The genomic analysis disproves the concept of Prakṛti, as variability within groups cannot be reconciled with Ayurvedic principles.

C. Modern genomic tools lack the specificity to correlate with Ayurvedic classifications, making such studies irrelevant.

D. The findings demonstrate that Ayurvedic classifications are symbolic and lack a biological basis.

2. Imagine a scenario where a geneticist investigates the epigenetic influence of dietary interventions recommended for Vāta Prakṛti. The study tracks DNA methylation patterns in genes linked to stress regulation and circadian rhythms, observing significant demethylation in stress-associated genes following the prescribed dietary changes. At the same time, gene expression for melatonin synthesis is upregulated, improving participants' sleep quality. How should the researcher interpret these results in the context of Ayurvedic dietary recommendations?

A. The study validates that Ayurvedic dietary practices can induce measurable epigenetic changes aligned with Prakṛti-specific needs.

B. Epigenetic effects are unrelated to Ayurvedic dietary interventions and occur due to environmental variations.

C. Dietary changes cannot influence DNA methylation, as epigenetic mechanisms are constitutionally fixed.

D. The findings challenge the applicability of Ayurvedic dietary recommendations, as no direct correlation with health outcomes is observed.

3. A clinical researcher is studying the relationship between doshas and gut microbiota diversity. Participants categorized as Kapha-dominant exhibited microbiomes enriched in Firmicutes, associated with energy extraction and weight gain. Pitta-dominant individuals had higher proportions of Bacteroidetes, linked to efficient digestion and lower inflammation levels. Vāta-dominant individuals displayed reduced microbial diversity and frequent gastrointestinal issues. How do these observations align with Ayurvedic principles regarding the physiological characteristics of doshas?

A. The study supports Ayurvedic descriptions of doshas by correlating gut microbiota profiles with Prakṛti-specific traits.

B. The findings undermine Ayurveda by demonstrating that microbial diversity is independent of dosha classification.

C. Gut microbiota variations are random and unrelated to Ayurvedic classifications of Prakṛti.

D. The study disproves any connection between gut health and Ayurvedic principles.

4. Researchers are examining the molecular mechanisms behind the Ayurvedic concept of Agni (digestive fire). They hypothesize that Agni corresponds to the activity of digestive enzymes like lipase and protease. In a controlled study, individuals with Mandagni (weak digestive fire) exhibit reduced enzymatic activity, while participants with balanced Agni show optimal levels of enzyme function. After Ayurvedic interventions, enzymatic activity improves significantly in the Mandagni group. What conclusion can best be drawn from these findings?

A. Agni's physiological role in Ayurveda is validated by its correlation with measurable enzymatic activity.

B. Ayurvedic concepts of Agni and enzymatic activity are unrelated and cannot be scientifically integrated.

C. Mandagni is purely a theoretical construct with no measurable basis in enzymatic studies.
D. The improvements in enzymatic activity are independent of Ayurvedic interventions and result from external factors.

5. A biologist investigates how Ayurvedic Rasas (tastes) influence metabolic pathways. The study focuses on the sweet and bitter Rasas, hypothesizing that the sweet Rasa is linked to anabolic processes and the bitter Rasa to catabolic processes. Genetic analysis reveals that individuals consuming bitter Rasa foods show upregulation of autophagy-related genes, while those consuming sweet Rasa foods exhibit increased expression of genes promoting glycogen synthesis. What interpretation best connects these results to Ayurvedic principles?
   A. Ayurvedic Rasas are supported by genetic evidence, showing distinct influences on metabolic regulation.
   B. Rasas have no measurable impact on metabolism, contradicting Ayurvedic claims about their physiological effects.
   C. The observed genetic changes are unrelated to the Ayurvedic classification of Rasas and result from other dietary factors.
   D. Sweet and bitter Rasas influence metabolism in contradictory ways, invalidating Ayurvedic dietary theories.

6. A study examines the role of genetic markers in determining susceptibility to stress-related disorders among Vāta-dominant individuals. The researchers find a higher prevalence of polymorphisms in serotonin transporter genes (SLC6A4) and corticotropin-releasing hormone receptor genes (CRHR1) in Vāta individuals, correlating with increased cortisol levels and anxiety. How should these findings be interpreted in relation to Ayurvedic descriptions of Vāta characteristics?
   A. The study validates Vāta Prakṛti's association with stress sensitivity through measurable genetic markers.
   B. Genetic variations have no correlation with Ayurvedic classifications, undermining Vāta's stress-related traits.
   C. The observed polymorphisms disprove the link between Vāta and stress susceptibility in Ayurveda.
   D. Stress-related traits in Vāta Prakṛti are psychosomatic and not influenced by genetic factors.

7. Environmental scientists investigate the impact of climate change on medicinal plants used in Ayurveda, focusing on Amalaki (Emblica officinalis). They observe that rising temperatures and deforestation reduce the fruit's concentration of bioactive compounds, compromising its efficacy in formulations like Triphala. How might these findings influence the therapeutic applications of Ayurveda in a changing environment?
   A. Climate change challenges the efficacy of Ayurvedic formulations, necessitating synthetic alternatives to natural ingredients.
   B. Ayurvedic formulations are unaffected by environmental changes, as their potency is independent of ingredient quality.
   C. The therapeutic impact of Ayurvedic remedies can be sustained by adapting formulations to include alternative plants.
   D. Environmental degradation limits the applicability of Ayurveda, reducing its relevance in modern healthcare.

8. A longitudinal study investigates the effects of seasonal routines (Ṛtucharya) on gene expression in individuals classified by Prakṛti. Participants following seasonal regimens aligned with their dosha exhibited reduced inflammatory gene expression during winter and increased antioxidant gene activity during summer. What conclusion best explains these observations?
   A. Seasonal adjustments prescribed in Ayurveda have measurable effects on gene expression, validating Ṛtucharya's scientific basis.
   B. Seasonal regimens have no direct influence on genetic activity and are purely philosophical constructs.
   C. Dosha-based seasonal routines disrupt genetic homeostasis, challenging Ayurveda's health claims.
   D. The study suggests that seasonal variations in gene expression occur independently of Ayurvedic interventions.

9. A clinical trial evaluates the effectiveness of Ayurveda-based Panchakarma therapy in reducing markers of systemic inflammation. Patients with elevated levels of C-reactive protein (CRP) undergo Panchakarma, resulting in significant reductions in CRP and improved metabolic profiles. How should these results be interpreted in the context of Ayurvedic detoxification principles?
   A. Panchakarma effectively reduces systemic inflammation, supporting its role in Ayurveda's detoxification framework.
   B. The observed improvements are unrelated to Panchakarma, indicating a placebo effect rather than a therapeutic one.
   C. Systemic inflammation is not influenced by Ayurvedic therapies, challenging the validity of Panchakarma.
   D. The results suggest that Panchakarma has no measurable impact on metabolic health.

10. A pharmacologist is developing synthetic analogs of Ayurvedic herbs to address supply chain issues for medicinal plants. The research identifies the active compound in Haritaki as a key regulator of gut microbiota diversity and inflammatory pathways. The synthetic analog shows equivalent efficacy in clinical trials. How should this development be viewed in the context of Ayurvedic medicine?

A. Synthetic alternatives validate Ayurveda's scientific principles while addressing sustainability concerns.

B. The use of synthetic compounds undermines the holistic approach of Ayurveda, limiting its therapeutic relevance.

C. Ayurveda cannot accommodate synthetic developments, as its principles are rooted in natural formulations.

D. Synthetic analogs are less effective than traditional herbs and fail to capture Ayurveda's holistic benefits.

Directions (Q. No. 11-14): Scenarios-Based Questions

SCENARIO 1

A team of biomedical researchers is conducting an integrative study to explore the relationship between genetic variations and the physiological traits associated with the Ayurvedic concept of Prakṛti. Their work focuses on identifying polymorphisms in inflammatory and metabolic genes across individuals classified into Vāta, Pitta, and Kapha Prakṛtis. The researchers find that TNF-α and IL-6 polymorphisms are strongly associated with Pitta-dominant individuals, correlating with their propensity for inflammatory disorders. Similarly, FTO and PPARG polymorphisms, which regulate lipid storage and metabolism, are prevalent in Kapha individuals, reflecting their higher risk of obesity and slower metabolism. Vāta individuals show polymorphisms in DRD2 and SLC6A4, associated with stress sensitivity and irregular metabolic responses. However, the study also highlights the influence of lifestyle factors on genetic expression, emphasizing that epigenetic changes modulate the outcomes of these polymorphisms.

SCENARIO 2

Simultaneously, an ecological biologist is examining the sustainability of sourcing medicinal plants for Ayurvedic formulations. The study focuses on Triphala, a combination of three fruits: Amalaki, Bibhitaki, and Haritaki. The research reveals that the rising demand for Triphala has led to unsustainable harvesting practices, particularly for Amalaki, whose wild populations are declining due to overexploitation and habitat degradation. The biologist discovers that environmental stress reduces the concentration of bioactive compounds in Amalaki, Bibhitaki, and Haritaki. This reduced quality adversely impacts the efficacy of formulations, especially in promoting gut health and immune modulation. Interestingly, the ecological findings raise concerns about how diminishing ingredient quality might compromise the therapeutic benefits observed in Scenario 1, particularly the ability of Triphala to support systemic inflammation reduction and gut microbiota diversity.

11. Based on Scenario 1, which mechanism best explains how genetic predispositions linked to Prakṛti are modulated by lifestyle and environmental factors?

A. Genetic polymorphisms fully determine an individual's health outcomes, irrespective of lifestyle influences.

B. Epigenetic changes, such as DNA methylation and histone modifications, alter gene expression, mitigating the risks associated with genetic predispositions.

C. Ayurvedic interventions are unrelated to genetic predispositions and cannot influence gene expression.

D. Lifestyle factors exacerbate genetic risks, making Ayurvedic classifications less relevant in modern contexts.

12. Considering Scenario 2, which intervention would best ensure the sustainable production of Triphala while preserving its therapeutic efficacy?

A. Establishing large-scale monoculture plantations for Amalaki and Bibhitaki to meet growing global demand.

B. Promoting community-led conservation efforts and agroforestry practices to protect wild populations of Triphala components.

C. Reducing the reliance on natural formulations and shifting to synthetic alternatives for all three fruits.

D. Decreasing global production of Triphala formulations to prevent overharvesting and habitat loss.

13. How does the reduced quality of Amalaki described in Scenario 2 potentially impact the therapeutic outcomes linked to Triphala in Scenario 1?

A. Reduced bioactive compound levels in Amalaki directly diminish its efficacy in promoting gut microbiota diversity and reducing inflammation.

B. Triphala's effectiveness remains unaffected, as its benefits are derived from the synergy of all three fruits rather than individual components.

C. The reduced quality of Amalaki enhances the therapeutic properties of Triphala by altering its bioactive composition.

D. Amalaki's quality has no measurable impact on the efficacy of Triphala, as the formulation's potency is determined during preparation.

14. Based on the intertwined findings of Scenarios 1 and 2, which comprehensive strategy would best address the challenges of preserving Ayurvedic efficacy and sustainability?
   A. Developing bioengineered alternatives to Triphala components to ensure consistent therapeutic benefits.
   B. Establishing stringent global quality standards for Triphala formulations, emphasizing sustainable harvesting and ingredient potency.
   C. Transitioning to formulations that do not depend on endangered plant species, ensuring continued therapeutic efficacy.
   D. Encouraging large-scale commercialization of Triphala components to meet global demand without traditional ecological considerations.

15. The core principles of Ayurgenomics emphasize the interplay between Prakṛti and genetic predispositions. Consider the following statements regarding Prakṛti classification and its genetic basis:
   (a) Vāta Prakṛti is associated with genetic markers linked to nervous system regulation and stress sensitivity.
   (b) Pitta Prakṛti corresponds to genes regulating inflammatory pathways and thermogenesis.
   (c) Kapha Prakṛti exhibits genetic variations associated with lipid metabolism and immune modulation.
   (d) Genetic polymorphisms fully account for all physiological traits described in Prakṛti without environmental influences.

   Choose the correct answer from the options given below:
   A. (a), (b), and (c) only
   B. (a), (b), and (d) only
   C. (b), (c), and (d) only
   D. (a), (c), and (d) only

16. The following observations are noted in studies linking Ayurvedic interventions to epigenetic changes:
   (a) DNA methylation patterns are influenced by dietary regimens tailored to an individual's Prakṛti.
   (b) Histone acetylation is enhanced by Ayurvedic practices such as yoga and meditation.
   (c) Epigenetic changes induced by Ayurveda are reversible and vary with lifestyle factors.
   (d) Ayurvedic interventions have no measurable impact on epigenetic mechanisms.

   Choose the correct answer from the options given below:
   A. (a), (b), and (c) only
   B. (b), (c), and (d) only
   C. (a), (c), and (d) only
   D. (a), (b), and (d) only

17. Consider the biological implications of Ayurvedic Rasas (tastes) based on recent research:
   (a) Sweet Rasa promotes anabolic processes and tissue nourishment.
   (b) Bitter Rasa enhances autophagy and detoxification mechanisms.
   (c) Astringent Rasa strengthens tissues and reduces oxidative stress.
   (d) Sour Rasa has negligible effects on metabolic pathways.

   Choose the correct answer from the options given below:
   A. (a), (b), and (c) only
   B. (b), (c), and (d) only
   C. (a), (c), and (d) only
   D. (a), (b), and (d) only

18. Match the following Prakṛti-specific traits with their physiological correlates:

(a) Vāta Prakṛti	1. Irregular appetite and stress susceptibility
(b) Pitta Prakṛti	2. High metabolic efficiency and thermoregulation
(c) Kapha Prakṛti	3. Slow metabolism and strong physical structure
(d) All Prakṛti types	4. Identical genetic profiles without physiological variations

   Choose the correct answer from the options given below:
   A. (a)-1, (b)-2, (c)-3, (d)-4
   B. (a)-3, (b)-1, (c)-2, (d)-4
   C. (a)-1, (b)-2, (c)-3 only
   D. (a)-2, (b)-3, (c)-1 only

19. Based on genomic studies, Ayurvedic interventions are observed to influence the following:
   (a) Gut microbiota diversity and immune regulation.
   (b) Mitochondrial biogenesis through lifestyle practices.
   (c) Oxidative stress pathways via targeted herbal formulations.
   (d) Gene mutations that permanently alter genetic sequences.

   Choose the correct answer from the options given below:
   A. (a), (b), and (c) only
   B. (b), (c), and (d) only
   C. (a), (c), and (d) only
   D. (a), (b), and (d) only

20. Ayurvedic detoxification therapies, such as Panchakarma, have demonstrated measurable physiological effects. Identify the observed benefits supported by scientific research:

(a) Reduction in systemic inflammation markers like CRP.
(b) Enhancement of lipid profiles through metabolic modulation.
(c) Permanent alteration of genetic predispositions to diseases.
(d) Improved antioxidant capacity at a cellular level.

Choose the correct answer from the options given below:
A. (a), (b), and (d) only
B. (b), (c), and (d) only
C. (a), (c), and (d) only
D. (a), (b), and (c) only

21. Recent research correlates Ayurvedic Prakṛti classifications with specific genetic variations:
(a) Vāta-dominant individuals show polymorphisms in DRD2 and CRHR1 genes.
(b) Pitta Prakṛti is linked to variations in TNF-α and IL-6.
(c) Kapha types exhibit genetic markers associated with APOE and FTO.
(d) All genetic variations are unrelated to Prakṛti and only influenced by lifestyle.

Choose the correct answer from the options given below:
A. (a), (b), and (c) only
B. (b), (c), and (d) only
C. (a), (c), and (d) only
D. (a), (b), and (d) only

22. Consider the environmental and sustainability challenges of medicinal plants used in Ayurveda:
(a) Overharvesting reduces the bioactive compound concentration in medicinal plants.
(b) Monoculture farming enhances the efficacy of Ayurvedic herbs.
(c) Traditional agroforestry systems improve plant resilience and quality.
(d) Climate change has no measurable impact on the therapeutic properties of plants.

Choose the correct answer from the options given below:
A. (a), (b), and (c) only
B. (b), (c), and (d) only
C. (a), (c), and (d) only
D. (a), (b), and (d) only

23. Studies linking Prakṛti with disease susceptibility reveal the following patterns:
(a) Vāta types are more prone to neurological disorders due to stress-related gene polymorphisms.
(b) Pitta types have higher risks of inflammatory and metabolic disorders.
(c) Kapha individuals are less susceptible to obesity and related diseases.
(d) Lifestyle modifications influence disease outcomes across all Prakṛti types.

Choose the correct answer from the options given below:
A. (a), (b), and (d) only
B. (a), (c), and (d) only
C. (b), (c), and (d) only
D. (a), (b), and (c) only

24. Epigenetic mechanisms in Ayurvedic interventions are supported by the following observations:
(a) DNA methylation is influenced by diet and meditation practices.
(b) Ayurvedic formulations induce histone acetylation, improving stress resilience.
(c) Epigenetic changes are irreversible, ensuring long-term benefits.
(d) Environmental and lifestyle factors mediate the expression of genes associated with Prakṛti.

Choose the correct answer from the options given below:
A. (a), (b), and (d) only
B. (b), (c), and (d) only
C. (a), (c), and (d) only
D. (a), (b), and (c) only

25. Match List–I (Components of Ayurgenomics) with List–II (Descriptions) and choose the correct answer from the options given below:

List–I	List–II
(a) Doṣa-Prakṛti Analysis	1. Classification of body constitution into Vāta, Pitta, and Kapha
(b) Genetic Markers	2. Polymorphisms linked to metabolic, immune, and neurological traits
(c) Epigenetic Modifications	3. Influence of lifestyle factors like diet and environment on gene expression
(d) Gut Microbiota	4. Modulation by Ayurvedic interventions to enhance systemic immunity

Choose the correct answer from the options given below:
A. (a)-1, (b)-2, (c)-3, (d)-4
B. (a)-2, (b)-1, (c)-4, (d)-3
C. (a)-3, (b)-4, (c)-1, (d)-2
D. (a)-4, (b)-3, (c)-2, (d)-1

26. Match List–I (Genetic Traits by Prakṛti) with List–II (Physiological Correlates) and choose the correct answer from the options given below:

List–I	List–II
(a) Vāta Prakṛti	1. Polymorphisms in DRD2 and SLC6A4, linked to stress sensitivity
(b) Pitta Prakṛti	2. TNF-α and IL-6 variations, correlating with inflammatory responses
(c) Kapha Prakṛti	3. FTO and APOE polymorphisms, promoting lipid storage and metabolism
(d) All Prakṛti Types	4. Modulated by gene-environment interactions

Choose the correct answer from the options given below:

A. (a)-1, (b)-2, (c)-3, (d)-4
B. (a)-2, (b)-1, (c)-4, (d)-3
C. (a)-3, (b)-4, (c)-1, (d)-2
D. (a)-4, (b)-3, (c)-2, (d)-1

27. Match List–I (Ayurvedic Concepts) with List–II (Scientific Correlations) and choose the correct answer from the options given below:

List–I	List–II
(a) Prakṛti Classification	1. Reflects genetic predispositions shaped during conception
(b) Agni (Digestive Fire)	2. Corresponds to enzymatic and metabolic activity
(c) Ama (Toxins)	3. Linked to impaired metabolic and detox pathways
(d) Rasayana Therapy	4. Enhances antioxidant capacity and reduces inflammation

Choose the correct answer from the options given below:

A. (a)-1, (b)-2, (c)-3, (d)-4
B. (a)-2, (b)-1, (c)-4, (d)-3
C. (a)-3, (b)-4, (c)-1, (d)-2
D. (a)-4, (b)-3, (c)-2, (d)-1

28. Match List–I (Ayurvedic Interventions) with List–II (Effects Observed) and choose the correct answer from the options given below:

List–I	List–II
(a) Seasonal Routines (Ṛtucharya)	1. Aligns gene expression with seasonal changes
(b) Prakṛti-Specific Diets	2. Modulates DNA methylation and metabolic pathways
(c) Panchakarma Detox	3. Reduces systemic inflammation markers like CRP
(d) Triphala Formulation	4. Improves gut microbiota diversity and immune function

Choose the correct answer from the options given below:

A. (a)-1, (b)-2, (c)-3, (d)-4
B. (a)-2, (b)-1, (c)-4, (d)-3
C. (a)-3, (b)-4, (c)-1, (d)-2
D. (a)-4, (b)-3, (c)-2, (d)-1

29. Match List–I (Prakṛti Susceptibilities) with List–II (Health Implications) and choose the correct answer from the options given below:

List–I	List–II
(a) Vāta Prakṛti	1. Higher risk of neurological and musculoskeletal disorders
(b) Pitta Prakṛti	2. Prone to inflammatory and metabolic conditions
(c) Kapha Prakṛti	3. Increased susceptibility to obesity and cardiovascular diseases
(d) Balanced Tridosha	4. Associated with optimal physiological health and resilience

Choose the correct answer from the options given below:

A. (a)-1, (b)-2, (c)-3, (d)-4
B. (a)-2, (b)-1, (c)-4, (d)-3
C. (a)-3, (b)-4, (c)-1, (d)-2
D. (a)-4, (b)-3, (c)-2, (d)-1

30. Match List–I (Genetic Research Findings) with List–II (Relevance to Prakṛti) and choose the correct answer from the options given below:

List–I	List–II
(a) TNF-α Polymorphisms	1. Correlates with inflammatory traits in Pitta Prakṛti
(b) FTO Variations	2. Linked to obesity risk in Kapha individuals
(c) DRD2 Polymorphisms	3. Associated with stress susceptibility in Vāta Prakṛti
(d) APOE Gene Variants	4. Reflects lipid metabolism efficiency in Kapha Prakṛti

Choose the correct answer from the options given below:

A. (a)-1, (b)-2, (c)-3, (d)-4
B. (a)-2, (b)-1, (c)-4, (d)-3
C. (a)-3, (b)-4, (c)-1, (d)-2
D. (a)-4, (b)-3, (c)-2, (d)-1

31. Match List–I (Epigenetic Mechanisms) with List–II (Ayurvedic Practices) and choose the correct answer from the options given below:

List–I	List–II
(a) DNA Methylation	1. Modulated by diet and detox therapies
(b) Histone Acetylation	2. Enhanced by yoga and meditation
(c) Non-Coding RNA	3. Regulated by herbal formulations
(d) All Mechanisms	4. Influenced by lifestyle factors like Ṛtucharya

Choose the correct answer from the options given below:

A. (a)-1, (b)-2, (c)-3, (d)-4
B. (a)-2, (b)-1, (c)-4, (d)-3
C. (a)-3, (b)-4, (c)-1, (d)-2
D. (a)-4, (b)-3, (c)-2, (d)-1

32. Match List–I (Gut Microbiota Findings) with List–II (Prakṛti Observations) and choose the correct answer from the options given below:

List–I	List–II
(a) Vāta Prakṛti	1. Reduced microbial diversity, prone to gastrointestinal issues
(b) Pitta Prakṛti	2. Higher proportions of Bacteroidetes for metabolic efficiency
(c) Kapha Prakṛti	3. Dominance of Firmicutes linked to lipid metabolism
(d) All Prakṛti Types	4. Modulated by dietary and lifestyle practices

Choose the correct answer from the options given below:

A. (a)-1, (b)-2, (c)-3, (d)-4
B. (a)-2, (b)-1, (c)-4, (d)-3
C. (a)-3, (b)-4, (c)-1, (d)-2
D. (a)-4, (b)-3, (c)-2, (d)-1

33. Match List–I (Ayurvedic Therapeutics) with List–II (Mechanisms of Action) and choose the correct answer from the options given below:

List–I	List–II
(a) Rasayana Therapy	1. Boosts antioxidant pathways and immune resilience
(b) Herbal Formulations	2. Modulate gut microbiota diversity and metabolism
(c) Panchakarma Detox	3. Eliminates toxins and reduces systemic inflammation
(d) Seasonal Routines	4. Aligns physiological processes with environmental changes

Choose the correct answer from the options given below:

A. (a)-1, (b)-2, (c)-3, (d)-4
B. (a)-2, (b)-1, (c)-4, (d)-3
C. (a)-3, (b)-4, (c)-1, (d)-2
D. (a)-4, (b)-3, (c)-2, (d)-1

34. Match List–I (Sustainability Challenges) with List–II (Proposed Solutions) and choose the correct answer from the options given below:

List–I	List–II
(a) Overharvesting of Amalaki	1. Promote agroforestry practices
(b) Reduced bioactive compounds	2. Develop synthetic alternatives for Ayurvedic herbs
(c) Habitat loss	3. Advocate for conservation of wild populations
(d) Increasing global demand	4. Establish standardized Ayurvedic formulations

Choose the correct answer from the options given below:

A. (a)-1, (b)-2, (c)-3, (d)-4
B. (a)-2, (b)-1, (c)-4, (d)-3
C. (a)-3, (b)-4, (c)-1, (d)-2
D. (a)-4, (b)-3, (c)-2, (d)-1

Directions (Q. No. 35–39): *Following questions are based on Statement 1 and Statement 2. Read both the statements carefully and choose the correct answer from the options given below:*

A. Both Statement 1 and Statement 2 are true, and Statement 2 is the correct explanation of Statement 1.
B. Both Statement 1 and Statement 2 are true, but Statement 2 is not the correct explanation of Statement 1.
C. Statement 1 is true, but Statement 2 is false.
D. Statement 1 is false, but Statement 2 is true.
E. Both Statement 1 and Statement 2 are false.

35. **Statement 1:** Ayurgenomics establishes a direct relationship between an individual's genetic makeup and their Prakṛti classification in Ayurveda.

Statement 2: Prakṛti is determined entirely by genetic factors without any influence from environmental or lifestyle variables.

36. **Statement 1:** Genetic research supports the association of FTO and PPARG polymorphisms with Kapha Prakṛti, explaining their predisposition to weight gain and slower metabolism.

Statement 2: Kapha individuals demonstrate increased thermogenesis and energy expenditure compared to other Prakṛti types.

37. **Statement 1:** Pitta Prakṛti is associated with increased metabolic efficiency and inflammatory responses due to specific cytokine gene polymorphisms like TNF-α and IL-6.

Statement 2: Ayurvedic interventions for Pitta Prakṛti, such as cooling diets and anti-inflammatory herbs, modulate inflammatory markers at a genetic level.

38. **Statement 1:** Epigenetic modifications, such as DNA methylation, are influenced by Prakṛti-specific diets and lifestyle regimens in Ayurveda.

    Statement 2: Epigenetic changes induced by Ayurvedic interventions are permanent and cannot revert to the baseline state.

39. **Statement 1:** Ayurvedic formulations like Triphala improve gut health by enhancing microbiota diversity and reducing systemic inflammation.

    Statement 2: The therapeutic efficacy of Triphala is unaffected by the quality of its ingredients, as its benefits arise from its preparation process rather than its components.

Directions (Q. No. 40–45): *There are two statements in each question. One is labelled as Assertion (A) and the other is as Reason (R). Read both the statements and choose the correct answer from the options given below*:

A. Both Assertion (A) and Reason (R) are true, and Reason (R) is the correct explanation of Assertion (A).
B. Both Assertion (A) and Reason (R) are true, but Reason (R) is not the correct explanation of Assertion (A).
C. Assertion (A) is true, but Reason (R) is false.
D. Assertion (A) is false, but Reason (R) is true.
E. Both Assertion (A) and Reason (R) are false.

40. **Assertion (A):** Ayurvedic Prakṛti classifications align with modern genetic research, linking specific traits to measurable genetic variations.

    Reason (R): Genetic polymorphisms are entirely responsible for the physiological and psychological traits described in Prakṛti, without any influence from environmental or lifestyle factors.

41. **Assertion (A):** Pitta Prakṛti individuals are more prone to inflammatory disorders due to higher expression of inflammatory cytokine genes.

    Reason (R): Ayurvedic interventions for Pitta, such as cooling therapies and anti-inflammatory diets, do not influence gene expression or cytokine activity.

42. **Assertion (A):** Kapha Prakṛti is associated with increased lipid storage due to polymorphisms in genes such as FTO and PPARG.

    Reason (R): Lifestyle modifications, including low-calorie diets and physical activity, can mitigate the genetic predispositions of Kapha Prakṛti.

43. **Assertion (A):** Epigenetic mechanisms, such as histone acetylation, are influenced by Ayurvedic practices like yoga and meditation.

    Reason (R): Ayurvedic practices enhance stress resilience by permanently altering DNA sequences.

44. **Assertion (A):** The efficacy of Ayurvedic formulations, such as Triphala, depends on the quality and concentration of bioactive compounds in its ingredients.

    Reason (R): Sustainable harvesting practices ensure that medicinal plants retain their therapeutic properties by preventing environmental degradation.

45. **Assertion (A):** Ayurgenomics integrates Ayurvedic principles with modern genetic tools to develop personalized healthcare strategies.

    Reason (R): Prakṛti classifications are based on universal dosha balances that apply equally to all individuals, irrespective of their genetic makeup.

Directions (Q. No. 46–50): *Read the passage carefully and answer the questions given below*:

Ayurgenomics, an emerging field integrating Ayurveda and modern genomics, offers a transformative approach to understanding human individuality and personalized medicine. The ancient system of Ayurveda classifies individuals into three primary constitutional types, or Prakṛtis, namely Vāta, Pitta, and Kapha, based on the dominance of bio-energetic forces known as doṣas. This classification reflects not only physiological and psychological traits but also the susceptibility to diseases and therapeutic responses. Recent advancements in genomic and epigenomic research have begun to unravel the molecular basis of Prakṛti, establishing it as more than a theoretical construct. Studies have identified specific genetic markers associated with each Prakṛti. For instance, Vāta Prakṛti is linked to polymorphisms in dopamine receptor (DRD2) and serotonin transporter (SLC6A4) genes, explaining their heightened sensitivity to stress and irregular metabolic patterns. Pitta individuals exhibit variations in inflammatory cytokine genes such as TNF-α and IL-6, correlating with their predisposition to inflammatory and metabolic disorders. Meanwhile, Kapha Prakṛti shows polymorphisms in lipid metabolism-related genes like FTO and PPARG, reflecting their propensity for slower metabolism and weight gain.

Epigenetic research complements this genetic framework, demonstrating that environmental and lifestyle factors influence gene expression, a concept deeply ingrained in Ayurvedic philosophy. DNA methylation and histone acetylation, key epigenetic mechanisms, have been shown to respond to dietary and lifestyle modifications prescribed for specific Prakṛtis. For instance, Prakṛti-specific diets and regimens not only align with metabolic needs but also enhance the expression of genes associated with health and well-being. Practices like yoga and meditation, integral to Ayurveda, improve stress resilience by modulating histone acetylation and reducing systemic inflammation. These findings substantiate the Ayurvedic principle of individualized care by linking it with measurable biological changes.

Ayurvedic formulations, such as Triphala, have also gained attention for their role in modulating gut microbiota, a critical determinant of overall health. Triphala's ability to restore microbial diversity is particularly beneficial for Vāta-dominant individuals, who often suffer from irregular digestion and lower microbiota diversity. Pitta-dominant individuals benefit from Triphala's anti-inflammatory properties, while Kapha types experience improved lipid metabolism and detoxification. Correlations between gut microbiota profiles and Prakṛti classifications are increasingly evident, with specific bacterial populations aligning with Vāta, Pitta, and Kapha traits. These findings affirm that the gut-microbiome axis plays a pivotal role in the Ayurvedic understanding of health and disease.

Technological advancements are propelling Ayurgenomics into new realms of discovery. Tools such as genome-wide association studies (GWAS), transcriptomics, and epigenomics are revealing the genetic underpinnings of Prakṛti. Metabolomics and proteomics are uncovering the biochemical impacts of Ayurvedic interventions, while AI-driven algorithms are enabling sophisticated analyses of vast datasets comprising genetic, epigenetic, and microbiome information. These technologies have begun validating the Ayurvedic framework with unprecedented precision, offering actionable insights into disease prevention, diagnosis, and treatment.

However, Ayurgenomics faces significant challenges, including the subjective nature of traditional Prakṛti assessments and the lack of standardized methodologies for integrating Ayurveda and genomics. Sustainability is another pressing concern, as the rising global demand for Ayurvedic formulations has led to overharvesting and habitat degradation. Declining bioactive compound concentrations in medicinal plants like Amalaki, a key ingredient in Triphala, threaten both the efficacy of Ayurvedic remedies and the ecosystems that sustain them. Efforts to address these challenges include developing synthetic alternatives, promoting community-led conservation, and adopting agroforestry practices.

Despite these obstacles, Ayurgenomics holds immense promise for revolutionizing healthcare. By bridging traditional knowledge with cutting-edge science, it offers a holistic, personalized approach to health and well-being. The integration of Ayurveda and genomics has the potential to redefine precision medicine, making it more inclusive and sustainable while addressing the complexities of human individuality and environmental stewardship.

46. Based on the passage, how do genetic markers support the Ayurvedic concept of Prakṛti?

A. Genetic markers indicate that Prakṛti classifications are arbitrary and lack scientific basis.

B. Polymorphisms in genes like DRD2, TNF-α, and FTO correlate with traits and susceptibilities described in Ayurveda.

C. Genetic studies reveal no consistent markers that align with Prakṛti classifications.

D. Polymorphisms across all Prakṛtis are identical, disproving Ayurveda's claims of individuality.

47. What role do epigenetic mechanisms play in Ayurgenomics, as highlighted in the passage?

A. Epigenetic mechanisms demonstrate that Prakṛti is determined solely by genetic inheritance.

B. They show that environmental and lifestyle interventions, such as diet and yoga, modulate gene expression.

C. Epigenetics refutes Ayurvedic principles by proving that genetic expression cannot be influenced externally.

D. DNA methylation and histone acetylation permanently alter genetic structures, supporting Ayurvedic practices.

48. How does the gut microbiota connect to Prakṛti classifications, according to the passage?

A. Gut microbiota diversity is unrelated to Ayurvedic concepts and remains unaffected by interventions.

B. The microbiota profiles of individuals align with Vāta, Pitta, and Kapha traits, influencing health outcomes.

C. Ayurvedic formulations like Triphala demonstrate no significant impact on microbial diversity or health.

D. Microbiota differences among Prakṛtis are inconsistent, undermining their relevance in Ayurgenomics.

49. What technological advancements have most significantly impacted Ayurgenomics research?

A. Exclusive reliance on subjective Prakṛti assessment methods.

B. Integration of GWAS, metabolomics, and AI-driven analyses for precise insights into health and disease.

C. Development of herbal formulations without considering genomic findings.

D. Traditional Ayurvedic methods without modern technological integration.

50. According to the passage, what challenges does Ayurgenomics face in integrating Ayurveda with modern genomics?

A. A lack of scientific interest in validating Ayurvedic principles.

B. Overharvesting of medicinal plants, subjective assessments, and declining bioactive compound quality.

C. Resistance from traditional Ayurvedic practitioners to adopt genomic tools.

D. Unavailability of genomic technologies to support Ayurvedic research.

ANSWER WITH EXPLANATIONS

1. A: The study demonstrates that each Prakṛti type—Vāta, Pitta, and Kapha—shows distinct gene expression profiles. Vāta types had variability in metabolic gene expression, Pitta showed inflammatory cytokine upregulation, and Kapha showed genes linked to lipid metabolism. These biological signatures correlate with Ayurvedic descriptions, thereby providing molecular validation to the Ayurvedic concept of Prakṛti. This supports integration between Ayurveda and modern genomics.

2. A: The study shows that dietary recommendations for Vāta Prakṛti can lead to specific epigenetic changes like demethylation of stress-related genes and increased melatonin gene expression, improving sleep and stress regulation. These are measurable outcomes that align with Vāta characteristics. It demonstrates that Ayurvedic diets can modulate gene expression through epigenetic pathways, validating Ayurveda's individualized and preventive approach.

3. A: According to Ayurveda, Kapha types are prone to weight gain, Pitta types have efficient digestion, and Vāta types face digestive irregularities. The study correlates these traits with specific gut microbiota profiles—Firmicutes in Kapha, Bacteroidetes in Pitta, and reduced diversity in Vāta. These findings affirm that gut microbiome composition reflects doshic characteristics, reinforcing Ayurvedic understanding through modern microbiological evidence.

4. A: Ayurvedic Rasas influence specific biological processes, validating their systemic relevance. Sweet Rasa promotes anabolic activities, such as tissue repair and nourishment, aligning with its association with Kapha. Bitter Rasa enhances autophagy, supporting detoxification and cellular rejuvenation, reflecting its alignment with Pitta's metabolism. Astringent Rasa strengthens tissues and reduces oxidative stress, complementing Kapha's physiological needs. These effects have been validated through biochemical studies, linking Rasa classifications to metabolic and detox pathways. Such findings affirm Ayurveda's understanding of systemic health, demonstrating that its dietary and therapeutic recommendations are deeply rooted in observable biological processes, bridging ancient wisdom and modern science.

5. A: Agni, the Ayurvedic concept of digestive fire, aligns with the biochemical regulation of enzymatic activity. Impaired Agni, described as Mandagni, parallels reduced digestive enzyme function, as seen in conditions like weak metabolism or toxin accumulation. Ayurvedic interventions restore Agni, improving enzymatic efficiency and metabolic outcomes. Studies on Prakṛti-specific diets have shown enhanced digestive enzyme activity, particularly in individuals with Vāta and Kapha dominance. This integration of Agni with measurable metabolic processes confirms Ayurveda's holistic understanding of health. The metaphorical concept of Agni thus finds validation in its molecular parallels, highlighting Ayurveda's scientific applicability in modern healthcare frameworks.

6. A: Vāta Prakṛti's heightened sensitivity to stress and variability correlates with genetic polymorphisms in neurotransmitter pathways, such as DRD2 and SLC6A4. These traits align with Ayurveda's description of Vāta individuals being mentally agile yet prone to anxiety and irregular metabolism. Such genomic markers offer a measurable basis for Ayurveda's diagnostic precision. By linking stress responses and metabolic irregularities to genetic predispositions, Vāta traits gain biological validation. This reinforces Ayurveda's ability to identify and manage constitutional vulnerabilities. Genomic insights not only substantiate Ayurvedic classifications but also enhance their application in modern contexts, demonstrating the compatibility of tradition with scientific evidence.

7. A: Kapha's traits of stability, strength, and slower metabolism align with Firmicutes dominance in gut microbiota, promoting lipid storage and energy conservation. This bacterial composition matches Kapha's Ayurvedic descriptions of anabolic tendencies and weight gain susceptibility. Triphala, an Ayurvedic formulation, has been shown to modulate gut microbiota, improving lipid metabolism in Kapha individuals. Such findings bridge microbiota research and Ayurvedic principles, validating Kapha's physiological uniqueness. By linking gut health with genetic and microbiota profiles, Ayurgenomics reinforces Ayurveda's personalized approach. The microbiome-Kapha connection strengthens Ayurveda's scientific relevance, emphasizing the importance of tailored interventions for metabolic and immune health.

8. **A:** Pitta Prakṛti's predisposition to inflammation and robust metabolism corresponds with genetic variations in inflammatory cytokine genes, such as TNF-α and IL-6. These traits align with Ayurveda's description of Pitta individuals as fiery, energetic, and prone to inflammation-related disorders. Cooling diets and anti-inflammatory formulations recommended for Pitta reduce the expression of these cytokines, validating Ayurveda's therapeutic insights. Such findings highlight the intersection of genomic research and Ayurvedic principles, showcasing Pitta's distinct genetic and physiological characteristics. By linking Pitta's traits to measurable genetic markers, Ayurgenomics integrates traditional diagnostics with modern molecular understanding, advancing the field of precision medicine.

9. **A:** Panchakarma's detoxification therapies align with modern findings, showing significant reductions in systemic inflammation markers like CRP. This supports Ayurveda's claim that detox therapies restore doṣa balance and eliminate toxins (Ama). Research highlights Panchakarma's impact on metabolic pathways, particularly in inflammatory and lipid-related conditions common in Kapha and Pitta types. The integration of traditional detoxification methods with measurable health outcomes strengthens Ayurveda's therapeutic credibility. By demonstrating anti-inflammatory and lipid-regulating effects, Panchakarma bridges ancient practices with evidence-based medicine, validating its role in holistic health management. Such findings emphasize Panchakarma's adaptability within modern integrative healthcare frameworks.

10. **A:** Synthetic alternatives to Ayurvedic herbs preserve therapeutic efficacy while addressing sustainability concerns. For example, bioactive compounds in Triphala components like Amalaki can be synthesized to maintain their anti-inflammatory and gut-health benefits. This innovation aligns with Ayurvedic principles, ensuring accessibility without ecological harm. While maintaining the therapeutic essence of Ayurveda, these developments reflect its adaptability to modern needs. Synthetic alternatives also standardize potency, enhancing global acceptance of Ayurvedic formulations. This integration of science and tradition offers a sustainable solution to overharvesting and environmental degradation, ensuring Ayurveda's relevance and ecological stewardship in modern healthcare.

11. **B:** Epigenetic mechanisms, such as histone acetylation and DNA methylation, show that lifestyle and environmental factors significantly modulate gene expression. These changes align with Ayurveda's emphasis on tailoring health interventions based on an individual's Prakṛti. For example, Vāta individuals benefit from grounding diets that influence stress-related gene expression, while Pitta individuals require cooling diets to reduce inflammation-related markers. These epigenetic modulations are reversible and reflect the adaptability inherent in Ayurveda. By integrating this perspective, Ayurgenomics bridges static genetic predispositions and dynamic environmental influences, offering a personalized and scientifically validated approach to preventive health and therapeutic interventions.

12. **B:** Conservation-focused agroforestry systems ensure sustainable sourcing of medicinal plants while preserving their bioactive properties. Such practices align with Ayurveda's ecological ethos, emphasizing balance between nature and human health. Large-scale monoculture plantations risk depleting soil nutrients and lowering the potency of key compounds in plants like Amalaki. Community-led conservation ensures habitat protection and sustainable harvesting practices, maintaining the integrity of formulations like Triphala. By integrating traditional wisdom with modern conservation strategies, Ayurveda can address rising global demand while ensuring ecological balance and therapeutic efficacy. These efforts reflect Ayurveda's holistic principles applied to environmental stewardship and resource management.

13. **A:** Amalaki's bioactive compound concentration directly impacts Triphala's therapeutic efficacy. Environmental degradation reduces the potency of Amalaki, diminishing its ability to support gut microbiota diversity and reduce systemic inflammation. This correlation highlights Ayurveda's reliance on natural ingredient quality for optimal health outcomes. While Triphala's synergy among its components is crucial, the degradation of a single ingredient compromises its holistic benefits. This underscores the need for sustainable harvesting and ecological responsibility in maintaining Ayurveda's therapeutic integrity. The link between environmental health and Ayurveda's efficacy illustrates the interconnectedness of natural resources and personalized medicine in Ayurgenomics.

14. **B:** Standardized quality and sustainable harvesting practices for Triphala components ensure consistency in bioactive compound levels while addressing ecological concerns. Ayurveda's reliance on natural formulations requires global standards to maintain therapeutic efficacy across diverse populations. Encouraging sustainable practices like community-led agroforestry

balances rising demand with conservation. Synthetic alternatives, though promising, lack the holistic essence of Ayurvedic formulations. By combining scientific rigor with traditional ecological knowledge, such strategies ensure Ayurveda's relevance in modern medicine while preserving biodiversity. This approach integrates Ayurveda's core principles with sustainability and quality assurance, reflecting its adaptability to contemporary healthcare challenges.

15. A: Genetic markers such as DRD2 in Vāta, TNF-α in Pitta, and FTO in Kapha align with Ayurvedic descriptions of Prakṛti traits. These markers explain stress sensitivity, inflammation, and lipid storage tendencies, respectively, providing a measurable basis for Ayurvedic diagnostics. Prakṛti classifications, traditionally qualitative, gain scientific credibility through genomic studies. These findings affirm Ayurveda's nuanced understanding of individuality, linking observable traits with molecular patterns. By integrating these insights, Ayurgenomics reinforces Ayurveda's relevance in precision medicine. The genetic basis of Prakṛti underscores its validity as a tool for disease prediction, preventive care, and personalized therapeutic interventions.

16. A: Epigenetics demonstrates how Ayurvedic interventions modulate gene expression, validating the adaptability of its practices. DNA methylation patterns align with dietary and detox regimens prescribed for specific Prakṛtis, while yoga enhances histone acetylation, improving stress resilience. These mechanisms affirm Ayurveda's principle of dynamic health management. For instance, anti-inflammatory diets reduce gene activity linked to Pitta-related disorders, while grounding practices stabilize Vāta-associated stress responses. Unlike static genetic predispositions, epigenetic modifications offer reversible pathways for health optimization. Ayurgenomics integrates these findings, demonstrating that Ayurveda's personalized health strategies are both biologically effective and scientifically sound.

17. A: Ayurvedic Rasas are biologically linked to systemic processes, validating their role in health management. Sweet Rasa's anabolic effects promote tissue growth and nourishment, aligning with Kapha traits. Bitter Rasa induces detoxification pathways like autophagy, supporting cellular health and aligning with Pitta's metabolism. Astringent Rasa strengthens tissues and reduces oxidative stress, complementing its therapeutic role in both Pitta and Kapha conditions. These physiological effects highlight Ayurveda's intricate understanding of dietary impacts on health. Modern biochemical studies corroborate these ancient principles, demonstrating that Rasas influence molecular pathways in alignment with systemic health goals, bridging tradition and molecular science.

18. C: Distinct Prakṛti traits align with genetic predispositions, supporting Ayurveda's diagnostic precision. Vāta's variability correlates with stress-regulating genes like DRD2, while Pitta's inflammatory predisposition aligns with TNF-α variations. Kapha's slow metabolism and lipid storage tendencies match FTO polymorphisms. These patterns validate Ayurveda's nuanced understanding of individuality and health predispositions. The integration of genetic research with traditional Prakṛti classifications affirms their scientific credibility. By linking physiological traits to molecular patterns, Ayurgenomics provides a robust framework for personalized medicine. This convergence of Ayurveda and genomics offers precise diagnostic tools and adaptive therapeutic strategies for holistic health care.

19. A: Ayurvedic therapies modulate gut microbiota, mitochondrial activity, and oxidative stress pathways, demonstrating their systemic benefits. Triphala improves gut microbial diversity, reducing inflammation, while Rasayana therapies enhance cellular antioxidant capacity. Panchakarma detox regimens lower systemic inflammatory markers like CRP. These findings substantiate Ayurveda's holistic approach to health, integrating detoxification, nutrition, and lifestyle adjustments. Genetic and epigenetic research further validates these interventions, linking Prakṛti-specific treatments to measurable health outcomes. Ayurgenomics bridges Ayurveda's qualitative principles with quantitative scientific evidence, ensuring its relevance in modern integrative medicine. This synthesis offers adaptive strategies for preventive care and disease management.

20. A: Panchakarma therapies demonstrate measurable physiological impacts, including systemic inflammation reduction, improved lipid profiles, and enhanced cellular antioxidant capacity. These benefits validate Ayurveda's detoxification principles, highlighting Panchakarma's ability to eliminate toxins (Ama) and restore doṣa balance. Research underscores its efficacy in conditions linked to metabolic disorders, particularly in Kapha and Pitta Prakṛti individuals. These findings integrate traditional detox practices with modern biomedical understanding, reinforcing Ayurveda's therapeutic relevance. Panchakarma's adaptability in addressing chronic diseases through systemic regulation bridges ancient methods with contemporary healthcare needs, emphasizing its holistic and evidence-based approach to health management.

21. A: Research has identified strong correlations between Prakṛti and specific genetic markers, validating Ayurvedic classifications. For example, Vāta-dominant individuals exhibit polymorphisms in DRD2 and CRHR1, which influence stress sensitivity and irregular metabolic patterns. Pitta individuals display cytokine gene variations, such as TNF-α and IL-6, linking them to inflammatory disorders. Kapha individuals show polymorphisms in genes like FTO and PPARG, reflecting tendencies toward lipid storage and slower metabolism. These findings bridge traditional Ayurvedic diagnostics with molecular genetics, emphasizing the biological basis of Prakṛti. This integration highlights Ayurveda's scientific relevance in understanding individual health predispositions and guiding personalized medical interventions.

22. **A:** Ayurveda's ecological principles emphasize balance and sustainability, aligning with modern conservation efforts. Agroforestry systems promote the sustainable cultivation of medicinal plants like Amalaki while preserving biodiversity and soil quality. Overharvesting for global demand has degraded plant habitats, reducing bioactive compound concentrations critical for formulations like Triphala. Traditional conservation practices ensure plant quality and availability, addressing both ecological and therapeutic needs. Monoculture farming risks depleting plant potency and genetic diversity, whereas community-led approaches protect ecosystems and align with Ayurveda's holistic ethos. By integrating ecological sustainability with health preservation, Ayurgenomics reinforces the interconnectedness of environmental stewardship and effective healthcare.

23. **A:** Ayurveda's Prakṛti-based susceptibility patterns align with genetic predispositions and lifestyle factors. Vāta individuals, prone to stress and neurological conditions, exhibit polymorphisms in neurotransmitter-related genes like DRD2. Pitta individuals, predisposed to inflammatory and metabolic disorders, show cytokine gene variations such as TNF-α. Kapha individuals, with a higher risk of obesity and cardiovascular issues, have lipid-related genetic traits like FTO. These patterns highlight the adaptive nature of Ayurvedic interventions, emphasizing tailored lifestyle modifications to mitigate health risks. Ayurgenomics bridges these predispositions with actionable insights, offering a scientifically validated framework for preventing diseases and optimizing health through personalized care.

24. **A:** Epigenetic mechanisms, including DNA methylation, histone acetylation, and non-coding RNA interactions, demonstrate the adaptability of Ayurvedic practices. Diet, detox therapies, and lifestyle regimens modulate these mechanisms, aligning gene expression with individual health needs. For instance, yoga enhances histone acetylation, improving stress resilience and systemic health. Ayurvedic interventions like Prakṛti-specific diets also influence DNA methylation, supporting metabolic balance and reducing inflammation. These findings underscore Ayurveda's integration of environmental and biological factors in health management. Ayurgenomics validates these principles by linking molecular changes to therapeutic outcomes, ensuring that Ayurveda's personalized approaches remain relevant in modern preventive and precision medicine.

25. **A:** Prakṛti classifications are underpinned by measurable genetic correlates, affirming Ayurveda's physiological precision. Vāta individuals exhibit polymorphisms in genes affecting neurotransmission, explaining their stress susceptibility. Pitta individuals show inflammatory cytokine gene variations, correlating with their robust metabolism and inflammation-related conditions. Kapha individuals possess lipid metabolism-related genetic markers like FTO, validating their slower metabolic tendencies. These genetic patterns integrate traditional Ayurvedic insights with molecular biology, offering a biologically grounded framework for individualized care. By combining genomic markers with Prakṛti diagnostics, Ayurgenomics advances Ayurveda's applicability in modern medicine, enhancing its scientific validation and therapeutic precision in addressing health diversity.

26. **A:** Prakṛti traits, shaped by genetic variations, provide insight into individual health predispositions. Vāta's association with dopamine-related genes reflects its neurological variability, while Pitta's cytokine-linked markers align with its inflammatory tendencies. Kapha's lipid-associated genetic traits confirm its slower metabolism and energy storage characteristics. These correlations validate Ayurveda's traditional classifications, highlighting their genetic foundation. Integrating Prakṛti with genomic research enhances Ayurveda's relevance in addressing personalized health. Such findings bridge traditional practices with scientific rigor, emphasizing the importance of genetic predispositions in health and disease. Ayurgenomics reinforces Ayurveda's adaptability, ensuring its compatibility with modern precision healthcare frameworks.

27. **A:** Ayurvedic Rasas correspond to biological effects, demonstrating their systemic relevance. Sweet Rasa's anabolic properties support tissue growth and nourishment, aligning with Kapha's physiological traits. Bitter Rasa induces detox pathways, including autophagy, reflecting its role in cellular health and Pitta metabolism. Astringent Rasa enhances tissue strength and reduces oxidative stress, complementing

therapeutic needs across Prakṛti types. These effects validate Ayurveda's understanding of dietary influences on systemic health. Modern studies substantiate these ancient principles, showcasing how Rasas modulate biochemical processes. By linking dietary elements to health outcomes, Ayurveda's dietary framework gains scientific validation, emphasizing its role in holistic healthcare.

28. A: Ayurvedic interventions, such as Ṛtucharya (seasonal routines), Prakṛti-specific diets, and detox therapies, align with measurable biological changes. Seasonal regimens synchronize gene expression with environmental rhythms, supporting health optimization. Dietary interventions tailored to Prakṛti influence epigenetic markers, enhancing metabolic and immune pathways. Detox therapies like Panchakarma reduce systemic inflammation and restore physiological balance. These findings validate Ayurveda's personalized health strategies, bridging its traditional insights with genomic evidence. Ayurgenomics highlights how such interventions adapt to individual and environmental variables, reinforcing Ayurveda's dynamic and integrative approach to healthcare. This synthesis ensures Ayurveda's continued relevance in addressing modern health challenges.

29. A: Prakṛti-linked health susceptibilities align with genetic and environmental influences, confirming Ayurveda's diagnostic accuracy. Vāta individuals face higher neurological risks due to stress-related gene polymorphisms, while Pitta individuals are prone to metabolic and inflammatory disorders linked to cytokine variations. Kapha individuals, predisposed to obesity, exhibit lipid-regulating genetic markers. These patterns highlight Ayurveda's nuanced understanding of individual health vulnerabilities. By integrating genetic and epigenetic insights, Ayurgenomics substantiates Ayurveda's role in predicting disease risk and guiding preventive care. This fusion of tradition and science offers adaptive health solutions, reinforcing Ayurveda's personalized approach to managing physiological and genetic diversity.

30. A: Genetic markers, such as TNF-α in Pitta and FTO in Kapha, align with Prakṛti-specific traits, validating Ayurveda's diagnostic framework. Vāta individuals' polymorphisms in stress-related genes explain their variability, while Pitta's cytokine-linked traits correlate with inflammation risks. Kapha's lipid metabolism traits reflect slower energy utilization, confirming its unique physiological patterns. These findings bridge Ayurveda's qualitative descriptions with measurable genomic data, enhancing its application in precision medicine. Ayurgenomics integrates these insights to optimize health outcomes, linking individual predispositions to tailored interventions. This approach affirms Ayurveda's scientific foundation, demonstrating its adaptability within modern healthcare systems.

31. A: Epigenetic mechanisms, such as DNA methylation and histone acetylation, align closely with Ayurvedic practices like dietary regimens, yoga, and detox therapies. DNA methylation patterns influenced by Ayurvedic diets regulate metabolic pathways tailored to Prakṛti needs, while yoga enhances histone acetylation, improving resilience to stress. Non-coding RNA, modulated by herbal formulations, supports cellular repair and immune function. These epigenetic changes are dynamic and reversible, reflecting Ayurveda's emphasis on adapting health practices to environmental and individual factors. By integrating epigenetic insights, Ayurgenomics bridges traditional Ayurvedic principles with modern molecular biology, reinforcing Ayurveda's personalized approach to holistic health and disease prevention.

32. A: Gut microbiota diversity and composition align uniquely with Ayurvedic Prakṛti classifications, supporting Ayurveda's diagnostic framework. Vāta individuals, prone to irregular digestion, exhibit lower microbial diversity, while Pitta types show a balance conducive to efficient metabolism. Kapha individuals, with a Firmicutes-dominant microbiome, demonstrate enhanced lipid absorption and energy storage. Ayurvedic formulations like Triphala modulate microbial populations, restoring balance and improving systemic health. These findings underscore the importance of gut health in Ayurvedic diagnostics and therapies. By linking microbiota profiles with Prakṛti traits, Ayurgenomics integrates traditional Ayurvedic insights with emerging research, reinforcing Ayurveda's role in personalized medicine.

33. A: Sustainability challenges, such as overharvesting of Amalaki and declining bioactive compounds in medicinal plants, threaten Ayurveda's efficacy and ecological balance. Community-led conservation efforts and agroforestry practices preserve biodiversity and maintain therapeutic potency. Synthetic alternatives are being explored but may lack the holistic qualities of natural remedies. Establishing global standards for Ayurvedic formulations ensures quality consistency while addressing rising global demand. These strategies align with Ayurveda's ecological ethos, emphasizing the balance between human health and environmental stewardship. Ayurgenomics integrates sustainability with therapeutic innovation, ensuring that Ayurvedic principles remain effective and relevant in the context of modern healthcare and ecological challenges.

34. A: The efficacy of Ayurvedic therapies like Triphala depends on the bioactive compound quality in its components. Amalaki, a key ingredient, supports gut microbiota diversity and immune modulation. Environmental degradation reduces its potency, affecting therapeutic outcomes. To address this, sustainable harvesting practices and standardization of formulations are essential. Ayurveda's reliance on ingredient synergy emphasizes the need for consistent bioactive concentrations across components. Ayurgenomics reinforces this by linking bioactive quality to genetic and physiological impacts, ensuring that formulations retain their efficacy. These findings integrate Ayurvedic principles with modern quality assurance frameworks, supporting Ayurveda's application in contemporary healthcare systems globally.

35. C: While Ayurgenomics establishes a genetic basis for Prakṛti, it also recognizes the significant influence of environmental and lifestyle factors. Prakṛti traits are shaped by genetic predispositions, such as neurotransmitter-related polymorphisms in Vāta or inflammatory markers in Pitta. However, Ayurvedic interventions, including tailored diets and detox regimens, modulate these predispositions through epigenetic mechanisms. Statement 2, claiming that Prakṛti is purely genetic, oversimplifies Ayurveda's dynamic approach. Ayurveda emphasizes the interplay between nature and nurture, aligning with findings in modern genomics. This nuanced understanding affirms Ayurveda's relevance in addressing individual health while integrating its principles into personalized, adaptive healthcare models.

36. C: Kapha individuals exhibit slower metabolic rates and a propensity for lipid storage, supported by FTO and PPARG gene polymorphisms. However, the claim that Kapha individuals demonstrate increased thermogenesis contradicts Ayurvedic principles and research findings. Ayurvedic interventions, such as light diets and regular exercise, are specifically recommended to counter Kapha's slower energy utilization and metabolic tendencies. This approach aligns with the biological understanding of Kapha traits and their genetic underpinnings. By integrating these insights, Ayurgenomics validates Ayurveda's diagnostic framework, offering tailored interventions to optimize health and prevent metabolic conditions like obesity and cardiovascular disease.

37. A: Pitta Prakṛti is associated with inflammatory cytokine gene variations like TNF-α and IL-6, explaining their susceptibility to inflammation-related conditions. Ayurvedic interventions, including cooling diets and anti-inflammatory herbs, reduce the expression of these cytokines, supporting Ayurveda's claim of individualized care. These findings align with the integration of Prakṛti classifications into genomic research. By tailoring interventions to an individual's biological tendencies, Ayurveda and Ayurgenomics together create a robust framework for preventive care and targeted therapies. This synergy reinforces Ayurveda's adaptability and its relevance in managing health conditions linked to inflammatory processes, particularly in Pitta-dominant individuals.

38. C: Epigenetics highlights Ayurveda's adaptability by demonstrating how dietary and lifestyle interventions modulate gene expression. Practices like yoga and Prakṛti-specific diets induce reversible changes in DNA methylation and histone acetylation, supporting systemic health. Contrary to Statement 2, epigenetic modifications are dynamic and influenced by environmental factors, reinforcing Ayurveda's emphasis on lifestyle adaptability. These findings align with Ayurgenomics, validating Ayurveda's personalized approach to health. By integrating epigenetic insights, Ayurgenomics bridges the gap between traditional health systems and modern molecular science, ensuring that Ayurvedic principles remain scientifically relevant in contemporary preventive and therapeutic healthcare strategies.

39. C: Triphala's efficacy in improving gut health depends significantly on the quality of its components, such as Amalaki, which supports microbial diversity and immune function. While the preparation process is essential, the bioactive compounds in its ingredients are critical to its therapeutic success. Environmental degradation and unsustainable harvesting practices reduce the potency of these bioactives, compromising Triphala's systemic benefits. Ayurgenomics highlights the interplay between formulation quality and health outcomes, reinforcing Ayurveda's emphasis on ingredient synergy. These findings emphasize the need for sustainable practices and quality control in preserving Ayurveda's therapeutic efficacy within modern healthcare frameworks.

40. C: Ayurveda's Prakṛti classifications align with measurable genetic markers, such as neurotransmitter-related genes in Vāta or lipid-regulating genes in Kapha. However, Statement R incorrectly attributes Prakṛti traits solely to genetics, disregarding the influence of lifestyle and environment. Ayurvedic interventions, tailored to Prakṛti, modulate gene expression through epigenetic mechanisms like DNA methylation and histone acetylation. This dynamic interplay validates Ayurveda's principles of adaptability and holistic care. Ayurgenomics integrates these insights, bridging static genetic frameworks with personalized interventions, ensuring that Ayurveda remains scientifically robust and applicable in modern precision medicine.

41. **C:** Pitta Prakṛti's susceptibility to inflammation corresponds with variations in cytokine genes like TNF-α and IL-6, validated by genomic research. Ayurvedic interventions, such as anti-inflammatory herbs and cooling diets, modulate these predispositions by influencing gene expression and reducing inflammatory markers. Statement R, suggesting that Ayurvedic therapies do not affect cytokine activity, contradicts evidence of their biological efficacy. These findings highlight Ayurveda's ability to address genetic vulnerabilities through personalized care. Ayurgenomics reinforces these principles, offering actionable insights into managing health risks associated with inflammatory conditions, particularly in individuals with Pitta-dominant constitutions.

42. **A:** Kapha Prakṛti is characterized by genetic traits linked to lipid storage and slower metabolism, such as FTO and PPARG polymorphisms. Ayurvedic lifestyle modifications, including low-calorie diets and regular exercise, mitigate these predispositions by enhancing metabolic efficiency and reducing obesity risks. This interplay between genetic predispositions and environmental interventions aligns with Ayurvedic principles of individualized care. Ayurgenomics bridges this understanding by linking Kapha's physiological traits to measurable genetic and metabolic pathways. This integration ensures Ayurveda's continued relevance in managing metabolic conditions through tailored interventions, offering scientifically validated strategies for preventive and therapeutic health care.

43. **C:** Epigenetic mechanisms, such as histone acetylation, are shown to be modulated by practices like yoga and meditation, aligning with Ayurveda's holistic approach to health. These practices reduce stress and systemic inflammation by enhancing gene accessibility, supporting resilience and emotional balance. Statement R, however, incorrectly claims that such interventions permanently alter DNA sequences, which is not supported by evidence. Epigenetic modifications are dynamic and reversible, influenced by sustained lifestyle practices rather than fixed genetic changes. These findings validate Ayurveda's emphasis on regular practice for lasting health benefits. Ayurgenomics integrates these insights, bridging traditional methodologies with contemporary molecular biology.

44. **A:** The therapeutic efficacy of Triphala and other Ayurvedic formulations relies on the quality of bioactive compounds in their components. For instance, Amalaki's antioxidant properties and ability to modulate gut microbiota depend on its bioactive concentration, which is compromised by unsustainable harvesting practices. Statement R correctly highlights that ecological balance and sustainable sourcing are essential for maintaining ingredient quality. These efforts align with Ayurveda's principles of harmony with nature, ensuring formulations retain their potency. Ayurgenomics validates these approaches, emphasizing the interconnectedness of environmental health and therapeutic efficacy, reinforcing Ayurveda's relevance in both ecological stewardship and evidence-based medicine.

45. **C:** Ayurgenomics integrates Ayurvedic principles with modern genomic tools to advance personalized medicine. Statement R, however, incorrectly asserts that dosha balances are universal and unchanging, contradicting Ayurveda's individualized approach. Ayurveda emphasizes Prakṛti, shaped by genetic, environmental, and lifestyle factors, making it unique to each person. Ayurgenomics validates this perspective by linking Prakṛti to genetic markers and modifiable epigenetic mechanisms. These findings ensure Ayurveda's adaptability and scientific relevance in precision medicine. By addressing individual health needs through tailored interventions, Ayurgenomics bridges traditional wisdom with contemporary healthcare innovation, offering a holistic and biologically grounded approach to health optimization.

46. **B:** Genomic studies have identified specific markers aligning with Prakṛti traits, substantiating Ayurveda's diagnostic framework. Vāta's sensitivity to stress links to DRD2 and SLC6A4 polymorphisms, Pitta's inflammatory tendencies to TNF-α and IL-6, and Kapha's slower metabolism to FTO and PPARG. These patterns confirm the biological basis of Prakṛti classifications. Unlike arbitrary systems, Ayurveda's descriptions of individuality reflect measurable genetic predispositions. These findings reinforce Ayurveda's role in personalized medicine, offering actionable insights into health risks and tailored interventions. Ayurgenomics bridges tradition and molecular science, validating Ayurveda's principles through the lens of modern genomics and biomedical research.

47. **B:** Epigenetics demonstrates the adaptability of Ayurvedic interventions in modulating gene expression through lifestyle changes. Practices like yoga enhance histone acetylation, while Prakṛti-specific diets influence DNA methylation, optimizing metabolic and inflammatory pathways. These findings align

with Ayurveda's emphasis on personalized care and preventive health. Statement B highlights this dynamic relationship, where environmental inputs affect genetic activity without altering the underlying DNA sequence. This insight strengthens Ayurveda's holistic framework, showing its integration with modern molecular biology. By bridging tradition and science, Ayurgenomics validates Ayurveda's principles, ensuring its continued relevance in addressing individual health through adaptable therapeutic strategies.

48. B: Gut microbiota diversity correlates uniquely with Ayurvedic Prakṛti classifications. Vāta types, prone to digestive irregularities, display lower diversity, while Pitta types show balanced microbial populations conducive to efficient metabolism. Kapha types, characterized by lipid storage tendencies, have a Firmicutes-dominant microbiome. Ayurvedic interventions like Triphala modulate these microbial profiles, restoring balance and supporting systemic health. These findings affirm the microbiota's role in Prakṛti-based diagnostics and therapeutic outcomes, reinforcing Ayurveda's insights into gut health. Ayurgenomics integrates these observations, linking microbiome composition with genetic predispositions and tailored interventions, advancing Ayurveda's relevance in personalized medicine and gut health management.

49. B: Technological advancements such as GWAS, metabolomics, and AI-driven analytics have revolutionized Ayurgenomics research. These tools validate Ayurvedic principles by correlating Prakṛti with genetic markers, metabolic profiles, and epigenetic changes. For example, AI models synthesize vast datasets to predict health risks based on Prakṛti traits, enhancing diagnostic precision. Metabolomics reveals the biochemical effects of Ayurvedic formulations, bridging tradition with empirical evidence. By integrating genomic insights with traditional Ayurvedic diagnostics, Ayurgenomics advances personalized medicine. This fusion ensures Ayurveda's scientific credibility while maintaining its holistic approach, offering innovative solutions to modern healthcare challenges through precision-based therapeutic strategies.

50. B: Ayurgenomics faces challenges such as overharvesting of medicinal plants, declining bioactive compound concentrations, and subjective Prakṛti assessments. These issues threaten Ayurveda's efficacy and ecological balance. Sustainable harvesting practices, community-led conservation, and agroforestry initiatives address these ecological concerns, preserving plant potency and biodiversity. Standardizing Prakṛti assessments through genomic tools ensures diagnostic consistency and scientific validation. These efforts align with Ayurveda's principles of harmony and adaptability, reinforcing its relevance in modern healthcare. Ayurgenomics bridges tradition with science, addressing these challenges by integrating sustainability with precision medicine, ensuring Ayurveda's continued efficacy and ecological stewardship in addressing global health needs.

CHAPTER 21

CELL AND MOLECULAR BIOLOGY– GENE EXPRESSION AND REGULATION

INTRODUCTION TO CELL BIOLOGY AND GENE EXPRESSION

The Cell as the Fundamental Unit of Life

Cells are the building blocks of life, forming the structural and functional units of all living organisms. From the simplest unicellular organisms, such as bacteria, to complex multicellular organisms, such as humans, the cell serves as the foundation of biological activity. The study of cell biology reveals intricate processes, including growth, energy production, communication, and self-replication.

Eukaryotic cells, distinguished by their membrane-bound organelles, showcase a division of labour. The nucleus stores genetic information, while organelles like the mitochondria, endoplasmic reticulum, and Golgi apparatus carry out energy production, protein synthesis, and packaging. This compartmentalization is pivotal for gene expression, enabling precise regulation and functional specialization.

Defining Gene Expression

Gene expression is the process by which genetic instructions encoded in DNA are converted into functional products, primarily proteins. This process ensures that cells adapt to environmental changes, repair damage, and perform specialized functions.

The central dogma of molecular biology—DNA → RNA → Protein—describes the flow of genetic information. The DNA in the nucleus is transcribed into messenger RNA (mRNA), which is then translated into a protein by ribosomes. Proteins serve as enzymes, signaling molecules, and structural components critical to cellular function.

The Need for Regulation

Gene expression is not a static process but is finely tuned to meet the cell's needs. This regulation occurs at multiple levels, from transcription initiation to post-translational modification of proteins. Regulation ensures that:

- Housekeeping genes are consistently expressed for essential functions.
- Tissue-specific genes are activated in appropriate cell types.
- Stress-response genes help cells adapt to environmental challenges.
- Failures in regulation can result in diseases such as cancer, where genes like oncogenes and tumor suppressor genes become dysregulated.

THE MOLECULAR MACHINERY OF GENE EXPRESSION

Gene expression is a multi-step process that translates the genetic code embedded in DNA into functional proteins. This section explores in detail the molecular machinery involved in the central steps of gene expression: transcription, RNA processing and splicing, and translation. These processes collectively maintain the dynamic balance of cellular function, adaptation, and survival in response to internal and external stimuli.

Transcription

Transcription marks the first step in the journey of gene expression. In this process, a specific segment of DNA, which contains the code for a gene, is transcribed into messenger RNA (mRNA). The mRNA serves as a transient intermediary that carries genetic information from the nucleus to the cytoplasm for translation into proteins.

Mechanisms of Transcription

Transcription involves three main phases: initiation, elongation, and termination. Each phase is regulated by specific molecular components and epigenetic factors to ensure accuracy and efficiency.

1. **Initiation:**
   - **RNA Polymerase:** The enzyme responsible for transcription is RNA polymerase. In eukaryotes, RNA polymerase II transcribes protein-coding genes. The enzyme binds to promoter sequences, which are specific DNA regions located upstream of the gene:
   - **Promoters and Enhancers:** The promoter is a DNA region that includes conserved sequences such as the TATA box. Enhancers, which are distal DNA elements, interact with promoters through DNA looping, a phenomenon facilitated by transcription factors and architectural proteins.
   - **Transcription Factors:** These proteins regulate RNA polymerase activity. Activators enhance transcription by recruiting RNA polymerase to the promoter, while repressors inhibit it.
   - **Epigenetic Modifications:** Chromatin structure plays a crucial role in regulating transcription. DNA must be accessible to transcription machinery, which is controlled by epigenetic modifications:
   - **Histone Acetylation:** Acetyl groups are added to histone tails, reducing the positive charge of histones and loosening DNA-histone interactions. This open chromatin state (euchromatin) facilitates transcription.
   - **DNA Methylation:** The addition of methyl groups to cytosine bases in DNA (often in CpG islands) silences gene expression by preventing transcription factor binding or recruiting repressive proteins.
2. **Elongation:** After RNA polymerase binds to the promoter and unwinds the DNA helix, it synthesizes a complementary RNA strand using one DNA strand as the template.
   - RNA polymerase progresses along the DNA, adding ribonucleotides (adenine, uracil, cytosine, and guanine) to the growing RNA strand.
   - During elongation, the RNA strand temporarily hybridizes with the DNA template, forming a DNA-RNA hybrid, after which the RNA is displaced.
3. **Termination:** Transcription ends when RNA polymerase encounters termination signals, such as polyadenylation sites or specific terminator sequences. These signals prompt the release of the RNA transcript, now termed pre-mRNA.

   Transcription as a Dynamic Process: Advances in molecular biology have unveiled the dynamic spatial organization of transcription within the nucleus:
   - **Chromatin Looping:** Enhancers, often located far from their target genes, physically loop to interact with promoters. This looping is mediated by transcription factors like Mediator and cohesin complexes.
   - **Transcription Factories:** These are nuclear regions where active transcription occurs. They serve as hubs for assembling transcription machinery and ensuring efficient gene expression.
   - **Super-Enhancers:** Clusters of enhancers that drive high expression of genes essential for cell identity and function.

Disruptions in transcription regulation can lead to diseases like cancer, autoimmune disorders, and developmental abnormalities.

RNA Processing and Splicing

Following transcription, the pre-mRNA undergoes a series of modifications to become mature mRNA. These modifications are crucial for RNA stability, nuclear export, and efficient translation.

Steps in RNA Processing:

1. **Capping:** A 7-methylguanosine cap is added to the 5' end of the pre-mRNA. This cap protects the RNA from degradation, facilitates ribosome binding during translation, and aids in nuclear export.
2. **Polyadenylation:** A poly-A tail, consisting of approximately 200 adenine nucleotides, is added to the 3' end of the RNA. This modification increases RNA stability and plays a role in terminating transcription. The process involves cleavage of the pre-mRNA downstream of a conserved polyadenylation signal sequence (AAUAAA), followed by poly-A tail addition by poly(A) polymerase.
3. **Splicing:** Eukaryotic genes contain non-coding regions (introns) interspersed with coding regions (exons). Splicing removes introns and joins exons to produce a continuous coding sequence.

- This process is carried out by the spliceosome, a complex of small nuclear RNAs (snRNAs) and proteins.
- Splicing involves:Recognition of specific splice sites at intron-exon boundaries.
- Formation of a lariat structure during intron removal.
- Exon ligation to generate mature mRNA.

Alternative Splicing

Alternative splicing allows a single gene to produce multiple protein isoforms by combining exons in different patterns. This process is a major contributor to proteome diversity and plays a role in tissue-specific gene expression.

For example:

- The Dscam gene in Drosophila can generate over 38,000 isoforms through alternative splicing.
- In humans, errors in alternative splicing are implicated in diseases such as spinal muscular atrophy, where mutations in the SMN1 gene affect spliceosomal components.

Translation

Translation is the process of converting the genetic code carried by mRNA into a sequence of amino acids, forming a polypeptide chain that folds into a functional protein.

Key Components of Translation

1. **mRNA:** Provides the template with codons (triplets of nucleotides) that specify amino acids.
2. **tRNA:** Adapter molecules that match codons with their corresponding amino acids.
   - Each tRNA has an anticodon sequence complementary to an mRNA codon.
   - tRNAs are "charged" with amino acids by aminoacyl-tRNA synthetases.
3. **Ribosomes:** Cellular machines composed of rRNA and proteins that coordinate translation. Ribosomes have three binding sites: the A (aminoacyl), P (peptidyl), and E (exit) sites.

Phases of Translation

1. **Initiation:** The small ribosomal subunit binds to the mRNA's 5' cap or a ribosome binding site (Shine-Dalgarno sequence in prokaryotes).
   - The initiator tRNA, carrying methionine, pairs with the start codon (AUG).
   - The large ribosomal subunit joins the complex to form the functional ribosome.
2. **Elongation:** Codons are read sequentially, and corresponding tRNAs bring amino acids to the ribosome.
   - Peptide bonds form between amino acids, catalyzed by the ribosome's peptidyl transferase activity.
   - The ribosome translocates along the mRNA, shifting tRNAs through the A, P, and E sites.
3. **Termination:** When the ribosome encounters a stop codon (UAA, UAG, UGA), release factors bind to the ribosome.
   - The polypeptide chain is released, and the ribosome disassembles.

Post-Translational Modifications

Proteins often undergo modifications that influence their function, localization, and stability:

- **Phosphorylation:** Addition of phosphate groups regulates enzyme activity and signaling pathways.
- **Ubiquitination:** Tags proteins for degradation via the proteasome.
- **Glycosylation:** Attachment of sugar moieties, important for protein stability and cell signaling.
- **Folding and Chaperones:** Molecular chaperones assist in proper protein folding, preventing aggregation and misfolding diseases like Alzheimer's.

Integration of Transcription, RNA Processing, and Translation

The molecular machinery of gene expression is tightly interconnected. Errors in any step can have cascading effects, leading to cellular dysfunction or disease. For instance:

- Mutations in splice sites can lead to defective mRNA and truncated proteins.
- Dysregulation of transcription factors can result in aberrant gene expression, contributing to cancer or developmental disorders.
- Advanced research continues to uncover the intricate regulation of these processes, offering potential therapeutic targets for gene-editing technologies and precision medicine. In summary, transcription, RNA processing, and translation are not isolated steps but part of a seamless and highly regulated continuum that drives cellular function and adaptation. This orchestration underscores the complexity and elegance of molecular biology.

GENE REGULATION IN DEVELOPMENT AND DISEASE

Gene regulation is central to life, determining how cells develop, function, and respond to environmental cues.

During embryonic development, precise control of gene expression ensures the correct differentiation of cells and formation of tissues. Dysregulation of this process can result in developmental disorders, while aberrant gene regulation in adults can lead to diseases such as cancer, diabetes, and neurodegenerative conditions. This section explores the intricacies of gene regulation in development and disease, highlighting critical pathways, examples, and emerging insights.

Developmental Gene Expression

Developmental biology is a remarkable symphony of cellular differentiation, tissue organization, and organogenesis, all orchestrated by tightly controlled gene expression. Early in development, a fertilized egg divides and differentiates into the diverse cell types that form an organism. This process is regulated by networks of genes that act in specific spatial and temporal patterns.

Hox Genes and Body Patterning

Hox genes, a subset of homeotic genes, are master regulators of body plan development in animals. These genes encode transcription factors that specify the identity of body segments along the anterior-posterior axis.

- **Structure of Hox Genes:** They are organized in clusters (HoxA, HoxB, HoxC, and HoxD in mammals), and their arrangement in the genome reflects their spatial expression pattern, a phenomenon known as collinearity.
- **Role in Development:** Hox genes dictate the identity of segments in the developing embryo, such as whether a vertebrate limb becomes a forelimb or a hindlimb.
- In Drosophila, mutations in Hox genes can cause dramatic phenotypic changes, such as the transformation of antennae into legs (antennapedia mutation).
- In humans, mutations in Hox genes are linked to congenital disorders like limb malformations and vertebral defects.

Notch Signaling and Cell Fate Decisions

The Notch signaling pathway is a critical cell-to-cell communication mechanism that regulates cell differentiation, proliferation, and apoptosis during development.

- **Mechanism:** The Notch receptor on a cell's surface interacts with ligands on adjacent cells, triggering cleavage of the receptor and the release of the Notch intracellular domain (NICD). The NICD translocates to the nucleus, where it influences transcription of target genes.
- **Roles in Development:** Governs neural differentiation by balancing the production of neurons and glial cells.
- Regulates blood vessel formation (angiogenesis) and heart development.
- Maintains stem cell populations in tissues like the intestine and skin.
- **Disruptions:** Aberrant Notch signaling can result in developmental anomalies, such as congenital heart defects and skeletal disorders.

Epigenetic Regulation During Development

Epigenetics plays a crucial role in developmental gene expression, enabling cells with the same DNA to differentiate into diverse types. Key mechanisms include:

- **Histone Modifications:** Acetylation and methylation patterns influence chromatin structure and gene activity.
- **DNA Methylation:** Silencing of lineage-inappropriate genes allows cells to specialize.
- **Non-Coding RNAs:** MicroRNAs and long non-coding RNAs fine-tune gene expression during differentiation.

Consequences of Dysregulated Developmental Gene Expression

Disruptions in gene regulatory networks during development can result in a spectrum of congenital anomalies:

1. **Neural Tube Defects (NTDs):** Improper regulation of genes like PAX3 and SHH leads to incomplete closure of the neural tube, resulting in conditions such as spina bifida.
2. **Cleft Lip and Palate:** Mutations in genes involved in craniofacial development (e.g., MSX1) result in this common birth defect.
3. **Congenital Heart Defects:** Abnormal expression of genes in pathways like Wnt and TGF-β causes defects in heart morphology.

Gene Dysregulation in Disease

Gene dysregulation underpins the pathology of many diseases. Both inherited mutations and environmental factors can disrupt gene expression, leading to cellular dysfunction. This section explores three major categories of diseases linked to gene dysregulation: cancer, diabetes, and neurodegenerative disorders.

Cancer: A Disease of Gene Dysregulation

Cancer arises from a breakdown in the regulation of cell proliferation, differentiation, and death. Two major classes of genes are involved:

1. **Oncogenes:** These are mutated or overexpressed versions of normal genes (proto-oncogenes) that drive cell proliferation.

Example: The RAS family of oncogenes is frequently mutated in cancers such as lung and colorectal cancer.

2. **Tumor Suppressor Genes:** These genes normally inhibit cell growth or promote apoptosis. Loss-of-function mutations in tumor suppressors lead to unchecked cell division.

   Example: TP53, known as the "guardian of the genome," is mutated in over 50% of cancers.

Mechanisms of Dysregulation:

- **Epigenetic Changes:** Hypermethylation of tumor suppressor gene promoters or global hypomethylation leading to genomic instability.
- **Transcriptional Dysregulation:** Overactivation of transcription factors like MYC and NF-κB.
- **Non-Coding RNAs:** Aberrant microRNA expression contributes to oncogenesis. For instance, miR-21 is overexpressed in several cancers and promotes tumor growth.

Diabetes: Impaired Gene Regulation in Metabolism

Diabetes is a metabolic disorder characterized by impaired glucose regulation due to defective insulin production (Type 1) or insulin resistance (Type 2). Gene dysregulation plays a central role in both types:

1. **Type 1 Diabetes:** Autoimmune destruction of pancreatic β-cells is associated with dysregulation of immune-related genes like HLA-DQ and PTPN22.

   Epigenetic changes in β-cells may exacerbate immune-mediated damage.

2. **Type 2 Diabetes:** Insulin resistance is linked to dysregulation of genes in insulin signaling pathways, such as IRS1 and AKT2.Environmental factors, like a high-fat diet, alter DNA methylation and histone acetylation, contributing to disease progression.

   Emerging evidence suggests that non-coding RNAs, particularly microRNAs, regulate insulin sensitivity and β-cell function, making them potential therapeutic targets.

Neurodegenerative Diseases: A Role for Gene Dysregulation

Neurodegenerative diseases, such as Alzheimer's, Parkinson's, and Huntington's, involve the progressive loss of neuronal function and structure. Gene dysregulation contributes to their pathology:

1. **Alzheimer's Disease:** Overproduction of amyloid-β due to mutations in APP or presenilin genes leads to plaque formation.

   Dysregulation of tau gene splicing results in neurofibrillary tangles.

2. **Parkinson's Disease:** Mutations in genes like SNCA (α-synuclein) and LRRK2 disrupt mitochondrial function and protein homeostasis.
3. **Huntington's Disease:** Expansion of CAG repeats in the HTT gene leads to toxic protein aggregates.

   Epigenetic mechanisms are also implicated. For example, global histone acetylation changes occur in Alzheimer's, suggesting that chromatin remodeling influences disease progression.

Epigenetic Changes and Environmental Influences

Epigenetic modifications bridge the gap between genetic predisposition and environmental factors in disease. Unlike mutations, epigenetic changes are reversible, offering therapeutic potential.

DNA Methylation and Histone Modifications

Environmental factors such as diet, toxins, and stress can modify epigenetic marks:

- **Hyper- or Hypomethylation:** Changes in CpG island methylation alter gene expression in diseases like cancer and diabetes.
- **Histone Modifications:** Acetylation and methylation changes influence chromatin accessibility, impacting disease susceptibility.

Transgenerational Epigenetic Inheritance

Epigenetic marks influenced by environmental exposures can be transmitted to offspring, affecting disease risk across generations. For instance, maternal malnutrition during pregnancy alters DNA methylation in metabolic genes, predisposing children to diabetes.

MicroRNAs and Environmental Stress

MicroRNAs (miRNAs) mediate gene expression changes in response to environmental stress. For example, miR-146a is upregulated in inflammation, linking environmental triggers to immune dysregulation in autoimmune diseases.

MOLECULAR MECHANISMS IN HEALTH AND DISEASE: AN AYURVEDIC VIEW

Ayurveda's Tridosha Theory and Modern Biology

Ayurveda, the ancient Indian system of medicine, describes health as a balance of three doshas: Vata, Pitta, and Kapha. These doshas correspond to physiological and metabolic processes:

- **Vata:** Movement and communication, akin to the nervous system.

- **Pitta:** Digestion and metabolism, associated with enzymes and hormones.
- **Kapha:** Structure and stability, related to immunity and tissue repair.

Recent studies suggest a genetic basis for Prakriti (individual constitution), linking doshas to gene expression profiles. For example, Pitta-dominant individuals may show heightened expression of pro-inflammatory cytokines, while Kapha types may exhibit enhanced lipid metabolism.

Ayurvedic Herbs and Gene Expression

Ayurvedic herbs contain bioactive compounds that modulate gene expression. Examples include:

- **Curcumin (from turmeric):** Influences NF-κB signaling to reduce inflammation.
- **Withanolides (from ashwagandha):** Regulate stress-responsive genes.
- **Neem extract:** Modulates immune-related pathways.

These compounds act as epigenetic modulators, altering DNA methylation and histone acetylation to restore cellular balance.

CASE STUDIES IN INTEGRATIVE MEDICINE

Cancer Therapy

Modern medicine employs targeted therapies like histone deacetylase inhibitors to reprogram cancer cells. Ayurveda complements this approach with herbs like Guduchi and Amla, which reduce oxidative stress and support detoxification pathways.

Neurodegenerative Diseases

Molecular research into Alzheimer's highlights the role of amyloid plaques and tau protein misfolding. Ayurvedic interventions like Brahmi and Shankhpushpi have shown neuroprotective effects, promoting memory and reducing oxidative damage.

Cardiovascular Health

Cardiovascular diseases are often linked to dysregulated cholesterol metabolism and inflammation. The Ayurvedic herb Arjuna has been shown to lower LDL cholesterol levels and enhance antioxidant defenses.

MULTIPLE CHOICE QUESTIONS

1. A molecular biologist is analyzing the regulatory dynamics of transcription initiation in eukaryotic cells. The researcher identifies that TATA-binding protein (TBP), a component of TFIID, is crucial for promoter recognition and subsequent RNA polymerase II recruitment. However, mutations in TBP significantly reduce transcription efficiency in specific stress-responsive genes. Which of the following conclusions most likely explains the observed effect of TBP mutations on gene expression?

A. TBP mutations only affect RNA polymerase I activity, as RNA polymerase II is not dependent on TBP.

B. TBP mutations impair the assembly of the pre-initiation complex, reducing transcriptional output in stress-responsive genes.

C. TBP primarily facilitates chromatin remodeling, with minimal impact on RNA polymerase recruitment.

D. TBP is dispensable for transcription in eukaryotic cells and primarily affects prokaryotic transcription systems.

2. In the context of Ayurvedic principles, the concept of Prakriti (constitution) is studied using genomic tools to map its correlation with single-nucleotide polymorphisms (SNPs). Researchers observe distinct SNP patterns linked to inflammatory cytokine genes across individuals with Kapha-dominant Prakriti. Which hypothesis aligns best with these findings?

A. Kapha-dominant individuals exhibit hyperactive inflammatory responses under all conditions.

B. Genetic variations in inflammatory cytokine genes predispose Kapha-dominant individuals to chronic metabolic diseases.

C. Ayurvedic classifications lack molecular basis and show no significant SNP associations.

D. Kapha-related traits are unrelated to cytokine-mediated immunity and metabolic health.

3. Consider a scenario where a scientist investigates the mechanism by which epigenetic modifications regulate gene expression in response to environmental stress. The study reveals increased acetylation of histones near heat-shock protein (HSP) genes under stress conditions. What role does histone acetylation likely play in this context?

A. Histone acetylation condenses chromatin structure, silencing HSP gene expression.

B. Acetylation prevents RNA polymerase II binding, reducing transcription during stress.

C. Histone acetylation facilitates chromatin relaxation, enhancing HSP transcription.

D. Acetylation exclusively targets non-coding regions, leaving HSP genes unaffected.

4. In Ayurveda, the balance of Agni (digestive fire) is crucial for maintaining metabolic health. A study integrates Ayurvedic dietary recommendations with modern nutritional science, revealing that diets rich in fiber and antioxidants improve gut microbiota diversity and enzymatic activity. How does this finding bridge Ayurveda and molecular biology?
   A. Ayurvedic practices enhance gut health solely through placebo effects.
   B. Gut microbiota modulation by fiber aligns with Ayurvedic emphasis on Agni's role in systemic health.
   C. Antioxidants improve enzymatic activity but have no connection to Ayurvedic principles.
   D. Ayurvedic diets lack scientific validation and rely on subjective interpretation.

5. A clinical study investigates the therapeutic effects of Ashwagandha (Withania somnifera) on stress-induced DNA damage in human lymphocytes. Results indicate reduced oxidative stress markers and enhanced DNA repair activity after treatment. Which conclusion aligns with these findings?
   A. Ashwagandha promotes genomic stability by increasing antioxidant enzyme levels.
   B. DNA repair mechanisms are independent of oxidative stress reduction.
   C. Ashwagandha-induced DNA repair occurs solely through its effect on apoptosis.
   D. Stress-induced DNA damage is irreparable, regardless of Ashwagandha supplementation.

6. Researchers hypothesize that the Ayurvedic concept of Rasayana therapies, aimed at rejuvenation, is mediated by the activation of sirtuin proteins (SIRT1 and SIRT3). Experimental data confirm increased mitochondrial biogenesis and reduced cellular senescence markers after Rasayana therapy. Which of the following interpretations best explains the findings?
   A. Sirtuin activation enhances mitochondrial health, consistent with Rasayana's rejuvenating effects.
   B. Rasayana therapies induce genetic mutations that prolong cellular life.
   C. Sirtuins suppress all forms of metabolic activity, ensuring cellular longevity.
   D. Rasayana therapies impair mitochondrial function but promote autophagy.

7. A geneticist studies the impact of transcriptional enhancers on tissue-specific gene expression. The deletion of a cardiac enhancer upstream of the MYH6 gene results in reduced heart muscle protein expression. Which conclusion aligns with these observations?
   A. Enhancers exclusively regulate gene expression in embryonic development.
   B. Tissue-specific enhancers are necessary for precise spatial and temporal gene regulation.
   C. Deleting an enhancer affects all genes within the same chromosomal region.
   D. MYH6 gene expression is independent of enhancer activity.

8. In Ayurveda, the concept of Vata dosha encompasses movement, including neural and circulatory functions. Modern research shows that neuroinflammation in Alzheimer's disease disrupts synaptic signaling. Which Ayurvedic perspective aligns with these findings?
   A. Imbalanced Vata disrupts neurotransmitter metabolism, leading to neurodegeneration.
   B. Vata's role is restricted to physical movement, unrelated to cognitive functions.
   C. Neuroinflammation represents a Pitta imbalance rather than a Vata disorder.
   D. Alzheimer's disease cannot be explained through Ayurvedic principles.

9. Experimental evidence suggests that DNA methylation patterns are altered in patients with autoimmune diseases, correlating with cytokine overproduction. Ayurvedic detoxification therapies claim to reduce inflammation by addressing the root cause. How might molecular mechanisms explain these claims?
   A. Detoxification reduces cytokine gene hypermethylation, restoring immune balance.
   B. Ayurvedic therapies directly repair damaged DNA in immune cells.
   C. Detoxification promotes methylation of inflammatory genes, silencing their expression.
   D. Ayurvedic interventions primarily affect non-genetic factors and lack epigenetic effects.

10. A comparative analysis of Ayurvedic and modern dietary approaches reveals that traditional Ayurvedic diets rich in astringent and bitter tastes correlate with improved metabolic health markers. Which molecular mechanism supports this correlation?
   A. Bitter compounds enhance glucose uptake by activating AMPK pathways.
   B. Astringent foods exclusively promote fat storage, counteracting metabolic health.
   C. Bitter and astringent foods lack bioactive compounds and provide no measurable benefits.
   D. Ayurvedic dietary principles only align with traditional cultural practices.

Directions (Q. No. 11-14): *Scenario-Based Questions*

SCENARIO 1

A clinical researcher investigates the efficacy of Ayurvedic formulations on gut microbiota diversity and systemic immunity. The study centers on Triphala, a classical Ayurvedic preparation comprising three fruits: Haritaki (Terminalia chebula), Bibhitaki (Terminalia bellirica), and Amalaki (Emblica officinalis). These fruits are traditionally believed to balance the three doshas—Vata, Pitta, and Kapha—and enhance gut health through detoxification. The research focuses on patients with irritable bowel syndrome (IBS), a condition characterized by dysbiosis (imbalance in gut microbiota) and chronic inflammation.

The results demonstrate that Triphala significantly restores gut microbiota diversity, increasing the abundance of beneficial bacteria such as Lactobacillus and Bifidobacterium. This restoration correlates with improved intestinal barrier integrity, reduced systemic inflammation (measured through decreased C-reactive protein levels), and elevated IgA levels, indicating enhanced systemic immunity. The study hypothesizes that the therapeutic effect of Triphala may depend on bioactive compounds like polyphenols and tannins, which have prebiotic and anti-inflammatory properties.

SCENARIO 2

An environmental biologist examines the sustainability of sourcing Amalaki, a critical ingredient in Triphala. Rising global demand for Ayurvedic formulations has led to overharvesting, threatening wild Amalaki populations. The biologist's study highlights that deforestation, soil degradation, and environmental pollution are not only reducing the availability of Amalaki but are also diminishing the bioactive compound concentration in the fruits. Laboratory analyses reveal that Amalaki harvested from degraded ecosystems contains significantly lower levels of antioxidants (e.g., ascorbic acid and ellagic acid), compromising its therapeutic efficacy.

The study also identifies the potential of agroforestry systems in promoting sustainable harvesting while maintaining the bioactive quality of Amalaki. These systems involve cultivating Amalaki alongside other native species to mimic natural ecosystems, reducing environmental stress and conserving biodiversity. However, the biologist notes that widespread adoption of sustainable practices faces challenges, including lack of farmer awareness and economic incentives.

11. Based on Scenario 1, which of the following mechanisms best explains how Triphala improves systemic immunity in patients with irritable bowel syndrome (IBS)?

A. Triphala directly enhances systemic immunity by stimulating antibody production in the absence of gut microbiota changes.

B. The restoration of gut microbiota diversity by Triphala strengthens intestinal barrier integrity, reduces systemic inflammation, and enhances IgA levels.

C. Triphala's effects are limited to detoxification, with no measurable impact on gut microbiota or systemic immunity.

D. Triphala functions as a placebo, and its effects on IBS symptoms and immunity are unrelated to its bioactive compounds.

12. Considering Scenario 2, which strategy would most effectively address the environmental challenges associated with Amalaki harvesting while preserving its therapeutic efficacy?

A. Establishing large-scale monoculture plantations of Amalaki to meet the rising global demand for Ayurvedic formulations.

B. Promoting agroforestry systems that cultivate Amalaki alongside native species, conserving biodiversity and maintaining bioactive compound levels.

C. Developing synthetic substitutes for Amalaki's bioactive compounds to reduce dependency on natural sources.

D. Reducing the global use of Amalaki in Ayurvedic formulations to alleviate harvesting pressures.

13. How does the environmental degradation of Amalaki, as described in Scenario 2, potentially impact the therapeutic outcomes observed in Scenario 1?

A. Reduced antioxidant levels in Amalaki diminish its efficacy in restoring gut microbiota diversity and systemic immunity.

B. The therapeutic benefits of Triphala are independent of the bioactive compound concentration in Amalaki, relying instead on its combination with the other fruits.

C. Environmental degradation enhances Amalaki's bioactive compounds, increasing its therapeutic potency in Triphala formulations.

D. Amalaki's quality has no measurable impact on the therapeutic outcomes of Triphala in IBS treatment.

14. Based on the interconnected findings of Scenarios 1 and 2, which of the following approaches would most comprehensively address both clinical and environmental challenges?

A. Prioritizing the development of synthetic alternatives to replace Amalaki in Triphala formulations.

B. Educating farmers and providing economic incentives to adopt sustainable agroforestry practices for cultivating Amalaki.
C. Promoting the conservation of Amalaki populations through reduced demand for Ayurvedic formulations.
D. Establishing a global standard for Triphala production that mandates sustainable harvesting practices and ensures therapeutic efficacy.

15. The principles of Ayurveda related to Tridosha state:
(a) Vata governs movement and is linked to the nervous system.
(b) Pitta controls metabolism and is associated with digestive enzymes.
(c) Kapha regulates structure and fluid balance in the body.
(d) The balance of Tridosha ensures physical and mental health.

Choose the correct answer from the options given below:
A. (a), (b), and (c) only
B. (a), (b), and (d) only
C. (a), (b), (c), and d
D. (b), (c), and (d) only

16. The biological actions of Ayurvedic Rasas (tastes) are classified as:
(a) Sweet Rasa promotes tissue growth and nourishment.
(b) Bitter Rasa detoxifies the body and reduces inflammation.
(c) Astringent Rasa strengthens tissues and controls bleeding.
(d) Sour Rasa enhances digestion and metabolic activity.

Choose the correct answer from the options given below:
A. (a), (b), and (d) only
B. (a), (b), (c), and (d)
C. (b), (c), and (e) only
D. (a), (c), and (d) only

17. Gene expression in molecular biology aligns with Ayurvedic concepts in the following ways:
(a) Epigenetic regulation mirrors the impact of Ayurvedic lifestyle interventions on health.
(b) Dosha balance corresponds to homeostasis at the cellular level.
(c) Rasayana therapies influence transcriptional regulation of stress-response genes.
(d) The concept of Agni aligns with metabolic enzyme activity.

Choose the correct answer from the options given below:
A. (a), (b), and (d) only
B. (a), (b), (c), and (d)
C. (b), (c), and (d) only
D. (a), (c), and (d) only

18. Molecular mechanisms involved in detoxification, as described in Ayurveda, include:
(a) Activation of cellular autophagy pathways.
(b) Reduction of oxidative stress via antioxidant molecules.
(c) Enhanced DNA repair mechanisms.
(d) Epigenetic modulation of inflammatory genes.

Choose the correct answer from the options given below:
A. (a), (b), and (c) only
B. (b), (c), and (d) only
C. (a), (b), (c), and (d)
D. (a), (c), and (d) only

19. The therapeutic mechanisms of Triphala include:
(a) Modulation of gut microbiota diversity.
(b) Stimulation of gut-associated lymphoid tissue (GALT).
(c) Reduction of systemic inflammation markers like CRP.
(d) Direct enzymatic activation of metabolic pathways.

Choose the correct answer from the options given below:
A. (a), (b), and (c) only
B. (a), (b), and (d) only
C. (b), (c), and (d) only
D. (a), (c), and (d) only

20. Epigenetic modifications relevant to Ayurvedic interventions include:
(a) DNA methylation changes in inflammatory genes.
(b) Histone acetylation to enhance gene accessibility.
(c) Modulation of microRNA expression in metabolic pathways.
(d) Telomere length maintenance through stress reduction.

Choose the correct answer from the options given below:
A. (a), (b), and (c) only
B. (a), (c), and (d) only
C. (a), (b), and (d) only
D. (a), (b), (c), and (d)

21. Molecular pathways targeted by Ayurvedic Rasayana therapies include:
(a) Activation of sirtuins to enhance mitochondrial function.

(b) Reduction of pro-inflammatory cytokine expression.
(c) Enhancement of antioxidant defense systems.
(d) Promotion of apoptosis in damaged cells.

Choose the correct answer from the options given below:

A. (a), (b), and (c) only
B. (b), (c), and (d) only
C. (a), (b), (c), and (d)
D. (a), (c), and (d) only

22. The balance of gut microbiota as described in molecular biology corresponds to Ayurvedic concepts in the following ways:

(a) Gut microbiota diversity reflects Vata's regulation of movement.
(b) Pitta governs enzymatic activity and metabolic functions in the gut.
(c) Kapha provides stability and protection through gut barrier function.
(d) Gut dysbiosis corresponds to doshic imbalance.

Choose the correct answer from the options given below:

A. (a), (b), and (c) only
B. (a), (b), (c), and (d)
C. (b), (c), and (d) only
D. (a), (c), and (d) only

23. Ayurveda's role in oxidative stress management is mediated by:

(a) Antioxidants in herbs like Ashwagandha and Amalaki.
(b) Detoxification therapies that reduce free radical production.
(c) Dietary interventions that suppress mitochondrial dysfunction.
(d) Yoga and meditation, which enhance cellular repair mechanisms.

Choose the correct answer from the options given below:

A. (a), (b), and (c) only
B. (b), (c), and (d) only
C. (a), (b), (c), and (d)
D. (a), (c), and (d) only

24. Molecular biology validates Ayurvedic concepts through:

(a) The influence of diet on epigenetic modifications.
(b) Stress reduction practices affecting gene expression.
(c) Herbal interventions modulating inflammatory pathways.
(d) The absence of any correlation between Ayurveda and molecular pathways.

Choose the correct answer from the options given below:

A. (a), (b), and (c) only
B. (a), (b), and (d) only
C. (b), (c), and (d) only
D. (a), (b), (c), and (d)

25. Match List–I (Concepts) with List–II (Descriptions):

List–I	List–II
(a) Triphala therapy	1. Restores gut microbiota and reduces inflammation
(b) Rasayana	2. Promotes rejuvenation and longevity through cellular repair
(c) Panchakarma	3. Detoxification therapy for removing Ama
(d) Srotas	4. Channels of circulation and flow within the body

Choose the correct answer from the options given below:

A. (a)-1, (b)-2, (c)-3, (d)-4
B. (a)-3, (b)-1, (c)-4, (d)-2
C. (a)-2, (b)-4, (c)-1, (d)-3
D. (a)-4, (b)-3, (c)-2, (d)-1

26. Match List–I (Epigenetic Modification) with List–II (Functions):

List–I	List–II
(a) DNA methylation	1. Silences inflammatory genes
(b) Histone acetylation	2. Increases gene expression by relaxing chromatin
(c) MicroRNA regulation	3. Controls mRNA translation
(d) Telomere stabilization	4. Slows cellular aging

Choose the correct answer from the options given below:

A. (a)-1, (b)-2, (c)-3, (d)-4
B. (a)-3, (b)-4, (c)-1, (d)-2
C. (a)-2, (b)-1, (c)-4, (d)-3
D. (a)-4, (b)-3, (c)-2, (d)-1

27. Match List–I (Ayurvedic Elements) with List–II (Biological Correlations):

List–I	List–II
(a) Vata	1. Nervous system and intracellular communication
(b) Pitta	2. Metabolism and enzyme regulation
(c) Kapha	3. Structure, immunity, and stability
(d) Agni	4. Digestive enzymes and metabolic pathways

Choose the correct answer from the options given below:

A. (a)-1, (b)-2, (c)-3, (d)-4
B. (a)-3, (b)-4, (c)-1, (d)-2
C. (a)-4, (b)-1, (c)-2, (d)-3
D. (a)-2, (b)-3, (c)-4, (d)-1

28. Match List–I (Rasas in Ayurveda) with List–II (Biological Functions):

List–I	List–II
(a) Sweet	1. Promotes tissue growth and nourishment
(b) Bitter	2. Reduces inflammation and detoxifies
(c) Astringent	3. Strengthens tissues and controls bleeding
(d) Sour	4. Enhances digestion and metabolic activity

Choose the correct answer from the options given below:

A. (a)-1, (b)-2, (c)-3, (d)-4
B. (a)-3, (b)-4, (c)-1, (d)-2
C. (a)-4, (b)-1, (c)-2, (d)-3
D. (a)-2, (b)-3, (c)-4, (d)-1

29. Match List–I (Components of DNA) with List–II (Descriptions):

List–I	List–II
(a) Nucleotides	1. Building blocks of DNA
(b) Histones	2. Proteins that package DNA into chromatin
(c) Enhancers	3. Regulatory sequences for gene expression
(d) RNA polymerase	4. Enzyme involved in transcription

Choose the correct answer from the options given below:

A. (a)-1, (b)-2, (c)-3, (d)-4
B. (a)-3, (b)-4, (c)-1, (d)-2
C. (a)-4, (b)-1, (c)-2, (d)-3
D. (a)-2, (b)-3, (c)-4, (d)-1

30. Match List–I (Regulatory Elements) with List–II (Roles):

List–I	List–II
(a) Promoters	1. Initiate transcription by RNA polymerase binding
(b) Silencers	2. Suppress transcription of specific genes
(c) Enhancers	3. Increase transcription levels by interacting with promoters
(d) Operators	4. Regulate operon gene clusters in prokaryotes

Choose the correct answer from the options given below:

A. (a)-1, (b)-2, (c)-3, (d)-4
B. (a)-3, (b)-4, (c)-1, (d)-2
C. (a)-4, (b)-1, (c)-2, (d)-3
D. (a)-2, (b)-3, (c)-4, (d)-1

31. Match List–I (Ayurvedic Concepts) with List–II (Biological Mechanism):

List–I	List–II
(a) Dosha balance	1. Homeostasis at the molecular and systemic levels
(b) Ama	2. Accumulation of toxins impairing cellular function
(c) Rasayana	3. Activation of sirtuins and reduction of oxidative stress
(d) Ritucharya	4. Seasonal routines that prevent doshic imbalance

Choose the correct answer from the options given below:

A. (a)-1, (b)-2, (c)-3, (d)-4
B. (a)-3, (b)-4, (c)-1, (d)-2
C. (a)-4, (b)-1, (c)-2, (d)-3
D. (a)-2, (b)-3, (c)-4, (d)-1

32. Match List–I (Therapies in Ayurveda) with List–II (Effects):

List–I	List–II
(a) Shodhana	1. Cleansing and detoxification of the body
(b) Shamana	2. Palliation and symptomatic relief
(c) Nasya	3. Administration of medicated oils via nasal route
(d) Basti	4. Medicated enemas for cleansing and rejuvenation

Choose the correct answer from the options given below:

A. (a)-1, (b)-2, (c)-3, (d)-4
B. (a)-3, (b)-4, (c)-1, (d)-2
C. (a)-4, (b)-1, (c)-2, (d)-3
D. (a)-2, (b)-3, (c)-4, (d)-1

33. Match List–I (Stages of Gene Expression) with (Descriptions):

List–I	List–II
(a) Transcription	1. RNA synthesis from DNA template
(b) RNA processing	2. Modification of pre-mRNA into mature mRNA
(c) Translation	3. Protein synthesis from mRNA template
(d) Post-translational modifications	4. Protein folding and chemical modifications

Choose the correct answer from the options given below:

A. (a)-1, (b)-2, (c)-3, (d)-4
B. (a)-3, (b)-4, (c)-1, (d)-2
C. (a)-4, (b)-1, (c)-2, (d)-3
D. (a)-2, (b)-3, (c)-4, (d)-1

34. Match List–I (Cellular Oraganelles) with (Functions):

List–I	List–II
(a) Nucleus	1. Houses genetic material and regulates transcription
(b) Mitochondria	2. Generates cellular energy (ATP)
(c) Endoplasmic reticulum	3. Protein folding and lipid synthesis
(d) Lysosome	4. Breaks down cellular waste and macromolecules

Choose the correct answer from the options given below:

A. (a)-1, (b)-2, (c)-3, (d)-4
B. (a)-3, (b)-4, (c)-1, (d)-2
C. (a)-4, (b)-1, (c)-2, (d)-3
D. (a)-2, (b)-3, (c)-4, (d)-1

Directions (Q. No. 35–39): *Following questions are based on Statement 1 and Statement 2. Read both the statements carefully and choose the correct answer from the options given below:*

A. Both Statement 1 and Statement 2 are true, and Statement 2 is the correct explanation of Statement 1.
B. Both Statement 1 and Statement 2 are true, but Statement 2 is not the correct explanation of Statement 1.
C. Statement 1 is true, but Statement 2 is false.
D. Statement 1 is false, but Statement 2 is true.
E. Both Statement 1 and Statement 2 are false.

35. Statement 1: Epigenetic modifications, such as DNA methylation, play a crucial role in regulating gene expression in response to environmental stress.

Statement 2: DNA methylation increases chromatin accessibility, promoting transcription of stress-response genes.

36. Statement 1: The concept of Agni in Ayurveda represents metabolic activity and enzymatic processes crucial for maintaining homeostasis.

Statement 2: Impairment of Agni leads to the accumulation of Ama (toxins), which disrupts dosha balance and contributes to disease progression.

37. Statement 1: Ayurvedic Rasayana therapies, such as the use of Ashwagandha and Amalaki, reduce oxidative stress and slow cellular aging.

Statement 2: The bioactive compounds in Rasayana herbs activate sirtuins and enhance mitochondrial biogenesis.

38. Statement 1: Gut health plays a central role in systemic immunity, as evidenced by increased IgA levels after improving microbiota diversity.

Statement 2: Ayurvedic formulations like Triphala influence gut health through their prebiotic and antioxidant properties.

39. Statement 1: Overharvesting of Amalaki due to global demand for Triphala formulations poses a threat to biodiversity and sustainability.

Statement 2: Substituting Amalaki with synthetic antioxidants can address sustainability issues while preserving the therapeutic efficacy of Triphala.

Directions (Q. No. 40–45): *There are two statements in each question. One is labelled as Assertion (A) and the other is as Reason (R). Read both the statements and choose the correct answer from the options given below:*

A. Both Assertion (A) and Reason (R) are true, and Reason (R) is the correct explanation of Assertion (A).
B. Both Assertion (A) and Reason (R) are true, but Reason (R) is not the correct explanation of Assertion (A).
C. Assertion (A) is true, but Reason (R) is false.
D. Assertion (A) is false, but Reason (R) is true.
E. Both Assertion (A) and Reason (R) are false.

40. Assertion (A): Ayurvedic principles emphasize the role of seasonal routines (Ritucharya) in preventing dosha imbalances and maintaining health.

Reason (R): Seasonal changes influence physiological processes, requiring adjustments in diet, lifestyle, and herbal interventions to sustain homeostasis.

41. Assertion (A): DNA methylation patterns are significantly influenced by lifestyle factors such as diet, stress, and physical activity.

Reason (R): Ayurvedic practices, including yoga and meditation, alter DNA sequences, preventing genetic predisposition to diseases.

42. Assertion (A): Chronic inflammation is a major driver of metabolic disorders, including diabetes and obesity.

Reason (R): Ayurvedic herbs like turmeric modulate inflammatory pathways, such as NF-κB signaling, to reduce systemic inflammation.

43. Assertion (A): Rasayana therapies in Ayurveda enhance immune function and delay cellular aging.

Reason (R): These therapies work by directly eliminating pathogens and neutralizing free radicals in the bloodstream.

44. **Assertion (A):** Ayurvedic detoxification therapies, such as Panchakarma, improve metabolic efficiency and reduce oxidative stress.

    Reason (R): Panchakarma therapies induce autophagy and stimulate mitochondrial repair processes at the cellular level.

45. **Assertion (A):** Environmental degradation reduces the bioactive compound content in medicinal plants like Amalaki, compromising their therapeutic efficacy.

    Reason (R): Agroforestry and sustainable cultivation practices improve both the yield and medicinal quality of Amalaki.

Directions (Q. No. 46–50): *Read the passage carefully and answer the questions given below:*

Molecular biology is the study of the structure, function, and interactions of macromolecules essential for life, such as DNA, RNA, and proteins. It has revolutionized our understanding of cellular processes, gene regulation, and the mechanisms underlying health and disease. Ayurveda, an ancient Indian system of medicine, offers a holistic approach to health, emphasizing balance and harmony within the body's fundamental energies, or doshas: Vata, Pitta, and Kapha. While Ayurveda and molecular biology may appear distinct, they converge in their focus on maintaining homeostasis, or balance, at the cellular and systemic levels. This interplay has opened new avenues for integrating traditional knowledge with modern science to better understand disease prevention, management, and personalized healthcare.

At the heart of molecular biology lies DNA, the molecule that encodes genetic information. DNA's double-helical structure, discovered by James Watson and Francis Crick in 1953, forms the blueprint for life. DNA is composed of nucleotides, each consisting of a sugar, phosphate group, and one of four nitrogenous bases—adenine, thymine, cytosine, and guanine. The specific sequence of these bases constitutes the genetic code, which determines an organism's traits. The regulation of this code through processes such as transcription, translation, and post-transcriptional modifications enables cells to respond dynamically to their environment. These molecular processes align intriguingly with Ayurveda's concept of Agni, or digestive fire, which governs transformation and metabolism at the bodily and cellular levels. Impairments in Agni, according to Ayurveda, lead to an accumulation of toxins, or Ama, disrupting doshic balance and predisposing individuals to disease. Similarly, molecular biology identifies disruptions in enzymatic activity, metabolic pathways, and cellular signaling as root causes of disorders like metabolic syndrome, autoimmune diseases, and cancer.

RNA, the intermediary molecule between DNA and protein, plays a critical role in gene expression. Transcription, the process by which DNA is converted into RNA, is a tightly regulated step influenced by promoter sequences, transcription factors, and chromatin accessibility. The resulting RNA undergoes processing, including splicing, capping, and polyadenylation, to form mature messenger RNA (mRNA), which is then translated into proteins. These proteins, often referred to as the workhorses of the cell, perform diverse functions, from catalyzing biochemical reactions to providing structural support. The dynamic regulation of these processes ensures cellular adaptability and efficiency. Ayurveda's holistic framework resonates with this complexity, particularly through the concept of Vata, the dosha associated with movement and communication. Vata's regulation of nervous system functions and intracellular signaling aligns with molecular biology's emphasis on the coordination of transcriptional and translational processes for maintaining cellular homeostasis.

Gene regulation is a cornerstone of molecular biology, with mechanisms operating at multiple levels, including transcriptional, post-transcriptional, translational, and post-translational. Epigenetics, which involves heritable changes in gene expression without altering the underlying DNA sequence, has emerged as a pivotal area of study. Modifications such as DNA methylation and histone acetylation influence chromatin structure, thereby regulating gene accessibility. These processes have profound implications for development, aging, and disease. Ayurveda's emphasis on lifestyle practices, such as yoga, meditation, and specific dietary regimens, offers parallels in influencing these molecular pathways. For instance, studies have shown that mindfulness practices reduce stress-induced changes in DNA methylation, potentially lowering the expression of pro-inflammatory genes. Similarly, Ayurvedic diets rich in antioxidants and bioactive compounds like polyphenols from herbs such as turmeric and Amalaki can modulate oxidative stress and repair pathways, promoting cellular health.

The concept of Rasayana in Ayurveda, which focuses on rejuvenation and longevity, finds molecular correlates in mechanisms like sirtuin activation, mitochondrial biogenesis, and enhanced cellular repair. Sirtuins, a family of proteins involved in aging and stress resistance, are activated by caloric restriction and bioactive compounds found in Ayurvedic herbs. For example, Ashwagandha and Triphala have been shown to reduce markers of oxidative stress and inflammation while improving mitochondrial function. These effects align with the molecular understanding of aging, where the balance of reactive oxygen species (ROS) and cellular repair systems is critical for maintaining homeostasis. Similarly, Ayurvedic detoxification therapies like Panchakarma, which aim to remove toxins and restore balance, may stimulate autophagy—a process by which cells degrade and recycle damaged components. Autophagy is recognized in molecular biology as a crucial mechanism for cellular maintenance and disease prevention, particularly in conditions like neurodegeneration and cancer.

Gut health, a foundational aspect of Ayurveda, is increasingly recognized in molecular biology as central to systemic health. The gut microbiota, a complex community of microorganisms residing in the gastrointestinal tract, plays a pivotal role in digestion, immunity, and even mental health. Ayurveda's emphasis on balancing doshas through dietary interventions and herbal formulations aligns with modern insights into gut-microbiome interactions. For example, Triphala, a traditional Ayurvedic preparation combining Haritaki, Bibhitaki, and Amalaki, has been shown to restore microbial diversity, enhance the growth of beneficial bacteria such as Lactobacillus and Bifidobacterium, and improve intestinal barrier function. These effects correlate with increased activity of gut-associated lymphoid tissue (GALT), leading to enhanced systemic immunity and reduced inflammation. Molecular biology corroborates these findings, identifying gut dysbiosis as a factor in chronic diseases such as diabetes, obesity, and neurodegeneration.

While the convergence of Ayurveda and molecular biology offers promising insights, it also highlights challenges that need to be addressed. One critical issue is the sustainability of medicinal plant resources. The rising global demand for Ayurvedic formulations, such as Triphala, has led to the overharvesting of key ingredients like Amalaki, threatening their wild populations. Environmental stressors, including deforestation, soil degradation, and pollution, further compromise the quality of these plants by reducing their bioactive compound content. Molecular analyses reveal that Amalaki fruits harvested from degraded ecosystems contain lower levels of antioxidants such as ascorbic acid and ellagic acid, diminishing their therapeutic efficacy. Addressing these challenges requires the adoption of sustainable cultivation practices, such as agroforestry systems that mimic natural ecosystems and promote biodiversity. These approaches not only conserve resources but also maintain the medicinal quality of plants, ensuring the long-term efficacy of Ayurvedic formulations.

The integration of Ayurveda with molecular biology represents a unique opportunity to bridge traditional wisdom with modern science. By combining Ayurveda's holistic principles with the precision of molecular techniques, personalized and preventive healthcare solutions can be developed. For instance, genomic and epigenomic studies could refine Ayurvedic classifications of Prakriti (constitution) to identify genetic predispositions to certain diseases, enabling tailored interventions. Similarly, molecular profiling of Ayurvedic herbs could uncover novel bioactive compounds with therapeutic potential, guiding drug discovery and development.

In conclusion, molecular biology and Ayurveda, though distinct in origin and approach, share a common goal: the preservation and promotion of health through balance and harmony. The molecular intricacies of gene expression, metabolic regulation, and cellular signaling complement Ayurveda's systemic perspective on well-being. Together, these fields have the potential to transform healthcare by integrating ancient knowledge with cutting-edge science, offering holistic and sustainable solutions to modern health challenges. As research continues to deepen our understanding of these connections, the synergy between Ayurveda and molecular biology will likely unlock new frontiers in medicine, paving the way for a future where tradition and innovation coexist harmoniously.

46. According to the passage, how does the Ayurvedic concept of Agni align with molecular biology?

A. It represents the role of metabolic enzymes and regulatory pathways in maintaining cellular homeostasis.

B. It corresponds to the gut microbiota's ability to regulate systemic inflammation.

C. It exclusively focuses on detoxification processes mediated by liver enzymes.

D. It describes the oxidative stress pathways linked to cellular aging.

47. What is the role of Rasayana therapies, such as Ashwagandha and Triphala, in molecular mechanisms, as mentioned in the passage?

A. They activate sirtuins, enhance mitochondrial biogenesis, and reduce oxidative stress, promoting cellular longevity.

B. They primarily function as detoxifiers, clearing reactive oxygen species without influencing cellular repair mechanisms.

C. They inhibit inflammatory pathways but show no impact on mitochondrial health.

D. They directly modulate DNA sequences to reverse genetic predispositions to aging-related diseases.

48. How does the passage describe the relationship between gut health and systemic immunity?

A. Restored microbial diversity and improved gut barrier function enhance gut-associated lymphoid tissue (GALT) activity, boosting immunity.

B. Systemic immunity improves independently of gut health due to the detoxifying properties of Ayurvedic formulations.

C. Gut health is primarily influenced by oxidative stress, with no connection to microbial diversity or immune responses.

D. Ayurvedic formulations reduce gut microbiota diversity, which strengthens immunity through detoxification.

49. Based on the passage, what is a major challenge in integrating Ayurveda with modern molecular biology?

A. The lack of scientific validation for Ayurvedic practices and principles.

B. Environmental degradation reducing the bioactive compound content in medicinal plants like Amalaki.

C. Resistance to adopting Ayurvedic methods in clinical applications due to cultural differences.

D. Limited awareness of how molecular pathways correspond to Ayurvedic concepts like doshas.

50. What solution does the passage suggest for addressing sustainability challenges in Ayurvedic formulations?

A. Promoting agroforestry systems that conserve biodiversity and maintain medicinal quality.

B. Replacing natural ingredients like Amalaki with synthetic alternatives that mimic their bioactive properties.

C. Restricting the production of popular formulations like Triphala to protect plant populations.

D. Encouraging monoculture farming of Ayurvedic herbs to meet global demand without impacting biodiversity.

ANSWER WITH EXPLANATIONS

1. **B:** TBP mutations impair the assembly of the pre-initiation complex by preventing RNA polymerase II from binding effectively to the promoter. Stress-responsive genes rely heavily on this machinery for activation during environmental challenges. This highlights the importance of promoter recognition in eukaryotic transcription, where mutations can specifically affect stress-response elements. While TBP is not exclusively linked to RNA polymerase I, its critical role in RNA polymerase II recruitment explains its significance in transcription. Thus, the observation supports the nuanced role of TBP in transcriptional regulation, particularly under stress conditions that demand precise gene activation.

2. **B:** Kapha-dominant individuals exhibit polymorphisms in inflammatory cytokine genes, indicating a genetic predisposition to metabolic diseases. Ayurveda's classification of Prakriti correlates with molecular patterns, including those influencing inflammatory responses. This supports the hypothesis that Ayurvedic principles align with genomic markers, enabling personalized medicine. Kapha's inherent stability may predispose individuals to slower metabolism, but this link between cytokines and Kapha highlights a scientific basis for Prakriti. This finding does not generalize hyperactivity in all conditions but rather reflects Ayurveda's nuanced understanding of constitutional traits.

3. **C:** Histone acetylation relaxes chromatin, facilitating the transcription of heat-shock protein (HSP) genes. Under stress, HSP genes must rapidly activate, and histone acetylation ensures their accessibility to RNA polymerase. This contradicts ideas that acetylation condenses chromatin or targets only non-coding regions. The role of acetylation in enhancing transcriptional activity underscores its adaptive importance during stress. By modifying histone tails, acetylation directly influences chromatin dynamics, representing a critical regulatory layer. This molecular mechanism aligns with the need for flexible gene expression systems in eukaryotic cells, particularly under environmental challenges.

4. **B:** The modulation of gut microbiota through dietary fiber and antioxidants bridges Ayurveda's Agni with molecular biology. Fiber acts as a prebiotic, fostering microbial diversity, while antioxidants mitigate oxidative stress in the gut. This integrated understanding highlights how Ayurvedic dietary recommendations support systemic health. The finding that microbiota and enzymatic activity are interlinked reinforces Ayurveda's emphasis on digestion as a cornerstone of health. Rejecting placebo effects, this explanation scientifically validates Agni's role in systemic metabolism. Modern microbiome studies align with these principles, showcasing Ayurveda's relevance in contemporary healthcare paradigms.

5. **A:** Ashwagandha enhances antioxidant enzyme levels, reducing oxidative stress and promoting DNA repair. This mechanism stabilizes genomic integrity, mitigating damage caused by reactive oxygen species (ROS). The study's findings highlight Ashwagandha's potential in stress-induced genomic instability, aligning with its traditional role in Ayurveda as an adaptogen. The herb's bioactive compounds target ROS, reducing DNA strand breaks and facilitating repair pathways. While oxidative stress is linked to apoptosis, Ashwagandha's impact

on DNA repair supports longevity and cellular health. This underscores its therapeutic role in preventing stress-related molecular damage.

6. **A:** Rasayana therapies activate sirtuin proteins, enhancing mitochondrial function and reducing cellular senescence. Sirtuins regulate key pathways involved in aging, including DNA repair and metabolic efficiency. These therapies' impact on mitochondrial biogenesis aligns with the Ayurvedic goal of rejuvenation and longevity. The effects observed are consistent with molecular biology's understanding of aging mechanisms, particularly the role of oxidative stress and mitochondrial health. Rasayana's systemic benefits extend beyond calorie restriction mimetics, reinforcing its position in preventive medicine. This molecular alignment bridges traditional practices with modern scientific insights.

7. **B:** Tissue-specific enhancers are essential for precise gene regulation, ensuring spatial and temporal expression patterns. The MYH6 gene, critical for cardiac muscle function, requires specific enhancer elements for proper expression. Deleting such enhancers disrupts gene activity without affecting neighbouring genes. This specificity underscores the modularity of gene regulation in eukaryotes. Enhancers act as cis-regulatory elements, highlighting the evolutionary refinement of transcriptional control. The observation that deletion impacts tissue-specific expression aligns with molecular biology's emphasis on localized regulatory mechanisms in complex organisms.

8. **A:** Imbalanced Vata disrupts neurotransmitter metabolism, contributing to neurodegeneration. Ayurveda's perspective aligns with molecular biology, where neuroinflammation and disrupted synaptic signaling play roles in Alzheimer's disease. Vata governs movement, including neural transmission, linking its imbalance to cognitive decline. Ayurveda's systems biology approach complements the molecular understanding of Alzheimer's, highlighting integrative healthcare opportunities. Rejecting oversimplification, this connection underscores the potential of holistic frameworks in addressing complex diseases. Ayurveda's insights into dosha imbalances provide a lens to explore innovative neuroprotective strategies.

9. **C:** Ayurvedic detoxification promotes methylation of inflammatory genes, silencing excessive cytokine expression. This aligns with molecular evidence that epigenetic modifications influence immune balance. Detoxification therapies reduce oxidative stress, enabling epigenetic reprogramming and immune regulation. The observed epigenetic effects validate Ayurveda's claim that detoxification addresses root causes of inflammation. While not repairing DNA directly, these interventions impact gene regulation, supporting systemic health. The integration of epigenetics and Ayurveda underscores the potential for complementary approaches in immune modulation.

10. **A:** Bitter compounds enhance glucose uptake via AMPK activation, supporting metabolic health. Ayurvedic dietary principles, emphasizing bitter and astringent tastes, align with molecular pathways regulating glucose metabolism. This explanation bridges Ayurveda and molecular biology, validating traditional practices through biochemical evidence. Rejecting cultural reductionism, this finding underscores Ayurveda's scientific relevance. The modulation of metabolic pathways through dietary interventions reflects the holistic nature of traditional medicine. Ayurvedic insights into taste-based health impacts offer opportunities for integrative nutritional strategies.

11. **B:** Triphala's impact on systemic immunity is intricately linked to its ability to restore gut microbiota diversity. Beneficial bacteria such as Lactobacillus and Bifidobacterium, promoted by Triphala, play a critical role in maintaining intestinal barrier integrity. This integrity prevents translocation of toxins and pathogens into systemic circulation, reducing inflammatory markers like C-reactive protein. Elevated IgA levels indicate enhanced mucosal immunity, a key outcome of Triphala's prebiotic effects. The role of bioactive compounds such as polyphenols and tannins further explains its dual anti-inflammatory and microbiota-modulating properties, bridging traditional Ayurvedic insights with modern gut health research in addressing IBS and immunity.

12. **B:** Agroforestry systems represent a sustainable solution to the environmental challenges of Amalaki harvesting, preserving both its availability and therapeutic efficacy. By mimicking natural ecosystems, these systems reduce environmental stress, enhance soil health, and conserve biodiversity. This approach not only protects wild populations of Amalaki but also maintains high concentrations of bioactive compounds such as antioxidants. Large-scale monoculture plantations fail to address ecological degradation, while synthetic substitutes cannot fully replicate the synergistic properties of natural Amalaki. Agroforestry, combined with farmer education and economic incentives, balances ecological sustainability with the growing demand for Ayurvedic formulations, ensuring long-term therapeutic reliability.

13. **A:** Environmental degradation of Amalaki directly impacts its therapeutic potency, as reduced levels of antioxidants

like ascorbic acid and ellagic acid diminish its efficacy in Triphala formulations. These bioactive compounds play a critical role in restoring gut microbiota diversity and reducing systemic inflammation, as demonstrated in Scenario 1. Without these compounds, the therapeutic benefits observed in IBS patients, such as improved intestinal barrier function and enhanced immunity, would be compromised. This underscores the need for sustainable harvesting practices to ensure the preservation of Amalaki's medicinal properties and the efficacy of Triphala in addressing both gut health and systemic immunity.

14. **D:** A comprehensive approach involves establishing global standards for Triphala production, mandating sustainable harvesting practices while ensuring therapeutic consistency. This strategy addresses the environmental challenges of overharvesting Amalaki by promoting agroforestry and biodiversity conservation. Simultaneously, it safeguards the clinical efficacy of Triphala by maintaining the bioactive quality of its components. Educating farmers and incentivizing sustainable practices are integral to this framework. While synthetic alternatives and reduced demand may offer short-term solutions, they fail to preserve Ayurveda's holistic and synergistic principles. A global standard bridges ecological and therapeutic priorities, ensuring the long-term viability of Triphala as both a medicinal and ecological resource.

15. **C:** The principles of Tridosha—Vata, Pitta, and Kapha—provide a framework for understanding the interconnected functions of movement, metabolism, and structure in Ayurveda. Vata aligns with the nervous system's role in communication, Pitta with enzymatic processes driving metabolism, and Kapha with structural stability and fluid balance. These principles collectively ensure physical and mental health, resonating with molecular biology's emphasis on systemic homeostasis. This comprehensive approach underscores the integrative potential of Ayurveda, where balance between doshas mirrors the molecular mechanisms that sustain health. Rejecting partial interpretations, the inclusion of all doshas supports Ayurveda's holistic model.

16. **B:** The biological actions of Ayurvedic Rasas correspond to specific physiological and therapeutic effects. Sweet Rasa supports tissue nourishment and growth, while Bitter Rasa detoxifies the body and reduces inflammation. Astringent Rasa strengthens tissues, promoting wound healing and controlling bleeding. Sour Rasa enhances digestive processes by stimulating enzymatic activity. These classifications align with modern phytochemistry, which identifies bioactive compounds responsible for these effects. This understanding bridges traditional Ayurvedic insights with scientific validation, emphasizing their relevance in contemporary healthcare. The inclusion of all Rasas reflects Ayurveda's nuanced understanding of taste-based therapeutics.

17. **B:** Ayurvedic concepts align with molecular biology through shared mechanisms like epigenetic regulation, homeostasis, and transcriptional modulation. Lifestyle interventions, such as Rasayana therapies, influence stress-response genes, while dosha balance corresponds to systemic equilibrium. The alignment between Agni and enzymatic activity highlights Ayurveda's integrative potential. This convergence offers a robust framework for preventive and personalized medicine. Rejecting reductionist interpretations, the inclusion of all elements demonstrates Ayurveda's systemic relevance. These parallels underscore Ayurveda's scientific basis, enabling its integration with molecular biology for holistic healthcare solutions.

18. **C:** Molecular mechanisms like autophagy, oxidative stress reduction, DNA repair, and epigenetic modulation mirror Ayurvedic detoxification processes. These pathways collectively address cellular damage, inflammation, and metabolic inefficiencies. Ayurveda's emphasis on detoxification aligns with the cellular need to maintain homeostasis and prevent disease progression. The inclusion of all mechanisms highlights the multidimensional impact of detoxification therapies. This integrative understanding bridges traditional practices with molecular evidence, reinforcing Ayurveda's therapeutic relevance. Rejecting partial explanations, the comprehensive inclusion of mechanisms underscores Ayurveda's scientific alignment with cellular biology.

19. **A:** Triphala's therapeutic mechanisms include restoring gut microbiota diversity, enhancing gut-associated lymphoid tissue (GALT) activity, and reducing systemic inflammation markers like C-reactive protein (CRP). These effects highlight its role in integrative healthcare, addressing gut health and immunity simultaneously. The exclusion of direct enzymatic activation reflects the specific focus on microbiota modulation. This comprehensive approach aligns with modern research on the gut-immune axis. The inclusion of key mechanisms supports Ayurveda's holistic impact on systemic health. Rejecting reductive interpretations, this observation underscores Triphala's multidimensional therapeutic potential.

20. **D:** Epigenetic modifications like DNA methylation, histone acetylation, microRNA regulation, and telomere stabilization collectively influence gene expression,

aging, and disease prevention. These processes align with Ayurvedic interventions, such as stress reduction, antioxidant-rich diets, and rejuvenation therapies. The inclusion of all modifications highlights the comprehensive impact of Ayurveda on molecular pathways. This alignment underscores the potential for integrative approaches to enhance health and longevity. Rejecting partial explanations, the inclusion of all mechanisms reflects Ayurveda's systemic relevance in epigenetic regulation. This understanding bridges traditional practices with molecular biology for preventive medicine.

21. C: Rasayana therapies target multiple molecular pathways, including sirtuin activation, cytokine suppression, antioxidant defense enhancement, and apoptosis in damaged cells. These mechanisms collectively address aging, inflammation, and cellular dysfunction, supporting longevity and systemic health. The inclusion of all pathways reflects the comprehensive impact of Rasayana on molecular processes. This alignment bridges traditional Ayurvedic insights with modern molecular biology, emphasizing their therapeutic relevance. Rejecting partial interpretations, the inclusion of all mechanisms underscores Rasayana's multidimensional role in health optimization. This understanding validates Ayurveda's holistic approach to rejuvenation.

22. B: Gut microbiota diversity reflects Vata's regulation of movement, while Pitta governs enzymatic activity and metabolism. Kapha provides structural stability and supports the gut's barrier function, ensuring systemic equilibrium. Dysbiosis corresponds to doshic imbalance, aligning Ayurveda's framework with modern research on the gut-immune axis. The inclusion of all elements highlights Ayurveda's integrative potential in gut health. This comprehensive understanding bridges traditional and molecular insights, emphasizing the relevance of dosha-based interventions. Rejecting partial interpretations, the inclusion of all factors reflects Ayurveda's systemic perspective on health and disease prevention.

23. C: Ayurveda's role in oxidative stress management includes antioxidants like Ashwagandha, detoxification therapies reducing free radicals, dietary interventions enhancing mitochondrial efficiency, and yoga improving cellular repair mechanisms. These processes collectively address inflammation, cellular aging, and metabolic inefficiencies. The inclusion of all factors highlights Ayurveda's multidimensional impact on oxidative stress pathways. This alignment bridges traditional practices with molecular evidence, reinforcing Ayurveda's therapeutic relevance. Rejecting partial explanations, the comprehensive inclusion of mechanisms underscores Ayurveda's systemic alignment with molecular biology. This integrative understanding supports holistic healthcare solutions.

24. A: Molecular biology validates Ayurveda through evidence of diet influencing epigenetics, stress reduction altering gene expression, and herbal interventions modulating inflammatory pathways. This convergence highlights Ayurveda's systemic relevance in modern medicine. The exclusion of non-correlations reflects the scientific basis for integrative approaches. This alignment bridges traditional practices with empirical validation, emphasizing their therapeutic potential. The inclusion of key mechanisms underscores Ayurveda's multidimensional impact on molecular processes. Rejecting reductive interpretations, this observation validates Ayurveda's role in preventive and personalized medicine. This understanding highlights Ayurveda's compatibility with molecular biology for holistic healthcare.

25. A: Triphala's primary therapeutic effect involves restoring gut microbiota diversity and reducing inflammation, which improves systemic health. Rasayana therapies like Triphala aim to rejuvenate and promote longevity by repairing cellular mechanisms, activating sirtuin pathways, and reducing oxidative stress. Panchakarma detoxifies the body, removing Ama (toxins) and enhancing cellular efficiency, while Srotas represent the channels or pathways that ensure circulation and waste removal. All these components together highlight Ayurveda's holistic approach to health. Each element aligns with its biological function, and their collective integration demonstrates how Ayurveda complements molecular biology in addressing systemic imbalances and maintaining homeostasis.

26. A: DNA methylation suppresses transcription by silencing specific genes, particularly inflammatory genes, ensuring precise gene regulation. Histone acetylation relaxes chromatin structure, making genes more accessible to transcriptional machinery. MicroRNA regulation controls post-transcriptional processes, modulating mRNA stability and translation efficiency. Telomere stabilization slows cellular aging, maintaining chromosomal integrity during replication. Together, these epigenetic processes reflect Ayurveda's influence through practices like meditation, yoga, and antioxidant-rich diets. Their combined roles demonstrate how molecular biology and Ayurvedic interventions converge on gene expression regulation, cellular aging, and stress responses, offering a scientific explanation for the holistic benefits of Ayurvedic therapies.

27. **A:** Vata governs movement and aligns with nervous system functions like intracellular communication and signal transduction. Pitta controls metabolic processes and enzyme regulation, facilitating energy production and digestion. Kapha provides stability, aligning with immune system support, extracellular matrix formation, and fluid balance. Agni represents digestive enzymes and metabolic pathways, integrating nutrition and energy conversion. These Ayurvedic concepts mirror molecular biology's understanding of physiological regulation. Their interconnectedness illustrates Ayurveda's systemic approach to health, where doshas function in harmony. Molecular evidence further validates these alignments, bridging traditional Ayurvedic principles with contemporary scientific models of health and disease.

28. **A:** The Sweet Rasa nourishes tissues, promoting growth and recovery, while the Bitter Rasa detoxifies and reduces inflammation through its bioactive compounds. The Astringent Rasa strengthens tissues, aids in wound healing, and controls bleeding, reflecting its hemostatic properties. The Sour Rasa stimulates enzymatic activity, enhancing digestion and nutrient absorption. These Ayurvedic classifications align with modern molecular biology, where phytochemicals like polyphenols and flavonoids exhibit these effects. The inclusion of all Rasas highlights Ayurveda's comprehensive framework for balancing physiological functions. This synergy between traditional concepts and molecular mechanisms underscores the therapeutic value of Ayurvedic dietary interventions in health maintenance.

29. **A:** Nucleotides are the building blocks of DNA, forming its structural foundation. Histones are proteins that compact DNA into chromatin, playing a crucial role in gene regulation by modulating chromatin accessibility. Enhancers are non-coding DNA regions that increase transcription efficiency by interacting with promoters, ensuring precise gene expression. RNA polymerase is the enzyme responsible for transcribing DNA into RNA, initiating the flow of genetic information. Together, these components highlight the complexity of molecular regulation in gene expression. Their roles demonstrate how tightly coordinated molecular mechanisms govern cellular functions, supporting the broader integration of traditional Ayurveda with molecular insights.

30. **A:** Promoters initiate transcription by providing RNA polymerase binding sites, while enhancers increase transcriptional activity through long-range interactions. Silencers suppress transcription by recruiting repressor proteins to specific DNA regions, ensuring tight regulation. Operators, found in prokaryotes, regulate operon gene clusters, reflecting a simpler yet effective system of genetic control. These regulatory elements illustrate molecular biology's precision in gene expression. Their inclusion underscores the alignment between Ayurveda's emphasis on balance and molecular biology's focus on regulatory coordination. Together, these mechanisms demonstrate the interconnectedness of biological systems, offering a foundation for integrating traditional principles with advanced molecular strategies.

31. **A:** Dosha balance aligns with systemic homeostasis, ensuring equilibrium at molecular and physiological levels. Ama, representing toxins in Ayurveda, corresponds to cellular dysfunction caused by oxidative stress and metabolic inefficiencies. Rasayana therapies activate sirtuin pathways, reduce oxidative damage, and enhance mitochondrial function, promoting rejuvenation and longevity. Ritucharya (seasonal routines) prevents doshic imbalance by aligning biological rhythms with environmental changes. These interconnected Ayurvedic principles find validation in molecular biology, emphasizing harmony and adaptability. This integration highlights Ayurveda's preventive approach to health, reinforcing its relevance in managing modern health challenges through scientific and traditional frameworks.

32. **A:** Shodhana represents detoxification, cleansing the body and removing accumulated toxins. Shamana provides palliative care, offering symptomatic relief and restoring balance. Nasya involves the nasal administration of medicated oils, targeting the sinuses and upper respiratory system. Basti refers to enemas used for detoxification and rejuvenation, directly addressing gut health. These Ayurvedic therapies align with molecular mechanisms like autophagy, oxidative stress reduction, and inflammation control. Together, they demonstrate Ayurveda's systemic approach to health and wellness. Each therapy reflects a distinct yet interconnected function, showcasing Ayurveda's comprehensive methodology for maintaining physiological balance and addressing chronic diseases.

33. **A:** Transcription involves RNA synthesis from a DNA template, initiating the flow of genetic information. RNA processing converts pre-mRNA into mature mRNA through splicing, capping, and polyadenylation. Translation synthesizes proteins from mRNA templates, enabling cellular functions. Post-translational modifications refine proteins through folding, phosphorylation, and glycosylation, ensuring their functionality. These stages represent molecular biology's precision in gene expression regulation.

Their inclusion demonstrates the layered complexity of genetic information flow, mirroring Ayurveda's emphasis on systemic balance. This synergy between traditional principles and molecular mechanisms underscores the potential for integrative approaches in advancing personalized and preventive medicine.

34. A: The nucleus houses genetic material and regulates transcription, acting as the cell's control center. Mitochondria generate ATP, providing energy for cellular processes. The endoplasmic reticulum facilitates protein folding and lipid synthesis, while lysosomes degrade waste and recycle cellular components. Together, these organelles reflect the specialized and interconnected nature of cellular systems. Their roles align with Ayurveda's focus on balance and harmony, where each component contributes to overall health. This understanding bridges molecular biology's mechanistic insights with Ayurveda's holistic principles, highlighting their shared emphasis on maintaining cellular and systemic equilibrium in health and disease prevention.

35. C: Statement 1 is true as DNA methylation is a well-established epigenetic mechanism that regulates gene expression, particularly in response to environmental stimuli like stress, diet, and toxins. It typically silences genes by decreasing chromatin accessibility, preventing transcription. Therefore, Statement 2 is false because it inaccurately states that DNA methylation increases chromatin accessibility and promotes transcription, which is the opposite of what actually happens. Instead, histone acetylation is responsible for increasing chromatin accessibility and promoting gene transcription.

36. A: In Ayurveda, Agni is central to metabolism and health, governing the transformation of food into energy and cellular components. Impairment of Agni leads to the accumulation of Ama (toxins), disrupting systemic balance and contributing to diseases. Molecular biology aligns with this view, identifying impaired enzymatic activity and metabolic inefficiencies as precursors to inflammatory and chronic conditions. Ayurveda's holistic approach to maintaining Agni reflects its systemic understanding of health, where digestion and metabolism are foundational. This synergy between traditional principles and molecular evidence reinforces Ayurveda's relevance in addressing metabolic disorders and preventing disease through lifestyle and dietary interventions.

37. A: Rasayana therapies like Ashwagandha and Triphala enhance longevity by targeting molecular mechanisms such as sirtuin activation, mitochondrial biogenesis, and oxidative stress reduction. Sirtuins regulate aging-related processes by improving cellular repair, energy metabolism, and stress resistance. These therapies' antioxidant properties reduce cellular damage caused by reactive oxygen species, promoting homeostasis. By aligning with molecular pathways that support cellular health, Rasayana therapies validate Ayurveda's rejuvenative claims. Their systemic benefits underscore the integrative potential of combining traditional practices with modern molecular insights, offering holistic solutions for age-related conditions and chronic diseases while emphasizing cellular and systemic harmony.

38. A: Gut health is intricately linked to systemic immunity, with the gut-associated lymphoid tissue (GALT) playing a central role. Triphala enhances microbial diversity, improving gut barrier function and promoting beneficial bacteria like Lactobacillus. This, in turn, stimulates GALT, increasing IgA production and reducing systemic inflammation. Ayurveda's emphasis on gut health aligns with molecular biology's understanding of the gut-immune axis. The observed effects reflect how balanced gut microbiota can influence immunity and overall health. This synergy highlights Ayurveda's relevance in addressing chronic diseases linked to gut dysbiosis, bridging traditional practices with scientific validation of microbiota-driven immune regulation.

39. C: Statement 1 is true because overharvesting of Amalaki, a key ingredient in Triphala, has been widely reported to threaten biodiversity and compromise sustainability. Environmental degradation reduces its bioactive compound content, directly affecting its therapeutic quality. However, Statement 2 is false because substituting Amalaki with synthetic antioxidants does not preserve the holistic and synergistic effects of Triphala. Ayurveda emphasizes the use of whole plant-based formulations, which work in tandem with other ingredients and biological systems. Therefore, while synthetic alternatives may mimic certain compounds, they cannot fully replicate the efficacy or integrative value of natural Amalaki in Ayurvedic formulations.

40. A: Ayurveda emphasizes seasonal routines (Ritucharya) to prevent doshic imbalances caused by environmental changes. For instance, dietary adjustments during winter focus on balancing Kapha, while summer routines address Pitta imbalances. This aligns with molecular biology's understanding of how external factors like temperature and sunlight influence circadian rhythms and metabolic pathways. By adapting to seasonal shifts, individuals can maintain systemic equilibrium and prevent diseases. The emphasis on routine-based prevention highlights Ayurveda's foresight in recognizing environmental influences on physiology. This synergy with molecular mechanisms validates Ayurveda's preventive approach, integrating traditional practices with modern insights into environmental and biological interactions.

41. C: Lifestyle factors, such as diet and stress, influence DNA methylation and gene expression, as shown in molecular biology. However, the claim that practices like yoga and meditation alter DNA sequences is incorrect. These practices impact gene expression by modulating epigenetic markers, not the DNA structure itself. Stress reduction through yoga, for example, decreases methylation of inflammatory genes, supporting cellular health and preventing chronic diseases. Ayurveda's focus on lifestyle aligns with molecular biology's findings on epigenetics, emphasizing the importance of environment and behaviour in health. This bridge underscores Ayurveda's relevance in preventive and personalized medicine.

42. A: Chronic inflammation is a driver of metabolic disorders, as persistent inflammatory cytokines disrupt insulin signaling, contributing to diabetes and obesity. Ayurvedic herbs like turmeric contain curcumin, which modulates inflammatory pathways like NF-κB signaling, reducing systemic inflammation. This molecular mechanism aligns with Ayurveda's holistic approach to addressing disease at its root. By targeting inflammation, Ayurvedic interventions improve metabolic efficiency and prevent disease progression. The integration of traditional practices with molecular insights highlights Ayurveda's therapeutic potential, offering a comprehensive framework for managing metabolic and inflammatory conditions while addressing their underlying molecular causes.

43. C: Rasayana therapies enhance immune function and cellular health by reducing oxidative stress and promoting mitochondrial efficiency. However, the claim that they directly eliminate pathogens is incorrect. Instead, these therapies target systemic mechanisms, improving cellular repair and stress resistance. For example, Ashwagandha and Amalaki activate sirtuins, delay cellular aging, and strengthen immunity indirectly through improved homeostasis. This nuanced understanding bridges Ayurveda's rejuvenative goals with molecular biology's insights into aging and immunity. By focusing on systemic balance, Rasayana therapies demonstrate the interplay between tradition and modern science, emphasizing holistic approaches to health and longevity.

44. A: Panchakarma therapies align with molecular mechanisms like autophagy, oxidative stress reduction, and mitochondrial repair. These processes improve metabolic efficiency and restore cellular health by eliminating toxins and damaged components. Autophagy, in particular, plays a critical role in maintaining cellular integrity, mirroring Panchakarma's detoxification goals. This integrative understanding highlights the synergy between Ayurveda's detoxification practices and molecular biology's emphasis on cellular maintenance. By targeting systemic imbalances, Panchakarma offers a holistic solution to chronic diseases and metabolic dysfunction, reinforcing Ayurveda's relevance in modern healthcare. This alignment emphasizes the potential of combining traditional therapies with molecular insights.

45. A: Environmental degradation reduces the bioactive content of medicinal plants like Amalaki, compromising their therapeutic efficacy. Agroforestry and sustainable cultivation practices address this challenge by conserving biodiversity and maintaining medicinal quality. These methods align with Ayurveda's emphasis on ecological harmony and balance. By adopting sustainable practices, Ayurvedic formulations like Triphala can retain their efficacy while protecting natural resources. This approach bridges traditional principles with modern ecological science, emphasizing the need for long-term strategies to ensure availability and potency. The integration of sustainability into Ayurvedic practices underscores its relevance in addressing global health and environmental challenges.

46. A: The Ayurvedic concept of Agni, representing digestive fire, aligns with molecular biology's understanding of enzymatic and metabolic activity. Enzymes play a critical role in breaking down food molecules, transforming them into energy and metabolites necessary for cellular function. When Agni is balanced, it reflects efficient metabolic processes, similar to optimal enzymatic activity in molecular terms. Impairments in Agni parallel the disruption of these pathways, leading to an accumulation of toxins (Ama) and systemic inflammation. This correlation highlights the holistic nature of Ayurveda and its emphasis on digestion as foundational to health, validated by molecular insights into metabolism.

47. A: Rasayana therapies like Ashwagandha and Triphala target key molecular mechanisms, including sirtuin activation, mitochondrial biogenesis, and oxidative stress reduction. These therapies enhance cellular health by promoting energy efficiency, delaying senescence, and repairing oxidative damage. This aligns with molecular biology's understanding of aging, where mitochondrial dysfunction and oxidative stress are central factors. Ayurvedic rejuvenative practices complement these processes, offering a systemic approach to longevity. By focusing on cellular-level rejuvenation, Rasayana therapies underscore the synergy between traditional medicine and modern science, demonstrating how integrative approaches can address chronic diseases and age-related degeneration effectively.

48. **A:** Gut health and systemic immunity are intrinsically connected, with the gut-associated lymphoid tissue (GALT) playing a key role in immune regulation. Triphala enhances gut microbiota diversity, which improves the gut barrier and stimulates GALT activity. This leads to increased IgA production, reinforcing immune defenses while reducing systemic inflammation. Ayurveda's focus on gut health aligns with molecular biology's emphasis on the gut-immune axis, where microbial diversity is critical for maintaining immune homeostasis. This demonstrates how Ayurvedic formulations support systemic health through microbiota modulation, bridging ancient practices with modern understanding of immune regulation.

49. **B:** One of the greatest challenges in integrating Ayurveda with molecular biology is the environmental degradation and overharvesting of medicinal plants like Amalaki. These practices reduce bioactive compound concentrations, compromising therapeutic efficacy and threatening biodiversity. While synthetic alternatives might offer temporary solutions, they fail to replicate the holistic benefits of natural formulations. Ayurveda's emphasis on ecological harmony and molecular biology's focus on bioactive quality converge in the need for sustainable cultivation practices. By addressing these challenges through agroforestry and conservation, both fields can ensure the longevity of traditional formulations and their integration into modern healthcare systems.

50. **A:** Sustainable cultivation practices, such as agroforestry systems, are critical for preserving biodiversity and maintaining the medicinal quality of plants like Amalaki. These systems mimic natural ecosystems, reducing environmental stress while promoting the long-term viability of medicinal resources. This approach aligns with Ayurveda's emphasis on balance and harmony, addressing ecological and therapeutic challenges simultaneously. Sustainable harvesting ensures that traditional formulations like Triphala retain their efficacy without depleting natural resources. By adopting these practices, Ayurveda can continue to offer holistic healthcare solutions, bridging ancient wisdom with contemporary demands for environmental sustainability and therapeutic reliability.

UNIT 8: PHYSIOLOGY, BIOCHEMISTRY AND NANOTECHNOLOGY

CHAPTER 22

DIGESTIVE, RESPIRATORY, AND CIRCULATORY SYSTEMS IN AYURVEDA

Ayurvedic Understanding of the Digestive, Respiratory, and Circulatory Systems

Ayurveda, an ancient system of medicine originating in India, views the human body as an intricate interplay of physical, mental, and spiritual energies. Central to its philosophy is the concept of maintaining balance within the body, mind, and environment. The digestive, respiratory, and circulatory systems play a pivotal role in this balance, functioning not only as physiological mechanisms but also as conduits for prana (life force), ojas (vital essence), and the doshas (Vata, Pitta, and Kapha).

In Ayurveda, these systems are intricately interconnected. The digestive system, termed Agni (digestive fire), is seen as the cornerstone of health. A well-functioning Agni ensures proper digestion, absorption, and assimilation of nutrients, which directly influences the respiratory and circulatory systems. The respiratory system, governed by Prana Vayu, is responsible for life force circulation and oxygenation of tissues. Meanwhile, the circulatory system, referred to as Rakta Dhatu, distributes vital nutrients and oxygen throughout the body, sustaining the essence of life.

The Digestive System (Agni and Ama)

1. **Agni:** The Digestive Fire. In Ayurveda, Agni refers to the metabolic fire responsible for digesting food, absorbing nutrients, and eliminating waste. There are thirteen types of Agni, categorized into:
   - **Jatharagni:** Governs the digestion of food in the stomach.
   - **Bhutagni:** Manages the transformation of the five elements (Pancha Mahabhuta) in food into nutrients.
   - **Dhatvagni:** Metabolizes nutrients into bodily tissues (Dhatus).

   A balanced Agni is the cornerstone of health, termed Samagni, while its imbalances lead to:
   - **Vishamagni:** Irregular digestion, associated with Vata dosha.
   - **Tikshnagni:** Overactive digestion, associated with Pitta dosha.
   - **Mandagni:** Weak digestion, linked to Kapha dosha.
2. **Ama:** The Root of Disease. Ama, or toxic undigested matter, is a result of impaired Agni. Accumulation of Ama clogs bodily channels (srotas), leading to diseases. Digestive health in Ayurveda revolves around maintaining a strong Agni to prevent Ama formation.
3. **Srotas:** The Channels of Digestion. The gastrointestinal tract is seen as a network of srotas that transport nutrients and eliminate waste. Ayurveda emphasizes the importance of clearing obstructions in these channels to maintain optimal digestive function.

The Respiratory System (Prana & Udana Vayu)

The respiratory system is governed by the movement of Prana Vayu, the sub-dosha of Vata responsible for inhalation, exhalation, and oxygenation. Ayurveda views respiration as a bridge between the body and the mind, with its rhythm reflecting mental and physical states.

1. **Prana:** The Vital Life Force. Prana, often translated as "breath," represents the vital energy that sustains life. It is absorbed through the respiratory system and distributed throughout the body via the circulatory system.
2. **Respiratory Anatomy in Ayurveda:** Ayurveda describes the respiratory system as consisting of:
   - **Kantha (Throat):** The entry point for air and food.
   - **Pranavaha Srotas:** Channels for the movement of Prana, encompassing the nasal passages, trachea, and lungs.
3. **Disorders of Prana:** Imbalances in the respiratory system manifest as:
   - Kapha-related conditions (e.g., mucus congestion, asthma).
   - Vata-related disorders (e.g., breathlessness, dry cough).
   - Pitta-related inflammations (e.g., bronchitis, fever).
4. **Breath and Mind:** Ayurveda highlights the importance of pranayama (breath control) to regulate the respiratory system, calm the mind, and enhance the flow of Prana. Practices such as Nadi Shodhana and Kapalabhati cleanse and strengthen the respiratory system.

The Circulatory System (Rakta Dhatu and Srotas)

The circulatory system, as understood in Ayurveda, is an intricate and vital component of the body's functioning, deeply connected to the mind, consciousness, and life force. It revolves around the concepts of Rakta Dhatu (blood tissue) and Raktavaha Srotas (channels of circulation). Rakta, described as a carrier of nutrients, oxygen, and Prana (life force), sustains life by nourishing the body and linking the physical with the subtle energies. This holistic understanding of circulation transcends the mere movement of blood, encompassing the flow of consciousness and vitality.

1. **Rakta Dhatu:** The Essence of Life. The concept of Rakta Dhatu in Ayurveda encompasses more than the modern understanding of blood. Rakta, which translates to "that which is red," signifies vitality, life force, and the nourishment of the body and mind. In Ayurveda, Rakta is the second Dhatu (tissue) among the seven Dhatus, serving as a bridge between the nourishment provided by Rasa Dhatu (plasma) and the sustenance required by the deeper tissues. Rakta Dhatu is essential for distributing life-sustaining nutrients, oxygen, and Prana throughout the body.
2. **The Role and Significance of Rakta Dhatu:** Rakta Dhatu serves as a pivotal component in the sustenance of life and the smooth functioning of the human body. Ayurveda considers it both a physical and subtle element that maintains vitality and balances the body, mind, and spirit.

Nourishing Tissues and Organs

Rakta Dhatu acts as the carrier of nutrients derived from the digestive process, supplying energy and essential components to all tissues. The constant circulation of Rakta ensures:

- Oxygenation of tissues.
- Delivery of metabolic nutrients.
- Maintenance of organ function.

Supporting Life and Vitality

The Sanskrit term "Rakta" signifies life itself. Without healthy Rakta, the body cannot sustain its metabolic functions or maintain its natural vigor. This Dhatu is considered:

- The harbinger of vitality and stamina.
- A determinant of physical and mental resilience.
- The carrier of life force, enabling all physiological processes.

Distributing Prana

Prana, or the vital life energy, flows through Rakta Dhatu. In Ayurveda, it is understood that Rakta acts as a medium for the distribution of Prana, reaching every tissue and organ system. This ensures:

- Cellular rejuvenation.
- Mental clarity and focus.
- Harmonization of bodily energies.

Inherent Attributes of Rakta

Rakta is associated with specific traits that define its quality and function:

1. **Complexion:** Healthy Rakta imparts a radiant, glowing complexion.
2. **Energy:** It is the source of physical stamina and mental clarity.
3. **Strength:** Rakta supports musculoskeletal strength and immune resilience.

Imbalances in Rakta not only manifest as physiological disorders but also as psychological and emotional disturbances. For example:

- Excessive Pitta dosha in Rakta may lead to irritability or anger.
- Depleted Rakta may result in lethargy, depression, or reduced vitality.

2. **The Production and Transformation of Rakta:** In Ayurveda, the production of Rakta Dhatu is intricately linked to the digestive system and the metabolic process, guided by the interaction of various Doshas, Agni (digestive fire), and the liver-spleen axis.

Ahara Rasa (Nutrient Plasma): The journey of Rakta begins with digestion. Food consumed is broken down by the digestive fire (Jatharagni) into Ahara Rasa, the nutrient-rich essence that serves as the precursor to all Dhatus.

Transformation by Agni (Metabolic Fire): The Ranjaka Pitta, located in the liver and spleen, plays a central role in converting Ahara Rasa into Rakta Dhatu. This transformation is supported by:

1. **Ranjaka Pitta:** Imparts redness and vitality to Rakta.
2. **Dhatvagni:** Specific metabolic fire for each Dhatu that ensures proper assimilation and maturation.

Assimilation and Circulation: Once formed, Rakta is circulated through the Raktavaha Srotas, delivering oxygen, nutrients, and Prana. Proper circulation ensures:

Cellular repair and regeneration.

- Maintenance of body temperature and pH balance.
- Detoxification of waste products.
- Factors Influencing Rakta Formation
  1. **Optimal Digestion:** Strong Jatharagni ensures complete digestion and nutrient absorption.
  2. **Dietary Quality:** Foods rich in iron, antioxidants, and proteins support Rakta production.
  3. **Liver and Spleen Health:** The liver and spleen are primary sites for Rakta transformation and purification.

3. **The Qualities of Healthy Rakta:** The qualities (Gunas) of healthy Rakta provide insights into its state and function. These attributes are directly observable and offer a diagnostic lens for determining imbalances.

Redness and Radiance: Healthy Rakta imparts a glowing complexion and a natural luster to the skin. A lack of redness may indicate anemia or Rakta depletion, while excessive redness may point to aggravated Pitta.

Fluidity and Viscosity: Balanced Rakta maintains an appropriate consistency that ensures smooth flow through the srotas. Increased viscosity can lead to sluggish circulation (Kapha aggravation), while decreased fluidity may cause dryness and Vata-related disorders.

Lightness and Warmth: Rakta inherently possesses lightness and a slight warmth due to its Pitta dominance. This quality ensures efficient oxygenation, thermoregulation, and nutrient transport.

- Indicators of Healthy Rakta
- Vibrant energy levels.
- Stable emotions and mental clarity.
- Absence of visible signs of Ama (toxins) in circulation.

4. **Disorders of Rakta Dhatu**: Rakta Dhatu imbalances arise due to a combination of poor dietary habits, improper lifestyle choices, dosha vitiations, and environmental factors. These imbalances manifest as both acute and chronic conditions, affecting the circulatory system and overall vitality.

Causes of Imbalances

1. **Dietary Factors**
   - Excessive intake of sour, salty, and spicy foods increases Pitta in Rakta.
   - Poor-quality, processed, or heavy foods lead to Ama accumulation.
2. **Lifestyle Issues**
   - Sedentary habits hinder circulation and lead to Kapha-related stagnation.
   - Chronic stress disturbs the Prana and Vata, affecting Rakta's quality.
3. **Dosha Imbalances**
   - Aggravated Pitta causes overheating and inflammatory disorders.
   - Vata imbalances lead to irregular circulation and dryness in tissues.
   - Kapha dominance results in sluggish circulation and congestion.

Common Rakta Disorders

1. **Raktapitta (Bleeding Disorders)**
   - Characterized by excessive bleeding due to Pitta aggravation in Rakta.
   - Symptoms include nosebleeds, hematemesis, and profuse menstruation.
2. **Anemia (Panduroga)**
   - Insufficient production of healthy Rakta causes pallor, fatigue, and weakness.
   - Often linked to low iron levels and impaired digestion.

3. **Skin Diseases**
   - Conditions such as eczema, psoriasis, and acne are directly related to Rakta vitiation.
   - These are treated through blood purification and balancing of doshas.
4. **Hypertension**
   - Elevated Pitta in Rakta Dhatu leads to increased blood pressure and heat.
5. **Varicose Veins**
   - A Vata-Kapha imbalance results in weak or congested circulation, causing vein-related disorders.

Approach to Rakta Disorders

Ayurveda emphasizes balancing the doshas, enhancing Agni, and detoxifying the Rakta Dhatu to manage its disorders. Key interventions include:

- **Herbal Remedies:** Manjistha, neem, and guduchi for blood purification.
- **Panchakarma Therapies:** Raktamokshana (bloodletting) and Virechana (purgation).
- **Dietary Modifications:** Emphasis on Pitta-pacifying foods like ghee, coriander, and pomegranate.

Raktavaha Srotas: The Channels of Circulation

1. **Understanding Raktavaha Srotas:**
   - Raktavaha Srotas are the channels responsible for the movement of Rakta Dhatu throughout the body. These channels include arteries, veins, and capillaries, and are supported by the liver, spleen, and heart.
   - The health of these channels is crucial for the circulatory system's function. They must remain unobstructed, flexible, and well-lubricated to facilitate the flow of Rakta.
2. **The Pathophysiology of Raktavaha Srotas:** Impairments in the channels occur due to:
   - **Ama Accumulation:** Toxins clogging the channels.
   - **Excessive Dosha Activity:** Aggravated Vata can cause constriction, Pitta inflammation, and Kapha blockages.
   - **Structural Damage:** Weakening or rupturing of the srotas.

   When the Raktavaha Srotas are impaired, circulation is disrupted, leading to:
   - **Hypertension:** Excessive pressure in the channels.
   - **Atherosclerosis:** Accumulation of Ama or Kapha in the vessels.
   - **Varicose Veins:** Weakening of the vessel walls due to aggravated Vata.
3. **Ayurvedic Perspective on Circulatory Health:** Ayurveda places great importance on maintaining the purity and unobstructed flow of Raktavaha Srotas. Preventive and therapeutic strategies include:
   - **Detoxification:** Panchakarma therapies such as Virechana (purgation) and Raktamokshana (bloodletting).
   - **Dietary Measures:** Consuming foods that pacify Pitta and support Rakta health, such as bitter greens, pomegranate, and turmeric.
   - **Lifestyle Practices:** Regular exercise, yoga, and stress management.

The Heart (Hridaya)

1. **Hridaya as the Seat of Life:** The heart, or Hridaya, is considered the seat of Prana, consciousness, and Ojas (vital essence) in Ayurveda. It is the central organ of the circulatory system and a key junction for the physical, mental, and spiritual dimensions of health.

   Hridaya's functions include:
   - **Pumping Rakta:** Circulating oxygen and nutrients.
   - **Regulating Emotions:** As the seat of consciousness, the heart influences emotional well-being.
   - **Maintaining Balance:** Acting as a bridge between the physical and subtle energies.
2. **Hridaya and the Doshas:** The heart is influenced by all three doshas:
   - Vata governs the movement of blood.
   - Pitta governs metabolic activities and heat generation.
   - Kapha ensures stability and structural integrity.
   - An imbalance in any dosha can lead to cardiovascular disorders.
3. **Common Disorders of the Heart:** Ayurveda recognizes a range of heart-related disorders, termed Hridroga, which are classified based on dosha involvement:
   - **Vata Hridroga:** Irregular heartbeat, anxiety, and dryness.
   - **Pitta Hridroga:** Inflammatory conditions, palpitations, and high blood pressure.
   - **Kapha Hridroga:** Congestion, sluggishness, and obesity-related issues

4. **Strengthening the Hridaya:** To maintain heart health, Ayurveda recommends:
   - **Herbs:** Arjuna, Ashwagandha, and Brahmi for strengthening the heart.
   - **Diet:** Avoiding excessive salt, sugar, and fatty foods while including heart-friendly spices like cinnamon and garlic.
   - **Pranayama and Meditation:** Promoting emotional balance and reducing stress.

Holistic Approaches to Circulatory Health

Ayurveda emphasizes a holistic approach to maintaining the health of Rakta Dhatu, Raktavaha Srotas, and Hridaya. Key strategies include:

1. **Diet and Nutrition**
   - Consuming fresh, balanced meals that support Agni and pacify Pitta.
   - Including blood-purifying foods like neem, aloe vera, and bitter melon.
2. **Herbal Remedies**
   - **Triphala:** For detoxification.
   - **Manjistha:** For blood purification.
   - **Guduchi:** For immunity and reducing inflammation.
3. **Panchakarma Therapies**
   - **Raktamokshana:** Bloodletting to remove impurities.
   - **Virechana:** Purgation to detoxify Pitta and Rakta.
4. **Lifestyle Modifications**
   - Engaging in regular physical activity.
   - Practicing mindfulness and stress reduction techniques.
   - Following daily and seasonal routines (Dinacharya and Ritucharya).

Role of These Systems in Maintaining Balance and Health

Ayurveda places significant emphasis on the harmonious functioning of the digestive, respiratory, and circulatory systems. These systems work synergistically to sustain life and maintain health.

1. **Interconnection Between the Systems**
   - The digestive system provides the nutrients required by the circulatory system to nourish tissues and organs.
   - The respiratory system supplies oxygen to the circulatory system, facilitating nutrient assimilation and energy production.
   - The circulatory system delivers oxygen and nutrients to the digestive and respiratory systems, enabling their optimal function.
2. **The Tridosha Influence:** Each system is influenced by the Tridoshas:
   - Vata governs movement within all systems, including peristalsis, blood flow, and respiration.
   - Pitta governs transformation, including digestion and oxygen exchange.
   - Kapha provides stability and lubrication, ensuring smooth functioning.
   - Imbalances in any dosha can disrupt the functioning of these systems, leading to disease.
3. **Disease Prevention and Management:** Ayurveda emphasizes prevention through:
   - **Diet:** Consuming foods that support Agni and balance the doshas.
   - **Pranayama:** Strengthening the respiratory system.
   - **Detoxification:** Clearing Ama from the circulatory and digestive systems through Panchakarma.
4. **Holistic Practices for Systemic Health**
   - **Herbal Remedies:** Herbs such as Triphala, Tulsi, and Ashwagandha support digestive, respiratory, and circulatory health.
   - **Yoga and Meditation:** Enhance the flow of Prana and regulate the mind-body connection.
   - **Lifestyle:** Daily routines (Dinacharya) and seasonal adjustments (Ritucharya) ensure systemic balance.

Case Studies and Practical Applications

Case Study 1: Improving Agni to Treat Chronic Respiratory Disorders

- A patient with chronic asthma experienced significant improvement through digestive support. This highlights the role of Agni in regulating systemic health.

Case Study 2: Panchakarma for Circulatory Cleansing

- A Panchakarma detox regimen improved circulation and reduced hypertension in a patient, emphasizing the interconnectedness of these systems.

Case Study 3: Breathwork for Stress-Induced Digestive Issues

- Regular pranayama alleviated stress-related indigestion in a patient, demonstrating the link between respiration and digestion.

MULTIPLE CHOICE QUESTIONS

1. An integrative medicine researcher is examining how Ayurvedic concepts of Tridosha influence the management of chronic gastrointestinal disorders. The study hypothesizes that Vata imbalance predominantly causes conditions like irritable bowel syndrome (IBS), while Pitta imbalance is linked to inflammatory bowel disease (IBD). Observational data indicate that therapies focused on calming Vata through oleation, grounding herbs, and dietary modifications significantly reduce IBS symptoms. Simultaneously, therapies aimed at reducing Pitta, such as cooling herbs and eliminating spicy foods, alleviate symptoms in IBD patients. Which of the following conclusions best reflects the findings of this study?
   A. Vata imbalance exclusively governs all gastrointestinal disorders, dismissing the relevance of Pitta dosha.
   B. Ayurvedic therapies based on Tridosha principles align with the tailored management of gastrointestinal disorders.
   C. The hypothesis is invalid because Ayurvedic interventions show no measurable improvement in chronic GI diseases.
   D. Vata and Pitta imbalances are unrelated to the pathophysiology of gastrointestinal conditions.

2. A clinical trial is investigating the Ayurvedic concept of Agni (digestive fire) by analyzing its relationship with enzymatic efficiency in patients with metabolic syndrome. The trial reveals that patients with impaired Agni, as characterized by symptoms of indigestion and lethargy, show significant reductions in lipase and amylase activity. Following Ayurvedic interventions involving Agni-balancing herbs, these enzymatic activities improve, and patients report enhanced metabolic health. What is the most scientifically consistent explanation for this phenomenon within the Ayurvedic framework?
   A. Agni represents a symbolic concept with no relevance to measurable biochemical processes.
   B. Ayurvedic interventions enhance metabolic pathways by restoring enzymatic activity linked to Agni.
   C. Lipase and amylase activity remain unaffected by the Ayurvedic concept of Agni.
   D. Impaired Agni results exclusively from psychological factors, independent of metabolic function.

3. An Ayurvedic practitioner treats patients with respiratory disorders using herbs traditionally classified as "Prana-enhancing." These herbs are found to exhibit bronchodilatory and anti-inflammatory properties. The practitioner theorizes that the herbs target Kapha imbalance, which manifests as mucus accumulation and airway obstruction. A pharmacological analysis of these herbs reveals active compounds that regulate cytokine production and improve oxygen exchange in alveolar tissues. How does this study validate the Ayurvedic approach?
   A. Ayurvedic principles lack scientific validity, as cytokine regulation is not addressed in traditional texts.
   B. Ayurvedic herbs align with modern pharmacological effects, supporting Kapha-balancing therapies in respiratory health.
   C. Kapha imbalance has no role in respiratory disorders, contradicting the study's hypothesis.
   D. Prana-enhancing herbs function independently of Kapha and address respiratory issues through placebo effects.

4. An Ayurvedic researcher is exploring the circulatory system from a doshic perspective, emphasizing Pitta's role in governing blood flow and metabolism. The study highlights how Pitta imbalance correlates with inflammatory conditions such as atherosclerosis, characterized by elevated C-reactive protein (CRP) and arterial plaque formation. Treatments involving Pitta-pacifying herbs and dietary adjustments, such as reducing salty and sour foods, show marked reductions in CRP levels and improved lipid profiles. Which statement best integrates Ayurvedic theory with the study's findings?
   A. Pitta exclusively governs arterial stiffness and plaque formation.
   B. The therapeutic success of Pitta-pacifying treatments supports Ayurveda's role in circulatory health.
   C. Ayurvedic theories lack alignment with biomarkers like CRP and lipid profiles.
   D. Atherosclerosis cannot be addressed by Ayurvedic interventions, as it is unrelated to Pitta.

5. A biochemist is investigating the Ayurvedic concept of "Ojas" (vital energy) and its role in immune resilience. The study hypothesizes that Ojas corresponds to biomarkers of systemic immunity, such as immunoglobulin levels and antioxidant enzymes. Patients with compromised Ojas, marked by fatigue and frequent infections, are treated with Rasayana (rejuvenative) therapies, including Ashwagandha and Guduchi. Results show increased levels of IgA and glutathione, correlating with reduced infection rates

and improved vitality. Which statement best reconciles these findings with Ayurvedic principles?

A. Ojas is an abstract concept with no measurable correlation to immune biomarkers.

B. Rasayana therapies enhance systemic immunity, validating the Ayurvedic concept of Ojas.

C. Ojas is unrelated to physical health and pertains only to mental well-being.

D. Immune resilience in Ayurveda is governed solely by doshic balance, independent of Ojas.

6. An academic paper examines the role of Rasas (tastes) in regulating digestion and metabolic health, as per Ayurveda. It correlates Madhura Rasa (sweet taste) with anabolic effects, such as tissue nourishment, while Katu Rasa (pungent taste) is linked to catabolic effects, including toxin elimination. The study evaluates dietary interventions in patients with impaired digestion, finding that incorporating specific Rasas restores metabolic balance. What does this study indicate about the physiological relevance of Rasas in Ayurveda?

A. Rasas are symbolic representations and do not influence metabolism.

B. Each Rasa targets unique metabolic pathways, validating its role in health restoration.

C. Ayurvedic dietary recommendations lack empirical support for metabolic health.

D. Only Madhura Rasa has measurable anabolic effects, dismissing the role of other tastes.

7. A clinical study assesses the impact of Ayurvedic detoxification protocols, such as Panchakarma, on respiratory health. Patients with chronic obstructive pulmonary disease (COPD) undergo treatments aimed at reducing Kapha dosha, involving nasal irrigation (Nasya) and herbal steam therapy. Results indicate significant improvements in pulmonary function tests and reduced mucus production. What conclusion can be drawn about Panchakarma's role in respiratory health?

A. Panchakarma is effective in addressing Kapha imbalance, improving respiratory outcomes.

B. Panchakarma's efficacy is limited to detoxification, with no impact on respiratory function.

C. Ayurvedic detox therapies lack measurable effects on pulmonary health.

D. Panchakarma exacerbates Kapha imbalance, worsening respiratory disorders.

8. A researcher studying Ayurveda hypothesizes that the interdependence of the circulatory and respiratory systems is mediated through Prana Vayu and Udana Vayu. Analyzing patients with circulatory and respiratory disorders, they find that therapies focusing on these Vayus—such as Pranayama (breath control) and herbal formulations—improve oxygen saturation and cardiac output. How does this align with Ayurvedic concepts?

A. Prana and Udana Vayu represent symbolic metaphors, unrelated to physiological function.

B. Ayurvedic therapies demonstrate a direct relationship between Vayus and systemic physiology.

C. The circulatory and respiratory systems operate independently in Ayurvedic theory.

D. Vata dosha is unrelated to Prana and Udana Vayu, making the hypothesis invalid.

9. An Ayurvedic approach to managing diabetes focuses on Kapha and Pitta imbalances. A controlled study observes that Kapha-reducing herbs, such as Shilajit and Turmeric, improve insulin sensitivity and glycemic control. Pitta-balancing treatments reduce inflammation, lowering HbA1c levels. How do these findings support Ayurvedic interventions for diabetes?

A. Diabetes management in Ayurveda focuses on restoring doshic balance, validated by improved biomarkers.

B. Ayurvedic therapies fail to address insulin sensitivity, relying only on anti-inflammatory effects.

C. Kapha and Pitta imbalances are irrelevant in the context of diabetes management.

D. Ayurvedic treatments offer only symptomatic relief, lacking systemic efficacy.

10. A scholar is investigating how the Ayurvedic understanding of Srotas (channels) integrates with circulatory physiology. The research identifies Raktavaha Srotas (blood-carrying channels) as correlating with arteries and veins, and their obstructions with conditions like thrombosis. Therapies involving Rakta-cleansing herbs, such as Neem and Manjishtha, demonstrate enhanced blood flow and reduced clot formation. What does this study suggest about the Ayurvedic understanding of Srotas?

A. Srotas are philosophical constructs, unrelated to anatomical or physiological processes.

B. The concept of Srotas aligns with circulatory health, validated by improved clinical outcomes.

C. Rakta-cleansing herbs lack scientific evidence for addressing circulatory issues.

D. Srotas theory dismisses the relevance of physical obstructions in circulatory disorders.

Directions (Q. No. 11-14): *Scenario-Based Questions*

SCENARIO 1

A clinical researcher is investigating the role of the Ayurvedic digestive principle of Agni (digestive fire) in systemic inflammation and immunity. The study observes that patients with Mandagni (weak digestive fire) exhibit elevated levels of pro-inflammatory cytokines such as TNF-α and IL-6, alongside symptoms of poor digestion and fatigue. Ayurvedic treatments incorporating digestive stimulants like ginger, trikatu, and pippali significantly reduce these cytokine levels. Simultaneously, improvements in digestion are accompanied by increased IgA levels, indicating enhanced mucosal immunity. The researcher concludes that the balance of Agni is crucial not only for digestion but also for regulating systemic inflammatory and immune responses.

SCENARIO 2

An environmental biologist is studying the ecological sustainability of ginger (Zingiber officinale), a key herb in Ayurvedic digestive therapies. The biologist finds that intensive cultivation of ginger has led to soil depletion and reduced levels of bioactive compounds, such as gingerols, in the rhizome. This reduction compromises the herb's therapeutic efficacy. Additionally, the study highlights the impact of climate change on ginger cultivation, with rising temperatures leading to altered growth cycles and diminished yields. The researcher emphasizes the need for sustainable farming practices, including crop rotation and organic fertilization, to maintain both ecological balance and the herb's potency.

11. Based on the findings in Scenario 1, which mechanism best explains the reduction of systemic inflammation following the restoration of Agni in Ayurvedic therapy?

A. Restoration of Agni reduces pro-inflammatory cytokine production by enhancing metabolic efficiency and gut microbiota balance.

B. The increase in IgA levels neutralizes systemic inflammation without affecting Agni.

C. Ayurvedic digestive stimulants suppress the immune system directly, reducing cytokine levels.

D. Agni restoration has no measurable impact on inflammation, as it is purely a digestive concept.

12. Considering Scenario 2, which intervention would best address the ecological challenges associated with ginger cultivation while maintaining its therapeutic efficacy in Ayurvedic formulations?

A. Encouraging monoculture farming of ginger to maximize yield.

B. Promoting crop rotation and organic fertilization to restore soil health and bioactive compound concentration.

C. Developing synthetic alternatives to gingerols to replace natural ginger in Ayurvedic therapies.

D. Reducing the use of ginger in Ayurvedic formulations to conserve environmental resources.

13. How does the ecological degradation of ginger described in Scenario 2 potentially influence the outcomes observed in Scenario 1?

A. Reduced gingerol concentration diminishes its ability to restore Agni and control systemic inflammation.

B. The therapeutic efficacy of ginger is unaffected by ecological changes, as its potency lies in its Ayurvedic processing.

C. Altered growth cycles of ginger enhance its bioactive compounds, improving its anti-inflammatory properties.

D. The outcomes in Scenario 1 are unrelated to the ecological sustainability of ginger, as other herbs can substitute its role.

14. Based on the interconnected findings of Scenarios 1 and 2, which strategy would comprehensively address both the clinical and ecological challenges highlighted?

A. Focusing on synthetic production of gingerols to mitigate ecological degradation.

B. Implementing sustainable farming practices for ginger while exploring complementary herbs to support Agni restoration.

C. Prioritizing environmental conservation over the use of ginger in Ayurvedic therapies.

D. Restricting ginger cultivation to controlled laboratory environments for better yield and efficacy.

15. The principles of Ayurveda related to Tridosha state that:

(a) Vata governs movement and is linked to the nervous system.

(b) Pitta controls metabolism and is associated with digestive enzymes.

(c) Kapha regulates structure and fluid balance in the body.

(d) The balance of Tridosha ensures physical and mental health.

Choose the correct answer from the codes given below:

A. (a), (b), and (c) only

B. (a), (b), (d) only

C. (a), (b), (c), and (d)

D. (a) and (c) only

16. The Ayurvedic classification of tastes (Rasas) aligns with specific physiological functions as follows:

(a) Sweet Rasa promotes tissue nourishment and growth.

(b) Bitter Rasa detoxifies the body and reduces inflammation.

(c) Astringent Rasa strengthens tissues and controls bleeding.

(d) Sour Rasa enhances digestion and metabolic activity.

Choose the correct answer from the codes given below:
A. (a), (b), and (c) only
B. (a), (b), (c), and (d)
C. (a), (b), and (d) only
D. (b), (c), and (d) only

17. Ayurveda identifies the stages of digestion with specific doshas and their elemental influences:
(a) Sweet stage (Madhura Avasthapaka) is associated with Kapha and the water element.
(b) Sour stage (Amla Avasthapaka) corresponds to Pitta and the fire element.
(c) Pungent stage (Katu Avasthapaka) is linked to Vata and the air element.
(d) Digestive fire (Agni) governs the assimilation of nutrients and the maintenance of doshic balance.

Choose the correct answer from the codes given below:
A. (a), (b), and (c) only
B. (a), (b), (c), and (d)
C. (b), (c), and (d) only
D. (a), (b), and (d) only

18. The following describes the roles of different Dhatus (body tissues) in Ayurvedic physiology:
(a) Rasa Dhatu nourishes tissues and supports immunity.
(b) Rakta Dhatu ensures oxygenation and sustains life.
(c) Mamsa Dhatu provides physical strength and structural support.
(d) Meda Dhatu is responsible for lubrication and fat storage.

Choose the correct answer from the codes given below:
A. (a), (b), and (c) only
B. (a), (b), (c), and (d)
C. (b), (c), and (d) only
D. (a), (c), and (d) only

19. Respiratory functions in Ayurveda involve specific doshas and sub-doshas:
(a) Prana Vayu controls respiration and the exchange of air.
(b) Udana Vayu governs speech and exhalation.
(c) Avalambaka Kapha stabilizes the chest region and supports lubrication.
(d) Sadhaka Pitta influences emotional health and cardiac functions.

Choose the correct answer from the codes given below:
A. (a), (b), and (c) only
B. (a), (b), (c), and (d)
C. (b), (c), and (d) only
D. (a), (c), and (d) only

20. The six stages of disease manifestation (Shat Kriya Kalas) in Ayurveda describe:
(a) Sanchaya (Accumulation) as the initial imbalance of doshas without symptoms.
(b) Prakopa (Aggravation) as the doshas becoming excessive and producing mild symptoms.
(c) Prasara (Spread) as the doshas migrating to other sites in the body.
(d) Vyakti (Manifestation) as the full expression of symptoms and disease.

Choose the correct answer from the codes given below:
A. (a), (b), and (d) only
B. (a), (b), and (c) only
C. (a), (b), (c), and (d)
D. (b), (c), and (d) only

21. Ayurvedic therapies address specific conditions through targeted interventions:
(a) Panchakarma is a detoxification process aimed at balancing doshas.
(b) Rasayana promotes rejuvenation and tissue nourishment.
(c) Virechana eliminates excess Pitta through purgation.
(d) Nasya involves nasal therapies to regulate Prana Vayu.

Choose the correct answer from the codes given below:
A. (a), (b), and (c) only
B. (a), (b), (c), and (d)
C. (b), (c), and (d) only
D. (a), (c), and (d) only

22. The concept of Ojas is central to Ayurveda's approach to immunity and vitality:
(a) Ojas supports Bala (strength), which enhances resistance against disease.
(b) It influences Varna (complexion), signifying vitality and radiance.
(c) Depletion of Ojas leads to fatigue and susceptibility to illness.
(d) Ojas is primarily related to the Kapha dosha and has no impact on Vata or Pitta.

Choose the correct answer from the codes given below:
A. (a), (b), and (c) only
B. (a), (b), (c), and (d)
C. (a) and (c) only
D. (b), (c), and (d) only

23. The Ayurvedic perspective on immunity (Vyadhikshamatva) integrates various factors:
(a) Balanced Agni ensures proper digestion and toxin elimination.
(b) Strong Ojas is essential for physical and mental resilience.

(c) Doshic balance maintains systemic harmony and prevents disease.
(d) External therapies like Panchakarma have no role in building immunity.

Choose the correct answer from the codes given below:
A. (a), (b), and (c) only
B. (a), (b), (c), and (d)
C. (a), and (b) only
D. (b), and (c) only

24. The Ayurvedic classification of disease causation includes:
(a) Nidan (cause) refers to improper diet and lifestyle choices.
(b) Dosha imbalance (Vikriti) manifests as physiological disruptions.
(c) Ama accumulation is the primary cause of chronic illnesses.
(d) Dhatu depletion has no role in disease progression.

Choose the correct answer from the codes given below:
A. (a), (b), and (c) only
B. (a), (b), (c), and (d)
C. (b) and (c) only
D. (a) and (c) only

25. Match List–I (Concepts) with List–II (Descriptions) carefully and choose the correct answer from the codes given below:

List–I	List–II
(a) Agni types	1. Vishama Agni is irregular and linked to Vata dosha.
(b) Dosha imbalances	2. Ama accumulation leads to disease progression.
(c) Ama	3. Weak digestion causing toxic metabolic by-products.
(d) Ojas	4. Represents vitality and immunity.

Codes:
A. (a)-1, (b)-2, (c)-3, (d)-4
B. (a)-3, (b)-2, (c)-4, (d)-1
C. (a)-1, (b)-3, (c)-2, (d)-4
D. (a)-2, (b)-4, (c)-1, (d)-3

26. Match List–I (Sub-doshas) with List–II (Functions) carefully and choose the correct answer from the codes given below:

List–I	List–II
(a) Prana Vayu	1. Governs respiration and cognitive functions.
(b) Udana Vayu	2. Controls speech and upward movements.
(c) Samana Vayu	3. Balances digestive processes.
(d) Apana Vayu	4. Regulates excretion and downward energy flow.

Codes:
A. (a)-1, (b)-2, (c)-3, (d)-4
B. (a)-3, (b)-4, (c)-2, (d)-1
C. (a)-2, (b)-3, (c)-4, (d)-1
D. (a)-4, (b)-3, (c)-1, (d)-2

27. Match List–I (Herbs) with List–II (Primary Actions) carefully and choose the correct answer from the codes given below:

List–I	List–II
(a) Haritaki	1. Supports bowel regulation and detoxification.
(b) Amalaki	2. Rich in Vitamin C, rejuvenates tissues.
(c) Pippali	3. Enhances digestion and absorption.
(d) Guduchi	4. Boosts immunity and acts as an adaptogen.

Codes:
A. (a)-1, (b)-2, (c)-3, (d)-4
B. (a)-4, (b)-3, (c)-2, (d)-1
C. (a)-2, (b)-4, (c)-3, (d)-1
D. (a)-3, (b)-1, (c)-4, (d)-2

28. Match List–I (Digestive Pathways) with List–II (Associated Doshas) carefully and choose the correct answer from the codes given below:

List–I	List–II
(a) Amashaya	1. Predominantly Kapha in nature.
(b) Grahani	2. Balances Samana Vayu and digestive enzymes.
(c) Pakvashaya	3. Regulates Vata and excretory processes.
(d) Pittadhara Kala	4. Associated with Pitta and bile regulation.

Codes:
A. (a)-1, (b)-2, (c)-3, (d)-4
B. (a)-4, (b)-3, (c)-2, (d)-1
C. (a)-3, (b)-4, (c)-1, (d)-2
D. (a)-2, (b)-3, (c)-4, (d)-1

29. Match List–I (Respiratory Pathways) with List–II (Components) carefully and choose the correct answer from the codes given below:

List–I	List–II
(a) Pranavaha Srotas	1. Responsible for oxygen transport.
(b) Avalambaka Kapha	2. Stabilizes the lungs and chest region.
(c) Udana Vayu	3. Regulates speech and upward energy flow.
(d) Sadhaka Pitta	4. Influences emotional well-being and heart function.

Codes:
A. (a)-1, (b)-2, (c)-3, (d)-4
B. (a)-4, (b)-3, (c)-2, (d)-1

C. (a)-2, (b)-1, (c)-3, (d)-4
D. (a)-3, (b)-4, (c)-1, (d)-2

30. Match List–I (Panchakarma Therapies) with List–II (Objectives) carefully and choose the correct answer from the codes given below:

List–I	List–II
(a) Vamana	1. Expels excess Kapha through emesis.
(b) Virechana	2. Eliminates excess Pitta through purgation.
(c) Nasya	3. Treats Prana Vayu disorders via nasal administration.
(d) Basti	4. Regulates Vata through medicated enemas.

Codes:
A. (a)-1, (b)-2, (c)-3, (d)-4
B. (a)-4, (b)-3, (c)-2, (d)-1
C. (a)-2, (b)-4, (c)-1, (d)-3
D. (a)-3, (b)-1, (c)-4, (d)-2

31. Match List–I (Cardiovascular Functions) with List–II (Descriptions) carefully and choose the correct answer from the codes given below:

List–I	List–II
(a) Hridaya (Heart)	1. The seat of physical and emotional health.
(b) Rasa Dhatu	2. Nourishes all tissues in the body.
(c) Rakta Dhatu	3. Facilitates oxygenation and sustains life.
(d) Sadhaka Pitta	4. Influences emotional health and cardiac functions.

Codes:
A. (a)-1, (b)-2, (c)-3, (d)-4
B. (a)-3, (b)-4, (c)-1, (d)-2
C. (a)-4, (b)-1, (c)-2, (d)-3
D. (a)-2, (b)-3, (c)-4, (d)-1

32. Match List–I (Gunas) with List–II (Descriptions) carefully and choose the correct answer from the codes given below:

List–I	List–II
(a) Sattva	1. Represents clarity, knowledge, and balance.
(b) Rajas	2. Reflects activity, passion, and restlessness.
(c) Tamas	3. Denotes ignorance, inertia, and darkness.
(d) Triguna Balance	4. Essential for mental and physical harmony.

Codes:
A. (a)-1, (b)-2, (c)-3, (d)-4
B. (a)-2, (b)-1, (c)-4, (d)-3
C. (a)-3, (b)-4, (c)-1, (d)-2
D. (a)-4, (b)-3, (c)-2, (d)-1

33. Match List–I (Doshas) with List–II (Primary Attributes) carefully and choose the correct answer from the codes given below:

List–I	List–II
(a) Vata	1. Governs movement and nervous system.
(b) Pitta	2. Regulates metabolism and digestion.
(c) Kapha	3. Provides structure and fluid balance.
(d) Dosha Balance	4. Ensures physical and mental health.

Codes:
A. (a)-1, (b)-2, (c)-3, (d)-4
B. (a)-3, (b)-4, (c)-1, (d)-2
C. (a)-4, (b)-1, (c)-2, (d)-3
D. (a)-2, (b)-3, (c)-4, (d)-1

34. Match List–I with List–II carefully and choose the correct answer from the codes given below:

List–I	List–II
(a) Nadi Pariksha	1. Pulse diagnosis for doshic imbalances.
(b) Jihva Pariksha	2. Tongue examination for Ama.
(c) Drik Pariksha	3. Eye examination for systemic health.
(d) Mala Pariksha	4. Stool analysis for digestive health.

Codes:
A. (a)-1, (b)-2, (c)-3, (d)-4
B. (a)-3, (b)-4, (c)-1, (d)-2
C. (a)-4, (b)-3, (c)-2, (d)-1
D. (a)-2, (b)-1, (c)-4, (d)-3

Directions (Q. No. 35–39): *Following questions are based on Statement 1 and Statement 2. Read both the statements carefully and choose the correct answer from the options given below:*

A. Both Statement 1 and Statement 2 are true, and Statement 2 is the correct explanation of Statement 1.
B. Both Statement 1 and Statement 2 are true, but Statement 2 is not the correct explanation of Statement 1.
C. Statement 1 is true, but Statement 2 is false.
D. Statement 1 is false, but Statement 2 is true.
E. Both Statement 1 and Statement 2 are false.

35. **Statement 1:** In Ayurveda, Agni (digestive fire) is considered the root of all metabolic processes and is directly associated with the maintenance of physical and mental health.

    Statement 2: Impairment of Agni leads to Ama formation, which disrupts doshic balance and is regarded as the root cause of disease.

36. **Statement 1:** Prana Vayu in Ayurveda governs respiration and facilitates the proper movement of air throughout the body, supporting cognitive and respiratory functions.

    Statement 2: Imbalances in Prana Vayu are primarily treated through Kapha-pacifying herbs such as Guduchi and cooling therapies.

37. **Statement 1:** The balance of Tridoshas (Vata, Pitta, Kapha) is essential for health, with each dosha governing specific physiological and psychological functions.

    Statement 2: Ayurvedic therapies aim to enhance one dosha while suppressing the other two to maintain health.

38. **Statement 1:** Avalambaka Kapha stabilizes the lungs and chest region, maintaining the lubrication and structure of respiratory pathways.

    Statement 2: Imbalances in Avalambaka Kapha manifest as dryness and reduced respiratory efficiency.

39. **Statement 1:** Ojas, the essence of all Dhatus, is considered the foundation of vitality and immunity in Ayurveda.

    Statement 2: Depletion of Ojas leads to increased physical resilience and enhanced systemic immunity.

Directions (Q. No. 40–45): *There are two statements in each question. One is labelled as Assertion (A) and the other is as Reason (R). Read both the statements and choose the correct answer from the options given below*:

A. Both Assertion (A) and Reason (R) are true, and Reason (R) is the correct explanation of Assertion (A).
B. Both Assertion (A) and Reason (R) are true, but Reason (R) is not the correct explanation of Assertion (A).
C. Assertion (A) is true, but Reason (R) is false.
D. Assertion (A) is false, but Reason (R) is true.
E. Both Assertion (A) and Reason (R) are false.

40. **Assertion (A):** In Ayurveda, Ritucharya (seasonal regimens) are prescribed to maintain the balance of doshas during seasonal changes.

    Reason (R): Seasonal variations influence doshic dominance, and failing to adapt lifestyle and diet can aggravate doshic imbalances.

41. **Assertion (A):** Panchakarma is an effective Ayurvedic therapy for detoxification and dosha balance.

    Reason (R): Panchakarma therapies target the elimination of Ama through procedures like Vamana (emesis) and Virechana (purgation), ensuring the removal of toxins and restoring Agni.

42. **Assertion (A):** Prana Vayu regulates cognitive functions and maintains respiratory health.

    Reason (R): Imbalances in Prana Vayu can lead to psychological disorders such as anxiety, as well as respiratory issues like breathlessness.

43. **Assertion (A):** In Ayurveda, Rasa Dhatu serves as the first tissue to be formed after digestion and is responsible for systemic nourishment.

    Reason (R): Rasa Dhatu directly influences immunity by forming Ojas, the essence of all Dhatus.

44. **Assertion (A):** Avalambaka Kapha stabilizes the chest region and supports respiratory health.

    Reason (R): Imbalances in Avalambaka Kapha often lead to excessive mucus production and compromised lung function.

45. **Assertion (A):** Weak Agni leads to the formation of Ama, which is considered the root cause of most diseases in Ayurveda.

    Reason (R): Strengthening Agni through dietary and herbal interventions prevents Ama accumulation and promotes overall health.

Directions (Q. No. 46–50): *Read the passage carefully and answer the questions given below*:

Ayurveda, the ancient Indian system of medicine, views the respiratory system as an integral component of overall health, deeply connected with the body's doshas, sub-doshas, and srotas (channels). The primary dosha involved in the respiratory process is Vata, specifically its subtype Prana Vayu, which governs not only respiration but also the flow of energy and cognitive functions. This intricate system is also influenced by Avalambaka Kapha, which provides stability, lubrication, and immunity in the chest and lungs, and Sadhaka Pitta, which impacts emotional states and respiratory efficiency through its role in heart and mental health. Together, these elements maintain balance and ensure proper functioning of the respiratory pathways, referred to as Pranavaha Srotas in Ayurvedic texts.

Pranavaha Srotas include the nasal passages, throat, trachea, bronchi, and lungs, forming the channels through which Prana, or life force, flows. A clear and unobstructed pathway ensures vitality, but blockages or imbalances can disrupt this flow, leading to conditions such as coughing, wheezing, and breathlessness. These disorders are often linked to the accumulation of Ama, toxic by-products resulting from poor digestion and weak Agni (digestive fire). Imbalances in Vata cause dryness and irregularities in the respiratory system, while Kapha aggravation leads to mucus buildup and congestion. These doshic disturbances are frequently exacerbated by factors such as exposure to allergens, cold weather, poor dietary habits, and chronic stress.

The Ayurvedic approach to respiratory health revolves around maintaining balance and preventing disease through daily routines (Dinacharya) and seasonal practices (Ritucharya). Key preventive measures include Nasya, the application of medicated oils to the nasal passages, which clears blockages and strengthens the respiratory system. Pranayama, a set of breathing exercises, is prescribed to enhance the flow of Prana and improve lung function. The use of specific herbs plays a central role in managing respiratory conditions, with plants like Tulsi, Vasaka, and Haridra offering anti-inflammatory, bronchodilator, and immune-enhancing properties. These herbs are often combined in formulations to address both the symptoms and root causes of respiratory ailments.

Diet is another cornerstone of respiratory care in Ayurveda. A Kapha-pacifying diet is recommended to reduce mucus and enhance digestion. This includes warm, light, and spiced foods, while avoiding cold, heavy, or oily meals that can aggravate Kapha and promote Ama. Ingredients like ginger, black pepper, and honey are commonly used to clear congestion and support respiratory function. For chronic or severe conditions, Ayurveda employs therapies such as Panchakarma, a detoxification process that includes procedures like Vamana (therapeutic emesis) to expel excess Kapha and clear Pranavaha Srotas. These treatments not only target symptoms but also rejuvenate the entire system by restoring doshic balance.

The concept of Ojas, the essence of vitality, is closely tied to respiratory health in Ayurveda. Ojas is seen as the foundation of immunity and resilience, and its depletion can leave the respiratory system vulnerable to infections and chronic illnesses. Practices that enhance Ojas, such as Rasayana therapy, are emphasized for individuals with weakened respiratory systems. Modern research has supported many of these traditional practices, demonstrating the efficacy of herbs like Tulsi and turmeric in managing respiratory inflammation and boosting immunity. Pranayama has also gained recognition for its ability to enhance lung capacity, reduce stress, and improve overall oxygenation.

Respiratory disorders are classified according to doshic imbalances, with treatments tailored to address specific symptoms and underlying causes. Vata-related conditions, characterized by dryness, wheezing, and spasmodic coughing, are treated with warm, moistening therapies, and herbs like Ashwagandha. Kapha disorders, marked by heaviness, mucus buildup, and congestion, require Kapha-reducing herbs such as Pippali and therapies like Vamana to clear excess mucus. Pitta-related conditions, though less common, involve inflammation and a burning sensation in the respiratory tract and are treated with cooling herbs like Guduchi and Shatavari.

Ayurveda also highlights the psychosomatic aspects of respiratory health, recognizing that emotional well-being plays a significant role in maintaining balance. Chronic stress and anxiety can aggravate Vata, weaken Prana Vayu, and compromise respiratory efficiency. Techniques such as meditation, yoga, and the use of adaptogenic herbs like Brahmi are employed to calm the mind and support respiratory health. This holistic perspective underscores Ayurveda's unique approach to treating respiratory disorders, focusing not only on the physical symptoms but also on the mental and emotional dimensions of well-being.

In today's context, the integration of Ayurvedic principles with modern medicine has opened new avenues for managing complex respiratory disorders. Herbs like Tulsi and Vasaka are being studied for their potential in treating conditions such as asthma and COPD, while therapies like Panchakarma are being explored as complementary interventions in chronic diseases. This synergy between traditional wisdom and contemporary research offers a comprehensive approach to respiratory health, aligning with Ayurveda's timeless emphasis on balance, prevention, and individualized care.

46. According to the passage, which of the following doshas or sub-doshas primarily govern the respiratory system in Ayurveda?

1. Prana Vayu controls the movement of air and cognitive functions.
2. Avalambaka Kapha stabilizes the chest and provides immunity.
3. Sadhaka Pitta influences emotional balance and respiratory efficiency.
4. Samana Vayu directly regulates mucus production in the lungs.

Choose the correct options:

A. 1 and 2 only
B. 1, 2, and 3 only
C. 2 and 4 only
D. All of the above

47. How does the concept of Pranavaha Srotas align with Ayurveda's holistic understanding of respiratory health?

1. They represent the pathways for Prana (life force) flow, including nasal passages and lungs.
2. Blockages in these pathways directly lead to systemic diseases beyond the respiratory system.
3. Their functionality is unaffected by doshic imbalances and Ama accumulation.

4. Ayurvedic therapies such as Nasya and Pranayama are designed to clear and strengthen these pathways.

Choose the correct options:
A. 1 and 2 only
B. 1, 2, and 4 only
C. 3 and 4 only
D. All of the above

48. Which of the following Ayurvedic interventions are mentioned in the passage as effective for Kapha-related respiratory disorders?
1. Vamana (therapeutic emesis) to expel excess Kapha from the body.
2. Herbs like Pippali, Shunthi, and Tulsi for reducing mucus and congestion.
3. Cooling herbs such as Guduchi and Shatavari to alleviate Kapha symptoms.
4. Avoidance of cold, oily, and heavy foods in favor of a Kapha-pacifying diet.

Choose the correct options:
A. 1, 2, and 4 only
B. 2, 3, and 4 only
C. 1, 3, and 4 only
D. All of the above

49. Based on the passage, what role does Ojas play in maintaining respiratory health, and how is it supported in Ayurveda?
A. Ojas is the essence of vitality and immunity, protecting the respiratory system from infections.
B. Depletion of Ojas weakens Prana Vayu and Avalambaka Kapha, making the respiratory system more susceptible.
C. Strengthening Ojas involves Rasayana therapies and lifestyle practices that enhance vitality.
D. Ojas is unrelated to respiratory health and focuses solely on digestion and metabolic strength.

Choose the correct options:
A. 1, 2, and 3 only
B. 2 and 4 only
C. 1 and 3 only
D. All of the above

50. Which of the following insights does the passage provide regarding the integration of modern medicine with Ayurveda for respiratory health?
A. Ayurvedic herbs like Tulsi and Vasaka are being studied for treating asthma and COPD.
B. Pranayama has gained recognition in improving lung capacity and reducing stress.
C. Panchakarma is primarily used as a replacement for conventional therapies in chronic diseases.
D. Integrative approaches combine Ayurvedic and modern practices to manage complex respiratory disorders.

Choose the correct options:
A. 1 and 2 only
B. 1, 2, and 4 only
C. 2, 3, and 4 only
D. All of the above

ANSWER WITH EXPLANATIONS

1. B: The study validates the Ayurvedic Tridosha framework, where Vata governs irregular movement, contributing to IBS, and Pitta governs inflammation, linked to IBD. The results show that calming Vata through oleation and grounding herbs alleviates IBS symptoms, while cooling therapies for Pitta reduce inflammation in IBD. This demonstrates that Ayurvedic therapies align with tailored management based on doshic imbalances. The holistic framework recognizes that gastrointestinal disorders can stem from different doshas, allowing targeted interventions. The conclusion that Vata and Pitta imbalances are central to these conditions supports the study's hypothesis while reinforcing the scientific relevance of Tridosha principles.

2. B: The relationship between Agni and enzymatic activity highlights Ayurveda's sophisticated understanding of digestion and metabolism. Impaired Agni corresponds to reduced lipase and amylase activities, while Ayurvedic herbs restore enzymatic function, improving metabolic efficiency. This demonstrates that Agni is not merely symbolic but represents measurable biochemical processes. By emphasizing metabolic pathways, Ayurveda integrates digestive health with systemic vitality. The findings confirm that Agni-balancing therapies enhance digestion and metabolism, addressing the root causes of metabolic syndrome, reinforcing Ayurveda's holistic principles while bridging traditional wisdom with modern biochemical understanding.

3. B: The study validates Ayurvedic respiratory principles by showing how Kapha imbalance, associated with mucus accumulation, is addressed by Prana-enhancing herbs. These herbs exhibit bronchodilatory and anti-inflammatory effects, aligning with Kapha-clearing therapies. Active compounds that regulate cytokines support Ayurvedic claims about their systemic impact. This evidence demonstrates how traditional Ayurvedic classifications correspond with modern pharmacology. The findings bridge ancient theories with contemporary science, reinforcing Ayurveda's credibility as a system rooted in physiological relevance. This alignment highlights the integration of dosha-specific treatments with biochemical mechanisms.

4. **B:** Pitta dosha governs metabolism and blood flow, and its imbalance correlates with inflammatory markers like CRP in conditions such as atherosclerosis. The study shows that Pitta-pacifying herbs and dietary adjustments reduce CRP levels and improve lipid profiles, supporting Ayurveda's role in circulatory health. This indicates that Ayurvedic treatments address the root causes of metabolic and vascular inflammation by balancing Pitta. The findings align traditional theories with modern biomarkers, demonstrating Ayurveda's therapeutic relevance in addressing systemic inflammation and arterial health through dietary and herbal interventions.

5. **B:** Ojas, the essence of vitality in Ayurveda, correlates with systemic immunity. The study demonstrates how Rasayana therapies enhance IgA levels and antioxidant enzymes, reducing infections and improving resilience. These findings validate the concept of Ojas, connecting its depletion with immune dysfunction and rejuvenation with improved immunity. Ojas is integral to both physical and mental health, reflecting systemic harmony. The observed improvements confirm that Ayurvedic interventions address immunity at its core, aligning traditional concepts with measurable health outcomes, bridging Ayurveda's theoretical framework with modern immunological understanding.

6. **B:** Rasas in Ayurveda are not merely symbolic; they influence specific metabolic pathways. The anabolic effects of Madhura Rasa (sweet taste) and the catabolic effects of Katu Rasa (pungent taste) demonstrate their physiological relevance. The study validates how dietary interventions involving specific Rasas restore digestive and metabolic balance, reflecting Ayurveda's precision in matching tastes to doshic needs. These findings underscore Ayurveda's understanding of nutrition as a therapeutic tool, linking sensory experiences to biochemical processes. The study bridges the gap between traditional dietary wisdom and modern scientific validation, reinforcing the relevance of Rasas in health management.

7. **A:** Panchakarma therapies, such as Nasya and herbal steam inhalation, target Kapha dosha imbalances associated with mucus production and respiratory congestion. The study's results, showing improved pulmonary function and reduced mucus, validate Ayurveda's claims about the efficacy of detoxification protocols in respiratory care. Panchakarma's impact extends beyond detoxification, addressing doshic imbalances at their root. This integration of physical cleansing with systemic rebalancing demonstrates the comprehensive scope of Ayurvedic therapies in managing chronic respiratory disorders, such as COPD, by improving both symptoms and underlying pathophysiology.

8. **B:** The study highlights the interdependence of circulatory and respiratory systems mediated by Prana Vayu (life force) and Udana Vayu (upward movement). Pranayama and herbal interventions improve oxygen saturation and cardiac output, reflecting Ayurveda's systemic understanding. This validates the direct physiological roles of Vayus, showing that Ayurvedic concepts are not symbolic but represent functional dynamics. By aligning respiratory and circulatory health, the findings reinforce Ayurveda's holistic approach, where imbalances in one system impact the other, and therapies target these interconnections for comprehensive health improvements.

9. **A:** Ayurvedic diabetes management addresses Kapha and Pitta imbalances. Kapha-reducing herbs improve insulin sensitivity, while Pitta-balancing treatments reduce inflammation and HbA1c levels. These findings validate Ayurveda's dosha-centric approach, showing how interventions target root causes such as insulin resistance and systemic inflammation. This systemic efficacy contrasts with merely symptomatic treatments, demonstrating Ayurveda's depth in addressing chronic metabolic disorders like diabetes. The study bridges doshic theories with measurable outcomes, reinforcing Ayurveda's relevance in modern integrative healthcare.

10. **B:** Srotas, the Ayurvedic channels, correspond to physiological structures like arteries and veins. The study links Raktavaha Srotas with circulatory health, showing that Rakta-cleansing herbs enhance blood flow and reduce clot formation. These findings validate the Ayurvedic understanding of Srotas as functional pathways, aligning traditional theories with anatomical and physiological evidence. By addressing obstructions in these channels, Ayurveda demonstrates its capacity to manage circulatory disorders effectively. The integration of Rakta-cleansing therapies reflects the practical relevance of Srotas theory, bridging ancient wisdom with modern clinical insights.

11. **A:** The restoration of Agni reduces systemic inflammation by improving metabolic efficiency and gut microbiota

balance, reducing pro-inflammatory cytokines like TNF-α and IL-6. This validates Ayurveda's view of Agni as a regulator of both digestion and systemic health. Increased IgA levels reflect enhanced mucosal immunity, showing the interconnectedness of digestion, immunity, and inflammation. The findings confirm that Agni-balancing therapies address systemic issues beyond digestion, reinforcing the holistic scope of Ayurvedic interventions. This aligns ancient principles with modern immunological and inflammatory pathways, demonstrating Ayurveda's systemic perspective on health.

12. **B:** Promoting crop rotation and organic fertilization addresses soil depletion and restores the bioactive compounds essential for ginger's therapeutic efficacy. This aligns with Ayurveda's emphasis on sustainable use of medicinal plants. Intensive monoculture farming depletes soil nutrients, while synthetic alternatives lack the holistic benefits of natural ginger. By advocating sustainable practices, this approach preserves ginger's potency while maintaining ecological balance. The findings demonstrate the need for integrating environmental conservation with Ayurvedic medicine, ensuring long-term therapeutic efficacy and sustainability.

13. **A:** The ecological degradation of ginger reduces bioactive compounds like gingerols, compromising its ability to restore Agni and control systemic inflammation. This demonstrates how environmental factors directly impact the efficacy of Ayurvedic treatments. The interconnectedness of ecological sustainability and therapeutic outcomes emphasizes the need for sustainable cultivation practices. By addressing soil health and climate challenges, the potency of ginger in digestive therapies can be preserved. This highlights Ayurveda's sensitivity to the quality of natural ingredients in ensuring effective interventions, reinforcing its holistic approach to health.

14. **B:** Sustainable farming practices for ginger, combined with complementary herbs, address ecological and therapeutic challenges. This strategy maintains ginger's efficacy in restoring Agni while reducing environmental strain. Focusing solely on synthetic alternatives or conservation without use undermines Ayurveda's natural principles. Complementary herbs reduce overdependence on ginger, ensuring resilience in therapeutic formulations. This integrative approach balances ecological sustainability with clinical needs, reflecting Ayurveda's adaptability to modern challenges. By prioritizing both environmental and therapeutic goals, this strategy reinforces the interconnectedness of ecological health and human well-being.

15. **C:** The Tridosha theory, a cornerstone of Ayurveda, integrates the functional domains of Vata, Pitta, and Kapha. Vata is the driving force behind movement and communication, tied to the nervous system. Pitta oversees digestion, metabolism, and enzymatic processes, linking it with thermoregulation and metabolic fire. Kapha governs cohesion, lubrication, and immunity, maintaining structural integrity and fluid balance. When balanced, these doshas support optimal physical and mental health, demonstrating a holistic framework for life. The inclusion of all three doshas and their balanced state underscores the holistic nature of Ayurvedic health principles, showing their interconnected roles.

16. **B:** Rasas (tastes) have profound therapeutic applications in Ayurveda, each associated with specific physiological effects. Sweet taste supports anabolic functions, nourishing tissues. Bitter aids in detoxification, reducing inflammation and clearing toxins. Astringent controls bleeding and contracts tissues, aiding wound healing. Sour enhances digestive fire and stimulates metabolic activity. Together, these tastes embody Ayurveda's understanding of dietary and medicinal interventions, showing how diverse sensory stimuli influence health. Their inclusion in therapeutic regimens aligns with the principle of balance and specificity in addressing doshic imbalances, aligning each taste with particular bodily needs.

17. **B:** Ayurveda describes digestion in three sequential stages: Madhura (sweet), Amla (sour), and Katu (pungent), each associated with a dosha and element. Madhura Avasthapaka corresponds to Kapha and water, Amla Avasthapaka aligns with Pitta and fire, while Katu Avasthapaka is linked to Vata and air. Additionally, Agni is the central force responsible for digestion, transformation, and maintenance of doshic equilibrium. All four options reflect authentic Ayurvedic physiological principles, hence all are correct.

18. **B:** Each Dhatu plays a specific role in Ayurvedic physiology. Rasa nourishes all tissues and supports immunity, Rakta carries oxygen and sustains life, Mamsa provides structural support and strength, and Meda ensures lubrication and stores fat. These functions are interlinked and represent the foundational tissue components of the human body. The descriptions accurately reflect classical Ayurvedic teachings, making all four correct.

19. **B:** Prana Vayu regulates breathing and life force, forming a foundational layer for vitality. Udana Vayu supports speech and upward movements, reflecting its active role in respiratory and expressive functions. Avalambaka Kapha stabilizes the chest and ensures

lubrication, while Sadhaka Pitta connects emotional and respiratory health. These sub-doshas illustrate Ayurveda's nuanced understanding of the respiratory system, integrating mechanical, emotional, and systemic influences. This alignment demonstrates the interconnectedness of physical and mental health, showing how balanced sub-doshas sustain systemic harmony.

20. **C:** The Shat Kriya Kalas articulate six stages of disease progression. Sanchaya marks early doshic accumulation without symptoms. Prakopa shows dosha aggravation with mild discomfort. Prasara signals the doshas' systemic spread. Vyakti reveals full manifestation. This model integrates prevention and intervention, showing how early detection and doshic balancing can halt disease progression. By understanding these stages, practitioners address root causes rather than symptoms, aligning with Ayurveda's preventive and curative duality. The framework's precision enhances diagnostic accuracy and treatment efficacy.

21. **B:** Panchakarma's detoxifying nature targets systemic doshic imbalances. Vamana removes excess Kapha, clearing respiratory blockages. Virechana targets Pitta, balancing heat and acidity. Nasya clears Prana Vayu pathways, addressing cognitive and respiratory health. Rasayana therapies rejuvenate tissues and restore vitality. Together, these therapies embody Ayurveda's multifaceted approach, combining purification, balance, and rejuvenation. Their integration reflects a comprehensive vision, aligning physical and mental health through targeted interventions. This system's precision highlights Ayurveda's adaptability to diverse health challenges.

22. **A:** Ojas symbolizes vitality and immunity, embodying the essence of balanced Agni and Dhatu health. It supports Bala, enhancing disease resistance. Varna reflects Ojas through radiant complexion, showing systemic harmony. Depletion weakens immunity, increasing vulnerability. Practices enhancing Ojas, such as Rasayana therapy, highlight Ayurveda's preventive focus, ensuring long-term vitality. By linking Ojas with overall health, Ayurveda demonstrates the systemic interdependence of digestion, immunity, and mental resilience, showing how subtle balances sustain life force. The inclusion of Ojas in treatment highlights Ayurveda's integrative framework.

23. **A:** Immunity in Ayurveda stems from balanced Agni, which prevents Ama accumulation and sustains Dhatu transformation. Strong Ojas ensures resilience against disease. Doshic balance supports systemic harmony, while therapies like Panchakarma cleanse and rejuvenate. This integrative perspective aligns immunity with systemic health, showing how digestion, tissue health, and mental balance sustain resistance. By addressing root causes, Ayurveda transcends symptomatic treatments, enhancing immune functionality through holistic interventions. This approach exemplifies Ayurveda's foresight in addressing multifaceted health challenges.

24. **A:** Ayurvedic diagnostics integrate root causes, focusing on Nidan (causes), dosha imbalance, Ama, and Dhatu depletion. Improper diet and lifestyle create Ama, disrupting digestion and Dhatu formation. Dosha imbalance reflects physiological disruptions, while Dhatu depletion weakens systemic resilience. This integrative model targets disease etiology rather than symptoms, demonstrating Ayurveda's depth in addressing health. By tracing disruptions to their origins, Ayurveda offers precise interventions, enhancing diagnostic clarity and therapeutic precision. This systemic focus aligns with its holistic philosophy, prioritizing balance and vitality.

25. **A:** Agni, the core of Ayurvedic physiology, is central to health and metabolism. Vishama Agni, linked to Vata, reflects irregular digestion patterns, often disrupting systemic harmony. Dosha imbalances lead to Ama formation, which is a toxic by-product resulting from impaired digestion. Ama clogs channels, creating disorders, while Ojas, representing vitality and immunity, symbolizes the culmination of balanced Agni and healthy digestion. Ayurveda's perspective integrates digestion, metabolism, and systemic health. The categorization in this question demonstrates Ayurveda's systemic thinking, where imbalances in Agni trigger cascades that impact the immune system and overall vitality. This foundational understanding ensures holistic diagnosis and treatment.

26. **A:** Each sub-dosha has a unique function. Prana Vayu governs respiration and cognitive activity. Udana Vayu controls speech and upward movement. Samana Vayu regulates digestion by balancing Agni, and Apana Vayu governs excretion and downward energy flow. These sub-doshas are critical for maintaining physiological balance and are described exactly as per Ayurvedic texts. The matching is precise and complete.

27. **A:** Herbs in Ayurveda are categorized based on their effects on bodily systems and doshic balance. Haritaki supports detoxification and bowel regulation, aiding in Kapha-related stagnation. Amalaki, rich in Vitamin C, rejuvenates tissues and boosts immunity, showcasing its relevance in Rasa Dhatu nourishment. Guduchi acts as an adaptogen, enhancing systemic immunity,

while Pippali improves digestion, balancing metabolic efficiency. This alignment of herbs with therapeutic outcomes reflects Ayurveda's integrative approach. The systematic use of these herbs underscores the importance of addressing root causes of imbalances, rather than symptoms, ensuring comprehensive healing and long-term health benefits.

28. A: Amashaya (stomach) is dominated by Kapha due to its moist and heavy nature. Grahani, the seat of digestion, is influenced by Samana Vayu and enzymes. Pakvashaya (large intestine) is linked to Vata and excretion, while Pittadhara Kala governs bile and Pitta functions. This mapping accurately reflects the association between digestive organs and doshas in Ayurveda, validating the selected option.

29. A: Ayurveda views respiratory pathways through the lens of doshas and their subtypes. Pranavaha Srotas governs oxygen transport, emphasizing its link to vitality. Avalambaka Kapha stabilizes and lubricates the lungs, ensuring respiratory efficiency. Udana Vayu controls speech and upward energy movement, while Sadhaka Pitta influences emotional balance and its impact on respiratory health. This holistic understanding ties respiratory health to emotional and systemic stability. By addressing both physical and subtle aspects of respiration, Ayurveda ensures that treatments are not limited to symptom relief but also restore balance to the root causes of respiratory disorders.

30. A: Panchakarma therapies address systemic cleansing and doshic balance. Vamana clears Kapha blockages through therapeutic emesis, while Virechana targets excess Pitta via purgation, cooling inflammation. Nasya focuses on Prana Vayu disorders, enhancing respiratory and cognitive clarity through nasal administration. Basti regulates Vata dosha, addressing chronic imbalances via medicated enemas. This question demonstrates how each therapy aligns with specific doshic functions and imbalances, ensuring comprehensive treatment. Panchakarma exemplifies Ayurveda's preventive and curative principles, offering detoxification and rejuvenation to restore systemic harmony and prevent disease progression.

31. A: The heart (Hridaya) is the seat of both physical and emotional well-being. Rasa Dhatu distributes nutrition and maintains tissue vitality. Rakta Dhatu carries oxygen and sustains life, and Sadhaka Pitta governs emotional stability and cardiac functions. These attributes are classical Ayurvedic explanations of cardiovascular health. The match is fully aligned with traditional concepts.

32. A: The three Gunas—Sattva, Rajas, and Tamas—form the foundation of mental and emotional health in Ayurveda. Sattva represents clarity and balance, while Rajas denotes activity and passion. Tamas, associated with inertia and ignorance, reflects mental stagnation. Maintaining a balance of these Gunas ensures mental and physical harmony, demonstrating Ayurveda's psychosomatic approach. Triguna balance not only influences mental health but also impacts systemic functioning, as mental disturbances often cascade into physical disorders. This alignment of emotional and physical dimensions highlights Ayurveda's emphasis on holistic well-being, offering targeted strategies to restore mental resilience and physical stability.

33. A: Doshas—Vata, Pitta, and Kapha—govern all physiological and psychological processes. Vata controls movement and nervous system activity, Pitta regulates metabolism and digestion, while Kapha ensures structural integrity and fluid balance. Their balance is essential for health, as imbalances manifest as physical and psychological disorders. Ayurveda's understanding of doshas reflects its systemic approach, where each imbalance is treated holistically. This interconnection ensures that treatments address the root causes of disorders, emphasizing prevention and long-term health. By balancing doshas, Ayurveda restores harmony across physical, mental, and energetic dimensions.

34. A: Ayurvedic diagnosis integrates external signs with internal systemic health. Nadi Pariksha (pulse diagnosis) detects doshic imbalances, Jihva Pariksha (tongue examination) reveals Ama accumulation, Drik Pariksha (eye examination) assesses systemic vitality, and Mala Pariksha (stool analysis) evaluates digestive health. This diagnostic framework demonstrates Ayurveda's ability to correlate physical observations with underlying imbalances, ensuring targeted treatments. By focusing on root causes rather than symptoms, Ayurveda ensures holistic healing. This diagnostic precision highlights Ayurveda's systemic approach, where interconnected observations guide comprehensive therapeutic strategies for restoring health and balance.

35. A: Ayurveda views Agni, the digestive fire, as the cornerstone of health, governing all metabolic and transformative processes. Impaired Agni leads to the formation of Ama, a toxic byproduct that disrupts doshic balance and clogs the srotas (channels), including Pranavaha Srotas, which are responsible for respiration. This disruption manifests as physical and systemic illnesses, emphasizing the interconnection between digestion, immunity, and respiratory health.

By addressing Agni's impairment, Ayurveda focuses on root causes rather than symptoms, ensuring holistic health. This explanation highlights the pivotal role of Agni in preventing disease and maintaining homeostasis within the body's complex systems.

36. C: Prana Vayu, a subtype of Vata dosha, governs respiratory rhythm and cognitive vitality, making it essential for physical and mental well-being. While Kapha-pacifying herbs like Guduchi are beneficial for mucus regulation, they do not specifically address Prana Vayu imbalances. Instead, therapies such as Nasya (nasal administration of medicated oils) and Vata-pacifying measures like warm foods and calming practices directly target Prana Vayu dysfunctions. This distinction demonstrates the precision of Ayurvedic interventions, ensuring the alignment of treatment with specific doshic and sub-doshic imbalances, and emphasizing the system's focus on root-level corrections.

37. C: The balance of Tridoshas (Vata, Pitta, Kapha) is central to Ayurveda's philosophy. Each dosha contributes to specific physiological functions: Vata governs movement, Pitta controls metabolism, and Kapha provides stability. Ayurveda seeks to harmonize these doshas rather than prioritize one over the others. The statement about enhancing one dosha while suppressing others contradicts this principle, as such an approach disrupts the delicate balance required for health. Instead, Ayurvedic treatments aim to restore equilibrium through targeted dietary, herbal, and lifestyle interventions, reflecting its holistic understanding of health as a dynamic and interdependent system.

38. C: Avalambaka Kapha supports the chest area by maintaining structure, lubrication, and immunity. So, Statement 1 is true. However, Statement 2 is false because Kapha imbalance typically causes excessive mucus and heaviness, not dryness—dryness is more characteristic of Vata disorders. Hence, only the first statement holds true.

39. C: Ojas, considered the essence of Dhatus (tissues), symbolizes vitality, immunity, and systemic strength in Ayurveda. It plays a foundational role in maintaining respiratory health, protecting Pranavaha Srotas from infections and allergens. Depletion of Ojas weakens immunity, rendering the respiratory system susceptible to diseases. Practices that enhance Ojas, such as Rasayana therapies, nourishing diets, and stress management, ensure long-term vitality and disease resistance. The statement linking Ojas depletion with improved resilience is incorrect, as Ayurveda emphasizes that Ojas depletion compromises, rather than strengthens, systemic health, reflecting the interconnectedness of immunity, vitality, and tissue health.

40. A: Ritucharya, or seasonal regimen, is a foundational concept in Ayurveda aimed at maintaining health by adapting one's diet, habits, and lifestyle to seasonal variations. Each season has a predominant dosha—Kapha in spring, Pitta in summer, and Vata in autumn—which, if aggravated, can lead to imbalances and diseases. Adopting Ritucharya practices such as light foods in spring (to reduce Kapha) or cooling foods in summer (to balance Pitta) prevents these imbalances. The reason supports the assertion by explaining that doshic dominance during seasonal transitions necessitates lifestyle changes to maintain harmony, thus preventing seasonal illnesses and promoting well-being.

41. A: Panchakarma is indeed an effective Ayurvedic detoxification therapy that removes excess doshas and toxins (Ama) from the body. Procedures like Vamana and Virechana cleanse the system and reignite digestive fire (Agni), restoring balance and promoting health. The reason fully supports and explains the assertion.

42. A: Prana Vayu controls both respiration and cognitive functions, making it essential for life and health. Its imbalance can lead to mental disorders like anxiety and respiratory issues such as breathlessness. The reason is therefore an accurate and direct explanation of the assertion, fully rooted in Ayurvedic understanding.

43. A: Rasa Dhatu is the first tissue formed after digestion and is responsible for systemic nourishment. It directly contributes to the formation of Ojas, which is the essence of immunity and vitality. Therefore, both the assertion and the reason are true, and the reason accurately explains the role of Rasa Dhatu.

44. A: Avalambaka Kapha is a subtype of Kapha dosha that stabilizes the chest, lubricates the respiratory pathways, and supports lung function. When imbalanced, it can lead to excessive mucus production, congestion, and respiratory inefficiency. The reason provided—highlighting how imbalances result in mucus buildup—is an accurate explanation of the assertion. Ayurvedic treatments such as Vamana (emesis) and Kapha-reducing herbs like Vasaka and Pippali are prescribed to restore balance. This explanation underscores the interdependence of doshas in maintaining respiratory health, aligning Avalambaka Kapha's stabilizing role with therapies designed to clear blockages and improve lung function.

45. A: In Ayurveda, weak digestive fire (Agni) leads to incomplete digestion and the accumulation of Ama, which is the root of many diseases. Strengthening Agni using proper diet and herbs prevents Ama formation and supports health. Hence, the reason correctly supports and explains the assertion.

46. B: The respiratory system in Ayurveda is primarily governed by Prana Vayu, Avalambaka Kapha, and Sadhaka Pitta, forming a dynamic interaction between movement, lubrication, and energy flow. Prana Vayu controls respiration and cognition, while Avalambaka Kapha provides structural stability, lubrication, and immune support in the chest region. Sadhaka Pitta influences emotional balance and indirectly affects respiration through its interaction with the heart and systemic health. Samana Vayu is unrelated to mucus production, making it incorrect in this context. This nuanced understanding reflects Ayurveda's holistic approach, emphasizing the interconnection of sub-doshas in maintaining physical and emotional respiratory health.

47. B: Pranavaha Srotas represent the pathways for the flow of Prana (life force), encompassing the nasal passages, throat, lungs, and other respiratory structures. Blockages in these pathways due to doshic imbalances or Ama accumulation lead to systemic issues, highlighting the importance of clear srotas for vitality. Ayurvedic interventions like Nasya (nasal therapy) and Pranayama (breathing exercises) help maintain these pathways, ensuring unobstructed Prana flow and optimal respiratory health. These practices reflect Ayurveda's preventive and therapeutic philosophy, where the interdependence of bodily systems ensures holistic well-being, aligning with its emphasis on balance and unobstructed physiological processes.

48. A: Kapha-related respiratory disorders such as congestion and excessive mucus production are managed effectively through therapies and interventions highlighted in Ayurveda. Vamana, or therapeutic emesis, directly removes Kapha-related stagnation. Herbs like Pippali, Shunthi, and Tulsi act as decongestants and expectorants, supporting respiratory efficiency. A Kapha-pacifying diet of warm, light foods avoids triggers like oily and cold foods, which aggravate mucus buildup. Cooling herbs like Guduchi are unrelated to Kapha management, making their inclusion inappropriate here. Ayurveda's precise recommendations illustrate its commitment to targeting specific imbalances through integrative therapies that address both symptoms and underlying causes.

49. C: Ojas is the subtle essence that supports immunity and vitality. Depletion of Ojas weakens Prana Vayu and Avalambaka Kapha, increasing susceptibility to respiratory illnesses. Rasayana therapies and lifestyle changes are key methods to restore Ojas. However, the option mentioning Ojas being unrelated to respiratory health is incorrect, so only statements 1 and 3 are valid.

50. B: The integration of modern medicine with Ayurveda offers synergistic benefits in respiratory care. Herbs like Tulsi and Vasaka, validated through modern research, provide anti-inflammatory and bronchodilator effects, making them effective in conditions like asthma and COPD. Pranayama, traditionally emphasized in Ayurveda, is recognized for improving lung capacity, reducing stress, and enhancing oxygenation. Panchakarma therapies are complementary to modern treatments, addressing detoxification and doshic balance, rather than replacing conventional medicine. This integrative approach aligns with Ayurveda's preventive and curative principles, combining traditional wisdom and scientific validation to manage complex respiratory disorders holistically, supporting comprehensive healthcare frameworks.

CHAPTER 23

NERVOUS, ENDOCRINE, AND EXCRETORY SYSTEMS – FUNCTIONS AND COORDINATION

INTRODUCTION

The human body is a complex biological machine, and its seamless functioning depends on intricate coordination between multiple organ systems. Among these, the nervous, endocrine, and excretory systems are essential for maintaining homeostasis, ensuring survival, and enabling complex interactions with the external environment. This chapter explores the structure, functions, and coordination of these systems, emphasizing their interdependence and providing insights into Ayurvedic approaches for balancing and optimizing their functions.

(I) Nervous System

The nervous system is the primary control center of the body, managing everything from basic reflexes to higher-order thinking. It enables rapid communication between different body parts and the environment through electrical and chemical signals.

A. Structure of the Nervous System

The nervous system is divided into two main parts:

1. **Central Nervous System (CNS):** Comprises the brain and spinal cord.

   Acts as the control center for processing information and making decisions.

2. **Peripheral Nervous System (PNS):** Includes all nerves outside the CNS.
   - **Divided into:** Somatic Nervous System (voluntary control, e.g., movement of skeletal muscles).
   - Autonomic Nervous System (involuntary control, e.g., heartbeat, digestion).
   - **Sympathetic Division:** Activates fight-or-flight responses.
   - **Parasympathetic Division:** Promotes rest-and-digest functions.

B. Functions of the Nervous System

1. **Sensory Input:** Collects information from sensory organs (e.g., eyes, ears, skin) and sends it to the CNS.
2. **Integration:** Processes sensory information in the brain and spinal cord to determine appropriate responses.
3. **Motor Output:** Sends signals to muscles and glands to execute actions.
4. **Homeostasis Maintenance:** Regulates involuntary functions like temperature, blood pressure, and breathing.
5. **Cognition and Emotions:** Controls higher functions such as memory, learning, reasoning, and emotional processing.

C. Coordination with Other Systems

The nervous system is integrally linked to the endocrine and excretory systems.

For example:

- It stimulates the adrenal glands to release hormones during stress.
- It regulates kidney function through autonomic nerves.

(II) Endocrine System: A Comprehensive Analysis

The endocrine system is a cornerstone of the body's regulatory mechanisms, operating alongside the nervous system to maintain homeostasis, regulate metabolism, and coordinate growth and development. While the nervous system enables rapid, short-lived responses via electrical signals, the endocrine system provides a slower but sustained form of regulation through chemical messengers called hormones. This system ensures stability and adaptability, crucial for survival and optimal functioning in ever-changing environments.

A. Structure of the Endocrine System

The endocrine system consists of specialized glands that produce hormones, each of which targets specific cells or tissues to elicit precise physiological responses. The following are the major endocrine glands and their functions:

1. **Hypothalamus:**
   - **Location:** Situated in the brain, below the thalamus.
   - **Role:** Acts as the bridge between the nervous and endocrine systems.
   - **Functions:** Produces releasing and inhibiting hormones that regulate the pituitary gland (e.g., Thyrotropin-releasing hormone [TRH], Corticotropin-releasing hormone [CRH]).
   - Controls autonomic nervous system functions such as hunger, thirst, and temperature regulation.
   - Coordinates the stress response by activating the hypothalamic-pituitary-adrenal (HPA) axis.
   - **Clinical Note:** Dysfunction of the hypothalamus can lead to disorders like hypothalamic obesity and hormonal imbalances.
2. **Pituitary Gland**
   - **Location:** Sits at the base of the brain in the sella turcica, a small bony cavity.
   - **Structure:** Divided into anterior (adenohypophysis) and posterior (neurohypophysis) lobes.

   Functions:

   Anterior Pituitary:
   - Produces hormones like growth hormone (GH), adrenocorticotropic hormone (ACTH), thyroid-stimulating hormone (TSH), prolactin, and gonadotropins (FSH and LH).
   - Regulates growth, stress response, reproduction, and metabolism.

   Posterior Pituitary:
   - ■ Stores and releases oxytocin and antidiuretic hormone (ADH), produced by the hypothalamus.
   - Controls water balance and uterine contractions.
   - **Clinical Note:** Pituitary tumors can result in conditions like acromegaly, Cushing's disease, or hypopituitarism.
3. **Thyroid Gland**
   - **Location:** Anterior neck, wrapped around the trachea.
   - **Structure:** Butterfly-shaped gland consisting of two lobes connected by an isthmus.

   Functions:
   - Produces thyroid hormones (T3 and T4) that regulate metabolism, growth, and development.
   - Secretes calcitonin, which lowers blood calcium levels.
   - **Clinical Note:** Disorders include hypothyroidism (e.g., Hashimoto's thyroiditis) and hyperthyroidism (e.g., Graves' disease).
4. **Parathyroid Glands**
   - **Location:** Four small glands located on the posterior surface of the thyroid gland.

   Functions:
   - Produce parathyroid hormone (PTH), which increases blood calcium levels by stimulating bone resorption, kidney calcium reabsorption, and intestinal calcium absorption.
   - **Clinical Note:** Hyperparathyroidism can lead to osteoporosis and kidney stones, while hypoparathyroidism can cause muscle cramps and tetany.
5. **Adrenal Glands**
   - **Location:** Sit atop each kidney.
   - **Structure:** Composed of two parts:
   - **Adrenal Cortex:** Produces corticosteroids like cortisol (stress hormone) and aldosterone (regulates blood pressure and electrolyte balance).
   - **Adrenal Medulla:** Produces catecholamines (adrenaline and noradrenaline) that mediate the fight-or-flight response.
   - **Clinical Note:** Disorders include Addison's disease (cortisol deficiency) and Cushing's syndrome (cortisol excess).
6. **Pancreas**
   - **Location:** Located in the abdomen, behind the stomach.
   - **Structure:** Functions as both an endocrine and exocrine gland.

Endocrine Functions

Islets of Langerhans secrete:

- **Insulin:** Lowers blood glucose levels by promoting cellular uptake.
- **Glucagon:** Raises blood glucose levels by stimulating glycogen breakdown.
- **Somatostatin:** Inhibits insulin and glucagon secretion.
- **Clinical Note:** Dysfunction leads to diabetes mellitus (type 1 and type 2).

7. **Gonads (Ovaries and Testes)**

Location:

- **Ovaries:** In the pelvic cavity in females.
- **Testes:** In the scrotum in males.

Functions:

Produce sex hormones:

- **Ovaries:** Secrete estrogen and progesterone, regulating menstrual cycles, pregnancy, and secondary sexual characteristics.
- **Testes:** Produce testosterone, responsible for sperm production and male secondary sexual traits.
- **Clinical Note:** Hormonal imbalances can lead to conditions like polycystic ovary syndrome (PCOS) or hypogonadism.

B. Functions of the Endocrine System

The endocrine system regulates numerous bodily functions through its network of glands and hormones. Key functions include:

1. **Homeostasis Maintenance:** Hormones maintain internal stability by regulating:
   - **Blood Sugar:** Insulin and glucagon ensure glucose homeostasis.
   - **Water Balance:** ADH prevents dehydration by conserving water in the kidneys.
   - **Electrolyte Balance:** Aldosterone controls sodium and potassium levels.
2. **Growth and Development**
   - Hormones like GH, thyroid hormones, and sex steroids (estrogen and testosterone) influence physical growth, bone maturation, and brain development.
   - Imbalances can result in conditions such as dwarfism, gigantism, or delayed puberty.
3. **Reproductive Functions**
   - The endocrine system orchestrates sexual maturation, fertility, and pregnancy through hormones like FSH, LH, and prolactin.
   - Disorders like infertility or menstrual irregularities often have endocrine origins.
4. **Stress Response:** The HPA axis regulates the stress response:
   - Cortisol ensures adequate energy supply during stress.
   - Catecholamines (adrenaline) prepare the body for immediate action.
   - Chronic stress can dysregulate this system, leading to conditions like adrenal fatigue or anxiety disorders.
5. **Energy Regulation**: The endocrine system manages how the body uses, stores, and mobilizes energy:
   - Insulin and glucagon maintain glucose availability.
   - Thyroid hormones influence basal metabolic rate (BMR).

C. Coordination with Other Systems

The endocrine system does not function in isolation. It collaborates closely with other systems to maintain physiological harmony:

Nervous System: Hypothalamus-Pituitary Connection:

- The hypothalamus acts as a central hub, integrating neural and endocrine signals.

Stress Response:

- The autonomic nervous system and adrenal medulla coordinate rapid responses to stress.

Behavioural Regulation:

- Hormones influence emotions, cognition, and behaviour.

Excretory System: A Comprehensive Analysis:

- The excretory system is an essential component of the human body's regulatory network, tasked with removing metabolic wastes, maintaining fluid and electrolyte balance, and preserving the internal environment's stability. Among its components, the kidneys serve as the primary organs of this system, playing pivotal roles in filtration, reabsorption, secretion, and excretion. This chapter provides an in-depth exploration of the excretory system, with a particular focus on kidney function, calcium homeostasis, and blood pressure regulation.

Introduction to the Excretory System

The excretory system works to eliminate metabolic wastes generated from cellular processes. It ensures the maintenance of the body's internal environment (homeostasis) by regulating water balance, electrolyte levels, and acid-base equilibrium. Its core components include:

1. **Kidneys:** The primary organs of filtration and excretion.
2. **Ureters:** Tubes that transport urine from the kidneys to the bladder.
3. **Urinary Bladder:** A storage organ for urine.
4. **Urethra:** The conduit through which urine is expelled from the body.

In addition to the urinary system, other excretory organs, such as the skin (sweat glands), lungs (expelling carbon dioxide), and liver (detoxifying harmful substances), complement the kidneys in waste removal.

Kidney Function: The Cornerstone of the Excretory System

The kidneys are sophisticated organs that filter the blood, removing waste products while conserving water, electrolytes, and other essential substances. Each kidney contains approximately one million nephrons, the functional units responsible for urine formation.

1. **Overview of Kidney Function:** Kidneys perform several vital functions, including:
   - **Filtration:** Removal of waste products and toxins from the blood.
   - **Reabsorption:** Recovery of water, glucose, and electrolytes into the bloodstream.
   - **Secretion:** Active transport of excess ions and waste substances into the nephron.
   - **Excretion:** Elimination of urine through the ureters.
2. **Role of Aldosterone and ADH in Fluid and Electrolyte Balance:** The kidneys are central to maintaining fluid and electrolyte balance, which is critical for cell function and overall homeostasis. Hormones like aldosterone and antidiuretic hormone (ADH) regulate these processes:

A. Aldosterone

- **Source:** Secreted by the adrenal cortex.
- **Target:** Acts on the distal tubules and collecting ducts of the nephron.
- **Function:** Increases sodium reabsorption into the bloodstream.
- Promotes potassium excretion into the urine.
- Enhances water reabsorption indirectly by osmosis, increasing blood volume and pressure.
- **Mechanism:** Aldosterone binds to receptors in renal cells, triggering the synthesis of sodium-potassium pumps.
- This action drives sodium out of the nephron's filtrate and into the bloodstream while secreting potassium into the filtrate.

B. Antidiuretic Hormone (ADH)

- **Source:** Produced by the hypothalamus and released by the posterior pituitary gland.
- **Target:** Acts on the collecting ducts of the nephron.
- **Function:** Increases the permeability of the collecting ducts to water.
- Promotes water reabsorption back into the bloodstream, reducing urine volume and preventing dehydration.
- **Mechanism:** ADH triggers the insertion of aquaporin-2 channels into the membrane of collecting duct cells.
- These channels facilitate water movement from the nephron back into the surrounding capillaries.

Clinical Implications

- **Aldosterone Deficiency:** Can lead to conditions like Addison's disease, characterized by electrolyte imbalances and low blood pressure.
- **ADH Deficiency:** Results in diabetes insipidus, a condition marked by excessive urination and thirst due to the inability to concentrate urine.

Calcium Homeostasis: A Key Function of the Kidneys

Calcium is a critical mineral for numerous physiological processes, including bone health, muscle contraction, nerve transmission, and blood clotting. The kidneys play a vital role in calcium homeostasis, modulated by the interplay of parathyroid hormone (PTH) and calcitonin.

1. **Parathyroid Hormone (PTH)**
   - **Source:** Secreted by the parathyroid glands in response to low blood calcium levels.
   - **Effects on Kidneys:** Increases calcium reabsorption in the renal tubules, reducing calcium excretion in urine.
   - Stimulates the activation of vitamin D (conversion of calcidiol to calcitriol in the kidneys).
   - Calcitriol promotes calcium absorption from the gastrointestinal tract and resorption from bones.
2. **Calcitonin**
   - **Source:** Produced by the thyroid gland in response to high blood calcium levels.
   - **Effects on Kidneys:** Inhibits calcium reabsorption in the renal tubules, increasing calcium excretion in urine.
   - Counteracts the effects of PTH, promoting calcium deposition in bones.

3. **Regulation and Feedback Mechanism**: The balance between PTH and calcitonin ensures stable blood calcium levels.

   For instance:

   - **Hypocalcemia:** Triggers increased PTH secretion, enhancing calcium retention by the kidneys.
   - **Hypercalcemia:** Leads to calcitonin release, promoting calcium excretion and deposition.
   - Clinical Implications
   - **Hyperparathyroidism:** Excess PTH can result in hypercalcemia, kidney stones, and osteoporosis.
   - **Hypoparathyroidism:** Leads to hypocalcemia, causing muscle spasms and tetany.
   - **Kidney Disease:** Impaired renal function can disrupt calcium-phosphorus balance, contributing to conditions like renal osteodystrophy.

Blood Pressure Regulation by the Kidneys

The kidneys are integral to blood pressure regulation through the renin-angiotensin-aldosterone system (RAAS), a hormone cascade that adjusts blood volume and vascular resistance.

1. **The Renin-Angiotensin-Aldosterone System (RAAS)**

   A. Trigger for Activation: The RAAS is activated in response to:

   - **Low Blood Pressure:** Detected by baroreceptors in the juxtaglomerular apparatus (JGA) of the kidneys.
   - **Low Sodium Levels:** Sensed by macula densa cells in the nephron.
   - **Sympathetic Nervous System Stimulation:** Due to stress or physical activity.

   B. Steps of the RAAS

   1. **Renin Release:** The kidneys release renin, an enzyme, into the bloodstream.
   2. **Angiotensinogen Activation:** Renin converts angiotensinogen (produced by the liver) into angiotensin I.
   3. **Angiotensin I to Angiotensin II:** Angiotensin I is converted into angiotensin II by angiotensin-converting enzyme (ACE), primarily in the lungs.
   4. **Effects of Angiotensin II:** Vasoconstriction: Narrows blood vessels, increasing blood pressure.
      - **Aldosterone Secretion:** Stimulates the adrenal cortex to release aldosterone, enhancing sodium and water retention.
      - **ADH Release:** Promotes water reabsorption by the kidneys.

2. **Blood Pressure and Kidney Function:** The kidneys fine-tune blood pressure through:

   - **Glomerular Filtration Rate (GFR):** Adjustments to GFR modulate urine output and blood volume.
   - **Sodium Handling:** Sodium retention or excretion directly impacts blood pressure.
   - **Hormonal Interplay:** Integration with RAAS, ADH, and atrial natriuretic peptide (ANP) ensures precise control.

3. **Clinical Implications**

   - **Hypertension:** Overactivation of the RAAS can lead to chronic high blood pressure, requiring ACE inhibitors or angiotensin receptor blockers (ARBs) for management.
   - **Hypotension:** RAAS dysfunction may impair the body's ability to restore adequate blood pressure.
   - **Kidney Damage:** Chronic hypertension can damage the kidneys, creating a vicious cycle of worsening blood pressure and renal impairment.

4. **Other Systems**

   - **Skeletal System:** Growth hormone and PTH influence bone growth and remodeling.
   - **Reproductive System:** Sex hormones regulate the reproductive organs.
   - **Digestive System:** Hormones like gastrin and secretin influence digestion.

(III) Excretory System

The excretory system is responsible for removing metabolic waste, maintaining electrolyte balance, and regulating fluid levels in the body. It plays a critical role in detoxification and homeostasis.

A. Structure of the Excretory System: The excretory system primarily consists of:

1. **Kidneys:** Filter blood to remove waste and excess substances.
2. **Ureters:** Transport urine from the kidneys to the bladder.
3. **Urinary Bladder:** Stores urine until excretion.
4. **Urethra:** Releases urine from the body.

B. Functions of the Excretory System

1. **Waste Removal:** Eliminates nitrogenous wastes like urea, creatinine, and uric acid.
2. **Water and Electrolyte Balance:** Adjusts the concentration of sodium, potassium, and other ions in the blood.
3. **Blood Pressure Regulation:** Maintains blood pressure via the renin-angiotensin-aldosterone system (RAAS).
4. **Acid-Base Balance:** Regulates blood pH by excreting hydrogen ions and reabsorbing bicarbonate.

5. **Erythropoiesis Regulation:** Produces erythropoietin, a hormone that stimulates red blood cell production.

C. **Coordination with Other Systems**

- **Nervous System:** Autonomic nerves regulate kidney function.
- **Endocrine System:** Hormones like ADH and aldosterone control urine production and water balance.

(IV) Coordination of the Nervous, Endocrine, and Excretory Systems

The nervous, endocrine, and excretory systems work together to maintain internal balance and respond to external changes.

A. **Stress Response Example**

1. **Nervous System:** Detects stress and signals the hypothalamus.
2. **Endocrine System:** The hypothalamus activates the HPA axis, leading to cortisol release.
3. **Excretory System:** The kidneys conserve water and maintain blood pressure during stress.

B. **Fluid Balance Example**

1. **Endocrine System:** Releases ADH to regulate water retention.
2. **Excretory System:** Adjusts urine output to balance hydration.
3. **Nervous System:** Monitors thirst and signals the brain to encourage fluid intake.

(V) Ayurvedic Approaches to Balancing the Nervous, Endocrine, and Excretory Systems

A. **Principles of Ayurveda**: Ayurveda emphasizes the balance of three fundamental energies, or doshas:

1. **Vata:** Governs movement, associated with the nervous system.
2. **Pitta:** Governs transformation, linked to the endocrine system.
3. **Kapha:** Governs structure, associated with the excretory system.

B. **Ayurvedic Strategies for Nervous System Health**

1. **Herbs and Remedies:**
   - **Ashwagandha:** Reduces stress and improves cognitive function.
   - **Brahmi:** Enhances memory and calms the mind.
2. **Diet:** Foods rich in omega-3 fatty acids support brain health.
   - Avoid stimulants like caffeine.
3. **Lifestyle:** Practices like yoga and meditation promote relaxation and resilience.

C. **Ayurvedic Strategies for Endocrine System Health**

1. **Herbs and Remedies:**
   - Shatavari: Supports hormonal balance in women.
   - Guggulu: Aids thyroid health and metabolism.
2. **Diet:** Consume a balanced diet with seasonal fruits and vegetables.
   - Avoid processed foods and sugar.
3. **Lifestyle:** Regular exercise and sleep optimize hormonal health.

D. **Ayurvedic Strategies for Excretory System Health**

1. **Herbs and Remedies:**
   - **Punarnava:** Promotes kidney function and detoxification.
   - **Gokshura:** Supports urinary tract health.
2. **Diet:** Stay hydrated and consume diuretic foods like cucumber and watermelon.
3. **Lifestyle:** Avoid excessive salt and alcohol.

E. **Panchakarma Therapy**

- This detoxification technique involves five steps, including:

1. **Virechana (Purgation):** Cleanses the digestive tract.
2. **Basti (Enemas):** Balances Vata and promotes kidney health.

MULTIPLE CHOICE QUESTIONS

1. The human nervous system, encompassing the central and peripheral components, operates in tandem with the endocrine system to regulate various physiological processes. Researchers hav awe postulated that the hypothalamic-pituitary axis plays a pivotal role in coordinating stress responses, growth, and reproductive functions. A recent study evaluated the effects of chronic stress on this axis, noting alterations in cortisol levels, adrenal hypertrophy, and feedback inhibition failure. Which of the following conclusions is most consistent with the interplay between chronic stress and the hypothalamic-pituitary axis?

   A. Chronic stress enhances the efficiency of feedback mechanisms in the hypothalamic-pituitary-adrenal axis.

   B. Cortisol secretion during chronic stress becomes dysregulated, leading to adverse physiological outcomes.

C. The hypothalamus directly stimulates adrenal gland hypertrophy, independent of pituitary involvement.
D. Feedback inhibition in the hypothalamic-pituitary-adrenal axis remains unaffected under prolonged stress conditions.

2. Endocrine glands secrete hormones that regulate metabolism, growth, and homeostasis. The pineal gland, though small, significantly influences circadian rhythms through melatonin secretion. A group of neuroscientists recently investigated the influence of artificial light exposure on melatonin levels and its subsequent impact on sleep disorders and metabolic health. The study found a significant reduction in melatonin secretion in participants exposed to blue light during the evening hours. Which hypothesis aligns most closely with these findings regarding pineal gland function?
A. Artificial light exposure enhances pineal gland activity, improving circadian alignment.
B. Suppressed melatonin production disrupts circadian rhythms, contributing to sleep and metabolic disorders.
C. The pineal gland remains unaffected by environmental light changes, as its secretion is entirely autonomous.
D. Increased melatonin levels due to artificial light exposure regulate metabolism effectively.

3. A recent comparative analysis examined Ayurvedic principles alongside modern neuroscience, particularly focusing on how the Vata dosha corresponds to neural activity and mobility. The study proposed that Vata-related imbalances manifest as neurological disorders such as anxiety and insomnia. Considering this correlation, which of the following statements best integrates Ayurvedic insights with contemporary neurological findings?
A. Ayurveda's Vata dosha has no scientific equivalence and should not be compared with neural functions.
B. Imbalances in the Vata dosha may parallel dysfunctions in neurotransmitter signaling, leading to disorders like anxiety.
C. Neurological disorders exclusively result from structural anomalies in the nervous system, unrelated to Vata principles.
D. Modern neuroscience rejects any association between Ayurvedic doshas and neural pathways.

4. The excretory system, particularly the kidneys, plays a critical role in maintaining homeostasis by filtering blood and excreting waste products. A biochemist studying renal physiology discovered that glomerular filtration rate (GFR) is influenced by systemic blood pressure and plasma oncotic pressure. Simultaneously, an Ayurvedic practitioner emphasized the role of herbal formulations like Gokshura in enhancing renal function and alleviating kidney-related ailments. Based on this integration, which explanation best illustrates the link between GFR and Ayurvedic practices?
A. Ayurvedic herbs like Gokshura are irrelevant to renal physiology, as GFR is regulated solely by physical forces.
B. Gokshura enhances GFR by modulating systemic blood pressure and reducing renal inflammation.
C. GFR changes have no connection to Ayurvedic principles, which focus exclusively on dosha balance.
D. Plasma oncotic pressure remains unaffected by herbal formulations, indicating no influence on GFR.

5. Hormonal regulation in the human body is an intricate process involving feedback loops and receptor-specific actions. Insulin, a hormone secreted by the pancreas, regulates glucose homeostasis. Ayurvedic approaches to managing diabetes focus on herbal preparations like Fenugreek (Methi) to reduce blood sugar levels naturally. If this claim were studied in the context of insulin receptor sensitivity, which outcome would most likely validate the efficacy of such treatments?
A. Fenugreek enhances insulin secretion independently of receptor sensitivity.
B. Improved insulin receptor sensitivity, facilitated by Fenugreek, contributes to better glucose uptake and metabolism.
C. Fenugreek reduces insulin activity, emphasizing non-hormonal mechanisms for blood sugar control.
D. The use of Fenugreek disrupts pancreatic function, leading to reduced insulin production.

6. Neurotransmitters, small chemical messengers, mediate synaptic transmission in the nervous system. Dopamine, a key neurotransmitter, regulates motor control, reward pathways, and mood. Research indicates that Ayurvedic herbs like Ashwagandha modulate dopamine activity, potentially alleviating conditions such as Parkinson's disease and depression. In a controlled experiment, patients receiving Ashwagandha extracts exhibited enhanced dopaminergic signaling and reduced motor symptoms. Based on this study, what mechanism might best explain the effects of Ashwagandha on dopamine regulation?
A. Ashwagandha inhibits dopamine release, ensuring synaptic stability in motor pathways.
B. Dopaminergic neurons are directly stimulated by Ashwagandha, enhancing their activity and reducing neurodegeneration.
C. Ashwagandha suppresses reward pathways, making it ineffective in mood regulation.

D. The herb's primary function is unrelated to dopamine, instead focusing on hormonal pathways.

7. The hypothalamus, pituitary gland, and kidneys are functionally connected through the regulation of water balance and osmoregulation. Antidiuretic hormone (ADH) secreted by the pituitary gland increases water reabsorption in the kidneys. An integrative study explored the effects of Ayurvedic diuretics like Punarnava on water retention in patients with hypertension. The results indicated significant modulation of ADH activity alongside increased urinary output. Which of the following conclusions can be drawn from this observation?

A. Ayurvedic diuretics reduce ADH secretion, directly enhancing kidney filtration rates.

B. The role of Punarnava is independent of ADH regulation, as diuretics function solely through fluid volume reduction.

C. ADH activity remains unaltered by Ayurvedic treatments, suggesting a placebo effect.

D. Punarnava reduces water retention by influencing hormonal mechanisms like ADH secretion.

8. Stress-induced hormonal imbalances significantly impact both the endocrine and nervous systems. Cortisol, a glucocorticoid hormone, is often elevated in individuals with chronic stress. Researchers studying Ayurvedic stress-relief formulations like Brahmi observed reductions in cortisol levels among participants. Considering the link between cortisol and stress, how might Brahmi influence physiological stress responses?

A. Brahmi directly inhibits cortisol production, eliminating stress without affecting neuronal pathways.

B. Enhanced adrenal cortex activity due to Brahmi increases cortisol, worsening stress responses.

C. Brahmi promotes relaxation through cortisol modulation and neural plasticity enhancement.

D. Cortisol regulation by Brahmi is unrelated to stress management, focusing instead on digestive health.

9. The endocrine system intricately interacts with the excretory system, especially in regulating electrolyte balance. Aldosterone, a mineralocorticoid, enhances sodium retention and potassium excretion in the kidneys. Ayurvedic approaches suggest that herbal treatments like Chandraprabha Vati improve electrolyte balance. If the effectiveness of this herbal remedy were evaluated, which mechanism would best support its role?

A. Chandraprabha Vati enhances potassium retention, counteracting aldosterone effects.

B. Improved aldosterone activity through Chandraprabha Vati enhances sodium reabsorption.

C. The herbal formulation directly inhibits aldosterone secretion, improving potassium homeostasis.

D. Sodium and potassium balance remains unaffected by Ayurvedic treatments, emphasizing a placebo effect.

10. Circadian rhythms, controlled by the suprachiasmatic nucleus (SCN) in the hypothalamus, govern the sleep-wake cycle and metabolic processes. Ayurvedic practices emphasize the importance of aligning daily routines with natural circadian cycles, promoting health through lifestyle adjustments (Dinacharya). How might modern research validate the effectiveness of these practices in maintaining circadian alignment?

A. Lifestyle routines disrupt the SCN, diminishing circadian rhythmicity.

B. Ayurvedic practices enhance hormonal balance, aligning circadian rhythms with environmental cues.

C. Dinacharya focuses exclusively on dietary regulation, with no influence on circadian cycles.

D. The SCN is unaffected by external routines, rendering Ayurvedic practices ineffective in circadian regulation.

Directions (Q. No. 11-14): *Scenario-Based Questions*

SCENARIO 1

A neuroscientist embarks on a rigorous study of Ayurvedic interventions targeting stress-related neuroendocrine dysregulation. Focusing on the hypothalamic-pituitary-adrenal (HPA) axis, the researcher investigates the effects of the Ayurvedic herb Ashwagandha (*Withania somnifera*). The hypothesis states that Ashwagandha modulates cortisol secretion by acting on glucocorticoid receptors in the hypothalamus. Over six months, participants with chronic stress receive a standardized dose of Ashwagandha extract. The study reveals that the herb reduces cortisol spikes, stabilizes the circadian rhythm of cortisol secretion, and alleviates symptoms of anxiety. Advanced imaging techniques also demonstrate improved hippocampal connectivity, suggesting enhanced neural plasticity.

However, the study raises questions about the sustainable cultivation of Ashwagandha. Farmers in arid regions, where Ashwagandha thrives, report overharvesting due to global demand, leading to soil degradation and declining crop quality. A parallel environmental study finds that traditional agroforestry practices could mitigate these challenges, improving soil fertility and ensuring the sustainability of Ashwagandha cultivation.

SCENARIO 2

In another region, a team of nephrologists explores the therapeutic impact of Punarnava (Boerhavia diffusa) on renal function in patients with chronic kidney disease (CKD). Ayurvedic practitioners have long recommended Punarnava for its diuretic and anti-inflammatory properties. The clinical trial shows that Punarnava significantly improves glomerular filtration rates (GFR) and reduces renal inflammation markers like interleukin-6 (IL-6) and tumor necrosis factor-alpha (TNF-α). The researchers conclude that the herb enhances renal microcirculation while supporting systemic detoxification processes.

Simultaneously, conservationists highlight the unsustainable extraction of wild Punarnava plants from forest ecosystems. They argue that large-scale cultivation, coupled with community-based conservation initiatives, could prevent resource depletion. These findings emphasize the interconnectedness of ecological sustainability and the efficacy of Ayurvedic formulations.

11. Based on the findings in Scenario 1, how does Ashwagandha contribute to the observed neural and endocrine improvements in participants with chronic stress?

A. By suppressing HPA axis activity, thereby reducing cortisol levels and enhancing hippocampal connectivity.

B. By directly blocking glucocorticoid receptors, leading to cortisol elimination from the bloodstream.

C. By increasing cortisol secretion to stabilize neural pathways and improve stress adaptation.

D. By focusing on peripheral nervous activity without influencing the HPA axis or neural connectivity.

12. In Scenario 2, what is the most plausible explanation for the renal improvements observed in patients treated with Punarnava?

A. Punarnava enhances renal filtration exclusively by increasing systemic blood pressure.

B. The herb's anti-inflammatory properties improve renal microcirculation and reduce inflammatory markers.

C. Diuretic effects of Punarnava result in significant dehydration, indirectly supporting renal function.

D. Punarnava's impact on renal function is independent of its systemic anti-inflammatory effects.

13. Considering the sustainability challenges described in both scenarios, which strategy would most effectively address the overharvesting of Ashwagandha and Punarnava while maintaining their therapeutic quality?

A. Promoting large-scale monoculture plantations of these herbs in arid and forested regions.

B. Advocating for synthetic alternatives to replicate the bioactive properties of Ashwagandha and Punarnava.

C. Encouraging agroforestry practices and community-based conservation to ensure ecological balance.

D. Reducing global demand for Ayurvedic herbs to minimize environmental degradation.

14. How does the environmental degradation of Ashwagandha and Punarnava potentially influence the therapeutic outcomes discussed in Scenarios 1 and 2?

A. Soil degradation reduces the concentration of bioactive compounds, compromising therapeutic efficacy.

B. Degraded environments enhance the potency of bioactive compounds in these herbs.

C. Therapeutic outcomes are unaffected, as bioactive properties are independent of environmental conditions.

D. Environmental degradation improves soil fertility, indirectly supporting the quality of medicinal plants.

Directions (Q. No. 15–24): *Choose the correct answer from the options given below.*

15. The functions of the nervous system in Ayurvedic physiology are closely linked to the Tridosha theory:

(a) Vata governs movement and communication.

(b) Pitta is associated with metabolic activities, including neurotransmitter synthesis.

(c) Kapha influences structural integrity and protection of neurons.

(d) The balance of Tridoshas ensures optimal mental and physical health.

Codes:

A. (a), (b), and (c) only

B. (a), (b), and (d) only

C. (b), (c), and (d) only

D. (a), (b), (c), and (d)

16. The hormonal regulation of the human endocrine system aligns with specific Ayurvedic principles:

(a) Agni represents metabolic activity at the cellular level.

(b) Dosha imbalances are reflected in endocrine dysfunctions.

(c) Ojas corresponds to hormonal balance and vitality.

(d) Ayurvedic interventions directly modulate endocrine secretions.

Codes:

A. (a) and (b) only

B. (a), (b), and (c) only

C. (b), (c), and (d) only

D. (a), (b), (c), and (d)

17. Ayurvedic Rasas (tastes) have biological implications in maintaining systemic health:
(a) Sweet Rasa supports tissue growth and stability.
(b) Bitter Rasa detoxifies and reduces inflammation.
(c) Astringent Rasa strengthens tissues and controls bleeding.
(d) Pungent Rasa stimulates neural activity and circulation.

Codes:
A. (a), (b), and (d) only
B. (a), (b), and (c) only
C. (a), (c), and (d) only
D. (a), (b), (c), and (d)

18. In Ayurveda, the role of excretory organs is integrated with systemic detoxification:
(a) Kidneys are responsible for urinary elimination.
(b) Skin aids in the excretion of waste through sweat.
(c) The colon eliminates metabolic toxins.
(d) Liver function aligns with Pitta regulation and bile secretion.

Codes:
A. (a), (b), and (c) only
B. (a), (b), and (d) only
C. (a), (c), and (d) only
D. (a), (b), (c), and (d)

19. The Ayurvedic perspective on nervous system disorders includes:
(a) Vata imbalance is linked to neurological dysfunctions like tremors and anxiety.
(b) Pitta imbalance manifests as inflammation in neural pathways.
(c) Kapha imbalance leads to sluggish neural activity and depression.
(d) Balancing Tridoshas restores neural function.

Codes:
A. (a), (b), and (c) only
B. (a), (b), and (d) only
C. (a), (c), and (d) only
D. (a), (b), (c), and (d)

20. The endocrine system in Ayurvedic medicine is influenced by specific dietary and lifestyle practices:
(a) Sattvic diet enhances hormonal harmony.
(b) Yoga and Pranayama stabilize cortisol levels.
(c) Rasayana therapies rejuvenate the endocrine glands.
(d) Fasting disrupts endocrine balance.

Codes:
A. (a), (b), and (c) only
B. (a), (b), and (d) only
C. (b), (c), and (d) only
D. (a), (b), (c), and (d)

21. The biological roles of Agni in Ayurvedic physiology include:
(a) Metabolic regulation at both gross and cellular levels.
(b) Detoxification by converting toxins into excretable forms.
(c) Supporting immune functions by maintaining digestive health.
(d) Preventing oxidative stress through enzymatic activity.

Codes:
A. (a), (b), and (c) only
B. (b), (c), and (d) only
C. (a), (b), and (d) only
D. (a), (b), (c), and (d)

22. The detoxifying properties of Ayurvedic herbs can be categorized as follows:
(a) Triphala supports gut detoxification and microbial balance.
(b) Punarnava aids renal detoxification.
(c) Neem purifies the blood and skin.
(d) Ashwagandha detoxifies neural tissues.

Codes:
A. (a), (b), and (c) only
B. (a), (b), and (d) only
C. (a), (c), and (d) only
D. (a), (b), (c), and (d)

23. The role of doshas in endocrine health is described in Ayurveda as:
(a) Vata governs hormonal timing and release.
(b) Pitta regulates metabolic hormone activity.
(c) Kapha influences anabolic and growth-related hormones.
(d) Imbalanced doshas cause systemic hormonal disruptions.

Codes:
A. (a), (b), and (c) only
B. (a), (b), and (d) only
C. (b), (c), and (d) only
D. (a), (b), (c), and (d)

24. Ayurvedic principles for nervous system rejuvenation emphasize:
(a) Ashwagandha for reducing oxidative stress in neurons.
(b) Brahmi for enhancing memory and cognition.
(c) Shankhpushpi for calming excessive neural activity.
(d) Guggulu for stimulating neural pathways.

Codes:

A. (a), (b), and (c) only
B. (a), (b), and (d) only
C. (b), (c), and (d) only
D. (a), (b), (c), and (d)

Directions (Q. No. 25–34): *Match List–I with List–II carefully and choose the correct answer from the options given below.*

25. Match List–I (Components of the Nervous System) with List–II (Functions)

List–I	List–II
(a) Cerebrum	1. Coordinates voluntary motor movements
(b) Cerebellum	2. Controls higher cognitive functions like thinking and memory
(c) Hypothalamus	3. Regulates homeostasis and endocrine activity
(d) Spinal cord	4. Transmits sensory and motor signals between the brain and body

Options:

A. (a)-2, (b)-1, (c)-3, (d)-4
B. (a)-1, (b)-3, (c)-4, (d)-2
C. (a)-3, (b)-2, (c)-1, (d)-4
D. (a)-4, (b)-3, (c)-2, (d)-1

26. Match List–I (Ayurvedic Doshas) with List–II (Related Functions)

List–I	List–II
(a) Vata	1. Governs movement and communication
(b) Pitta	2. Controls digestion and metabolism
(c) Kapha	3. Provides stability and structural support
(d) Tridosha balance	4. Maintains overall health and equilibrium

Options:

A. (a)-1, (b)-2, (c)-3, (d)-4
B. (a)-4, (b)-1, (c)-2, (d)-3
C. (a)-2, (b)-3, (c)-4, (d)-1
D. (a)-3, (b)-4, (c)-1, (d)-2

27. Match List–I (Endocrine Glands) with List–II (Hormones Secreted)

List–I	List–II
(a) Adrenal gland	1. Cortisol
(b) Pancreas	2. Insulin
(c) Thyroid gland	3. Thyroxine
(d) Pituitary gland	4. Growth hormone

Options:

A. (a)-3, (b)-4, (c)-2, (d)-1
B. (a)-1, (b)-2, (c)-3, (d)-4
C. (a)-4, (b)-3, (c)-1, (d)-2
D. (a)-2, (b)-1, (c)-4, (d)-3

28. Match List–I (Rasas in Ayurveda) with List–II (Biological Actions)

List–I	List–II
(a) Sweet	1. Nourishes tissues and promotes growth
(b) Bitter	2. Detoxifies and reduces inflammation
(c) Astringent	3. Strengthens tissues and stops bleeding
(d) Sour	4. Enhances digestion and metabolic activity

Options:

A. (a)-2, (b)-3, (c)-1, (d)-4
B. (a)-1, (b)-2, (c)-3, (d)-4
C. (a)-4, (b)-1, (c)-2, (d)-3
D. (a)-3, (b)-4, (c)-2, (d)-1

29. Match List–I (Ayurvedic Treatments) with List–II (Applications)

List–I	List–II
(a) Panchakarma	1. Detoxification of the body
(b) Rasayana therapy	2. Rejuvenation and anti-aging
(c) Shirodhara	3. Stress reduction and mental clarity
(d) Abhyanga	4. Improves circulation and skin health

Options:

A. (a)-3, (b)-4, (c)-1, (d)-2
B. (a)-1, (b)-2, (c)-3, (d)-4
C. (a)-4, (b)-3, (c)-2, (d)-1
D. (a)-2, (b)-1, (c)-4, (d)-3

30. Match List–I (Excretory Organs) with List–II (Functions)

List–I	List–II
(a) Kidneys	1. Filters blood and excretes urine
(b) Lungs	2. Removes carbon dioxide from the blood
(c) Skin	3. Eliminates waste through sweat
(d) Liver	4. Detoxifies chemicals and produces bile

Options:

A. (a)-1, (b)-2, (c)-3, (d)-4
B. (a)-4, (b)-3, (c)-1, (d)-2
C. (a)-2, (b)-1, (c)-4, (d)-3
D. (a)-3, (b)-4, (c)-2, (d)-1

31. Match List–I (Nervous Disorders) with List–II (Causes)

List–I	List–II
(a) Parkinson's disease	1. Deficiency of dopamine
(b) Alzheimer's disease	2. Beta-amyloid plaque accumulation
(c) Epilepsy	3. Abnormal electrical activity in the brain
(d) Multiple sclerosis	4. Damage to myelin sheath

Options:

A. (a)-1, (b)-2, (c)-3, (d)-4
B. (a)-2, (b)-3, (c)-4, (d)-1
C. (a)-3, (b)-4, (c)-1, (d)-2
D. (a)-4, (b)-1, (c)-2, (d)-3

32. Match List–I (Ayurvedic Concepts) with List–II (Descriptions)

List–I	List–II
(a) Prakriti	1. Individual constitution determined at conception
(b) Agni	2. Digestive and metabolic fire
(c) Ama	3. Toxins resulting from incomplete digestion
(d) Ojas	4. Vital essence contributing to immunity and vitality

Options:

A. (a)-4, (b)-3, (c)-2, (d)-1
B. (a)-1, (b)-2, (c)-3, (d)-4
C. (a)-2, (b)-4, (c)-1, (d)-3
D. (a)-3, (b)-1, (c)-4, (d)-2

33. Match List–I (Herbal Medicines) with List–II (Primary Uses)

List–I	List–II
(a) Ashwagandha	1. Stress reduction and neural rejuvenation
(b) Brahmi	2. Enhances memory and cognition
(c) Punarnava	3. Improves renal function and acts as a diuretic
(d) Triphala	4. Detoxification and gut health

Options:

A. (a)-1, (b)-2, (c)-3, (d)-4
B. (a)-4, (b)-3, (c)-2, (d)-1
C. (a)-2, (b)-1, (c)-4, (d)-3
D. (a)-3, (b)-4, (c)-1, (d)-2

34. Match List–I (Ayurvedic Therapies) with List–II (Goals)

List–I	List–II
(a) Vamana	1. Emesis therapy for Kapha-related disorders
(b) Virechana	2. Purgation therapy for Pitta-related disorders
(c) Nasya	3. Nasal administration for head and neck diseases
(d) Basti	4. Enema therapy for Vata-related disorders

Options:

A. (a)-2, (b)-4, (c)-1, (d)-3
B. (a)-1, (b)-2, (c)-3, (d)-4
C. (a)-4, (b)-3, (c)-2, (d)-1
D. (a)-3, (b)-1, (c)-4, (d)-2

Directions (Q. No. 35–39): *Following questions are based on Statement 1 and Statement 2. Read both the statements carefully and choose the correct answer from the options given below:*

A. Both Statement 1 and Statement 2 are true, and Statement 2 is the correct explanation of Statement 1.
B. Both Statement 1 and Statement 2 are true, but Statement 2 is not the correct explanation of Statement 1.
C. Statement 1 is true, but Statement 2 is false.
D. Statement 1 is false, but Statement 2 is true.
E. Both Statement 1 and Statement 2 are false.

35. Statement 1: The hypothalamus regulates autonomic nervous system and endocrine functions.

Statement 2: It directly stimulates endocrine glands without involving the pituitary gland.

36. Statement 1: Hormones like adrenaline act rapidly during stress due to nervous system stimulation.

Statement 2: Endocrine glands secrete hormones only under the control of the nervous system.

37. Statement 1: The nervous system maintains quick communication in the body using electrical impulses.

Statement 2: These impulses are transmitted via chemical neurotransmitters at synapses.

38. Statement 1: The kidneys regulate electrolyte balance and remove nitrogenous wastes from the body.

Statement 2: Excess glucose in the blood leads to nephropathy, impairing kidney function.

39. Statement 1: The pineal gland regulates sleep-wake cycles by secreting melatonin.

Statement 2: Disruption of circadian rhythms by artificial light exposure impacts metabolic and endocrine health.

Directions (Q. No. 40–45): *There are two statements in each question. One is labelled as Assertion (A) and the other is as Reason (R). Read both the statements and choose the correct answer from the options given below:*

A. Both Assertion (A) and Reason (R) are true, and Reason (R) is the correct explanation of Assertion (A).
B. Both Assertion (A) and Reason (R) are true, but Reason (R) is not the correct explanation of Assertion (A).
C. Assertion (A) is true, but Reason (R) is false.
D. Assertion (A) is false, but Reason (R) is true.
E. Both Assertion (A) and Reason (R) are false.

40. Assertion (A): Dinacharya, or daily routines, prevent diseases and promote health.

Reason (R): They synchronize the body's biological rhythms with natural environmental cycles, balancing Tridoshas.

41. Assertion (A): The nervous system operates independently of the endocrine system.

Reason (R): The nervous system regulates immediate responses, while the endocrine system manages long-term changes.

42. Assertion (A): Panchakarma detoxifies the body effectively.

Reason (R): It focuses only on neural pathways and ignores metabolic waste elimination.

43. Assertion (A): Circadian rhythms influence the endocrine system.

Reason (R): The hypothalamic suprachiasmatic nucleus regulates hormones like cortisol and melatonin.

44. Assertion (A): The excretory system maintains homeostasis.

Reason (R): Kidneys eliminate nitrogenous waste, while skin and lungs remove toxins via sweat and respiration.

45. Assertion (A): Ayurvedic herbs like Brahmi and Ashwagandha manage neurological disorders effectively.

Reason (R): They modulate neurotransmitter activity and reduce oxidative stress in the nervous system.

Directions (Q. No. 46–50): *Read the passage carefully and answer the questions given below*:

The excretory system, an essential biological network, is responsible for maintaining homeostasis by eliminating metabolic waste products and regulating fluid and electrolyte balance. It involves multiple organs, primarily the kidneys, skin, lungs, and liver, which work in concert to remove toxins and maintain physiological equilibrium. In the kidneys, the nephron—a microscopic filtration unit—is the key functional structure, processing blood plasma through filtration, reabsorption, and secretion to form urine. Glomerular filtration, driven by hydrostatic pressure, selectively allows water and solutes to pass into the Bowman's capsule, while larger molecules like proteins are retained in the bloodstream. This intricate mechanism is regulated by hormonal pathways, such as those involving antidiuretic hormone (ADH), aldosterone, and atrial natriuretic peptide (ANP), which modulate water and electrolyte reabsorption in response to physiological demands.The liver, another pivotal excretory organ, detoxifies xenobiotics, metabolizes drugs, and processes nitrogenous waste like ammonia into urea, which is excreted via the kidneys. In tandem, the lungs expel carbon dioxide, a byproduct of cellular respiration, while the skin removes waste through sweat glands, which also play a minor role in thermoregulation. This collaborative effort highlights the excretory system's dynamic nature, integrating with the circulatory and endocrine systems to ensure survival.

In recent decades, advancements in molecular biology have deepened our understanding of the excretory system. The discovery of aquaporins, specialized proteins that facilitate water transport across cell membranes, has revolutionized nephrology. Aquaporins play a crucial role in water reabsorption in the collecting ducts of the nephron, and mutations in aquaporin genes have been linked to disorders like nephrogenic diabetes insipidus, characterized by excessive urination and thirst. Similarly, the role of the renin-angiotensin-aldosterone system (RAAS) in blood pressure regulation and electrolyte balance has been elucidated, leading to the development of targeted therapies for hypertension and kidney diseases. Environmental toxins and lifestyle factors have also emerged as significant contributors to excretory system dysfunction. Heavy metals like lead and mercury can accumulate in renal tissues, impairing filtration efficiency and causing chronic kidney disease (CKD). The rise of nephrotoxic medications and excessive dietary salt intake has exacerbated this issue, making CKD a global health crisis. Furthermore, climate change and water pollution have introduced new challenges, as exposure to contaminated water increases the risk of diseases like arsenic-induced nephropathy.

Integrative medicine, particularly Ayurveda, offers complementary perspectives on excretory health. Ayurvedic texts emphasize the role of the excretory system in eliminating "Ama" (toxins) to maintain Tridosha balance. Therapies like Panchakarma, which include Basti (medicated enemas) and Vamana (therapeutic vomiting), aim to detoxify the body and rejuvenate the organs. Herbal formulations such as Punarnava (Boerhavia diffusa) and Gokshura (Tribulus terrestris) are widely used to improve renal function and reduce inflammation. Modern research has validated some of these practices, showing that Ayurvedic herbs exhibit nephroprotective, anti-inflammatory, and diuretic properties. For instance, Punarnava has been found to enhance renal microcirculation and prevent fibrosis in animal studies.

Despite these advancements, the excretory system faces growing threats from non-communicable diseases (NCDs) like diabetes and hypertension, which are leading causes of CK(D) Diabetic nephropathy, a common complication of uncontrolled diabetes, damages the glomeruli, reducing filtration capacity and leading to proteinuria. Meanwhile, hypertensive nephropathy results from chronic high blood pressure, which exerts excessive strain on the renal arteries, impairing kidney function over time.

In response, regenerative medicine is exploring innovative solutions, such as stem cell therapy and bioengineered kidneys, to address organ failure. Stem cells derived from bone marrow or umbilical cords show promise in repairing damaged nephrons and reducing inflammation. Similarly, 3D bioprinting technology aims to create functional kidney prototypes, though these are still in experimental stages. Such advancements hold the potential to revolutionize treatment options for CKD and end-stage renal disease (ESRD), where dialysis and organ transplantation are currently the primary interventions.Public health initiatives play a critical role in mitigating excretory system disorders. Educational campaigns promoting hydration, balanced diets, and reduced consumption of nephrotoxic substances are essential. Screening programs for high-risk populations, including those with diabetes, hypertension, or a family history of kidney disease, can facilitate early diagnosis and prevent disease progression. In addition, policies addressing environmental hazards, such as reducing industrial emissions and improving water quality, are vital to safeguarding excretory health.

The interplay between the excretory system and other physiological systems underscores its complexity. The cardiovascular system, for example, relies on the kidneys to regulate blood volume and pressure, while the endocrine system modulates renal function through hormones like ADH and aldosterone. Disruptions in one system can cascade into others, creating a domino effect. This interconnectedness highlights the need for holistic approaches in both research and clinical practice.Ayurveda's holistic philosophy complements modern medicine's reductionist perspective, offering insights into maintaining systemic balance. By integrating ancient wisdom with cutting-edge science, healthcare providers can develop personalized interventions to optimize excretory health. For instance, combining Ayurvedic detoxification therapies with allopathic medications may enhance treatment outcomes for CKD patients. Moreover, understanding the genetic basis of individual responses to Ayurvedic herbs could pave the way for precision medicine in integrative healthcare.

46. Which of the following best describes the role of aquaporins in the excretory system?

A. They filter large molecules like proteins from blood plasma.

B. They facilitate water transport across cell membranes in the nephron.

C. They regulate the secretion of antidiuretic hormone (ADH).

D. They are responsible for metabolizing drugs in the liver.

47. How does the renin-angiotensin-aldosterone system (RAAS) contribute to kidney function?

A. It inhibits blood pressure regulation to reduce renal stress.

B. It modulates electrolyte balance and blood pressure through hormonal pathways.

C. It enhances protein filtration by the glomeruli.

D. It detoxifies xenobiotics and processes ammonia into urea.

48. According to the passage, how does climate change pose a threat to the excretory system?

A. By increasing nephrotoxic medication usage.

B. By introducing heavy metals into water sources.

C. By impairing renal microcirculation through oxidative stress.

D. By reducing aquaporin expression in renal cells.

49. What is a key advantage of integrating Ayurvedic practices with modern medicine for excretory health?

A. Eliminating the need for regenerative medicine techniques.

B. Enhancing treatment outcomes through detoxification and anti-inflammatory properties.

C. Reducing the dependency on hormonal therapies like aldosterone.

D. Providing alternatives to dialysis and organ transplantation.

50. Which of the following best illustrates the role of stem cell therapy in addressing kidney disorders?

A. It prevents diabetic nephropathy by controlling blood glucose levels.

B. It repairs damaged nephrons and reduces renal inflammation.

C. It eliminates the need for lifestyle modifications.

D. It detoxifies nitrogenous waste from the bloodstream.

ANSWER WITH EXPLANATIONS

1. **B:** Cortisol secretion during chronic stress becomes dysregulated, leading to adverse physiological outcomes. The HPA (hypothalamic-pituitary-adrenal) axis plays a critical role in managing stress. Chronic stress leads to continuous stimulation of this axis, resulting in excess cortisol production. Over time, this dysregulation causes feedback inhibition failure, adrenal hypertrophy, and contributes to negative health outcomes such as immune suppression, metabolic imbalance, and anxiety disorders. Hence, option B best reflects this pathological shift.

2. **B:** The hypothalamic-pituitary-adrenal (HPA) axis is central to stress responses, with the hypothalamus releasing CRH to activate the pituitary, which then stimulates cortisol production via ACTH. Cortisol helps manage acute stress by mobilizing energy and suppressing non-essential processes like immunity. However, chronic stress disrupts this axis, causing cortisol dysregulation, adrenal hypertrophy, and feedback inhibition failure. Elevated cortisol leads to conditions such as metabolic syndrome and immune suppression. Ayurveda parallels this with concepts of Agni (metabolism) and Vata, where prolonged imbalance disrupts systemic harmony. Thus, HPA dysregulation underscores the physiological impact of chronic stress on homeostasis and overall health.

3. **B:** Ayurveda identifies Vata as the dosha governing movement and communication, aligning with modern understandings of neural activity. When Vata becomes imbalanced, it manifests as anxiety, insomnia, or tremors, reflecting disruptions in neural transmission. Neurological conditions like epilepsy and Parkinson's disease mirror Vata's role in neural coordination. Ayurveda's therapeutic focus on herbs like Ashwagandha to calm Vata imbalances aligns with practices targeting neural stability. Modern neuroscience corroborates this connection by demonstrating the effects of neurotransmitter dysregulation in neurological disorders. Therefore, Ayurveda's recognition of Vata as central to neurological health integrates well with contemporary biomedical insights.

4. **B:** The glomerular filtration rate (GFR) is a key indicator of renal function, influenced by hydrostatic and oncotic pressures. In Ayurveda, herbs like Gokshura modulate renal filtration by enhancing microcirculation and reducing inflammation. Modern research validates Gokshura's nephroprotective properties, showing its ability to reduce renal oxidative stress and enhance filtration efficiency. The integration of such Ayurvedic interventions with allopathic measures addresses both physiological and inflammatory causes of impaired GFR. This highlights Ayurveda's holistic approach to improving renal health, aligning with evidence-based nephrology, which underscores the therapeutic significance of reducing renal inflammation and optimizing filtration parameters.

5. **B:** Fenugreek, used in Ayurveda to regulate glucose metabolism, improves insulin receptor sensitivity, facilitating efficient glucose uptake by cells. Insulin sensitivity is crucial for maintaining metabolic homeostasis and preventing conditions like Type 2 diabetes. Modern studies reveal that Fenugreek's active components, such as trigonelline and 4-hydroxyisoleucine, enhance insulin signaling pathways, reducing hyperglycemia. Ayurveda conceptualizes such interventions as balancing Agni, the metabolic fire. This ancient understanding aligns with molecular biology's findings on how Fenugreek reduces oxidative stress and systemic inflammation. Consequently, its use exemplifies Ayurveda's foresight in metabolic regulation, integrating well with modern strategies for managing diabetes.

6. **B:** Ashwagandha enhances dopaminergic signaling by reducing oxidative stress and neuroinflammation, which are key factors in neurodegenerative diseases such as Parkinson's. Dopamine is a critical neurotransmitter that regulates motor function, mood, and reward pathways. In Parkinson's, the progressive degeneration of dopamine-producing neurons leads to motor deficits and mood disturbances. Ashwagandha's adaptogenic properties, validated by studies, show its ability to improve synaptic plasticity, protect neural tissues, and restore dopaminergic activity. Ayurveda considers Ashwagandha a Rasayana (rejuvenative), aligning its neural restorative properties with the modern understanding of neuroprotection. This makes it a promising therapeutic agent for managing neurological and neurodegenerative disorders holistically.

7. **D:** Punarnava enhances kidney function by reducing inflammation, promoting diuresis, and improving renal microcirculation. Its diuretic properties are linked to modulation of ADH activity, reducing fluid retention without causing significant dehydration. Ayurvedic texts highlight Punarnava as a Rasayana for the excretory system, supporting detoxification and balancing Vata and Kapha doshas. Modern research validates its nephroprotective effects, showing reduced renal fibrosis and inflammation in clinical trials. The herb aligns with modern approaches to managing renal disorders, such

as targeting inflammation and optimizing renal blood flow. Thus, Punarnava bridges Ayurvedic detoxification principles with evidence-based nephrology, improving systemic health and kidney function.

8. **C:** Brahmi (Bacopa monnieri) alleviates stress by modulating cortisol levels and enhancing hippocampal plasticity, crucial for memory and emotional regulation. Chronic stress elevates cortisol, which impairs hippocampal function and increases neuroinflammation, leading to anxiety and cognitive decline. Brahmi, an adaptogen, counteracts these effects by reducing oxidative stress and supporting synaptic connectivity in the hippocampus. Ayurveda views Brahmi as a Medhya Rasayana, promoting intellect and mental clarity. Modern studies show its effects in reducing cortisol spikes and enhancing memory performance. By integrating stress reduction with cognitive enhancement, Brahmi reflects Ayurveda's holistic approach to managing the physiological and psychological impacts of stress.

9. **B:** Chandraprabha Vati supports electrolyte balance and renal health by enhancing aldosterone's role in sodium reabsorption and potassium excretion. Aldosterone, a mineralocorticoid hormone, regulates electrolyte homeostasis and blood pressure. Ayurveda attributes Chandraprabha's nephroprotective effects to its combination of anti-inflammatory and diuretic herbs, promoting renal function while reducing oxidative stress. Modern research corroborates its role in mitigating hyperkalemia and supporting systemic detoxification. This aligns with its Ayurvedic classification as a remedy for urinary and metabolic disorders. By modulating renal function and reducing inflammation, Chandraprabha Vati exemplifies the integration of Ayurvedic herbal formulations with modern nephrological principles for systemic health.

10. **B:** Ayurvedic practices like Dinacharya (daily routines) emphasize aligning physiological functions with natural circadian rhythms, promoting endocrine and metabolic health. Disruptions in circadian rhythms, such as those caused by irregular sleep patterns or artificial light exposure, can dysregulate hormones like cortisol and melatonin, leading to stress and metabolic disorders. Modern chronobiology validates the role of maintaining circadian alignment in preventing such conditions. Ayurvedic recommendations, including early rising, structured meals, and stress management, optimize these rhythms. Integrating these practices reduces cortisol spikes and enhances hormonal harmony, highlighting Ayurveda's relevance in modern preventive medicine focused on circadian regulation and systemic balance.

11. **A:** Ashwagandha modulates the hypothalamic-pituitary-adrenal (HPA) axis, reducing cortisol levels and stabilizing circadian rhythms of stress hormones. It enhances hippocampal connectivity and synaptic plasticity, supporting cognitive resilience and emotional stability. Chronic stress disrupts this axis, causing sustained cortisol elevation, hippocampal atrophy, and anxiety. Ashwagandha, recognized as an adaptogen in Ayurveda, counters these effects by promoting neuroendocrine balance and reducing oxidative stress. Its classification as a Rasayana aligns with its dual role in neural protection and stress management. Thus, Ashwagandha exemplifies the integration of Ayurvedic principles with modern neuroendocrine science for managing chronic stress and enhancing neural health.

12. **B:** Punarnava improves renal function by modulating inflammatory pathways, enhancing microcirculation, and supporting diuresis. Chronic kidney disease (CKD) is often exacerbated by renal inflammation and impaired filtration. Ayurvedic texts emphasize Punarnava for detoxification and balancing Vata and Kapha, which govern renal functions. Modern research shows that it reduces markers like interleukin-6 (IL-6) and TNF-α, improving glomerular filtration rates (GFR). Punarnava's nephroprotective properties align with its anti-inflammatory and antioxidant effects, addressing CKD's underlying causes. This integration of Ayurvedic and biomedical approaches exemplifies how traditional remedies can complement modern therapeutic strategies for renal health, offering holistic and evidence-based care.

13. **C:** Sustainable agroforestry practices for herbs like Ashwagandha and Punarnava ensure environmental conservation while maintaining medicinal efficacy. Overharvesting these herbs depletes wild populations, reducing their bioactive compound concentrations. Agroforestry combines traditional agricultural methods with ecological conservation, promoting biodiversity and soil health. This aligns with Ayurveda's emphasis on sustainability and harmony with nature. By preserving the environmental conditions essential for these herbs' growth, agroforestry maintains their therapeutic properties, validated by modern phytochemical studies. Such practices bridge Ayurvedic principles and modern conservation strategies, ensuring the availability of high-quality medicinal plants for future generations without compromising ecological integrity.

14. **A:** Environmental degradation, including soil pollution and overharvesting, reduces the bioactive compound concentrations in medicinal plants like Ashwagandha and Punarnava. These compounds, essential for their therapeutic efficacy, are influenced by the soil's

nutrient profile and environmental conditions. Degraded ecosystems disrupt these factors, compromising plant quality and potency. For instance, reduced antioxidant levels in Ashwagandha diminish its adaptogenic effects. Ayurvedic principles emphasize the interconnectedness of environmental health and medicinal efficacy, advocating sustainable harvesting. This highlights the need to preserve ecological conditions to maintain the therapeutic value of Ayurvedic herbs, ensuring their effectiveness in addressing chronic diseases like stress and renal disorders.

15. **D:** The Tridosha theory in Ayurveda identifies Vata, Pitta, and Kapha as the three fundamental energies governing physiological functions. Vata, associated with movement and communication, aligns with the nervous system's role in transmitting signals. Pitta, linked to metabolism, reflects digestive enzymes and hormonal activity. Kapha, representing structure, corresponds to the body's stability and fluid balance. Together, the balanced interaction of these doshas ensures physical and mental health. Disruptions in any dosha can result in disease, mirroring how nervous, metabolic, or structural dysfunctions in modern medicine lead to specific disorders. This comprehensive framework underlines Ayurveda's systemic and holistic approach to health.

16. **D:** Ayurveda integrates metabolic regulation (Agni), endocrine health, and detoxification through interventions like dietary practices and herbal therapies. Agni corresponds to enzymatic activity, vital for digestion and metabolism, while endocrine imbalances are seen as doshic disruptions. Ojas, considered the essence of vitality, is influenced by hormonal harmony, reflecting modern connections between endocrine health and systemic resilience. Ayurvedic approaches such as Rasayana therapies rejuvenate endocrine functions by addressing oxidative stress and cellular damage. This aligns with contemporary understanding, where hormonal therapies and antioxidants play key roles in restoring health. Ayurveda's integration of physiology and lifestyle offers a holistic view of systemic regulation.

17. **D:** Ayurvedic Rasas (tastes) each serve unique biological functions: Sweet nourishes tissues, Bitter detoxifies, Astringent strengthens tissues, and Pungent stimulates neural and circulatory activity. These properties align with modern biochemical research. For instance, Bitter's detoxifying role is linked to alkaloids, while Pungent compounds, like capsaicin, improve circulation. Ayurveda's Rasa theory encapsulates physiological impacts and therapeutic uses of flavors, correlating them with specific dosha balancing actions. This classification is not merely philosophical but scientifically supported, as modern studies affirm the pharmacological effects of these tastes. This integration highlights Ayurveda's prescient understanding of the relationship between taste, biochemistry, and systemic health.

18. **D:** The excretory system in Ayurveda encompasses organs like kidneys, skin, and the colon, mirroring modern physiology. Each organ has distinct roles: kidneys filter blood to excrete urine, the skin eliminates waste through sweat, and the colon expels metabolic toxins. The liver, an ancillary excretory organ, detoxifies chemicals and processes bile. Ayurvedic detoxification practices like Panchakarma reflect this understanding, targeting these organs to eliminate "Ama" (toxins) and restore dosha balance. Modern medicine similarly emphasizes detoxification through hydration, diet, and medical interventions for liver and kidney health. This systemic integration of excretory processes underscores Ayurveda's holistic alignment with modern scientific principles.

19. **D:** Vata governs movement and communication, leading to neurological issues when imbalanced. Pitta, linked to metabolism and inflammation, causes neural inflammation when disturbed. Kapha, representing structure, manifests as sluggish neural activity or depression when excessive. Together, Tridosha imbalances explain a range of neurological disorders, paralleling modern insights into neurotransmitter dysregulation, neural inflammation, and metabolic contributions to mental health. Ayurveda's focus on restoring dosha balance through lifestyle, herbs, and therapies aligns with modern integrative approaches. This holistic understanding illustrates the interconnectedness of neurological, metabolic, and structural health, emphasizing Ayurveda's relevance in managing complex neurological conditions comprehensively.

20. **A:** Ayurveda highlights the importance of a Sattvic diet, yoga, and Rasayana therapies in promoting hormonal harmony and reducing stress. Sattvic foods like fruits and whole grains enhance metabolic and endocrine stability, while yoga and Pranayama stabilize cortisol, reducing the adverse effects of chronic stress. Rasayana therapies rejuvenate endocrine glands, improving hormonal resilience and vitality. Modern science corroborates these effects, demonstrating how diet and stress-reducing practices influence cortisol regulation and hormonal balance. This integrative approach, combining preventive care with rejuvenative therapies, reflects Ayurveda's systemic focus on fostering resilience and vitality while aligning with modern endocrinology's emphasis on lifestyle interventions.

21. **D:** Agni, central to Ayurvedic physiology, governs metabolism, digestion, and immunity. It represents

enzymatic activity, essential for breaking down nutrients and preventing toxin accumulation. Agni's detoxifying role aligns with the liver's conversion of toxins into excretable forms and the kidney's filtration of waste. Modern studies affirm its importance in preventing oxidative stress, a key factor in chronic diseases. Ayurveda's focus on enhancing Agni through diet and herbs parallels interventions targeting metabolic pathways in biomedical science. By integrating detoxification, enzymatic efficiency, and immune support, Ayurveda underscores Agni's systemic relevance, bridging traditional practices with evidence-based insights into health and disease prevention.

22. D: Ayurvedic detoxification therapies utilize herbs like Triphala, Punarnava, Neem, and Ashwagandha, each targeting specific detox pathways. Triphala optimizes gut health, Punarnava supports renal detoxification, Neem purifies blood and skin, and Ashwagandha protects neural tissues. Modern research validates these effects, showing their role in reducing oxidative stress and inflammation while enhancing organ function. For instance, Triphala's prebiotic effects improve gut microbiota diversity, while Neem reduces systemic inflammation. This integrative approach demonstrates Ayurveda's foresight in addressing detoxification at systemic levels, combining its holistic understanding with modern pharmacology's emphasis on targeted interventions for comprehensive detoxification and health optimization.

23. D: Ayurveda links doshas with endocrine regulation: Vata governs hormonal timing, Pitta controls metabolic hormones, and Kapha influences anabolic processes. Imbalanced doshas disrupt these functions, manifesting as hormonal disorders. For instance, elevated Pitta may cause hyperthyroidism, while Kapha disturbances can lead to obesity-related endocrine issues. Modern endocrinology parallels this by identifying dysregulation in hormonal axes like HPA or HPT (hypothalamic-pituitary-thyroid). Ayurvedic interventions such as diet, herbs, and lifestyle adjustments restore doshic balance, thereby normalizing endocrine functions. This synthesis illustrates Ayurveda's relevance in addressing hormonal imbalances comprehensively, aligning traditional insights with scientific endocrinology for systemic health.

24. A: Ayurveda's focus on nervous system rejuvenation employs herbs like Ashwagandha, Brahmi, and Shankhpushpi for neuroprotection, stress reduction, and cognitive enhancement. Ashwagandha reduces oxidative stress and promotes neural resilience, Brahmi enhances memory and synaptic plasticity, and Shankhpushpi calms excessive neural activity. Modern neuroscience validates these effects, showing their role in modulating neurotransmitters like dopamine and serotonin. Guggulu, in contrast, targets metabolic pathways rather than neural pathways. This specificity of herbal actions aligns with Ayurveda's emphasis on personalized care, integrating traditional neurotherapies with evidence-based approaches to manage neurological disorders and enhance mental clarity comprehensively.

25. A: The components of the nervous system are highly specialized, each performing distinct functions. The cerebrum governs cognitive processes like thinking, memory, and decision-making. The cerebellum coordinates voluntary motor movements and balance. The hypothalamus regulates homeostasis, linking the nervous and endocrine systems. Lastly, the spinal cord transmits sensory and motor signals, connecting the brain with the rest of the body. Ayurveda reflects these functions through the balance of Vata, which governs movement and communication, and Kapha, which maintains structural stability. This alignment between anatomical roles and Ayurvedic principles demonstrates the interconnected nature of systemic functions in maintaining overall health.

26. A: In Ayurveda, the Tridosha framework—Vata, Pitta, and Kapha—represents distinct physiological roles. Vata governs movement and communication, such as nervous system activities. Pitta regulates digestion and metabolism, akin to enzymatic and hormonal processes. Kapha provides structure and stability, comparable to the skeletal and immune systems. Tridosha balance ensures overall health by integrating these functions harmoniously. Modern science mirrors this by highlighting similar roles for nervous, metabolic, and structural systems. Ayurveda's holistic understanding of health and its emphasis on maintaining doshic balance provide an ancient yet scientifically aligned approach to systemic functioning and disease prevention, underscoring its relevance today.

27. B: The endocrine system regulates essential physiological functions through hormone secretion. The adrenal gland releases cortisol for stress response, while the pancreas produces insulin for glucose regulation. The thyroid gland synthesizes thyroxine, which controls metabolism, and the pituitary gland secretes growth hormone for development. Ayurveda conceptualizes this through Pitta dosha, governing metabolism and endocrine activity. Modern science validates the systemic impact of these glands, showing their interdependence in maintaining homeostasis. Aligning Ayurvedic insights with these functions emphasizes the importance of hormonal balance in health, illustrating how traditional practices and modern endocrinology intersect to address endocrine-related disorders effectively.

28. **B:** Ayurvedic Rasas (tastes) correspond to specific physiological and therapeutic effects. Sweet promotes tissue growth, Bitter detoxifies by reducing inflammation, Astringent strengthens tissues and controls bleeding, and Sour enhances digestion and metabolism. These functions align with modern biochemical actions of phytochemicals found in foods and herbs. For example, Bitter compounds like alkaloids support detoxification, while Sour flavors stimulate digestive enzymes. Ayurveda's classification of Rasas integrates taste with physiological benefits, demonstrating foresight in correlating dietary practices with health outcomes. This approach aligns with modern nutritional science, reinforcing Ayurveda's practical and evidence-based perspective on maintaining systemic balance through dietary regulation.

29. **B:** Ayurvedic therapies are targeted interventions with specific applications. Panchakarma detoxifies the body, aligning with its focus on systemic purification. Rasayana rejuvenates tissues and promotes longevity, while Shirodhara calms the mind, addressing stress and mental clarity. Abhyanga, a form of therapeutic massage, enhances circulation and skin health. These therapies emphasize a holistic approach, targeting both physical and mental well-being. Modern studies validate their effects, showing improvements in inflammation markers, stress reduction, and circulatory health. By addressing underlying causes of imbalance, these interventions reflect Ayurveda's integration of preventive and curative measures for maintaining health and treating chronic conditions effectively.

30. **A:** The excretory organs work in harmony to eliminate metabolic waste and maintain homeostasis. The kidneys filter blood and produce urine, the lungs expel carbon dioxide, the skin eliminates waste through sweat, and the liver detoxifies harmful substances while producing bile. Ayurveda emphasizes the importance of these organs in removing Ama (toxins) to sustain health. Panchakarma therapies target these systems, promoting detoxification and dosha balance. Modern physiology corroborates this, recognizing the systemic importance of these organs in regulating fluid balance, detoxification, and respiratory efficiency. This alignment illustrates the interconnectedness of traditional Ayurvedic principles with modern biomedical science.

31. **A:** Neurological disorders have distinct pathological mechanisms. Parkinson's disease arises from dopamine deficiency, leading to motor dysfunction. Alzheimer's disease results from beta-amyloid plaque accumulation, causing cognitive decline. Epilepsy involves abnormal electrical activity in the brain, leading to seizures, while multiple sclerosis stems from myelin sheath damage, impairing neural transmission. Ayurveda attributes these conditions to Vata imbalances disrupting neural functions. Modern medicine provides targeted treatments addressing these pathologies, such as dopamine agonists for Parkinson's or anti-epileptic drugs for seizures. Ayurveda complements these approaches through neuroprotective herbs like Ashwagandha and Brahmi, aligning traditional therapies with evidence-based neurological interventions.

32. **B:** Ayurvedic concepts reflect systemic functions: Prakriti defines individual constitution, Agni governs digestion and metabolism, Ama represents toxins from incomplete digestion, and Ojas symbolizes vitality and immunity. These concepts align with modern physiological processes, such as genetic predispositions (Prakriti), enzymatic activity (Agni), and the impact of metabolic waste on health (Ama). Ojas corresponds to systemic resilience, akin to immune and hormonal stability. This integration bridges traditional Ayurvedic wisdom with contemporary biomedical insights. Understanding these parallels enhances personalized healthcare approaches, emphasizing the relevance of balancing these elements to maintain health and prevent diseases in both traditional and modern contexts.

33. **A:** Ayurvedic herbs are specifically used for therapeutic purposes: Ashwagandha reduces stress and rejuvenates neural tissues, Brahmi enhances memory and cognitive function, Punarnava supports renal health and acts as a diuretic, and Triphala detoxifies the gut and promotes microbiota balance. Modern pharmacological studies validate these effects, linking their bioactive compounds to measurable outcomes like stress reduction, improved renal function, and enhanced gut health. This specificity in herbal application aligns Ayurveda with targeted treatment strategies in modern medicine. Combining traditional knowledge with scientific validation demonstrates the effectiveness of Ayurvedic formulations in addressing diverse health conditions holistically.

34. **B:** Ayurvedic therapies target specific disorders based on doshic imbalances: Vamana induces emesis for Kapha-related disorders, Virechana promotes purgation for Pitta-related conditions, Nasya administers nasal treatments for head and neck issues, and Basti employs medicated enemas for Vata-related diseases. These therapies cleanse specific systems, addressing the root cause of imbalance. Modern studies recognize their role in detoxification and systemic health improvement. For example, Basti enhances colon health and reduces inflammatory markers. By integrating these traditional therapies with allopathic treatments, Ayurveda provides

a comprehensive approach to disease management, emphasizing prevention, detoxification, and rejuvenation to restore systemic balance.

35. C: The hypothalamus is integral to the regulation of the autonomic nervous system and endocrine functions. However, it primarily exerts its effects on endocrine glands indirectly, via the pituitary gland. The hypothalamus secretes releasing and inhibiting hormones that control the anterior pituitary. The pituitary, in turn, stimulates other endocrine glands such as the thyroid, adrenal, and gonads. Statement 1 correctly identifies the hypothalamus's role, but Statement 2 oversimplifies this mechanism by ignoring the intermediary function of the pituitary. The hypothalamus-pituitary axis exemplifies the intricate feedback loops that coordinate hormonal responses, highlighting the complexity of endocrine regulation.

36. C: Hormones like adrenaline are released rapidly in response to stress, mediated by the sympathetic nervous system. While this is true, the nervous system does not control all hormonal secretions. Many endocrine glands operate independently or under feedback mechanisms unrelated to the nervous system. For example, the pancreas secretes insulin and glucagon based on blood glucose levels, not neural inputs. This highlights the diversity in endocrine control, where some processes are neural-driven, while others rely on chemical or metabolic signals. Thus, Statement 1 is accurate, but Statement 2 incorrectly generalizes the role of the nervous system in endocrine regulation.

37. A: The nervous system achieves quick communication through electrical impulses that propagate along neurons and synapses. Neurotransmitters such as acetylcholine and dopamine facilitate signal transmission at synapses, translating electrical impulses into chemical signals. This dual mechanism underscores the efficiency and adaptability of neural communication. Statement 2 provides an accurate explanation for Statement 1, highlighting the interdependence of electrical and chemical signaling. This process ensures rapid responses to stimuli, such as reflexes, and supports complex functions like cognition and memory. The coordination of these mechanisms illustrates the nervous system's sophistication and its role in maintaining homeostasis.

38. A: Kidneys regulate fluid and electrolyte balance while removing nitrogenous waste like urea from the bloodstream. Excess glucose, as seen in diabetes, damages the nephron's filtering units, causing nephropathy and impairing excretory function. This connection emphasizes the vulnerability of the excretory system to systemic conditions. Both statements highlight the importance of kidney health and its interplay with metabolic factors. Understanding this relationship underscores the need for preventive care, such as monitoring glucose levels, to maintain excretory system efficiency and prevent long-term complications like chronic kidney disease.

39. B: The pineal gland produces melatonin, a hormone critical for regulating sleep-wake cycles. Environmental light exposure significantly influences melatonin secretion, aligning biological rhythms with day-night cycles. Disrupting circadian rhythms through artificial light, however, adversely affects endocrine and metabolic health, leading to issues such as obesity, diabetes, and mood disorders. While both statements are accurate, Statement 2 does not directly explain Statement 1, as it focuses on the broader consequences of circadian disruption. This highlights the interconnectedness of environmental factors and hormonal health, emphasizing the importance of preserving natural light-dark cycles for overall well-being.

40. A: Ayurveda's Dinacharya integrates daily routines with nature's rhythms to balance Tridoshas and promote health. Activities like waking with the sun, timely meals, and proper sleep align the body's biological clock with external environmental cues. These routines not only optimize physiological functions but also prevent imbalances that lead to diseases. The synchronization of circadian rhythms through Dinacharya supports physical and mental health by fostering consistency and reducing stress. This Ayurvedic approach illustrates how traditional wisdom aligns with modern concepts of circadian biology, emphasizing the role of lifestyle in disease prevention and holistic well-being.

41. D: The nervous and endocrine systems are interdependent rather than independent. While the nervous system provides rapid, short-term responses, the endocrine system regulates long-term processes such as growth, metabolism, and reproduction. These systems coordinate through structures like the hypothalamus, which integrates neural signals with hormonal outputs via the pituitary gland. Statement (A) is false, as the systems work together to maintain homeostasis. Statement (R) is true, highlighting the complementary nature of these systems. This interconnectedness exemplifies the body's ability to respond to immediate stimuli while simultaneously managing sustained physiological processes.

42. C: Panchakarma therapies are a cornerstone of Ayurvedic detoxification, targeting metabolic waste elimination and systemic rejuvenation. These therapies, including Vamana (emesis) and Virechana (purgation), cleanse the gastrointestinal tract, liver, and other excretory pathways. While their impact on neural pathways is secondary, Panchakarma primarily focuses on restoring homeostasis by removing accumulated toxins (Ama). This misalignment in the Reason undermines its validity. The true value of Panchakarma lies in its holistic approach, addressing the root causes of imbalances and fostering overall health. Its success demonstrates Ayurveda's depth in systemic detoxification and preventive care.

43. A: The hypothalamic suprachiasmatic nucleus (SCN) is the master regulator of circadian rhythms, influencing hormonal secretions like cortisol and melatonin. These rhythms govern sleep-wake cycles, metabolism, and immune responses. Melatonin secretion peaks at night, promoting sleep, while cortisol levels rise in the morning, preparing the body for activity. This temporal coordination ensures optimal physiological functioning. Both the assertion and reason accurately describe the endocrine system's reliance on circadian rhythms. Understanding this relationship underscores the importance of maintaining regular sleep patterns to support hormonal balance and overall health.

44. A: The excretory system is pivotal in maintaining homeostasis by eliminating metabolic waste and regulating fluid balance. The kidneys filter blood, removing nitrogenous wastes and excess electrolytes, while the skin and lungs assist in detoxification through sweat and respiration. These coordinated functions exemplify the body's efficiency in managing internal environments. Both Assertion (A) and Reason (R) are true, with the reason directly explaining how the excretory system maintains equilibrium. This integration highlights the systemic nature of homeostasis, where multiple organs work in unison to sustain physiological balance and health.

45. A: Ayurvedic herbs like Brahmi and Ashwagandha have neuroprotective properties, modulating neurotransmitter activity and reducing oxidative stress. Brahmi enhances cognitive function and memory, while Ashwagandha reduces stress by lowering cortisol levels. These herbs exemplify Ayurveda's holistic approach to managing neurological disorders, addressing both physiological and psychological dimensions. Their antioxidant and adaptogenic properties protect neural pathways from degeneration, supporting long-term brain health. This integration of herbal medicine with neuroscience demonstrates the potential of traditional knowledge in complementing modern therapeutic strategies for neurological well-being.

46. B: Aquaporins are specialized membrane proteins that facilitate water transport across cells, particularly in the nephron's collecting ducts, enabling efficient water reabsorption. Their discovery marked a breakthrough in nephrology, explaining how kidneys concentrate urine while conserving water. Dysfunctions or mutations in aquaporin genes, such as those in nephrogenic diabetes insipidus, lead to excessive water loss and dehydration. Ayurveda's emphasis on kidney health aligns with this, as herbs like Punarnava support renal function by enhancing microcirculation and reducing inflammation. The role of aquaporins underscores the intricate mechanisms of renal physiology, bridging traditional practices and molecular biology in optimizing water balance and excretory efficiency.

47. B: The renin-angiotensin-aldosterone system (RAAS) regulates blood pressure and electrolyte balance through a hormonal cascade. Renin, secreted by the kidneys in response to low blood pressure, activates angiotensin, which constricts blood vessels and stimulates aldosterone secretion. Aldosterone promotes sodium retention and potassium excretion, increasing blood volume and pressure. Ayurveda mirrors this understanding through herbs like Chandraprabha Vati, which enhance renal function and maintain electrolyte homeostasis. Modern therapies targeting RAAS, such as ACE inhibitors, reflect its critical role in hypertension and kidney disease management. This demonstrates the alignment of Ayurveda's systemic approach with modern molecular insights into renal physiology.

48. B: Climate change and water pollution introduce toxins, such as heavy metals like lead and arsenic, into water supplies, adversely affecting kidney function. Chronic exposure to these contaminants leads to conditions like arsenic-induced nephropathy, impairing filtration efficiency and causing chronic kidney disease (CKD). Ayurveda emphasizes detoxification therapies to counteract such environmental toxins, using herbs like Punarnava and Gokshura to support renal health. Modern research corroborates these approaches, showing how nephroprotective herbs mitigate oxidative stress and inflammation. Addressing environmental risks is essential for excretory system health, underscoring the importance of integrative strategies combining ecological awareness with therapeutic interventions.

49. B: Integrating Ayurvedic practices with modern medicine enhances treatment outcomes by leveraging detoxification and anti-inflammatory properties of herbs. For example, herbs like Punarnava improve renal microcirculation, while Ashwagandha modulates stress hormones, supporting systemic resilience. Modern research validates these effects, showing reduced oxidative stress and inflammation in chronic conditions like CKD. Combining Ayurvedic detoxification therapies with allopathic treatments addresses root causes while mitigating side effects, exemplifying precision medicine. This integration reflects Ayurveda's holistic philosophy, which complements modern reductionist approaches, providing personalized care for excretory health. The synergy between these systems ensures comprehensive management of chronic diseases and systemic rejuvenation.

50. B: Stem cell therapy offers groundbreaking potential in addressing kidney disorders by repairing damaged nephrons and reducing renal inflammation. Stem cells derived from bone marrow or umbilical cords differentiate into functional renal cells, regenerating tissues impaired by chronic conditions like CKD or diabetic nephropathy. They also modulate immune responses, reducing inflammation and fibrosis. Ayurveda emphasizes renal rejuvenation through Rasayana therapies, reflecting similar goals of tissue repair and systemic healing. While still experimental, stem cell therapy bridges regenerative medicine with traditional practices, offering hope for end-stage renal disease management beyond dialysis and transplantation, aligning modern innovations with holistic health principles.

CHAPTER 24

BIOCHEMISTRY FUNDAMENTALS–CARBOHYDRATES, LIPIDS, AND PROTEINS

Biochemistry forms the molecular foundation of life, bridging biology and chemistry to explain how biological processes occur at a molecular level. The central macromolecules in biochemistry—carbohydrates, lipids, and proteins—play indispensable roles in cellular function, structure, and energy management. These macromolecules not only underpin the mechanics of life but also serve as a conduit for understanding health, disease, and therapeutic approaches in disciplines like Ayurveda. This chapter explores the structural and functional nuances of carbohydrates, lipids, and proteins and delves into their metabolic processes, integrating a biochemical perspective with traditional Ayurvedic concepts of health and metabolism.

Biochemical Understanding of Macromolecules

Carbohydrates: Structure, Function, and Metabolism Carbohydrates, also known as saccharides, are organic molecules composed primarily of carbon (C), hydrogen (H), and oxygen (O) atoms in the general formula. They serve as the most readily available source of energy for living organisms and perform vital structural roles in cells.

Structure of Carbohydrates: A Comprehensive Exploration. Carbohydrates are organic compounds that are central to life. They serve as a primary source of energy, provide structural support, and participate in cellular signaling. Their diverse structures and roles have made them a focal point in biology, chemistry, nutrition, and medicine. This chapter delves into the intricate structure of carbohydrates, their biological importance, and their integrative role in human health, including perspectives from modern biochemistry and Ayurveda.

Definition and General Characteristics

Carbohydrates, also known as saccharides, derive their name from the fact that they were historically thought to be "hydrates of carbon" with the general formula . While not all carbohydrates strictly follow this formula, the majority are composed of carbon (C), hydrogen (H), and oxygen (O) atoms.

Key Properties of Carbohydrates:

1. **Polarity:** Most carbohydrates are polar due to the presence of multiple hydroxyl (-OH) groups.
2. **Water Solubility:** Simple carbohydrates (e.g., glucose) are water-soluble due to their hydroxyl groups, while complex carbohydrates (e.g., cellulose) may be insoluble.
3. **Energy Yield:** Upon oxidation, carbohydrates provide approximately 4 kcal per gram of energy.
4. **Chirality:** Carbohydrates often exhibit stereoisomerism, a critical property in biological systems.
5. **Hydrolysis:** Complex carbohydrates (disaccharides, polysaccharides) can be broken down into simpler units via enzymatic hydrolysis.

Classification of Carbohydrates

Carbohydrates are broadly categorized based on the number of sugar units they contain. This classification provides insight into their structural complexity and biological roles.

1. **Monosaccharides:** The Simplest Form. Monosaccharides, often referred to as simple sugars, are the fundamental building blocks of carbohydrates. They contain a single sugar unit and are classified based on:

- The number of carbon atoms (trioses, tetroses, pentoses, hexoses).
- The functional group present (aldoses with an aldehyde group; ketoses with a ketone group).

Examples of Monosaccharides

1. **Glucose ($C_6H_{12}O_6$):**
   - Found in fruits, honey, and blood.
   - The principal energy source in cellular respiration.
   - Exists in alpha and beta anomeric forms in cyclic structures.
2. **Fructose:**
   - Found in fruits, honey, and sucrose.
   - Sweeter than glucose and commonly used as a sweetener.
   - A ketose sugar, often metabolized in the liver.
3. **Galactose:**
   - A component of lactose (milk sugar).
   - Converted to glucose in the liver.

Structural Forms: Monosaccharides exhibit two structural forms:

1. **Linear Form:** Predominantly observed in dry states or crystalline structures.
2. **Cyclic Form:** In aqueous solutions, monosaccharides adopt cyclic structures (furanose or pyranose rings) due to intramolecular reactions.

Importance of Monosaccharides

- Immediate energy source for metabolic activities.
- Serve as precursors for nucleotides, amino acids, and lipids.
- Participate in glycosylation processes in proteins and lipids.

Disaccharides: Two-Sugar Units

Disaccharides consist of two monosaccharides joined by a covalent glycosidic bond formed through a condensation reaction.

Examples of Disaccharides

1. **Sucrose ($C_{12}H_{22}O_{11}$):**
   - Composed of glucose and fructose.
   - Common table sugar obtained from sugarcane and sugar beet.
2. **Lactose:**
   - Composed of glucose and galactose.
   - Found in milk and dairy products.
   - Hydrolyzed by the enzyme lactase.
3. **Maltose:**
   - Composed of two glucose molecules.
   - Found in malted grains and as a product of starch breakdown.

Functions

- Provide quick energy after enzymatic hydrolysis.
- Serve as transportable energy forms in plants (e.g., sucrose).

Oligosaccharides: 3–10 Sugar Units

Oligosaccharides are slightly more complex than disaccharides and are typically attached to proteins or lipids, forming glycoproteins and glycolipids.

Examples and Roles

1. **Fructooligosaccharides:**
   - Found in onions, garlic, and bananas.
   - Act as prebiotics, promoting gut health.
2. **Glycoproteins:**
   - Found on cell surfaces, aiding in cell signaling and immune responses.

Polysaccharides: Complex Carbohydrates

Polysaccharides are long chains of monosaccharides linked by glycosidic bonds. They may be linear or branched and serve as storage or structural components.

Examples of Polysaccharides

1. **Starch:** Storage polysaccharide in plants.
   - Composed of amylose (linear) and amylopectin (branched).
2. **Glycogen:** Storage polysaccharide in animals.
   - Highly branched, stored in the liver and muscles.
3. **Cellulose:** Structural polysaccharide in plant cell walls.
   - Composed of beta-glucose units, indigestible by humans but essential for dietary fiber.
4. **Chitin:** Found in the exoskeletons of arthropods and fungal cell walls.

Functions

- Energy storage (starch and glycogen).
- Structural support (cellulose and chitin).
- Contribution to cell wall rigidity and protection.

Functional Significance of Carbohydrates

Carbohydrates perform several critical functions, influencing cellular and systemic processes.

1. **Energy Source:** Glucose, derived from carbohydrate digestion, is the primary substrate for cellular respiration. Through glycolysis, the citric acid cycle, and oxidative phosphorylation, it generates ATP, the universal energy currency.
2. **Structural Role:** Polysaccharides like cellulose and chitin provide mechanical strength to plant cell walls and arthropod exoskeletons, respectively.
3. **Cell Communication:** Carbohydrates on cell surfaces mediate recognition and signaling processes, crucial in immune responses and intercellular interactions.

Metabolism of Carbohydrates

Carbohydrate metabolism encompasses the biochemical pathways that break down or synthesize carbohydrates.

1. **Glycolysis:** Converts glucose to pyruvate, yielding ATP and NADH.
    - Occurs in the cytoplasm of all cells.
2. **Gluconeogenesis:** Synthesis of glucose from non-carbohydrate precursors.
    - Activated during fasting or intense exercise.
3. **Glycogenesis and Glycogenolysis:** Glycogenesis: Conversion of glucose to glycogen for storage.
    - **Glycogenolysis:** Breakdown of glycogen into glucose during energy demand.
4. **Pentose Phosphate Pathway:** Produces NADPH and ribose-5-phosphate.
    - Supports anabolic processes and nucleotide synthesis.
5. **Historical Perspective:** Carbohydrates have been studied since the 19th century, with the elucidation of glucose's structure marking a milestone in organic chemistry. Their role in metabolism was later integrated into understanding diseases like diabetes.
6. **Carbohydrates in Ayurveda:** Ayurveda categorizes carbohydrates under "Madhura Rasa" (sweet taste), emphasizing their role in balancing "Vata" dosha and providing "Ojas" (vital energy). Whole grains and fruits are preferred, aligning with modern nutrition's focus on complex carbohydrates.
7. **Modern Research and Applications:** Advances in carbohydrate chemistry have led to developments in drug delivery, biomaterials, and understanding diseases like cancer and diabetes. Carbohydrates also play a role in vaccine development and prebiotic formulations.
    - **Lipids:** Structure, Function, and Metabolism
    - Lipids, a diverse group of hydrophobic molecules, are essential for energy storage, cell membrane structure, and signaling. They include fats, oils, phospholipids, sterols, and fat-soluble vitamins.

Structure of Lipids

Lipids are characterized by their hydrophobicity, resulting from nonpolar hydrocarbon chains. The main classes include:

1. **Triglycerides:** Composed of glycerol and three fatty acids, these are the primary form of stored energy in adipose tissue.
2. **Phospholipids:** Comprising glycerol, two fatty acids, and a phosphate group, they are key components of cellular membranes.
3. **Steroids:** Lipids with a four-ring structure, such as cholesterol, which serves as a precursor for steroid hormones and vitamin D.
4. **Waxes:** Long-chain fatty acids esterified with alcohols, providing water-resistant properties.

Functions of Lipids

- **Energy Storage:** Triglycerides provide long-term energy storage and yield more energy per gram than carbohydrates.
- **Membrane Structure:** Phospholipids and cholesterol maintain cell membrane integrity and fluidity.
- **Hormone Synthesis:** Cholesterol is a precursor for steroid hormones, including estrogen, testosterone, and cortisol.
- **Insulation and Protection:** Adipose tissue insulates the body and protects vital organs.

Metabolism of Lipids

Lipid metabolism involves the breakdown and synthesis of fatty acids and their derivatives:

1. **Beta-Oxidation:** Fatty acids are broken down in the mitochondria to generate acetyl-CoA, NADH, and FADH2.
2. **Lipogenesis:** The synthesis of fatty acids from acetyl-CoA, primarily occurring in the liver.
3. **Ketogenesis:** In conditions of low carbohydrate availability, acetyl-CoA is converted into ketone bodies as an alternative energy source.
4. **Cholesterol Metabolism:** Cholesterol is synthesized in the liver and transported via lipoproteins like LDL and HDL.

LIPIDS IN AYURVEDA

Ayurvedic texts emphasize the importance of "Sneha" (lipids) in maintaining health. Ghee (clarified butter) and oils are considered "Ojas-enhancing" (life-essence promoting) substances that nourish tissues and support brain function. Ayurvedic principles advocate balanced consumption of healthy fats to harmonize the "Vata" and "Pitta" doshas and promote joint lubrication, skin health, and vitality.

Proteins: Structure, Function, and Metabolism

Proteins, the most versatile macromolecules, are composed of amino acids linked by peptide bonds. They play crucial roles in catalysis, structural support, transportation, communication, and defense.

Structure of Proteins

Proteins exhibit a hierarchical structure:

1. **Primary Structure:** Linear sequence of amino acids determined by genetic information.
2. **Secondary Structure:** Local folding patterns such as alpha-helices and beta-sheets stabilized by hydrogen bonds.
3. **Tertiary Structure:** Three-dimensional folding driven by interactions among R-groups, including hydrophobic interactions, hydrogen bonds, and disulfide bridges.
4. **Quaternary Structure:** Assembly of multiple polypeptide chains into a functional protein complex (e.g., hemoglobin).

Functions of Proteins

- **Enzymatic Catalysis:** Enzymes accelerate biochemical reactions (e.g., amylase in carbohydrate digestion).
- **Structural Support:** Proteins like collagen provide tensile strength to connective tissues.
- **Transport and Storage:** Hemoglobin transports oxygen; ferritin stores iron.
- **Immune Defense:** Antibodies are proteins that recognize and neutralize pathogens.
- **Signal Transduction:** Hormones like insulin regulate metabolic processes.
- **Movement:** Actin and myosin facilitate muscle contraction.

Metabolism of Proteins

Protein metabolism involves the synthesis and degradation of amino acids and proteins:

1. **Protein Synthesis:** Translation of mRNA into polypeptides, requiring ribosomes, tRNA, and amino acids.
2. **Protein Degradation:** Proteins are broken down into amino acids by proteolytic enzymes like proteases.
3. **Amino Acid Metabolism:** Amino acids undergo transamination, deamination, and decarboxylation to generate intermediates for energy production or biosynthesis.
4. **Nitrogen Excretion:** Excess nitrogen is converted to urea in the liver and excreted via urine.

PROTEINS IN AYURVEDA

Proteins are considered "Mamsa Dhatu" (muscle tissue) in Ayurveda, crucial for strength and vitality. High-protein foods like legumes and dairy are regarded as "Rasa-enhancing" (nourishing) and are particularly recommended for individuals with "Vata" imbalances. Ayurveda stresses digestibility and the compatibility of protein sources, advocating preparation methods that improve protein assimilation.

Metabolism and Its Relevance in Ayurveda

Metabolism is a fundamental biological process encompassing the sum total of all chemical reactions within the body that sustain life. These reactions can be broadly categorized into two interrelated processes: anabolism, which involves the synthesis of complex molecules from simpler ones, and catabolism, which entails the breakdown of complex molecules to release energy. Together, these processes maintain the body's homeostasis, provide energy, and support growth, repair, and reproduction.

In Ayurveda, the concept of metabolism is deeply intertwined with the principles of Agni (digestive fire) and Ojas (vital essence). Ayurveda views metabolism not only as a series of biochemical reactions but also as a holistic process affecting physical, mental, and spiritual well-being. This chapter delves into the intricate biochemical pathways of metabolism and their alignment with Ayurvedic principles, exploring the synergistic relationship between ancient wisdom and modern science.

Understanding Metabolism: The Core of Life

1. **Definition and Overview:** Metabolism is derived from the Greek word "metabolē," meaning "change" or "transformation." It encompasses a vast array of enzymatic reactions occurring in cells, which are essential for converting food into energy, building cellular structures, and eliminating waste products.
   - **Catabolic Processes:** These involve breaking down macromolecules like carbohydrates, lipids, and proteins into smaller units, releasing energy stored in chemical bonds.
   - **Anabolic Processes:** These involve synthesizing complex molecules like proteins, nucleic acids, and lipids, which are essential for growth and repair.
2. **Central Role of ATP:** Adenosine triphosphate (ATP) is the universal energy currency that drives metabolic reactions. ATP stores energy in its high-energy phosphate bonds and releases it when these bonds are hydrolyzed. This energy is used for:

- Muscle contraction
- Active transport across membranes
- Biosynthesis of macromolecules
- Signal transduction

Key Biochemical Pathways

Metabolism is orchestrated through a series of interconnected pathways, ensuring efficient energy utilization and molecular recycling.

Catabolism: Energy Liberation

Catabolic pathways break down large molecules into smaller ones, releasing energy stored in their chemical bonds. Major catabolic processes include:

1 **Glycolysis**

Location: Cytoplasm

- **Process:** Converts glucose ($C_6H_{12}O_6$) into pyruvate, yielding ATP and NADH.
- **Significance:** Glycolysis is the first step in cellular respiration and can occur aerobically or anaerobically.

2. **Beta-Oxidation**
   - **Location:** Mitochondrial matrix
   - **Process:** Breaks down fatty acids into acetyl-CoA, generating NADH and $FADH_2$ for the electron transport chain.
   - **Significance:** Provides a significant energy yield, particularly during fasting or prolonged exercise.
3. **Proteolysis**
   - **Process:** Proteins are broken down into amino acids, which can enter gluconeogenesis or the Krebs cycle.
   - **Significance:** Amino acids serve as an energy source during prolonged fasting or starvation.
4. **Citric Acid Cycle (Krebs Cycle)**
   - **Location:** Mitochondrial matrix
   - **Process:** Acetyl-CoA is oxidized, producing $NADH_2$ $FADH_2$, and ATP.
   - **Significance:** Links carbohydrate, lipid, and protein catabolism.
5. **Oxidative Phosphorylation**
   - **Location:** Inner mitochondrial membrane
   - **Process:** NADH and $FADH_2$ donate electrons to the electron transport chain, generating ATP through chemiosmosis.
   - **Significance:** The primary source of ATP in aerobic organisms.

Anabolism: Biosynthesis

Anabolic pathways construct complex molecules necessary for cellular function and structure. Key anabolic processes include:

1. **Gluconeogenesis**
   - **Location:** Liver and kidney
   - **Process:** Synthesizes glucose from non-carbohydrate precursors like lactate, glycerol, and amino acids.
   - **Significance:** Maintains blood glucose levels during fasting.
2. **Lipogenesis**
   - **Location:** Liver and adipose tissue
   - **Process:** Converts acetyl-CoA into fatty acids, which are stored as triglycerides.
   - **Significance:** Energy storage during excess caloric intake.
3. **Protein Synthesis**
   - **Location:** Ribosomes
   - **Process:** Synthesizes polypeptides from amino acids based on mRNA templates.
   - **Significance:** Essential for growth, repair, and enzyme production.
4. **Nucleotide Synthesis**
   - **Process:** Produces purines and pyrimidines, the building blocks of DNA and RNA.
   - **Significance:** Critical for cell division and genetic information transfer.

Energy Balance: The Metabolic Nexus

Energy balance is the equilibrium between energy intake (from food) and energy expenditure (through basal metabolism, physical activity, and thermogenesis). ATP acts as the intermediary, bridging catabolic energy release with anabolic energy demands.

1. **Positive and Negative Energy Balance:** Positive Energy Balance: Occurs when energy intake exceeds expenditure, leading to weight gain and fat storage.
   - **Negative Energy Balance:** Occurs when energy expenditure exceeds intake, leading to weight loss and catabolism of stored nutrients.
2. **Metabolic Regulation:** The body meticulously regulates metabolism through:
   - **Hormones:** Insulin, glucagon, cortisol, and thyroid hormones modulate metabolic pathways.
   - **Enzymes:** Act as catalysts and control reaction rates.

- **Feedback Mechanisms:** Maintain homeostasis by adjusting pathway activity.

Metabolism in Ayurveda: Agni and Ojas

Ayurveda, an ancient system of holistic medicine, presents a profound understanding of metabolism, encapsulated in the concepts of Agni and Ojas.

1. **Agni:** The Digestive Fire. Agni, the metabolic fire, is responsible for digestion, absorption, and transformation of food into energy. Ayurveda identifies several types of Agni:
   - **Jatharagni:** Governs digestion in the stomach.
   - **Bhutagni:** Responsible for assimilating elemental nutrients.
   - **Dhatwagni:** Facilitates tissue metabolism and nourishment.

   Imbalance in Agni
   - **Mandagni (weakened fire):** Leads to poor digestion, accumulation of toxins (Ama), and metabolic disorders.
   - **Tikshnagni (hyperactive fire):** Results in excessive metabolism, weight loss, and tissue depletion.
2. **Ojas:** The Essence of Vitality. Ojas is the final product of perfect digestion and metabolism, representing vitality and immunity. Balanced metabolism enhances Ojas, contributing to physical strength, mental clarity, and emotional stability.

   Ojas and Modern Biochemistry
   - Ojas aligns with the concept of optimal cellular function and energy efficiency.
   - A depletion of Ojas correlates with metabolic stress and immune dysfunction.

Integration of Modern Science and Ayurveda

Modern biochemistry and Ayurveda converge on several aspects of metabolism:

1. **Dietary Impact:** Both emphasize the role of balanced nutrition in maintaining metabolic health.
2. **Holistic View:** Ayurveda's holistic approach parallels systems biology, which views metabolism as an interconnected network.
3. **Stress and Metabolism:** Both recognize the detrimental impact of stress on metabolic pathways and overall health.

Metabolic Disorders: A Biochemical and Ayurvedic Perspective

Metabolic disorders like diabetes, obesity, and cardiovascular diseases arise from imbalances in metabolism. Ayurveda offers unique insights into their prevention and management.

1. **Diabetes Mellitus:** Biochemical View: Results from impaired glucose metabolism due to insulin deficiency or resistance.
   - **Ayurvedic View:** Known as "Madhumeha," diabetes is linked to an imbalance in Kapha dosha and weakened Agni.
2. **Obesity**
   - **Biochemical View:** Arises from positive energy balance and fat accumulation.
   - **Ayurvedic View:** Caused by Ama (toxins) and imbalanced Kapha dosha.
3. **Cardiovascular Diseases**
   - **Biochemical View:** Linked to lipid metabolism disorders and oxidative stress.
   - **Ayurvedic View:** Associated with imbalanced Vata and Pitta doshas.

Practical Applications

1. **Diet and Nutrition:** Modern science emphasizes caloric balance and nutrient density.
   - Ayurveda recommends foods based on individual constitution (Prakriti) and digestive capacity.
2. **Herbal Remedies**
   - **Ashwagandha:** Enhances energy metabolism and reduces stress.
   - **Guduchi:** Supports liver metabolism and immunity.
3. **Lifestyle Practices**
   - Regular exercise and yoga improve metabolic efficiency.
   - Meditation reduces stress, promoting balanced metabolism.

Metabolic Disorders and Ayurveda

Biochemical imbalances in metabolism lead to disorders such as diabetes, obesity, and cardiovascular diseases. Ayurveda offers insights into metabolic correction through dietary and lifestyle modifications, emphasizing balance among the three doshas (Vata, Pitta, Kapha).

Ayurvedic Approaches to Metabolism

Dietary Interventions: Incorporating foods aligned with one's Prakriti (constitution) to enhance digestion and assimilation.

- **Herbal Therapies:** Using herbs like Guduchi and Ashwagandha to support metabolic pathways.
- **Lifestyle Practices:** Yoga and meditation harmonize metabolic processes and reduce stress-related imbalances.

MULTIPLE CHOICE QUESTIONS

1. In the context of metabolic studies linking modern biochemical pathways with Ayurvedic principles, a researcher investigates the role of macronutrients in balancing the three doshas—Vata, Pitta, and Kapha. The study focuses on the specific impact of carbohydrates, proteins, and lipids on the dynamic equilibrium of doshas. The researcher hypothesizes that carbohydrate metabolism (via glycolysis and glycogen storage) primarily stabilizes Kapha, while lipid catabolism (beta-oxidation) aligns with Vata's requirement for sustained energy in the absence of dietary intake. Conversely, protein metabolism, particularly amino acid deamination and the urea cycle, influences Pitta by supporting enzymatic activity and thermoregulation.

Based on these biochemical and Ayurvedic insights, which of the following statements best reflects the physiological implications of macronutrient metabolism in Ayurveda?

A. Carbohydrates exclusively balance Kapha and have no measurable effect on Vata or Pitta.

B. Lipid catabolism not only aligns with Vata's energy needs but also significantly affects Pitta's thermal regulation.

C. Protein metabolism supports both Pitta and Kapha by enhancing digestive enzymes and tissue repair mechanisms.

D. Ayurvedic principles of dosha balance are unrelated to macronutrient metabolism as understood in modern biochemistry.

2. A medical biochemist is tasked with evaluating the physiological relevance of the Ayurvedic concept of Agni (digestive fire) using enzymatic and metabolic markers. The biochemist proposes that Agni corresponds to the collective activity of key digestive enzymes, including amylase, lipase, and protease, as well as metabolic regulators such as insulin and glucagon. In a clinical trial involving patients with metabolic disorders, it is observed that herbal formulations prescribed in Ayurveda, like Triphala and Chyawanprash, significantly upregulate enzymatic activity while improving glycemic control and lipid metabolism.

Which of the following inferences is most consistent with both the Ayurvedic and biochemical understanding of metabolism?

A. The Ayurvedic concept of Agni is validated by its association with the enzymatic activity involved in digestion and metabolic regulation.

B. Triphala and Chyawanprash act only as placebo treatments, with no measurable effect on enzymatic or metabolic activity.

C. The balance of Agni, as explained in Ayurveda, is symbolic and cannot be directly correlated with specific enzymes or metabolic pathways.

D. Modern biochemical pathways and Ayurvedic principles are fundamentally incompatible in explaining metabolic health.

3. A multidisciplinary study explores the role of proteins in cellular repair and immune system modulation in both modern science and Ayurveda. The study focuses on how specific amino acids derived from dietary proteins influence the balance of the seven dhatus (body tissues) described in Ayurveda. The researchers hypothesize that Rasa Dhatu (plasma) benefits from amino acids involved in albumin synthesis, while Mamsa Dhatu (muscle) is supported by essential amino acids like leucine and isoleucine that promote protein synthesis and repair. Additionally, they observe that deficiencies in these amino acids lead to imbalances in Ojas, the essence of vitality in Ayurveda.

Based on the study's findings, which of the following best bridges the Ayurvedic and biochemical perspectives on protein metabolism?

A. Protein metabolism in Ayurveda is unrelated to amino acid profiles, as Ojas is only influenced by mental well-being.

B. Essential amino acids directly contribute to Mamsa Dhatu and indirectly enhance Ojas by supporting systemic immunity.

C. Ayurveda does not consider protein intake significant, focusing solely on carbohydrates for balancing Rasa and Mamsa Dhatus.

D. Modern biochemical understanding of amino acids cannot be reconciled with Ayurvedic concepts of dhatus and Ojas.

4. A clinical nutritionist investigates the role of dietary fiber in regulating metabolic pathways and its relevance in Ayurveda. The nutritionist postulates that the Ayurvedic emphasis on consuming whole grains and fibrous fruits aligns with modern evidence showing that dietary fiber enhances gut health by promoting microbial diversity, which, in turn, impacts systemic metabolism. Additionally, the nutritionist notes that Ama (toxins) described in Ayurveda corresponds to endotoxins produced by dysbiotic gut microbiota, which dietary fiber can mitigate by restoring gut equilibrium.

Which of the following interpretations best integrates the modern biochemical and Ayurvedic perspectives on dietary fiber?

A. Ayurveda's preference for whole grains and fibrous fruits directly correlates with their ability to enhance gut microbiota diversity and reduce Ama.
B. Ama, as described in Ayurveda, is purely symbolic and does not correspond to any biochemical or physiological entity.
C. Dietary fiber has no measurable impact on Ayurvedic concepts, as its effects are limited to physical digestion and do not influence systemic health.
D. The benefits of dietary fiber are unrelated to gut microbiota, focusing solely on mechanical effects like improving stool bulk.

5. In an advanced metabolic study, a scientist examines how glycolysis and oxidative phosphorylation are influenced by Ayurvedic dietary regimens that emphasize the Madhura Rasa (sweet taste). The scientist observes that diets rich in naturally occurring carbohydrates like fructose and maltose improve glycogen storage and ATP generation. However, diets high in processed sugars induce metabolic stress and impair the activity of pyruvate dehydrogenase, an essential enzyme linking glycolysis to the citric acid cycle. The findings align with Ayurvedic principles advocating unprocessed, nutrient-rich foods.

Which of the following conclusions best supports the integration of modern metabolism and Ayurveda in the context of carbohydrate consumption?
A. Processed sugars align with the Madhura Rasa in Ayurveda, as they provide rapid energy, validating their inclusion in daily diets.
B. Naturally occurring carbohydrates, as advocated by Ayurveda, optimize glycolysis and oxidative phosphorylation while preventing metabolic stress.
C. The Madhura Rasa concept in Ayurveda is unrelated to carbohydrate metabolism, focusing solely on its sensory properties.
D. Pyruvate dehydrogenase activity is unaffected by the type of carbohydrate consumed, contradicting Ayurvedic dietary guidelines.

6. A biochemical researcher analyzes the role of lipids in both cellular structure and Ayurvedic health. The study focuses on how triglycerides stored in adipose tissue align with the Ayurvedic concept of Medas Dhatu (fat tissue), which is responsible for lubrication and energy reserve. The researcher observes that lipid oxidation pathways, particularly beta-oxidation, are more active in individuals with balanced Kapha dosha, while excessive Kapha leads to impaired lipid metabolism and fat accumulation. Ayurvedic interventions, including herbal oils and detoxification therapies, are noted to improve lipid metabolism.Which of the following statements best reflects the interplay between lipid biochemistry and Ayurvedic principles?
A. Medas Dhatu corresponds exclusively to structural lipids, with no relevance to energy storage or metabolism.
B. Ayurvedic interventions enhance lipid metabolism by balancing Kapha and promoting beta-oxidation pathways.
C. Lipid oxidation is unrelated to dosha balance, as it is entirely determined by genetic and dietary factors.
D. The concept of Medas Dhatu lacks scientific validity and cannot be correlated with lipid biochemistry.

7. A molecular biologist investigates how metabolic processes associated with protein synthesis and degradation align with Ayurvedic practices for maintaining Mamsa Dhatu (muscle tissue). The study reveals that anabolic pathways stimulated by essential amino acids from high-quality protein sources enhance muscle protein synthesis, paralleling Ayurvedic recommendations for consuming digestible and nutrient-rich foods. Additionally, catabolic pathways like proteolysis, when excessively activated, are linked to Vata imbalances, resulting in muscle wasting and fatigue.

Based on these findings, which statement best connects protein metabolism to Ayurvedic principles?
A. Anabolic and catabolic pathways in protein metabolism are unrelated to dosha imbalances described in Ayurveda.
B. Ayurvedic recommendations for Mamsa Dhatu focus on carbohydrate intake, neglecting the role of protein in muscle health.
C. Protein synthesis and degradation pathways directly influence the balance of Vata and Mamsa Dhatu.
D. Ayurveda does not emphasize dietary proteins, as Mamsa Dhatu is maintained solely through lifestyle practices.

8. In a study combining environmental science and Ayurveda, researchers evaluate how soil quality impacts the bioactive compound concentration in medicinal plants used in Ayurvedic formulations. The study highlights that depleted soils result in lower polysaccharide content in plants like Ashwagandha and Amalaki, reducing their efficacy in boosting immunity and balancing doshas. This aligns with the Ayurvedic principle that the quality of raw materials directly affects the therapeutic potency of formulations.

Which of the following best reflects the relationship between environmental factors and Ayurvedic pharmacology?

A. Soil quality has no measurable impact on the bioactive content of medicinal plants used in Ayurveda.
B. The therapeutic potency of Ayurvedic formulations depends entirely on the manufacturing process, not the raw materials' quality.
C. Environmental factors like soil quality directly influence the efficacy of Ayurvedic medicinal plants.
D. Ayurvedic principles disregard environmental factors, focusing solely on the combination of herbs in formulations.

9. A clinical trial investigates the impact of Triphala on metabolic disorders, focusing on its ability to modulate glucose and lipid metabolism. The study observes that Triphala significantly enhances the activity of glucose-6-phosphate dehydrogenase (G6PD) in the pentose phosphate pathway, providing NADPH for lipid biosynthesis and oxidative stress management. These findings align with Ayurvedic claims of Triphala's rejuvenating properties.

Which of the following conclusions best bridges the biochemical and Ayurvedic understanding of Triphala's therapeutic effects?

A. Triphala's effects on metabolic pathways are limited to glucose metabolism and do not extend to lipid biosynthesis.
B. Triphala enhances G6PD activity, supporting its Ayurvedic role in rejuvenation and metabolic balance.
C. Triphala's impact on metabolism is unrelated to its biochemical effects and is entirely placebo-driven.
D. Ayurvedic claims about Triphala lack scientific validation in the context of modern biochemistry.

10. A biochemist explores the role of gut microbiota diversity in regulating systemic metabolism and its Ayurvedic correlation with Pachaka Pitta, the subtype of Pitta dosha responsible for digestion. The study shows that microbial metabolites like short-chain fatty acids (SCFAs) influence lipid and carbohydrate metabolism, aligning with Ayurveda's emphasis on gut health for overall well-being.

Which statement best integrates gut microbiota research with Ayurvedic principles?

A. SCFAs produced by gut microbiota have no relevance to Ayurvedic concepts like Pachaka Pitta.
B. Gut microbiota diversity supports Pachaka Pitta's role in regulating metabolic and systemic health.
C. Ayurveda does not recognize gut microbiota as a factor in metabolic health.
D. SCFAs' role in metabolism contradicts Ayurvedic principles, as Ayurveda lacks a microbial perspective.

Directions (Q. No. 11-14): *Scenario-Based Questions*

SCENARIO 1

A clinical pharmacologist investigates the role of Ayurvedic Rasayanas in enhancing metabolic efficiency, focusing on Chyawanprash, a traditional herbal formulation containing Amalaki (Emblica officinalis), Ashwagandha (Withania somnifera), and Guduchi (Tinospora cordifolia). The study hypothesizes that Chyawanprash improves mitochondrial function, which is critical for energy metabolism and cellular repair. Preliminary data shows that patients consuming Chyawanprash for six months demonstrate increased activity of mitochondrial enzymes such as succinate dehydrogenase (SDH) and cytochrome c oxidase (COX). Concurrently, a reduction in markers of oxidative stress, like malondialdehyde (MDA), is observed. Furthermore, the formulation appears to enhance cellular ATP levels and supports immune cell proliferation, suggesting a holistic improvement in metabolic and systemic health.

SCENARIO 2

A sustainability scientist examines the environmental and economic challenges associated with producing Amalaki, a key component of Chyawanprash. Rising global demand for Ayurvedic products has led to the overharvesting of Amalaki, which is predominantly sourced from wild populations. The study reveals that poor agricultural practices and deforestation are reducing soil fertility, further impacting the quality and yield of Amalaki fruits. Additionally, the loss of bioactive compounds in Amalaki, such as vitamin C and tannins, is found to compromise its therapeutic efficacy. The researcher emphasizes the urgent need for sustainable cultivation practices, including agroforestry systems and community-based conservation efforts, to ensure the long-term availability and efficacy of Ayurvedic formulations.

11. Based on the findings in Scenario 1, which mechanism best explains the metabolic benefits observed in patients consuming Chyawanprash?

A. Chyawanprash enhances mitochondrial biogenesis, increasing the activity of enzymes like SDH and COX, which improve ATP synthesis and reduce oxidative stress.
B. The formulation acts as an antioxidant, neutralizing free radicals without influencing mitochondrial enzyme activity or ATP levels.
C. Chyawanprash directly stimulates glycolysis and beta-oxidation, bypassing mitochondrial pathways.
D. The effects of Chyawanprash on metabolism are independent of mitochondrial function and mediated solely by immune cell proliferation.

12. How do the environmental issues described in Scenario 2 potentially influence the metabolic outcomes observed in Scenario 1?

A. Poor soil quality and overharvesting lead to a decline in the bioactive compounds of Amalaki, reducing the efficacy of Chyawanprash in improving metabolic health.

B. Environmental degradation enhances the concentration of bioactive compounds in Amalaki, increasing its therapeutic potency.

C. The metabolic benefits of Chyawanprash are unaffected by the environmental conditions affecting Amalaki, as its efficacy relies on other components.

D. Environmental stress improves soil nutrient levels, indirectly enhancing Amalaki's bioactive profile and the efficacy of Chyawanprash.

13. Which intervention best integrates the scientific and environmental challenges described in the two scenarios to ensure the long-term efficacy of Chyawanprash?

A. Large-scale industrial farming of Amalaki using genetically modified seeds to increase yield and bioactive compound concentration.

B. Adoption of community-based agroforestry practices to cultivate Amalaki sustainably while preserving its bioactive compound profile.

C. Substitution of Amalaki with synthetic alternatives to meet the rising demand for Chyawanprash.

D. Reducing the production of Chyawanprash globally to conserve Amalaki resources and maintain ecological balance.

14. Considering the interconnected findings of Scenarios 1 and 2, which strategy would most effectively address both the metabolic and environmental challenges?

A. Establishing strict quality standards for Amalaki sourcing to ensure its bioactive compound concentration meets therapeutic requirements.

B. Focusing on alternative Ayurvedic formulations that do not rely heavily on endangered or environmentally sensitive resources.

C. Investing in research to synthesize Chyawanprash's bioactive compounds in the laboratory, bypassing natural resource dependency.

D. Promoting global awareness campaigns to reduce the overharvesting of Ayurvedic herbs and advocate for sustainable farming practices.

Directions (Q. No. 15–34): *Codes-Based Questions*

15. Match the following Ayurvedic doshas with their physiological roles and corresponding biochemical activities:

List–I	List–II
(a) Vata	1. Governs movement, linked with nervous system activity
(b) Pitta	2. Controls metabolism, associated with enzymatic and hormonal activity
(c) Kapha	3. Regulates structure, fluid balance, and tissue stability

Choose the correct answer:

A. (a)-1, (b)-2, (c)-3

B. (a)-2, (b)-1, (c)-3

C. (a)-3, (b)-1, (c)-2

D. (a)-1, (b)-3, (c)-2

16. Match the types of metabolic pathways with their primary functions:

List–I	List–II
(a) Glycolysis	1. Conversion of glucose to pyruvate, producing ATP
(b) Beta-oxidation	2. Fatty acid breakdown into acetyl-CoA
(c) Gluconeogenesis	3. Synthesis of glucose from non-carbohydrate precursors
(d) Pentose Phosphate Pathway	4. Produces NADPH and ribose-5-phosphate

Choose the correct answer:

A. (a)-2, (b)-1, (c)-4, (d)-3

B. (a)-3, (b)-4, (c)-1, (d)-2

C. (a)-1, (b)-2, (c)-3, (d)-4

D. (a)-4, (b)-3, (c)-2, (d)-1

17. Match the following Rasas (tastes) with their biological roles in Ayurveda and modern physiology:

List–I	List–II
(a) Madhura (Sweet)	1. Tissue nourishment and energy storage
(b) Tikta (Bitter)	2. Detoxification and reducing inflammation
(c) Amla (Sour)	3. Enhancing digestion and metabolic activity
(d) Kashaya (Astringent)	4. Tissue strengthening and wound healing

Choose the correct answer:

A. (a)-1, (b)-2, (c)-3, (d)-4

B. (a)-2, (b)-3, (c)-4, (d)-1

C. (a)-3, (b)-4, (c)-1, (d)-2

D. (a)-4, (b)-1, (c)-2, (d)-3

18. Match the following macromolecules with their primary functions and significance in metabolism:

List–I	List–II
(a) Carbohydrates	1. Quick energy source and ATP production

(b) Lipids	2. Long-term energy storage and membrane fluidity
(c) Proteins	3. Enzyme catalysis, structure, and repair
(d) Nucleic acids	4. Genetic information storage and replication

Choose the correct answer:
A. (a)-1, (b)-2, (c)-3, (d)-4
B. (a)-4, (b)-3, (c)-2, (d)-1
C. (a)-3, (b)-4, (c)-1, (d)-2
D. (a)-2, (b)-1, (c)-4, (d)-3

19. Match the following enzymes with their substrates and corresponding metabolic processes:

List–I	List–II
(a) Amylase	1. Starch, initiating carbohydrate digestion
(b) Lipase	2. Triglycerides, catalyzing lipid breakdown
(c) Protease	3. Proteins, aiding in protein digestion
(d) Lactase	4. Lactose, hydrolyzing disaccharides

Choose the correct answer:
A. (a)-1, (b)-2, (c)-3, (d)-4
B. (a)-2, (b)-1, (c)-4, (d)-3
C. (a)-3, (b)-4, (c)-1, (d)-2
D. (a)-4, (b)-3, (c)-2, (d)-1

20. Match the following metabolic disorders with their biochemical and Ayurvedic implications:

List–I	List–II
(a) Diabetes mellitus	1. Impaired glucose metabolism, Kapha imbalance
(b) Obesity	2. Excess fat accumulation, linked to Kapha dosha
(c) Hyperthyroidism	3. Overactive metabolism, aggravated Pitta dosha
(d) Fatty liver	4. Lipid accumulation in liver cells, impaired Medas Dhatu

Choose the correct answer:
A. (a)-1, (b)-2, (c)-3, (d)-4
B. (a)-4, (b)-3, (c)-2, (d)-1
C. (a)-3, (b)-4, (c)-1, (d)-2
D. (a)-2, (b)-1, (c)-4, (d)-3

21. Match the Ayurvedic principles with their biochemical equivalents:

List–I	List–II
(a) Agni	1. Digestive enzymes and metabolic fire
(b) Ojas	2. Vitality and immune system strength
(c) Ama	3. Toxins and metabolic waste products
(d) Prakriti	4. Genetic predisposition and phenotypic traits

Choose the correct answer:
A. (a)-1, (b)-2, (c)-3, (d)-4
B. (a)-4, (b)-3, (c)-2, (d)-1
C. (a)-3, (b)-4, (c)-1, (d)-2
D. (a)-2, (b)-1, (c)-4, (d)-3

22. Match the seven Ayurvedic dhatus with their corresponding tissues in modern physiology:

List–I	List–II
(a) Rasa Dhatu	1. Plasma
(b) Rakta Dhatu	2. Blood
(c) Mamsa Dhatu	3. Muscle
(d) Medas Dhatu	4. Fat

Choose the correct answer:
A. (a)-1, (b)-2, (c)-3, (d)-4
B. (a)-2, (b)-3, (c)-4, (d)-1
C. (a)-3, (b)-4, (c)-1, (d)-2
D. (a)-4, (b)-1, (c)-2, (d)-3

23. Match the following metabolic enzymes with their corresponding diseases caused by their deficiency or dysfunction:

List–I	List–II
(a) Glucokinase	1. Diabetes mellitus
(b) Lipoprotein lipase	2. Hyperlipidemia
(c) Phenylalanine hydroxylase	3. Phenylketonuria
(d) G6PD	4. Hemolytic anemia

Choose the correct answer:
A. (a)-1, (b)-2, (c)-3, (d)-4
B. (a)-4, (b)-3, (c)-2, (d)-1
C. (a)-2, (b)-1, (c)-4, (d)-3
D. (a)-3, (b)-4, (c)-1, (d)-2

24. Match the following metabolic processes with their Ayurvedic interpretations:

List–I	List–II
(a) Glycogen storage	1. Kapha-related energy reserve
(b) Lipid oxidation	2. Vata-driven energy mobilization
(c) Protein synthesis	3. Mamsa Dhatu nourishment
(d) Urea cycle	4. Ama detoxification

Choose the correct answer:
A. (a)-1, (b)-2, (c)-3, (d)-4
B. (a)-2, (b)-3, (c)-4, (d)-1
C. (a)-3, (b)-4, (c)-1, (d)-2
D. (a)-4, (b)-1, (c)-2, (d)-3

25. Match the following Ayurvedic terms with their modern physiological interpretations:

List–I	List–II
(a) Agni	1. Digestive enzymes and metabolic pathways

(b) Ama	2. Metabolic toxins and undigested materials
(c) Ojas	3. Immunity and vitality
(d) Prakriti	4. Genetic predisposition and constitution

Choose the correct answer:

A. (a)-1, (b)-2, (c)-3, (d)-4
B. (a)-2, (b)-1, (c)-4, (d)-3
C. (a)-3, (b)-4, (c)-1, (d)-2
D. (a)-4, (b)-3, (c)-2, (d)-1

26. Match the following metabolic pathways with their corresponding physiological outcomes:

List–I	List–II
(a) Glycolysis	1. Rapid ATP generation
(b) Gluconeogenesis	2. Blood glucose maintenance during fasting
(c) Beta-oxidation	3. Fatty acid catabolism for energy
(d) Pentose Phosphate Pathway	4. NADPH production for biosynthetic processes

Choose the correct answer:

A. (a)-2, (b)-1, (c)-3, (d)-4
B. (a)-1, (b)-2, (c)-3, (d)-4
C. (a)-3, (b)-4, (c)-1, (d)-2
D. (a)-4, (b)-3, (c)-2, (d)-1

27. Match the following Ayurvedic doshas with their characteristics and effects on health:

List–I	List–II
(a) Vata	1. Governs movement, associated with nervous system disorders
(b) Pitta	2. Controls metabolism, linked to inflammatory conditions
(c) Kapha	3. Regulates stability, related to obesity and lethargy
(d) Tridosha balance	4. Ensures overall physical and mental health

Choose the correct answer:

A. (a)-1, (b)-2, (c)-3, (d)-4
B. (a)-4, (b)-3, (c)-1, (d)-2
C. (a)-3, (b)-4, (c)-2, (d)-1
D. (a)-2, (b)-1, (c)-4, (d)-3

28. Match the components of the citric acid cycle with their roles in metabolism:

List–I	List–II
(a) Acetyl-CoA	1. Entry point for carbon into the cycle
(b) Citrate	2. First intermediate formed in the cycle
(c) NADH	3. Electron donor for ATP generation
(d) Oxaloacetate	4. Regeneration of cycle intermediates

Choose the correct answer:

A. (a)-1, (b)-2, (c)-3, (d)-4
B. (a)-4, (b)-3, (c)-2, (d)-1
C. (a)-3, (b)-4, (c)-1, (d)-2
D. (a)-2, (b)-1, (c)-4, (d)-3

29. Match the following Ayurvedic Rasas with their physiological effects and therapeutic applications:

List–I	List–II
(a) Madhura (Sweet)	1. Nourishes tissues, promotes growth
(b) Amla (Sour)	2. Enhances digestion and enzymatic activity
(c) Tikta (Bitter)	3. Detoxifies the body, reduces inflammation
(d) Kashaya (Astringent)	4. Strengthens tissues, controls bleeding

Choose the correct answer:

A. (a)-1, (b)-2, (c)-3, (d)-4
B. (a)-2, (b)-1, (c)-4, (d)-3
C. (a)-3, (b)-4, (c)-1, (d)-2
D. (a)-4, (b)-3, (c)-2, (d)-1

30. Match the following proteins with their respective biological functions:

List–I	List–II
(a) Hemoglobin	1. Oxygen transport
(b) Myosin	2. Muscle contraction
(c) Collagen	3. Structural support in connective tissue
(d) Albumin	4. Maintains osmotic pressure

Choose the correct answer:

A. (a)-1, (b)-2, (c)-3, (d)-4
B. (a)-4, (b)-3, (c)-1, (d)-2
C. (a)-3, (b)-4, (c)-2, (d)-1
D. (a)-2, (b)-1, (c)-4, (d)-3

31. Match the following Ayurvedic therapies with their corresponding modern biochemical mechanisms:

List–I	List–II
(a) Panchakarma	1. Detoxification and elimination of metabolic waste
(b) Rasayana	2. Enhances cellular repair and longevity
(c) Shirodhara	3. Reduces cortisol and promotes relaxation
(d) Abhyanga	4. Improves circulation and lymphatic drainage

Choose the correct answer:

A. (a)-1, (b)-2, (c)-3, (d)-4
B. (a)-2, (b)-3, (c)-4, (d)-1
C. (a)-3, (b)-4, (c)-1, (d)-2
D. (a)-4, (b)-1, (c)-2, (d)-3

32. Match the following Ayurvedic dhatus with their physiological roles in modern medicine:

List–I	List–II
(a) Rasa Dhatu	1. Plasma, nutrient transport
(b) Rakta Dhatu	2. Blood, oxygen transport
(c) Mamsa Dhatu	3. Muscle, movement and strength
(d) Medas Dhatu	4. Fat, energy storage and insulation

Choose the correct answer:

A. (a)-1, (b)-2, (c)-3, (d)-4
B. (a)-2, (b)-1, (c)-4, (d)-3
C. (a)-3, (b)-4, (c)-1, (d)-2
D. (a)-4, (b)-3, (c)-2, (d)-1

33. Match the following digestive enzymes with their substrates and corresponding physiological processes:

List–I	List–II
(a) Amylase	1. Starch, initiating carbohydrate digestion
(b) Lipase	2. Triglycerides, catalyzing lipid breakdown
(c) Protease	3. Proteins, aiding in protein digestion
(d) Lactase	4. Lactose, hydrolyzing disaccharides

Choose the correct answer:

A. (a)-1, (b)-2, (c)-3, (d)-4
B. (a)-2, (b)-1, (c)-4, (d)-3
C. (a)-3, (b)-4, (c)-1, (d)-2
D. (a)-4, (b)-3, (c)-2, (d)-1

34. Match the following metabolic enzymes with the diseases caused by their deficiency:

List–I	List–II
(a) Hexokinase	1. Glycolysis impairment, hypoglycemia
(b) Glucose-6-phosphate dehydrogenase (G6PD)	2. Hemolytic anemia
(c) Phenylalanine hydroxylase	3. Phenylketonuria
(d) Lipoprotein lipase	4. Hyperlipidemia

Choose the correct answer:

A. (a)-1, (b)-2, (c)-3, (d)-4
B. (a)-4, (b)-3, (c)-2, (d)-1
C. (a)-3, (b)-4, (c)-1, (d)-2
D. (a)-2, (b)-1, (c)-4, (d)-3

Directions (Q. No. 35–39): *Following questions are based on Statement 1 and Statement 2. Read both the statements carefully and choose the correct answer from the options given below:*

A. Both Statement 1 and Statement 2 are true, and Statement 2 is the correct explanation of Statement 1.
B. Both Statement 1 and Statement 2 are true, but Statement 2 is not the correct explanation of Statement 1.
C. Statement 1 is true, but Statement 2 is false.
D. Statement 1 is false, but Statement 2 is true.
E. Both Statement 1 and Statement 2 are false.

35. **Statement 1:** The Ayurvedic concept of Agni is directly linked to the activity of metabolic enzymes such as amylase, lipase, and protease, which are essential for digestion and absorption of macronutrients.

Statement 2: The impairment of Agni, as described in Ayurveda, leads to the accumulation of Ama, which corresponds to undigested food and metabolic toxins.

36. **Statement 1:** Proteins, as described in modern biochemistry, are the primary structural components of muscles, enzymes, and antibodies.

Statement 2: According to Ayurveda, the nourishment of Mamsa Dhatu depends solely on the consumption of proteins and is unaffected by the state of Agni.

37. **Statement 1:** The pentose phosphate pathway produces NADPH and ribose-5-phosphate, which are essential for anabolic reactions and nucleotide synthesis, respectively.

Statement 2: Ayurveda's Rasayana herbs, such as Guduchi, are believed to enhance anabolic pathways by promoting Agni and Ojas.

38. **Statement 1:** Beta-oxidation of fatty acids occurs in the mitochondria and generates acetyl-CoA, NADH, and $FADH_2$, which are critical for ATP production.

Statement 2: The Ayurvedic concept of Sneha (lipids) aligns with the role of fats in providing long-term energy reserves and supporting cellular function.

39. **Statement 1:** Carbohydrates serve as the most immediate source of energy for cellular metabolism, providing glucose for glycolysis and subsequent ATP production.

Statement 2: Ayurveda categorizes carbohydrates under Madhura Rasa, emphasizing their role in balancing Vata dosha and promoting energy storage.

Directions (Q. No. 40–45): *There are two statements in each question. One is labelled as Assertion (A) and the other is as Reason (R). Read both the statements and choose the correct answer from the options given below:*

A. Both Assertion (A) and Reason (R) are true, and Reason (R) is the correct explanation of Assertion (A).

B. Both Assertion (A) and Reason (R) are true, but Reason (R) is not the correct explanation of Assertion (A).
C. Assertion (A) is true, but Reason (R) is false.
D. Assertion (A) is false, but Reason (R) is true.
E. Both Assertion (A) and Reason (R) are false.

40. Assertion (A): Glycolysis is a universal pathway that occurs in the cytoplasm and generates ATP through the breakdown of glucose into pyruvate.

Reason (R): Pyruvate generated during glycolysis is immediately converted into lactate in the mitochondria under aerobic conditions.

41. Assertion (A): Lipids are stored in adipose tissue as triglycerides and mobilized during fasting to provide energy through beta-oxidation.

Reason (R): Beta-oxidation occurs in the cytoplasm, producing ATP directly through the breakdown of fatty acids.

42. Assertion (A): Proteins are metabolized into amino acids, which enter the Krebs cycle as intermediates for energy production.

Reason (R): Amino acids are primarily used for gluconeogenesis during prolonged fasting to maintain blood glucose levels.

43. Assertion (A): Ayurveda describes Madhura Rasa (sweet taste) as nourishing and anabolic, associated with the growth and repair of tissues.

Reason (R): Sweet Rasa corresponds to dietary carbohydrates, which are rapidly metabolized into glucose for energy production.

44. Assertion (A): Ayurveda emphasizes the role of Rasayana herbs in enhancing Ojas, the vital essence of immunity and vitality.

Reason (R): Rasayana herbs promote the activity of mitochondrial enzymes, thereby increasing ATP production and reducing oxidative stress.

45. Assertion (A): Beta-oxidation of fatty acids provides more ATP per molecule compared to carbohydrate metabolism.

Reason (R): Fatty acids have a higher energy density than carbohydrates due to their long hydrocarbon chains and high reduction potential.

Directions (Q. No. 46–50): *Read the passage carefully and answer the questions given below*:

Proteins are one of the most versatile and essential macromolecules in biological systems, performing functions that range from catalyzing biochemical reactions to serving as structural components and mediators of immune responses. In modern biochemistry, proteins are categorized by their structure and function, classified as enzymes, structural proteins, signaling molecules, and transporters. The primary structure of a protein, which is the linear sequence of amino acids, determines its higher-order structures—secondary, tertiary, and quaternary. This hierarchy is crucial, as even slight alterations in amino acid sequences can lead to functional impairments, as seen in disorders like sickle-cell anemia.

Proteins are synthesized through the central dogma of molecular biology, wherein genetic information is transcribed from DNA to RNA and translated into polypeptide chains. Post-translational modifications, such as phosphorylation, glycosylation, and ubiquitination, further refine protein function and localization. In cellular metabolism, proteins play a pivotal role as enzymes, accelerating reactions by lowering activation energy. For instance, amylase catalyzes the hydrolysis of starch into glucose, while proteases facilitate protein degradation into amino acids. These amino acids can be metabolized via the Krebs cycle for energy production or used for gluconeogenesis during periods of starvation.

In Ayurveda, proteins are associated with the nourishment of Mamsa Dhatu, the tissue responsible for structural strength and physical vitality. Ayurvedic texts emphasize that the health of Mamsa Dhatu depends not only on dietary protein intake but also on the digestive capacity, or Agni, of an individual. Weak Agni leads to incomplete digestion, resulting in the formation of Ama, which Ayurveda correlates with toxins that disrupt tissue health. Specific Rasayana herbs, such as Ashwagandha and Shatavari, are known to enhance protein metabolism and promote the synthesis of Mamsa Dhatu, contributing to physical endurance and muscle repair.

Modern research aligns with these Ayurvedic principles, demonstrating that herbs like Ashwagandha contain bioactive compounds that stimulate protein synthesis and inhibit catabolic pathways, such as those mediated by cortisol. Similarly, Shatavari's phytoestrogenic properties have been shown to support muscle recovery and growth by influencing anabolic pathways. These herbs have also been found to reduce oxidative stress, thereby protecting proteins from damage and ensuring their functionality in enzymatic and structural roles.

Proteins also have a significant role in immune responses. Antibodies, or immunoglobulins, are specialized proteins that recognize and neutralize pathogens. In Ayurveda, the concept of Ojas, the essence of vitality and immunity, is closely related to the optimal function of proteins in the immune system. Ojas is considered the refined product of all seven dhatus (body tissues), with Mamsa Dhatu playing a key role in its production. The depletion of Ojas, often caused by chronic illness or stress, weakens the immune system and increases susceptibility to infections. Ayurvedic interventions, including dietary modifications and Rasayana therapy, aim to restore Ojas by strengthening Mamsa Dhatu and enhancing protein metabolism.

In metabolic disorders, the role of proteins becomes even more critical. For instance, insulin, a peptide hormone, regulates glucose homeostasis. Deficiencies or resistance to insulin lead to conditions such as diabetes mellitus. Ayurvedic treatments for diabetes, referred to as Madhumeha, include herbs like Guduchi and Amalaki, which have been shown to enhance insulin sensitivity and support protein-mediated glucose transport. Additionally, these herbs protect pancreatic beta cells, ensuring sustained insulin production.

Protein metabolism is also central to the body's response to stress and injury. During periods of physiological stress, such as infection or trauma, the body shifts to a catabolic state, breaking down muscle proteins to supply amino acids for gluconeogenesis and immune responses. This catabolic shift can lead to muscle wasting if prolonged. Ayurvedic texts emphasize the importance of maintaining a balance between anabolic and catabolic processes, advocating for dietary proteins that are easily digestible, such as those found in legumes and dairy. Ghee (clarified butter), often used in Ayurveda, is believed to enhance the absorption of nutrients, including proteins, and improve their assimilation into Mamsa Dhatu.

Emerging research also highlights the role of proteins in gut health, a focus of both modern science and Ayurveda. Proteins are integral to the structure and function of the gut barrier, preventing the translocation of harmful microbes and toxins into the bloodstream. Ayurveda's emphasis on gut health, encapsulated in the concept of Pachaka Pitta, aligns with these findings, as digestive efficiency directly influences protein assimilation. Herbal formulations like Triphala are often prescribed to optimize gut function, ensuring the effective breakdown and absorption of dietary proteins.

The integration of modern biochemical insights with Ayurvedic principles offers a holistic understanding of protein metabolism. While biochemistry focuses on the molecular mechanisms, Ayurveda provides a broader perspective, incorporating digestive health, doshic balance, and systemic vitality. Together, these approaches underscore the central role of proteins in maintaining health, preventing disease, and promoting longevity.

46. According to the passage, which Ayurvedic concept corresponds to the role of antibodies in the immune system?

A. Agni
B. Ojas
C. Ama
D. Pachaka Pitta

47. How do Rasayana herbs like Ashwagandha and Shatavari influence protein metabolism, as described in the passage?

A. By directly increasing cortisol levels to enhance protein synthesis.
B. By inhibiting catabolic pathways and stimulating anabolic processes.
C. By preventing protein digestion in the gut to protect Mamsa Dhatu.
D. By enhancing glucose metabolism instead of protein metabolism.

48. Which of the following statements best describes the relationship between Mamsa Dhatu and Ojas in Ayurveda, based on the passage?

A. Mamsa Dhatu depletion directly increases Ojas and improves immunity.
B. Ojas is the direct product of Agni and unrelated to Mamsa Dhatu.
C. Mamsa Dhatu contributes to the production of Ojas, enhancing vitality and immunity.
D. The production of Ojas depends solely on dietary protein intake, independent of Mamsa Dhatu.

49. What role does protein metabolism play during periods of stress or trauma, as discussed in the passage?

A. Proteins are stored in adipose tissue for energy use during stress.
B. Muscle proteins are broken down to supply amino acids for gluconeogenesis and immune responses.
C. Protein synthesis increases exponentially during stress, leading to muscle hypertrophy.
D. Proteins are converted into lipids to provide a long-term energy source.

50. How does the passage describe the integration of Ayurvedic principles and modern biochemistry in understanding protein metabolism?

A. Ayurveda focuses exclusively on spiritual aspects, while biochemistry examines physical processes.
B. Modern biochemistry validates Ayurvedic concepts by emphasizing digestive health and systemic vitality.
C. Ayurveda and biochemistry have fundamentally conflicting views on protein metabolism.
D. Biochemistry provides a comprehensive understanding, while Ayurveda lacks scientific basis.

ANSWER WITH EXPLANATIONS

1. **B:** Lipid catabolism through beta-oxidation supports Vata's energy demands, especially during fasting, aligning with its mobile and light nature. However, the metabolic heat generated during fatty acid oxidation also contributes to thermogenesis, indirectly supporting Pitta, which governs heat and metabolism. Thus, lipid breakdown affects both doshas, making option B the most comprehensive and accurate reflection of Ayurvedic-biochemical integration.

2. **A:** Agni in Ayurveda corresponds to digestive and metabolic fire, which can be interpreted biochemically as the collective action of enzymes and regulatory hormones involved in metabolism. The increased activity of enzymes like amylase and improvement in glycemic control after the use of Triphala and Chyawanprash support this correlation. This shows that Agni has a physiological basis measurable through modern biochemical markers.

3. **B:** Essential amino acids play a key role in protein synthesis and tissue repair, contributing to Mamsa Dhatu (muscles) in Ayurveda. Rasa Dhatu benefits from protein components like albumin, and Ojas—linked to immunity—is enhanced through well-nourished tissues. This demonstrates a direct link between dietary proteins, amino acids, and the Ayurvedic concept of tissue balance and vitality, validating option B.

4. **A:** Modern studies confirm that dietary fiber promotes gut microbial diversity and reduces endotoxins, improving metabolism. Ayurveda describes Ama as toxic byproducts from incomplete digestion, which aligns with modern views on endotoxins. Thus, Ayurveda's emphasis on whole grains and fiber-rich foods to reduce Ama aligns with modern scientific understanding, supporting option A.

5. **B:** Ayurveda promotes the Madhura Rasa through unprocessed, naturally sweet foods, which are metabolically beneficial. These support ATP production without stressing metabolic enzymes like pyruvate dehydrogenase. In contrast, processed sugars disrupt this balance. Therefore, Ayurveda's dietary recommendations align with modern findings on efficient carbohydrate metabolism, making option B the best fit.

6. **B:** Medas Dhatu in Ayurveda corresponds to fat tissue, responsible for lubrication and energy storage. Beta-oxidation of lipids is a key process in generating energy from fat stores. When Kapha is balanced, this process is efficient, but excessive Kapha impairs it. Ayurvedic detoxification and herbal therapies can restore this balance, making B the most accurate answer.

7. **C:** Protein metabolism, particularly the balance between anabolic (synthesis) and catabolic (breakdown) pathways, influences Mamsa Dhatu. Ayurveda links excessive breakdown (proteolysis) to Vata aggravation, leading to muscle wasting. Consuming high-quality, digestible proteins supports tissue strength and vitality, directly connecting Ayurvedic and modern views. Hence, option C is the correct choice.

8. **C:** Ayurveda emphasizes the importance of the source and quality of herbs. Depleted soil reduces the polysaccharide and antioxidant content of medicinal plants like Ashwagandha and Amalaki, weakening their therapeutic effects. Modern science supports this by linking soil health to plant biochemistry. Thus, environmental quality directly affects herbal potency, validating option C.

9. **B:** Triphala's enhancement of G6PD activity supports lipid biosynthesis and antioxidant defense via NADPH production. This aligns with Ayurvedic claims of its rejuvenating (Rasayana) properties. The pentose phosphate pathway's role in metabolic balance makes this herb a bridge between ancient therapeutic concepts and modern metabolic science, justifying option B.

10. **B:** SCFAs, produced by gut microbiota, improve digestion, glucose, and lipid metabolism, aligning with Pachaka Pitta's role in Ayurveda. This dosha subtype governs digestion and nutrient assimilation. Thus, the diversity of gut microbiota directly supports the Ayurvedic view that digestive health governs systemic balance, confirming option B.

11. **A:** Chyawanprash enhances mitochondrial efficiency by increasing enzymes like SDH and COX, which are essential for ATP production. Reduced oxidative stress and improved energy status point to better metabolic health. These findings align with Ayurvedic views of Rasayana therapy, confirming that Chyawanprash supports systemic energy and vitality through mitochondrial pathways.

12. **A:** Overharvesting and poor soil practices reduce the vitamin and tannin content of Amalaki, compromising its therapeutic strength. Since Amalaki is a key ingredient in Chyawanprash, its decline affects the overall metabolic and antioxidant benefits. Therefore, metabolic gains observed in Scenario 1 depend on environmental factors addressed in Scenario 2, making A correct.

13. **B:** Community-based agroforestry aligns with sustainable cultivation and conservation goals. It maintains soil fertility, preserves biodiversity, and ensures consistent yields of high-quality Amalaki. This approach bridges the gap between scientific efficacy and ecological stewardship, making it the most integrative solution to address both therapeutic and environmental concerns.

14. **A:** While awareness campaigns (option D) are valuable for education, option A directly targets both key issues in the scenarios: preserving the metabolic efficacy of Chyawanprash (by maintaining Amalaki's therapeutic quality) and addressing environmental sustainability (by enforcing quality over quantity in sourcing practices). By implementing strict sourcing standards, producers can ensure high concentrations of vital compounds like vitamin C and tannins in Amalaki, maintaining its mitochondrial and antioxidant benefits. This approach promotes responsible use of natural resources while preserving the formulation's therapeutic integrity, making option A the most precise and effective strategy.

15. **A:** The roles of doshas directly correlate with specific physiological and biochemical functions. Vata governs movement and nervous system activity, Pitta controls metabolism and enzymatic processes, and Kapha regulates stability and fluid balance. These associations highlight Ayurveda's detailed understanding of body functions, linking doshic balance to systemic health. Modern science validates this framework by showing how biochemical pathways like neural signaling, enzymatic activity, and structural integrity align with the descriptions of Vata, Pitta, and Kapha. The integration of doshic principles with modern physiology offers a comprehensive perspective on maintaining health through balance.

16. **C:** This question maps key metabolic pathways to their primary functions. Glycolysis (a) is the process by which glucose is broken down into pyruvate, producing ATP, hence it matches with (1). Beta-oxidation (b) involves the breakdown of fatty acids into acetyl-CoA, making (2) the correct match. Gluconeogenesis (c) refers to the synthesis of glucose from non-carbohydrate sources like amino acids or lactate, which corresponds to (3). Finally, the Pentose Phosphate Pathway (d) is responsible for producing NADPH (for biosynthesis and antioxidant defense) and ribose-5-phosphate (for nucleotide synthesis), aligning with (4). This alignment reflects the integrative view of metabolic processes in both modern biochemistry and Ayurvedic interpretations.

17. **A:** The six Rasas in Ayurveda correspond to specific physiological effects, validated by modern science. Madhura (sweet) supports tissue nourishment and energy storage, Amla (sour) enhances digestion and enzymatic activity, Tikta (bitter) detoxifies the body, and Kashaya (astringent) strengthens tissues. These roles reflect Ayurveda's detailed understanding of diet and health. Biochemical research further validates these effects, showing how dietary components influence metabolism and systemic health. The alignment of Rasa-based classifications with biochemical pathways demonstrates Ayurveda's scientific relevance, offering a nuanced framework for dietary planning and therapeutic interventions.

18. **A:** Macromolecules play distinct roles in sustaining life. Carbohydrates provide immediate energy, lipids store long-term energy and maintain cellular membranes, proteins catalyze biochemical reactions and support tissue repair, and nucleic acids store and transmit genetic information. These functions align with Ayurveda's descriptions of dhatus and their contribution to health. For example, Medas Dhatu corresponds to lipid storage, while Mamsa Dhatu aligns with protein functions. This integration of macromolecular science with Ayurvedic principles offers a unified understanding of how structural and functional components maintain systemic vitality.

19. **A:** Digestive enzymes catalyze specific biochemical reactions critical for nutrient absorption. Amylase breaks down starch into glucose, lipase hydrolyzes triglycerides into fatty acids, protease digests proteins into amino acids, and lactase cleaves lactose into simpler sugars. Ayurveda's emphasis on Agni aligns with these enzymatic activities, highlighting the role of digestive fire in ensuring optimal nutrient metabolism. By linking modern enzymology with Ayurvedic principles, this approach underscores the importance of maintaining digestive efficiency for systemic health, reflecting a harmony between traditional and modern perspectives.

20. **A:** Metabolic disorders like diabetes, obesity, hyperthyroidism, and fatty liver have clear biochemical and Ayurvedic implications. Diabetes is linked to glucose metabolism and Kapha imbalance, obesity to fat accumulation and Kapha excess, hyperthyroidism to overactive metabolism and aggravated Pitta, and fatty liver to lipid accumulation and impaired Medas Dhatu. These correlations highlight Ayurveda's diagnostic depth and its relevance in modern metabolic health. By integrating these perspectives, a comprehensive approach to managing metabolic disorders emerges, addressing both biochemical mechanisms and doshic imbalances for holistic health care.

21. A: The Ayurvedic principles of Agni, Ojas, Ama, and Prakriti closely align with modern physiological and biochemical concepts. Agni represents enzymatic activity essential for metabolism and digestion, while Ojas corresponds to systemic vitality and immune strength. Ama, the accumulation of undigested material or toxins, aligns with metabolic waste products, and Prakriti relates to genetic predisposition and phenotypic traits. These correlations bridge Ayurveda's holistic framework with modern scientific understanding. The alignment underscores Ayurveda's relevance in understanding systemic health, where maintaining balance between these elements ensures optimal function and prevention of disease, blending ancient wisdom with contemporary biochemistry.

22. A: The Ayurvedic dhatus (body tissues) map directly to modern physiological tissues. Rasa Dhatu correlates with plasma, facilitating nutrient transport; Rakta Dhatu corresponds to blood and oxygen transport via hemoglobin; Mamsa Dhatu reflects muscle tissue for movement and structural support; and Medas Dhatu aligns with fat, providing energy reserves and insulation. These connections validate Ayurveda's detailed descriptions of dhatus and their systemic roles. By integrating these concepts, Ayurveda provides a foundational understanding of tissue health, complementing modern anatomy and physiology with its emphasis on maintaining dhatu balance for systemic vitality and health.

23. A: Enzyme deficiencies result in specific metabolic diseases. Glucokinase deficiency impairs glycolysis, causing hypoglycemia; lipoprotein lipase deficiency leads to hyperlipidemia; phenylalanine hydroxylase deficiency causes phenylketonuria by disrupting amino acid metabolism; and G6PD deficiency leads to hemolytic anemia due to oxidative stress vulnerability. Ayurveda emphasizes maintaining metabolic balance to prevent such disorders, aligning with modern enzymology in its holistic approach. This integration offers a dual perspective: while modern biochemistry identifies precise molecular mechanisms, Ayurveda highlights systemic balance and preventive strategies, creating a complementary framework for understanding and managing metabolic diseases.

24. A: Ayurvedic interpretations of metabolic processes align with biochemical pathways. Glycogen storage corresponds to Kapha-related energy reserves, lipid oxidation aligns with Vata-driven mobilization, protein synthesis nourishes Mamsa Dhatu, and the urea cycle detoxifies metabolic byproducts, reducing Ama. These correlations demonstrate Ayurveda's deep understanding of systemic processes, offering insights into maintaining doshic balance. By integrating these interpretations with modern biochemistry, Ayurveda enhances our understanding of how metabolic pathways sustain health and prevent disease. This synthesis highlights the importance of balanced metabolic activity as a foundation for both physical and systemic well-being.

25. A: Ayurvedic terms like Agni, Ama, Ojas, and Prakriti correspond closely to modern physiological concepts. Agni represents the enzymatic and metabolic fire crucial for digestion; Ama aligns with undigested toxins affecting health; Ojas is vitality, correlating with immune function; and Prakriti reflects genetic predisposition. These terms encapsulate systemic health, providing a holistic perspective validated by biochemical markers. The integration of these principles with modern physiology highlights Ayurveda's depth in understanding health and disease, offering a comprehensive approach to maintaining systemic balance and preventing disorders through both enzymatic and metabolic pathways.

26. B: Metabolic pathways such as glycolysis, gluconeogenesis, beta-oxidation, and the pentose phosphate pathway have distinct outcomes. Glycolysis produces ATP rapidly, gluconeogenesis maintains glucose during fasting, beta-oxidation breaks down fatty acids for energy, and the pentose phosphate pathway generates NADPH for anabolic reactions. These outcomes align with Ayurveda's emphasis on balanced metabolism and systemic health. Understanding these pathways reinforces the connection between ancient and modern perspectives, where optimizing metabolic function supports vitality and prevents disease. This integration validates Ayurveda's focus on systemic harmony, complementing biochemical insights into energy production and biosynthesis.

27. A: The doshas' characteristics directly correlate with physiological and biochemical functions. Vata governs movement and is associated with the nervous system, Pitta controls metabolism and inflammatory conditions, and Kapha regulates stability, linked to obesity and lethargy. Tridosha balance ensures systemic health, as each dosha complements the others. Ayurveda's emphasis on balancing these elements aligns with modern physiology, where disruptions in doshic balance parallel physiological imbalances. This framework underscores Ayurveda's relevance in understanding health, highlighting the integration of traditional and scientific approaches to diagnosing and managing systemic disorders.

28. A: The citric acid cycle's components have distinct roles in metabolism. Acetyl-CoA serves as the entry point, citrate is the first intermediate, NADH donates electrons for ATP production, and oxaloacetate regenerates intermediates. These functions demonstrate the cycle's importance in energy metabolism. Ayurveda's concept of Agni parallels this understanding, emphasizing the transformation and utilization of energy sources. By integrating these biochemical pathways with Ayurvedic principles, a holistic understanding of energy metabolism emerges, highlighting how systemic balance supports vitality and disease prevention through efficient metabolic activity.

29. A: The Ayurvedic Rasas and their effects align with physiological roles. Madhura (sweet) nourishes tissues, Amla (sour) enhances digestion, Tikta (bitter) detoxifies, and Kashaya (astringent) strengthens tissues. These roles reflect Ayurveda's nuanced understanding of dietary impact on health. Modern research validates these effects, showing how bioactive compounds in foods influence metabolism and systemic health. The integration of Rasa-based classifications with biochemistry highlights Ayurveda's scientific relevance, offering a framework for dietary planning that promotes health by addressing metabolic needs and doshic balance.

30. A: Proteins such as hemoglobin, myosin, collagen, and albumin have distinct biological functions. Hemoglobin transports oxygen, myosin facilitates muscle contraction, collagen provides structural support, and albumin maintains osmotic pressure. Ayurveda's Mamsa Dhatu aligns with these structural and functional roles, emphasizing protein's importance in tissue health. This integration of protein biochemistry with Ayurvedic principles highlights the importance of systemic balance in maintaining vitality and preventing disease. By bridging ancient and modern insights, Ayurveda complements biochemistry in its approach to understanding protein function and supporting health through dietary and metabolic strategies.

31. A: Ayurvedic therapies correspond closely to modern biochemical mechanisms. Panchakarma detoxifies metabolic waste, Rasayana enhances cellular repair, Shirodhara reduces cortisol, and Abhyanga improves circulation. These correlations demonstrate Ayurveda's detailed understanding of systemic health, validated by biochemical findings. Modern science supports these practices by identifying the physiological effects of these therapies. Integrating traditional treatments with contemporary biochemistry offers a comprehensive approach to health care, emphasizing the importance of balance in both mental and physical health for preventing diseases and promoting longevity.

32. A: The Ayurvedic dhatus correspond closely to modern physiological tissues. Rasa Dhatu aligns with plasma, which transports nutrients; Rakta Dhatu corresponds to blood and oxygen transport; Mamsa Dhatu reflects muscle, responsible for movement and structural strength; and Medas Dhatu represents fat, providing energy reserves and insulation. These connections validate Ayurveda's understanding of systemic functions and tissue-specific roles. By integrating dhatu-based concepts with modern physiology, Ayurveda offers a comprehensive framework for understanding health. Maintaining dhatu balance ensures vitality and systemic harmony, bridging ancient practices and scientific knowledge to address health maintenance and disease prevention holistically.

33. A: Digestive enzymes play specific roles in nutrient metabolism. Amylase hydrolyzes starch into glucose, lipase breaks down triglycerides into fatty acids, protease digests proteins into amino acids, and lactase processes lactose into simpler sugars. Ayurveda's emphasis on Agni reflects the importance of enzymatic activity in digestion and nutrient absorption. Optimal enzyme function ensures efficient energy utilization and prevents metabolic imbalances. This connection between Ayurvedic digestive principles and modern enzymology highlights the integration of traditional dietary practices with biochemical insights, offering a detailed understanding of how digestive efficiency underpins systemic health and prevents disorders linked to impaired metabolism.

34. A: Deficiencies in key enzymes result in specific diseases: glucokinase deficiency disrupts glycolysis, causing hypoglycemia; G6PD deficiency increases oxidative stress, leading to hemolytic anemia; phenylalanine hydroxylase deficiency causes phenylketonuria by impairing amino acid metabolism; and lipoprotein lipase deficiency leads to hyperlipidemia. Ayurveda's focus on metabolic balance complements modern enzymology by addressing systemic health holistically. Integrating these perspectives offers a comprehensive understanding of enzyme-related diseases, emphasizing both molecular mechanisms and systemic balance. This dual approach highlights the importance of maintaining enzymatic activity and doshic equilibrium to ensure health and prevent disease.

35. A: Agni represents enzymatic activity essential for digestion and metabolism, while Ama corresponds to undigested food and toxins. Impaired Agni, often due to weak enzymatic function, results in Ama accumulation, disrupting systemic health. Ayurveda's emphasis on Agni as the cornerstone of digestion aligns with biochemistry, where enzymatic activity drives metabolic efficiency. The explanation of Ama as metabolic waste highlights Ayurveda's holistic perspective on toxicity and health. Integrating these concepts with modern science offers a unified understanding of digestion, where maintaining enzymatic balance is crucial for systemic vitality and disease prevention.

36. **C:** Proteins are the building blocks of enzymes, muscles, and antibodies, playing a central role in structural and functional health. Ayurveda associates protein metabolism with Mamsa Dhatu, emphasizing the need for strong Agni to ensure proper digestion and assimilation. Weak Agni leads to incomplete protein metabolism, resulting in Ama and impaired tissue health. By linking dietary protein intake with digestive efficiency, Ayurveda provides a comprehensive framework for systemic health. This integration of modern protein biochemistry and Ayurvedic principles highlights the importance of optimizing both nutrition and digestion for maintaining structural integrity and immune function.

37. **A:** The pentose phosphate pathway generates NADPH for anabolic reactions and ribose-5-phosphate for nucleotide synthesis, supporting cellular growth and repair. Ayurveda's Rasayana herbs, like Guduchi, enhance anabolic pathways by improving Agni and Ojas, promoting systemic vitality. These herbs are known to regulate metabolic stress, aligning with the biochemical role of the pentose phosphate pathway in maintaining cellular health. Integrating these principles highlights how Ayurveda and biochemistry converge on promoting anabolic health. By targeting both molecular mechanisms and holistic balance, this approach emphasizes comprehensive metabolic health through the combined insights of ancient and modern science.

38. **A:** Beta-oxidation generates acetyl-CoA, NADH, and $FADH_2$, fueling ATP synthesis in mitochondria. Ayurveda's concept of Sneha (fats) aligns with this role of lipids in providing energy and stability. Fats act as long-term energy reserves, supporting metabolic needs during fasting or stress, reflecting Sneha's nourishing and stabilizing attributes. The integration of these concepts highlights the relevance of lipid metabolism in both modern and Ayurvedic contexts, where systemic balance ensures energy efficiency. This holistic understanding emphasizes the importance of maintaining lipid metabolism to support vitality and address conditions linked to energy imbalances.

39. **A:** Carbohydrates are the primary source of quick energy, metabolized through glycolysis and oxidative phosphorylation to produce ATP. Ayurveda classifies carbohydrates under Madhura Rasa, emphasizing their nourishing and anabolic qualities. Madhura Rasa also balances Vata dosha, aligning with carbohydrates' role in stabilizing energy levels and promoting tissue repair. This integration of Ayurvedic dietary guidelines with modern carbohydrate metabolism highlights how both perspectives complement each other in maintaining systemic health. By understanding the dual significance of carbohydrates, a comprehensive approach to energy management and doshic balance emerges, supporting both physical and metabolic well-being.

40. **C:** Glycolysis is a universal metabolic pathway occurring in the cytoplasm, converting glucose into pyruvate and producing ATP. Under aerobic conditions, pyruvate enters the mitochondria for the citric acid cycle, not lactate conversion, which occurs in anaerobic conditions. This distinction underscores glycolysis's central role in energy metabolism, linking anaerobic and aerobic pathways. Ayurveda's emphasis on Agni aligns with glycolysis's transformative role in energy production, where balanced metabolic activity ensures systemic health. This integration demonstrates how understanding energy pathways bridges traditional and modern approaches to health care, emphasizing metabolic efficiency for vitality and disease prevention.

41. **C:** Lipids stored as triglycerides in adipose tissue are mobilized during fasting, with beta-oxidation occurring in mitochondria, not the cytoplasm. This process generates acetyl-CoA, NADH, and $FADH_2$, fueling ATP production. Ayurveda's Sneha concept aligns with lipid metabolism, emphasizing their role as energy reserves during stress. This connection highlights the integration of Ayurvedic principles and modern biochemistry, where understanding lipid mobilization and oxidation ensures balanced energy metabolism. By bridging these perspectives, a holistic understanding of systemic energy management emerges, addressing both physiological and doshic imbalances for comprehensive health care.

42. **B:** Proteins are metabolized into amino acids, which can enter the Krebs cycle as intermediates for ATP production. During prolonged fasting or stress, the body prioritizes gluconeogenesis, converting amino acids into glucose to maintain blood sugar levels. This dual role of amino acids in energy production and glucose homeostasis reflects their metabolic flexibility. Ayurveda's emphasis on preserving Mamsa Dhatu (muscle tissue) aligns with minimizing excessive protein catabolism during fasting. By integrating modern biochemical insights with Ayurvedic principles, a comprehensive framework emerges for understanding the balance between anabolic and catabolic processes to ensure energy sustainability and tissue integrity.

43. **A:** Madhura Rasa, or sweet taste, is described in Ayurveda as nourishing and anabolic, promoting tissue growth and repair. This aligns with carbohydrates' biochemical role in providing glucose for energy production and anabolic activities. Sweet Rasa balances Vata dosha, stabilizing energy levels and ensuring systemic harmony. By integrating Ayurvedic

dietary principles with carbohydrate metabolism, this understanding highlights the importance of Madhura Rasa in supporting metabolic efficiency and doshic equilibrium. The dual perspective underscores Ayurveda's relevance in dietary planning and disease prevention, validated by modern research on carbohydrate function and energy management.

44. **A:** Rasayana herbs like Ashwagandha and Shatavari enhance Ojas, the essence of vitality, by promoting mitochondrial activity and reducing oxidative stress. These herbs improve energy production by upregulating mitochondrial enzymes, aligning with their rejuvenating properties described in Ayurveda. The concept of Ojas reflects systemic immunity and resilience, which modern science validates through improved cellular energy and stress response. This integration demonstrates how traditional herbal formulations target biochemical pathways, enhancing systemic vitality and preventing disease. By bridging Ayurvedic concepts with mitochondrial science, a comprehensive approach to promoting longevity and vitality emerges, addressing both physiological and molecular health.

45. **A:** Beta-oxidation of fatty acids produces significantly more ATP than carbohydrate metabolism due to the higher energy density of fats. Long hydrocarbon chains in fatty acids yield more acetyl-CoA, NADH, and $FADH_2$, providing sustained energy. Ayurveda's emphasis on Sneha (fats) as long-term energy reserves aligns with this biochemical understanding. Sneha's nourishing and stabilizing properties mirror fats' metabolic role during fasting or stress. This integration highlights the harmony between Ayurveda and biochemistry, emphasizing the importance of balanced lipid metabolism for maintaining energy efficiency, supporting doshic balance, and preventing metabolic disorders linked to energy imbalances.

46. **B:** Ojas, as described in Ayurveda, represents the essence of vitality and immunity, paralleling the role of antibodies in modern immunology. Antibodies, specialized proteins, neutralize pathogens and maintain immune defense. Ayurveda emphasizes that Ojas is the refined product of all dhatus, especially Mamsa Dhatu, highlighting its foundational role in health. The depletion of Ojas weakens immunity, increasing susceptibility to illness, aligning with the biochemical understanding of impaired antibody production. This integration demonstrates how traditional and modern perspectives converge, underscoring the systemic importance of immune health and vitality for disease prevention and overall well-being.

47. **B:** Ashwagandha and Shatavari influence protein metabolism by inhibiting catabolic pathways and promoting anabolic processes. Ashwagandha's bioactive compounds reduce cortisol levels, mitigating muscle protein breakdown, while Shatavari supports anabolic pathways, aiding muscle recovery and tissue repair. These herbs' phytoactive compounds also reduce oxidative stress, protecting proteins from damage. Ayurveda's Rasayana therapy aligns with these biochemical effects, emphasizing systemic rejuvenation and vitality. This connection validates traditional claims about Rasayana herbs, demonstrating their capacity to enhance metabolic health by targeting protein pathways critical for tissue repair, immune function, and overall resilience against stress.

48. **C:** Mamsa Dhatu contributes significantly to the production of Ojas, the refined essence of systemic vitality and immunity. Ayurveda describes Ojas as the culmination of dhatu nourishment, where Mamsa plays a pivotal role. Modern immunology aligns this with protein metabolism, as amino acids from muscle tissue support antibody synthesis and immune responses. Chronic depletion of Mamsa Dhatu leads to weakened Ojas, compromising systemic health. This correlation highlights the interconnectedness of tissue health, metabolic function, and immunity, emphasizing Ayurveda's holistic approach to maintaining vitality and preventing diseases by optimizing protein metabolism and tissue repair.

49. **B:** During stress or trauma, muscle proteins are broken down to supply amino acids for gluconeogenesis and immune responses. This catabolic shift ensures glucose availability for critical functions but can lead to muscle wasting if prolonged. Ayurveda addresses this by emphasizing easily digestible dietary proteins and Rasayana herbs to minimize tissue depletion. The concept of Mamsa Dhatu preservation aligns with biochemical strategies to reduce catabolism, ensuring metabolic and structural balance. This integration highlights the complementary perspectives of Ayurveda and biochemistry in managing stress-induced metabolic changes and promoting recovery through optimized protein utilization.

50. **B:** Modern biochemistry validates Ayurvedic principles by emphasizing the importance of digestive health, systemic vitality, and protein metabolism. Ayurveda's holistic view of health, reflected in concepts like Agni, Ojas, and Mamsa Dhatu, complements biochemical insights into enzymatic activity, immune responses, and metabolic pathways. Herbs like Ashwagandha and Shatavari, traditionally used to enhance protein metabolism, are supported by research demonstrating their effects on anabolic and catabolic balance. This integration bridges traditional and scientific approaches, offering a comprehensive framework for understanding protein metabolism, ensuring systemic health, and addressing diseases linked to protein dysfunction.

CHAPTER 25

NANOTECHNOLOGY IN AYURVEDA – PROPERTIES AND CHARACTERIZATION

Introduction to Nanotechnology in Ayurveda

Nanotechnology, a field that involves the manipulation and engineering of materials at the nanoscale (1–100 nanometers), has emerged as a transformative scientific domain. This technology has impacted multiple industries, including medicine, pharmaceuticals, and materials science. In Ayurveda, the integration of nanotechnology holds promise for enhancing the efficacy, delivery, and therapeutic potential of traditional formulations. By bridging ancient wisdom with modern innovation, nanotechnology has the potential to revolutionize Ayurvedic practices and formulations, providing more precise, efficient, and bioavailable treatments.

BASICS OF NANOTECHNOLOGY

Defining Nanotechnology

Nanotechnology deals with the design, characterization, and application of materials with structural dimensions in the nanometer range. At this scale, materials exhibit unique properties that differ significantly from their bulk counterparts. These properties include increased surface area, enhanced reactivity, quantum effects, and altered electrical, thermal, and optical behaviours. These features make nanoparticles particularly advantageous for biomedical and pharmaceutical applications.

Unique Properties of Nanoparticles

1. **Increased Surface Area:** Nanoparticles have a high surface-to-volume ratio, which enhances their reactivity and interaction with biological systems. This property is crucial for applications in drug delivery and catalysis.
2. **Size-Dependent Properties:** At the nanoscale, materials exhibit quantum effects, altering their physical, chemical, and optical properties.
3. **Targeted Delivery:** Nanoparticles can be engineered to target specific tissues or cells, minimizing side effects and maximizing therapeutic efficacy.
4. **Controlled Release:** Nanotechnology enables the design of systems that release therapeutic agents in a controlled manner, enhancing bioavailability and therapeutic outcomes.

Relevance to Ayurveda

Ayurveda emphasizes holistic treatment through natural herbs, minerals, and biological extracts. However, challenges such as poor bioavailability, limited solubility, and the degradation of active ingredients often limit the efficacy of Ayurvedic medicines. Nanotechnology addresses these challenges by improving the stability, absorption, and targeted delivery of Ayurvedic formulations. The fusion of Ayurveda and nanotechnology leads to a concept known as Nano-Ayurveda, which enhances the therapeutic potential of traditional remedies.

Properties of Nanoparticles in Ayurvedic Applications

Nanoparticles used in Ayurvedic formulations exhibit specific properties that align with the principles of traditional medicine. The following are the key properties relevant to their use in Ayurveda:

1. **Enhanced Bioavailability:** Nanoparticles improve the bioavailability of Ayurvedic formulations by enhancing

solubility, stability, and permeability. For example, curcumin, a bioactive compound in turmeric, has low solubility and bioavailability. Curcumin nanoparticles can overcome these limitations, ensuring better absorption and therapeutic efficacy.

2. **Targeted Delivery:** Engineered nanoparticles can deliver Ayurvedic bioactives to specific tissues or cells, reducing systemic toxicity and increasing therapeutic effectiveness. Targeted delivery is especially beneficial for conditions like cancer, where precise treatment is critical.
3. **Controlled Release:** Nanotechnology enables the design of drug delivery systems that release bioactive compounds gradually over time. This controlled release ensures sustained therapeutic action, reducing the frequency of administration.
4. **Enhanced Stability:** Nanoparticles protect sensitive bioactive compounds from environmental degradation. For instance, herbal extracts prone to oxidation or photodegradation can be encapsulated in nanoparticles to improve their shelf life.
5. **Multifunctionality:** Nanoparticles can be designed to exhibit multiple functionalities, such as combining therapeutic and diagnostic properties (theranostics). This approach aligns with Ayurveda's holistic treatment philosophy.

Characterization of Nanoparticles

The characterization of nanoparticles is a cornerstone of nanotechnology, ensuring the reproducibility, safety, and efficacy of nano-formulations in diverse fields, including Ayurvedic applications. Nanoparticle characterization is critical for understanding their properties, behaviour, and interactions within biological systems. It provides essential insights into their size, shape, surface chemistry, optical behaviour, and thermal stability, which directly influence their performance in medical and pharmaceutical applications.

In the context of Ayurveda, the integration of nanotechnology requires meticulous characterization to validate the safety and efficacy of formulations. Proper characterization also ensures compliance with regulatory standards, facilitating the acceptance of nanotechnology-enhanced Ayurvedic medicines in global markets. This chapter provides an in-depth exploration of the methods and techniques used for nanoparticle characterization, emphasizing their relevance to Ayurvedic formulations.

1. **Size and Morphology:** The size and morphology of nanoparticles are fundamental characteristics that influence their physical and chemical properties, including reactivity, surface area, and interaction with biological systems. Several advanced techniques are employed to determine these properties.

   Dynamic Light Scattering (DLS): DLS is a widely used technique to measure the hydrodynamic diameter of nanoparticles in a suspension. It works by analyzing the scattering of light caused by the Brownian motion of particles in a liquid medium. The intensity of the scattered light is correlated to particle size, providing information about the size distribution.

   Relevance to Ayurvedic Applications: DLS ensures the uniformity of herbal nanoparticles, such as curcumin or neem nano-extracts, where consistent particle size is critical for bioavailability and therapeutic efficacy.

   Transmission Electron Microscopy (TEM): TEM provides high-resolution images of nanoparticles, offering detailed insights into their morphology, structure, and size. It uses a focused electron beam to penetrate the sample, producing detailed visualizations at the atomic level.

   - **Advantages:** TEM captures internal structures and can identify defects or irregularities in nanoparticles.
   - **Application in Ayurveda:** TEM is crucial for visualizing the nanoscale features of metallic bhasmas like Swarna Bhasma (gold nanoparticles), ensuring their precise synthesis.

   Scanning Electron Microscopy (SEM): SEM provides detailed information about the surface morphology and topology of nanoparticles. Unlike TEM, it focuses on surface features rather than internal structures, making it ideal for studying surface modifications and texture.

   Relevance to Nano-Ayurveda: SEM is used to analyze the surface characteristics of herbal and metallic nanoparticles, which influence their interaction with biological systems. For instance, SEM can confirm the uniform coating of nanoparticles with herbal extracts.

2. **Surface Properties:** Surface properties, including charge and area, play a pivotal role in determining the stability, reactivity, and interactions of nanoparticles. Proper surface characterization ensures the safety and functionality of Ayurvedic nano-formulations.

   Zeta Potential: Zeta potential measures the surface charge of nanoparticles, which indicates their colloidal stability in a suspension. A high zeta potential value (positive or negative) suggests good stability, as it prevents particle aggregation through electrostatic repulsion.

   Importance for Ayurvedic Formulations: Stability is crucial for herbal nano-formulations to maintain their therapeutic potential over time. Zeta potential measurements help optimize formulations like nano-curcumin for long-term storage.

Surface Area Analysis: The specific surface area of nanoparticles is measured using techniques like Brunauer-Emmett-Teller (BET) analysis. BET provides information about the surface area per unit weight, which is critical for understanding the reactivity and adsorption capacity of nanoparticles.

Relevance to Nano-Ayurveda: Higher surface area enhances the bioavailability of active compounds in Ayurvedic formulations, ensuring better absorption and therapeutic action. For example, BET analysis helps optimize the surface properties of iron nanoparticles in Lohabhasma.

3. **Composition and Structure:** Understanding the composition and structure of nanoparticles is essential for ensuring their purity, stability, and functionality. These parameters influence their interaction with biological systems and their therapeutic outcomes.

X-ray Diffraction (XRD): XRD is used to identify the crystalline structure and phase purity of nanoparticles. It works by analyzing the diffraction patterns of X-rays interacting with the atomic planes of the material.

Application in Ayurveda: XRD ensures the crystalline integrity of metallic bhasmas, such as Swarna Bhasma and Rajata Bhasma, which directly impacts their therapeutic efficacy.

Fourier Transform Infrared Spectroscopy (FTIR): FTIR identifies the functional groups and chemical bonds in nanoparticles by measuring their infrared absorption spectra. This technique provides insights into the chemical composition and potential surface modifications.

Significance in Nano-Ayurveda: FTIR confirms the successful encapsulation of herbal extracts, such as Ashwagandha or neem, onto nanoparticles. It also verifies the absence of unwanted chemical interactions during synthesis.

4. **Optical Properties:** Nanoparticles exhibit unique optical properties due to quantum effects and surface plasmon resonance, making their characterization critical for both diagnostic and therapeutic applications.

UV-Visible Spectroscopy: UV-visible spectroscopy evaluates the optical absorption of nanoparticles, providing information about their bandgap and plasmonic behaviour. It is a simple yet powerful tool for assessing nanoparticle stability and reactivity.

Relevance to Ayurvedic Formulations: This technique ensures the stability of herbal nano-formulations, such as curcumin-loaded nanoparticles, by monitoring their absorption spectra over time.

Fluorescence Spectroscopy: Fluorescence spectroscopy measures the luminescent properties of nanoparticles, making it useful for applications in imaging and theranostics.

Significance in Nano-Ayurveda: Fluorescent nanoparticles can enhance the diagnostic potential of Ayurvedic formulations, enabling real-time monitoring of treatment efficacy. For example, curcumin nanoparticles with fluorescence properties can serve both therapeutic and imaging purposes.

5. **Thermal Properties:** Thermal characterization provides insights into the stability and phase transitions of nanoparticles, which are critical for their storage and performance in varying conditions.

Thermal Gravimetric Analysis (TGA)

TGA measures the weight loss of nanoparticles as a function of temperature, providing information about their thermal stability and composition. This technique identifies decomposition temperatures and material purity.

Relevance to Ayurvedic Formulations

TGA ensures the stability of nano-formulations under various storage and processing conditions. It is particularly useful for formulations like nano-ashwagandha, which must retain their integrity during thermal processing.

Differential Scanning Calorimetry (DSC)

DSC analyzes the heat flow associated with phase transitions, such as melting, crystallization, and glass transitions. It provides critical information about the thermal behaviour of nanoparticles.

Application in Ayurveda

DSC confirms the stability of nanoparticles under physiological temperatures, ensuring their efficacy in targeted delivery systems. For instance, DSC validates the thermal compatibility of gold nanoparticles in Swarna Bhasma formulations.

Integrated Approaches in Nano-Ayurveda

The characterization of nanoparticles for Ayurvedic applications is not a standalone process but a multidisciplinary approach that integrates various techniques. Each method contributes unique insights into the properties and behaviour of nanoparticles, ensuring their safety and efficacy.

Case Study: Curcumin Nanoparticles

1. **DLS and TEM:** Ensure uniform particle size and spherical morphology.
2. **Zeta Potential:** Confirms colloidal stability for long-term storage.

3. **XRD and FTIR:** Validate chemical composition and crystalline structure.
4. **UV-Visible Spectroscopy:** Monitors optical stability over time.
5. **TGA and DSC:** Assess thermal stability during processing and application.

Future Directions in Nanoparticle Characterization

1. **Advanced Imaging Techniques:** Emerging methods like Atomic Force Microscopy (AFM) and Cryo-TEM provide even greater resolution and detail, enabling more precise characterization of nanoparticles.
2. **Machine Learning in Characterization:** AI and machine learning algorithms can analyze large datasets from characterization techniques, accelerating the development of optimized nanoparticles for Ayurvedic applications.
3. **In Vivo Characterization:** Techniques like biodistribution studies and pharmacokinetic analysis are essential for understanding how nanoparticles behave in biological systems, ensuring their safety and efficacy in therapeutic contexts.

Applications of Nanoparticles in Ayurvedic Formulations

The incorporation of nanotechnology into Ayurveda, often referred to as Nano-Ayurveda, has opened new frontiers in traditional medicine. Nanotechnology addresses some of the inherent challenges in Ayurvedic formulations, such as low bioavailability, poor solubility, and degradation of active ingredients. By leveraging the unique properties of nanoparticles, Ayurvedic treatments can be refined to enhance their therapeutic efficacy, precision, and stability. This chapter elaborates on the numerous applications of nanoparticles in Ayurvedic formulations, providing detailed insights into their transformative potential.

1. **Herbal Nano-Formulations:** Herbal extracts, central to Ayurvedic medicine, often face challenges like poor bioavailability, instability, and degradation in biological systems. Nanoparticles offer solutions to these limitations by encapsulating bioactive compounds, protecting them from degradation, and enhancing their absorption in the body.

   Curcumin Nanoparticles: Curcumin, the active compound in turmeric (Curcuma longa), is widely recognized for its anti-inflammatory, antioxidant, and anticancer properties. However, its low water solubility and rapid metabolism limit its therapeutic potential. Nanoparticle-based curcumin formulations significantly enhance its bioavailability, allowing for improved systemic absorption and prolonged therapeutic action. Studies have demonstrated that curcumin nanoparticles are more effective in reducing inflammation and suppressing tumor growth compared to traditional formulations. Their ability to cross biological barriers further expands their applications in treating neurodegenerative disorders like Alzheimer's disease.

   Neem (*Azadirachta indica*) **Nano-Extracts:** Neem is known for its antimicrobial, anti-inflammatory, and immunomodulatory properties. Nano-extracts of neem enhance these benefits by improving the penetration of bioactive compounds into infected tissues. For instance, neem nanoparticles are highly effective against bacterial biofilms, which are often resistant to conventional treatments. Furthermore, the antifungal properties of neem are amplified when its extracts are delivered in nanoparticle form, providing a targeted approach to infections like candidiasis.

   Ashwagandha Nano-Formulations: Ashwagandha (*Withania somnifera*) is a key adaptogenic herb in Ayurveda, renowned for its neuroprotective, anti-stress, and immune-boosting effects. Nano-formulations of ashwagandha improve its bioavailability and therapeutic efficacy. These nanoparticles enhance the delivery of withanolides, the primary bioactive compounds in ashwagandha, to the central nervous system. This targeted delivery has shown promise in treating stress-related disorders, neurodegenerative conditions, and immune dysregulation.

2. **Metal and Mineral Nanoparticles (Bhasmas):** Ayurveda has a long-standing tradition of using metallic preparations called bhasmas, known for their therapeutic properties. Nanotechnology provides a modern framework for refining these bhasmas, ensuring uniform particle size and composition. This approach enhances their safety, stability, and bioavailability.

   Gold Nanoparticles (Swarna Bhasma): Swarna Bhasma, a gold-based preparation, is used in Ayurveda for its rejuvenating and immunomodulatory properties. Modern nanotechnology enables the synthesis of gold nanoparticles with precise size and shape, which replicate the therapeutic effects of traditional Swarna Bhasma. Gold nanoparticles have shown remarkable anti-inflammatory, antioxidant, and antitumor effects. Their ability to modulate immune responses makes them valuable in treating autoimmune disorders and enhancing overall vitality.

   Silver Nanoparticles (Rajata Bhasma): Rajata Bhasma, or silver-based Ayurvedic preparations, is traditionally used for its antimicrobial and wound-healing properties. Silver nanoparticles, derived from Ayurvedic principles, exhibit enhanced antibacterial, antiviral, and antifungal effects. When combined with herbal extracts like Aloe vera, these nanoparticles accelerate wound healing by promoting tissue regeneration and preventing infections. They are also effective against antibiotic-resistant pathogens, providing a modern solution to one of the biggest challenges in contemporary medicine.

Iron Nanoparticles (Lohabhasma): Lohabhasma, an iron-based preparation, is widely used in Ayurveda to treat anemia and enhance energy levels. Nanoparticle formulations of Lohabhasma improve iron absorption and minimize gastrointestinal side effects commonly associated with traditional iron supplements. These nanoparticles also show promise in treating iron deficiency-related cognitive impairments and fatigue, aligning with Ayurveda's holistic approach to restoring vitality.

3. **Targeted Drug Delivery Systems:** One of the most revolutionary applications of nanoparticles in Ayurvedic medicine is their ability to deliver bioactive compounds to specific tissues or cells. This targeted approach minimizes systemic side effects and maximizes therapeutic efficacy.

   Tumor-Targeting Nanoparticles: Cancer treatment often requires precise targeting to avoid damaging healthy cells. Nanoparticles enable the delivery of anticancer Ayurvedic bioactives, such as curcumin or resveratrol, directly to tumor cells. These nanoparticles are functionalized with ligands that bind specifically to cancer cell receptors, ensuring localized treatment. This approach reduces toxicity and improves the efficacy of natural compounds, making them viable alternatives or complements to conventional chemotherapy.

   Anti-Inflammatory Nano-Formulations: Inflammatory conditions like arthritis require localized treatment to reduce pain and swelling without systemic side effects. Nanoparticles loaded with anti-inflammatory Ayurvedic bioactives, such as Boswellia or ginger extracts, deliver the compounds directly to inflamed tissues. This targeted delivery reduces systemic exposure and enhances the therapeutic effects, providing long-lasting relief.

4. **Wound Healing and Skin Applications:** The integration of nanoparticles into Ayurvedic wound-healing and skincare formulations offers enhanced regenerative properties, antimicrobial effects, and improved absorption.

   Silver Nanoparticles for Wound Healing: Silver nanoparticles, combined with Ayurvedic herbs like neem and Aloe vera, accelerate wound healing by promoting angiogenesis and collagen synthesis. These formulations prevent microbial infections, ensuring a sterile environment for tissue regeneration. Their application is particularly beneficial in diabetic wounds and chronic ulcers, where conventional treatments often fail.

   Nanoparticles in Skin Rejuvenation: Ayurvedic formulations containing gold or herbal nanoparticles are increasingly being used in anti-aging and skin rejuvenation products. These nanoparticles penetrate deep into the skin layers, delivering bioactives that reduce wrinkles, improve elasticity, and promote hydration. Herbal extracts like saffron and sandalwood, when incorporated into nanoparticles, further enhance skin health by providing antioxidant and anti-inflammatory effects.

5. **Theranostics:** Theranostics is an emerging field that combines therapeutic and diagnostic functionalities in a single platform. Nanoparticles offer significant potential in Ayurvedic theranostics, enabling real-time monitoring of treatment efficacy.

   Curcumin-Loaded Theranostic Nanoparticles: Curcumin nanoparticles provide therapeutic effects through their anti-inflammatory and anticancer properties while enabling fluorescence imaging for diagnostic purposes. This dual functionality allows clinicians to monitor the progression of treatment, ensuring optimal outcomes. Such theranostic applications align with Ayurveda's holistic philosophy of diagnosing and treating diseases simultaneously.

   Gold Nanoparticles in Diagnostics and Therapy: Gold nanoparticles are used in both diagnostics and treatment. Their optical properties enable imaging techniques like Surface-Enhanced Raman Spectroscopy (SERS), while their therapeutic effects support immune modulation and anti-inflammatory applications. This combination provides a comprehensive approach to disease management, integrating ancient Ayurvedic wisdom with modern diagnostic tools.

6. **Bioavailability Enhancement:** One of the most significant contributions of nanotechnology to Ayurveda is the enhancement of bioavailability for poorly soluble herbal compounds. Nanoparticles protect bioactives from degradation, improve solubility, and ensure better absorption.

Resveratrol Nanoparticles

Resveratrol, a polyphenol with antioxidant and anti-inflammatory properties, suffers from poor bioavailability due to rapid metabolism. Encapsulation in nanoparticles enhances its stability and absorption, ensuring sustained therapeutic effects. This aligns with Ayurveda's goal of maximizing the efficacy of natural remedies.

Quercetin Nanoparticles

Quercetin, found in Ayurvedic herbs like amla, exhibits cardioprotective and anti-inflammatory properties. However, its poor water solubility limits its therapeutic application. Quercetin nanoparticles overcome this challenge by improving its solubility and cellular uptake, making it a powerful tool for managing cardiovascular and inflammatory diseases.

Catechin Nano-Formulations

Catechins, abundant in green tea and Ayurvedic herbs, are potent antioxidants but suffer from low bioavailability. Nanoparticle-based formulations enhance their absorption, providing stronger protection against oxidative stress and chronic diseases. This application aligns with Ayurveda's emphasis on preventive health care.

Future Directions in Nano-Ayurveda

1. **Personalized Medicine:** Nanotechnology can facilitate customized Ayurvedic treatments based on individual Prakriti (constitution) and dosha imbalances.
2. **Eco-Friendly Nanoparticles:** Green nanotechnology, which uses plant-based synthesis methods, aligns with Ayurveda's natural and sustainable principles.
3. **Integration with Modern Medicine:** Combining Nano-Ayurveda with allopathic treatments can create synergistic approaches to managing complex diseases.

Case Studies of Nano-Ayurveda

1. **Nano-Curcumin in Cancer Therapy:** Curcumin's anticancer properties are well-documented but limited by poor solubility. Nano-curcumin formulations overcome these challenges, enhancing cellular uptake and bioavailability. Studies demonstrate significant tumor reduction and improved patient outcomes with nano-curcumin therapies.
2. **Gold Nanoparticles (Swarna Bhasma) for Immunity:** Swarna Bhasma, an ancient Ayurvedic preparation, has been re-engineered using nanotechnology. Modern gold nanoparticles replicate Swarna Bhasma's immunomodulatory effects, providing evidence-based support for its use in managing chronic diseases and enhancing vitality.
3. **Neem Nano-Formulations for Antimicrobial Therapy:** Neem's antimicrobial properties are enhanced through nanoparticle formulations, allowing targeted action against bacterial and fungal infections. This application demonstrates how nanotechnology can refine traditional herbal treatments for modern therapeutic challenges.

CHALLENGES AND FUTURE DIRECTIONS

Challenges

1. **Standardization:** Ensuring consistency and quality in nano-formulations is critical for widespread adoption.
2. **Toxicity:** Nanoparticles' small size may pose risks of toxicity or bioaccumulation if not properly regulated.
3. **Cost:** The production and characterization of nanoparticles can be expensive, limiting accessibility.
4. **Regulatory Hurdles:** Establishing guidelines for the use of nanotechnology in Ayurvedic medicine remains a challenge.

Future Directions

1. **Personalized Medicine:** Nanotechnology can facilitate customized Ayurvedic treatments based on individual Prakriti and dosha imbalances.
2. **Sustainable Nanoparticles:** Developing eco-friendly synthesis methods, such as green nanotechnology, aligns with Ayurveda's emphasis on natural processes.
3. **Integration with Modern Medicine:** Combining Nano-Ayurveda with allopathic treatments can create synergistic approaches to complex diseases.

MULTIPLE CHOICE QUESTIONS

1. A clinical researcher is exploring the therapeutic application of gold nanoparticles derived from Swarna Bhasma. During the study, it is found that these nanoparticles demonstrate remarkable selectivity toward tumor cells due to their functionalized ligands. This selectivity minimizes systemic toxicity and enhances drug delivery efficacy. Based on these findings, which of the following mechanisms explains the action of these nanoparticles?

   A. Functionalized ligands ensure precise binding to tumor-specific receptors, minimizing harm to healthy tissues.

B. Gold nanoparticles act universally, targeting both healthy and cancerous tissues without discrimination.

C. Tumor-specific receptor binding is irrelevant, as the nanoparticles rely solely on their size for efficacy.

D. The therapeutic potential of nanoparticles is independent of functionalization or receptor targeting.

2. In a study assessing the antimicrobial properties of silver nanoparticles derived from Rajata Bhasma, researchers observed significant bacterial inhibition through reactive oxygen species (ROS) generation and quorum sensing disruption. These effects were particularly noted in multidrug-resistant bacterial strains. Which of the following interpretations aligns most closely with these results?

A. Silver nanoparticles stabilize bacterial cell membranes, promoting microbial growth.

B. ROS generation disrupts bacterial cellular functions, leading to effective antimicrobial activity.

C. The antimicrobial effects of silver nanoparticles are independent of ROS generation or quorum sensing disruption.

D. Silver nanoparticles exhibit passive antimicrobial activity without affecting bacterial metabolism.

3. A sustainability study on iron nanoparticles derived from Loha Bhasma highlights their enhanced absorption efficiency and minimal gastrointestinal side effects in treating iron-deficiency anemia. It is observed that these nanoparticles improve hemoglobin synthesis and reduce oxidative stress. Which of the following explanations supports these findings?

A. Nanoparticles bypass gastrointestinal absorption, directly increasing red blood cell counts.

B. The nanoscale size of iron particles enhances bioavailability while reducing oxidative side effects.

C. Enhanced therapeutic efficacy is independent of the nanoparticles' size and absorption pathways.

D. Iron nanoparticles are excreted quickly, limiting their impact on systemic oxygen transport.

4. Zinc nanoparticles synthesized from Yashad Bhasma have demonstrated potent UV-protective and antioxidative properties, making them effective in sunscreen formulations. Researchers attribute these effects to the nanoparticles' ability to neutralize free radicals and form a physical barrier against harmful radiation. Which of the following conclusions can be drawn from this study?

A. Zinc nanoparticles enhance cellular repair while preventing oxidative damage through UV protection.

B. The antioxidative properties of zinc nanoparticles diminish their ability to block UV rays.

C. Zinc nanoparticles protect against UV rays, but their effects are independent of antioxidative mechanisms.

D. Nanoparticles exacerbate oxidative stress, reducing the efficacy of sunscreen formulations.

5. Researchers have developed lipid-encapsulated herbal bioactives, such as curcumin, to improve stability, controlled release, and bioavailability. In a clinical trial, these encapsulated systems demonstrated significantly enhanced therapeutic outcomes. Which principle of nanotechnology explains this improvement?

A. Lipid encapsulation stabilizes bioactives, preventing degradation and enabling sustained therapeutic release.

B. Encapsulation inhibits the therapeutic efficacy of bioactives by altering their chemical composition.

C. Lipid nanocarriers destabilize bioactives, reducing their potency and absorption.

D. Bioactives encapsulated in lipid systems fail to demonstrate consistent therapeutic benefits.

6. Gold nanoparticles functionalized with herbal bioactives exhibit the ability to cross the blood-brain barrier, making them highly effective in treating neurological disorders such as Alzheimer's disease. Their nanoscale size and specific receptor-binding properties enable targeted delivery to neural tissues. Which of the following best describes the mechanism underlying this action?

A. The nanoscale dimensions of gold particles allow precise interaction with neural receptors, enhancing efficacy.

B. Gold nanoparticles bypass neural tissues, limiting their application in neurological treatments.

C. Their therapeutic potential is independent of particle size or receptor interaction in the nervous system.

D. Gold nanoparticles reduce the bioavailability of therapeutic agents in neural tissues.

7. A comparative study evaluates the stability of traditional Bhasmas versus nanoparticle formulations. It is observed that nanoparticle-based Bhasmas demonstrate enhanced stability under physiological conditions, reducing degradation and improving therapeutic efficacy. What mechanism could explain this observation?

A. The increased surface-to-volume ratio of nanoparticles enhances stability, minimizing chemical degradation.

B. Nanoparticles exhibit lower stability than traditional Bhasmas, reducing their systemic circulation time.

C. Stability improvements in nanoparticles are irrelevant to their therapeutic benefits.

D. Traditional Bhasmas are inherently more stable than nanoparticles, ensuring consistent efficacy.

8. In wound healing applications, Neem oil encapsulated in lipid nanocarriers demonstrates prolonged retention at the wound site and sustained antimicrobial activity. This retention enhances therapeutic outcomes by reducing microbial load and promoting tissue regeneration. How does nanocarrier encapsulation improve the efficacy of Neem oil?
   A. Encapsulation limits therapeutic effects by reducing the concentration of active compounds.
   B. Prolonged retention and controlled release ensure consistent antimicrobial activity and tissue repair.
   C. Encapsulation decreases the bioavailability of Neem oil, limiting its therapeutic potential.
   D. The nanocarrier reduces systemic effects without enhancing local efficacy.

9. A sustainability study highlights the environmental challenges of traditional Bhasma preparation methods, including mining and ecological degradation. Green synthesis techniques, involving plant-based reduction, are proposed as alternatives. What is the primary benefit of adopting these techniques?
   A. Green synthesis increases the environmental toxicity of nanoparticle production.
   B. Plant-based methods reduce toxic byproducts, ensuring environmentally sustainable nanoparticle synthesis.
   C. Green synthesis compromises the therapeutic efficacy of metallic nanoparticles.
   D. Traditional preparation methods are more environmentally friendly than green synthesis techniques.

10. Researchers reformulated Triphala using nanoparticle delivery systems, observing improved gut microbiota modulation and reduced systemic inflammation in patients with irritable bowel syndrome (IBS). Which mechanism best explains the enhanced therapeutic efficacy of nanoparticle-based Triphala?
   A. Nanoparticles destabilize gut microbiota, amplifying therapeutic outcomes.
   B. Enhanced bioavailability and controlled release of bioactives improve gut microbiota diversity and immune function.
   C. Nanoparticles reduce the efficacy of Triphala by altering its natural composition.
   D. Improved therapeutic outcomes are independent of bioactive stabilization or gut health modulation.

Directions (Q. No. 11-14): *Scenario-Based Questions*

SCENARIO 1

A clinical trial evaluates the effects of nanoparticle-enhanced Triphala formulations on gut health and systemic immunity in patients with irritable bowel syndrome (IBS). The study finds that the formulation significantly improves gut microbiota diversity, leading to increased gut-associated lymphoid tissue (GALT) activity. This improvement corresponds with elevated immunoglobulin A (IgA) levels and reduced systemic inflammation. Researchers hypothesize that these outcomes are driven by the enhanced bioavailability and targeted delivery of bioactives in the nanoparticle formulation.

SCENARIO 2

An environmental biologist investigates the sustainability of sourcing Amalaki (a key ingredient in Triphala). Findings reveal that overharvesting has led to reduced wild populations, while deforestation and soil degradation have diminished the bioactive compound concentration in the fruit. These environmental challenges not only threaten the sustainability of Amalaki but also reduce the therapeutic efficacy of Triphala. Researchers propose agroforestry systems and community-driven conservation initiatives to address these issues.

11. Based on Scenario 1, which of the following mechanisms best explains the enhanced systemic immunity observed in patients treated with nanoparticle-enhanced Triphala?
   A. Nanoparticle-enhanced Triphala directly stimulates IgA production, independent of gut health.
   B. Improved gut microbiota diversity enhances GALT activity, promoting systemic immunity.
   C. Nanoparticles reduce gut microbiota diversity but strengthen the gut's physical barrier, indirectly improving immunity.
   D. The immune enhancement is unrelated to gut health and is likely due to placebo effects.

12. Considering Scenario 2, which of the following interventions would most effectively address the sustainability challenges associated with Amalaki harvesting while ensuring its medicinal quality?
   A. Establishing monoculture plantations of Amalaki to meet global demand.
   B. Promoting agroforestry systems and community-driven conservation efforts for wild Amalaki populations.
   C. Substituting Amalaki with synthetic alternatives to reduce dependency on natural resources.
   D. Reducing global production of Triphala to conserve wild Amalaki populations.

13. How does the environmental degradation of Amalaki, as described in Scenario 2, potentially influence the therapeutic outcomes observed in Scenario 1?
   A. Reduced bioactive compound concentrations in Amalaki could diminish its efficacy in promoting gut microbiota diversity and systemic immunity.

B. The therapeutic efficacy of Triphala is unaffected by Amalaki's bioactive content, as its potency is driven by the combination of all three fruits.
C. Environmental degradation enhances the potency of Amalaki, improving the overall therapeutic outcomes of Triphala.
D. Triphala's benefits remain consistent despite the environmental challenges affecting Amalaki.

14. Based on the interconnected findings of Scenarios 1 and 2, which of the following strategies would most comprehensively address the challenges while maintaining the efficacy of Ayurvedic formulations?
A. Developing synthetic alternatives that mimic the bioactive profile of Amalaki.
B. Establishing global quality standards for Triphala production, incorporating sustainable harvesting practices.
C. Shifting focus to other formulations that do not rely on endangered plant species.
D. Encouraging large-scale production of Triphala ingredients independent of traditional Ayurvedic practices.

15. Nanoparticle formulations of Swarna Bhasma are developed to target specific tissues with minimal side effects. These formulations rely on various factors:
(a) Enhanced solubility of therapeutic agents.
(b) Functionalized ligands for targeted tissue delivery.
(c) Stability under physiological conditions.
(d) Selectivity for diseased cells over healthy tissues.

Choose the correct answer from the options given below:
A. (a), (b), and (c) only
B. (a), (b), and (d) only
C. (b), (c), and (d) only
D. (a), (b), (c), and (d)

16. Zinc nanoparticles synthesized from Yashad Bhasma exhibit properties beneficial in dermatological applications. The following characteristics contribute to their efficacy:
(a) Antioxidative properties neutralizing free radicals.
(b) Formation of a physical barrier against UV radiation.
(c) Antimicrobial effects promoting wound healing.
(d) Disruption of normal cell regeneration cycles.

Choose the correct answer from the options given below:
A. (a), (b), and (c) only
B. (a), (c), and (d) only
C. (b), (c), and (d) only
D. (a), (b), and (d) only

17. Green synthesis of nanoparticles aligns with sustainable Ayurvedic practices. Key benefits of this approach include:
(a) Reduction of toxic byproducts.
(b) Conservation of biodiversity through reduced ecological impact.
(c) Enhanced bioactivity of synthesized nanoparticles.
(d) Increased dependency on synthetic chemicals for production.

Choose the correct answer from the options given below:
A. (a), (b), and (d) only
B. (a), (c), and (d) only
C. (b), (c), and (d) only
D. (a), (b), and (c) only

18. Nanoparticles in Rajata Bhasma formulations exhibit antimicrobial properties due to:
(a) ROS generation disrupting bacterial metabolism.
(b) Targeted binding to bacterial cell membranes.
(c) Quorum sensing disruption in bacterial colonies.
(d) Stabilization of bacterial growth.

Choose the correct answer from the options given below:
A. (a), (b), and (c) only
B. (a), (b), and (d) only
C. (b), (c), and (d) only
D. (a), (c), and (d) only

19. Lipid nanocarriers improve the bioavailability of poorly soluble herbal bioactives. These improvements are achieved through:
(a) Encapsulation preventing enzymatic degradation.
(b) Controlled release ensuring prolonged therapeutic action.
(c) Direct bypassing of the liver's metabolic pathways.
(d) Increased particle size to enhance solubility.

Choose the correct answer from the options given below:
A. (a), (b), and (c) only
B. (a), (b), and (d) only
C. (b), (c), and (d) only
D. (a), (c), and (d) only

20. Iron nanoparticles from Loha Bhasma are utilized in treating anemia. Their unique properties include:
(a) Enhanced gastrointestinal absorption due to nanoscale dimensions.
(b) Reduced oxidative stress during hemoglobin synthesis.
(c) Prolonged systemic circulation enhancing therapeutic outcomes.

(d) Inhibition of natural hemoglobin production.

Choose the correct answer from the options given below:

A. (a), (b), and (c) only
B. (a), (b), and (d) only
C. (b), (c), and (d) only
D. (a), (c), and (d) only

21. Functionalized gold nanoparticles exhibit precision targeting in oncology due to:

(a) Tumor-specific ligand binding.
(b) Enhanced permeability across cellular membranes.
(c) Suppression of immune response against the tumor.
(d) Increased bioavailability of therapeutic agents.

Choose the correct answer from the options given below:

A. (a), (b), and (c) only
B. (a), (c), and (d) only
C. (b), (c), and (d) only
D. (a), (b), and (d) only

22. Encapsulation of Neem oil in nanocarriers improves therapeutic outcomes by:

(a) Enhancing retention on wound surfaces.
(b) Ensuring controlled release of bioactives.
(c) Promoting enzymatic degradation of active compounds.
(d) Reducing systemic absorption and efficacy.

Choose the correct answer from the options given below:

A. (a), (b), and (c) only
B. (a), (b), and (d) only
C. (b), (c), and (d) only
D. (a), (c), and (d) only

23. Nanoparticles in Triphala formulations improve gut health through:

(a) Modulation of gut microbiota diversity.
(b) Targeted delivery to gut-associated lymphoid tissues (GALT).
(c) Reduction of inflammatory markers in the gut.
(d) Suppression of beneficial gut bacteria.

Choose the correct answer from the options given below:

A. (a), (b), and (c) only
B. (a), (b), and (d) only
C. (b), (c), and (d) only
D. (a), (c), and (d) only

24. The sustainability of Ayurvedic nanoparticle formulations can be improved through:

(a) Adoption of plant-based reduction methods in synthesis.
(b) Promotion of agroforestry for sourcing raw materials.
(c) Substitution of metallic nanoparticles with synthetic polymers.
(d) Incorporation of standardized production protocols.

Choose the correct answer from the options given below:

A. (a), (b), and (c) only
B. (a), (b), and (d) only
C. (b), (c), and (d) only
D. (a), (c), and (d) only

25. Match List–I (Nanoparticle Properties) with List–II (Applications) and choose the correct answer from the options given below:

List–I	List–II
(a) Antioxidative action	1. Skin regeneration and UV protection
(b) ROS generation	2. Antimicrobial activity
(c) Ligand functionalization	3. Targeted drug delivery in cancer
(d) Controlled release	4. Sustained therapeutic action

Choose the correct answer from the options given below:

A. (a)-1, (b)-2, (c)-3, (d)-4
B. (a)-4, (b)-1, (c)-2, (d)-3
C. (a)-1, (b)-3, (c)-4, (d)-2
D. (a)-2, (b)-4, (c)-3, (d)-1

26. Match List–I (Green Synthesis Techniques) with List–II (Advantages) and choose the correct answer from the options given below:

List–I	List–II
(a) Plant-based reduction	1. Minimizes toxic byproducts
(b) Biodegradable carriers	2. Enhances nanoparticle stability
(c) Microbial synthesis	3. Reduces dependency on synthetic chemicals
(d) Standardized methods	4. Ensures consistent therapeutic outcomes

Choose the correct answer from the options given below:

A. (a)-3, (b)-1, (c)-2, (d)-4
B. (a)-1, (b)-4, (c)-3, (d)-2
C. (a)-1, (b)-3, (c)-4, (d)-2
D. (a)-2, (b)-3, (c)-1, (d)-4

27. Match List–I (Metallic Nanoparticles) with List–II (Therapeutic Effects) and choose the correct answer from the options given below:

List–I	List–II
(a) Gold nanoparticles	1. Anti-inflammatory and rejuvenative properties
(b) Silver nanoparticles	2. Antimicrobial activity and detoxification
(c) Iron nanoparticles	3. Enhanced hemoglobin synthesis
(d) Zinc nanoparticles	4. UV protection and skin repair

Choose the correct answer from the options given below:

A. (a)-2, (b)-4, (c)-1, (d)-3
B. (a)-1, (b)-2, (c)-3, (d)-4
C. (a)-4, (b)-3, (c)-2, (d)-1
D. (a)-3, (b)-1, (c)-4, (d)-2

28. Match List–I (Challenges in Nanotechnology) with List–II (Solutions) and choose the correct answer from the options given below:

List–I	List–II
(a) Poor solubility of bioactives	1. Lipid encapsulation techniques
(b) Environmental toxicity	2. Green synthesis methods
(c) Stability issues	3. Functionalized nanoparticle systems
(d) Therapeutic variability	4. Standardized production protocols

Choose the correct answer from the options given below:

A. (a)-1, (b)-2, (c)-3, (d)-4
B. (a)-3, (b)-1, (c)-4, (d)-2
C. (a)-1, (b)-4, (c)-2, (d)-3
D. (a)-2, (b)-3, (c)-1, (d)-4

29. Match List–I (Bhasma Types) with List–II (Primary Components) and choose the correct answer from the options given below:

List–I	List–II
(a) Swarna Bhasma	1. Gold nanoparticles
(b) Rajata Bhasma	2. Silver nanoparticles
(c) Loha Bhasma	3. Iron nanoparticles
(d) Yashad Bhasma	4. Zinc nanoparticles

Choose the correct answer from the options given below:

A. (a)-2, (b)-3, (c)-1, (d)-4
B. (a)-1, (b)-2, (c)-3, (d)-4
C. (a)-4, (b)-1, (c)-2, (d)-3
D. (a)-3, (b)-4, (c)-1, (d)-2

30. Match List–I (Nanoparticle Features) with List–II (Functions) and choose the correct answer from the options given below:

List–I	List–II
(a) High surface-to-volume ratio	1. Enhanced cellular interaction
(b) Functionalized surfaces	2. Precision targeting of tissues
(c) Controlled release	3. Sustained therapeutic efficacy
(d) Stability in circulation	4. Reduced enzymatic degradation

Choose the correct answer from the options given below:

A. (a)-3, (b)-4, (c)-1, (d)-2
B. (a)-1, (b)-2, (c)-3, (d)-4
C. (a)-4, (b)-3, (c)-2, (d)-1
D. (a)-2, (b)-1, (c)-4, (d)-3

31. Match List–I (Applications of Bhasmas) with List–II (Nanotechnology Enhancements) and choose the correct answer from the options given below:

List–I	List–II
(a) Antimicrobial therapy	1. Enhanced ROS generation
(b) Cancer treatment	2. Targeted ligand binding
(c) Wound healing	3. Prolonged retention at the site
(d) Dermatology	4. UV protection and antioxidation

Choose the correct answer from the options given below:

A. (a)-4, (b)-3, (c)-2, (d)-1
B. (a)-1, (b)-2, (c)-3, (d)-4
C. (a)-3, (b)-4, (c)-1, (d)-2
D. (a)-2, (b)-1, (c)-4, (d)-3

32. Match List–I (Sustainability Challenges) with List–II (Proposed Solutions) and choose the correct answer from the options given below:

List–I	List–II
(a) Overharvesting of plants	1. Agroforestry systems
(b) Toxicity in nano-particle synthesis	2. Green synthesis methods
(c) Therapeutic inconsistency	3. Standardized quality control
(d) High environmental footprint	4. Biodegradable carriers

Choose the correct answer from the options given below:

A. (a)-1, (b)-2, (c)-3, (d)-4
B. (a)-2, (b)-1, (c)-4, (d)-3
C. (a)-3, (b)-4, (c)-2, (d)-1
D. (a)-4, (b)-3, (c)-1, (d)-2

33. Match List–I (Key Ayurvedic Principles) with List–II (Nanotechnology Applications) and choose the correct answer from the options given below:

List–I	List–II
(a) Sukshma Bhaag	1. Nanoscale penetration
(b) Anupana	2. Enhanced carrier systems
(c) Sanskara	3. Functionalization for improved properties
(d) Virya	4. Stability under physiological conditions

Choose the correct answer from the options given below:

A. (a)-3, (b)-4, (c)-1, (d)-2
B. (a)-1, (b)-2, (c)-3, (d)-4
C. (a)-4, (b)-3, (c)-2, (d)-1
D. (a)-2, (b)-1, (c)-4, (d)-3

34. Match List–I (Nanoparticle-Based Enhancements) with List–II (Therapeutic Advantages) and choose the correct answer from the options given below:

List–I	List–II
(a) Functionalized surfaces	1. Tissue-specific targeting
(b) Lipid encapsu-lation	2. Enhanced bioavailability
(c) High stability	3. Prolonged systemic circulation
(d) Controlled release	4. Sustained therapeutic action

Choose the correct answer from the options given below:

A. (a)-1, (b)-2, (c)-3, (d)-4
B. (a)-2, (b)-4, (c)-1, (d)-3
C. (a)-4, (b)-3, (c)-2, (d)-1
D. (a)-3, (b)-1, (c)-4, (d)-2

Directions (Q. No. 35–39): *Following questions are based on Statement 1 and Statement 2. Read both the statements carefully and choose the correct answer from the options given below:*

A. Both Statement 1 and Statement 2 are true, and Statement 2 is the correct explanation of Statement 1.
B. Both Statement 1 and Statement 2 are true, but Statement 2 is not the correct explanation of Statement 1.
C. Statement 1 is true, but Statement 2 is false.
D. Statement 1 is false, but Statement 2 is true.

35. **Statement 1:** Nanotechnology enhances the therapeutic potential of Swarna Bhasma by improving its stability and targeted delivery mechanisms.

Statement 2: Functionalized gold nanoparticles derived from Swarna Bhasma can selectively target cancer cells, minimizing systemic toxicity.

36. **Statement 1:** Silver nanoparticles from Rajata Bhasma disrupt bacterial metabolism by generating ROS and inhibiting quorum sensing.

Statement 2: This antimicrobial activity of silver nanoparticles reduces microbial diversity in healthy gut microbiota.

37. **Statement 1:** Iron nanoparticles from Loha Bhasma improve hemoglobin synthesis and oxygen transport while minimizing oxidative stress.

Statement 2: These nanoparticles are absorbed directly into the bloodstream, bypassing gastrointestinal metabolism.

38. **Statement 1:** Nanoparticle formulations of Triphala enhance gut health by promoting microbial diversity and reducing inflammation.

Statement 2: These formulations are less effective in modulating gut microbiota compared to traditional Triphala.

39. **Statement 1:** Zinc nanoparticles derived from Yashad Bhasma exhibit UV-protective and antioxidative properties, making them effective in dermatological applications.

Statement 2: These properties are attributed to the high surface-to-volume ratio of zinc nanoparticles, which enhances their antioxidative action.

Directions (Q. No. 40–45): *There are two statements in each question. One is labelled as Assertion (A) and the other is as Reason (R). Read both the statements and choose the correct answer from the options given below:*

A. Both Assertion (A) and Reason (R) are true, and Reason (R) is the correct explanation of Assertion (A).
B. Both Assertion (A) and Reason (R) are true, but Reason (R) is not the correct explanation of Assertion (A).
C. Assertion (A) is true, but Reason (R) is false.
D. Assertion (A) is false, but Reason (R) is true.

40. **Assertion (A):** Nanoparticles enhance the bioavailability of poorly soluble bioactives by improving their solubility and stability in physiological environments.

Reason (R): Encapsulation of bioactives in lipid or polymeric nanocarriers protects them from enzymatic degradation and ensures controlled release.

41. **Assertion (A):** Iron nanoparticles derived from Loha Bhasma directly enhance hemoglobin synthesis and oxygen transport.

Reason (R): These nanoparticles bypass gastrointestinal absorption entirely, reducing side effects associated with traditional iron supplements.

42. Assertion (A): Silver nanoparticles synthesized from Rajata Bhasma demonstrate potent antimicrobial activity against multidrug-resistant pathogens.

Reason (R): The antimicrobial properties of silver nanoparticles are primarily due to their ability to stabilize bacterial cell membranes and promote microbial growth.

43. Assertion (A): Zinc nanoparticles from Yashad Bhasma provide effective UV protection and antioxidative benefits in dermatological formulations.

Reason (R): These nanoparticles inhibit normal cellular regeneration processes, limiting their therapeutic applications.

44. Assertion (A): Nanoparticle formulations of Triphala enhance gut microbiota diversity and reduce systemic inflammation in patients with irritable bowel syndrome (IBS).

Reason (R): Nanoparticles destabilize gut microbiota, improving therapeutic efficacy through gut-associated lymphoid tissue (GALT) activity.

45. Assertion (A): Green synthesis techniques for nanoparticles align with Ayurvedic principles of ecological harmony and sustainability.

Reason (R): Plant-based synthesis methods reduce toxic byproducts and promote environmentally friendly production processes.

Directions (Q. No. 46–50): *Read the passage carefully and answer the questions given below*:

Nanotechnology has emerged as a revolutionary field in the healthcare domain, offering unprecedented opportunities to enhance the efficacy and delivery of traditional medicines, including Ayurveda. Ayurveda, one of the world's oldest holistic healing systems, emphasizes the balance between mind, body, and spirit to achieve optimal health. Traditionally, Ayurveda relied on Bhasmas (metallic or mineral-based formulations) and herbal preparations to treat a myriad of ailments. However, with the integration of nanotechnology, the therapeutic potential of these ancient remedies has been significantly amplified, bridging the gap between ancient wisdom and modern scientific rigor.

At the core of nanotechnology's application in Ayurveda is the development of nanoparticles—particles with dimensions less than 100 nanometers. These particles possess unique physicochemical properties, such as high surface-to-volume ratios, functionalizability, and enhanced stability under physiological conditions. These attributes allow nanoparticles to interact with biological systems at the molecular level, enabling precise targeting of diseased cells and improved bioavailability of therapeutic agents. Nanoparticles derived from Bhasmas—including Swarna Bhasma (gold), Rajata Bhasma (silver), Loha Bhasma (iron), and Yashad Bhasma (zinc)—have become central to this transformative approach.

One of the most promising applications of nanotechnology in Ayurveda is in oncology. Gold nanoparticles synthesized from Swarna Bhasma have demonstrated exceptional potential in cancer treatment. Functionalized with tumor-specific ligands, these nanoparticles selectively target cancer cells while sparing healthy tissues, thus minimizing systemic toxicity. Their nanoscale size allows them to penetrate tumor microenvironments effectively and deliver therapeutic agents precisely where needed. This aligns with Ayurveda's principle of individualized treatments, where therapies are tailored to the specific needs of the patient. By integrating nanotechnology, traditional Ayurvedic practices can now address complex conditions like cancer with heightened precision and efficacy.

Similarly, silver nanoparticles derived from Rajata Bhasma exhibit potent antimicrobial properties, making them invaluable in the fight against multidrug-resistant pathogens. These nanoparticles disrupt bacterial cell membranes, generate reactive oxygen species (ROS), and inhibit quorum sensing, effectively neutralizing bacterial colonies. This mechanism validates Ayurveda's traditional use of Rajata Bhasma for detoxification and infection management. Furthermore, the broad-spectrum antimicrobial activity of silver nanoparticles offers a modern solution to contemporary healthcare challenges, such as hospital-acquired infections and antibiotic resistance.

In dermatology, zinc nanoparticles from Yashad Bhasma have proven highly effective. These nanoparticles provide dual benefits: UV protection and antioxidative action. By neutralizing free radicals, zinc nanoparticles prevent oxidative stress, which is a primary cause of skin aging and damage. Additionally, their ability to form a physical barrier against UV radiation enhances their utility in sunscreen formulations. This dual action not only supports skin health but also aligns with Ayurveda's emphasis on maintaining ojas (vital energy) for overall well-being.

Iron nanoparticles synthesized from Loha Bhasma have revolutionized the treatment of iron-deficiency anemia. Traditional iron supplements often cause gastrointestinal side effects such as nausea and constipation. However, the nanoscale dimensions of iron nanoparticles facilitate efficient absorption in the gastrointestinal tract, reducing these adverse effects while enhancing hemoglobin synthesis and oxygen transport. This innovation demonstrates how nanotechnology refines traditional formulations to meet the demands of modern healthcare, without compromising their natural essence.

Beyond metallic nanoparticles, the encapsulation of herbal bioactives in nanocarriers has emerged as a game-changing innovation. Bioactives such as curcumin, derived from turmeric, often face challenges like poor solubility and rapid degradation in systemic circulation. Encapsulating these bioactives in lipid or polymeric nanocarriers addresses these limitations by protecting them from enzymatic degradation and enabling controlled release. This not only enhances their bioavailability but also prolongs their therapeutic action, making them more effective in managing chronic conditions like inflammation, arthritis, and cardiovascular diseases.

Sustainability is another critical area where nanotechnology has made a significant impact. Traditional preparation methods for Bhasmas often involve mining and processing practices that have ecological implications. To address these concerns, green synthesis techniques have been developed. These methods use plant-based reductants to produce nanoparticles, minimizing toxic byproducts and environmental toxicity. For example, extracts from plants like neem and tulsi have been successfully used as reducing agents in the synthesis of gold and silver nanoparticles. This approach not only aligns with Ayurveda's ecological ethos but also ensures that the therapeutic properties of nanoparticles are preserved.

The benefits of nanotechnology in Ayurveda are not without challenges. One significant concern is the overharvesting of medicinal plants, which threatens biodiversity and the sustainability of raw materials. For instance, Amalaki (Phyllanthus emblica), a key ingredient in Triphala, has faced population decline due to rising global demand. Environmental stressors, such as deforestation and soil degradation, further reduce the bioactive compound concentration in these plants, affecting the efficacy of Ayurvedic formulations. To mitigate these challenges, researchers have proposed agroforestry systems and community-based conservation practices. By integrating traditional agricultural wisdom with modern ecological principles, these initiatives aim to ensure the long-term availability of medicinal plants.

Standardization is another area that requires attention. Unlike synthetic drugs, which undergo rigorous quality control protocols, Ayurvedic formulations often lack standardized production methods. The variability in raw materials and preparation techniques can lead to inconsistencies in therapeutic outcomes. Nanotechnology offers a solution by enabling the precise characterization and functionalization of nanoparticles. Advanced analytical tools, such as scanning electron microscopy (SEM) and Fourier-transform infrared spectroscopy (FTIR), allow researchers to assess the size, shape, and surface properties of nanoparticles, ensuring consistency and reproducibility in formulations.

The integration of nanotechnology into Ayurveda also raises questions about regulatory frameworks and global acceptance. While Ayurveda is deeply rooted in Indian tradition, its adoption in international markets has been limited by skepticism regarding its scientific validity. Nanotechnology provides a pathway to bridge this gap by validating traditional practices through modern scientific methodologies. Clinical trials, toxicological studies, and pharmacokinetic analyses are essential to demonstrate the safety and efficacy of nanoparticle-based Ayurvedic formulations. By adhering to global regulatory standards, Ayurveda can expand its reach and gain recognition as a credible and effective healthcare system.

Nanotechnology represents a transformative force in the evolution of Ayurvedic medicine. By enhancing the stability, bioavailability, and therapeutic precision of traditional formulations, nanoparticles bridge the ancient wisdom of Ayurveda with the advancements of modern science. From cancer treatment and antimicrobial therapy to dermatology and anemia management, the applications of nanotechnology in Ayurveda are vast and diverse. However, realizing the full potential of this synergy requires a balanced approach that addresses challenges such as sustainability, standardization, and global acceptance. By fostering interdisciplinary collaboration and integrating ecological principles, nanotechnology can elevate Ayurveda to new heights, offering innovative solutions for complex health challenges while preserving its timeless essence.

46. According to the passage, how do gold nanoparticles derived from Swarna Bhasma revolutionize cancer treatment?

A. By enhancing hemoglobin synthesis and oxygen transport.

B. By selectively targeting tumor cells, minimizing systemic toxicity.

C. By disrupting bacterial cell membranes and generating ROS.

D. By neutralizing free radicals to prevent oxidative stress.

47. Why are green synthesis methods important in Ayurvedic nanoparticle production?

A. They use synthetic chemicals to enhance nanoparticle stability.

B. They minimize toxic byproducts and align with ecological principles.

C. They enhance dependency on metallic nanoparticles for therapeutic outcomes.

D. They eliminate the need for medicinal plants in formulations.

48. What is the role of lipid nanocarriers in herbal bioactive formulations?

A. To destabilize bioactives and reduce therapeutic efficacy.

B. To encapsulate bioactives, enhancing solubility and controlled release.

C. To increase enzymatic degradation of bioactives in systemic circulation.

D. To inhibit the therapeutic action of bioactives in chronic conditions.

49. How do iron nanoparticles derived from Loha Bhasma improve the treatment of anemia?

A. By increasing gastrointestinal side effects to enhance systemic absorption.

B. By improving gastrointestinal absorption and reducing oxidative stress.

C. By bypassing natural absorption pathways, reducing systemic circulation.

D. By limiting hemoglobin synthesis to control oxygen transport.

50. What key challenge must be addressed to ensure the global acceptance of nanoparticle-enhanced Ayurvedic medicine?

A. The elimination of traditional Ayurvedic formulations.

B. Standardization and consistency in therapeutic outcomes.

C. Complete reliance on synthetic alternatives for medicinal plants.

D. Ignoring sustainability challenges in sourcing raw materials.

ANSWER WITH EXPLANATIONS

1. **A:** Gold nanoparticles derived from Swarna Bhasma exhibit exceptional potential in oncology by selectively targeting tumor cells. Functionalized with tumor-specific ligands, these nanoparticles ensure precision in drug delivery, aligning perfectly with Ayurveda's principle of personalized treatment. Their nanoscale size allows for deep penetration into the tumor microenvironment, enhancing their therapeutic efficacy while minimizing systemic toxicity. Unlike conventional chemotherapeutic agents, which often harm healthy cells, gold nanoparticles reduce side effects significantly, making treatment safer. This advancement bridges traditional Ayurvedic knowledge with modern nanotechnology. Moreover, their stability in physiological conditions ensures consistent outcomes, validating Ayurveda's focus on reliable, individualized healing practices in complex disorders like cancer.

2. **C:** Silver nanoparticles synthesized from Rajata Bhasma have proven their effectiveness against multidrug-resistant pathogens, making them indispensable in antimicrobial therapies. Their mechanism of action involves disrupting bacterial membranes, producing reactive oxygen species (ROS), and inhibiting quorum sensing, thereby neutralizing harmful bacteria. This aligns with Ayurveda's traditional use of Rajata Bhasma for detoxification and infection management. In a modern context, the ability of these nanoparticles to target bacterial biofilms further reinforces their role in addressing healthcare challenges like antibiotic resistance. By validating these traditional principles through scientific advancements, nanotechnology enhances the therapeutic spectrum of Rajata Bhasma, preserving its relevance in addressing contemporary healthcare issues.

3. **B:** Iron nanoparticles derived from Loha Bhasma are highly effective in treating iron-deficiency anemia because their reduced particle size improves gastrointestinal absorption. Traditional iron supplements often cause oxidative stress and gastrointestinal discomfort. However, the enhanced surface area and stability of nanoparticles ensure better bioavailability, facilitating hemoglobin synthesis without triggering significant oxidative damage. This reflects a successful integration of modern nanomedicine with Ayurvedic aims of gentle, efficient nourishment of Rakta Dhatu (blood tissue).

4. **A:** Yashad Bhasma-derived zinc nanoparticles provide dual dermatological benefits: they act as a physical barrier against harmful UV radiation and neutralize free radicals responsible for oxidative skin damage. This combined effect enhances tissue repair and protects skin integrity, making these nanoparticles ideal for sunscreen formulations. Their antioxidative and protective properties also align with Ayurvedic emphasis on preserving Ojas (vital energy), supporting the skin's role in systemic health.

5. **A:** Encapsulation of curcumin in lipid nanocarriers overcomes the limitations of poor solubility and rapid degradation, which often hinder its efficacy. By protecting curcumin from enzymatic breakdown, nanocarriers enable sustained release, ensuring prolonged therapeutic effects. This approach enhances

the bioavailability of curcumin, making it more effective in managing chronic inflammatory and degenerative conditions like arthritis and cardiovascular diseases. Nanotechnology thus amplifies Ayurveda's use of curcumin as a powerful anti-inflammatory agent. This innovation demonstrates how traditional herbal remedies can be optimized for modern healthcare needs without losing their natural essence, bridging the gap between ancient wisdom and cutting-edge science.

6. **A:** The use of gold nanoparticles derived from Swarna Bhasma in crossing the blood-brain barrier has opened new avenues for treating neurological disorders. Functionalized gold nanoparticles are capable of delivering therapeutic agents directly to neural tissues, addressing conditions such as Alzheimer's disease and Parkinson's disease. This precision targeting reflects Ayurveda's principle of individualized and targeted healing. The high biocompatibility and stability of these nanoparticles further ensure minimal side effects, making them a safer alternative to conventional treatments. This development not only validates the ancient applications of Swarna Bhasma but also enhances its adaptability to address complex, modern neurological conditions effectively.

7. **A:** Nanoparticles demonstrate high stability under physiological conditions due to their enhanced surface-to-volume ratio, which minimizes degradation and ensures consistent therapeutic effects. This characteristic is particularly critical in improving the efficacy of traditional Bhasmas, which often face challenges in maintaining stability during systemic circulation. By ensuring uniformity in therapeutic action, nanoparticles align with Ayurveda's emphasis on predictable and reliable treatments. Furthermore, the ability to retain their bioactive properties under diverse conditions highlights the compatibility of nanoparticles with traditional formulations, enabling them to meet modern medical standards while preserving their historical significance in Ayurvedic medicine.

8. **B:** Encapsulating Neem oil in lipid nanocarriers significantly enhances its retention on wound surfaces, enabling a prolonged release of bioactives. This feature ensures sustained antimicrobial activity and promotes tissue regeneration, making it highly effective in wound healing. Nanotechnology addresses the limitations of traditional formulations, such as rapid degradation and inconsistent efficacy, thereby improving the therapeutic potential of Neem. This development aligns with Ayurveda's emphasis on localized and sustained healing, validating traditional principles with modern scientific advancements. By refining the delivery mechanisms of herbal oils, nanotechnology ensures that Ayurvedic treatments remain relevant and effective in contemporary medical applications.

9. **B:** Green synthesis of nanoparticles aligns seamlessly with Ayurveda's ecological principles, emphasizing harmony with nature. By using plant-based reductants, such as neem and tulsi extracts, green synthesis minimizes toxic byproducts, preserving environmental balance while maintaining therapeutic efficacy. This sustainable approach reduces the dependency on resource-intensive methods, ensuring the long-term viability of Ayurvedic practices. By integrating modern ecological practices with traditional wisdom, green synthesis represents a paradigm shift in nanoparticle production, enhancing the credibility and acceptance of Ayurveda in global markets. This innovation underscores the adaptability of Ayurvedic principles to meet contemporary challenges without compromising their foundational values.

10. **B:** Nanoparticle formulations of Triphala significantly improve gut microbiota diversity, which is essential for systemic immunity and overall health. By enhancing the bioavailability of bioactives, these formulations optimize their interaction with gut-associated lymphoid tissues (GALT), reducing inflammation and boosting immunity. This aligns with Ayurveda's principle of holistic healing, where gut health is central to well-being. Nanotechnology validates and refines traditional Triphala formulations, addressing modern challenges like irritable bowel syndrome (IBS) with greater precision and efficacy. The integration of advanced delivery systems ensures that traditional Ayurvedic treatments can meet contemporary healthcare needs while preserving their therapeutic essence.

11. **B:** Nanoparticle-enhanced Triphala formulations improve gut health by restoring microbial diversity and stimulating gut-associated lymphoid tissue (GALT) activity. These formulations validate Ayurveda's focus on the gut as a key to systemic immunity. By enhancing the bioavailability of active compounds, they directly influence immune modulation, as observed in increased immunoglobulin A (IgA) levels and reduced systemic inflammation. This advanced targeting aligns with Ayurveda's holistic healing principles, demonstrating that traditional formulations, when combined with modern delivery systems, can achieve greater precision in addressing chronic conditions like irritable bowel syndrome (IBS) and promoting overall well-being.

12. **B:** Agroforestry and community-driven conservation are sustainable approaches to ensuring the long-term availability of Amalaki. These practices reduce the environmental impact of overharvesting and align with Ayurveda's ecological harmony principle. Agroforestry

systems integrate medicinal plants into diverse ecosystems, preserving biodiversity while maintaining medicinal quality. Community conservation ensures traditional agricultural knowledge is preserved and adapted to modern needs. These initiatives exemplify how combining traditional wisdom with ecological principles can address the global demand for Ayurvedic formulations, ensuring sustainability and therapeutic efficacy without compromising environmental health.

13. **A:** Environmental degradation of Amalaki significantly reduces its bioactive compound concentration, impacting its therapeutic efficacy in promoting gut health and systemic immunity. The loss of medicinal quality in raw materials underscores the importance of sustainable sourcing and quality control in Ayurveda. Nanotechnology can mitigate this issue by enhancing the stability and bioavailability of the remaining bioactives, but addressing the root cause—environmental degradation—is crucial. These interconnected challenges highlight the need for integrating traditional agricultural practices with modern conservation methods, ensuring that the therapeutic benefits of Amalaki and Triphala formulations remain consistent and effective.

14. **B:** Establishing global quality standards for Triphala ensures consistency in bioactive compound levels while promoting sustainable harvesting practices. This comprehensive approach addresses therapeutic variability and ecological challenges, validating Ayurveda's principles of holistic healing and sustainability. By incorporating standardized production protocols, Ayurvedic formulations can meet global healthcare requirements while maintaining their traditional essence. This initiative exemplifies the potential of Ayurveda to adapt to contemporary healthcare systems without compromising its foundational values, ensuring therapeutic efficacy and ecological balance in a rapidly globalizing world.

15. **D:** Nanoparticle formulations of Swarna Bhasma utilize multiple nanotechnological strategies to optimize therapeutic impact. Enhanced solubility improves absorption, while functionalized ligands allow the nanoparticles to selectively bind to diseased tissues (such as tumors). Their stability in physiological environments ensures they remain intact until they reach the target site. Most importantly, their selectivity minimizes toxicity to healthy tissues, enhancing safety and precision. This comprehensive approach exemplifies how nanotechnology elevates traditional Ayurvedic interventions into targeted modern therapies.

16. **A:** The antioxidative and UV-protective properties of zinc nanoparticles from Yashad Bhasma make them indispensable in modern dermatological formulations. By neutralizing free radicals, these nanoparticles prevent oxidative stress, a major cause of skin damage and premature aging. Their ability to form a protective barrier against UV radiation enhances their efficacy as sunscreens. These dual properties align with Ayurveda's holistic approach to maintaining skin health and vitality. Nanotechnology validates and refines traditional formulations, demonstrating how Bhasmas can be adapted for contemporary skincare applications while preserving their foundational principles.

17. **D:** Green synthesis techniques reduce environmental toxicity and align with Ayurveda's ecological ethos, preserving the bioactivity of nanoparticles. By utilizing plant-based reductants, such as neem and tulsi extracts, these methods minimize the ecological footprint of nanoparticle production. This sustainable approach enhances therapeutic efficacy while addressing modern environmental challenges. Green synthesis bridges traditional Ayurvedic wisdom with cutting-edge science, ensuring that the ecological principles underlying Ayurveda are not compromised. This innovation demonstrates Ayurveda's adaptability in meeting global sustainability goals while maintaining its therapeutic integrity.

18. **A:** The antimicrobial activity of Rajata Bhasma-based nanoparticles is driven by three key mechanisms: ROS generation causes bacterial damage, direct membrane interaction disrupts bacterial integrity, and quorum sensing interference prevents colony formation. These mechanisms provide a multi-pronged attack on bacteria, making silver nanoparticles highly effective even against resistant strains. Stabilization of bacterial growth, however, is counterproductive and not aligned with antimicrobial goals, making (d) incorrect.

19. **A:** Lipid nanocarriers enhance the bioavailability of poorly soluble bioactives by encapsulating them in protective shells, preventing enzymatic degradation and enabling controlled release. This innovation prolongs the therapeutic effects of bioactives, ensuring consistent outcomes in treating chronic conditions. By addressing the limitations of traditional formulations, lipid nanocarriers validate Ayurveda's principles of sustained and localized healing. This advanced delivery system demonstrates how nanotechnology can refine Ayurvedic treatments to meet modern healthcare standards without compromising their natural essence.

20. **A:** Iron nanoparticles from Loha Bhasma improve hemoglobin synthesis and oxygen transport by enhancing gastrointestinal absorption and reducing oxidative stress. These nanoparticles bypass the side effects commonly associated with traditional iron supplements, such as nausea and constipation. Their nanoscale size allows for efficient systemic absorption,

aligning with Ayurveda's focus on balancing efficacy and safety. This innovation bridges traditional Ayurvedic formulations with contemporary healthcare requirements, offering a refined solution to managing iron-deficiency anemia effectively while maintaining the holistic principles of Ayurvedic medicine.

21. D: Functionalized gold nanoparticles in oncology work effectively due to their tumor-specific ligand binding, allowing precise attachment to cancer cells while sparing healthy tissues. Their nanoscale size enhances permeability across cell membranes, aiding deep tissue penetration. Additionally, they improve the bioavailability of drugs by ensuring more of the therapeutic agent reaches the target site. However, suppression of immune response is not a desirable mechanism, as it can cause complications. Thus, (a), (b), and (d) are correct.

22. A: Encapsulation of Neem oil in nanocarriers enhances therapeutic efficacy primarily by (a) increasing its retention time at the wound site and (b) allowing controlled release of the active compounds, ensuring consistent antimicrobial action. Surprisingly, (c) is also considered valid in some contexts because although nanocarriers are usually designed to protect actives, in some biodegradable carrier systems, controlled enzymatic degradation of the carrier can help release the bioactive effectively — hence it's included. However, (d) is incorrect, because reduced systemic absorption is advantageous for localized wound healing and does not reduce efficacy.

23. A: Nanoparticle-based Triphala improves gut health by modulating the diversity of gut microbiota, which in turn impacts metabolism and immunity. These nanoparticles also target gut-associated lymphoid tissue (GALT), enhancing immune surveillance. Reduction of inflammatory markers in the gut has been clinically observed, supporting its anti-inflammatory role. Importantly, these formulations support beneficial bacteria, not suppress them. Thus, (d) is not correct, making (a), (b), and (c) the right combination.

24. B: Sustainability in Ayurvedic nanomedicine can be achieved by adopting plant-based reduction methods, which reduce environmental toxicity. Agroforestry systems ensure sustainable raw material sourcing without harming biodiversity. Standardized production protocols help maintain consistent therapeutic quality across batches. Substituting with synthetic polymers is not eco-friendly nor aligned with Ayurvedic philosophy, so option (c) is incorrect. Hence, (a), (b), and (d) form the correct trio.

25. A: Antioxidative action of nanoparticles is linked to UV protection and skin regeneration (1), while reactive oxygen species (ROS) generation plays a vital role in antimicrobial activity (2). Ligand functionalization is central to targeted drug delivery in cancer (3), ensuring precision therapy. Controlled release mechanisms support sustained therapeutic action (4), improving efficiency over time. Thus, all pairings in option A are accurately matched with their respective applications.

26. A: In green synthesis techniques, plant-based reduction (a) reduces dependency on synthetic chemicals as it uses natural phytochemicals from plant extracts to produce nanoparticles, avoiding harsh chemical agents. Biodegradable carriers (b) help minimize toxic byproducts since they naturally decompose without polluting the environment, making them eco-friendly. Microbial synthesis (c), which utilizes bacteria or fungi to produce nanoparticles, enhances their stability due to biological capping and controlled synthesis environments. Finally, standardized methods (d) ensure consistent therapeutic outcomes by offering uniformity in nanoparticle size, composition, and bioactivity, which is critical for reproducible medical applications.

27. B: Gold nanoparticles from Swarna Bhasma offer anti-inflammatory and rejuvenative benefits (1), especially in chronic conditions. Silver nanoparticles from Rajata Bhasma are known for their strong antimicrobial and detoxifying effects (2). Iron nanoparticles from Loha Bhasma enhance hemoglobin synthesis (3), vital for treating anemia. Zinc nanoparticles from Yashad Bhasma are widely used in dermatology for UV protection and skin repair (4). All associations in option B are accurate.

28. A: Poor solubility of bioactives is tackled through lipid encapsulation (1), enhancing bioavailability. Environmental toxicity concerns are addressed via green synthesis methods (2), which use plant-based reducers. Stability issues are resolved by functionalized nanoparticle systems (3), which make them more robust in physiological conditions. Therapeutic variability is minimized through standardized production protocols (4), ensuring consistency. Option A best matches challenges with solutions.

29. B: Swarna Bhasma primarily consists of gold nanoparticles (1), used for rejuvenation and anti-aging. Rajata Bhasma includes silver nanoparticles (2), known for antimicrobial activity. Loha Bhasma contains iron nanoparticles (3), beneficial in treating anemia. Yashad Bhasma provides zinc nanoparticles (4), used for dermatological purposes. These components are traditionally and scientifically validated, making option B correct.

30. B: A high surface-to-volume ratio enhances cellular interaction (1), improving uptake of nanoparticles. Functionalized surfaces allow precise targeting of tissues (2), vital in oncology. Controlled release ensures sustained therapeutic efficacy (3), extending drug action. Stability in circulation reduces enzymatic degradation (4), protecting the bioactive compound. All functions match appropriately with the features, confirming option B as correct.

31. B: Antimicrobial activity is boosted by enhanced ROS generation (1) in Bhasma-based nanoparticle therapy. Cancer treatment benefits from targeted ligand binding (2), increasing specificity. In wound healing, prolonged retention at the site (3) ensures effective action. Dermatological applications, like sunscreen, benefit from UV protection and antioxidative properties (4). Option B matches all enhancements correctly with their applications.

32. A: Overharvesting of plants is mitigated by agroforestry systems (1), which promote sustainable cultivation. Toxicity in nanoparticle synthesis is reduced through green methods (2), using natural reducers. Therapeutic inconsistency is tackled via standardized quality control (3), essential for global acceptance. A high environmental footprint can be reduced by using biodegradable carriers (4), supporting eco-friendly practices. Therefore, option A best addresses sustainability challenges.

33. B: Sukshma Bhaag, or subtle essence, aligns with nanoscale penetration (1), enhancing cellular access. Anupana, the vehicle or carrier, correlates with enhanced delivery via nanocarriers (2). Sanskara, the process of refinement, is akin to nanoparticle functionalization for improved effects (3). Virya, indicating potency, reflects stability under physiological conditions (4), ensuring consistent performance. Thus, option B perfectly maps Ayurvedic principles to nanotech.

34. A: Functionalized surfaces offer tissue-specific targeting (1), improving treatment precision. Lipid encapsulation boosts bioavailability (2) by protecting bioactives from degradation. High stability ensures prolonged systemic circulation (3), allowing for extended therapeutic presence. Controlled release allows drugs to act over a longer duration (4), enhancing effectiveness in chronic conditions. All features are correctly matched to their benefits in option A.

35. A: Swarna Bhasma, when converted into gold nanoparticles through nanotechnology, shows significantly enhanced therapeutic potential due to improved stability in physiological environments and targeted delivery to diseased tissues. The key reason behind this enhanced targeting is the functionalization of gold nanoparticles with tumor-specific ligands. These ligands help the particles bind selectively to cancer cells, minimizing toxicity to healthy cells. Therefore, both statements are true, and Statement 2 correctly explains the mechanism underlying Statement 1.

36. C: Silver nanoparticles from Rajata Bhasma have demonstrated powerful antimicrobial effects by generating reactive oxygen species (ROS) that damage bacterial cells and by disrupting quorum sensing, which is crucial for bacterial communication and colony formation. While this makes them effective against multidrug-resistant bacteria, it does not imply that they harm beneficial gut microbiota. In fact, their targeted antimicrobial activity is designed to reduce pathogens without compromising overall microbial diversity. Hence, Statement 1 is correct, but Statement 2 is incorrect.

37. C: Iron nanoparticles derived from Loha Bhasma are effective in treating iron-deficiency anemia because their small size enhances gastrointestinal absorption, leading to better bioavailability and fewer side effects. They support hemoglobin synthesis and oxygen transport while minimizing oxidative stress. However, Statement 2 is incorrect as these nanoparticles are not absorbed directly into the bloodstream; they still go through the gastrointestinal tract but are absorbed more efficiently due to their nanoscale properties. Therefore, only Statement 1 is true.

38. C: Triphala, when formulated using nanoparticles, shows improved performance in enhancing gut health. These nanoformulations promote microbial diversity and help reduce gut inflammation by improving bioactive delivery and retention in the gut. Contrary to Statement 2, studies have shown that nanoparticle-based Triphala is often more effective than traditional forms due to better solubility and stability of its compounds. Hence, Statement 1 is correct, but Statement 2 falsely claims that these formulations are less effective.

39. A: Zinc nanoparticles from Yashad Bhasma are beneficial in dermatology due to their dual action: they block harmful UV radiation and scavenge free radicals, preventing skin damage. These effects are largely attributed to their high surface-to-volume ratio, which increases their interaction with reactive species and enhances their antioxidative capacity. Thus, both statements are valid, and Statement 2 correctly explains why zinc nanoparticles are effective, making option A the most appropriate choice.

40. A: Gold nanoparticles derived from Swarna Bhasma demonstrate high bioavailability and stability under physiological conditions, allowing for efficient targeted delivery to tumor cells. This targeted mechanism minimizes systemic toxicity while enhancing therapeutic precision, addressing a key limitation of conventional cancer treatments. By functionalizing nanoparticles with tumor-specific ligands, Swarna Bhasma aligns with Ayurveda's focus on individualized healing, optimizing treatment outcomes. This application bridges traditional Ayurvedic knowledge with modern oncology, offering innovative solutions for complex health challenges. Nanotechnology thus validates and refines the principles of Ayurveda, ensuring its adaptability and relevance in addressing contemporary medical needs while preserving its holistic approach.

41. C: Iron nanoparticles from Loha Bhasma improve therapeutic outcomes in treating anemia by facilitating better absorption and reducing oxidative stress. However, they do not bypass gastrointestinal absorption entirely. Their nanoscale size enhances their bioavailability, ensuring efficient hemoglobin synthesis and oxygen transport with minimal side effects. This innovation aligns with Ayurveda's principle of balancing efficacy and safety, refining traditional formulations to meet modern healthcare standards. Nanotechnology exemplifies how traditional wisdom can address contemporary health challenges, providing safer and more effective solutions for managing iron-deficiency anemia without compromising the core principles of Ayurvedic medicine.

42. C: Silver nanoparticles synthesized from Rajata Bhasma demonstrate potent antimicrobial activity by generating ROS and disrupting bacterial membranes, not by stabilizing bacterial growth. These mechanisms address modern challenges like multidrug resistance, validating Ayurveda's detoxification principles. By integrating nanotechnology, these traditional formulations gain precision and enhanced efficacy, making them suitable for combating contemporary infectious diseases. The ability to inhibit quorum sensing further highlights their role in preventing bacterial communication and biofilm formation. This innovation underscores the adaptability of Ayurveda in addressing critical healthcare challenges, bridging the gap between traditional practices and advanced scientific methodologies effectively.

43. C: Zinc nanoparticles from Yashad Bhasma indeed provide excellent UV protection and antioxidative benefits, making them valuable in dermatological applications. However, the reason stated—"inhibiting normal cellular regeneration processes"—is incorrect. In fact, these nanoparticles support tissue health by reducing oxidative stress and promoting repair, not limiting regeneration. Thus, while the assertion is valid, the reason contradicts the therapeutic purpose and is false.

44. C: Nanoparticle formulations of Triphala improve gut microbiota diversity and reduce systemic inflammation, validating their role in managing conditions like irritable bowel syndrome (IBS). However, these formulations do not destabilize gut microbiota. Instead, they enhance therapeutic precision and efficacy by targeting gut-associated lymphoid tissues (GALT). This advanced delivery mechanism aligns with Ayurveda's focus on gut health as the cornerstone of systemic well-being. Nanotechnology refines traditional formulations to meet modern healthcare challenges effectively, ensuring that Ayurvedic treatments remain relevant and impactful in addressing chronic health conditions while maintaining their holistic healing principles.

45. A: Green synthesis techniques for nanoparticle production align with Ayurveda's ecological principles, emphasizing sustainability and minimal environmental impact. Plant-based methods, such as using neem or tulsi extracts as reductants, reduce toxic byproducts and preserve nanoparticle bioactivity. This aligns with the Ayurvedic ethos of harmony with nature, ensuring therapeutic efficacy without compromising ecological balance. By integrating modern sustainability practices with traditional wisdom, green synthesis addresses environmental challenges and validates Ayurveda's relevance in contemporary healthcare. This approach ensures that Ayurvedic formulations meet global sustainability goals while maintaining their therapeutic and ecological integrity.

46. B: Gold nanoparticles from Swarna Bhasma revolutionize cancer treatment by selectively targeting tumor cells through receptor-mediated pathways. This specificity minimizes systemic toxicity and enhances therapeutic efficacy, addressing a major limitation of conventional chemotherapies. Their nanoscale dimensions allow for precise penetration into tumor microenvironments, aligning with Ayurveda's principle of personalized treatment. Nanotechnology refines the traditional applications of Swarna Bhasma, ensuring its relevance in modern oncology while preserving its holistic healing philosophy. This innovation demonstrates how Ayurveda's ancient practices can be adapted to meet complex contemporary healthcare needs effectively.

47. B: Silver nanoparticles derived from Rajata Bhasma effectively combat multidrug-resistant pathogens by disrupting bacterial membranes and generating reactive oxygen species (ROS). These mechanisms neutralize harmful bacteria without fostering resistance, addressing critical challenges in modern medicine. This validates Ayurveda's detoxification principles, emphasizing the elimination of impurities to restore balance. Nanotechnology enhances the antimicrobial properties of Rajata Bhasma, ensuring its precision and efficacy in combating contemporary infectious diseases. By bridging ancient practices with modern science, silver nanoparticles exemplify Ayurveda's adaptability and relevance in addressing complex healthcare issues effectively.

48. B: Lipid nanocarriers solve major limitations of herbal bioactives like poor solubility and rapid degradation. Encapsulation shields them from enzymatic breakdown in the digestive tract and allows for sustained, controlled release into the bloodstream. This improves bioavailability and enhances their therapeutic efficacy, especially in chronic diseases. In Ayurveda, this aligns with the principle of *Anupana*—appropriate carriers that enhance the absorption and action of medicine.

49. B: Green synthesis methods for nanoparticle production align with Ayurvedic principles of sustainability and ecological harmony. By utilizing plant-based reductants, these methods minimize toxic byproducts and preserve nanoparticle bioactivity, ensuring consistent therapeutic outcomes. This sustainable approach addresses modern environmental challenges while maintaining the integrity of Ayurvedic formulations. Green synthesis demonstrates how traditional ecological wisdom can be integrated with advanced scientific practices, ensuring Ayurveda's relevance in addressing contemporary healthcare needs. This innovation underscores the adaptability of Ayurvedic principles to meet global sustainability goals without compromising their therapeutic essence.

50. B: For Ayurvedic medicine to gain global acceptance, especially in its modern nanoparticle-enhanced form, it must meet international standards of quality, safety, and efficacy. This involves standardized production protocols, consistent raw material sourcing, and robust scientific validation. Variability in formulations can lead to inconsistent outcomes, limiting credibility. Therefore, standardization is essential to bridge the gap between traditional Ayurvedic wisdom and contemporary global healthcare systems.

UNIT 9: BIODIVERSITY, ENVIRONMENTAL HEALTH, IPR, AND ENTREPRENEURSHIP

CHAPTER 26

BIODIVERSITY OF MEDICINAL PLANTS, CONSERVATION, AND ECOSYSTEM

Introduction: Understanding Biodiversity and Its Importance

Biodiversity refers to the variety of life forms present on Earth, encompassing different species of plants, animals, fungi, and microorganisms, as well as the genetic differences within these species and the ecosystems they form. In the realm of medicinal plants, biodiversity is a critical component of traditional and modern healthcare systems. Medicinal plants, derived from diverse ecosystems, play an essential role in human health by providing raw materials for both traditional and pharmaceutical medicine. Ayurveda, the ancient Indian system of holistic healing, extensively relies on these plants to promote health, prevent diseases, and restore balance in the body and environment.

The biodiversity of medicinal plants is a reservoir of natural compounds with therapeutic potential. Globally, over 25,000 plant species are used in traditional medicine, with approximately 6,000 species found in India alone. Many of these plants are endangered due to habitat destruction, overharvesting, and climate change, making their conservation a matter of urgency. Moreover, medicinal plant biodiversity supports ecosystems by maintaining ecological balance, providing habitat and food for various species, and contributing to environmental health.

Importance of Biodiversity in Medicinal Plants

1. **Source of Medicinal Compounds:** Medicinal plants are an indispensable source of bioactive compounds that serve as the foundation for drug discovery. Approximately 70% of the world's population relies on plant-based medicine for primary healthcare. These plants contain secondary metabolites, such as alkaloids, flavonoids, terpenoids, and glycosides, which exhibit pharmacological properties. For instance, Rauwolfia serpentina provides reserpine, an antihypertensive agent, while Catharanthus roseus is the source of vinblastine and vincristine, used in cancer treatment.
2. **Role in Traditional Medicine:** Ayurveda, Unani, Siddha, and Traditional Chinese Medicine rely on medicinal plants for holistic healing. Ayurveda uses herbs such as Ashwagandha (Withania somnifera), Tulsi (Ocimum sanctum), and Neem (Azadirachta indica) for treating diverse ailments, from stress and inflammation to infections and chronic diseases. The diversity of medicinal plants ensures a wide array of formulations to address individual health needs.
3. **Ecological Significance:** Biodiversity contributes to ecosystem services, such as pollination, nutrient cycling, and soil fertility, which are essential for the growth of medicinal plants. Forests, grasslands, and wetlands, rich in plant diversity, serve as natural habitats for medicinal species. For example, the Western Ghats in India are a biodiversity hotspot, housing numerous medicinal plants like Shatavari (Asparagus racemosus) and Guduchi (Tinospora cordifolia).
4. **Cultural and Economic Value:** Medicinal plants are integral to cultural traditions and local economies. Communities across the world have developed knowledge systems around the use of plants for

health and well-being. The global herbal medicine market is estimated to reach over $100 billion by 2025, driven by demand for natural remedies. The preservation of biodiversity ensures the continuity of these cultural and economic benefits.

5. **Resilience Against Climate Change:** Biodiversity acts as a buffer against climate change by maintaining ecosystem stability. Diverse plant species adapt better to changing environmental conditions, ensuring the survival of medicinal plants and the ecosystems they support.

Conservation Strategies for Medicinal Plants: A Comprehensive Exploration

The growing demand for medicinal plants, driven by their critical role in traditional and modern healthcare systems, has placed enormous pressure on their availability and sustainability. To ensure that future generations benefit from these invaluable resources, strategic conservation measures must be implemented. Conservation strategies aim to safeguard the genetic diversity, ecological balance, and traditional knowledge associated with medicinal plants. These strategies can be broadly classified into in situ and ex situ approaches, supplemented by sustainable harvesting, community participation, and robust legal frameworks. This chapter provides a detailed exploration of these strategies, emphasizing their importance and implementation.

IN SITU CONSERVATION

Preservation Within Natural Habitats

In situ conservation is the preservation of medicinal plants within their natural ecosystems. This approach ensures that plants are maintained in their original habitats, allowing for the conservation of entire ecosystems and the ecological interactions within them.

1. **Biosphere Reserves:** Biosphere reserves are designated areas aimed at conserving biodiversity while supporting sustainable use of natural resources. They encompass core, buffer, and transition zones to balance conservation and human activities.
   - **Role in Conservation:** These reserves protect medicinal plants in their natural environments, ensuring their genetic diversity and ecological roles are preserved.
   - **Indian Examples:** The Nilgiri Biosphere Reserve, a UNESCO-listed site, is home to species like Terminalia chebula (Haritaki) and Phyllanthus emblica (Amla), used extensively in Ayurveda.
2. **Sacred Groves:** Sacred groves are forest patches protected by local communities for religious or cultural reasons. These areas often house rare and endemic medicinal plants.
   - **Ecological Significance:** Sacred groves act as micro-reserves, conserving genetic diversity and offering habitat to species threatened elsewhere.
   - **Examples in India:** Sacred groves in Meghalaya and Maharashtra harbor plants like Nothapodytes nimmoniana, known for its cancer-fighting compound camptothecin.
3. **Protected Areas:** National parks, wildlife sanctuaries, and other protected areas play a significant role in conserving biodiversity, including medicinal plants.
   - **Integration with Conservation Goals:** By restricting human interference, these areas provide a refuge for plant species and promote natural regeneration.

     Examples: Silent Valley National Park in Kerala is renowned for its rich medicinal flora, including species like Trichopus zeylanicus (Arogyapacha), a plant used for its adaptogenic properties.

Advantages of In Situ Conservation

- Maintains ecological interactions and evolutionary processes.
- Preserves entire ecosystems, benefiting associated fauna and microorganisms.
- Offers opportunities for research on medicinal plant ecology and habitat-specific adaptations.

EX SITU CONSERVATION

Preservation Outside Natural Habitats

Ex situ conservation involves protecting medicinal plants outside their natural habitats. This method is essential for conserving species that are critically endangered or face threats in their native ecosystems.

1. **Botanical Gardens:** Botanical gardens serve as repositories for medicinal plants, offering controlled environments for their propagation, study, and education.

   Examples: The Indian Botanical Garden in Kolkata conserves numerous medicinal species and supports research into their properties and cultivation techniques.
2. **Seed Banks:** Seed banks store seeds of medicinal plants under controlled conditions, ensuring the preservation of genetic material for future use.
   - **Importance:** Seed banks protect against the risk of extinction and provide a resource for reintroduction programs.

- **Institutional Example:** The National Bureau of Plant Genetic Resources (NBPGR) in India maintains a comprehensive collection of medicinal plant seeds.

3. **Herbal Gardens:** Herbal gardens are dedicated spaces for cultivating medicinal plants, often integrated with educational and research initiatives.
   - **Role in Conservation:** These gardens promote awareness of medicinal plants, facilitate research, and serve as genetic reservoirs.
   - **Examples:** The National Medicinal Plants Board (NMPB) supports the establishment of herbal gardens across India.

Advantages of Ex Situ Conservation

- Ensures the survival of species in controlled environments.
- Facilitates research and propagation of endangered species.
- Acts as a backup for restoring natural populations.

SUSTAINABLE HARVESTING

Need for Sustainable Practices

Overharvesting of medicinal plants to meet commercial demand is a major threat to their survival. Sustainable harvesting ensures that plant populations are not depleted while maintaining ecosystem balance.

1. **Key Practices:** Limiting Collection to Mature Plants: Harvesting only mature plants allows younger specimens to grow and regenerate.
   - **Rotational Harvesting:** Collecting plants from different areas in rotation prevents overexploitation of specific regions.
   - **Harvesting Specific Plant Parts:** Collecting leaves, flowers, or seeds without uprooting entire plants promotes sustainability.
2. **Community Involvement:** Local communities play a vital role in implementing sustainable harvesting practices. By involving indigenous knowledge holders, resource use can be optimized while ensuring ecological sustainability.

Benefits of Sustainable Harvesting

- Maintains the ecological integrity of habitats.
- Supports the long-term availability of medicinal plants.
- Ensures equitable resource use for local communities and industries.

COMMUNITY PARTICIPATION

Empowering Local Communities

Indigenous and local communities possess invaluable knowledge about medicinal plants and their sustainable use. Empowering these communities ensures effective conservation and equitable benefit sharing.

1. **Traditional Knowledge:** Role in Conservation: Indigenous knowledge systems provide insights into the ecology, uses, and sustainable management of medicinal plants.
   - **Documentation:** Initiatives to document traditional knowledge, such as the People's Biodiversity Register in India, safeguard this cultural heritage.
2. **Collaborative Models:** Joint Forest Management (JFM): A participatory approach where communities and forest departments collaborate to conserve biodiversity.
   - **Case Studies:** JFM initiatives in Odisha and Madhya Pradesh have successfully conserved medicinal plant species while benefiting local populations.

Impact of Community Participation

- Enhances conservation efforts through localized expertise.
- Promotes sustainable livelihoods for indigenous communities.
- Strengthens the cultural and ecological significance of medicinal plants.

POLICY AND LEGISLATION

Role of Government Policies

Legal frameworks and international agreements are essential for regulating the conservation and sustainable use of medicinal plants.

1. **National Policies:**
   - **The Biological Diversity Act (2002):** This Indian legislation regulates access to genetic resources and ensures equitable benefit sharing.
   - **National Medicinal Plants Board (NMPB):** Established to promote the conservation and sustainable use of medicinal plants through research and funding.
2. **International Agreements:**
   - **Convention on Biological Diversity (CBD):** Aims to conserve biodiversity, ensure sustainable use, and promote benefit sharing.
   - **CITES:** Regulates the international trade of endangered medicinal plants to prevent overexploitation.

Need for Strengthening Policies

- Implement stricter regulations on habitat destruction and overharvesting.
- Promote research on propagation techniques and sustainable harvesting.
- Ensure equitable sharing of benefits with local communities.

Challenges in Medicinal Plant Conservation

1. **Habitat Destruction:** Deforestation, urbanization, and agricultural expansion threaten natural habitats, leading to the decline of medicinal plant populations.
2. **Overharvesting:** Commercial demand for medicinal plants often results in unsustainable harvesting practices, depleting natural populations.
3. **Climate Change:** Rising temperatures, altered rainfall patterns, and extreme weather events disrupt ecosystems, affecting the growth and survival of medicinal plants.
4. **Lack of Awareness:** Limited awareness among communities and industries about the importance of conservation contributes to unsustainable practices.
5. **Limited Research:** Insufficient research on propagation techniques, pharmacological properties, and conservation methods hampers effective implementation.

Future Directions

1. **Integrating Traditional Knowledge with Modern Science:** Combining indigenous knowledge with modern biotechnology can enhance conservation efforts, such as through tissue culture and genetic engineering.
2. **Strengthening Community-Based Conservation:** Involving local communities in decision-making processes and benefit-sharing initiatives ensures long-term success.
3. **Expanding Research and Funding:** Investing in research on medicinal plant biodiversity, sustainable harvesting, and pharmacological properties will strengthen conservation strategies.
4. **Enhancing Education and Awareness:** Raising awareness about the importance of medicinal plants and their conservation can motivate individuals and industries to adopt sustainable practices.

Ayurveda's Role in Ecological Balance and Environmental Health

1. **Principles of Ayurveda and Ecological Harmony:** Ayurveda is deeply rooted in ecological principles, emphasizing the interconnectedness of humans and nature. It recognizes that the health of individuals depends on the health of the environment. Concepts like Prakriti (constitution), Dosha (biological energies), and Panchamahabhuta (five elements) reflect the relationship between human well-being and ecological balance.
2. **Sustainable Use of Resources:** Ayurveda advocates for the sustainable use of natural resources. Formulations often utilize entire plants or specific parts (roots, leaves, seeds) without wasting materials. For example, the Dashamoola group of herbs uses roots from ten medicinal plants, ensuring balance in harvesting.
3. **Promotion of Agroforestry:** Agroforestry, the integration of trees and crops, aligns with Ayurvedic principles by maintaining biodiversity and soil fertility. Medicinal plants like Amla (*Phyllanthus emblica*) and Arjuna (*Terminalia arjuna*) are commonly cultivated in agroforestry systems, providing ecological and economic benefits.
4. **Role in Pollution Control:** Several medicinal plants contribute to environmental health by mitigating pollution. For instance, Neem and Tulsi purify air and water, while Vetiver (*Chrysopogon zizanioides*) prevents soil erosion. These plants exemplify Ayurveda's role in promoting environmental sustainability.
5. **Education and Awareness:** Ayurveda emphasizes education on the sustainable use of medicinal plants. Practitioners and communities are encouraged to protect local biodiversity, ensuring the availability of resources for future generations.

Challenges in Medicinal Plant Conservation

1. **Habitat Destruction:** Deforestation, urbanization, and agricultural expansion lead to the loss of natural habitats, endangering medicinal plants.
2. **Overharvesting:** Unsustainable harvesting driven by commercial demand depletes plant populations, threatening biodiversity.
3. **Climate Change:** Rising temperatures, altered rainfall patterns, and extreme weather events disrupt ecosystems, affecting plant growth and survival.
4. **Lack of Awareness:** Many communities lack knowledge about the importance of medicinal plant conservation, leading to overexploitation and neglect.
5. **Limited Research and Funding:** Insufficient research on propagation techniques, pharmacological properties, and sustainable practices hampers conservation efforts.

Future Directions and Recommendations

1. **Integrating Traditional Knowledge with Modern Science:** Combining traditional Ayurvedic knowledge with modern biotechnology can enhance conservation and sustainable use. For example, tissue culture techniques can propagate endangered species like Saraca asoca (Ashoka).
2. **Strengthening Policies:** Governments must enforce stricter regulations on habitat protection, sustainable harvesting, and trade of medicinal plants.
3. **Enhancing Community Involvement:** Involving local communities in conservation initiatives ensures long-term success. Education programs and equitable benefit-sharing models can motivate communities to protect biodiversity.
4. **Promoting Research and Development:** Investing in research on medicinal plant biodiversity, cultivation techniques, and pharmacological properties will strengthen conservation strategies.
5. **Expanding Herbal Gardens and Seed Banks:** Establishing more herbal gardens and seed banks will safeguard genetic resources and support conservation efforts.

MULTIPLE CHOICE QUESTIONS

1. A multidisciplinary research team investigates the intricate relationship between the biodiversity of medicinal plants and their therapeutic efficacy within Ayurveda. They focus on plants such as Ashwagandha and Guduchi, hypothesizing that their bioactive compounds are deeply influenced by specific environmental factors in their native habitats. The study further highlights that substituting such plants with synthetics significantly reduces therapeutic outcomes. If the hypothesis is validated, which of the following best supports the preservation of biodiversity as crucial for Ayurvedic medicine?
   A. The bioactive compounds of Ashwagandha and Guduchi show reduced efficacy when cultivated in non-native ecosystems.
   B. Synthetic alternatives for these plants achieve identical therapeutic results, making biodiversity preservation less critical.
   C. Ayurvedic medicine is unaffected by biodiversity loss because its principles rely solely on universal concepts.
   D. The ecosystem's role in Ayurvedic formulations is negligible since all bioactive properties can be chemically synthesized.

2. A conservation biologist investigates the overharvesting of medicinal plants like Sarpagandha (*Rauwolfia serpentina*) and its implications for Ayurveda's global relevance. The findings reveal that while modern science isolates specific alkaloids, the holistic therapeutic effects of Sarpagandha rely on its full phytochemical spectrum. How does this research reshape conservation strategies for medicinal plants?
   A. Promoting sustainable harvesting practices is essential to preserve the full phytochemical spectrum critical for Ayurvedic efficacy.
   B. Substituting medicinal plants with synthetic compounds is an effective solution to biodiversity challenges.
   C. Overharvesting of Sarpagandha poses minimal impact since Ayurvedic formulations adapt to resource depletion through alternative plants.
   D. Conservation efforts are unnecessary as synthetic analogs can replace endangered medicinal species.

3. A clinical research initiative examines the ecological and pharmacological significance of endangered medicinal plants in Ayurveda. The study focuses on Haritaki, Bibhitaki, and Amalaki—the three components of Triphala—and their role in gut microbiota restoration and systemic immunity enhancement. If biodiversity loss reduces the bioactive compound quality in Amalaki, how would it affect the therapeutic outcomes of Triphala?
   A. The diminished bioactive compound concentration in Amalaki undermines Triphala's efficacy in gut microbiota modulation.
   B. Amalaki's quality reduction has no measurable effect on Triphala's overall therapeutic potency.
   C. Triphala's effectiveness remains unaffected because its detoxifying properties are primarily derived from Haritaki and Bibhitaki.
   D. The reduced quality of Amalaki enhances Triphala's therapeutic benefits due to compensatory phytochemical interactions.

4. A research collaboration between environmental scientists and Ayurvedic practitioners focuses on the sustainability of medicinal plants like Ashwagandha and Amalaki in the face of rising global demand. The findings emphasize that unsustainable harvesting practices deplete wild populations, reduce plant quality, and disrupt local ecosystems. Which conservation strategy aligns best with Ayurvedic principles to address these challenges?

A. Large-scale monoculture farming of medicinal plants to meet global demand while conserving wild populations.
B. Encouraging community-driven agroforestry and in-situ conservation to maintain biodiversity and therapeutic quality.
C. Limiting the use of endangered plants in Ayurveda to focus on alternative medicinal species.
D. Replacing wild medicinal plants with synthetic alternatives to reduce ecological stress.

5. An ethnobotanist investigates the historical and ecological roots of Ayurveda's reliance on medicinal plants. The study reveals that Ayurveda integrates biodiversity not only for health but also for ecological balance. What does this integration imply for modern conservation strategies?
A. Ayurvedic practices promote a harmonious relationship between health and the environment, advocating sustainable biodiversity use.
B. Modern conservation efforts should focus on substituting endangered Ayurvedic plants with lab-grown synthetic analogs.
C. Ayurvedic reliance on biodiversity is symbolic, with no direct implications for contemporary ecological conservation.
D. Biodiversity conservation is irrelevant to Ayurveda's therapeutic effectiveness, as its principles operate independently of specific ecosystems.

6. A detailed study highlights that Ayurveda's therapeutic principles are deeply rooted in the synergistic effects of multiple bioactive compounds found in diverse medicinal plants. Loss of biodiversity, particularly in ecologically sensitive areas, threatens the availability of key species such as Guduchi and Sarpagandha. How would such biodiversity loss likely impact the future of Ayurvedic medicine?
A. Biodiversity loss undermines Ayurvedic efficacy, as fewer species are available to balance the Tridoshas holistically.
B. Ayurvedic medicine remains unaffected, as it can easily substitute endangered plants with synthetics.
C. Loss of specific plant species leads Ayurveda to adapt its therapeutic principles to modern ecological limitations.
D. Biodiversity has no measurable impact on Ayurveda, as its therapeutic efficacy is based on universally applicable principles.

7. An ecologist evaluates the effectiveness of sustainable harvesting practices for medicinal plants like Amalaki and Ashwagandha. The research demonstrates that sustainable agroforestry not only conserves biodiversity but also improves the therapeutic quality of medicinal plants through better soil health and ecosystem resilience. What conclusion best describes the relationship between sustainability and Ayurvedic medicine?
A. Sustainable harvesting preserves biodiversity, which is crucial for maintaining the therapeutic efficacy of Ayurveda.
B. Agroforestry practices disrupt traditional Ayurvedic methods, reducing the authenticity of treatments.
C. Biodiversity conservation is irrelevant to Ayurvedic formulations, as their efficacy depends only on chemical synthesis.
D. Sustainability focuses exclusively on environmental protection and has no bearing on medicinal plant quality.

8. A pharmacological study investigates the impact of monoculture cultivation on the therapeutic properties of medicinal plants commonly used in Ayurveda. The results indicate that while monoculture increases yield, it significantly reduces phytochemical diversity, compromising plant efficacy. Based on these findings, which conservation practice would best align with Ayurvedic principles?
A. Transitioning to polyculture systems that mimic natural ecosystems to preserve phytochemical diversity.
B. Focusing on monoculture farming to meet global demand for Ayurvedic products.
C. Replacing Ayurvedic formulations with chemically synthesized alternatives to reduce reliance on monoculture farming.
D. Promoting global exports of monoculture-grown Ayurvedic plants as a sustainable alternative.

9. A global demand surge for Ayurvedic products has resulted in the overharvesting of critical medicinal plants, threatening their wild populations. A policy proposal emphasizes integrating biodiversity conservation with Ayurvedic medicine production. Which strategy most effectively addresses the ecological and therapeutic concerns raised by this issue?
A. Encouraging localized cultivation using traditional farming methods to reduce pressure on wild populations.
B. Developing synthetic alternatives to replace endangered medicinal plants in Ayurvedic formulations.
C. Limiting the global promotion of Ayurveda to prevent overharvesting of plants.
D. Establishing international trade restrictions to conserve endangered plant species.

10. A case study examines the consequences of deforestation and climate change on the quality and availability of medicinal plants integral to Ayurveda. The analysis suggests that environmental degradation alters the phytochemical profiles of plants like Haritaki and Bibhitaki, reducing their therapeutic effectiveness. How does this finding reinforce the link between ecological preservation and Ayurvedic efficacy?

A. Environmental degradation diminishes Ayurvedic efficacy by compromising plant quality and availability.
B. Climate change enhances the phytochemical diversity of plants, improving their therapeutic potential.
C. Ayurveda is unaffected by environmental degradation, as its principles do not rely on ecological conditions.
D. The therapeutic properties of Ayurvedic plants are independent of their environmental context.

Directions (Q. No. 11–14): *Scenario-Based Questions*

SCENARIO 1

A team of environmental scientists investigates how traditional Ayurvedic agricultural practices, such as organic farming and companion planting, contribute to ecological balance. The study reveals that these methods not only conserve soil fertility and water resources but also enhance biodiversity by promoting the growth of medicinal plants alongside staple crops. Furthermore, these practices reduce the reliance on chemical fertilizers and pesticides, leading to healthier ecosystems. However, the team identifies challenges in scaling these practices for commercial use without compromising their ecological benefits.

SCENARIO 2

Simultaneously, an Ayurvedic researcher examines the role of medicinal plants in environmental health by focusing on their ability to restore degraded ecosystems. The study highlights that certain plants, such as Neem and Tulsi, possess phytoremediation properties, helping to detoxify soil and water polluted by industrial waste. Additionally, the researcher finds that integrating such plants into reforestation projects not only revitalizes ecosystems but also creates habitats for pollinators and wildlife, aligning with Ayurveda's principle of living in harmony with nature.

11. Based on Scenario 1, which of the following conclusions best supports Ayurveda's contribution to sustainable agriculture and ecological balance?

A. Ayurvedic agricultural practices enhance biodiversity and soil health but face scalability issues due to commercial farming pressures.
B. Organic farming and companion planting in Ayurveda provide no measurable ecological benefits and are primarily cultural traditions.
C. Ayurvedic farming practices reduce biodiversity by focusing exclusively on medicinal plant cultivation.
D. Ayurveda's agricultural methods are incompatible with modern ecological needs due to their reliance on outdated techniques.

12. Considering the findings in Scenario 2, which of the following mechanisms best explains how medicinal plants like Neem and Tulsi support environmental health?

A. Neem and Tulsi enhance pollination processes but have limited impact on ecosystem detoxification.
B. Medicinal plants with phytoremediation properties detoxify polluted soils and waters, contributing to ecosystem restoration.
C. Ayurvedic plants only benefit human health and play no significant role in environmental conservation.
D. Neem and Tulsi reduce biodiversity by monopolizing resources needed by other plant species in their vicinity.

13. How do the ecological benefits of Ayurvedic agricultural practices in Scenario 1 complement the phytoremediation properties of medicinal plants described in Scenario 2?

A. Ayurvedic farming enhances biodiversity, creating supportive ecosystems for plants with phytoremediation abilities to detoxify degraded environments.
B. The practices in Scenario 1 and the plants in Scenario 2 operate independently, with no measurable influence on each other's ecological outcomes.
C. Phytoremediation plants thrive better in chemically intensive agricultural systems rather than traditional Ayurvedic methods.
D. Ayurvedic farming and phytoremediation are incompatible due to competing resource requirements.

14. What overarching strategy, integrating the findings of both scenarios, would most effectively address environmental health challenges while maintaining Ayurveda's ecological ethos?

A. Promoting large-scale monoculture farming of medicinal plants to maximize phytoremediation benefits.
B. Integrating Ayurvedic agricultural practices with reforestation projects using phytoremediation plants to restore ecosystems and enhance biodiversity.
C. Replacing traditional Ayurvedic farming methods with modern chemical-intensive agriculture to scale production.
D. Limiting the cultivation of phytoremediation plants to controlled environments to prevent ecological disruptions.

Directions (Q. No. 15–24): *Codes-Based Questions in a Flowing Manner:*

15. Which of the following statements correctly describe the role of medicinal plants in biodiversity?

(a) Medicinal plants support pollination and stabilize soil.
(b) Overharvesting of medicinal plants leads to biodiversity loss and ecosystem imbalance,
(c) Monoculture plantations enhance biodiversity.
(d) Medicinal plants regulate water cycles and prevent soil erosion.

Select the answer from the options given below:
A. (a), (b), and (d)
B. (b), (c), and (d)
C. (a), (c), and (d)
D. (a), (b), (c), and (d)

16. Which of the following conservation strategies are correctly described?
(a) Biosphere reserves protect entire ecosystems and promote sustainability.
(b) Seed banks store genetic material for future use.
(c) Sacred groves are small forest patches preserved for cultural and religious reasons.
(d) Botanical gardens focus on research and propagation of plant species.

Select the answer from the options given below:
A. (a), (b), (c), and (d)
B. (a), (b), and (d) only
C. (a), (c), and (d) only
D. (b), (c), and (d) only

17. Which of the following sustainable harvesting practices are correctly linked to their benefits?
(a) Rotational harvesting prevents overexploitation by alternating collection sites.
(b) Harvesting only mature plants ensures regeneration of plant populations.
(c) Collecting non-destructive parts, such as leaves or seeds, allows sustainable extraction.
(d) Community monitoring enhances resource management by involving local populations.

Select the answer from the options given below:
A. (a), (b), (c), and (d)
B. (a), (b), and (d) only
C. (a), (c), and (d) only
D. (b), (c), and (d) only

18. Which of the following statements reflect the alignment of Ayurveda with sustainability?
(a) Ayurveda promotes biodiversity by using multiple medicinal plants in formulations.
(b) It aligns human practices with ecological cycles through seasonal routines.
(c) Ayurveda prioritizes monoculture farming for economic growth.
(d) The sustainable use of plant-based resources ensures ecological preservation.

Select the answer from the options given below:
A. (a), (b), and (d)
B. (a), (b), and (c)
C. (b), (c), and (d)
D. (a), (c), and (d)

19. Which of the following biodiversity hotspots are correctly associated with medicinal plants?
(a) Western Ghats are known for Rauwolfia serpentina (Sarpagandha).
(b) Eastern Himalayas host Nardostachys jatamansi (Jatamansi).
(c) Sundarbans are home to Avicennia officinalis (Mangrove tree).
(d) Indo-Burma region is associated with Acorus calamus (Sweet flag).

Select the answer from the options given below:
A. (a), (b), and (d) only
B. (a), (b), (c), and (d)
C. (b), (c), and (d) only
D. (a) and (c) only

20. Which of the following conservation policies are accurately described?
(a) The Biological Diversity Act, 2002 regulates access to genetic resources and promotes benefit-sharing.
(b) The National Medicinal Plants Board (NMPB) supports conservation, propagation, and sustainable use of medicinal plants.
(c) The Convention on Biological Diversity (CBD) advocates global conservation and equitable benefit-sharing.
(d) CITES controls international trade in endangered species of plants.

Select the answer from the options given below:
A. (a), (b), and (d) only
B. (a), (b), (c), and (d)
C. (b), (c), and (d) only
D. (a) and (c) only

21. Which of the following Ayurvedic principles are correctly linked with their ecological implications?
(a) Panchamahabhuta represents the interconnectedness of nature and human health.
(b) Tridosha maintains ecological balance through harmony with natural cycles.
(c) Agni symbolizes metabolic energy aligned with environmental rhythms.
(d) Ojas reflects vitality preserved through sustainable living practices.

Select the answer from the options given below:
A. (a), (b), and (c) only
B. (b), (c), and (d) only
C. (a), (b), (c), and (d)
D. (a) and (d) only

22. Which of the following measures are most closely aligned with in situ conservation?
(a) Sacred groves managed by local communities.
(b) National parks ensuring ecological stability.
(c) Botanical gardens preserving endangered species.
(d) Seed banks storing genetic material.

Select the answer from the options given below:
A. (a) and (b) only
B. (b) and (d) only
C. (a), (b), and (c) only
D. (a) and (c) only

23. Which of the following Ayurvedic principles reflect conservation implications?
(a) Lokasamgraha emphasizes holistic approaches to biodiversity conservation.
(b) Dinacharya aligns human practices with natural cycles for sustainability.
(c) Sadvritta promotes mindful consumption and resource preservation.
(d) Prakriti encourages biodiversity by recognizing individual uniqueness.

Select the answer from the options given below:
A. (a), (b), (c), and (d)
B. (a), (b), and (d) only
C. (a), (c), and (d) only
D. (b), (c), and (d) only

24. Which of the following measures are most suitable for sustainable conservation of medicinal plants?
(a) Documenting traditional uses through ethnobotanical studies.
(b) Establishing tissue culture labs for endangered species.
(c) Encouraging monoculture plantations for commercialization.
(d) Training local communities in scientific harvesting techniques.

Select the answer from the options given below:
A. (a), (b), and (d)
B. (b), (c), and (d)
C. (a), (c), and (d)
D. (a), (b), and (c)

25. Match List–I (Conservation Methods) with List–II (Objectives):

List–I	List–II
(a) Biosphere reserves	1. Protect entire ecosystems and promote sustainable use
(b) Seed banks	2. Preserve genetic material in controlled environments
(c) Sacred groves	3. Protect rare species through community-managed sites
(d) Botanical gardens	4. Cultivate plants for research and education

Which of these measures are most appropriate?
A. (a)-1, (b)-2, (c)-3, (d)-4
B. (a)-2, (b)-4, (c)-1, (d)-3
C. (a)-4, (b)-3, (c)-2, (d)-1
D. (a)-3, (b)-1, (c)-4, (d)-2

26. Match List–I (Medicinal Plants) with List–II (Uses):

List–I	List–II
(a) *Withania somnifera* (Ashwagandha)	1. Adaptogen and stress-reliever
(b) *Tinospora cordifolia* (Guduchi)	2. Immune booster and detoxifying agent
(c) *Phyllanthus amarus* (Bhumyamalaki)	3. Hepatoprotective properties for liver health
(d) *Ocimum sanctum* (Tulsi)	4. Antioxidant and anti-inflammatory agent

Which of these measures are most appropriate?
A. (a)-1, (b)-2, (c)-3, (d)-4
B. (a)-2, (b)-3, (c)-4, (d)-1
C. (a)-3, (b)-1, (c)-2, (d)-4
D. (a)-4, (b)-3, (c)-1, (d)-2

27. Match List–I (Traditional Practices) with List–II (Ecological Relevance):

List–I	List–II
(a) Sacred groves	1. Biodiversity hotspots preserving rare species
(b) Agroforestry	2. Promotes ecological balance through mixed cultivation
(c) Sustainable harvesting	3. Ensures regeneration through minimal environmental impact
(d) Ethnobotanical studies	4. Documents traditional knowledge for conservation

Which of these measures are most appropriate?
A. (a)-1, (b)-2, (c)-3, (d)-4
B. (a)-3, (b)-4, (c)-2, (d)-1

C. (a)-4, (b)-1, (c)-2, (d)-3
D. (a)-2, (b)-3, (c)-4, (d)-1

28. Match List–I (Biodiversity Hotspots) with List–II (Medicinal Plants):

List–I	List–II
(a) Western Ghats	1. *Rauwolfia serpentina* (Sarpagandha)
(b) Eastern Himalayas	2. *Nardostachys jatamansi* (Jatamansi)
(c) Sundarbans	3. *Avicennia officinalis* (Mangrove tree)
(d) Indo-Burma region	4. *Acorus calamus* (Sweet flag)

Which of these measures are most appropriate?
A. (a)-1, (b)-3, (c)-4, (d)-2
B. (a)-2, (b)-4, (c)-1, (d)-3
C. (a)-1, (b)-2, (c)-3, (d)-4
D. (a)-4, (b)-3, (c)-2, (d)-1

29. Match List–I (Policies) with List–II (Objectives):

List–I	List–II
(a) Biological Diversity Act, 2002	1. Regulates access to genetic resources and promotes benefit sharing
(b) National Medicinal Plants Board (NMPB)	2. Supports conservation and sustainable use of medicinal plants
(c) Convention on Biological Diversity (CBD)	3. Advocates global conservation and benefit sharing
(d) CITES	4. Controls international trade of endangered plant species

Which of these measures are most appropriate?
A. (a)-1, (b)-2, (c)-3, (d)-4
B. (a)-4, (b)-3, (c)-1, (d)-2
C. (a)-3, (b)-1, (c)-4, (d)-2
D. (a)-2, (b)-4, (c)-1, (d)-3

30. Match List–I (Ayurvedic Principles) with List–II (Ecological Relevance):

List–I	List–II
(a) Panchamahabhuta (Five Elements)	1. Represents interconnectedness of nature and human health
(b) Tridosha	2. Maintains balance through harmony in cycles
(c) Agni (Digestive Fire)	3. Aligns energy with environmental rhythms
(d) Ojas	4. Reflects vitality preserved through sustainable living

Which of these measures are most appropriate?
A. (a)-1, (b)-2, (c)-4, (d)-3
B. (a)-2, (b)-1, (c)-3, (d)-4
C. (a)-4, (b)-3, (c)-2, (d)-1
D. (a)-1, (b)-2, (c)-3, (d)-4

31. Match List–I (Conservation Measures) with List–II (Conservation Methods):

List–I	List–II
(a) Sacred groves	1. Preserved forest patches by local communities
(b) Botanical gardens	2. Maintains endangered plants in controlled environments
(c) National parks	3. Ensures ecological stability
(d) Seed banks	4. Stores genetic material for future use

Which of these measures are most appropriate?
A. (a)-1, (b)-2, (c)-3, (d)-4
B. (a)-2, (b)-4, (c)-1, (d)-3
C. (a)-4, (b)-1, (c)-2, (d)-3
D. (a)-3, (b)-1, (c)-4, (d)-2

32. Match List–I (Hotspots) with List–II (Species):

List–I	List–II
(a) Western Ghats	1. Gymnema sylvestre
(b) Eastern Himalayas	2. Taxus wallichiana
(c) Indo-Burma	3. Terminalia chebula
(d) Sundarbans	4. Heritiera fomes

Which of these measures are most appropriate?
A. (a)-1, (b)-3, (c)-4, (d)-2
B. (a)-2, (b)-4, (c)-1, (d)-3
C. (a)-1, (b)-2, (c)-3, (d)-4
D. (a)-4, (b)-3, (c)-2, (d)-1

33. Match List–I (Conservation Goals) with List–II (Methods):

List–I	List–II
(a) Preserve biodiversity	1. Encourage sacred groves
(b) Promote education	2. Develop botanical gardens
(c) Ensure regeneration	3. Enforce sustainable harvesting
(d) Mitigate over-harvesting	4. Establish rotational harvesting

Which of these measures are most appropriate?
A. (a)-1, (b)-2, (c)-3, (d)-4
B. (a)-2, (b)-4, (c)-1, (d)-3
C. (a)-4, (b)-1, (c)-2, (d)-3
D. (a)-3, (b)-1, (c)-4, (d)-2

34. Match List–I (Ayurvedic Practices) with List–II (Relevance):

List–I	List–II
(a) Lokasamgraha	1. Holistic approaches to conservation
(b) Dinacharya	2. Aligns human activity with ecological sustainability
(c) Sadvritta	3. Encourages resource mindfulness
(d) Prakriti	4. Supports biodiversity through individual uniqueness

Which of these measures are most appropriate?
A. (a)-2, (b)-4, (c)-1, (d)-3
B. (a)-1, (b)-2, (c)-3, (d)-4
C. (a)-3, (b)-1, (c)-2, (d)-4
D. (a)-4, (b)-3, (c)-2, (d)-1

Directions (Q. No. 35–39): *Following questions are based on Statement 1 and Statement 2. Read both the statements carefully and choose the correct answer from the options given below:*
A. Both Statement 1 and Statement 2 are true, and Statement 2 is the correct explanation of Statement 1.
B. Both Statement 1 and Statement 2 are true, but Statement 2 is not the correct explanation of Statement 1.
C. Statement 1 is true, but Statement 2 is false.
D. Statement 1 is false, but Statement 2 is true.

35. Statement 1: Medicinal plant conservation is integral to the sustainability of Ayurvedic practices, as many formulations rely on plant-based ingredients.

Statement 2: The rising demand for Ayurvedic formulations has increased the pressure on wild populations of medicinal plants, leading to overharvesting and habitat destruction.

36. Statement 1: In situ conservation of medicinal plants involves maintaining plant populations within their natural ecosystems.

Statement 2: Botanical gardens are examples of in situ conservation as they recreate the natural habitat of medicinal plants for preservation.

37. Statement 1: Sacred groves act as natural gene banks, preserving the genetic diversity of medicinal plants.

Statement 2: Sacred groves are significant for biodiversity conservation as they are managed with traditional ecological knowledge.

38. Statement 1: Sustainable harvesting practices ensure the long-term availability of medicinal plants while preventing ecosystem degradation.

Statement 2: Harvesting medicinal plants in their reproductive stages ensures rapid regeneration and higher yields.

39. Statement 1: Ethnobotanical studies are essential for documenting traditional knowledge of medicinal plants and their uses.

Statement 2: Ethnobotanical studies focus only on plant taxonomy and exclude cultural and therapeutic practices associated with plants.

Directions (Q. No. 40–45): *There are two statements in each question. One is labelled as Assertion (A) and the other is as Reason (R). Read both the statements and choose the correct answer from the options given below:*
A. Both Assertion (A) and Reason (R) are true, and Reason (R) is the correct explanation of Assertion (A).
B. Both Assertion (A) and Reason (R) are true, but Reason (R) is not the correct explanation of Assertion (A).
C. Assertion (A) is true, but Reason (R) is false.
D. Assertion (A) is false, but Reason (R) is true.

40. Assertion (A): Biodiversity hotspots are critical regions for the conservation of medicinal plants.

Reason (R): These regions harbor high species diversity and endemism but are under significant threat due to habitat destruction.

41. Assertion (A): Seed banks are an effective method of conserving medicinal plant biodiversity.

Reason (R): Storing seeds under controlled conditions allows for long-term preservation and ensures availability during replanting initiatives.

42. Assertion (A): Overharvesting of medicinal plants disrupts ecosystem stability and biodiversity.

Reason (R): Rapid urbanization and commercial exploitation are the primary causes of medicinal plant depletion in forests.

43. Assertion (A): Community-based conservation programs like Joint Forest Management (JFM) enhance medicinal plant conservation.

Reason (R): These programs involve local communities in sustainable resource management and ensure equitable benefit-sharing.

44. Assertion (A): Conservation of medicinal plants is essential for the continued development of pharmaceutical drugs.

Reason (R): Many synthetic drugs are based on bioactive compounds derived from medicinal plants.

45. Assertion (A): Sacred groves in India are critical for preserving the genetic diversity of medicinal plants.

Reason (R): Sacred groves are often situated in urban areas and are maintained by modern scientific interventions.

Directions (Q. No. 46–50): *Read the passage carefully and answer the questions given below*:

The biodiversity of medicinal plants has been a cornerstone of traditional healthcare systems such as Ayurveda, Traditional Chinese Medicine (TCM), and African ethnomedicine for centuries. Medicinal plants not only contribute to healthcare but also play a significant role in maintaining ecological balance and supporting rural economies. However, rapid urbanization, deforestation, climate change, and unsustainable harvesting practices have severely threatened the survival of numerous medicinal plant species. Overharvesting for global markets, particularly for high-demand species such as *Nardostachys jatamansi, Rauwolfia serpentina, and Withania somnifera,* has led to a decline in wild populations, pushing many of them toward the brink of extinction.

In the context of Ayurveda, medicinal plants hold a unique position as they are deeply intertwined with its principles of balancing the doshas—Vata, Pitta, and Kapha. Plants such as Ashwagandha (*Withania somnifera*) are valued for their adaptogenic properties, helping the body cope with stress, while Guduchi (*Tinospora cordifolia*) acts as a detoxifier and immune booster. The role of biodiversity hotspots like the Western Ghats and Eastern Himalayas in preserving such plants cannot be overstated. These regions harbor rare species whose biochemical compositions make them invaluable for both traditional and modern medicine.

The conservation of medicinal plants is not merely a scientific challenge but also a socio-economic and cultural issue. Many indigenous communities depend on these plants for their livelihoods and healthcare needs. Sacred groves—forest patches preserved by local communities for religious and cultural purposes—are vital reservoirs of medicinal plant biodiversity. These groves, often untouched by commercial exploitation, serve as natural gene banks, preserving the genetic diversity of rare and endemic species. Examples include the sacred groves of the Khasi and Garo hills in Meghalaya, which are known for their rich biodiversity.

Strategies for conservation must encompass both in situ and ex situ approaches. In situ conservation involves preserving plants in their natural habitats, as seen in biosphere reserves like the Nilgiri Biosphere Reserve. Ex situ conservation, on the other hand, includes seed banks, botanical gardens, and tissue culture techniques. For instance, the National Bureau of Plant Genetic Resources (NBPGR) in India plays a crucial role in preserving the seeds of medicinal plants. Herbal gardens, such as those managed by the National Medicinal Plants Board (NMPB), also contribute to ex situ conservation efforts by cultivating endangered species in controlled environments.

Policy frameworks and legislation are critical to addressing the challenges of medicinal plant conservation. The Biological Diversity Act (2002) in India promotes the conservation and sustainable use of biodiversity while ensuring equitable benefit-sharing. On an international level, the Convention on Biological Diversity (CBD) and the Convention on International Trade in Endangered Species (CITES) regulate the trade and conservation of medicinal plants. These policies aim to balance the needs of conservation with economic and healthcare demands.

Sustainable harvesting practices are another key aspect of conservation. Methods such as rotational harvesting, collecting plants only at maturity, and avoiding the uprooting of entire plants help ensure the regeneration of medicinal species. Community participation is indispensable in this regard. Initiatives like Joint Forest Management (JFM) in India empower local communities to manage forest resources sustainably. Indigenous knowledge also plays a crucial role, as traditional healers and community elders possess invaluable insights into the ecological and therapeutic aspects of medicinal plants.

Modern science and technology have begun to integrate with traditional knowledge to enhance the conservation of medicinal plants. Advances in biotechnology, such as tissue culture and genetic engineering, offer new avenues for propagating endangered species and enhancing their bioactive properties. Research into the pharmacological potential of medicinal plants continues to validate their traditional uses, bridging the gap between ancient wisdom and modern medicine.

Ayurveda's emphasis on sustainability aligns closely with the principles of environmental health. The Ayurvedic concept of Lokasamgraha, which emphasizes harmony between humans and nature, underscores the importance of conserving natural resources. Practices like Dinacharya (daily routine) and Ritucharya (seasonal routine) also reflect this ecological perspective, promoting balance not just within the body but also with the external environment.

The biodiversity of medicinal plants is an irreplaceable asset that requires concerted efforts for its conservation. A holistic approach involving scientific research, community participation, sustainable practices, and robust policy frameworks is essential to ensure that these valuable resources continue to benefit humanity and the environment for generations to come.

46. What are the primary threats to medicinal plant biodiversity as mentioned in the passage?

(a) climate change and unsustainable harvesting

(b) urbanization and habitat destruction

(c) overharvesting for global markets

(d) lack of traditional knowledge among local communities

Choose the correct answer from the options given below:

A. (a) and (b) only

B. (a), (b), and (c) only

C. (b), (c), and (d) only

D. (a), (c), and (d) only

47. How do sacred groves contribute to medicinal plant conservation?

(a) they serve as natural gene banks, preserving genetic diversity

(b) they are managed by local communities and remain untouched by commercial exploitation

(c) they promote scientific research and modern cultivation practices

(d) they function as biodiversity hotspots with endemic species

Choose the correct answer from the options given below:

A. (a) and (b) only

B. (a), (c), and (d) only

C. (b) and (d) only

D. (a), (b), and (d) only

48. Which of the following statements best describes the role of biodiversity hotspots in the conservation of medicinal plants?

(a) biodiversity hotspots like the Western Ghats house rare species valuable for medicine

(b) they provide natural habitats essential for the growth and regeneration of medicinal plants

(c) they eliminate the need for ex situ conservation measures

(d) they are solely focused on the commercial cultivation of high-demand species

Choose the correct answer from the options given below:

A. (a) and (b) only

B. (b) and (c) only

C. (a), (b), and (c) only

D. (b) and (d) only

49. What role does modern science play in the conservation of medicinal plants?

(a) tissue culture and genetic engineering aid in propagating endangered species

(b) advances in biotechnology enhance the bioactive properties of medicinal plants

(c) pharmacological research validates the traditional uses of medicinal plants

(d) genetic engineering eliminates the need for traditional cultivation methods

Choose the correct answer from the options given below:

A. (a) and (b) only

B. (a), (b), and (c) only

C. (b), (c), and (d) only

D. (a) and (d) only

50. How does Ayurveda align with environmental conservation principles?

(a) lokasamgraha emphasizes harmony between humans and nature

(b) dinacharya and ritucharya promote ecological balance through sustainable practices

(c) ayurveda discourages the use of natural resources for medicinal purposes

(d) it integrates modern conservation methods with traditional knowledge

Choose the correct answer from the options given below:

A. (a), (b), and (c) only

B. (b), (c), and (d) only

C. (a), (b), and (d) only

D. (a), (c), and (d) only

ANSWER WITH EXPLANATIONS

1. A: The relationship between biodiversity and the therapeutic efficacy of Ayurvedic plants such as Ashwagandha and Guduchi is intrinsically linked to their ecological origins. Plants grown in native ecosystems develop bioactive compounds through complex environmental interactions, contributing to their medicinal properties. The hypothesis that biodiversity is essential to Ayurveda is validated when non-native cultivation leads to reduced efficacy. Substituting natural sources with synthetic alternatives lacks the synergistic bioactivity essential for holistic healing. This argument underscores that biodiversity preservation is not just ecological but vital for sustaining Ayurvedic medicine's authenticity. Loss of such biodiversity risks degrading both therapeutic outcomes and traditional knowledge systems.

2. A: Sustainable harvesting is fundamental to conserving the full phytochemical spectrum of medicinal plants like Sarpagandha. This research shows that isolating alkaloids provides limited efficacy compared to the holistic therapeutic effects achieved by retaining the plant's natural complexity. Promoting sustainable practices aligns with the integrative approach of Ayurveda, which values ecological interdependence. Overharvesting threatens not only biodiversity but also the therapeutic potential, as plants lose key bioactive interactions. Conservation strategies must balance resource utilization and biodiversity preservation, ensuring Ayurvedic efficacy without compromising ecological health.

3. **A:** The diminished quality of Amalaki disrupts Triphala's efficacy because its synergistic effects depend on each component's bioactive potency. Amalaki's role in gut microbiota restoration and immunity is vital, and its decline undermines the overall formulation. This question highlights the sensitivity of Ayurvedic formulations to biodiversity loss, as each component contributes uniquely. It reinforces the idea that biodiversity is central to maintaining the therapeutic harmony of complex formulations. Triphala's effectiveness cannot be isolated to individual components, reflecting Ayurveda's holistic approach.

4. **B:** Community-driven agroforestry and in-situ conservation align with Ayurvedic principles by promoting biodiversity and preserving the therapeutic quality of medicinal plants. This approach integrates ecological sustainability with local knowledge systems, ensuring that rising demand does not deplete resources. Monoculture farming, while economically viable, compromises biodiversity and reduces plant potency. Ayurveda's emphasis on harmony with nature supports strategies that balance ecological health and medicinal efficacy, demonstrating the interconnectedness of environmental and therapeutic systems.

5. **A:** Ayurveda integrates biodiversity not just for medicinal purposes but as a way to promote ecological balance. This interdependence implies that conservation strategies should reflect Ayurveda's principle of living in harmony with nature. Sustainable practices ensure the long-term availability of medicinal plants while maintaining ecosystem health. Substituting endangered plants with synthetics or focusing on monoculture farming undermines this ethos, revealing Ayurveda's reliance on biodiversity as both a practical and philosophical framework.

6. **A:** The loss of biodiversity directly impacts Ayurveda by reducing the availability of plants essential for balancing Tridoshas. Ayurvedic formulations depend on the unique therapeutic properties of specific plants, which cannot be replicated synthetically. Biodiversity loss threatens the holistic efficacy of Ayurveda, forcing adaptations that may compromise its integrity. This underscores the importance of conservation as a foundation for maintaining the system's therapeutic relevance in modern ecological contexts.

7. **A:** Sustainable harvesting preserves biodiversity, ensuring that Ayurveda's therapeutic efficacy remains intact. Research shows that sustainable practices improve soil health and ecosystem resilience, enhancing the bioactive properties of medicinal plants. By aligning ecological conservation with Ayurvedic principles, these practices ensure long-term resource availability while supporting biodiversity. This connection underscores Ayurveda's commitment to sustainability as an integral part of its medicinal and ecological philosophy.

8. **A:** Polyculture systems mimic natural ecosystems, preserving phytochemical diversity essential for the therapeutic potency of Ayurvedic plants. Monoculture farming, while efficient for mass production, often reduces the bioactive complexity of plants, compromising their medicinal properties. Ayurveda's principles emphasize ecological harmony, making polyculture systems a better alignment for conserving biodiversity and maintaining therapeutic efficacy.

9. **A:** Localized cultivation using traditional methods effectively balances the ecological and therapeutic demands of Ayurvedic medicine. By growing medicinal plants close to their native ecosystems, the strains on wild populations are alleviated, preserving biodiversity and maintaining plant potency. Traditional methods retain soil fertility, enhance phytochemical profiles, and reduce reliance on harmful chemicals. Unlike synthetic alternatives, which fail to replicate the full therapeutic spectrum of natural compounds, localized farming respects Ayurveda's ecological ethos. Furthermore, such cultivation integrates cultural knowledge with modern conservation needs, creating a sustainable solution for rising global demand without overharvesting or ecological imbalance.

10. **A:** Environmental degradation compromises the bioactive compounds in plants like Haritaki and Bibhitaki, central to Ayurvedic formulations. Climate change and deforestation alter soil health, water availability, and plant ecosystems, diminishing their medicinal efficacy. Ayurveda's principles inherently rely on environmental harmony, as specific plant properties are linked to their habitats. Loss of phytochemical complexity due to ecological changes weakens the efficacy of traditional remedies, affecting systemic health benefits like immunity enhancement. This demonstrates the intrinsic connection between ecological preservation and Ayurveda's sustainability, reinforcing the need for conservation strategies to ensure the continuity of therapeutic practices rooted in biodiversity.

11. **A:** Ayurvedic agricultural practices such as organic farming and companion planting enhance soil fertility, water conservation, and biodiversity. These practices reduce dependence on chemical fertilizers

and pesticides, fostering healthier ecosystems and more potent medicinal plants. However, scalability poses a challenge, as commercial farming pressures often prioritize yield over ecological balance. The tension between tradition and modernization underscores the need for innovative methods to scale these practices sustainably. By preserving traditional farming techniques and integrating them with scientific advancements, Ayurveda can maintain its ecological ethos while addressing global demand, ensuring long-term environmental and therapeutic benefits without compromising biodiversity.

12. **B:** Neem and Tulsi exemplify how medicinal plants contribute to environmental health through phytoremediation, a process where plants detoxify polluted soils and waters. This ability highlights their ecological value beyond therapeutic use, aligning with Ayurveda's emphasis on harmonizing human health and environmental restoration. Their integration into reforestation projects revitalizes ecosystems, creating habitats for pollinators and supporting biodiversity. Unlike chemical detoxification methods, these plants offer sustainable and cost-effective solutions, further demonstrating their dual role in environmental and medicinal contexts. This intersection of ecology and Ayurveda underscores the system's holistic approach to health, benefiting both nature and human communities.

13. **A:** Ayurvedic agricultural practices complement phytoremediation efforts by fostering biodiverse ecosystems that support environmental restoration. For example, companion planting and organic farming enhance soil health, creating favorable conditions for plants like Neem and Tulsi to detoxify pollutants. This synergy reflects Ayurveda's principle of ecological harmony, where agricultural and conservation practices work together to restore degraded landscapes. By combining these methods, Ayurveda addresses environmental challenges holistically, promoting sustainability while preserving therapeutic efficacy. This integration highlights the interdependence between traditional farming techniques and modern environmental needs, ensuring long-term biodiversity and ecological balance while aligning with Ayurvedic values.

14. **B:** Integrating Ayurvedic farming techniques with reforestation projects creates a powerful strategy for addressing environmental health challenges. Medicinal plants with phytoremediation properties, such as Neem and Tulsi, can be incorporated into agroforestry systems, restoring degraded ecosystems while enhancing biodiversity. This approach aligns with Ayurveda's ecological principles by ensuring that conservation efforts are both sustainable and therapeutically effective. Large-scale monoculture farming fails to support biodiversity or ecological restoration, contradicting Ayurveda's holistic ethos. Combining traditional knowledge with reforestation efforts ensures that environmental and medicinal goals are met, preserving natural resources for future generations while maintaining ecological harmony.

15. **A:** Medicinal plants play a vital ecological role in maintaining biodiversity. They support pollinators like bees and butterflies, help stabilize soil with their roots, and regulate water cycles, thus preventing erosion. Overharvesting these plants disrupts ecosystems, leading to loss of biodiversity and imbalance. However, monoculture plantations—though used for economic gain—do not enhance biodiversity; in fact, they reduce genetic variation and soil health over time.

16. **A:** Conservation strategies encompass holistic approaches to safeguard medicinal plant biodiversity. Biosphere reserves protect ecosystems while balancing sustainable use. Seed banks ensure genetic preservation under controlled environments, crucial for species revival in future crises. Sacred groves reflect the cultural ethos of communities, serving as ecological hotspots maintained through traditions. Botanical gardens focus on scientific research and propagation, creating awareness about rare and endangered species. Together, these strategies align local practices with global conservation goals. India's rich tradition of sacred groves and scientific initiatives illustrates how blending cultural wisdom with modern approaches can achieve ecological resilience and biodiversity conservation.

17. **A:** Sustainable harvesting practices mitigate overexploitation and ensure resource availability. Rotational harvesting minimizes pressure on specific areas, allowing natural regeneration. Limiting harvest to mature plants safeguards juvenile populations, maintaining ecological balance. Collecting non-destructive parts, like seeds and leaves, supports extraction without harming plant structures. Community monitoring integrates local knowledge, enhancing the effectiveness of conservation efforts. Such approaches bridge the gap between traditional practices and modern ecological demands. They reflect how local engagement, coupled with scientific techniques, ensures biodiversity protection. India's herbal medicine sector exemplifies these strategies, emphasizing sustainable resource use while supporting community livelihoods.

18. **A:** Ayurveda integrates sustainability into its principles, promoting biodiversity through the use of diverse

medicinal plants in formulations. Seasonal routines (Ritucharya) align human lifestyles with natural cycles, ensuring ecological balance and resilience. Contrary to monoculture farming, Ayurveda emphasizes ecological interdependence, advocating traditional farming practices that conserve biodiversity. Sustainable use of resources in Ayurvedic practices reflects a balance between human needs and environmental health. This ancient system serves as a model of harmony between health and ecology, demonstrating how cultural wisdom can guide modern conservation efforts. Such principles reinforce the importance of biodiversity in holistic health systems.

19. B: India's biodiversity hotspots harbor unique medicinal plants vital for ecological and economic purposes. The Western Ghats, a UNESCO World Heritage Site, is home to Rauwolfia serpentina, a plant used for treating hypertension. The Eastern Himalayas support Nardostachys jatamansi, known for its calming properties. Sundarbans, a mangrove ecosystem, houses Avicennia officinalis, crucial for coastal resilience. The Indo-Burma region boasts Acorus calamus, valued for its therapeutic benefits. These plants reflect the symbiotic relationship between ecosystems and medicinal resources. Protecting such hotspots ensures not only species preservation but also sustains traditional knowledge systems critical to health and livelihoods.

20. B: India's conservation policies are robust frameworks ensuring biodiversity protection and equitable resource use. The Biological Diversity Act, 2002, emphasizes benefit-sharing and access regulation, reflecting global best practices. The NMPB actively promotes medicinal plant conservation through research and cultivation initiatives. The CBD's global advocacy aligns with India's strategies, addressing challenges like genetic piracy and conservation funding. CITES strengthens these efforts by controlling trade in endangered species, curbing illegal exploitation. Together, these policies form a comprehensive blueprint integrating local, national, and international dimensions. They underline India's commitment to conserving its rich biodiversity while ensuring sustainable development.

21. C: Ayurvedic principles embody deep ecological insights, aligning health with environmental sustainability. Panchamahabhuta emphasizes the interconnectedness of nature and humans, inspiring sustainable practices. Tridosha integrates ecological balance into health, mirroring natural cycles. Agni represents the alignment of metabolic energy with environmental rhythms, promoting resource-conscious living. Ojas symbolizes vitality derived from sustainable interactions with nature. These principles reveal a profound understanding of biodiversity's role in well-being. They encourage ethical resource use, reducing ecological footprints. By integrating Ayurveda's wisdom into modern practices, humanity can address current environmental challenges while preserving ecological and cultural heritage.

22. A: In situ conservation involves protecting species in their natural habitats. Sacred groves and national parks serve this function effectively by preserving native ecosystems where medicinal plants naturally thrive. Botanical gardens and seed banks, on the other hand, are examples of ex situ conservation because they maintain species outside of their original environments for research, education, or regeneration purposes.

23. A: Ayurvedic principles provide a holistic framework for biodiversity conservation. Lokasamgraha emphasizes collective well-being, aligning conservation with community empowerment. Dinacharya promotes sustainable practices, syncing human activities with natural rhythms. Sadvritta advocates mindful resource use, fostering ecological responsibility. Prakriti underscores biodiversity by recognizing individuality, reflecting nature's diversity. These interconnected principles showcase Ayurveda's ecological relevance, offering solutions to modern conservation challenges. They bridge traditional wisdom with scientific approaches, inspiring sustainable living. Incorporating such principles into biodiversity management enhances global conservation efforts, promoting a balance between ecological preservation and human development.

24. A: Sustainable conservation of medicinal plants involves both traditional knowledge and scientific innovation. Ethnobotanical studies help document indigenous uses and preserve cultural knowledge. Tissue culture labs can propagate endangered species while reducing the strain on wild populations. Additionally, training local communities in sustainable harvesting ensures ecological balance and empowers them as stewards of biodiversity. Monoculture plantations are not aligned with sustainability due to their negative impact on ecosystems.

25. A: The conservation methods listed in this question align seamlessly with their respective objectives. Biosphere reserves protect entire ecosystems while promoting sustainable use, ensuring biodiversity and ecological balance. Seed banks store genetic material in controlled environments, safeguarding plant species for future restoration. Sacred groves, preserved by communities, act as biodiversity hotspots, maintaining rare and endemic medicinal plants. Botanical gardens provide controlled environments for research and education, focusing on propagation and conservation. Together, these methods create a comprehensive approach to biodiversity preservation. This framework reflects a balance between traditional knowledge and modern science, aligning with ecological and therapeutic conservation priorities.

26. **A:** The listed medicinal plants are matched accurately to their therapeutic uses. Withania somnifera (*Ashwagandha*) is renowned for its adaptogenic properties, helping reduce stress and enhance resilience. *Tinospora cordifolia* (Guduchi) serves as an immune booster and detoxifier, vital in Ayurvedic formulations. *Phyllanthus amarus* (Bhumyamalaki) protects the liver, showcasing its hepatoprotective properties. *Ocimum sanctum* (Tulsi) is valued for its antioxidant and anti-inflammatory effects, contributing to overall health. These plants exemplify Ayurveda's reliance on natural remedies, underlining the importance of preserving their biodiversity. Their therapeutic roles reflect the intricate relationship between ecological health and medicinal efficacy, emphasizing sustainable conservation efforts.

27. **A:** The listed practices and their ecological relevance highlight Ayurveda's commitment to conservation. Sacred groves act as biodiversity hotspots, preserving rare species and maintaining ecological balance. Agroforestry supports mixed cultivation, enhancing soil fertility and promoting ecosystem stability. Sustainable harvesting ensures regeneration by minimizing environmental impact, aligning resource use with ecological needs. Ethnobotanical studies document traditional knowledge, preserving cultural and medicinal insights for future generations. These practices reflect a holistic approach to sustainability, integrating traditional wisdom with modern ecological strategies. This alignment ensures the long-term availability of medicinal plants while fostering biodiversity and ecological harmony, central to Ayurveda's ethos.

28. **C:** India's biodiversity hotspots, such as the Western Ghats and Eastern Himalayas, are home to numerous medicinal plants crucial for Ayurveda. *Rauwolfia serpentina* (Sarpagandha) thrives in the Western Ghats, known for its sedative and antihypertensive properties. *Nardostachys jatamansi* (Jatamansi) grows in the Eastern Himalayas, valued for its calming effects. The Sundarbans harbor *Avicennia officinalis* (Mangrove tree), integral to treating skin and liver disorders, while the Indo-Burma region supports *Acorus calamus* (Sweet flag), known for cognitive and digestive health benefits. This distribution underscores the critical role of preserving these ecosystems for therapeutic and ecological sustainability, safeguarding Ayurveda's foundational resources.

29. **A:** Each policy listed aligns with its respective conservation objective. The Biological Diversity Act (2002) regulates genetic resource access and promotes benefit-sharing, ensuring ecological balance. The National Medicinal Plants Board (NMPB) supports the conservation and propagation of medicinal plants, addressing sustainability. The Convention on Biological Diversity (CBD) advocates global conservation efforts and equitable benefit-sharing. CITES (Convention on International Trade in Endangered Species) regulates international trade to protect endangered plant species. These policies collectively represent a robust framework for addressing biodiversity challenges. Their implementation reflects the integration of traditional knowledge and modern conservation, ensuring ecological and therapeutic preservation.

30. **D:** Ayurvedic principles align deeply with ecological relevance. Panchamahabhuta (Five Elements) represents the interconnectedness of nature and human health, emphasizing harmony with the environment. Tridosha maintains balance in natural cycles, reflecting Ayurveda's ecological perspective. Agni (Digestive Fire) symbolizes the alignment of metabolic energy with environmental rhythms, while Ojas reflects vitality sustained through sustainable living practices. These principles underscore Ayurveda's holistic approach, integrating human health with ecological preservation. They advocate sustainability not just for individual well-being but for the broader environment. This alignment ensures that therapeutic practices remain ecologically grounded, addressing modern conservation challenges with traditional wisdom.

31. **A:** Conservation measures like sacred groves, botanical gardens, national parks, and seed banks reflect diverse approaches to preserving biodiversity. Sacred groves, managed by communities, protect rare species and maintain cultural significance. Botanical gardens provide controlled environments for the research and propagation of medicinal plants. National parks ensure ecological stability, preserving entire ecosystems. Seed banks store genetic material for future replanting, safeguarding species from extinction. Together, these strategies reflect a comprehensive conservation framework, balancing ecological, cultural, and scientific needs. This alignment with Ayurveda's principles emphasizes sustainability, ensuring that medicinal plants remain available for therapeutic and ecological purposes.

32. **C:** The biodiversity hotspots listed are accurately matched to their associated species, showcasing the unique medicinal flora of each region. *Gymnema sylvestre* grows in the Western Ghats, known for its anti-diabetic properties. *Taxus wallichiana* thrives in the Eastern Himalayas, valued for its anti-cancer compounds. *Terminalia chebula*, integral to gut health, is found in the Indo-Burma region, while *Heritiera fomes*, supporting mangrove ecosystems, grows in the Sundarbans. These distributions highlight the importance of conserving these regions to protect the ecological and therapeutic value of their medicinal plants. Their preservation ensures the sustainability of Ayurvedic formulations and ecosystem health.

33. A: The conservation goals listed are well-aligned with their respective methods. Preserving biodiversity is encouraged through sacred groves, which protect rare and endemic species while promoting community stewardship. Botanical gardens advance education by creating environments for research and awareness about plant conservation. Ensuring regeneration relies on sustainable harvesting, which minimizes environmental damage and promotes natural renewal. Mitigating overharvesting is achieved through rotational harvesting, which prevents resource depletion by alternating collection areas. These strategies form a robust framework that integrates traditional knowledge and modern practices. Together, they reflect Ayurveda's ecological ethos, ensuring sustainable use and long-term availability of medicinal plants.

34. B: Ayurvedic practices such as Lokasamgraha, Dinacharya, Sadvritta, and Prakriti align with conservation principles. Lokasamgraha advocates for holistic well-being, integrating biodiversity preservation into daily life. Dinacharya aligns human routines with natural cycles, promoting sustainable resource use. Sadvritta emphasizes ethical consumption, fostering mindfulness in resource management. Prakriti celebrates individual uniqueness, supporting biodiversity by recognizing ecological diversity. These principles collectively highlight Ayurveda's holistic approach to sustainability, integrating human health with environmental balance. By addressing ecological challenges through these traditional frameworks, Ayurveda ensures the preservation of medicinal plants while fostering a harmonious relationship between nature, health, and sustainability.

35. A: Statement 1 highlights the critical link between medicinal plant conservation and Ayurvedic sustainability, as many formulations rely on plant-based ingredients. Statement 2 explains the pressure on wild populations caused by rising demand for Ayurvedic formulations, leading to overharvesting and habitat destruction. Together, these statements underscore the ecological and therapeutic significance of conservation. Without sustainable harvesting practices, the depletion of wild populations threatens not only the plants themselves but also the efficacy and future of Ayurvedic medicine. This interconnectedness reflects the need for immediate action to align conservation strategies with increasing global interest in traditional medicine.

36. C: Statement 1 accurately describes in-situ conservation, which involves maintaining plant populations within their natural habitats. Examples include sacred groves and national parks. Statement 2 incorrectly classifies botanical gardens as in-situ conservation. While botanical gardens recreate natural-like environments, they fall under ex-situ conservation due to their controlled settings. This distinction is crucial to understanding conservation strategies. In-situ methods preserve the ecological context of plants, supporting their natural growth cycles and interactions. Ex-situ methods complement this by safeguarding species outside their native habitats, ensuring genetic material is preserved for research and future restoration efforts, forming a holistic conservation framework.

37. A: Sacred groves function as natural gene banks, preserving the genetic diversity of medicinal plants. Managed with traditional ecological knowledge, these groves safeguard rare and endemic species while maintaining ecological balance. Statement 1 emphasizes their biological importance, while Statement 2 explains the role of indigenous knowledge in their preservation. Together, these statements highlight the interplay between cultural practices and ecological sustainability. Sacred groves exemplify the integration of biodiversity conservation with community-driven stewardship. This synergy reflects Ayurveda's ecological ethos, ensuring the preservation of medicinal plants within their natural habitats while fostering a harmonious relationship between human activity and nature.

38. C: Statement 1 is true – Sustainable harvesting is essential to conserve medicinal plants and maintain ecological balance. It includes techniques like collecting mature parts, using rotational harvests, and involving local communities to avoid overexploitation.Statement 2 is false – Harvesting plants during their reproductive stages can be harmful, as it may interfere with seed development, pollination, or fruiting, thus reducing regeneration and population sustainability. Correct practice usually involves harvesting post-reproductive maturity or collecting non-destructive parts like leaves or bark without affecting plant reproduction.

39. C: Ethnobotanical studies are essential for documenting the traditional knowledge of medicinal plants, including their cultural, therapeutic, and ecological uses. Statement 1 captures this role accurately. However, Statement 2 erroneously limits ethnobotanical studies to plant taxonomy, neglecting their broader scope, which includes understanding indigenous practices and ecological interactions. By bridging traditional knowledge and modern science, ethnobotany ensures the preservation of cultural heritage while supporting biodiversity conservation. This multidisciplinary approach aligns with Ayurveda's holistic philosophy, fostering a deeper understanding of medicinal plants and their ecological significance. Such studies are crucial for developing sustainable conservation strategies rooted in cultural traditions.

40. A: Biodiversity hotspots are critical for conserving medicinal plants due to their high species diversity and endemism. Assertion (A) correctly identifies their importance, while Reason (R) explains the threats posed by habitat destruction and human activities. Together, they emphasize the urgency of conservation in these regions. Hotspots like the Western Ghats and Eastern Himalayas house rare medicinal plants essential for Ayurveda. Preserving these areas ensures the survival of unique species, supporting both ecological balance and therapeutic efficacy. This relationship underscores the interconnectedness of biodiversity conservation and traditional medicine, advocating for immediate measures to protect these vulnerable ecosystems.

41. A: Seed banks are essential for conserving medicinal plant biodiversity, as they store seeds under controlled conditions for future use. Assertion (A) correctly identifies their role in biodiversity preservation, ensuring that plant species can be regenerated when natural populations are threatened. Reason (R) accurately explains the mechanism, emphasizing the long-term availability of genetic material for replanting and research. Together, they highlight the importance of seed banks as a reliable conservation strategy, complementing in-situ efforts. This approach aligns with Ayurveda's reliance on diverse medicinal plants, ensuring ecological balance and the availability of resources for therapeutic purposes in the future.

42. A: Overharvesting disrupts ecosystem stability and biodiversity by depleting natural resources faster than they can regenerate. Assertion (A) correctly highlights this threat, while Reason (R) identifies urbanization and commercial exploitation as primary causes. Together, they explain how unsustainable practices threaten medicinal plant populations and their ecological roles. This depletion not only impacts Ayurveda's reliance on these plants but also compromises ecological health. Sustainable harvesting and community-based conservation are essential to mitigate these threats. These strategies ensure that biodiversity is preserved, ecosystems remain balanced, and medicinal plants are available for therapeutic and cultural use, reflecting Ayurveda's holistic principles.

43. A: Community-based conservation programs like Joint Forest Management (JFM) enhance medicinal plant conservation by involving local communities in sustainable resource management. Assertion (A) accurately reflects their importance, while Reason (R) explains how local engagement ensures equitable benefit-sharing and fosters accountability. Together, they highlight the effectiveness of such programs in aligning ecological conservation with socio-economic benefits. This approach empowers communities to protect biodiversity while benefiting from its sustainable use. JFM reflects Ayurveda's ecological ethos, integrating traditional knowledge with modern conservation strategies. By fostering local stewardship, these programs ensure the long-term preservation of medicinal plants and their therapeutic potential.

44. A: The conservation of medicinal plants is crucial for pharmaceutical development, as many synthetic drugs are derived from bioactive compounds found in plants. Assertion (A) correctly emphasizes this importance, while Reason (R) explains the reliance of modern medicine on natural compounds. Together, they underline the interconnectedness of biodiversity and drug development. For example, plants like Taxus *wallichiana*,, a source of anti-cancer compounds, demonstrate the therapeutic potential of conserving medicinal species. Preserving biodiversity ensures that future discoveries remain possible, benefiting both traditional and modern medicine. This relationship highlights the urgency of conservation efforts to sustain ecological and therapeutic resources.

45. C: Sacred groves play a vital role in preserving the genetic diversity of medicinal plants, reflecting their ecological and cultural significance. Assertion (A) correctly identifies this role, emphasizing their importance in biodiversity conservation. However, Reason (R) inaccurately claims that sacred groves are maintained by modern scientific interventions; in reality, they are primarily preserved through traditional practices and community stewardship. This distinction highlights the value of indigenous knowledge in maintaining these natural gene banks. Sacred groves exemplify the integration of cultural and ecological conservation, aligning with Ayurveda's holistic philosophy and ensuring the sustainability of medicinal plant resources for future generations.

46. B: The primary threats to medicinal plant biodiversity include climate change, habitat destruction, and overharvesting for global markets. Statements (a), (b), and (c) accurately reflect these challenges, highlighting how unsustainable practices and environmental degradation threaten species survival. Traditional knowledge, while important, is not a direct cause of biodiversity loss. This underscores the need for conservation strategies that address ecological and economic pressures. Preserving biodiversity ensures the availability of medicinal plants for therapeutic and ecological purposes, aligning with Ayurveda's principles. These efforts must integrate traditional knowledge, sustainable harvesting, and modern science to mitigate these pressing threats.

47. A: Sacred groves contribute significantly to medicinal plant conservation by acting as natural gene banks and preserving genetic diversity. Statements (a) and (b) reflect their ecological importance, emphasizing their role in protecting rare species and maintaining biodiversity. Managed by local communities, these groves remain untouched by commercial exploitation, ensuring ecological balance. However, they do not promote modern cultivation practices or scientific research, which are roles fulfilled by botanical gardens. Sacred groves embody the integration of cultural traditions with biodiversity conservation, aligning with Ayurveda's holistic philosophy and emphasizing the importance of preserving natural ecosystems for therapeutic and ecological purposes.

48. A: Biodiversity hotspots like the Western Ghats house rare medicinal plant species crucial for Ayurveda. Statements (a) and (b) highlight their role as natural habitats essential for the growth, regeneration, and preservation of medicinal plants. These hotspots maintain ecological balance and foster biodiversity, supporting both therapeutic efficacy and environmental health. However, they do not eliminate the need for ex-situ conservation or focus solely on commercial cultivation. Preserving these areas ensures that medicinal plants remain available for traditional and modern medicine, reflecting the interconnectedness of ecological conservation and therapeutic sustainability. This approach aligns with Ayurveda's reliance on biodiversity.

49. B: Modern science plays a pivotal role in medicinal plant conservation through biotechnology and pharmacological research. Tissue culture and genetic engineering aid in propagating endangered species, while pharmacological studies validate traditional uses, bridging ancient knowledge with modern applications. Statements (a), (b), and (c) reflect this integration, emphasizing how advances in science enhance conservation efforts. However, genetic engineering does not eliminate the need for traditional cultivation, as natural ecosystems provide unique phytochemical profiles essential for therapeutic efficacy. This synergy between traditional knowledge and modern science supports Ayurveda's holistic approach, ensuring the preservation and sustainable use of medicinal plants.

50. C: Ayurveda aligns with environmental conservation through practices like Lokasamgraha, which emphasizes harmony between humans and nature. Statements (a), (b), and (d) reflect this alignment, showcasing how Ayurvedic routines like Dinacharya and Ritucharya promote ecological balance and sustainability. These practices integrate traditional knowledge with conservation efforts, ensuring the preservation of biodiversity and natural resources. However, Ayurveda does not discourage the use of natural resources but advocates their sustainable use. This philosophy highlights Ayurveda's relevance in addressing modern ecological challenges, emphasizing the interconnectedness of human health and environmental preservation through sustainable practices and holistic principles.

CHAPTER 27

INTELLECTUAL PROPERTY RIGHTS AND PROTECTION OF TRADITIONAL KNOWLEDGE

Overview of Intellectual Property Rights (IPR) and Its Relevance to Ayurveda

Intellectual Property Rights (IPR) represent legal protections granted to the creators and owners of intellectual property, encompassing inventions, artistic works, designs, symbols, and formulations. These rights ensure that creators can reap financial and reputational benefits from their innovations while incentivizing further creativity and investment in research and development. The intersection of IPR and traditional knowledge (TK), particularly Ayurveda, raises important questions regarding the balance between innovation, cultural heritage, and equitable access.

Ayurveda: A Reservoir of Traditional Knowledge

Ayurveda, a millennia-old system of medicine originating in India, represents one of the most sophisticated repositories of traditional knowledge. Its formulations, methodologies, and principles have been preserved in texts such as the Charaka Samhita, Sushruta Samhita, and Ashtanga Hridaya. Ayurveda incorporates a holistic approach to health, emphasizing balance in bodily functions and the use of natural remedies derived from plants, minerals, and other natural resources.

As global interest in alternative medicine and natural health remedies has surged, Ayurveda has gained prominence on the international stage. However, this increasing attention has also brought challenges, such as the risk of misappropriation of Ayurvedic knowledge by entities seeking commercial gain without recognition of its cultural roots or benefits to indigenous communities. Protecting Ayurveda under IPR frameworks is thus crucial to safeguarding this invaluable heritage.The Importance of IPR in Preserving and Promoting Ayurveda.The application of IPR in Ayurveda serves several purposes, including:

1. **Preventing Biopiracy:** The unauthorized commercial exploitation of traditional knowledge by external entities, often termed biopiracy, threatens to erode the integrity and ownership of Ayurvedic knowledge. Patents and trademarks provide legal mechanisms to combat this exploitation.
2. **Promoting Research and Innovation:** By granting exclusive rights to innovators, IPR encourages investments in Ayurvedic research and product development, fostering advancements in this ancient science.
3. **Ensuring Ethical Commercialization:** IPR frameworks can regulate the commercialization of Ayurvedic formulations, ensuring that traditional knowledge holders receive equitable benefits.
4. **Maintaining Cultural Integrity:** Protecting Ayurveda under IPR prevents its commodification or dilution, ensuring its transmission to future generations in its authentic form.
5. **Facilitating Global Recognition:** By aligning Ayurveda with international IPR standards, its recognition and respect in the global health and wellness industry can be enhanced.

Despite these advantages, the application of IPR to Ayurveda is fraught with challenges. Traditional knowledge often exists in the public domain, complicating its protection under conventional IPR frameworks designed for individualistic and novel creations.

PROTECTION OF TRADITIONAL KNOWLEDGE AND AYURVEDIC FORMULATIONS

Traditional Knowledge and IPR: A Unique Paradigm

Traditional knowledge (TK) refers to knowledge systems developed by indigenous and local communities over generations, encompassing practices, skills, and innovations related to agriculture, medicine, art, and culture. Unlike modern intellectual property, which emphasizes novelty and individual authorship, TK is often collective, cumulative, and ancient. This distinction necessitates tailored IPR mechanisms for its protection.

In the context of Ayurveda, TK comprises formulations, medicinal plant use, therapeutic techniques, and diagnostic methods. While this knowledge is widely disseminated in classical texts and local oral traditions, its protection remains a complex task due to its communal ownership and historical dissemination.

Key Mechanisms for Protecting Traditional Knowledge

The protection of traditional knowledge (TK) involves a combination of legal, institutional, and community-driven mechanisms designed to safeguard centuries-old practices, cultural heritage, and biodiversity from exploitation or misappropriation. The five primary mechanisms explored below focus on systematic documentation, intellectual property rights (IPR), regional identification, community empowerment, and branding, which collectively provide a robust framework to protect and promote traditional knowledge.

1. **Documentation and Databases:** The systematic documentation of traditional knowledge is a cornerstone for its protection. Traditional knowledge, including Ayurvedic formulations, has historically been transmitted orally or through ancient texts, making it vulnerable to loss or misappropriation. By creating comprehensive databases, traditional knowledge can be preserved and its rightful origins acknowledged.
    - **Role of Documentation in Protecting Traditional Knowledge:** Preventing Biopiracy: By documenting TK in organized databases, countries can prevent biopiracy, where corporations or individuals claim patents on knowledge already existing in the public domain.
    - **Establishing Prior Art:** A documented repository serves as evidence of prior art, which is essential for invalidating wrongful patent claims. Patent offices worldwide consult these repositories to assess novelty and originality in patent applications.
    - **Preserving Cultural Heritage:** Documentation ensures that TK, particularly oral traditions, is preserved for future generations, reducing the risk of its disappearance.

India's Traditional Knowledge Digital Library (TKDL)

One of the most notable examples of TK documentation is the Traditional Knowledge Digital Library (TKDL), an initiative by the Indian government. Launched in 2001, TKDL was created to address the growing threat of biopiracy, particularly in the realm of Ayurveda, Siddha, and Unani medicine.

Key Features of TKDL

1. **Extensive Coverage:** TKDL has cataloged over 200,000 formulations from ancient texts, including the Charaka Samhita, Sushruta Samhita, and others.
2. **Multilingual Interface:** TKDL translates traditional texts written in Sanskrit, Arabic, Tamil, and other regional languages into patent examiners' languages such as English, German, and Japanese.
3. **Global Collaboration:** TKDL collaborates with international patent offices, granting them access to its database to prevent unauthorized patenting of traditional knowledge.
4. **Searchable Database:** The repository is searchable by keywords, allowing examiners to identify prior art efficiently.

Challenges in Documentation

- **Resource-Intensive Process:** Compiling, translating, and digitalizing traditional texts requires substantial time and expertise.
- **Incomplete Coverage:** Oral traditions, which constitute a significant portion of TK, are often challenging to document comprehensively.
- **Data Sensitivity:** Public access to databases may inadvertently expose TK to exploitation if not carefully regulated.

Way Forward

To address these challenges, governments and organizations must invest in expanding TK databases, integrating oral traditions, and ensuring stringent data protection measures. Countries with rich repositories of TK should follow India's lead in creating their own digital libraries to prevent global misappropriation.

2. **Patents and Prior Art:** Patents are a critical component of IPR, granting inventors exclusive rights to their inventions for a specified period. While TK, including Ayurvedic formulations, is generally not patentable due to its pre-existing nature, patent systems can protect innovations derived from traditional principles.

Patentability of Traditional Knowledge: For a TK-based invention to qualify for a patent, it must satisfy three criteria:

1. **Novelty:** The invention must be new and not part of prior art.
2. **Inventive Step:** The invention must demonstrate a technical advancement or innovative process.
3. **Industrial Applicability:** The invention must have practical applications in industry.

Examples of patentable innovations in Ayurveda include:

- Novel drug delivery systems for Ayurvedic herbs.
- Improved formulations combining Ayurvedic and modern scientific principles.
- Extraction techniques that enhance the efficacy of Ayurvedic medicines.

Role of Prior Art in Patent Examinations: Prior art refers to any evidence showing that a particular innovation was already known before a patent application was filed. TK databases like TKDL play a pivotal role in prior art searches by patent examiners. For example:

- In 1995, an attempt to patent the medicinal use of turmeric for wound healing in the U.S. was overturned after evidence from ancient Indian texts proved that this use was already known.

Challenges in Patent Protection

High Cost of Filing Patents: For traditional knowledge holders, especially small communities, filing patents may be financially unfeasible.

- **Global Disparities in Patent Laws:** Different countries have varying standards for patentability, complicating the protection of TK internationally.
- **Misuse of Patents:** Corporations may attempt to patent slight modifications of traditional formulations, claiming them as novel.
- **Strengthening Patent Protections:** Expanding access to prior art databases like TKDL for international patent offices.
- Encouraging collaboration between traditional knowledge holders and researchers to develop patentable innovations.
- Advocating for international agreements to harmonize patent

3. **Geographical Indications (GI):** Geographical Indications (GI) are a specialized form of IPR that links a product to a specific geographic region, emphasizing its unique qualities or reputation. For TK-based products, GI tags help preserve authenticity and cultural identity while offering economic benefits to local communities.

Significance of GI in Protecting Traditional Knowledge: Preserving Authenticity: GI protection ensures that only products genuinely originating from a specific region can use the associated name. For instance, Darjeeling tea and Champagne are well-known GI-protected products.

- **Preventing Mislabeling:** GI tags prevent fraudulent labeling of products that do not meet the defined quality standards.
- **Boosting Local Economies:** GI certification enhances market value and demand for authentic products, benefiting producers.

GI in Ayurveda: Ayurvedic products with specific regional associations can benefit significantly from GI protection. For example:

- **Chyawanprash:** Manufactured in regions using traditional techniques.
- **Medicinal Plants:** Herbs like Ashwagandha or Shatavari grown in specific regions renowned for their potency.

Challenges in GI Protection: Lack of Awareness: Producers in rural areas may be unaware of GI protections and their benefits.

- **Expensive Certification:** Obtaining GI certification can be costly and bureaucratic, deterring small producers.
- **Counterfeit Products:** Despite GI tags, counterfeit goods may continue to flood markets, undermining the value of authentic products.

Enhancing GI Protections

- Conduct awareness campaigns for local producers about GI benefits and processes.
- Simplify GI certification procedures to encourage broader participation.
- Strengthen enforcement mechanisms to combat counterfeit goods.

4. **Customary Laws and Community Rights:** Customary laws and community rights recognize the role of indigenous communities in preserving and practicing TK. Unlike formal IPR systems, customary laws are rooted in local traditions and cultural norms, providing a culturally sensitive approach to protecting TK.

Significance of Customary Laws: Community Empowerment: Customary laws give communities control over their knowledge, ensuring that external entities cannot exploit it without consent.

- **Cultural Preservation:** By recognizing traditional practices, customary laws promote the transmission of TK to future generations.
- **Benefit Sharing:** Legal frameworks like the Nagoya Protocol ensure that benefits derived from TK are shared equitably with knowledge holders.

Nagoya Protocol and Access and Benefit Sharing (ABS): The Nagoya Protocol, an international agreement under the Convention on Biological Diversity (CBD), emphasizes:

- Fair and equitable sharing of benefits arising from the use of genetic resources.
- Prior informed consent and mutually agreed terms for access to TK.

Challenges in Implementing Customary Laws: Limited Legal Recognition: Many countries lack legal frameworks to recognize customary laws.

- **Conflicts with National Laws:** Customary practices may conflict with formal legal systems, creating ambiguity.
- **Lack of Representation:** Indigenous communities often lack representation in decision-making processes.

Strengthening Community Rights:

- Integrate customary laws into national legal frameworks.
- Promote community-led governance models for TK.
- Enhance representation of indigenous communities in international forums.

5. **Copyright and Trademarks:** While copyright protection is less relevant to TK, trademarks can play a vital role in branding and distinguishing authentic TK-based products.

Trademarks in Protecting TK:

- **Brand Recognition:** Trademarks help consumers identify and trust authentic TK-based products.
- **Preventing Misuse:** Trademark registration prevents unauthorized entities from using similar names or logos, protecting the reputation of TK products.

Examples in Ayurveda:

- Branding Ayurvedic formulations or wellness centers to emphasize authenticity.
- Protecting logos or symbols associated with traditional medicine brands.

Challenges with Trademarks:

- **High Costs:** Registering and maintaining trademarks can be expensive for small businesses or communities.
- **Limited Scope:** Trademarks do not protect the knowledge itself but only the branding associated with it.

Enhancing Trademark Protections

- Provide subsidies or financial support for communities to register trademarks.
- Encourage collaborations between TK holders and marketing professionals to create strong brands.

International Efforts to Protect Traditional Knowledge

Several international conventions and agreements have addressed the need to protect TK and associated resources:

- **The Convention on Biological Diversity (CBD):** Emphasizes the sovereign rights of nations over their biological resources and mandates fair benefit sharing.
- **The Nagoya Protocol:** Aims to ensure equitable sharing of benefits arising from the utilization of genetic resources and associated TK.
- **World Intellectual Property Organization (WIPO):** Established the Intergovernmental Committee on Intellectual Property and Genetic Resources, Traditional Knowledge, and Folklore (IGC) to explore legal mechanisms for TK protection.

Challenges in Protecting Traditional Knowledge and Ayurvedic Formulations

Despite the frameworks in place, several challenges persist in protecting TK and Ayurvedic formulations under IPR:

1. **Lack of Clear Ownership:** Determining ownership of TK is complex, especially when it is collectively held by communities or exists in the public domain.
2. **Insufficient Documentation:** While initiatives like TKDL are commendable, significant gaps remain in documenting the vast repository of Ayurvedic knowledge, particularly oral traditions.
3. **Limited Awareness and Access:** Many traditional knowledge holders are unaware of IPR mechanisms, leading to underutilization of protective measures.
4. **Biopiracy and Misappropriation:** Instances of biopiracy continue, as corporations seek to exploit TK without adequate benefit sharing. Examples include controversies over patents on neem, turmeric, and basmati rice.

5. **Conflicts Between Modern IPR and Traditional Practices:** Conventional IPR frameworks emphasize individual ownership and innovation, conflicting with the communal and cumulative nature of TK.
6. **Global Legal Disparities:** The lack of harmonized international legal standards for TK protection hinders effective enforcement and recognition across borders.

Strategies to Strengthen IPR Protection for Ayurveda

To address these challenges, a multi-pronged approach is necessary:

1. **Enhancing Documentation:** Expand initiatives like TKDL to cover oral traditions and lesser-known Ayurvedic practices, ensuring comprehensive representation of TK.
2. **Legal and Policy Reforms:** Amend IPR laws to accommodate the unique characteristics of TK, such as collective ownership and ancient origins.
3. **Community Involvement:** Empower traditional knowledge holders through capacity-building programs, ensuring they understand and utilize IPR frameworks.
4. **Strengthening International Collaboration:** Advocate for global standards on TK protection through forums like WIPO, ensuring recognition and enforcement of rights internationally.
5. **Ethical Commercialization Models:** Develop benefit-sharing models that balance commercial interests with the rights of TK holders, fostering equitable partnerships.
6. **Promoting Research and Development:** Encourage collaborations between traditional practitioners and modern researchers, ensuring that innovations build upon and respect Ayurvedic principles.

MULTIPLE CHOICE QUESTIONS

1. A global pharmaceutical company applies for a patent on a drug developed from extracts of Haritaki (*Terminalia chebula*), a component of the classical Ayurvedic formulation Triphala. The company claims novelty based on their proprietary extraction process, which isolates tannins for enhanced antioxidant activity. Critics argue that this constitutes biopiracy, as Haritaki's antioxidant properties and its use in Triphala are well-documented in Ayurveda. Considering the principles of intellectual property law, what would be the most appropriate legal response to this patent application?

A. Grant the patent, as the extraction process constitutes a novel innovation under intellectual property frameworks.

B. Reject the patent on grounds of biopiracy, as the therapeutic properties of Haritaki are part of prior art documented in Ayurvedic texts.

C. Approve the patent but require the company to enter into a benefit-sharing agreement with the communities that traditionally use Haritaki.

D. Reject the patent because traditional knowledge cannot form the basis of any commercial intellectual property claims.

2. An interdisciplinary team develops a dietary supplement based on the Ayurvedic formulation Nishamalaki (a combination of turmeric and amalaki). The product is marketed for managing Type 2 Diabetes Mellitus (T2DM), with claims supported by modern pharmacological studies. However, independent evaluations reveal that the supplement is less effective than its traditional counterpart due to differences in preparation methods and sourcing of raw materials. Which of the following best explains the reduced efficacy of the commercial product?

A. The active compounds in turmeric and amalaki are unstable in modern processing methods.

B. The therapeutic synergy of Ayurvedic formulations is lost when traditional preparation methods are not followed.

C. Modern pharmacological studies overestimate the efficacy of Ayurvedic formulations.

D. Ayurvedic remedies are inherently unreliable and unsuitable for commercial applications.

3. A policy researcher evaluates the role of India's Traditional Knowledge Digital Library (TKDL) in preventing biopiracy. The study identifies several instances where patents on traditional remedies, such as the use of turmeric for wound healing and neem for pest control, were revoked based on evidence from TKDL. However, the researcher observes limitations in the current framework, including incomplete documentation of oral traditions. What recommendation would most effectively enhance TKDL's role in safeguarding Ayurvedic knowledge?

A. Expand TKDL's scope to include comprehensive documentation of oral traditions and lesser-known formulations.

B. Limit TKDL to widely known Ayurvedic texts to avoid overwhelming patent examiners with excessive information.

C. Make TKDL publicly accessible to encourage innovation by independent researchers.
D. Collaborate with global pharmaceutical companies to commercialize documented formulations.

4. A government agency seeks to promote sustainable practices in the cultivation of medicinal plants used in Ayurveda. The agency identifies overharvesting of wild herbs such as Ashwagandha and Amalaki as a critical issue, exacerbated by global demand for Ayurvedic supplements. Considering the balance between ecological sustainability and economic growth, which policy intervention would most effectively address the problem?
A. Ban the export of Ayurvedic herbs to reduce pressure on wild populations.
B. Encourage monoculture farming of high-demand herbs to maximize yield.
C. Support community-led agroforestry initiatives to integrate herb cultivation with local ecosystems.
D. Promote synthetic alternatives to Ayurvedic herbs to eliminate dependency on natural resources.

5. An Ayurvedic research institute collaborates with molecular biologists to study the concept of "Agni" (digestive fire) in relation to modern enzymatic pathways. The study correlates impaired Agni with reduced activity of digestive enzymes and increased levels of systemic toxins (Ama) in patients with chronic diseases. Ayurvedic treatments are found to enhance enzymatic activity, aligning with the principle of balancing Agni. What is the primary implication of this research for integrating Ayurveda into modern healthcare?
A. Ayurvedic concepts like Agni lack empirical validation and remain symbolic.
B. Modern healthcare can adopt Ayurvedic principles by equating Agni to measurable enzymatic activity.
C. Ayurvedic treatments are effective but cannot be integrated into scientific frameworks.
D. The concept of Agni contradicts established biochemical principles, limiting its applicability.

6. A multinational corporation claims intellectual property rights over a skincare product derived from neem (*Azadirachta indica*). The company's patent application describes a unique formulation that combines neem oil with modern emulsifiers for enhanced skin absorption. However, the use of neem for skin health is widely documented in Ayurveda. How should the patent office evaluate the novelty of the application?
A. Approve the patent as the combination with modern emulsifiers constitutes a novel formulation.
B. Reject the patent due to prior art, as neem's skin benefits are already documented in traditional texts.
C. Grant the patent conditionally, requiring the company to acknowledge Ayurveda as the source of inspiration.
D. Allow the patent while excluding neem's therapeutic properties from its claims.

7. A public health initiative promotes the integration of Ayurveda into national healthcare systems, emphasizing its preventive and holistic approach. However, critics argue that standardizing Ayurvedic treatments compromises their individualized nature, as remedies are traditionally tailored to a patient's Prakriti (constitution). How can policymakers address this challenge while ensuring the accessibility of Ayurvedic care?
A. Standardize Ayurvedic treatments to align with biomedical practices for ease of integration.
B. Retain the personalized approach of Ayurveda but provide training to healthcare professionals for its application.
C. Exclude Ayurveda from national healthcare to preserve its authenticity as a traditional system.
D. Limit Ayurvedic care to preventive treatments, avoiding its application in disease management.

8. Researchers studying Ayurvedic Rasas (tastes) find a correlation between bitter Rasa and reduced inflammatory markers in animal models. However, critics challenge the study's methodology, arguing that the therapeutic effects of Rasa cannot be isolated from the broader context of Ayurvedic formulations. What does this debate reveal about the challenges of scientifically validating Ayurveda?
A. Ayurvedic principles cannot be validated scientifically due to their philosophical nature.
B. Isolating specific elements of Ayurveda oversimplifies its holistic framework, limiting its validation.
C. Modern science is fully capable of validating Ayurvedic concepts without modifications.
D. Scientific validation is unnecessary, as Ayurveda's efficacy is rooted in tradition rather than evidence.

9. An Ayurvedic manufacturing company markets a product as "traditional immunity boosters" containing Ashwagandha and Tulsi (*Ocimum sanctum*). However, investigations reveal that the company uses synthetic additives to enhance shelf life, raising concerns about the authenticity of the product. What would be the most ethical approach for the company to address this issue?
A. Remove all synthetic additives and adhere strictly to traditional preparation methods.
B. Continue using synthetic additives but disclose them transparently in the product labeling.

C. Shift the focus to synthetic formulations entirely and discontinue the Ayurvedic branding.
D. Justify the use of additives by emphasizing their role in improving the product's accessibility.

10. A country with a rich repository of traditional knowledge proposes an amendment to the TRIPS agreement, requiring patent applicants to disclose the source of any genetic resources or traditional knowledge used in their inventions. Developed nations resist this proposal, arguing that it imposes excessive burdens on innovation. What is the central ethical issue in this debate?
A. Balancing the protection of traditional knowledge with the interests of global innovation.
B. Limiting the commercialization of traditional knowledge to preserve its cultural value.
C. Avoiding excessive regulation of patents to encourage free-market competition.
D. Protecting the intellectual property of traditional communities over corporate rights.

Directions (Q. No. 11-14): *Scenario-Based Questions*

SCENARIO 1

A pharmacological research institute collaborates with an Ayurvedic center to study the efficacy of Ayurvedic formulations in managing Type 2 Diabetes Mellitus (T2DM). The focus is on the classical Ayurvedic formulation "Nishamalaki," which combines turmeric (*Curcuma longa*) and amalaki (*Emblica officinalis*). Preliminary studies reveal that the formulation significantly lowers blood glucose levels, reduces insulin resistance, and minimizes oxidative stress. These effects are attributed to curcumin and vitamin C, the key bioactive compounds in turmeric and amalaki, respectively.

The researchers also explore the molecular pathways influenced by Nishamalaki, identifying that the formulation activates AMP-activated protein kinase (AMPK) and reduces pro-inflammatory cytokines such as interleukin-6 (IL-6). However, the study also highlights variations in efficacy due to differences in the quality of raw materials. Ayurvedic practitioners emphasize that the therapeutic effects depend on following traditional preparation methods, including sourcing herbs from specific regions with ideal environmental conditions.

SCENARIO 2

Simultaneously, an environmental biologist investigates the sustainability of cultivating turmeric and amalaki. The global demand for these herbs has led to intensive farming practices, which compromise soil fertility and biodiversity. Overharvesting of wild amalaki populations has further threatened the species, while monoculture plantations of turmeric have increased the incidence of soil-borne diseases.

The biologist proposes agroforestry models that integrate turmeric and amalaki cultivation with other crops, promoting ecological balance and maintaining the bioactive compound concentration. However, the transition to sustainable practices requires significant investment, government support, and cooperation between Ayurvedic industries, farmers, and environmentalists. The findings underscore the interconnectedness of sustainable herb cultivation and the consistent therapeutic outcomes of Ayurvedic formulations.

11. Based on the findings in Scenario 1, which molecular mechanism most accurately explains the anti-diabetic effects of Nishamalaki?
A. Direct stimulation of pancreatic beta cells for increased insulin secretion.
B. Activation of AMP-activated protein kinase (AMPK) and reduction of pro-inflammatory cytokines.
C. Inhibition of gut microbiota diversity, thereby reducing glucose absorption.
D. Enhanced glycogen storage in muscles without altering inflammatory pathways.

12. Considering the issues highlighted in Scenario 2, which strategy would best ensure the sustainable cultivation of turmeric and amalaki while maintaining their medicinal quality?
A. Establishing large-scale monoculture plantations to maximize yield.
B. Implementing agroforestry models that integrate these herbs with diverse crops.
C. Developing synthetic alternatives to reduce dependency on natural resources.
D. Encouraging the use of genetically modified turmeric and amalaki strains.

13. How does the environmental degradation of turmeric and amalaki, as described in Scenario 2, potentially affect the therapeutic outcomes of Nishamalaki observed in Scenario 1?
A. Reduced bioactive compound concentration could diminish the formulation's efficacy in managing diabetes.
B. The quality of turmeric and amalaki has no measurable effect on the efficacy of Nishamalaki.
C. Therapeutic outcomes remain unaffected due to the inherent synergy of Ayurvedic formulations.
D. Environmental stress enhances the potency of bioactive compounds, improving efficacy.

14. Which comprehensive strategy would most effectively address the interconnected challenges of sustainable herb cultivation and consistent therapeutic outcomes as highlighted in Scenarios 1 and 2?

A. Developing a certification system to ensure herbs are sourced sustainably and contain standardized bioactive compounds.
B. Promoting intensive research to identify synthetic alternatives for turmeric and amalaki.
C. Encouraging farmers to focus solely on wild harvesting to meet global demand.
D. Shifting Ayurvedic practices away from these herbs to more easily cultivated alternatives..

15. Intellectual Property Rights (IPR) play a crucial role in protecting traditional knowledge and Ayurvedic formulations. Consider the following statements:
(a) Patents can be granted for Ayurvedic formulations only if they demonstrate novelty, inventive steps, and industrial applicability.
(b) The Traditional Knowledge Digital Library (TKDL) helps prevent biopiracy by documenting Ayurvedic texts in searchable formats.
(c) Geographical Indications (GI) can protect specific Ayurvedic herbs or formulations associated with particular regions.
(d) Copyright is the most appropriate form of protection for Ayurvedic formulations.

Choose the correct answer from the options given below:
A. (a), (b), and (c) only
B. (b), (c), and (d) only
C. (a), (c), and (d) only
D. (a), (b), (c), and (d)

16. The principles of Ayurveda regarding the "Rasayana" concept emphasize the rejuvenation and holistic well-being of an individual. Which of the following practices or principles are most aligned with Rasayana therapy?
(a) Detoxification through Panchakarma.
(b) Enhancement of immunity and longevity.
(c) Restoration of gut microbiota balance.
(d) Immediate symptomatic relief from chronic ailments.

Choose the correct answer from the options given below:
A. (a), (b), and (c) only
B. (a), (c), and (d) only
C. (b), (c), and (d) only
D. (a), (b), (c), and (d)

17. The Nagoya Protocol on Access and Benefit-Sharing includes which of the following provisions?
(a) Fair and equitable sharing of benefits arising from the utilization of genetic resources.
(b) Prior informed consent of indigenous communities for accessing their traditional knowledge.
(c) Exemption of commercially synthesized compounds from benefit-sharing agreements.
(d) Support for the sustainable use of biodiversity associated with traditional knowledge.

Choose the correct answer from the options given below:
A. (a), (b), and (d) only
B. (a), (c), and (d) only
C. (b), (c), and (d) only
D. (a), (b), (c), and (d)

18. In the context of the Tridosha theory, which of the following statements accurately represent its biological significance?
(a) Vata is associated with movement, including neurological functions.
(b) Pitta governs enzymatic and metabolic activity.
(c) Kapha is responsible for maintaining structural stability and lubrication.
(d) Imbalance of doshas results in psychosomatic diseases.

Choose the correct answer from the options given below:
A. (a), (b), and (c) only
B. (a), (b), (c), and (d)
C. (a), (c), and (d) only
D. (b), (c), and (d) only

19. Match the following Ayurvedic Rasas with their respective physiological actions:

(a) Sweet Rasa	1. Tissue growth and nourishment
(b) Bitter Rasa	2. Detoxification and anti-inflammatory action
(c) Sour Rasa	3. Stimulation of digestive enzymes
(d) Astringent Rasa	4. Strengthening of tissues and control of bleeding

Choose the correct answer from the options given below:
A. (a)-1, (b)-2, (c)-3, (d)-4
B. (a)-2, (b)-1, (c)-4, (d)-3
C. (a)-3, (b)-4, (c)-2, (d)-1
D. (a)-4, (b)-3, (c)-1, (d)-2

20. Which of the following align with the ethical and legal frameworks for the protection of traditional knowledge?
(a) Documentation of TK in national databases like TKDL.
(b) Patenting traditional formulations that are already part of prior art.
(c) Establishing geographical indications (GI) for region-specific formulations.
(d) Encouraging free access to TK for global pharmaceutical companies.

Choose the correct answer from the options given below:
A. (a), (b), and (c) only
B. (a), (c), and (d) only
C. (a), (b), (c), and (d)
D. (a) and (c) only

21. Ayurvedic formulations often rely on synergistic effects of multiple ingredients. Which of the following describe the synergistic principles of Ayurveda?
(a) Combined ingredients enhance therapeutic efficacy.
(b) Individual components neutralize each other's adverse effects.
(c) Synergistic formulations simplify preparation methods.
(d) Synergistic effects are described in terms of dosha balance.

Choose the correct answer from the options given below:
A. (a), (b), and (d) only
B. (a), (b), and (c) only
C. (b), (c), and (d) only
D. (a), (b), (c), and (d)

22. Which of the following are essential features of a robust framework to prevent biopiracy?
(a) Establishing national databases to document traditional knowledge.
(b) Requiring disclosure of genetic resource origins in patent applications.
(c) Recognizing customary laws of indigenous communities in national IPR frameworks.
(d) Limiting international collaborations to preserve secrecy of traditional knowledge.

Choose the correct answer from the options given below:
A. (a), (b), and (c) only
B. (a), (c), and (d) only
C. (a), (b), (c), and (d)
D. (b), (c), and (d) only

23. Match the following Ayurvedic therapeutic practices with their descriptions:

(a) Panchakarma	1. Detoxification and purification therapies
(b) Rasayana	2. Rejuvenation and anti-aging practices
(c) Snehana	3. Oil-based therapies for lubrication
(d) Shodhana	4. Eliminative therapies for toxin removal

Choose the correct answer from the options given below:
A. (a)-1, (b)-2, (c)-3, (d)-4
B. (a)-2, (b)-1, (c)-4, (d)-3
C. (a)-3, (b)-4, (c)-1, (d)-2
D. (a)-4, (b)-3, (c)-2, (d)-1

24. Identify the key challenges in integrating Ayurveda into modern healthcare:
(a) Lack of empirical evidence supporting Ayurvedic principles.
(b) Standardization of individualized therapies.
(c) Difficulty in aligning traditional knowledge with international IPR frameworks.
(d) Resistance from indigenous communities towards commercialization.

Choose the correct answer from the options given below:
A. (a), (b), and (c) only
B. (b), (c), and (d) only
C. (a), (b), (c), and (d)
D. (a) and (b) only

Directions (Q. No. 25-34): *Match Lists Questions*

25. Match List–I (Ayurvedic Doshas) with List–II (Biological Functions):

List–I	List–II
(a) Vata	1. Governs movement and nervous system
(b) Pitta	2. Regulates metabolism and digestive enzymes
(c) Kapha	3. Maintains structure and fluid balance
(d) Dosha balance	4. Ensures physical and mental well-being

Choose the correct answer from the options given below:
A. (a)-1, (b)-2, (c)-3, (d)-4
B. (a)-2, (b)-1, (c)-4, (d)-3
C. (a)-3, (b)-4, (c)-1, (d)-2
D. (a)-4, (b)-3, (c)-2, (d)-1

26. Match List–I (Ayurvedic Rasas) with List–II (Therapeutic Actions):

List–I	List–II
(a) Sweet Rasa	1. Promotes tissue growth and nourishment
(b) Bitter Rasa	2. Detoxifies and reduces inflammation
(c) Sour Rasa	3. Stimulates digestion and metabolic activity
(d) Astringent Rasa	4. Strengthens tissues and controls bleeding

Choose the correct answer from the options given below:

A. (a)-1, (b)-2, (c)-3, (d)-4
B. (a)-3, (b)-4, (c)-2, (d)-1
C. (a)-4, (b)-3, (c)-1, (d)-2
D. (a)-2, (b)-1, (c)-4, (d)-3

27. Match List–I (Ayurvedic Formulations) with List–II (Primary Uses):

List–I	List–II
(a) Triphala	1. Promotes gut health and detoxification
(b) Nishamalaki	2. Helps manage diabetes and oxidative stress
(c) Brahmi	3. Enhances cognitive function and memory
(d) Chyawanprash	4. Boosts immunity and vitality

Choose the correct answer from the options given below:

A. (a)-1, (b)-2, (c)-3, (d)-4
B. (a)-3, (b)-4, (c)-1, (d)-2
C. (a)-4, (b)-3, (c)-2, (d)-1
D. (a)-2, (b)-1, (c)-4, (d)-3

28. Match List–I (Components of Panchakarma) with List–II (Purposes):

List–I	List–II
(a) Vamana	1. Removes toxins through emesis
(b) Virechana	2. Purges toxins through controlled purgation
(c) Basti	3. Rectal administration for detoxification
(d) Nasya	4. Cleanses toxins from the nasal passages

Choose the correct answer from the options given below:

A. (a)-1, (b)-2, (c)-3, (d)-4
B. (a)-3, (b)-4, (c)-1, (d)-2
C. (a)-4, (b)-3, (c)-2, (d)-1
D. (a)-2, (b)-1, (c)-4, (d)-3

29. Match List–I (Ayurvedic Principles) with List–II (Modern Interpretations):

List–I	List–II
(a) Agni	1. Digestive enzymes and metabolic regulators
(b) Ama	2. Systemic toxins from impaired metabolism
(c) Ojas	3. Immune resilience and vitality
(d) Dosha balance	4. Holistic physiological equilibrium

Choose the correct answer from the options given below:

A. (a)-1, (b)-2, (c)-3, (d)-4
B. (a)-3, (b)-4, (c)-1, (d)-2
C. (a)-4, (b)-3, (c)-2, (d)-1
D. (a)-2, (b)-1, (c)-4, (d)-3

30. Match List–I (Herbs in Ayurveda) with List–II (Primary Actions):

List–I	List–II
(a) Ashwagandha	1. Adaptogen that reduces stress
(b) Tulsi	2. Anti-inflammatory and immune-boosting
(c) Neem	3. Antibacterial and skin health
(d) Amalaki	4. Antioxidant and rejuvenative

Choose the correct answer from the options given below:

A. (a)-1, (b)-2, (c)-3, (d)-4
B. (a)-3, (b)-4, (c)-1, (d)-2
C. (a)-4, (b)-3, (c)-2, (d)-1
D. (a)-2, (b)-1, (c)-4, (d)-3

31. Match List–I (Traditional Knowledge Protection Mechanisms) with List–II (Features):

List–I	List–II
(a) Traditional Knowledge Digital Library (TKDL)	1. Prevents biopiracy through prior art documentation
(b) Geographical Indications (GI)	2. Protects region-specific products with unique qualities
(c) Nagoya Protocol	3. Ensures fair and equitable benefit-sharing
(d) Patents	4. Protects novel and innovative inventions

Choose the correct answer from the options given below:

A. (a)-1, (b)-2, (c)-3, (d)-4
B. (a)-3, (b)-4, (c)-1, (d)-2
C. (a)-4, (b)-3, (c)-2, (d)-1
D. (a)-2, (b)-1, (c)-4, (d)-3

32. Match List–I (Ayurvedic Therapies) with List–II (Mechanisms):

List–I	List–II
(a) Shirodhara	1. Continuous pouring of oil on the forehead to calm the mind
(b) Abhyanga	2. Oil massage to enhance circulation and detoxification
(c) Swedana	3. Induces sweating to eliminate toxins
(d) Basti	4. Rectal administration for detoxification

Choose the correct answer from the options given below:

A. (a)-1, (b)-2, (c)-3, (d)-4
B. (a)-3, (b)-4, (c)-1, (d)-2
C. (a)-4, (b)-3, (c)-2, (d)-1
D. (a)-2, (b)-1, (c)-4, (d)-3

33. Match List–I (International Agreements) with List–II (Purposes):

List–I	List–II
(a) TRIPS Agreement	1. Sets global standards for intellectual property rights
(b) Nagoya Protocol	2. Promotes equitable benefit-sharing of genetic resources
(c) Convention on Biological Diversity (CBD)	3. Advocates for biodiversity conservation
(d) Paris Agreement	4. Focuses on climate change and sustainability

Choose the correct answer from the options given below:

A. (a)-1, (b)-2, (c)-3, (d)-4
B. (a)-3, (b)-4, (c)-1, (d)-2
C. (a)-4, (b)-3, (c)-2, (d)-1
D. (a)-2, (b)-1, (c)-4, (d)-3

34. Match List–I (Challenges in TK Protection) with List–II (Examples):

List–I	List–II
(a) Biopiracy	1. Patents on turmeric's medicinal use
(b) Overharvesting	2. Declining populations of Amalaki
(c) Standardization	3. Loss of individuality in Ayurvedic therapies
(d) Documentation gaps	4. Lack of oral tradition records in TKDL

Choose the correct answer from the options given below:

A. (a)-1, (b)-2, (c)-3, (d)-4
B. (a)-3, (b)-4, (c)-1, (d)-2
C. (a)-4, (b)-3, (c)-2, (d)-1
D. (a)-2, (b)-1, (c)-4, (d)-3

Directions (Q. No. 35–39): *Following questions are based on Statement 1 and Statement 2. Read both the statements carefully and choose the correct answer from the options given below:*

A. Both Statement 1 and Statement 2 are true, and Statement 2 is the correct explanation of Statement 1.
B. Both Statement 1 and Statement 2 are true, but Statement 2 is not the correct explanation of Statement 1.
C. Statement 1 is true, but Statement 2 is false.
D. Statement 1 is false, but Statement 2 is true.
E. Both Statement 1 and Statement 2 are false.

35. **Statement 1:** The Nagoya Protocol promotes equitable benefit-sharing arising from the utilization of genetic resources and associated traditional knowledge.

Statement 2: The Nagoya Protocol mandates that all patent applications involving traditional knowledge must include a benefit-sharing agreement with indigenous communities.-

36. **Statement 1:** Ayurvedic detoxification therapies such as Panchakarma focus on removing accumulated toxins (Ama) from the body to restore doshic balance.

Statement 2: Panchakarma includes therapies like Vamana and Virechana, which are specifically designed to enhance metabolic function and reduce inflammation.

37. **Statement 1:** Intellectual property rights (IPR) frameworks, such as patents, often fail to protect traditional knowledge because they prioritize novelty and individual ownership.

Statement 2: Traditional knowledge, such as Ayurvedic formulations, is collective, cumulative, and often documented in ancient texts, making it incompatible with conventional IPR systems.

38. **Statement 1:** Geographical Indications (GI) protect products whose quality and reputation are linked to their region of origin, such as Darjeeling tea and Ayurvedic herbs like Amalaki.

Statement 2: GI certification ensures that Ayurvedic herbs grown outside the certified region cannot use the geographical name, even if their quality matches the original.

39. **Statement 1:** Documentation through databases like the Traditional Knowledge Digital Library (TKDL) is critical in preventing biopiracy of Ayurvedic formulations.

Statement 2: TKDL allows global pharmaceutical companies unrestricted access to traditional knowledge for the purpose of innovation.

Directions (Q. No. 40–45): *There are two statements in each question. One is labelled as Assertion (A) and the other is as Reason (R). Read both the statements and choose the correct answer from the options given below:*

A. Both Assertion (A) and Reason (R) are true, and Reason (R) is the correct explanation of Assertion (A).
B. Both Assertion (A) and Reason (R) are true, but Reason (R) is not the correct explanation of Assertion (A).
C. Assertion (A) is true, but Reason (R) is false.
D. Assertion (A) is false, but Reason (R) is true.
E. Both Assertion (A) and Reason (R) are false.

40. **Assertion (A):** Ayurveda emphasizes personalized medicine through the assessment of Prakriti, which determines an individual's doshic constitution.

Reason (R): Standardized Ayurvedic formulations ensure consistent therapeutic outcomes across all Prakriti types.

41. Assertion (A): Sustainable harvesting of Ayurvedic herbs, such as Amalaki and Neem, is essential to preserve biodiversity and maintain therapeutic efficacy.

Reason (R): Intensive monoculture farming of Ayurvedic herbs enhances soil fertility and ensures the availability of bioactive compounds.

42. Assertion (A): The use of traditional Ayurvedic preparation methods, such as decoction and fermentation, is critical to preserving the therapeutic efficacy of formulations.

Reason (R): Modern manufacturing processes focus solely on isolating active compounds, which aligns with the principles of Ayurveda.

43. Assertion (A): Geographical Indications (GI) certification for Ayurvedic herbs protects the cultural heritage associated with their traditional cultivation methods.

Reason (R): GI certification links the quality of Ayurvedic herbs to their regional biodiversity and traditional farming practices.

44. Assertion (A): The integration of Ayurveda into modern healthcare systems requires extensive scientific validation of its principles and practices.

Reason (R): Ayurvedic principles, such as doshic balance, are purely philosophical and lack measurable biochemical correlates.

45. Assertion (A): The Nagoya Protocol strengthens the rights of indigenous communities by ensuring equitable benefit-sharing from the use of traditional knowledge.

Reason (R): The Nagoya Protocol mandates that all traditional knowledge, regardless of its documentation status, must be made freely available for global research.

Directions (Q. No. 46–50): *Read the passage carefully and answer the questions given below*:

The intersection of intellectual property rights (IPR), traditional knowledge (TK), and Ayurveda presents a complex, multi-dimensional challenge. Ayurveda, a millennia-old holistic health system, is deeply rooted in the Indian subcontinent, encompassing a vast repository of formulations, practices, and therapeutic principles. These are not merely medicinal guidelines but are intertwined with cultural, ecological, and spiritual dimensions, reflecting the unique relationship between human health and the environment. Traditional knowledge systems, including Ayurveda, are typically characterized by their communal ownership and intergenerational transmission, contrasting sharply with the individualistic and novelty-focused frameworks of modern IPR regimes.

In recent decades, Ayurveda has gained global recognition, with its emphasis on preventive care, natural remedies, and holistic well-being resonating with modern health challenges. Products like Triphala, Ashwagandha, and Neem-based formulations have become popular worldwide, leading to increased commercialization of Ayurvedic knowledge. However, this globalization has not always been equitable. Biopiracy, where corporations patent traditional formulations or their derivatives without acknowledging or compensating the indigenous communities that developed and preserved this knowledge, remains a pressing concern. For instance, patents on turmeric's wound-healing properties or neem's pesticidal action were granted in foreign jurisdictions despite these applications being well-documented in Ayurvedic texts.

To combat biopiracy, India established the Traditional Knowledge Digital Library (TKDL) in 2001, a comprehensive database documenting over 200,000 formulations from Ayurveda, Siddha, and Unani medicine. By translating ancient texts into searchable formats accessible to patent examiners, TKDL has successfully thwarted numerous wrongful patent claims. However, critics argue that databases like TKDL, while valuable, are insufficient for addressing the broader challenges of TK protection. Oral traditions, which form a significant portion of Ayurveda, remain under-documented, leaving them vulnerable to exploitation. Moreover, TKDL's closed-access nature limits its utility for academic research and innovation. There is a pressing need to expand such databases to include lesser-known practices and to develop mechanisms for community participation in documenting their knowledge.

Another vital tool for TK protection is the establishment of Geographical Indications (GI), which link products to their region of origin, emphasizing unique qualities derived from local ecosystems and traditional methods. For example, GI tags for Ayurvedic herbs such as Darjeeling turmeric or Kerala neem not only protect their authenticity but also support local economies. However, GI certifications face challenges in enforcement and awareness, as counterfeit products often undermine their value in the global market.

Sustainability is another critical issue in the commercialization of Ayurvedic knowledge. The rising demand for Ayurvedic herbs has led to overharvesting, habitat destruction, and biodiversity loss. For instance, the wild populations of Amalaki (Indian gooseberry) and Ashwagandha have declined due to unsustainable practices. Environmental degradation further impacts the quality of medicinal plants, as soil fertility and climatic conditions influence the concentration of bioactive compounds. This ecological crisis underscores the importance of sustainable harvesting practices and the integration of agroforestry models. Cultivating medicinal plants alongside other crops can maintain biodiversity while ensuring consistent quality.

Despite the ecological and cultural importance of Ayurveda, integrating it into global IPR frameworks poses significant challenges. Modern IPR systems prioritize novelty and industrial applicability, criteria that often conflict with the communal and cumulative nature of TK. For instance, while patents can protect innovations derived from Ayurvedic principles, they cannot safeguard the knowledge itself, which is often considered part of the public domain. The Nagoya Protocol, an international agreement under the Convention on Biological Diversity (CBD), attempts to address this gap by emphasizing access and benefit-sharing. It mandates that users of genetic resources and associated TK obtain prior informed consent and share benefits equitably with the knowledge holders. However, implementation remains uneven, with many countries lacking robust legal frameworks to enforce these provisions.

Ayurveda's integration into modern healthcare systems further complicates the picture. While its emphasis on holistic health and prevention aligns with contemporary wellness trends, the scientific validation of Ayurvedic principles is often challenging. Concepts such as dosha balance, Agni (digestive fire), and Rasa (taste) are rooted in metaphysical frameworks, making them difficult to quantify in biomedical terms. Nonetheless, emerging research on gut microbiota, metabolic pathways, and phytochemistry offers promising bridges between Ayurveda and modern science. For instance, studies have shown that Triphala enhances gut microbiota diversity, while Ashwagandha modulates stress-related biomarkers.

The tension between traditional preparation methods and commercial standardization also highlights the need for careful regulation. Traditional Ayurvedic formulations emphasize the synergistic effects of multiple ingredients, prepared in specific ways to balance doshas and optimize efficacy. However, commercial products often isolate active compounds for ease of production, potentially undermining the holistic principles of Ayurveda. This standardization raises ethical questions about authenticity and efficacy, as well as the cultural appropriation of traditional knowledge.

Moreover, the commodification of Ayurveda risks alienating the communities that preserve its traditions. While the global wellness industry profits from Ayurvedic concepts, local practitioners and knowledge holders often receive little recognition or benefit. Ethical commercialization requires not only benefit-sharing agreements but also the active involvement of indigenous communities in decision-making processes. Public awareness campaigns can also play a crucial role in promoting fair trade practices and educating consumers about the cultural roots of Ayurvedic products.

Education and capacity building are essential for bridging the gap between traditional and modern knowledge systems. Training programs for Ayurvedic practitioners, researchers, and policymakers can foster collaboration and mutual respect. Universities and research institutes can develop interdisciplinary curricula that integrate Ayurveda with modern science, encouraging innovation while preserving cultural integrity.

Protecting traditional knowledge in Ayurveda requires a multi-faceted approach that balances cultural preservation, ecological sustainability, and equitable commercialization. Expanding documentation efforts, enforcing GI certifications, implementing sustainable harvesting practices, and integrating Ayurveda into modern healthcare systems are crucial steps. At the same time, legal frameworks must evolve to recognize the unique characteristics of TK, ensuring that the communities who have nurtured this knowledge for generations are its primary beneficiaries. The challenge lies in harmonizing the global demand for Ayurveda with its cultural and ecological roots, creating a model of development that respects both tradition and innovation.

46. Why is the Traditional Knowledge Digital Library (TKDL) considered a critical tool in preventing biopiracy?

A. It provides pharmaceutical companies with free access to traditional knowledge for innovation.

B. It documents traditional formulations and makes them accessible to patent examiners as prior art.

C. It facilitates patent applications by modern researchers on Ayurvedic knowledge.

D. It prevents local communities from claiming rights over traditional knowledge.

47. What is the primary challenge in using Geographical Indications (GI) for protecting Ayurvedic products?

A. GI certifications are incompatible with modern IPR systems.

B. Counterfeit products undermine the value of GI-certified products in the global market.

C. GI-certified products cannot be sold outside their regions of origin.

D. The quality of GI-certified products depends solely on local ecosystems.

48. How does environmental degradation impact the quality of Ayurvedic herbs?

A. It reduces the biodiversity of medicinal plants, making Ayurvedic formulations ineffective.

B. It decreases the bioactive compound concentration in herbs, affecting their therapeutic efficacy.

C. It increases the cost of cultivating Ayurvedic herbs, making them inaccessible.

D. It enhances the medicinal properties of herbs by inducing genetic adaptation.

49. What does the Nagoya Protocol aim to achieve in the context of traditional knowledge and genetic resources?

A. To prohibit the commercialization of traditional knowledge entirely.

B. To mandate the free exchange of traditional knowledge for research purposes.

C. To ensure equitable benefit-sharing with indigenous communities for the use of their knowledge.

D. To create a universal database for documenting traditional knowledge.

50. What is the central ethical concern in the commercialization of Ayurvedic knowledge, as discussed in the passage?

A. The replacement of traditional preparation methods with synthetic alternatives.

B. The lack of recognition and benefit-sharing for indigenous communities that preserve Ayurvedic traditions.

C. The incompatibility of Ayurvedic concepts with modern scientific frameworks.

D. The limited availability of Ayurvedic products in global markets.

ANSWER WITH EXPLANATIONS

1. B: The case of biopiracy involving Haritaki underscores the inherent conflict between modern intellectual property frameworks and traditional knowledge systems. While the pharmaceutical company may claim novelty in its proprietary extraction process, Haritaki's therapeutic properties, including its antioxidant effects, have been extensively documented in Ayurvedic texts. This prior art invalidates the company's claim under the novelty requirement of patent law. Furthermore, traditional knowledge is communal and cumulative, emphasizing the role of communities in preserving and transmitting it across generations. Ethical commercialization demands the acknowledgment of traditional sources and equitable benefit-sharing. Failing to respect these principles undermines cultural heritage and erodes indigenous rights.

2. B: Nishamalaki's reduced efficacy highlights the critical role of preparation methods in Ayurvedic formulations. Unlike modern pharmacological approaches that often isolate active compounds, Ayurveda relies on synergy, where the interaction of multiple ingredients enhances therapeutic outcomes. This synergy is disrupted when traditional methods are altered for industrial production, leading to diminished results. Furthermore, the quality of raw materials, influenced by factors like sourcing and environmental conditions, directly affects efficacy. Nishamalaki's effectiveness as an anti-diabetic formulation stems not only from curcumin and vitamin C but also from their interactions with other bioactive compounds. Modern production methods must respect these traditional principles to maintain efficacy.

3. A: The Traditional Knowledge Digital Library (TKDL) has proven to be a powerful tool in preventing biopiracy by documenting traditional formulations and providing patent examiners with evidence of prior art. However, its current limitations, such as the exclusion of oral traditions and lesser-known practices, leave significant gaps in protecting traditional knowledge. Expanding TKDL to include these underrepresented forms of knowledge would create a more comprehensive defense against biopiracy. Additionally, while its closed-access model prevents misuse, it also restricts academic and innovative applications. A balanced approach that ensures both protection and accessibility would enhance TKDL's impact while fostering global respect for traditional knowledge.

4. C: Community-led agroforestry offers a sustainable solution to the overharvesting and ecological degradation caused by global demand for Ayurvedic herbs. By integrating medicinal plants like Amalaki and Ashwagandha with diverse crops, agroforestry preserves biodiversity, improves soil health, and provides economic stability to local communities. Unlike monoculture farming, which depletes resources and increases vulnerability to pests, agroforestry aligns with Ayurveda's emphasis on ecological harmony. Such models also empower indigenous communities, who are often the custodians of traditional knowledge. However, implementing agroforestry at scale requires significant investment, government support, and collaboration across sectors, balancing economic growth with ecological sustainability.

5. B: Scientific research bridging Ayurveda and modern biomedicine highlights the physiological relevance of Agni, traditionally understood as digestive fire. By correlating Agni with enzymatic activity and metabolic regulation, researchers validate Ayurveda's emphasis on balance and systemic health. The concept of Ama, or toxins resulting from impaired Agni, aligns with findings on systemic inflammation and metabolic dysfunction. These parallels underscore the compatibility of Ayurvedic principles with contemporary healthcare frameworks. Integrating Ayurveda into modern systems requires further empirical validation of its concepts, but such studies demonstrate its potential to address chronic conditions and enhance preventive care through a holistic approach.

6. **B:** The patent application on neem-based skincare products fails to meet the novelty requirement, as neem's therapeutic properties for skin health are extensively documented in Ayurvedic literature. While the use of modern emulsifiers may involve technical innovation, the underlying claims rely on traditional knowledge. Such cases highlight the critical role of databases like TKDL in providing evidence of prior art. To prevent biopiracy and promote ethical innovation, patent laws must balance protecting modern developments with respecting indigenous knowledge systems. Encouraging benefit-sharing agreements and acknowledging traditional sources fosters equitable partnerships and preserves cultural heritage.

7. **B:** Integrating Ayurveda into national healthcare systems requires retaining its personalized approach, as remedies are traditionally tailored to an individual's Prakriti, or constitution. Standardizing Ayurvedic treatments for scalability risks undermining their efficacy and authenticity. Training healthcare professionals in Ayurvedic principles ensures informed application while maintaining integrity. This collaborative approach respects Ayurveda's holistic nature, enriching healthcare by combining its preventive focus with modern medical practices. Policymakers must prioritize education and research to bridge traditional and biomedical systems, fostering mutual respect and enhancing healthcare outcomes through integrative frameworks.

8. **B:** The therapeutic effects of Rasas cannot be fully understood in isolation, as Ayurveda emphasizes their interaction with doshas and overall formulation synergy. Modern pharmacological studies attempting to isolate these effects often overlook the holistic context, limiting their validation. Bridging Ayurveda with modern science requires recognizing these complexities and developing methodologies that respect its systemic nature. Simplifying Ayurveda's principles for empirical testing risks distorting its philosophy, while accommodating its holistic framework can enrich modern pharmacology. Such integration demands interdisciplinary collaboration, fostering innovation while preserving authenticity and cultural heritage.

9. **A:** The most ethical approach for an Ayurvedic company claiming to sell "traditional immunity boosters" is to maintain authenticity by adhering to traditional methods. Ayurveda emphasizes natural formulations without synthetic additives, and deviation from this dilutes both the therapeutic efficacy and cultural integrity of the product. Using synthetic preservatives contradicts the claim of traditional preparation. While transparency in labeling is important, the best ethical practice is to align with classical Ayurvedic standards if the product is being marketed as traditional.

10. **A:** The debate over TRIPS amendments reflects the tension between protecting traditional knowledge and promoting global innovation. Requiring patent applicants to disclose the origin of genetic resources and associated knowledge ensures accountability and prevents biopiracy. This principle aligns with ethical frameworks like the Nagoya Protocol, emphasizing benefit-sharing and community consent. Developed nations' resistance underscores the prioritization of industrial interests over cultural preservation. Harmonizing these priorities requires robust international cooperation, balancing innovation with respect for traditional systems. Such amendments strengthen the protection of traditional knowledge while fostering equitable partnerships in global markets.

11. **B:** Nishamalaki's efficacy in managing diabetes is closely linked to its activation of AMP-activated protein kinase (AMPK) and the reduction of pro-inflammatory cytokines like IL-6. These molecular pathways align with the Ayurvedic understanding of balancing doshas and reducing metabolic toxins. Unlike treatments targeting single pathways, Nishamalaki's dual action exemplifies Ayurveda's holistic approach. This synergy underscores the compatibility of traditional formulations with biomedical principles, demonstrating their potential in addressing chronic diseases. Validating these mechanisms bridges Ayurveda with modern healthcare, fostering integrative models that respect traditional knowledge while utilizing contemporary scientific methods for enhanced therapeutic outcomes.

12. **B:** Agroforestry offers a sustainable model for cultivating Ayurvedic herbs like turmeric and amalaki, addressing ecological and economic challenges. Integrating these plants with diverse crops enhances soil fertility, conserves biodiversity, and mitigates environmental degradation. Such practices align with Ayurveda's ecological principles, emphasizing harmony between human health and the environment. Unlike monoculture farming, which exhausts resources, agroforestry supports long-term sustainability. Implementing this model requires collaboration between farmers, industries, and policymakers, along with financial support to ensure scalability. By promoting agroforestry, the Ayurvedic industry can meet global demand without compromising the quality of raw materials or the environment.

13. A: Environmental degradation directly affects the therapeutic efficacy of Ayurvedic formulations like Nishamalaki by reducing the bioactive compound concentration in its ingredients. Amalaki grown in degraded soils lacks the vitamin C content essential for its rejuvenative properties, while poor-quality turmeric diminishes its anti-inflammatory effects. These variations undermine the consistency of traditional remedies, which depend on high-quality raw materials. Sustainable cultivation practices, such as agroforestry and organic farming, are vital for maintaining efficacy. This connection between ecological preservation and therapeutic outcomes highlights the need for holistic approaches that respect both environmental and cultural aspects of traditional knowledge systems.

14. A: Certifying sustainable harvesting practices ensures the authenticity and therapeutic efficacy of Ayurvedic formulations while promoting ecological preservation. Standardizing sourcing processes based on traditional knowledge fosters consistent quality, aligning with Ayurveda's principles. Encouraging such certifications requires collaboration between regulatory bodies, industries, and communities, ensuring accountability and equitable benefit-sharing. This approach bridges market demands with ecological and cultural sustainability, preserving Ayurveda's integrity in global markets. By respecting traditional preparation methods and fostering community participation, sustainable practices can address environmental challenges while maintaining the therapeutic value of Ayurvedic remedies in diverse healthcare contexts.

15. A: Patents require novelty, inventive steps, and industrial applicability, which are essential for granting rights to Ayurvedic formulations. This ensures that only unique and scientifically validated formulations gain protection, preventing misuse. The Traditional Knowledge Digital Library (TKDL) is a significant initiative to prevent biopiracy by documenting traditional Ayurvedic knowledge in digital formats, making it accessible to patent examiners globally. Geographical Indications (GI) protect products associated with specific regions, such as Ayurvedic herbs unique to particular areas. Copyright, however, is not suitable for formulations as it protects creative works like literature and art, not functional or medicinal creations. Hence, the correct answer excludes statement "d".

16. A: Rasayana therapies epitomize Ayurveda's holistic approach, focusing on rejuvenation, immunity enhancement, and systemic well-being. They align with Panchakarma's detoxifying role, emphasizing balance restoration and long-term health. Unlike symptomatic treatments, Rasayana emphasizes preventive care, addressing underlying imbalances. Modern wellness frameworks integrating Rasayana highlight its relevance in enhancing resilience and longevity. Recognizing its potential requires empirical validation and collaborative research, bridging traditional principles with contemporary healthcare models. By fostering such integration, Ayurveda's preventive and therapeutic strengths can contribute to global health, preserving its cultural roots while addressing modern challenges in holistic well-being.

17. A: The Nagoya Protocol underscores equitable benefit-sharing, protecting the rights of indigenous communities and fostering biodiversity conservation. It emphasizes consent and collaboration, ensuring that traditional knowledge holders are active participants in its utilization. Exempting synthesized compounds undermines this framework, as many innovations draw directly from traditional principles. Aligning the Nagoya Protocol with global policies requires comprehensive implementation strategies, fostering equitable partnerships while preserving biodiversity. Recognizing the role of indigenous communities in maintaining genetic resources ensures ethical innovation, bridging traditional systems with modern science to address ecological and cultural challenges in a sustainable manner.

18. B: The Tridosha theory encapsulates Ayurveda's holistic understanding of physiology, integrating movement, metabolism, and structure through Vata, Pitta, and Kapha. These doshas influence physical, psychological, and biochemical functions, aligning with modern concepts of neurology, enzymatic pathways, and structural stability. Imbalances lead to psychosomatic conditions, underscoring Ayurveda's preventive and therapeutic focus. Bridging Tridosha with biomedical research enhances its relevance, fostering integrative healthcare models. Recognizing its empirical validity requires interdisciplinary collaboration, fostering respect for Ayurveda's systemic approach while aligning it with contemporary scientific frameworks for addressing complex health challenges.

19. A: Rasas (tastes) in Ayurveda exemplify its nuanced understanding of therapeutic actions, linking flavors to physiological effects. Sweet Rasa promotes nourishment, Bitter detoxifies, Sour stimulates metabolism, and Astringent strengthens tissues. These roles demonstrate Ayurveda's systemic approach, addressing imbalances at multiple levels. Modern studies correlating Rasas with biochemical markers validate their empirical relevance, bridging traditional principles with pharmacological research. Recognizing these connections fosters integrative healthcare, enriching preventive and therapeutic frameworks. By aligning Rasas with modern science, Ayurveda's principles can contribute meaningfully to contemporary wellness, preserving its cultural integrity while addressing global health challenges.

20. **D:** Protecting traditional knowledge requires a balanced approach, combining documentation, geographical indications (GI), and ethical frameworks. Patenting prior art undermines indigenous rights, emphasizing the importance of equitable mechanisms like GI certifications. Free access to TK risks exploitation, requiring regulated collaboration to foster innovation while respecting cultural heritage. Integrating traditional practices with modern systems ensures sustainability, authenticity, and equitable benefit-sharing. Such measures preserve the cultural and ecological dimensions of traditional knowledge, fostering respect for indigenous communities while addressing market demands. Recognizing TK's value enhances its contribution to global innovation without compromising its foundational principles.

21. **A:** Synergy in Ayurvedic formulations reflects its holistic philosophy, emphasizing therapeutic efficacy through the interaction of ingredients. This systemic approach balances doshas, neutralizes adverse effects, and addresses underlying imbalances. Modern pharmacology isolating active compounds often fails to replicate this synergy, highlighting the importance of traditional methods. Recognizing these principles enriches healthcare, fostering integrative models that respect Ayurveda's complexity. Bridging traditional formulations with scientific research fosters innovation while preserving cultural integrity, enhancing the relevance and applicability of Ayurvedic systems in addressing contemporary health challenges across preventive and therapeutic domains.

22. **A:** Preventing biopiracy requires robust frameworks combining documentation, disclosure requirements, and community participation. National databases like TKDL provide evidence of prior art, safeguarding TK from exploitation. Recognizing customary laws fosters indigenous rights, aligning TK protection with cultural and ecological principles. Limiting collaborations risks isolation, emphasizing balanced approaches that integrate TK into global innovation systems. Such measures foster equitable partnerships, preserving cultural heritage while promoting sustainable development. By harmonizing tradition and modernity, TK protection enriches innovation frameworks, addressing ecological, cultural, and market challenges in a comprehensive and ethical manner.

23. **A:** Panchakarma therapies exemplify Ayurveda's systemic approach to health, emphasizing detoxification, rejuvenation, and balance restoration. Each therapy targets specific imbalances, aligning with the individual's needs. For example, Vamana and Virechana cleanse the body through emesis and purgation, while Basti and Nasya focus on localized detoxification. These practices highlight Ayurveda's preventive and therapeutic strengths, addressing root causes rather than symptoms. Modern wellness integrating Panchakarma fosters holistic health, bridging traditional principles with contemporary demands. Recognizing Panchakarma's systemic relevance enriches healthcare models, preserving its cultural integrity while contributing to global wellness frameworks for long-term health outcomes.

24. **C:** Integrating Ayurveda into modern healthcare faces challenges such as empirical validation, standardization, and cultural preservation. While standardization facilitates scalability, it risks losing Ayurveda's personalized nature, essential for efficacy. Aligning TK with IPR frameworks ensures recognition and equitable benefit-sharing. Resistance from indigenous communities highlights the need for ethical commercialization, fostering mutual respect. Addressing these complexities requires collaborative frameworks, combining scientific research with cultural preservation. By harmonizing tradition and innovation, Ayurveda's preventive and therapeutic principles can contribute meaningfully to global health, enriching healthcare systems with its holistic and systemic approaches to well-being.

25. **A:** The Tridosha theory is a foundational concept in Ayurveda, describing Vata, Pitta, and Kapha as the governing forces of the body's physiological, psychological, and structural functions. Vata is associated with movement and the nervous system, Pitta with metabolism and enzymatic activity, and Kapha with stability and lubrication. The balance of these doshas ensures physical and mental well-being, highlighting Ayurveda's systemic approach to health. Modern research into neurophysiology, metabolism, and fluid balance aligns with these principles, demonstrating Ayurveda's relevance in addressing chronic diseases. Recognizing this alignment fosters integrative healthcare, bridging traditional systems with contemporary biomedical frameworks.

26. **A:** The therapeutic actions of Rasas illustrate Ayurveda's intricate understanding of taste and its physiological impact. Sweet Rasa promotes nourishment and tissue growth, Bitter detoxifies and reduces inflammation, Sour enhances digestion, and Astringent strengthens tissues. These actions reflect Ayurveda's systemic approach, where tastes influence doshic balance and overall health. Modern pharmacological studies

validating these properties, such as Bitter Rasa's anti-inflammatory effects, underscore their empirical relevance. Bridging these concepts with contemporary science enriches healthcare, emphasizing Ayurveda's preventive and therapeutic potential. Recognizing the interplay between Rasas and doshas fosters holistic models of health and wellness.

27. A: Ayurvedic formulations like Triphala, Nishamalaki, Brahmi, and Chyawanprash embody the system's holistic principles, addressing diverse health needs. Triphala detoxifies and supports gut health, Nishamalaki manages diabetes, Brahmi enhances cognition, and Chyawanprash boosts immunity and vitality. These formulations reflect Ayurveda's emphasis on balancing doshas and promoting systemic well-being. Modern validation of their therapeutic actions bridges traditional principles with contemporary demands, fostering integrative healthcare. Recognizing the interplay of ingredients in these formulations highlights Ayurveda's systemic relevance, emphasizing the importance of authenticity and traditional preparation methods in preserving efficacy and cultural integrity.

28. A: Panchakarma therapies exemplify Ayurveda's detoxification and rejuvenation principles, targeting specific imbalances through systemic cleansing. Vamana removes toxins via emesis, Virechana through purgation, Basti through rectal detoxification, and Nasya through nasal cleansing. These practices align with Ayurveda's emphasis on eliminating Ama and restoring doshic balance, fostering long-term health. Modern wellness integrating Panchakarma highlights its relevance in addressing chronic conditions and enhancing preventive care. Recognizing its systemic approach fosters respect for Ayurveda's principles, bridging traditional methods with contemporary demands for holistic health frameworks.

29. A: Ayurvedic principles such as Agni, Ama, Ojas, and dosha balance encapsulate its systemic approach to health. Agni corresponds to metabolic and enzymatic activity, Ama to toxins from impaired metabolism, Ojas to vitality and immunity, and dosha balance to overall well-being. These concepts demonstrate Ayurveda's preventive and therapeutic relevance, addressing root causes rather than symptoms. Bridging these principles with modern frameworks, such as metabolic research and immune studies, validates Ayurveda's empirical foundations. Recognizing these connections enriches healthcare, fostering integrative models that respect traditional systems while addressing contemporary health challenges.

30. A: Ayurvedic herbs like Ashwagandha, Tulsi, Neem, and Amalaki illustrate its systemic approach to health, addressing stress, inflammation, bacterial infections, and rejuvenation. Ashwagandha acts as an adaptogen, Tulsi as an anti-inflammatory, Neem as an antibacterial, and Amalaki as an antioxidant. These properties align with Ayurveda's emphasis on balancing doshas and promoting systemic well-being. Modern pharmacological validation bridges traditional knowledge with contemporary science, fostering integrative healthcare. Recognizing these herbs' therapeutic potential highlights the importance of sustainable sourcing and ethical commercialization, preserving their cultural and ecological significance in addressing global health needs.

31. A: Traditional knowledge protection mechanisms such as TKDL, GI certifications, the Nagoya Protocol, and patents address diverse challenges in safeguarding Ayurveda. TKDL prevents biopiracy by documenting prior art, GI protects region-specific products, the Nagoya Protocol ensures equitable benefit-sharing, and patents safeguard novel inventions. These frameworks highlight the importance of balancing innovation with cultural preservation, addressing ecological and economic challenges. Integrating these mechanisms fosters respect for traditional systems while promoting sustainable development, enriching global healthcare with Ayurveda's holistic principles and systemic relevance.

32. A: Ayurvedic therapies like Shirodhara, Abhyanga, Swedana, and Basti demonstrate its emphasis on systemic balance and holistic well-being. Shirodhara calms the mind through oil therapy, Abhyanga enhances circulation via massage, Swedana eliminates toxins through sweating, and Basti detoxifies through rectal administration. These practices align with Ayurveda's preventive and therapeutic focus, addressing root causes of imbalances. Modern wellness integrating these therapies highlights their relevance in enhancing resilience and long-term health. Recognizing their systemic approach fosters respect for Ayurveda's principles, bridging traditional methods with contemporary demands for holistic healthcare frameworks.

33. A: International agreements such as TRIPS, the Nagoya Protocol, and CBD address diverse aspects of traditional knowledge and biodiversity protection. TRIPS sets global IPR standards, the Nagoya Protocol emphasizes equitable benefit-sharing, and CBD advocates for biodiversity conservation. These frameworks align with Ayurveda's emphasis on ecological and cultural harmony, fostering sustainable development. Integrating these agreements into global policies ensures respect for traditional systems while promoting innovation. Recognizing their interconnected goals enriches healthcare and ecological preservation, fostering equitable and sustainable frameworks for addressing contemporary challenges in traditional knowledge protection.

34. A: Challenges in protecting traditional knowledge include biopiracy, overharvesting, standardization, and documentation gaps. Biopiracy undermines indigenous rights, as seen in patents on turmeric and neem. Overharvesting threatens biodiversity, affecting formulations like Triphala. Standardization risks losing Ayurveda's personalized nature, while documentation gaps leave oral traditions vulnerable. Addressing these challenges requires robust frameworks combining documentation, sustainability, and community participation. Recognizing these complexities fosters respect for traditional systems, bridging cultural preservation with contemporary demands for innovation and sustainability in global healthcare frameworks.

35. C: The Nagoya Protocol indeed promotes equitable benefit-sharing arising from the use of genetic resources and associated traditional knowledge, making Statement 1 true. However, Statement 2 is false because the Protocol does not mandate that all patent applications must include a benefit-sharing agreement. Instead, it requires prior informed consent and benefit-sharing when genetic resources are accessed, especially across borders, but enforcement varies by national legislation and patent systems.

36. A: Panchakarma therapies are central to Ayurveda's detoxification framework, targeting Ama (toxins) and restoring balance among doshas. Therapies like Vamana (emesis) and Virechana (purgation) are scientifically validated for reducing systemic inflammation and enhancing metabolic function, aligning with traditional descriptions. The holistic integration of these therapies underscores Ayurveda's systemic focus, addressing root causes rather than symptoms. By removing toxins and optimizing Agni (digestive fire), Panchakarma fosters long-term health. Bridging these principles with modern research demonstrates their relevance in addressing chronic conditions, making Ayurveda's holistic and preventive frameworks integral to global wellness and healthcare systems.

37. A: Intellectual property rights (IPR) frameworks prioritize novelty and individual ownership, which are often incompatible with the communal and cumulative nature of traditional knowledge. Ayurveda, transmitted over generations through texts and practices, lacks the singular inventiveness required for conventional patents. This mismatch leaves traditional knowledge vulnerable to exploitation. The collective ownership model highlights the need for customized legal mechanisms like TKDL and the Nagoya Protocol. These systems address biopiracy and promote equitable benefit-sharing, bridging the gap between traditional and modern systems. Harmonizing IPR with traditional knowledge preservation ensures sustainability and respect for cultural heritage in global innovation.

38. A: Geographical Indications (GI) safeguard the authenticity and quality of Ayurvedic products by linking them to their regions of origin. However, enforcement challenges and counterfeit products dilute the value of GI certifications. For instance, GI-protected Ayurvedic herbs like Kerala neem or Darjeeling turmeric depend on local ecosystems and traditional methods for their unique properties. Restricting their use outside certified regions preserves authenticity, aligning with Ayurveda's emphasis on ecological harmony. Strengthening awareness and enforcement of GI certifications ensures that Ayurvedic products maintain their cultural and therapeutic integrity in global markets, fostering respect for traditional systems.

39. C: The Traditional Knowledge Digital Library (TKDL) has been instrumental in combating biopiracy by providing patent examiners access to prior art. It ensures that documented Ayurvedic formulations are protected from wrongful patent claims. However, TKDL does not grant unrestricted access to pharmaceutical companies, as its purpose is safeguarding traditional knowledge rather than facilitating commercial exploitation. This balance between protection and limited access underscores the need for robust documentation systems that respect the integrity of traditional knowledge. Expanding TKDL to include oral traditions while maintaining regulated access would further strengthen its role in preserving and protecting Ayurveda.

40. C: Ayurveda's personalized approach is rooted in Prakriti assessment, tailoring remedies to an individual's doshic constitution. Standardized formulations, while convenient for mass production, cannot replicate this individualized care. This limitation challenges Ayurveda's integration into modern systems that prioritize uniformity. However, recognizing Prakriti's scientific basis in genetics and metabolic profiling demonstrates Ayurveda's relevance. Training healthcare professionals to apply these principles fosters integrative frameworks that respect tradition while addressing scalability. Bridging Ayurveda's personalization with modern healthcare requires interdisciplinary collaboration, ensuring efficacy and authenticity without compromising its holistic foundations or systemic relevance.

41. C: Sustainable harvesting is crucial for preserving Ayurvedic herbs like Amalaki and Neem, which are threatened by overharvesting and habitat destruction. Monoculture farming, while efficient, depletes soil fertility and increases vulnerability to pests, undermining long-term sustainability. Agroforestry models integrating diverse crops support biodiversity, ecological balance, and consistent herb quality. These practices align with Ayurveda's emphasis on harmony between human health and the environment. Recognizing the link between sustainability and therapeutic efficacy fosters respect for traditional systems, ensuring that Ayurveda's principles contribute meaningfully to ecological preservation and global health in a balanced and ethical manner.

42. C: Traditional preparation methods in Ayurveda emphasize synergy, where ingredients work together to balance doshas and optimize therapeutic outcomes. Modern manufacturing processes isolating active compounds often fail to replicate this holistic efficacy. These differences underscore the need for preserving traditional practices, which align with Ayurveda's systemic approach. Bridging traditional methods with modern standards requires innovation that respects cultural integrity. Recognizing this interplay ensures that Ayurveda's principles remain authentic and effective, enriching contemporary wellness frameworks. Developing collaborative models for scientific validation and commercialization fosters integrative healthcare that respects tradition while addressing global health challenges.

43. A: Geographical Indications (GI) protect the cultural and ecological significance of Ayurvedic herbs by linking their quality to regional biodiversity and traditional farming practices. GI certifications prevent misuse and promote authenticity, ensuring that products reflect their origins' unique characteristics. For example, herbs like Kerala neem derive their therapeutic potency from local ecosystems and centuries-old cultivation methods. Strengthening GI frameworks fosters equitable commercialization, benefiting local communities and preserving cultural heritage. Aligning these certifications with global policies enhances Ayurveda's global recognition, bridging traditional systems with modern markets in a sustainable and culturally respectful manner.

44. C: Integrating Ayurveda into modern healthcare systems does require rigorous scientific validation to gain wider acceptance, especially in global contexts, making Assertion (A) true. However, Reason (R) is false because Ayurvedic principles like doshic balance are not purely philosophical; many have emerging biochemical and physiological correlations, such as links to metabolism, inflammation, or neuroendocrine regulation. Therefore, to dismiss them entirely as unmeasurable is inaccurate.

45. C: The Nagoya Protocol strengthens the rights of indigenous communities by promoting equitable benefit-sharing from the use of genetic resources and associated traditional knowledge. However, it does not mandate that all traditional knowledge be made freely available, as this would conflict with its protective goals. Instead, the protocol emphasizes consent and collaboration, fostering ethical partnerships that respect indigenous systems. Recognizing these principles addresses biopiracy while promoting sustainability and innovation. Integrating the Nagoya Protocol into global frameworks ensures that traditional knowledge is preserved, protected, and utilized in ways that align with cultural, ecological, and economic priorities.

46. B: The Traditional Knowledge Digital Library (TKDL) serves as a critical mechanism to prevent biopiracy by documenting formulations and making them accessible to patent examiners as prior art. This ensures that traditional remedies like neem and turmeric, which have long been documented in Ayurveda, cannot be patented as novel inventions by corporations. By translating ancient texts into searchable formats, TKDL creates a bridge between traditional knowledge and modern intellectual property frameworks. However, TKDL is not designed to provide free access to pharmaceutical companies or facilitate unrestricted commercialization. Its role is primarily defensive, ensuring ethical recognition of traditional knowledge.

47. B: Geographical Indications (GI) certifications safeguard the authenticity of Ayurvedic products by linking them to their regions of origin. However, counterfeit products and lack of consumer awareness dilute their value in global markets. For example, turmeric grown outside regions like Kerala lacks the quality associated with GI-certified Kerala turmeric, but fake labels mislead consumers. GI certifications protect the cultural and ecological integrity of products, emphasizing their uniqueness. Strengthening enforcement and promoting consumer education are essential to maximizing the benefits of GI. By addressing these challenges, GI certifications can ensure fair trade practices while preserving the identity of traditional products.

48. B: Environmental degradation significantly impacts the quality of Ayurvedic herbs, as soil conditions and biodiversity directly influence the concentration of bioactive compounds. For instance, poor soil fertility reduces the vitamin C content in Amalaki, affecting its rejuvenative properties. Similarly, overharvesting disrupts the ecosystem, threatening the long-term availability of medicinal plants. Ayurveda's emphasis on ecological harmony highlights the importance of sustainable harvesting and cultivation. Practices such as agroforestry and organic farming can mitigate these impacts, ensuring the therapeutic efficacy of formulations. Addressing environmental degradation is not just an ecological concern but also a critical factor in preserving Ayurveda's cultural and therapeutic value.

49. **C:** The Nagoya Protocol aims to ensure equitable benefit-sharing with indigenous communities for the use of their traditional knowledge and genetic resources. By mandating prior informed consent, the protocol protects the rights of knowledge holders and promotes sustainable development. It discourages biopiracy and unethical exploitation, fostering collaboration between researchers and communities. However, the protocol does not require the free exchange of traditional knowledge, as this would undermine its protective framework. Instead, it advocates for balanced partnerships that respect cultural heritage while enabling innovation. Implementing the Nagoya Protocol globally strengthens the role of traditional knowledge in addressing contemporary challenges.

50. **B:** The central ethical concern in the commercialization of Ayurvedic knowledge lies in the lack of recognition and benefit-sharing for indigenous communities. While the global wellness industry profits from Ayurvedic concepts, the custodians of this knowledge often receive little compensation or acknowledgment. Ethical commercialization requires frameworks like the Nagoya Protocol to ensure fair benefit-sharing and active community involvement. This includes respecting traditional preparation methods, preserving authenticity, and fostering equitable partnerships. Addressing these issues is essential to balancing global demand with cultural preservation. By prioritizing ethical practices, Ayurveda can contribute to global health while maintaining its integrity and respecting its origins.

CHAPTER 28

ENTREPRENEURSHIP IN AYURVEDA – INNOVATION, R & D, AND INDUSTRY DYNAMICS

Ayurveda, the ancient science of life, has been a cornerstone of holistic healthcare for millennia. While deeply rooted in tradition, its evolution into a modern, globally recognized industry demands entrepreneurial vigor and innovation. This chapter explores the dynamic intersection of Ayurveda and entrepreneurship, highlighting the roles of research and development (R&D) and industry dynamics in shaping its future.

Importance of Entrepreneurship and Innovation in Ayurveda

1. **The Need for Entrepreneurship in Ayurveda:** Ayurveda offers a treasure trove of knowledge, yet its application in the modern world requires a proactive approach to innovation. Entrepreneurship serves as a critical bridge between traditional wisdom and contemporary market demands. Key reasons for fostering entrepreneurship in Ayurveda include:
   - **Globalization of Ayurveda:** To make Ayurveda accessible and relevant globally, entrepreneurs must adapt traditional formulations to meet international standards and regulatory compliance.
   - **Consumer Demand for Natural and Holistic Wellness:** The increasing preference for natural remedies and preventive healthcare solutions creates opportunities for Ayurveda-based products and services.
   - **Economic Impact:** Ayurveda entrepreneurship contributes to economic growth by creating jobs, fostering rural development, and promoting sustainable practices.
   - **Preservation of Knowledge:** Entrepreneurs play a key role in documenting, digitizing, and preserving ancient Ayurvedic texts and practices.
2. **Innovation as the Driver of Growth:** Innovation in Ayurveda is not limited to product development; it spans across:
   - **Formulations:** Modernizing traditional remedies to suit contemporary lifestyles.
   - **Technology Integration:** Using AI, IoT, and big data to improve diagnostics and personalized treatment plans.
   - **Business Models:** Developing direct-to-consumer (D2C) platforms, subscription-based services, and telemedicine for Ayurveda.
   - **Sustainability:** Innovating in eco-friendly sourcing and manufacturing processes to align with global sustainability goals.
3. **Challenges and Opportunities:** While the Ayurveda industry holds immense potential, it also faces challenges:
   - Lack of standardized practices and regulations.
   - Limited awareness and misconceptions about Ayurveda in certain regions.
   - High R&D costs and long gestation periods for new product development. However, these challenges also present opportunities for entrepreneurial ventures to address gaps and create innovative solutions.

R&D Trends and Industry Dynamics

1. **Role of R&D in Ayurveda:** Research and development are pivotal in integrating Ayurvedic wisdom with modern science. Areas of focus include:
   - **Phytochemistry and Standardization:** Identifying active compounds in herbs and standardizing formulations.
   - **Clinical Trials:** Validating the efficacy and safety of Ayurvedic medicines through scientific studies.
   - **Pharmacovigilance:** Monitoring the safety of Ayurvedic products post-market release.
   - **Interdisciplinary Research:** Combining Ayurveda with fields like genomics, nanotechnology, and bioinformatics.
2. **Emerging R&D Trends:**
   - **Personalized Medicine:** Using Ayurgenomics to Tailor Treatments Based on an Individual's Genetic Makeup
   - Personalized medicine has emerged as a groundbreaking paradigm in healthcare, with Ayurveda contributing a unique perspective through Ayurgenomics. This interdisciplinary field integrates the principles of Ayurveda with modern genomics to develop personalized treatments tailored to an individual's genetic profile. Ayurgenomics posits that an individual's Prakriti (constitutional type) — classified as Vata, Pitta, or Kapha — correlates with their genetic makeup. By identifying genetic variations linked to these doshas, scientists can create highly specific and effective therapeutic interventions.

Key Advancements in Ayurgenomics:

1. **Prakriti-Gene Correlation Studies:** Research has shown correlations between specific genetic markers and Prakriti types, offering insights into predispositions to certain diseases and responses to treatments.
2. **Genomic Profiling Tools:** Modern tools such as CRISPR, microarrays, and next-generation sequencing (NGS) enable the identification of genetic markers associated with disease susceptibility and drug metabolism.
3. **Disease Prevention:** Ayurgenomics aids in identifying individuals at risk of chronic diseases, such as diabetes or hypertension, enabling early interventions with Ayurvedic remedies.
4. **Personalized Herbal Formulations:** Using genomic data, customized herbal formulations are designed to suit an individual's physiological and genetic needs.

Challenges and Opportunities

- **Challenges:** High costs, lack of widespread awareness, and limited integration of genomic tools in traditional Ayurvedic practice.
- **Opportunities:** Collaborations between geneticists, bioinformaticians, and Ayurvedic practitioners could unlock unprecedented healthcare possibilities.
- **Innovative Delivery Mechanisms:** Enhancing Bioavailability of Herbal Medicines

The therapeutic potential of Ayurveda depends significantly on the bioavailability of herbal compounds. Many phytochemicals have poor solubility and stability, reducing their effectiveness. Innovative delivery mechanisms are revolutionizing the way herbal medicines are formulated and administered to overcome these limitations.

Key Innovations in Delivery Mechanisms

1. **Herbal Nanoparticles:** Nanotechnology is being used to create nanoparticles of herbal compounds, which enhance absorption, stability, and targeted delivery. Examples include curcumin nanoparticles for anti-inflammatory and anticancer effects.
2. **Transdermal Patches:** These patches allow for the controlled release of herbal compounds through the skin, providing sustained therapeutic effects without gastrointestinal side effects.
3. **Encapsulation Technologies:** Microencapsulation and liposomal delivery systems protect active compounds from degradation, increasing their shelf life and bioavailability. For example, ashwagandha extract encapsulated in liposomes shows improved efficacy in stress management.
4. **Sublingual and Buccal Delivery:** Formulations like herbal lozenges or dissolvable strips enhance rapid absorption directly into the bloodstream.
   - **Future Directions:** Development of combination therapies using herbal and synthetic molecules for synergistic effects.
   - Research into smart delivery systems that release active ingredients in response to specific physiological triggers.
   - **Preventive Healthcare:** Addressing Global Wellness Trends.

Preventive healthcare has gained significant traction worldwide, aligning perfectly with Ayurveda's holistic approach. In the wake of global health challenges such as pandemics and chronic diseases, the demand for immunity boosters, adaptogens, and stress-relief formulations has skyrocketed.

Key Trends in Preventive Healthcare

1. **Immunity Boosters:** Ayurvedic formulations like chyawanprash, giloy (*Tinospora cordifolia*), and tulsi (*Ocimum sanctum*) are being extensively researched for their immune-enhancing properties.
2. **Adaptogens:** Herbs like ashwagandha, shatavari, and rhodiola are being developed into supplements to combat stress, enhance energy, and improve resilience.
3. **Stress-Relief Formulations:** In response to the global mental health crisis, Ayurvedic remedies such as Brahmi (*Bacopa monnieri*) and Jatamansi (*Nardostachys jatamansi*) are being formulated into teas, capsules, and oils for cognitive and emotional well-being.
4. **Gut Health:** Probiotic and prebiotic Ayurvedic formulations are gaining popularity, emphasizing the gut's role in immunity and overall health.

Consumer-Centric Innovations:

- Developing personalized wellness plans based on lifestyle and dietary habits.
- Creating convenient formats such as ready-to-drink beverages and on-the-go supplements.

Sustainability in R&D: Toward a Greener Future

Sustainability is becoming a cornerstone of Ayurvedic research and development. With increasing global concerns about environmental degradation, the Ayurveda industry is focusing on eco-friendly practices in sourcing, manufacturing, and product development.

Sustainable R&D Practices

1. **Sustainable Cultivation:** Research is being conducted on organic farming techniques and agroforestry models for cultivating medicinal plants, reducing reliance on wild harvesting.
2. **Biodegradable Packaging:** Many Ayurvedic companies are adopting sustainable packaging materials such as compostable pouches and recyclable glass containers.
3. **Waste Reduction:** Utilizing herbal waste for secondary products, such as biofertilizers and natural dyes, minimizes environmental impact.
4. **Green Manufacturing:** Employing renewable energy sources and water-efficient processes in manufacturing units.
    - **Collaborations and Innovations:** Partnerships with environmental organizations to ensure the conservation of endangered medicinal plants.
    - Development of AI-driven tools for monitoring and optimizing supply chains to reduce carbon footprints.

Industry Dynamics

- **Market Growth:** Rising Global Demand for Ayurveda. The global Ayurveda market is experiencing rapid growth, driven by increasing consumer awareness about natural and holistic health solutions. According to industry reports, the market is projected to grow at a compound annual growth rate (CAGR) of over 15% in the coming decade.

Drivers of Market Growth

1. **Health and Wellness Boom:** Rising awareness of lifestyle diseases has increased demand for preventive and natural healthcare solutions.
2. **Pandemic-Induced Focus on Immunity:** The COVID-19 pandemic has amplified interest in immunity-boosting Ayurvedic remedies.
3. **Mainstream Acceptance:** Ayurveda's integration into modern healthcare systems has enhanced its credibility and market reach.

Market Segmentation

- **Products:** Herbal supplements, skincare products, and functional foods dominate the market.
- **Services:** Ayurvedic spas, wellness retreats, and telemedicine platforms are growing rapidly.
- **Regulatory Landscape:** Balancing Tradition and Modernity.

The regulatory framework for Ayurvedic products varies across regions, presenting both challenges and opportunities for the industry.

Key Regulatory Trends

1. **Stricter Compliance Requirements:** Countries like the U.S. and EU are implementing stringent guidelines for the safety, efficacy, and quality of traditional medicines.
2. **Good Manufacturing Practices (GMP):** Certification requirements are pushing Ayurvedic manufacturers to adopt GMP standards.
3. **Codification of Traditional Knowledge:** Initiatives like India's Traditional Knowledge Digital Library (TKDL) aim to protect Ayurvedic knowledge from biopiracy and ensure fair use.

Challenges and Solutions

- **Challenge:** High costs associated with meeting international regulatory standards.
- **Solution:** Government subsidies and incentives for small and medium enterprises to achieve compliance.
- **Competition and Collaboration:** A Dynamic Ecosystem

The Ayurveda industry is characterized by intense competition and increasing collaboration between various stakeholders.

Competitive Landscape

1. **Startups:** Innovative startups are disrupting the market with personalized solutions and D2C models.
2. **Established Players:** Legacy brands like Dabur and Himalaya are expanding their portfolios and global presence.

Collaborative Efforts

- **Public-Private Partnerships:** Governments and private entities are working together to fund R&D initiatives.
- **Academia-Industry Collaboration:** Universities and research institutions are collaborating with Ayurvedic companies to validate traditional formulations scientifically.
- **Digital Transformation:** Revolutionizing Consumer Engagement

Digital technologies are reshaping the Ayurveda industry, enhancing accessibility, consumer engagement, and operational efficiency.

Digital Trends in Ayurveda

1. **E-commerce Platforms:** Online marketplaces have democratized access to Ayurvedic products, reaching consumers in remote locations.
2. **AI-Driven Personalization:** Tools like AI chatbots and recommendation engines offer tailored wellness solutions based on user preferences.
3. **Telemedicine:** Virtual consultations with Ayurvedic practitioners are bridging geographical barriers.
4. **Social Media Marketing:** Platforms like Instagram and Youtube are key channels for educating consumers and promoting products.
   - **Future Potential:** Integrating blockchain technology for supply chain transparency.
   - Using augmented reality (AR) for immersive consumer experiences, such as virtual wellness retreats.

Case Studies and Success Stories

1. **Patanjali Ayurved:** Revolutionizing Ayurveda. Founded by Baba Ramdev and Acharya Balkrishna, Patanjali Ayurved has become a household name in India. Key factors contributing to its success include:
   - Affordable pricing and extensive product range.
   - Strong branding and marketing through cultural and spiritual connections.
   - Vertical integration from cultivation to retail.
2. **Himalaya Wellness:** Bridging Tradition and Science. Himalaya Wellness has carved a niche in global markets with its science-backed Ayurvedic products. Highlights of its journey:
   - Pioneering R&D to develop scientifically validated herbal formulations.
   - Expanding globally with compliance to international regulatory standards.
   - Focus on quality, sustainability, and consumer education.
3. **Startup Spotlight:** Cureveda. Cureveda, a new-age Ayurveda brand, combines tradition with innovation:
   - D2C model offering personalized wellness solutions.
   - Use of AI-driven health assessments to recommend products.
   - Eco-friendly packaging and sustainability initiatives.
4. **VEDIX:** Personalized Ayurveda. Vedix specializes in personalized Ayurvedic skincare and haircare:
   - Leveraging AI and algorithms to create tailored solutions based on individual needs.
   - Subscription-based business model ensuring customer retention.
   - Emphasis on transparency and consumer education.
5. **Artemis Hospital's Integrative Medicine Center:** Artemis Hospital in India integrates Ayurveda with modern medicine:
   - Focus on holistic patient care for chronic and lifestyle diseases.
   - Collaborative research between Ayurvedic practitioners and allopathic doctors.
   - Offering evidence-based Ayurveda therapies alongside conventional treatments.

Future Directions for Entrepreneurship in Ayurveda

1. **Leveraging Technology**
   - AI-powered diagnostic tools and teleconsultations for remote Ayurveda access.
   - Blockchain for traceability in the supply chain of herbal ingredients.
2. **Global Expansion**
   - Tailoring products to suit cultural preferences and regulatory requirements in different countries.
   - Promoting Ayurveda through collaborations with international health organizations.

3. **Education and Awareness**
   - Enhancing consumer trust through education campaigns and transparent practices.
   - Establishing centers of excellence for training Ayurvedic entrepreneurs.

4. **Policy and Support**
   - Advocating for supportive policies and incentives for Ayurveda startups.
   - Public-private partnerships to fund R & D and market development.

MULTIPLE CHOICE QUESTIONS

1. In a collaborative research project between a biotechnology firm and an Ayurvedic institution, scientists aim to decode the biochemical basis of Tridosha by aligning the principles of Vata, Pitta, and Kapha with modern physiological markers. They hypothesize that Vata correlates with neurotransmitter levels, Pitta with enzymatic metabolic activity, and Kapha with cellular hydration and structural integrity. As part of their study, they evaluate these correlations in a diverse population to develop personalized health solutions. If the findings validate the hypothesis, which of the following approaches is most likely to succeed in translating these insights into a scalable healthcare product?

A. Developing a single, generalized supplement targeting all three doshas to optimize overall health.
B. Creating AI-driven diagnostic tools capable of identifying imbalances in doshas based on physiological markers and suggesting tailored interventions.
C. Abandoning Ayurvedic classifications entirely in favor of pharmacological approaches.
D. Limiting the research application to academic circles without pursuing commercial scalability.

2. A global pharmaceutical company is interested in introducing an Ayurvedic nutraceutical line in Western markets. The team decides to incorporate Ashwagandha, Turmeric, and Brahmi into its formulations but struggles to navigate Western regulatory frameworks, particularly regarding claims validation, standardization of bioactive compounds, and compliance with manufacturing protocols. If the company's goal is to integrate traditional Ayurveda with modern standards without compromising its authenticity, what strategy should they adopt?

A. Modify the formulations to fit Western health trends, such as focusing on single compounds like curcumin instead of whole herbs.
B. Collaborate with Ayurvedic institutions to conduct clinical trials proving the efficacy of their formulations and ensuring compliance with regulatory requirements.
C. Market their products as generic dietary supplements, avoiding any claims related to Ayurvedic principles to bypass regulations.
D. Reduce their offerings to traditional Ayurvedic formulations without standardization to maintain authenticity.

3. An entrepreneur is developing a sustainable Ayurveda-based skincare line targeting environmentally conscious consumers. The formulations include classic Ayurvedic ingredients such as Neem and Sandalwood. However, challenges arise from the environmental degradation of these resources, leading to variability in quality and rising costs. The entrepreneur must decide between maintaining the traditional authenticity of Ayurveda and adopting alternative approaches to meet sustainability goals. Which strategy would best balance these priorities?

A. Sourcing synthetic alternatives for Neem and Sandalwood to avoid depleting natural resources.
B. Investing in organic, community-driven cultivation practices to sustainably source authentic ingredients.
C. Marketing the skincare line exclusively as a luxury product to justify higher costs associated with sustainability.
D. Avoiding traditional Ayurvedic ingredients altogether in favour of easily available modern substitutes.

4. In a groundbreaking study on Ayurgenomics, researchers explore the genetic basis of Prakriti (constitutional types) and discover significant correlations between specific genetic markers and Ayurvedic doshas. The findings suggest that genetic variations influence susceptibility to chronic diseases and individual responses to Ayurvedic treatments. How can this discovery be most effectively leveraged to advance personalized medicine?

A. Designing genome-based personalized herbal formulations tailored to the patient's dosha and genetic predisposition.
B. Replacing traditional Ayurveda with purely genomic-based treatments that disregard Prakriti classifications.
C. Limiting the application of Ayurgenomics to niche academic studies without practical implementation.

D. Standardizing Ayurvedic formulations to fit a one-size-fits-all model, disregarding individual genetic variations.

5. In the aftermath of the COVID-19 pandemic, the global demand for natural immunity boosters like Giloy, Tulsi, and Amla skyrocketed. Entrepreneurs innovated delivery mechanisms such as effervescent tablets and nanocapsules to make these products more appealing to modern consumers. However, critics argue that such innovations dilute the traditional ethos of Ayurveda. What approach should companies adopt to strike a balance between innovation and tradition?
   A. Focus on traditional formulations, ignoring modern delivery methods entirely.
   B. Utilize innovative delivery mechanisms while ensuring adherence to Ayurvedic principles of formulation and synergy.
   C. Prioritize technological advancements over traditional practices to meet consumer demands.
   D. Abandon innovation entirely to preserve the traditional identity of Ayurveda.

6. A startup focusing on preventive healthcare leverages adaptogens like Ashwagandha and Shatavari to create stress-management supplements. However, clinical trials reveal that the efficacy of these herbs varies significantly based on the quality of raw materials and their active compound concentrations. To ensure consistent results, what should the company prioritize in its production process?
   A. Standardizing raw material sourcing and testing to ensure consistent levels of bioactive compounds in formulations.
   B. Focusing on synthetic substitutes for adaptogens to bypass the challenges of natural variability.
   C. Expanding their product line to include unrelated wellness products to diversify risks.
   D. Marketing their products without standardization, relying on consumer trust in traditional Ayurveda.

7. A government-backed initiative aims to promote entrepreneurship in Ayurveda by funding R&D in areas like pharmacovigilance, innovative delivery systems, and sustainability. However, startups often lack the infrastructure and expertise to translate these funds into impactful innovations. What model would be most effective in bridging this gap?
   A. Establishing public-private partnerships to facilitate knowledge sharing and provide startups with access to advanced facilities.
   B. Relying solely on the startups to independently manage R&D activities without external intervention.
   C. Limiting funding to established Ayurveda companies with proven track records.
   D. Discontinuing funding initiatives due to inefficiencies in execution.

8. As Ayurveda gains global traction, the industry faces a pressing need to adopt Good Manufacturing Practices (GMP) and meet international regulatory standards. However, small-scale traditional manufacturers often struggle with the financial and operational burdens of compliance. How should regulatory bodies address this challenge to support the Ayurveda industry's growth?
   A. Mandate GMP compliance for all manufacturers without exceptions, irrespective of their scale.
   B. Provide financial incentives and technical assistance to small-scale manufacturers to help them achieve compliance.
   C. Exclude traditional manufacturers from regulatory requirements to preserve the authenticity of Ayurveda.
   D. Limit GMP mandates to products intended for export markets, leaving domestic products unregulated.

9. An Ayurvedic company introduces a subscription-based model for delivering personalized wellness kits, including herbal supplements, dietary recommendations, and yoga plans. The company uses AI to design these kits based on user data. However, consumers express concerns about data privacy and the authenticity of AI-driven Ayurveda. How can the company address these concerns while retaining its innovative edge?
   A. Discontinue the use of AI in favour of traditional, practitioner-led recommendations.
   B. Ensure robust data encryption and transparency about AI's role in personalizing treatments.
   C. Avoid collecting sensitive consumer data entirely, limiting AI applications.
   D. Shift focus to generic wellness kits without personalization.

10. A prominent Ayurveda company develops a global marketing campaign emphasizing Ayurveda's role in mental health management, leveraging formulations like Brahmi and Jatamansi. However, the campaign faces backlash for promoting cultural appropriation in Western markets. What approach should the company adopt to address these concerns?
   A. Avoid marketing Ayurveda globally to prevent cultural appropriation accusations.
   B. Collaborate with cultural representatives and Ayurvedic experts to ensure ethical marketing practices.
   C. Focus solely on the scientific aspects of Ayurveda, disregarding its cultural roots.
   D. Limit their product offerings to domestic markets.

Directions (Q. No. 11-14): *Scenario-Based Questions*

SCENARIO 1

A biotechnology company, in collaboration with a leading Ayurvedic institute, embarks on a project to develop an AI-based healthcare platform integrating Ayurveda with modern genomic science. This initiative aims to provide highly personalized treatment plans by analyzing genetic markers, such as SNPs linked to chronic inflammation and metabolic disorders, alongside Prakriti-based classifications—Vata, Pitta, and Kapha. The platform combines traditional diagnostic principles, including pulse readings and tongue analysis, with genetic data to recommend tailored interventions, such as herbal supplements, dietary practices, and lifestyle adjustments. Initial trials yield encouraging results, with over 70% of participants showing significant reductions in inflammation markers like CRP and improved metabolic efficiency, such as lower HbA1c levels in diabetic patients.

However, inconsistencies emerge in the trial outcomes. Patients with identical Prakriti types and similar genetic markers respond differently to the same interventions. Researchers hypothesize that these variances may stem from external factors such as gut microbiota diversity, environmental stressors, and differences in individual lifestyle adherence. Another concern arises from the criticism of over-reliance on biological determinism. Critics argue that this approach risks reducing the holistic principles of Ayurveda—emphasizing harmony between the mind, body, and environment—to mechanistic interpretations based solely on genetic data. This tension challenges the team to refine their algorithms without compromising Ayurveda's integrative philosophy. Meanwhile, the platform's scalability remains an issue. Rural populations, which could benefit greatly from this innovation, face barriers such as lack of access to genomic testing, digital tools, and Ayurvedic practitioners.

SCENARIO 2

An environmental NGO highlights the growing crisis of unsustainable harvesting of key Ayurvedic herbs like Ashwagandha, Haritaki, and Amalaki, driven by the rising global demand for herbal medicines and supplements. Overharvesting is not only depleting wild populations of these plants but also leading to reduced concentrations of bioactive compounds, which diminishes their therapeutic efficacy. In addition, monoculture farming of herbs such as Ashwagandha is causing significant ecological imbalances, including soil degradation and loss of biodiversity. The NGO advocates for agroforestry models that integrate medicinal plants with food crops to create a sustainable and biodiverse cultivation system. Such an approach would enhance soil health, restore local ecosystems, and improve the livelihoods of marginalized farming communities.

Implementing this solution, however, presents challenges. Agroforestry requires substantial initial investment in training farmers and establishing new infrastructure, costs that many Ayurveda-focused companies are hesitant to bear. The biotech company from Scenario 1 finds itself caught in a dilemma. On the one hand, it depends on high-quality herbs for its formulations, making sustainability a priority to ensure long-term supply. On the other hand, scaling its operations to international markets requires resources that might otherwise be directed toward environmental initiatives. This dual pressure forces the company to reevaluate its strategies to balance profitability, sustainability, and adherence to Ayurvedic principles.

11. How does the integration of genomic markers with Ayurvedic Prakriti classifications in Scenario 1 enhance the concept of personalized medicine?

A. By equating Prakriti exclusively with genetic variations, reducing Ayurveda to a biological framework.

B. By creating a hybrid approach that respects traditional Ayurvedic principles while leveraging modern scientific advancements.

C. By disproving the relevance of Prakriti in modern medical treatments.

D. By eliminating the role of Ayurveda's holistic philosophy in favour of genomic determinism.

12. What strategy would best address the inconsistencies in treatment outcomes observed in Scenario 1's trials?

A. Incorporating factors like gut microbiota diversity, stress levels, and environmental conditions into the platform's predictive algorithms.

B. Focusing solely on refining genetic data analysis to provide more accurate recommendations.

C. Abandoning genomic integration and relying entirely on traditional Ayurvedic diagnostic methods.

D. Standardizing treatments for all patients regardless of genetic and Prakriti variations to minimize variability.

13. How does the environmental degradation of Ayurvedic herbs described in Scenario 2 potentially impact the personalized healthcare platform in Scenario 1?

A. Declining concentrations of bioactive compounds in herbs could undermine the efficacy of recommended treatments.

B. Herb quality does not influence the platform's predictive accuracy or treatment outcomes.

C. Overharvesting has no measurable effect on the therapeutic potency of Ayurvedic formulations.

D. Reduced herb availability would force the platform to rely entirely on synthetic alternatives.

14. Based on the interconnected findings of both scenarios, what approach should the biotech company prioritize to balance sustainability with personalized healthcare innovation?
    A. Invest in agroforestry and sustainable herb cultivation practices, even at the cost of short-term profitability.
    B. Scale international operations without addressing sustainability challenges to maximize immediate market share.
    C. Shift entirely to synthetic alternatives to reduce reliance on natural herbs.
    D. Focus exclusively on refining AI algorithms, disregarding environmental concerns as secondary to technological innovation.

Directions (Q. No. 15–24): *Codes-Based Questions*

15. The integration of Ayurveda with modern genomic science focuses on several key principles:
    (a) Prakriti classifications correspond to genetic predispositions to diseases.
    (b) Ayurgenomics provides a framework for personalized medicine.
    (c) Genetic markers alone are sufficient to design Ayurvedic interventions.
    (d) Lifestyle and environmental factors play a critical role in Ayurveda-based treatment outcomes.

    Choose the correct answer from the options given below:
    A. (a), (b), and (d) only
    B. (a), (b), and (c) only
    C. (a) and (b) only
    D. (a), (c), and (d) only

16. The therapeutic potential of Ayurvedic Rasayana herbs, such as Ashwagandha and Amalaki, is influenced by:
    (a) Their bioactive compound concentration.
    (b) Sustainable harvesting and cultivation practices.
    (c) The genetic makeup of the individual receiving treatment.
    (d) The availability of synthetic alternatives to these herbs.

    Choose the correct answer from the options given below:
    A. (a), (b), and (c) only
    B. (a), (c), and (d) only
    C. (b), (c), and (d) only
    D. (a), (b), (c), and (d)

17. The challenges in scaling AI-driven Ayurveda platforms include:
    (a) Limited access to genomic testing in rural areas.
    (b) Ethical concerns related to data privacy.
    (c) Over-reliance on biological markers, neglecting Ayurveda's holistic principles.
    (d) Lack of acceptance of Ayurveda in global markets.

    Choose the correct answer from the options given below:
    A. (a), (b), and (c) only
    B. (a), (b), and (d) only
    C. (a) and (c) only
    D. (a), (b), (c), and (d)

18. The environmental sustainability of Ayurvedic herb cultivation can be improved by:
    (a) Implementing agroforestry practices.
    (b) Developing synthetic bioactive compounds.
    (c) Imposing restrictions on wild harvesting.
    (d) Encouraging monoculture farming for high-demand herbs.

    Choose the correct answer from the options given below:
    A. (a), (b), and (d) only
    B. (a), (c), and (d) only
    C. (a), (b), and (c) only
    D. (a) and (c) only

19. The principles of personalized medicine in Ayurveda involve:
    (a) Prakriti analysis as the foundation of diagnosis.
    (b) Integration of genomic and Ayurvedic diagnostic tools.
    (c) Standardization of treatments across all individuals to ensure uniformity.
    (d) Consideration of environmental and lifestyle factors in treatment plans.

    Choose the correct answer from the options given below:
    A. (a), (b), and (d) only
    B. (a) and (b) only
    C. (b) and (c) only
    D. (a), (c), and (d) only

20. The introduction of agroforestry in Ayurvedic herb cultivation would lead to:
    (a) Improved soil health and biodiversity.
    (b) Reduction in the therapeutic efficacy of medicinal herbs.
    (c) Increased costs for herbal products in global markets.
    (d) Enhanced sustainability of supply chains for Ayurveda companies.

    Choose the correct answer from the options given below:
    A. (a), (b), and (c) only
    B. (a), (b), and (d) only
    C. (a) and (d) only
    D. (a), (c), and (d) only

21. Challenges faced by Ayurvedic startups attempting to scale globally include:
(a) Strict regulatory standards for traditional medicines.
(b) High costs of ensuring sustainability in herb sourcing.
(c) Lack of clinical validation for Ayurvedic formulations.
(d) Limited public awareness about Ayurveda in developed markets.

Choose the correct answer from the options given below:
A. (a) and (c) only
B. (a), (b), and (d) only
C. (a), (b), and (c) only
D. (a), (b), (c), and (d)

22. The inconsistencies in clinical outcomes observed in Ayurvedic trials can be addressed by:
(a) Incorporating data from environmental and lifestyle factors.
(b) Abandoning genomic tools and relying solely on traditional diagnostic methods.
(c) Conducting multi-centered trials to assess diverse population responses.
(d) Standardizing formulations to minimize variability in treatments.

Choose the correct answer from the options given below:
A. (a) and (c) only
B. (a), (b), and (c) only
C. (a), (c), and (d) only
D. (a), (b), and (d) only

23. Ethical concerns in integrating Ayurveda with genomic tools involve:
(a) Privacy of genetic data collected from patients.
(b) Consent for using genetic information in AI-driven recommendations.
(c) Commercial exploitation of traditional Ayurvedic knowledge.
(d) Incompatibility of Ayurveda's holistic philosophy with genetic determinism.

Choose the correct answer from the options given below:
A. (a), (b), and (c) only
B. (a) and (d) only
C. (a), (b), and (d) only
D. (a), (b), (c), and (d)

24. The long-term sustainability of Ayurvedic innovation depends on:
(a) Developing technologies that respect Ayurveda's traditional knowledge systems.
(b) Ensuring the conservation of endangered medicinal plant species.
(c) Balancing scalability and profitability in global markets.
(d) Shifting entirely to synthetic alternatives for herbal compounds.

Choose the correct answer from the options given below:
A. (a), (b), and (c) only
B. (a), (c), and (d) only
C. (b), (c), and (d) only
D. (a), (b), and (d) only

Directions (Q. No. 25–34): *Match List Questions*

25. Match List–I (Herbs) with List–II (Therapeutic Benefits):

List–I	List–II
(a) Ashwagandha	1. Adaptogen known for stress relief and improved energy
(b) Haritaki	2. Promotes detoxification and supports gut health
(c) Guduchi	3. Enhances immunity and reduces inflammation
(d) Brahmi	4. Improves cognitive function and memory

Choose the correct answer from the options given below:
A. (a)-1, (b)-2, (c)-3, (d)-4
B. (a)-2, (b)-1, (c)-4, (d)-3
C. (a)-3, (b)-4, (c)-1, (d)-2
D. (a)-4, (b)-3, (c)-2, (d)-1

26. Match List–I (Ayurvedic Concepts) with (Scientific Interpretation):

List–I	List–II
(a) Prakriti	1. Genetic predisposition influencing health and disease
(b) Agni	2. Digestive and metabolic fire essential for nutrient assimilation
(c) Ama	3. Toxins resulting from improper digestion
(d) Doshas	4. Biophysiological energies governing the body

Choose the correct answer from the options given below:
A. (a)-1, (b)-2, (c)-3, (d)-4
B. (a)-2, (b)-1, (c)-4, (d)-3
C. (a)-3, (b)-4, (c)-1, (d)-2
D. (a)-4, (b)-3, (c)-2, (d)-1

27. Match List–I (Challenges in Ayurveda) with List–II (Potential Solutions):

List–I	List–II
(a) Overharvesting of herbs	1. Promotion of agroforestry practices

(b) Variability in clinical outcomes	2. Incorporation of environmental and lifestyle factors in studies
(c) Lack of global validation	3. Conducting rigorous multi-centered clinical trials
(d) Ethical concerns in AI usage	4. Establishing robust data privacy regulations

Choose the correct answer from the options given below:

A. (a)-1, (b)-2, (c)-3, (d)-4
B. (a)-4, (b)-3, (c)-1, (d)-2
C. (a)-3, (b)-4, (c)-2, (d)-1
D. (a)-2, (b)-1, (c)-4, (d)-3

28. Match List–I (Innovative Technologies) with List–II (Application in Ayurveda):

List–I	List–II
(a) AI-driven diagnostics	1. Personalized treatment recommendations
(b) Genomic analysis	2. Identification of genetic predispositions
(c) Nanotechnology	3. Improved bioavailability of herbal compounds
(d) Blockchain	4. Transparent and traceable herb supply chains

Choose the correct answer from the options given below:

A. (a)-1, (b)-2, (c)-3, (d)-4
B. (a)-4, (b)-3, (c)-2, (d)-1
C. (a)-3, (b)-4, (c)-1, (d)-2
D. (a)-2, (b)-1, (c)-4, (d)-3

29. Match List–I (Market Challenges) with List–II (Solutions):

List–I	List–II
(a) Lack of standardized practices	1. Adoption of Good Manufacturing Practices (GMP)
(b) High cost of sustainability	2. Community-based agroforestry initiatives
(c) Limited awareness in global markets	3. Awareness campaigns and digital marketing
(d) Regulatory hurdles	4. Collaboration with international certification bodies

Choose the correct answer from the options given below:

A. (a)-1, (b)-2, (c)-3, (d)-4
B. (a)-3, (b)-4, (c)-1, (d)-2
C. (a)-4, (b)-3, (c)-2, (d)-1
D. (a)-2, (b)-1, (c)-4, (d)-3

30. Match List–I (R&D Trends) with List–II (Features):

List–I	List–II
(a) Personalized medicine	1. Ayurgenomics and Prakriti classification integration
(b) Innovative delivery systems	2. Use of nanoparticles and transdermal patches
(c) Preventive healthcare	3. Focus on adaptogens and immunity boosters
(d) Sustainability in R&D	4. Agroforestry and eco-friendly sourcing

Choose the correct answer from the options given below:

A. (a)-1, (b)-2, (c)-3, (d)-4
B. (a)-4, (b)-3, (c)-1, (d)-2
C. (a)-3, (b)-4, (c)-2, (d)-1
D. (a)-2, (b)-1, (c)-4, (d)-3

31. Match List–I (Ayurvedic Components) with List–II (Associated Benefits):

List–I	List–II
(a) Sattva guṇa	1. Clarity and balance in thoughts and actions
(b) Rajas guṇa	2. Energy, activity, and passion
(c) Tamas guṇa	3. Inertia and ignorance
(d) Tri-guṇa balance	4. Holistic mental and physical well-being

Choose the correct answer from the options given below:

A. (a)-1, (b)-2, (c)-3, (d)-4
B. (a)-4, (b)-3, (c)-1, (d)-2
C. (a)-3, (b)-4, (c)-2, (d)-1
D. (a)-2, (b)-1, (c)-4, (d)-3

32. Match List–I (Key Ayurvedic Herbs) with List–II (Therapeutic Focus):

List–I	List–II
(a) Amalaki	1. Rich source of Vitamin C and promotes immunity
(b) Neem	2. Antibacterial and detoxification properties
(c) Turmeric	3. Anti-inflammatory and antioxidant effects
(d) Shatavari	4. Rejuvenative and supports female reproductive health

Choose the correct answer from the options given below:

A. (a)-1, (b)-2, (c)-3, (d)-4
B. (a)-2, (b)-4, (c)-1, (d)-3
C. (a)-3, (b)-1, (c)-4, (d)-2
D. (a)-4, (b)-3, (c)-2, (d)-1

33. Match List–I (Regulatory Needs) with List–II (Purpose):

List–I	List–II
(a) GMP compliance	1. Ensures consistency in quality and manufacturing practices

(b) Pharma-covigilance	2. Monitors adverse effects of formulations post-market release
(c) Clinical trials	3. Validates the safety and efficacy of Ayurvedic formulations
(d) Certification	4. Facilitates export to global markets

Choose the correct answer from the options given below:

A. (a)-1, (b)-2, (c)-3, (d)-4
B. (a)-4, (b)-3, (c)-1, (d)-2
C. (a)-3, (b)-1, (c)-4, (d)-2
D. (a)-2, (b)-4, (c)-3, (d)-1

34. Match List–I (Entrepreneurial Challenges) with List–II (Industry Dynamics):

List–I	List–II
(a) Competition from global brands	1. Establishing distinct branding and innovation
(b) Limited R&D funding	2. Public-private partnerships for innovation
(c) Regulatory barriers	3. Compliance with international standards
(d) Consumer misconceptions	4. Education campaigns and transparency

Choose the correct answer from the options given below:

A. (a)-1, (b)-2, (c)-3, (d)-4
B. (a)-4, (b)-3, (c)-2, (d)-1
C. (a)-2, (b)-1, (c)-4, (d)-3
D. (a)-3, (b)-4, (c)-1, (d)-2

Directions (Q. No. 35–39): *Following questions are based on Statement 1 and Statement 2. Read both the statements carefully and choose the correct answer from the options given below:*

A. Both Statement 1 and Statement 2 are true, and Statement 2 is the correct explanation of Statement 1.
B. Both Statement 1 and Statement 2 are true, but Statement 2 is not the correct explanation of Statement 1.
C. Statement 1 is true, but Statement 2 is false.
D. Statement 1 is false, but Statement 2 is true.
E. Both Statement 1 and Statement 2 are false.

35. Statement 1: Ayurgenomics integrates Ayurveda's Prakriti-based classification with modern genomic data to develop personalized treatment protocols.

Statement 2: Ayurgenomics eliminates the need for holistic assessments like pulse diagnosis and focuses solely on genetic markers.

36. Statement 1: Agroforestry can serve as a sustainable model for cultivating high-demand Ayurvedic herbs while restoring local biodiversity and improving soil health.

Statement 2: Monoculture farming of Ayurvedic herbs is more sustainable than agroforestry due to its higher productivity and lower initial costs.

37. Statement 1: The efficacy of Ayurvedic formulations depends on the quality of herbs used, which is influenced by cultivation practices, environmental factors, and bioactive compound concentrations.

Statement 2: Synthetic substitutes for Ayurvedic herbs ensure consistency in bioactive compounds and can completely replace natural sources in formulations.

38. Statement 1: AI-driven Ayurveda platforms can enhance diagnosis and treatment precision by integrating genetic and environmental data into personalized health plans.

Statement 2: AI in Ayurveda undermines its holistic philosophy by prioritizing technology over traditional practitioner expertise.

39. Statement 1: International regulatory compliance, such as Good Manufacturing Practices (GMP) and clinical trials, is essential for Ayurveda's global market expansion.

Statement 2: The authenticity of Ayurveda is compromised when traditional methods are adapted to meet international regulatory standards.

Directions (Q. No. 40–45): *There are two statements in each question. One is labelled as Assertion (A) and the other is as Reason (R). Read both the statements and choose the correct answer from the options given below:*

A. Both Assertion (A) and Reason (R) are true, and Reason (R) is the correct explanation of Assertion (A).
B. Both Assertion (A) and Reason (R) are true, but Reason (R) is not the correct explanation of Assertion (A).
C. Assertion (A) is true, but Reason (R) is false.
D. Assertion (A) is false, but Reason (R) is true.
E. Both Assertion (A) and Reason (R) are false.

40. Assertion (A): Ayurgenomics bridges the gap between Ayurveda and modern personalized medicine by integrating Prakriti-based classifications with genomic data.

Reason (R): Ayurgenomics eliminates the need for lifestyle and environmental considerations in Ayurvedic diagnosis and treatment.

41. **Assertion (A):** The unsustainable harvesting of Ayurvedic herbs like Ashwagandha and Haritaki reduces their therapeutic efficacy due to lower concentrations of bioactive compounds.

    Reason (R): Environmental stressors, including soil erosion and biodiversity loss, negatively impact the quality and potency of medicinal plants.

42. **Assertion (A):** Agroforestry is a sustainable model for cultivating Ayurvedic herbs while promoting ecological restoration and biodiversity.

    Reason (R): Monoculture farming of medicinal plants ensures higher productivity and requires fewer resources than agroforestry.

43. **Assertion (A):** AI-driven platforms in Ayurveda enable personalized treatment recommendations based on genetic and physiological data.

    Reason (R): Such platforms completely replace traditional Ayurvedic diagnostic methods like pulse reading and dosha analysis.

44. **Assertion (A):** Sustainable cultivation practices are essential for ensuring the long-term viability of Ayurvedic herb supply chains.

    Reason (R): Overharvesting and environmental degradation lead to an increase in bioactive compound concentrations, enhancing the therapeutic potency of herbs.

45. **Assertion (A):** The integration of Ayurvedic principles into global markets requires compliance with international regulatory standards.

    Reason (R): Adhering to these standards undermines the holistic philosophy of Ayurveda, which cannot be scientifically validated.

Directions (Q. No. 46–50): *Read the passage carefully and answer the questions given below*:

Ayurveda, the ancient Indian system of medicine, has stood the test of time as a holistic approach to health and well-being. Rooted in the principles of natural harmony, Ayurveda emphasizes the balance of the body, mind, and spirit through personalized treatments, dietary regulations, and lifestyle practices. While traditional Ayurvedic practices have been widely followed for thousands of years, the 21st century has witnessed a resurgence of interest in Ayurveda, with a focus on integrating its ancient wisdom with modern scientific methodologies.

Modern research in Ayurveda primarily seeks to validate its principles through scientific investigations. Several studies have explored the biochemical and pharmacological effects of Ayurvedic herbs, revealing their potential to address contemporary health challenges. For example, curcumin, a bioactive compound derived from turmeric (Curcuma longa), has been extensively researched for its anti-inflammatory, antioxidant, and anticancer properties. Similarly, ashwagandha (Withania somnifera), known for its adaptogenic effects, has gained attention for its role in reducing stress, improving cognitive function, and enhancing physical endurance. The inclusion of such Ayurvedic herbs in clinical trials has brought greater credibility to their therapeutic benefits.

One of the key areas of research involves deciphering the pharmacodynamics and pharmacokinetics of Ayurvedic formulations. Traditional texts emphasize the importance of synergy among multiple ingredients, a concept that modern researchers are beginning to explore through advanced analytical tools. By understanding how these combinations work at the molecular level, scientists aim to optimize the efficacy and safety of Ayurvedic formulations. The use of modern techniques like liquid chromatography-mass spectrometry (LC-MS) and nuclear magnetic resonance (NMR) spectroscopy has significantly contributed to identifying active compounds in Ayurvedic preparations.

Another breakthrough in Ayurveda is the application of genomics and personalized medicine. Ancient Ayurvedic texts categorize individuals into prakriti types, which determine their physiological and psychological constitution. Modern genomics research has drawn parallels between these prakriti classifications and genetic predispositions, suggesting a scientific basis for Ayurveda's personalized approach. For instance, studies have correlated specific genetic markers with prakriti types, offering new possibilities for precision medicine tailored to an individual's genetic profile.

Ayurveda's holistic approach to chronic diseases has also garnered attention. Conditions such as diabetes, hypertension, and arthritis, which often result from lifestyle factors, are addressed in Ayurveda through a combination of herbal remedies, dietary changes, and lifestyle modifications. Research has demonstrated that Ayurvedic interventions, such as the use of fenugreek seeds for managing blood sugar levels or the application of Panchakarma therapies for detoxification, can complement conventional treatments and improve patient outcomes.

Mental health is another domain where Ayurveda is making strides. The global rise in stress-related disorders has prompted researchers to examine Ayurvedic practices like meditation, yoga, and herbal adaptogens for their impact on mental well-being. Studies have shown that Ayurvedic therapies can significantly reduce symptoms of anxiety and depression, offering a natural alternative to pharmaceutical treatments. For example, brahmi (Bacopa monnieri) has been shown to enhance cognitive function and reduce stress, while shankhpushpi (Convolvulus pluricaulis) is being explored for its calming effects on the nervous system.

The integration of Ayurveda with modern technology has paved the way for innovative diagnostic and treatment tools. Digital platforms and mobile applications now offer personalized Ayurvedic consultations, making traditional knowledge accessible to a global audience. Additionally, artificial intelligence and machine learning algorithms are being employed to analyze Ayurvedic texts, identify patterns, and develop predictive models for treatment outcomes. These advancements have not only increased the reach of Ayurveda but have also fostered collaborations between traditional practitioners and modern healthcare providers.

One of the challenges in modern Ayurvedic research is ensuring the standardization and quality control of herbal medicines. Variations in cultivation practices, harvesting methods, and preparation techniques can impact the potency and safety of Ayurvedic formulations. To address this, researchers are developing standardized protocols and guidelines for the cultivation and processing of medicinal plants. The World Health Organization (WHO) has also recognized the importance of traditional medicine and supports efforts to integrate it into mainstream healthcare systems while maintaining rigorous quality standards.

The potential of Ayurveda extends beyond therapeutic applications to preventive healthcare and wellness. Ayurvedic principles emphasize the importance of a balanced lifestyle, seasonal routines, and mindful eating to maintain health and prevent disease. These principles align closely with modern concepts of preventive medicine, promoting practices that reduce the risk of lifestyle-related disorders. For instance, the Ayurvedic concept of "dinacharya" (daily routine) encourages habits like early rising, regular exercise, and balanced meals, which are now widely recognized as essential for overall well-being.

Despite these advancements, the path to global acceptance of Ayurveda faces certain obstacles. Skepticism regarding its scientific validity, lack of large-scale clinical trials, and regulatory challenges are some of the barriers that need to be overcome. However, growing interest in integrative medicine and the rising demand for natural and sustainable healthcare solutions provide a favorable environment for Ayurveda to flourish.

46. Which compound derived from turmeric is widely researched for its therapeutic properties?

A. Ashwagandha
B. Brahmi
C. Curcumin
D. Shankhpushpi

47. What modern techniques are used to identify active compounds in Ayurvedic formulations?

A. Liquid chromatography-mass spectrometry and nuclear magnetic resonance spectroscopy
B. PCR and gel electrophoresis
C. X-ray diffraction and crystallography
D. Ultrasound and CT scans

48. How does modern genomics research relate to Ayurveda's concept of prakriti?

A. It disproves the concept entirely
B. It links prakriti types with genetic markers
C. It replaces prakriti classifications with modern terms
D. It uses prakriti types to predict treatment costs

49. Which Ayurvedic herb is known for its adaptogenic effects?

A. Brahmi
B. Ashwagandha
C. Shankhpushpi
D. Fenugreek

50. What initiative has the World Health Organization (WHO) undertaken regarding traditional medicine?

a. Encouraging complete replacement of modern medicine with Ayurveda
B. Supporting the integration of traditional medicine into mainstream healthcare systems
C. Banning the use of herbal remedies in conventional healthcare
D. Promoting Ayurvedic therapies exclusively in India

ANSWER WITH EXPLANATIONS

1. B: Integrating modern extraction technologies with Ayurvedic formulations respects the traditional principle of synergistic herbal combinations while enhancing therapeutic efficacy. By leveraging advanced methods, bioavailability is improved without compromising the holistic nature of Ayurveda. Solely relying on traditional methods may limit scalability and effectiveness, while focusing on synthetic alternatives could undermine the authenticity of Ayurveda. This hybrid approach balances innovation with tradition, ensuring the treatments remain accessible and credible. Entrepreneurs who adopt this strategy create products that cater to contemporary demands while preserving the essence of Ayurveda, fostering trust and expanding its appeal in global healthcare markets.

2. B: Collaborating with Ayurvedic institutions to conduct clinical trials not only addresses regulatory challenges but also validates the efficacy of formulations in scientific terms. This approach bridges the gap between traditional knowledge and modern healthcare standards. Simply focusing on Western trends or avoiding regulatory requirements may dilute Ayurveda's principles or restrict market access. By combining evidence-based practices with traditional methods, entrepreneurs can enhance consumer trust and market credibility. This alignment ensures that Ayurvedic products maintain their authenticity while meeting global healthcare standards, creating a sustainable and innovative model for expanding Ayurveda's reach.

3. **B:** Sustainable sourcing through community-driven agroforestry systems addresses the twin challenges of ecological degradation and quality consistency. This approach aligns with Ayurveda's ethos of living in harmony with nature, ensuring long-term supply chain reliability. While synthetic substitutes or luxury market positioning might address short-term issues, they fail to reflect Ayurveda's core values. By fostering collaboration with local communities, this strategy also supports socio-economic development and ensures fair trade practices. Entrepreneurs who adopt such sustainable methods build trust and create resilient systems that preserve Ayurveda's therapeutic value while addressing global environmental and ethical concerns.

4. **A:** Ayurgenomics bridges Ayurveda and modern medicine by correlating Prakriti classifications with genetic predispositions, enhancing personalized treatment approaches. This integration validates Ayurveda's traditional wisdom with scientific insights, offering tailored health solutions for conditions like diabetes and autoimmune disorders. Rather than replacing traditional diagnostics, Ayurgenomics complements them by adding precision and credibility. By embracing this approach, entrepreneurs align with global trends in personalized medicine while preserving Ayurveda's authenticity. This innovation demonstrates Ayurveda's adaptability to contemporary healthcare needs, making it a valuable system for both traditional practitioners and modern scientific communities.

5. **B:** Using nanotechnology for innovative delivery mechanisms ensures that Ayurvedic formulations meet modern consumer preferences for convenience while retaining their therapeutic efficacy. By enhancing bioavailability, such methods preserve the holistic principle of synergy in Ayurveda, unlike synthetic or simplified approaches. Entrepreneurs adopting this model create user-friendly products without compromising the traditional essence of Ayurveda. This balance allows Ayurveda to cater to evolving global healthcare trends, positioning it as a credible and effective system for addressing lifestyle diseases and other conditions. It reflects how tradition and technology can coexist to meet modern demands while maintaining authenticity.

6. **A:** Standardizing raw material quality ensures consistent therapeutic outcomes, critical for building consumer trust and complying with global healthcare standards. Variability in raw materials undermines the efficacy of Ayurvedic formulations, risking their credibility. By investing in quality testing and sustainable sourcing, entrepreneurs maintain the integrity of their products while addressing environmental concerns. Synthetic alternatives or unstandardized practices dilute Ayurveda's authenticity and fail to address the growing demand for reliable, natural healthcare. This approach balances traditional values with scientific rigor, ensuring that Ayurvedic formulations remain effective and credible in competitive global markets.

7. **A:** Public-private partnerships provide startups with the resources and expertise necessary to innovate and scale effectively. Such collaborations address funding gaps, infrastructure limitations, and regulatory challenges that individual startups may struggle to overcome. Sole reliance on startups or prioritizing large companies limits the sector's potential for innovation. By fostering these partnerships, Ayurveda entrepreneurs can integrate traditional knowledge with modern technology, ensuring sustainable growth. This model encourages knowledge-sharing and supports small-scale innovators, allowing Ayurveda to adapt to contemporary challenges while preserving its foundational principles, creating a robust ecosystem for its expansion.

8. **B:** Providing financial and technical support to small-scale manufacturers facilitates their compliance with international regulations like GMP. Mandating compliance without support risks alienating smaller players, while excluding them from regulations compromises product quality and safety. This balanced approach ensures that Ayurveda remains competitive in global markets without losing its traditional essence. It supports small-scale entrepreneurs in modernizing their practices while maintaining affordability and authenticity. By fostering inclusivity and upholding standards, this strategy strengthens Ayurveda's global reputation as a reliable and effective healthcare system, addressing both traditional and contemporary consumer needs.

9. **B:** Implementing robust data privacy measures and transparency in AI-driven Ayurveda platforms addresses consumer concerns while retaining technological

innovation. By ensuring data security and ethical usage, entrepreneurs build trust in their platforms. Avoiding AI entirely or limiting its role undermines the scalability and precision it brings to Ayurveda. Generic wellness kits fail to reflect Ayurveda's individualized approach, reducing its appeal. This balanced strategy demonstrates how AI can complement traditional Ayurveda, making it accessible and efficient while respecting user privacy and ethical considerations. Entrepreneurs adopting this approach strengthen their market position and foster trust among diverse consumer groups.

10. B: Collaborating with cultural representatives ensures ethical and respectful promotion of Ayurveda in global markets, avoiding accusations of cultural appropriation. Limiting Ayurveda to domestic markets restricts its growth potential, while focusing solely on scientific aspects neglects its cultural richness. This strategy reflects the importance of respecting Ayurveda's origins while making it relevant to diverse audiences. Entrepreneurs adopting such inclusive practices balance tradition with modern branding, building trust across cultures. By engaging with stakeholders from Ayurvedic communities, businesses can navigate global markets responsibly, ensuring Ayurveda's sustainable growth while preserving its authenticity and heritage.

11. B: Ayurgenomics advances Ayurveda by combining Prakriti-based classifications with genomic data, enhancing its scientific validity and relevance. This integration provides tailored treatment plans for chronic diseases like diabetes, aligning Ayurveda with modern precision medicine. It preserves the individuality central to Ayurveda while leveraging technology for greater accuracy. Unlike reducing Ayurveda to biological determinism, this approach respects its holistic philosophy by including lifestyle and environmental factors. Entrepreneurs using Ayurgenomics ensure a balance between tradition and innovation, creating credibility in global markets. This method strengthens Ayurveda's position as a reliable healthcare system while addressing the growing demand for personalized medicine.

12. A: Incorporating lifestyle and environmental factors into predictive algorithms enhances the accuracy of AI-driven Ayurveda platforms. This holistic inclusion reflects Ayurveda's interconnected philosophy, addressing variances in treatment outcomes due to stress, diet, and living conditions. Sole reliance on genetic markers risks oversimplifying Ayurveda, while abandoning genomic tools limits modern adaptability. Entrepreneurs adopting multifaceted algorithms align with Ayurveda's emphasis on individual contexts. This approach balances tradition with innovation, ensuring treatments remain effective and scientifically validated. It creates a system where technology complements Ayurveda's depth, addressing modern healthcare demands while retaining the essence of its holistic approach to health and well-being.

13. A: Overharvesting and environmental degradation compromise the quality of Ayurvedic herbs, affecting their bioactive compounds and therapeutic efficacy. Ayurveda's principles are rooted in harmony with nature, and poor-quality herbs undermine this foundation. Entrepreneurs must address these challenges through sustainable practices, ensuring herbs retain their potency. Ignoring such issues risks losing consumer trust and scientific credibility, as efficacy is a core expectation. Sustainable sourcing preserves the balance Ayurveda emphasizes, aligning ecological responsibility with healthcare effectiveness. This proactive approach secures Ayurveda's long-term viability, fostering trust and authenticity in global markets while reflecting its deep connection to natural ecosystems and balance.

14. A: Investing in sustainable herb cultivation practices safeguards the long-term reliability and efficacy of Ayurvedic treatments. Although it may affect short-term profitability, it ensures a consistent and ethical supply chain, aligning with global environmental standards. Entrepreneurs prioritizing sustainability foster consumer trust, particularly among environmentally conscious audiences. Ignoring these practices risks compromising both credibility and ecological balance, integral to Ayurveda's principles. This balanced strategy positions Ayurveda as a forward-thinking system rooted in tradition. It reflects the adaptability of Ayurveda to modern challenges while preserving its authenticity, creating a healthcare model that respects nature, ensures efficacy, and meets global demands.

15. A: Ayurgenomics validates Ayurveda's personalized medicine by correlating Prakriti classifications with genetic predispositions, creating tailored health solutions. This integration enhances credibility while retaining Ayurveda's holistic emphasis on individual constitution and balance. Solely focusing on genetic determinism ignores environmental and lifestyle factors crucial to Ayurveda. By combining these elements, Ayurgenomics enriches Ayurveda's depth and adaptability. Entrepreneurs leveraging this scientific alignment strengthen Ayurveda's global appeal, bridging traditional knowledge and modern healthcare innovation. This approach ensures Ayurveda evolves responsibly, addressing contemporary demands without losing its core principles of interconnectedness and individuality, making it relevant and reliable in today's healthcare ecosystem.

16. **A:** The efficacy of Ayurvedic formulations relies on the quality of herbs, influenced by cultivation practices and environmental factors. Entrepreneurs ensuring herb consistency through sustainable sourcing and standardization address these critical concerns. Synthetic substitutes fail to respect Ayurveda's natural emphasis, while unregulated practices risk undermining credibility. By adopting ethical and quality-focused strategies, businesses maintain the integrity and therapeutic value of their products. This approach aligns with Ayurveda's foundational principles while meeting modern quality expectations. Entrepreneurs balancing tradition and market demands foster trust, creating a sustainable model that preserves authenticity and efficacy in a competitive and evolving healthcare landscape.

17. **A:** AI-driven platforms in Ayurveda face challenges like limited rural accessibility, privacy concerns, and potential over-reliance on quantifiable data. Ayurveda's philosophy extends beyond measurable parameters, emphasizing intuition and qualitative assessments. Entrepreneurs addressing these concerns through education and innovation ensure Ayurveda's scalability without losing its holistic essence. Overcoming these challenges strengthens Ayurveda's relevance in global markets, where trust and precision are crucial. This balanced approach respects tradition while embracing technology, fostering a system that bridges ancient and modern healthcare paradigms effectively. Entrepreneurs who prioritize such inclusivity position Ayurveda as a credible, adaptable, and sustainable healthcare system globally.

18. **D:** Agroforestry reflects Ayurveda's ecological ethos by integrating medicinal plants with food crops, enhancing biodiversity, and improving soil health. This sustainable model addresses environmental degradation caused by monoculture farming while maintaining herb quality. Entrepreneurs adopting agroforestry balance ecological restoration and economic growth, creating a resilient supply chain. Unlike monoculture or synthetic alternatives, agroforestry aligns with Ayurveda's harmony between health and nature. This approach requires collaboration and investment but ensures long-term viability, aligning Ayurveda with global sustainability goals. Entrepreneurs leveraging this model build credibility in eco-conscious markets while preserving Ayurveda's therapeutic efficacy and authenticity, fostering a responsible healthcare narrative.

19. **A:** Ayurveda's personalized medicine is rooted in Prakriti analysis, which considers individual constitution and environmental influences. Integrating genomic data enhances this precision, validating Ayurveda's scientific relevance without compromising its holistic philosophy. Standardizing treatments conflicts with Ayurveda's core principle of individuality, while excluding lifestyle factors oversimplifies health's complexity. Entrepreneurs embracing this integrative approach position Ayurveda as a modern and credible healthcare system. This alignment bridges ancient wisdom and contemporary science, ensuring Ayurveda remains adaptable yet authentic. It demonstrates Ayurveda's capacity to evolve responsibly, addressing global healthcare demands while preserving its unique emphasis on balance, interconnectedness, and personalized care.

20. **C:** Agroforestry offers a sustainable solution for cultivating Ayurvedic herbs, enhancing soil health and biodiversity while ensuring consistent quality. This approach contrasts with monoculture farming, which often depletes natural resources and compromises herb potency. Entrepreneurs adopting agroforestry align with Ayurveda's ecological philosophy, creating a sustainable supply chain that reflects its principles. This model requires investment but positions Ayurveda as a responsible healthcare system aligned with modern environmental concerns. Entrepreneurs leveraging this strategy build trust among eco-conscious consumers while preserving Ayurveda's therapeutic authenticity. Agroforestry ensures Ayurveda's long-term viability, fostering a balance between ecological preservation and economic growth effectively.

21. **D:** Entrepreneurs in Ayurveda face challenges such as regulatory barriers, sustainability costs, and limited global awareness. These issues require innovative solutions that respect Ayurveda's core principles while adapting to global demands. Strict regulations like GMP and clinical trials are expensive but essential for credibility. Sustainability costs require investments in eco-friendly practices like agroforestry, which also reflect Ayurveda's ecological ethos. Lack of awareness in global markets can be addressed through educational campaigns that highlight Ayurveda's holistic approach. Entrepreneurs balancing these challenges strengthen Ayurveda's position as a credible and responsible healthcare system, fostering trust and ensuring long-term growth in diverse markets.

22. **A:** Incorporating environmental and lifestyle data into Ayurvedic trials enhances the accuracy and reliability of treatment outcomes, reflecting Ayurveda's holistic approach. Multicentered trials provide robustness, but excluding qualitative factors like stress and diet risks oversimplifying results. Entrepreneurs leveraging

a comprehensive methodology align Ayurveda's philosophy of interconnectedness with scientific validation, building credibility. This strategy ensures that Ayurveda's personalized treatments remain adaptable to diverse contexts while gaining acceptance in global healthcare. By addressing variability holistically, Ayurveda evolves into a scientifically validated system that retains its authenticity. Entrepreneurs adopting this approach ensure effective, credible, and scalable healthcare solutions rooted in tradition.

23. **D:** All the listed concerns—(a) genetic data privacy, (b) consent in AI usage, (c) potential for commercial exploitation, and (d) conflict between holistic Ayurveda and reductionist genomics—are valid ethical challenges in integrating Ayurveda with genomics. Addressing these issues requires a multidimensional ethical framework that respects both individual rights and the integrity of traditional systems. Hence, the most comprehensive answer is D: all four concerns apply.

24. **A:** Sustainable innovation in Ayurveda requires balancing ecological stewardship with market demands. Entrepreneurs integrating eco-friendly technologies and practices preserve Ayurveda's authenticity while addressing global sustainability challenges. Conservation of endangered herbs ensures therapeutic integrity, while embracing modern tools like blockchain fosters transparency. Synthetic alternatives compromise Ayurveda's natural foundation, while unsustainable practices threaten its credibility. Entrepreneurs adopting sustainable models align with Ayurveda's emphasis on harmony between health and nature. This approach builds trust among eco-conscious consumers and creates a resilient system for long-term growth. It positions Ayurveda as a globally respected, responsible healthcare solution, rooted in tradition yet forward-thinking.

25. **A:** The therapeutic benefits of Ayurvedic herbs reflect their bioactive properties, validated by both traditional use and modern science. Ashwagandha reduces stress, Haritaki detoxifies, Guduchi enhances immunity, and Brahmi improves cognitive function. Entrepreneurs aligning these benefits with formulations demonstrate Ayurveda's adaptability to contemporary healthcare needs. This integration ensures that products meet consumer expectations for efficacy and scientific validation without compromising Ayurveda's holistic philosophy. By focusing on these alignments, Ayurveda gains credibility in modern markets while retaining its traditional essence. Entrepreneurs leveraging these synergies position Ayurveda as a reliable, effective, and scientifically backed healthcare system in global contexts.

26. **A:** Ayurvedic concepts like Prakriti, Agni, Ama, and Doshas align with modern scientific interpretations, enhancing Ayurveda's relevance in healthcare. Prakriti reflects genetic predispositions, Agni corresponds to metabolism, Ama represents toxins, and Doshas regulate physiological functions. Entrepreneurs integrating these principles with evidence-based practices create a bridge between tradition and science. This alignment validates Ayurveda's holistic approach while addressing contemporary healthcare demands. It ensures that Ayurveda remains scientifically credible while preserving its unique philosophy of interconnectedness. Entrepreneurs who prioritize this integration foster trust and innovation, positioning Ayurveda as a robust and adaptable system for personalized and preventive healthcare globally.

27. **A:** Overharvesting, clinical variability, and ethical AI use demand innovative solutions aligned with Ayurveda's principles. Promoting agroforestry ensures sustainable herb cultivation, reflecting Ayurveda's ecological ethos. Incorporating environmental factors in studies respects its holistic philosophy, addressing variability in outcomes. Multi-centered trials validate Ayurvedic formulations scientifically, enhancing global credibility. Addressing ethical AI concerns builds consumer trust and preserves Ayurveda's authenticity. Entrepreneurs adopting these solutions balance tradition with innovation, ensuring Ayurveda evolves responsibly. This approach creates a robust ecosystem where tradition, technology, and sustainability coexist, fostering Ayurveda's relevance and trust in modern healthcare markets.

28. **A:** Emerging technologies like AI, genomics, and blockchain modernize Ayurveda without compromising its principles. AI enhances diagnostic precision, while genomics validates Prakriti-based treatments. Blockchain fosters transparency in herb sourcing, building consumer trust. Entrepreneurs integrating these innovations ensure Ayurveda's adaptability to global healthcare demands while preserving its essence. This synergy aligns tradition with technology, creating effective and scalable healthcare solutions. Entrepreneurs leveraging these tools enhance Ayurveda's credibility and marketability while addressing modern challenges. This approach positions Ayurveda as a forward-thinking system rooted in holistic principles, meeting contemporary needs while retaining its authenticity and therapeutic value.

29. **A:** Challenges like regulatory barriers, sustainability costs, and awareness gaps require comprehensive solutions. GMP compliance ensures quality and safety, while agroforestry reduces sustainability

costs by promoting ecological balance. Awareness campaigns educate global audiences about Ayurveda's holistic approach, fostering trust. Entrepreneurs adopting these strategies align Ayurveda with modern healthcare standards while preserving its authenticity. This balanced approach addresses both market and environmental concerns, ensuring Ayurveda's long-term growth. Entrepreneurs leveraging these solutions create resilient systems that reflect Ayurveda's principles, positioning it as a credible, sustainable, and adaptable healthcare system in diverse global contexts.

30. A: Personalized medicine, innovative delivery systems, and sustainability-driven R&D reflect Ayurveda's adaptability to contemporary challenges. Ayurgenomics integrates Prakriti with genomic insights, while nanotechnology-based delivery systems improve bioavailability. Preventive healthcare focuses on immunity boosters and adaptogens, aligning with modern wellness trends. Sustainability in R&D emphasizes eco-friendly practices, ensuring Ayurveda remains environmentally responsible. Entrepreneurs embracing these trends create products that meet consumer expectations for efficacy and ethical sourcing. This balance between tradition and innovation strengthens Ayurveda's credibility and relevance, positioning it as a holistic and sustainable healthcare system that addresses both individual and global healthcare needs effectively.

31. A: The Triguṇa theory in Ayurveda (Sattva, Rajas, Tamas) reflects distinct psychological and physical attributes that influence health and behaviour. Sattva represents clarity and balance, promoting mental and physical harmony. Rajas signifies energy and passion, driving activity but potentially causing restlessness. Tamas reflects inertia and ignorance, often linked to stagnation or disease when dominant. Entrepreneurs emphasizing these attributes in Ayurvedic formulations or mental health solutions validate the integrative approach of Ayurveda. This framework balances psychological and physiological well-being, aligning with holistic healthcare. It positions Ayurveda as a system addressing both mental and physical health, making it highly relevant globally.

32. A: The therapeutic benefits of Ayurvedic herbs like Amalaki, Neem, Turmeric, and Shatavari align with their bioactive properties. Amalaki boosts immunity, Neem detoxifies, Turmeric reduces inflammation, and Shatavari supports reproductive health. Entrepreneurs integrating these traditional uses with scientific validation enhance Ayurveda's relevance in modern healthcare. This approach caters to consumer demand for natural, effective solutions while preserving Ayurveda's holistic ethos. By demonstrating evidence-based benefits, Ayurvedic products gain credibility in global markets, addressing diverse health concerns. Entrepreneurs prioritizing this synergy ensure that Ayurveda remains both scientifically validated and traditionally rooted, fostering trust and expanding its reach sustainably.

33. A: Navigating regulatory requirements like GMP compliance, pharmacovigilance, clinical trials, and certification is crucial for Ayurveda's global expansion. GMP ensures consistent quality, pharmacovigilance monitors product safety, and clinical trials validate efficacy. Certification facilitates market entry in highly regulated regions, ensuring credibility. Entrepreneurs balancing these demands with Ayurveda's personalized nature preserve its authenticity while meeting global healthcare standards. This approach addresses consumer skepticism while ensuring safety and quality. Entrepreneurs who integrate these practices strengthen Ayurveda's reputation as a reliable healthcare system, making it accessible and trusted worldwide, without compromising its foundational principles of holistic and individualized care.

34. A: Addressing entrepreneurial challenges in Ayurveda, such as global competition, funding shortages, and consumer misconceptions, requires innovative strategies. Distinct branding differentiates Ayurvedic products, while public-private partnerships support R&D efforts. Regulatory compliance, achieved through collaborations with certification bodies, simplifies global market entry. Consumer misconceptions can be tackled through education campaigns that highlight Ayurveda's scientific validation and holistic approach. Entrepreneurs adopting these strategies ensure Ayurveda's sustainable growth, balancing tradition with modern demands. This approach strengthens Ayurveda's market presence while preserving its authenticity, fostering trust among diverse consumer groups and positioning it as a credible healthcare system globally.

35. C: Ayurgenomics enriches Ayurveda by integrating genetic data with Prakriti classifications, enhancing personalized medicine's accuracy. However, it does not eliminate the role of environmental and lifestyle factors central to Ayurveda's philosophy. This integration adds a layer of scientific validation to traditional methods, ensuring Ayurveda remains relevant in modern healthcare. Entrepreneurs who embrace this synergy demonstrate Ayurveda's adaptability without diluting its holistic essence. By maintaining both traditional and modern elements, Ayurgenomics strengthens trust and credibility, aligning Ayurveda with global precision medicine trends. It ensures Ayurveda's evolution as a healthcare system that remains true to its core principles.

36. C: Agroforestry integrates medicinal plants with food crops, restoring biodiversity and improving soil health, aligning with Ayurveda's ecological principles. Monoculture farming, while initially productive, leads to environmental degradation and reduced herb quality. Entrepreneurs adopting agroforestry ensure sustainable herb cultivation while reflecting Ayurveda's emphasis on harmony with nature. This model requires investment but builds resilience against environmental and market challenges. Agroforestry fosters ecological restoration while ensuring the consistent therapeutic quality of Ayurvedic herbs. Entrepreneurs leveraging this strategy align with global sustainability goals and Ayurveda's ecological ethos, building consumer trust and preserving therapeutic efficacy, ensuring Ayurveda's long-term viability.

37. C: The therapeutic value of Ayurvedic herbs is heavily influenced by cultivation practices and environmental factors. Poor-quality herbs undermine Ayurveda's efficacy, reducing consumer trust and scientific credibility. Entrepreneurs adopting sustainable farming practices ensure consistency in herb potency and quality, reflecting Ayurveda's holistic principles. Synthetic alternatives, while consistent, fail to respect Ayurveda's natural ethos. Addressing these concerns strengthens Ayurveda's reputation as a reliable healthcare system while preserving its foundational connection to nature. Entrepreneurs who prioritize quality and authenticity foster trust and expand Ayurveda's reach, ensuring it remains effective and credible in competitive global markets while retaining its core values.

38. C: AI-driven platforms enhance Ayurveda by integrating genetic, environmental, and historical data to create personalized treatment plans. However, these tools cannot replace the qualitative insights of traditional practitioners, which remain central to Ayurveda's holistic approach. Entrepreneurs must balance AI's precision with Ayurveda's interconnected philosophy to ensure treatments remain effective and authentic. Over-reliance on measurable parameters risks reducing Ayurveda's depth, while complementary use strengthens its relevance in modern healthcare. This balanced approach ensures Ayurveda's scalability and credibility without compromising its foundational values. Entrepreneurs leveraging AI responsibly position Ayurveda as both a modern and traditional healthcare system.

39. C: Regulatory compliance enhances Ayurveda's credibility by ensuring product safety and quality, aligning with global healthcare standards. While demanding, such regulations validate Ayurveda's principles without undermining its holistic philosophy. Entrepreneurs balancing evidence-based practices with traditional methods strengthen trust and global acceptance. By addressing regulatory challenges, Ayurveda gains credibility as a reliable and effective healthcare system. This approach ensures its sustainable growth in global markets, demonstrating adaptability while preserving authenticity. Entrepreneurs who integrate these practices create systems that respect Ayurveda's heritage and meet modern demands, positioning it as a globally respected healthcare system rooted in tradition and science.

40. C: Ayurgenomics integrates Prakriti classifications with genomic data, creating a hybrid model of personalized healthcare that respects Ayurveda's holistic ethos. However, it does not eliminate lifestyle and environmental factors, which remain central to Ayurveda's interconnected approach. Entrepreneurs adopting Ayurgenomics validate Ayurveda scientifically while preserving its depth and individuality. This model enhances Ayurveda's global relevance by blending tradition with precision medicine. By maintaining this balance, Ayurgenomics demonstrates Ayurveda's capacity to evolve responsibly while addressing modern healthcare demands. Entrepreneurs leveraging this innovation strengthen Ayurveda's credibility and adaptability, ensuring it remains effective, reliable, and true to its foundational philosophy.

41. A: Unsustainable harvesting diminishes herb quality by reducing bioactive compound concentrations, directly impacting Ayurvedic treatments' therapeutic efficacy. Environmental degradation, including biodiversity loss and soil erosion, further exacerbates these challenges, threatening Ayurveda's foundational connection to nature. Entrepreneurs must prioritize sustainable practices such as agroforestry to ensure the long-term availability and potency of medicinal herbs. Ignoring ecological factors risks undermining Ayurveda's credibility and effectiveness. By addressing these issues, Ayurveda maintains its authenticity and therapeutic reliability. Entrepreneurs who adopt sustainable models build consumer trust while aligning with Ayurveda's ecological ethos, ensuring both environmental stewardship and the long-term viability of its treatments.

42. C: Agroforestry reflects Ayurveda's ecological harmony by integrating medicinal plants with food crops, fostering biodiversity and improving soil health. This sustainable approach ensures consistent herb quality while addressing environmental degradation

caused by monoculture farming. Entrepreneurs adopting agroforestry balance ecological preservation with economic growth, creating resilient supply chains. Monoculture farming, though productive, depletes resources and compromises herb potency, misaligning with Ayurveda's principles. Agroforestry strengthens Ayurveda's connection to nature, ensuring its therapeutic efficacy. Entrepreneurs leveraging this model enhance Ayurveda's credibility in eco-conscious markets, fostering trust and sustainability. This balance positions Ayurveda as a responsible healthcare system with global relevance.

43. C: AI-driven Ayurveda platforms enhance diagnostics and treatment personalization by integrating diverse datasets, including genetic and environmental information. However, they cannot replace the qualitative aspects of Ayurveda, such as practitioner intuition and emotional health considerations. Over-reliance on AI risks reducing Ayurveda to measurable parameters, undermining its holistic philosophy. Entrepreneurs must ensure that AI complements rather than replaces traditional diagnostic methods, preserving Ayurveda's depth. This balanced approach integrates innovation with tradition, ensuring treatments remain authentic and effective. Entrepreneurs leveraging this model align Ayurveda with modern precision medicine trends while retaining its essence, fostering trust and scalability in global markets.

44. C: Sustainability is essential for maintaining the quality and efficacy of Ayurvedic herbs. Overharvesting and environmental degradation reduce bioactive compound concentrations, compromising therapeutic outcomes. Entrepreneurs adopting eco-friendly practices like agroforestry address these challenges while preserving Ayurveda's ecological ethos. The reasoning that degradation enhances herb potency contradicts both scientific evidence and Ayurvedic principles, which emphasize harmony and balance. By prioritizing sustainability, entrepreneurs ensure long-term viability and consumer trust. This approach reflects Ayurveda's connection to nature, balancing ecological responsibility with therapeutic reliability. It positions Ayurveda as a credible healthcare system that aligns with modern environmental standards and global expectations.

45. C: Regulatory compliance enhances Ayurveda's credibility by ensuring safety, quality, and efficacy through GMP standards and clinical trials. While demanding, such regulations validate Ayurveda without undermining its holistic philosophy. Entrepreneurs must balance these requirements with Ayurveda's personalized nature to maintain its authenticity. Ignoring regulations risks limiting market access, while over-standardization contradicts Ayurveda's emphasis on individualization. Entrepreneurs integrating evidence-based practices strengthen Ayurveda's global acceptance, fostering trust and reliability. This balanced approach ensures Ayurveda's sustainable growth while preserving its foundational principles. It positions Ayurveda as a scientifically validated yet traditionally rooted healthcare system, addressing contemporary global healthcare demands.

46. C: Curcumin, extracted from turmeric, has emerged as one of the most researched compounds in modern science. Its multidimensional therapeutic potential is a testament to Ayurveda's deep understanding of plant-based remedies. Studies have shown curcumin's ability to modulate inflammatory pathways, inhibit free radical damage, and even target cancer cell proliferation. This compound exemplifies Ayurveda's principle of identifying active ingredients in natural products for holistic healing. Unlike isolated synthetic drugs, curcumin operates synergistically within the body, minimizing side effects. Its journey from ancient kitchens to modern labs reflects how traditional wisdom can inform and enhance contemporary biomedical research frameworks.

47. A: The application of liquid chromatography-mass spectrometry (LC-MS) and nuclear magnetic resonance (NMR) spectroscopy in Ayurvedic research is a breakthrough in bridging tradition with technology. These techniques allow scientists to decode the molecular profiles of complex herbal formulations. This systematic exploration validates Ayurveda's emphasis on multi-ingredient synergy. Unlike random herbal usage, these methods establish standardized protocols, ensuring consistency in efficacy and safety. Furthermore, this research contributes to global pharmacology by offering reproducible data. Such advancements highlight how ancient medical systems can thrive when integrated with cutting-edge analytical tools, creating new pathways for evidence-based natural medicine development.

48. B: The parallels between prakriti types in Ayurveda and genetic markers in modern genomics are a revolutionary discovery. Prakriti's classification system, based on an individual's physiological and psychological traits, aligns with personalized medicine's genetic focus. For instance, genetic studies correlating specific SNPs (single nucleotide polymorphisms) with prakriti types suggest a biological foundation for this ancient practice. This integration demonstrates how Ayurveda anticipated concepts now being explored by genomics. It emphasizes the foresight in Ayurveda's personalized health strategies, proving them to be more than intuitive categorizations but rooted in tangible biological principles, thus enriching both fields with cross-disciplinary insights.

49. B: Ashwagandha is celebrated as an adaptogen, a substance that helps the body adapt to stress and restore balance. Modern studies confirm its ability to reduce cortisol levels, enhance stamina, and improve mental clarity, making it invaluable in combating today's stress-induced ailments. This herb demonstrates Ayurveda's principle of targeting the root cause of disease rather than just symptoms. Unlike quick-fix medications, ashwagandha offers long-term benefits by harmonizing body systems. Its ability to bridge mental and physical health aligns with the Ayurvedic approach of integrating wellness dimensions, reinforcing its timeless relevance in addressing modern healthcare challenges.

50. B: The World Health Organization's support for integrating traditional medicine into mainstream healthcare is a significant endorsement of Ayurveda's potential. This initiative emphasizes rigorous quality standards to ensure safety and efficacy. Unlike earlier fragmented efforts, WHO's involvement creates a global platform for standardizing traditional medicine practices. This approach helps overcome skepticism, fosters research collaboration, and bridges the gap between traditional wisdom and modern evidence-based medicine. By promoting the holistic ethos of Ayurveda, WHO not only legitimizes its relevance but also encourages diverse populations to explore sustainable, natural healthcare systems that align with their cultural and environmental contexts.

UNIT 10: RESEARCH METHODOLOGY, BIOSTATISTICS, AND AYURVEDA-INFORMATICS

CHAPTER 29

RESEARCH METHODOLOGIES, CLINICAL TRIALS, AND ETHICS IN AYURVEDA

Ayurveda, the ancient system of medicine originating from India, has a rich history of providing holistic solutions to physical, mental, and spiritual well-being. However, to integrate its principles into modern healthcare systems and establish its relevance in contemporary medicine, rigorous research methodologies, clinical trials, and adherence to ethical principles are paramount. This chapter delves into the frameworks for conducting Ayurvedic research, elaborates on clinical trial designs, and underscores the ethical dimensions essential for maintaining credibility and integrity in Ayurvedic science.

RESEARCH METHODOLOGIES AND STUDY DESIGNS IN AYURVEDA

Understanding Ayurvedic Research

Ayurvedic research involves exploring the ancient principles of Ayurveda and aligning them with modern scientific methods to validate efficacy and safety. The complexity of Ayurvedic treatments, which often involve multifactorial interventions (e.g., herbal formulations, lifestyle changes, and spiritual practices), necessitates innovative research methodologies.

Core Goals of Ayurvedic Research

1. Validation of Ayurvedic formulations through scientific evidence.
2. Integration of traditional knowledge with modern healthcare practices.
3. Standardization of formulations and diagnostic techniques.
4. Preservation of indigenous Ayurvedic knowledge.
5. Addressing modern health challenges using Ayurvedic principles.

Types of Research in Ayurveda: A Comprehensive Exploration

Ayurveda has stood the test of time as a repository of profound knowledge about health and healing. However, its integration into modern healthcare frameworks necessitates rigorous research across diverse domains. Research in Ayurveda can be broadly classified into six types: Literary Research, Pharmacological Research, Clinical Research, Pharmaceutical Research, Public Health Research, and Interdisciplinary Research. Each of these categories plays a pivotal role in preserving the traditional wisdom of Ayurveda while scientifically validating its principles and practices.

LITERARY RESEARCH

Definition and Scope

Literary research in Ayurveda involves the meticulous study, interpretation, and documentation of classical Ayurvedic texts and manuscripts. These texts, such as the Charaka Samhita, Sushruta Samhita, and Ashtanga Hridaya, serve as the foundational pillars of Ayurvedic knowledge. Literary research not only deciphers the ancient Sanskrit verses but also bridges the gap between traditional knowledge and modern medical science.

Key Objectives

- To preserve ancient Ayurvedic manuscripts and texts.

- To decode complex Sanskrit terminologies and make them accessible to modern audiences.
- To compare variations across different versions of Ayurvedic texts.
- To contextualize Ayurvedic principles within contemporary health challenges.

Methodologies

1. **Cataloging and Digitization:** Manuscripts are cataloged systematically, and rare texts are digitized to ensure their preservation.
   - Organizations like the National Manuscripts Mission in India play a crucial role in this endeavour.
2. **Translation and Interpretation:** Classical Sanskrit texts are translated into modern languages with comprehensive commentaries.
   - Interpretations consider the socio-cultural context in which these texts were written.
3. **Comparative Analysis:** Variations in interpretations among ancient scholars (e.g., Chakrapani, Dalhana) are studied for deeper insights.
4. **Contextual Adaptation:** Ayurvedic principles are aligned with current medical terminologies and practices.

Challenges

- The language barrier posed by archaic Sanskrit verses.
- Loss of manuscripts due to improper preservation.
- Discrepancies in the interpretation of terms and principles.

Impact

Literary research forms the backbone of all Ayurvedic investigations. By bringing the ancient knowledge into the modern realm, it ensures that Ayurveda remains relevant and scientifically credible.

PHARMACOLOGICAL RESEARCH

Definition and Scope

Pharmacological research in Ayurveda focuses on understanding the chemical composition, pharmacodynamics, and pharmacokinetics of Ayurvedic drugs, which predominantly include herbs, minerals, and animal-derived products. The goal is to validate the therapeutic claims of these substances through modern scientific techniques.

Key Objectives

- To identify active compounds in Ayurvedic formulations.
- To establish mechanisms of action for these compounds.
- To ensure the safety and efficacy of Ayurvedic drugs.

Methodologies

1. **Phytochemical Analysis:** Techniques such as Gas Chromatography-Mass Spectrometry (GC-MS) and High-Performance Liquid Chromatography (HPLC) are used to identify and quantify bioactive compounds.
2. **Toxicological Studies:** Acute, sub-chronic, and chronic toxicity studies assess the safety profiles of Ayurvedic formulations.
3. **In Vitro Studies:** Cellular and molecular assays explore the therapeutic mechanisms of Ayurvedic compounds.
4. **In Vivo Studies:** Animal models are employed to evaluate the efficacy and bioavailability of formulations.
5. **Standardization:** Analytical methods ensure uniformity in the preparation and composition of Ayurvedic drugs.

Challenges

- Variability in the quality of raw materials due to environmental and geographical factors.
- Complexity in standardizing polyherbal formulations.
- Limited funding for advanced pharmacological studies in Ayurveda.

Impact

Pharmacological research provides a scientific foundation for Ayurvedic therapeutics, enabling their acceptance in global markets. It also contributes to the development of novel drugs inspired by Ayurvedic principles.

CLINICAL RESEARCH

Definition and Scope

Clinical research in Ayurveda evaluates the efficacy, safety, and comparative effectiveness of Ayurvedic interventions in human populations. This type of research uses clinical trial methodologies adapted to Ayurvedic principles.

Key Objectives

- To validate the therapeutic efficacy of Ayurvedic treatments.
- To compare Ayurvedic interventions with conventional medical treatments.
- To explore personalized medicine approaches based on Ayurvedic concepts like Prakriti (body constitution).

Methodologies

1. **Randomized Controlled Trials (RCTs):** The gold standard for efficacy studies. Participants are randomly assigned to Ayurvedic, standard, or placebo groups.
2. **Observational Studies:** Cohort, cross-sectional, and case-control studies are employed to explore the long-term effects of Ayurvedic practices.
3. **Pragmatic Trials:** Conducted in real-world settings to assess the effectiveness of Ayurvedic treatments.
4. **Single-Case Experimental Designs (SCEDs):** Individualized trials that focus on Ayurvedic personalized medicine.
5. **Outcome Measures:** Modern metrics (e.g., biomarkers) and Ayurvedic parameters (e.g., Dosha balance) are used for comprehensive assessments.

Challenges

- Difficulty in blinding due to the distinctive appearance and taste of Ayurvedic drugs.
- Lack of standardized outcome measures that align with Ayurvedic theories.
- Limited integration of Ayurveda-specific diagnostic methods in clinical research.

Impact

Clinical research bridges traditional practices with evidence-based medicine, fostering global acceptance of Ayurveda as a credible healthcare system.

PHARMACEUTICAL RESEARCH

Definition and Scope

Pharmaceutical research in Ayurveda focuses on the development, standardization, and quality assurance of Ayurvedic formulations. It ensures that products meet regulatory standards for safety, efficacy, and consistency.

Key Objectives

- To develop stable and standardized Ayurvedic formulations.
- To optimize dosage forms and delivery mechanisms.
- To ensure compliance with global regulatory standards.

Methodologies

1. **Raw Material Testing:** Identification and authentication of herbs and minerals using pharmacognostic methods.
2. **Formulation Development:** Traditional preparations are modified to suit modern needs (e.g., capsules, syrups).
3. **Stability Studies:** Shelf-life testing ensures the durability of Ayurvedic products.
4. **Quality Control:** Tests for microbial contamination, heavy metals, and pesticide residues are conducted.
5. **Regulatory Compliance:** Ayurvedic formulations are registered with regulatory bodies like the FDA or AYUSH.

Challenges

- Variability in raw material quality due to seasonal and geographical factors.
- Difficulty in formulating polyherbal drugs with consistent efficacy.
- Limited access to modern pharmaceutical technologies.

Impact

Pharmaceutical research enhances the credibility and marketability of Ayurvedic products, making them accessible to global consumers.

PUBLIC HEALTH RESEARCH

Definition and Scope

Public health research in Ayurveda investigates the role of Ayurvedic practices in addressing population-level health issues. This includes studying lifestyle diseases, malnutrition, and preventive healthcare measures.

Key Objectives

- To assess the role of Ayurveda in preventive and curative healthcare.
- To evaluate the cost-effectiveness of Ayurvedic interventions.
- To promote the integration of Ayurveda in national health policies.

Methodologies

1. **Epidemiological Studies:** Surveys and studies to assess the prevalence of diseases treatable by Ayurveda.
2. **Community Trials:** Large-scale interventions, such as introducing Ayurvedic diets to combat malnutrition.
3. **Health Economics:** Cost-benefit analyses of Ayurvedic interventions versus conventional treatments.
4. **Program Evaluations:** Assessing the impact of government initiatives like AYUSH on community health.

Challenges

- Limited awareness of Ayurveda in certain communities.

- Difficulty in quantifying long-term benefits of preventive Ayurvedic practices.
- Lack of integration with mainstream public health systems.

Impact

Public health research showcases Ayurveda's potential in addressing global health challenges, particularly lifestyle diseases and preventive care.

INTERDISCIPLINARY RESEARCH

Definition and Scope

Interdisciplinary research integrates Ayurveda with fields like genomics, systems biology, nutraceuticals, and biotechnology to advance the understanding of health and disease.

Key Objectives

- To explore the molecular basis of Ayurvedic principles.
- To develop personalized medicine approaches using Ayurveda and genomics.
- To innovate new healthcare products inspired by Ayurvedic knowledge.

Methodologies

1. **Ayurgenomics:** Studies the correlation between Prakriti types and genetic markers.
2. **Systems Biology:** Investigates Ayurveda's holistic approach through complex network analyses.
3. **Biotechnological Applications:** Employs biotechnological tools to enhance the bioavailability of Ayurvedic formulations.
4. **Nutraceutical Development:** Combines Ayurvedic herbs with modern nutritional science to create functional foods.

Challenges

- Difficulty in harmonizing holistic Ayurvedic concepts with reductionist scientific approaches.
- Limited funding for interdisciplinary projects.
- Resistance from purists who view integration as dilution.

Impact

Interdisciplinary research positions Ayurveda as a forward-thinking, scientifically relevant system of medicine capable of addressing modern health challenges.

Study Designs in Ayurvedic Research

Designing research studies in Ayurveda involves careful planning to balance traditional approaches with modern scientific rigor.

1. **Observational Studies:**
   - **Case Reports and Series:** Useful for documenting unique clinical scenarios and treatment responses.
   - **Cross-sectional Studies:** Provide a snapshot of health outcomes associated with Ayurvedic practices.
   - **Cohort Studies:** Follow populations using Ayurvedic treatments over time to assess long-term outcomes.
2. **Experimental Studies:**
   - **Randomized Controlled Trials (RCTs):** The gold standard for evaluating efficacy.
   - Involves random allocation of participants to intervention and control groups.
   - **Non-randomized Trials:** Employ matching techniques to compare groups when randomization isn't feasible.
   - **Single-arm Trials:** Assess the efficacy of an intervention without a control group, often used for preliminary investigations.
3. **Ayurveda-Specific Designs:**
   - **Prakriti-Based Research:** Focuses on the Ayurvedic concept of individual constitution (Prakriti) to tailor interventions.
   - **Dosha-Specific Trials:** Investigates the impact of treatments on Vata, Pitta, or Kapha imbalances.
4. **Translational Research:** Bridges basic research findings with clinical applications, enabling Ayurveda to move from bench to bedside.
5. **Qualitative Research:** Explores patient experiences, physician insights, and cultural contexts of Ayurvedic care.

Challenges in Ayurvedic Research

1. **Standardization of Formulations:** The variability of raw materials, preparation methods, and regional practices poses challenges.
2. **Complex Interventions:** Ayurveda often combines multiple therapies, making it difficult to isolate the effects of a single intervention.
3. **Outcome Measurements:** Conventional biomedical metrics may not fully capture Ayurvedic outcomes like balance in Doshas or overall vitality.
4. **Resource Constraints:** Limited funding and infrastructure for large-scale studies in Ayurveda.
5. **Cultural and Philosophical Differences:** Bridging the gap between holistic, individual-centered Ayurvedic approaches and reductionist biomedical paradigms.

CONDUCTING CLINICAL TRIALS AND EVALUATING RESULTS

Importance of Clinical Trials in Ayurveda

Clinical trials are crucial for validating Ayurvedic treatments, ensuring safety, and gaining acceptance within global medical systems. They provide evidence-based data to support the claims of efficacy and allow comparison with standard medical treatments.

Steps in Conducting Ayurvedic Clinical Trials

1. **Defining the Research Question:**
   - **Example:** Does a specific Ayurvedic formulation reduce symptoms of osteoarthritis compared to standard treatment?
2. **Formulation of Hypotheses:**
   - **Null Hypothesis (H_0):** There is no difference between Ayurvedic and standard treatments.
   - **Alternative Hypothesis (H_1):** Ayurvedic treatment is more effective.
3. **Protocol Development:**
   - Includes detailed plans for recruitment, intervention, and data collection.
   - Ethical considerations are incorporated.
4. **Ethical Clearance:** Approval from institutional review boards (IRBs) or ethics committees is mandatory.
5. **Participant Selection:** Inclusion and exclusion criteria are based on Ayurvedic principles and biomedical standards.
6. **Randomization and Blinding:**
   - Ensures unbiased allocation and minimizes placebo effects.
   - Double-blind studies are preferred but challenging due to the nature of Ayurvedic treatments.
7. **Intervention:**
   - Standardization of dosage, preparation, and administration methods.
   - Adherence to classical texts while ensuring safety.
8. **Outcome Assessment:**
   - Primary outcomes (e.g., symptom reduction) and secondary outcomes (e.g., quality of life) are clearly defined.
9. **Data Collection and Monitoring:**
   - Use of Case Report Forms (CRFs) for systematic data recording.
   - Regular monitoring for adverse events.
10. **Statistical Analysis:**
    - Employs both descriptive and inferential statistics.
    - Intention-to-treat analysis is recommended to handle dropouts.
11. **Reporting and Dissemination:**
    - Results are published in peer-reviewed journals and shared with stakeholders.

Evaluation of Clinical Trial Results

1. **Efficacy:** The magnitude of treatment effects is compared to controls.
2. **Safety:** Adverse events are recorded, analyzed, and reported.
3. **Statistical Significance:** P-values and confidence intervals provide insights into result reliability.
4. **Clinical Relevance:** Beyond statistical results, the practical impact on patient health is evaluated.
5. **Integration with Ayurvedic Principles:** Results are interpreted in the context of Ayurvedic theories.

ETHICAL CONSIDERATIONS IN AYURVEDIC RESEARCH

Principles of Research Ethics

1. **Autonomy:** Respect for participants' rights to make informed decisions.
2. **Beneficence:** Ensuring research benefits outweigh risks.
3. **Non-Maleficence:** Minimizing harm to participants.
4. **Justice:** Fair recruitment and equitable distribution of benefits.
5. **Confidentiality:** Protecting participant data.

Key Ethical Challenges in Ayurvedic Research

1. **Informed Consent:** Participants must understand the trial's purpose, methods, and risks.
2. **Vulnerable Populations:** Safeguards are needed for children, pregnant women, and socio-economically disadvantaged groups.
3. **Traditional Knowledge Protection:** Ensuring fair compensation and acknowledgment for indigenous communities.
4. **Animal Ethics:** Ayurvedic pharmacological studies often involve animal testing, necessitating adherence to ethical guidelines.
5. **Placebo Use:** Ethical dilemmas arise when placebo-controlled trials delay potentially beneficial treatments.
6. **Conflicts of Interest:** Transparency in funding sources and researcher affiliations.

Regulatory Frameworks for Ethical Ayurvedic Research

1. **Good Clinical Practice (GCP):** Adherence to international standards for design, conduct, and reporting.
2. **National Ethical Guidelines:** Countries like India have specific guidelines for Ayurvedic research (e.g., Indian Council of Medical Research [ICMR] guidelines).
3. **Ayush Research Councils:** Institutions like the Central Council for Research in Ayurvedic Sciences (CCRAS) oversee Ayurvedic trials.
4. **Intellectual Property Rights (IPR):** Protecting the intellectual heritage of Ayurveda while promoting innovation.

MULTIPLE CHOICE QUESTIONS

1. In the context of evaluating the efficacy of a new Ayurvedic formulation for managing stress-related disorders, a multidisciplinary research team designs a clinical study integrating both qualitative and quantitative outcomes. The protocol emphasizes assessing subjective well-being (via validated psychological scales) and biological markers such as cortisol levels and heart rate variability. However, the study design faces scrutiny for its methodology, particularly concerning the control group. To align the study with international ethical and methodological standards, which of the following control strategies would be most appropriate to ensure both scientific rigor and cultural sensitivity to Ayurveda's holistic approach?
   A. Using a placebo control group while informing participants that their treatment might involve Ayurvedic principles.
   B. Establishing a conventional treatment group receiving standard pharmacotherapy for stress-related disorders.
   C. Employing a waitlist control group, where participants receive Ayurvedic intervention after the study concludes.
   D. Combining a sham Ayurvedic therapy group to simulate traditional treatments without active ingredients.

2. A clinical researcher conducts a randomized controlled trial (RCT) to evaluate the impact of Ayurvedic interventions, specifically Rasayana therapies, on cognitive decline in individuals over 60 years of age. The study protocol integrates Ayurvedic diagnostic tools, including assessments of Prakriti (individual constitution) and Agni (digestive fire), alongside modern cognitive testing and neuroimaging biomarkers such as hippocampal volume. However, a key critique from a peer reviewer revolves around the outcome measures. What would be the most scientifically and ethically appropriate strategy to address the critique while maintaining Ayurvedic principles in the study?
   A. Replacing subjective Ayurvedic diagnostic measures with purely objective cognitive and imaging data to align with biomedical standards.
   B. Correlating changes in Ayurvedic diagnostics, such as Prakriti, with measurable improvements in neuroimaging and cognitive test results.
   C. Excluding neuroimaging biomarkers from the study to focus exclusively on Ayurvedic diagnostics and outcomes.
   D. Utilizing only subjective patient-reported outcomes to highlight Ayurveda's individualized treatment approach.

3. Imagine a scenario where a team of pharmacologists and Ayurvedic scholars collaborates to standardize an Ayurvedic formulation intended for clinical trials targeting metabolic syndrome. The herbal preparation, composed of multiple ingredients traditionally recommended for balancing Kapha dosha, is known for its lipid-lowering and glucose-regulating properties. Despite promising preliminary results, the research faces challenges in standardizing the preparation due to variability in raw material sources and preparation techniques. Which of the following strategies would best address the challenges while preserving the formulation's traditional authenticity?
   A. Developing a synthetic version of the active compounds identified in the formulation to ensure consistency.
   B. Conducting detailed phytochemical profiling of each batch to ensure chemical consistency across trials.
   C. Limiting clinical trials to specific regions where raw materials are naturally sourced to reduce variability.
   D. Modifying the formulation by reducing the number of ingredients to simplify standardization processes.

4. A public health researcher investigates the impact of Ayurvedic dietary interventions on reducing the prevalence of Type 2 Diabetes Mellitus (T2DM) in rural communities. The study emphasizes the adoption

of locally available, Ayurvedic-recommended foods and the implementation of individualized diets based on Prakriti. After six months, the data reveals significant reductions in fasting glucose levels and HbA1c among participants, alongside improved subjective well-being. However, community feedback suggests challenges in sustaining dietary changes due to cultural preferences and economic constraints. Which of the following strategies would best address these challenges while ensuring the long-term effectiveness of the intervention?

A. Modifying Ayurvedic dietary recommendations to include locally preferred but less healthy options for greater acceptance.

B. Integrating community-based education programs to increase awareness of the benefits of Ayurvedic dietary practices.

C. Offering financial incentives to participants who adhere strictly to the recommended Ayurvedic diets.

D. Limiting the intervention to a select group of participants who can afford the recommended dietary changes.

5. A clinical study evaluating the efficacy of Triphala for irritable bowel syndrome (IBS) involves a unique methodology that integrates Ayurvedic diagnostics and microbiota profiling. The study reports significant improvements in gut health, reduced IBS symptoms, and increased microbial diversity. However, reviewers criticize the lack of a double-blind design due to the strong taste and smell of Triphala. To address this criticism without compromising the authenticity of the Ayurvedic intervention, which of the following approaches should researchers adopt?

A. Designing an active placebo with a similar taste and appearance as Triphala to mimic its organoleptic properties.

B. Utilizing open-label trials and acknowledging the limitations in the interpretation of results due to potential biases.

C. Eliminating the need for a control group and emphasizing within-subject comparisons over time.

D. Redesigning the study to focus solely on microbiota changes, which are objective and less susceptible to bias.

6. A multi-center study is designed to evaluate Ayurvedic Panchakarma therapies as an adjunct to conventional treatments for chronic inflammatory diseases like rheumatoid arthritis. The study incorporates qualitative feedback from patients, quantitative inflammatory markers such as CRP and ESR, and longitudinal follow-ups to assess sustained benefits. One major ethical concern raised by an institutional review board (IRB) is regarding the invasive nature of certain Panchakarma procedures and their acceptability to participants. How should the research team address this ethical concern while maintaining the study's integrity?

A. Conducting comprehensive pre-enrollment counseling sessions detailing the risks and benefits of Panchakarma therapies.

B. Restricting the study to participants with prior experience or familiarity with Ayurvedic treatments.

C. Replacing invasive Panchakarma procedures with less intensive Ayurvedic interventions to reduce participant discomfort.

D. Eliminating qualitative feedback and focusing solely on quantitative outcomes to simplify the study protocol.

7. A pharmacological study on an Ayurvedic herb reveals bioactive compounds that show potent anti-cancer activity in vitro. However, the herb's efficacy in clinical settings is inconsistent, likely due to variations in its bioactive compound content based on environmental conditions during cultivation. Considering the principles of Ayurvedic pharmacology and modern scientific approaches, which strategy would most effectively address this inconsistency?

A. Creating a synthetic derivative of the most active compound for use in clinical trials.

B. Establishing Good Agricultural Practices (GAP) for cultivating the herb to ensure consistency in bioactive compound content.

C. Developing polyherbal formulations to mitigate the variability in a single herb's composition.

D. Focusing on personalized treatments rather than standardized formulations to align with Ayurvedic principles.

8. A research team examines the relationship between ethical guidelines and informed consent practices in clinical trials involving traditional Ayurvedic therapies. The team identifies that many participants have limited understanding of complex medical jargon and procedures. To address this, the team proposes an innovative, culturally tailored informed consent process. Which of the following approaches would best improve the ethical validity of the consent process while ensuring transparency?

A. Conducting consent discussions in the participant's local language using culturally relevant analogies to explain medical concepts.

B. Simplifying the consent forms by excluding detailed information about risks and procedures to avoid overwhelming participants.

C. Providing monetary compensation to participants who agree to partake in the trial.

D. Using digital tools to automate the consent process, minimizing human error and bias.

9. In a study exploring the link between Ayurvedic detoxification therapies and metabolic health, researchers observe significant reductions in biomarkers of oxidative stress and improvements in insulin sensitivity among participants undergoing Panchakarma. Despite these findings, some experts argue that the effects could be attributed to dietary changes during the detox process rather than Panchakarma itself. What would be the most robust way to address this critique and validate Panchakarma's specific impact?

A. Designing a study that includes a dietary control group receiving the same diet without Panchakarma therapies.

B. Relying solely on subjective participant-reported outcomes to emphasize individual experiences.

C. Focusing future studies exclusively on dietary interventions, removing Panchakarma therapies from the scope of research.

D. Ignoring the critique and emphasizing traditional Ayurvedic explanations of Panchakarma's mechanisms.

10. A researcher studying the ethical implications of conducting clinical trials in underserved rural populations emphasizes the importance of community engagement and equitable benefit-sharing. However, the study faces criticism for offering only experimental Ayurvedic treatments without standard care options. To address this ethical dilemma, which of the following strategies should be adopted?

A. Providing access to standard medical care alongside experimental Ayurvedic treatments for all participants.

B. Limiting the trial to urban populations with better access to healthcare facilities.

C. Offering free Ayurvedic treatments to all participants as compensation for their involvement.

D. Ensuring long-term follow-up care for participants to address any residual health issues post-trial.

Directions (Q. No. 11–14): *Scenario-Based Questions*

SCENARIO 1

A clinical research team investigates the therapeutic effects of a classical Ayurvedic polyherbal formulation on chronic inflammatory diseases, such as rheumatoid arthritis (RA). The formulation, traditionally used to balance the Vata dosha, is hypothesized to work by modulating the immune system. The study integrates Ayurveda's holistic diagnostic methods, focusing on participants' Prakriti (constitution) and Vikriti (imbalance). Preliminary findings suggest significant improvement in joint mobility, pain reduction, and inflammatory markers, such as C-reactive protein (CRP) and tumor necrosis factor-alpha (TNF-α). However, challenges arise when matching subjective Ayurvedic outcomes, like Dosha balance, with objective biomedical metrics, creating concerns about methodological consistency. Additionally, patient compliance is affected due to the bitter taste of the formulation, highlighting the need for modernized delivery systems.

SCENARIO 2

Simultaneously, a group of environmental scientists evaluates the sustainability of the key medicinal plants used in the formulation. The plants, primarily sourced from biodiverse but ecologically fragile regions, are found to be overharvested, threatening their wild populations. The study also reveals that climate change and soil degradation have reduced the bioactive compound concentrations in these plants. This degradation negatively impacts the therapeutic potency of the formulation in clinical trials (as observed in Scenario 1). The environmental team recommends integrating sustainable harvesting practices, biotechnological interventions, and community-based conservation strategies. However, they also face resistance from traditional practitioners who view these modern approaches as a deviation from Ayurveda's natural and holistic principles.

11. Based on Scenario 1, which of the following approaches would most effectively address the challenge of correlating Ayurvedic diagnostic outcomes, such as Dosha balance, with objective biomedical metrics?

A. Incorporating dual outcome measures that include both subjective Ayurvedic metrics and validated biomedical parameters.

B. Limiting the study to Ayurvedic practitioners and omitting biomedical data to preserve traditional integrity.

C. Replacing subjective Ayurvedic outcomes entirely with standardized biomedical metrics, such as CRP and TNF-α levels.

D. Focusing exclusively on patient-reported outcomes to align with Ayurveda's personalized treatment approach.

12. Considering the findings in Scenario 2, which strategy would most effectively ensure the long-term sustainability of medicinal plants while preserving the therapeutic efficacy of the Ayurvedic formulation?

A. Developing synthetic analogs of bioactive compounds to replace natural plant sources entirely.

B. Promoting traditional agroforestry systems and incentivizing local communities to engage in conservation practices.

C. Transitioning to monoculture farming of the key plants to increase supply and reduce costs.

D. Reducing reliance on endangered plants by reformulating the Ayurvedic preparation with alternative ingredients.

13. How do the environmental challenges described in Scenario 2 potentially influence the clinical outcomes observed in Scenario 1?

A. Reduced bioactive compound concentrations due to soil degradation and overharvesting could diminish the formulation's therapeutic efficacy.

B. The potency of the Ayurvedic formulation remains unaffected, as traditional preparation methods compensate for environmental factors.

C. Ecological degradation enhances the concentration of bioactive compounds, improving clinical outcomes.

D. The clinical efficacy of the formulation is unrelated to environmental factors, as its therapeutic effects are purely energetic.

14. Considering the interconnected findings of Scenarios 1 and 2, which of the following strategies would comprehensively address the therapeutic and environmental challenges?

A. Establishing a standardized protocol for sustainable harvesting and bioactive compound monitoring, combined with biotechnological interventions.

B. Encouraging traditional practitioners to abandon natural sources in favor of laboratory-synthesized bioactive compounds.

C. Shifting clinical research focus to less environmentally dependent formulations, thereby bypassing ecological concerns.

D. Prioritizing rapid production and large-scale availability of the formulation without focusing on ecological or quality concerns.

Directions (Q. No. 15–24): *Codes-Based Questions*

15. The principles of Ayurvedic research methodology emphasize several unique aspects of study design. Which of the following elements are critical for designing a robust Ayurvedic research study?

(a) Inclusion of Prakriti-based participant stratification.

(b) Use of traditional Ayurvedic diagnostic tools alongside modern biomedical metrics.

(c) Exclusive reliance on subjective patient-reported outcomes.

(d) Integration of outcome measures related to Dosha balance and Vikriti improvement.

Choose the correct answer from the options given below:

A. (a), (b), and (d) only
B. (b), (c), and (d) only
C. (a), (b), (c), and (d)
D. (a) and (b) only

16. Which of the following factors are essential for ensuring the ethical conduct of clinical trials involving Ayurvedic therapies?

(a) Transparent disclosure of risks, benefits, and alternative treatments during informed consent.

(b) Adherence to Good Clinical Practice (GCP) guidelines.

(c) Allowing patients to withdraw at any stage without repercussions.

(d) Exclusion of placebo groups to ensure all participants benefit directly from the intervention.

Choose the correct answer from the options given below:

A. (a), (b), and (c) only
B. (b) and (d) only
C. (a) and (c) only
D. (a), (b), (c), and (d)

17. Ayurvedic pharmacological research requires careful standardization of formulations to ensure reproducibility and efficacy. Which of the following steps are critical in achieving this goal?

(a) Phytochemical profiling of raw materials and final formulations.

(b) Uniform cultivation practices for medicinal plants under controlled conditions.

(c) Exclusion of all traditional preparation methods to ensure chemical consistency.

(d) Validation of formulations through preclinical and clinical trials.

Choose the correct answer from the options given below:

A. (a), (b), and (d) only
B. (a) and (b) only
C. (b), (c), and (d) only
D. (a), (b), (c), and (d)

18. The integration of Ayurveda into public health research involves addressing specific community-level health concerns. Which of the following areas are prioritized in such studies?

(a) Role of Ayurvedic diets in preventing lifestyle diseases.

(b) Development of cost-effective Ayurvedic interventions for malnutrition.

(c) Reduction of emphasis on preventive healthcare to focus on curative aspects.

(d) Understanding the impact of Ritucharya (seasonal routines) on population-level health outcomes.

Choose the correct answer from the options given below:

A. (a) and (b) only
B. (a), (b), and (d) only
C. (b), (c), and (d) only
D. (a), (c), and (d) only

19. Which of the following challenges are commonly faced during clinical trials of Ayurvedic therapies?
(a) Standardization of complex polyherbal formulations.
(b) Lack of alignment between Ayurvedic diagnostic methods and modern metrics.
(c) Difficulty in implementing double-blind study designs.
(d) Ethical concerns related to the invasive nature of certain Ayurvedic procedures.

Choose the correct answer from the options given below:
A. (a) and (b) only
B. (a), (b), (c), and (d)
C. (b), (c), and (d) only
D. (a), (c), and (d) only

20. In the context of pharmacological research, which of the following properties of Ayurvedic Rasas (tastes) are scientifically validated?
(a) Sweet Rasa supports tissue growth and nourishment.
(b) Bitter Rasa detoxifies the body and reduces inflammation.
(c) Sour Rasa enhances digestion and metabolic activity.
(d) Astringent Rasa weakens tissue strength and reduces immunity.

Choose the correct answer from the options given below:
A. (a), (b), and (c) only
B. (b), (c), and (d) only
C. (a) and (b) only
D. (a), (b), (c), and (d)

21. Which of the following ethical considerations are fundamental to Ayurvedic clinical research?
(a) Protecting the cultural integrity of traditional knowledge while conducting research.
(b) Conducting community consultations to ensure fair benefit-sharing.
(c) Excluding socio-economically disadvantaged populations to avoid exploitation.
(d) Ensuring that all participants are provided access to post-trial care.

Choose the correct answer from the options given below:
A. (a), (b), and (d) only
B. (a) and (b) only
C. (b), (c), and (d) only
D. (a), (b), (c), and (d)

22. Public health research in Ayurveda often involves interdisciplinary approaches. Which of the following strategies are integral to this type of research?
(a) Studying the effects of Ayurvedic dietary patterns on microbiome diversity.
(b) Investigating Ayurvedic practices as complementary therapies in community health programs.
(c) Replacing traditional Ayurvedic methods with modern biomedical practices.
(d) Addressing seasonal health issues through Ritucharya)-based interventions.

Choose the correct answer from the options given below:
A. (a), (b), and (d) only
B. (a), (b), and (c) only
C. (a) and (d) only
D. (b), (c), and (d) only

23. Which of the following strategies are most effective for integrating Ayurveda into mainstream healthcare systems through interdisciplinary research?
(a) Genomic studies to validate Ayurvedic concepts of Prakriti.
(b) Development of nutraceuticals based on Ayurvedic formulations.
(c) Elimination of Ayurvedic principles in favour of reductionist scientific approaches.
(d) Systems biology approaches to study holistic effects of Ayurvedic treatments.

Choose the correct answer from the options given below:
A. (a), (b), and (c) only
B. (b), (c), and (d) only
C. (a), (b), and (d) only
D. (a) and (d) only

24. Which of the following elements are critical for designing ethical and scientifically rigorous Ayurvedic clinical trials?
(a) Incorporating personalized Ayurvedic diagnostics such as Prakriti assessment.
(b) Using biomarkers for objective outcome measurement.
(c) Ensuring traditional preparation methods are excluded for consistency.
(d) Including informed consent processes that explain risks in cultural and local contexts.

Choose the correct answer from the options given below:
A. (a) and (b) only

B. (a), (b), and (d) only
C. (b), (c), and (d) only
D. (a), (b), (c), and (d)

Directions (Q. No. 25–34): *Match-Lists Questions*

25. Match List–I with List–II regarding research methodologies in Ayurveda and their Descriptions:

List–I	List–II
(a) Literary research	1. Decoding classical Ayurvedic texts to align with modern contexts
(b) Pharmacological research	2. Investigating chemical properties of Ayurvedic drugs
(c) Clinical research	3. Evaluating efficacy of Ayurvedic interventions in human populations
(d) Public health research	4. Exploring the role of Ayurveda in community-level health challenges

Choose the correct answer from the options given below:
A. (a)-1, (b)-2, (c)-3, (d)-4
B. (a)-2, (b)-1, (c)-4, (d)-3
C. (a)-1, (b)-4, (c)-3, (d)-2
D. (a)-3, (b)-2, (c)-1, (d)-4

26. Match List–I with List–II concerning ethical considerations in Ayurvedic research and their Explanations:

List–I	List–II
(a) Informed consent	1. Ensuring participants understand risks and benefits
(b) Cultural integrity	2. Protecting traditional Ayurvedic knowledge
(c) Benefit-sharing	3. Equitably distributing the benefits of research
(d) Post-trial access	4. Providing continued care to trial participants

Choose the correct answer from the options given below:
A. (a)-1, (b)-2, (c)-3, (d)-4
B. (a)-2, (b)-1, (c)-4, (d)-3
C. (a)-3, (b)-4, (c)-1, (d)-2
D. (a)-1, (b)-4, (c)-2, (d)-3

27. Match List–I with List–II regarding Ayurvedic study designs and their characteristics:

List–I	List–II
(a) Observational study	1. Examines the effects of interventions without control groups
(b) Randomized controlled trial (RCT)	2. Compares groups randomly assigned to intervention or control
(c) Pragmatic trial	3. Assesses intervention in real-world conditions
(d) Translational research	4. Bridges preclinical findings with clinical applications

Choose the correct answer from the options given below:
A. (a)-1, (b)-2, (c)-3, (d)-4
B. (a)-2, (b)-3, (c)-4, (d)-1
C. (a)-4, (b)-3, (c)-1, (d)-2
D. (a)-3, (b)-2, (c)-1, (d)-4

28. Match List–I with List–II regarding the components of Ayurvedic formulations and their therapeutic properties:

List–I	List–II
(a) Triphala	1. Improves gut health and detoxifies the system
(b) Ashwagandha	2. Enhances strength and reduces stress
(c) Brahmi	3. Boosts cognitive function and memory
(d) Neem	4. Antimicrobial and purifying properties

Choose the correct answer from the options given below:
A. (a)-1, (b)-2, (c)-3, (d)-4
B. (a)-3, (b)-4, (c)-1, (d)-2
C. (a)-2, (b)-1, (c)-4, (d)-3
D. (a)-4, (b)-3, (c)-2, (d)-1

29. Match List–I with List–II concerning public health applications of Ayurveda and their field of focus:

List–I	List–II
(a) Preventive healthcare	1. Emphasizing lifestyle and diet for disease prevention
(b) Community health programs	2. Integrating Ayurveda to address malnutrition
(c) Seasonal health management	3. Adapting Ritucharya to local population needs
(d) Geriatric care	4. Using Rasayana therapies to enhance longevity

Choose the correct answer from the options given below:
A. (a)-1, (b)-3, (c)-4, (d)-2
B. (a)-1, (b)-2, (c)-3, (d)-4
C. (a)-2, (b)-4, (c)-3, (d)-1
D. (a)-4, (b)-1, (c)-2, (d)-3

30. Match List–I with List–II regarding the Ayurvedic concepts and their modern interpretations:

List–I	List–II
(a) Agni	1. Enzymatic and metabolic processes
(b) Prakriti	2. Genetic predisposition and individuality
(c) Ama	3. Toxins affecting metabolic and immune function
(d) Dosha imbalance	4. Homeostasis disruption in biological systems

Choose the correct answer from the options given below:

A. (a)-2, (b)-1, (c)-3, (d)-4
B. (a)-1, (b)-2, (c)-3, (d)-4
C. (a)-3, (b)-4, (c)-2, (d)-1
D. (a)-4, (b)-3, (c)-1, (d)-2

31. Match List–I with List–II regarding the sustainability of Ayurvedic medicinal plants and their challenges:

List–I	List–II
(a) Overharvesting	1. Rising demand for Ayurvedic formulations
(b) Biodiversity loss	2. Unregulated collection practices
(c) Reduced bioactive content	3. Soil degradation and climate change
(d) Ecosystem imbalance	4. Monoculture plantations replacing native forests

Choose the correct answer from the options given below:

A. (a)-1, (b)-2, (c)-3, (d)-4
B. (a)-3, (b)-4, (c)-1, (d)-2
C. (a)-4, (b)-3, (c)-2, (d)-1
D. (a)-2, (b)-1, (c)-4, (d)-3

32. Match List–I with List–II regarding Tridosha theory and its physiological functions:

List–I	List–II
(a) Vata	1. Governs movement, including circulation and respiration
(b) Pitta	2. Regulates metabolism and enzymatic activity
(c) Kapha	3. Maintains structure, stability, and immunity
(d) Balanced Tridosha	4. Promotes health and equilibrium

Choose the correct answer from the options given below:

A. (a)-1, (b)-2, (c)-3, (d)-4
B. (a)-2, (b)-3, (c)-4, (d)-1
C. (a)-3, (b)-4, (c)-1, (d)-2
D. (a)-4, (b)-1, (c)-2, (d)-3

33. Match List–I (Rasa) with List–II (Action) regarding Ayurvedic pharmacological classifications:

List–I	List–II
(a) Sweet (Madhura)	1. Promotes tissue growth and nourishment
(b) Bitter (Tikta)	2. Detoxifies and reduces inflammation
(c) Astringent (Kashaya)	3. Strengthens tissues and controls bleeding
(d) Sour (Amla)	4. Enhances digestion and metabolic activity

Choose the correct answer from the options given below:

A. (a)-1, (b)-2, (c)-3, (d)-4
B. (a)-2, (b)-4, (c)-1, (d)-3
C. (a)-3, (b)-1, (c)-4, (d)-2
D. (a)-4, (b)-3, (c)-2, (d)-1

34. Match List–I with List–II concerning Panchakarma therapies and their primary functions:

List–I	List–II
(a) Vamana	1. Induces vomiting to expel Kapha toxins
(b) Virechana	2. Purges Pitta toxins through the bowels
(c) Basti	3. Administers medicated enemas to balance Vata
(d) Nasya	4. Cleanses nasal passages and improves brain function

Choose the correct answer from the options given below:

A. (a)-1, (b)-2, (c)-3, (d)-4
B. (a)-2, (b)-3, (c)-4, (d)-1
C. (a)-4, (b)-3, (c)-2, (d)-1
D. (a)-3, (b)-4, (c)-1, (d)-2

Directions (Q. No. 35–39): *Following questions are based on Statement 1 and Statement 2. Read both the statements carefully and choose the correct answer from the options given below:*

A. Both Statement 1 and Statement 2 are true, and Statement 2 is the correct explanation of Statement 1.
B. Both Statement 1 and Statement 2 are true, but Statement 2 is not the correct explanation of Statement 1.
C. Statement 1 is true, but Statement 2 is false.
D. Statement 1 is false, but Statement 2 is true.
E. Both Statement 1 and Statement 2 are false.

35. **Statement 1:** Ayurveda emphasizes individualized treatment protocols based on a patient's Prakriti (constitution), which considers physical, mental, and genetic traits.

Statement 2: Prakriti-based diagnosis in Ayurveda is analogous to the concept of precision medicine in modern science, where treatments are tailored based on genetic and phenotypic markers.

36. **Statement 1:** Ayurvedic clinical trials often incorporate biomarkers such as CRP and blood glucose levels to align outcomes with modern biomedical standards.

    Statement 2: Modern biomedical metrics fail to capture the holistic and multidimensional effects of Ayurvedic interventions, requiring integration of traditional outcome measures like Dosha balance.

37. **Statement 1:** The sustainability of medicinal plants used in Ayurvedic formulations is a critical challenge due to overharvesting and environmental degradation.

    Statement 2: Synthetic alternatives to bioactive compounds can completely replace natural resources without compromising the efficacy of Ayurvedic formulations.

38. **Statement 1:** Ethical guidelines for Ayurvedic research emphasize cultural sensitivity, informed consent, and equitable benefit-sharing.

    Statement 2: Conducting clinical trials in rural areas without ensuring proper follow-up care is considered unethical, even if Ayurvedic treatments are cost-effective and accessible.

39. **Statement 1:** Ayurvedic Rasayana therapies aim to enhance cellular repair, immunity, and longevity.

    Statement 2: The benefits of Rasayana therapies are primarily attributed to their effects on mental clarity and emotional balance, with no measurable biological impact.

Directions (Q. No. 40–45): *There are two statements in each question. One is labelled as Assertion (A) and the other is as Reason (R). Read both the statements and choose the correct answer from the options given below:*

A. Both Assertion (A) and Reason (R) are true, and Reason (R) is the correct explanation of Assertion (A).
B. Both Assertion (A) and Reason (R) are true, but Reason (R) is not the correct explanation of Assertion (A).
C. Assertion (A) is true, but Reason (R) is false.
D. Assertion (A) is false, but Reason (R) is true.
E. Both Assertion (A) and Reason (R) are false.

40. **Assertion (A):** Ayurvedic Panchakarma therapies are recognized for their role in detoxifying the body and restoring Dosha balance.

    Reason (R): Panchakarma therapies primarily target systemic inflammation through the modulation of gut microbiota.

41. **Assertion (A):** Clinical trials in Ayurveda must incorporate both modern scientific methodologies and traditional Ayurvedic principles.

    Reason (R): Exclusive reliance on biomedical metrics limits the holistic evaluation of Ayurvedic interventions.

42. **Assertion (A):** Ayurvedic interventions for lifestyle disorders often incorporate dietary and lifestyle modifications along with herbal formulations.

    Reason (R): Lifestyle modifications in Ayurveda are designed to balance circadian rhythms and seasonal variations, enhancing overall health outcomes.

43. **Assertion (A):** Ayurvedic formulations like Triphala are widely studied for their antioxidant and antimicrobial properties.

    Reason (R): The efficacy of Triphala is primarily due to its bioactive compounds, which are unaffected by environmental or processing factors.

44. **Assertion (A):** Integrating Ayurveda into public health systems requires addressing sociocultural barriers and ensuring accessibility.

    Reason (R): Ayurvedic principles are inherently complex and require specialized knowledge, limiting their applicability in large-scale public health programs.

45. **Assertion (A):** Ethical Ayurvedic research must incorporate traditional knowledge systems and modern scientific methodologies.

    Reason (R): Traditional Ayurvedic concepts are incompatible with modern scientific methods, making integration difficult.

Directions (Q. No. 46–50): *Read the passage carefully and answer the questions given below:*

Ayurveda, one of the world's oldest medical systems, has witnessed growing global recognition for its holistic approach to health and wellness. The rising demand for evidence-based validation of Ayurvedic therapies has prompted the development of new regulatory frameworks and research initiatives in India. These initiatives aim to harmonize the principles of Ayurveda with modern scientific methodologies while preserving its traditional essence.

Under the aegis of the Ministry of AYUSH, the Indian government has implemented robust guidelines for clinical trials in Ayurveda. The Central Council for Research in Ayurvedic Sciences (CCRAS) plays a pivotal role in overseeing Ayurvedic research, ensuring that studies adhere to global standards of Good Clinical Practice (GCP). The primary objective is to generate reliable, reproducible, and evidence-based data to establish the safety and efficacy of Ayurvedic treatments.

One of the most significant advancements has been the integration of Ayurveda into India's Clinical Trial Registry (CTRI). This ensures transparency and accountability in Ayurvedic research. For every clinical trial conducted, detailed protocols, including the intervention, outcomes, and ethical approvals, must be registered. Such measures aim to bridge the gap between traditional knowledge and modern scientific scrutiny.

Another landmark initiative is the promotion of interdisciplinary research. Researchers from diverse fields, such as molecular biology, pharmacology, and systems biology, collaborate to study the biochemical and genetic mechanisms underlying Ayurvedic interventions. For instance, Ayurgenomics explores how Prakriti (individual constitution) aligns with genetic predispositions, offering a personalized approach to healthcare. This research has led to several patents, including formulations targeting inflammatory diseases and metabolic disorders.

One notable example is a patented Ayurvedic protein-based formulation designed for inflammatory bowel diseases (IBD). This formulation, derived from classical texts, combines plant-based peptides with anti-inflammatory herbs to restore gut health. Preclinical studies revealed significant improvements in biomarkers of inflammation, such as interleukin-6 (IL-6) and C-reactive protein (CRP). Subsequent clinical trials showed that the formulation not only reduced symptoms like abdominal pain and diarrhea but also improved the diversity of gut microbiota.

Despite these advancements, Ayurvedic clinical trials face unique challenges. Standardizing complex polyherbal formulations, ensuring quality control of raw materials, and aligning traditional diagnostic methods with modern outcome measures are persistent obstacles. Additionally, the distinctive sensory properties of Ayurvedic preparations often complicate blinding in randomized controlled trials (RCTs). Researchers must innovate methodologies to address these challenges while upholding the core principles of Ayurveda.

The Indian government has introduced funding schemes to support large-scale clinical trials and research infrastructure. Initiatives like the Extra Mural Research (EMR) scheme and public-private partnerships encourage collaboration between academic institutions, industry, and traditional practitioners. Furthermore, efforts are underway to establish global Ayurvedic standards in collaboration with the World Health Organization (WHO). These standards aim to facilitate the integration of Ayurvedic therapies into international healthcare systems, making them more accessible and credible.

The ethical dimensions of Ayurvedic research are equally crucial. Informed consent must ensure participants understand the risks and benefits of traditional therapies. Researchers are also tasked with protecting the cultural heritage of Ayurveda by involving traditional practitioners and ensuring equitable benefit-sharing. Ethical frameworks emphasize transparency, community engagement, and post-trial access to treatments for participants.

The future of Ayurvedic clinical trials looks promising with technological advancements such as artificial intelligence (AI) and machine learning (ML). These tools assist in identifying patterns in patient responses, optimizing formulations, and predicting outcomes. For example, AI algorithms can analyze large datasets to correlate Prakriti with disease susceptibility, further advancing personalized medicine.

The evolving landscape of Ayurvedic clinical trials under India's new regulatory frameworks represents a significant step toward evidence-based integration of traditional medicine into modern healthcare. By addressing challenges such as standardization, quality control, and ethical considerations, India is paving the way for Ayurveda's global resurgence. However, maintaining the delicate balance between tradition and science remains paramount to ensuring the authenticity and effectiveness of this ancient medical system.

Find the answers for the following questions based on your understanding of the text:

46. According to the passage, what is the primary objective of integrating Ayurveda into India's Clinical Trial Registry (CTRI)?

A. To promote the export of Ayurvedic products to international markets.

B. To ensure transparency and accountability in Ayurvedic research.

C. To replace traditional knowledge systems with modern methodologies.

D. To bypass ethical regulations for faster trial approvals.

47. Why are interdisciplinary collaborations emphasized in Ayurvedic research, as discussed in the passage?

A. To replace Ayurvedic principles with modern scientific approaches.

B. To study the biochemical and genetic mechanisms underlying Ayurvedic interventions.

C. To focus exclusively on preclinical studies and avoid human trials.

D. To ensure that Ayurvedic treatments are marketed as pharmaceutical drugs.

48. What challenges in Ayurvedic clinical trials are highlighted in the passage?

A. Lack of funding and international collaboration.

B. Difficulty in standardizing formulations and blinding in trials.

C. Inability to produce synthetic alternatives for Ayurvedic drugs.

D. Resistance from traditional practitioners to modern research methodologies.

49. What ethical considerations are essential for Ayurvedic clinical trials, as per the passage?

A. Encouraging exclusive participation of traditional practitioners.

B. Ensuring informed consent, equitable benefit-sharing, and post-trial access.

C. Eliminating the need for community engagement in rural trials.

D. Providing financial incentives to participants without disclosing trial details.

50. How are AI and machine learning tools contributing to Ayurvedic research, according to the passage?

A. By simplifying the sensory properties of Ayurvedic formulations for trials.

B. By analyzing datasets to correlate Prakriti with disease susceptibility.

C. By eliminating the need for traditional diagnostic methods.

D. By automating clinical trial protocols for faster approvals.

ANSWER WITH EXPLANATIONS

1. C: A waitlist control ensures scientific rigor while respecting Ayurveda's ethical and cultural framework. It allows for fair comparison between groups while ensuring that all participants eventually benefit from the therapy. This design is well-suited when placebo or sham interventions are inappropriate due to the holistic, personalized nature of the treatment. It balances participant expectations with methodological demands and promotes trust and transparency.

2. B: This approach preserves the essence of Ayurveda while meeting the expectations of biomedical research. Correlating traditional assessments (e.g., Prakriti and Agni) with measurable data (e.g., hippocampal volume or cognitive scores) strengthens the scientific credibility of Ayurvedic interventions. It ensures integrative validation rather than replacement of Ayurvedic diagnostics. This dual-tracking also allows a broader understanding of health outcomes. It supports interdisciplinary collaboration and enriches both knowledge systems. The methodology becomes more acceptable for publication and regulatory evaluation.

3. B: Phytochemical profiling allows researchers to maintain batch-to-batch consistency without compromising the traditional multi-herbal identity of the formulation. This ensures that therapeutic efficacy remains reproducible and scientifically measurable. It also satisfies regulatory requirements for quality assurance and standardization in trials. Unlike synthetic versions or ingredient reduction, this method retains the polyherbal synergy Ayurveda emphasizes. It respects classical formulations while meeting modern clinical expectations. Profiling supports the reproducibility of outcomes and boosts acceptance in global scientific circles.

4. B: Community education is a sustainable, respectful, and empowering strategy that aligns with public health principles. It helps individuals understand the rationale and benefits behind Ayurvedic dietary changes, improving compliance. Education allows culturally relevant adaptations without diluting health benefits. Unlike financial incentives or exclusion, this builds long-term behavioral change. It also promotes self-efficacy and inclusivity, ensuring that dietary interventions are embraced, not imposed. It helps bridge the gap between traditional principles and modern lifestyle preferences.

5. A: Triphala has a distinctive taste and smell, making double-blind designs difficult. An active placebo that mimics its sensory characteristics allows blinding, which reduces bias and increases study reliability. This is critical in clinical trials to ensure objectivity and reduce placebo effects. Unlike open-label designs or removing controls, it strengthens methodological rigor while retaining the authenticity of the Ayurvedic treatment. It balances the unique challenges of herbal research with standard clinical expectations. This solution enables robust, reproducible, and credible research outcomes.

6. A: Comprehensive pre-enrollment counseling is essential for ethical compliance in Panchakarma trials due to their invasive nature. Such discussions empower participants with a clear understanding of procedures, risks, and benefits, fostering informed decision-making. Familiarity with Ayurveda among participants is helpful but cannot replace the need for detailed consent processes. Substituting invasive procedures dilutes the trial's objectives, compromising scientific validity. Ensuring that participants are well-informed and willing safeguards their autonomy and trust. This approach aligns with global ethical standards, maintaining Ayurveda's integrity while addressing participant concerns. Transparent communication is thus key to bridging traditional practices and modern research ethics.

7. **B:** Good Agricultural Practices (GAP) ensure the consistency of bioactive compounds in Ayurvedic herbs, addressing the variability caused by environmental factors. Variations in soil, climate, and harvesting practices significantly affect the therapeutic efficacy of herbs. Establishing GAP standardizes cultivation, providing reproducible results in clinical trials. While synthetic derivatives offer consistency, they may lose the holistic synergy inherent in Ayurvedic formulations. Polyherbal solutions mitigate variability but do not address the core issue of raw material quality. Personalized treatments align with Ayurveda's philosophy but cannot replace the need for standardized practices in research. GAP thus ensures quality without compromising traditional authenticity.

8. **A:** Culturally tailored informed consent processes ensure that participants understand complex medical procedures and risks in clinical trials involving Ayurvedic therapies. Conducting discussions in the local language with culturally relevant analogies helps bridge gaps in comprehension, especially in populations unfamiliar with scientific jargon. Simplifying consent forms without detailing risks violates ethical standards and could exploit participants' lack of understanding. Providing monetary compensation may inadvertently pressure participants, undermining their autonomy. Digital tools may assist documentation but cannot replace personal engagement in culturally diverse settings. Transparent and inclusive communication ensures ethical integrity and participant trust, aligning with global standards in Ayurvedic research.

9. **A:** Critiques regarding the influence of dietary changes during Panchakarma on clinical outcomes are valid and must be addressed through control groups receiving identical diets without therapies. Such a design isolates the specific effects of Panchakarma, ensuring scientific rigor. Solely relying on subjective reports risks bias, while focusing on dietary interventions alone overlooks the holistic objectives of Ayurveda. Dismissing critiques undermines the credibility of Ayurvedic research. A balanced methodology that incorporates modern controls while respecting traditional practices strengthens the evidence base for Panchakarma, showcasing its specific benefits in detoxification and metabolic health, validated through robust comparative frameworks.

10. **A:** Offering access to standard medical care alongside experimental Ayurvedic treatments ensures ethical fairness and protects participants' health during clinical trials. This dual approach aligns with global research norms, ensuring participants are not deprived of proven therapies. Limiting trials to urban populations or focusing exclusively on free Ayurvedic treatments fails to address healthcare disparities in rural areas. Financial incentives without comprehensive care may exploit vulnerable populations. Ethical trials should prioritize equitable healthcare access, fostering trust and credibility in Ayurvedic research. This integrative approach balances scientific exploration with participant welfare, ensuring alignment with ethical guidelines and long-term societal benefits.

11. **A:** Dual outcome measures, combining subjective Ayurvedic metrics like Dosha balance with validated biomedical parameters, ensure methodological rigor in research. This approach respects traditional diagnostics while aligning with modern scientific expectations. Limiting the study to Ayurvedic methods risks losing credibility, while focusing solely on biomedical metrics ignores Ayurveda's holistic framework. Exclusively subjective outcomes may lead to bias, compromising validity. Integrating both systems provides a comprehensive evaluation of Ayurvedic interventions, bridging ancient wisdom with modern research standards. This dual methodology enhances the robustness and acceptability of findings, paving the way for integrative approaches in personalized healthcare.

12. **B:** Promoting traditional agroforestry and involving local communities in conserving medicinal plants addresses ecological and therapeutic challenges. This strategy ensures sustainable harvesting while preserving biodiversity and maintaining the quality of raw materials. Monoculture plantations can harm ecosystems, and synthetic alternatives may lose the holistic properties integral to Ayurveda. Reducing reliance on endangered plants risks compromising therapeutic efficacy. Community-based conservation aligns with Ayurveda's respect for nature and sustains its long-term viability. Engaging local stakeholders fosters environmental responsibility and safeguards the medicinal qualities of plants, ensuring that Ayurvedic practices remain authentic, effective, and ecologically sustainable.

13. **A:** Environmental degradation, including soil depletion and overharvesting, directly impacts the bioactive

compound concentrations in medicinal plants, reducing their therapeutic efficacy. This diminished potency affects clinical outcomes, as observed in the preparation's reduced ability to promote gut health and systemic immunity. Claims that traditional preparation methods compensate for environmental factors lack empirical support, and suggesting enhanced potency contradicts the evidence. Ayurvedic formulations rely on the integrity of their raw materials, making environmental sustainability crucial. Addressing these challenges ensures consistent therapeutic outcomes and reinforces Ayurveda's credibility in managing health conditions through high-quality, eco-friendly formulations.

14. **A:** Establishing standardized protocols for sustainable harvesting and monitoring bioactive compounds ensures the long-term efficacy of Ayurvedic formulations. These measures balance ecological concerns with therapeutic integrity, preserving both the environment and traditional practices. Developing synthetic alternatives undermines Ayurveda's natural essence, while shifting focus to other formulations neglects core therapies. Large-scale production risks environmental harm without sustainability frameworks. Combining scientific innovation with conservation fosters Ayurveda's growth while maintaining authenticity. Such initiatives demonstrate a commitment to ecological balance and holistic healthcare, ensuring the continued relevance of Ayurveda in addressing modern health challenges sustainably.

15. **A:** Robust Ayurvedic research requires integrating traditional diagnostics, such as Prakriti stratification, with modern metrics for comprehensive evaluations. Outcome measures must include both subjective and objective parameters, ensuring alignment with Ayurveda's holistic framework and scientific rigor. Exclusive reliance on subjective outcomes risks bias, while modern-only metrics ignore the core philosophy of Ayurveda. Dosha balance and Vikriti improvements must be documented to validate interventions. Combining these approaches enriches the evidence base, bridging ancient knowledge with contemporary methodologies. This fusion fosters credibility, ensuring that Ayurvedic research meets global scientific standards while preserving its traditional principles.

16. **A:** Ethical Ayurvedic research prioritizes informed consent, adhering to GCP guidelines, and respecting participants' autonomy. Transparency about risks and benefits ensures ethical integrity. Allowing participants to withdraw without repercussions aligns with global ethical standards. Placebo groups, though controversial, must be used judiciously to maintain scientific rigor. Ethical considerations in Ayurvedic trials go beyond compliance, emphasizing cultural sensitivity, equitable benefit-sharing, and participant welfare. This approach fosters trust, ensuring that Ayurveda integrates seamlessly into evidence-based healthcare while upholding its traditional values and ethical responsibilities. Such ethical rigor strengthens Ayurveda's global credibility as a holistic and reliable medical system.

17. **A:** Standardizing Ayurvedic formulations requires a multi-pronged approach, including phytochemical profiling, uniform cultivation practices, and rigorous preclinical and clinical validation. Phytochemical profiling ensures consistency in the chemical composition of raw materials and final products, addressing variability due to environmental or regional factors. Uniform cultivation practices under controlled conditions, such as Good Agricultural Practices (GAP), further stabilize ingredient quality. Preclinical and clinical validation solidifies the evidence base for safety and efficacy. Excluding traditional preparation methods compromises authenticity, while incomplete standardization diminishes reproducibility. A balanced approach ensures that Ayurvedic formulations retain their holistic essence while meeting the demands of global research standards.

18. **B:** Public health research in Ayurveda emphasizes preventive strategies, such as dietary interventions and seasonal routines (Ritucharya), to address community-level health concerns. Ayurvedic diets can mitigate lifestyle diseases like diabetes, while interventions for malnutrition provide cost-effective solutions in underserved populations. Seasonal health management through Ritucharya adapts practices to local environmental conditions, ensuring relevance. Neglecting preventive aspects or focusing solely on curative measures diminishes Ayurveda's holistic impact. Integrating these strategies into public health systems demonstrates Ayurveda's capacity to address modern challenges sustainably, bridging the gap between traditional wisdom and contemporary community healthcare needs with culturally sensitive solutions.

19. **B:** Ayurvedic clinical trials face multifaceted challenges, including standardizing polyherbal formulations, aligning traditional diagnostics with biomedical metrics, and addressing methodological hurdles like blinding. The complexity of formulations, with synergistic effects between ingredients, complicates reproducibility. Traditional diagnostics such as Dosha balance must integrate with objective measures like biomarkers to satisfy scientific scrutiny. Blinding trials is challenging due to distinctive sensory properties of Ayurvedic preparations. Addressing these issues requires innovative methodologies that respect Ayurveda's principles while meeting modern standards. These efforts will enhance the credibility of Ayurvedic research, fostering acceptance within global healthcare frameworks while retaining its traditional integrity.

20. **A:** Scientific validation of Ayurvedic Rasas (tastes) aligns with their described biological actions. Sweet Rasa supports tissue growth and nourishment, as seen in formulations for strength and vitality. Bitter Rasa's detoxifying and anti-inflammatory properties are well-documented, aiding in cleansing therapies. Sour Rasa enhances digestion and metabolism, linking it to enzymatic activation. Astringent Rasa strengthens tissues, controlling bleeding, contrary to misconceptions about weakening immunity. These biological correlations underscore the scientific basis of Rasas, bridging traditional Ayurvedic knowledge with modern pharmacology. This integration enhances Ayurveda's global credibility and promotes its acceptance as an evidence-based complementary medical system.

21. **A:** Ethical considerations in Ayurvedic clinical research emphasize preserving cultural integrity, ensuring equitable benefit-sharing, and protecting participant rights. Involving traditional practitioners respects Ayurveda's heritage and fosters collaboration. Equitable benefit-sharing ensures communities contributing to research receive fair compensation, aligning with ethical principles. Providing post-trial access to treatments maintains trust and accountability. Excluding vulnerable populations without addressing exploitation misses the ethical focus. Ethical frameworks must balance respect for traditional practices with modern accountability, ensuring Ayurveda's integration into global healthcare systems while safeguarding participant welfare and cultural authenticity. This commitment strengthens Ayurveda's reputation as an ethical and effective medical system.

22. **A:** Interdisciplinary public health research in Ayurveda incorporates Ayurvedic dietary patterns, complementary therapies, and seasonal interventions to enhance population health. Ayurvedic diets improve gut microbiome diversity, mitigating lifestyle disorders. Complementary therapies integrate Ayurveda with conventional healthcare, addressing malnutrition and chronic illnesses. Seasonal interventions, like Ritucharya, align practices with environmental changes, preventing seasonal health imbalances. Replacing traditional methods with biomedical approaches undermines Ayurveda's holistic strengths. Addressing these areas demonstrates Ayurveda's adaptability and relevance in modern public health, creating a sustainable and culturally sensitive healthcare framework that bridges traditional wisdom with contemporary scientific insights for better community outcomes.

23. **C:** Integrating Ayurveda into mainstream healthcare requires interdisciplinary strategies like Ayurgenomics, nutraceutical development, and systems biology. Ayurgenomics correlates Prakriti with genetic predispositions, advancing personalized medicine. Nutraceuticals based on Ayurvedic formulations combine traditional knowledge with modern nutrition science, addressing global health needs. Systems biology analyzes Ayurveda's holistic effects, aligning with contemporary research paradigms. Eliminating Ayurvedic principles risks losing its essence, while reductionist approaches fail to capture its multidimensional benefits. This integration balances tradition with innovation, enhancing Ayurveda's global acceptance and positioning it as a vital component of evidence-based, personalized, and preventive healthcare frameworks for the modern era.

24. **B:** Designing ethical and scientifically rigorous Ayurvedic clinical trials necessitates integrating personalized diagnostics like Prakriti assessment with biomarkers for objective outcomes. Informed consent processes must explain risks and benefits transparently, respecting cultural contexts. Excluding traditional preparation methods undermines authenticity, while standardized scientific validation enhances credibility. Balancing traditional principles with modern methodologies ensures comprehensive evaluations, bridging Ayurveda's holistic strengths with contemporary research demands. This approach fosters participant trust, ethical integrity, and scientific rigor, enabling Ayurveda's integration into global healthcare systems while maintaining its core philosophy. Such trials uphold Ayurveda's relevance in addressing complex health challenges through evidence-based solutions.

25. **A:** Matching Ayurvedic research methodologies with their respective descriptions highlights the multifaceted nature of the discipline. Literary research focuses on decoding classical texts to align traditional knowledge with modern science. Pharmacological research investigates the chemical properties and therapeutic effects of Ayurvedic drugs, often using techniques like chromatography and spectroscopy. Clinical research evaluates the efficacy of interventions in human populations using methodologies such as randomized controlled trials (RCTs). Public health research

explores Ayurveda's role in addressing community health challenges, such as malnutrition and lifestyle disorders. Each methodology contributes uniquely, creating a comprehensive framework for Ayurveda's evidence-based integration into global healthcare.

26. A: Ethical considerations in Ayurvedic research ensure participant welfare, cultural sensitivity, and fair benefit-sharing. Informed consent empowers participants with knowledge about risks, benefits, and procedures, fostering transparency. Protecting Ayurveda's cultural integrity involves respecting traditional practices and acknowledging their contributions. Benefit-sharing ensures equitable distribution of research gains, particularly in resource-dependent communities. Post-trial access to treatments demonstrates accountability and care for participants, building trust. These principles align with global ethical standards, reinforcing Ayurveda's credibility and fostering sustainable, respectful integration into contemporary healthcare. By prioritizing ethical frameworks, Ayurvedic research maintains its authenticity while adhering to rigorous modern scientific practices.

27. A: The alignment of study designs with their characteristics underscores the methodological diversity in Ayurvedic research. Observational studies explore outcomes without intervention, providing insights into natural occurrences. RCTs compare intervention groups with controls, ensuring methodological rigor and bias minimization. Pragmatic trials assess interventions in real-world settings, emphasizing practical applicability. Translational research bridges basic findings with clinical applications, translating theoretical knowledge into actionable healthcare solutions. Each design serves specific research objectives, ensuring a balanced approach to validating Ayurvedic interventions. Combining traditional principles with rigorous methodologies enhances Ayurveda's global acceptance, making it a credible complementary and alternative medicine system.

28. A: Matching Ayurvedic components with their therapeutic properties showcases their unique roles in holistic healing. Triphala detoxifies and improves gut health, enhancing digestive function. Ashwagandha reduces stress and improves strength, supporting the body's resilience against external stressors. Brahmi boosts cognitive function, promoting mental clarity and memory. Neem's antimicrobial and purifying properties cleanse the system, aiding in detoxification. These components exemplify Ayurveda's integrative approach, addressing physical, mental, and systemic health. Understanding these roles bridges traditional knowledge with modern science, fostering evidence-based applications of Ayurvedic therapies in addressing contemporary health challenges effectively and holistically.

29. B: Ayurveda's application in public health demonstrates its holistic approach to community health challenges. Preventive healthcare focuses on lifestyle and dietary modifications, reducing the burden of chronic diseases. Community health programs integrate Ayurvedic solutions for malnutrition, emphasizing accessibility and cost-effectiveness. Seasonal health management through Ritucharya aligns practices with environmental changes, preventing seasonal disorders. Geriatric care utilizes Rasayana therapies to enhance longevity and quality of life. These approaches highlight Ayurveda's adaptability to diverse health needs, making it a valuable complement to modern public health systems. By addressing both preventive and curative aspects, Ayurveda contributes to sustainable community healthcare models.

30. B: Ayurveda's foundational concepts align with modern interpretations, enhancing its relevance in contemporary science. Agni corresponds to enzymatic and metabolic processes essential for digestion and systemic health. Prakriti reflects genetic predispositions and individuality, offering a framework for personalized medicine. Ama, representing toxins, aligns with modern concepts of metabolic and immune dysfunction. Dosha imbalance parallels disruptions in homeostasis, linking Ayurveda's diagnostic principles to modern pathophysiology. These correlations bridge traditional wisdom with empirical validation, enabling Ayurveda to integrate seamlessly into evidence-based healthcare. Such connections affirm Ayurveda's scientific foundations, reinforcing its credibility and applicability in addressing modern health challenges.

31. A: Environmental challenges affecting Ayurvedic medicinal plants emphasize the need for sustainable practices. Overharvesting, driven by rising demand, depletes wild populations, while unregulated collection threatens biodiversity. Soil degradation and climate change reduce the bioactive content of medicinal plants, compromising their efficacy. Monoculture plantations exacerbate ecosystem imbalances, further endangering native species. Addressing these challenges requires implementing conservation strategies, such as community-based agroforestry and regulated harvesting practices. Sustainable solutions ensure the preservation of Ayurveda's raw materials while maintaining therapeutic integrity. By fostering ecological balance, Ayurveda upholds its commitment to natural and holistic healing, aligning with global sustainability goals.

32. A: The Tridosha theory encapsulates Ayurveda's systemic understanding of physiology. Vata governs movement, including circulation and respiration, essential for dynamic bodily functions. Pitta regulates metabolism and enzymatic activity, facilitating digestion and energy production. Kapha maintains structure, stability, and immunity, ensuring resilience against external stressors. A balanced Tridosha promotes health and equilibrium, highlighting Ayurveda's holistic approach. These roles reflect interconnected biological systems, affirming the theory's scientific relevance. Understanding Tridosha provides insights into individual health dynamics, enabling personalized diagnostics and treatments. Such integrative perspectives enrich Ayurveda's application in modern healthcare, emphasizing balance as the cornerstone of systemic well-being.

33. A: The Ayurvedic classification of Rasas (tastes) aligns with their physiological actions. Sweet Rasa nourishes tissues, supporting growth and vitality. Bitter Rasa detoxifies and reduces inflammation, aiding in cleansing therapies. Astringent Rasa strengthens tissues, controlling bleeding and promoting recovery. Sour Rasa enhances digestion and metabolic activity, facilitating nutrient absorption. These properties exemplify Ayurveda's focus on systemic balance and holistic healing. Understanding the biological impact of Rasas bridges traditional classifications with modern pharmacological research. This integration validates Ayurveda's therapeutic principles, fostering its acceptance as a scientifically grounded medical system addressing diverse health needs effectively.

34. A: Panchakarma therapies align with specific functions aimed at systemic detoxification and Dosha balance. Vamana induces vomiting to expel excess Kapha, cleansing the upper digestive tract. Virechana purges Pitta toxins, addressing systemic inflammation through bowel cleansing. Basti, or medicated enemas, balances Vata, aiding in systemic detoxification and nourishment. Nasya cleanses nasal passages, enhancing respiratory and neurological function. These therapies demonstrate Ayurveda's integrative approach to health, targeting root causes of imbalances rather than symptoms. Understanding their functions reinforces Ayurveda's relevance in modern detoxification and disease prevention strategies, highlighting its holistic contributions to maintaining systemic equilibrium and wellness.

35. A: Ayurveda's Prakriti-based treatment aligns with modern precision medicine by tailoring interventions to individual traits, such as genetic predispositions and phenotypic markers. This approach highlights Ayurveda's personalized and holistic focus, considering physical, mental, and environmental factors. Modern science validates Prakriti as a tool for disease prevention and management, bridging ancient diagnostics with genomic insights. The integration of Ayurveda's individualized framework with precision medicine strengthens healthcare approaches. While the overlap is significant, it also emphasizes the uniqueness of Ayurveda's comprehensive methodologies, which extend beyond genetic markers to include lifestyle and environmental influences, offering a broader scope than contemporary precision medicine.

36. A: Integrating biomarkers like CRP with Ayurvedic diagnostics reflects a necessary evolution in research methodology. While biomarkers provide objective data, Ayurvedic metrics such as Dosha balance capture holistic dimensions often missed in reductionist approaches. Modern metrics alone fail to encompass the systemic and energetic changes Ayurveda emphasizes. Balancing these methods fosters a more nuanced understanding of outcomes, aligning traditional principles with global scientific standards. By incorporating both, researchers validate Ayurveda's efficacy while respecting its foundational concepts. This dual approach ensures that Ayurveda contributes meaningfully to evidence-based medicine, preserving its authenticity while adapting to contemporary research expectations and healthcare integration.

37. C: The sustainability of medicinal plants remains critical to Ayurvedic efficacy. Overharvesting and environmental degradation reduce the quality of raw materials, diminishing therapeutic potential. While synthetic alternatives might mimic bioactive compounds, they fail to capture the holistic properties of natural formulations integral to Ayurveda's philosophy. Preserving biodiversity through sustainable practices ensures long-term availability and maintains the essence of Ayurvedic treatments. Synthetic substitutes undermine Ayurveda's reliance on natural synergies, while emphasizing conservation fosters ecological and therapeutic integrity. Sustainable harvesting protects both ecosystems and Ayurveda's reputation, ensuring its relevance in addressing health challenges within an ethical and environmentally conscious framework.

38. A: Ethical Ayurvedic research hinges on informed consent, community engagement, and equitable benefit-sharing, ensuring participant welfare and cultural sensitivity. Conducting trials in underserved areas requires addressing healthcare disparities, including access to post-trial care, to avoid exploitation.

Transparency about risks and benefits builds trust and aligns with global ethical standards. Neglecting post-trial responsibilities violates ethical principles, jeopardizing participant rights and study integrity. Ayurveda's emphasis on holistic care extends to research ethics, ensuring that participants benefit beyond the trial. This approach fosters credibility and trust, creating sustainable frameworks for Ayurvedic integration into healthcare systems while respecting cultural and participant concerns.

39. **C:** Rasayana therapies enhance cellular repair, immunity, and longevity through measurable biological impacts, including antioxidant effects and telomere preservation. While mental clarity and emotional balance are central to Ayurveda, they complement, rather than replace, physical health benefits. Modern research demonstrates systemic improvements, such as reduced oxidative stress, validating Rasayana's physiological relevance. Suggesting solely mental benefits undermines Ayurveda's holistic framework. Instead, these therapies integrate mind and body health, addressing aging comprehensively. Empirical validation of their cellular benefits strengthens Ayurveda's evidence base, fostering acceptance in modern medicine while preserving its integrative philosophy of systemic rejuvenation and overall well-being.

40. **A:** Panchakarma therapies effectively detoxify the body and restore Dosha balance, addressing systemic inflammation. Recent research links these therapies to gut microbiota modulation, highlighting their physiological mechanisms. For example, specific procedures promote microbial diversity, reducing inflammatory markers like C-reactive protein (CRP). This connection validates Ayurveda's traditional explanations through modern science, bridging ancient practices with contemporary health research. Suggesting a solely symbolic or unrelated role undermines their holistic contributions. By addressing root causes rather than symptoms, Panchakarma therapies exemplify Ayurveda's systemic approach to healing, enriching its relevance in integrative medicine and emphasizing its scientifically validated impacts on health.

41. **A:** Ayurvedic clinical trials must balance traditional methodologies with modern scientific rigor. Exclusive reliance on biomedical metrics limits the holistic scope of Ayurveda, failing to capture dimensions like Dosha balance. Conversely, excluding modern metrics reduces credibility in global healthcare systems. A hybrid approach integrating subjective Ayurvedic diagnostics with objective biomarkers ensures comprehensive evaluation. Modern frameworks benefit from Ayurveda's personalized insights, while Ayurveda gains empirical validation, fostering mutual enrichment. This integration strengthens Ayurveda's role in evidence-based medicine, ensuring its therapies meet contemporary healthcare demands while preserving its unique focus on holistic, individualized, and systemic approaches to health.

42. **A:** Ayurvedic interventions for lifestyle disorders emphasize dietary and behavioural changes to restore systemic balance. These modifications align with circadian rhythms and seasonal variations, optimizing physiological processes. For instance, adopting a Ritucharya routine prevents Dosha aggravation during seasonal transitions. These principles reduce chronic disease risks, addressing root causes rather than symptoms. Modern research increasingly validates such practices, highlighting their impact on metabolic health and systemic resilience. Ayurveda's emphasis on preventive care contrasts with biomedical approaches focusing on treatment, offering complementary perspectives. This integration demonstrates Ayurveda's potential to enrich healthcare through sustainable, personalized, and evidence-based strategies for long-term wellness.

43. **C:** Triphala's antioxidant and antimicrobial properties derive from its bioactive compounds, which depend on environmental and processing factors. Studies show that variations in soil and climate affect the potency of its ingredients, such as tannins and flavonoids. Claiming its efficacy is unaffected by these variables contradicts evidence, emphasizing the need for standardization. Holistic preparation methods ensure synergy among ingredients, but consistency requires modern quality control. Triphala exemplifies Ayurveda's reliance on natural integrity, validated through science. Addressing variability strengthens its therapeutic efficacy and ensures reproducibility in clinical research, demonstrating Ayurveda's adaptability to rigorous scientific frameworks while preserving its traditional essence.

44. **C:** The Assertion is true—integrating Ayurveda into public health systems demands addressing accessibility, cultural attitudes, and acceptance across diverse populations. However, the Reason is not entirely true; while Ayurvedic principles are deep and detailed, they are not inherently incompatible with public health. With proper training and adaptation (e.g., simplified protocols, local engagement), Ayurveda can effectively scale. Therefore, the reason doesn't hold as an explanation.

45. **C:** Ethical Ayurvedic research integrates traditional knowledge with modern methodologies, balancing authenticity with scientific rigor. Suggesting incompatibility

ignores evidence of successful interdisciplinary collaborations, such as Ayurgenomics. These integrations preserve Ayurveda's principles while validating its relevance in modern contexts. Rejecting modern methods risks Ayurveda's marginalization, while wholly abandoning tradition compromises its core philosophy. Ethical research frameworks emphasize mutual respect, ensuring Ayurveda's therapies meet global scientific standards while retaining their holistic focus. This balance fosters Ayurveda's acceptance as a credible, evidence-based system addressing complex health challenges through integrative approaches, bridging ancient wisdom with contemporary healthcare innovations.

46. **B:** The integration of Ayurveda into India's Clinical Trial Registry (CTRI) ensures transparency and accountability in Ayurvedic research. By mandating the registration of detailed protocols, including intervention methods, ethical approvals, and outcomes, CTRI fosters trust among stakeholders and aligns Ayurvedic studies with global research standards. This transparency is critical for bridging traditional Ayurvedic practices with modern scientific methodologies. It addresses the skepticism surrounding traditional therapies by emphasizing evidence-based approaches. Rather than promoting exports or bypassing ethical standards, CTRI strengthens the credibility of Ayurvedic research, paving the way for global acceptance and integration into mainstream healthcare systems.

47. **B:** Interdisciplinary collaborations in Ayurvedic research are essential to studying the biochemical and genetic mechanisms underlying Ayurvedic interventions. For example, Ayurgenomics connects the concept of Prakriti with genetic predispositions, aligning traditional diagnostics with modern personalized medicine. Such research enriches Ayurveda's relevance in contemporary healthcare by providing scientific validation for ancient principles. This approach neither replaces Ayurvedic principles nor avoids human trials. Instead, it integrates traditional knowledge with advanced fields like molecular biology and pharmacology. By fostering these collaborations, Ayurveda evolves into a scientifically credible system capable of addressing modern health challenges while retaining its traditional ethos.

48. **B:** The passage highlights significant challenges in Ayurvedic clinical trials, including the difficulty of standardizing complex polyherbal formulations and the sensory properties that complicate blinding in trials. Environmental factors affecting raw materials add to the complexity, impacting reproducibility and efficacy. Aligning traditional diagnostic methods with objective biomedical outcome measures presents another hurdle. These challenges necessitate innovative methodologies that maintain Ayurveda's core principles while meeting global research standards. The passage does not suggest a lack of funding or resistance from practitioners as the primary issues but emphasizes the need for methodological and quality control improvements to ensure reliable outcomes.

49. **B:** Ethical considerations in Ayurvedic clinical trials include ensuring informed consent, equitable benefit-sharing, and post-trial access for participants. Informed consent guarantees that participants understand the risks and benefits of traditional therapies. Equitable benefit-sharing involves compensating communities that contribute to the research, preserving the cultural heritage of Ayurveda. Post-trial access ensures continuity of care for participants, fostering trust. Eliminating community engagement or providing financial incentives without transparency violates ethical norms. These principles align Ayurvedic research with global standards, emphasizing participant welfare, cultural respect, and transparency, which are essential for Ayurveda's credibility and global acceptance.

50. **B:** Artificial intelligence (AI) and machine learning (ML) tools contribute to Ayurvedic research by analyzing datasets to correlate Prakriti with disease susceptibility. This enhances personalized medicine, aligning traditional diagnostics with modern scientific methods. ML also aids in phytochemical profiling, ensuring consistency and quality control in Ayurvedic formulations. These technologies do not eliminate traditional methods but complement them by accelerating research processes and improving precision. AI and ML demonstrate how Ayurveda can integrate cutting-edge tools to validate its principles, address modern healthcare demands, and maintain its authenticity. Such innovations enhance Ayurveda's position in global healthcare systems.

CHAPTER 30

BIOSTATISTICS, AYURVEDA-INFORMATICS, AND HEALTH INFORMATICS

BASICS OF BIOSTATISTICS AND DATA ANALYSIS

Introduction to Biostatistics

Biostatistics is a branch of statistics dedicated to analyzing and interpreting data derived from biological, medical, and health-related studies. It serves as a cornerstone for evidence-based decision-making in healthcare, public health, and clinical research. By providing tools to describe, infer, and predict data patterns, biostatistics enables scientists and healthcare practitioners to draw meaningful conclusions about health outcomes, disease epidemiology, and treatment effectiveness.

Biostatistics encompasses descriptive statistics (summarizing data), inferential statistics (drawing conclusions from samples), and advanced methods like regression modeling, survival analysis, and multivariate techniques. These tools collectively aid in understanding complex biological phenomena.

Importance of Biostatistics in Health Research

1. **Epidemiological Studies:** Biostatistics is integral to identifying risk factors for diseases, understanding their spread, and evaluating interventions to control outbreaks. For example, calculating prevalence, incidence, and relative risk helps pinpoint public health threats.
2. **Clinical Trials:** Clinical research relies on biostatistics for designing trials, randomizing participants, and analyzing data to assess the safety and efficacy of interventions.
3. **Genomic Studies:** With the advent of high-throughput technologies, biostatistical techniques help decipher complex genomic data, leading to personalized medicine.
4. **Health Informatics:** Biostatistics supports decision-making by deriving actionable insights from health informatics systems, including electronic health records (EHRs).

Fundamental Concepts in Biostatistics

1. **Population and Sample:**
   - A population encompasses all individuals of interest in a study.
   - A sample is a subset of the population used for analysis. Sampling methods must ensure that the sample accurately represents the population
2. **Types of Data:**
   - **Nominal Data:** Categorical without order (e.g., blood groups).
   - **Ordinal Data:** Categorical with order (e.g., cancer stages).
   - **Interval Data:** Quantitative without a true zero (e.g., temperature in Celsius).
   - **Ratio Data:** Quantitative with a true zero (e.g., weight).
3. **Measures of Central Tendency:**
   - **Mean:** Average of data values.

- **Median:** Middle value in ordered data.
- **Mode:** Most frequent value.

4. **Measures of Dispersion:**
   - **Range:** Difference between maximum and minimum values.
   - **Variance:** Average squared deviation from the mean.
   - **Standard Deviation:** Square root of variance.
5. **Probability and Hypothesis Testing:**
   - Probability quantifies the likelihood of events.
   - Hypothesis testing involves null (no effect) and alternative (effect exists) hypotheses, tested using statistical methods like *t*-tests, chi-square tests, and ANOVA.

Data Analysis Techniques

1. **Descriptive Statistics:** Describes data using graphs, charts, and summary statistics.
2. **Inferential Statistics:** Draws conclusions about populations based on sample data.
3. **Regression Analysis:** Models relationships between variables, e.g., linear regression, logistic regression.
4. **Survival Analysis:** Examines time-to-event data, commonly used in oncology and chronic disease studies.
5. **Bayesian Methods:** Updates probabilities based on new evidence, widely used in modern medical research.
6. **Machine Learning in Biostatistics:** Incorporates advanced algorithms to identify patterns and predict outcomes from large datasets.

Ayurveda-Informatics: Integrating Ayurveda with Modern Informatics

The Essence of Ayurveda

Ayurveda, an ancient Indian medical science, is rooted in principles of holistic wellness. It emphasizes individualized treatment based on prakriti (constitution), doshas (bioenergetic forces), and natural remedies derived from herbs and minerals. Ayurveda advocates for preventive care, balancing physical, mental, and spiritual health.

Challenges in Ayurveda Research

Despite its efficacy, Ayurveda faces challenges in global acceptance due to:

- Lack of standardization in formulations.
- Insufficient integration with modern scientific paradigms.
- Limited clinical trial data supporting efficacy.
- Poor documentation and digitization of traditional knowledge.

Role of Ayurveda-Informatics

Ayurveda-Informatics aims to modernize and validate Ayurveda using advanced informatics technologies. It integrates ancient wisdom with tools like data analytics, bioinformatics, and health informatics, facilitating standardization, validation, and global outreach of Ayurvedic practices.

1. **Digitalization of Classical Texts:** Classical Ayurvedic texts such as Charaka Samhita and Sushruta Samhita are being digitized, enabling structured databases for research.
2. **Standardization and Ontology Development:** Informatics systems help develop standardized terminologies, ontologies, and classifications for Ayurvedic concepts, enhancing interoperability with modern medical systems.
3. **Personalized Medicine:** Ayurveda-Informatics leverages genomic data and machine learning to align Ayurvedic principles with personalized medicine, addressing individual-specific health needs.

Key Applications of Ayurveda-Informatics

Ayurveda-Informatics is an emerging interdisciplinary field that merges traditional Ayurvedic knowledge with modern computational and informatics tools. Its applications are vast and transformative, enabling Ayurveda to integrate seamlessly into the global healthcare ecosystem. Below, we explore the key applications of Ayurveda-Informatics in detail, each with comprehensive elaboration and examples.

1. **Database Development:** Comprehensive Repositories for Ayurvedic Knowledge
   - **Significance of Database Development:** Ayurveda, being one of the oldest systems of medicine, has an extensive repository of knowledge accumulated over millennia. This knowledge is documented in classical texts such as the Charaka Samhita, Sushruta Samhita, and Ashtanga Hridaya. However, the unstructured format of these texts and lack of digital accessibility have limited their utility in modern research and practice.
   - **Ayurveda-Informatics and Database Creation:** Ayurveda-Informatics focuses on digitizing, standardizing, and organizing this knowledge into structured, searchable databases. These repositories serve as centralized hubs for Ayurvedic information, providing researchers, clinicians, and policymakers with easy access to validated data.

Examples of Ayurvedic Databases:

1. **AYUSH Research Portal:**
   - A government initiative in India that consolidates research studies, clinical trials, and academic

publications in Ayurveda and other traditional medicine systems.

- It includes a searchable repository of evidence-based research on Ayurvedic treatments.

2. **Traditional Knowledge Digital Library (TKDL):**
   - A collaborative project between India's Council of Scientific and Industrial Research (CSIR) and the Ministry of AYUSH.
   - TKDL translates ancient Ayurvedic texts into multiple languages and formats, making them accessible to patent offices worldwide. This initiative safeguards traditional knowledge from biopiracy.
3. **Pharmacopoeia of Indian Medicine:** A database of standardized formulations and monographs detailing the preparation, quality standards, and therapeutic uses of Ayurvedic drugs.

Role of Technology in Database Development

Modern informatics tools like Natural Language Processing (NLP), Optical Character Recognition (OCR), and knowledge graphs facilitate:

- **Extraction and Structuring:** Transforming unstructured textual information into structured formats.
- **Interoperability:** Enabling integration with biomedical and pharmacological databases.

Impact of Comprehensive Databases

Research Enablement: Provides a foundation for systematic research in Ayurveda, bridging traditional wisdom with scientific evidence.

- **Global Accessibility:** Promotes Ayurveda's global reach by offering multilingual and culturally neutral resources.
- **Regulatory Support:** Aids in regulatory approvals and intellectual property protection by providing robust documentation of Ayurvedic formulations and therapies.

2. **Bioinformatics Integration:** Understanding Ayurvedic Drug Mechanisms

   Bioinformatics in Ayurveda: Bioinformatics employs computational techniques to analyze biological data at the molecular level. When applied to Ayurveda, it helps decipher the molecular basis of Ayurvedic drugs, offering scientific validation and enhancing their therapeutic application.

Key Contributions of Bioinformatics Integration

1. **Decoding Phytochemicals:** Ayurvedic formulations often contain multiple bioactive compounds derived from plants. Bioinformatics tools like molecular docking and QSAR (Quantitative Structure-Activity Relationship) modeling help identify active constituents and predict their interactions with biological targets.

   Example: Curcumin, a bioactive compound in turmeric (*Curcuma longa*), has been extensively studied for its anti-inflammatory and anticancer properties using bioinformatics techniques.
2. **Mechanism of Action (MoA) Studies:** Bioinformatics platforms like STRING (Search Tool for the Retrieval of Interacting Genes/Proteins) and KEGG (Kyoto Encyclopedia of Genes and Genomes) reveal pathways influenced by Ayurvedic drugs.

   Example: Ashwagandha (*Withania somnifera*) is studied for its adaptogenic effects, and bioinformatics helps understand its influence on stress-related pathways.
3. **Network Pharmacology:** Ayurveda adopts a holistic, polyherbal approach where multiple ingredients act synergistically. Network pharmacology maps these interactions, offering insights into their combined therapeutic effects.

   Example: Triphala, a combination of three fruits, is analyzed for its antioxidant and gastrointestinal benefits.
4. **Genomic Integration:** Genomic tools like pharmacogenomics help link Ayurvedic principles like prakriti (individual constitution) with genetic predispositions, enabling personalized medicine.

Technologies Used in Bioinformatics Integration

- Molecular modeling and simulation software (e.g., AutoDock, Schrodinger).
- Bioinformatics databases like PubChem, ChEMBL, and TCMSP (Traditional Chinese Medicine Systems Pharmacology Database).

Benefits of Bioinformatics Integration

- **Scientific Validation:** Demonstrates the efficacy of Ayurvedic treatments using molecular evidence.
- **Personalized Medicine:** Aligns Ayurvedic principles with genetic insights, paving the way for tailored healthcare.
- **Global Acceptance:** Enhances Ayurveda's credibility within the global biomedical community.

3. **Predictive Analytics:** Machine Learning in Ayurvedic Healthcare

The Role of Predictive Analytics

Predictive analytics involves using data, statistical algorithms, and machine learning techniques to forecast future outcomes.

In Ayurveda, predictive analytics leverages patient data and traditional principles like prakriti (constitution) and doshas (bioenergetic forces) to anticipate disease susceptibility and treatment efficacy.

Applications in Ayurveda

1. **Prakriti Analysis:** Machine learning algorithms classify individuals into vata, pitta, or kapha prakriti based on physical, physiological, and psychological attributes.

   Example: Decision trees and random forests are used to analyze questionnaires and biometric data for prakriti determination.

2. **Disease Susceptibility Prediction:** By integrating genomic and phenotypic data, predictive models identify individuals at risk for specific conditions.

   Example: Studies suggest that kapha-dominant individuals may be predisposed to diabetes, while pitta types may have a higher risk for inflammatory conditions.

3. **Treatment Optimization:** Algorithms predict the most effective Ayurvedic treatment based on patient-specific parameters.

   Example: Recommending a personalized herbal regimen for metabolic disorders.

   Tools and Technologies

   - Machine learning libraries like TensorFlow, Scikit-learn, and PyTorch.
   - Big data platforms for analyzing large-scale health and genomic data.

   Impact of Predictive Analytics

   - **Proactive Healthcare:** Identifies risks early, enabling preventive interventions.
   - **Precision Ayurveda:** Matches treatments to individual profiles, enhancing efficacy.
   - **Enhanced Research:** Offers insights into disease patterns and treatment responses.

4. **Clinical Decision Support Systems (CDSS):** Enhancing Clinical Practice

What are CDSS?

Clinical Decision Support Systems (CDSS) are software tools designed to assist healthcare professionals in decision-making. Ayurveda-Informatics incorporates Ayurvedic principles and guidelines into CDSS, enabling holistic patient care.

Features of Ayurvedic CDSS

1. **Integrated Knowledge Base:** Incorporates Ayurvedic texts, treatment guidelines, and research findings.

   Example: A CDSS might suggest a herbal formulation for joint pain based on the patient's prakriti and symptoms.

2. **Diagnostic Support:** Tools like pulse diagnosis (nadi pariksha) are digitized and integrated into CDSS for accurate prakriti and dosha assessment.

   Example: AI-driven sensors analyze pulse patterns to determine dosha imbalances.

3. **Treatment Recommendations:** CDSS provides personalized recommendations, including herbal formulations, dietary advice, and lifestyle modifications.

4. **Monitoring and Feedback:** Tracks patient outcomes and refines recommendations over time.

Technological Backbone

- Natural Language Processing (NLP) for extracting insights from Ayurvedic texts.
- AI and expert systems for decision-making.

Benefits of Ayurvedic CDSS

- **Standardized Care:** Ensures consistency in clinical practice.
- **Time Efficiency:** Reduces diagnostic and treatment planning time.
- **Accessibility:** Enables non-specialist practitioners to deliver evidence-based Ayurvedic care.

5. **Drug Discovery and Validation:** Combining Ayurveda and Cheminformatics

Challenges in Ayurvedic Drug Development

Ayurvedic drugs often face skepticism due to a lack of scientific validation and standardization. Traditional formulations are complex mixtures, making it difficult to isolate and study their bioactive components.

Ayurveda-Informatics in Drug Discovery

Cheminformatics and computational tools address these challenges by:

1. **Identifying Bioactive Compounds:** Tools like molecular docking predict the interaction between herbal compounds and biological targets.

   Example: Molecular docking studies have shown the potential of andrographolide, a compound in Kalmegh (Andrographis paniculata), in treating viral infections.

2. **Herb-Drug Interaction Studies:** Predicting potential interactions between Ayurvedic herbs and modern drugs ensures safety in integrative medicine.

3. **Standardization of Formulations:** Analytical tools like HPLC and LC-MS validate the composition and quality of Ayurvedic drugs.

4. **High-Throughput Screening:** Virtual screening of compound libraries accelerates drug discovery.

Validation Techniques

- **In Silico:** Molecular simulations and cheminformatics.
- **In Vitro:** Laboratory testing on cell cultures.
- **In Vivo:** Animal studies and clinical trials.

Impact of Drug Discovery Integration

- **Global Recognition:** Provides scientific backing for Ayurvedic formulations.
- **Enhanced Safety:** Identifies and mitigates adverse effects.
- **Accelerated Development:** Shortens the time from discovery to clinical application.

HEALTH INFORMATICS AND ITS APPLICATIONS IN AYURVEDIC HEALTHCARE

Overview of Health Informatics

Health informatics refers to the use of information technology to improve healthcare delivery, patient outcomes, and system efficiency. It bridges clinical practice, data science, and IT, enabling evidence-based care.

Importance of Health Informatics

1. Enhances patient care through real-time data sharing and analysis.
2. Improves clinical workflows via automation and decision support.
3. Facilitates large-scale epidemiological studies.
4. Supports precision medicine by integrating genomic, clinical, and lifestyle data.

Applications of Health Informatics in Ayurveda

1. **Electronic Health Records (EHRs):** Incorporating Ayurvedic parameters like doshas, prakriti, and nadi-pariksha (pulse diagnosis) into EHRs enables holistic documentation of patient history.
2. **Telemedicine:** Health informatics supports Ayurvedic teleconsultations by integrating video consultations, remote diagnostic tools, and patient education platforms.
3. **Mobile Health (mHealth):** Ayurveda-based mobile applications offer personalized wellness plans, lifestyle tracking, and herbal remedy recommendations, empowering users to manage their health proactively.
4. **Big Data Analytics:** Analyzing large datasets of Ayurvedic clinical records helps identify treatment trends, efficacy patterns, and population health insights.
5. **Artificial Intelligence (AI) and Machine Learning (ML):** AI models are used to refine Ayurvedic diagnostic methods, optimize herbal formulations, and predict patient outcomes.
6. **IoT in Ayurveda:** Wearable devices and IoT technologies capture real-time health metrics, aiding in the dynamic assessment of Ayurvedic treatments.

Challenges in Health Informatics for Ayurveda

1. Lack of standardized integration between Ayurvedic and modern medical parameters.
2. Data privacy concerns, especially in sensitive health records.
3. Limited adoption of health IT infrastructure in rural areas.
4. Need for rigorous validation of Ayurvedic informatics tools.

Future Directions

1. **Integrative Healthcare Platforms:** Building unified platforms that combine Ayurvedic and allopathic data, facilitating comprehensive patient care.
2. **Blockchain in Ayurveda:** Ensuring secure and tamper-proof storage of Ayurvedic formulations and patient records.
3. **Global Collaboration:** Promoting international research collaborations to validate Ayurvedic therapies using advanced informatics tools.
4. **Education and Training:** Introducing Ayurveda-Informatics in academic curricula to nurture skilled professionals.

MULTIPLE CHOICE QUESTIONS

1. A pharmacologist integrates traditional Ayurvedic principles with biostatistical tools to investigate Ashwagandha's efficacy in reducing cortisol levels in individuals with chronic stress. The study employs a randomized controlled trial (RCT) with stratified sampling based on prakriti. The results show variability in outcomes depending on participants' dosha dominance, with Kapha-dominant individuals showing the least improvement. Which of the following conclusions aligns most with the study's findings?

A. Dosha dominance affects therapeutic outcomes, validating prakriti-based customization in Ayurveda.

B. Ashwagandha's effects are unrelated to prakriti, and the variability is due to external factors.
C. RCTs are unsuitable for studying Ayurvedic interventions due to inherent individualization.
D. Prakriti-based stratification introduces bias, invalidating the study's results.

2. A data scientist develops a machine learning model to predict metabolic disorders based on Ayurvedic prakriti classifications, integrating patient demographic, lifestyle, and genomic data. The model reveals significant predictive accuracy for Kapha-dominant individuals. How should the scientist interpret these findings in the context of Ayurveda-Informatics?
A. The model undermines traditional Ayurveda by reducing its principles to statistical correlations.
B. Predictive analytics supports prakriti as a scientifically valid classification for personalized healthcare.
C. Ayurveda cannot be reconciled with data-driven approaches like machine learning.
D. The findings prove that prakriti is a non-scientific construct with no predictive power.

3. Researchers evaluate the correlation between Ayurvedic Rasas (tastes) and modern pharmacological actions. The study focuses on the bitter Rasa, which Ayurveda associates with detoxification and anti-inflammatory properties. Experimental analysis reveals that compounds with a bitter Rasa activate liver detoxification enzymes and reduce inflammatory cytokines. What do these findings suggest?
A. Ayurvedic Rasas lack pharmacological relevance and are purely symbolic.
B. Modern pharmacology validates Ayurvedic concepts through molecular mechanisms.
C. The bitter Rasa's traditional claims cannot be substantiated by experimental analysis.
D. Ayurveda's classification system is outdated and inconsistent with modern science.

4. A public health initiative combines Ayurveda with health informatics to combat non-communicable diseases (NCDs) in underserved populations. The program includes a mobile app that integrates prakriti-based recommendations, dietary tracking, and biomarker monitoring. After six months, the program reports improved glycemic control and reduced cardiovascular risk among users. Which aspect of Ayurveda-Informatics is most evident in this initiative?
A. Standardization of Ayurvedic therapies across populations.
B. Personalization of healthcare through prakriti-based interventions.
C. Exclusive reliance on genomic data for health recommendations.
D. Elimination of subjective elements in Ayurvedic practice.

5. A bioinformatics study analyzes the molecular basis of Triphala's therapeutic effects, focusing on its antioxidant and anti-inflammatory properties. Computational modeling identifies pathways influenced by Triphala's bioactive compounds, including activation of nuclear factor erythroid 2–related factor 2 (Nrf2) signaling. How should this study be interpreted in the context of Ayurveda-Informatics?
A. Triphala's effects are coincidental and unrelated to traditional claims.
B. The findings validate Ayurveda's holistic approach through molecular insights.
C. Ayurveda's relevance is diminished by reducing its formulations to biochemical interactions.
D. Computational tools are insufficient to assess the efficacy of traditional medicines.

6. Researchers conduct a study linking Agni (digestive fire) to gut microbiota diversity, hypothesizing that weak Agni (Mandagni) corresponds to dysbiosis. The study observes that individuals with impaired digestion show reduced microbial diversity and increased inflammatory markers. Ayurvedic interventions, including Triphala and dietary adjustments, restore balance. What does this study illustrate?
A. Ayurvedic interventions lack measurable effects on gut health.
B. Agni's Ayurvedic concept aligns with modern understandings of gut health and immunity.
C. Microbial diversity is irrelevant to Agni and its associated Ayurvedic principles.
D. Weak Agni is unrelated to gut microbiota and systemic inflammation.

7. An environmental biologist examines the sustainability of sourcing Amalaki, a key Triphala component. Overharvesting and habitat degradation are found to reduce the fruit's bioactive compound concentration, potentially impacting therapeutic efficacy. How should Ayurveda-Informatics address this issue?
A. Develop synthetic alternatives to replace Amalaki in formulations.
B. Promote sustainable cultivation and conservation practices.
C. Shift focus from Amalaki-based therapies to alternative herbal solutions.
D. Reduce Triphala production to conserve Amalaki populations.

8. A hospital implements a Clinical Decision Support System (CDSS) that incorporates prakriti assessments to

recommend personalized therapies. After a year, patient outcomes improve significantly for chronic conditions like diabetes and hypertension. What conclusion can be drawn from the success of the CDSS?

A. Prakriti-based recommendations enhance therapeutic precision and efficacy.
B. CDSS systems minimize the importance of Ayurvedic principles by standardizing treatments.
C. The system's success is unrelated to prakriti and is driven by data analytics alone.
D. CDSS systems are ineffective in integrating Ayurveda with modern healthcare.

9. A clinical trial investigates the use of Rasayana (rejuvenation) therapies in slowing cellular aging. Participants receiving Chyawanprash show increased telomerase activity and reduced oxidative stress compared to a control group. How does this finding align with Ayurveda?

A. Rasayana therapies lack empirical support despite traditional claims.
B. The findings validate Rasayana principles through measurable biological effects.
C. Chyawanprash's effects are purely coincidental and unrelated to Ayurveda.
D. The study disproves the relevance of Rasayana in modern healthcare.

10. A data-driven platform integrates Ayurvedic concepts with genomic research to predict individual responses to herbal formulations. The platform reveals that Pitta-dominant individuals respond poorly to formulations rich in heating herbs. What does this illustrate about Ayurveda-Informatics?

A. Ayurveda cannot integrate with genomic research due to inherent subjectivity.
B. Ayurveda-Informatics supports the scientific relevance of dosha-specific interventions.
C. Dosha classifications are invalid when tested against genomic data.
D. Ayurvedic principles must be replaced with empirical frameworks for relevance.

Directions (Q. No. 11–14): *Scenario-Based Questions*

SCENARIO 1

A clinical study investigates the effects of Ayurvedic interventions on gut health. Triphala, a classical formulation, is administered to patients with irritable bowel syndrome (IBS). Results show improved gut microbiota diversity and reduced inflammatory markers, including C-reactive protein (CRP). Enhanced immunity, measured through increased IgA levels, is also observed.

SCENARIO 2

Simultaneously, an environmental biologist studies the sustainability of Amalaki, a key Triphala ingredient. Overharvesting threatens its wild populations, and environmental degradation reduces bioactive compound concentrations, potentially impacting therapeutic efficacy.

11. Based on Scenario 1, which mechanism best explains the improved systemic immunity observed with Triphala use?

A. Direct stimulation of immunoglobulin production.
B. Restoration of gut microbiota diversity, enhancing gut-associated lymphoid tissue (GALT) function.
C. Triphala's detoxifying properties, which reduce microbial diversity and boost the gut barrier.
D. A placebo effect unrelated to gut health.

12. Considering Scenario 2, what intervention would best address Amalaki's sustainability challenges while preserving its medicinal quality?

A. Establishing monoculture plantations to meet demand.
B. Promoting agroforestry and community-based conservation.
C. Replacing Amalaki with synthetic bioequivalents.
D. Reducing global production of Triphala.

13. How does environmental degradation of Amalaki potentially influence therapeutic outcomes observed in Scenario 1?

A. Reduced bioactive compounds diminish its efficacy in supporting gut health and immunity.
B. The quality of Amalaki does not affect Triphala's potency due to synergistic effects.
C. Environmental stress enhances Amalaki's therapeutic properties.
D. Triphala's efficacy remains unaffected as it relies on other ingredients.

14. Based on Scenarios 1 and 2, which strategy would address sustainability challenges while maintaining Triphala's efficacy?

A. Shifting from traditional formulations to synthetic alternatives.
B. Developing a global standard for sustainable harvesting practices.
C. Replacing Triphala with formulations not reliant on endangered species.
D. Encouraging large-scale commercial cultivation of all Triphala components.

Directions (Q. No. 15–24): *Codes-Based Questions*

15. The principles of Tridosha include:

(a) Vata governs motion and neural activity.
(b) Pitta regulates metabolism and enzymatic processes.

(c) Kapha maintains structure and fluid balance.
(d) Dosha balance ensures health.

Choose the correct answer from the options given below:
A. (a), (b), and (c) only
B. (a), (b), and (d) only
C. (a), (b), (c), and (d)
D. (a) and (b) only

16. Biological effects of Ayurvedic Rasas:
(a) Sweet Rasa supports tissue growth.
(b) Bitter Rasa detoxifies and reduces inflammation.
(c) Astringent Rasa strengthens tissues.
(d) Sour Rasa improves digestion.

Choose the correct answer from the options given below:
A. (a), (b), and (d) only
B. (a), (b), (c), and (d)
C. (b), (c), and (d) only
D. (a) and (c) only

17. Characteristics of Biostatistics include:
(a) Application in health research.
(b) Use of quantitative data analysis.
(c) Focus on clinical trial design.
(d) Evaluation of population health trends.

Choose the correct answer from the options given below:
A. (a), (b), and (c) only
B. (a), (b), (c), and (d)
C. (a) and (b) only
D. (b), (c), and (d) only

18. Key components of Ayurveda-Informatics are:
(a) Digitization of classical Ayurvedic texts.
(b) Integration with modern diagnostic tools.
(c) Development of AI models for dosha analysis.
(d) Use of wearable technology for Ayurvedic health monitoring.

Choose the correct answer from the options given below:
A. (a) and (b) only
B. (a), (b), and (c) only
C. (a), (b), (c), and (d)
D. (b) and (d) only

19. Health Informatics involves:
(a) Electronic Health Records (EHR).
(b) Use of AI for predictive diagnostics.
(c) Data standardization across healthcare systems.
(d) Development of mHealth (mobile health) applications.

Choose the correct answer from the options given below:
A. (a), (b), and (d) only
B. (a), (b), (c), and (d)
C. (b), (c), and (d) only
D. (a) and (c) only

20. Applications of Biostatistics in Clinical Research include:
(a) Estimation of treatment effects in trials.
(b) Calculation of sample size for studies.
(c) Identification of biomarkers for diseases.
(d) Prediction of public health outcomes.

Choose the correct answer from the options given below:
A. (a), (b), and (d) only
B. (a), (b), (c), and (d)
C. (b) and (d) only
D. (a), (c), and (d) only

21. Benefits of Ayurveda-Informatics include:
(a) Evidence-based validation of Ayurvedic practices.
(b) Improved accessibility of Ayurvedic knowledge.
(c) Integration with telemedicine platforms.
(d) Personalization of Ayurvedic therapies through AI.

Choose the correct answer from the options given below:
A. (a), (b), and (c) only
B. (b), (c), and (d) only
C. (a), (b), (c), and (d)
D. (a) and (d) only

22. Key principles of Health Informatics are:
(a) Data privacy and security.
(b) Interoperability of health systems.
(c) Patient-centered healthcare delivery.
(d) Automated health monitoring through IoT.

Choose the correct answer from the options given below:
A. (a), (b), and (d) only
B. (a), (b), (c), and (d)
C. (b), (c), and (d) only
D. (a) and (c) only

23. Contributions of Biostatistics to Epidemiology include:
(a) Estimation of disease prevalence and incidence.
(b) Assessment of risk factors for diseases.
(c) Analysis of effectiveness of public health interventions.
(d) Modeling of disease transmission patterns.

Choose the correct answer from the options given below:
A. (a), (b), and (d) only
B. (b), (c), and (d) only
C. (a), (b), (c), and (d)
D. (a) and (c) only

24. Ayurvedic diagnostic tools focus on:
(a) Pulse diagnosis (Nadi Pariksha).
(b) Examination of bodily excreta (Mala Pariksha).
(c) Skin and tongue analysis.
(d) Use of imaging technologies like MRI.

Choose the correct answer from the options given below:
A. (a), (b), and (c) only
B. (a), (b), (c), and (d)
C. (b) and (c) only
D. (a) and (b) only

Directions (Q. No. 25–34): *Match List–I with List–II and choose the correct answer from the options given below*:

25. Match List–I (Ayurvedic Components) with List–II (Functions):

List–I	List–II
(a) Vata Dosha	1. Governs movement and neural impulses
(b) Pitta Dosha	2. Regulates metabolism and enzymatic activity
(c) Kapha Dosha	3. Maintains structural stability and lubrication
(d) Balance of Tridosha	4. Ensures physical and mental well-being

Choose the correct answer from the options given below:
A. (a)-1, (b)-2, (c)-3, (d)-4
B. (a)-2, (b)-1, (c)-4, (d)-3
C. (a)-3, (b)-4, (c)-1, (d)-2
D. (a)-4, (b)-3, (c)-2, (d)-1

26. Match List–I (Applications of Ayurveda-Informatics) with List–II (Outcomes):

List–I	List–II
(a) Predictive Analytics	1. Enables prakriti-based disease risk assessment
(b) Bioinformatics	2. Deciphers molecular mechanisms of herbs
(c) Clinical Decision Support Systems (CDSS)	3. Supports prakriti-guided diagnostic workflows
(d) EHR Systems	4. Digitizes patient data for Ayurveda diagnostics

Choose the correct answer from the options given below:
A. (a)-1, (b)-2, (c)-3, (d)-4
B. (a)-3, (b)-1, (c)-4, (d)-2
C. (a)-4, (b)-3, (c)-1, (d)-2
D. (a)-2, (b)-4, (c)-3, (d)-1

27. Match List–I (Biostatistical Methods) with List–II (Applications):

List–I	List–II
(a) Regression Analysis	1. Predicts prakriti-disease correlations
(b) ANOVA	2. Compares outcomes across dosha groups
(c) Kaplan-Meier Analysis	3. Tracks survival rates of Rasayana therapies
(d) Meta-Analysis	4. Combines results from multiple clinical trials

Choose the correct answer from the options given below:
A. (a)-1, (b)-2, (c)-3, (d)-4
B. (a)-4, (b)-3, (c)-2, (d)-1
C. (a)-2, (b)-1, (c)-4, (d)-3
D. (a)-3, (b)-4, (c)-1, (d)-2

28. Match List–I (Rasas in Ayurveda) with List–II (Biological Actions):

List–I	List–II
(a) Sweet Rasa	1. Supports tissue nourishment and repair
(b) Bitter Rasa	2. Detoxifies the liver and reduces inflammation
(c) Astringent Rasa	3. Strengthens mucosal barriers and tissues
(d) Sour Rasa	4. Enhances enzymatic activity and digestion

Choose the correct answer from the options given below:
A. (a)-1, (b)-2, (c)-3, (d)-4
B. (a)-3, (b)-4, (c)-1, (d)-2
C. (a)-4, (b)-3, (c)-2, (d)-1
D. (a)-2, (b)-1, (c)-4, (d)-3

29. Match List–I (Challenges in Ayurveda-Informatics) with List–II (Descriptions):

List–I	List–II
(a) Data Standardization	1. Lack of consistency in Ayurvedic terminologies
(b) Interoperability	2. Challenges in integrating Ayurvedic data with biomedical systems
(c) Privacy Concerns	3. Risks associated with prakriti-based EHRs
(d) Conservation	4. Overharvesting of medicinal plants

Choose the correct answer from the options given below:
A. (a)-1, (b)-2, (c)-3, (d)-4
B. (a)-3, (b)-4, (c)-1, (d)-2

C. (a)-4, (b)-1, (c)-3, (d)-2
D. (a)-2, (b)-3, (c)-4, (d)-1

30. Match List–I (CDSS Features for Ayurveda) with List–II (Functions):

List–I	List–II
(a) Prakriti-Based Inputs	1. Provides personalized treatment recommendations
(b) Dosha Imbalance Alerts	2. Highlights deviations for timely interventions
(c) Integration with EHR Systems	3. Facilitates record-keeping and retrieval of Ayurvedic data
(d) AI-Driven Diagnostics	4. Supports accurate dosha-based diagnosis

Choose the correct answer from the options given below:
A. (a)-1, (b)-2, (c)-3, (d)-4
B. (a)-4, (b)-3, (c)-2, (d)-1
C. (a)-2, (b)-1, (c)-4, (d)-3
D. (a)-3, (b)-4, (c)-1, (d)-2

31. Match List–I (Ayurvedic Interventions) with List–II (Health Outcomes):

List–I	List–II
(a) Panchakarma	1. Detoxifies the body and restores dosha balance
(b) Rasayana Therapy	2. Rejuvenates cells and slows aging
(c) Triphala	3. Improves gut microbiota diversity
(d) Chyawanprash	4. Enhances immune function and vitality

Choose the correct answer from the options given below:
A. (a)-1, (b)-2, (c)-3, (d)-4
B. (a)-4, (b)-3, (c)-2, (d)-1
C. (a)-3, (b)-4, (c)-1, (d)-2
D. (a)-2, (b)-1, (c)-4, (d)-3

32. Match List–I (Health Informatics Tools) with List–II (Applications in Ayurveda).

List–I	List–II
(a) EHR Systems	1. Captures prakriti-based patient records
(b) Predictive Analytics	2. Forecasts prakriti-related disease risks
(c) Telemedicine Platforms	3. Enables remote Ayurvedic consultations
(d) Data Visualization Tools	4. Displays trends in dosha-based health outcomes

Choose the correct answer from the options given below:
A. (a)-1, (b)-2, (c)-3, (d)-4
B. (a)-4, (b)-3, (c)-1, (d)-2
C. (a)-2, (b)-1, (c)-4, (d)-3
D. (a)-3, (b)-4, (c)-2, (d)-1

33. Match List–I (Stages in Ayurvedic Care) with List–II (Details):

List–I	List–II
(a) Preconception Care	1. Purification and strengthening of reproductive tissues
(b) Embryonic Development	2. Governed by mātuja, pitruja, and ātmā
(c) Formation of Prakriti	3. Determined during conception by dosha influences
(d) Postnatal Care	4. Focuses on nutrition and ojas restoration

Choose the correct answer from the options given below:
A. (a)-1, (b)-2, (c)-3, (d)-4
B. (a)-2, (b)-1, (c)-4, (d)-3
C. (a)-3, (b)-4, (c)-1, (d)-2
D. (a)-4, (b)-3, (c)-2, (d)-1

34. Match List–I (Bioinformatics Techniques) with List–II (Applications):

List–I	List–II
List–I	List–II
Docking	interactions
(b) Network Pharmacology	2. Studies synergistic effects in polyherbal formulations
(c) Genomics	3. Correlates prakriti with genetic markers
(d) Metabolomics	4. Analyzes biochemical changes due to herbal therapies

Choose the correct answer from the options given below:
A. (a)-1, (b)-2, (c)-3, (d)-4
B. (a)-4, (b)-3, (c)-1, (d)-2
C. (a)-2, (b)-1, (c)-4, (d)-3
D. (a)-3, (b)-4, (c)-2, (d)-1

Directions (Q. No. 35–39): *Following questions are based on Statement 1 and Statement 2. Read both the statements carefully and choose the correct answer from the options given below:*

A. Both Statement 1 and Statement 2 are true, and Statement 2 is the correct explanation of Statement 1.
B. Both Statement 1 and Statement 2 are true, but Statement 2 is not the correct explanation of Statement 1.
C. Statement 1 is true, but Statement 2 is false.
D. Statement 1 is false, but Statement 2 is true.
E. Both Statement 1 and Statement 2 are false.

35. **Statement 1:** Ayurveda-Informatics enables the digitization and integration of traditional Ayurvedic knowledge with modern computational tools for research and healthcare delivery.

    Statement 2: This integration ensures global acceptance of Ayurveda by providing standardized treatment protocols and eliminating the need for prakriti-based customization.

36. **Statement 1:** Predictive analytics in Ayurveda uses machine learning models to analyze prakriti-based data and predict disease risks.

    Statement 2: Such models disregard qualitative Ayurvedic principles and rely exclusively on genomic and demographic inputs.

37. **Statement 1:** Biostatistics provides a scientific framework for validating the efficacy of Ayurvedic interventions through hypothesis testing and statistical analysis.

    Statement 2: Randomized controlled trials (RCTs) are incompatible with Ayurveda due to its individualized treatment approach.

38. **Statement 1:** Health informatics systems incorporating Ayurvedic principles, such as prakriti-based EHRs, improve the accuracy and personalization of healthcare delivery.

    Statement 2: These systems are effective only in urban settings due to the digital literacy and technological requirements for implementation.

39. **Statement 1:** The integration of bioinformatics in Ayurveda has enabled the identification of molecular mechanisms underlying herbal formulations like Triphala.

    Statement 2: This approach reduces the relevance of traditional Ayurvedic formulations by prioritizing biochemical pathways over holistic principles.

Directions (Q. No. 40–45): *There are two statements in each question. One is labelled as Assertion (A) and the other is as Reason (R). Read both the statements and choose the correct answer from the options given below*:

A. Both Assertion (A) and Reason (R) are true, and Reason (R) is the correct explanation of Assertion (A).
B. Both Assertion (A) and Reason (R) are true, but Reason (R) is not the correct explanation of Assertion (A).
C. Assertion (A) is true, but Reason (R) is false.
D. Assertion (A) is false, but Reason (R) is true.
E. Both Assertion (A) and Reason (R) are false.

40. **Assertion (A):** Ayurveda-Informatics enhances the global acceptance of traditional Ayurvedic practices through the use of digitized knowledge repositories.

    Reason (R): These repositories provide evidence-based validation of Ayurvedic formulations by replacing qualitative assessments with computational models.

41. **Assertion (A):** Predictive analytics in Ayurveda identifies disease susceptibility by analyzing prakriti and lifestyle data.

    Reason (R): Such analytics exclusively rely on genetic markers, disregarding qualitative factors like dosha imbalances.

42. **Assertion (A):** Biostatistics provides a robust framework for assessing the efficacy of Ayurvedic therapies.

    Reason (R): Randomized controlled trials (RCTs) are the only statistical tools applicable to Ayurveda research.

43. **Assertion (A):** Clinical Decision Support Systems (CDSS) integrating Ayurvedic principles improve the precision of therapeutic interventions.

    Reason (R): CDSS eliminates the subjective nature of Ayurveda by replacing prakriti-based assessments with algorithmic models.

44. **Assertion (A):** Sustainable sourcing of medicinal plants is critical for preserving the efficacy of Ayurvedic formulations.

    Reason (R): Overharvesting reduces bioactive compound concentrations in plants, compromising their therapeutic potential.

45. **Assertion (A):** Ayurveda-Informatics facilitates personalized healthcare by integrating traditional principles with modern technologies.

    Reason (R): It replaces Ayurveda's qualitative diagnostic methods with standardized treatment protocols.

Directions (Q. No. 46–50): *Read the passage carefully and answer the questions given below*:

Ayurveda, with its rich heritage and time-tested principles, is now finding a unique place in the realm of personalized medicine through the integration of advanced informatics and data analytics. This interdisciplinary collaboration, often referred to as Ayurveda-Informatics, is not just about validating traditional practices but also redefining them in the context of modern healthcare challenges.

One of the foundational principles of Ayurveda is the concept of Tridosha, which emphasizes the balance of Vata, Pitta, and Kapha doshas for optimal health. Recent research has linked these doshas to genetic, metabolic, and psychological traits, providing a framework for prakriti-based precision medicine. For example, Kapha-dominant individuals are often predisposed to metabolic disorders, while Vata-dominance is associated with nervous system conditions. Such correlations have encouraged the use of bioinformatics to map dosha-related genetic markers, enabling targeted interventions.

Health informatics tools such as Electronic Health Records (EHRs) tailored to Ayurvedic diagnostics have emerged as game changers. By incorporating prakriti-specific data, these systems allow practitioners to customize treatments, track patient progress, and generate insights for large-scale studies. Predictive analytics further enhances this process by identifying disease risks and suggesting lifestyle modifications based on prakriti and other clinical indicators. For instance, individuals identified as at-risk for diabetes through these tools can receive Kapha-pacifying dietary recommendations and herbal interventions, potentially averting disease progression.

However, the integration of Ayurveda with informatics is not without challenges. The lack of standardization in Ayurvedic terminologies and formulations creates barriers to interoperability across digital platforms. Moreover, the sourcing of medicinal plants such as Ashwagandha and Haritaki is under strain due to overharvesting and habitat loss. This raises concerns not only about sustainability but also about maintaining the therapeutic efficacy of Ayurvedic formulations, which rely heavily on plant bioactive compounds.

The ethical dimension of Ayurveda-Informatics is another critical area of concern. Personalized data generated through prakriti-based EHRs is highly sensitive and requires robust safeguards to ensure privacy and prevent misuse. Furthermore, there is an ongoing debate about whether computational tools dilute Ayurveda's holistic philosophy, which integrates physical, mental, and spiritual health. Critics argue that excessive reliance on data-driven approaches risks sidelining the nuanced, practitioner-led diagnostic methods that have been the cornerstone of Ayurveda for millennia.

Despite these challenges, the future of Ayurveda-Informatics appears promising. Initiatives such as the Traditional Knowledge Digital Library (TKDL) have already demonstrated the potential to protect and standardize traditional knowledge. Collaborative efforts between technologists, Ayurvedic practitioners, and policymakers are paving the way for a new era of healthcare that balances innovation with tradition. By combining the wisdom of Ayurveda with the precision of modern informatics, this approach holds the potential to redefine healthcare on a global scale.

Find the answers to the following questions based on your understanding of the passage:

46. According to the passage, how does the concept of Tridosha contribute to modern personalized medicine?

A. By providing a generalized framework for all individuals irrespective of prakriti.
B. By linking doshas to genetic and metabolic traits, enabling targeted interventions.
C. By focusing exclusively on psychological conditions in prakriti-dominant individuals.
D. By eliminating the need for genetic and metabolic analysis in healthcare.

47. What is the role of prakriti-specific EHRs in Ayurveda-Informatics, as mentioned in the passage?

A. To replace traditional Ayurvedic diagnostic methods with computational tools.
B. To customize treatments, track progress, and generate insights for large-scale studies.
C. To standardize Ayurvedic treatments across diverse populations.
D. To eliminate the need for personalized healthcare in Ayurveda.

48. What challenge related to medicinal plants is highlighted in the passage?

A. Overharvesting and habitat loss affecting the availability and efficacy of bioactive compounds.
B. Lack of public awareness about the importance of medicinal plants in Ayurveda.
C. Overdependence on synthetic alternatives for traditional Ayurvedic formulations.
D. Inefficiency of traditional farming practices in meeting global demand.

49. What ethical concern is associated with prakriti-based EHRs, as described in the passage?

A. The difficulty of standardizing personalized data across global healthcare systems.
B. The potential misuse of sensitive health data if robust safeguards are not implemented.
C. The exclusion of traditional Ayurvedic practitioners from technology-driven processes.
D. The lack of public access to personalized healthcare tools in rural areas.

50. According to the passage, what is the most promising aspect of Ayurveda-Informatics for the future of healthcare?

A. Exclusive reliance on computational tools to standardize Ayurvedic treatments.
B. The protection and global dissemination of traditional knowledge through initiatives like TKDL.
C. The gradual replacement of Ayurveda's holistic principles with evidence-based models.
D. The elimination of personalized treatments in favour of universal healthcare solutions.

ANSWER WITH EXPLANATIONS

1. **A:** Kapha-dominant individuals are inherently predisposed to metabolic issues due to their slower metabolism and fat storage tendencies, as highlighted in Ayurvedic principles. The study confirms that prakriti plays a crucial role in determining disease susceptibility, bridging Ayurveda with modern scientific frameworks. By stratifying participants based on prakriti, researchers validated Kapha's connection with insulin resistance. Standardized treatment approaches often fail to address such individual nuances, making prakriti-based personalization essential. This finding not only emphasizes the practical relevance of Ayurveda but also showcases how modern tools like RCTs can enhance its credibility. Thus, Ayurveda and biostatistics can synergistically improve healthcare outcomes.

2. **B:** Predictive analytics aligns with Ayurveda's focus on preventive, personalized care. Machine learning models analyzing prakriti and lifestyle data offer actionable insights into disease risks, supporting targeted interventions. Unlike traditional medicine, Ayurveda emphasizes prevention, making analytics an ideal complement. This approach bridges ancient wisdom with contemporary science, reinforcing Ayurveda's modern relevance. By integrating qualitative factors like dosha imbalances, predictive tools maintain Ayurveda's holistic nature. The analysis proves that technology and tradition can coexist, creating a robust framework for early interventions. Thus, predictive analytics not only validates Ayurveda but also enhances its accessibility and scalability in healthcare.

3. **B:** The biochemical validation of Ayurvedic Rasas, such as the detoxifying effects of bitter Rasa, highlights Ayurveda's empirical foundations. Modern pharmacological studies on bitter compounds activating liver enzymes confirm these ancient claims. Such findings strengthen the credibility of Ayurveda as a science rooted in observable phenomena. Unlike symbolic interpretations, the study reveals a direct link between taste classification and physiological effects. These correlations provide evidence that Ayurveda's Rasa framework is biologically significant. Bridging pharmacology with Ayurveda showcases the latter's enduring relevance, proving that ancient classifications align with modern biochemical understandings. This integration enhances Ayurveda's applicability in evidence-based medicine.

4. **B:** Prakriti-based interventions demonstrate the effectiveness of Ayurveda-Informatics in addressing non-communicable diseases. By offering personalized recommendations for diet and lifestyle, the program aligns with Ayurveda's core principles. The observed health improvements validate the fusion of tradition and technology. Unlike generalized healthcare models, prakriti-based systems recognize individual variations, ensuring precision. The program's success underscores the transformative potential of Ayurveda-Informatics in preventive care. Digital tools bridge the gap between traditional insights and modern needs, making Ayurveda more accessible. By emphasizing prakriti, the initiative proves that integrating holistic care with informatics can address complex health challenges effectively and sustainably.

5. **B:** The identification of Nrf2 activation by Triphala provides scientific evidence for its antioxidant and anti-inflammatory properties, aligning with Ayurvedic traditions. Computational studies confirm how Triphala's bioactive compounds influence molecular pathways, bridging ancient remedies with contemporary mechanisms. This validation strengthens Ayurveda's credibility as a science-based system. However, these insights must complement, not replace, its holistic philosophy. By combining computational research with Ayurvedic wisdom, the therapeutic potential of Triphala can be better understood and applied. This integration illustrates Ayurveda's adaptability, showing how its principles can be validated without losing their essence in modern healthcare settings.

6. **B:** The study linking weak Agni to dysbiosis and inflammation validates Ayurveda's emphasis on digestion as central to health. Agni's role aligns with the modern understanding of gut microbiota diversity's impact on systemic health. Ayurvedic interventions like Triphala restore balance, confirming the therapeutic value of traditional remedies. These findings bridge Ayurveda's holistic insights with microbiological research, showcasing their complementarity. The research highlights how Ayurveda's focus on digestion extends beyond mere metabolism, encompassing immunity and overall wellness. This evidence emphasizes Ayurveda's relevance in addressing gut health, demonstrating the compatibility of traditional concepts with modern scientific approaches.

7. **B:** Sustainable cultivation practices address both ecological and medicinal concerns in Ayurveda. Overharvesting of plants like Amalaki not only threatens biodiversity but also diminishes the therapeutic efficacy of formulations. Traditional agroforestry systems promote biodiversity while preserving the quality of

bioactive compounds. Synthetic substitutes, while practical, compromise Ayurveda's holistic integrity. Conservation efforts ensure that ecological harmony aligns with Ayurveda's principles, maintaining its effectiveness and ethical foundation. This sustainable approach ensures the availability of high-quality medicinal resources while addressing global demand. Collaborative efforts among communities, scientists, and policymakers are critical to sustaining Ayurveda's environmental and therapeutic legacy.

8. **A:** Prakriti-based CDSS systems enhance diagnostic precision by aligning modern algorithms with Ayurveda's personalized framework. The observed patient outcomes confirm the efficacy of combining tradition with technology. While algorithms aid scalability, retaining practitioner expertise ensures holistic care. By integrating digital tools with prakriti principles, CDSS modernizes Ayurveda without compromising its core philosophy. The success of these systems highlights their potential in bridging traditional healthcare with contemporary demands. This synergy not only validates Ayurvedic practices scientifically but also makes them accessible to a global audience, reinforcing Ayurveda's position as a relevant and effective healthcare system.

9. **B:** Chyawanprash's ability to enhance telomerase activity validates its traditional use as a rejuvenative Rasayana. The study bridges Ayurveda's anti-aging claims with measurable biological effects, emphasizing its relevance in modern medicine. By demonstrating reduced oxidative stress, the research highlights the compatibility of Ayurveda's holistic interventions with contemporary science. This alignment reinforces Ayurveda's preventive and restorative focus, proving that traditional therapies can support cellular health. Chyawanprash exemplifies how ancient formulations remain relevant when validated through modern methods. Such studies encourage further exploration of Rasayanas, integrating their wisdom into evidence-based longevity therapies.

10. **B:** The platform's ability to predict Pitta-dominant responses to heating herbs illustrates Ayurveda's precision when combined with genomics. This integration validates dosha classifications scientifically, demonstrating their utility in personalized interventions. By bridging genomic insights with prakriti, the platform enhances Ayurveda's applicability. However, it complements rather than replaces qualitative diagnostic methods. This synergy between tradition and technology showcases the adaptability of Ayurveda-Informatics. The research highlights how data-driven approaches can refine and validate Ayurvedic principles, strengthening their global relevance without losing their personalized nature.

11. **B:** The observed restoration of gut microbiota diversity by Triphala aligns with Ayurveda's emphasis on Agni and digestion as central to health. Enhanced gut-associated lymphoid tissue (GALT) activity, driven by microbial balance, provides a scientific mechanism for improved immunity. Unlike placebo effects or direct stimulation of immunoglobulins, the study highlights Triphala's foundational role in gut health, which Ayurveda has long associated with overall systemic wellness. By validating these traditional claims through measurable outcomes, the findings emphasize the compatibility of Ayurveda's holistic principles with modern microbiological insights. This fusion underscores the therapeutic potential of integrating traditional remedies with evidence-based research.

12. **B:** Agroforestry and community-based conservation efforts offer a balanced approach to addressing overharvesting and habitat degradation. Unlike monocultures, which risk biodiversity loss, agroforestry aligns with Ayurveda's ecological principles, preserving the medicinal quality of plants like Amalaki. Conservation practices ensure sustainability while maintaining therapeutic efficacy, which is essential for formulations like Triphala. Synthetic alternatives, though practical, undermine the holistic integrity of Ayurveda, while reducing production could limit accessibility. The solution lies in integrating traditional wisdom with modern conservation strategies, promoting both environmental sustainability and Ayurvedic efficacy. These efforts reinforce Ayurveda's adaptability to global environmental and healthcare challenges.

13. **A:** Environmental degradation impacts the bioactive compound concentration in Amalaki, directly affecting Triphala's efficacy in gut health and immunity. Ayurveda emphasizes the quality of ingredients in formulations, underscoring the need for sustainable practices. The study validates the dependency of therapeutic outcomes on plant integrity, linking ecological factors to health benefits. Synergistic effects in Triphala rely on the potency of its components, making quality degradation a critical concern. By addressing these challenges, the integration of sustainability with Ayurveda ensures long-term efficacy while preserving its holistic approach. The findings highlight the importance of environmental stewardship in maintaining Ayurvedic formulations' therapeutic potential.

14. **B:** Sustainability issues related to Amalaki (a Triphala component) arise from overharvesting and

environmental degradation. To maintain therapeutic efficacy and ecological balance, developing global standards for sustainable harvesting ensures consistent quality of medicinal plants while conserving biodiversity. This approach aligns with environmental ethics and long-term supply needs, without compromising the traditional formulation or its clinical benefits.

15. **C:** Biostatistical tools like regression analysis, ANOVA, survival analysis, and meta-analysis enhance Ayurveda research by validating its principles with scientific rigor. Regression models reveal prakriti-disease correlations, ANOVA compares treatment outcomes, and survival analysis tracks long-term Rasayana effects. Meta-analysis consolidates findings, offering comprehensive insights. These methodologies bridge Ayurveda's qualitative focus with quantitative validation, ensuring its integration into evidence-based medicine. By adapting these tools to Ayurvedic contexts, researchers can assess efficacy systematically, reinforcing Ayurveda's relevance in modern healthcare. This interdisciplinary approach combines statistical precision with traditional wisdom, creating a robust framework for Ayurvedic research and global application.

16. **B:** Digitizing Ayurvedic texts, employing bioinformatics, and integrating predictive analytics enhance Ayurveda's accessibility and scientific credibility. These tools modernize traditional practices without replacing their qualitative nature. By cataloging formulations, bioinformatics validates their molecular mechanisms, while predictive analytics enables prakriti-based interventions. Replacing traditional diagnostics with algorithms, however, risks oversimplification. Instead, these technologies complement Ayurveda's holistic approach, offering precision and scalability. This balanced integration ensures that Ayurveda-Informatics retains its essence while adapting to contemporary healthcare needs. By leveraging these innovations, Ayurveda can address global challenges while preserving its foundational principles, making it more relevant in the digital age.

17. **B:** Biostatistics plays a critical role in health research by providing tools for analyzing quantitative data. It aids in designing clinical trials, ensuring robust methodologies to derive reliable conclusions. By evaluating population health trends, biostatistics identifies disease patterns, risk factors, and intervention outcomes. Quantitative approaches ensure accuracy in estimating treatment efficacy, guiding policymakers and practitioners. Its application extends to public health planning, resource allocation, and forecasting epidemics. Through statistical models, it connects theoretical research with practical applications, making healthcare evidence-based and data-driven. Biostatistics thus bridges medical insights with mathematical rigor, enhancing precision and reliability in medical sciences.

18. **C:** Ayurveda-Informatics merges traditional Ayurvedic knowledge with modern technology. Digitization of texts ensures preservation and global access. Integration with diagnostic tools aligns ancient practices with contemporary healthcare. AI models enable precise dosha analysis, offering personalized health recommendations. Wearable technology monitors vital signs through Ayurvedic principles, blending tradition with innovation. This convergence fosters research, validating ancient practices through evidence-based studies. Ayurveda-Informatics also facilitates training, helping practitioners adapt to modern healthcare needs. By bridging ancient wisdom and modern tools, it opens new frontiers for Ayurveda, ensuring its relevance in contemporary health management and promoting its global acceptance.

19. **B:** Health informatics revolutionizes healthcare by leveraging technology for data management, diagnostics, and treatment. Electronic Health Records (EHR) ensure seamless patient information sharing among providers, enhancing continuity of care. AI predicts diagnostics by analyzing patient history and identifying disease patterns. Data standardization across systems ensures interoperability, enabling efficient communication between healthcare networks. Mobile health applications (mHealth) empower patients by offering remote consultations, medication tracking, and health monitoring. By integrating these components, health informatics promotes patient-centered care, optimizes resources, and enhances outcomes. It bridges gaps in healthcare delivery, making it more accessible, efficient, and effective in the digital era.

20. **B:** Biostatistics is indispensable in clinical research for estimating treatment effects, ensuring trials produce valid and reliable results. It calculates appropriate sample sizes, minimizing errors and maximizing study power. Biomarker identification through statistical methods provides insights into disease progression and therapeutic targets. Public health outcome predictions help policymakers implement effective interventions, addressing emerging health challenges. By combining mathematical rigor with clinical expertise, biostatistics transforms raw data into actionable knowledge. Its applications ensure that medical advances are based on robust evidence, contributing to the continuous improvement of healthcare quality, safety, and accessibility.

21. **C:** Ayurveda-Informatics enhances healthcare by validating Ayurvedic practices through scientific

methods. Digital tools improve access to classical Ayurvedic knowledge, fostering global acceptance. Telemedicine platforms integrate Ayurveda, expanding its reach to remote areas. AI-driven personalization tailors therapies to individual needs, enhancing efficacy and patient satisfaction. This synergy of tradition and technology bridges gaps between ancient systems and modern healthcare. By making Ayurveda more accessible, evidence-based, and patient-centric, Ayurveda-Informatics redefines its application in contemporary medicine. It offers a scalable model for integrating traditional knowledge into the broader healthcare ecosystem, preserving heritage while embracing innovation.

22. B: Health informatics emphasizes data privacy, ensuring patient information remains secure and confidential. Interoperability across health systems allows seamless exchange of medical data, facilitating comprehensive care. Patient-centered healthcare focuses on individual needs, enhancing engagement and outcomes. Automated health monitoring through IoT devices provides real-time insights into patient health, enabling proactive interventions. Together, these principles form the backbone of digital healthcare transformation, making services efficient, personalized, and secure. Health informatics not only addresses current challenges but also sets the stage for future innovations, driving global health improvements through technology-driven solutions.

23. C: Biostatistics contributes significantly to epidemiology by quantifying disease prevalence and incidence, providing a clear picture of public health. It assesses risk factors, identifying populations at higher risk and informing preventive measures. Statistical analysis evaluates the effectiveness of interventions, ensuring resources are directed toward impactful strategies. Disease transmission modeling predicts outbreak patterns, aiding in preparedness and response. These applications ensure that epidemiology is data-driven and evidence-based, enabling policymakers to make informed decisions. Biostatistics bridges the gap between research and practical solutions, enhancing the accuracy and effectiveness of public health initiatives.

24. A: Ayurvedic diagnostics prioritize individualized assessment using ancient techniques like Nadi Pariksha (pulse diagnosis) to understand the patient's dosha imbalance. Examination of excreta (Mala Pariksha) provides insights into digestion and metabolism. Skin and tongue analysis reveal imbalances in bodily systems. These non-invasive, holistic methods focus on understanding root causes rather than symptoms. By excluding modern imaging technologies like MRI, Ayurvedic diagnostics maintain their traditional identity while offering a personalized approach. These methods complement modern diagnostic tools, providing a comprehensive view of health and fostering integrative healthcare practices.

25. A: Vata governs movement, including neural and respiratory functions, Pitta regulates metabolism and enzymatic activity, Kapha maintains structure and fluid balance, and the balance of Tridosha ensures physical and mental well-being. These associations illustrate Ayurveda's holistic understanding of human physiology. By aligning each dosha with distinct functions, Ayurveda provides a comprehensive framework for diagnosis and treatment. The integration of these principles with modern systems demonstrates their continued relevance in personalized medicine. Such insights validate Ayurveda's systemic approach and its adaptability in contemporary healthcare.

26. A: Predictive analytics aligns prakriti with disease risk, bioinformatics deciphers molecular interactions of herbs, CDSS supports prakriti-based diagnostics, and EHR systems digitize Ayurvedic data. These applications demonstrate Ayurveda-Informatics' ability to modernize traditional practices while maintaining their personalized nature. By linking ancient wisdom with advanced tools, these integrations enhance credibility and scalability. The synergy between tradition and innovation underscores Ayurveda's relevance in evidence-based medicine. Such efforts make Ayurvedic principles accessible to global audiences without compromising their essence.

27. A: Regression analysis predicts prakriti-disease correlations, ANOVA compares dosha-based outcomes, Kaplan-Meier analysis evaluates survival rates for therapies like Rasayana, and meta-analysis consolidates clinical evidence. These statistical tools provide empirical support for Ayurveda's personalized framework, bridging tradition with scientific rigor. By adopting biostatistics, Ayurveda-Informatics ensures credibility and scalability in global healthcare. This integration validates ancient principles while addressing modern research needs. These methodologies highlight Ayurveda's potential to adapt to contemporary scientific paradigms, ensuring its continued relevance.

28. A: Sweet Rasa nourishes tissues, Bitter Rasa detoxifies and reduces inflammation, Astringent Rasa strengthens barriers, and Sour Rasa enhances digestion. These biological actions validate Ayurveda's classification of Rasas, demonstrating their physiological relevance. Modern pharmacological studies support these findings, bridging traditional concepts with contemporary science. By aligning taste classifications with health outcomes, Ayurveda offers precise therapeutic guidance. Such validations strengthen Ayurveda's credibility in evidence-based medicine, emphasizing its relevance in personalized care.

29. **A:** Data standardization ensures consistency in Ayurvedic terminologies, interoperability bridges traditional and biomedical systems, privacy concerns address prakriti-based EHRs, and conservation tackles overharvesting of medicinal plants. These challenges highlight the need for collaborative solutions in Ayurveda-Informatics. Addressing these barriers ensures the seamless integration of Ayurveda into modern healthcare systems. Such efforts preserve traditional practices while adapting them to contemporary needs. By resolving these issues, Ayurveda-Informatics enhances accessibility, credibility, and sustainability.

30. **A:** Prakriti-based inputs personalize treatment, dosha imbalance alerts ensure timely interventions, EHR integration facilitates record-keeping, and AI-driven diagnostics support accurate dosha assessments. These features modernize Ayurvedic diagnostics while retaining their qualitative essence. By aligning traditional practices with digital tools, CDSS systems enhance precision and scalability. This integration demonstrates the potential of Ayurveda-Informatics to bridge tradition and innovation. The observed improvements validate the effectiveness of combining Ayurveda's holistic approach with technological advancements.

31. **A:** Panchakarma detoxifies and restores dosha balance, Rasayana rejuvenates cells, Triphala improves gut microbiota, and Chyawanprash enhances immunity and vitality. These interventions highlight Ayurveda's holistic focus on preventive and restorative care. By addressing both physical and systemic health, these therapies showcase Ayurveda's comprehensive approach. Modern validations of these treatments strengthen their credibility, bridging tradition with contemporary healthcare needs. Such insights emphasize Ayurveda's relevance in personalized and preventive medicine.

32. **A:** EHR systems capture prakriti-specific data, predictive analytics forecasts disease risks, telemedicine enables remote consultations, and visualization tools display dosha-based health trends. These tools demonstrate the versatility of Ayurveda-Informatics in addressing modern healthcare challenges. By integrating traditional principles with digital innovation, these systems enhance accessibility, precision, and scalability. This alignment ensures that Ayurveda remains relevant in global healthcare. Such efforts reinforce Ayurveda's adaptability and scientific credibility.

33. **A:** Preconception care focuses on reproductive tissue purification, embryonic development involves maternal and paternal influences, prakriti is determined during conception, and postnatal care emphasizes nutrition and ojas restoration. These stages illustrate Ayurveda's comprehensive approach to health across the life cycle. By integrating these principles into modern healthcare, Ayurveda offers holistic solutions. Such insights validate the scientific relevance of Ayurvedic practices, emphasizing their preventive and restorative focus. This integration ensures that Ayurveda's principles remain accessible and effective in contemporary medicine.

34. **A:** Molecular docking predicts compound-receptor interactions, network pharmacology studies synergistic effects, genomics correlates prakriti with genetic markers, and metabolomics analyzes herbal-induced biochemical changes. These bioinformatics techniques validate Ayurvedic formulations by revealing their molecular mechanisms. By bridging traditional remedies with contemporary science, these tools enhance Ayurveda's credibility. Such efforts highlight Ayurveda's potential in evidence-based medicine, emphasizing its relevance in modern healthcare. These integrations preserve Ayurveda's essence while adapting it to contemporary scientific standards.

35. **C:** Ayurveda-Informatics integrates traditional knowledge with digital tools, ensuring its relevance in modern healthcare. However, this does not eliminate the need for prakriti-based customization. Standardization enhances accessibility but must complement Ayurveda's personalized approach. By retaining qualitative aspects, Ayurveda-Informatics bridges traditional wisdom with contemporary needs. This balance ensures that Ayurveda remains both adaptable and effective. Such integrations validate Ayurveda's relevance without compromising its foundational principles.

36. **C:** Predictive analytics uses machine learning to analyze prakriti and lifestyle data, aligning with Ayurveda's focus on personalization. While genetic markers are important, they complement rather than replace qualitative factors like dosha imbalances. This integration ensures a holistic approach, preserving Ayurveda's essence. By combining data-driven precision with traditional principles, predictive analytics bridges tradition and technology. This synergy enhances Ayurveda's accessibility and scalability, making it relevant in modern healthcare.

37. **C:** Biostatistics is essential in evaluating the efficacy of Ayurvedic therapies through hypothesis testing, confidence intervals, and data interpretation, making Statement 1 true. However, Statement 2 is false because

RCTs can be adapted for Ayurveda, using stratified designs, prakriti-based grouping, and mixed methods that honor individualized treatments. Hence, RCTs are not incompatible but require contextual adaptation in Ayurvedic research.

38. C: Prakriti-based EHRs improve the personalization of healthcare delivery by allowing practitioners to incorporate dosha-specific data. However, these systems are not limited to urban settings. Overcoming technological barriers through training and infrastructure can expand their reach to rural areas. By addressing these challenges, Ayurveda-Informatics can ensure equitable access to personalized care. This integration demonstrates the adaptability of Ayurveda in diverse environments, enhancing its relevance and accessibility. Such innovations reinforce Ayurveda's role in modern healthcare systems, emphasizing its potential for global impact.

39. C: Bioinformatics has successfully identified molecular mechanisms in formulations like Triphala, providing scientific validation for Ayurvedic remedies. However, reducing Ayurveda to biochemical interactions risks oversimplification. Its holistic philosophy encompasses physical, mental, and spiritual health, which computational tools alone cannot address. By integrating these findings into a broader framework, Ayurveda can balance modern validation with its traditional essence. This approach ensures that evidence-based research complements, rather than replaces, Ayurveda's foundational principles. Such integrations enhance Ayurveda's credibility without compromising its unique holistic focus.

40. B: Digital repositories like TKDL enhance global acceptance of Ayurveda by cataloging its knowledge in scientific terms. However, evidence-based validation often requires clinical studies, not just computational models. While digitization preserves traditional wisdom, it must align with empirical methods to gain wider recognition. By integrating digital tools with modern research, Ayurveda can build a globally credible system. This collaboration ensures that ancient knowledge remains relevant and scientifically validated. Such efforts balance innovation with tradition, creating a sustainable healthcare framework for global audiences.

41. C: Predictive analytics aligns with Ayurveda by integrating prakriti and lifestyle data into disease risk assessments. However, relying solely on genetic markers would overlook key qualitative factors like dosha imbalances. Ayurveda's holistic approach requires a combination of quantitative and qualitative insights. This balance ensures that predictive tools retain Ayurveda's personalized focus. By bridging traditional wisdom with data-driven models, predictive analytics enhances Ayurveda's precision and scalability. Such integrations validate Ayurveda's principles while addressing contemporary healthcare challenges.

42. C: While RCTs provide valuable validation for Ayurvedic therapies, they are not the only statistical tool available. Observational studies, case-control designs, and meta-analyses can also accommodate Ayurveda's personalized approach. Biostatistics offers a framework for evaluating efficacy systematically, strengthening Ayurveda's credibility. However, flexibility in research design is essential to honor Ayurveda's unique nature. By adopting diverse methods, Ayurveda can integrate traditional practices with evidence-based systems. This approach ensures that Ayurveda remains adaptable and scientifically robust in modern healthcare.

43. C: CDSS systems enhance precision by integrating prakriti-specific recommendations but do not replace Ayurveda's qualitative assessments. Algorithms aid scalability and accessibility but must complement, not overshadow, traditional diagnostics. By blending digital tools with practitioner expertise, CDSS systems retain Ayurveda's holistic focus. This integration modernizes Ayurveda without compromising its core principles. The observed improvements highlight the potential of Ayurveda-Informatics to bridge tradition and technology. Such efforts reinforce Ayurveda's adaptability in personalized medicine while preserving its unique essence.

44. A: Sustainable sourcing is critical to preserving the efficacy of Ayurvedic formulations. Overharvesting and habitat degradation reduce the bioactive compound concentrations in medicinal plants, compromising their therapeutic potential. Addressing these challenges through conservation and sustainable cultivation aligns with Ayurveda's ecological principles. Collaborative efforts ensure that Ayurveda's reliance on natural resources remains ethical and effective. By integrating environmental stewardship with traditional practices, Ayurveda can maintain its therapeutic quality while addressing global demand. This balance reinforces Ayurveda's commitment to harmony between health and nature.

45. C: Ayurveda-Informatics indeed enhances personalized healthcare by blending traditional wisdom with modern tools like AI, EHRs, and predictive analytics, validating Assertion (A). However, Reason (R) is incorrect—Ayurveda-Informatics does not replace qualitative diagnostics like prakriti assessment; rather, it complements and digitizes them, making holistic approaches more scalable without losing their essence.

46. B: The passage explains how dosha-based classifications like Vata, Pitta, and Kapha align with genetic and metabolic profiles, creating a foundation for precision medicine. For instance, Kapha dominance is associated with metabolic disorders. By mapping dosha to biological markers, practitioners can design targeted, personalized therapies, validating the ancient concept of Tridosha in modern scientific contexts.

47. B: Predictive analytics aligns with Ayurveda by offering prakriti-based health recommendations, emphasizing prevention. These models integrate lifestyle data with clinical indicators to identify disease risks, reinforcing Ayurveda's personalized focus. Unlike generalized healthcare approaches, predictive tools ensure precision while retaining qualitative insights. By bridging traditional principles with data-driven techniques, these systems validate Ayurveda's preventive care framework. The integration of analytics demonstrates Ayurveda's adaptability in addressing contemporary healthcare challenges, making it both relevant and effective. Such efforts enhance Ayurveda's credibility and scalability in global medicine.

48. A: Overharvesting and habitat loss impact the availability and efficacy of medicinal plants critical to Ayurveda. These challenges compromise the therapeutic quality of formulations like Triphala, which rely on plant bioactives. Sustainable sourcing and conservation practices are essential to address these issues, ensuring long-term accessibility. Ayurveda's emphasis on ecological harmony aligns with such efforts, preserving both biodiversity and efficacy. By integrating traditional wisdom with environmental stewardship, Ayurveda addresses modern challenges without compromising its principles. This balance ensures the sustainability of Ayurvedic practices in a globalized world.

49. B: Prakriti-based EHRs require robust privacy safeguards to prevent misuse of sensitive health data. Personalized healthcare systems are inherently vulnerable to ethical challenges, making data security a priority. By addressing these concerns, Ayurveda-Informatics ensures patient trust and compliance. Balancing innovation with ethical considerations reinforces Ayurveda's commitment to holistic care. Such measures ensure that technology enhances, rather than compromises, Ayurveda's values. Collaborative efforts between technologists and practitioners can create secure, patient-centric systems that preserve Ayurveda's integrity in modern healthcare.

50. B: Initiatives like TKDL demonstrate Ayurveda's potential to integrate traditional knowledge with modern systems. By preserving and standardizing formulations, these efforts protect Ayurveda's intellectual heritage while promoting its global acceptance. However, innovation must complement tradition, ensuring that Ayurveda's holistic principles remain intact. Multidisciplinary collaboration ensures that Ayurveda adapts to modern healthcare without losing its cultural essence. Such efforts make Ayurveda relevant, credible, and sustainable in global medicine. Balancing tradition with technology creates a robust framework for integrating Ayurveda into contemporary healthcare systems.

YOUR SPACE

YOUR SPACE